# Strategic Management

# FIFTH EDITION

# Strategic Management

## Awareness and Change

**John Thompson**

University of Huddersfield

**with Frank Martin**

University of Stirling

SOUTH-WESTERN
CENGAGE Learning

Australia • Brazil • Japan • Korea • Mexico • Singapore • Spain • United Kingdom • United States

**Strategic Management, 5th Edition**
John Thompson with Frank Martin

Publishing Director: John Yates
Commissioning Editor: Thomas Rennie
Manufacturing Manager: Helen Mason
Marketing Manager: Rossella Proscia
Typesetter: Saxon Graphics, Derby
Cover design: Jackie Wrout
Text design: Design Deluxe, Bath, UK

For product information and technology assistance, contact **emea.info@cengage.com**.

For permission to use material from this text or product, and for permission queries, email **clsuk.permissions@cengage.com**

British Library Cataloguing-in-Publication Data
A catalogue record for this book is available from the British Library.

ISBN:978-1-84480-083-4

**Cengage Learning EMEA**
High Holborn House, 50-51 Bedford Row
London WC1R 4LR

Cengage Learning products are represented in Canada by Nelson Education Ltd.

For your lifelong learning solutions, visit
**www.cengage.co.uk**

Purchase e-books or e-chapters at:
**http://estore.bized.co.uk**

Printed by C & C Offset, China
4 5 6 7 8 9 10 – 10 09 08

# Brief contents

# Contents

# List of Minicases

Many Minicases have an international flavour. The country or countries of company origin that the Minicase refers to have been indicated with country codes as follows:

GB   Great Britain
Eur   Europe
US   United States of America
ANZ  Australia/New Zealand
Ind   Indian subcontinent
AS   Asia, including Japan
SA   South America
Int   these Minicases have an international flavour

# Preface

## About this book

This book is about strategic awareness, strategic analysis and the management of strategic change. It is designed for use by students who will become future managers and for managers in practice; after all, in some way or another, *all managers are strategy makers*. It looks at how managers become strategically aware of their company's position and potential opportunities for change, at how changes often happen in reality, and at how the process might be managed more effectively.

Strategic management is concerned with the actions that organizations take to deal with the changes, opportunities, threats, challenges and surprises in their external and internal environments. Put simply, strategies are means to ends. How, then, do organizations:

- determine desired outcomes?
- understand the circumstances and events affecting these outcomes and the means of attaining them?
- decide upon actions that they intend to take?
- implement these desired strategies through a series of tactical moves and changes?
- evaluate progress and relative success?

These are the broad themes addressed in this book.

Since the first edition was written some 15 years ago the subject of strategic management has been developed and our understanding of certain aspects has changed. In addition, the world of business has been transformed by the rapid growth of the Internet and the emergence of the new and entrepreneurial dot.com organizations. Indeed, entrepreneurship as a subject has also increased in popularity and significance and it is not realistic to treat it as completely divorced from strategy as the two are very clearly related. While some of these changes were reflected in the second, third and fourth editions, this fifth edition sees major revisions to both the structure and content to bring both the text and the case material fully up to date. In addition, and for the first time, John Thompson has worked with a co-author – Frank Martin from the University of Stirling.

### Thinking strategically

Strategy is about how an organization sets about getting to where it wants to get – it is about setting, pursuing and achieving its mission and objectives. In the early stages of a company's development, this is usually straightforward – it is not difficult for everyone concerned to appreciate the desired end points and the routes forward. As the business grows and diversifies then it separates into different parts and these have to be co-ordinated. Strategy takes on a different complexity. The ideal outcome is synergistic – the sum of the achievements of the various parts exceeds what they might be expected to achieve individually and independently. At this stage issues of strategy and structure (including managing and controlling within the structure) have to be dealt with together. The ability to implement strategic ideas holds the key to prosperity.

If something goes wrong it could be that the organization has made a strategic mis-judgement – it has attempted to do something for which it is inadequately or inappro-priately resourced, for example – or it could be that it makes mistakes in implementation – it underestimates the reaction of its competitors, maybe.

Uncertainty (and therefore risk) is always prevalent in strategy. Organizations will plan to some extent, and they will vary in the extent to which they do plan. But managers can never plan for every eventuality and possibility. Strategies emerge as managers and organizations react to the world around them. They attempt to counter threats and seize opportunities. Flexibility is essential. How they do this comes down to the style and approach of the person in ultimate charge – the strategic leader. But in some way or other every manager is (potentially) a strategy maker.

Strategy may involve planning, plans and even formal documentation, but fundamen-tally it is a way of thinking and behaving.

In the end it is probably true that 'everything in strategy is simple, but nothing in strategy is very easy'. It is a mistake to over-complicate things. It is also a mistake to underestimate competition – in part because new competitors can enter an industry quickly and surprisingly – or to ignore change pressures and become complacent.

It has to be tempting, though, to sit back and enjoy the fruits of success once an organization has become an industry leader – and maybe a global organization in the process. But size and success is no guarantee of permanency. Corporate history (like military history) contains numerous stories of once-great, once-dominant corporations that have fallen by the wayside. It is vital that stasis and inertia is avoided. Again, it is an attitude of mind.

Prolonged success, then, in part, depends upon how organizations deal with crises when they occur. Astute companies will have made preparations for dealing with possible crises, but they will still have to be dealt with when they happen. Yet again, this comes down to an ability to think things through and to stay vigilant and flexible.

Of course, from time to time there will be changes of strategic leadership. When these changes happen, it is likely that newcomers will want to change strategies and/or structures. There is always the potential to improve things – but it is equally possible to destroy something that works well.

From this short and cryptic explanation of strategy, you will see why we subtitle our book 'Awareness and Change'!

## How to use this book

### Structure and content

The content follows the established Analysis, Choice, Implementation model that is used in most strategy texts, and is structured in five parts, which systematically deal with a series of 12 key questions.

Part One: *Understanding Strategy and Strategic Management* looks at the strategy process as a whole and includes a comprehensive framework of the process around which the book is structured. A special supplement at the end of Part 1 (pp. 109–37) incorporates an introduction to the key strategic themes which are developed throughout the book and, for this reason, it could be seen in part as a reference section. A second (new) reference supplement (pp. 138–41) lists the various tools and techniques that can be used to carry out a strategic analysis of any organization. These are then developed throughout the book, but this supplement is useful for assignments and case analyses. Part One includes a chapter on the business model, mission and objectives and it therefore addresses the following question:

■ Where is the organization going – and how might this have to be changed?

*Content:*
Chapter 1 Introducing the Strategy Process
Chapter 2 The Business Model, the Organizational Mission and Objectives
Supplement: Key Strategic Concerns
Supplement: Strategic Analysis Frameworks

Part Two: *Strategic Analysis* looks at three distinct but clearly related approaches to strategy: market- or opportunity-driven; resource-based; and competitor influenced strategic management. Part Two includes a number of tools and techniques which help us to understand the current competitive situation. This part also looks at strategic positioning and competitive advantage. It also includes a chapter on strategic success, culture and values. Culture is a vital element of our study as it determines how strategies and changes are determined and implemented.
We ask:

■ Where are the future opportunities and threats for the organization?
■ How might it capitalize on its strengths, competencies and capabilities, and reduce any key weaknesses?
■ How can its competitiveness be improved and strengthened?
■ How is the organization doing? Where is it doing well and where is it doing less well?
■ How good is the organization's information management?

*Content:*
Chapter 3 Strategic Thinking, Environmental Influences and Synergy
Chapter 4 Environmental Analysis and Strategic Positioning
Chapter 5 Resource-led Strategy
Chapter 6 The Dynamics of Competition

Part Three: *Strategy Creation* describes and evaluates the different ways in which strategies are formulated and created. Several valuable planning models and techniques are discussed. We also look at both entrepreneurship and intrapreneurship. We therefore continue to ask:

■ How might the organization be developed in the future?
■ How can its competitiveness be strengthened?

*Content:*
Chapter 7 Success, Culture and Values

Chapter 8 An Introduction to Strategy Creation
Chapter 9 Strategic Planning
Chapter 10 Strategic Leadership, Entrepreneurship and Intrapreneurship

Part Four: *Corporate Strategy* begins with a study of the various strategic alternatives that a firm might consider and with the determinants of a good choice. It deals with both growth and retrenchment issues. There is also a discussion of business failure and a chapter on international strategy. The relevant questions are:

- What corporate strategic alternatives are available and worthy of serious consideration?
- What can, cannot, should and should not the organization do in the future?

*Content:*
Chapter 11 Strategic Alternatives, Strategy Evaluation and Strategy Selection
Chapter 12 Strategic Growth
Chapter 13 International Strategy
Chapter 14 Failure, Consolidation and Recovery Strategies

Part Five: *Strategy Implementation* evaluates the issues involved in strategy implementation. Organization structures, resource management and the complexities of managing change are included, as are issues of risk and crisis management. The following questions are therefore addressed:

- What criteria affect the proposed change decisions, how and why?
- How might the proposed changes be implemented and managed?

*Content:*
Chapter 15 Strategy Implementation
Chapter 16 Managing Strategy in the Organization
Chapter 17 Leading Change
Chapter 18 Final Thoughts: The Purpose of Strategy?

Strategic management is a complex and dynamic subject and, as we said at the beginning of this Preface, since the first four editions of this book were published a number of new ideas and views have emerged. In addition, certain practices and priorities have changed to reflect developments around the world. Consequently, the whole text has been reviewed and restructured. Most chapters have been substantially rewritten and some have been consolidated. Many of the Minicases are new. Existing readers will appreciate how the basic structure of the book has been changed. The *significant* new content of individual chapters is explained very briefly below. There are many other changes.

- Chapters 1 and 2 explain The Business Model and argue that successful companies have a clear, understood model which embraces what they do, for whom they do it and what their compelling reason for buying is.
- Chapters 1 and 8 have special sections on military strategy. Our study of this subject has its origins in warfare and therefore it is appropriate to show the links between business and military strategy, albeit briefly.
- Part One has two special supplements which are clearly identifiable and which can be used as reference chapters at any time. They cover, first, key themes in strategic management and, second, important strategic analysis frameworks.

- Chapter 6 is refocused on competitive *strategy*. Studying competitive advantage as part of a strategy course is ubiquitous – but it is important to go further. Competition and competitive pressures drive the tactics of many organizations, who have to respond if they are to thrive and prosper in a climate of change.

- Chapter 10 links together strategic leadership, entrepreneurship and intrapreneurship. Strategic leaders drive the processes through which organizations create, change and implement strategies. Again in an environment of change it is important there is the ability to spot and exploit new opportunities. Innovation is vital.

- Chapter 13 provides a more detailed treatment of international strategy.

The long cases that have been a feature at the end of previous editions have been taken out and placed on the support web site.

# Key themes

## Strategy in practice

The book contains over 100 Minicases within the various chapters. Around a half of these are UK cases; 25 use well-known American companies, whose names are generally recognized around the world. The remainder are from Europe, the Far East and Australasia. Additional full-length cases are available on the book's web site. All the cases cover large and small businesses, both national and international in scope, manufacturing and service, and the private, public and non-profit sectors. The retail, leisure, financial and transport service industries are included, as are several non-profit and charity organizations. We have included a large number of retail examples for several reasons. First, they are mostly recognizable companies that students can readily visit and experience at first hand. Second, they sell products that many readers will buy regularly. Third, they are in an industry that is subject to fashion and innovation; strategies change frequently. We have also included several Minicases from industries that place a heavy reliance on the Internet. In part this is because they are typically very contemporary, but again it is because students can easily access them for follow-up material. Some of the cases have been included in earlier editions of this book, but where this is the case, they have been either updated or rewritten for this new edition.

## Differing perspectives

It must be emphasized that no single approach, model or theory can explain the realities of strategic change in practice for all organizations; different organizations and managers will find certain approaches much more relevant to their circumstances and style. All approaches will have both supporters and critics. It is therefore important to study the various approaches within a sound intellectual framework so that they can be evaluated by students and other readers.

Students of business and management and practising managers must work out for themselves the intricacies and difficulties of managing organizations at the corporate level and of managing strategic change at all levels of the organization. It is no good being told how to be prescriptive when it is patently obvious that there is no universal model. Observations of practice in isolation are equally limited in their usefulness.

However, an attempt to find explanations that can be utilized does make sense. Testing and evaluating reality against a theoretical framework helps this process.

## Key features

**Cases and examples**  In addition to numerous references in the main text to organizations and events, as we mentioned above, over 100 short Minicase examples are included. The cases are designed to illustrate points in the main text. They are also intended to supplement the reader's own experiences and investigation. Each chapter begins with a carefully written Minicase which represents the main themes of the chapter. There are specific questions at the end of every Minicase and relevant web site addresses are provided to enable easy follow-up. Inevitably some of the cases will date during the life of the text, in the sense that the strategies and fortunes of the companies featured in the examples will change. Strategies have life cycles, and strategies that prove effective at certain times will not always remain so. Companies that fail to change their strategies at the right time are likely to experience declining fortunes. Questions are included at the ends of chapters to encourage the reader to research and analyse the subsequent fortunes of companies included as cases.

Additionally, full-length cases are also included on the accompanying web site.

**Learning objectives**  These appear at the start of every chapter to help you monitor your understanding and progress through the chapter.

**Boxes**  Boxes are used in the text and featured separately within the relevant chapter for special emphasis and easy reference. They cover three tasks:

1. Some define *Key Concepts* in strategy and also explain significant contributions which underpin an understanding of strategic management.
2. Others are *Discussions* and they feature particular debates where there are differing opinions.
3. Boxes covering *Strategy in Action* provide annotated applications of particular ideas and concepts.

**Finance in Action**  At the end of certain chapters, and in the form of appendices, there are Finance in Action supplements which expand upon points introduced in the text. They provide more detail than some readers will require; for others they enhance key aspects of strategic analysis.

**Figures**  A comprehensive set of figures, which are either new or redrawn, illustrate and explain the issues covered in the text.

**Quotations**  Short and pithy quotations from a variety of senior managers in the private and the public sectors are sprinkled throughout the text to illustrate a spectrum of opinions. These are useful for provoking class discussion and examination questions.

**Chapter summaries**  An outline summary of the content and main points is given at the end of every chapter. This can help readers to check that they appreciate the main points and issues before reading on.

**Questions and research assignments** These are included at the end of each chapter. Some questions relate to the ideas contained in the text and the illustrative cases, and some are examples of the type that feature in non-case study examinations of this subject.

Several research projects, both library and Internet based, are included to encourage the reader to develop his or her knowledge and understanding further. The web site provides a gateway of links to sites that are helpful in researching the Internet projects.

**Further reading** At the end of the chapters we include a short list of further reading references. It consists in part of 'classic' journal articles, some of which have been cited in the main text. These are spread over several years – as the subject has emerged – and we appreciate that some readers may find it difficult to access some of the older ones through their libraries. We therefore also include a number of more recent articles. It should be appreciated that although fresh articles are being published all the time, only a very small number add anything *really new* to our understanding of strategy and strategic management.

**Glossary** The book also includes a glossary, including definitions of well over 100 key terms. For ease of reference words that are included in the glossary are highlighted in purple in the text.

## Web site

An extensive accompanying web site (accessible from http://www.cengage.co.uk) provides a comprehensive set of additional resources for both students and lecturers. It includes additional material and examples about strategic management, links to companies and further information sources, guidance for lecturers and interactive resources for students. Full details are given below.

### For students
- Integrative web-based case that mirrors the major sections in the book and includes tasks to take you through the strategic management process
- Interactive multiple choice questions for each chapter to help test your learning
- Chapter overviews for each chapter that focus on the 'why' not the 'what' to help deepen your understanding
- Seven full length cases to allow more detailed study
- Links to useful company, news and other relevant sites
- Online glossary to explain key terms
- Student guide to analysing case studies
- Student guide to referencing your work correctly

### For lecturers
- Downloadable tutor notes
- Downloadable PowerPoint™ slides
- Case study library

- Guide to using case studies in your teaching
- Guide to the use of the web in your teaching

# Advice for lecturers

## Teaching aims

The main purpose of the book is to help students who aim to become managers, and managers in practice, to:

- develop their strategic awareness
- increase their understanding of how the functional areas of management (in which they are most likely to work) contribute to strategic management and to strategic changes within organizations
- appreciate how strategic change is managed in organizations.

The content is broad and the treatment is both academic and practical, in order to provide value for practising managers as well as full- and part-time students. The subject matter included is taught in a wide variety of courses, including undergraduate courses in business studies and related areas, MBA and other postgraduate master's degrees, post-experience management courses and courses for a number of professional qualifications. The subject can be entitled strategic management, business policy, corporate strategy or business planning.

The material is relevant for all types of organization: large and small businesses, manufacturing and service organizations, and both the public and private sectors. The examples included relate to all of these. Although the topics discussed are broadly applicable, certain issues are sector specific, and these are discussed individually.

This edition has been written and structured in 18 chapters to support courses that last a full academic year. Clearly, some lecturers will opt to spend longer than a single week or session on some topics or possibly switch the order of the chapters marginally. Neither of these should present any problems and suggested course outlines are provided on the website for different types of course. Some courses in strategy run for a only a single semester, focusing more on the analytical aspects of the subject. A careful selection of chapters, in a logical sequence, can underpin such courses quite readily and a suggested outline is provided on the companion website.

# Advice for students

## Studying strategy

Strategic management is concerned with understanding, as well as choosing and implementing, the strategy or strategies that an organization follows. It is a complex process that can be considered from a number of different perspectives. For example, one can design prescriptive models based on a series of logical stages that look at how to choose and implement strategies aimed at achieving some form of long-term success for the organization. This is a systematic approach designed to bring about optimum results. An alternative paradigm, or conceptual framework, is a systemic approach that concerns understanding what is happening in reality and thinking about how things might be improved. The emphasis is on learning about how strategic management is practised by looking at what organizations actually do and by examining the decisions that they make and carry out.

In this book both perspectives are considered and linked together. While it is always useful to develop models that attempt to provide optimizing solutions, this approach is inadequate if it fails to explain reality. Strategic management and strategic change are dynamic, often the result of responses to environmental pressures, and frequently not the product of extensive deliberations involving all affected managers.

Managers should be aware of the issues and questions that must be addressed if changes in strategy are to be formulated and implemented effectively. At the same time, they should be aware of the managerial and behavioural processes taking place within organizations in order that they can understand how changes actually come about.

Prescriptive models are found quite frequently in business and management teaching. For example, there are models for rational decision-making built around the clear recognition and definition of a problem and the careful and objective analysis and evaluation of the alternative solutions. There are economic models of various market structures showing how an organization can maximize profit. However, decision-making invariably involves subjectivity and short cuts, and organizations do not always seek profit maximization as their top priority. Although organizations and individuals rarely follow these models slavishly – quite often they cannot, and sometimes they choose not to – this does not render them worthless. Far from it: they provide an excellent framework or yardstick for evaluating how people reach their decisions, what objectives are being pursued and how situations might be improved. The argument is that if managers observe what is happening and seek to explain it and evaluate it against some more ideal state then they will see ways of managing things more effectively. In this way managerial performance can be improved. Note the use of the expression 'more effectively'. For a whole variety of reasons situations cannot be managed *perfectly*.

The reader with personal experience of organizations, management and change (whether it is limited or extensive, broad or specialized) should use this experience to complement the examples and cases described in the book. Ideally the experience and the cases will be used jointly to evaluate the theories and concepts discussed. There is no universal approach to the management of strategy and strategic change. An individual must establish what approaches and decisions are likely to prove most effective in particular circumstances, and why. This learning experience can be enhanced:

- by evaluating the theoretical and conceptual contributions of various authors
- by considering practical examples of what has proved successful and unsuccessful for organizations
- by examining these two aspects in combination to see which theories and concepts best help an understanding of reality.

*The manager's job is change. It is what we live with. It is what we are to create. If we cannot do that, then we are not good at the job. It is our basic job to have the nerve to keep changing and changing and changing again.*

Sir Peter Parker

Pressures to change are always present in the form of opportunities and threats. At any point in time the significance of these pressures will vary markedly from industry to industry and from organization to organization. Managers may be aware of them and seek to respond positively; they may recognize opportunities and threats and choose to do little about them other than perhaps to avert crises; or they may be totally unaware of them. A lack of awareness can mean that potentially good opportunities are also lost; it may mean that businesses fail if they are not able to react and respond to the threats and problems when they arise. All businesses must react to pressures from the environment such as supply shortages, new products from competitors or new retailing opportunities, but some will be very proactive and thereby seek to manage their environment.

It is important to point out that students of strategic management may not be, or may not become, key strategic decision-makers in their organizations but instead may specialize in one particular function, such as marketing, production or finance. Similarly, their experience may be with only one product or one division if their employer is a multiproduct or multidivisional organization. Nevertheless, the decisions that they make or to which they contribute can affect the strategy for a particular product or service and in turn affect the organization. It is vital that they appreciate exactly how their function operates within an organizational context, and how decisions made in their area of interest can affect both other functions and the organization as a whole.

Finally, and to reinforce this last point, students occasionally ask whether 'strategic management' is about the management of strategy in organizations or about how people can manage strategically – an interesting point! The focus here is on the management of strategy in organizations but, by studying and applying the theory, and reflecting on its relevance in the context of personal observations and experience, readers should be able to improve their effectiveness as managers. In essence they will benefit – as will any organization in which they work – by being better placed to take a strategic perspective and to use it to inform decisions and actions. Remember, there are no finite answers to the decisions and actions that should be taken. Organizations, and many of the problem issues they have to deal with, are complex and ill-defined. After all, if strategy were straightforward, the relative success rate of organizations of every type and size would be much greater than it is.

> *Experience is a wonderful thing, but not a useful one. When you are young, you don't trust others' experience – for if you do, this can paralyse you. When you get old, it is too late to use it – and you cannot transmit it for the reasons outlined.*
>
> Jacques Calvet, Le President du Directoire, PSA Peugeot Citroën.

## Acknowledgements

The publisher would like to thank the following reviewers for their contribution:

David Pollard, University of Abertay; Carsten Scheibye, Copenhagen Business School; Kent Springdal, Kingston University; and Jan Stiles, Henley Management College.

# Guided tour of the book

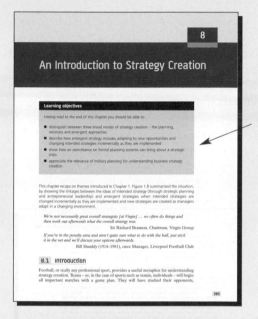

**Learning Objectives** – appear at the start of every chapter to help you monitor your understanding and progress through the chapter. Each chapter also ends with a conclusion section that recaps the key content for revision purposes

**Minicases** – more than 100 minicases throughout the book show how each chapter's main issues are applied in real-life business situations in different types of international and national companies. Each minicase is accompanied by questions to help you test your understanding of the issues.

**Boxes** – these perform three different functions throughout the text: *key concepts* (highlighting significant contributions/themes within the field); *strategy in action* (providing applications of particular ideas and concepts) and *discussion* (featuring particular debates where there are differing opinions).

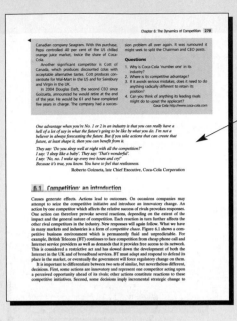

**Quotes** – short quotes from senior managers in the private and public sectors are used throughout the text to illustrate a spectrum of opinions; these are ideal for provoking class discussion and examination questions.

**Glossary Terms** – key terms are highlighted in colour throughout and explained in full in a glossary at the end of the book, enabling you to find explanations of key terms quickly.

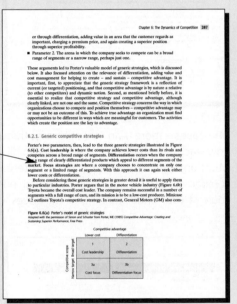

**Summaries** – each chapter ends with a comprehensive summary that provides a thorough re-cap of the key issues in each chapter, helping you to assess your understanding and revise key content.

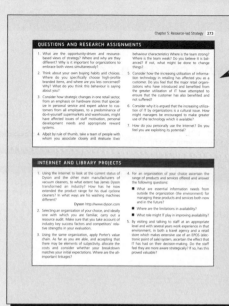

**Questions and
Research Assignments** – provided at the end of each chapter, these help reinforce and test your knowledge and understanding, and provide a basis for group discussions and activities.

**Further Reading and References** – comprehensive references and often annotated further reading at the end of each chapter allows you to explore the subject further, and acts as a starting-point for projects and assignments.

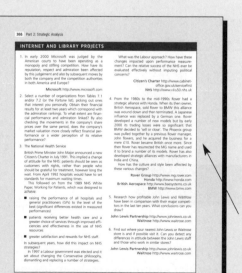

**Internet and Library Projects** – these more detailed questions and activities encourage you to further develop and build on your knowledge and understanding through online or library-based research and project work.

# Supplementary Resources

## Visit the companion website at www.cengage.co.uk

### For students

- Integrative web-based case that mirrors the major sections in the book and includes tasks to take you through the strategic management process
- Interactive multiple choice questions for each chapter to help test your learning
- Chapter overviews for each chapter that focus on the 'why' not the 'what' to help deepen your understanding
- Seven full length cases to allow more detailed study
- Links to useful company, news and other relevant sites
- Online glossary to explain key terms
- Student guide to analysing case studies
- Student guide to referencing your work correctly

### For lecturers

- Downloadable tutor notes
- Downloadable PowerPoint™ slides
- Case study library
- Guide to using case studies in your teaching
- Guide to the use of the web in your teaching

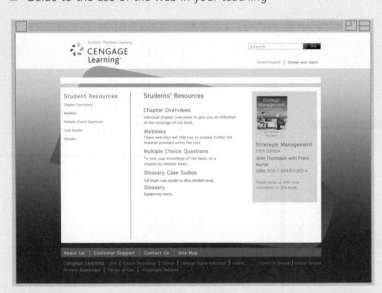

## ExamView® testbank

This testbank and test generator provides a huge amount of different types of questions, allowing lecturers to create online, paper and local area network (LAN) tests. This CD-based product is only available from your Cengage sales representative.

# Understanding Strategy and Strategic Management

Organizations, their strategies, their structures and the management of them become ever more complex. Among the reasons for this are the increasing turbulence and propensity to change in the business environment, and the tendency for multiproduct multinational organizations to become commonplace. Organizations need to know where they are, where they are going and how to manage the changes. Managers in these organizations need to know where their roles fit in relation to the whole and how they can contribute to strategic developments and changes. These are the issues addressed by a study of strategic management.

This first part is designed to provide a broad appreciation of strategic management and to develop the framework used in the book in order to:

■ outline the scope and complexity of the study area

■ provide an initial overview of some major contributors to the subject to illustrate what is meant by, and included in, strategic management, and to demonstrate that there is no single universally accepted approach

■ develop a framework which will provide a model for the structure and content of the book

■ explain the significance of a robust business model

■ examine what is meant by purpose, direction and objectives and consider how these might be set and used

■ help you think and act in a strategic way.

A number of key strategic issues and topics are raised in two reference supplements to Part One and then explored in greater depth in the following chapters.

Chapter 2, then, is followed by two useful supplements which readers are encouraged to use for reference purposes. The first supplement introduces a number of important strategic concepts which affect strategy creation and implementation in every organization, and which crop up in numerous places throughout the book. It concludes with an introduction to some of the important issues, dilemmas and challenges in strategy which affect many of the decisions that must be taken. It is the existence of these dilemmas that ensures there are no 'right answers' in the world of strategy. The second supplement outlines the important strategic analysis frameworks which are useful for exploring strategy in organizations, including those written up as case studies.

# Introducing the Strategy Process

## Learning objectives

Having read to the end of this chapter you should be able to:

- define strategic management and strategic change
- distinguish between corporate, competitive and functional strategies
- summarize strategic management in terms of three interrelated aspects – awareness, choice and implementation
- appreciate that there are five complementary perspectives of strategy – vision, plan, tactics, position and pattern
- clarify the three broad approaches to strategy creation, namely visionary ideas, planning and emergence
- show how strategy has military origins
- understand the place of strategy in small businesses, the public sector and non-profit organizations.

Strategies are means to ends. All organizations, large and small, profit-seeking and not-for-profit, private and public sector, have a purpose, which may or may not be articulated in the form of a mission and/or vision statement. Strategies relate to the pursuit of this purpose. Strategies must be created and implemented, and it is these issues which are addressed by our study of strategic management. This opening chapter begins by outlining how successful organizations manage their strategies, and what they achieve, before exploring the meaning of strategy in greater detail. It then continues with an explanation of the strategic management process in the context of the framework upon which this book is structured before explaining the different ways in which strategies are created. Next it describes how the subject of strategic management has developed in the last 30 years, before concluding with a brief consideration of the similarities and differences in strategic management in various types of organization.

## Minicase 1.1 The Low-price, No-frills Airlines   GB  Eur  US  Int

This opening case features the three best-known airlines in this sector of the industry. They have all been growing in recent years and their success has been earned at a time when the world's leading full-service carriers have all experienced problems. Their strategies may all be similar, but their stories, and the strategic leaders behind them, are quite different.

Herb Kelleher began Southwest Air in 1971 with a simple intention – 'fly people safely, cheaply and conveniently between Dallas, Houston and San Antonio' – three key cities in Texas. Kelleher set out to compete against coach and car travel rather than the other airlines. He had been a champion college athlete and a successful Texas lawyer before he started the airline when he was 40 years old. The idea for Southwest, however, had come from a client (and co-founder of the business) who spotted the gap in the market.

Southwest has prospered and grown to become the fifth largest carrier in the USA. After 30 successful years it served over 50 cities in 27 states and had some 2500 flights every day. Kelleher's strategy, competitive advantage and success has always been based on a number of factors:

- frequent and reliable departures
- relatively short journeys by American standards, now averaging 450 miles but with the average having increased as the airline has grown in size and destinations
- the choice of smaller airports nearer to city centres where relevant, in preference to international airports which are further away from the centre
- very low prices
- automated ticketing and direct bookings (without travel agents), and now using the Internet extensively
- limited *frills*, limited refreshments, no videos and just one class of seating – if airlines serve only soft drinks rather than coffee and tea (with the inevitable milk, sugar and stirrer) it is

easier to collect passenger rubbish and thus speed up cabin cleaning between flights

- no seat assignments – which encourages passengers to turn up early so they can be towards the front of the boarding line, which in turn means planes are likely to take off on time
- fast gate turnarounds, to maximize the time the planes are in the air
- a standardized fleet of Boeing 737s, to simplify maintenance.

Southwest is clearly America's leading short-distance, point-to-point carrier. Others have preceded it and others have joined the industry, but none of these has been able to make the equivalent impact. Southwest has won the US Department of Transport's coveted 'Triple Crown' award of best on-time record, best baggage handling and fewest customer complaints on several occasions. Every new route and destination is immediately popular and, as a result, Southwest has been consistently profitable for some 30 years, a unique record for an airline anywhere in the world.

Kelleher is a renowned 'people person'. Through profit-sharing schemes, employees own over 10 per cent of the company's stock, and he has made 'working in the airline industry an adventure'. Southwest is dynamic and responsive; employees accept empowerment and are motivated to work hard and deliver high levels of service consistently. Rules and regulations are minimized to allow staff the freedom to deal with issues as they arise. 'Ask employees what's important to them. Ask customers what's important to them. Then do it. It's that simple', says Kelleher. The frequent flyer programme, unusually, rewards passengers for the number of individual flights, not the miles flown.

But it is never that simple! Southwest is also renowned as 'one of the zaniest companies in history'. From the very beginning, Kelleher encouraged flight attendants to crack jokes during in-flight emergency briefings, but, at the same time, operate with very high safety standards. He was

▶

**Southwest Air** Air attendant © David Woo

determined that passengers would enjoy their flights. Some of the planes are decorated externally to reinforce the fun image. Three of them, promoting major sponsor Sea World, are flying killer whales; one is painted with the Texas flag; another is christened Arizona One, a spoof of Air Force One. Flight attendants have been known to hide in the overhead lockers as passengers come on board, startling them as they open up the lockers. Kelleher often appears in fancy dress for certain flights and special occasions. A special prize for the passenger with the biggest hole in his sock is quite typical.

Consequently, a sense of humour has become a key element in the recruitment process. During their training, employees are given a book with sections on jokes, games and songs – but they are all encouraged to develop an individual style. 'At Southwest we don't want clones – everyone is expected to colour outside the lines.' Kelleher is dedicated and focused and in possession of a strong ego. He is creative and innovative and he understands the contribution that people can make. He has always had the courage to be different. When he was introduced to an idea he appreciated the opportunity and activated it. Truly profit-orientated, he has been extremely successful in a dynamic and cruel industry, where many competing airlines have failed.

One of the largest and best-known European low-price, no-frills airlines is easyJet, begun in 1995 by a 28-year-old Greek entrepreneur, Stelios

Haji-Ioannou, the son of a wealthy shipping magnate. He intended to 'make flying in Europe affordable for more and more people'. Parodying British Airways' claim to be 'The World's Favourite Airline', easyJet now calls itself 'The Web's Favourite Airline'. Over 75 per cent of its bookings come via the Internet; the rest are direct over the telephone. There are no commissioned travel agency bookings, no tickets and no on-board meals. When passengers with a reservation check in at the airport, they are allocated a number, based on their time of check in, not when they prebooked, and this determines the order in which they board the aircraft. There are no seat reservations. easyJet's first hub airports in the UK were (relatively uncongested and quick turnaround) Luton and Liverpool; and destinations are concentrated in Scotland and continental Europe, including Athens, Barcelona, Geneva and Nice. All the aeroplanes are relatively new Boeing 737s, painted white and orange and featuring easyJet's telephone number on the side. The airline became profitable for the first time in 1998. More recently easyJet acquired Go, the no frills competitor set up by British Airways. This meant a new hub at Stansted, the UK base of rival Ryanair, and rapid expansion. Early problems in co-ordinating the operations of the two carriers affceted profitability.

Stelios had studied in the UK, at the London School of Economics and City University, and then worked for his father for a short while. He began his first business, Stelmar Tankers, in 1992. easyJet's strategy was modelled on Southwest Air, but Stelios claimed he had been inspired by Richard Branson and Virgin Atlantic (see Minicase 1.3). His approach to customers and people mirrors that of Branson. Commuting from Nice – his main home is in Monte Carlo – he flies on his own planes several times a week and talks to the passengers. A television 'docusoap' on easyJet which began in 1998 showed that Stelios was regularly present at Luton (his headquarters) and willing to help resolve passenger problems.

*I lead by example. I believe that people will do things if they see their boss doing exactly the same things … the best way to motivate a team is to convince them they're always under*

▶

*attack ... having an external enemy is the best way of focusing their mind on results, rather than fighting each other and becoming complacent ... I'm keen that important information is available to everybody in the company ... there are no secrets.*

The easyJet product is, in reality, a package of services, many subcontracted in. easyJet provides the planes and their crews, and markets and sells the flights. As a company, it is focused. Check-in and information services, snacks (for passengers to buy before they board the aeroplane), baggage handling and fleet maintenance are all bought in from specialists.

Stelios recruited Ray Webster, a senior executive from Air New Zealand, to be the chief executive of easyJet – and in 2002 he announced that he would relinquish the chairman's role so he could focus his energy and efforts on his other businesses. Sir Colin Chandler, who had been the strategic leader at defence giant Vickers, replaced him. easyJet has planes on order from both Boeing (more 737s) and Airbus Industrie; when the fleet comprises two different aircraft easyJet will have a different business model from that of Southwest Air and its main European rival, Ryanair.

Stelios is a serial entrepreneur and he has begun a number of other businesses since the lauch of easyJet. See Minicase 8.1. None of them has been consistently profitable though. They include:

- easyInternet café
- easyCar – low-cost car rental, mainly at airports
- easyValue – a price comparison site on the web
- easyMoney – an Internet bank
- easyCinema – a cut-price cinema seat business
- easy Pizza – pizza delivery service.

easyJet's main rival is Ryanair, which was started by the Ryan family in Dublin in 1985 as a direct rival to Aer Lingus. A full-service carrier, it failed to grow into a profitable business. Michael O'Leary, a tax accountant, joined the business in 1991 and he soon became the strategic leader. O'Leary went to America to learn about Southwest Air and re-launched Ryanair as a no-frills, low-cost carrier. Again he has only used Boeing 737s; and Ryanair always looks for airports with relatively low charges even if they are several miles outside the city they serve. For example, the one serving Brussels is 40 kms to the south of the city; the commute to Stockholm is 100 kms; and the one designated Copenhagen is actually over the border in Sweden. This provides a cost saving when compared with easyJet. Ryanair recently acquired Buzz, a rival low-cost carrier started by the Dutch airline KLM. Whereas Stelios retained most of the Go operations when he acquired that business, O'Leary has retained only certain Buzz routes and very few of the staff. Both Ryanair and easyJet carry over 20 million passengers each year. Ryanair is more profitable than easyJet and the various full-service carriers in Western Europe.

Michael O'Leary's very successful strategy is based on defining a rival-beating price for a route, undercutting easyJet wherever they compete for a route, and then making sure costs are driven down to allow that route to be profitable. 'Everything we do is designed to pass on lower fares.' Like easyJet most promotions feature low fares. Ryanair claim the first 70 per cent of seats on every flight are available at the two lowest fares – for later bookings the prices can rise substantially.

Ryanair is the cost leader in the European industry. O'Leary manages to keep the costs at two thirds of easyJet's, which means Ryanair's costs are 60 per cent of those incurred by UK holiday charter airlines and 50 per cent of those attributable to the leading full-service domestic carriers. O'Leary achieves savings in a number of ways, in particular:

- Buying aircraft when the manufacturers are experiencing trading problems, thus driving down the price
- Selling costs – there are only direct Internet sales. Outlawing travel agents can mean a saving of up to 15 per cent
- Passenger services provided – there are no tickets in the normal sense and no air bridges

– passengers have to walk out to the aircraft. There is a charge for any soft drinks served on board

- Crew costs – pay rates are lower than rivals, and there are just three cabin crew on every flight, low for an aircraft of this size: however, they are not there to serve food and drinks but to look after passenger safety

- Ground handling – in part by not worrying how far away from cities airports are, and obtaining huge discounts by using airports which are chasing business

- Seat density – Ryanair packs 15 per cent more passengers in its Boeings

- Ryanair designs its own advertisements, ignoring specialist agencies. One irreverent ad featured the Pope and the phrase *Psst ... want to know the 4th secret of Fatima* which upset the Catholic Church but earned a huge amount of free publicity. By allowing other brands to be advertised on the outside of its planes Ryanair earns additional revenue.

By striking alliances with local hotels and transport providers (such as car hire firms) Ryanair earns commissions, which constitute some 15 per cent of its net profits.

There are other less obvious reductions in the services provided by the no-frills airlines. Ryanair, for example, only have a relatively small customer services activity. The low-cost model means they are likely to be less sympathetic than the full-service carriers if passengers miss their flight or the flight has to be cancelled.

The no-frills carriers have certainly had a major impact upon the airline industry and their success has in part been at the expense of the full-service carriers, such as British Airways in the UK, who have had to respond. There is a proportion of passengers who will always opt for the lowest price; others will never compromise on service. In-between people have a choice to make, and BA for one is working hard to trim its costs and reduce its fares in order to narrow the price gap.

**Task**

This Minicase introduces a number of important issues. Amongst them are:

- New competitors can dramatically change an industry
- Rivals compete to establish and maintain a competitive edge
- The role of a strategic leader is critical
- The Internet has offered new strategic opportunities.

Either think about or discuss with colleagues what you think the key messages are in relation to these issues.

The quotations from Stelios Haji-Ioannou are extracted from: Maitland, A (1998) No frills and lots of feedback, *Financial Times*, 17 September.

**easyJet** http://www.easyjet.com
**Southwest Airlines** http://www.southwest.com
**Ryanair** http://www.ryanair .com
Photographer: Charles Falk

## 1.1 Strategy explained

*The flame of competition has changed from smokey yellow to intense white heat. For companies to survive and prosper they will have to have a vision, a mission and strategy. They will pursue the action arising from that strategy with entrepreneurial skill and total dedication and commitment to win.*

Peter B Ellwood, Chief Executive, Lloyds TSB Group

*Far too many companies either have no goals at all, other than cost reduction, or their boss hides them in his head. There's no hope for companies in Britain unless more top managements accept the need for a widely communicated set of clear objectives.*

Peter Beck, ex-Chairman, The Strategic Planning Society, 1987

### 1.1.1 Introducing strategy

At their simplest, strategies help to explain the things that managers and organizations do. These actions or activities are designed and carried out in order to fulfil certain designated purposes, some of them short term in nature, others longer term. The organization has a direction and broad purpose, which should always be clear, articulated and understood, and which sometimes will be summarized in the form of a mission statement. More specific **milestones** and targets (**objectives**) can help to guide specific actions and measure progress.

**Strategies, then, are means to ends.**

They are relevant for the organization as a whole, and for the individual businesses and/or functions that comprise the organization. They are created and changed in a variety of ways. They have, however, one common feature: they all have life cycles and need changing, either marginally or dramatically, at certain times.

While strategic management incorporates major changes of direction for the whole business, such as **diversification** and growth overseas, it also involves smaller changes in strategies for individual products and services and in particular functions such as marketing and operations. Decisions by managers in relation to their particular areas of product or functional responsibility have a strategic impact and contribute to strategic change.

**To some extent all managers are strategy-makers.**

Strategic management is a complex and fascinating subject with straightforward underlying principles but no 'right answers'. **Strategy** is about issues and perspectives on problems – there is no single, prescriptive doctrine which satisfies everyone's views.

Companies succeed if their strategies are appropriate for the circumstances they face, feasible in respect of their resources, skills and capabilities, and desirable to their important **stakeholders** – those individuals and groups, both internal and external, who have a stake in and an influence over the business. Simply, strategy is fundamentally about a fit between the organization's resources and the markets it targets – plus, of course, the ability to sustain fit over time and in changing circumstances.

Companies fail when their strategies fail to meet the expectations of these stakeholders or produce outcomes which are undesirable to them. To succeed long term, companies must compete effectively and outperform their rivals in a dynamic, and often turbulent, environment. To accomplish this they must find suitable ways for creating and **adding value** for their customers. A **culture** of internal co-operation and customer orientation, together with a willingness to learn, adapt and change, is ideal. Alliances and good working relationships with suppliers, distributors and customers are often critically important as well.

Morrison and Lee (1979) concluded that successful companies seem to be distinguished from their less successful competitors by a common pattern of management practices:

- First, they identify more effectively than their competitors the key success factors inherent in the economics of each business. For example in the airline industry, with its high fixed costs and relatively inflexible route allocations, a high load factor is critical to success. It is important, though, that high load factors are not at the expense of healthy sales of more expensive seats, and this requires skilful marketing.

WH Smith, desiring growth beyond the scope offered from its (then) current business lines (wholesaling and retailing newspapers and magazines, stationery, books and sounds), diversified into do-it-yourself with a chain of Do-It-All stores, introduced travel agencies into a number of its existing stores and acquired related interests in Canada and America. Travel was later divested, along with investments in cable television, to enable greater concentration on sounds, videos and consumer and office stationery. Important acquisitions included the Our Price and Virgin music stores and the Waterstone's chain of specialist booksellers. Do-It-All became a joint venture with Boots, but it struggled to be profitable with strong competition from B & Q and Texas. It was acquired by Sainsbury's in the mid-1990s. In 1996 WH Smith divested its office stationery businesses. Later in the 1990s both Waterstone's and Our Price were also divested, and the book publisher, Hodder Headline, was acquired. This has now been sold again. These are all examples of corporate strategic change.

In October 1995 WH Smith, responding to the willingness of the leading supermarket chains to sell newspapers, magazines and a carefully selected range of books – with discounted prices for current bestsellers – began to discount books from a number of publishers. This was an important change of competitive strategy as, previously, Smiths had been a staunch supporter of the Net Book Agreement. This long-standing agreement between publishers and booksellers was designed to prevent intense price competition.

**WH Smith** http://www.whsmith.co.uk

The Burton Group sold the last of its manufacturing interests in 1988. Once one of the leading men's clothing manufacturers in Europe the group (renamed Arcadia), by a series of related acquisitions and divestments, became essentially a major retailer of fashion goods for both men and women. In recent years Burton acquired – and later divested – Debenham's. Arcadia is now owned by the entrepreneur and specialist in corporate turnarounds, Philip Green.

**Arcadia (Burton Group)** http://www.arcadia.co.uk

UK building societies, restrained by legislation until the mid-1980s, expanded their financial services to include current accounts with cheque books and cash-dispensing machines – to compete more aggressively with the high-street banks – and diversified into such linked activities as estate agencies and insurance. Mergers took place between, for example, the Halifax and Leeds Permanent societies and Abbey National and National & Provincial, to strengthen their positions as diversified financial institutions. Moreover, the largest ones (notably Abbey National and the Halifax) have given up their mutual status and become quoted companies. Halifax has now merged with Bank of Scotland and Abbey has been bought by the Spanish bank, Santander.

Some time later a number of the leading supermarket groups opted to diversify into financial services, utilizing their customer databases and information for carefully targeted marketing. In a quite different (and more evolutionary way) the decision by high-street banks to open on Saturdays for a limited range of services was strategic change. Here the banks were copying the building societies and reacting to increased competition.

**Abbey National** http://www.abbeynational.co.uk
**Halifax** http://www.halifax.co.uk

National Bus Company was privatized during the mid-1980s, mostly by splitting it up into small local or regional companies which were then bought out by their existing management teams. The sector has since become more concentrated as certain growth-orientated operators such as Stagecoach and First Bus (a name change from Badgerline) have bought out other smaller companies – following a mixed strategy of organic growth and acquisition. One major challenge for these aggressive companies has been to try and avoid intervention from the UK regulatory authorities, concerned with competition in the industry. Having acquired a number of local bus franchises in the UK, Stagecoach has also expanded overseas and bought a minority shareholding (49 per cent) in Virgin Rail.

**Stagecoach** http://www.stagecoachholdings.com

Fourth is the ability to manage *strategic change*, both continuous, gradual, incremental changes and more dramatic, discontinuous changes. Innovation and change concern the strategy process in an organization.

Sound implementation and innovation should enable an organization to thrive and prosper in a dynamic, global environment, but in turn they depend on competencies in strategic awareness and learning. Organizations must understand the strategic value of the resources that they employ and deploy, and how they can be used to satisfy the needs and expectations of customers and other stakeholders while outperforming competitors.

*Strategy is about actions, not plans – specifically the commitment of resources to achieving strategic ends … concrete steps that immediately affect people's lives, not abstract intentions.*

Andrew S Grove, CEO, Intel

Many of these points were evident in Minicase 1.1, The Low-price, No-frills Airlines, which showed that:

- newcomers can change an industry – by being creative, innovative and different
- new competitors can, and will, find ways of breaking down apparent barriers to entry
- companies need to find some clear and distinct competitive advantage, something which is both attractive to customers and profitable
- this advantage will come from what organizations do: their distinctive competencies and capabilities
- charismatic and visible strategic leaders often have a major impact on the choice and implementation of key strategies
- people are critically important if strategies are to be implemented effectively
- the Internet is becoming increasingly important; and
- business can be fun!

It is, however, also important to realize that in many organizations certain parts may be 'world class' and highly profitable while other businesses are not. Good practices in the strong businesses can be discerned, transferred and learned, but this may not be enough. Some industries and competitive environments are simply less friendly and premium profits are unlikely. The real danger occurs if the weaker businesses threaten to bring down the strong ones that are forced to subsidize them. It is an irony that companies in real difficulty, possibly through strategic weaknesses, need to turn in an excellent performance if they are to survive.

Finally, it must be realized that past and current success is no guarantee of success in the future. Companies are not guaranteed, or entitled to, continued prosperity. They must adapt and change in a dynamic environment. Many fail to do this, for all sorts of reasons, and disappear. Some close down; others are acquired. Minicase 1.2, Marks and Spencer, shows how this previously outstanding company has lost its way in recent years. The points are also brought out in Minicase 1.4, McDonald's, at the end of this chapter.

In summary, it is no longer adequate for organizations to have strong, professional management – they also need good change management. What works effectively today may not be appropriate tomorrow. Organizations need new visions for the future and

## Minicase 1.2  Marks and Spencer plc    (GB)

Marks and Spencer (M&S) is a well-known and revered high-street retailer in the UK. The early growth of M&S was built around clothing, and its reputation owes much to the popularity of its underwear! M&S introduced us to lycra and Y-fronts. It built a second reputation for foods, pioneering chilled fresh varieties and bringing the avocado pear to the UK mass market. Always gradually, other ranges such as cosmetics, homewear, gifts and furniture have been added systematically. A home-delivery service for furniture has been expanded to include other items. Every shopping centre developer wants M&S to open a store, as they always attract customers.

The original foundations of the business lay with a young, Jewish immigrant and his Leeds market stall. Michael Marks had a poor grasp of English, a clear disadvantage for a trader in a noisy street market! Opportunistically, he turned his disadvantage into a strength. He had a sign on his stall: *Don't Ask The Price – It's a Penny*, and for a penny he provided the widest range and best-quality items he could find. This philosophy of *value for money* has pervaded through the generations and been sustained with innovation and change – but the focus on value has never been lost. The market stall led to a store, and then to stores on most high streets in Britain. The Spencer in the name came from Marks' first business partner, an accountant. However the Marks family became related to the Sieff family through marriage, and it is these two families together who have controlled the business through most of its history. Indeed Simon Marks (strategic leader from 1916 to 1964 and the man who really established and cemented in place Marks and Spencer's high street dominance), and his successor Marcus Sieff, have both been described as 'retail genius'.

The strategy of M&S, then, is concerned with diversification of their product ranges within these broad product groups, but at the same time seeking to specialize where their own St Michael label could be used effectively. All M&S products have traditionally carried the M&S name and quite often the St Michael brand. At the beginning of the new millennium a decision was made to reduce the emphasis on using the St Michael brand name and emphasize the company name more prominently. M&S seeks to innovate whilst upgrading and adding value to its existing ranges. Over the years, M&S has found that many of its long-established stores in town and city centres are simply too small. An expansion programme has therefore developed along several lines. Adjacent units have been acquired when practical and new larger stores created, especially in new out-of-town shopping centres; if land has been available, buildings have been extended; and new sales floors have been opened up by converting stockrooms and moving stock to outside warehouses. This brings its own logistics problems. Satellite stores – smaller branches some distance away from the main branch – have been opened in certain towns. These satellites typically carry complete ranges – it might be men's fashions, ladies' clothes or children's items. The choice depends on the square footage available and the local prospects for particular lines. In a similar vein, in towns considered too small to support a full branch, specialist stores, perhaps just for food, have been opened. The selection of products within the whole M&S range varies between stores.

Other strategic changes are:

- Constant improvements in displays, partly to present products better and also to get more items into the stores. 'Sales per square foot' is a vital measure of success.

- Electronic point-of-sale (EPOS). Information technology has been harnessed to improve productivity and to enable M&S to respond more quickly to market changes, particularly relevant for fashion items. Thanks in part to technology, M&S staff costs as a percentage of their turnover are less than those of many competitors, but the quality of service has remained high.

- The development of support financial services, such as unit trusts, building upon the success

▶

of the M&S Chargecard, the third most popular credit card in the UK. The business has now been sold.

■ International growth in, for example, France, Belgium, Canada, the US and Hong Kong. The development has been gradual, with one of the objectives being to introduce new types of competition. Some mistakes have been made as part of the learning process, and sales in some countries have been disappointing, but the risks have been contained in order not to threaten the UK interests. Recently there have been some withdrawals and attempted withdrawals – M&S tried but failed to sell the Kings supermarket chain it owns in America, for example.

In the 1930s M&S pioneered a new form of inventory control when it designed perforated tags in two identical halves. Half was torn off at the point-of-sale, dropped in a box and then sent to the Baker Street (London) head office, where it was used to direct store replenishment. Over time this enabled M&S to introduce sophisticated replenishment from out-of-town warehouses and reduce the in-store stockrooms in favour of more direct selling space.

M&S possesses a number of identifiable strategic resources which have been instrumental in meeting customer key success factors, and thereby providing long-term profitable returns for shareholders. They include:

| | |
|---|---|
| *Physical resources* | The wide range of value-for-money, own-brand products |
| | The sites and store displays |
| *Intangible resources* | Image and reputation |
| | Staff knowledge, expertise and commitment to service |
| *Capabilities/processes* | Supply-chain management. |

While there have been, and continue to be, strategic changes, the fundamental principles or values upon which the business grew and prospered have remained constant until the last few years. These are:

■ high-quality, dependable products, styled conservatively and offering good value for money
■ good relations with employees, customers, suppliers and other stakeholders
■ simple operations
■ comfortable stores
■ financial prudence (most properties, for example, are freehold – they have not been sold and leased back to fund the expansion).

The foundation for the unique (St Michael) products and competitive prices was the M&S system of supply-chain relationships, a considerable proportion of these being with UK manufacturers for much of its history. In recent years M&S has, somewhat controversially, included more and more goods sourced overseas, sometimes for particular quality issues, but mostly for lower costs. In general, where they have been successful, the arrangements with suppliers have been long term and non-contractual. They are based on mutual trust and common understanding. M&S is actively involved in product specification, input management (to their suppliers), quality control and production scheduling. M&S is frequently the supplier's most important customer. Why has it worked so effectively? The M&S reputation for fair dealing – with its suppliers, customers and employees – has for many years been seen as too valuable to put at risk.

But, at the end of the 1990s, this long-established business was suffering declines in sales and profits. Critics argued that too many product ranges were no longer the winners that people associated with the company, and its management needed strengthening at all levels. Interestingly, this setback occurred in the decade when the company had, for the first time in its history, a chief executive who was not a descendant of one of the Marks or Sieff families.

Simply, Marks and Spencer had:

- 'Taken its eye off' its customers and become over-reliant on its image and reputation
- Become too reliant on (typically UK-based) suppliers whose costs were relatively uncompetitive in global terms and at the same time
- Allowed margins to increase gradually, tarnishing the long-standing value for money image
- Lost some of the fashion element in its key clothing ranges.

Peter Drucker (1985) had earlier summarized M&S as

*probably more entrepreneurial and innovative than any other company in Western Europe these last fifty years … may have had a greater impact on the British economy, and even on British society, than any other change agent in Britain, and arguably more than government or laws.*

Was it conceivable that this visible and successful business was under real threat for the first time? Clara Freeman (2000), at that time an M&S executive, admitted that M&S

*lost the pace, lost the focus … no-one saw it coming. It was the classic management story – everything is going swimmingly and you don't tinker with a successful formula. After sales and profits declined, M&S put the magnifying lens on the business and asked what was wrong. Staff and customers told us that the quality was not as consistent as it used to be, and the service needs to be better than it is.*

In 1999 the current Chairman and Chief Executive, Richard Greenbury, announced he would retire early and, after a very visible and acrimonious internal wrangle, a new Chief Executive (Peter Salsbury) was appointed from inside the business. Later, a new Executive Chairman, Luc Vandevelde, previously the head of a major French supermarket chain, was recruited. Several ranges were quickly revamped and successful stock trials accelerated. M&S began to use more demographic and customer data to determine the product ranges for each store – previously stores of roughly the same size had carried similar ranges, regardless of their location. Sales did not pick up as rapidly as had been hoped, and rumours of possible takeover bids appeared in the press. Salsbury resigned as Chief Executive, to be replaced by Roger Holmes, recruited from Kingfisher.

Under Holmes, product ranges were changed again. Clothing is designed for people who prefer classic styles and for those who prefer the latest fashions. Lesiure clothing has become more prominent. At the same time the branded Per Una range, designed and sourced by George Davies, the entrepreneur responsible for the growth of the Next chain and the introduction of the George clothing range to Asda, has been added. David Beckham endorses a range of children's clothing. A number of stores have been sold and leased back to raise cash. A new format for furniture and furnishings, designed by Victor Radice, recruited from Selfridges, was trialled. More and more products are sourced overseas. Staffing levels are tighter than in the past. Sales and profits – and the share price – all improved but not dramatically. Holmes vowed that the company would never be complacent again.

In 2004 the entrepreneur Philip Green (owner of Arcadia and Bhs – Minicase 10.4) made a bid for the company, but the M&S Board rejected his offer. Some institutional shareholders were willing to accept his offer. The Board was provoked, however, to make changes. Vandevelde left, along with Holmes and Radice. The new CEO is Stuart Rose, who had previously been responsible for the turnaround at Arcadia before its sale to Philip Green. Radice's new home store format was dropped and Rose negotiated to sell M&S' financial services business.

## References

Drucker, PF (1985) *Innovation and Entrepreneurship*, Heinemann.

Freeman, C (2000) Interview, *Management Today*, January.

◀

the capability to deliver them. They require open communications and a team approach, a willingness to listen and respond to customers, the delegation of real **power**, the ability to share learning across the organization and the ability to use culture to convey aims and values. Change is seen as an opportunity, not a threat. This sometimes implies an entrepreneurial **strategic leader**. It invariably requires flexibility and innovation, which implies intrapreneurial managers who accept responsibility for driving the change initiatives. Typically such managers will exhibit the following skills and attributes:

- A tolerance of calculated risks
- A combination of leadership, general management and financial skills
- Planning, time and project management skills
- Receptiveness to innovation
- A commitment to continuous learning
- A willingness to delegate
- Motivated by factors other than financial gain
- Self-confident, resilient and persevering
- Good communication skills.

### 1.1.3 Five perspectives on strategy

More than anyone else, Henry Mintzberg has been responsible for drawing attention to alternative views and perspectives on strategy, all of them legitimate. Mintzberg *et al.* (1998) provide an excellent summary of his work on this topic.

The top oval in Figure 1.1 suggests that strategies can be seen in a **visionary** context. Here it is implied that strategy can be considered as a clear strategic purpose, intent and direction for the organization, but without the detail worked out. In a dynamic **environment**, managers would then determine more detailed and specific strategies in 'real time' rather than exclusively in advance. However, they would always have a framework of direction to guide their decision-making and help them to determine what is appropriate. In addition, some strategies come from a visionary input from an entrepreneurial manager, or strategic leader, who spots an opportunity and is minded to act on it.

This contrasts with some people's thinking that strategy and *planning* are synonymous. Certainly, as we shall see later in this chapter, **strategic planning** has a crucial role in **strategy creation**, but it does not fully explain how strategies are changed. Both the visionary and planning perspective are concerned with thinking ahead as far as it might be sensible to think and **plan**. While the *tactical* view is also about the future, it is really

**Figure 1.1** Five views of strategy

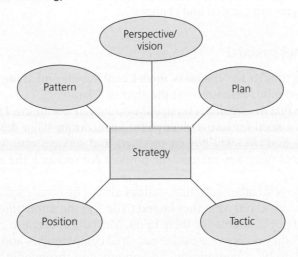

about the immediate future. The assumption being made here is that competitors in a dynamic market will constantly adopt new ploys in an attempt to steal a short-term gain or advantage. Their **tactics** may be easily copied, but there can be some temporary advantage when rivals are caught by surprise and need time to react.

Metaphorically, we can relate these ideas to a game of competitive football. There will be a broad purpose concerned with finishing at a certain level in a league or winning a cup competition, and this will influence the fundamental approach to every game. Sometimes a win would be seen as essential; on other occasions a 'clean sheet' would be more desirable or a draw could be perfectly satisfactory. From this, more detailed game plans will be devised for every match. But, inevitably, 'the best laid schemes o' mice and men gang aft a gley'. Early goals by the opposition can imply a setback and demand that plans are quickly revised and tactics changed. This is always possible at half-time, but during the match the team will have to rely on shouted instructions from the touchline and leadership from the team captain as play continues. Individual players will always be allowed some freedom of movement and the opportunity to show off their particular skills. New tactics will emerge as players regroup and adapt to the circumstances, but quite often games will be turned around by the individual vision, inspiration and brilliance of key players.

These three views all concern the future and imply change; the notion of *position* is akin to the idea of freezing time momentarily. It relates to strategic fit and the organization's competitive position at the present time. It is, in effect, a statement of what is happening; and it can be vital for 'taking stock', realizing and clarifying a situation so that future changes are based on clear knowledge rather than assumption.

Of course, organizations come to their present position as a result of decisions taken previously; plans have been implemented and tactics adjusted as events have unfolded. It is again crucial to analyse and understand this evolving *pattern*, appreciating just what has happened, why and how. This can be a valuable foundation for future decisions, plans and actions but, although history can be a guide to the future, rarely in strategy are events repeated without some amendment. The importance of clarifying the pattern from the various decisions and changes also explains why strategy has irreverently been described as a 'series of, mindless, random events, rationalized in retrospect'!

Our understanding of these alternative perspectives will be strengthened when we look at how strategies are created and changed.

### 1.1.4 The business model

This brief introduction to the **business model** explains the meaning of the term; the subject is developed more extensively at the start of Chapter 2.

When we argue that an organization needs a sound, or a winning, business model we mean that there is a need for a very clear picture concerning what the organization is – and what it isn't – and who will buy its products and services and why. The business model thus embraces three key themes: the product (or service); the market; the 'compelling reason to buy'.

It is important to remember here that strategy always involves choices. Organizations have to make decisions about what they intend to do – at the same time ruling out things it is less appropriate or desirable for them to do. Maybe it is because competition is too intense; or perhaps they do not possess the required competencies and capabilities. This picture then needs to be communicated and understood throughout the organization. Moreover, the model – and the strategies which underpin it – need to be reviewed constantly. The picture should embrace the business as it is now, and how it will be in the future – where and how it will change and grow.

One interesting example of choice and timing is the high technology start-up which offered its Internet systems to BT, whose engineers were truly enthusiastic about the prospects. However, in BT it was the marketing and sales people who bought new systems and they felt the product was too far ahead of its time, and, as a consequence, they would be unable to sell it to BT customers. As a result it took 18 months for the market to catch up with the technology.

Minicase 1.1 provides an ideal example of a business model – that for the low-cost, no-frills airline. This model may have been pioneered by Southwest Air but it has been copied extensively by others, including easyJet and Ryanair. It is important to realize that the business models for these two competitors, whilst similar, are different. Ryanair looks to be low cost in every activity whilst easyJet chooses to incur some higher costs to offer a slightly different service. In particular easyJet opts for main airports in the cities it flies to, whilst Ryanair invariably chooses the cheapest available in the vicinity. Passengers are likely to have to travel further to catch their flights. In addition, easyJet broke ranks with the basic model when it decided to use more than one plane, adding Airbuses to its Boeing fleet.

The fundamental underpinning to the model is a low-cost culture with a constant search for savings to allow ever-lower prices, but without reducing passenger safety. This demands that only those aspects of the service that are seen as essential or important are included; others that are offered by the traditional full-service airlines are dropped. The market is anyone – business, holiday or general passengers – who wants low prices and will trade off certain aspects of service to get them.

The model then has to be delivered and implemented; and this is where we come down to the operational details that support the model. The choice of a single type of aircraft and the selection of fringe airports are typical actions that make up the strategy to deliver the model.

By contrast, Manchester United is far more than a successful football club. It is a collection of diversified but related activities that can be associated with a distinctive brand – a brand which signifies success, such that association with it automatically implies being part of something that is successful. It reflects high **quality** – and consequently customers expect to have to pay premium prices to buy this association. The 'core market' might be the 60,000 plus fans who turn up at Old Trafford for Premier League matches, but there are many more people all round the world who are interested in having some part of this success story. In Porter terminology, Manchester United is very clearly differentiated – and very profitable.

More examples are provided in Chapter 2.

Drawing upon this introduction to the business model we can restate strategy as a set of four visions or articulated pictures – for:

- The businesses and industries the organization should be in – its corporate strategy
- How it will compete in each one in its search for advantage – which takes in its targeted customers
- How every activity which supports these strategies can be linked effectively to create synergy and avoid fragmentation
- How and when to change strategies.

It will be appreciated that all of these support the essential purpose of the organization.

### 1.1.5 Functional, competitive and corporate strategies

Figure 1.2 reflects that there are three distinct perspectives of strategic analysis:

1. The strategic environment
2. The competing organization
3. The individual strategist.

The diagram summarizes three distinct, but interrelated and interdependent, levels of strategy: corporate (the whole organization), competitive (the distinct strategy for each constituent business, product or service in the organization) and functional (the activities which underpin the competitive strategies).

**Figure 1.2** Levels of strategy

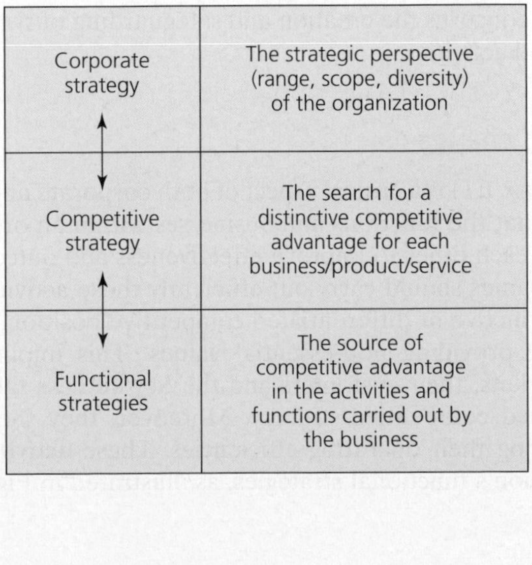

| | |
|---|---|
| Corporate strategy ↕ | The strategic perspective (range, scope, diversity) of the organization |
| Competitive strategy ↕ | The search for a distinctive competitive advantage for each business/product/service |
| Functional strategies | The source of competitive advantage in the activities and functions carried out by the business |

Simply, most organizations choose to produce one or more related or unrelated products or services for one or more markets or market segments. Consequently, the organization should be structured to encompass this range of product markets or service markets. As the number and diversity of products increases the structure is likely to be centred on divisions which are sometimes referred to as **strategic business units** (SBUs). Such SBUs are responsible individually for developing, manufacturing and marketing their own product or group of products. Each SBU will therefore have a strategy, which Porter (1980) calls a **competitive strategy**. Competitive strategy is concerned with 'creating and maintaining a competitive advantage in each and every area of business' (Porter, 1980). It can be achieved through any one function, although it is likely to be achieved through a unique and distinctive combination of functional activities. For each functional area of the business, such as production, marketing and human resources, the company will have a functional strategy. It is important that **functional strategies** are designed and managed in a co-ordinated way so that they interrelate with each other and at the same time collectively allow the competitive strategy to be implemented properly.

Successful competitive and functional strategies add value in ways which are perceived to be important by the company's stakeholders, especially its customers, and which help to distinguish the company from its competitors. Adding value is explained and discussed further in the supplement to Part One. Mathur and Kenyon (1998) reinforce these points. They contend that **competitive advantage** is fundamentally about the positioning and fit of an organization in its industry or market, and that success is based on distinct differences and sound cost management.

**Corporate strategy**, essentially and simply, is deciding what businesses the organization should be in and how the overall group of activities should be structured and managed. It has been described by Porter as 'the overall plan for a diversified business', although it is perfectly acceptable for a business to elect to stay focused on only one product or service range. This does happen in many companies, especially small businesses. In this case the corporate and competitive strategies are synonymous. Corporate strategy for a multibusiness group is concerned with maintaining or improving overall growth and **profit** performance through **acquisition**, organic investment (internally funded growth), **divestment** and closure. The term strategic perspective is often used to describe the range and diversity of business activities, in other words the corporate strategy. Each business activity then has a competitive position or strategy. The management of corporate strategy concerns the creation and safeguarding of *synergies* from the portfolio of businesses and activities.

### 1.1.6 Synergy and change

Synergy (defined in Box 1.1) is a critical aspect of both corporate and competitive strategies. It is important that the functions and businesses within an organization work collectively and support each other to improve effectiveness and outcomes.

At all times, companies should carry out efficiently those activities which are essential for creating a distinctive or differentiated competitive position, and avoid incurring unnecessary costs by providing non-essential values. This implies that they clearly understand their markets, their customers and the **key success factors** that they must meet, i.e. their defined competitive strategy. Moreover, they should constantly seek improvement by driving their operating efficiencies. These **activities** will be encapsulated in the organization's functional strategies, as illustrated in Figure 1.3.

**Figure 1.3** Strategic success through complementary activities

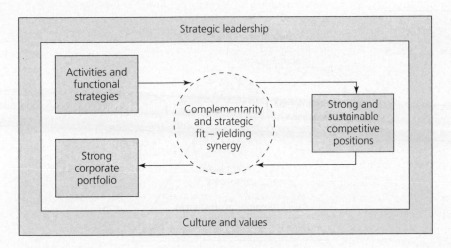

Figure 1.3 highlights that these functional strategies must fit a defined, clear competitive strategic position and complement each other to achieve internal synergy. Where they fail to complement each other the company's competitive position will inevitably be weakened. The outcome will be a strong competitive position which can only be sustained by innovation and improvement, and sometimes by the move to a new competitive **paradigm**. Managing these changes effectively is very dependent upon the style and approach of the strategic leader and the culture and values of the organization. Michael Porter (1996) has argued along similar lines.

It is important to remember, though, that people are often naturally competitive and their competitive energy should be directed against external rivals rather than members of their own organization. Carefully managed, internal competition for scarce resources can, of course, sharpen managerial skills.

## 1.2   Strategic management

### 1.2.1  The strategic management process

*All newly appointed chief executives should ask five key questions:*

- *What are the basic goals of the company?*
- *What is the strategy for achieving these goals?*
- *What are the fundamental issues facing the company?*
- *What is its culture?*
- *And is the company organized in a way to support the goals, issues and culture?*

Bob Bauman, ex-chief executive of SmithKline Beecham

*When Sir Ian MacGregor took over the ailing British Steel Corporation he met each senior executive face-to-face and asked him to justify the existence of his part of the organization. Each one was given a maximum of ten minutes.*

**Figure 1.4** Strategic management

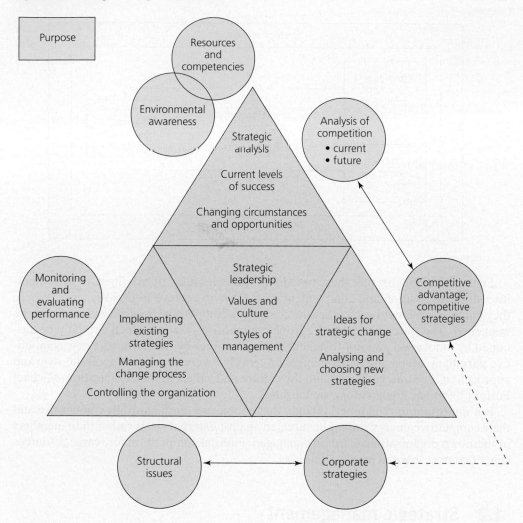

Traditionally, courses in strategic management have been built around three important elements:

■ strategic *analysis*
■ strategy *creation and choice*
■ strategy *implementation*.

These three elements are shown in Figure 1.4, together with the key aspects of strategy that relate to them.

In this book, however, we typically use the term 'strategic awareness' to embrace the analysis of the current situation and an assessment of the routes forward that are available, and 'strategic change' to reflect the selection of the route to follow and its implementation. All within the overall purpose of the organization.

Strategic management, then, involves awareness of how successful and strong the organization and its strategies are, and of how circumstances are changing. At any time, previously sound products, services and strategies are likely to be in decline, or threatened by competition. As this happens, new 'windows of opportunity' are opening for the vigilant and proactive companies.

New strategies, which may be changes to the corporate portfolio or changes at the competitive level, must be created. Sometimes these strategic ideas will emerge from formal planning processes; at other times, and particularly in the case of functional and competitive strategies, changes will emerge as managers throughout the organization try out new ideas.

The actual strategies being pursued at any time reflect the organization's strategy content, and the important issues are:

■ the ability of the organization to add value in meaningful ways, which exploit organizational resources to achieve synergy, and at the same time

■ satisfy the needs of the organization's major stakeholders, particularly its shareholders and customers.

The selection of new strategies must take account of these criteria.

Existing and new strategies must be implemented. A strategy is only useful when it has been implemented, and hence the organization must have an appropriate structure, clear and contributory functional strategies and systems which ensure that the organization behaves in a cohesive rather than a fragmented way. The larger or more diverse the organization becomes, the more likely it is that this becomes a problem. In multiproduct, **multinational** organizations with considerable interdependence between the products or services and between subsidiaries, for example, divisions may become competitive with each other and not pull together.

The processes involved in designing and carrying through any changes must be managed, monitored and controlled.

These process themes can be captured in relevant frameworks for studying strategy, such as the one featured in Figure 1.5 (a), which all tend to follow a pattern:

**Figure 1.5(a)** Strategic management: awareness and change

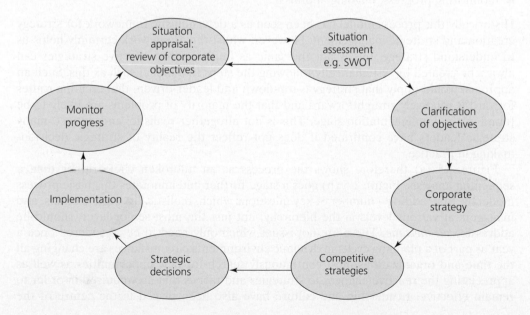

**Figure 1.5(b)** Strategic management:awareness and change

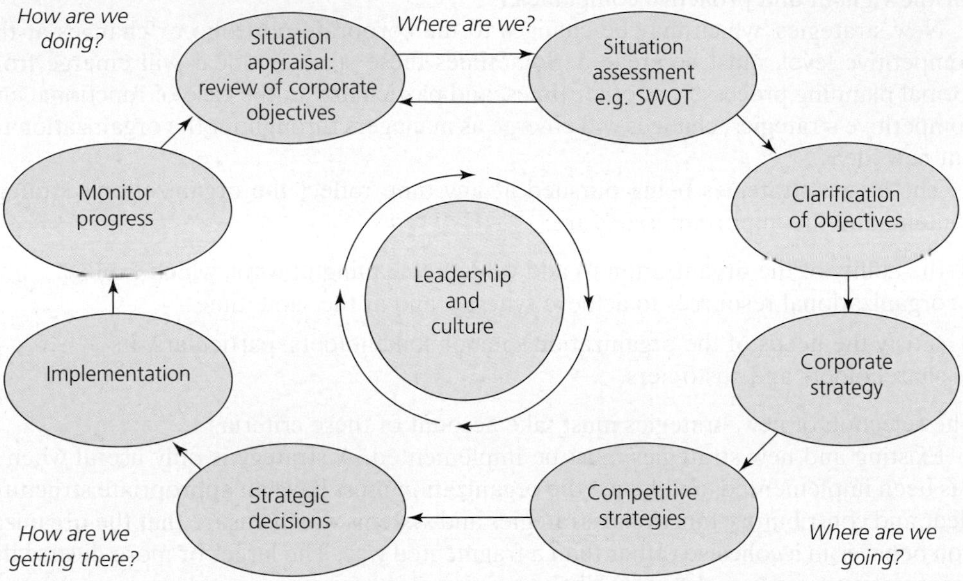

- appraisal of the current situation and current strategies, invariably using a SWOT (strengths, weaknesses, opportunities and threats) analysis, which itself is likely to be informed by a number of other external and internal analysis frameworks
- determination of desirable changes to objectives and/or strategies – at all levels, corporate, competitive, functional
- a search for, and choice of, suitable courses of action
- implementation of the changes
- monitoring progress; ongoing appraisal.

Historically this process model has been seen as a deterministic framework for strategy creation and strategic management. However, whilst this framework certainly helps us to understand strategy, this is not the same as implying that effective strategies can always be created by systematically following the steps in a model such as this. Such an approach would imply that strategy is top-down and leader-driven, that creating routes forward is relatively straightforward and that the majority of problems are likely to be found at the implementation stage. This is not altogether realistic; and, in fact, many strategic leaders have confirmed it does not reflect the reality of strategic decision-making in practice.

Figure 1.5 (a) therefore shows the process as an unbroken circle rather than a sequential analysis. Figure 1.5 (b) goes a stage further and annotates this basic process model by, first, adding a number of key questions which, realistically, organizations, and managers at various levels in the hierarchy, not just the most senior layer, should be addressing *all the time*. These are not issues which only need to be considered once a year as part of a planning cycle; in dynamic environments circumstances are changing all the time and organizations must continuously search for new opportunities as well as appreciating the reactive changes to strategies and tactics that are required in order to remain effective. Leadership and culture have also been placed in the centre of the diagram, illustrating their critical impact on strategic decision making and strategic performance. Arguably, strategy and strategic change in organizations cannot be understood without some understanding of the contribution of the strategic leader and the way in which the culture acts either as stimulus or constraint on the necessary changes.

The way that an organization is structured into divisions and/or functions, and the amount of authority delegated to individual managers must inevitably influence day-to-day decision-making. These 'coal-face' decisions determine the actual strategies pursued and the levels of success. The objectives that an organization is pursuing in reality therefore stem from **strategy implementation**. In order to properly appreciate just how well an organization is doing relative to both its objectives and its competitors, to explore opportunities and threats, to appraise strengths and weaknesses, to evaluate alternative courses of action and so on, it is vital to have an effective information system. How an organization gathers and uses information is therefore another important aspect of strategic management.

### 1.2.2  A Strategic Management Framework

*The most important management technique is to understand the real situation in which you are operating.*

(Sir Paul Girolami, Chairman, Glaxo, 1987)

*The best way to predict the future is to invent it.*

(John Sculley, when Chairman, Apple Computers)

Figure 1.6, re-presents the constituent elements of strategy as a set of 12 questions concerning strategic awareness and strategic change.

Moving from left to right, the questions follow a logical sequence. If an organization needs to take stock of just where it is placed at the moment to evaluate emerging opportunities and threats before clarifying a set of objectives for which strategies, both corporate and competitive, can be evaluated, selected and implemented, then the model can be used in a sequential, and possibly iterative, way. It will be seen that information (the bottom box) implies monitoring and continuity.

However, these questions can also be thought of as a set of important issues that managers everywhere in the organization should be addressing all the time in a turbulent environment. Nevertheless, they still need to be presented in a clear framework to ensure that any issues emerging can be placed in context, and any proposed changes assessed for their impact on other issues.

If managers seek answers to these questions continuously, and make and carry out appropriate strategic decisions, they will improve the performance and effectiveness of their organization by:

- generating increased strategic awareness
- ensuring that functional managers appreciate the strategic environment and the implications of decisions concerning individual products, services and markets; and
- making decisions about the need for, and appropriateness of, particular change opportunities.

**Figure 1.6** A strategy framework based on a series of questions

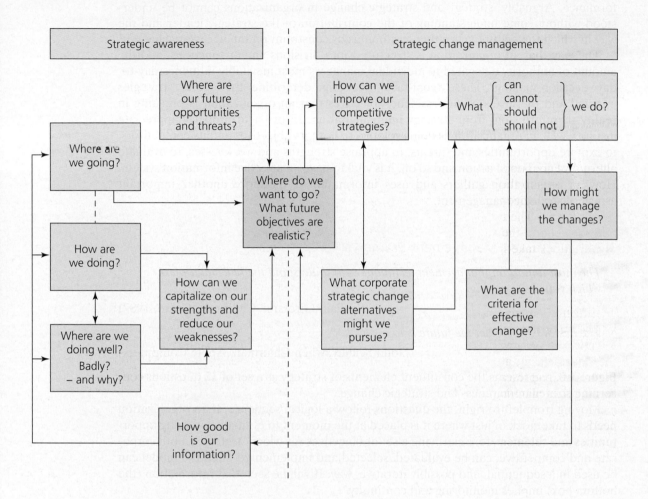

## 1.3 Strategy Creation

This section looks in greater detail at how strategies are changed and new strategies created – points discussed in the earlier sections are now taken up.

### 1.3.1 Opportunities for change

It is vital that managers are strategically aware both of potentially threatening developments and of opportunities for profitable change, and that they seek to match and improve the fit between the environment and the organization's resources.

*A wise man will make more opportunities than he finds.*

(Francis Bacon)

There is, however, no single recommended approach for seeking out and pursuing new opportunities. There is a broad spectrum ranging from what might be termed

**Figure 1.7** Strategic change

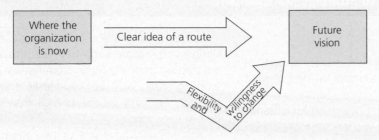

entrepreneurial opportunism to what Quinn (1980) calls '**logical incrementalism**'. These are analogous to the bird and squirrel approaches described in Box 1.3.

Strategic change can be relatively evolutionary or gradual, or much more dramatic or revolutionary. The nature of the opportunities (and threats) is directly related to both the general and the specific industry environments; and the approach that particular organizations take in seeking to match resources to the environment is dependent on the basic values of the organization and the style of the strategic leader. However, as will be seen, it does not follow that the strategic leader is the sole manager of strategic change.

Effectively managed change requires a vision of the future – where the organization is heading or wants to go – together with the means for creating and reaching this future. Planning a way forward from where the organization is now may not be enough to create the future vision; at the same time, when there is a vision, it is illogical to set off in pursuit without the appropriate 'equipment'. There must be a clear vision of a route, and this requires planning; on the way, managers should stay alert for dangers and opportunity (see Figure 1.7). Well-tracked routes (strategies that have proved successful in the past) and experience can both be beneficial, but in a dynamic environment there will always be an element of the unknown.

## 1.3.2  Planning and strategy creation

All managers plan. They plan how they might achieve objectives. Planning is essential to provide direction and to ensure that the appropriate resources are available where and when they are needed for the pursuit of objectives. Sometimes the planning process is detailed and formal; on other occasions planning may be informal, unstructured and essentially 'in the mind'. In the context of strategy formulation a clear distinction needs to be made between the cerebral activity of informal planning (planning strategy) and formalized planning systems (strategic planning).

Formal strategic planning systems are most useful in stable conditions. Environmental opportunities and threats are forecast, and then, as we saw earlier, strategies are planned and implemented. Strategies which are appropriate, feasible and desirable are most likely to help the organization to achieve its mission and objectives.

Where the environment is more turbulent and less predictable, strategic success requires flexibility, and the ability to learn about new opportunities and introduce appropriate changes continuously. Planning systems can still make a valuable contribution, but the plans must not be inflexible.

In addition, it is important not to discount the contribution of visionary strategic leaders who become aware of opportunities – and on occasions, create new

## Box 1.3  Approaches to Strategic Management

### The bird approach

Start with the entire world – scan it for opportunities to seize upon, trying to make the best of what you find.

You will resemble a bird, searching for a branch to land on in a large tree. You will see more opportunities than you can think of. You will have an almost unlimited choice.

But your decision, because you cannot stay up in the air for ever, is likely to be arbitrary, and because it is arbitrary, it will be risky.

### The squirrel approach

Start with yourself and your company – where you are at with the skills and the experience you have – and what you can do best.

In this approach you will resemble a squirrel climbing that same large tree. But this time you are starting from the trunk, from familiar territory, working your way up cautiously, treefork by treefork, deciding on the branch that suits you best at each fork.

You will only have one or two alternatives to choose from at a time – but your decision, because it is made on a limited number of options, is likely to be more informed and less risky.

In contrast to the bird who makes single big decisions, the squirrel makes many small ones. The squirrel may never become aware of some of the opportunities that the bird sees, but he is more likely to know where he is going.

Adapted from Cohen, P (1974) *The Gospel According to the Harvard Business School*, Penguin. Originally published by Doubleday, New York, 1973.

opportunities – and take risks based on their awareness and insight of markets and customers. Stelios Haji-Ioannou (Minicase 1.1), founder of easyJet and various other ventures – such as easyCinema and easyPizza – is an ideal example.

Formal strategic planning implies determined actions for achieving stated and desired objectives. For many organizations these objectives will focus on sales growth and **profitability**. A detailed analysis of the strategic situation will be used to create a number of strategic alternatives, and then certain options will be chosen and implemented.

Planning systems are useful, and arguably essential, for complex or diversified organizations with a large number of businesses that need integrating. There are several possible approaches. Head office can delegate the detailed planning to each division, offering advice and making sure that the plans can be co-ordinated into a sensible total package. Alternatively, the planning system can be controlled centrally in order to establish priorities for resource allocation.

While the discipline of planning and setting priorities is valuable, the plans must not be inflexible and incapable of being changed in a dynamic competitive environment. During implementation it is quite likely that some plans will be discarded and others modified.

### 1.3.3  Visionary and entrepreneurial leadership

Strategic planning systems imply that strategies are selected carefully and systematically from an analytical process. In other instances major strategic changes will be decided upon without lengthy formal analysis. Typically such changes will reflect strong, entrepreneurial leadership and be visionary and discontinuous: I have seen the future and this is it! A good example is provided by Richard Branson and Virgin, Minicase 1.3.

# Minicase 1.3  Richard Branson and Virgin　　GB

Sir Richard Branson is unquestionably a legend in his own lifetime. His name and presence are associated closely with all the Virgin activities and businesses, and he has demonstrated a unique ability to exploit a brand name and apply it to a range of diversified products and services. He *is* Virgin – so, will he leave a lasting business legacy like Ray Kroc (McDonald's – Minicase 1.4) has done? Can this diverse business outlive its founder? Or would Virgin be split up into its many constituent businesses without Branson to lead it?

Branson is creative, opportunistic and dedicated to those activities in which he engages. Possessed of a strong ego, he is an excellent self-publicist. Popular with customers and employees, he has created a hugely successful people-driven business. His determination to succeed and his willingness to take risks are manifest in his transatlantic power boating and round-the-world ballooning exploits. Although he has said that he 'wouldn't do this if I didn't think I'd survive', the *Financial Times* has commented that 'all those associated with Mr. Branson have to accept that he is an adventurer ... he takes risks few of us would contemplate'. He has chosen to enter and compete in industries dominated by large and powerful corporations. Having challenged British Airways very visibly, for example, Coca-Cola has also been a target. Significantly, and not unexpectedly, his name comes up frequently when other business people are asked to name the person they most admire.

Now over 50 years old, Branson has been running businesses for more than 30 years. He began *Student* magazine when he was a 16-year-old public schoolboy, selling advertising from a public phone booth. Ever opportunistic, he incorporated a mail-order record business, buying the records from wholesalers once he had a firm order and cash in advance. Thwarted by a two-month postal strike, Branson decided to enter retailing. Realizing the importance of location, he started looking for something along Oxford Street in London. Spotting an unused first floor above a shoe shop, he persuaded the owner to let him use it rent free until a paying tenant came along, on the grounds that if he was successful he would generate extra business for the shoe shop! He had a queue stretching 100 yards when it opened and never looked back – characteristically, he had turned a threat into an opportunity. The London record shop was followed by record production: Branson signed and released Mike Oldfield's extremely successful *Tubular Bells* after Oldfield had been turned down by all of the leading record companies. Branson was always an astute and visionary businessman, carefully recruiting people with the necessary expertise to manage the detail of his various enterprises. His main skill has been in networking, finding opportunities and securing the resources necessary for their exploitation. In this he has had to show courage and flexibility.

He decided to begin a transatlantic airline in 1984. The move had been prompted by an American who approached him with a proposal for an all-business-class transatlantic service. Although Branson rejected this particular focus, he took just a few weeks to make his decision. In this short period Branson analysed why small airlines had previously failed with similar ventures. In particular he focused on Freddie Laker's Skytrain, which had competed with a basic service and low prices. When the major airlines reduced their prices Skytrain was driven from the market because it had no other competitive advantage. Branson saw an opportunity: Virgin Atlantic Airways would offer added value and superior service at competitive prices, and concentrate on a limited number of the most lucrative routes. Branson had both a vision and many critics, who argued that he lacked the requisite skills.

He set about implementing his vision, initially leasing two Boeing 747 jumbo jets, and ensured that he generated publicity and notoriety for his initiative. More detailed planning came later after he began recruiting people with expertise in the industry. In this case the planning concentrated on the implementation of a visionary strategy. The airline has grown steadily since its creation and has won a number of awards for the quality of its

▶

service. Additional aircraft have been leased and bought, and new routes added. The growth has been in limited, incremental steps as Virgin Atlantic has learnt from experience in a very dynamic environment. The major carriers such as British Airways have clearly seen Virgin as a threat – but realistically only after Branson's early successes – and have been forced to respond. When Virgin broke into the transatlantic market with its innovative new service, it took the existing carriers by surprise; this was competition from an unexpected source. A successful holiday business has also been developed alongside the airline.

Over many years Branson has successfully marketed a range of products and services by systematically applying the Virgin brand name. The products and services may have been diversified – holidays, consumer products such as Virgin Vodka and Virgin Cola, cinemas, a radio station, mobile phones, financial services and Virgin Railways are examples – but the customer-focused brand image has remained constant.

Virgin was floated in 1986 but later reprivatized; Branson had been uncomfortable with the accountability expectations of institutional shareholders. Since then he has used joint ventures, minority partners and divestments (such as the sales of his music business and record shops) to raise money for new ventures and changes of direction. In 1999 Branson sold a 49 per cent stake in the airline to Singapore Airlines, partly to strengthen its competitiveness, but also to raise money for investment in further new ventures. A similar percentage of Virgin Railways was sold to the bus and train operator, Stagecoach. When Virgin Music was sold to Thorn EMI the general belief was that the money was required to subsidize the growing airline. More recently profits from the successful airline have allegedly been used to shore up other Virgin businesses.

Describing itself as a 'branded venture capital company', Virgin has created well over 200 businesses; and Branson has recently decided to increase his presence in electronic commerce and the Internet, believing that a vast range of products and services can be sold this way under the Virgin umbrella. A typical success story has been Virgin Wine. When BA and Air France decided, in 2003, to stop all Concorde flights, Branson was interested in continuing them with the Virgin brand.

Branson's business philosophy is built around quality products and services, value for money, innovation and an element of fun. 'I never let accountants get in the way of business. You only live once and you might as well have a fun time while you're living.' By focusing on customers and service he has frequently been able to add value where larger competitors have developed a degree of complacency. 'The challenge of learning and trying to do something better than in the past is irresistible.' Branson always realized that this would be impossible without the appropriate people and created an organization with a devolved and informal culture. Business ideas can, and do, come from anywhere in Virgin. And from people outside the organization. Employees with ideas that Branson likes will be given encouragement and development capital. Once a venture reaches a certain size it is freed to operate as an independent business within the Virgin Group, and the intrapreneur retains an equity stake. Branson runs Virgin from a large house in London's Holland Park, having outgrown the canal narrow boat that he used for many years. There has never been a traditional head office infrastructure.

## Questions

1. What are Richard Branson's strengths and limitations as a strategic leader?
2. How have they been manifested as Virgin has developed?
3. Can this diverse business outlive its founder?
4. Or would Virgin be split up into its many constituent businesses without Branson to lead it?
5. What are the similarities and differences between the Branson/Virgin Atlantic strategy and those of the low-price, no-frills airlines such as Southwest and easyJet?
6. What routes has Branson added to his original transatlantic services?

**Virgin Group** http://www.virgin.com

To an outsider it can often appear that the organization is pursuing growth with high-risk strategies, which are more reliant on luck than serious thought. This can underestimate the thinking that is involved, because quite often these entrepreneurs and visionary leaders have an instinctive feel for the products, services and markets involved, and enjoy a clear awareness and insight of the opportunities and risks.

This mode of strategy creation is most viable when the strategic leader has the full confidence of the organization, and he or she can persuade others to follow his or her ideas and implement the strategies successfully. Implementation requires more detailed planning and incremental changes with learning: initially it is the broad strategic idea that is formulated entrepreneurially.

Formal planning and/or visionary leadership will invariably determine important changes to corporate strategies; competitive and functional level changes are more likely to involve **emergent strategy** in the form of adaptive and incremental changes. The actual implementation of corporate level decisions is also likely to be incremental.

It is clear from the experiences of many organizations that planning and visionary leadership do not, in themselves, explain strategy creation, as the following story illustrates.

Richard T. Pascale of Stanford University (1984) has described how a number of Honda executives arrived in Los Angeles from Japan in 1959 to establish an American subsidiary. Their original aim (intended strategy) was to focus on selling 250cc and 350cc machines, rather than 50cc Honda cubs, which were a big hit in Japan. Their instinct told them that the Honda 50s were not suitable for the US market, where everything was bigger and more luxurious than in Japan.

However, sales of the 250cc and 350cc bikes were sluggish, and the bikes themselves were plagued by mechanical failure. It looked as though Honda's strategy was going to fail. At the same time the Japanese executives were using the Honda 50s to run errands

**Honda Motorcycles** – Sold by Sears to an untapped market

around Los Angeles, attracting a lot of attention. One day they got a call from a Sears Roebuck buyer who wanted to sell them to a broad market of Americans who were not necessarily already motorcycle enthusiasts. The Honda executives were very hesitant to sell the 50cc bikes for fear of alienating serious bikers, who might then associate Honda with 'wimp' machines. In the end they were pushed into doing so by the failure of the 250cc and 350cc machines. The rest is history. Honda had stumbled on a previously untouched market segment that was to prove huge. It had also found a previously untried channel of distribution: general retailers rather than speciality motorbike stores. By 1964 nearly one out of every two motorcycles sold in the US was a Honda.

Gladwell (2000) would refer to the call from Sears Roebuck as a 'tipping point', where some unexpected and unpredictable event has a major impact. A similar event happened to Hush Puppies in the mid-1990s. This brand of casual shoe had declined markedly in popularity and its owners were barely supporting it. However, a number of young people in New York started wearing them as something of a fashion statement, and mainly because nobody else was wearing them. They were spotted and copied and suddenly there was a resurgence in the popularity of the brand. It had nothing to do with any marketing by the manufacturers.

The critical point that emerges from the Honda and Hush Puppies examples is that in contrast to the view that strategies are planned, successful strategies can emerge without prior planning.

Other classic business school examples of emergent or unintended strategies are Xerox, who set out to sell photocopiers when customers only really wanted the copies not the machines, and Gillette actively promoting shavers when the real desire of the customer is for a shave. The razor blade is what is wanted by the consumer. Arguably it is better to give the razor away if this ensures you sell the blades.

We can now argue that there are two distinct elements to emergent strategic change.

### 1.3.4 Incremental strategic change

In dynamic and turbulent competitive environments, detailed formal planning is seen to be problematic. The plans are only as good as any forecasts, which must be uncertain. It can make sense, therefore, not to rely on detailed plans, but instead to plan broad strategies within a clearly defined mission and purpose.

Having provided this direction, the strategic leader will allow strategies to emerge in a decentralized organization structure. Managers will meet regularly, both formally and informally, to discuss progress and changing trends; they will plan new courses of action and then try them out: a form of 'real-time planning'.

> *When I was younger I always conceived of a room where all these [strategic] concepts were worked out for the whole company. Later I didn't find any such room... . The strategy [of the company] may not even exist in the mind of one man. I certainly don't know where it is written down. It is simply transmitted in the series of decisions made.*

> James B Quinn, 1980

Quinn argues that organizations test out relatively small changes and develop with this approach rather than go for major changes. An example would be Marks and Spencer testing a proposed new line in a selected and limited number of stores before deciding to launch it nationally. Lex Service Group (see Box 1.2) followed an incremental approach when it diversified into hotels, building and buying properties one by one rather than acquiring a chain of hotels.

## 1.3.5 Adaptive strategic change

Some organizations will be characterized by extensive **decentralization**, **empowerment** and accountability. Here, managers throughout the organization are being encouraged to look for opportunities and threats and to innovate. The underlying argument is that managers 'at the coal face' are closest to the key changes in the organization's environment and should, therefore, be in a position where they can, on the one hand, react quickly and, on the other hand, be proactive or intrapreneurial in attempting to change or manage the external environment. Managers will be encouraged and empowered to make changes in their areas of responsibility and, ideally, rewarded for their initiatives. The implication is that functional changes will impact upon competitive strategies in a positive way as the organization adapts to its changing environment. Conceptually this is similar to incremental change.

Proponents of chaos theory such as Ralph Stacey (1993) argue that intentional strategies are, per se, 'too inflexible for unknown futures'. Relying on this approach is a 'recipe for stagnation and failure because of the extent of the complexity'. Companies must seek to 'achieve a state of creative tension on the edge of instability'. These theorists accept that organizational hierarchies and planning are needed to control day-to-day operations but, in the long term, strategies must be allowed to emerge from the 'self-organizing activities of loose, informal, destabilizing networks'.

In summary, therefore, strategy can result from a stream of decisions and information fed upwards from the lower management levels of the organization. Quinn contends that this is sensible, logical and positive:

*The most effective strategies of major enterprises tend to emerge step by step from an iterative process in which the organization probes the future, experiments and learns from a series of partial (incremental) commitments rather than through global formulations of total strategies. Good managers are aware of this process and they consciously intervene in it. They use it to improve the information available for decisions and to build the psychological identification essential to successful strategies. The process is both logical and incremental. Such logical incrementalism is not 'muddling' as most people understand that word. Properly managed it is a conscious, purposeful, proactive, executive practice.*

Teamworking and learning are at the heart of the adaptive and incremental modes. Managers must learn about new opportunities and threats; they should also learn from the successes and mistakes of other managers. Managers must be willing to take measured risks; for this to happen understandable mistakes and errors of judgement should not be sanctioned harshly.

Change is gradual and comes from experimentation; new strategies involve an element of trial and error. Success is very dependent upon communications. Managers must know of the opportunities and threats facing them; the organization must be able to synthesize all changes into a meaningful pattern, and spread learning and best practice.

Mintzberg (1989) argues that organizations should be structured and managed to ensure that formulators of strategies (managers whose decisions lead to strategic changes) have information, and that the implementers of strategies and changes have the appropriate degree of power to ensure that the desired changes are brought about.

Figure 1.8 pulls these ideas together and highlights that it is quite normal to find all of these modes in evidence simultaneously in an organization, although there is likely to

**Figure 1.8** Strategy creation

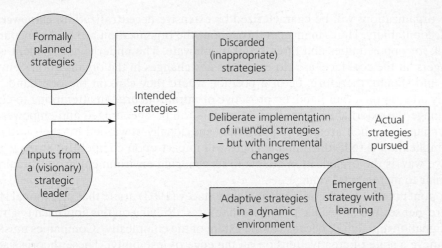

be one dominant mode. Moreover, different managers in the same organization will not necessarily agree on the relative significance of each mode; their perceptions of what is actually happening will vary.

The message for managers is that they need to recognize this process of emergence and to intervene where appropriate, killing off bad emergent strategies but nurturing potentially good ones. To make such decisions, however, managers must be able to judge the worth of emergent strategies. They must be able to think strategically. This viewpoint is probably the best argument for the continued use of the rationalist approach.

*Strategy is necessarily incremental and adaptive, but that does not in any way imply that its evolution cannot be, or should not be, analyzed, managed, and controlled.*

Pascale, 1984

## 1.4 The emergence of strategic management

*All men can see the tactics by which I conquer, but what none can see is the strategy out of which great victory is evolved.*

SunTzu, *The Art of War*, 400 BC

*Strategy is the evolution of the original guiding idea according to continually changing circumstance.*

Helmuth Moltke, Prussian General and Chief of Staff, 1858–1888

### 1.4.1 Origins in military strategy

Strategy has always had military roots and *Webster's New World Dictionary* defines strategy as 'the science of planning and directing military operations'. Strategic manoeuvres use the principles of **military strategy**, a theme taken up by James (1984).

*To survive you have to learn to fight by the rules of the game. The rules of the business game have changed in response to economic, technological and social dislocation and require new approaches to market combat. The companies that will survive and prosper [in the 1980s and beyond] will be those which recognise the new rules of the market-place and adopt end-game strategies which reflect the combative nature of the market-place. Those companies which continue to use game plans which are not conflict orientated will have a less-than-even chance of survival.*

Thus, strategy would be seen as the set of **policies** used for the conduct of conflict and the securing of an advantage over the competition.

We do however need to be careful with the usefulness of the military analogy: a business cannot vanquish all its foes and go home. Business is there for the long haul. Modern warfare is based on the destruction of opposing forces and on the use of resources which are greater than that of the enemy so as to give an overwhelming advantage, presenting the victor with the opportunity to destroy the enemy. This seldom happens in business – although the use by British Airways of its resources to help destroy Freddie Laker, an issue explored in Minicase 14.1, is one worth considering in this light.

*Success in business is usually about adding value of your own, not diminishing that of your competitors, and is based on distinctive capability, not destructive capacity. … The second area in which the military analogy misleads is in inviting excessive emphasis on leadership, vision, and determination. … If General Custer or Lord Raglan had been businessmen, would we have been so keen to become their employees or to buy shares in their business. … Fighting against overwhelming odds may sometimes be a necessary military strategy. It is almost always not a sensible business strategy.*

Kay 1993

**The military in action**    ©Peter Turnley/Corbis

Hinterhuber and Popp (1992) provide another example of the military analogy in the context of trying to identify the qualities needed to be a strategic manager. They contend that perhaps the greatest strategist of all time was not a business executive or an **entrepreneur** but a general ... Helmuth von Moltke, chief of the Prussian and German general staffs from 1858 to 1888, engineered the strategy behind the military victories that allowed Otto von Bismarck to assemble a loose league of German states into a powerful empire. Moltke possessed two important characteristics that made him into a superior strategist:

1. The ability to understand the significance of events without being influenced by current opinion, changing attitudes, or his own prejudices.
2. The ability to make decisions quickly and to take the indicated action without being deterred by a perceived danger.

The two characteristics support each other and apply to managers and entrepreneurs as much as to generals and national leaders.

> *Moltke issued directive guidelines for autonomous decision making. In the past, Prussian officers were discouraged from acting on their own. Moltke turned such tradition on its head by expecting the officers to show individual initiative. According to Moltke, strategy is applied common sense and cannot be taught. Moltke's general conception of strategy – viewing all obvious factors in the right perspective – cannot be learned in any school.*

Of course, a fundamental difference between military and business strategy is that business strategy is formulated, implemented, and evaluated with an assumption of competition, whereas military strategy is based on the assumption of conflict. Nonetheless, military conflict and business competition are so similar that many techniques for the formulating, implementing and evaluating of strategies apply to both.

Another important military metaphor relates strategy and tactics to guerrilla warfare, which is particularly relevant for understanding strategy and the small business. The small business owner usually lacks resources and is often competing with organizations much larger than himself.

This lack of resources usually takes the form of deficiencies in strategic management **knowledge**, lack of functional managerial skills, and insufficient capital to exploit external opportunities. The owner manager often is forced to adopt a day-to-day cognitive frame of reference. Fundamentally, this is the scenario of the guerrilla fighter. Resources need to be obtained and husbanded. Human and financial resources are often scarce and the 'enemy' is often much larger and well entrenched. The guerrilla, if he is to survive and prosper, must use resources wisely and pick the time and place of battle so as to make the best use of these scarce resources. The role of the 'military adviser' has always been important in such a campaign. Consider the success of the Vietcong against the greatest military power on earth – acknowledged to be the only war the United States of America has ever lost. Arguably the Vietcong would never be able to defeat, in a formal military sense, the United States. What the Vietcong set out to do was to make the war one the Americans could never win conventionally. They therefore sought to 'sicken' the US and to achieve success (that is to win the war) in the only way they could. In this case it was the winning of the public relations campaign. The US was portrayed as the giant, the aggressor, and the poor Vietcong as the victims fighting a titanic struggle against the odds. True or false it worked with the turning away, within America, of populist support for the war.

An earlier example of a successful guerrilla campaign is that of Robin Hood and the Sheriff of Nottingham. Robin and his so-called Merry Men had limited resources with which to take on a much bigger enemy. However, by winning popular support and not antagonizing too many key players in the external environment, the band were able to survive and prosper.

These points are expanded in Box 1.4.

## Box 1.4  Strategy – the Military Perspective

*War is a means to an end – just as business strategy is. The end might be a desired one (either power or economic wealth) or it might be survival when under threat.*

*Like business strategy, it is characterized by uncertainty and threat. The downside, losing, can be very unpleasant.*

The military strategist – just like a strategic leader – has control over the resources and must deploy them. He or she must also make sure there is resource development and innovation, and mastermind the supply chain.

Visionary and motivational leadership at various levels is vital, as is individual enterprise (individual acts of heroism) within the boundaries of a framework of discipline.

We have all studied military history in school, even if only at a superficial level. We may have read books; we have almost certainly seen movies, ranging from Shakespeare's *Henry V* to John Wayne winning the war in the Pacific! If we can think of key aspects of conflict and warfare we can clarify a number of themes and concepts that are vital for our study of strategy in a business context. In warfare, as in business, there are lessons from defeat and lessons from success. Simply, military ideas can help us to be more effective strategic thinkers.

### Important elements and themes

- Strategic intent – a broad plan
- Positioning and tactical ploys
- Detailed but flexible action plans – Napoleon, for example, seemed to plan by algorithm and always prepare for a variety of possibilities and contingencies
- Capability – resource adequacy and replenishment
- Competency – skills and weaponry represent technical and process competencies and capabilities
- Focus – so there are few diversions or distractions from the main thrust
- Thinking ahead – to develop new resources and technologies first
- 'The rules of the game' can always be changed with a new weapon or tactics – witness the potential of biological weapons
- Guerrilla fighters always imply a hidden, surprise threat – they are innovative and entrepreneurial
- Allies and alliances are likely to be essential – as with nations, it can sometimes be in a company's interests to form an alliance with a past or even an existing rival (enemy) to guard against an even greater enemy
- Fear is an important competitive weapon. Some actions are deterred or delayed because of the fear of competitive reaction. The Cold War typified this. Image matters. It is possible to win without engaging in conflict if your reputation frightens people off. Image and reputation are thus a barrier to entry
- Self-belief is also vital. There has to be a will to win and a belief that winning is possible. This comes from envisioning and values-driven leadership

**DISCUSSION**

▶

■ In this context, people will die to help their colleagues – team belongingness is a key element

■ This is particularly poignant in war when new team members have to be integrated quickly to replace those who have been lost

■ Flexibility must be maintained. Anyone can be caught out by surprise

■ All the time, gathering performance data and spotting new, emerging, developments and trends cannot be over-valued. This may be directly and indirectly related to the main focus of current activity

■ With the military, of course, spying and hiding the competitor information you do have is a legitimate tactic. Industrial espionage goes on, but it is not perceived as ethical.

### Important rules of war

■ Never engage a superior force without a clear plan of action that has a real chance of success. Until you have this plan, defend!

■ Don't waste time and resources attacking a place that has no strategic or other value. Stay focused

■ When you have made progress, reinforce to protect your back and flanks and prevent counter-attack as you continue onwards

■ Whenever you can, stay on the move and keep reinforcing your advantage.

### Reference

The material in this box has been sourced in part from:
Davies, P *Military Strategy* in Jenkins, M and Ambrosini, V (2002) *Strategic Management – A Multi-perspective Approach,* Palgrave.

### Further reading

Clausewitz, C von (1982) *On War,* Penguin.
Howard, M (2002) *Clausewitz: A Very Short Introduction,* Oxford University Press.
Sun Tzu (1981) *The Art of War,* Hodder & Stoughton.

## 1.4.2 Evolving views of strategy

In this section we refer to a number of approaches to strategic management, all of which are discussed in detail at different points in the book, where they are referenced more fully.

Since the 1960s, when we really began to study strategic management, the strategic planning framework has provided a valuable base for the understanding of the subject. Since then several other approaches have been added. They are all relevant and help to shed further light on this complex topic. If strategy were easy to understand and practise, then more organizations would be successful and sustain this success over time. However, although it is based in many ways on some simple points and common sense, strategy remains enigmatic.

Figure 1.9 shows that when Porter (1980, 1985) drew attention to the subject of competitive advantage, and the significance of strategic positioning, an important second layer was added to the planning foundation. The next important contribution was the clarification that many strategies emerge as decisions are taken all the time in dynamic circumstances, highlighting that while planning plays an important role, it is a partial one.

The general thrust of these approaches is market driven, based on the argument that organizations must react in a dynamic environment, seizing new opportunities and

**Figure 1.9** Emerging views of strategic management

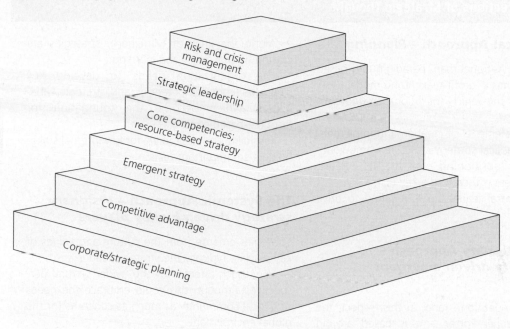

avoiding major potential threats. Responding to customers, suppliers and competitors will always be vital, but an alternative perspective is also relevant. This **resource-based strategy** argues that organizations must discern their critical strategic strengths and look for ways of building and exploiting them in order to mould the competitive environment. In the supplement to this Part we look at the relevant issues of core competency and **strategic capability**. Successful organizations will blend both the market and resource perspectives so that they do not overlook potentially good opportunities.

In recent years the subject of strategic leadership has received greater prominence, stimulated in part by the media. Business success stories have been popular items for newspapers and magazines, especially where there is a high-profile figure who can be identified with the organization and the story. In addition, the fall from grace of some very high-profile business people has proved newsworthy. The accompanying autobiographies of some of these people have added to this understanding.

Box 1.5 provides an alternative perspective on these important approaches.

Most recently, **risk management** and **crisis management** have joined the debate. Organizations have recognized that **scenario** building can help their understanding of uncertainty, where the future may depend in part on the past but will not replicate it. For some industries, such as pharmaceuticals (where huge investments in new drugs are required but carry no guarantee of success) and electronic commerce (which is changing by the day) serious risk assessment is vital. The environment is busy with information and triggers, never more so than now, thanks to the Internet, but discerning the real commercial opportunities is probably harder rather than easier than it was in the past. Organizational fortunes can, therefore, change rapidly, and crises can arise suddenly to catch out the unwary organization. The study of learning, and the involvement of people in an empowered and intrapreneurial culture, is a key element both of this topic and of emergent strategy.

**DISCUSSION**

## Box 1.5 Directions of Strategic Thought

### The Classical Approach – *Planning*

Driven by the 'rational man' paradigm and based on the economists' profit-maximizing model.

Planning is the vehicle for rational strategy creation.

There are elements of creation and implementation, the classical strategy-structure framework.

Strategic positioning is at its heart. Appropriateness is therefore a key test.

Strong central leadership is required to drive the process.

### The Evolutionary Approach – *Opportunity-driven emergent strategy*

Driven by competition – and, in this respect, the work of Michael Porter – it is based around responding to identified opportunities and threats.

The idea is that only the best performers survive in a dynamic world, accepting there is always an element of luck and chance.

The approach questions whether organizations can create differences by a largely rational approach.

'Strategizing' – or thinking long term – can be dangerous if it reduces organizational flexibility.

Rather strategy is about tactical moves (changes) in response to external events.

The appropriate resources are essential to put the organization in a position to 'engage the enemy'.

Appropriateness and feasibility are the key tests.

### The Processual Approach – *resource-based emergent planning*

This is driven by internal stakeholders and assumes that adaptation to the outside world is through internal political bargaining, compromise and accommodation.

Along the lines of Mintzberg, strategies are crafted by trial, error and learning.

The organization needs to develop key strengths (core competencies and strategic capabilities) which become the foundation for resource-based strategies

Feasibility and desirability for key internal stakeholders are important tests.

### The Systemic Approach – *Visionary strategy driven by key players*

Strategies emerge from the culture and values of key players, typically the strategic leader.

Very much affected by the 'wider picture' perspective, although this could embrace the needs of a local community as much as concerns for the global environment.

In some economies the systemic approach can correspond to the profit-seeking paradigm behind the classical approach.

Developed from: Whittington, R (1993) *What Is Strategy – And Does It Matter?* International Thomson.

### Commentary

Whittington sees the Classical and Processual approaches as internally-driven, on the grounds that the classical approach is driven by an internal desire to maximize profits. Evolutionary and Systemic are then external.

However we might argue that the Classical approach (like the Evolutionary) is external, as they are both based on a search for economic opportunities in a competitive environment.

The Systemic (like the Processual) is internal, because it is based on the values of powerful strategic leaders.

The following discussion on strategic disturbances and groupthink supports the significance of this sixth layer in Figure 1.9.

**Strategic disturbance** Stacey (1993) advocates that strategy is about handling disturbance, and this is related to changing both competitive advantage and competitive capability. We can see how disturbances constitute risk and mishandled, crises.

To Stacey, strategy is not about a comprehensive and integrated set of actions or routes to objectives … instead it is about a comprehensive and integrated total control system, which will enable the strategic leader to deal with unforeseeable disturbances, changes in competitive advantage and capability as they occur. Handling disturbance effectively is, therefore, a question of control in its widest sense.

*The starting point is not the mission, and certainly not detailed long term objectives, but the appropriate style of control.*

This argument reinforces the significance of placing leadership and culture at the centre of Figure 1.5(b).

Disturbances can arise from anywhere and everywhere. The basic business flows of orders/requisitions, inputs/outputs and money, all give rise to disturbances; machine breakdowns, material shortages, unpaid debts, rising stock levels and changes in the pattern of orders, also give rise to disturbances. The environment impacts on the flows, feeding disturbances into the organization – through, for example, the loss of a major customer, changing customer tastes and the appearance of a new competitor. The environment also feeds disturbances directly to the instruments of control – public opinion, changes in work culture, pressures to install training, reward pressures and so on. The environment could also directly contribute disturbance – changes in taxation, changes in health and safety requirements, trade union law, environmental legislation imposing uniform standards throughout the EU and so on. The instruments of control can directly contribute disturbance – new staff and managers may join the company with different cultural values. Roles can directly contribute disturbance through individual dissatisfaction with roles or a poor fit of people to their roles.

Disturbances are continuously bombarding the business from all directions, and wherever they come from they have to be handled at the core of the control system by managers and workers who apply processes to control elements. The outcome is some form of action. This action is based on structured thinking, but not an analytical straitjacket.

One serious drawback to the formal planning approach then, is the problem of trying to foresee strategic disturbance over a period which extends much into the future. We all know that the early years of this century will see a rapid growth in the age group of 60 and over in most industrialized countries. We know that this group will be healthier and wealthier than ever before in history. But just what does this mean for business? What will these rich, healthy pensioners be looking for – Club 65+ instead of Club 18–30? Moreover, when does it make sense for anyone to do anything about it? This major demographic change is a strategic disturbance, but should an entrepreneur start building holiday villas now?

**Groupthink** Social psychologist Irving L. Janis (1972) argues 'groupthink' occurs when a group of decision-makers embark on a course of action without questioning underlying assumptions. The group coalesces around a person or a policy. It ignores or filters out information which could be used to question that policy and develops after-the-fact rationalization for its decision.

Williams (1976) has analysed the problem of groupthink and crisis management in the nuclear age. Two main themes emerged from his work. Not only does a group strive for unanimity but there also can be the additional problem of this striving for unanimity overriding the group's motivation to realistically appraise alternative courses of action. This might mean that the group is willing to take a level of risk that individually they would not take, and that members of the decision-making unit exude great self-confidence, firmly believing that the policy they adopt is almost bound to succeed.

Williams argues that the Bay of Pigs invasion and the escalation of the Vietnam war under President Johnson are both classic examples of overconfidence in one's own plans and underestimation of the capabilities and resourcefulness of the enemy.

An excellent example of the difficulty of trying to remain objective during a crisis and to make a rational decision based on the facts rather than follow a narrow decision path, is the Cuban Missile Crisis in 1962. This is discussed by Williams (1976), but a valuable insight into what it might have been like at this time can be seen in the film made of the crisis, *Thirteen Days* (Hollywood Pictures), which features Kevin Costner as President Kennedy's principal adviser. The heavy pressure placed on Kennedy by the US military for a strike on Cuba is well depicted; however, the President resists this pressure and arrives at the blockade decision which ultimately proved successful. In this instance, groupthink was clearly resisted.

## 1.5   Mission, strategy, objectives and tactics

These four terms were all defined in Box 1.1 and they have either been introduced in brief or discussed in detail in this chapter. Figure 1.10 shows how they interrelate hierarchically, and looks at them in the context of intended and emergent strategy creation.

Strategies are means to ends. Where they are planned in some detail they will relate to specific objectives or targets. Both objectives and strategies set and pursued should help to achieve, or at least to pursue, the purpose or mission of the organization. Tactics and actions, carried out everywhere in the organization by various managers and other staff, represent on the one hand the implementation of **intended strategies** and, on the other hand new strategic ideas being tried out by empowered managers.

The left-hand section of Figure 1.10 highlights how, with intended strategies, the mission is used to establish objectives, which in turn lead to strategies and tactics. With emergent strategy – the right-hand section of the diagram – managers are expected to appreciate and support the broad purpose and direction of the organization, and it is a key role of the strategic leader to ensure that they actually do this. Within this context they are then empowered to decide upon, and try out, new strategic ideas. What they do determines the level of achievement and performance of the organization. Here we can see how tactical successes drive strategy and performance. In both cases environmental and resource considerations will guide decision-making, but the information will be used by different people at different levels in the hierarchy.

With intended strategies, performance evaluation straightforwardly concerns the achievement (or not) of stated objectives with the strategies and tactics used. In the case

**Figure 1.10** The strategy process

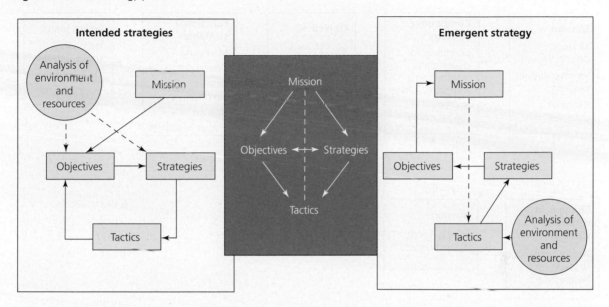

of emergent strategy, performance evaluation is really an assessment of what has been achieved in the context of the mission.

Finally, it is important to recognize that specific issues and events will be perceived differently at different levels of the organizational hierarchy, partly because individual businesses in a diverse organization can – and often will – have their own **mission statements**. While they may differ, they should be complementary.

We have already seen how strategy has its origins in warfare, and a recent military example provides a useful illustration of these points. In the Second World War the mission of the British government was, quite simply, to win the war. This required contributions from each of the armed services and from others. Winning the Battle of Britain was, consequently, one objective, supported by various strategies concerned with, for example, training pilots and building aircraft. The recruitment of women to work in the aeroplane factories was one of many tactics. An individual front line squadron would, however, define its mission differently. It might, for example, have been concerned with shooting down enemy planes and minimizing losses. To the government, with a higher level purpose, this would be seen as an objective. Similarly, advancing against the enemy and capturing a hill might be the current mission for a group of soldiers; to them at the time nothing else would matter. In the context of the war as a whole, however, this would be a very low-level and short-term tactic.

## 1.6   Strategy statements

Before we finish this chapter with a look at strategic management in different contexts, it is useful to draw together many of the points we have made by showing them in the form of a strategy statement, illustrated in Figure 1.11.

**Figure 1.11** Strategy statements

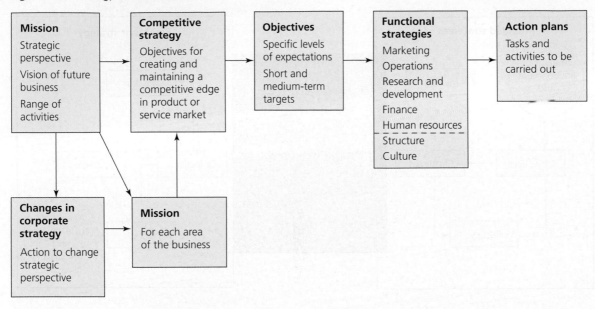

The argument would be that all managers in an organization should be in a position to produce such a statement for their organization, and understand the interconnections.

The overall mission or purpose may or may not change over time; a great deal depends upon the extent to which it allows the organization to develop and change its strategic perspective. Each business or division within the organization is likely to have its own mission, from which will be derived an appropriate competitive strategy. This leads on to the establishment of specific objectives and firm levels of expectation in respect of sales, profits, production and so on. Functional strategies will be developed to ensure that these targets are achieved and that the appropriate action plans, or tasks to be carried out, are defined. Although not explicitly shown on the strategy statement, there should be monitoring and control systems to assess performance against targets.

## 1.7 Strategic management in specific contexts

Strategic ideas are relevant for all types of organization, and many of the key issues are the same, although they may differ in their relative significance. At the same time there are some important differences, which are introduced in this section. Throughout the book an attempt is made to use examples and cases that reflect a range of different types and size of organization but, inevitably, large manufacturing and service businesses feature most prominently, largely because they are the organizations and brand names that most readers will recognize and relate to easily.

### 1.7.1 Small businesses

Typically, small businesses will focus on a single product or service, or at least a restricted range of related products and services, targeted at a defined market niche.

Competitive and functional strategies are important, but many of the corporate strategy issues discussed herein will not be relevant until the organization grows larger, assuming that it does so. In addition, their customers may be concentrated in a single geographical area, but this will certainly not always be the case. In some large organizations, the structure is designed to encourage the individual businesses to behave as a typical small business in some of its operations.

There is generally a great reliance on the owner–manager for all major strategic decisions. The advantage can be speed, as decisions need not become lost or slowed down in discussion or committee; the corresponding disadvantage can be an overreliance on one person who may become overstretched as the business develops. Hence, there is an emphasis on visionary strategy creation and on emergence, as new ideas are tried out. Sophisticated analysis and planning is less likely, and sometimes a lack of attention to detail can constitute another weakness.

The real challenge for small businesses is to develop and strengthen their resources once they start growing: if they fail they will lose their competitiveness. Some never possess any real competitive advantage in the first place and, while they may survive if they are run efficiently, they are unlikely to grow to any significant size.

Where a small business fails to grow it will always be dependent on the actions of others. Both its suppliers and customers could be larger and consequently more powerful. In this case it could be paying cash for its supplies and giving extended credit to its customers, resulting in cash-flow problems. It is also likely to be very reactive to competitor initiatives until it can become more prominent and proactive. The helpful publicity and visibility given to larger organizations may be withheld, even at a local level. High-quality managers and employees, who could fuel the growth, may not find a small, and perceptually inconsequential company, attractive to work for. Nevertheless, all companies start small: they are, after all, the seedbed for those successful entrepreneurs who create growth businesses.

The success, or lack of it, then, will be hugely dependent on the strategic leader and his or her culture and style. The future will be dictated by their skill and also by their ability to acquire resources, particularly in terms of finance. A lack of capital can often be a real restraint to growth. Banks often demand security and collateral and venture capitalists often only become interested once the business has reached a certain size and proved itself. We saw earlier how guerrilla warfare provides a useful metaphor for the strategic use of tactics by small businesses.

This traditional logic concerning small businesses, however, has to some degree been turned on its head in the case of many new Internet or '**dot.com**' companies who have been able to raise millions of pounds on the strength of a barely proven idea that appeared to offer a golden opportunity. Financiers have taken risks that they would previously have shunned because of the speed and growth of this sector and its inherent uncertainty.

### 1.7.2 Global companies

Here the emphasis is very much on corporate strategy: diversity, geographical scope and co-ordinating the countries where products are made with the countries where they are sold. Using low-cost labour factories in Eastern Europe and the Far East can prove controversial while still being an economic necessity. In addition, these are often very powerful companies whose annual turnover exceeds the gross national product (GNP) of many of the world's smaller countries. Nevertheless, issues of competitiveness and competitive advantage are as relevant as they are for a small business. One key complication can be currency fluctuations when component supplies and finished goods are moved around the world.

The major dilemma for many global companies concerns their need to achieve global-scale economies from concentrating production in large plants whilst not sacrificing their local identity and relevance in the various markets. To accomplish this they must stay close to their customers and markets, whose specific tastes and preferences may differ markedly, even though they are buying essentially the same product.

The organizational structure can be, and often is, just as important as the strategy. This, in turn, raises a number of important people issues. People may be switched from business to business and from country to country as part of their personal progression. This movement also helps the whole organization to transfer skills and knowledge and to learn good practices from different parts of the business.

Global corporations also need to develop expertise in financial management. Attractive development grants and packages will be available in certain countries and influence strategic developments. Interest rates are not the same around the world, and consequently loans can be more attractive in certain countries and not in others. Moreover, tax rates vary and it can be very beneficial to be seen to be earning profits in low-tax countries instead of high-tax ones.

### 1.7.3 Not-for-profit organizations

Organizations such as churches and charities clearly fit into this sector very well, but certain other profit-generating businesses, such as museums, zoos and local theatres, are relatively closely aligned. In the case of the latter examples, the profit objective is often designed to create a 'war chest' for future investment rather than to reward an owner or a group of investors. For this reason there are many common characteristics. Money may be perceived differently in not-for-profit organizations than in profit-seeking businesses, but there is still a need to create a positive cash flow. A charity, for example, can only spend on good causes if it can generate funds. For this reason, churches and charities can legitimately appear very commercial in their outlook, and this must be accepted alongside the cause that they are targeting.

These not-for-profit organizations need social entrepreneurs or strategic leaders who, in many ways, will be similar to those found in the profit-seeking sector. They will possess similar **entrepreneurial** and leadership qualities, but they will be driven by a cause, which attracts them to the particular organization and sector. This, in turn, guides the mission, purpose and culture. In addition, there is likely to be a greater reliance on voluntary helpers and possibly managers and others who readily accept salaries and wages below those that they might earn in the profit sector.

There are likely to be variations on the modes of strategy creation discussed herein. There is likely to be some committee structure, involving both salaried employees and unpaid volunteers, the latter often in senior roles. Decision-making can be slow and political in nature, although clearly it does not have to be this way. However, strong and dominant leaders (either paid or unpaid) quite often emerge and are at the heart of strategy-making. Because there is a need for accountability for the funds raised, planning systems are likely to be prominent.

## 1.7.4 Public sector organizations

In many countries around the world the composition of this sector has changed over recent years. Typically essential service industries, such as telecommunications, gas, electricity, water, and air, bus and rail transport, have been privatized, often resulting in the creation of a number of complementary or even competing businesses. The outcome in each industry has been one or more private companies, some of which have since merged or been acquired, sometimes by overseas parents. In the case of the UK this privatization programme has also included individual companies such as British Airports Authority (BAA), which manages several airports but is largely a retail organization. Outside direct government control, BAA has expanded overseas and now manages a number of other airports around the world.

In every case there is some form of regulation and government influence, as distinct from the direct government control of the past. The trend towards privatization has gathered momentum for many reasons, one factor in Europe being the stronger stance on government subsidies to individual industries by the European Commission. The key appears to lie in the effectiveness of the regulation, which must attempt to balance the needs of all key stakeholders: customers, employees and investors.

As a result, we now tend to think of local authorities and public health and emergency services as the archetypal public sector organizations. Clearly these are service businesses, and ones which will always have to choose and prioritize between different needs and stakeholders. In general, they will always be able to achieve more outcomes if they can acquire more resources. However, they remain largely dependent on central government for their resources and are therefore influenced by the political agenda of the day. Increasingly, some have greater involvement with the private sector than was the case in the past. The British National Health Service works alongside the private health-care sector and, although their roles and remits differ, the same consultants operate in both sectors. Many services in local communities were subjected to compulsory competitive tendering (CCT) during the early and mid-1990s and, as a result, were outsourced to providers in the private, profit-seeking sector. CCT has now been replaced by the need to find and deliver 'best value'.

Decision-making and style features some element of bureaucracy, in part because of the role of governing bodies, be they elected (local councillors) or appointed (e.g. NHS Trust Boards). As accountability has become increasingly public in recent years, analysis and planning will also be very prominent. Again, however, strong leaders can, and will, make an impact; and, as the public sector environment is no more stable than the one affecting commercial businesses, emergent strategy is also very important.

The closing case in this chapter, Minicase 1.4 on McDonald's, features many of the points we have discussed. McDonald's grew very rapidly around a winning business model and became a world leader in its industry. The brand was ubiquitous, visible and identifiable everywhere. However, in recent years, the company has lost its way and the brand has become tarnished. If it is to survive and restore its previous high growth, McDonald's will have to change certain aspects of its strategy fundamentally. We see that a previously successful strategic leader has been tempted out of retirement to champion the necessary transformation.

## Minicase 1.4 McDonald's       US  Int

McDonald's, built by a visionary, the late Ray Kroc, has become a very successful international company, with outlets in some 120 countries. Its products are popular with large numbers of customers, and certainly not just children. In 1996, according to Interbrand consultants, McDonald's ousted Coca-Cola as the world's best-known brand. But recently the company recorded its first ever trading loss.

Ray Kroc has been described by *Time Magazine* as 'one of the most influential builders of the twentieth century'. Few children refuse a McDonald's burger – and its golden arches logo became a symbol of American enterprise. Kroc was a truly opportunistic and focused entrepreneur who built an organizational network of dedicated franchisees. Yet his entrepreneurial contribution began late in life and the McDonald's chain of hamburger restaurants was certainly not his own invention. Instead he saw – really he stumbled on – an opportunity where others missed the true potential for an idea. Once he had seen the opportunity he rigorously applied business acumen and techniques to focus on providing value for his customers. By standardizing his product and restaurants he was able to guarantee high and consistent quality at relatively low cost. Kroc was also wise enough to use the expertise that his franchisees were developing. The golden arches brand and the Ronald McDonald character became ubiquitous.

In 1955, at the age of 52, Ray Kroc completed 30 years as a salesman, mainly selling milkshake machines to various types of restaurant across America, including hamburger joints. His customers included the McDonald brothers who, having moved from New Hampshire to Hollywood, but failing to make any headway in the movie business, had opened a small drive-through restaurant in San Bernadino, California. They offered a limited menu, paper plates and plastic cups, and guaranteed the food in 60 seconds. When their success drove them to buy eight milkshake machines, instead of the two their small size would logically suggest, Ray Kroc's interest was alerted and he set off to see the restaurant. Kroc's vision was for a national chain which could benefit from organization and business techniques. He bought out the McDonald brothers and set about building a global empire. After he officially retired from running the business, and until his death in 1984, Ray Kroc stayed on as President and visited two or three different restaurants every week. He saw himself as the 'company's conscience', checking standards against his QSCV vision – quality food, fast and friendly service, clean restaurants and value for money.

The McDonald's empire grew to be 30,000 restaurants worldwide serving 40 million people everyday; America always remained the biggest market. At one stage up to 3000 new venues were being opened in a single year. The basic formula has worked as well in Moscow and Beijing as it has in the US. Although the products available are broadly similar in the US and Europe, menus are seen as flexible in other parts of the world. Japanese stores, for example, feature teriyaki burgers, sausage patties with teriyaki sauce. Many of the stores are franchises; the rest are mainly joint ventures but some 2500 are company owned.

The growth and success in an industry where 'fast food is a by-word for low wages and an unskilled temporary workforce' is not accidental. It has been very carefully planned and managed, although McDonald's relies a lot on the people at the sharp end. Employees are often young; they work a closely prescribed system, operating internationally established rules and procedures for preparing, storing and selling food. Various incentive schemes are practised. Labour turnover is high, however, and consequently McDonald's has its critics as well as its supporters. Nevertheless, it is obvious that some competitors seek to emulate McDonald's in a number of ways: products, systems and employee attitudes.

*Our competitors can copy many of our secrets, but they cannot duplicate our pride, our enthusiasm and our dedication for this business.*

McDonald's has been profitable because it is efficient and productive; and it has stayed ahead of its competitors by being innovative and looking for new opportunities.

A lot of the developments are planned and imaginative. McDonald's does not move into new countries without thorough investigation of the potential; the same is true for new locations. There are now McDonald's branches in American hospitals, military bases and zoos; worldwide they can be found in airport terminals, motorway service stations, supermarkets (Tesco), and on board cruise ships and Swiss trains.

McDonald's relies heavily on its suppliers for fresh food; again, arrangements are carefully planned, monitored and controlled. The in-store systems for cooking and running branches are very tight, to ensure that products and service standards are the same worldwide. New product development has utilized all of the group's resources. The Big Mac, which was introduced nationally in the USA in 1968, was the idea of a Pittsburgh franchisee who had seen a similar product elsewhere. The aim was to broaden the customer base and make McDonald's more adult orientated. The company allowed the franchisee to try the product in his restaurant in 1967, although there was some initial resistance amongst executives who wished to retain a narrow product line, and it proved highly successful.

Egg McMuffins in the early 1970s were a response to a perceived opportunity – a breakfast menu and earlier opening times. Previously the restaurants opened at 11.00 a.m. Although the opportunity was appreciated the development of the product took place over four years, and the final launch version was created by a Santa Barbara franchisee who had to invent a new cooking utensil.

When Chicken McNuggets were launched in 1982 it was the first time that small boneless pieces of chicken had been mass produced. The difficult development of the product was carried out in conjunction with a supplier and there was immediate competitive advantage. The product was not readily copied. From being essentially a hamburger chain McDonald's quickly became second to Kentucky Fried Chicken for fast-food chicken meals.

McDonald's continually tries out new menus, such as pizzas, in order to extend its share of the overall fast-food market, but for many years it avoided any diversification, nor did it offer any different 'food concept'. To enhance its image of good value, and to compete in a very dynamic industry, McDonald's offers 'extra-value meals', special combinations at low prices. However, McDonald's has been criticized for increasing portion sizes as a marketing tool – which might seem like extra value but is, at the same time, encouraging greater consumption of fast food at any one time.

In addition, McDonald's is a 'penny profit' business. It takes hard work and attention to detail to be financially successful. Store managers must do two things well: control costs and increase sales. Increased sales come from the products, certainly, but also from service. Cost control is vital, but it must not be achieved by compromising product quality, customer service or restaurant appearance. Instead, it requires a focus on productivity and attention to detail. Success with these strategies has been achieved partly through serious attempts to share learning and best practice throughout the global network.

The company became an industry leader and contends there were six main reasons behind this:

- Visibility: to this end substantial resources are devoted to marketing. The golden arches symbol is instantly recognizable.

- Ownership or control of real-estate sites: McDonald's argues that this factor differentiates it from its competitors who lease more.

- Its commitment to franchising and supplier partnerships.

- It is worldwide, with restaurants in some 120 countries, and uses local managers and employees.

■ The structure is very decentralized but lines of responsibility and accountability are clear.

■ It is a growth company – or at least it has been for most of its existence.

By the mid-1990s, with the company still growing rapidly, the 'early warning signs' began to appear for the first time. The company held 40 per cent of the US market for its products, and yet its burgers were not coming out as superior to Wendy's and Burger King in taste tests. In addition, a special promotion in America, based around burgers for 55 cents each, did not prove successful because of the conditions attached to the offer. A new spicier – and premium price – burger for adults, the Arch Deluxe, had not taken off. New restaurants in the US were beginning to take sales away from existing ones, rather than generating new business. Established franchisees were hardly delighted! One complained, sued and won $16 million in damages. A leading franchisee pressure group expressed the view that the entrepreneurial drive of founder Ray Kroc (who died in 1984) had been lost and replaced by a non-entrepreneurial bureaucracy. This change of culture was one reason why McDonald's recently pursued a libel action in the UK against two environmentalists: a case where McDonald's won the legal argument but lost the accompanying public-relations battle.

After a period of criticism and disappointing results McDonald's began to fight back. With franchisees paying half the costs, new computerized kitchen equipment has been systematically installed in its 30,000 restaurants, allowing fast cooking to order. Ready-to-serve meals no longer have to stand for a few minutes on heated trays. In addition, McDonald's began to experiment with new low-risk opportunities for its competencies in supply-chain management, franchising, promotion and merchandizing by acquiring new restaurant chains. Included were a group of Mexican restaurants in Colorado, a chain of pizza outlets in Ohio, 23 Aroma coffee shops in London and the Boston Market chain of chicken restaurants. The US operations were split into five independent geographical regions.

But all of these initiatives failed to stop McDonald's starting to trade at a loss for the first time in 2002. Also for the first time, restaurants were closed down – some 700 in all, expecially where there was unnecessary duplication – as a response to falling sales. The share price tumbled. Jim Cantalupo, a retired strategic leader, was tempted back to try and restore the past glory. Was this possible – or was the brand at the beginning of the end of its life cycle? Interestingly, McDonald's fastest growing competitior was Subway, which markets fresh sandwiches and is perceived to be offering a far healthier alternative.

Cantalupo's strategy had a number of important elements:

■ The focus was to be on new customers rather than new restaurants.

■ In part this will be achieved through healthier food options. This will be achieved in the content and the preparation; at the same time people will be encouraged to eat more healthily.

■ Existing customers will be encouraged to visit the restaurants more often – and to support this, service must get better. Fresh, hot food must be available within a three minute promise. The toilets must be spotless at all times, however busy the restaurant is. Underpinning this will be a renewed emphasis on staff training.

■ New products will feature more imagination and innovation. There is now (in America in particular) a wider range of salads and new desserts, including bagged fresh fruit. For the adult taste, Mexican burgers are beginning to make inroads.

Both sales and profitability are up again, but it is perhaps too early to argue that McDonald's is truly turned around – not least because Jim Cantalupo died suddenly in 2004 and another strategic leader had to be found.

## Questions

1. How does McDonald's create value for its customers?

2. How might it create new values in the future?

3. What are its important competencies and capabilities?

4. To what extent do you think issues of strategic leadership and culture have influenced its growth and prosperity?

McDonald's http://www.mcdonalds.com

## Task

Find out who replaced Cantalupo and what changes were subsequently made.

# SUMMARY

Strategies are means to ends – they are the means through which organizations seek to achieve objectives and fulfil their mission or purpose.

All managers can be strategy makers because of their influence in both strategy creation and strategy implementation.

Strategic management is a process which embraces the strategies together with the themes of excellence in their implementation, creativity and innovation when they are changed and the effective and timely management of these changes.

There is evidence that strategic thinking, and hence strategic management, could be improved in many companies by:

- *segmenting* and *targeting* markets more crisply and definitively
- appreciating clearly what the *key success factors* are in the targeted markets and segments
- creating real *competitive advantage*
- out-thinking rivals.

There are three levels of strategy:

- *corporate* – the overall portfolio of businesses within an organization
- *competitive* – the search for, and maintenance of, competitive advantage in each and every business, product and/or service
- *functional* – the activities that deliver the competitive advantage.

These activities, products, services and businesses should not be analysed exclusively at an individual 'ring-fenced' level, but also in terms of the whole organization. Links should be forged wherever possible to generate *synergies*.

Strategies should not be thought of as having one single definition or perspective. Five have been discussed: visionary strategies, planned strategies and tactics, all of which address the future; present strategic positions, and patterns that have emerged with past decisions and strategies.

The strategic management process comprises three broad stages: analysis, creation and choice, and implementation. This three-stage approach can be linked to the popular and well-established concept of *strategic planning*.

Additional themes complement, but do not replace, strategic planning in the understanding of the realities of strategic management and strategic change, namely competitive advantage, emergent strategy creation, strategic competency, strategic leadership, and risk and crisis management.

There are three ways in which strategies are created: with visionary leadership, from a planning process and adaptively and incrementally as new decisions are taken in real time.

Strategy and strategic management in different sectors, such as small and global businesses, the public sector and not-for-profit organizations, have many similarities, but there are clear differences, especially of emphasis.

## QUESTIONS AND RESEARCH ASSIGNMENTS

1. What exactly is a strategy? What have you learned about different perspectives, levels and ways in which they are changed?

2. What are the key elements in the strategic management process?

3. How have Marks and Spencer sought to attain and maintain competitive advantage? What do you think their objectives might have been?

4. From your background knowledge, what might be the key success factors required for success in the airline business? How do you feel Virgin and easyJet have embraced these? How important a factor is 'risk taking'?

# INTERNET AND LIBRARY PROJECTS

1. Sainsbury's first became UK market leader for 'packaged groceries' in 1983, with some 16 per cent market share. Tesco and the Co-op each had 14.5 per cent and ASDA 8 per cent.

   The company's shares continued to outperform the *Financial Times* Index of top shares throughout the 1980s, and an editorial in the *Financial Times* commented that Sainsbury's 'performance combines profitability, productivity and a sense of social purpose.'

   However, there did not appear to be any 'grand strategy'.

   *We did not sit down in the early 70s and work out any corporate plan, or say that by a particular time we intended to be in a particular business, or to be of a particular size.*

   Roy Griffiths, Managing Director

   Rather, Griffiths claimed, Sainsbury's had 'identified and obsessively pursued' opportunities that fitted the company's corporate values, the 'basics of the business'.

   These were:

   ■ selling quality products at competitive (although not necessarily the cheapest) prices

   ■ exacting quality-control standards

   ■ extensive research into competitors and customers

   ■ strict financial management

   ■ tight control of suppliers

   ■ planned staff involvement.

   In recent years Tesco has overtaken Sainsbury to become the UK market leader. Why?

   Try to identify the successful strategies pursued by Tesco and the comparative shortcomings in the Sainsbury strategy.

   Can you identify any influence from changes in strategic leadership?

   ASDA http://www.asda.com
   J. Sainsbury plc http://www.j-sainsbury.co.uk
   Sainsbury's http://www.sainsburys.com
   Tesco http://www.tesco.com

2. The American engineering contractor, Bechtel, has acquired a reputation for its ability to rescue major public-sector projects which have either been in difficulty or behind schedule, or had cost over-runs. Specific examples of successful intervention by Bechtel as project managers include the following.

   | Appointment date | Project | Cost (£ billion) |
   | --- | --- | --- |
   | 1990 | Channel Tunnel | 10 |
   | 1993 | Cardiff Bay Barrage | 200 |
   | 1996 | Channel Tunnel Rail Link | 5.8 |
   | 1998 | Jubilee Line Extension | 3.5 |

   What are the competencies and capabilities possessed and exploited by Bechtel to create this record of success?

   Bechtel http://www.bechtel.com
   Cardiff Bay Barrage http://www.uwc.ca/pearson/ensy/mega/stephen/stephen.htm
   Channel Tunnel Rail Link http://www.ctrl.co.uk
   Eurotunnel http://www.eurotunnel.co.uk
   Jubilee Line Extension http://www.railway-technology.com/projects/jubilee

3. easyCinema is a recent venture of Stelios Haji-Ioannou. What is the basic vision or business model behind this new venture? To what extent is this vision similar to or different from his original vision for easyJet?

   Background details for easyJet can be found in Minicase 1.1.

   easyCinema http://www.easycinema.com

# Further reading

Houlden, EB (1986) Developing a company's strategic management capability, *Long Range Planning*, 19 (5).

Mintzberg, H (1987) The strategy concept 1: Five P's for strategy, *California Management Review*, Fall.

Henderson, BD (1989) The origin of strategy, *Harvard Business Review*, November–December.

Mintzberg, H (1990) The design school – reconsidering the basic premises of strategic management, *Strategic Management Journal*, 11.

Prahalad, CK and Hamel, G (1990) The core competency of the corporation, *Harvard Business Review*, May–June.

Ansoff, HI (1991) Critique of Henry Mintzberg's the design school – reconsidering the basic premises of strategic management, *Strategic Management Journal*, 12.

Stalk, G, Evans, P and Shulman (1992) Competing on capabilities – the new rules of corporate strategy, *Harvard Business Review*, March–April.

Hamel, G and Prahalad, CK (1993) Strategy as stretch and leverage, *Harvard Business Review*, March–April.

## References

Gladwell, M (2000) *The Tipping Point – How Little Things Can Make a Big Difference,* Little Brown.

Hinterhuber, H and Popp, W (1992) Are you a strategist or just a manager? *Harvard Business Review*, January–February.

James, B (1984) *Business Wargames,* Penguin.

Janis, IL (1972) *Victims of Groupthink,* 2nd edn, Houghton Mifflin.

Mathur, SS and Kenyon, A (1998) *Creating Value: Shaping Tomorrow's Business*, Butterworth-Heinemann.

Mintzberg, H, Ahlstrand, B and Lampel, J (1998) *Strategy Safari*, Prentice Hall.

Mintzberg, H (1989) *Mintzberg on Management*, Free Press.

Morrison, R and Lee, J (1979) From planning to clearer strategic thinking, *Financial Times*, 27 July.

Pascale, RT (1984) Perspectives on strategy – the real story behind Honda's success, *California Management Review*, 26.

Porter, ME (1980) *Competitive Strategy*, Free Press.

Porter, ME (1985) *Competitive Advantage*, Free Press.

Porter, ME (1996) What is strategy? *Harvard Business Review*, November–December.

Quinn, JB (1980) *Strategies for Change: Logical Incrementalism*, Irwin.

Stacey, RD (1993) *Strategic Management and Organizational Dynamics*, Pitman.

Williams, P (1976) *Crisis Management – Confrontations and Diplomacy in the Nuclear Age,* Martin Robertson.

# 2

# The Business Model, the Organizational Mission and Objectives

Strategies are means to ends – this chapter is about these ends. Organizations undertake purposeful activity; what they do is not without purpose. Ideally, that purpose will be understood, shared and supported by everyone in the organization such that there is a clear, if broad, direction for the activities and strategies. Establishing the purpose and direction is a key role of the strategic leader; and it will provide a basis for the more detailed objectives and performance targets for individual managers and employees. This does not imply that everyone always shares the more detailed objectives; indeed, there can often be internal conflicts over these. Moreover, what individual people actually do and achieve affects organizational performance. Hence, this chapter looks at the idea of purposeful activity by considering the organizational mission and objectives.

To achieve the purpose, we need a clear business model and so we begin this chapter with a more detailed look at this important foundation of strategy.

A number of economic and behavioural theories contributes to our understanding of this subject. Considered here are the potentially conflicting expectations of different stakeholders, the role of institutional shareholders, and whether the profit motive should be the key driving force. A separate section looks at inherent conflicts of interest in certain not-for-profit organizations and later at issues of social responsibility and business ethics which also affect behaviour, performance and outcomes in a variety of ways. The chapter opens with a case on Ben and Jerry's ice cream, a company which has always been proud of its commitment to social and environmental causes and which has recently been acquired by the Anglo-Dutch multinational corporation Unilever.

## Minicase 2.1 Ben and Jerry's Ice Cream                                                    US

This idiosyncratic business was founded and developed by two partners, both entrepreneurs but, at face value, unlikely businessmen. Ben Cohen was a college dropout who had become a potter. His friend from his schooldays was Jerry Greenfield, a laboratory assistant who had failed to make it into medical school. They had become 'seventies hippies with few real job prospects'. They decided they wanted to do something themselves and 'looked for something they might succeed at'. They 'liked food, so food it was!' They could not afford the machinery for making bagels, their first choice, but ice cream was affordable. In 1977 they opened an ice-cream parlour in Burlington, Vermont, where there were 'lots of students and no real competition'. They fostered a relaxed, hippy atmosphere and employed a blues pianist. Their ice cream was different, with large and unusual chunks.

They were instantly successful in their first summer, but sales fell off in the fall and winter when the snow arrived. They realized they would have to find outlets outside Vermont if they were to survive. Ben went on the road. Always dressed casually, he would arrive somewhere around 4.00 a.m. and then sleep in his car until a potential distributor opened. He was able to 'charm the distributors' and the business began to grow. Ben and Jerry's success provoked a response from the dominant market leader, Häagen Dazs, owned by Pillsbury. Their market share was 70 per cent of the luxury ice-cream market. Häagen Dazs threatened to withdraw their product from any distributors who also handled Ben and Jerry's. The two partners employed a lawyer and threatened legal action, but their real weapon was a publicity campaign targeted at Pillsbury itself, and its famous 'dough boy' logo. 'What's the Dough Boy afraid

of?' they asked. Their gimmicks generated massive publicity and they received an out-of-court settlement. More significantly, the publicity created new demand for luxury ice cream, and the company began to grow more rapidly than had ever been envisaged. A threat had been turned into a massive opportunity. Soon Ben and Jerry's had a segment market share of 39 per cent, just 4 per cent behind Häagen Dazs. The company has expanded internationally with mixed success. They have enjoyed only limited success in the UK 'because there was only limited marketing support'.

Perhaps not unexpectedly, given their background, Ben and Jerry have created a values-driven business; some of their ice creams have been linked to causes and interests they support and promote. Rainforest Crunch ice cream features nuts from Brazil; the key ingredients for Chocolate Fudge Brownie are produced by an inner-city bakery in Yonkers, New York; and they favour Vermont's dairy-farming industry. When the business needed equity capital to support its growth, local Vermont residents were given priority treatment. Ben and Jerry argue they are committed to their employees who 'bring their hearts and souls as well as their bodies and minds to work' but acknowledge that their internal opinion surveys show a degree of dissatisfaction with the amount of profits (7.5 per cent) given away every year to good causes.

The two realists with an unusual but definite ego drive later dropped out of day-to-day management '... the company needed a greater breadth of management than we had ...' and were content to be 'two casual, portly, middle-aged hippies'.

In early Spring 2000 the business was acquired by Unilever, the multinational foods, detergents and cosmetics business. Unilever already owned the UK market leader, Walls ice cream. Unilever and Walls had recently been investigated by the UK competition authorities because of their strategy of insisting that retailers only stock Walls ice cream if Unilever provide them with a freezer cabinet on loan.

**Questions**

1. Do you think the objectives of Ben and Jerry's will have had to change after this acquisition?

2. Do you think it will now feel like 'a different place to work', with different priorities?

**Ben and Jerry's** http://www.benjerry.com

*If you don't know where you are going, any road will take you there.*

Raymond G Viault, when Chief Executive Officer, Jacobs Suchard, Switzerland

*A voyage of a thousand miles begins with a single step. It is important that that step is in the right direction.*

Old Chinese saying, updated

*How can we go forward when we don't know which way we are facing?*

John Lennon, 1972

*Life can only be understood backward, but it must be lived forward.*

S Kierkegaard

## 2.1 Introduction

This chapter is about the idea of strategic direction and objectives – what is meant by the terminology used and the implications. First, and critically important, an organization needs a concise business model which clearly relates to its purpose and which is shared and understood. Objectives (in some form or another) should be set and communicated so that people know where the strategic leader wants the organization to be at some time in the future. At the same time it is essential that the objectives currently being pursued are clearly understood. Because of incremental changes in strategies the actual or implicit objectives may have changed from those that were established and made explicit sometime in the past. Objectives, therefore, establish direction, and in some cases set specific end points. They should have timescales or end dates attached to them. The attainment of them should be measurable in some way, and ideally they will encourage and motivate people.

It is important, straight away, to distinguish between the idea of a broad purpose and specific, measurable, milestones. The organization needs direction in terms of where the strategic leader wants it to go, and how he or she would wish it to develop. This is really related to the *mission* of the organization, and/or possibly a visionary statement concerning the future. This mission is likely to be stated broadly and generally, and it is unlikely that it can ever be achieved completely. Thus, the organization pursues the mission, looking for new opportunities and new ways of building value for customers, dealing with problems and seeking to progress continually in the chosen direction. Improvements in the overall situation towards the stated mission are the appropriate measure of performance.

Managers at all levels are likely to be set specific objectives to achieve. These, logically, are quantifiable targets for sales, profit, productivity or output, and performance against them is measured and evaluated. Objectives then become measurable points which indicate how the organization is making definite progress towards its broad purpose or mission.

Intended strategies are developed from the mission and the desired objectives as they are the means of achieving them. Hence, a change of objectives is likely to result in changes of strategy. At the same time it is important to realize that incremental, adaptive and emergent changes in strategy, whether the result of internal or external pressure, affect the levels of performance of the organization, i.e. the growth, profit or market share, and these performance levels should be related to the objectives actually being pursued.

The central theme of the chapter is that it is essential that the most senior managers in an organization understand clearly where their company is going, and why. Ideally, all managers will appreciate the overall mission, the business model and how their own role contributes to their attainment. The strategies being followed may be different to those that were originally stated, and there may be good reasons for this. Thus, the situation should be reviewed constantly and the strategic leader should seek to remain informed and aware of what is happening.

## 2.2 The business model

The business model provides an explanation of an organization's 'recipe for success', and it contains those factors that essentially define the business. It is, in many respects, the vehicle for delivering the purpose or mission. It encapsulates both 'big picture' and 'little picture' elements and it can be applied to both the present and the future. Over time the model, and the strategies it encapsulates, are likely to change, even if the basic purpose remains constant. Put simply, the business model should clearly show how the business is going to make money. Many dot.com business essentially failed because they did not address the issue of how they were going to make money. They offered technology to deliver a product that customers simply were not prepared to pay for – they failed to blend business and technology innovation.

Every organization is practicing a model, even though it may not have thought it through in any depth. Where this is the case, any success could well be short-lived as it implies there is a reliance on good fortune rather than analytical insight. One might argue that if the model can't be articulated or written down, then the organization's managers don't know what the model is.

As we saw in Chapter 1, the basic themes of the business model are products (or services), customers and competitive logic – the compelling reason for people to buy the products and services. It is, of course, important to recognize that good ideas and a plausible outline model are relatively easy to imagine and define … the secret lies in delivering the model and implementing the strategies. In military terms, tactics can be trickier than the grand strategy – even though we clearly need both.

The business model is outlined in Figure 2.1 and the elements of this diagram are discussed below.

The three fundamental elements of the model itself are shown at the top, metaphorically mounted on an important base.

**Figure 2.1** The business model

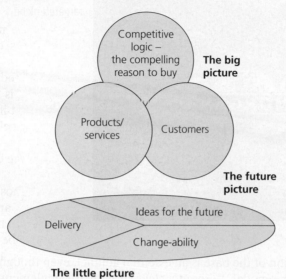

The little picture

*Products and services* constitute *what* the organization produces or markets. The range can be broad or narrow, focused or diversified. The choice, like the selection of target customers and competitive strategies, implies a decision concerning what to do and what not to do. There needs to be a clear strategic logic for what is in the range. Every one should be able to make a contribution to the business; none of them should be in a position where they bring harm to any of the others because, perhaps, they are underperforming and demanding cash subsidies.

*Customers* make up markets – they are the *who* in the model. Again the coverage can be narrow or broad. The scope of the business can be localized, national or international. And these can vary between the various products.

The link between products and customers represents the organization's strategic or competitive position. If it is a strong, or a winning, position, then there is a good reason for this.

When we add the third element, *competitive logic*, we have our *why*, our compelling reason to buy. These three together constitute the organizational 'big picture'. The competitive logic can be based on price; equally it can be based on difference.

We shall see later, in Chapter 6, that there are four basic approaches to the positioning element of the model:

- A narrow product (or service) range for a broad range of customers – the basics of the business model for Starbucks and the low-cost airlines

- A broad product range for a defined segment of the market – Harrods provides a vast choice of items for those people who are willing to pay premium prices and who enjoy being seen out with a Harrods bag

- A narrow range for a targeted niche – hand-made Morgan cars appeal to a limited number of people who want a sports car with an essentially pre-war style and who are willing to join a waiting list of some four years duration

- A broad range for a wide market – Amazon.com has added a diverse range of products to its original books and it sells to anyone who is interested in buying online.

**Morgan cars** A narrow range for a targeted niche

The *delivery* section of the base is an essential adjunct, even though it may not strictly be part of the outline model. Without a clear strategy for implementing and delivering the model the organization will be compromising on **efficiency** and effectiveness. This, then is the *how* element, and it includes the structure of the organization and the operations and activities carried out by people within the structure. Cost management and synergy are key themes. Unnecessary costs should be avoided; equally it can be a mistake to 'penny-pinch' on things that really matter to customers. At the same time it can be helpful if the activities complement and support each other. This is the 'little picture' behind the 'big picture'.

What works successfully today cannot be guaranteed to work for ever. Business models and strategies have life cycles and therefore organizations must address *when* they might need to make changes. They need an appreciation of a 'future picture', concerning changes to *what, how and for whom.* This is the *future model.*

Essentially the right model changes with circumstances. Therefore developing and adapting the business model is the key to business success. Getting it right is essentially the main test for the top management of any business. When they get the business model wrong profits suffer. In 2003, out of town retailer Matalan had ceased to get it right. Chief Executive John King is quoted as saying: 'I've come to the conclusion the value wasn't good enough, we have not been aggressive enough on price and we went on promotion too late.' As a result, Matalan was forced to cut prices by 50 per cent before Christmas and 75 per cent in the New Year.

We can use Matalan to reprise the main elements of an effective business model. The business model must clearly show and prove how you are going to make money. It must address and answer the following questions.

- What is different about our value proposition?
- Who are our customers?
- What do customers value today?
- What will customers value tomorrow?

The questions asked of customers should also be addressed of investors. The capital markets need to be convinced that a business understands the needs of investors. If not they will not buy into the business model.

Ensuring the future model can also be delivered when it is needed means that the organization needs *change-ability*, which in turn will be very dependent upon its strategic leadership.

Hamel (2000) argues that new business models are emerging all the time as fresh opportunities are found. Amongst the examples he cites are:

1. Consolidation in the small and medium-sized enterprises (SME) sector as large organizations grow bigger by systematically absorbing a series of small (and sometimes local) businesses. Examples include funeral services and Hanson, the UK-based aggregates business which operates mainly in the US and UK

2. Throwaway varieties of such products as watches and cameras

3. Individual customizing. Collector's editions of the ubiquitous Barbie doll appeal to certain enthusiasts and command a premium price. Apple's iPod allows people to download music of their own choosing to compile a CD of their favourites.

Minicase 2.2 on Enterprise Cars provides an illustration of a very successful business model and the following examples provide an insight into the reality that there is any number of possible models – some of which imply clear choices and compromises – and their relative value diminishes over time.

**William Morrison**  The William Morrison supermarket group, strongest in the north of England and still a family company in many respects, competes successfully with Tesco, Sainsbury and ASDA. Founded in Bradford and led by the septuagenarian entrepreneur Sir Ken Morrison, and prior to its acquisition of Safeway (Case 4.5), Morrisons had approaching a 20 per cent share of the food retailing market in Yorkshire, although across the country as a whole it was nearer 4 per cent. The market leader, Tesco, now has 18 per cent of the UK market.

Fundamentally the large supermarket chains offer broadly the same product ranges, although there will be some clear differences. Across a wide range of goods there are the leading brands and own-label alternatives, which normally are cheaper.

Morrisons' customers are not going to be markedly different from those who pick Tesco or ASDA. They all emphasize competitive prices. Location, of course, and convenience will influence customer choice. Sainsbury is somewhat different as their prices overall are slightly higher. Waitrose (owned by John Lewis) and Marks and Spencer, with a focus on premium products and higher prices, have a different market appeal. So where is the Morrisons 'compelling reason to buy'?

The Morrison strategy is not identical to those of its rivals. Morrison focuses on a composite package of 'everyday low prices' (which itself isn't unique – both ASDA and Tesco claim the same), multi-buys and special offers. It is this combination that makes it distinctive. Unusually it also manufactures a substantial proportion of its own food products, even owning its own abattoirs. It packages most of its own fresh food and displays these in-store as they would feature in a traditional open street market. This is very deliberate and it reflects Morrisons' origins as market traders. In addition, every store looks the same. Bananas are hung up to keep them fresh, when normally they will be laid out in trays. Again unusually, it owns its own delivery fleet rather than relying on specialist logistics companies. In a Morrisons store you will see fishmongers and butchers in white hats and striped aprons – which is pretty ubiquitous – but they will be found in a section of the store which is designed to feel like an open street market. The focus is on food; Morrisons is less interested than its main rivals in clothing and other non-food products. There are no online sales and no loyalty cards.

In this respect we can see Morrisons' northern roots being strongly reflected in its ambience and culture. Some would argue that these northern roots are also reflected in Morrisons taking more trade credit days from its suppliers than any of its leading rivals.

**Dell** It has been said that Michael Dell, founder and CEO of Dell Computer, is fast becoming the Henry Ford of the information age – as a mass producer of standardized products. Dell assembles and sells PCs and laptops and, more recently, servers and storage hardware. The company began when Dell was a university student some 20 years ago. In the early days Dell sold only to the business market, and, although this remains his dominant market, home consumers are a growth area. The business model is simple and powerful – and unusual for the industry.

Dell buys in standardized components in order to minimize the need for any expensive R&D. Sales are direct to customers, typically over the Internet. Together with a telephone helpline, this alleviates the need for middlemen and the consequential distributor margins. Dell builds to order and carries very little inventory of finished products. This cannot happen effectively without strict attention to detail and constant process re-engineering.

As a result Dell has relatively low costs. It then adopts a very aggressive pricing policy in order to seize market share from any competitor who has taken its eye off the ball and

---

## Minicase 2.2 Enterprise Cars

Enterprise Cars was founded in St Louis, Missouri, in 1957 as a car leasing business. Rentals began in 1963. Today, with a turnover of US$6 billion, it is the largest car rental business in the US and growing in Europe. It is still a private business controlled by the founding family. The company has 500,000 vehicles, making it the largest buyer of cars in America. The real growth has occurred in the 1990s when the market began to realize the value of the Enterprise business model – which is different from the other majors like Alamo, Avis and Hertz.

### The product and the demand

Whereas most car rental businesses specialize in the travelling public, Enterprise focuses on those car owners who have been parted from their own vehicles. This segment has generally been avoided by the other leading competitors. Enterprise customers' cars might be in a garage for service; more likely they have been subject to accident or breakdown. Enterprise staff collect customers from whichever garage they leave their car and drive them to their own compound.

### The customers

Some customers can plan and book in advance, but most are making an inevitable late booking. Consequently they are often people experiencing some sort of distress and agitation because of the uncertainty. In addition, the actual customer might be an insurance company rather than the car owner himself.

### Operational aspects

Enterprise is decentralized into 5000 individual offices with an average of 10 employees each. They are all profit centres. There is extensive monitoring and tracking of cash and profit and customer satisfaction. The stated intention is to make every office feel like a local family business with staff who are 'passionate about service'. There is an extensive graduate recruitment programme to find able young people to work alongside mature, experienced front-line staff. Coffee and doughnuts are provided whilst customers fill in their paperwork.

Enterprise Cars http://www.enterprise.com

let its costs increase. The assumption is that this business model can be used for other consumer electrical products such as digital music players and flat screen televisions. Some critics argue that the model has to be limited as a substantial proportion of consumers would be unwilling to buy without being able to inspect a model in a store. But the logic of this argument becomes thinner as more and more of us know people who have bought a Dell – we can inspect theirs.

**Avon**  Like Dell, Avon's business model is also built around direct selling. Avon was 117 years old in 2003, having started life as the California Perfume Company. Most of us would recognize the brand from the 'army' of Avon ladies who deliver catalogues to their customers every few weeks, take their orders and later deliver their choices. Customers pay their local agent. The products themselves are manufactured in various countries around the world.

Although the direct selling remains constant, other elements of the model are constantly changing. Existing product ranges are likely to change at any time; and new products are added, often replacing poor-selling items. Packaging often changes to freshen the appearance of products. No two catalogues are identical, although some products do appear regularly; and there are always special offers. More recently 'well-ness' products for health- and fitness-conscious customers have been included. These range from vitamin supplements to yoga mats. Avon 'Cosmeceuticals', brands endorsed by dermatologists, fit somewhere between medications and cosmetics.

Avon has also diversified to widen its overall customer appeal. It became prominent as a convenient supplier to middle class mothers who were short of time for personal shopping, but this is no longer adequate. Although the average age of Avon's customers is around 39, this average is falling slowly. In part this is affected by the wider product choices; it is also enhanced by the choice of younger role models to promote the products. Model Yasmin le Bon and tennis stars, Serena and Venus Williams are included here. In addition, in the US, Avon has developed its new Mark range for 16–24 year old customers.

Like Ikea, Avon has seen the benefit of moving into China and Russia, two huge consumer markets. However, direct selling is illegal in China and so Avon trades through specialist boutiques.

**London Zoo**  In the case of London Zoo – see Minicase 2.5 – we see evidence of difficult decisions concerning 'products' and customers. Without at least some retailing activities London Zoo would be out of business. A part of the Zoological Society of London, the zoo has a key scientific purpose related to conservation and the preservation of endangered species. However, those animals that are particularly attractive to most paying visitors are often not the most endangered. Moreover, there is a duty to educate as a large proportion of the visitors are children. Many national animal collections around the world are much more heavily subsidized, but in recent years London Zoo has not been allowed to become grant-dependent. It has had to establish a revenue-generating business model without losing sight of its origins and fundamental purpose – within the constraint of its location in a Royal Park which seriously affects any possibility of expansion. London Zoo has therefore had to build a model which balances conservation, education and entertainment.

**The Opera**  Globally, opera can only survive if it is subsidized, so again the business model must embrace this. The subsidy can be from government – in the UK The Arts

Council, which, for example, accounts for 30 per cent of the budget at The Royal Opera House – or corporate and private donors.

Customers are willing to pay very high prices for the best seats as long as the quality performance merits it. And many operagoers are discerning. In part opera is expensive because it demands a large number of singers and musicians. In the UK, prices for the Royal Opera House Covent Garden rise to £160.00 – although the cheapest restricted view seats can sometimes be bought for £3.00. The Metropolitan in New York is more expensive, with top prices of US$280.00. But opera houses have to be maintained through the year and orchestras retained. They are not going to be full of customers every night of the year. The market is too limited for that.

Opera has long enjoyed an elitist image; operagoers are so-called aficionados. And yet the reality has changed in recent years. The opera 'product' now extends well beyond the world's leading opera houses. The change began when *Nessun Dorma* was used as the theme music for the 1990 football World Cup and, on the back of this, the concert by 'The Three Tenors' was broadcast to the world on television and the accompanying CD became the best-selling classical album of all time. More recently more populist singers like Lesley Garrett and Russell Watson have brought operatic arias to an ever-wider audience. And who will ever forget Julia Roberts being introduced to the opera in the film *Pretty Woman* and being so moved she almost 'peed in her pants'!

In other words, the opera 'product' now encapsulates CD and popular television as well as actual performances for a growing and changing market. The leading singers have been very carefully 'packaged' and marketed to give them a wider appeal.

**Invensys** Invensys began life as BTR and was later absorbed by another engineering conglomerate, Siebe. When Sir Owen Green stepped down as strategic leader in 1993

**The Opera** Metropolitan Opera House, New York © Bettman/Corbis

BTR had enjoyed some thirty years of acquisition, diversification and growth. It was the seventh largest company in the UK. Ten years later Invensys was relegated from the FTSE 100, the share price had collapsed and the debt was regarded as 'junk'. Things began to go downhill when the once successful business model was no longer appropriate. Interestingly Hanson, a very similar business to BTR in many respects, was deliberately split into five separate businesses. BTR did not opt for such radical change and has paid a penalty.

The BTR business model relied on control through cash. Companies, typically anything involving engineering of some form, were bought if they were undervalued and capable of some rejuvenation. Overheads were reduced and parts might be sold on as the company was split up. Prices were increased because many customers are captive in the short term. Strategic leaders of business units were rewarded for profit success – but there was a penalty for failure! Cash was repatriated from the individual businesses to BTR's head office and invested selectively in those businesses that could provide the highest returns. Synergy and linkages between the businesses was not high on the agenda.

However, as the productivity reforms of the Thatcher government took hold the number of undervalued businesses declined. They were driven out of business altogether. When the economy stagnated, the ability to generate cash as BTR had been able to do in the past was also reduced. This led to less investment in the businesses, which became less competitive as a result. BTR was now in a downward spiral.

A new business model was based on divestment and selective acquisition to build a different empire of related businesses – but the company has never been able to restore its cash-generating successes of the 1980s and early 1990s. Invensys now has its fifth strategic leader in ten years.

## 2.3  Definitions, terminology and examples

Box 2.1 defines the terms *vision*, *mission* and *objectives* and provides a range of examples from the private and public sectors. Figure 2.2 shows the relationships between these terms, highlighting their key constituents. The examples in Box 2.1 were selected to illustrate the relevant points, not because they are superior or inferior to those of other organizations; they should be evaluated in this light.

The word 'values' is important in both the mission and vision statement, but with a different emphasis. It is important that a mission statement captures how an organization will create and add value for its customers; the vision relates to the corporate values that should be held by employees and visible to the outside world.

The expression *aims* is sometimes used as an alternative to mission. The term *goals* is seen as synonymous with objectives, and in this book the terms are used interchangeably. Specifically, where other works are being referred to and those authors have used the term goal as opposed to objective, their terminology is retained. It is also important to distinguish between long-term and short-term objectives or goals. Thompson and Strickland (1980) provide a useful distinction. They argue that objectives overall define the specific kinds of performance and results that the organization seeks to produce through its activities. The *long term objectives* relate to the desired performance and results on an ongoing basis; *short-term objectives* are concerned with the near-term performance targets that the organization desires to reach in progressing towards its

**Figure 2.2** Vision and mission statements and objectives

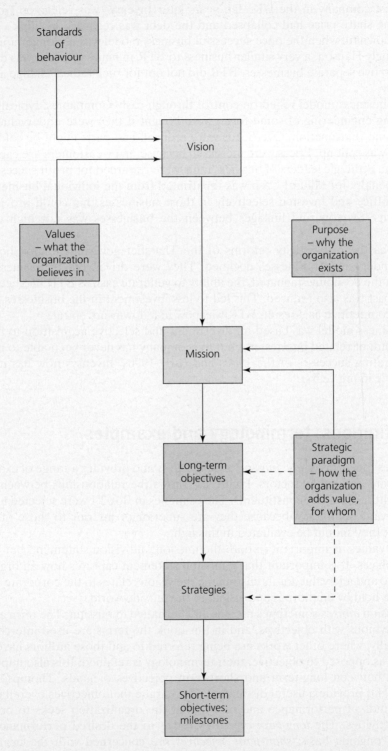

## Box 2.1  Examples of Vision, Mission and Objectives Statements

### Vision statements

A vision statement describes what the company is to become in the (long-term) future.

### The Sony spirit

*'Sony doesn't serve markets; Sony makes markets.'*

Sony is a trail blazer, always a seeker of the unknown. Sony will never follow old trails, yet to be trod. Through this progress Sony wants to serve mankind.

**Sony** http://www.sony.com

### WH Smith (1995)

*'There's nowhere quite like WH Smith. It's full of energy and colour and excitement.'*

*'Just when you think you know them, they surprise you. Everywhere you look there are fresh, inspired ideas.'*

*'Smith's is an essential part of life. It's a unique blend of information, inspiration and just plain fun.'*

*'Everything is chosen with thought, designed with care and presented with imagination.'*

*'Customer service is instinctive. It's the right help at the right time, by people who know what they're saying and love what they're doing.'*

*'Smith's builds its reputation day by day, product by product and customer by customer.'*

*'Always in front.'*

We can see represented here: adding new values, innovation, products which match customer needs, effective presentation, service and constant improvement. Given the recent performance of the company it is debatable whether this has been achieved.

**WH Smith** http://www.whsmith.co.uk

### British Airways

*'The world's favourite airline'.*

This vision, first adopted in the 1990s, focuses on employees and customers. The related mission emphasized BA's desire to be the world's first truly global airline, which in turn generated a corporate strategy of carefully selected alliances. To be feasible, however, it has always been essential that BA staff believe in the vision and act accordingly. In recent years staff trust and morale has declined as costs have been cut dramatically and the airline's profitability has declined.

**British Airways** http://www.britishairways.com

### Mission statements

The mission reflects the essential purpose of the organization, concerning particularly why it is in existence, the nature of the business(es) it is in, and the customers it seeks to serve and satisfy.

### The Girl Guides Association

*'To help a girl reach her highest potential.'*

These eight words cut straight to the heart of the movement; there is a clear and direct statement of purpose.

**Girl Guides Association** http://www.wagggsworld.org

### *Financial Times* Conferences

*'The mission of the FTC is to organize conferences on subjects of interest to the international business community, using the highest calibre speakers and providing attending delegates with the finest service, thereby providing a low-cost and time-efficient means of both obtaining impartial quality information and making senior-level industry contacts.'*

We can see a clear definition of the business, a formulation of objectives, delivery strategies, means of differentiating the service and stakeholder relevance.

***Financial Times*** http://www.news.ft.com

**KEY CONCEPTS**

### Virgin Atlantic Airways

*'As the UK's second long-haul carrier, to build an intercontinental network concentrating on those routes with a substantial established market and clear indication of growth potential, by offering the highest possible service and lowest possible cost.'*

Not particularly elegant in style, but it does clarify both the target markets and the source of competitive advantage.

**Virgin Atlantic** http://www.virgin-atlantic.com

### Long-term objectives

Objectives are desired states or results linked to particular timescales and concerning such things as size or type of organization, the nature and variety of the areas of interest and levels of success.

### British Airports Authority (BAA): Open objectives

*'BAA aims to enhance the value of the shareholders' investments by achieving steady and remunerative long-term growth. Its strategy for developing and operating world-class international airports that are safe, secure, efficient and profitable is based on a commitment to continuously enhancing the quality of service to passengers and business partners alike. This process of constant improvement includes cost-effective investment in new airport facilities closely matched to customer demand.'*

These are in the context of a stated mission to 'make BAA the most successful airport company in the world'.

**British Airports Authority** http://www.baa.co.uk

### HP Bulmer Holdings: Multiple stakeholder objectives

For many years HP Bulmer listed several specific objectives in its Annual Report, from which the following has been reproduced with permission from the company. The list and the commitment behind them are clearly laudable, but, having said that, company performance deteriorated in 2001 and 2002 and the business was acquired by Scottish and Newcastle Breweries. Objectives will not always be achieved.

*'Our mission is to remain the world's most successful cider company. We will continue to measure our success in terms of market leadership, product quality, increasing shareholder value, and rewarding employment opportunities for our employees. This will be achieved by attaining the following objectives:*

1. *Lead and grow the UK and international cider markets through meeting consumer needs by superior marketing and sustained high levels of customer service.*
2. *Maintain lowest industry costs and ensure the most economical supply of essential and quality raw materials.*
3. *Be dedicated to fulfilling the requirements of all our customers through achieving excellence in our products, operations and service.*
4. *Adopt best practice across all of our activities through an innovative approach to product, process development and information technology.*
5. *Foster a culture of continuous improvement through self-motivation, team work and acceptance of change.*
6. *Provide competitive pay, employee share ownership and single status employment while achieving a link between performance, reward and shareholder interests.*
7. *Give all employees the opportunity to develop skills and potential through actively improving their own and the company's performance. Promote from within whenever appropriate.*
8. *Keep employees informed of policy, plans and performance. Invite comments and feedback and, through employee involvement, show how individual and team efforts contribute towards the company's success.*

9.  *Provide a high quality working environment taking all appropriate steps to ensure the health and safety of our employees, customers and the community.*

10. *Preserve the quality of life and environment in our everyday work and to benefit our local communities whenever an affordable opportunity arises.'*

Multiple objectives, stated in this form, will demand priorities and trade-offs at different times, but their value is that they draw attention to the potentially conflicting needs of all the major stakeholders.

**HP Bulmer Holdings** http://www.bulmer.co.uk

### Kirin Brewery (Japan): Closed objectives

*'For the decade of the 1990s:*

■ *Increase sales from 1250 billion yen (1990) to 1700 billion (2000)*

■ *Increase sales of non-beer products to 60 per cent of total revenue*

■ *Diversifying (further) into biotechnology, construction engineering, information systems and service industries*

■ *Become a global corporation.'*

**Kirin Brewery** http://www.kirin.co.jp/english/index.html

Measurement can be straightforward for an objective such as 'the achievement of a minimum return of 20 per cent of net capital employed in the business, but with a target of 25 per cent, in the next 12 months'. If the objective is less specific, for example, 'continued customer satisfaction, a competitive return on capital employed and real growth in earnings per share next year', measurement is still possible but requires a comparison of competitor returns and the monitoring of customer satisfaction through, say, the number of complaints received. Richards (1978) uses the terms 'open' and 'closed' to distinguish between objectives that are clearly measurable and typically finance based (closed) and those that are less specific and essentially continuing.

long-term objectives. Making use of such techniques as management by objectives, these performance targets can be agreed with individual managers, who are then given responsibility for their attainment and held accountable.

## 2.3.1  Vision statements

While mission statements have become increasingly popular for organizations, *vision statements* are less prevalent. The lack of a published statement, of course, is not necessarily an indication of a lack of vision. Where they exist they reflect the company's vision of some future state, which ideally the organization will achieve. Terminology and themes such as a world-class manufacturer, a quality organization, a provider of legendary service and a stimulating, rewarding place to work might well appear. The essential elements focus on those values to which the organization is committed and appropriate standards of behaviour for all employees. Possible improvement paths, employee development programmes and measures or indicators of progress should be established for each element of the vision.

*Strategy development is like driving around a roundabout. The signposts are only useful if you know where you want to go. Some exits lead uphill, some downhill – most are one-way streets and some have very heavy traffic indeed. The trick is in picking the journey's end before you set out – otherwise you go around in circles or pick the wrong road.*

Gerry M Murphy, when Chief Executive Officer, Greencore plc, Ireland

*Arne Ness said, when he climbed Everest: I had a dream. I reached it. I lost the dream and I miss it. When we reached our dream we didn't have another long-term objective. So people started to produce their own new objectives, not a common objective, but different objectives depending on where they were in the organization. I learned that before you reach an objective you must be ready with a new one, and you must start to communicate it to the organization. But it is not the goal itself that is important … it is the fight to get there.*

Jan Carlzon, when Chairman and Chief Executive Officer, Scandinavian Airlines System

### 2.3.2 Mission statements

The corporate mission is the overriding *raison d'être* for the business. Ackoff (1986), however, claimed that many corporate mission statements prove worthless, one reason being that they consist of loose expressions such as 'maximize growth potential' or 'provide products of the highest quality'. How, he queries, can a company determine whether it has attained its maximum growth potential or highest quality? His points are still valid today. Primarily, the mission statement should not address what an organization must do in order to survive, but what it has chosen to do in order to thrive. It should be positive, visionary and motivating.

Ackoff suggests that a good mission statement has five characteristics.

■ It will contain a formulation of objectives that enables progress towards them to be measured.

■ It differentiates the company from its competitors.

■ It defines the business(es) that the company wants to be in, not necessarily is in.

■ It is relevant to all stakeholders in the firm, not just shareholders and managers.

■ It is exciting and inspiring.

Campbell (1989) argues that to be valuable mission statements must reflect corporate values, and the strategic leader and the organization as a whole should be visibly pursuing the mission. He takes a wider perspective than Ackoff by including aspects of the corporate vision and arguing that there are four key issues involved in developing a useful mission.

First, it is important to clarify the purpose of the organization – why it exists. Hanson plc, for example, which is referred to at various stages in this book, was led by Lord James Hanson for some 25 years and he stated:

*It is the central tenet of my faith that the shareholder is king. My aim is to advance the shareholder's interest by increasing earnings per share.*

By contrast, and at the same time, Lex Service Group published an alternative view:

*We will exercise responsibility in our dealings with all our stakeholders and, in the case of conflict, balance the interest of the employees and shareholders on an equal basis over time.*

The implications of these contrasting perspectives are discussed in the next section of this chapter.

Second, the mission statement should describe the business and its activities, and the position that it wants to achieve in its field. Third, the organization's values should be stated. How does the company intend to treat its employees, customers and suppliers, for example? Finally, it is important to ensure that the organization behaves in the way that it promises it will. This is important because it can inspire trust in employees and others who significantly influence the organization.

It is generally accepted that in successful companies middle and junior managers know where the strategic leaders are taking the company and why. In less successful organizations there is often confusion about this.

Mission statements, like vision statements, can all too easily just 'state the obvious' and as a result have little real value. The secret lies in clarifying what makes a company different and a more effective competitor, rather than simply restating those requirements that are essential for meeting key success factors. A mission (or vision) statement which could easily be used by another business, whether in the same industry or not – as many can be – is, simply, of no great value. Companies that succeed long term are those which create competitive advantages and sustain their strong positions with flexibility and improvement. The vision and mission should support this.

The principal purpose of these statements is communication, both externally and internally and, arguably, a major benefit for organizations is the thinking they are forced to do in order to establish sound statements. Nevertheless, many are still worded poorly. In addition, it is essential that the mission (or vision) is more than a plaque in a foyer; employees have to make the words mean something through their actions. For this to happen, employees must feel that the organization actually means what it is saying in the mission and vision statements. There must be an element of trust, for without it the desired outcomes will not be achieved.

The mission clearly corresponds closely to the basic philosophy or vision underlying the business, and if there is a sound philosophy, strategies that generate success will be derived from it. Sock Shop was founded in 1983, with a simple vision. One newspaper has summarized it as, 'shopping in big stores for basic items like stockings is a fag, but nipping into an attractive kiosk at an Underground station, British Rail concourse or busy high street is quick, convenient and can be fun'. From this have emerged six key marketing features or strategies, which have become the foundations of the company's success and rapid growth:

- shops located within areas of heavy pedestrian traffic
- easily accessible products
- friendly and efficient service
- a wide range of quality products designed to meet the needs of customers
- attractive presentations
- competitive selling prices.

In 1989, after a number of years of growth and success, Sock Shop began to lose money. The hot summer weather and the London Underground strikes were blamed for falling sales. Increasing interest rates caused additional financial problems. Moreover, Sock Shop expanded into the US and this had proved costly. However, in February 1990 Sock Shop founder, Sophie Mirman, commented: 'We provide everyday necessities in a fashionable manner ... our concept remains sound. Our merchandise continues to be not merely "lifestyle".' Sophie Mirman has since lost control of Sock Shop but her vision prevails.

## 2.4  Objectives: issues and perspectives

A full consideration of objectives incorporates three aspects:

- an appreciation of the objectives that the organization is actually pursuing and achieving – where it is going and why
- the objectives that it might pursue, and the freedom and opportunity it has to make changes
- specific objectives for the future.

This chapter looks at the issues that affect and determine the first two of these. Decisions about specific future objectives are considered later in the book (Chapter 9). We begin, though, by looking briefly at a number of theories of business organizations and considering the role and importance of stakeholders.

### 2.4.1  Market models

Basic microeconomic theory states that firms should seek to maximize profits and that this is achieved where marginal revenue is equal to marginal cost. A number of assumptions underpin this theory, including the assumptions that firms clearly understand the nature of the demand for their products, and why people buy, and that they are willing and able to control production and sales as the model demands. In reality, decision makers do not have perfect knowledge and production and sales are affected by suppliers and distributors.

However, this basic theory has resulted in the development of four market models (Table 2.1), and the characteristics of these in respect of barriers to entry into the industry and the marketing opportunities (differentiation potential; price and non-price competition) determine whether or not there is a real opportunity to achieve significant profits.

In markets which approach pure competition (pure competition as such is theoretical), firms will only make 'normal' profits, the amount required for them to stay in the industry. Products are 'commodities', not differentiated, and so premium prices for certain brands are not possible. There are no major barriers to entry into the industry and so new suppliers are attracted if there are profits to be made. Competition results, and if supply exceeds demand the ruling market price is forced down and only the efficient firms survive.

In monopolistic competition there are again several suppliers, some large, many small, but products are differentiated. However, as there are once more no major barriers to entry the above situation concerning profits applies. Newcomers increase supply and although those firms with distinctive products can charge some premium they will still have to move in line with market prices generally, and this will have a dampening effect on profits.

Only in **oligopoly** and monopoly markets, where a small number of large firms is dominant, is there real opportunity for 'supernormal' profits, in excess of what is required to stay in business. However, in oligopoly the small number of large firms tend

**Table 2.1** Structural characteristics of four market models

| Market | Number of firms | Type of product | Control over price by supplier | Entry conditions | Non-price competition[*] | Examples[†] |
|---|---|---|---|---|---|---|
| Pure competition | Large | Standardized Identical or almost identical | None | Free | None | Agricultural products; some chemicals; printing; laundry services |
| Monopolistic competition | Large | Differentiated | Some | Relatively easy | Yes | Clothing; furniture; soft drinks; plumbers restaurants |
| Oligopoly[**] | Few or a few dominant | Standardized or differentiated | Limited by mutual interdependence Considerable if collusion takes place | Difficult | Yes | Standardized: cement; sugar; fertilizers Differentiated: margarine; soaps; detergents |
| Pure monopoly | One | Unique | Considerable | Blocked | Yes | British Gas (domestic consumers); water companies in their regions; local bus companies in certain towns |

[*]Non-price competition occurs in many ways, e.g. by attempts to increase the extent of product differentiation and buyer preference through advertising, brand names, trade marks, promotions, distribution outlets; by new product launch and innovation, etc.
[†]Useful further reading: Doyle, P and Gidengil, ZB (1977) An empirical study of market structures. *Journal of Management Studies*, 14(3), October, 316–28. Some of the examples are taken from this.
[**]There are many oligopoly models of collusive and non-collusive type. They make varying behavioural and structural assumptions.
*Journal of Management Studies* http://www.blackwellpublishers.co.uk/journals/JOMS

to be wary of each other and prices are held back to some extent for fear of losing market share. Suppliers are interdependent and fear that a price decrease will be met by competitors (thus reducing profits) and price increases will not (hence market share will be threatened). There are two types of oligopoly, depending on whether opportunities exist for significant differentiation. In all of these models competition is a major determinant of profit potential and therefore objectives must be set with competitors in mind. In a monopoly (again somewhat theoretical in a pure sense) excess profits could be made if government did not act as a restraint. In the UK, although such **public sector**

**organizations** as British Gas and British Telecom have been privatized, their actions in terms of supply and pricing are monitored and regulated.

### 2.4.2 Stakeholder theory

The influence of external stakeholders will be examined again in Chapter 4, which looks at the business environment, but it is important to introduce the topic at this stage. A further assumption of profit-maximizing theory is that shareholders in the business should be given first priority and be the major consideration in decision-making, and this arose because early economic theorists saw owners and managers as being synonymous. This assumption no longer holds, however. A study of market models demonstrates the important role played by competitors and by government as a restraining force, and it was also suggested that organizations must pay some regard to their suppliers and distributors. In addition, managers and employees must be considered. The decisions taken by managers which create incremental change will be influenced by the objectives and values that they believe are important. Managers are paid employees, and whilst concerned about profits, they will also regard growth and security as important.

These are all *stakeholders*. Freeman (1984) defines stakeholders as any group or individual who can affect, or is affected by, the performance of the organization. Newbould and Luffman (1979) argue that current and future strategies are affected by:

- external pressures from the marketplace, including competitors, buyers and suppliers; shareholders; pressure groups; and government
- internal pressures from existing commitments, managers, employees and their trade unions
- the personal ethical and moral perspectives of senior managers.

Stakeholder theory, then, postulates that the objectives of an organization will take account of the various needs of these different interested parties who will represent some type of informal coalition. Their relative power will be a key variable, and the organization will on occasions 'trade off' one against the other, establishing a hierarchy of relative importance. Stakeholders see different things as being important and receive benefits or rewards in a variety of ways, as featured in Table 2.2.

Stakeholder interests are not always consistent. For example, investment in new technology might improve product quality and as a result lead to increased profits. While customers who are shareholders might perceptively benefit, if the investment implies lost jobs then employees, possibly managers, and their trade unions may be dissatisfied. If the scale of redundancy is large and results in militant resistance, the government may become involved.

The various stakeholders are not affected in the same way by every strategic decision and, consequently, their relative influence will vary from decision to decision. In 1995 Shell, one of Europe's most successful and respected companies, was forced to change an important strategic decision following a high-profile campaign by a leading pressure group. Shell wanted to sink its redundant Brent Spar oil platform in deep seas some 150 miles west of Scotland. It had reached an agreement with the UK government that, scientifically, this was the most appropriate means of disposal for the platform. Greenpeace objected and protesters boarded the platform, claiming that it still contained 5000 tonnes of oil which would eventually be released to pollute the sea. The ensuing and professionally orchestrated publicity fuelled public opinion, and there were

**Table 2.2** Examples of stakeholder interests

| | |
|---|---|
| Shareholders | Annual dividends; increasing the value of their investment in the company as the share price increases. Both are affected by growth and profits<br>Institutional shareholders may balance high-risk investments and their anticipated high returns with more stable investments in their portfolio |
| Managers | Salaries and bonuses; perks; status from working for a well-known and successful organization; responsibility; challenge; security |
| Employees | Wages; holidays; conditions and job satisfaction; security – influenced by trade union involvement |
| Consumers | Desirable and quality products; competitive prices – very much in relation to competition; new products at appropriate times |
| Distributors | On time and reliable deliveries |
| Suppliers | Consistent orders; payment on time |
| Financiers | Interest payments and loan repayments; like payment for supplies, affected by cash flow |
| Government | Payment of taxes and provision of employment; contribution to the nation's exports |
| Society in general | Socially responsible actions – sometimes reflected in pressure groups |

Note: This is not intended to constitute a complete list.

protests in a number of European countries, including attacks on petrol stations in Germany. Shell backed down and agreed to investigate other possibilities for disposal. The UK government expressed both anger and disappointment with this decision. Independent inspectors later proved that Greenpeace's claims were gross exaggerations – the residual oil was much, much less than 5000 tonnes. The press concluded: 'Shell went wrong in spending too much time convincing government of the case for sea-bed dumping, but not attaching enough importance to consulting other stakeholder groups.'

Shell had been made to appear socially irresponsible, yet the ethics of the Greenpeace campaign are questionable; these issues are explored further at the end of this chapter.

Waterman (1994) contends that successful companies do not automatically make shareholders their first priority. Instead, they pay primary attention to employees and customers and, as a result, they perform more effectively than their rivals. The outcome is superior profits and wealth creation for the shareholders. Simon (1964) argues that one of the main reasons for an organization's collapse is a failure to incorporate the important motivational concerns of key stakeholders. Small businesses, for example, are generally weak in relation to their suppliers, especially if these are larger well-established concerns; and if they neglect managing their cash flow and fail to pay their accounts on time they will find their deliveries stopped. For any organization, if new products or services fail to provide consumers with what they are looking for, however well produced or low priced they might be, they will not sell.

A 1999 survey by Deloitte Consulting confirmed that 'customer-centric' manufacturing companies worldwide are 60 per cent more profitable than those that are less committed to customers. In addition, they enjoy lower operating costs. Customer-centricity is seen as a 'systematic process which sets objectives for customer loyalty and retention and then tracks performance towards those goals'. It should facilitate the development of higher added value, premium-price products.

**Figure 2.3** Satisfying stakeholders

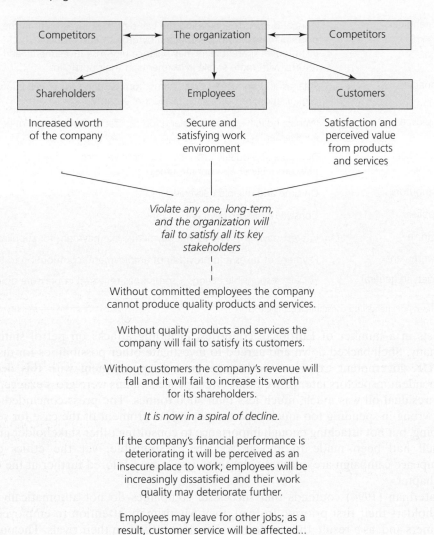

Figure 2.3 shows that shareholders, employees and customers are the three key stakeholders that the organization must satisfy, but invariably in a competitive environment: if they fail with any group long term they will place the organization in jeopardy through a spiral of decline. Figure 2.4 is an alternative presentation of the same points. On the left is a virtuous circle of growth and prosperity. Satisfied, perhaps even delighted, customers enable high financial returns, which can be used in part to reward employees. A perception of fairness here can be instrumental for motivating employees to keep customers satisfied and thus sustain the circle. The issues of measuring performance in relation to all of the stakeholders will be taken up in Chapter 7. The right-hand side clarifies that the needs of customers can sometimes conflict with the demands of some shareholders, especially those who are willing to trade off long-term achievement for short-term financial returns. Competitors are always trying to persuade customers to switch allegiance and thus impact on an organization's success.

**Figure 2.4** Complementary or conflicting measures

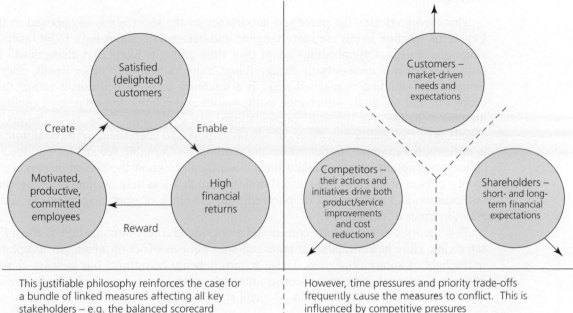

This justifiable philosophy reinforces the case for a bundle of linked measures affecting all key stakeholders – e.g. the balanced scorecard

However, time pressures and priority trade-offs frequently cause the measures to conflict. This is influenced by competitive pressures

While these arguments are, in themselves, convincing, many organizations still fail to satisfy their stakeholders long term. The following theories provide some insight into this reality.

*The investor and the employee are in the same position, but sometimes the employee is more important, because he will be there a long time, whereas an investor will often get in and out on a whim in order to make a profit. The worker's mission is to contribute to the company's welfare, and his own, every day. All of his working life he is really needed.*

Akio Morita, Joint Founder, Sony

### 2.4.3 Cyert and March's behavioural theory

Stakeholder theory is closely related to the ideas in Cyert and March's *A Behavioural Theory of the Firm* (1963). Cyert and March argue that the goals of an organization are a *compromise* between members of a coalition comprising the parties affecting an organization. The word compromise is used as the actual choice is linked to relative power and there are inevitably conflicts of interest. Cyert and March argue that there are essentially five directional pulls to consider:

■ production-related, and encapsulating stable employment, ease of control and scheduling

■ inventory-related – customers and sales staff push for high stocks and wide choice, management accountants complain about the cost of too much stock

■ sales-related – obtaining and satisfying orders

■ market share, which yields power relative to competitors

■ profit, which concerns shareholders, senior management and the providers of loan capital.

This theory stresses the perceived importance of the short term, as opposed to the long term, because issues are more tangible and because decisions have to be taken as situations change. Organizations adapt over time and it is likely that changes will be limited unless it is necessary to change things more radically. In other words, once a compromise situation is reached there is a tendency to seek to retain it rather than change it, and the goals will change as the values and relative importance of coalition members change. As a result, organizational slack develops. This is 'payments to members of the coalition in excess of what is required to keep them in the coalition'. It is difficult, for example, to determine the minimum acceptable reward for employees; assets are generally underexploited since it is difficult to know the maximum productivity of a person or machine; and uncertainties mean that less than optimal price, product and promotional policies will be pursued. The existence of slack does allow for extra effort in times of emergency.

This theory can be usefully considered alongside Herbert Simon's (1964) theory of satisficing. Here he contends that managers seek courses of action which are acceptable in the light of known objectives. These actions may not be optimal but they are chosen because of internal and external constraints such as time pressure, a lack of information and the vested interests of certain powerful stakeholders.

### 2.4.4 Objectives and constraints

Simon (1964) also makes an important distinction between objectives and constraints. Some of the ends that strategies are designed to achieve are not freely set objectives but constraints imposed on the organization by powerful stakeholders or agencies. Simply, organizational freedom – to set objectives – is constrained. For example, an animal food company might wish to offer low priced feeds for livestock but be constrained by dietary requirements which, by determining ingredients, influence costs and hence prices.

In recent years, many of the world's leading drug companies have changed their strategies as a result of external constraints. Governments have been increasingly reluctant to fund expensive drugs and treatments. Some companies have closed plants, while others have relocated for lower costs. There has been an increased research focus on treatments that are most likely to receive funding, arguably at the expense of potential breakthroughs in other areas. Priorities and strategies in the UK National Health Service (NHS) are affected by the government's waiting-list targets. Network Rail (which manages and maintains the UK railway infrastructure for the government) has an independent regulator who imposes specific requirements and targets for safety which inevitably affect costs and borrowing needs.

A number of other authors have offered theories in an attempt to explain the behaviour of organizations and the objectives they seek.

### 2.4.5 Baumol's theory of sales maximization

Baumol (1959) argues that firms seek to maximize sales rather than profits, but within the constraint of a minimum acceptable profit level. It can be demonstrated that profit maximizing is achieved at a level of output below that which would maximize sales revenue and that, as sales and revenue increase beyond profit maximizing, profits are sacrificed. Firms will increase sales and revenue as long as they are making profits in excess of what they regard as an acceptable minimum. Businessmen, Baumol argues, attach great importance to sales as salaries are often linked to the scale of operations. 'Whenever executives are asked "How's business?", the typical reply is that sales have been increasing or decreasing.'

### 2.4.6 Williamson's model of managerial discretion

Williamson (1964) argues that managers can set their own objectives, that these will be different from those of shareholders and that managerial satisfaction is the key. Satisfaction increases if a manager has a large staff reporting to him or her, if there are lavish perks and if profits exceed the level required for the essential development of the business and the necessary replacement of equipment. This extra profit can be used for pet projects or the pursuit of non-profit objectives. The manner in which managers reward themselves for success is discretionary.

### 2.4.7 Marris's theory of managerial capitalism

Marris (1964) again postulates growth as a key concern, as managers derive utility from growth in the form of enhanced salaries, power and status. The constraint is one of security. If, as a result of growth strategies pursued by the firm, profits are held down, say because of interest charges, the market value of the firm's shares may fall relative to the book value of the assets. In such a case the firm may become increasingly vulnerable to takeover, and managers wish to avoid this situation.

### 2.4.8 Penrose's theory of growth

Penrose (1959) has offered another growth theory, arguing that an organization will seek to achieve the full potential from all its resources. Firms grow as long as there are unused resources, diversifying when they can no longer grow with existing products, services and markets. Growth continues until it is halted. A major limit, for example, could be production facilities either in terms of total output or because of a bottleneck in one part of the operation. Changes can free the limit, and growth continues until the next limiting factor appears. Another limit is the capacity of managers to plan and implement growth strategies. If managers are stretched, extra people can be employed, but the remedy is not immediate. New people have to be trained and integrated, and this takes up some of the time of existing managers. Penrose refers to this issue as the 'receding managerial limit' because again the limiting factor decreases over a period of time. In a climate of reasonably constant growth and change managers learn how to cope with the dynamics of change; and properly managed, given that overambition is constrained and that market opportunities exist, firms can enjoy steady and continuous growth.

### 2.4.9 Galbraith's views on technocracy

Finally, Galbraith (1969) highlighted the particular role of large corporations, whose pursuit of size requires very large investments associated with long-term commitments. Because of these financial commitments the corporations seek to control their environment as far as they possibly can, influencing both government and consumer, and they

DISCUSSION

### Box 2.2 Profit

A business school is likely to teach that an organization must be good to people because then they will work harder; and if they work harder the business will make a profit.

They will also teach that a firm should strive to produce better products and services, because with better products the firm will make greater profits.

**What if they told the story the other way round?**

What if they taught managers: you have got to make a profit, because if you do not make a profit you cannot build offices that are pleasant to be in. Without profit you cannot pay decent wages.

Without profit you cannot satisfy a lot of the needs of your employees. You have got to make a profit because without a profit you will never be able to develop a better product.

The profit would still be made. People would still get decent wages. Most employers would still make an effort to improve their products as they do now.

*'But you would have a whole new ball game.'*

Adapted from Cohen, P (1974) *The Gospel According to the Harvard Business School*, Penguin. Originally published by Doubleday, New York, 1973.

**Harvard Business School** http://www.hbs.edu

in turn are controlled by what Galbraith calls 'technocrats' – teams of powerful experts and specialists. Their purposes are, first, to protect as well as control the organization, and hence they seek financial security and profit, and, second, to 'affirm' the organization through growth, expansion and market share. As is typical of oligopolists, price competition is not seen to be in their interests, and hence aggressive marketing and non-price competition are stressed. In addition, such firms will seek to influence or even control (by acquisition) suppliers and distributors, and they may well see the world, rather than just the UK, as their market. These issues are all explored later in the book.

Galbraith (1963) also identified the growth of 'countervailing power' to limit this technocracy. The growth of trade unions in the past is an example of this, but, as seen in recent years, the technocrats have fought back successfully. The increasing size and power of grocery retailers such as Sainsbury and Tesco, and their success with own-label brands, has put pressure on all product manufacturers, especially those whose products are not the brand leader. As a consequence the owners of the strongest brands have invested heavily to promote their brands and ensure that they are selected, even though there may be cheaper alternatives. Moreover, there have been mergers within retailing in an attempt to strengthen power bases. Tesco has expanded from the UK into Europe, while Wal-Mart has acquired ASDA. Simply, over time there are swings in relative power and, as a result, the potential for consumer exploitation is checked and available profits are shared more widely.

### 2.4.10 Profit as an objective

Box 2.2 discusses whether profit is the ultimate objective of profit-seeking business organizations or whether it is merely a means to other ends, which themselves constitute the real objectives. Not-for-profit organizations are considered separately later in this chapter.

Ackoff (1986) argues that both profit and growth are means to other ends rather than objectives in themselves. He argues that profit is necessary for the survival of a business enterprise, but is neither the reason for which the business is formed nor the reason why it stays in existence. Instead, Ackoff contends,

*Those who manage organizations do so primarily to provide themselves with the quality of work life and standard of living they desire ... their behaviour can be better understood by assuming this than by assuming that their objective is to maximize profit or growth.*

However, it is also important to consider the quality of life of investors (shareholders), customers, suppliers and distributors, as well as other employees of the firm who are not involved in decision-making. Developing earlier points, it can be argued that employees are the major stakeholders, because if the firm goes out of business they incur the greatest losses.

In many respects it does not matter whether profit is seen as an objective or as a means of providing service and satisfaction to stakeholders, as long as both are considered and not seen as mutually exclusive. However, the 'feel' and culture of an organization will be affected. In simple terms an organization will succeed if it survives and meets the expectations of its stakeholders. If its objectives relate to the stakeholders, it is successful if it attains its objectives.

*The purpose of industry is to serve the public by creating services to meet their needs. It is not to make profits for shareholders, nor to create salaries and wages for the industrial community. These are necessary conditions for success, but not its purpose.*

Dr George Carey, retired Archbishop of Canterbury

*The responsibility of business is not to create profits but to create live, vibrant, honourable organizations with a real commitment to the community.*

Anita Roddick, founder, The Body Shop

### 2.4.11  The influence of shareholders

Some commentators hold the view that too many companies are still encouraged to seek short-term profits in order to please their major institutional shareholders, and that it is only by considering the long term and the interests of all stakeholders that companies will become more effective competitors in world markets. In the UK, for example, Constable (1980) stated: 'Britain's steady relative industrial decline over the past 30 years is related to an insistence on setting purely financial objectives which have been operated in relatively short time scales.' Institutions such as pension funds effectively control the UK's largest companies through the sizeable blocks of shares that they own; in contested takeovers, for example, individual pension fund managers will be instrumental in determining the outcome. These managers have a remit to earn the best returns that they can obtain for their members. Since the mid-1990s there has been a drive to increase the transparency of these large shareholder blocks, and companies have been required to publish more information.

The issue of short-termism is complex, however, and Box 2.3 investigates the debate. Companies, obviously, cannot disregard powerful institutional shareholders. What is crucial is to ensure that there is dialogue and mutual understanding and agreement concerning the best interests of the company, its shareholders and other stakeholders.

In his debate on the short- and long-term perspective, Constable (Table 2.3), contrasts two sets of objectives, ranked in order of priority. He contends that company B is

**Table 2.3** Contrasting company objectives

| Company A | Company B |
| --- | --- |
| 1. Return on net assets, 1–3 year time horizon | 1. Maintenance and growth of market share |
| 2. Cash flow | 2. Maintenance and growth of employment |
| 3. Maintenance and growth of market share | 3. Cash flow |
| 4. Maintenance and growth of employment | 4. Return on net assets |

## Box 2.3 Long- and Short-termism: The Debate

DISCUSSION

Laing (1987) has argued that where owners and managers are the same people, the goals and means of achieving them are not in conflict; but institutional fund managers, themselves under pressure to perform in the short term, have often put pressure on public companies to pursue strategies that may be incompatible with sound long-term management. It is, however, generally acknowledged that companies must pursue strategies that increase the long-term value of the business for its shareholders, or eventually they are likely to be under threat of acquisition. It is also often argued that many companies believe that they are likely to be under threat from powerful institutional shareholders if short-term performance is poor, i.e. if sales and profits fail to grow. The result can be a reluctance to undertake costly and risky investments, say, in research and development (R&D), if the payback is uncertain.

Thus, it would follow that if a manufacturing business were seeking to boost short-term profits and earnings per share for reasons of expedience, it might well reduce quality and service and fail to invest adequately for the future. The price for this would be inevitable decline. This tendency could be worsened if the company were under threat of takeover and thus anxious to improve its immediate performance. For businesses in countries such as Germany and Japan, where historically 'the Damoclean sword of hostile takeovers was virtually unknown' (Laing, 1987) this has been less likely than in the UK.

Institutional shareholders must clearly want to be able to exercise some control or influence over large companies where they have substantial equity interests. One dilemma is that while they want to rein in powerful and risk-orientated strategic leaders, they do not want to forsake the potential benefits of strong, entrepreneurial leadership. They can exert influence by:

■ pushing for the roles of chairman and chief executive to be separated, and arguing for a high proportion of carefully selected non-executive (external part-time) directors

■ attempting to replace senior managers whose performance is poor or lacklustre, but this can be difficult (it is often argued that shareholders are too passive about this option)

■ selling their shares to predatory bidders.

While this final option is a perpetual threat, and the biggest fear of many strategic leaders, not all companies are prevented from investing in R&D. Logically, those which are well managed are in command of where they are going to invest. In addition, institutions argue that they are objective about their investments and turn down more offers for their shares than they accept.

In essence, 'managers should not be discouraged by their owners, their shareholders, from taking risks, from undertaking research and from investing in innovation' (Laing, 1987).

A more recent analysis by the *Financial Times* (Martinson, 1998) suggests that large institutional shareholders do take a long-term view but rarely make helpful comments on strategy. When they exercise their voting power it is generally clear and visible, rather than covert. Many fund managers were seen as professional but, at the same time,

▶

'ill-informed fund managers are making increasing demands on executive time'.

Undoubtedly more communication between directors and their shareholders concerning results, plans and philosophies would be desirable in many cases. Would this resolve the difficulties, or is something more drastic still required?

Lipton (1990) has controversially suggested that Boards should be subject to quinquennial reviews of their performance (partially conducted by independent outsiders) and their plans for the next five years. Hostile bids could be considered at the same time, but not between reviews. Boards may or may not be re-elected, depending on their relative performance. The idea is to generate more stability and to 'unite directors and shareholders behind the goal of maximizing long-term profits'.

The late Lord White of Hanson plc (1990) stated his disagreement, arguing that if institutional shareholders are willing to sell their shares it is usually the result of poor management generally, and not merely a reluctance to invest in R&D. 'Under-performing companies are frequently typified by high top salaries, share options confined to a handful of apparatchiks and generous golden parachutes.' Such companies are often legitimate takeover targets, and inevitably the bids are likely to be perceived as hostile.

In summary, long-term success requires that companies and their strategic leaders are properly accountable for their performance and, for many businesses, this really has to be to their shareholders. At the same time, shareholders must be objective and take a long-term perspective, and they must be active, not passive, about replacing poor managers and about intervening when they feel that the corporate strategy is wrong.

The dilemmas relate to the implementation of these ideas and to the issue of whether institutions have advisers with enough detailed, industry-specific, knowledge to make an objective judgement.

**Footnote**

The references used in this box may be dated but the arguments still remain. The issue has never been truly resolved. However, more recently, shareholder power has also been exercised in other ways. Institutional shareholders – partly as a reaction to media and public opinion – have joined the debate about director rewards. It is not unusual for CEOs to have two or three year rolling contracts, such that if they resign or are fired, they receive handsome 'golden handshakes'. WH Smith is a case in point. In 2003 Kate Swann became the new CEO, joining them from a similar role at Argos. She was given a 'golden hello' as compensation for lost share options at her previous employer. At the same time, Retail Director Beverley Hodson was also paid compensation for being overlooked for the job. Soon afterwards she resigned and received a generous payoff. Some shareholders were unhappy as they blamed her for the company's deteriorating performance in 2003.

Later in the chapter we also see how shareholders are increasingly concerned that companies come clean on any ethical risks involved in the business.

**Sources**

Laing, H (1987) quoted in *First*, 1 (2).
Lipton, M (1990) An end to hostile takeovers and short-termism, *Financial Times*, 27 June.
Martinson, J (1998) Companies say big shareholders take long view, *Financial Times*, 27 April.
White, G (1990) Why management must be accountable, *Financial Times*, 12 July.

**Financial Times** http://www.ft.com
**Hanson plc** http://www.hansonplc.com
**ASDA** http://www.asda.com

likely to grow at the expense of company A, and that these objective sets, A and B, are essentially those adopted by large UK and Japanese companies, respectively, for much of the period since the Second World War. To suggest that Japanese success rests solely on a particular set of objectives is oversimplifying reality, but it has certainly contributed.

**Table 2.4** Perceptions of stakeholder importance

| Stakeholder | Prioritization by industry strategic leaders | Prioritization by analysts with institutional investors |
|---|---|---|
| Existing customers | 1 | 1 |
| Existing employees | 2 | 3 |
| Potential customers | 3 | 2 |
| Institutional investors | 4 | 4 |
| Suppliers | 5 | 7 |
| Potential employees | 6 | 6 |
| City analysts | 7 | 5 |
| Private (individual) shareholders | 8 | 10 |
| Business media | 9 | 9 |
| General media | 10 | 11 |
| Local communities | 11 | 12 |
| Members of Parliament/Local Authorities | 12 | 8 |

Source: Based on research by MORI (2000).
**Mori** http://www.mori.com

In Japan and Germany, however, shareholders do not exert pressure in the same way as they do in the UK. Cross-shareholding between companies in Japan means that only 25 per cent of shares in Japanese businesses are for trading and speculation, and this generates greater stability. In Germany the companies hold a higher proportion of their own shares, and banks act as proxy voters for private investors. Banks thereby control some 60 per cent of the tradeable shares, again generating stability. German companies also adopt a two-tier board structure. A supervisory board has overall control and reports to shareholders and employee unions; reporting to this board is a management board, elected for up to five years.

Table 2.4 pulls together a number of the points discussed here by showing how organizational strategic leaders and institutional investors do not share completely the same perspective on stakeholder priorities, although there are clear similarities with the most important stakeholders. Interestingly, suppliers, key partners in the **supply chain**, receive a higher priority from strategic leaders, while the institutions rate politicians more highly than do organizational leaders. It is both significant and realistic, that small, individual shareholders are not particularly powerful, because they are generally too disparate to become organized. Individually, they may be able to embarrass an organization with difficult questions at its Annual General Meeting, but this is far from an expression of ongoing power.

## 2.4.12   The importance of the strategic leader

To conclude this section it is useful to emphasize the key role of the strategic leader, and his or her values, in establishing the main objectives and the direction in which they take the organization. Personal ambitions to build a large conglomerate or a multinational company may fuel growth; a determination to be socially responsible may restrain certain activities that other organizations would undertake; a commitment to high quality will influence the design, cost and marketing approach for products. A strong orientation towards employee welfare, as is illustrated in Minicase 2.3 on ASDA, will again influence objectives quite markedly.

The objectives and values of the strategic leader are a particularly important consideration in the case of small firms. While it is possible for small firms to enjoy competitive advantage, say by providing products or services with values added to appeal to local customers in a limited geographical area, many are not distinctive in any marked way. Where this is the case, and where competition is strong, small firms will be price takers, and their profits and growth will be influenced substantially by external forces. Some small firm owners will be entrepreneurial, willing to take risks and determined to build a bigger business, whereas others will be content to stay small. Some small businesses are started by people who essentially want to work for themselves rather than for a larger corporation, and their objectives could well be concerned with survival and the establishment of a sound business which can be passed on to the next generation of their family.

Each of the ideas and theories discussed in this section provides food for thought, but individually none of them explains fully what happens, or what should happen, in organizations. In the authors' experience certain organizations are highly growth orientated, willing to diversify and take risks, while others, constrained by the difficulties of coping with rapid growth and implementing diversification strategies, are less ambitious in this respect. Each can be appropriate in certain circumstances and lead to high performance, but in different circumstances they may be the wrong strategy.

Stakeholder theory is extremely relevant conceptually, but organizations are affected by the stakeholders in a variety of ways. Priorities must be decided for companies on an individual basis. Moreover, the strategic leader, and in turn the organization, will seek to satisfy particular stakeholders rather than others because of their personal backgrounds and values. There is no right or wrong list of priorities. However, while priorities can and will be established, all stakeholders must be satisfied to some minimum level. In the final analysis the essential requirement is congruence among environment, values and resources.

So far this chapter has concentrated on profit-seeking organizations and considered just how important the profit motive might be. Not-for-profit organizations may be growth conscious, quality conscious or committed to employee welfare in the same way as profit seekers, but there are certain differences which require that they are considered separately.

Archie Norman is the entrepreneurial strategic leader who 'made a difference' at ASDA by pioneering change and instilling a new culture. ASDA, now owned by Wal-Mart of America (the world's largest retailer), is the UK's second largest supermarket group, behind Tesco and ahead of Sainsbury's. Its early growth and success came in the 1960s when it began to open out-of-town supermarkets – large stores for that time, but relatively small in today's terms – largely in the north of England, where the company has always been strongest. The Head Office is still in Leeds, but the company has now developed nationally. In the 1980s, ASDA began to diversify, first into furniture retailing and then into carpets. This was followed by the acquisition of kitchen supplier MFI in 1985; two years later MFI became a management buyout when the promised synergies proved illusory. Shortly after this, ASDA bought 60 stores from Gateway and struck a deal with George Davies (the entrepreneur behind the growth and temporary fall of Next) which gave ASDA the exclusive rights on a range of George-branded clothing. By the early 1990s ASDA was, however, trading at a loss. Analysts concluded that the company lacked a strong corporate identity and it had become a reactive follower in its main industry.

A new chairman was appointed in 1991 and he recruited Archie Norman to be the new Chief Executive. At this time Norman was 37 years old and was originally a McKinsey consultant, where he had worked with William Hague, the ex-leader of the Conservative Party. He was then Group Finance Director with the retail group Kingfisher. When Norman became non-executive Chairman in 1997, after being elected a Conservative MP for Tunbridge Wells, ASDA had regained its popularity and profitability. Together with his deputy, and later successor, Allan Leighton, Norman had transformed the company. Although Norman 'took best practice from elsewhere and ASDA-ized it', it was always believed that he used Wal-Mart as his model, and so perhaps it was no surprise when Wal-Mart acquired ASDA in 1999. David Glass, Chief Executive of Wal-Mart, commented of ASDA:

'I have not seen such passion for a company amongst its employees – except at Wal-Mart.'

What exactly had Norman and Leighton done? Furniture and carpets had been divested at the earliest opportunity. The business had been split into two distinct parts: the (large) supermarkets – ASDA owns some of the largest food stores in the UK – where the non-food ranges were strengthened; and smaller, local, Dales stores with a limited range of grocery products. The whole business was refocused on 'ordinary working people who demand value': advertising used the slogan 'That's ASDA Price!' to reinforce an average saving of some 5 per cent against Tesco and Sainsbury prices.

High productivity and high levels of service have been derived from a committed and involved staff, who have seen many changes in their working lives. People became known as 'colleagues'. A new suggestion scheme, 'Tell Archie!', generated 45,000 suggestions in five years, and Norman claimed to have read them all. Incentives are linked in to the scheme, and employees can also benefit from share options and training at the ASDA Academy. Since 1995, Colleague Circles have also provided an effective forum for staff involvement in customer service innovation. At Head Office there are no reserved car parking spaces and everyone works in large, open-plan offices. Staff are encouraged to wear ASDA baseball caps when they do not want to be disturbed by their colleagues. In relative terms, store management has grown at the expense of head-office staffing.

Norman initially became non-executive Chairman when he became an MP, but once he had negotiated the sale to Wal-Mart he resigned.

*We refer to ASDA on a number of occasions in the book. The next key reference is in Chapter 4, when we look at SWOT (strengths, weaknesses, opportunities, threats) analysis of the company. See Figure 4.5.

### Question

1. How is ASDA attempting to ensure that its employees deliver the virtuous circle of growth and prosperity illustrated in Figure 2.4?

ASDA http://www.asda.com

## 2.5  Objectives of public sector and not-for-profit organizations

In order to understand the objectives of not-for-profit organizations and appreciate where they are aiming to go, a number of points need to be considered.

- Stakeholders are important, particularly those who are providers of financial support.
- There will be a number of potentially conflicting objectives, and quite typically the financial ones will not be seen as the most essential in terms of the mission.
- While there will be a mix of quantitative (financial) and qualitative objectives, the former will be easier to measure, although the latter relate more closely to the mission of the organization.
- For this reason the efficient use of resources becomes an important objective.

These points will now be examined in greater depth, making reference to Minicases 2.4 and 2.5 (the National Theatre and London Zoo) together with a number of other examples, as public sector and not-for-profit organizations are many and varied.

Historically, and at one extreme, certainly in terms of size, *nationalized industries* with essentially monopoly markets have been seen as both public sector and non-profit. Throughout their existence different governments have strived to establish acceptable and effective measures of performance for them. At various times both **break-even** and return on capital employed have been stressed. There has always been an inbuilt objectives conflict between social needs (many of them provided essential services) and a requirement that the very substantial resources involved were managed commercially in order to avoid waste. The Conservative government of the 1980s followed a policy of privatizing certain nationalized industries partly on the grounds that in some cases more competition will be stimulating and create greater efficiency.

In Britain, the NHS can be viewed similarly. Fundamentally, its purpose relates to the health and well-being of the nation, and attention can be focused on both prevention and cure. The role of the police in terms of crime prevention and the solution of crimes that have taken place can be seen as synonymous. The health service can spend any money it is offered, as science continually improves what can be done for people. In a sense it is a chicken and egg situation. Resources improve treatments and open up new opportunities for prevention; and these in turn stimulate demand, particularly where they concern illnesses or diseases which historically have not been easily treated. However, these developments are often very expensive, and decisions have then to be made about where funds should be allocated. Quite simply, the decisions relate to priorities.

Customers of the health service are concerned with such things as the waiting time for admission to hospital and for operations, the quality of care as affected by staff attitudes and numbers, and arguably privacy in small wards, cleanliness and food. Doctors generally are concerned with the amount of resources and their ability to cope with demand; some consultants are anxious to work at the leading edge of their specialism; while administrators must ensure that resources are used efficiently.

The government funds the NHS, and as the major source of funds it is a key influence. It is very concerned with the political fallout from perceived weaknesses in the service, and inevitably its priorities are affected by this. It has been reported that the

## Minicase 2.4 The National Theatre

**GB**

The National Theatre is in fact three theatres in one building on the south bank of the river Thames in London. A substantial proportion of revenue has to be allocated to cover the overheads on the building. The specially-built theatre opened in 1976. Despite its name, and although its 'company' does at times tour the country, it does not attract a national audience. The plays it offers are generally different from those in the more commercial non-subsidized theatres in London's West End, and it attracts a mixture of regular theatregoers from the south-east of England, foreign tourists and occasional visitors.

The National receives a grant from the Arts Council, which is funded by the Treasury. At certain times during the 1980s and 1990s the grant increased at less than the rate of inflation, a reflection of government policy concerning support for the arts and their belief that more private support was required. In addition, the National receives private sponsorship and earns money from the box office, catering and other front-of-house sales. Sponsorship and subsidies allow ticket prices to be lower than they otherwise would.

Some stakeholders, such as directors and actors, might hold the view that as the National is prestigious it should seek to offer the 'best of everything' – plays, actors, costumes and scenery – and that it should experiment and seek to be innovative. At the same time it has at least to break even, although the types of play and musical which earn the most revenue at the box office are not necessarily those that the National will seek to produce.

Sir Peter Hall, Director from 1976 to 1988, has said that his main aim was to provide working conditions where actors can be at their most creative. Audiences and money matter, but they are not the primary goal.

How, then, is success measured? Audiences and revenue can certainly be measured, but 'success is something you can feel and smell when you are with an audience'.

### Questions

1. Is it possible for the National Theatre to satisfy all of its stakeholders at any one time?
2. What do you think the priorities should be?
3. Has the National Theatre adopted a policy of putting on more commercial productions in recent years?

**National Theatre** http://www.nt-online.org

Labour government's emphasis on waiting lists, a key pledge in its 1997 election manifesto, has distorted clinical priorities, such that many minor ailments have been given priority for treatment over more major ones. Pfeffer (1981) has argued that the relative power of influencers is related to the funds that they provide. The less funding that is provided by customers, the weaker is their influence over decisions. Hence, a not-for-profit organization such as the NHS may be less customer orientated than a private competitive firm. Some would argue that the private medical sector is more marketing conscious. Without question, and in simple terms, the NHS is about patient care within imposed budgetary constraints. The issue really concerns whether patients perceive that it feels like a service driven by a culture of care or by a culture of resource-management efficiency.

All organizations will seek to measure performance in some way. It was stated earlier in the chapter that performance against quantitative objectives can be measured directly, whereas performance against qualitative objectives is typically indirect and more difficult. If attention is focused on the aspects that are most easily measured there is a danger that these come to be perceived as the most important objectives. Hospital

## Minicase 2.5   London Zoo    **GB**

London Zoo, in Regent's Park, is one of two zoological gardens which are controlled and administered by the Zoological Society of London (ZSL). The other is Whipsnade Park, in Bedfordshire, and this covers 600 acres compared with just 36 acres in London.

The Society's original charter laid down its primary purpose as 'the advancement of zoology and animal physiology, and the introduction of new and curious subjects of the animal kingdom', but this has been modified in the current mission. ZSL now exists to 'achieve and promote the worldwide conservation of animals and their habitats'. This is pursued by:

- Keeping and presenting animals at the two zoos
- Prioritizing threatened species
- Helping people become more aware of animal welfare and conservation issues
- Maintaining an education programme
- Undertaking both conservation work and serious zoological research
- Publishing activities.

However, ZSL has to generate an income from visitors to supplement its other sources of revenue. Therefore from the mission must stem a fundamental dilemma: how much is a zoo a place of entertainment and relaxation, with customers paramount, and how much is it an organization with primarily educational and scientific purposes? One commercial constraint for London Zoo is the fact that Regent's Park is a Royal Park, and that by-laws restrict certain activities such as on-site advertising.

There are basically five main activities: London Zoo, Whipsnade Park, The Institute of Zoology (conferencing and publishing), conservation programmes and the world-renowned library.

At times in the past the zoo has received a series of annual grants from the Department of the Environment, and in 1988 it was given £10 million as a designated one-off payment 'to put it on a firm financial footing'. It remains 'the only national collection in the world not publically funded on a regular basis'.

Income is essentially from visitors, the majority of whom live within comfortable travelling distance of London, through membership and admission fees and merchandising, but there are some research grants. Many of the visitors are on organized school trips, and weather conditions are very important in attracting or deterring people.

Many visitors are attracted by big animals, as evidenced by the commercial success of safari parks, but these are costly and dangerous, and well researched and relatively safe as far as endangered species go. Quite often the most endangered species are relatively unattractive to visitors. Whipsnade is regarded as more ideal for big animals. London Zoo for many years has had no hippos (since the 1960s – although there are pygmy hippos in the collection) and no bears (since 1986), but more recently some large animals have been brought back to counter visitor criticism. There are, for example, giraffes, lions, tigers and leopards. However, in 2001, and following an incident with a visitor, London Zoo's elephants were moved to Whipsnade. Visitors can drive around Whipsnade, parking in various places en route, but it is not a safari park. There are some 650 species at London Zoo, of which 112 can be classified as 'threatened'. There are breeding programmes for 130 species.

Critics have sometimes argued that London Zoo's management has failed to fully exploit the zoo's conservation work by featuring it in informative displays and that much of the zoo's important and scientifically renowned research is not recognized by the general public. This may be correct, but the fact remains that much of the important conservation work involves species which are relatively uninteresting for many public visitors, for example the rare Rodriguez fruit bat.

The Department of the Environment paid for a report by independent consultants (1987–8) and concluded that 'management at London Zoo did not reflect the commercial emphasis which was

▶

essential for survival and prosperity without a permanent subsidy'. They recommended the establishment of a new company to manage London and Whipsnade Zoos, separate from the scientific research of the Zoological Society. This company was established in October 1988, with the aim of reversing the falling trend in admissions and returning the zoo to profit in three years.

The numbers of visitors did increase in 1989 and 1990, but below the level required to break even. In April 1991 newspapers first reported that London Zoo might have to close, with some animals destroyed and others moved to Whipsnade. The government refused further financial assistance, not wholly convinced of the need for urban zoos. Cost reduction per se was ruled out as this was likely to provoke a new fall in admissions. Instead, rescue plans concentrated on a smaller zoo with a new concept: natural habitats such as an African rainforest complete with gorillas, and a Chinese mountain featuring the pandas. There would be less emphasis on caged animals. These developments have taken place but there have still been criticisms from some groups that the space for gorillas is inadequate when compared with the facilities they enjoy in some other zoos. The reality is, of course, that only so much can be done in 36 acres whilst still retaining a collection that is attractive to visitors.

Although changes were made, attendances continued to fall. The zoo's closure was announced formally in June 1992. New external funding has since provided a reprieve.

Since 1992 the zoo has secured its survival by emphasizing its role as a conservation centre, breeding endangered species and returning them to the wild. During the 1990s ZSL managed to break even by using publicity more effectively to attract some one million visitors a year.

More recently the zoo has stopped providing pony rides for children, declaring that this is not an appropriate form of entertainment. The Mappin Café was renovated in 2002; and plans are in hand for a new aquatic centre at Silverton Quays in London's Docklands. Whilst some changes in the last 20 years have been forced on the zoo by external pressures, others have been voluntary. In the end London Zoo has to find a business model that attracts sufficient visitors and revenue in the face of competition from a wide range of other tourist attractions.

In 2002/3 ZSL had incoming resources of £34 million. £13.1 million came from members' subscriptions and admission charges; £4.2 million from merchandising and catering and £3.7 million from grants. These grants did not amount to public subsidies. Half of the total was HEFCE (Higher Education Funding Council) research funding chanelled through the University of Cambridge; most of the other half came from individual grants related to specific projects. £7.5 million was recovered VAT payments – which partly explains why income had increased from £21 million in 2001/2. Profit after tax was £1.4 million, up from £1.2 million.

In this year there were 815,000 paying visitors at London Zoo, with a further 445,000 at Whipsnade.

## Questions

1. What should the objectives of London Zoo be?
2. Who are the major stakeholders, and how important are they?
3. If you were in charge (and remembering the constraints) what strategies would you recommend?

**London Zoo** http://www.londonzoo.co.uk

administrators can easily measure the number of admissions, the utilization of beds and theatres, the cost of laundry and food and so on. Fundamentally more important is who is being treated relative to the real needs of the community. Are the most urgent and needy cases receiving the priorities they deserve? How is this measured? Performance measures therefore tend to concentrate on the efficient use of resources rather than the effectiveness of the organization. Although profit may not be an important consideration, costs are. In addition, these measures may well be a source of conflict between medical and administrative staff, and this is a reflection of the fact that there is likely to be disagreement and confusion about what the key objectives are.

Given this, the objectives that are perceived as important and are pursued at any time are very dependent on the relative power of the influencers and their ability to exercise power. Linked to this point is the relationship between hospitals and whatever area and regional health authorities are in existence at any time. Similarly, where not-for-profit organizations have advisory bodies, or boards of trustees, the relationship and relative power are important.

Tourist attractions such as London Zoo (Minicase 2.5) and leading museums (including the British Museum, the Natural History Museum and the Victoria and Albert, which is the National Museum of Art and Design) have a potential conflict of objectives concerning their inevitable educational and scientific orientations and the requirement that they address commercial issues. Museums can earn money from shops and cafeterias and they receive some private funding, but to a great extent they are reliant on government grants. In the 1980s these grants did not keep pace with their monetary demands and hence it became necessary for them to seek additional revenue as well as manage resources and costs more efficiently. Admission charges were introduced by some museums and, perhaps inevitably, they became a controversial issue in the UK. In November 1985 the Victoria and Albert Museum introduced voluntary admission charges, and in April 1987 the Natural History Museum started charging for entry. Some potential visitors are always going to be lost as they refuse to pay, and this has implications for the educational objective. It was reported that by 1987 admissions to the Victoria and Albert had fallen to one million a year from a peak of 1.75 million in 1983, but they began to increase again after 1988 as people became more accustomed to charging. However, the museum was criticized by some arts lovers for a poster campaign describing it as 'an ace caff with quite a nice museum attached', although museum staff claimed that this was a major reason for the increase in attendances. Some museums, including the British Museum, adamantly opposed charging. The new Tate Modern, opened in 2000, did not charge for admission. In the last few years admission charges to London's main museums have largely been dropped as new grants and subsidies have been provided. However, it is still arguable that with either admission charges or larger grants the museums could employ more curators and provide an enhanced service. More exhibits could be put on show; exhibitions could be changed more often, for example. In the end a balance has to be found between level of service and the number of visitors. Is quality or quantity more important.

At the National Theatre (Minicase 2.4) the issue addresses art and finance. Subsidized theatres perceive their role to be different from that of commercial theatres and a number of them, including the Royal Shakespeare Company, English National Opera and the Royal Opera House, Covent Garden, compete for a percentage of Arts Council funding. When the Arts Council, as a major stakeholder and provider of funds, attempts to influence the strategies of the theatres they are often accused of meddling. Again there is a potential chicken and egg situation. If the theatres, under pressure from reduced subsidies (in real terms), raise more revenue and reduce their costs, they may find that this results in permanently reduced subsidies. Hence, as an alternative, they may choose to restrain their commercial orientation.

*Cathedrals* face a similar dilemma. The costs of repairs and maintenance are forcing some to charge visitors fixed amounts rather than rely on voluntary donations. Their mission is concerned with religion and charity but they are not immune from commercial realities.

*Charities* frequently have sets of interdependent commercial and non-commercial objectives. Oxfam's mission concerns the provision of relief and the provision of aid where it is most needed throughout the world. Additional objectives relate to teaching people how to look after themselves better through, say, irrigation and better farming techniques and to obtaining publicity to draw public attention to the plight of the needy. Their ability to pursue these objectives is constrained by resource availability. Consequently, Oxfam have fund-raising objectives, and strategies (including retailing through Oxfam shops) to achieve them. It is difficult to say which receives most priority as they are so interdependent.

While the coverage of not-for-profit organizations in this section has been partial, as many other organizations such as schools and universities are fundamentally non-profitable, the points are representative of the sector.

The issue of the displacement of objectives has been discussed in some not-for-profit organizations. Attention is centred on quantitative measures as they are relatively easily carried out. The efficient use of resources replaces profit as the commercial objective, and while this may not be an essential aspect of the mission, it will be seen as important by certain stakeholders. In reality attention has switched from evaluating outputs and outcomes (the real objectives) to measuring inputs (resources) because it is easier to do. Where the stakeholders are major sponsors, and particularly in the case of government departments, there will be an insistence upon cost-effectiveness. Many of the organizations mentioned in this section are managed by people whose training and natural orientation is towards arts or science, and this can result in feelings of conflict with regard to objectives. Quite typically the organization will pursue certain objectives for a period of time, satisfying the most influential stakeholders in the coalition, and then change as the preferences of stakeholders, or their relative power and influence, change.

While profit-seeking and not-for-profit organizations have essentially different missions, the issue of profit-making is complex. Some not-for-profit organizations rely on subsidies and these enable prices to be kept below what they would otherwise be. In nationalized industries the element of customer service has been seen to be important, with prices controlled or at least influenced by government. An independent regulator has been appointed when nationalized businesses have been privatized. However, unless the providers of grants and subsidies are willing to bear commercial trading losses and at the same time finance any necessary investment, there is a necessity for the organizations to generate revenue at least equal to the costs incurred. Where investment finance also needs to be generated a surplus of income over expenditure is important. This basically is profit. While profit may not therefore be an essential part of the mission, it is still required.

*The objectives pursued by organizations frequently differ from those proclaimed. Some years ago I assumed that the principal objective of universities was the education of students. Armed with this assumption I could make no sense of their behaviour. I learned that education, like profit, is a requirement not an objective and that the principal objective is to provide their faculties with the quality of work life and the standard of living they desire. That's why professors do so little teaching, give the same courses over and over again, arrange classes at their convenience, not that of their students, teach subjects they want to teach rather than students want to learn and skip classes to give lectures [elsewhere] for a fee.*

Russell Ackoff, 1986

## 2.6  The impact of personal objectives

It has already been established that organizations are generally too large and complex to have only one objective. As a result, and influenced by stakeholders, there are typically several objectives with varying degrees of relative importance. It is now appropriate to consider why organizations cannot be treated separately from the people who work in them.

Objectives can be set (and changed) in any one of three ways:

- The strategic leader decides.
- Managers throughout the organization are either consulted or influence the objectives by their decisions and actions.
- All or some of the external stakeholders influence or constrain the organization in some way.

The second of these is addressed in this section. With emergent strategy the decisions made by managers determine the actual strategies pursued, and in turn revised, implicit, objectives replace those that were previously declared as intended objectives. The incidence or likelihood of this is affected by the culture of the organization, the relative power bases of managers, communication systems, and whether or not there are rigid policies and procedures or more informal management processes that allow managers considerable freedom. Box 2.4 defines policies and discusses their role in strategy implementation. The following brief example illustrates the impact of policies. Consider a multiple store that sells compact discs as one of its products and has nearby a small independent competitor that appeals to different customers. If the small store closed down there could be new opportunities for the manager of the multiple store if he changed his competitive strategy for CDs by changing his displays, improved his stock levels and supported these moves with window displays promoting the changes. Head-office merchandising policies concerning stocks and displays may or may not allow him this freedom.

In the case of intended strategy, the strategic leader determines and states the objectives, strategies and proposed changes for the organization. In arriving at decisions he or she may be influenced in a minor or major way by stakeholders outside the organization and the managers consulted. In order to ensure that the strategies are implemented (and the objectives achieved) the strategic leader will design and build an organization structure – which may restrict managers or allow them considerable freedom – and will determine policies which may be mandatory or advisory. This will tie in to the culture of the organization and will be influenced by the style and values of the strategic leader.

However, the types of policy and the authority and freedom delegated to managers guide, influence and constrain decision-making. The motives, values and relative power of individual managers, the relative importance of particular functions, divisions or strategic business units in the organization, and the system of communications are also influential. The stated or *official objectives* may or may not be achieved; there may be appropriate incremental decisions which reflect changes in the environment; or managers may be pursuing personal objectives, which Perrow (1961) has termed *operative goals*. This is happening when the behaviour taking place cannot be accounted for by official company objectives and policies. The aggregation of these various decisions determines the emergent strategic changes, the actual objectives followed and the results achieved.

**KEY CONCEPTS**

## Box 2.4 Policies

*You must provide a framework in which people can act. For example, we have said that our first priority is safety, second is punctuality, and third is other services. So if you risk flight safety by leaving on time, you have acted outside the framework of your authority. The same is true if you don't leave on time because you are missing two catering boxes of meat. That's what I mean by a framework. You give people a framework, and within the framework you let people act.*

Jan Carlzon, when President and Chief Executive Officer, SAS (Scandinavian Airlines System)

■ *Policies* are guidelines relating to decisions and approaches which support organizational efforts to achieve stated and intended objectives.

■ They are basically *guides to thoughts* (about how things might or should be done) and *actions*.

■ They are therefore *guides to decision-making*. For example, a policy which states that for supplies of a particular item three quotations should be sought and the cheapest selected, or a policy not to advertise in certain newspapers, or a policy not to trade with particular countries – all influence decisions. Policies are particularly useful for routine repetitive decisions.

■ Policies can be at corporate, divisional (or strategic business unit [SBU]) or functional level, and they are normally stated in terms of management (of people), marketing, production, finance and research and development.

■ If stated objectives are to be achieved, and the strategies designed to accomplish this implemented, the appropriate policies must be there in support. In other words, the behaviour of managers and the decisions that they make should be supportive of what the organization is seeking to achieve. Policies guide and constrain their actions.

■ Policies can be mandatory (rules which allow little freedom for original thought or action) or advisory. The more rigid they are the less freedom managers have to change things with delegated authority, and this can be good or bad depending on change pressures from the environment.

■ *It is vital to balance consistency and co-ordination* (between the various divisions, SBUs and departments in the organization) *with flexibility*.

■ Policies need not be written down. They can be passed on verbally as part of the culture.

■ Policies *must* be widely understood if they are to be useful.

Operative goals may complement official goals or they may conflict. A complementary situation would exist if the stated objective was in terms of a target return on capital employed, and if this was achieved through operative goals of managers and decisions taken by them regarding delivery times, quality and so on. If, however, a sales manager was favouring particular customers with discounts or priority deliveries on low-profit orders, or a production manager was setting unnecessarily high quality standards (as far as customers are concerned) which resulted in substantial rejections and high operating costs, profits would be threatened. In such cases operative goals would conflict with official goals.

In this context, a report from the Public Management Foundation (1999) highlights a dilemma. Arguing that the UK government was feeling frustrated by the slow speed at which the public sector was embracing certain objectives and strategies from the profit-seeking private sector, the Foundation discovered a 'public sector ethos' amongst its managers. They are driven to 'make a difference for the community'. Improving local services and increasing user satisfaction are their personal priorities. There are occasions when this conflicts with the prioritization, rather than the actual existence, of stated, intended objectives for cutting costs and improving efficiencies. There is also a perception among many public-sector managers that their funders prefer centralized management **controls**, while they would like more autonomy and delegated authority. The situation is confused further when changing political pressures and necessities impact upon objectives and priorities.

## 2.7   Social responsibility and business Ethics

Having looked at some of the theories which are relevant for a study of objectives, and at typical objectives that organizations pursue and why, it is appropriate to conclude this chapter with a consideration of wider societal aspects. Objectives that relate to **social responsibility** may be affected by stakeholders; in some cases they result from legislation, but often they are voluntary actions. The issue is one of how responsible a firm might choose to be, and why – simply, firms can be socially responsible (proactive) or socially responsive (reactive to pressure). Again, the particular values of the strategic leader will be very influential. There is, though, often an interesting 'Catch-22' at work. Starbucks promotes itself as a socially responsible business, citing its dealings with coffee growers and pickers in developing countries. That it makes a serious effort is not in doubt. And yet Starbucks gets singled out by environmental and other campaigners – because they believe that a company which promotes itself as responsible is a softer target and more easily influenced than one that is either hostile or ambivalent.

There are numerous ways in which a firm can behave responsibly in the interests of society, and examples are given below. It should not be thought, however, that social responsibility is a one-way process; organizations can benefit considerably from it. Social responsibility and profitability can be improved simultaneously (The Performance Group, 1999).

- Product safety: This can be the result of design or production and includes aspects of supply and supplier selection to obtain safe materials or components. Product safety will be influenced to an extent by legislation, but an organization can build in more safety features than the law requires. Some cars are an example of this, such as Volvo which is promoted and perceived as a relatively safe car. Product safety will have cost implications. Sometimes the safety is reflected in perceived higher quality, which adds value that the customer is willing to pay a premium for, but at other times it will be the result of the organization's choosing to sacrifice some potential profit.

- Working conditions: Linked to the previous point, these can include safety at work, which again is affected by legislation which sets minimum standards. Aspects of job design to improve working conditions and training to improve employees' prospects are further examples.

- Honesty, including not offering or accepting bribes.

- Avoiding pollution.

- Avoiding discrimination.

The above points are all subject to some legislation.

- Community action: This is a very broad category with numerous opportunities, ranging from charitable activities to concerted action to promote industry and jobs in areas which have suffered from economic recession. Many large organizations release executives on a temporary basis to help with specific community projects.

- Industry location: Organizations may locate new plants in areas of high unemployment for a variety of reasons. While aspects of social responsibility may be involved, the decision may well be more economic. Grants and rate concessions may be important.

- Other environmental concerns: These include recycling, waste disposal, protecting the ozone layer and energy efficiency. Box 2.5 illustrates a number of specific examples.

Porter (1995) contends that many companies mistakenly see environmental legislation as a threat, something to be resisted. Instead, he argues, they should see regulation as an indication the company is not using its resources efficiently. Toxic materials and discarded packaging are waste. The costs incurred in eliminating a number of environmental problems can be more than offset by other savings and improvements in product quality. Companies should be innovative and not reluctantly just complying with their legal requirements. However, the European chemical industry has argued that bulk chemical manufacture has been largely driven out of EU countries by the costs of complying with environmental regulation. Standards in many Far Eastern countries are less restrictive.

- Attitude of food retailers: For example, accurate labelling (country of origin), free-range eggs, organic vegetables, biodegradable packaging, CFC-free aerosols and products containing certain dubious E-number additives. It is a moot point whether retailers or consumers should decide on these issues.

Objectives of this nature become part of the organization culture. Social responsibility is at the heart of activities and objectives because it is felt that the organization has an obligation both to the community and to society in general. However, it must not be assumed that the approach receives universal support. Milton Friedman (1979), the economist, argues that 'the business of business is business … the organization's only social responsibility is to increase its profit'. Friedman also comments that donations to charity and sponsorship of the arts are 'fundamentally subversive' and not in the best interests of the shareholders. Social responsibility would then be the result of legislation. Drucker (1974) argues businesses have a role in society which is 'to supply goods and services to customers and an economic surplus to society … rather than to supply jobs to workers and managers, or even dividends to shareholders'. The latter, he argues, are means not ends. Drucker contends that it is mismanagement to forget that a hospital exists for its patients and a university for its students. This contrasts with the comments by Russell Ackoff about university academics quoted earlier.

The topic is complex, and although the outcome of certain decisions can be seen to be bringing benefit to the community or employees the decision may have been influenced by legislation or perceived organizational benefit (enlightened self-interest) rather than a social conscience. One could argue that the organization will benefit if it looks after its employees; equally one could argue that it will suffer if it fails to consider employee welfare. The two approaches are philosophically different, but they may

## Box 2.5  Examples of Environmental Strategies

1  **McDonald's** took an equity stake in a new venture for recycling the waste collected at their restaurants. Some plastic containers which cannot be recycled have been withdrawn; food scraps are used for making compost. **Sainsbury's** give a one-penny refund for every plastic carrier that customers reuse. This saves the retailer the cost of providing a new bag; it also reduces the amount of waste plastic.

2  **Marks and Spencer** has worked with campaign groups to identify damaging pesticides and stopped its suppliers from using them.

3  **Electricity generating** has gradually switched to gas and cleaner coal (with a low sulphur content) because coal has been shown to cause acid rain.

4  **Packaging**. Smaller, lighter packages use fewer raw materials and they are cheaper to transport. **Procter and Gamble** and **Unilever** have both introduced more concentrated versions of their detergent brands which, ironically, many consumers have seen as poor value for money because they have been unconvinced by the instructions to use less of the product! Soft drinks manufacturers have switched to fully recyclable aluminium cans and plastic bottles. In 2003 the **Co-op** and **Somerfield** pioneered degradable plastic carrier bags which self-destruct to gas, water and a little mineral matter after a period of months. Tesco followed their lead in 2004.

5  **ICI** invested in the challenge to find a replacement for chlorofluorocarbons (CFCs), gases which are used extensively in aerosols and refrigeration equipment, and which are widely blamed for depleting the ozone layer.

6  **The Body Shop** produces a comprehensive, externally audited, environmental report, its Green Book. The emphasis on such factors as energy waste and product stewardship drives improvements. Among other initiatives, The Body Shop has sought to eliminate its use of polyvinylchloride (PVC) because of the environmental impact of such packaging.

7  **The motor vehicle industry.** Historically, car manufacturers exploited an opportunity very successfully: increased affluence and the desire for individual freedom had generated a demand for private cars. Their success in increasing levels of ownership created a number of threats: traffic density, pollution from exhaust emissions, material waste through obsolescence, the 'waste' of scarce resources in high-consumption, inefficient, engines, and safety problems arising from the sheer volume of traffic, congestion and hurry.

A response was needed, and this has involved both manufacturers and government:

■ Legislation made catalytic converters compulsory on all new cars after January 1993.

■ New models invariably feature improvements in design and technology which reduce waste and increase fuel efficiency.

■ Some new plants feature strategies for reducing energy consumption, water consumption and solvent emissions.

■ New concept vehicles are being developed, including electric cars and others which mix the traditionally contradictory high performance with environmental friendliness. These have a long-term timescale.

■ Links between different forms of transport (road, rail, air and water) are being strengthened. BMW, for example, has pioneered co-operative ventures in Munich, where research has shown that in one square kilometre of the city centre in busy periods drivers of 50 per cent of the cars on the move are driving round looking for parking spaces.

■ Old parts are being recycled. In France both Peugeot and Renault opened plants for this, followed by other European manufacturers, but these initiatives remain small ventures in relation to the total numbers of cars being scrapped.

■ In 1998 Mazda promised to plant five trees for every Demio model it sold: more than enough to compensate for the carbon emissions from the cars, as trees absorb carbon dioxide.

**Body Shop** http://www.bodyshop.com
**ICI** http://www.ici.com
**McDonald's** http://www.mcdonalds.com
**Procter and Gamble** http://www.pg.com
**Sainsbury's** http://www.sainsburys.com

generate similar results. Some organizations feature their community role extensively in corporate advertising campaigns designed to bring them recognition and develop a caring, responsible image.

### 2.7.1 Business ethics

Disasters such as the explosion at the chemical plant in Bhopal, India, in 1984 have long raised the question of how far companies should go in pursuit of profits. More recent cases, such as Tyco and Enron, have raised different but related issues of ethical behaviour. The CEO of Tyco has been prosecuted for using corporate funds to provide a lavish personal lifestyle – at the same time as sponsoring a number of creative accounting practices to hide the company's true financial performance. Enron lost huge sums of shareholder money as it developed futures trading for energy.

Ethics is defined as 'the discipline dealing with what is good and bad and right and wrong or with moral duty and obligation' (*Webster's Third New International Dictionary*). Houlden (1988) suggests that **business ethics** encompasses the views of people throughout society concerning the morality of business, and not just the views of the particular business and the people who work in it.

Issues such as golden handshakes, insider dealing and very substantial salary increases for company chairmen and chief executives are topical and controversial. But is it ethical for large companies to pursue high-risk strategies which might leave several small company suppliers financially exposed? Again, when some large (and smaller) companies come to grief (often through ill-advised or ill-judged strategic choices) many employees may find their pension funds have disappeared. Is this also an ethical issue?

The high-profile case of British Airways and Virgin Atlantic, where BA was accused of using privileged information to evaluate Virgin's route profitability and to persuade Virgin customers to switch airlines, suggested that BA acted unethically. In contrast, Hewlett-Packard, the US electronics multinational which is widely regarded as being highly ethical, operates an internal ban on the use of improper means for obtaining competitor information. The company also insists that any statements about its competitors must be fair, factual and complete.

Public attention is drawn to these issues, and people's perceptions of businesses generally and individually are affected. However, their responses differ markedly. Some people feel disgruntled but do nothing, whereas others take more positive actions. Managers, however, should not ignore the potential for resistance or opposition by their customers, who may refuse to buy their products or use their services.

Another ethical concern is individual managers or employees who adopt practices which senior managers or the strategic leader would consider unethical. These need to be identified and stopped. If they remain unchecked they are likely to spread, with the argument that 'everyone does it'. Sales staff using questionable methods of persuasion, even lying, would be an example. However, it does not follow that such practices would always be seen as unethical by senior managers – in some organizations they will be at least condoned, and possibly even encouraged.

Minicase 2.6 on the Co-operative Bank highlights how one organization has used an ethical stance to create a competitive advantage.

## 2.7.2 Ethical dilemmas

One classic ethical dilemma concerns the employee who works for a competitor, is interviewed for a job, and who promises to bring confidential information if he is offered the post. Should the proposition be accepted or not? The issue, featured at the beginning of this section, is how far companies should go in pursuit of profits. In such a case as this, long-term considerations are important as well as potential short-term benefits. If the

---

### Box 2.6 Three Ethical Dilemmas

A well-established European pharmaceutical company (X), in a country with a moderate but not large Catholic community, has developed and patented a new drug which safely induces abortion and has demonstrable health-care benefits for women seeking an abortion. For a variety of reasons, largely economic (health-care savings, benefit reductions and corporation tax revenues), its government is encouraging it to launch the drug in the home country and around the world at the earliest opportunity. Profits to the company would be good, but they would not have a dramatic impact on the company's overall profits. They would, however, ensure the future viability of a small production plant in an area of high unemployment. However, a sizeable block of the company's shares (but not a controlling interest) has recently been acquired by a foreign mini-conglomerate whose chief executive is a Catholic and opposed to the drug on religious grounds. As X's managing director you also know from your personal experience that if you launch the drug in America, one of your key export markets, you can expect protests from demonstrators opposed to abortion. What should you do?

A business manager for a well-known high street bank is told by her manager that her function is shortly to be moved to a new regional centre some 25 miles away and that her own position is secure. She is personally delighted as her travel-to-work commute will be reduced, but she knows that there will be redundancies. Under instruction that for the moment the news is embargoed from other staff, she is concerned when her personal assistant approaches her a few days later. She has heard unsubstantiated rumours on the bank's grapevine and she would, for family reasons, be unable to move. She wants to know what she should do as she is about to pay a deposit on a new house. What should the business manager do? What is 'right by her employer' and what is 'right by her subordinate'?

A young consultant with a relatively new and small but fast-growing management consultancy is invited out of the blue to be joint presenter (with the senior partner) of a bid to a potentially very large client. He is surprised; he has had no involvement in preparing the bid. Moreover, it is not in his area of expertise. Flattered with the wonderful opportunity, but at the same time concerned, he discusses the request with his mentor in the consultancy. He is informed that the contact person in the client organization is, like him, from an ethnic minority background. The senior partner felt that the client would like to see that the consultancy's only non-white consultant was a key member of the team. How should he react?

Developed from material in Badaracco, JL Jr (1997) *Defining Moments – When Managers Must Choose Between Right and Right*, Harvard Business School Press.

DISCUSSION

competitor who loses the confidential information realizes what has happened it may seek to retaliate in some way. Arguably, the best interests of the industry as a whole should be considered. Box 2.6 presents three more ethical dilemmas.

Another example is the company with a plant that is surplus to requirements and which it would like to sell. The company knows the land beneath the plant contains radioactive waste. Legally it need not disclose this fact to prospective buyers, but is it ethical to keep quiet? Research commissioned by the Rowntree Foundation (see Taylor, 1997) concluded that housebuilders and estate agents generally do not warn buyers when new homes are built on previously contaminated industrial land. Pet food manufacturers, looking to expand their sales, would logically seek to differentiate their products by featuring particular benefits and satisfied, friendly pets, but they will also hope to persuade more people to become owners. Given the publicity on potentially dangerous breeds of dog, and the numbers of abandoned pets, particularly after Christmas, what would constitute an ethical approach to promotion? In 1991 a small number of ministers in the Church of England questioned whether the Church Commissioners, with £3 billion to invest to cover the future salaries and pensions of clergy, should be free to invest the money anywhere (in an attempt to maximize earnings) or whether they should be restricted to organizations which were known to be ethical in their business dealings. Interestingly, Martinson (1998) reported that the shares of companies widely perceived to be ethical in their strategies, policies and behaviour do not underperform when measured against the equity markets overall. In this context community involvement is seen as positive; any involvement with tobacco, alcohol or military equipment is negative.

Badaracco and Webb (1995) also highlight how internal decisions can be influenced by unethical practices. They quote instances of invented market-research findings, and

## Minicase 2.6 The Co-operative Bank

Retail banking in the UK has become extremely competitive as traditional building societies and foreign banks have entered the sector. To compete, charges have been kept relatively low, leaving the banks with too many unprofitable accounts. Their challenge: attracting the 'right customers', those who will retain a sizeable current account balance and also purchase other products such as insurance policies. A typical 'good customer' would be 25–40 years old and a member of the ABC1 social groupings.

The Co-op Bank, owned by the Co-operative Wholesale Society, began an advertising campaign in the early 1990s which concentrated on the bank's ethical stance towards business. The bank stated it would not deal with tobacco companies, cosmetics companies which used animals for testing, companies involved in blood sports, factory farming and animal fur products, and any business which caused pollution. Some corporate accounts were closed.

Almost immediately, the volume of retail deposits increased by over 10 per cent, with new customers actively citing the advertising campaign. Profits accrued after two years of losses. Many customers also took out the bank's new gold credit card.

The bank began to develop a customer profile which featured a disproportionate percentage of ABC1s. The Managing Director at the time, Terry Thomas, commented: 'After all, what bank would want to attract low income, badly-educated, ignorant people?'

### Questions

1. Did it make sense for the Co-operative Bank to trade off corporate clients for new personal accounts in this way?
2. Do you know whether the strategy is still in place?

**Co-operative Bank** http://www.co-operativebank.co.uk

altered investment returns which imply, erroneously, that the organization is meeting its published targets. They distinguish between 'expedient actions' and 'right actions'.

In contrast, a serious dilemma faces individuals in an organization who feel that their managers are pursuing unethical practices. There are several examples of individuals who have acted and suffered as a result of their actions. An accountant with an insurance company exposed a case of tax evasion by his bosses and jeopardized his career. Stanley Adams, an employee of Hoffman la Roche, the Swiss drug company, believed that his firm was making excessive profits and divulged commercially sensitive information to the European Commission. He also lost his career and suffered financially. There are similar examples of engineers who felt that design compromises were threatening consumer safety, complained, and lost their jobs.

Many of the ethical issues that affect strategic decisions are regulated directly by legislation. Equally, many companies do not operate in sensitive environments where serious ethical issues require thought and attention. However, some companies and their strategic leaders do need a clear policy regarding business ethics. Often they have to decide whether to increase costs in the short run, say to improve safety factors, on the assumption that this will bring longer-term benefits. Short-term profitability, important to shareholders, could be affected. Increased safety beyond minimum legal requirements, for example, would increase the construction costs of a new chemical plant. If safety were compromised to save money, nothing might actually go wrong and profits would be higher. However, an explosion or other disaster results in loss of life, personal injury, compensation and legal costs, lost production, adverse publicity and tension between the business and local community. The long-term losses can be substantial.

Reidenbach and Robin (1995) have produced a spectrum of five ethical/unethical responses.

- *Amoral companies* seek to 'win at all costs'; anything is seen as acceptable. The secret lies in not being found out.
- *Legalistic companies* obey the law and no more. There is no code of ethics; companies act only when it is essential.
- *Responsive companies* accept that being ethical can pay off.
- *Ethically engaged companies* actively want to 'do the right thing' and to be seen to be doing so. Ethical codes will exist, but ethical behaviour will not necessarily be a planned activity and fully integrated into the culture.
- *Ethical companies* such as Body Shop have ethics as a core value, supported by appropriate strategies and actions which permeate the whole organization.

Because ethical standards and beliefs are aspects of the corporate culture, they are influenced markedly by the lead set by the strategic leader and his or her awareness of behaviour throughout the organization. If a proper lead is not provided, managers will be left to 'second guess' what would be seen as appropriate behaviour. Power, then, can be used ethically or unethically by individual managers.

Frederick (1988) contends that the corporate culture is the main source of any ethical problems. He argues that managers are encouraged to focus their professional energies on productivity, efficiency and leadership, and that their corporate values lead them to act in ways which place the company interests ahead of those of consumers or society.

To guard against this it can be useful for a company to publish a corporate code of ethics, which all managers are expected to follow. Typically, large US companies have been more progressive with such codes than those in the UK. In the early 1990s, some 30 per cent of large companies in the UK had published codes, but the number has since been growing all the time.

The typical issues covered in an ethics code include relationships with employees (the most prevalent factor in the UK codes of ethics), government (more important in the US), the community and the environment.

Drawing on earlier points, attitudes towards bribery and inducement, and the use of privileged information, could also be incorporated in any code. Attention might also be paid to practices which are commonplace but arguably unethical. Examples would include a deliberate policy not to pay invoices on time, and creative accounting, presenting information in the most favourable light. The extent to which audited company accounts can be wholly relied upon is another interesting issue.

Tucker and Maitland (2004) report that the Association of British Insurers (representing shareholders who own 20 per cent of the shares traded on the London Stock Exchange) are putting increasing pressure on businesses to disclose any relevant social, ethical and environmental concerns. Issues that might raise concern would include those linked to pollution and climate change, fast food and obesity and working conditions in developing countries. Perhaps there is an element of enlightened self-interest, a fear of the impact of litigation on share prices if something goes wrong – but perhaps it is the outcome rather than the motive that really matters. The final case in this chapter, Minicase 2.7 on Nike, addresses this point.

Business ethics is arguably important and worthy of serious attention. However, a consideration of ethical issues in strategic decisions typically requires that a long-term perspective is adopted. Objectives and strategies should be realistic and achievable rather than overambitious and very difficult to attain. In the latter case individual managers may be set high targets which encourage them to behave unethically, possibly making them feel uneasy. Results may be massaged, for instance, or deliberately presented with inaccuracies. Such practices spread quickly and dishonesty becomes acceptable. The longer-term perspective can reduce the need for immediate results and targets which managers feel have to be met at all costs. However, pressure from certain stakeholders, particularly institutional shareholders, may focus attention on the short term and on results which surpass those of the previous year. The longer-term perspective additionally allows for concern with processes and behaviour, and with how the results are obtained. The drive for results is not allowed to override ethical and behavioural concerns.

Houlden (1988) concludes that strategic leaders should be objective about how society views their company and its products, and wherever possible should avoid actions that can damage its image. If an action or decision that certain stakeholders might view as unethical is unavoidable, such as the closure of a plant, it is important to use public relations to explain fully why the decision has been taken. The need for a good corporate image should not be underestimated.

Later chapters (particularly Chapter 6) include discussions on how organizations might achieve competitive advantage. Ethical considerations can make a significant contribution to this. A commitment to keeping promises about quality standards and delivery times, or not making promises which cannot be met, would be one example. If employees are honest and committed, and rewarded appropriately for this, then costs are likely to be contained and the overall level of customer service high, thereby improving profits.

To summarize briefly, this chapter has been about direction and about ends, the ends which help to determine the strategies that organizations select and pursue. A number of key terms have been defined and a number of important conflicts of interest explained. The next two chapters look first at how we might measure performance against these desired end points and then at issues of organizational culture, which provide an important guide to why organizations pick particular strategies and follow certain routes.

## Minicase 2.7  Nike                                                         (US) (Int)

The Nike brand name is most commonly associated with trainers, but Nike produces a range of leisure and sports gear. Several leading sports personalities endorse its products. The company is profitable, and, arguably in part for this reason, has been targeted by environmentalists and other campaign groups. Nike, like its leading competitors such as Adidas and Reebok, focuses on design and marketing and outsources manufacturing from around the world. In fact, Nike purchases supplies from 700 different factories in 50 countries. It is typical and perhaps logical to use low-cost labour around the world, as long as exploitation is not an issue. Lower production costs allow for lower prices – but then there is the issue of what constitutes an acceptable margin for the brand owner.

Nike has been accused of condoning worker exploitation in some of these factories. Under-age child labour and sexual harassment have been cited. Nike has, not unexpectedly, been worried by the allegations, flagging how campaigners have been making greater use of the Internet to spread their allegations and generate adverse publicity for the company. Moreover, Nike employees in the US have been targeted, when realistically they can have little personal influence on working conditions in developing countries. However, such targeting makes for an effective campaign to which the company must react. And Nike has admitted that making trainers is routine and tedious.

One story that became prominent concerned a student customer who wanted to take up Nike's offer of customizing his trainers. The student wanted 'Sweatshop' printing on his shoes. Nike refused. The customer appeared to accept the rejection, but then e-mailed the company with a letter that he also put on the Internet – he asked for a photograph of the 10-year old Vietnamese girl who made his shoes.

Nike has responded.

■ It has required subcontract manufacturers to stipulate a minimum age for workers it employs

■ It has helped to set up and part-funded the Global Alliance for Workers and Communities, which monitors and criticizes some of the practices it sees – experience shows it does not spare its funders

■ It has invested in training for factory managers and supervisors, highlighting employees rights but really focusing on the links between productivity and employee satisfaction.

Source Skapinker, M (2002) Why Nike has broken into a sweat, *Financial Times*, 7 March.

### Questions

1. Do you think Nike is sufficiently responsible and ethical?
2. If not, what else do you think it should do?

**Nike** http://www.nike.com

CASE

## SUMMARY

The business model addresses what a company does (its products and services), who its target customers are, and what their compelling reason to buy is. We should be able to discern a clear business model for any organization.

The corporate *mission* represents the overriding purpose for the business, and ideally it should explain why the organization is different and set it apart from its main rivals. It should not be a statement that other organizations can readily adopt. Its main purpose is communication.

It is useful to separate the mission statement from a statement of corporate *vision* which concerns 'what the organization is to become'.

Both can provide a valuable starting point for more specific *objectives* and strategies. Shorter-term objectives will normally have timescales or end-dates attached to them and ideally they will be 'owned' by individual managers.

It is, therefore, feasible to argue that organizations (as a whole) have a purpose and individual managers have objectives.

Mission, vision and objectives all relate to the *direction* that the organization is taking – the ends from which strategies are derived.

It is not, however, feasible to assume that the organization will always be free to set these objectives for its managers: there may be constraints from key stakeholders. A number of theories and models, mainly from a study of economics, can help us to understand why organizations do the things they do.

In addition, individuals will have *personal objectives* that they wish (and intend) to pursue, which should not be allowed to work against the best interests of the organization.

External *stakeholders* also have expectations for the organization. These will not always be in accord with each other, and important trade-offs and priorities must be established. There is always the potential for conflicts of interest. As a result, the organization will be seen to have a multitude of objectives, but all contributory to a single purpose.

Profit is necessary for profit-seeking businesses; a positive cash flow is essential for not-for-profit organizations. Profit (or cash) can, however, be seen as either a means or an end, and this will impact upon the 'feel' or culture of the organization.

Regardless, there is a virtuous circle of financial returns, motivated employees and satisfied customers.

Issues of *social responsibility* and *business ethics* are important for all organizations. They will be seen by some organizations as a threat or constraint and encourage a strategy of compliance. Other organizations will perceive them as an opportunity to create a difference and in turn a positive image. They are becoming increasingly visible, issues which organizations should take seriously and not ignore.

## QUESTIONS AND RESEARCH ASSIGNMENTS

1. Using the Ben and Jerry's case (or another case from Chapter 1 if you prefer) clarify what you think the business model is.

2. Think of any organization with which you have personal experience. Do you believe that profit (or cash in the case of a non-profit organization) is seen as a means or an end by the key decision-makers? Do they all agree on this?

3. What key issues do you believe should be incorporated in a company statement on ethics?

## INTERNET AND LIBRARY PROJECTS

1. First consider how the objectives of HP Bulmer Holdings, detailed in Box 2.1, might be ranked in order of priority. Is there a difference between an ideal ranking and the likely ranking in practice? Then find out what happened to the business. Did the company get its priorities wrong and was this why the business was sold to Scottish and Newcastle. Note: Prior to the acquisition, members of the Bulmer family held over 50 per cent of the ordinary shares.

2. From the FT Fast Track web site, pick a rapidly growing business of your choice from within the top ten businesses listed. In 400 words or less can you describe the business model of that business. http://www.fasttrack100.co.uk/

3. When Tottenham Hotspur became the first English Football League club with a stock exchange listing (in 1983) the issue prospectus said: 'The Directors intend to ensure that the Club remains one of the leading football clubs in the country. They will seek to increase the Group's income by improving the return from existing assets and by establishing new sources of revenue in the leisure field.'

(a) Research the strategies followed by Tottenham Hotspur plc since 1983. Do you believe that the interests of a plc and a professional football club are compatible or inevitably conflicting?

(b) Which other clubs have followed Tottenham? Have they chosen similar or different strategies? How have they performed as businesses?

(c) In view of the comments about social responsibility, how do you view the fact that football clubs generally invest far more money in players (wages and transfer fees) than they do in their grounds (amenities and safety)?

4. Have the objectives (in particular the order of priorities) of the Natural History Museum changed since the introduction (and later abandonment) of compulsory admission charges in April 1987?

5. In view of the findings after the *Herald of Free Enterprise* disaster at Zeebrugge in March 1987 and the *Estonia* disaster in 1994, how does a company such as P&O (the owners of the *Herald*) balance the extra costs involved in additional safety measures with the need to be competitive internationally, and the time added on to voyages by more rigorous safety procedures with customer irritation if they are delayed unnecessarily?

**Natural History Museum** http://www.nhm.ac.uk
**P&O Group** http://www.p-and-o.com
**Tottenham Hotspur plc**
http://www.spurs.co.uk/index.asp
**Zoological Society of London/London Zoo**
http://www.londonzoo.co.uk

## Further reading

Simon, HA (1964) On the concept of organizational goal, *Administrative Science Quarterly*, 9 (1).

Drucker, PF (1989) What business can learn from non–profits, *Harvard Business Review*, July–August.

Andrews, KR (1989) Ethics in practice, *Harvard Business Review*, September–October.

Campbell, A and Yeung, S (1991) Creating a sense of mission, *Long Range Planning*, August.

Chan Kim, W and Mauborgne, R (2002) Charting your company's future, *Harvard Business Review*, May–June.

## References

Ackoff, RL (1986) *Management in Small Doses*, John Wiley.

Badaracco, JL and Webb, A (1995) Business ethics: a view from the trenches, *California Management Review*, 37 (2), Winter.

Baumol, WJ (1959) *Business Behaviour, Value and Growth*, Macmillan.

Campbell, A (1989) Research findings discussed in Skapinker, M (1989) Mission accomplished or ignored? *Financial Times*, 11 January. See also: Campbell, A and Nash, L (1992) *A Sense of Mission: Defining Direction for the Large Corporation*, Addison-Wesley.

Constable, J (1980) The nature of company objectives. Unpublished paper, Cranfield School of Management.

Cyert, RM and March, JG (1963) *A Behavioural Theory of the Firm*, Prentice-Hall.

Deloitte (1999) *Making Customer Loyalty Real – A Global Manufacturing Study*, Deloitte Consulting and Deloitte & Touche, http://www.dc.com/research

Drucker, PF (1974) *Management: Tasks, Responsibilities, Practices*, Harper & Row.

Frederick, WC (1988) An ethics roundtable: the culprit is culture, *Management Review*, August.

Freeman, RE (1984) *Strategic Management: A Stakeholder Approach*, Pitman.

Friedman, M (1979) The social responsibility of business is to increase its profits. In *Business Policy and Strategy* (eds DJ McCarthy, RJ Minichiello and JR Curran), Irwin.

Galbraith, JK (1963) *American Capitalism. The Concept of Countervailing Power*, Penguin.

Galbraith, JK (1969) *The New Industrial State*, Penguin.

Hamel, G (2000) *Leading the Revolution*, Harvard Business School Press.

Houlden, B (1988) The corporate conscience, *Management Today*, August.

Marris, R (1964) *The Economic Theory of Managerial Capitalism*, Macmillan.

Martinson, J (1998) Ethical equities perform well, *Financial Times*, 21 July.

Newbould, GD and Luffman, GA (1979) *Successful Business Policies*, Gower.

Penrose, E (1959) *The Theory of the Growth of the Firm*, Blackwell.

Performance Group, The (1999) *Sustainable Strategies for Value Creation*, Oslo, Norway.

Perrow, C (1961) The analysis of goals in complex organizations, *American Sociological Review*, 26, December.

Pfeffer, J (1981) *Power in Organizations*, Pitman.

Porter, ME (1995) Interviewed for the Green Management letter, *Euromanagement*, June.

Public Management Foundation (1999) *Wasted Values*, London.

Reidenbach, E and Robin, D (1995) Quoted in Drummond, J: Saints and sinners, *Financial Times*, 23 March.

Richards, MD (1978) *Organizational Goal Structures*, West.

Simon, HA (1964) On the concept of organizational goal, *Administrative Science Quarterly*, 9 (1).

Taylor, A (1997) Home buyers unaware of contamination, *Financial Times*, 24 October.

Thompson, AA and Strickland, AJ (1980) *Strategy Formulation and Implementation*, Irwin.

Tucker, S and Maitland, A (2004), Business put under pressure to disclose ethical risks, *Financial Times*, 26 February.

Waterman, R (1994) *The Frontiers of Excellence: Learning from Companies that Put People First*, Nicholas Brealey Publishing.

Williamson, OE (1964) *Economics of Discretionary Behaviour: Managerial Objectives in a Theory of the Firm*, Kershaw.

# Supplements

There are two supplements to Part One. They are a distinctive feature of this book.

The first supplement introduces, outlines and explains a number of key terms, themes and concepts, all of which are taken up and developed in greater detail at various points in the text. These pages are designed to be a reference section so that you can find your way back to check your understanding of the concepts at any time.

The second supplement is another reference section. It provides a concise summary of the key frameworks that can be used to carry out a strategic analysis. Again, all the frameworks are developed in detail in the main text.

# Key Strategic Concerns

## Learning objectives

Having read to the end of these supplements you should be able to:

- appreciate how leadership, culture and values are at the heart of strategic decision-making
- understand the importance of strategic positioning and how two important approaches to strategy – market-driven and resource-based – impact upon it
- define key success factors and give examples of these
- explain the term competitive advantage
- appreciate the significance of adding value, core competencies, strategic capabilities and strategic architecture
- explain what is meant by E–V–R congruency
- explain why the strategic challenge for organizations concerns decisions about content and process within the context of a set of important issues and dilemmas
- be aware of the existence of a number of useful strategic analysis frameworks.

The purpose of the first section of this supplement is to introduce, outline and explain a number of key terms, themes and concepts which run through the book and help our understanding of strategy and strategic management. They will all be taken up and developed in greater detail at various points in the text. These pages are easily referenced so that you can find your way back to check your understanding of the concepts at any time.

## 1.S.1 Strategic leadership

It has been pointed out that a major aim of this book is to encourage readers to be more strategically aware. Long-term strategic success requires that the efforts of managers are co-ordinated. This is the task of the chief executive or managing director of the whole organization and in turn of general managers of subsidiaries or divisions in the case of large complex organizations. For simplicity in this book the term *strategic leader* is used to refer to this role.

The role is analogous to that of the captain of a ship. In a sailing race, for example, the captain must sail the ship possibly in uncertain or dangerous waters, with one or more clear goals in sight. The chosen strategy or strategies will be decided upon in the light of these goals, and the risks of any actions will be assessed. Nevertheless the captain's success will depend on the crew. It is essential that the crew acts in a co-ordinated way, and therefore it is crucial that the strategies are communicated and understood. For an excellent example of this see Cranwell-Ward *et al.* (2002).

One of the most visible strategic leaders of recent years has been Jack Welch, who is often described as transformational, because of his success in turning around and rejuvenating General Electric. Under Welch, GE grew to become the most valuable corporation in the world, when measured by corporate assets. GE also remained substantially diversified when many other corporations were becoming more focused. Welch groomed three possible successors before he retired; only one could get the job. The other two left. One has successfully turned around retail giant, Home Depot. All these cases are discussed in the book.

The strategic leader must build and lead a team of managers, and establish the goals or objectives. Styles will vary enormously, as will the scope of the objectives. Some leaders will be autocratic, others entrepreneurial. Some, arguably like Henry Ford of Ford Motor Company and Ray Kroc who built McDonald's, will be visionaries, whereas others will set more modest goals. Others, such as Richard Branson (Minicase 1.3) are not only idiosyncratic role models, they *are* their organization. The person and the business cannot be realistically separated.

The leader and his or her managers should be clear about where the organization is going, where they want to go and how they are going to get there. This requires an appreciation of the environment and an understanding of the organization's resources.

## 1.S.2 Culture and values

Schein (1985) defines culture as 'the deeper level of basic assumptions and beliefs that are shared by members of an organization, that operate unconsciously, and that define in a basic "taken for granted" fashion an organization's view of itself and its environment'.

Culture is

> *A pattern of basic assumptions that works well enough to be considered valid, and therefore is taught to new [organization] members as the correct way to perceive, think and feel in relation to problems of external adaptation and internal integration. … [it is] learned, evolves with new experiences, and can be changed if one understands the dynamics of the learning process.*

In the simplest terms it is the way that organizational members behave and the values that are important to them and it dictates the way that decisions are made, the objectives of the organization, the type of competitive advantage sought, the organization structure and systems of management, functional strategies and policies, attitudes towards managing people and information systems. Many of these are interrelated.

In the late 1980s, Woolworth's (the high-street retailer which subsequently became part of the Kingfisher Group) identified that customer service, when compared with their main rivals, was a relative weakness and a major contributor to their disappointing performance. People, they concluded, are a major strategic resource, and they reflect the values of the organization. In common with many other service organizations, Woolworth's introduced a customer-care training programme entitled 'Excellence', and linked it to staff rewards. There have been two achievements: customer perception of staff helpfulness increased, and there were immediate financial gains.

For these reasons, styles of corporate decision-making, leadership and values are a central driving force in the model in Figure 1.4. They are always important, and they are not easily changed without the appointment of a new chief executive.

## 1.S.3 Environmental fit and stakeholder satisfaction

Several authors have defined strategy in terms of the relationship between an organization and its environment. One such definition is:

*The positioning and relating of the firm/organization to its environment in a way which will assure its continued success and make it secure from surprises.*

Ansoff, 1984

The organization is influenced by the strategic leader, and in the context of an ideally clear vision and direction, the organization draws its resources (employees, managers, plant, supplies, finance, etc.) from a competitive business environment. It has to compete with other firms for labour, supplies, loans, etc., and it operates in a network which includes its suppliers and financial backers, with whom one would expect it to have strong and robust relationships. With strategies and activities, it must then use these inputs in some organized way to produce products and services which can be marketed effectively and, where appropriate, profitably – thus generating outcomes which satisfy all key stakeholders. It must invariably succeed in a competitive marketplace. As well as appreciating market demand and the strengths, weaknesses and strategies of its competitors, it must respond to fundamental changes in society and the economy. Over time people's tastes change, their discretionary purchasing power rises and falls, luxuries can become necessities and previously popular products can become unfashionable. The economy is not static, and it is strongly affected by government policy. Whilst some companies influence government policy, many do not. A **PEST** (political, economic, social and technical) analysis can provide a straightforward and useful framework for analysing the external environment (see Chapter 4).

Therefore, strategic management involves the following:

- a clear awareness of environmental forces and the ways in which they are changing
- an appreciation of potential and future threats and opportunities
- decisions on appropriate products and services for clearly defined markets
- the effective management of resources to develop and produce these products for the market, achieving the right quality for the right price at the right time
- appreciating how key strategic resources might be redeployed and exploited to create new market opportunities.

Strategic management, then, is effective when resources match stakeholder needs and expectations and change to maintain a fit in a turbulent environment. As we have seen, the external environment consists of suppliers, distributors and customers as well as bankers and other financial institutions and shareholders. It also includes competitors and sometimes the government. These stakeholders all expect something from a business in return for their support. If organizations are to be successful – and in many cases, profitable – they have to meet the needs and expectations of all their external stakeholders. It is also essential that the interests, needs and expectations of internal stakeholders, the employees, are not overlooked; after all, it is these employees who create the outcomes that satisfy external stakeholders. The relative demands of all the stakeholders determine what it is that a business must do well, and invariably their different requirements imply some difficult choices and trade-offs.

*Innovation* is an important element in maintaining fit as environmental forces and competitor strategies change. An innovative organization fosters learning which leads to continuous, managed change to products, services and processes. In turn, this demands an organization-wide commitment to improvement and change, together with the ability and willingness of managers to spot and seize change opportunities, factors again dependent upon leadership and cultural issues. Effective innovation is thus about people and the exploitation of the organization's knowledge and intelligence.

## 1.S.4  Strategic positioning

A straightforward, popular and well-known technique, a **SWOT** (strengths, weaknesses, opportunities, threats) analysis, implies that an organization's resources (which constitute its strengths and weaknesses) should match the demands and pressures from its external environment (manifest as a set of opportunities and threats) as effectively as possible and, with change, stay matched in dynamic and turbulent times. The overlap of products and services (the outcome of the use of the organization's resources) with market needs is shown as strategic fit in Figure S.1.

Here we can see illustrated two different, but complementary, approaches to strategy creation and strategic change.

**Market-driven strategy** (or **opportunity-driven strategy**) reflects the adoption of the marketing concept, and implies that strategies are designed – and resources developed and deployed – with customer and consumer needs in mind. Carefully and creatively

**Figure S.1** Strategic positioning

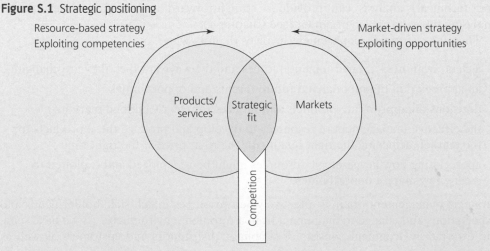

defining the industry or industries in which an organization competes can influence its perspective on the products and services it supplies. Marketing students will always remember that railway companies are in the transportation business! The approach is market-pull, and the value of a distinct competitive advantage is clearly synonymous with this approach. It should, however, never be forgotten that different sectors of the same industry require different competencies, and that the demands of creating new competencies may be readily underestimated.

Although it is convenient to see resources as organizational strengths and weaknesses (which they very clearly are) and the environment as the source of opportunities and threats, this is too simplistic. Resources can also constitute both opportunities and strengths. Resource-based strategy implies that the organization clarifies its core strategic competencies and capabilities and seeks to exploit these by finding new market opportunities where they can be used to create new values and competitive advantage. The assumption is that the organization can mould and develop its market with innovatory new ideas, sometimes changing the rules of competition in an industry. This can imply the creation of new customer preferences and perspectives in the process.

Resources which are central to an organization's success can be a threat if they could be lost. Particular people can be a major asset, and a key reason for organizational success, and people can be lost. Although rare, one reality is that they could die, but more realistically they could leave and join a competitor. Obvious instances are professional footballers and restaurant chefs. Some football clubs lose star players to rivals, sometimes for a transfer fee, sometimes when they are out of contract. Although this can affect the playing fortunes of the club, it is unlikely that fans will follow them. Loyalty goes too deep. The same cannot be said of chefs, however. Top-quality chefs can be the reason customers frequent a particular restaurant, and if they move, customers may well go with them.

All the time competitors will be attempting to accomplish the same ends. Hence, while a company is trying to create a stronger fit between itself and its customers, its competitors will be attempting to force them apart by offering something superior which draws customers away and destroys fit. Hence, a third and more tactical approach to strategy is **competitor influenced**, which implies short-term vigilance to deal with any threatening competitor initiatives. Whilst significant, it is important that an organization does not become over-reliant upon this tactical approach.

Moreover, emerging opportunities can attract competitors with different backgrounds and motives. Developments in computer software and hardware (high-quality monitors, scanners and printers) have opened up an opportunity for digital cameras. Kodak were interested because of their dependency on the photographic industry and the potential long-term threat to film-based photography. Canon and Hewlett-Packard were both interested as they could see a new opportunity for exploiting technological competencies that they already possessed. The challenge for each rival was quite different.

It is now appropriate to look further at market needs as key success factors for an organization, and at resources in the context of competency and capability. From that the concept of added value can be explored. It is this value that provides strategic fit and competitive advantage.

## 1.S.5 Key success factors

A company will have to produce to high and consistent quality levels and meet delivery promises to customers. Delivery times have been reducing gradually in very competitive industries. Suppliers and subcontractors expect regular orders and accurate forecasting when very quick deliveries are demanded from them. Without such support **just in time** production systems are impractical. Just in time systems rely on regular and reliable deliveries from suppliers in order to maintain constant production without the need for high parts inventories.

Companies will try to minimize their stockholding because this helps both cash flow and costs. Conglomerate subsidiaries will have to generate a positive cash flow in order to meet the financial expectations of the parent company who, in effect, act as its bankers. Costs have to be controlled so that companies remain price competitive, although low prices are not always a marketing weapon.

These stakeholder requirements represent *key success factors*, those things that an organization must do well if it is to be an effective competitor and thrive. In addition, many companies have to be innovative and improve both their product range and their customer service if they are to remain a leading competitor in a changing industry.

Some key success factors will be industry- and sector-specific. For example, successful consumer goods manufacturers will need skills in brand management. Charities need skills in fund-raising and public relations. There is intense competition between charities for donations, and consequently they must be run as businesses. They can only spend what they can raise. It is also essential that they use their money appropriately, are seen to be doing so and are recognized for their efforts. The differing demands of fund-raising and aid provision lead to complex cultures and organizations.

BUPA, a private medical organization based in the UK, has a similar dilemma. Typical of such organizations around the world, the business comprises two parts: insurance, with a strong commercial culture and orientation, and hospitals, which are naturally more of a caring community.

Resources must be managed with stakeholder needs in mind. Consequently, it is important that everyone in the organization recognizes and is committed to meeting key success factors, and is additionally responsive to change pressures in a dynamic and competitive environment. Without this commitment companies will be unable to sustain a match with the environment as it changes.

Figure S.2 illustrates that if organizations are to satisfy their stakeholders, especially their customers, while outperforming their rivals, their competitive offering should comprise:

■ the ability to meet the recognized key success factors for the relevant industry or market

■ distinctive competencies and capabilities which yield some form of competitive advantage, and

■ the ability and willingness to deploy these competencies and capabilities to satisfy the special requirements of individual customers, for which a premium price can often be charged. Hall (1992) suggests using the term 'customerizing' instead of marketing to reflect the importance of customers as individuals rather than as a generic group who constitute a market.

As an example, Table S.1 lists the key success factors – together with the company's relative abilities – for a number of different activities within The Crysalis Group before parts of the business were sold to Thorn EMI.

**Figure S.2** The competitive offering: criteria for effectiveness

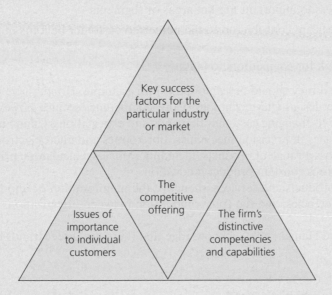

**Table S.1** Chrysalis Group: key success factors and situation analysis in four business sectors

| Activity | Key success factors | Situation analysis |
| --- | --- | --- |
| Music | Artists | Small roster |
| | Repertoire/music | Few awards in later 1980s; previously more successful |
| | Promotion | Poor performance in US |
| Facilities (production factilities for music, videos etc.) | Latest technology | Heavy investment in latest technology |
| | Technical skills | Highly skilled and innovative |
| | Location | International |
| | | Complementary to main activity of music, but very competitive and there is over-capacity |
| Machines | *Juke boxes* | |
| | Site and content | UK market leader |
| | *Fruit machines* | |
| | Site and novelty | No. 3 in market Very profitable, but subject to rapid changes |
| Property development | Saleable acquisitions | Joint venture with builder (successful) |
| | | Profitable |
| | | Good for cash utilization |

## 1.S.6  Core competencies

In order to meet their key success factors organizations must develop **core competencies** (Prahalad and Hamel 1990). These are distinctive skills which yield competitive advantage, and ideally they:

- provide access to important market areas or segments
- make a significant contribution to the perceived customer benefits of the product or service
- prove difficult for competitors to imitate.

Once developed they should be exploited as, for example, Honda have exploited their skills at engine design and technology. Core competencies must, however, be flexible and responsive to changing customer demands and expectations. Canon have developed core competencies in precision mechanics, fibre optics and microelectronics, and these are spread across a range of products, including cameras, calculators, printers and photocopiers. There is constant product innovation.

Successful products and services, then, are the manifestation of important, underlying core competencies; and the true competition between organizations is at this competency level.

Prahalad and Hamel (1990) acknowledge that there are three strands to core competency:

- technologies
- processes (or capabilities) and
- strategic architecture.

Different competitors in the same industry may well build their success by emphasizing different key competencies. While the particular expertise may be different, they all need to be competent in a number of key activities, the key success factors. In the global oil industry, for example, Exxon has long been renowned for its financial expertise, crucial when huge speculative and high-risk investments are required for exploration and developing new fields. In contrast, British Petroleum (BP) has historically relied heavily on its exploration skills. It was BP who developed the huge Forties Field in the North Sea and the fields off the hostile North Coast of Alaska, aided by the imaginative trans-Alaska pipeline. Royal Dutch Shell, a joint Anglo-Dutch company with two head offices in the UK and the Netherlands, has developed a valuable competency in managing a decentralized and diversified global business. Mobil's outstanding competency was in the related field of lubricants produced from the oil. Later in the book we will look at how the oil industry has been consolidating in recent years as the industry environment has become more demanding.

## 1.S.7  Strategic capabilities

Stalk *et al.* (1992) argue that strategic success is based on capabilities – processes that enable the company to be an effective competitor. Distribution networks that achieve both high service levels (effectiveness) and low costs (efficiency) would be an example. Typically these processes will cut across whole organizations, rather than be product-specific, and they will rely heavily on information systems and technology. In many respects Stalk's capabilities are the processes embedded in Hamel and Prahalad's core competencies. Whilst it is optional whether they are separated, or all seen as core competencies, we think that a valuable distinction can be made between competencies that are largely rooted in technologies and process-based capabilities. Although delivering similar outcomes, conceptually they are very different.

Retailers such as Boots in the UK (which has encompassed high-street department stores, specialist pharmacies, optical retailing, Halfords car products and service bays, Fads, Homestyle and Do-It-All DIY at various times) operate a number of different retail formats, capitalizing on their expertise in supply chain, information and service management.

Hamel and Prahalad (1993) developed these ideas further when they argued that understanding processes should generate intelligence that can be used to create added or greater value from resources, in order to strengthen or enhance competitiveness. They refer to this as *stretching resources*. The ability to stretch resources is very dependent on strategic **architecture**, which is discussed next.

Kay (1993) further stresses that, to be beneficial, both core competencies and strategic capabilities must be capable of exploitation and be *appropriable*. In other words, the firm must be able to realize the benefits of the competencies and capabilities for the company itself, rather than the main beneficiaries being its suppliers, customers or competitors. (John Kay is referenced in more than one section of this supplement. The strategy framework that he proposed is outlined in the second supplement but the various elements are dealt with at different points in the book where they fit best.)

## 1.S.8  Strategic architecture competencies

Strategic success requires:

- the organization to behave in a co-ordinated, synergy-creating manner, integrating functions and businesses
- the value-adding network (links between manufacturers, retailers, suppliers and intermediate distributors) to be managed as an effective, integrated, system.

Kay (1993) refers to the ability to achieve these demands as strategic architecture. The ability to build and control a successful architecture is facilitated by strong technological competency and effective functional process competencies.

Honda is renowned for its expertise in engine design and technology. However, its success as an international company has also been dependent on its ability to establish an effective distribution (dealer) network for all of its products. This has been enhanced by sound, information technology (IT)-supported, communications and control systems. As another example, Marks and Spencer's functional competencies and brand technology create both an image and a capability which enable it to trade in clothes, foods, cosmetics, household furnishings and credit. These competencies also bestow on the company the power to demand and obtain from its suppliers worldwide both a strict adherence to Marks' technological specifications and very keen prices.

The important themes in architecture are:

- internally: 'systemic thinking', which leads to synergy from the fostering of interdependencies between people, functions and divisions in organizations; and

■ externally: the establishment of linkages or even alliances between organizations at different stages of the added **value chain**.

Successful internal architecture requires that managers think 'organizationally' rather than put themselves first or promote their particular part of the organization to the detriment of other parts. Synergy from internal architecture also depends on the ability of the divisions or businesses in a conglomerate to support each other, transferring skills, competencies and capabilities, and sometimes sharing common resources. This, in turn, is partially dependent on the ability of the organization to learn, and share learning. It is also affected by the actual portfolio of businesses managed by a corporation. Goold *et al.* (1994) use the term '**heartland**' to describe that range of businesses to which a corporate head office can add value, rather than see value destroyed through too much complexity and diversity.

Alliances enable companies to focus on their core skills and competencies. Nike, for example, a leading company in sporting and leisure footwear, focuses on product design, marketing and personality endorsements; it avoids manufacturing, which it subcontracts to specialists worldwide. Partners have to support each other, however, and understand each other's various needs and expectations. The main benefits will come from sharing information, which in turn should enable companies to respond more quickly to new opportunities and threats. **Alliance** partners can also be an excellent means of overcoming relative weaknesses.

## 1.S.9 Leveraging resources

Hamel and Prahalad (1993) also emphasize the need to manage the organization's strategic resources to achieve ambitious, stretching objectives. Productivity can be improved by gaining the same output from fewer resources – this is downsizing (sometimes called **rightsizing**) – and by leveraging, achieving more output from given resources.

Clearly, internal and external architecture are both important for leveraging resources. In addition, organizations can benefit by ensuring that there is a clear and understood focus for the efforts. This could take the form of a properly communicated mission or purpose, which is acknowledged and understood. British Airways would claim that much of its success historically has been based around a commitment to the slogan 'The World's Favourite Airline'. This example again emphasizes the significance of corporate image.

## 1.S.10 Adding value

A business must add value if it is to be successful. As supply potential has grown to exceed global demand in the majority of industries, adding value has become increasingly important. In simple terms the extent of the value added is the difference between the value of the outputs from an organization and the cost of the inputs or resources used. Two fundamental questions are being addressed: what is the value created and what is the cost?

The traditional paradigm, based on the accountancy measure, is that prices reflect costs plus a profit margin. The lack of differentiation, for which a higher price can be charged, implies enormous downward pressures on costs. Performance measurement is then based upon economy of scale (low input costs) and efficiency (minimizing the actual and attributed costs of the resources used for adding further value).

While it is important to use all resources efficiently and properly, it is also critical to ensure that the potential value of the outputs is maximized by ensuring that they fully meet the needs of the customers for whom they are intended. An organization achieves this when it sees its customers' objectives as its own objectives and enables its customers to easily add more value or, in the case of final consumers, feel that they are gaining true value for money.

In the new paradigm, the key is value for the customer; if resources are used to provide real value for customers, they will pay a price which reflects its worth to them.

John Kay (1993) researched the most successful European companies during the 1980s, measured by their average costs per unit of net output. He found that each company had developed an individual strategy for adding value and creating competitive success. Glaxo (number one in the ten) successfully exploited the international potential for its patented antiulcer drug Zantac. LVMH (Louis Vuitton, Moët Hennessy), sixth in the list, generated synergy from the global distribution of a diverse range of high-quality, premium-brand products. Benetton, second, enjoyed beneficially close links with its suppliers and distributors, again worldwide. Marks and Spencer (tenth, and Minicase 1.2 in the previous chapter) was also expert at supply-chain management and further benefited from its value-for-money image and **reputation**. In contrast, low-price food retailer Kwik Save, fifth in the list, was selling its products with a low margin but enjoying a relatively very high turnover to capital employed. BTR (number nine) had expertise in the management of a diversified conglomerate. Many of Kay's leading companies are featured in short cases in this book, and it is important to emphasize that the relative fortunes of some of these organizations have declined. It was shown in Chapter 1 that Marks and Spencer has recently fallen from grace; the demise of both BTR and Kwik Save has been greater. Simply, it cannot be assumed that what constitutes value for customers at some point in time will always constitute value. When needs and requirements change, companies must find new ways of creating high added value. Here will lie a future challenge for the no-frills, cut-price airlines.

The important elements in adding value are:

- understanding and being close to customers, in particular understanding their perception of value
- a commitment to quality
- a high level of all-round service
- speedy reaction to competitive opportunities and threats
- innovation.

Organizations can seek to add value by, first, adding positive features, such as air conditioning, comfortable bucket seats and CD players in cars and, second, by removing any features perceived as negatives or drawbacks. Antilock braking systems and four-wheel drive gearboxes reduce the concerns that some people have about driving in bad weather, while extended warranty schemes remove the fear of unknown future repair costs. Each of these additions has a value for which some customers – not all – will pay a premium.

**Figure S.3** Adding value for customers

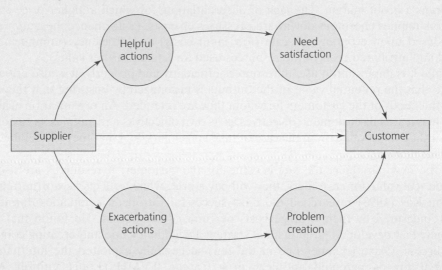

It is quite conceivable that organizations are pursuing strategies or policies which make life harder for their customers. Minimum order quantities and, possibly, volume discounts, may force or encourage customers to buy more than they need or can afford to stock. Obsolescence can then become an issue. Organizations could evaluate the merit of discounts based on annual sales rather than only on individual orders. Simply, organizations should be looking to ensure that they follow the top loop of Figure S.3 and not the bottom one.

Organizations that truly understand their customers can create competitive advantage and thereby benefit from higher prices and loyalty. High-capacity utilization can then help to reduce costs.

As an example, the prices of airline seats are related to the value that they have for customers and the benefits they offer, not simply the airline's cost for providing the seat and the associated service. With full-service airlines, the first-class cabin has traditionally offered space, comfortable seats which can be reclined almost to the horizontal, and high-quality food and service. Business class is based on similar principles but to a more limited degree. Now airlines have introduced sleeper seats, which can be converted into a horizontal bed, in these cabins for long-haul overnight flights. Both classes are quieter than the economy section, offering some opportunity for business travellers to work, and reservations can be changed. Economy seats at full fare allow for late bookings, open tickets to allow for flexible return schedules, upstairs seats on Boeing 747s with some airlines and special sections of the cabin on others, and, clearly, more chance of an upgrade. Reduced advance-purchase fares can be very good value for money, but they are inflexible. Travellers must stay for a prescribed period, flights and tickets cannot be altered and sometimes payment must be made early and in full.

One important key success factor for any airline is the ability to sell the right mix of tickets to maximize the revenue potential from every flight. Empty seats imply lost revenue; at the same time, if every ticket is sold at a discounted price, the flight is unlikely to be profitable. After flipping from profit to loss at the end of the 1990s, British Airways switched its emphasis and increased the size of its premium-price business class cabins at the expense of low-margin economy seating. Consequently, the airline performance measures include load factors, passenger kilometres (the numbers of passengers multiplied by the distance flown), and the revenue per passenger kilometre.

It is quite typical of airlines, both full-service and the no-frills carriers, to increase the seat price as the flight fills. Only a certain proportion of seats are available at the lowest prices. Early bookers get prices that are denied to others. However, if a flight is not full it is sometimes, but certainly not always, possible to get distress prices at the last minute. But it can be a mistake for a customer to hold out for these – they may never become available.

Opportunities for adding value which attracts customers must be sought and exploited. Numerous possible opportunities exist at corporate, competitive and functional strategy levels. Resources must be deployed to exploit these opportunities. Pümpin (1991) argues that multiplication, i.e. strategic consistency and performance improvement by concentrating on certain important strategies and learning how to implement them more effectively, promotes growth. The matching process is led and championed by the strategic leader, who is responsible for establishing the key values. While striving to improve performance with existing strategies the organization must constantly search for new windows of opportunity. McDonald's (Minicase 1.4) provides an excellent example. Ray Kroc spotted an opportunity in the growing fast-food market and exploited it by concentrating on new product ideas and franchised outlets, supported by a culture that promoted 'quality, service, cleanliness and value'.

Figures S.4 and S.5 summarize these arguments about strategic competency and competitive success. Figure S.4 shows that organizations must add value, and continue to find new ways of adding fresh value, for their customers. They achieve this by developing, changing and exploiting core resource-based technological competencies. This exploitation involves organizational processes and capabilities, together with strong linkages with other companies in the supply chain (strategic architecture), in order to create differentiation and effective cost control and, thus, establish a superior competitive position. The situation is always fluid, though; organizations cannot assume that currently successful products, services and competitive strategies will be equally

**Figure S.4** Adding value for sustained competitive advantage

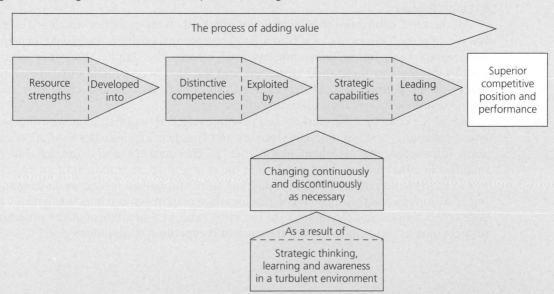

**Figure S.5** Changing strategies
Based on ideas in KPMG (1999) *Change the Game, Change the Rules of the Game,*
www.kpmg.co.uk/kmpg/services/manage/ebook.change

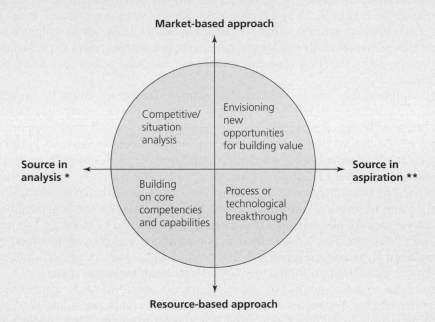

Analysis * – *includes strategic planning systems and routine decision-making.*
Aspiration ** – *ranges from entrepreneurially visionary inputs to new ideas which result in emergent change.*

successful in the future. They must be changed at appropriate times. In turn, this requires competency in awareness, thinking and learning. Realizing which competencies are most important for long-term success, concentrating attention on them, developing them and measuring the desired improvements is a critically important task for the strategic leader.

All the time, companies should carry out efficiently those activities which are essential for creating a distinctive or differentiated competitive position, and avoid incurring unnecessary costs by providing non-essential values. This implies that they clearly understand their markets, their customers and the key success factors that they must meet – their defined competitive strategy. Moreover, they should constantly seek improvement by driving their operating efficiencies.

Figure S.5 combines the market- and resource-based views of strategy with the analytical (planning) and aspirational (visionary and emergent) approaches to strategy creation introduced and explained in Chapter 1. The market-based approach can be manifest in either an analytical insight into the competitive environment or an endeavour to envision new opportunities for building value through an instinctive understanding of customers and their needs. The resource-based approach can build analytically on core competencies and capabilities. At the same time, real breakthroughs in processes or technologies can help to rewrite the rules of competition in an industry.

# 1.S.11  Competitive advantage

Ohmae (1982) contends that business strategy is all about competitive advantage. He argues that without competitors there would be no need for strategy, for the sole purpose of strategic management is to enable the company to gain, as effectively as possible, a sustainable edge over its competitors – to alter a company's strength relative to that of its competitors in the most efficient way. Actions affecting the health of a business (value engineering or improved cash flow which improve profitability) widen the range of alternative strategies that the company may choose to adopt vis-à-vis its competitors.

A good strategy is one by which a company can gain significant ground on its competitors at an acceptable cost to itself. There are basically four ways:

■ Identify the key success factors in an industry and concentrate resources in a particular area where the company sees an opportunity to gain the most significant strategic advantage over its competitors.

■ Exploit any area where a company enjoys relative superiority. This could include using technology or the sales network developed elsewhere in the organization for other products or services.

■ Aggressively attempt to change the key success factors by challenging the accepted assumptions concerning the ways in which business is conducted in the industry or market.

■ Innovate: open up new markets or develop new products.

The principal concern is to avoid doing the same thing, on the same battleground, as the competition. The aim is to attain a competitive situation in which a company can

■ gain a relative advantage through measures that its competitors will find hard to follow, and

■ extend that advantage further.

Competitive advantage is more than the idea of a competitive strategy, which may or may not prove distinctive. Porter (1985), the author most commonly associated with this topic, has shown how companies can seek broad advantage within an industry or focus on one or a number of distinct segments. He argues that advantage can accrue from particular **generic strategies** which are available to all competitors in an industry:

■ **cost leadership**, whereby a company prices around the average for the market (with a middle-of-the-road product or service) and enjoys superior profits because its costs are lower than those of its rivals

■ **differentiation**, where value is added in areas of real significance for customers, who are then willing to pay a premium price for the distinctiveness. A range of differentiated products (or services), each designed to appeal to a different segment, is possible, as is focus on just one segment.

In addition, *speed* (quicker new **product development** and fast reaction to opportunities and threats) can provide advantage, essentially by reducing costs and differentiating.

Real competitive advantage implies that companies are able to satisfy customer needs more effectively than their competitors. Because few individual sources of advantage are sustainable in the long run, the most successful companies innovate and continually seek new forms of advantage in order to open up a competitive gap and then maintain their lead. Successfully achieving this is a cultural issue.

Ohmae (1982) offers an alternative, but clearly related, framework to that of Michael Porter for studying competitive advantage. Ohmae focuses on three Cs: customers, competitors and the corporation.

- *Customers* will ultimately decide whether or not the business is successful by buying or not buying the product or service. However, customers cannot be treated en masse. Specific preferences should be sought and targeted. Products should be differentiated to appeal to defined market segments.

- *Competitors* will similarly differentiate their products, goods and services, and again incur costs in doing so. Competition can be based on price, image, reputation, proven quality, particular performance characteristics, distribution or after-sales service, for example.

- *Corporations* are organized around particular functions (production, marketing, etc.). The way that they are structured and managed determines the cost of the product or service.

There are opportunities to create competitive advantage in several areas of business, such as product design, packaging, delivery, service and customizing. Such opportunities achieve differentiation, but they can increase costs. Costs must be related to the price that customers are willing to pay for the particular product, based to some extent upon how they perceive its qualities, again in relation to competitors.

Strategic success, in the end, requires a clear understanding of the needs of the market, especially its segments, and the satisfaction of targeted customers more effectively and more profitably than by competitors.

## 1.S.12 Achieving competitive advantage

Competitive advantage, then, does not come from simply being different. It is achieved if and when real value is added for customers. This often requires companies to *stretch their resources* to achieve higher returns (Hamel and Prahalad 1993). Improved productivity may be involved; ideally employees will come up with innovations, new and better ways of doing things for customers.

This innovation can result in lower costs, differentiation or a faster response to opportunities and threats, the bases of competitive advantage; and it is most likely to happen when the organization succeeds in harnessing and exploiting its core competencies and capabilities.

It also requires that employees are empowered. Authority, responsibility and accountability will be decentralized, allowing employees to make decisions for themselves. They should be able and willing to look for improvements. When this is managed well, a company may succeed in changing the rules of competition. Basically, organizations should seek to encourage 'ordinary people to achieve extraordinary results'.

This will only happen if achievement is properly recognized, and initiative and success are rewarded. Some people are naturally reticent about taking risks. 3M, which developed Post-It Notes, Sony, Hewlett-Packard and Motorola are four organizations which are recognized as being highly creative and innovative. In each case employees are actively encouraged to look for, and try out, new ideas. In such businesses the majority of products in the corporate portfolio will have only existed for a few years. Effective empowerment can bring continual growth to successful companies and also provide ideas for turning around companies in decline.

Competitive advantage is also facilitated by good internal and external communications, achieving one of the potential benefits of linkages. Without this businesses cannot share and *learn* best practice. Moreover, information is a fundamental aspect of organizational control. Companies can learn from suppliers, from distributors, from customers, from other members of a large organization, and from competitors.

Companies should never overlook opportunities for communicating their achievements, strengths and successes. Image and reputation are vitally important, as they help to retain business.

## 1.S.13   E-V-R congruence

If one wished to claim that an organization was being managed effectively from a strategic point of view, one would have to show, first, that its managers appreciated fully the dynamics, opportunities and threats present in their competitive environment, and that they were paying due regard to wider societal issues; second, that the organization's resources (inputs) were being managed strategically, taking into account its strengths and weaknesses, and that the organization was taking advantage of its opportunities. Key success factors and core competencies would be matched.

The factors behind these matching issues are ubiquitously listed in the form of a SWOT analysis, a simple framework that most readers will already be familiar with. SWOT stands for

Strengths
Weaknesses            } the (internal) resource themes

Opportunities
Threats               } the (external) environmental themes.

Effective matching will not just happen, though. It needs to be managed. Moreover, potential new opportunities need to be sought and resources developed. It is also important, therefore, that the values of the organization match the needs of the environment and the key success factors. It is the values and culture that determine whether the environment and resources are currently matched, and whether they stay congruent in changing circumstances.

Values are traditionally subsumed as a resource in a SWOT analysis, but it is useful to separate them out. The notion of E–V–R (environment–values–resources) congruence, then, is an integration of these issues. Basically, there is an overlap between the environment (key success factors) and resources (competencies and capabilities), and the organization is committed to sustaining this overlap with effective strategic change initiatives. This notion of E–V–R congruence is illustrated in the top left diagram in Figure S.6 and Minicase S.1 on The National Trust.

The value of E–V–R analysis is that it provides a straightforward framework for assessing the organization's existing strategies and strategic needs. It is crystal clear at a conceptual level what organizations have to achieve and sustain strategically; the challenge then is to use the logic to explore and create opportunities and ways for achieving

**Figure S.6** E–V–R congruence

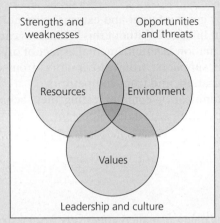

Strengths and weaknesses

Opportunities and threats

Resources

Environment

Values

Leadership and culture

E–V–R congruence

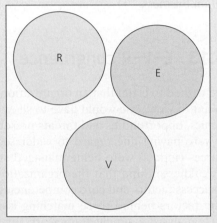

R

E

V

The lost organization

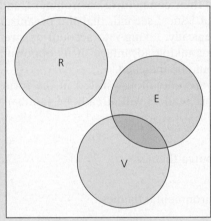

R

E

V

The consciously incompetent organization

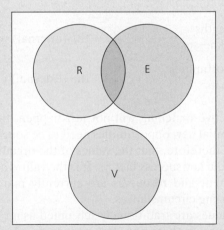

R

E

V

The unconsciously competent organization

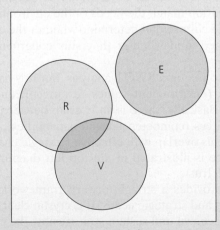

E

R

V

Strategic drift

and sustaining congruence by dealing with the various, but different, risks that organizations have to manage if they are to avoid crises in the face of uncertainty.

If we conclude that an organization does enjoy E–V–R congruence it is important to test its robustness. Conceptually the three circles can merely overlay each other, and be easily pulled apart. Alternatively, like the old magician's trick, they can seem like interlocking circles which appear difficult to separate.

The other four illustrations in Figure S.6 feature alternative instances of incongruence. E–V–R analysis can be applied at more than one level; and consequently different managers should be in positions where they can address which of the alternatives in Figure S.6 best represents their organization and their individual business. Having selected the one that they feel best sums up the present situation, they can immediately see the direction and thrust of the changes that are needed to create or restore congruency.

Managers at the individual business level might find it more expedient to recast the mnemonic E–V–R with three Cs – Customer expectations (for E); Competencies and capabilities (for R); and Culture (for V).

Working downwards from the top left in the figure, a 'lost organization' is seen next. Possibly there was congruency at some time, but now products, services and markets are out of alignment and the values inappropriate. Without major changes to strategy, structure and style, almost certainly involving a change of strategic leader, an organization in this situation has no future. This degree of incongruence would be relatively unusual, but the other three possibilities are not.

The 'consciously incompetent' organization is aware of the needs for success in its marketplace, and managers appreciate the importance of satisfying its customers, but it is simply not achieving the desired level of service and quality. Managers may well have some insight into what might be improved but not be in a position to achieve this improvement. Maybe there is a key resource shortage of some form or a lack of investment, or a person or people with key skills have left and not been replaced. Possibly too many managers are unwilling to grasp the changes that are needed and accept empowerment and responsibility. It is typical for a company in this situation to be constantly fighting crises and problems. Because of the customer orientation, there will be a commitment to resolving the problems and difficulties and, for this reason, some customers may be somewhat tolerant. However, the organization is likely to be highly reactive and, consequently, again the position cannot be sustained indefinitely. A more proactive and entrepreneurial approach will be required to strengthen the resource base and restore congruency with a fresh strategic position.

In contrast, the 'unconsciously competent' organization enjoys **strategic positioning** without any real commitment, especially to improvement and change. Things are working, at a surface level and possibly with some element of luck. Any success is taken for granted. The organization is unable to exploit its strengths and, if it fails to address this, then E and R will drift apart over time, possibly sooner rather than later, to create a lost organization. The required change in culture and values probably implies a change of leadership, certainly of leadership style, to increase decentralization and empowerment.

'Strategic drift' is commonplace. An organization which is internally cohesive simply loses touch with its environment. Demands may change, and fresh competition may make the company's products and services less attractive than in the past. The challenge then concerns realignment in a dynamic environment, which certainly requires a change in management style and, possibly again, leadership. This organization desperately

## Minicase S.1  The National Trust  GB

The National Trust acquires and preserves country-side and historic places of interest in the UK 'for the benefit of us all', generally allowing access to members and fee-paying visitors. The National Trust is now responsible for over half a million acres of land, 600 miles of coastline and some 250 houses and gardens. The Trust relies heavily on members' subscriptions to help to fund its various activities; and gifts and endowments, together with limited government funding, enable new acquisitions. Maintenance standards are high and expensive, and conservation is seen as more important than commercial exploitation, and, where necessary, access. On occasions, but not very often, the numbers of visitors will be restricted either directly or indirectly by, for example, limiting the parking facilities. National Trust membership doubled from 1 million to 2 million during the 1980s and continued to grow, albeit at a slower rate, during the 1990s. Generally The National Trust displays E–V–R congruence but a dilemma and a new challenge for the National Trust would arise if a more commercial orientation became necessary in order to fund desired activities.

### Environment

The stakeholders and interested parties – those whose interests the Trust must serve – are:

- National Trust members and visitors
- donors of properties
- conservation agencies and ramblers' associations
- financial benefactors
- National Trust employees
- government, and
- the nation as a whole.

### Resources

The skills required are:

- property management – both upkeep of the buildings and the management of land resources; large areas of farmland are leased
- expertise in arts and furnishings
- public relations and marketing.

### Values

The National Trust has proved successful in developing and deploying resources to meet the needs and expectations of its stakeholders. Staff are typically more property management-orientated than they are marketing-orientated, but they are knowledgeable and expert. Preservation and the presentation of the properties to the standard maintained by their original owners are seen as important aspects of the service by both the Trust employees and its members. Theme parks and activities have no place in the National Trust; and there is a high moral tone to every activity, including the National Trust shops which tend to sell high-quality selected products at premium prices.

In addition, Trust staff appear to share an ethos (typically shared by people who work for other charities) which combines the feeling of working for a good cause, clear identification with its purpose and principles, and a certain readiness to accept lower rewards than those normally earned in manufacturing and service businesses.

### Question

Membership now exceeds 3 million but costs are rising faster than revenue. In 2003/4 profits amounted to £4 million from a turnover of £300 million. To maintain its E-V-R, what should the National Trust do?

**The National Trust** http://www.nationaltrust.org.uk

needs new ideas, which may already be available inside the organization, but have not been captured.

An article by Peter Drucker (1994) complements both this model and these arguments when he states that all organizations have implicit or explicit 'theories' for their business, incorporating:

- assumptions about the environment, specifically markets, customers and important technologies
- assumptions about its mission or purpose, and
- assumptions about the core (content) competencies required to fulfil the mission.

These assumptions, at any time, must be realistic, congruent, communicated and understood; to achieve this they must be evaluated regularly and rigorously.

Pümpin (1987) uses the term strategic excellence positions (SEPs) to describe 'capabilities which enable an organization to produce better-than-average results over the longer term compared with its competitors'. SEPs imply that organizations appreciate the views of customers and develop the capabilities required to satisfy these needs. Moreover, they are perceived by their customers to be a superior competitor because of their skills and accomplishments.

It is important to deploy resources and to focus the drive for excellence (an aspect of the organization's culture) on issues which matter to customers. IBM, for example, have succeeded historically by concentrating on service, Rolls Royce motor cars on image and quality, and Procter and Gamble on advertising and **branding**.

Businesses should seek to develop competitive advantage and a strategic excellence position for each product and service. Overall **E–V–R congruence** then depends on these SEPs together with any corporate benefits from linkages and interrelationships.

The development of SEPs and E–V–R congruence takes time, and requires that all functional areas of the business appreciate which factors are most significant to customers. Once achieved, however, it cannot be assumed that long-term success is guaranteed. Situations change and new windows of opportunity open (Abell, 1978). The demand for guaranteed overnight parcel deliveries anywhere in the country, and immediate services within cities, opened up the opportunity for couriers; new technologies used in laptop computers, facsimile machines and the Internet have created demand and behaviour changes. Competitors may behave unexpectedly, and consequently there is a need for strategic awareness and for monitoring potential change situations.

Handy (1994) also stresses that timing plays a crucial role in the management of strategic change. He uses the sigmoid curve (Figure S.7) to illustrate that organizations must change when they are successful, not when it is too late. His argument is that change should be initiated at point A, not point B. At point A there is time to be positive and embed change before a situation deteriorates too far, thus maintaining a generally positive momentum. If the change is delayed to point B, then there is a real chance that the organization will go into decline, albeit temporarily, and appear very reactive. The shaded area thus represents a period of uncertainty and turbulence, with 'old' and 'new' operating side by side.

Vigilance should help an organization to decide where it should be concentrating its resources at the moment, how it might usefully invest for the future, and where it needs to divest as existing windows of opportunity start to close. New market needs may imply a change of values, and this again will take time and prove challenging. It is not easy, for instance, to change a strong cost culture into one that is more innovatory.

**Figure S.7** Timing strategic change

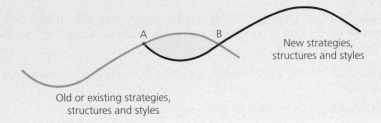

A    B

New strategies, structures and styles

Old or existing strategies, structures and styles

Bettis and Prahalad (1995) argue that business decisions are affected by a 'dominant logic', championed by the strategic leader and communicated through the organization. This could be an articulated vision or a culturally integrated paradigm concerning 'what the business is about and how things get done'. It is shown next how **strategic regeneration** implies that this logic needs to be changed. IBM's growth and early industry dominance was built on a belief that mainframe computers were essential for organizations. Competitors such as Microsoft, which concentrated on software, highlighted that IBM's logic was outdated and it needed to be 'unlearned'. New products and new processes alone would prove inadequate. The new logic is one of decentralized personal computers in the hands of knowledgeable workers.

Organizations, therefore, should build on their past successes while always realizing that the past may not be the best guide to the future.

The concept of E-V-R convergence is revisited on a number of occasions throughout the text.

## 1.S.14  Strategic regeneration and transformational change

*The future was predictable – though very few predicted it!*

Alan Kay, when Research Fellow, Apple Computer

Organizations have to deal with dynamic and uncertain environments, some of which are more turbulent than others. Organizations should actively and continuously look for opportunities to exploit their competencies and strategic abilities, adapt and seek improvements in every area of the business: gradual change, building on an awareness and understanding of current strategies and successes. One difficulty is the fact that organizations are not always able to clarify exactly why they are successful. At the same time it is also valuable if they can think ahead discontinuously, trying to understand future demand, needs and expectations. By doing this they will be aiming to be the first competitor with solutions. Enormous benefits are available to the companies which succeed by, in effect, rewriting the rules of competition in an industry.

Hamel (1997) argues that a changing business (or external) environment opens up the possibility for finding new business and competitive opportunities all the time. There are opportunities for entrepreneurs and the entrepreneurially-minded organization; for the others there are threats. He cites globalization, shorter product and service life cycles (linked to technology improvements and to consumer willingness to change more frequently than in the past) and faster, more sophisticated communication networks as typical sources of opportunity. He explains that there are known and visible areas of opportunity, such as gene-engineered drugs, non-branch banking and multimedia, but stresses that the secret lies in finding the 'right' strategic position to exploit the opportunity. Because of the constant environmental turbulence any strategic position must be seen as temporary and sensitive to unexpected events; innovation is needed to reinforce and defend a position of strength.

Some years ago the economist Joseph Schumpeter (1949) described those entrepreneurs who create or stumble upon something which is radically different as 'alpha innovators'. Their achievements have secondary – 'beta' – effects upon a wide range of businesses and industries as new entrepreneurial opportunities are opened up. Many new businesses are started. Fresh improvements trigger further activity. Steam engines, petrol engines and microprocessors are examples of alpha innovations.

Without constant improvement, renewal and **intrapreneurship** there are obvious dangers in this changing environment, but alone this may well prove inadequate. The most entrepreneurial companies will, at the same time, be searching for new ways of competing. Linked to this is the difficulty for many organizations that future competitive threats are as likely to come from unknown or unexpected organizations currently outside the industry as they are from existing, known rivals. In the early 1980s it is highly likely that British Airways (BA) was particularly concerned with the possible actions over routes and fares by its main American and European rivals; it seems much more improbable that they anticipated the threat that Richard Branson and Virgin Atlantic was going to pose. BA may well have recognized the potential for new competitors as deregulation changed the air-travel environment, but predicting the source was another matter. The outsider Direct Line had the same impact on the insurance industry.

In a sense this process is an attempt to invent the future, and the resources of the organization, its people and technologies will need to be applied creatively. Companies should imagine new product opportunities and strive to develop new products and services because they believe that customers will value them if they are available (Hamel and Prahalad 1991). The idea for the notebook computer, using an electronic pen to input data, came to Mitchell Kapor (the founder of Lotus) and Jerry Kaplan (a consultant) when they shared an airplane trip and Kapor was bemoaning how long it took him every evening to update his pocket organiser (which had a traditional keyboard) with the notes he had jotted down during the day. They envisioned a product and then systematically worked through the issues and problems.

Developments like this are based on ideas and dreams rather than merely attempting to improve existing products. Asking customers is not enough: companies must be able both to understand them and to think at least one jump ahead. There is a danger when companies follow their nose but fail to truly understand their markets. In such cases, research and development may drive product development down an inappropriate track. In addition, caution is necessary when ideas are implemented, because markets and customers are likely to resist changes that seem too radical.

To minimize the risk, 'expeditionary marketing' – low-risk incursions into the market to test out new features or new performances – can be useful. Here, organizations are really attempting to create markets ahead of competitors and just slightly ahead of customers.

In summary, organizations are searching for E–V–R congruence:

- long-term product or service leadership, which is dictated by the *environment*
- long-term cost leadership, which is *resource dependent*

■ product and service excellence, doing things more quickly than competitors without sacrificing quality – essential *values*.

Strategic regeneration refers to simultaneous changes to strategies and structures (organizational processes) in this search.

Strategies have to be reinvented. New products and services should be created by questioning how and why existing ones are popular and successful, and looking for new ways of adding extra value. Electronic publishing and CD-ROM technology, for example, have offered enormous potential for dramatically changing the ways in which people learn. Rewards have been available for those companies which have learnt how to exploit these environmental opportunities.

In thinking ahead, companies should consider both products (or services) and core competencies. Concentrating on products encourages a search for new competitive opportunities; thinking creatively about competencies (which transcend individual products and businesses) can generate radically new opportunities for adding value and establishing a different, future 'competitive high ground'.

Structural changes are designed to improve resource efficiency and effectiveness. Recent trends have been:

■ **downsizing** – splitting the organization into small, autonomous, decentralized units. Those organizations that have taken this too far have inadvertently lost key resources which were critical for their competitiveness. Consequently, the notion of 'rightsizing' is the important one.

■ **delayering** – using the power and potential of IT to reduce the number of layers of managers, in order to speed up decision-making, and

■ **business process re-engineering** – reviewing and redesigning processes in order that tasks can be performed better and more rapidly.

Simply, changes are required to the structure of the organization, the nature and scope of jobs and the network of communications.

Empowerment and teamworking are also seen as essential for creating the values necessary to enable this degree of change.

On paper, the idea of strategic regeneration can be justified as essential, exciting and rewarding but, not unexpectedly, there are likely to be major barriers when applying the ideas. The most obvious hurdles are:

■ the quality of leadership required to provide the necessary drive and direction

■ an inability to create an internal culture of change – the most powerful inhibitors will be experienced, established managers who have become out of date

■ uncertainty about changing needs and competitor activities.

Pascale (1992) uses the word transformational to describe organizations which succeed with simultaneous strategic and structural change. They become learning organizations which Senge (1991) says

*encourage continuous learning and knowledge generation at all levels, have processes which can move knowledge around the organization easily to where it is needed, and can translate that knowledge quickly into changes in the way the organization acts, both internally and externally.*

Senge 1991

Successful entrepreneurs and entrepreneurial organizations often find new products and new needs ahead of both their rivals and their customers. Market research can tap into issues that are important for customers, but it is unlikely to provide the answers. Creativity, insight and innovation stimulated within the organization are more likely to achieve this. Entrepreneurs and entrepreneurial organizations thus create proprietary foresight from public knowledge by synthesizing information and environmental signals and creating new patterns and opportunities.

This intellectual foresight has a number of possible sources, according to Hamel and Prahalad (1994):

- It can be a personal restlessness with the existing status quo.
- It can be a natural curiosity (which the education system does not manage to stifle!) that leads to creativity. Sometimes the entrepreneurial people concerned have a childlike innocence in the questions they ask, and the process is stimulated by a wide network of contacts.
- It may be a willingness on the part of certain individuals to speculate and manage the risk of investigation. Invention has to precede learning.
- It is sometimes a desire to change things and 'leave footprints'.
- Often there is an empathy with the industry and market concerned, coupled with
- The ability to conceptualize what does not yet exist: 'you can't create a future you can't imagine'.

**Table S.2**  Strategic issues and dilemmas

| 1 | Build on the past | *or* | Learn from the past and realign |
|---|---|---|---|
| 2 | Deliberate strategy | *or* | Emergent strategy |
| 3 | Hands-on-leadership | *or* | Direction-only leadership |
| 4 | Build on strengths – resource-based | *or* | Search out new opportunities – market-driven |
| 5 | Differentiate for high added-value | *or* | Beat competitors on cost |
| 6 | Diversity | *or* | Focus |
| 7 | Size for critical mass | *or* | Small and entrepreneurial |
| 8 | Profit for shareholders | *or* | Consensus outcomes for multiple stakeholders |
| 9 | Mass market | *or* | Niche market |
| 10 | Global | *or* | Local |
| 11 | Culture of stability | *or* | Culture of chaos |
| 12 | Centralized for control | *or* | Decentralized for flexibility |
| 13 | Constant change, acting quickly | *or* | Limited and controlled change to protect reliability and quality |
| 14 | Relying on logic and investing when others have gone before | *or* | Being creative, innovative and pioneering – accepting the risks |
| 15 | Reacting to competition and events | *or* | Shaping events and markets |
| 16 | Revolutionary change | *or* | Incremental, emergent change |

## The strategic challenge

Organizations must manage and change their strategies within the context of a set of **strategic issues** and dilemmas. The stances that they choose to deal with these issues and dilemmas, and the strategies, structures and styles that result from their decisions, will determine their overall effectiveness.

Table S.2 lists 16 issues which are developed at various stages throughout the text, and the commentary below explains the dilemmas that they imply for managers and organizations. While this discussion introduces the topic, it is not intended to be fully comprehensive of all the issues and dilemmas faced by an organization.

## 1.S.15  Strategic issues and dilemmas

Organizations and managers must be able to clarify the learning from their past experiences, and pass this on to help future decisions (Issue 1). Successes can be built on; past mistakes and misjudgements should not be repeated. For many organizations, however, it would be a dangerous assumption that history will be repeated in the future. Things change too quickly, and in many industries future success will come from breaking past rules and being different. Future competition may come from unexpected sources such as organizations currently outside the industry. The dilemma concerns just what knowledge from the past provides ideal building blocks, and how it should be used. Ironically, those organizations which are most successful in sustaining a strong competitive position with constant improvement may be the ones who find that radical, discontinuous change is not synonymous with their culture (Issue 16).

It was shown in Chapter 1 that strategic change decisions come from entrepreneurial (or visionary) inputs, planning and emergence. Finding the right balance between these, and for managers to share a common perspective on their relative significance, constitutes a second dilemma (Issue 2). This leads on to a debate about strategic leadership style, something that will be taken up later. To what extent should the strategic leader be hands-on and actively involved in strategic decision-making, and at what level of detail, and how much should he or she step back, provide clear direction and delegate responsibility (Issue 3)?

The need to take both a market and a resource-based view of strategy simultaneously (Issue 4) was discussed earlier in this supplement. Also in this supplement differentiation and effective cost management were discussed as two key approaches to competitive advantage (Issue 5). Although the two are clearly linked, it is important that organizations are clear about whether they are attempting to compete on clear differences or superior cost management.

Another crucial issue is size. It is now quite normal to read that 'big is no longer beautiful', that it implies too much diversity and complexity. However, the issue of diversity (Issue 6) is itself complex. Clearly, many large, diverse conglomerates have chosen to divest and focus or, in cases such as ICI, split the organization into separate medium-sized parts. The question remains: is a strategy of conglomerate diversification by nature a poor choice, or is it that many organizations are unable to implement the strategy and create a structure whereby corporate headquarters can add value and foster the synergies which they believe exist? Focus can be achieved by concentrating on a limited number of clearly related (by marketing or technology) businesses. Some organizations are choosing to go further and divest activities and processes which are seen as non-core or non-essential. This is unlikely to mean they are no longer required at all, and consequently this strategy implies a need to develop a capability in managing networks and alliances.

Small meanwhile is dubbed innovative, creative and entrepreneurial. Small companies, though, are often fragile financially, often (not always) using low technology and featuring relatively poor working conditions. Successful ones grow to become medium-sized. The challenge for large organizations, searching for power, market share and **critical mass** is not to lose the creativity, flexibility and spontaneity of the small organization as they become bigger and more formal (Issue 7), such that they are able to manage the demands for discontinuous change and corporate renewal.

A further challenge is the attempt to balance and satisfy the needs and expectations of all the stakeholders (Issue 8). Shareholders, customers and employees have requirements which may conflict; moreover, they can sometimes sharpen the tension between the short- and long-term perspectives. Most people would agree that a business must ensure that it looks after its shareholders' investments and financial interests, but it would appear that organizations which balance the needs of all their stakeholders perform better (for their shareholders) in the long run. While thinking about the various internal and external stakeholders, the organization must never lose sight of what competitors are doing.

Other tensions concern the issues of mass marketing or niche marketing (Issue 9), and, in the case of larger businesses, how to balance global and local issues (Issue 10). Here, again, one challenge for larger companies concerns the potential benefits to be gained from thinking and behaving like fast-moving, flexible small organizations while obtaining the scale and synergy benefits that can accrue from size.

Many businesses need to develop a culture of change orientation without losing internal cohesion and stability (Issue 11). This implies an explicit and shared vision of where the organization is heading.

There is also a need to decentralize and give managers more delegated authority while not losing sight (at chief executive level) of the changes that they are introducing. This involves a difficult trade-off between such empowerment (delegating real responsibility in order to make the business more effective in its relations with all of its stakeholders) and the greater efficiencies often yielded by centralized control and systems which harness the latest IT (Issue 12). The revelation, in September 1995, that the estate agency subsidiary of the Halifax Building Society was paying its staff a bonus if they could sell houses by persuading clients to accept reduced prices, sparked an outcry. The incident provoked an internal investigation and the outcome was likely to lead to changes in the autonomy given to subsidiaries or stronger guidance on policy-making.

Organizations must be able to act quickly in response to opportunities and threats, but not at the expense of product and service quality: achieving high quality at the same time as cutting costs and improving efficiency (Issue 13). On occasions there will always be the dilemma of a recession. Organizations must cut back, control their costs and accept lower margins when supply potential exceeds demand in an economic downturn. Profits fall. Paradoxically, those competitors which are able to consolidate and invest strategically during a recession will be best prepared for the economic upturn. Some organizations will always be reticent about 'blue sky' investment in radical and innovatory ideas, while others will be willing to pioneer such change (Issue 14).

Finally, the organization must be able simultaneously to be reactive and proactive, planned and flexible, able to deal with pressures for both continuous and discontinuous change (Issue 15).

These issues reinforce the paradox of stability and instability. Stability concerns running existing businesses efficiently and effectively, exploiting strategic abilities and continually looking to create higher returns from the committed resources. Instability refers to the search for the new competitive high ground ahead of one's rivals. Stable organizations may come to rely on their ability to manage issues and potential crises as they arise. The danger for them is that they can easily become complacent and maybe even change-resistant. When this happens there is an argument that an internal crisis should be created in order to provoke action and renewal before the situation becomes unrecoverable.

Dealing with these issues and dilemmas in a dynamic and unpredictable environment is clearly difficult; there are no easy answers and the situation is always fluid. Achieving success, therefore, again implies the creation and exploitation of key strategic competencies. All of these issues are dealt with at various stages in the book and the implications are also reviewed in the final chapter.

Collins and Porras (1995) analysed a number of American companies which have proved to be resilient to the problems which hit them from time to time. Many Western companies have a life expectancy of less than 50 years; a select minority not only survives but thrives on change pressures. We appear to be able to take for granted that successful companies will be dedicated to customer service and all-round quality; they also typically feature an open culture with 'restless enquiry, learning and constant innovation'. Underpinning this is a strategic leader who is able to build an organization with appropriate values, principles and ways of thinking that will last through generations of shifting strategies. He or she need not be individually charismatic, although some clearly are.

Collins and Porras cite Walt Disney Corporation as a leading example. Walt Disney himself was charismatic, but the organization has survived and prospered since his death. The success of its theme parks, recent box-office blockbusters such as *The Lion King*, *Pocahontas* and *Hercules* and the 1995 acquisition of ABC, one of the USA's leading three television networks, are testimony to this. But there have been major setbacks at the same time, which Disney has had to weather. Jeffrey Katzenberg, head of the studios and the man responsible for several major film successes, left in 1994 when he was passed over for a promotion; he sought the number two post of President, vacant after the incumbent was killed in a helicopter accident. This happened shortly after the chief executive, Michael Eisner, had major heart surgery. Katzenberg later sued Disney for a settlement which reflected the value of future earnings from strategies pursued whilst he was employed and for which he was responsible. In 1995 Disney abandoned its plans for a new Civil War theme park in Virginia, following an intensive protest campaign by environmentalists. During the early 1990s EuroDisney experienced severe financial difficulties before being turned around. At the moment Disney is experiencing new challenges as its theme parks are allegedly beginning to seem dated for the high-tech expectations of some children used to sophisticated computer games.

Disney, according to Collins and Porras, relies more on experimentation than formal strategic planning; moreover, it effectively balances stability and change, integration and autonomy.

# References

Abell, DF (1978) Strategic windows, *Journal of Marketing*, 42 July.

Ansoff, HI (1984) *Implanting Strategic Management*, Prentice Hall.

Bettis, R and Prahalad, CK (1995) The dominant logic: retrospective and extension, *Strategic Management Journal*, volume 16, January.

Collins, J and Porras, J (1995) *Built to Last*, Century Business.

Cranwell-Ward, J, Bacon, A and Mackie, R (2002) *Inspiring Leadership: Staying Afloat in Turbulent Times,* Thomson.

Drucker, PF (1994) The theory of business, *Harvard Business Review*, September–October.

Goold, M, Campbell, A and Alexander, M (1994) *Corporate Level Strategy*, John Wiley.

Hall, D (1992) *The Hallmarks for Successful Business*, Mercury Books.

Hamel, G (1997) Address to a Strategic Planning Society Conference, London.

Hamel, G and Prahalad, CK (1991) Corporate imagination and expeditionary marketing, *Harvard Business Review*, July–August.

Hamel, G and Prahalad, CK (1993) Strategy as stretch and leverage, *Harvard Business Review*, March–April.

Hamel, G and Prahalad, CK (1994) *Competing for the Future*, Harvard Business School Press.

Handy, C (1994) *The Empty Raincoat*, Hutchinson.

Kay, JA (1993) *Foundations of Corporate Success*, Oxford University Press.

Ohmae, K (1982) *The Mind of the Strategist*, McGraw-Hill.

Pascale, RT (1992) Paper presented at the Strategic Renaissance Conference, Strategic Planning Society, London, October.

Porter, ME (1985) *Competitive Advantage*, Free Press.

Prahalad, CK and Hamel, G (1990) The core competence of the corporation, *Harvard Business Review*, May–June.

Pümpin, C (1987) *The Essence of Corporate Strategy*, Gower.

Pümpin, C (1991) *Corporate Dynamism*, Gower.

Schein, EH (1985) *Organization Culture and Leadership*, Jossey Bass.

Schumpeter, J (1949) *The Theory of Economic Development,* Harvard Business School Press.

Senge, P (1991) *The Fifth Discipline: The Art and Practise of the Learning Organization*, Doubleday.

Stalk, G, Evans, P and Shulman, LE (1992) Competing on capabilities: the new rules of corporate strategy, *Harvard Business Review*, March–April.

# Strategic Analysis Frameworks

This second supplement to Part One lists and cross-references a number of frameworks that can all be adopted for carrying out a strategic analysis of an organization. Different people will have personal preferences and may opt not to use all of them – especially as there is some clear overlap in a number of cases. These frameworks all help us to understand:

■ Where the organization – or a selected part of it – is at the moment

■ Where it might seek to develop in the future, given the circumstances it faces.

However, the key decisions an organization faces concern *what* changes to make and *how* to implement the chosen strategic decisions. Whilst analytical frameworks can provide valuable insight into these issues, by themselves they cannot provide the answers. Consequently the final framework provides three key tests for evaluating the effectiveness of current and proposed strategies.

The techniques and concepts outlined here are all developed in greater detail throughout the book, but readers may wish to refer back to this summary at any stage – and particularly if they are required to carry out a strategic analysis of a case study.

1. **MOST analysis – Chapter 2**

   **Mission – Objectives – Strategies – Tactics**

   The key check issues are:

   ■ Are M and O explicit, widely appreciated and shared?

   ■ Are M, O and S externally consistent and do they fit environmental and stakeholder needs?

   ■ Are O and S – the important ends and means – internally consistent? Do they make the most effective use of resources and capabilities?

   ■ Do the potential benefits from S and T justify the inherent risks and uncertainties?

## External analysis frameworks

2. **PEST or PESTLE analysis – Chapter 4**

   **Political – Economic – Social – Technological – Legal – Ethical issues**

   This framework enables the evaluation of key environmental variables or forces in an attempt to judge their potential future impact upon the organization.

It also informs the opportunities and threats elements of a SWOT analysis.

3. **Five forces industry analysis (Porter 1980) – Chapter 4**
   - The threat of new entrants
   - The threat of substitute products and services
   - The bargaining power of suppliers
   - The bargaining power of buyers
   - Rivalry amongst existing firms in the industry.

   Provides an assessment of how attractive – potentially profitable – an industry is.

4. **Key success factors – Chapter 4 and Part 1 Supplement 1**

   The things an organization must be able to perform both efficiently and effectively if it is to compete in an industry. The strengths, competencies and capabilities it has to have.

5. **Generic strategies (Porter 1985) – Chapter 6**

   Introduces cost leadership and differentiation as key drivers of competitive advantage. This framework enables an organization to check the logic of its current competitive strategy or begin a search for new competitive opportunities.

6. **Stakeholder analysis – Chapter 2**

   Assessing and prioritizing the needs and expectations of both external and internal stakeholders to ensure nothing of consequence is overlooked.

## Internal analysis frameworks

7. **Resource audits – Chapter 5**

   A straightforward analysis of the relative strengths and weaknesses of the organization. Typically based on a framework of functions and key activities – marketing, operations, human resources etc.

8. **The McKinsey 7-S framework (Peters and Waterman 1982)**

   An alternative (or additional) framework for analysing resources, based on seven interrelated internal elements:
   - Strategy – in particular functional strategies such as operations, marketing, innovation, research and development, human resources
   - Structure – internal structures and processes
   - Systems – external linkages and processes
   - Style – of leadership and management
   - Staff – 'people'
   - Skills – competencies and capabilities
   - Shared values – relating to the culture of the organization.

9. **Distinctive competencies (Kay 1993) – Chapter 5**

   A framework for exploring those distinctive competencies that separate strong and successful organizations from their weaker competitors.
   - Architecture – internal and external links and processes

- Strategic assets – factors (such as industry structure) which enable the organization to enjoy competitive advantage through, say, cost leadership or differentiation
- Reputation – the value of a distinctive image and brand
- Innovation – harnessing the change agenda.

10. **The value chain (Porter 1985) – Chapter 5**

Provides a framework for evaluating the relative significance of various activities undertaken by an organization – from the perspectives of cost and value added.

11. **Activity mapping (Porter 1996) – Chapter 6**

A diagrammatic approach to the interrelationships of the organization's activities.

12. **Financial analysis – Supplements to Chapters 7 and 11**
- The ability to raise capital and use it to generate higher returns
- Performance and profitability
- Solvency and liquidity.

These resource-based frameworks all inform the strengths and weaknesses element of a SWOT analysis.

13. **SWOT analysis – Chapter 4**

Strengths – Weaknesses – Opportunities – Threats

14. **Scenarios – Chapter 4**

Conceptual possibilities of possible future events and circumstances, used to add creativity to the opportunities and threats elements of a SWOT. Has the added advantage of helping managers think through how they might react if events unfold in unexpected ways.

15. **The culture grid – Chapter 7**

Analyses the culture of the organization in a framework of three clusters of criteria: manifestations; people; and power.

Informs the values element of E–V–R congruence to supplement the SWOT.

16. **E–V–R congruence – Part 1 Supplement and throughout the book**

Adds 'values' to a traditional SWOT analysis to capture the theme that effective strategic positions have to be both managed and changed.

17. **Portfolio analyses – Chapter 9**

Grids which allow a range of businesses, products or services to be plotted against certain criteria – providing an indication of appropriate strategies.

Some plot the attractiveness of an industry on one axis and the relative competitive strength of an organization on the other, thus utilizing Frameworks 3 and 5 above.

18. **Strategic value drivers – Chapters 4, 5 and 6**

Links to *key success factors*, and examines those factors that characterise a particular industry and highlight the implications of being a competitor in that industry. Examples might include:

- Growth rates and investment needs
- Planning horizons for investment and linked capital requirements
- Operating profit margins and sales volume requirements
- Credit given and taken, and cash requirements
- Perceived risk and the **cost of capital**.

### 19. The Ansoff grid – Chapter 9

A simple grid attributed to H. Igor Ansoff (1987) which provides a valuable framework to explore possible directions for strategic growth.

Based on existing and new markets and existing and new products/services it provides basic strategies for **market penetration**, **market development**, product development and diversification.

## Strategy evaluation – Chapter 11

If we review these 19 frameworks we can see three questions emerge, and these are fundamental for the success of any strategic choice:

- Is there a market opportunity?
- Does the organization have the necessary competencies and capabilities?
- Does the organization have the requisite financial resources?

But the personal preference element should not be overlooked. The strategic leader – possibly the owner of the business, perhaps the strategic leader and his or her senior team – must be fully committed. Moreover the strategy must fit the culture and values of the organization unless there is a drive to change these. There are, then, three fundamental issues to consider in strategy evaluation – and where there are choices to be made it is rare that one alternative comes out on top on all three. The fifteen frameworks above can all inform the following criteria:

- **Appropriateness** – in the context of environmental and competitive forces
- **Feasibility** – relative to resources, competencies and capabilities
- **Desirability** – the preferences of key decision-makers and the fit with the existing culture.

It will be realized that these three themes are closely linked to E–V–R congruence, which, as a framework, has the advantage of spanning the analysis and choice elements of strategic management.

## References

Ansoff, HI (1987) *Corporate Strategy,* revised edn, Penguin.

Kay, JA (1993) *Foundations of Corporate Success: How Business Strategies Add Value,* Oxford University Press.

Peters, TJ and Waterman, RH Jr (1982) *In Search of Excellence: Lessons from America's Best Run Companies,* Harper and Row.

Porter, ME (1980) *Competitive Strategy: Techniques for Analysing Industries and Competitors,* Free Press.

Porter, ME (1985) *Competitive Advantage: Creating and Sustaining Superior Performance,* Free Press.

Porter, ME (1996) What is strategy? *Harvard Business Review,* November–December.

# Strategic Analysis

In Part One the concept of environmental fit and a PEST (political, economic, social and technical) analysis was introduced to illustrate the presence, absence or loss of strategic positioning, competitiveness and strategic effectiveness. It was argued that culture and values hold the key to the existence and sustenance of positioning, competitiveness and effectiveness. This part looks in much greater detail at positioning and competitiveness, and useful techniques for carrying out the appropriate analyses are explained. Chapter 3, which begins Part Two, introduces the important concepts of strategic thinking and synergy, which are relevant for the whole book.

There are three distinct approaches to strategy and strategy creation. They should not be seen as opposing approaches, however, but as complementary approaches to opportunity finding. The entrepreneurial organization will certainly take account of all three, placing an appropriate emphasis on each one. They are:

■ **Market-driven.** The market-based approach implies an active search for new product and marketing opportunities in the external environment. These might be found in industries in which the organization already competes or in new ones.

■ **Resource-based.** Here the organization clarifies its distinctive core competencies and strategic capabilities – perhaps technologies and processes – which set it apart from its competitors in ways that customers value. It then seeks to build on these competencies and capabilities to build new values for both existing and new customers. This approach has the advantage of encouraging the organization to focus on what it can do well – as long as there is a market for it.

■ **Competitor-influenced.** This is a more tactical approach which implies short-term vigilance. Whilst seeking to build the future, an organization must never lose sight of the present day. Its existing positions must be protected against active competition. This means an ability to react to competitor moves and proactive initiatives designed to surprise competitors. Of course, it is important not to become over-reliant on this tactical approach as this is likely to make the organization more reactive rather than proactive.

Organizations should be looking for ways of being different from their competitors. This is unlikely to come from imitation, from monitoring and copying what rivals do – although this approach can be seen in many organizations. In the end such mimicry will make all competing organizations look remarkably similar, making it difficult for customers to distinguish between them and placing too much emphasis on price competition. Instead organizations should be looking to innovate to achieve two purposes – one intention is to always be ahead of rivals with new ideas; the second intention is to draw apart from competitors with radical differences that they find hard to imitate in the short term. There are two important provisos. First, the differences should mean something positive to customers; it is not simply a question of being different for the sake of being different. Second, it should never be assumed that any gap or advantage is anything but temporary; all ideas can be copied eventually, and all good ones will be!

We look at these three approaches in Part Two before developing our understanding of culture and values.

# 3

# Strategic Thinking, Environmental Influences and Synergy

**Learning objectives**

Having read to the end of this chapter you should be able to:

- explain the difference between the market- or opportunity-driven, resource-based and competitor-influenced views of strategy, appreciate the three views are frequently integrated in strategy creation and understand that some strategies are tactical responses to competition in a dynamic external environment
- explain why thinking is vital in strategy creation and implementation
- define synergy and explain its significance in both competitive and corporate strategy.

This is a short introductory chapter to Part Two. It explains strategic thinking and synergy, two key strategic issues which impact upon the opportunity-driven and resource-based approaches to strategy.

## 3.1 Introduction

Good ideas for the future can either start inside the organization or be obtained from external contacts, and the ability to synthesize and exploit the information that is available to develop new products, new services and new strategic positions is a reflection of the organization's *strategic thinking* capabilities.

At one level, matching, exploiting and changing the linkages between resource competency and environmental opportunity is an expression of organizational competitiveness, and the presence (or absence) of competitive advantage. It was shown earlier (Chapter 1) how it is essential for organizations to seek competitive advantage for every product, service and business in their portfolios. Competitiveness comes from functions and activities, and the effectiveness of the links between them. This is one aspect of *synergy*. The second aspect of synergy is the relatedness and interdependency of the different products, services and businesses and their ability to support each other in some way. Synergy is covered in this chapter, although corporate strategic logic is not explored until Part Five.

**Figure 3.1** The business environment

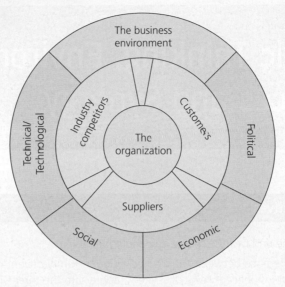

**Figure 3.2** Competitive strategy: A summary of techniques

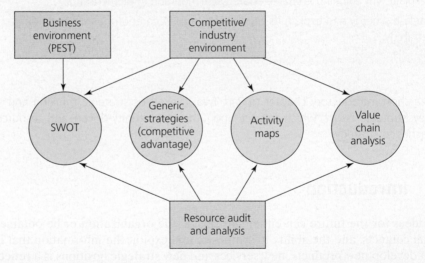

Figure 3.1 illustrates the organization in the context of its external environment. Its suppliers and customers, upon whom it depends, and its competitors – both existing and new-in-the-future – are shown as having an immediate impact. Wider environmental forces bear on all the 'players' in the industry, and these are shown in the outer circle as political, economic, social and technological (PEST) forces.

The forces and influences have been deliberately shown in concentric circles. It is quite typical for us to think of the organization as a group of activities (and/or functions) and then to place everything and everyone else, including suppliers and customers, in a so-called external business environment. Increasingly, it makes considerable sense for the organization to see itself working in partnership with its suppliers, distributors and customers. When this perspective is adopted, then only competitors from the middle ring would be placed in the external environment, together with the general forces which impact upon the whole industry.

Figure 3.2 extends this point, and shows the various concepts and techniques discussed in this part of the book in diagrammatic form.

## 3.2  Strategic thinking

Strategic thinking embraces the past, present and future. Understanding patterns and lessons from the past will certainly inform the future – but given the dynamic, turbulent and uncertain business environments that affect many industries and organizations, it would be dangerous to assume that the future will reflect the past and be a continuation of either past or existing trends.

Figure 3.3 shows (bottom triangle) how strategies which link competencies with a strategic vision for the future embrace learning from the past, an awareness of existing competencies and some insight into likely future trends. The top part of the figure highlights that *organizational learning* is required to build the future and that it encompasses:

**Figure 3.3** Organizational learning

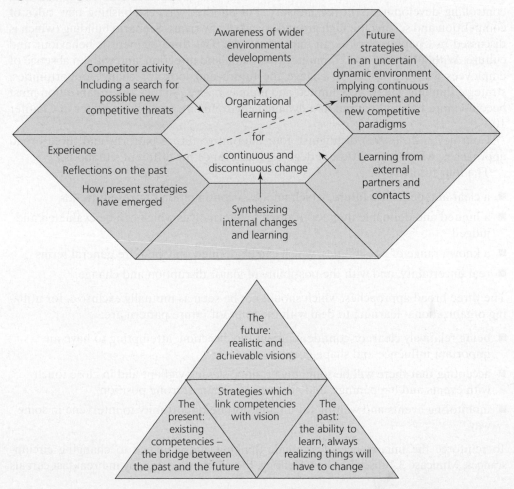

- a reflection on how present strategies have emerged over time
- an understanding of current competencies and the strategic value of particular resources and the linkages between them
- knowledge of existing competitors and what they are doing at the moment – and preparing to do in the future
- an appreciation of possible new sources of competition
- an awareness of wider environmental opportunities and threats
- an ability to share information with, and thus learn from, external partners and contacts, including suppliers, distributors and customers.

The effective organization will synthesize this learning into insightful strategies for dealing with future uncertainties.

Campbell and Alexander (1997) offer a different, but clearly related, approach to strategic thinking. They delineate three elements. First, insight into operating issues: with **benchmarking** other organizations (searching for good practices), process re-engineering and total quality management organizations should look for opportunities to improve continuously the way they do things. Second, future-gazing: exponents of chaos theory warn of the need always to be ready for the unexpected and unpredictable; and so here the emphasis is on discontinuous change, and the idea of reinventing and thus controlling developments in the industry. Put another way, establishing new rules of competition and seizing the high ground ahead of any rivals. Scenario building (which is discussed in Chapter 4) plays an important role. The third element is behaviour and culture. Without a clear and communicated vision and direction, and with an absence of employees who are willing to engage the future and look for change opportunities, strategic thinking will be very limited and unimaginative. Simply, the organization must become more entrepreneurial in a dynamic environment, as discussed later in Chapter 10.

Courtney *et al.* (1997) distinguish four alternative future patterns and three broad approaches, which have different degrees of relevance for different situations.

The four futures are:

- a clear and definable future, which implies a continuation of present trends
- a limited and definable number of discrete alternatives which can be evaluated and judged
- a known range of possibilities, which can be defined only in more general terms
- real uncertainty, and with the possibility of major disruption and change.

The three broad approaches, which should not be seen as mutually exclusive, for utilizing organizational learning to deal with the relevant future pattern are:

- being relatively clear, or confident, about the direction, attempting to have an important influence and shape events
- accepting that there will be some uncertainty, staying vigilant and in close touch with events and happenings, and adapting to retain a strong position
- monitoring events and waiting for an appropriate opportunity to intervene in some way.

To reinforce the importance of strategic thinking and vigilance to changing circumstances, Minicase 3.1 discusses how Kellogg, the dominant company in breakfast cereals

**Figure 3.4** Strategic thinking – purposes and elements
Based on: Rhodes, J and Thame, S (1988) Colours of Your Mind, Harper Collins

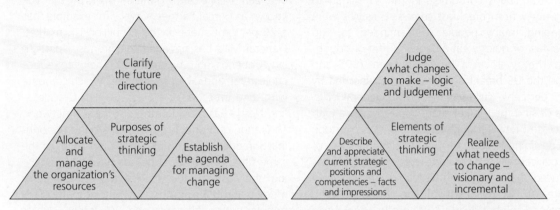

all round the world, has been adversely affected by increased competition combined with changing consumer tastes.

Figure 3.4 completes this section and summarizes the purposes and broad elements of strategic thinking.

Throughout this section on strategic thinking, the emphasis has been on the ability to take a holistic view and synthesize information. We need to synthesize information from the past and present and combine it with a view of the future. This embraces information which originates inside the organization and information that can be obtained from external partners and contacts. Synergy, which is discussed next, explains the importance of linkages and synthesis.

## Minicase 3.1  Kellogg's Cereals

CASE

Kellogg, with its well-known and very valuable brand name, had been the clear market leader for breakfast cereals throughout the world for many years when, at the end of the 1970s and into the early 1980s, it experienced declining market share in the US for the first time. Between 1979 and 1983 market share in the US fell from 42 per cent to 38 per cent in a market which was then growing at only 2 per cent per year, compared with 7 per cent a decade earlier. A key issue at the time was public pressure against foods with a high sugar content.

It was anticipated that Kellogg, like their main rivals in the cereals market, would choose to diversify into other foods. Kellogg did begin to diversify, but only on a relatively small scale, preferring to concentrate on grain-based products which it knows best. New products were developed and launched on a regular basis, some featuring artifi-

cial sweeteners. As well as new brands of breakfast cereal, these have included Nutri-Grain bars and fruit Pop Tarts, and more recently Rice Krispies snacks have been launched very successfully. Because of the declining birth rate, the new products were often aimed at adults as well as children. Fibre content was seen as an important factor for this. Kellogg, though, has been careful not to target products too narrowly on the grounds that once they are in a house any member of the family is likely to eat them. There have been a number of successes, and some failures.

As a result, Kellogg's market share of 42 per cent was restored in 1985. Sometime later Kellogg, along with its main rivals, increased prices and provoked a consumer switch to supermarket own-label brands, which Kellogg refused to manufacture. Its share then declined again.

In the 1990s consumers in the US began to turn away from breakfast cereals. Lifestyles were changing; many people were minded to skip breakfast or quickly eat a bagel, muffin or doughnut. They were in a hurry. Between 1995 and 2000 the US breakfast cereal market declined by 12.5 per cent. Kellogg's main rival, General Mills, was closing the market share gap in America with successful new products and in 1998 it overtook the declining Kellogg for the first time. Its share of 32 per cent was 1 per cent higher than Kellogg's reduced share. Although Kellogg, with an overall share of 40 per cent of the world market, remained global leader, its profits had been severely affected. In early 2000 Kellogg announced the closure of its manufacturing plant in Battle Creek, Michigan, the city where the business began over 100 years ago. The headquarters would remain there.

In 2001 Kellogg diversified into cookies and crackers by acquiring Keebler. By 2003 Kellogg was still world leader for cereals with sales in excess of $8 billion. There are over 40 varieties, plants in 19 countries and sales in 160 countries.

## Breakfast cereals in Europe

In Europe, Kellogg is the market leader with several best-selling brands. Its share has been as high as 50 per cent in recent years. British consumers eat more cereal per head than any other country, including the US, but other European countries, which tend to prefer breads, meats and cheeses for breakfast, have begun to provide a real opportunity as people have become more health conscious. In the 1990s, for example, the French market for breakfast cereals grew at over 20 per cent per year.

British Weetabix has traditionally held second place, but this is no longer the case. The market has become more competitive and Kellogg has faced an important challenge from a joint venture between Nestlé and General Mills of the US, known as Cereal Partners which, for example, has a 25 per cent share of the £1 billion UK market. General Mills has provided the brands – particularly Cheerios, an oat cereal which helps to reduce cholesterol, and Golden Grahams, which compete with (and preceded) Kellogg's Golden Crackles – and Nestlé has provided the distribution network. The range of products developed around the original Shredded Wheat is also in the portfolio. At the same time, private-label brands have been enjoying the fastest rate of growth, especially for mueslis and bran products, which are particularly popular with adult consumers. Weetabix – which also produces Alpen – is the leading UK producer.

In February 2000 Kellogg agreed to produce a special range of cereals for the German discount retailer, Aldi – the first time it had ever produced own-label products.

The continuing challenge for Kellogg lies in creating new product ideas for a market which is growing in certain parts of the world and declining in others, and the generation of a strong enough cash flow to fund the necessary advertising budgets, both for supporting existing brands and for launching the new cereal products. Each cereal product needs to be promoted individually.

## Questions

1. Visit a supermarket and look for the various Kellogg products. How many different breakfast cereal products can you spot? Do they all have directly competing brand alternatives? To what extent are they aimed at different market segments?

2. What are the non-cereal products?

3. Do they appear robust enough to compensate for any long-term decline in the breakfast cereal market?

**Kelloggs** http://www.kelloggs.com

# 3.3  Synergy

Synergy is either a path to sustained growth or a 'bridge too far' for organizations. It is concerned with the returns that are obtained from resources. Ansoff (1968) argues that resources should be combined and managed in such a way that the benefits which accrue exceed those which would result if the parts were kept separate, describing synergy as the $2 + 2 = 5$ effect. Simply, the combination of the parts produces results of greater magnitude than would be the case if the parts operated independently.

There are three basic synergy opportunities:

- *functional* – sharing facilities, competencies, ideas and best practice
- *strategic* – complementary competitive strategies across a corporate portfolio: even in a diversified conglomerate some sharing is possible
- *managerial* – compatible styles of management and values in different functions and businesses.

Sometimes the synergy is obtained by transferring people between different parts of an organization, possibly for a period of secondment, in order to facilitate the sharing.

In simple terms, if an organization manufactures and markets six different products, the organization should be structured to yield the benefits that might be possible from combining these different interests. For example, central purchasing for all products might yield **economies of scale**; factory rationalization might increase productivity or lower production costs; sales staff might be able to obtain more or larger orders if they are selling more than one product; each product might gain from name association with the others; and distributors might be more satisfied than if the company offered only a very limited range or a single product. Some of the benefits are clearly measurable, whereas others are more subjective; and the search for synergy clearly embraces structural as well as strategic decisions.

Similarly, if functions, products or business units were not co-ordinated, then efforts may well be duplicated, or delays might be built into the organization system because of a lack of understanding.

Corporate strategy decisions, such as acquisitions, alliances or divestments, should be made in the light of the overall synergistic implications of the change. Some – strategically sound – changes imply increased synergy opportunities, while others imply complexity, fragmentation and lost synergy. The synergy impact is seen in the competitive strategies and competitive success for each relevant activity. Simply, where an organization is considering increasing its range of products and services, or merging with or acquiring another company, synergy is an important consideration. In the case of an acquisition the combination of the companies should produce greater returns than the two on their own. Adding new products or services should not affect existing products or services in any adverse way, unless they are intended to be replacements. When such strategic changes take place the deployment of resources should be re-evaluated to ensure that they are being utilized both efficiently and effectively.

Obtaining synergy may well imply the sharing of knowledge and other resources between divisions or business units, possibly attempting to disseminate best practice. This is only feasible if resource efficiencies are measured and compared in order to identify which practices are best. Internal rivalries may prevent the attainment of the potential benefits from sharing. Synergy is more likely to occur if all the relevant activities are linked in such a way that the organization as a whole is managed effectively, which Drucker (1973) has defined as 'doing the right things'. Individual business units and functions must themselves be managed efficiently or, as Drucker would say, they must be 'doing things right'. It will be seen in Chapter 7 that resource efficiency considers how well resources are being utilized and the returns being obtained from them. Effectiveness incorporates an evaluation of whether the resources are being deployed in the most beneficial manner.

There are four key elements which must come together if potential synergy is to be achieved:

- *effective leadership* – which emphasizes the importance of co-operation, sharing, transfer and learning throughout the organization
- *facilitative structure* – which allows co-operation and inhibits internal conflict
- *supportive systems* – which encourage sharing and transfer. Examples include cross-functional and cross-business project teams and the provision of opportunities for managers to spend time in other parts of an organization
- *appropriate rewards* – such that parts of an organization can benefit from helping others.

Figure 3.5 pulls these themes together and shows how synergy potential must be examined inside a framework of strategic resources, strategic thinking and the relevant business environment. Potential exists from effectively combining the various functions and activities in each business, from sharing and learning between businesses and from the overall corporate strategic logic.

At the same time, though, it must be realized that the anticipated synergy from strategic changes is easily overestimated and quite frequently it does not accrue. Potential benefits from adding new activities may be misjudged. After all, there is always an element of subjective anticipation and promise – the synergy is justified with strategic logic but delivered through people and their behaviour – and this should not be an excuse for delusion. Admitting to strategic misjudgements rarely comes easy to strategic leaders and managers and, as a result, the appropriate exit or withdrawal when synergy is not obtained, may not happen when it should. Internal politics and conflicts, because

**Figure 3.5** Strategic thinking and synergy

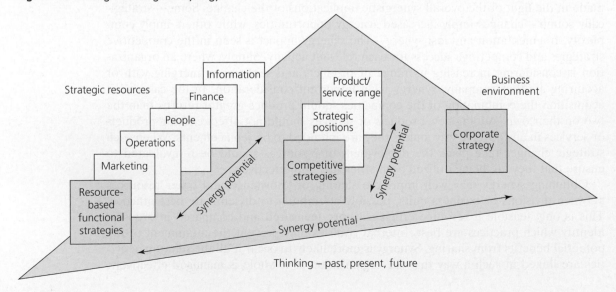

businesses and divisions see themselves as rivals rather than partners, all too often inhibit synergy.

### 3.3.1 Searching for synergy – three examples

**Sony** A number of Japanese electronics companies (specifically manufacturers of 'hardware' – televisions, videos and hi-fi equipment) have sought links with the US makers of music and films, the related 'software', arguing that there is potential synergy from merging the two. An array of new products continues to become technologically feasible and the manufacturers want to secure their commercial exploitation. Such developments have included high-definition and digital televisions, flat-screen TVs (both large and small for mounting on walls, like a picture, and carrying around), personal video disc players the same size as personal cassette players, miniaturized compact discs (CDs) and CD players and digital versatile discs (DVDs). Films can also be the basis for computer games. The large film companies have huge film libraries for video and games exploitation, both growth markets. The strategy is similar to that of the manufacturers of razors who have derived benefits and synergy from also manufacturing razor blades. From this they decided that they were better placed to make revenues selling blades and would be well advised to either cut the price of the razors or even give the razors away to sell more blades.

Not every product was a success, of course. Record companies were always reluctant to release music in the new high-technology digital audio tape (DAT) format when it was introduced. While Sony pioneered the hardware, its subsidiary CBS chose not to break industry ranks. DAT has never really taken off.

Sony acquired CBS Records in 1987 and Columbia Pictures from Coca-Cola in 1989. Previously, Coca-Cola had anticipated synergy from linking soft drinks and entertainment, but it had not accrued. Matsushita acquired MCA (Universal Pictures, record labels and part-ownership of a network TV station) in 1990. Toshiba negotiated a **joint venture** with Time Warner. Earlier, Rupert Murdoch had bought Twentieth Century Fox to exploit the film library on his cable and satellite TV networks worldwide.

The strategy has been defended with logical arguments. It has been suggested that if Sony had owned Columbia in the 1970s their Betamax video format would have proved more successful because more prerecorded videos would have been available in this format rather than the successful VHS – developed by Matsushita who were more resourceful in striking agreements with video makers. Similarly, CBS would prove a useful vehicle for forcing the pace of the switch from records to CDs.

Sceptics always argued that the synergy would not accrue, contending that the typical Japanese company and Hollywood film-makers have dramatically different cultures which would not prove compatible. Moreover, Japan was not noted for creativity in entertainment especially in the large corporate dimension. This is not however the case when it comes to computer games and certain forms of computer animations, such as the recently (2003) highly successful computer animation, 'Sprited Away'.

**LVMH – Louis Vuitton Moët Hennessy** LVMH, which describes itself as the world's leading luxury products group, 'brings together a unique collection of crafts and brands well known in prestige circles: champagne, cognac, luggage, watches, jewellery, perfumes and haute couture'. LVMH brands include: Moët and Chandon, Veuve Clicquot, Hennessy, Hine, Tag Heuer, Zenith, Christian Dior, Givenchy and Christian Lacroix, as well as the Louis Vuitton leather products. In 1993 LVMH sold its Roc Skincare subsidiary to Johnson & Johnson, as its products did not fit properly since they sell exclusively through pharmacies. More recently LVMH expanded into selective retailing with the purchase of chains such as Le Bon Marché, Duty Free and Sephora (cosmetics).

In 1999 LVMH acquired a 34 per cent shareholding in Gucci but was thwarted in its later attempt to buy the whole business – but LVMH made a substantial profit when the shares were sold. In 2001 the Italian fashion house, Fendi, was added to the empire. Also in 2001 the loss-making retail activities were declared 'non-core', but there was no immediate intention to sell them.

LVMH brands are all products with a global appeal, albeit to relatively limited market niches. For such products, the marketing/selling network has to be extensive or it cannot support the global distribution; consequently, there can be major benefits from linking together an appropriate range of products and brands. LVMH's synergistic benefits are:

- name association, particularly with fashion and perfumes
- advertising – savings by advertising several brands in the same magazines
- distribution – although there are specialist outlets for different products, large department stores sell many LVMH brands. Because the LVMH range as a whole is vital for these stores, LVMH can command premium positions and displays
- sales – a worldwide sales force and network yields savings.

In November 1999 LVMH had appeared to depart from its traditional pattern of acquisitions and bought Phillips, the world's third largest fine art auction house. Could it see hidden synergy potential here? Perhaps not: Phillips was divested in a management buy-out in 2002.

**Johnson & Johnson** Johnson & Johnson is a leading American health-care business with over 200 subsidiary businesses in three broad activities: pharmaceuticals, medical devices and consumer products. It is probably best known for its baby products and Band Aids, but most of its profits come from pharmaceuticals.

The company proclaims it is about 'people, values and environment'. All acquisitions must fit this culture-based credo. Between 1989 and 2002, when the company was run by Ralph Larsen, there were in excess of 50 acquisitions, many of them emerging biotechnology companies with innovatory ideas. Larsen was convinced that the Johnson & Johnson culture and style ensured most of the biotech founders stayed with the business after it was acquired, thus retaining a critical resource. Given that the style implies a decentralized structure, the synergy challenge lies in forging effective linkages between the relatively autonomous businesses.

Obviously, Sony, LMVH and Johnson & Johnson are very big organizations. Often such organizations can survive a number of bad decisions and perhaps one or more underperforming chief executives. However, over time no organization, however large, can survive a failure to plan. They do need to get it right at least some or most of the time. This is a theme we will return to in later parts of this book with organizations such as Marks and Spencer and Sainsbury's.

## 3.4   Concluding comments

We have introduced in this chapter the concept of strategic thinking and how that is often translated into attempts by organizations to achieve strategic synergy. Business strategy in organizations can too often become a 'me too'-type activity as the latest strategic concept to reach corporate boardrooms becomes widely accepted. For example: related diversification versus unrelated diversification, **vertical** versus **horizontal integration** and so on. Often a strategy is created post hoc from a series of actions which in reality only sought to provide a response to the tactics of rival organizations. However it is clear that if an organization does not change in some way, the standard momentum, over time, is downwards through getting an even smaller slice of a declining cake!

No organization deliberately plans to fail but many do fail to plan. We introduce in Part Two of the book the concept of the **learning organization** (Chapter 5) and in Chapter 7 a discussion on the merits of efficiency versus effectiveness. Basically effectiveness is crucial. Any organization, if it is to be successful, needs to 'do the right thing'. It can only do this through strategic thinking. This book provides the strategist with a range of strategic tools with which to guide their thinking. In the next chapter (Chapter 4) we will examine how strategy can be influenced by external environmental forces.

## SUMMARY

Strategic thinking relates to an organization's ability to gather, harness and utilize relevant information from inside the organization and from the (changing) external environment. The desired outcome is strong competitive strategies.

The external environment can usefully be seen as 'layered'. Suppliers, customers and competitors comprise the inner layer; the PEST (political, economic, social and technological) factors are the outer layer – because they affect the whole industry.

Strategic thinking demands an ability to learn from the past, to understand the present and to think ahead.

Effective thinking can be used to generate synergy, where the total achievements of the whole organization exceed what would be achieved if the various parts were working independently.

Synergy can be derived from sharing amongst the various functions of the organization, from complementary competitive strategies and from a cohesive management style.

## QUESTIONS AND RESEARCH ASSIGNMENTS

1. Synergy has been summarized as the '2 + 2 = 5' effect. Can you think of instances from your own experiences (maybe in a sporting context) where it has been in evidence?

Questions on the environmental influences discussed are to be found in later chapters.

## INTERNET AND LIBRARY PROJECTS

1. In September 2004 Sony acquired the MGM film library. What exactly did Sony buy and what benefits did Sony executives believed would accrue? Would this strengthen synergy? Were there any downside risks that you can see?

   **Sony** http://www.sony.com

2. Is the 'luxury brand' logic offered by LVMH a genuine synergy opportunity? How difficult might it be to generate the potential synergy in question?

   **LVMH** http://www.lvmh.com

## Further reading

Campbell, A and Alexander, M (1997) What's wrong with strategy?, *Harvard Business Review*, November–December.

Courtney, H *et al.* (2001) Strategy under uncertainty, *Harvard Business Review*, March–April.

## References

Ansoff, HI (1968) *Corporate Strategy*, Penguin (originally published by McGraw Hill in 1965).

Campbell, A and Alexander, M (1997) What's wrong with strategy? *Harvard Business Review*, November–December.

Courtney, H, Kirkland, J and Viguerie, P (1997) Strategy under uncertainty, *Harvard Business Review*, November–December.

Drucker, PF (1973) *Management*, Harper and Row.

# 4

# Environmental Analysis and Strategic Positioning

The notion of strategic positioning helps us understand the fit between an organization and its external environment. The opening case on the European pharmaceutical industry shows how company strategies have been influenced by such external environmental forces. Positions are related to the organization's ability to create and add value and consequently added value is discussed in relation to a SWOT (strengths, weaknesses, opportunities and threats) analysis. The chapter begins by examining the nature of the business environment, followed by a consideration of the impact of competition regulations on industry and company strategies. Positions, also, have to be changed, as seen in the discussion of E–V–R congruence. Sometimes the change is continuous and incremental; sometimes it is more dramatic or discontinuous. To help our understanding of the latter, the chapter concludes with a discussion of scenario building.

## Minicase 4.1 The European Pharmaceutical Industry    Eur

The global drugs industry is dominated by powerful American companies, perhaps not unexpectedly as the US has the world's highest spending ratio for health as a proportion of gross domestic product. But no single company is in a truly dominant position, although individual companies dominate particular segments with patented treatments. There is, in addition, a number of sizeable pharmaceutical companies in the UK, Germany, Sweden, Switzerland and France.

Past, and inevitable, government interest and involvement makes pharmaceuticals a politically sensitive industry. Individual consumers have relatively little influence on the choice of a particular drug, which is prescribed by doctors who are often working under constraints or limitations imposed by their respective governments. This affects the research and marketing strategies of the drug manufacturers. Governments across Europe have frequently agreed favourable prices with international companies who locate and invest in their countries, which has led to the establishment of more plants than are really needed and some loss of production efficiencies. The total spend on prescription drugs rose throughout western Europe in the 1980s and early 1990s. Between 1989 and 1992 it grew by nearly 50 per cent in real terms and almost all of the cost is borne by the public purse. The main reasons for the growth were ageing populations and medical advances.

However, in the economic recession, governments have become less and less willing to meet an ever-increasing bill; and in 1993 drug spending was deliberately curbed. The pharmaceutical companies have been forced to respond, and they have reacted in a number of ways. It will be seen in the following examples that national borders are no constraint in this industry.

■ Workforces have been reduced and sites closed. Hoechst and Bayer (Germany), Glaxo Wellcome and Fisons (UK) and Ciba (Switzerland) have all followed this strategy.

■ In addition, there has been a number of strategic acquisitions and divestments. Two of

the UK's leading companies were sold, Fisons to Rhône-Poulenc Rorer and the manufacturing interests of Boots to BASF. Wellcome was taken over by Glaxo, following a contested bid. In 1998, the two dominant UK companies, Glaxo Wellcome and SmithKline Beecham, were poised to merge, but the two chief executives could not reach agreement on strategic leadership of the new group. However, the strategic logic was always there and the merger went ahead in 2000. Other mergers include:
Sandoz and CIBA (both Swiss)
American Home Products, Monsanto and Pharmacia (in two stages)
Pfizer and Warner Lambert (both US)
Astra (Sweden) and Zeneca (UK and a spin-off from ICI)
Astra-Zeneca and Novartis (Switzerland).

As a result, Glaxo SmithKline became 'number one', with a 7.5 per cent share of the world market, followed by Pfizer-Warner Lambert with 6.5 per cent and Merck with 5 per cent.

■ As a form of industry restructuring both SmithKline Beecham (Anglo-American) and Merck (US) acquired leading American drugs wholesalers.

■ New marketing strategies have been developed, actively promoting to doctors and hospitals those drugs that governments are still willing to pay for. This applies particularly to drugs which are differentiated, protected by patent and not subject to intense competition. Sales forces have also been rationalized.

■ Research and development has been redirected to focus on:

(i) programmes which could lead to innovative and high-revenue drugs. The development of 'me-too' brands, which must be sold with lower margins in more competitive markets, is now seen as only low priority. Glaxo SmithKline has recently established six independent internal biotechnology research centres which work autonomously in their prescribed areas. Their role is to develop new drugs to a proof of concept stage, when they are handed over to a centralized unit which manages the final comprehensive testing. The intention is to encourage entrepreneurship, and each group is free to forge alliances with outside research agencies such as universities anywhere in the world.

(ii) generic (unbranded) drugs where patents have expired. Margins are low but generic drugs are popular with governments.

- European companies have forged alliances with US companies to obtain their greater expertise in cost management and in the research and development of generic products.

- New joint venture businesses have been set up, such as Rhône-Poulenc (France) and Merck's Animal Health Products division in London and then Rhône-Poulenc with Hoechst (Germany) for all the pharmaceutical interests of these two diversified conglomerates.

In the mid-1990s, the UK could claim 40 per cent of those employed in contract research in Europe and was continuing to attract new investment by overseas companies. When Sweden's Pharmacia merged with Upjohn of the US in 1995, a new corporate head office was opened in London. More recently, Pfizer opened a major research centre in Kent. However, others such as Roche have left the UK to focus their research elsewhere. There were four main reasons why London became 'the centre of the globe in terms of the pharmaceutical industry':

- UK scientists are as good as those in France, Germany, Switzerland and the US, but the total cost of employing them is lower

- the UK government's regulatory scheme differs from those of certain other countries and allows the drug companies to make between 17 per cent and 21 per cent return on capital employed, thus encouraging more investment

- strong UK capital markets have supported the blossoming biotechnology industry and

- the UK is home to the European Medicines Evaluation Agency, which issues drug licences for the whole of the EU.

By 2002/3 it was becoming apparent that the cost of developing and testing new drugs was on the increase. The total R&D spend had increased but the number of new drugs had declined. There were a number of causes, the relative significance of which is hard to quantify. Legislative requirements have tightened; because of past developments, incremental improvements and further breakthroughs become more complex and therefore expensive, despite the benefits and potential of biotechnology; some technically possible new drugs will not be able to recover the development costs because of the implied research costs. The cost of developing a new drug is now in the region of $800 million to $1.4 billion – to which a further $200 million launch costs can be added. Because patents are taken out before the final clinical trials, the rigorous testing regime means the drug companies have only 8 to 10 years of patent protection, in which time they have to recoup their research, development and launch costs in their prices. After this they are subject to competition from generic drugs.

The general approach to regulation in the UK has typically been one of regulating company profits and not the price of individual drugs, ensuring that companies which do invest in research and development can recover their costs while enjoying patent protection for a period of years. However, the new Labour government (elected in 1997) threatened to rein in drug expenditure. The leading companies countered by saying they would relocate abroad. In addition, the formation of a National Institute for Clinical Excellence (NICE) which licenses new drugs provided a new opportunity (for more effective monitoring) but, at the same time, a threat. In 1999 NICE refused a licence for Glaxo Wellcome's new influenza drug, Relenza, as it had not been tested on enough elderly people, those most vulnerable to flu. The drug has since received approval from NICE.

## Questions

1. How might the UK ensure it retains a leading position in this dynamic, turbulent but very important global industry?
2. What approach would you suggest any future British government should take?
3. Competition authorities in the UK have recommended that resale price maintenance (where manufacturers dictate retail prices) for over the counter non-prescription drugs should be abolished. If retailers are free to set their own prices it is assumed that the supermarkets will grow their share of the market at the expense of independent pharmacists. Should this happen, what impact might it have on the drug manufacturers themselves? The public will benefit in terms of prices, but is the situation more complex?

**AstraZeneca** http://www.astrazeneca.com
**Fisons (Aventis)** http://www.aventis.com
**Glaxo Wellcome** http://www.gsk.co.uk
**ICI** http://www.ici.com
**Pfizer** http://www.pfizer.com
**Pharmacia and Upjohn** http://www.pharmacia.com
**SmithKline Beecham** http://www.sb.com

*One thing is clear. Even if you're on the right track, you'll get run over if you just sit there!*

Sir Allen Sheppard, when Chairman, Grand Metropolitan plc (now Diageo)

## 4.1 Analysing the business environment

### 4.1.1 Managing in an increasingly turbulent world

This chapter examines in detail the environment in which the organization operates and considers how the forces present in the environment pose both opportunities and threats. The topic of stakeholders is developed further, as several of the environmental forces which affect the organization clearly have a stake in the business. Simply, stakeholders should be categorized in terms of their power and their interest. Those with power must be satisfied, especially if they are also interested in the activities of the organization. Those with relatively low power but high interest should certainly be kept informed. Competitors inevitably constitute a major influence on corporate, competitive and functional strategies and they are the subject of Chapter 6.

If a firm is to control its growth, change and development it must seek to control the forces that provide the opportunities for growth and change, and those that pose threats and demand responses. Not only must managers be aware of environmental forces and environmental change, they must manage the organization's resources to take advantage of opportunities and counter threats. In turn, the strategic leader should ensure that this happens and that the values and culture of the organization are appropriate for satisfying the key success factors. Quite simply, the environment delivers shocks to an organization, and the way in which resources are deployed and managed determines the ability to handle these shocks. This relates to E–V–R (environment–values–resources) congruence.

Over time, paradigms concerning 'what will work' to bring about success in a particular industry or competitive environment will be created and maintained. However, as environmental and competitive forces change, the current reality (at any time) of what is required for competitive success may be drifting away from the organization's paradigm; consequently, a new paradigm will be essential. In an age of discontinuity, paradigms will need changing more frequently and more dramatically; expediting these changes is a key managerial task.

Put another way, in a turbulent environment, the organization must change its strategies and possibly its beliefs if it is to maintain E–V–R congruence. A number of key themes underpin the issues discussed in this chapter:

- Traditional industries such as manufacturing and mining have given way to new, more technological – and frequently electronics-based – industries which demand new labour skills, and where 'knowledge workers' are of prime importance.

- New technologies can generate opportunities for substitutability, different forms of competition and the emergence of new competitors in an industry.

- In addition to changing skills demands, there have been other changes in the labour markets of developed countries. Many families have joint wage earners and more women are working. More and more people work from their homes, at least for part of their time.

- Many managers and employees are more time constrained and have less spare time than they would like. Not only does this imply less time for shopping (hence the potential for **e-commerce**), but demand has increased for convenient, time-saving products.

- People are living longer and, coupled with periods of lower birth rates, the average age of the population and the number of retired people are both increasing. These groups have more leisure time than working people.

- The Internet continues to change how we access information in a quite remarkable way.

- Multinational businesses have grown in strength and significance and they have become the norm for manufacturing industries.

- Manufacturers from the UK, US, Germany, Japan and other nations with a long-standing tradition in manufacturing have been willing to relocate factories in developing countries with lower wage costs. Technology which allows increasing levels of output from the same size factory has facilitated these changes. Hornby, which manufactures model railways and Scalextric racing car systems, switched production to China to enable it to devote more than two labour hours for every one utilized in the UK. The outcome is visibly higher quality for the same market price. There has been a resurgence of sales and fortunes at the company.

- Consequently, the competitive arena has been changing with, recently, the highest economic growth being enjoyed by the US, although during the early and mid-1990s it was the Pacific Rim countries. In many industries, global supply potential exceeds demand, placing downward pressures on real prices.

- Product and service markets, supply chains, capital markets and communication systems have become global in nature.

- The speed of change in most industries and markets has increased and product life cycles have shortened. For some companies, success can be very transient: a classic example of this being the computer games industry for both hardware and software.

- Governments have masterminded increasing degrees of deregulation. Other countries have followed the UK's lead and privatized public-sector utilities; air travel and telecommunications markets have been opened up to more competition.

■ Consumers are more aware and more knowledgeable; environmental groups have begun to wield increasing influence.

■ Changes in politics and regimes in different parts of the world, such as Eastern Europe and the Far East, have introduced an element of chaos and greater unpredictability. Opportunities open up but carry a significant downside risk.

Simply, environments are more turbulent; managing them and managing *in* them demand more flexibility and more discontinuity than in the past.

*There is no doubt that the world is becoming one marketplace. Capital markets, products and services, management and manufacturing techniques have all become global in nature. As a result, companies increasingly find that they must compete all over the world – in the global marketplace.*

Maurice Saatchi, when Chairman, Saatchi and Saatchi Company plc

*In my experience, corporate life-threatening problems in large manufacturing companies have developed over a long period. These problems should never have been permitted to grow so large, but they were allowed to do so by top management who were lethargic and self-satisfied, who engaged in self-delusion and congratulated themselves on their exalted status. In short, the managements were the problem.*

Eugene Anderson, ex-Chairman and Chief Executive, Ferranti International plc

**Figure 4.1** World class strategic performance

Developed by John Thompson from ideas in Kanter, RM (1996) *World Class – Thriving Locally in the Global Economy*, Simon and Schuster.

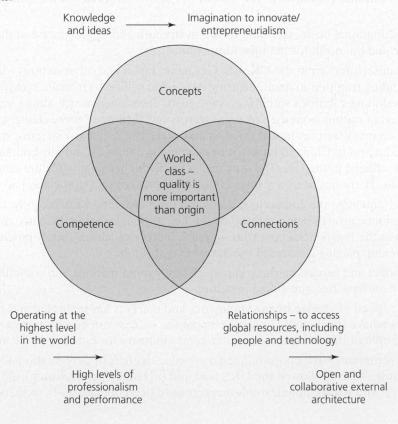

*How can we expect to succeed when we are playing cricket and the rest of the world is practising karate?*

Sir Edwin Nixon, when Chairman, Amersham International

Figure 4.1 emphasizes that as industries and markets become increasingly global, quality is more important than origin. People in Britain might like to claim 'British is best' – as might other people in other countries – but a statement such as this is meaningless unless it can be demonstrate that British (or other) products and services really are world class. To achieve world-class quality and reputation, companies must use knowledge and ideas to be innovative, operate at the level of the best in the world and form international networks and partnerships to access the best resources from around the world.

In this dynamic environment, the US has become the most competitive nation because it has taken a lead in technically advanced industries and transformed itself into a service economy. It has found ways of generating the private-sector finances required for investment in new and relatively high-risk sectors, and it has ensured that regulations do not inhibit labour-force flexibility. The US also has a compelling cultural will to win, the importance of which should never be underestimated. Europe is generally more restrictive, although practices do vary between countries, even within the European Union.

Although the following examples are British in origin and used to illustrate an important theme, similar stories can readily be told of other parts of the world. When the former British Prime Minister, Margaret Thatcher, came to power in 1979 she quickly identified a wide productivity gap between many British companies and those perceived to be the best in the world. She set about reducing the gap for both large and small companies – and she was successful, although in many industries a gap remains, albeit smaller than it would otherwise have been. In some industries Britain does have 'best in the world' companies, but relatively few industry-wide centres of excellence. In motor cars, really only two truly British companies remain. These, Morgan and TVR, are very small niche players. Rover is manufacturing again, having been divested by BMW, but it is financially weak with vehicles dependent upon competitors' technology. Ford now owns Jaguar and Land Rover; Vauxhall is a subsidiary of General Motors. Peugeot, Honda, Nissan and Toyota all assemble vehicles in UK factories. Nissan's Sunderland factory is their most productive plant.

In a complex deal Volkswagen bought Rolls Royce Vickers from Vickers without realizing the Rolls Royce name belonged to BMW. Bentleys are now manufactured in Crewe, Rolls Royces in Sussex. VW has rejuvenated Bentley, including reviving the company's sporting heritage. The cars competed very successfully at Le Mans in 2003, the first time in over 70 years they had raced there. Meanwhile BMW launched a new £200,000 Rolls Royce model in 2003. Target sales for the 20 foot long 2.4 tonne car are 1000 a year.

Yet, at the same time, British companies are dominant in the high-profile, advanced technology segment of Formula One racing. UK-based McLaren and Williams have only one serious rival, Ferrari – and Ferrari's technical development base is in the UK. Television assembly is similar in principle, with British plants owned and operated by French and Japanese manufacturers.

Where there are individual world-class companies in an industry, there is also often a long tail of low performers. Most significantly, though, average productivity in Britain remains below the average for many of its leading competitors. Simply, while British companies have improved, so too have most others! Britain may have reduced the productivity gap, and may seem able and committed to it not widening again, but the gap has not been closed, and rivals have certainly not been overtaken.

The competitive future for the UK, however, or any other equivalent developed country, does not lie in reducing wages to compete with the Far East and Eastern Europe, and thus creating a downward spiral of expectation; rather it lies in finding new ways of innovating, adding value, differentiating and *leading* consumers.

Notwithstanding this, some cutting back to create and maintain trim and efficient organizations will always be essential. These points are explored further in Box 4.1.

There are several frameworks for studying the environment of an organization. In addition to considering the company's *stakeholders* in terms of their relative power, influence, needs and expectations, a PEST analysis (discussed in detail later in this chapter) can prove useful. This is an objective and straightforward consideration of changing political, economic, social and technological influences. This review should help to clarify changing opportunities and threats.

The nature of the stakeholders and the environmental forces is a useful indicator of the most appropriate strategic approach for the organization to take. Where the environment is complex, turbulent and uncertain it will be necessary for the organization to be vigilant and speedily reactive. A carefully planned approach is ideal in stable and predictable circumstances, and a positive and proactive approach should be adopted where the environment can be changed or influenced.

## Box 4.1 Competitive Advantage and Strategy in the late 1990s

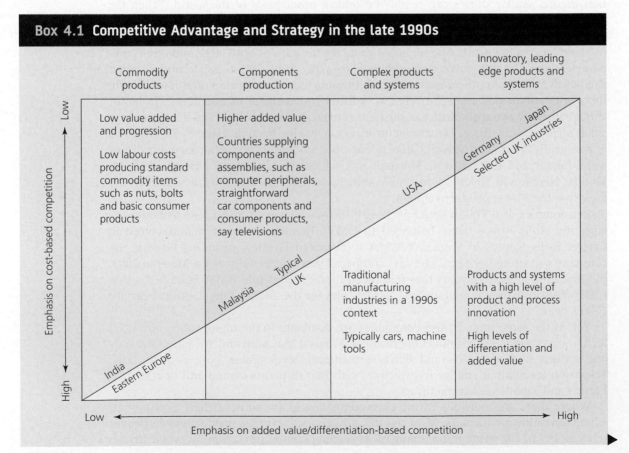

- Countries progress up and down the diagonal over time.

- Within each country different industries will be in different sectors. The position shown here on the diagonal is that with which the country is typically associated.

- The UK has drifted down to 'components' by offering incentives and relatively low labour costs to attract inward investments. However, with, for example aerospace and pharmaceuticals the UK is clearly in the innovatory sector.

- Arguably the UK should focus more intently on innovation to reverse the trend – otherwise the UK will increasingly become a mere supplier to the industry leaders and drivers. However, innovation requires managerial and workforce strengths and skills which the UK may not have.

- Innovation relates to products and services (radical improvements in value, reconceiving form and function) and market boundaries (attracting new customers, providing new values by satisfying individual needs more effectively).

Based on ideas in Kruse, G and Berry, C (1997) A nation of shopkeepers, *Management Today*, April.

## 4.1.2 Uncertainty, complexity and dynamism

Duncan (1972) argued that the environment is more uncertain the more complex or the more dynamic it is. An example of an organization facing a generally stable, non-dynamic and hence fairly certain environment is a small rural village post office. While most organizations face far more uncertainty, their managers also enjoy more challenges. In recent years the position of small village post offices has become more uncertain and many have closed. At the same time, however, the Post Office has looked at the possibility of offering a new range of banking services. The Post Office has realized that there is a window of opportunity as high-street banks consolidate and shut small branches. Moreover, they already have branches in every town and city that possess both spare capacity and a secure environment for handling cash. This development is not feasible without support and co-operation from the main clearing banks who, on the one hand, could benefit from the beneficial publicity, but, on the other hand, might see it constituting a new form of competition for some of their services. So far the banks have only co-operated reluctantly. The government has also announced plans for new computers which will allow post offices to become Internet centres with access to information on a variety of government services. If trials are successful this could enable more and more rural post offices to stay open.

While windows of opportunity are opening all the time, windows also close. In Spring 2000 the Dutch retail chain C & A announced that it was to close all its branches in the UK. The stores and their ranges had become unfashionable for many customers at a time when retail spending was pretty static, electronic commerce was increasing and new, more focused rivals, together with supermarkets such as ASDA, through clothes under the George label, were selling 'bottom end' fashionable designs at low prices.

**The dynamic environment**  Dynamism can be increased by a number of factors. Rapid technological change involving either products, processes or uses will mean that changes are likely to occur quickly and that organizations must stay aware of the activities of their suppliers and potential suppliers, customers and competitors. Where competition is on a global scale the pace of change may vary in different markets, and competition may be harder to monitor. In such cases the future is likely to be uncertain.

Risk-taking and creative entrepreneurial leadership may well be required as strategies pursued in the past, or modifications of them, may no longer be appropriate.

**The complex environment** An environment is complex where the forces and the changes involving them are difficult to understand. Quite often complexity and dynamism occur together. Technology-based industries and Internet-based businesses are excellent examples of this. The structure of the organization, the degree of decentralization and the responsibility and authority delegated to managers throughout the organization, and information systems can render complexity more manageable. Managers will need to be open and responsive to the need for change and flexible in their approach if they are to handle complexity successfully.

Managerial awareness and the approach to the management of change are therefore key issues in uncertain environments. If managers are strategically aware, and flexible and responsive concerning change, then they will perceive the complex and dynamic conditions as manageable. Other less aware managers may find the conditions so uncertain that they are always responding to pressures placed on the organization rather than appearing to be in control and managing the environment. Hence a crucial aspect of strategic management is understanding and negotiating with the environment in order to influence and ideally to control events.

Minicase 4.2 looks at issues of dynamism and complexity in the music industry.

**CASE**

## Minicase 4.2 The Recorded Music Industry

The recorded music industry has enjoyed a period of growth since the emergent popularity of Elvis Presley and The Beatles. From the mid 1980s to the mid 1990s the growth and prosperity was boosted by people's willingness to rebuild their collections by replacing their vinyl LPs and cassettes with compact discs. Since 1997, however, the popularity of singles has declined whilst sales of compilation albums and classical music has increased. Global revenues reached almost $40 billion dollars in 1999 but by 2003 these had declined by almost 20 per cent to $32 billion.

There are many forces at work driven by the public perception that they were paying too much for the product:

- People were downloading music from the Internet, sometimes legally, sometimes illegally. Eventually legal action would be taken to restrain the activities of Napster, a leading provider of online free downloads. The Internet also provided the opportunity to purchase CDs at significant discounts on high street prices.

- Pirate copies of CDs were increasingly available – some on the black market, some inadvertently through legitimate channels.

- The CD replacement market has matured as people have rebuilt their collections.

- More recently people have been able to make good home copies of their friends' CDs by purchasing a CD burner for the personal computer. To complete the task, CD labels can be downloaded from the Internet!

- The ways and means that people listen to music have changed to iPod and other MP3 players. Computer game-playing and satellite television have competed for the same leisure time. In the past people would play CDs time and time again; now many people only play them infrequently. New cars typically provide a CD player and yet there are also more radio stations to tune in to.

▶

- Young people – teenagers and others not in full-time employment – have often switched their discretionary purchasing away from music to their mobile phones.

- Retail competition has increased, stimulated in part by supermarkets increasing their sales of best sellers. As a result prices and margins have declined.

- Some analysts believe there is less creative talent being discovered than was the case in the past. Assuming this is true, there are potential causes. The industry is dominated by global conglomerates; the significance of small and entrepreneurial independent record labels has declined, although they are still around. The growth in popularity of television programmes designed to find new artistes and to form new boy and girl bands has also, for some, been a negative force. The real test is often whether sales of second and third albums exceed or fall below those of debut albums. In the past the successful groups and artistes saw sales grow; now it is less likely to happen.

By 2002 five companies controlled some 75 per cent of the global market, with the following market shares:

| Company | Share of global market (%) |
|---|---|
| Universal (MCA and Polygram) | 25.9 |
| Sony Music | 14.1 |
| EMI (incl. Virgin) | 11.9 |
| Warner Music | 11.1 |
| Bertelsmann (BMG) | 12.0 |

There were rumours that EMI was seriously interested in acquiring Warner Music from Time Warner Corporation, but in the end the business was sold to a financial consortium. Meanwhile Bertelsmann and Sony started planning a joint alliance which subsequently became a merger. Together they were roughly the same size as Universal.

**Questions**

1. What future changes do you foresee – and will these have a predominantly positive or negative impact on (a) consumers and (b) the record companies?

2. How have your own musical tastes and listening habits been changing in recent years?

Universal http://www.umusic.com
Sony Music http://www.sonymusic.com
EMI http://emirecords.co.uk
Bertelsmann http://www.sonybmg.com
Warner Music http://www.wmg.com

## 4.1.3 Environmental influences

Figure 3.1 showed how the organization is typically one of a number of competitors in an industry; and to a greater or lesser degree these competitors will be affected by the decisions, competitive strategies and innovation of the others. These interdependencies are crucial, and consequently strategic decisions should always involve some assessment of their impact on other companies, and their likely reaction. Equally, a company should seek to be fully aware of what competitors are doing at any time.

Furthermore, this industry will be linked to, and dependent on, other industries: industries from which it buys supplies, and industries to which it markets products and services. Essentially this relates to Porter's model of the forces that determine industry profitability, the subject of the next section in this chapter.

The relationships between a firm and its buyers and suppliers are again crucial for a number of reasons. Suppliers might be performing badly and as a result future supplies might be threatened; equally they might be working on innovations that will impact on organizations to which they supply. Buyers might be under pressure from competitors to switch suppliers. It is important to be strategically aware, and to seek to exert influence over organizations where there are dependencies.

These industries and the firms that comprise them are additionally part of a wider environment. This environment is composed of forces that influence the organizations, and which in turn can be influenced by them. Particular forces will be more or less important for individual organizations and in certain circumstances. It is important that managers appreciate the existence of these forces, how they might influence the organization, and how they might be influenced.

Mintzberg (1987) has used the term 'crafting strategy' to explain how managers learn by experience and by doing and adapting strategies to environmental needs. He sees the process as being analogous to a potter moulding clay and creating a finished object. If an organization embarks upon a determined change of strategy, certain aspects of implementation will be changed as it becomes increasingly clear with experience how best to manage the environmental forces. Equally, managers adapt existing competitive and functional strategies as they see opportunities and threats and gradually change things. In each case the aim is to ensure that the organization's resources and values are matched with the changing environment.

### 4.1.4 External forces: a PEST analysis

A PEST analysis is merely a framework that categorizes environmental influences as political, economic, social and technological forces. Sometimes two additional factors, environmental and legal, will be added to make a PESTEL analysis, but these themes can easily be subsumed in the others.

*Economic conditions* affect how easy or how difficult it is to be successful and profitable at any time because they affect both capital availability and cost, and demand. If demand is buoyant, for example, and the cost of capital is low, it will be attractive for firms to invest and grow with expectations of being profitable. In opposite circumstances firms might find that profitability throughout the industry is low. The timing and relative success of particular strategies can be influenced by economic conditions. When the economy as a whole or certain sectors of the economy are growing, demand may exist for a product or service which would not be in demand in more depressed circumstances. Similarly, the opportunity to exploit a particular strategy successfully may depend on demand which exists in growth conditions and does not in recession. Although a depressed economy will generally be a threat which results in a number of organizations going out of business, it can provide opportunities for some.

Economic conditions are influenced by *politics and government policy*; equally, they are a major influence affecting government decisions. The issue of whether European countries join, or remain outside, the single European currency is a case in point. At any one time either exported or imported goods can seem expensive or inexpensive, dependent upon currency exchange rates. There are many other ways, however, in which government decisions will affect organizations both directly and indirectly as they provide both opportunities and threats.

While economic conditions and government policy are closely related, they both influence a number of other environmental forces that can affect organizations. Capital markets determine the conditions for alternative types of funding for organizations; they can be subject to government controls, and they will be guided by the prevailing economic conditions. The rate of interest charged for loans will be affected by inflation and by international economics and, although the determining rate may be fixed by a central bank (as it is, for example, by the Bank of England) it will always be influenced by stated government priorities. Government spending can increase the money supply and make capital markets more buoyant. The expectations of shareholders with regard to company performance, their willingness to provide more equity funding or their willingness to sell their shares will also be affected.

The labour market reflects the availability of particular skills at national and regional levels; this is affected by training, which is influenced by government and other regional agencies. Labour costs will be influenced by inflation and by general trends in other industries, and by the role and power of trade unions.

The *sociocultural environment* encapsulates demand and tastes, which vary with fashion and disposable income, and general changes can again provide both opportunities and threats for particular firms. Over time most products change from being a novelty to a situation of market saturation, and as this happens pricing and promotion strategies have to change. Similarly, some products and services will sell around the world with little variation, but these are relatively unusual. Figure 4.2 shows how washing-machine designs are different for different European countries to reflect consumer preferences. Organizations should be aware of demographic changes as the structure of the population by ages, affluence, regions, numbers working and so on can have

**Figure 4.2** European preferences for washing machines

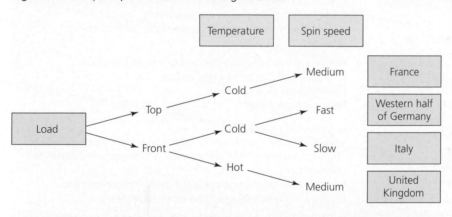

---

## Box 4.2  A PEST Analysis of the Credit-card Industry

| | |
|---|---|
| Political | Legislation allowing young people to own credit cards. The threat of restrictions on Internet trading. |
| Economic | The future presence – or not – of the UK, Denmark and Sweden in the Euro-Zone and the European single currency, and the impact of the single currency on interest rates generally. Future economic trends which will affect demand for consumption and credit. Freedom for, or restrictions on, new entrants to the industry. |
| Social | The willingness or reluctance to buy on credit – while credit is readily available for many people, there can be a rebellion against high interest charges. The increasing acceptance of Internet shopping, which depends on credit-card transactions – possibly affected by the age profile of the population. |
| Technical | Internet and e-business possibilities – and security. |

**Table 4.1** Environmental influences

| Influence | Examples of threats and opportunities |
| --- | --- |
| The economy | The strength of the economy influences the availability of credit and the willingness of people to borrow. This affects the level of demand. Interest rates and currency fluctuations affect both the cost and demand of imports and exports |
| Capital markets | This includes shareholders, and their satisfaction with company success. Are they willing to buy more shares if offered them to increase equity funding? Would they willingly sell if someone bid for the organization? Also included are the banking system, and the cost and availability of loan capital |
| Labour market | Changes in structure with an ageing population and more women seeking work<br>Availability of skills, possibly in particular regions<br>Influence of trade unions<br>Contribution of government training schemes |
| Technology | Robotics in manufacturing in industries such as car assembly<br>Computers for design and manufacturing<br>Information technology such as electronic point of sale in retailing |
| Sociocultural environment | Pressure groups affecting demand or industry location<br>Changing population – by age groups<br>Changing tastes and values<br>Regional movements |
| Government | Regional aid policies<br>Special industry initiatives, e.g. where high technology is involved<br>The legal environment is part of this, including the regulation of competition<br>Restraints on car exhaust emissions (pollution control) and labelling requirements would be other examples |
| Suppliers | Availability and cost of supplies, possibly involving vertical integration and decisions concerning whether to make or buy-in essential components |
| Customers | Changes in preferences and purchasing power<br>Changes in the distribution system |
| Competitors | Changes in competitive strategies<br>Innovation |
| The media | Effects of good and bad publicity, drawing attention to companies, products and services |

an important bearing on demand as a whole and on demand for particular products and services. Threats to existing products might be increasing; opportunities for differentiation and **market segmentation** might be emerging.

*Technology* in one respect is part of the organization and the industry part of the model as it is used for the creation of competitive advantage. However, technology external to the industry can also be captured and used, and this again can be influenced by government support and encouragement. Technological breakthroughs can create new industries which might prove a threat to existing organizations whose products or services might be rendered redundant, and those firms which might be affected in this way should be alert to the possibility. Equally, new technology could provide a useful input, perhaps in both manufacturing and service industries, but in turn its purchase will require funding and possibly employee training before it can be used.

The examples referred to here are only a sample of many, and individual managers need to appreciate how these general forces affect their organization in particular ways. Table 4.1 provides a general list of environmental influences and forces. To provide a specific example, Box 4.2 includes a short and very selective PEST analysis of environmental forces affecting the credit-card industry and picks out a number of key influences. It will be realized how such an analysis can be useful for helping to identify emerging opportunities and threats.

For any organization certain environmental influences will constitute powerful forces which affect decision-making significantly. For some manufacturing and service businesses the most powerful force will be customers; for others it may be competition.

In some situations suppliers can be crucial. In the case of some small businesses external forces can dictate whether the business stays solvent or not. A major problem for many small businesses concerns the management of cash flow – being able to pay bills when they are due for payment and being strong enough mentally to persuade customers to pay their invoices on time. In the UK, the National Health Service (NHS) is similarly very dependent upon government policies which affect all decision areas. Consultants' salaries, nurses' pay, new hospitals and wards, and new equipment are substantially determined by government decisions, which they will seek to influence.

## 4.1.5 Ansoff's model

Ansoff (1987) contends that 'to survive and succeed in an industry, the firm must match the aggressiveness of its operating and strategic behaviours to the changeability of demands and opportunities in the marketplace'. The extent to which the environment is changeable or turbulent depends on six factors:

- changeability of the market environment
- speed of change
- intensity of competition
- fertility of technology
- discrimination by customers
- pressures from governments and influence groups.

Ansoff suggests that the more turbulent the environment is, the more aggressive the firm must be in terms of competitive strategies and entrepreneurialism or change orientation if it is to succeed. The firms in an industry will be distributed such that a small number is insufficiently aggressive for the requirements of the industry, and as a result they are unprofitable or go out of business. Another small number will be above average in terms of success because they are best able to match the demands of the environment. Many will achieve results above average; and some others may also fail because they are too aggressive and try to change things too quickly through lack of awareness.

Where an organization is multiproduct or multinational, the various parts of the business are likely to experience some common environmental influences and some which are distinctive, which reinforces the need for managers who are closest to the market and to competitors to be able to change things.

Ansoff suggests that the environment should be analysed in terms of competition and entrepreneurship or change. The degree of competitive and entrepreneurial turbulence can be calculated by attributing scores to various factors. The competitive environment is affected by market structure and profitability, the intensity of competitive rivalry and the degree of differentiation, market growth, the stage in the life of the products or services in question and the frequency of new product launches, capital intensity and economies of scale. Certain of these factors, namely market growth, the stage in the life of the product and profitability, also help to determine the extent to which the environment is entrepreneurial. Changes in structure and technology, social pressures and innovation are also influential.

The culture of the organization and managerial competencies should then be examined to see whether they match and be changed as appropriate if they do not. Again, scores are attributed to various factors. Culture encompasses factors such as values, reaction and response to change, and risk orientation. Problem-solving approaches, information systems, environmental forecasting and surveillance, and management systems are included in the competencies. Ansoff is really arguing that the resources of the organization and the values must be congruent with the needs of the environment.

## 4.2 Analysing an industry

Porter (1980) argues that five forces determine the profitability of an industry. They are featured in Figure 4.3. At the heart of the industry are rivals and their competitive strategies linked to, say, pricing or advertising; but, he contends, it is important to look beyond one's immediate competitors as there are other determinants of profitability. Specifically there might be competition from substitute products or services. These alternatives may be perceived as substitutes by buyers even though they are part of a different industry. An example would be plastic bottles, cans and glass bottles for packaging soft drinks. There may also be a potential threat of new entrants, although some competitors will see this as an opportunity to strengthen their position in the market by

**Figure 4.3** Determining industry profitability – the five forces
Adapted from Porter, ME (1980) *Competitive Strategy: Techniques for Analysing Industries and Competitors*, Free Press.

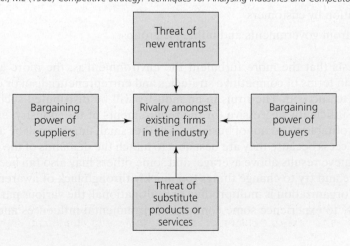

ensuring, as far as they can, customer loyalty. Finally it is important to appreciate that companies purchase from suppliers and sell to buyers. If they are powerful they are in a position to bargain profits away through reduced margins, by forcing either cost increases or price decreases. This relates to the strategic option of **vertical integration** which will be considered in detail later in the book. Vertical integration occurs where a company acquires, or merges with, a supplier or customer and thereby gains greater control over the chain of activities which leads from basic materials through to final consumption.

Any company must seek to understand the nature of its competitive environment if it is to be successful in achieving its objectives and in establishing appropriate strategies. If a company fully understands the nature of the five forces, and particularly appreciates which one is the most important, it will be in a stronger position to defend itself against any threats and to influence the forces with its strategy. The situation, of course, is fluid, and the nature and relative power of the forces will change. Consequently the need to monitor and stay aware is continuous.

## 4.2.1  The threat of new entrants: barriers to entry

Where barriers to entry are high new entrants are likely to be deterred, and if they do attempt entry they are likely to provoke a quick reaction from existing competitors. Low barriers generally mean that responses will be slower, offering more opportunities. A number of factors can create barriers:

- **Economies of scale**: Some of the possible ways of achieving economies of scale have been considered earlier. In addition the **experience curve** (see the supplement to this chapter) can be important. If there is a need for substantial investment to allow a new entrant to achieve cost parity with existing firms this may well be a deterrent. In such a case if a newcomer enters the market with only limited investment and is not able to achieve comparable economies of scale, he or she will be at a cost disadvantage from the start, in which case substantial differentiation will be required, but this introduces another issue.

- **Product differentiation**: If consumers perceive rival products or services to be clearly differentiated then newcomers must also seek to establish a distinct identity. Newcomers will therefore have to invest in advertising and promotion to establish their new brand, and this may be expensive. The major brewers and chocolate manufacturers, for example, spend millions of pounds each year promoting specific products and brands.

- **Capital requirements**: Any requirement for substantial investment capital in order to enter a market is a barrier to entry. The investment may be on capital equipment, research and development, or advertising to establish a market presence, and it may deter many aspiring competitors. However, large multi-product companies who wish to break into a market may finance the necessary investment with profits from other areas of the business. Drugs is one industry we have already mentioned where huge investments are required to develop and test possible new products over several years. Whilst patent protection allows the costs to be recouped through prices, the investment is all 'up front'.

- **Switching costs:** These are not costs incurred by the company wishing to enter the market but by the existing customers. If a buyer were to change his supplier from an established manufacturer to a newcomer costs may be incurred in a number of ways. New handling equipment and employee training are examples. Buyers may not be willing to change their suppliers because of these costs, thereby making it very difficult for any newcomer to poach existing business.

- **Access to distribution channels:** Existing relationships and agreements between manufacturers and the key distributors in a market may also create barriers to entry. Some manufacturers may be vertically integrated and own or control their distributors. Other distributors may have established and successful working relationships with particular manufacturers and have little incentive to change. Companies aspiring to enter a market may look for unique distribution opportunities to provide both access and immediate differentiation.

- **Cost advantages independent of scale:** This represents factors which are valuable to existing companies in an industry and which newcomers may not be able to replicate. Essential technology may be protected by patent; the supply of necessary raw materials may be controlled; or favourable locations near to supplies or markets may not be accessible. Government restrictions on competition may apply in certain circumstances.

Minicase 4.3 illustrates both weak and powerful barriers to entry in two completely different industries, DVD rentals and champagne.

Potential entrants, attracted by high margins in an industry and not detracted by any of the above barriers, must try and gauge any likely retaliation by existing manufacturers; and Porter argues that this can be assessed by examining:

- past behaviour when newcomers have entered or tried to enter the market;
- the resource capabilities of existing companies which will affect their ability to retaliate;
- the investment and commitment of existing companies which may make retaliation inevitable if they are to protect their investment and position;
- the rate of growth of the industry – the faster it is the more possibilities for a newcomer to be absorbed.

Existing firms may be prepared to reduce prices to deter entry and protect their market shares, especially if supply already exceeds demand. As a result, even in an oligopoly, profitability can be contained.

## 4.2.2 The bargaining power of suppliers

The behaviour of suppliers, and their relative power, can squeeze industry profits. Equally the ability of a firm to control its supplies by vertical integration (acquiring its suppliers) or long-term supply arrangements can be very beneficial. The relative power is affected by five major factors:

- Concentration amongst suppliers vis-à-vis the industry they sell to: if the supply industry is very concentrated then buyers have little opportunity for bargaining on prices and deliveries as suppliers recognize that their opportunities for switching suppliers are limited.

CASE

## Minicase 4.3  Barriers to Entry: DVD Rentals and the Champagne Industry  US  Eur

### Netflix

Netflix is an online DVD rental site begun by entrepreneur Reed Haslings in America in 1998. There is a monthly subscription of $19.95 (£12.50) and for this customers can borrow DVDs and keep them for as long as they like. There are about 12,000 titles to choose from, and these are mailed out with return envelopes. Typically customers have to wait between two and five days after e-mailing their order. By 2002, when 30 per cent of US households had a DVD player, Netflix had enrolled some 750,000 subscribers, and this number was growing at the rate of 100,000 every quarter. One can soon calculate this implies a revenue of $180 million every year.

The leading competitor, although not offering the same service, would be Blockbuster video, which rents videos to some 48 million customers through its ubiquitous retail outlets. Blockbuster will rent and even post out DVDs, but there is an individual item charge. It is a different business model. Netflix believes it has a competitive advantage because it can post summaries and reviews of all its DVDs on its web site, which all its customers have to use.

However, in 2002, a new and very powerful rival opted to enter the market and there was little Netflix could do in retaliation. Wal-Mart, which already sold DVDs, set up a rival service, undercutting Netflix's price by 10 per cent.

### Champagne

Several barriers to entry have acted to preserve the exclusiveness of the champagne industry. In most countries, and with the notable exceptions of the US and Russia, the term champagne can be applied only to wines made from grapes grown in one area, Champagne, in north-west France. The best grapes for champagne are grown on a particular type of chalky soil found only in this region. In addition strict (and enforced) French government rules require that only three varieties of grape may be used; and after the first fermentation the wine must be matured in the bottle for at least a year to generate the bubbles.

The business is carefully regulated, generally in favour of the 19,000 growers. Growers, who operate in co-operatives, historically have accounted for approximately one-third of the champagne that is manufactured; the rest has been produced by merchants who buy the grapes from the growers at prices fixed contractually every six years.

During the early and mid-1980s demand and sales grew by some 70 per cent. As a result grape prices rose and growers particularly started to manufacture more. These events attracted competitors who looked for ways of overcoming the entry barriers. The real threat came from other premium quality sparkling wines manufactured in countries such as Spain. The grower/merchant price agreement broke down in 1990, roughly at the time demand fell back. In an attempt to reinforce the image of superiority and exclusivity, and in response to the competition from other sparkling wines, champagne prices were increased deliberately. 'Quality and image is more important than quantity.'

The most influential company in the industry is LVMH (Louis Vuitton Moët Hennessy) whose brands (including Moët & Chandon, Dom Perignon, Veuve Clicquot, Mercier and Pommery – very popular in Japan) command around a 25 per cent market share. LVMH owns 1500 prime hectares out of the region's total of 35,000 hectares.

### Questions

1. Check the progress of Netflix and evaluate how this entrepreneurial business dealt with the threat from Wal-Mart.
2. Using LVMH as a starting point, look into the barriers to entry in the perfumes industry. Other companies to track are Estée Lauder, L'Oréal and Unilever. How successful have these leading companies been in controlling the distribution of their products through selected retailers?

Netflix http://www.netflix.com
LVMH http://www.lmvh.com

- The degree of substitutability between the products of various suppliers and the amount of product differentiation: a buyer could be tied to a particular supplier if his or her requirements cannot be met by other suppliers.

- The amount of, and potential for, vertical integration which might be initiated by either the supplier or the buyer: again government regulation on competition may prevent this.

- The extent to which the buyer is important to the supplier: if a buyer is regarded as a key customer he or she may well receive preferential treatment.

- Any switching costs that might be incurred by buyers will strengthen the position of suppliers.

### 4.2.3 The bargaining power of buyers

Any competitive action by buyers will act to depress industry profits, but specific arrangements with distributors or customers can be mutually beneficial. Vertical integration is again a possibility. The major supermarket grocery stores with their multiple outlets nationwide are in a very strong bargaining position with most of their suppliers.

This power has been strengthened by the success of private label brands, whose prices can be up to 60 per cent below those for the recognized major brands. Private labels have grown to over one third of UK retail food sales. They have proved most successful with chilled meals, frozen vegetables, fruit juices and cheese; and least successful with pet foods, sugar, coffee and, for a long time, breakfast cereals. Barriers against private label products are provided by innovation and aggressive marketing and promotion.

As the market for overseas travel grew in the UK, the power of the leading travel agency groups also grew vis-à-vis the tour operators – it is, after all, the travel agency that actually sells the holiday and has direct contact with customers, who they are able to influence. As a consequence the leading tour operators (Thomson and Airtours, subsequently renamed My Travel) sought to acquire their own agencies and exercise greater control over the supply chain. At the same time, industry rationalization has meant that a small number of tour operators (all of whom also own their own airline) dominate the market. In recent years there has been a reaction from the airlines. The low-cost carriers chose to sell direct in order to avoid agency commissions; now the leading full-service airlines such as BA have reduced the commissions they are willing to pay for tickets issued by travel agents.

The bargaining power of buyers is determined by:

- the concentration and size of buyer
- the importance to the buyer of the purchase in terms of both cost and quality (the more important it is the more he or she must ensure good relations with the supplier)
- the degree of product standardization, which affects substitutability
- the costs, practicability and opportunity for buyers to switch supplier
- the possibility of vertical integration, initiated by either the supplier or the buyer.

### 4.2.4 The threat of product substitutes

The existence or non-existence of close substitutes helps to determine the elasticity of demand for a product or service. In simple terms this is price sensitivity. If there are close substitutes, demand for a particular brand will increase or decrease as its price moves downwards or upwards relative to competitors. Price changes can be initiated by any firm, but other competitors will be affected and forced to react. If products are not seen as close substitutes then they will be less price sensitive to competitor price changes.

For this reason firms will seek to establish clear product or service differentiation in order to create customer preference and loyalty and thereby make their product or service less price sensitive. Where this is accomplished industry profits are likely to rise, which of course may be attractive to prospective newcomers who will seek to create further differentiation in order to encourage customers to switch to them and enable them to establish a presence in the market.

Products and services can be substituted for something completely different, reflecting the ever-present possibility that new competitors can change the 'rules of competition' in a market or industry. The music industry is in flux today. The sales of record CDs are in decline due to downloading from Internet music sites. CDs are expensive relative to the cost of production. Additionally the technology is now available to easily trawl for and capture music tracks on the Internet for a fraction of the cost of legally buying a CD. The music industry must come up with a solution to this problem which is more than just regulatory. It must suit the consumer!

### 4.2.5 Rivalry amongst existing competitors

Porter terms rivalry amongst existing competitors 'jockeying for position'. Competition may take the form of price competition, advertising and promotion, innovation, or service during and after sale. Where competitive firms are mutually interdependent, retaliation is a key issue. Before deciding upon aggressive competitive actions firms must attempt to predict how their competitors will react; when other firms are proactive an organization must at least be defensive in order to protect market share and profitability. The intensity of competition is affected by the market structure and depends on the following:

- the number of competitors and the degree of concentration
- the rate of growth of the industry – slow growth increases the pressure upon competitors to fight for market share
- the degree of differentiation – the less there is the more likely is price competition
- cost structures – where fixed costs are high relative to variable costs companies are very sensitive around the break-even point. Profits are very dependent upon volume.

As passenger aircraft become larger and more technologically sophisticated, the cost of buying (or leasing) and insuring them grows. The operating cost per seat mile – and break-even loadings – increases steadily, but with international overcapacity and competition, the revenue per seat mile has been falling. Some airlines have closed or been acquired; others have had to reduce salaries and numbers of employees.

**Table 4.2** A checklist for industry analysis

How many firms are in the industry, and what size are they?

How concentrated is the industry?

To what degree are products substitutes?

Is the industry growing or contracting?

What are the relative powers of suppliers? Buyers? Competitors?

What are the prevailing competitive strategies?

What entry barriers exist?

What economies of scale are present?

What experience/learning curve effects are important?

What exit barriers exist (if any)?

What important external factors affect competition?

An example of dedicated assets which have no obvious alternative use is multiplex cinema complexes. As the number of these has grown, cinema audiences have also grown, and an industry in decline has been given a new lease of life. In addition, it is quite normal for several fast food and retail outlets to open alongside the cinemas, helping to boost their traffic. But what would happen to the cinema buildings if audiences declined again? Additionally it could be argued that cinema going is now becoming expensive. The early alternative product offering in the market is easyCinema.com. History would suggest that is might just be the start of new competitive pressures in this industry.

Manufacturers of consumer electronics products have to invest continually to maintain the technology required for the necessary product improvements. To generate revenues to fund further investment they need volume sales; to create these they price with low, competitive margins. Profits are very slim, but the sunk costs are such that the cycle continues; it is too costly to come out of the industry. The cycle is reinforced by consumer purchasing behaviour. Consumers know which brands they are happy to consider, their shortlist depending upon the quality and differentiation they are seeking. They then buy on price, seeing certain brands as interchangeable. Inevitably, the retailers also earn only low margins.

Table 4.2 provides a summary checklist of factors for industry analysis, and Box 4.3 analyses the supermarket industry against Porter's model of five forces.

The rivalry factors discussed above, and the rivalry strategies, are both affected by any slowing down in the rate of industry growth, by acquisitions, and by changes in the marketing strategy of any one competitor resulting from the perception of new opportunities for differentiation or segmentation.

To be an effective competitor, a company must:

- appreciate which of the five forces is the most significant (it can be different for different industries) and concentrate strategic attention in this area
- position itself for the best possible defence against any threats from rivals
- influence the forces detailed above through its own corporate and competitive strategies

## Box 4.3  Industry Analysis – Supermarkets

### Threat of new entrants

Barriers to entry are very high, because of the necessary supply network and distribution infrastructure. The continual investment in EPOS (electronic point-of-sale) and EDI (electronic data interchange) systems creates further barriers. In addition, it is very difficult and very expensive to acquire new sites in prime positions. It is possible, given financial reserves, to build a position in selected market niches.

Of course, powerful companies, able to command huge financial resources, can break in with an acquisition, as we saw when Wal-Mart bought ASDA.

### Relative strength of suppliers

Supply agreements with major retail chains, using EDI, make the leading suppliers and supermarkets more and more interdependent. Ownership of a leading brand yields power, but secondary and tertiary brands must be more vulnerable. Further interdependency with own-label supply agreements.

### Relative strength of buyers

Invariably buyers will have more than one supermarket that they can access, especially if they are car owners. The power of the Internet to promote home deliveries also opens up choice. There will be some loyalty, but only if prices and service are competitive.

### Threat of substitutes

Small independent stores have a niche and a role, but the supermarkets are dominant. However, they are vulnerable on price for those products/brands offered by smaller, discount stores, especially where customers are willing to multi-shop. Home shopping via IT continues to be a sector of the market the supermarkets must develop rather than relinquish.

### Existing rivalries

The industry is very competitive, with four or five chains competing for the family shopping budget. Sainsbury, Tesco, ASDA (Wal-Mart) and Morrisons/Safeway have different competitive strategies (product ranges, pricing strategies, etc.) and have differing appeals, but they remain largely interchangeable. These companies must all invest to try and create differences as well as pricing competitively. The relatively speedy demise of the Co-op to a predominantly niche role illustrates how intense the rivalry is.

### Summary

| | |
|---|---|
| Barriers to entry | high |
| Power of suppliers | medium |
| Power of buyers | medium/high |
| Threat of substitutes | medium |
| Existing rivalries | intense |

■ anticipate changes or shifts in the forces – the factors that are generating success in the short term may not succeed long term.

Much will depend upon the strategic leader, the quality of management in the organization and the prevailing culture.

## 4.2.6  The role of government

Rather than incorporation as a separate sixth factor, Porter maintains the importance of government lies in an ability to affect the other five forces through changes in policy and new legislation. The examples below are not exhaustive.

1. The introduction of competition and an internal market in the National Health Service, a Conservative policy abandoned by the Blair Labour government.

2. A series of privatizations during the 1980s and 1990s, including British Aerospace, Rolls Royce, British Airways, British Telecom, British Rail and British Steel, along with the critically important gas, water and electricity utility industries. See also Minicase 4.4.

To prevent the businesses becoming national or local monopolies in private ownership, with enormous potential to exploit their customers, industry regulators have been appointed in a number of cases. The regulators and the newly privatized businesses have at times disagreed over important strategic issues. Individual regulators are given freedom to establish specific guidelines within clear broad principles, and some would argue that this makes conflict between them and the regulated businesses inevitable. One of the reasons for the diversification strategies by privatized companies is that they create business activities which are outside the direct control of the regulator. Given a general trend away from diversification to a concentration on core businesses and competencies, this has sometimes proved to be risky. Maybe the impact of the regulators also needs regulating.

## Minicase 4.4 Deregulation and the International Airline Industry

When governments regulated their airline industries, in order to control both national and international competition, new airlines were prevented from entering markets, existing companies could not simply offer flights into or out of any airport of their choice, routes could not be poached and prices for specified routes were fixed.

This regulation has been systematically reduced since the late 1970s. At this time in the US, where flying is as commonplace as bus and train journeys, and airline seats are perceived as essentially a commodity product, domestic competition was opened up. This has unleashed the underlying competitive nature of the industry with dramatic effects. The industry is characterized by chaos.

It is relatively easy to break into the industry once companies are allowed to do so. Planes can be leased and funded from revenue; maintenance can be bought in. Normally both fuel and planes are easily obtained. A company can enter by offering a limited service and concentrating on particular cities. Deregulation in the US attracted such companies; and existing large airlines sought to expand their routes. Buyers were generally

willing to fly with the airline which offered a flight at the time they wanted to travel, not differentiating, rather than building their arrangements around the schedule of their first-choice airline.

The British government has sought competition rather than monopoly control in the UK, privatizing British Airways in 1987. In 1991 the CAA (Civil Aviation Authority) relaxed certain rules, allowing new airlines to fly into and out of Heathrow for the first time since 1977. This intensified transatlantic competition as two strong US airlines (American and United, the two largest airlines in the world), which were restricted to Gatwick, acquired Heathrow/America routes from two weaker competitors, TWA and Pan Am respectively. At the same time Virgin Atlantic was: allowed to operate from Heathrow as well as Gatwick; allowed to fly to more American destinations; and given a number of BA's slots on the lucrative Heathrow to Tokyo route. All of these changes increased the competition for BA.

In 1992 European Union transport ministers agreed plans for a new 'open skies' policy, eventually featuring:

- Freer access for airlines to new routes throughout Europe. Previously many routes were protected by governments to prevent competition with their national carriers. One difficulty in implementing this is the ability of air traffic controllers to cope with more flights; European air traffic control is not fully co-ordinated and is overstretched.

- Greater freedom for airlines to set their own seat prices, within certain protective safeguards. This did not imply that prices would fall quickly because operating costs are already high, with many flights operating below capacity.

- Lower barriers to entry for new carriers.

Deregulation began in Australia in 1990, when controls on prices and schedules were removed, resulting in domestic price warfare, cost-cutting measures and the entry of a new national airline, 'the first for decades'. British Airways was allowed to buy a substantial shareholding in Qantas, Australia's leading international airline.

## Effects

- New route strategies based on a 'hub and spokes' – flights are concentrated around particular regional centres. American control 65 per cent of the slots at Dallas; United own 68 per cent of the slots at Washington National and 48 per cent of Chicago; and Delta 70 per cent of Atlanta. Internationally carriers expect the same control at the major airport in their home country, but many are now seeking to establish further hubs around the world.

- Company winners and losers. In 1991 in the US, for example, two previously major competitors, Eastern and Pan Am, went out of business. Earlier People Express, founded in the US in the early 1980s (following deregulation) to offer cheaper price flights, also failed after rapid growth and profitability. Companies such as American, United and Delta, less well-known before deregulation, have grown dramatically.

More recently United has opened negotiations to acquire smaller rival, US Air.

- New, small, focused airlines have also proved successful. We saw earlier how Southwest Air, based in Dallas, flies point-to-point (not hub-and-spoke) on short-haul routes, offering low fares, no pre-assigned seating and calling at secondary airports. Empowered employees deliver high service – founder Herb Kelleher has 'made working in this business an adventure for the employees'. The company uses only one type of aircraft, Boeing 737s, and avoids computer reservation systems in travel agencies; it prefers direct sales to its customers. Southwest has been consistently profitable; its operating ratios confirm that it outperforms most other US airlines. The Southwest strategy has been followed to varying degrees in the UK and Europe by competitors such as easyJet and Ryanair, as well as by Go (BA) and Buzz (KLM of the Netherlands) before they were acquired by easyJet and Ryanair respectively.

- New joint venture agreements and cross-shareholdings. In July 1992 BA reached an agreement with financially-troubled US Air (the fourth largest US carrier) to acquire a shareholding, and thereby gain access to US domestic routes. This arrangement collapsed when BA and American began to discuss a strategic alliance. The alliance they proposed has never materialized, although there are code-sharing links between the two airlines. More recently BA has formed an alliance with Iberia of Spain.

- Increased competitiveness with job losses during recession. Events like the 1991 Gulf War and 9/11 can have a major impact if people are deterred from flying.

- Greater reliance on information technology to allow pricing flexibility in order to maximize load factors. However, the increasing number of 'price wars' and special low-fare promotions has led to non-optimum fare mixes and unprofitable flights. In 1994 in the US, for example, 92 per cent of passengers flew on discount tickets and the average fare paid was just 35 per cent of the published full fare. During the 1990s the real cost of transatlantic flights halved. It is hardly surprising that customers have become increasingly confused. At the end of the 1990s BA chose to change its strategy and increase the number of its premium-price business and first class seats (at the expense of cheaper economy seats) in an attempt to increase the average fare and revenue yield of each flight. This has been partially successful.

At the same time …

■ Greater emphasis on service quality, especially punctuality and reliability, to try and establish customer loyalty. After all, expectations continue to rise despite the low fares.

■ The introduction of frequent flyer promotions (free flights on particular airlines for regular travellers who accumulate points for miles). This is also aimed at generating more loyalty. The end result has been a potent mix of poor profits, leading to corporate failures, disgruntled employees who are either laid off or forced to accept pay cuts, and unhappy passengers who are affected by the inevitable overbooking as airlines try to ensure every plane flies full.

■ The industry has exhibited one aspect of classic oligopoly behaviour with deregulation. When American Airlines tried to lead fares back up, it failed.

Perversely, at the same time, there is considerable regulation. The alliance between BA and American has become embroiled in the long running negotiations for an open-sky agreement between the UK and US, whereby individual airlines are allowed freer access to routes and airports. A proposal (in early 2000) for the acquisition of KLM by BA was immediately seized upon by the European Union competition regulators. Almost immediately it was suggested that BA and KLM would be required to divest their respective low-cost carriers, Go and Buzz.

### Questions

1. Why, then, deregulate?
2. Are governments too readily impressed by the seductive cost savings for passengers?
3. Would some regulation be more sensible than full deregulation?

## 4.3 Competition and the structure and regulation of industry

The four economic models of pure or perfect competition, monopolistic competition, oligopoly and monopoly were introduced in Chapter 2, when it was pointed out that the opportunity for substantial profits was most likely to be found in oligopoly and **monopoly structures**. Competition in the other models, resulting mainly from lower barriers to entry, has the effect of reducing profit margins. It is now useful to consider which models are dominant in the UK, and most other developed nations, as this influences the ways in which firms compete. Specifically, it affects the opportunities for differentiation and for the achievement of cost advantages which, as will be seen in Chapter 6, are major determinants of competitive advantage.

### 4.3.1 Monopoly power

It is important to point out here that as far as the regulatory authorities are concerned, a 25 per cent market share offers opportunities for a company to exploit monopoly power. Hence, although the model of pure monopoly assumes only one producer with absolute power in the marketplace, a large producer with a substantial share will be regarded as having **monopoly power**. It does not follow that such power will be used against the consumer; on the contrary, it can be to the consumer's advantage. Large companies with market shares in excess of their rivals may be able to produce at lower cost (and sell at lower prices) for any one of several reasons, including the ability to invest in high-output, low unit cost-technology; the ability to buy supplies in bulk and receive discounts; the ability to achieve distribution savings; and the opportunity to improve productivity as more and more units are produced. In fact, savings are possible in every area of the business. Economists call these savings economies of scale, and they are related to the notion of the experience or learning curve, which is explained in a Finance in Action supplement to this chapter.

It is quite normal to find an industry with a limited number (perhaps three, four or five) large mass market competitors with a broad product range and a number of much smaller niche producers. Interestingly if the largest companies control their costs well, then there will be a reduction in margin as market shares decline. The largest market shares will correspond to the highest margins. Conversely those competitors whose products are very specialist and with very limited market appeal to clearly defined niches or segments will enjoy higher margins than other niche producers whose products are less specialized. Here margin declines as market share increases.

A cost advantage, then, can be a major source of competitive advantage, and this point will be developed in greater detail later. The producer who is able to produce at a lower cost than his or her rivals may choose to price very competitively with a view to driving competitors out of the market and thereby increasing market share. Equally he or she may not; and by charging a higher price can make a greater profit per unit and thereby seek profit in preference to market share. In the first case the consumer benefits from lower prices and therefore monopoly power is not being used against the consumer. However, once a firm has built up a truly dominant market share it might seek to change its strategy and exploit its power more. This is when governments need to intervene in some way. This is the basis of the moves by both the EC and the US government to curb the power of Microsoft.

## 4.3.2 Concentration

Concentration is the measure of control exercised by organizations. There are two types.

*Aggregate concentration*, which will be mentioned only briefly, considers the power of the largest privately owned manufacturing firms in the economy as a whole.

*Sectoral or market concentration* traditionally considers the percentage of net output or employment (assets, sales or profits can also be measured) controlled by the largest firms in a particular industry, be it manufacturing or service. High **concentration ratio** figures tend to encourage monopoly or oligopoly behaviour, most probably the latter, which implies substantial emphasis on differentiation and non-price competition, with rivals seeing themselves as interdependent.

Many industries worldwide are essentially oligopolistic in structure, with a limited number of major competitors and barriers to entry in individual countries. In general, competition will be non-price rather than price, but price competition will be seen in situations where supply exceeds demand and there is aggressive competition for market share.

There may well be marketing and distribution advantages for companies which belong to conglomerates and this could increase their relative market power. Similarly, products which dominate particular market segments will yield advantages. Consequently, there is still opportunity for smaller companies to compete successfully in certain oligopoly markets, especially if they can differentiate their product so that it has appeal for particular segments of the market.

In the UK chocolate industry Thornton's has been successful with a limited range of high-quality chocolate products distributed through the company's own specialist outlets.

The dilemma for any government is to encourage firms to grow in size and become powerful competitive forces in world markets but at the same time to ensure that such size and power are not used to exploit their consumers. A recent example of this is the case of the Royal Bank of Scotland and its performance in 2003. The Royal Bank, in terms of its market capitalization, is now the fifth largest bank in the world. In early 2004 the bank posted a pre-tax profit figure of £6.16 billion, up 29 per cent on 2003. The bank makes £300 profit from every one of its private customers and it has been accused of both misleading and confusing its customers into taking on high interest-bearing credit cards.

### 4.3.3 The regulation of monopoly power

It is generally accepted in many countries that it is the state's role to monitor the forces of competition, to minimize any waste of resources due to economic inefficiency, to guard against any exploitation of relatively weak buyers or suppliers, and to ensure that powerful companies do not seek to eliminate their competitors purely to gain monopoly power.

Regulations are passed and implemented to police these issues. This section uses the situation in the UK to illustrate the point, but the principles and general approach are not unique to the UK. A new UK Competition Bill, passed in 1997 and operational in 1999, put the following structure in place.

In ultimate charge is the Department (or Minister) for Trade and Industry (DTI). The Office of Fair Trading (OFT), headed by a Director-General, has powers to carry out preliminary investigations of all proposed mergers or takeovers involving market shares of 25 per cent or more, or combined assets in excess of £75 million. If the OFT believes that major competition concerns are present, then it can refer the proposal to a second body, the Competition Commission, for further investigation. The Competition Commission is the delegated arbiter of referrals; in the past it has been the DTI.

Each case is considered on merit, and the presumption is not automatically that monopoly power is against the public interest. High profitability is considered acceptable if it reflects efficiency, but not if it is sustained by artificial barriers to entry. The OFT also investigates cartels.

The delay involved in an investigation can be important strategically. The process is likely to take at least six months and in that time a company which opposes the takeover bid against it will work hard to improve its performance and prospects. If this results in a substantial increase in the share price, the acquisitive company may withdraw on the grounds that the cost has become too high. Companies may seek to prevent a reference by undertaking to sell off part of the businesses involved in an acquisition if competition concerns are raised. Recently the UK government has mused about legislation to make company executives personally liable for competitive misdemeanours, but it has not been passed.

Since September 1990 the European Commission has also been able to influence the growing number of corporate mergers and acquisitions in the European Union (EU). Mergers are exempted, though, if each company has more than two-thirds of its EU-wide turnover in any one EU country. The intervention of the European authorities has been controversial and some judgements have been criticized. There is a voice of opinion in the US that the EC is hostile to American mergers where the companies enjoy substantial sales in Europe. The EU in effect prevented General Electric acquiring another American business, Honeywell.

### 4.3.4 Examples of intervention

In February 2000 the Competition Commission in the UK ruled that Unilever should be banned from distributing its own Wall's ice cream direct to retailers. Wall's ice-cream products hold the largest market share in the UK, in excess of 50 per cent. The argument was that a newly formed subsidiary, Wall's Direct, was undermining independent wholesalers and, as a consequence, competitors such as Nestlé and Mars were being squeezed out of the supply chain. The DTI chose to water down the ban and recommended a capping of the scope and extent of the distribution operation. Unilever, however, concluded that a cap was not feasible and it began to wind down its distribution.

In parallel with this investigation the Competition Commission had also looked at Unilever's practice of providing retailers with free freezer cabinets but insisting that they were used only for Wall's products. Small retailers, with room for just one freezer cabinet, were effectively prevented from stocking other brands. The Commission recommended that retailers should be allowed to fill up to half of the cabinet with rival products.

In July 2003 Manchester United, JJB (the UK's leading sportswear retailer) and Umbro (sportswear manufacturer) were all fined for colluding to fix the retail prices of replica football kits. Those concerned all denied the allegations. In a case brought in 2003 and ruled on in 2004, Ryanair fell foul of the Commission for accepting unfair landing subsidies from municipal airports in Europe.

Minicase 4.5 describes how the battle to acquire Safeway was largely determined by the Competition Commission.

Highlighting the global nature of competition regulation, Microsoft, dominant in personal computer operating systems, has been judged by an American court to be exploiting its monopoly power. In early 2000 it was ruled that the basic operating systems (based on Windows) and the applications (Microsoft Office and Internet Explorer) should be separated into two separate businesses, and that Microsoft should also be required to give away to its competitors some of its operating systems code. The contention was that Microsoft had driven Netscape out of the Internet browser market by tying its own browser, Explorer, to Windows. Inevitably the company appealed against the ruling, and after a Democratic President was replaced by a more sympathetic to business Republican, this requirement was relaxed. Microsoft could stay intact. However, the European competition authority has also been taking a very firm line, convinced that Microsoft has exploited its monopoly power. The *Financial Times* commented at one stage: 'Surely, most seriously of all, is that at a time Microsoft should be focusing all its talent on keeping up with technological innovation, it is hamstrung by this case.'

Box 4.4 describes the impact of regulation on the structure of the UK brewing industry over a period of years. Sometimes regulation produces unexpected and unpredicted outcomes: it is a grey world.

CASE

## Minicase 4.5  Bidding for Safeway  GB

Safeway, which began in California, entered the UK in 1962. Some forty years later it was the fourth largest supermarket chain in the UK. The company had grown steadily during its first 25 years before it was sold as a chain of 133 shops to rival group Argyll in 1987. The Safeway name, however, was retained. Later the business adopted a strategy of selected low price loss leaders with reasonable margins on everything else, but its stores were relatively small for the industry. Critics argued that it never had the right critical mass for the strategy it followed. In January 2003 William Morrison made an agreed £2.9 billion equity-based takeover bid.

Morrison was smaller and particularly strong in its home region of Yorkshire, where it was the largest supermarket chain. The company was controlled by 73-year-old Sir Ken Morrison who had taken over the business his father had started as a market stall in1899. The company had a distinctive business model (see Chapter 2) which yielded high sales per square foot and very competitive prices. With the takeover Morrison would become number four in the industry with a stronger geographic coverage.

It soon became apparent that the leading supermarkets – Tesco, ASDA and Sainsbury – would not stand idly by and let this happen unchallenged. Entrepreneur Philip Green – who had acquired and turned round both Arcadia and Bhs – also lurked in the wings and he might make an all-cash bid. It seemed inevitable that at least some of these bids would have to be subject to scrutiny. No large supermarket would be allowed to buy Safeway without at least some store disposals. In the end every supermarket bid – including Morrisons – was referred to the Competition Commission. Philip Green waited for the outcome.

Grocery sales and market shares were as follows in 2002:

| | Market share (%) | Stores | Sales (£ bn) |
|---|---|---|---|
| Tesco | 19.3 | 759 | 26.3 |
| Sainsbury | 12.7 | 485 | 18.2 |
| ASDA (Wal-Mart) | 10.8 | 263 | 16.0 |
| Safeway | 7.9 | 479 | 8.6 |
| Somerfield | 4.2 | | |
| Morrison | 3.9 | 119 | 4.3 |

When non-grocery sales are also factored in, Sainsbury is number three behind ASDA. Of the leading groups Sainsbury is the only one that doesn't compete aggressively on price (see Minicase 4.7).

The criteria that informed the evaluation were:

- Whether to focus on groceries or look at all items sold through supermarkets
- National market share
- Local store overlaps
- The impact on suppliers and the supply chain
- Company pricing strategies.

A leading retail analyst speculated that Morrison would be required to divest 41 of the 479 Safeway stores because of local duplication if its bid was approved. The figures for ASDA, Sainsbury and Tesco were 100, 208 and 233 stores respectively. The companies themselves maintained these were overestimates.

The Competition Commission approved the Morrison bid in September 2003 – as long as arrangements were first put in hand to dispose of 53 stores. The others were all blocked but they might be able to buy selected Safeway stores.

The original Morrison bid had valued Safeway at £2.9 billion. Assuming Morrison bid again, what would the price be this time? After all the group

▶

would be 53 stores smaller. Moreover, the share price had increased during the year. In December 2003 Safeway shares traded at 225 pence each. Having reached 320p by February 2003 they were 290p in October 2003. And, of course, Philip Green continued to wait – but he also had a problem. If he wanted to buy Safeway and break it up there would be restrictions on which groups he could sell stores to.

**Questions**

1. If you were Sir Ken Morrison, what would your reaction to the ruling have been?
2. Use the Internet to ascertain what did happen … do you support the actions of Morrison and Green?
3. In the end, who has been best served by the outcome – shareholders, employees, customers?

**Morrisons** http://www.morrisons.co.uk

## Box 4.4 Regulation and the Brewing Industry

When governments interfere in industries, there will be forced changes which often open up new opportunities. After all, detailed reports from the UK Competition Commission often contain significant information which becomes freely available to competitors and industry outsiders.

An investigation by the Monopolies and Mergers Commission (the predecessor to the Competition Commission) into brewing resulted in the 1991 Beer Orders. The investigation was prompted by four brewers controlling 60 per cent of brewing and 80 per cent of the UK's 60,000 public houses. The Beer Orders required that brewers with over 2000 pubs had to divest half their estate. In addition, all pubs they retained had to offer 'guest beers', ones not produced by the owner–brewer. The intention was to break the tied link whereby particular beers could be forced onto tenants by the powerful brewers.

In response, the leading brewers set up independent companies to buy out their own pubs, typically with links back to the brewers who were loaning the money. Naturally, the brewers retained the most lucrative pubs in their estates. In reality, the tied link was never truly broken. At the same time, the brewers began to diversify into hotels and restaurants because they were unable to open any new pubs. Bass acquired Holiday Inn, for example. Bass also owns Harvester restaurants and Britvic soft drinks. Whitbread similarly built a portfolio which included Travel Inn, Marriott Hotels (in the UK), Beefeater, Brewers Fayre, Bella Pasta, TGI Friday (UK franchise) and Pizza Hut (another UK franchise) restaurants, and the wine and spirits retailers Wine Rack, Threshers and Victoria Wine.

The Beer Orders provided new opportunities for entrepreneurial outsiders. The guest beer requirement, for example, led to the growth of micro-breweries, which produce only very limited quantities of generally very strong ales. Some pubs brew their own beer on-site. One manager with the Japanese bank, Nomura, came up with an idea to buy 2000 pubs from Bass for £2 billion. The bank had no interest in running pubs, but it was interested in property which could earn it some £300 million per year in rent. The bank raised the money for the deal by issuing bonds with a 10 per cent annual interest. Simply, the bank raised £2 billion for an annual interest payment of £200 million and earned £300 million in rents – a £100 million annual profit. Simple, really, if you have the idea and the resources to back the deal!

By 1999 the situation was:

| | Percentage of UK beer sales | |
| --- | --- | --- |
| | On-trade | Take home |
| Scottish and Newcastle | 27 | 22 |
| Bass | 23 | 17 |
| Whitbread | 14 | 20 |
| Carlsberg-Tetley | 13 | 9 |
| Other companies | 23 | 32 |

The activity profile (percentages of total turnover) of the four leading brewers was as follows:

|  | Bass | Whitbread | Scottish and Newcastle | Carlsberg-Tetley |
|---|---|---|---|---|
| Brewing | 33 | 22 | 61 | 77 |
| Retail | 30 | 30 | 27 | 0 |
| Soft drinks | 11 | 10 | 0 | 8 |
| Other leisure activities | 26 | 38 | 12 | 15 |

Shortly afterwards, both Bass and Whitbread announced that they were to withdraw from brewing in favour of other leisure activities. In 1997 the then Monopolies and Mergers Commission had approved a proposed merger between Bass and Carlsberg Tetley, but Secretary of State Margaret Beckett had intervened and stopped it. The Belgian brewer of Stella Artois, Interbrew, expressed interest in acquiring breweries from both companies – and would thus become the UK market leader. This was also stopped, but allowed on appeal – as long as the Carling, Caffrey's and Worthington brands were sold on. Meanwhile, Scottish and Newcastle (S&N) acquired Kronenbourg to become Europe's second largest brewer, second only to Heineken. S&N also owned Lodge Inns, Chef and Brewer restaurants, and the Center Parcs and Pontin's holiday resorts. In 2000 S&N was looking to divest its least profitable pubs and Center Parcs.

Since then Whitbread has joined Bass in divesting brewing in favour of other leisure activities. In 2003 S&N opted to leave the pub trade and agreed to sell its interests to the fast-growing pub chain, Spirit, one of a number of new operators. Other names were Enterprise Inns and Punch Taverns. All three had built up sizeable market shares through acquisition in recent years.

It is generally acknowledged that beer prices have risen more than the overall cost of living during this period – when supermarkets have also increased their presence in the industry. Of course, taxation policy cannot be ignored in considering this issue. It is clear that many motorists have discovered they can save money by crossing the Channel to France and buying beer and spirits in quantity there.

**Carlsberg-Tetley** http://www.carlsberg.com
**Heineken** http://www.heineken.com
**Interbrew** http://www.interbrew.com
**Scottish and Newcastle** http://www.scottish-newcastle.com
**Whitbread** http://www.whitbread.co.uk

**Whitbread and Bass** have joined forces to create new pub ventures

## 4.4  Strategic positioning and adding value

Strategic positioning and added value were defined and explained in Part One, and this section builds on that introduction.

### 4.4.1 Strategic positioning

Figure 4.4 emphasizes that effective strategic positions ensure that corporate strategic resources meet and satisfy key (or critical) success factors for customers and markets. Strategically valuable resources translate into core competencies and strategic capabilities (as explained in Part One), which are then manifest in a whole range of activities that the organization undertakes. The idea of activity mapping is developed in Chapter 5.

Competencies and capabilities can be separated by thinking of core competencies being built around technologies and technological skills, and strategic capabilities referring to processes and ways of doing things. Capabilities thus exploit the competencies; technology must, however, be developed to a particular level for a company to be influential in an industry or market. Hence, while the real competitive strength of an organization can be built around either competencies or capabilities, both must be present for relative success. Over time, both competency and capability must be improved with innovation. In Chapter 10 it is shown that people, learning and information are critical elements of this innovation. In addition, companies can benefit markedly from exploiting the linkages and relationships that they have with their suppliers and distributors.

It will be appreciated that an emphasis on key success factors – with a search for efficient, effective and imaginatively different ways of satisfying them – represents the market- or opportunity-driven approach to strategy, while exploiting competencies and capabilities is the resource-based approach. The market-driven approach places customers first, clarifying their needs and looking for new and different ways of satisfying them. The emphasis is on finding opportunities that competitors have yet to realize, and which ideally they will not be able to copy quickly. The resource-based approach is a search for better ways of utilizing and exploiting the strategic resources possessed by the organization. The two cases of Flying Flowers (Minicase 4.6) and Sainsbury (Minicase 4.7 later) illustrate the resource-based and opportunity-driven approaches respectively. Flying Flowers shows how underutilized resources can be exploited to develop a new market; and the Sainsbury case shows how competition has also impacted on the strategy and fortunes.

**Figure 4.4** Strategic positioning revisited

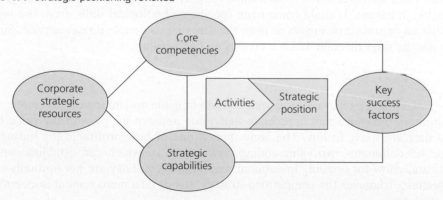

## Minicase 4.6  Flying Flowers                    GB

Flying Flowers, as the name suggests, sells flowers by post. The company was set up in Jersey in the Channel Islands in the early 1980s to save a struggling glasshouse business – a loss-making nursery needed and created a new opportunity. By 1996 turnover had grown to £35 million, with pre-tax profits of £4 million.

There are several key elements to the strategy and the success. First, the company holds only low stocks of the actual flowers, many of which it buys in cheaply from countries such as Colombia: flowers *from* Jersey does not have to mean flowers grown in Jersey!

Demand fluctuates markedly, peaking twice, at Christmas and Mother's Day, when the company typically receives 15,000 postal and 5000 telephone orders per day for a short period. Christmas sales amount to 5 million carnations in 330,000 boxed deliveries. Coping with this surge in demand is critical for success. The second key element therefore is staffing and staff management. As tourism is a leading source of employment in Jersey, and is strongest during the summer months, Flying Flowers is able to use casual hotel and restaurant staff. They are relatively plentiful on an island of scarce labour resources, and critically they are often laid off temporarily over Christmas and Mother's Day when tourism falls off.

Third, the company uses a disused glasshouse to house a noisy, steam-breathing machine which produces polystyrene boxes every working day of the year. These are then piled high to ensure that any demand peak can be catered for.

Fourth, and very critically, Flying Flowers has invested in IT to support both control and marketing. It holds a database on one million people and carefully targets its direct mail, analysing all responses and orders in detail. It has opened a telephone call centre in Witham, Essex.

Flying Flowers as a concept adds value for customers – high-quality, fresh flowers delivered directly to the door. Its operating costs are relatively low for the reasons described above and, of course, there are no returns to deal with.

The skills and competencies have been further exploited with the acquisition of other businesses. Flying Flowers bought Gardening Direct (mail-order bedding plants), Stanley Gibbons (publisher and stamp supplier) and another supplier of first-day covers.

### Questions

1. How does Flying Flowers add value?
2. What is the nature of its strategic position?
3. Did the acquisitions make sense in relation to its competencies and capabilities?

**Flying Flowers** http://www.jersey.co.uk/flyingflowers

It should be understood that strategic positioning, per se, is not a source of competitive advantage. Any relative advantage enjoyed by the organization comes from the resources and activities which establish and support the position. This can be tangible or intangible in nature. It could come from specific technological skills, from the reputation that an organization enjoys or from the way that its people deliver service. Simply, these are the ways through which it creates and adds value.

### 4.4.2  Added value

An organization uses its various resources, both tangible and intangible, to create value. If customers recognize and appreciate that value and are happy with the price being asked they are likely to buy. The issue then is one of how profitable the business is. Figure 4.5 delineates two value-adding cycles, both of which can establish superior profits and allow for ongoing investment and innovation. They are not mutually exclusive because, whatever the competitive strategy, strong cost management is essential.

**Figure 4.5** Adding value

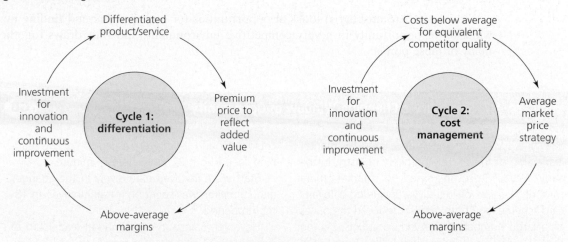

To be successful, products and services must fit into markets. Marketing and operations strategies are critical elements of competitive strategy but it is assumed that most readers will have already studied these topics elsewhere. These could be global or local markets, mass or niche markets. The products could be essentially commodities or substantially customized. The market (or the relevant niche) could be growing, static or declining. Each one can be profitable, but in different ways, with different strategies. Companies which target new markets, segments or niches may find that they are hard to penetrate, unless they have developed something radically new and different which is seen as a valuable alternative by customers. After all, most successful companies have realized that it is more expensive to win new business than it is to retain existing customers and, as a result, look after their customers. While patents can provide a barrier to new entrants and new rivals, so too can loyal customers!

However, some markets may equally be difficult to defend. This would be the case where the wider business environment is dynamic and turbulent, where the organization enjoys only a relatively weak strategic fit and where the service being provided is below the level expected. Hence, positioning and fit can be improved with customer care, product and service innovation and improvement, and by developing new products. All of this requires that companies take their competitors seriously, defend against any initiatives that they start and, on occasion, attack them. This can imply any or all of the following:

- finding and opening new windows of opportunity
- product and service development, improvement and enhancement
- direct attacks, such as price wars, either 'all-out' and sustained or short-term and guerrilla. Special discount promotions would be an example of the latter
- attempting to change the 'rules of engagement or competition' either openly (with genuinely new ideas) or more deviously (lobbying government for new regulations or buying out a key supplier or competitor)
- a 'war of words', seeking publicity for your activities and carefully disparaging your competitors. Sir Richard Branson was able to strengthen the image and position of Virgin Atlantic when he drew attention to British Airways' so-called 'dirty tricks' campaign to win over Virgin customers

■ networking and collaboration with key partners in the supply chain.

Minicase 4.7 (Sainsbury's) looks at opportunities for adding value and finding new windows of opportunity in a very competitive environment, and thus draws together many of these points.

## Minicase 4.7  Sainsbury's Changing Window of Opportunity  (GB)

Sainsbury's vies with ASDA and Tesco for market leadership of the UK retail grocery industry. In the early 1990s Tesco increased its market share through a series of initiatives, including a loyalty card scheme, and both retailers reduced the prices of a large number of everyday products. During the 1980s Sainsbury's, again like Tesco, had invested heavily in new superstores. A key challenge, critical for competitive advantage in the 1900s, was – and still is – customer service.

*Our strategy is about giving better quality, about value for money. Our customers come in every week, perhaps twice a week, and buy a huge range of products. If we are not performing, that is seen very quickly.*

David Sainsbury, when Chairman

Sainsbury began to address service more aggressively in the early 1990s. Head-office jobs were cut, but the number of staff in the stores was increased. Advertising was strengthened. A more extensive customer research programme revealed that shoppers were happy with Sainsbury's products but not its service. The major irritant was 'wonky' trolleys which prove difficult to steer in a straight line, followed by a lack of tills, the consequential long queues at the tills, product locations being changed too frequently, flimsy carrier bags, and fruit and vegetable bags which are difficult to open when they are removed from a roll. There were also complaints that checkout operators were scanning items more quickly than customers could pack them.

Sainsbury's introduced new policies. Once a checkout queue reached a certain size, another till would be opened. Customers asking about the location of a product were to be taken personally to the shelf rather than merely told where an item could be found. Staff were asked to cut the scanning speed from 22 to 18 items a minute.

Staff were involved extensively in the changes and £9 million was spent on retraining over an 18-month period.

However, Sainsbury's lost market leadership to Tesco in 1994 and has not regained it. Moreover, ASDA (now Wal-Mart) has been closing the gap on the two leaders during the past five years. Sainsbury's profits have been affected – 1995 proved to be a 'high'.

Analysts contend that Sainsbury's costs are higher, reflected in margins of just 4 per cent, while its rivals achieve 6 per cent. It has underperformed. They argue that the stores and distribution systems need streamlining. The average age of Sainsbury's retail depots is nearly 25 years, and its IT systems are over 10 years old. Building and opening new stores is not enough.

Sainsbury still believes that it must retain a brand which stands for quality and value, and that these must be delivered and be seen to be delivered – but without any further price cuts, which would threaten margins further. Whether Sainsbury's can achieve and retain this, and stay a mainstream rather than a more niched competitor, is the key issue and the key challenge. Sainsbury's has been described as a 'mass retailer with a niche market strategy' trapped between the lower prices of Tesco and ASDA and the more upmarket Marks and Spencer and Waitrose.

Although the Sainsbury family retains a large shareholding in the business, the company is no longer run by a Sainsbury. This ceased when Lord David Sainsbury left (in the late 1990s) to join the Blair government. In 2003 a new Chief Executive was appointed. Justin King had originally held a senior position at ASDA, but more recently he had headed the Food Division for Marks and Spencer.

▶

Would he seek to reposition Sainsbury, and if so, how and where? His initial promise was for price cuts in 2004.

Issues of leadership at Sainsbury are discussed in greater depth in a follow-up case in Chapter 10.

**Question**

1. Tesco and Wal-Mart have been investing more aggressively and now enjoy a higher margin cushion. Is there a way back for Sainsbury's?

**Sainsbury's** http://www.sainsburys.com

To summarize this section, Markides (1999) provides a list of six factors for competitive and strategic success. These are:

1. Choose a potentially winning position. This requires understanding *who* your customers are, *what* they require and expect and *how* they can be reached. This corresponds with Porter's (1996) view that it is essential to focus on certain activities and ignore others, not attempting to be 'all things to all people'.
2. Make this choice by a proper exploration of options, which implies.
3. An active search for opportunities to be different in a meaningful way, not just adopting a strategy because it seems to work.
4. Ensure all the support activities work together effectively and synergistically.
5. Create a real strategic fit and position which links the organization with its customers.
6. Ensure there is flexibility in both the activities and the fit so that innovation and change can sustain competitiveness.

### 4.4.3 Appropriability

Kay (1993) uses the term **'appropriability'** to make the point that organizations must seek to ensure that they see the benefits of the value which they create and add. After all, few things cannot be copied and some positions of advantage will be transient without improvement.

Value can be provided for customers in a whole variety of ways, but unless they are willing to pay a premium price which at least offsets the cost of adding the value, then it is the customer and not the organization that benefits. Even if a premium price can be charged, if this is then used to reward suppliers and employees, additional profits may not accrue. Sometimes higher profits are used primarily to reward shareholders, or owner–managers in the case of small organizations. All of these possibilities imply that the organization is not creating and sustaining a position where it makes superior profits and uses these (at least in part) to reinvest and help to build new values through improvement and innovation. Quite simply, the ideal scenario is a virtuous one, where every stakeholder benefits.

Regulation of railways in the UK provides an excellent example of the inherent tensions. The network and infrastructure provider (originally Railtrack, but Network Rail since the government effectively reprivatized this part of the industry, and which essentially maintains the lines, signalling and stations) and the train operating companies (such as Virgin Rail, National Express and GNER who provide the actual train services) are independent businesses. The picture is complex. Bus and coach operator Stagecoach, for example, has substantial stakes in more than one franchise, including

Virgin Rail. In addition, there is a Rail Regulator to oversee the whole industry – and he has removed franchises from underperforming businesses such as the French company, Connex, which ran commuter trains in the south-east.

Sometimes customers travel on services provided by just one train operator, but many journeys mean that customers are shared. Standards of reliability and service do vary. The government wants more people to use the railways (and other forms of public transport) to reduce traffic on the roads. This will only happen if services are good and prices acceptable. But attractive wages, required to recruit and retain a high calibre of employee, impact on costs and prices. So too do requirements for investment in new infrastructure (to improve services) and safety, particularly after a series of high-profile crashes. If investment demands, together with restraints on prices and profits imposed by the rail regulator, result in reduced profits and dividends, the individual train companies will find it increasingly difficult to generate and raise the funds they need for ongoing investment and improvement. Without the improvement, of course, they are likely to be fined by the regulator, making the profit situation even more precarious. There could very easily be a vicious rather than a virtuous circle.

## 4.5  SWOT (strengths, weaknesses, opportunities and threats) analysis

Environmental opportunities are only potential opportunities unless the organization can utilize resources to take advantage of them and until the strategic leader decides that it is appropriate to pursue the opportunity. It is therefore important to evaluate environmental opportunities in relation to the strengths and weaknesses of the organization's resources, and in relation to the organizational culture. Real opportunities exist when there is a close fit between environment, values and resources. Similarly, the resources and culture will determine the extent to which any potential threat becomes a real threat. This is E–V–R congruence, which was explained in Part One.

All of the resources at the disposal of the organization can be deployed strategically, including strategic leadership. It is therefore useful to consider the resources in terms of where they are strong and where they are weak as this will provide an indication of their strategic value. However, this should not be seen as a list of absolute strengths and weaknesses seen from an internal perspective; rather, the evaluation should consider the strengths and weaknesses in relation to the needs of the environment and in relation to competition. The views of external stakeholders may differ from those of internal managers (who in turn may disagree among themselves) when evaluating the relative strength of a particular product, resource or skill. Resources should be evaluated for their relative strengths and weaknesses in the light of key success factors.

Even though an organization may be strong or weak in a particular function, the corresponding position of its major competitors must also be taken into account. For example, it might have sophisticated computer-controlled machine tools in its factory, but if its competitors have the same or even better equipment, the plant should not be seen as a relative strength. This issue refers to distinctive competencies – relative strengths which can be used to create competitive advantage. As any resource can be deployed strategically, competitive advantage can be gained from any area of the total business.

An evaluation of an organization's strengths and weaknesses in relation to environmental opportunities and threats is generally referred to as a SWOT analysis.

**Figure 4.6** ASDA – analysis, early 1990s

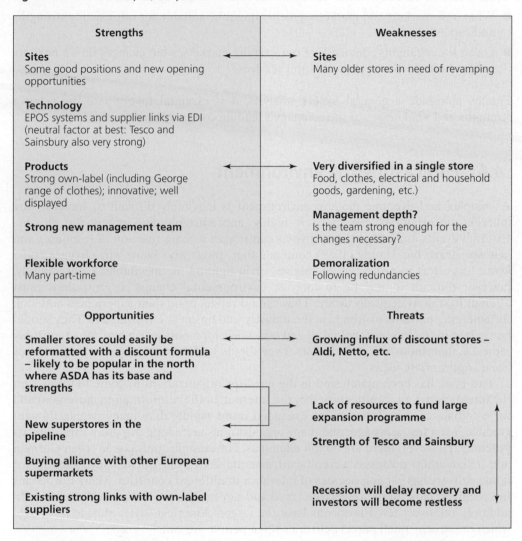

| Strengths | Weaknesses |
|---|---|
| **Sites**<br>Some good positions and new opening opportunities | **Sites**<br>Many older stores in need of revamping |
| **Technology**<br>EPOS systems and supplier links via EDI (neutral factor at best: Tesco and Sainsbury also very strong) | |
| **Products**<br>Strong own-label (including George range of clothes); innovative; well displayed | **Very diversified in a single store**<br>Food, clothes, electrical and household goods, gardening, etc.) |
| **Strong new management team** | **Management depth?**<br>Is the team strong enough for the changes necessary? |
| **Flexible workforce**<br>Many part-time | **Demoralization**<br>Following redundancies |

| Opportunities | Threats |
|---|---|
| **Smaller stores could easily be reformatted with a discount formula – likely to be popular in the north where ASDA has its base and strengths** | **Growing influx of discount stores – Aldi, Netto, etc.** |
| **New superstores in the pipeline** | **Lack of resources to fund large expansion programme**<br><br>**Strength of Tesco and Sainsbury** |
| **Buying alliance with other European supermarkets** | |
| **Existing strong links with own-label suppliers** | **Recession will delay recovery and investors will become restless** |

Figure 4.6 illustrates a popular and useful framework for a SWOT analysis applied to ASDA earlier in the 1990s, before the introduction of new strategies focusing on the product ranges, in-store layouts and a clear distinction between large ASDA superstores and smaller units with a limited range and discounted prices and finally its acquisition by Wal-Mart. The chart highlights how certain issues can be considered as either a strength or a weakness, an opportunity or a threat, depending on how they are managed in the future.

Once all of the important *strategic issues* have been teased out from a long list of strengths, weaknesses, opportunities and threats, the following questions should be asked.

■ How can we either neutralize critical weaknesses or convert them into strengths?

■ Similarly, can we neutralize critical threats or even build them into new opportunities?

- How can we best exploit our strengths in relation to our opportunities?
- What new markets and market segments might be suitable for our existing strengths and capabilities?
- Given the (changing) demands of our existing markets, what changes do we need to make to our products, processes and services?

Finally, alongside a general SWOT analysis, it is essential to evaluate the relative strengths and weaknesses of the company's leading competitors.

## 4.6 Forecasting the environment

A complex and dynamic modern environment is inevitably difficult to forecast; the inherent uncertainties can make it highly unpredictable and potentially chaotic. External events and competitor activities can trigger a chain reaction of responses and new scenarios; but Handy (1989) contends that 'those who know why changes come waste less effort in protecting themselves or in fighting the inevitable'. Consequently, however difficult it may be to forecast environmental change, organizations must attempt to stay strategically aware. They should reflect upon their experiences and look for emerging patterns or trends in the industry and business environment. They should be vigilant in tracking technological and other developments which may affect, possibly radically, their industries and markets. They should look for, and maybe even borrow or 'steal', appropriate ideas.

This issue has been manifested in the need for organizations to come to terms with the threats and opportunities posed by the Internet, both for information movement and for e-commerce. The Internet has expanded more rapidly than many people thought credible just a few years ago, and many organizations are a long way from exploiting its potential. However, there are inbuilt dilemmas. For example, only one in seven German and Italian adults possesses a credit card, essential for buying online. Buying online for home delivery has varying degrees of relevance in different countries. Many Europeans live relatively close to the shops concerned and can easily fetch the goods themselves. In addition, relatively few Europeans have the larger, American-style, outside postboxes which can accept small parcel deliveries when people are out.

> *Don't try to eliminate uncertainty … embrace it. Despite overwhelming evidence to the contrary many of us still view the future as an extension of the past.*
>
> Clem Sunter, Anglo American Corporation of South Africa (the world's largest mining group)

> *The world's changing. People in the US and Europe aren't going to live the way they do 100 years from now unless they do a lot of things differently. Who says that because we have 240 million people on this big piece of land [USA] we should have two cars and second homes, while 800 million people in India and 1 billion in China should live the way they live? We've only been wealthy in this country for 70 years. Who said we ought to have all this? Is it ordained?*
>
> John F. Welch, Chairman and former CEO, General Electric

# 4.7  Scenario planning

Scenario planning was first properly used in a business context by Shell some 30 years ago, however it still remains a fringe activity for many organizations.

Scenarios are often used in strategic management to explore future possibilities. Possible happenings and events are considered by looking at potential outcomes from particular causes and seeking to explain why things might occur. The value is in increased awareness by exploring possibilities and asking and attempting to answer 'what if' questions. Although scenario planning can be predictive and can be used to plan strategic changes, it can also help decision-making by providing managers with insight so that they can react better when things happen or change. It can also be helpful for conceptualizing possible new competitive paradigms.

Environments for many organizations have become – and continue to become – increasingly dynamic, turbulent and uncertain. They feature an element of competitive chaos, where companies continually thrust and parry with new ploys and stratagems in an attempt to, at the very least, 'stay in the game' and, ideally, get ahead of their rivals. Scenarios and scenario planning concern the medium- or long-term future and they embrace the possibility of real and dramatic change. Anticipation and creativity can be invaluable in dealing with the turbulence and uncertainty. By considering and evaluating future possibilities, organizations can put themselves in positions where they might be better placed to deal with the unpredictable challenges of the future. Put another way: simply engaging in the process of acknowledging and anticipating change enables managers to be less shocked by whatever change does occur.

Three central themes underpin effective scenario planning:

- It is important to clarify just what a business can and cannot change. Small farmers, for example, cannot enjoy the scale economies of large farms, nor can they affect the climate. They can, within reason, improve their soil and they can change their crops.
- What seems trivial or a pipe-dream today could be crucial in the future. In 1874, Western Union in America turned down Alexander Graham Bell's prototype telephone!
- Multiple scenarios need to be explored and then *held* as real possibilities. Shell, which pioneered scenario planning, is arguably ready to respond quickly to shocks which affect supply or prevailing prices.

The scenarios considered may involve modified versions of current competitive paradigms (the future is not the past, but at least the two are related) or radically new paradigms (everything changes in the end). The implications of the scenarios will tend towards one of two themes: first, there will be environmental changes but organizations can learn to cope with, and influence or manage events, and thereby enjoy some degree of relative stability; second, the environmental turbulence will be so great that the competitive situation will become ever more chaotic in nature.

Readers might like to consider a number of emerging issues in the UK, evaluate their significance and implications and, where appropriate, consider how they might apply in their own countries.

- People are living longer; there is an ageing population. But will the more recent trend of people retiring earlier, many on good pensions, continue? As people are healthier, is it not logical for them to work longer, as long as employers do not discriminate on age grounds? Of course, for some jobs skills can become outdated and people do become less useful. There is also the key dilemma of pensions. If people retire relatively early and live longer, there are two implications: one is that they will have to accept lower pensions; the other is that those people still in employment will have to pay far higher contributions to build up and sustain the pension funds.

■ According to most published statistics, unemployment is coming down, yet, at the same time, there are growing skills shortages. Developing the point above, raising the retirement age could help here, but only for some jobs. In a knowledge-based society, does the need for skill retraining and updating become more critical through a person's working life?

■ The NHS is stretched and private medicine is expensive. This could become more problematical as people live longer and especially if pensions are reduced. Hence, economically, people might need to work longer.

■ However, if the relative balance between salaried and 'permanent' career posts and self-employed people who contract themselves to various organizations continues to change, this issue of the length of working lives could be exacerbated.

■ In addition, it is becoming increasingly difficult for many families to prepare for retirement because of the increasing costs of educating their children. In turn, this increases the number of two-income families and creates a larger number of childcare positions.

In a wider context it might also be valuable to look at the implications of global climate change, the ever-increasing power of computing technology and the growth of new economies, such as China.

### 4.7.1 Developing useful scenarios

Organizations should really be looking to develop a number of scenarios that can be used to provoke debate among managers and possibly generate new creative ideas in the process – ideas that can be used as a basis for new strategies and action plans. As Schwartz (2003) points out, most future predictions will prove to be wrong – the real test of scenario planning is whether or not it changes how people manage their businesses, not whether the predictions are right.

The first step is to clarify the *key strategic issues*, mainly external, which will impact on the future that the company will face. Internally, many managers will already have formed views, which may not always accord, and which may be partial rather than com-prehensive, but these preliminary views will have caused the development of current working assumptions about future trends. It is invariably invaluable to also consult outside experts.

There are three types of issue to consider:

■ *predetermined elements* – for example, *social* changes to the size and structure of the population, lifestyles and values

■ *key uncertainties* – *political* changes and the inevitable *economic* changes which accompany it; the entry of new competitors; possible changes of corporate ownership

■ *driving forces* – developments in *technology* and education.

The link to a PEST analysis will be clearly seen.

The next step is to examine a number of *plausible outcomes* from the various key issues. It is particularly important to debate issues of positive and negative synergy, specifically the impact of interconnectedness. The discussions should generate some consensus, or possibly, and more realistically, accommodation on priorities, in the form of *viable scenarios* to test further.

These will often be presented as *stories*, illustrated creatively to generate interest and enthusiasm.

The *tests* against which they will be ultimately evaluated are:

■ What has been left out? – in effect, the extent of the comprehensiveness and the absence of key omissions – and

■ Do they lead to clearer understanding which informs future decisions and actions, while winning the commitment of everyone involved?

Yet in our rapidly changing world can even well-meaning scenario planning work? Box 4.5 provides an example of this. The BA planners probably thought they had it covered.

## Box 4.5  Scenario Planning at British Airways (BA)

BA believes that annual planning meetings (which are valuable and have a role to play) 'do not help people think about what might happen a decade from now'. Moreover, 'people have difficulty envisaging dramatic change'.

Consequently, in the mid-1990s, BA created two scenarios for the period to 2005, which it used in management meetings to provoke discussion about the implications of possible changes. These are known as *Wild Gardens* and *New Structures*.

*Wild Gardens* postulates a world where market forces are unleashed. Asian markets in particular grow rapidly and, early in the twenty-first century, after a period of strong growth, the US falls into a long recession. The 1996/97 general election in the UK is won for a fifth consecutive time by the Conservatives; the country remains divided over Europe. The EU is enlarged to bring in more Eastern European countries, but there is no single currency. The European Commission takes over negotiation of airline agreements from member governments, and concludes an Atlantic open-skies agreement which gives free access to transatlantic routes to carriers from both Europe and the US. Access to domestic airports in Europe and the US is widened.

The *New Structures* scenario is more stable, and gives greater control to individual governments. Asia's rise proves to be slower than initially anticipated, and Asian investment is reduced. Labour comes to power in the UK and joins France and Germany in promoting stronger European integration. A single currency (the Euromarque) is agreed, together with integrated air traffic control and a European high-speed rail network. There is increased commitment to the environment. In the US, President Clinton remains in power and reaches agreement with the Republicans to work together to increase investment and productivity. Taxes are increased; defence expenditure is reduced. North Korea provokes a security crisis in Asia and China suffers unrest after the death of Deng Xiaoping.

**British Airways** http://www.britishairways.com

### Reference

Moyer, K (1996) Scenario planning at British Airways – a case study, *Long Range Planning*, 29(2).

**STRATEGY IN ACTION**

However, 9/11 blew this out of the water – alongside some pretty poor election forecasting in the UK and a major US presidential change.

## 4.7.2 The dream society

Jensen (1999) contends that we shall soon be living in a 'dream society' where the stories attributed to products and services – their image and reputation – will be an increasingly significant aspect of competitive advantage. Examples might relate to free-range eggs, organic vegetables and celebrity-endorsed training shoes. Simply, the story adds value.

Jensen provides a number of themes for those organizations interested in creating 'dreams';

- *Adventure* Involvement in the 'great outdoors' or leisure activities. Manchester United branded clothing appears to combine both
- *Networks* BT (British Telecom) capitalized on this with its 'family and friends' name for its discounted call scheme as well as the television advertisements which feature ET and which, for example, link an absent father with his son for a game of chess
- *Self-discovery* Linked to products which allow people to say something about themselves. This theme has been exploited by VW (Volkswagen) with advertisements for the Golf which claim the only statement it needs to make is 'gone shopping'
- *Peace of mind* Security, often linked to the perceived safety of the known past. Perhaps this explains why VW has been able to relaunch the Beetle model and BMW a new Mini (a model that it acquired when it owned Rover)
- *Caring* Businesses can exploit their community links and programmes
- *Convictions* Ethical and environmental concerns are prominent. The Body Shop built a successful business around this, as shown in Chapter 7.

We conclude this chapter with a case on eBay – Minicase 4.8. eBay developed resources to seize a new opportunity that was being offered by the Internet. Typical of most of the truly successful Internet businesses to date, eBay provides a service rather than selling a specific product.

---

**CASE**

## Minicase 4.8 eBay　　　　　　　　　　　　　　　( US ) ( Int )

eBay has overtaken Amazon as the world's favourite e-commerce web site. It is fundamentally an online auction house, dealing in almost anything. The most popular products are cars and motor cycles, computers, books, music and electronic goods – but eBay once sold a Gulfstream jet aircraft for $4.9 million. Altogether there are 16,000 categories and it is not unusual for 5 million items a day to be featured.

Described as an online flea market in the late 1990s, eBay had actually started life in 1995 when its founder, French-born computer programmer Pierre Omidyar, set up a site so that his wife, who collected Pez sweet distributors, could make contact with other collectors around the world. It was not the first online auction house – and, unlike a number of its rivals, it has always charged a commission rather than provided a free service. Omidyar was another Silicon Valley resident and he also went in search of venture capital to expand the business in 1997. He raised $6.7 million for a third of his business. Similar to Google, most of this has never been used. The company was and always has been profitable. By 2002 it could boast 38 million customers and deals amounting to $9.4 billion a year. eBay's revenue target is $3 billion by 2005.

Head-hunters found Meg Whitman for Omidyar and she joined as CEO in 1998. Whitman had a corporate background – she had been working for Hasbro, the toy company, where she was running the Mr Potato Head franchise and masterminding the import into America of the Teletubbies. She recalls that she found a black and white web site with a single typeface – courier. Despite the fact the company was successful and growing, she believed the web site was 'confused'. She set about changing all this. She built up a fresh, strong management team and prepared the business for an initial public offering (IPO) of shares. When this happened late in 1998 it was the fifth most successful ever in US corporate history. Whitman has made the company international – it trades in 18 countries. Where sales have been disappointing – the case in Japan – she has simply closed the country site down. eBay arrived in the UK in December 1999. Its competitors now include Yahoo and Amazon, powerful names in Internet commerce.

On-line auctions have an interesting business model. There are no supply costs and there is no inventory. Goods are never handled – they simply move from seller to buyer. Once established there is little need to advertise and overall very little capital expenditure is required. Regular customers spend an average of 90 minutes when they are surfing the site – but they will make other quick visits to check progress when they are bidding for an item. Countless small businesses have found eBay a useful opportunity for selling their products. Success has to depend on satisfied customers and eBay invests in customer feedback, which is collected for every transaction and made available as data for other customers to access. Whitman is strong on performance orientation. eBay maintains that it has always listened to its customers and responded whenever appropriate. Interestingly there is little evidence of dishonest customer activity. Very few cheques ever seem to bounce, for example. Moreover, customers are very quick to respond if they notice any apparently rogue products being offered for sale – alleviating the need for eBay to invest heavily in security monitoring.

Approximately 40 per cent of the transactions are now online and eBay has had to develop the necessary competency. In July 2002 eBay bought PayPal, the world's largest online payment system. It is clearly possible to expand the scope of the business by offering the facility for customers to offer their products at a fixed price through the site – but this is different from the concept of an auction.

## Questions

1. Use the eBay web site to track the bidding for a product that interests you. You could, if you wished, sell something via eBay as an alternative. Why do you think this simple business concept has been so successful?
2. Examine eBay in terms of scenario planning. What could possibly happen to affect eBay in the future?

**ebay** http://www.ebay.com

# SUMMARY

Organizations operate with external environments that spring surprises on them from time to time. Indeed, many industries and markets are characterized by a form of 'competitive chaos' which arises from the natural dynamism, turbulence and uncertainty of both the industry and the environment.

It can make sense for the organization to see its boundary with the environment as relatively fluid. While suppliers, distributors and customers can be seen as outside the organizational boundary, they can also be identified as partners in a collaborative network which, more holistically, bounds with a number of external influences and forces.

Organizations must be able to react to the change pressures imposed by their environment (potential threats) and, at the same time, take advantage of opportunities which seem worthwhile. But this is arguably not enough. Leading organizations will create and sustain positions of strength by seeking to influence – and maybe even manage – their external environment.

A PEST (political, economic, social and technological forces) analysis provides a valuable framework for analysing relevant environmental forces.

All organizations should seek to understand the industries in which they compete. Industry attractiveness affects profitability and it can be assessed by considering five forces: barriers to entry; the relative power of suppliers; the relative power of buyers; the potential for substitutability; and inter-firm rivalry. Governments affect all five.

Over time, strong competitors create and seek to hold positions of power in markets and industries. For this reason governments everywhere will seek to exercise some degree of control. In the UK the relevant bodies are the Office of Fair Trading and the Competition Commission. However, in certain instances, UK companies will also be subject to regulation by the European Union.

Regulation is rarely clear-cut or black and white and sometimes the outcomes are not quite the ones desired.

To manage, and manage in, its environment an organization will need strong strategic positions. This implies finding and exploiting opportunities for adding value, in ways that consumers value and for which they will reward the organization with prices that imply superior margins.

Here we are talking about finding an effective blend between the opportunity-driven approach to strategy creation and the resource-based approach.

As organizations seek to exploit their *core competencies* and *strategic capabilities* to add value in this way, it is important that the value is appropriable. In other words, the benefits should not all go to shareholders (through high dividends), consumers (in, say, the form of relatively low prices) or employees (generous remuneration) such that the organization has inadequate resources for investment to build new ways of adding value for the future.

A SWOT (strengths, weaknesses, opportunities and threats) analysis is a second valuable framework for evaluating the position of an organization in relation to its environment. It is, however, important that the SWOT analysis is used to create ideas and is not just seen as a static statement of position.

It is important that organizations attempt to forecast their environment, however difficult this may prove. *Scenario planning* can make a very valuable contribution here if well done!

## QUESTIONS AND RESEARCH ASSIGNMENTS

1. Draw a diagram incorporating the environmental influences and stakeholders for any pub, discotheque or nightclub with which you are familiar.

   Do the same for London Zoo (Chapter 2).

   **Zoological Society of London/London Zoo**
   http://www.londonzoo.co.uk

2. From this evaluation, develop a SWOT analysis and consider the strategic implications.

3. One of the growth sectors in the UK economy has been in the area of call centres. Many thousands of people are employed in UK call centres. Many of these jobs are now being threatened with removal to India and other cheaper wage areas. How should the managers and workers of UK call centres respond?

4. Possibly in a group discussion, build a scenario relevant for the motor vehicle industry in ten years' time. How will people be using their cars? What will they expect in terms of size, performance, and external and interior design?

## INTERNET AND LIBRARY PROJECTS

1. How have changes in competition from around the world affected the UK footwear industry? What are the strategies of the leading, remaining manufacturers?

   You may wish to use a leading manufacturer such as C&J Clark as a key reference point. You should also look at a specialist such as Grenson or Church's. You might also investigate the source of your personal wardrobe of shoes, boots and trainers.

   **C&J Clark** http://www.clarks.com
   **Church's** http://www.churchsshoes.com
   **Grenson** http://www.grensonshoes.co.uk

2. How has Steve Pateman, owner of a family boot and shoe business in Northamptonshire, dealt with the pressures for change in this industry? How has the company diversified, and what do you think the implications are?

3. From your own experience, and from newspaper and other articles you have read or seen, list examples of where monopoly power and restrictive practices have been investigated, and where proposed mergers have been considered by the Competition Commission (or its predecessor the Monopolies and Mergers Commission). Evaluate the recommendations and outcomes. If you wish to follow up any of these investigations, all of the reports are published by HMSO.

   **Monopolies and Mergers Commission UK**
   http://www.coi.gov.uk/coi/depts/GMM/GMM.html
   **HMSO UK** http://www.hmso.gov.uk

4. Take an industry of your choice, perhaps the one you work for, and assess it in terms of

   (a) concentration

   (b) Porter's model of five forces.

   From this analyse one or more of the major competitors in terms of their chosen competitive strategies.

   As well as the Internet he following library sources might prove useful sources of information:

   ■ Business Monitors (PA and PQ series)

   ■ Annual Report of the Director General of Fair Trading (as a source of ideas)

   ■ Monopolies and Mergers Commission reports, and Competition Commission reports, which usually feature a comprehensive industry analysis

   ■ McCarthy's (or similar) Index (press cutting service for firms and industries).

5. How could Porter's five forces model be applied to Camelot, the monopoly supplier of the UK's lottery? On the one hand, Camelot operates under licence for a fixed period of years without any direct competition; on the other hand, it provides only one gambling opportunity amongst many. Why has Camelot needed to introduce several new games during the period of its licence?

## Further reading

Emery, FE and Trist, EL (1965) The causal texture of organisational environments, *Human Relations*, 18.

Whipple, W (1989) Evaluating alternative strategies using scenarios, *Long Range Planning*, 22 (3).

Ginter, P and Duncan, J (1990) Macroenvironmental analysis, *Long Range Planning*, December.

## References

Ansoff, HI (1987) *Corporate Strategy*, Penguin.

Benoit, B (1999) Nearing 50, hale and hearty on home ground – a corporate profile of SAGA, *Financial Times*, 23 November.

Duncan, R (1972) Characteristics of organizational environments and perceived environmental uncertainty, *Administrative Science Quarterly*, 313–27.

Handy, C (1989) *The Age Of Unreason*, Hutchinson.

Jensen, R (1999) *The Dream Society*, McGraw Hill.

Kay, JA (1993) *Foundations of Corporate Success*, Oxford University Press.

Markides, C (1999) Six principles of breakthrough strategy, *Business Strategy Review*, 10(2).

Mintzberg, H (1987) Crafting strategy, *Harvard Business Review*, July–August.

Porter, ME (1980) *Competitive Strategy: Techniques for Analyzing Industries and Competitors,* Free Press.

Porter, ME (1996) What is strategy?, *Harvard Business Review*, November–December.

Schwartz, P (2003) *Inevitable Surprises: Thinking Ahead in Times of Turbulence,* Gotham Books.

# Finance in Action: The Experience Curve

A large size, relative to competitors, can bring benefits. In particular, if a company has a market share substantially greater than its competitors it has opportunities to achieve greater profitability. Lower costs can be achieved if the company is managed well and takes advantage of the opportunities offered by being larger. These lower costs can be passed on to the consumer in the form of lower prices, which in turn puts pressure on competitors' profit margins and strengthens the position of the market leader.

Lower costs are achieved through economies of scale and the experience or learning effect. In the 1960s the Boston Consulting Group in the US estimated that the cost of production decreases by between 10 per cent and 30 per cent each time that a company's experience in producing the product or service doubles, as long as the company is managed well. In other words, as cumulative production increases over time there is a potential cost reduction at a predictable rate. The company learns how to do things better. The savings are spread across all value-added costs: manufacturing, administration, sales, marketing and distribution. In addition, the cost of supplies decreases as suppliers experience the same learning benefits.

The experience effect has been observed in high- and low-technology industries, in new and mature industries, in both manufacturing and service businesses, and in relation to consumer and industrial markets. Specific examples are cars, semiconductors, petrochemicals, long-distance telephone calls, synthetic fibres, airline transportation, crushed limestone and the cost of administering life insurance.

The experience curve is illustrated by plotting on a graph the cumulative number of units produced over time (the horizontal axis) and the cost per unit (the vertical axis), as shown in Exhibit 1. This particular curve is called an '85 per cent experience curve' as

**Exhibit 1** An 85 per cent experience curve plotted on a normal scale

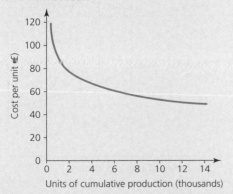

**Exhibit 2** The same 85 per cent experience curve plotted in log form

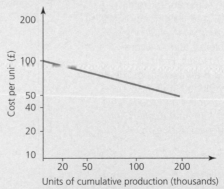

every time output is doubled the cost per unit falls to 85 per cent of what it was. In reality, the plot will be of a least-squares line but the trend will be clear. However, it is more common to plot the data on logarithmic scales on both axes, and this shows the straight-line effect illustrated in Exhibit 2.

Sources of the experience effect:

- increased labour efficiency through learning and consequent skills improvement
- the opportunity for greater specialization in production methods
- innovations in the production process
- greater productivity from equipment as people learn how to use it more efficiently
- improved resource mix as products are redesigned with cost savings in mind.

This is not an exhaustive list and the savings will not occur naturally. They result from good management.

## Pricing decisions and the experience effect

A market leader or other large producer who enjoys a cost advantage as a result of accumulated experience will use this as the basis for a pricing strategy linked to his or her objectives, which might be profit or growth and market share orientated. Exhibit 3 illustrates one way in which industry prices might be forced down (in real terms, after accounting for inflation) as the market leader benefits from lower costs. Initially, prices are below costs incurred because of the cost of development. As demand, sales and production increase prices fall, but at a slower rate than costs; the producer is enjoying a higher profit margin. This will be attractive to any competitors or potential competitors who feel that they can compete at this price even if their costs are higher. If competition becomes intensive and the major producer(s) wish to assert authority over the market they will decrease prices quickly and force out manufacturers whose costs are substantially above theirs. Stability might then be restored.

Companies with large market shares can therefore dictate what happens in a market, but there is a need for caution. If a company ruthlessly chases a cost advantage via the experience effect the implication could be ever-increasing efficiency as a result of less flexibility. The whole operating system is geared towards efficiency and cost savings. If demand changes or competitors innovate unexpectedly the strategy will have run out of time, as we have already seen. Companies should ensure that they are flexible enough to respond.

This material has mainly
  been summarized from:
Abell, DF and Hammond, JS (1979)
  *Strategic Market Planning:
  Problems, and Analytical
  Approaches*, Prentice-Hall.
Exhibit 3 is adapted from The Boston
  Consulting Group (1972)
  *Perspectives on Experience.
  Environmental Analysis and
  Strategic Positioning.*

**Exhibit 3** Pricing in relation to costs and the experience effect

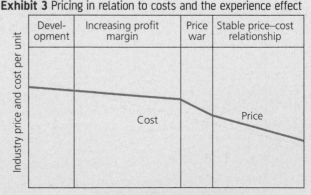

# Resource-led Strategy

The resource-based view of strategy gradually emerged during the 1980s and 1990s with a series of important contributions, in particular work on core competency from Prahalad and Hamel (1990) and on added value by Kay (1993). This view helps to explain why some organizations succeed in creating competitive advantage and earning superior profits, while others do not. Consequently, it looks at strategies which can be identified with an individual company as distinct from those that are available to all competitors through an understanding of industries and markets. In other words, market opportunities have to be identified and then satisfied in an individual and distinctive way. Supporters of the resource-based view put forward a number of arguments. As long as there are opportunities which can be identified, it will normally be easier and less risky for organizations to exploit their existing resources in new ways than to seek to acquire and learn new skills and competencies. Innovation matters and new ways of exploiting resources must be found to sustain any competitive advantage. Relative differences which separate a company from its rivals are critical: just having a resource is not enough. For this reason, it can be useful if particular strengths are not easily learned and imitated by rivals. The opening case on Dyson shows how innovation and new ways of creating and adding value through design can markedly change an industry. In this particular case, innovation allowed a newcomer to establish a position of market dominance and force a reaction from established manufacturers.

This chapter looks first and briefly at the idea of a resource audit before considering resource linkages and synergy through architecture and the notion of the value chain. The chapter concludes with a section on reputation and branding, key intangible assets. Before reading this chapter you might usefully re-read the sections on core competencies and leveraging resources in the Part One supplement.

## Minicase 5.1  James Dyson

James Dyson is an entrepreneur who challenged the industry giants, in his case with a revolutionary vacuum cleaner. His dual cyclone cleaner now has a UK market share in excess of 50 per cent and international sales are blooming: Dyson vacuum cleaners are now available in 37 countries. A Hoover spokesman has said on the BBC's *Money Programme*: 'I regret Hoover as a company did not take the product technology of Dyson … it would have been lain on a shelf and not been used.' Dyson has been compared by Professor Christopher Frayling, Rector of the Royal College of Art, with 'the great Victorian ironmasters… a one-man attempt to revive British manufacturing industry through design'. Dyson is creative, innovative, totally focused on customers and driven by a desire to improve everyday products. His dedication and ego drive is reflected in the following comment: 'the only way to make a genuine breakthrough is to pursue a vision with a single-minded determination in the face of criticism …' and this is exactly what he has done. Clearly a risk taker, he invested all of his resources in his venture. In the end his rise to fame and fortune came quickly, but the preceding years had been painful and protracted, and characterized by courage and persistence. They reflect the adage that 'instant success takes time'.

James Dyson's schoolmaster father died when he was just nine years old. The public school to which he was then sent 'made him a fighter'. At school he excelled in running, practising by running cross-countries on his own; and it was on these runs that he began to appreciate the magnificence of the railway bridges constructed by Brunel in the nineteenth century, an experience which helped to form his personal vision. An early leap in the dark came when he volunteered to play bassoon in the school orchestra, without ever having seen a bassoon! Naturally artistic, he won a painting competition sponsored by the *Eagle* comic when he was ten years old. Art became a passion and he later went on to complete a degree in interior design. Dyson may be an inventor, but he has no formal engineering background.

Dyson's first successful product and business was a flat-bottomed boat, the Sea Truck. At this time he learnt how a spherical plastic ball could be moulded, an idea that he turned to good use in the wild garden of his new home. His wheelbarrow was inadequate as the wheels sunk into the ground, so he substituted the wheel with a light plastic ball and thus invented the Ballbarrow. Backed by his brother-in-law on a 50:50 basis, Dyson invested in his new idea. Made of colourful, light plastic the barrow was offered to garden centres and the building trade, both of whom were less than enthusiastic. With a switch to direct mail via newspaper advertisements, the business took off. A new sales manager was appointed but his renewed attempt to sell the barrow through more traditional retail channels was again a failure. The financial penalty was the need for external investors, who later persuaded Dyson's brother-in-law to sell the business. A second painful experience came when the sales manager took the idea and design to the US, where Dyson later failed with a legal action against him.

Dyson's idea for a dual cyclone household cleaner came in 1979, when he was 31 years old. Again, it was a case of a need creating an opportunity. He was converting his old house and becoming frustrated that his vacuum cleaner would not clear all of the dust that he was creating. Particles were clogging the pores of the dust bags and reducing the suction capability of the cleaner. Needing something to collect paint particles from his plastic spraying operation for the ballbarrows, Dyson had developed a smaller version of the large industrial cyclone machines, which separate particles from air by using centrifugal forces in spinning cylinders. He believed that this technology could be adapted for home vacuum cleaners, removing the need for bags, but his partners in the Ballbarrow business failed to share his enthusiasm. Out of work when the business was sold, his previous employer, Jeremy Fry (for whom he had developed the Sea Truck), loaned him £25,000. Dyson matched this by selling his vegetable garden for £18,000 and taking out an additional £7000 overdraft on his house. Working from home, risking everything and drawing just £10,000 a year to keep himself, his wife and three children, he pursued his idea. Over the years he produced 5127 different prototypes.

When he ultimately approached the established manufacturers his idea was, perhaps predictably, rejected. Replacement dust bags are an important source of additional revenue. A series of discussions with potential partners who might license his idea brought mixed results. Fresh legal actions in the US for patent infringement – 'with hindsight I didn't patent enough features' – were only partially offset by a deal with Apex of Japan. Dyson designed the G-Force upright cleaner which Apex manufactured and sold to a niche in the Japanese market for the equivalent of £1200 per machine, from which Dyson received just £20. At least there was now an income stream, but this had taken seven years to achieve. Finally, in 1991 Lloyds Bank provided finance for the design and manufacture of a machine in the UK. Several venture capitalists and the Welsh Development Agency had turned him down. Dyson was determined to give his latest version the looks of NASA technology, but further setbacks were still to occur. Dyson was let down by the plastic moulder and assembler with whom he contracted, and was eventually forced to set up his own plant. Early sales through mail-order catalogues were followed by deals with John Lewis and eventually (in 1995) with Comet and Curry's. In this year a cylinder version joined the upright. Dyson continues to improve the designs to extend his patent protection. By 1999 his personal wealth was estimated to be £500 million.

Dyson has always seen himself as more of an inventor than a businessman. He established two separate businesses, both in Malmesbury, Wiltshire, and he kept Dyson Manufacturing and Dyson Research (design and patenting) apart. The dress code for employees is perpetually informal and communications are predominantly face-to-face. Memos are banned and even e-mails discouraged. Every employee is encouraged to be creative and contribute ideas. Most new employees are young – 'not contaminated by other employers' – and they all begin by assembling their own vacuum cleaner, which they can then buy for £20. There are over 60 designers, who work on improvements to the dual cyclone cleaners as well as new product ideas. In July 2001 Dyson unveiled the world's first robotic vacuum cleaner, DC06: 18 months of home trials provided invaluable information for Dyson to develop the concept further. Dyson is currently working on a new robot that incorporates improved DC06 technology and Root™ Cyclone cleaning power to deliver a truly autonomous alternative to manual vacuuming. Late in 2000 Dyson launched the two-drums washing machine – Dyson engineers noticed that 15 minutes of handwashing produced cleaner clothes than 67 minutes in the best washing machine. This discovery led onto the patented two-drums technology. Dyson two-drums has a unique wash action with two aligned drums that rotate in opposite directions (replicating that of a hand wash). The two-drums allergy washing machine is also the only washing machine to have the British Allergy Foundation Seal of Approval. This time, however, Dyson had his own resources to launch the product. Moreover Dyson controls 100 per cent of the shares in the business. He has learnt some painful lessons but is now enjoying the rewards of his dogged determination.

However, in recent years Dyson has transferred the majority of his manufacturing to lower cost plants in Malaysia. Perhaps inevitably this was opposed by the UK workforce and it has brought him adverse publicity.

**Questions**

1. Thinking about the issues of core competency and strategic capability, what is the 'secret' of James Dyson's competitive advantage?

2. Has he been able to appropriate the rewards of the value he has added?

**Dyson**: http://www.dyson.com

**James Dyson**

*People feel the best about their work when they do a high-quality job! Getting a job done quickly is satisfying. Getting a job done at low cost is rewarding. But getting a job done quickly, at low cost and with high quality is exciting!*

Robert C Stempel, when Chairman, General Motors Corporation

## 5.1  Auditing strategic resources

Chapter 4 looked at organizations in the context of their environments, somewhat artificially separating their general and competitive environments. Environments spring surprises on organizations from time to time. Sometimes the surprises constitute opportunities; at other times, threats. The most vigilant and aware organizations will be better placed to respond. Success lies in seeing opportunities 'ahead of the game' and responding in some individual way, ideally one that is genuinely different, appreciated by customers and not easily copied by rivals. The ability to do this comes down to individual, specific to the organization competencies and capabilities, which in turn emanate from the organization's resources. Resources, therefore, make the difference. In this chapter this argument is explored in greater depth and frameworks are provided which can help us to audit and evaluate strategic resources.

It does not follow that every resource an organization possesses is strategically significant. Sometimes it is tempting to list every positive resource as a strength, but this may be illusory. When we evaluate the resources of an organization in terms of their strategic significance, five factors matter:

1. Competitive superiority. The relative value when compared to rival organizations. A resource is not really a competitive strength if it is possessed by every competitor.
2. Barriers to replication. It is useful if rivals can be stopped from imitating or replicating any valuable resources.
3. Durability. Basically a time advantage relating to 1 and 2.
4. Substitutability. Can competitors neutralize the value of a resource by substituting an alternative?
5. Appropriability. Kay (1993) contends that it is essential that the organization possessing the resource benefits from it, rather than the real benefit accruing to someone else, such as a supplier or distributor.

The relationship between environmental forces and internal resources is at the heart of Figure 5.1, which has been adapted from the Harvard Business School approach to strategy (Kelly and Kelly, 1987). Here, selected products, services and markets are seen as environment driven and the competitive environment and stakeholders are shown with resources and values as four key strategic elements linked to corporate objectives. These elements can be changed, but in many cases not readily and not quickly, and consequently at any point in time they are reasonably fixed.

Six operating elements are also incorporated. *Marketing* relates to how the various products and services are positioned in relation to competitors, and how they are priced, advertised and distributed. *Manufacturing* involves the types of production process, location issues and technology utilization. *Finance* incorporates both performance targets

**Figure 5.1** Matching the organization and the environment

Adapted from Kelly, FJ and Kelly, HM (1987) *What They Really Teach You at the Harvard Business School*. Piatkus

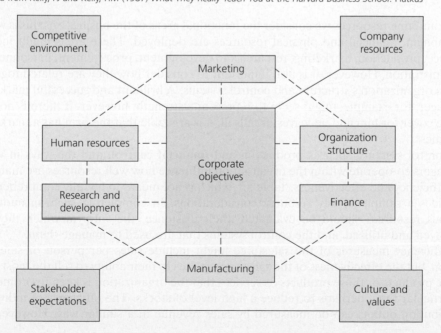

and sources of funding. *Research and development* considers how much to spend on research and development and whether the perspective is short or long term. *Human resources* relates to the types of people utilized and how they are rewarded. The *organization structure* encompasses how these functions are co-ordinated and controlled.

These operating elements determine whether or not the corporate objectives are achieved. The different functions in the organization are affected to varying degrees by different stakeholders, and certain stakeholders who have a significant impact on certain functions may have little direct importance for others. Equally, the specific stakeholders may influence individual functions in quite different ways. Their impact upon the whole organization is therefore affected by the organization structure and relative power and influence within the firm. The figure also highlights the strategic value of functional managers taking a more holistic view of the organization and their role and contribution.

How, then, might we audit and evaluate these operating elements or strategic resources?

An internal analysis should be a three-stage process:

1. an evaluation of the profile of the principal skills and resources of an organization
2. a comparison of this resource base with the requirements for competitive success in the industry
3. a comparison with competitors to determine the relative strengths and weaknesses and any significant comparative advantage.

Where internal managers carry out this analysis, it is inevitable that there will be some subjective judgement and it will be affected by their position in the organization.

In a SWOT (strengths, weaknesses, opportunities and threats) analysis, then, the strengths and weaknesses of resources must be considered in relative and not absolute terms. It is important to consider whether they are being managed effectively as well as efficiently. Resources, therefore, are not strong or weak purely because they exist or do not exist. Rather, their value depends on how they are being managed, controlled and used.

In auditing resources we consider the functional areas of the business, as this is where the human, financial and physical resources are deployed. These areas might include finance, production, marketing, research and development, procurement, personnel and administration. However, it is also important to consider how they are related together in the organization's structure and control systems. A brilliant and successful marketing manager, for example, might seem to represent a strength; however, if there is no adequate cover for him and he leaves or falls ill, it is arguable that the firm has a marketing weakness.

Control systems, such as production and **financial control**, and the ways in which managers co-operate within the organization influence how well resources are managed for efficiency and effectiveness. Table 5.1, which is not meant to be fully comprehensive, provides a sample of key resource considerations. In completing such an audit the various resources should be evaluated: their existence, the ways in which they are deployed and utilized, and the control systems that are used to manage them.

Efficiency measures of the salesforce might include sales per person or sales per region, but the effectiveness of the salesforce relates to their ability to sell the most profitable products or those products or services that the organization is keen to promote at a particular time, perhaps to reduce a high level of stocks. The efficiency of individual distribution outlets can be measured by sales revenue in a similar way. However, the

**Table 5.1** Aspects of the resource audit

| Resource/function | Key considerations |
|---|---|
| Marketing | Products and services: range, brand names and stage in life cycle |
| | Patents |
| | Strength of sales force |
| | Distribution channels |
| | Market information |
| Operations | Location and plant |
| | Capital equipment |
| | Capacity |
| | Processes |
| | Planning and manufacturing systems |
| | Quality control |
| | Supplies |
| Research and development | Annual budget |
| | Technology support |
| | Quality of researchers |
| | Record of success and reputation |
| | Spending in relation to industry norm |
| Information | Organizational knowledge and extent of sharing |
| | Information systems |
| | Problem-solving capabilities and procedures |
| Finance | Capital structure |
| | Working capital |
| | Cash flow |
| | Costing systems and variances |
| | Nature of shareholders |
| | Relations with bankers |
| Human resources | Numbers and qualifications |
| | Skills and experience |
| | Age profile |
| | Labour turnover and absenteeism |
| | Flexibility |
| | Development and training record and policies |
| | Motivation and culture |
| | Managerial competencies and capacity |

effectiveness of the distribution activity relates to exactly which products are being sold and to whom, whether they are available where customers expect them, and how much investment in stock is required to maintain the outlets. The efficiency of plant and equipment is linked to percentage utilization. The effectiveness involves an assessment of which products are being manufactured in relation to orders and delivery requirements, to what quality and with what rejection levels.

It is also important to assess the relative strengths and weaknesses in relation to competition.

Managers must be aware of and must address strategic issues if the resources are to be used for creating and sustaining competitive advantage. *Marketing* can be looked at from the point of view of managing the activities which comprise the marketing function. Product design and pricing, advertising, selling and distribution would be included here. However, if an organization is marketing orientated there is an implication that employees throughout the organization are aware of consumers and customers, their needs, and how they might be satisfied effectively while enabling the organization to achieve its objectives. Consumer concern becomes part of the culture and values. Consumers and customers are mentioned separately because for many organizations, particularly the manufacturers of products for consumer markets, their customers are distributors and their ultimate consumers are customers of the retailers that they supply.

Innovation and quality can be seen as aspects of production or *operations management*. Again, it is helpful if these factors become part of the culture. An innovatory organization is ready for change, and looking to make positive changes, in order to get ahead and stay ahead of competition. A concern for quality in all activities will affect both costs and consumer satisfaction.

In *human resources management* values are communicated and spread throughout the organization.

*Financial management* includes the control of costs so that profit is achieved and value is added to products and services primarily in areas that matter to consumers. This should provide differentiation and competitive advantage.

Lower costs and differentiation are important themes in competitive strategy. They relate to both an awareness of consumer needs and the management of resources to satisfy these needs effectively and, where relevant, profitably. Marketing orientation and the effective management of production and operations, people and finance are all essential aspects of the creation and maintenance of competitive strength and advantage.

Functional and competitive strategies are important for an understanding of strategic management in all types of organization, and they are especially important for a large proportion of small businesses and many not-for-profit organizations. Corporate strategic changes such as major diversification and acquisition, divestment of business units which are underperforming or international expansion may not be relevant for small firms with a limited range of products or services and a primarily local market, or for not-for-profit organizations with very specific missions. However, these organizations must compete effectively, operate efficiently and provide their customers and clients with products and services that satisfy their needs. Competitive and functional strategies are therefore the relevant issue.

As the Internet becomes more pervasive in our lives some organizations and industries are being presented with wonderful opportunities and, at the same time, real threats. Book retailing has changed with the growth of Amazon.com and the opening of online bookshops by the leading book retailers. Similarly, domestic banking has been changed with the growth of ATMs (automated teller machines or 'holes in the wall'), telephone call centres and Internet accounts. Competitors have had to develop new skills, competencies and capabilities in order to survive, let alone thrive. The challenge, though, did not stop here. It has also been necessary to clarify the key success factors for those customers who opted to avoid the Internet and stick with a personal service. What exactly are their needs and preferences? How can they be satisfied 'wonderfully well'? How can costs be trimmed in the process?

Success, then, depends upon understanding and linking with customers, and these points are explored further through the remainder of this chapter.

### 5.1.1 Kay's framework

Kay (1993) proposed a three-strand framework for evaluating or auditing strategic resources. He proposed the following factors:

- Architecture – internal and external relationships and links
- Reputation – the value and power of the organization's reputation, including branding
- Innovation – continually improving everything the organization does – products, services and processes – partially in response to competition and partially to drive competitiveness in the industry.

We look at both architecture and reputation in this chapter. Innovation is discussed in Chapter 10 when we look at strategic leadership, entrepreneurship and intrapreneurship, but evidence of it can be seen in the Levi's case later in this chapter and the Schick v Gillette case in Chapter 6 – Minicase 6.4.

## 5.2  Strategic architecture

Kay (1993) adopted the word 'architecture' to emphasize the importance of corporate networks and relationships. He argued that companies depend upon their people for their competitiveness and success, but strong and capable individuals, while important, are not enough. They must work together well and synergistically. Football clubs, and their need for skilled individuals to be moulded into a strong, winning team, provide a valuable metaphor. In addition, people's natural energies should not be focused on internal rivalries but on managing external demands. Success here can be enhanced through effective links between an organization, its suppliers, its distributors and its ultimate customers.

In summary, we should consider:

- The way managers and other employees co-operate within the organization. Communications and co-operation should work both horizontally and vertically. Transfer pricing arrangements and poorly crafted internal performance measures can all too easily set division against division and department against department, and create real internal competition for resources. Where managers find delight when another manager, department or division finds itself in trouble, something is wrong. But it still happens. Similarly, in some organizations, there is a reliance on top-down communications for issuing instructions coupled with an ability for managers lower down the organization to feed only good news upwards and suppress bad news. The valuable ideas that some junior and middle managers have are, consequently, neither sought nor listened to by their superiors. Kay calls this 'internal architecture'.
- Suppliers, organizations, distributors and final customers and consumers working together supportively in a 'seamless' chain which builds and provides value for all the participants, or 'external architecture'. Members of this value chain can make life either relatively easy or problematic for the other members, depending on their philosophy. The ideal outcome is one where everyone feels they are gaining some benefit rather than they are being exploited by someone who is ruthless or selfish. It is a feeling of 'win–win' rather than 'I win, you lose' or 'you win at my

**Figure 5.2** Effective supply chain management

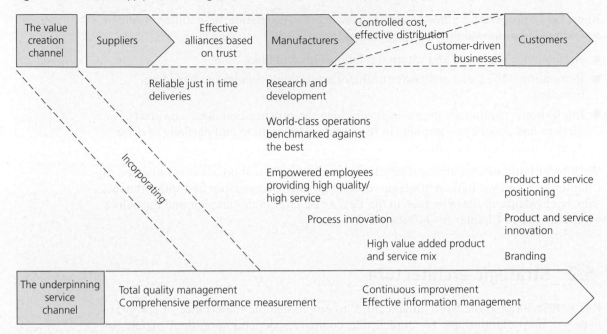

expense', which happens in many negotiations and deals. Sometimes the members of such a value chain will establish formalized partnerships or alliances to seal the relationship more firmly.

The outcome should be shared knowledge, co-operation and the development of trust and trusted routines, as illustrated in Figure 5.2 and Minicase 5.2 on Benetton. All parties should feel that they could rely on each other.

*The driving force in all the world's markets is competition. And the most aggressive drivers are the Japanese. Their competitive strength and ambitions are apparent around the world. Ultimately the only way to succeed is to be fully competitive in the marketplace. Fundamentally this means offering products with utility, style and value that the buyers want, making them with world-class productivity and quality, and serving the customers better than anyone else.*

John F Smith Jr, when Vice Chairman (International Operations), General Motors Corporation

A number of useful examples highlight the benefit of strong strategic architecture:

■ For many years Japanese organizations have benefited from membership of corporate families or *keiretsu*. Businesses, typically those clustered together in a geographical area, will all own shares in each other. Their directors will hold part-time directorships in other organizations in the *keiretsu*. The whole philosophy will be one of helping each other with either preferred supplier arrangements or the provision of help and advice. It will be realized how a base like this can foster benchmarking and the exchange of ideas and good practice, and the ability to exploit just in time supply arrangement. Here, manufacturers can avoid inventory costs by relying on their suppliers to deliver the quantities they need exactly when they are required for production.

## Minicase 5.2 Benetton

Eur Int

Benetton was founded in Italy in 1965 by a brother and sister to distribute home-made sweaters to retailers. Luciano Benetton had wholesaling experience, and his sister, Guiliana, design skills. Two other brothers joined later. The first Benetton store was opened in 1968. By 1978 there were 1000, and by 1988 over 5000 franchised outlets worldwide. After 1978 more and more manufacturing was subcontracted. Benetton has also diversified into related goods such as shirts, jeans, gloves, shoes and perfume. The business is still run from a headquarters in Italy.

Europe is seen as the home market, with production and marketing in both the West and East. However, Benetton is well established in the US and Canada, and growing in Japan and the Pacific Rim.

In 1972 Benetton started dyeing assembled garments rather than just the yarn; and this has enabled it to develop competitive advantage through a speedier response to fashion changes. If an item is selling unexpectedly well in one particular shop, and additional stocks are wanted, Benetton aims to provide the additional stocks more quickly than its competitors could. Requests are relayed through terminals to Benetton's mainframe computer, which also carries comprehensive product details and production requirements – the benefit of using computer-aided design and manufacture (CAD and CAM) extensively. Production requirements can therefore be fed quickly into the manufacturing system, even though a lot of work is subcontracted. Finished products are stored in one central warehouse, run by robots and just a handful of people. A quarter of a million items can be handled daily. Benetton aims to replenish its shops with popular items in one week ex-stock, four weeks including production. Production costs are increased by dyeing finished goods, but stock management overall (raw materials, semi-finished and finished items) is efficient.

*Much has changed in the world since Benetton was started in 1965, but not our mission: to satisfy people's needs with young, colourful, comfortable and easy-to-wear*

*products. This has been our route to world leadership in the design, production and distribution of clothing, accessories and footwear for men, women and children. Our range has been constantly enriched over time by intensive research into new materials and designs – and further additions will follow.*

Benetton is an international company with a global brand image, which has been built around the theme 'The United Colors of Benetton'. This international image is boosted by a strong association with motor racing. Benetton won both the Formula One drivers' and constructors' championships in 1995.

*Colour makes Benetton unique. The secret lies in presenting a broad spectrum of shades, creatively mixed and matched – new and different every time. The study of colour is our greatest research commitment as we constantly seek out new tones.*

Advertising features the same central message and choice of media throughout the world, although the actual themes of the advertisements vary. On occasions, some examples have proved controversial in certain countries. Benetton's approach is based on the premise that customers in different countries use clothing and accessories to express personal lifestyle preferences, with a tendency to demand increasingly higher quality goods. Advertising campaigns 'feature simplified, unambiguous images that convey meaning to the largest possible number of people and cultures throughout the world'.

### Competencies and capabilities

Benetton provides a range of popular and attractive garments and achieves some 20 per cent production cost savings compared with its main competitors. Its franchised retailers offer a high level of customer service with responsive and helpful employees. There is some local customization but, in the main, the same colourful, fashionable and classic garments are available worldwide.

▶

To achieve these outcomes, Benetton exploits a number of important competencies and capabilities:

- Dyeing skills are retained in-house.
- The basic grey colour lends itself readily to later colour changes.
- For many years Guiliana Benetton has controlled the design activities, which have again been retained in-house.
- Benetton retains classic designs and saves costs by avoiding too much variety.
- Eighty per cent of manufacturing is undertaken by independent suppliers.
- There are strong contractual arrangements with key suppliers around the world, some of whom work exclusively for Benetton.
- Benetton dictate tight technical specification for their supplies.
- Sophisticated IT systems are utilized in both design and manufacture.
- Most suppliers are small businesses, and in many instances Benetton loans money to finance them.
- Benetton's success is frequently seen by their suppliers as their own success, a relationship issue which clearly works in Benetton's favour.
- Periodically Benetton 'releases' suppliers, which keeps the rest on their toes.
- Purchasing is centralized and in bulk.
- A small army of agents oversees the franchised retailers and controls the company's image.
- Retailers are contracted to stock only Benetton's own brand products, although they have some local autonomy on ranges and colours.

- Benetton strictly controls the design, layout, ambience and prices in every store.
- Sophisticated IT systems link retailers with Benetton and in turn its suppliers to provide a fast response to demand patterns without unnecessary stockholding.
- Standard worldwide advertising features 'The United Colors of Benetton'.
- The company carefully sponsors events such as Formula One which have a young and smart image.

All quotations extracted from Benetton Annual Reports

## Questions

1. What is Benetton's competitive strategy?
2. How does it achieve competitive advantage?
3. How does Benetton use networks and partnerships to great effect?
4. In what ways would it be difficult for competitors to try and copy the success?

**Benetton** http://www.benetton.com

**Benetton advertising** campaigns have on occasions been met with controversy Photo: David Sims

- For many years Marks and Spencer was credited with having a valuable portfolio of key suppliers, many of them British, who were committed to it. Typically, M&S would take a substantial proportion of a supplier's annual output and would work with it on designs and quality. M&S knew that it was buying reliable, quality products; the suppliers knew they were working with one of the UK's strongest retailers. Customers were equally satisfied. M&S standards and expectations were exacting, but the mutual rewards were high and shared. Towards the end of the 1990s, as M&S was accused of having 'tired' ranges and manufacturing costs in Britain for many clothing and food products seemed relatively expensive, some of these arrangements broke down. One clothing supplier, William Baird, sued M&S for alleged breach of contract.

- The legendary Silicon Valley, heart of the American, and arguably the global, computer and semiconductor industries, has long benefited from networks and alliances. Companies spin-off from each other, sometimes as rivals, but more often to develop new products or to supply each other. In the early days of the industry young entrepreneurs readily shared their ideas and knowledge. As a result, Silicon Valley as a whole became an opportunity which attracted people with ideas and ambition.

Sometimes the value and constituency of these networks and partnerships can be hard to quantify or even explain. They owe a lot to people and to their history. They are relationships which emerge and strengthen over many years and are dependent upon personal relations and interactions. This often serves to make them even more powerful as they are automatically difficult to replicate. Consequently, architecture can be a vital element of competitive advantage.

As more and more organizations opt to focus on core strengths, activities and competencies, and divest those that are peripheral, the significance of architecture is reinforced and increased. When companies outsource important services such as information technology (IT) or payroll management, or choose to buy in key components they once made for themselves, they need to be able to rely upon, and trust, their new suppliers. Managing relationships, therefore, becomes an important new capability.

Some organizations, of course, have chosen to **outsource** their manufacturing. Dyson (Minicase 5.1) has switched its manufacturing to Malaysia to reduce costs. Royal Doulton (china) now focuses on design and marketing and outsources production from Indonesia. Dr Martens boots and shoes are made in China. Hornby, manufacturer of model electric trains and Scalextrix car racing systems, also manufactures in China. However, this move was not directed at reducing costs, per se. Hornby found it could devote two labour hours for every one used in the UK and thus produce models with much higher quality and detail at the same total cost. Without changing its prices, Hornby has seen its sales grow rapidly because of the greater authenticity. At the same time the company has been innovatory with new products. For example, both Eurostar and the Hogwarts Express from the Harry Potter stories provided new sales opportunities.

Buckingham and Coffman (1999) also draw attention to the importance of architecture in their delineation of four levels of customer service. Level 1 is accuracy and level 2, availability. These, they argue, have to be seen as the relatively easy levels, and are generally taken for granted. In other words, without them, a company cannot hope to win repeated business. Levels 3 and 4 are working partnerships and the provision of advice and support. These relate to strategic architecture.

Porter also made a contribution to strategic architecture by providing a value chain framework for helping to identify valuable differences and manage cost drivers. This is looked at in the Value Chain section later in the chapter.

Before we look in depth at the value chain, however, we next consider two critically important strategic resources: people and information. We are concentrating on these as they are key drivers of change as well as being crucially important in the implementation of chosen strategies.

# 5.3 Human resource strategies

### 5.3.1 The 'people contribution'

Successful organizations meet the needs and expectations of their customers more effectively than their competitors; at the same time, they generate acceptable financial returns. Achieving these outcomes requires competent and committed people. People, then, are critically important strategic resources. Successful companies will be able to attract, motivate, develop, reward and keep skilled and competent managers and other employees. They will be able to create and implement strategic changes in a supportive culture. People need to be used and stretched to get the best out of them but, correspondingly, they need to be looked after and rewarded. However, even successful companies have lean periods, and when these occur, they will again be able to retain their most important people. There is no one best way of achieving this.

Everything that an organization does, in the end, depends on people. Although technology and IT can make a major strategic impact, it is people who exploit their potential. Managers and employees are needed to implement strategies and to this end they must understand and share the values of the organization. They must be committed to the organization and they must work together well. At the same time, where an organization is decentralized and operating in a turbulent environment, the strategic leader will rely on people to spot opportunities and threats, to adapt and create new strategies.

Consequently, it is people who ultimately determine whether or not competitive advantage is created and sustained. Adding new values with innovation, they can be an opportunity and a source of competitive advantage; equally, unenthusiastic, uncommitted, untrained employees can act as a constraint. People's capabilities are infinite and resourceful in the appropriate organizational climate. The basic test of their value concerns how much they – and their contribution – would be missed if they left or, possibly worse, left and joined a competitor. They could take customers with them and not be easily replaced.

Achieving the highest level of outcomes that people are capable of producing will therefore depend upon the human resource practices adopted by the organization. While the issues are clear and straightforward – they involve selection, training, rewards and work organization – there is no single best approach to the challenge. A relatively formal, 'hard' approach can prove very successful in certain circumstances; other organizations will derive significant benefits from a 'softer', more empowered style. One issue here is whether the business is being driven by a small number of identifiable, key decision-makers or by the employees collectively.

Minicase 5.3 tells the remarkable story of Ricardo Semler, who took over the family engineering business in Brazil and transformed its fortunes by releasing the abilities and energies of its people. It is worth considering whether either of the market-driven (the E in E–V–R Congruence) and resource-based (R) views of strategy truly explain what has happened as Semco. Arguably the real driving force behind the changes has been values. Semler, in effect, deregulated Semco, allowing people the freedom to choose how they would work. Certain policies regarding competitiveness guided appropriate behaviour.

To bring out the best in people, they have to be managed well, and this requires leadership. A useful metaphor is that of an orchestra. Every member (manager/employee) is a specialist, with some making a unique contribution which, on occasions, can take the form of a solo performance. Nevertheless, all the contributions must be synthesized to create harmony (synergy), which is the role of the conductor (strategic leader). A single musician (weak link) can destroy a performance; a chain is only as strong as its weakest link.

A successful organization, therefore, needs people with appropriate skills and competencies who can work together effectively. People must be:

■ committed (commitment can be improved)

## Minicase 5.3  Ricardo Semler and Semco    SA

Ricardo Semler was just 21 years old when he took over as chief executive of his family's business, Semco. This Brazilian company manufactured pumps, food mixers, meat-slicing equipment and dishwashers. Brazil is a country characterized by high inflation and a massive relative wealth gap between the rich and the poor. His father believed that if he handed over the reins when Ricardo was still young, 'he could make his mistakes while he was still around to fix them!' His father had run the business along traditional and autocratic lines; Ricardo was to change everything, and the company has thrived and prospered.

Although he has an MBA from Harvard, Ricardo Semler's stated business philosophy is: 'follow your intuition'. He inherited a company where 'people did not want to come to work and managers watched everything and everybody constantly, trusting nobody', and transformed it into one which is 'ultimately democratic' and based on 'freedom, respect, trust and commitment'. Things did not happen instantaneously; many new approaches and experimental methods were tried and abandoned. However, in a ten-year period from the mid-1980s Semco achieved 900 per cent growth.

There is no reception area, no secretaries and no offices. Managers walk around constantly to provide help and assistance when it is requested; the workers organize their own flexible working time arrangements. Employees work in small clusters, and they can also rearrange their working space and environment as they wish. Semco has come to believe that clusters of no more than ten are required if this approach is to work effectively. Twelve layers of a management and supervisory hierarchy have been reduced to three. The appointment of any manager has to be approved by the workforce, and managers are subjected to regular assessment by their subordinates and shopfloor employees. People talk openly and 'when someone says they'll do something, they do it'. Consequently, managers also feel that they can spend time away from the plant, with customers and suppliers.

Profit sharing is by consultation and negotiation – 23 per cent of after-tax profits is available for the workforce – and all employees are trained to ensure that they can read the company accounts. There is no longer a formal chief executive post for Ricardo, who is now President. Instead, there is an informal board of six associates (the most senior managers) who elect a nominal chief executive for a six-month period. Ricardo sometimes attends their meetings as an adviser.

Ricardo has recently taken his ideas further, encouraging employees to consider starting up satellite supply companies and subcontracting for Semco. Those who have opted for this entrepreneurial route have been allowed to take Semco machines with them, leasing them on favourable terms. One advantage for Semco is the fact that it is no longer responsible for the maintenance and safety of the equipment. In addition, there is an opportunity for the machinery to be used more effectively as the satellite companies are free to work for other organizations; their efficiency gains can be passed through in the form of lower prices.

▶

If the venture fails, Semco takes back the equipment and the people. It is a relatively low and managed risk for all concerned.

Ricardo Semler has not been a man who has hidden his achievements! He has written the story of his role at Semco with the title *Maverick*. Like Julian Richer of Richer Sounds in the UK, he helps other companies as a consultant and he has become a recognized member of the management guru circuit around the world. He has also campaigned against corruption in Brazil, and he has exposed government officials who have been demanding bribes for domestic planning permission. As a result, he has generated hostility from certain prominent people in his country.

'Successful companies will be the ones that put quality of life first. Do this and the rest – quality of product, productivity of workers, profits for all – will follow.'

## Questions

1. Is Ricardo Semler really a 'maverick'?

2. Have these changes been sustainable?

3. Has Semco become even more 'maverick' or has it mellowed?

http://www.thunderbird.edu/pdf/
about_us/case_series/a15980024.pdf

## Sources

Semler, R (1993) *Maverick*, Century
Semler, R (2003) *The Seven Day Weekend*, Century

**Ricardo Semler** © James Leynse/Corbis

---

## Box 5.1 Empowerment

Empowerment means freeing employees from instructions and controls and allowing them to take decisions themselves. Total quality management implies constant improvement; to achieve this employees should be contributing to the best of their ability. Proponents argue that rules stifle innovation and that future success relies not on past results but on the continuing ability to manage change pressures. Managers must be free to make appropriate changes in a decentralized structure.

There are three main objectives of empowerment:

- to make organizations more responsive to external pressures

- to 'de-layer' organizations in order to make them more cost effective. British Airways, for example, now has five layers of management between the chief executive and the front line

who interface with customers. It used to be nine. Managers become responsible for more employees, who they are expected to coach and support rather than direct

- to create employee networks featuring teamworking, collaboration and horizontal communications. This implies changes in the ways in which decisions are made.

The important questions are why, how and when. The leading retailers, for example, benefited from increasing centralization throughout the 1980s. Information technology enabled cost savings and efficiencies from centrally controlled buying, store and shelf layouts, stocking policies and reordering. In the 1990s there was little support for changing this in any marked way and delegating these decisions to store level. In its early years, Waterstone's delegated book-buying responsibility to individual store managers, and this was regarded as exceptional. Once the company was acquired by WH Smith this decentralization was systematically removed. At the same time individual stores are judged in part on the quality of service provided to their customers; and it is in this area that there has always been considerable scope for empowering managers. However, in 2000, in an attempt to win back market share, Marks and Spencer has begun to decentralize purchasing and stock decisions and give store managers more opportunity to ensure that they stock ranges which best match local needs.

After C&A announced it was closing all its stores it allowed individual store managers the freedom to stock and sell what they thought was appropriate locally. Both sales and profits improved!

As empowerment is increased it is important that employees are adequately informed and knowledgeable, that they are motivated to exercise power, and that they are rewarded for successful outcomes. In flatter organization structures there are fewer opportunities for promotion.

There are, then, three basic empowerment options:

■ Employees can be encouraged to contribute ideas. As seen in Minicase 1.4, several new product ideas for McDonald's have come from individual franchisees. In reality, however, this may represent only token empowerment.

■ Employees work in teams which share and manage their own work, but within clearly defined policies and limits. This should increase both efficiency and job satisfaction.

■ More extensive decentralization means that individuals are much freer to change certain parameters and strategies. Evaluating outcomes is seen as the important control mechanism rather than rules and guidelines. An important distinction here is between making people accountable for their individual actions and making them accountable for the overall result. Constructive accountability gives people freedom to make decisions and demands that they accept responsibility for the consequences. This requires strong

leadership, a clear mission and effective communications, rewards and sanctions. Information must flow openly upwards and sideways as well as downwards. In many organizations there is a tendency for bad news to be selectively hidden, with perhaps two-thirds not flowing up to the next layer. Many potential threats are thereby not shared within the company. This would be unacceptable in an empowered organization.

For many organizations empowerment implies that the core organization strategies are decided centrally, with individual managers delegated a discretionary layer around the core (as shown below).

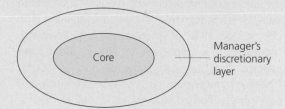

It is crucial first to find the right balance between the core and discretionary elements, and second to ensure that managers support and own the core strategy.

The deciding factors are:

■ The competitive strategies and the relative importance of close linkages with customers in order to differentiate and provide high levels of service. When this becomes essential empowerment may imply an inverted pyramid structure. The structure exists to support front-line managers, as shown below.

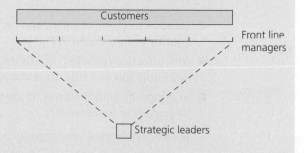

- Successful empowerment means putting the 'right' people in place and ensuring that they are able to do their job, which they understand and own. In this way they feel important.

- The extent to which the environment is turbulent and decisions are varied rather than routine.

- The expectations and preferences of managers and employees, and their ability and willingness to accept responsibility. Not everyone wants accountability and high visibility. If empowerment is mishandled it is possible that work will be simply pushed down a shorter hierarchy as managers seek to avoid responsibility.

Successful empowerment requires appropriate skills, which in turn frequently implies training. The appropriate style of management is coaching. Moreover, it is important to link in monitoring systems together with rewards and sanctions. Finally, empowerment must be taken seriously and not simply limited to non-essential decisions. Empowerment implies risk-taking, and any mistakes, while not overlooked, must be handled carefully.

*Empowerment is a powerful motivator as long as it does not suddenly stop when the really important and interesting decisions have to be taken.*

Jeremy Soper, ex Retail Sales Director, WH Smith

## Wal-Mart's strategies for empowering people

- Every project has a clear end-date.

- Everybody must experience success. Success can be built on success and people must never become complacent. People are therefore moved from clearly successful to less successful activities, so they can experience elements of both success and relative failure. In this way, 'winners' help others improve their standards and confidence; and people who are experiencing disappointment are moved into positions where morale is much higher. Linked to this,

- There is a no-blame culture and no victims.

- By moving around, people also become more multiskilled and thereby grow personally.

- People are encouraged to become involved in several, small, improvemental projects – many of them driven by ideas from customers.

- New ideas are tried out locally before being rolled-out more extensively.

- People are required to 'think, react and break down barriers'.

- There is a philosophy that: *Track record + Empathy = Credibility*. Empathy develops as people 'get out', network and meet people so they can better understand their needs. It is credibility that 'gets things done'.

- To get ahead and stay ahead, speed is 'everything'.

### Source for Wal-Mart material

Turner, K (1999) *The Wal-Mart Experience*, Presentation to a Retail Solutions International Conference, May.

Wal-Mart http://www.walmart.com

- competent (competencies can be developed, and can bring improved product quality and productivity)
- cost-effective (ideally costs should be low and performance high, although this does not imply low rewards for success)
- in sympathy with the aims of the organization (are the values and expectations of all parties in agreement?)

*Where people grow, profits grow.*

Dr Alex Krauer, when Chairman and Managing Director, Ciba-Geigy

## 5.3.2 Involving and empowering people

There are two recognized approaches to human resource management: the 'hard' approach and the 'soft' approach. The key tension or dilemma that is being addressed is the balance between centralization for control and decentralization for greater empowerment. The two approaches imply contrasting styles, but they can both be appropriate in certain circumstances. Moreover, companies can be hard on certain aspects and soft on others. In addition, the style may alter with the strategic demands placed on an organization. When times are difficult and a company must rationalize and downsize, a hard approach may prove to be appropriate for driving through the changes quickly. However, a softer, more empowered style may be required to rejuvenate the company and bring new sources of competitive advantage.

Hard human resource management assumes that:

- people are viewed as a resource and, like all resources, companies gain competitive advantage by using them efficiently and effectively
- the deployment and development of employees – who are essentially there to implement corporate and competitive strategies – is delegated to line managers who are responsible for groups of people
- scientific management principles and systems can be useful but should be used cautiously.

Soft human resource management assumes that:

- workers are most productive if they are committed to the company, informed about its mission, strategies and current levels of success, and
- involved in teams which collectively decide how things are to be done
- employees have to be trusted to take the right decisions rather than controlled at every stage by managers above them.

Soft human resource management argues that people are different from other resources (and often more costly) but they can create added value and **sustainable competitive advantage** from the other resources. Therefore, soft human resource management places greater emphasis on control through review and evaluation of outcomes, such that employees are led rather than managed.

*Empowerment* is explored more fully in Box 5.1, which also describes the Wal-Mart approach. United Airlines in the US provides another but quite different example. In 1994, the employees of United Airlines, the largest airline in the world, agreed to accept paycuts in exchange for majority control of the company, which was experiencing financial difficulties. As an outcome, decision-making was decentralized more. One example was the bringing together of 350 pilots, flight attendants, mechanics and other employees to plan the development of a new, low-cost, short-haul shuttle service on the west coast. United had to achieve very high service levels and low prices to compete with Southwest Airlines. The new venture was established reportedly 'without a single flaw'. However successful these changes may have been, they did not prevent United Airlines from going into financial administration when revenues and profits suffered after 9/11, when reduced passenger numbers on many routes led to overcapacity in the industry.

In an instance such as this, people who normally deal with problems and 'firefight', with a tactical perspective, are being encouraged to think more operationally and strategically in order to design a new service and the necessary systems whereby, ideally, many of the problems with which they are familiar are eliminated at the design stage.

Many organizations, however, still prefer more rigid controls from the centre, even though they may have reduced the number of layers in the organizational hierarchy and widened managers' spans of control. This, they believe, is the way to achieve efficiency and managed costs. Tighter systems inevitably constrain innovation and employee development; but, they assume, new ideas and people can be bought in or recruited.

### 5.3.3 Manager competency

Simply, some companies will seek to develop their employees and managers, invariably promoting from within. A strong culture and vision should foster both commitment and continuous, emergent change. Necessary new competencies are *learned*. In such organizations, team-working and networking are likely to be prominent. Other organizations prefer to search for the best people who might be available; they willingly recruit outsiders. They are seeking to *buy in* the new competencies that they require. People may feel less committed to such organizations in the long term, and consequently there will be a greater reliance on individualism and individual contributions.

The challenge for companies growing from within is that they need to become and stay very aware strategically if they are to remain ahead of their rivals; they will actively benchmark and look for new ideas that might be helpful. Companies securing new skills and competencies from outside face a different dilemma. If the competencies are available, and can be bought by any competitor, how can they ensure that they find the best ideas and people, and how can they generate some unique competency and competitive advantage?

Some companies will look to do both, finding, in the process, an appropriate balance. An analogy would be a leading football club which buys expensive, talented players in the transfer market while, at the same time, nurturing young players. There are many instances where highly skilled, experienced players do not fit in at a new club, certainly not at first; and when several arrive at once, it can be very disruptive until they are moulded into an effective team.

Capelli and Crocker-Hefter (1995) further distinguish between companies that seek to compete by moving quickly, perhaps by necessity, responding speedily to new opportunities, and those that have developed a more sustainable advantage in a long-standing market. They conclude that organizations competing on flexibility will typically find it more appropriate to recruit from outside. A reliance on developing new competencies internally may mean that they are too slow to gain early advantage from new opportunities. By contrast, organizations competing in established markets with long-standing relationships are more likely to rely on internally developed, organization-specific skills and strong internal and external architecture.

There are, inevitably, implications. In general, industries and markets are becoming more dynamic and turbulent, demanding that companies develop new product and market niche opportunities. This appears to imply an increasing reliance on recruiting strong, competent people from outside. In turn, this means that internal relationships and the culture may be under constant pressure to change. Companies are recruiting and rewarding individual experts; at the same time, synergistic opportunities demand strong internal architecture and co-operation. This is another organizational dilemma. Companies that succeed in establishing a strong, cohesive and motivating culture while developing new competencies flexibly and quickly are likely to be the future high performers.

**Figure 5.3** Five managerial mindsets

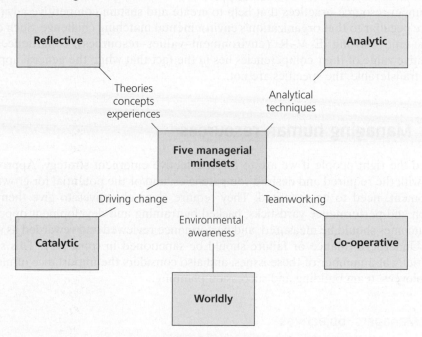

Reinforcing points from earlier chapters, this demands effective strategic leadership and a shared, understood vision for the organization. The extent to which an organization can become a 'learning organization', discussed later in this chapter, is of great significance.

Figure 5.3 repackages the notion of manager competency in the form of five distinct mindsets. Managers, in different degrees, will and must possess all of these abilities. The issues concern the balance and the opportunity. Some managers will be extremely competent in certain areas, but their profile, approach and style may not be appropriate for the demands placed on them. In addition, and given the way in which managers work with constant interruptions, and performing a series of short, pragmatic tasks, it can be difficult for them to find time to think, reflect and challenge. Short-termism and 'more-of-the-same' can all too readily be the result.

Many books have been written, and continue to be written, describing the behaviour patterns and practices of successful organizations. While there is inevitably some element of idiosyncrasy and uniqueness, this approach is interesting and valuable. It can be a rich source of ideas. However, it is not the same as identifying those competencies which have been shown empirically to be associated with the creation of superior performance.

*A real manager has to be a good leader in the sense that he has to embody an open-minded attitude of leadership in himself, in his fellow managers and even in the heads of each employee of his organization. Leadership, therefore, means to enable and help people to act as individual entrepreneurs within the frame of a commonly born vision of the business. A bad manager, on the other hand, is more an administrator who follows severe rules and customs within a stiff bureaucratic hierarchy.*

Dr Hugo M Sekyra, CEO and Chairman, Austrian Industries

It is because these questions are complex that some organizations will adopt and build human resource practices that help to create and sustain competitive advantage. They are peculiar to that organization's environmental matching challenge. Such organizations enjoy strong E–V–R (environment–values–resources) congruence. The competitive value of their competencies lies in the fact that while the general approach may be transferable, the specifics are not.

# 5.4 Managing human resources

We need the right people if we are to foster effective emergent strategy. Appropriate people with the required and desired competencies, and/or the potential for growth and development, need to be recruited. They require clear objectives to give them both direction and performance yardsticks, backed by training and development opportunities. Outcomes should be measured, and performance reviewed and rewarded as appropriate. Underperformance or failure should be sanctioned in some way. This section looks briefly at a number of these issues, and also considers the importance of motivating employees, team building and succession planning.

## 5.4.1 Managers' objectives

Hersey and Blanchard (1982) contend that organizational success and performance are affected by the congruence between the objectives of managers and those of their subordinates. They argue that the organization can only accomplish its objectives if those of managers and subordinates are supportive of each other and of the organization. Moreover, McGregor (1960) has argued that people need objectives to direct their efforts, and that if objectives are not provided by the organization they will create their own. This may not necessarily be disadvantageous for the organization, as Schein (1983) has suggested that managers are generally orientated towards economic goals and see profit as being important. However, personal objectives, which were discussed in Chapter 2, are likely to be allowed more freedom if managers are not given clear objectives. Porter *et al.* (1975) contend that individual behaviour is affected by people's perceptions of what is expected of them; and hence it could be argued that objectives pursued by managers will be dependent on:

- personal motives
- their understanding and perception of what the strategic leader and their colleagues expect them to contribute (expectations, although still subject to some interpretation, may or may not be made clear to managers)
- the culture of the organization.

Various systems and policies for setting and agreeing managers' objectives are available, but they are outside the scope of this book. Ideally, the resultant objectives will be 'SMART': specific, measurable, achievable, realistic and with a timescale.

While objective setting is important for dealing with tasks and priorities, it should never be forgotten that managing people effectively also involves communicating and interacting, and making sure there is always time and opportunity available for dealing with unexpected events.

**Figure 5.4** Alternative rewards

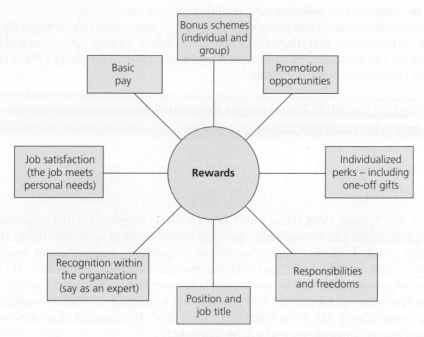

## 5.4.2 Rewards

Rewards are an important motivator, but it is important to appreciate that an individual may feel rewarded by things other than money or promotion (see Figure 5.4). The demands and responsibilities of a job, and the freedom that people are given to decide how to do things, can be rewarding. In addition, working with a particular group of people, especially if they are seen to be successful, can be rewarding. If people feel that their efforts are being rewarded and that future efforts will also be rewarded, their quality of work is likely to improve. In this way, total quality can be improved. Moreover, where **incremental strategic change** is dependent on individual managers seeing, and acting upon, opportunities and threats, the reward system must be appropriate and motivating.

A number of organizations, including BP, WH Smith and Federal Express, have at times experimented with formalized upward feedback as well as manager/subordinate appraisal. Although difficult to implement successfully, as these companies have all found, such systems can be very useful for increasing managers' awareness concerning their style and effectiveness. It is crucial that any performance evaluation systems which influence or determine rewards are open and fair, and perceived as such.

Rewards depend upon the success of the organization as a whole as well as individual contributions. Hence, individual motivation and the issues involved in building successful management teams are looked at next.

## 5.4.3 Involving and motivating people

If people are to be committed to the organization, and to the achievement of key objectives, they must be involved. Employees at the so-called grass-roots level are likely to know the details of the business and what really happens better than their superiors and managers. If they are involved and encouraged to contribute their ideas for improvements, the result can be innovation or quality improvement.

Moreover, if managers and other employees are to make effective strategic contributions it is important that they feel motivated. While money and position in the organization can motivate, there are other essential factors. Hertzberg (1968) emphasized the importance of the following:

- the potential to contribute and achieve through the job
- recognition for effort and success
- promotion opportunities
- interesting work
- responsibility.

David McClelland (McClelland and Winter, 1971) emphasizes the importance of knowing colleagues and subordinates and understanding what motivates them. He contends that people have three needs in varying proportions – achievement, power and affiliation – and individual profiles of the balance between these needs vary. He argues that managers should attempt to understand how much their subordinates desire power, look for opportunities where they can achieve, and want close or friendly working relationships, manifested, say, by not working in isolation. If managers then seek to meet these needs, subordinates can and will be motivated.

One major motivational challenge concerns downsizing. When organizations are cutting back, and people are being made redundant, it is both essential and difficult to maintain the commitment of those remaining. After all, they are the people upon whom new competitive advantages will depend, and without this the company cannot successfully rejuvenate.

Research by Roffey Park Management Centre (1995) established that while there is considerable enthusiasm among authors, consultants and senior managers for teamworking, empowerment and flexibility, many employees remain 'cynical, overworked, insecure and despondent' about the impact of flatter organization structures and the consequent reduction in promotion prospects. Employees frequently perceive delayering to be a cost-cutting exercise which actually reduces morale. When such rationalization is essential, and often it is, the real challenge comes afterwards, in encouraging the remaining managers to look for innovative new ways of adding value and to take risks, albeit limited and measured risks. This reinforces the critical importance of finding the most appropriate reward systems, together with mechanisms for involving, managing and leading people to achieve superior levels of performance.

### 5.4.4 Succession issues

Succession problems can concern both strategic leadership and managerial positions throughout the organization. Small firms whose growth and success have been dependent upon one person, most probably the founder, often experience problems when he or she retires, especially where there has been a failure to develop a successor in readiness. Some very large organizations also experience problems when particularly charismatic and influential strategic leaders resign or retire. Although they may be replaced by other strong leaders there may be changes to either or both the strategy or culture which do not prove successful.

However, succession problems can be seen with key people in any specialism and at any level of the organization. Firms need management in depth in order to cope with growth and with people leaving or being promoted. This implies that people are being developed constantly in line with, and in readiness for, strategic change; and this relates back to appraisal and reward systems. Many global companies deliberately move managers between countries and product groups as part of their management planning. This, they claim, opens the company up to 'different ideas and outside perceptions'.

### 5.4.5 Team building

Both formal and informal teams exist within organizations. Formal teams comprise sections or departments of people who work directly together on a continuous basis and in pursuit of particular specified objectives, and teams of senior managers who meet on a regular basis with an agreed agenda. Informal teams can relate to managers from different departments, or even divisions, who agree informally to meet to discuss and deal with a particular issue, or who are charged with forming a temporary group to handle an organization-wide problem. In both cases relationships determine effectiveness. Ideally, all members will contribute and support each other, and synergy will result from their interactions. Simply putting a group of people together in a meeting, however, does not ensure that they will necessarily work well together and form an effective and successful team.

A successful team needs:

- shared and agreed objectives
- a working language, or effective communications
- the ability to manage both the tasks and the relationships.

Cummings (1981) contends that individual contributions to the overall team effort are determined by personal growth needs (for achievement and personal development) and social needs – perceived benefits from working with others to complete tasks, rather than working alone.

Within any team, therefore, there will be a variety of skills, abilities and commitments. Some people will be natural hard workers who need little supervision or external motivation; others, who may be diligent and committed, may need all aspects of their task spelt out clearly; the major contribution of particular members might be in terms of their creativity and ideas. Meredith Belbin (1981) argues that a good team of people will have compensating strengths and weaknesses, and that as a group they will be able to perform a series of necessary and related tasks. Belbin has identified a number of characteristics or contributions that individuals make to teams. They relate to the provision of ideas, leadership, the resolution of conflict, the gathering and analysing of data and information, carrying out certain detailed work which might be regarded as boring by certain members, organizing people to make their most useful contributions, and developing relationships within the group. Individuals will contribute in a number of areas, not just one or two, but they will often be particularly strong in some and weak in others. A balance is required if the team is to work well together and complete the task satisfactorily.

Whoever is responsible for leading the team – it might be the strategic leader and his or her team of senior managers, or department managers – should consider the various

**Figure 5.5** The learning organization – leadership and vision
Based on the ideas of Charles Handy

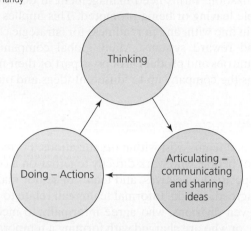

strengths and weaknesses of people and seek to develop them into an effective and cohesive team. If any essential areas of contribution are missing this should be dealt with, and any potential conflicts of strong personalities should be determined early.

### 5.4.6 The 'learning organization'

When we think of building strong, cohesive and integrated teams, we generally, and quite rightly, think of small groups of employees. However, the same themes can be extended to the scale of the whole organization. Where all the parts can be integrated effectively, share with each other and learn from each other we have what Senge (1991) has called a 'learning organization' – which is explained in Box 5.2. Simply, as shown in Figure 5.5, the whole organization is able to think strategically and create synergy by sharing its knowledge and ideas and generating actions which contribute to the interests of the whole. The process is self-reinforcing as managers objectively review their progress.

## Box 5.2 **The Learning Organization**

**KEY CONCEPTS**

The basic arguments are as follows:

- When quality, technology and product/service variety are all becoming widely available at relatively low cost, speed of change is essential for sustained competitive advantage.

- If an organization, therefore, fails to keep up with, or ahead of, the rate of change in its environment it will either be destroyed by stronger competitors, or lapse into sudden death or slow decline. The ideal is to be marginally ahead of competitors – opening up too wide a gap might unsettle customers.

- An organization can only adapt if it is first able to learn, and this learning must be cross-functional as well as specialist.

*Hence a learning organization encourages continuous learning and knowledge generation at all levels, has processes which can move knowledge around the organization easily to where it is needed, and can translate that knowledge quickly into changes in the way the organization acts, both internally and externally.*

Senge, 1991

Strategically important information, together with lessons and best practice, will thus be spread around; and ideally this learning will also be protected from competitors.

## Essential requirements

■ Systemic thinking, such that decision-makers will be able to use the perspective of the whole organization; and there will be significant environmental awareness and internal co-operation. For many organizations the systemic perspective will be widened to incorporate collaboration and strategic alliances with other organizations in the added value chain.

■ Management development and personal growth – to enable effective empowerment and leadership throughout the organization, and in turn allow managers to respond to perceived environmental changes and opportunities.

■ A shared vision and clarity about both core competencies and key success factors. Changes should be consistent through strategic and operational levels.

■ Appropriate values and corporate culture – to exploit core competencies fully and satisfy key success factors.

■ A commitment to customer service, quality and continuous improvement.

■ Kotter and Heskett (1992) argue that the appropriate culture is one which is capable of constant adaptation as the needs of customers, shareholders and employees change.

■ Team learning within the organization through problem sharing and discussion.

These points have been used to develop the following matrix which draws together a number of issues discussed in this chapter and relates them to key issues of change management.

| | Individuals and tasks | Teams and integration |
|---|---|---|
| **Empowerment and development** | Effectiveness oriented<br><br>Focus on problem-solving approach<br><br><br>Change accepted | The learning organization<br><br>Innovative, intrapreneurial, risk-taking<br><br>Change initiated |
| **Orientation towards efficiency and results** | Concentration on resource efficiency<br><br>Consistent and systematic<br><br><br>Change resisted | Supportive organization<br><br>Cross-functional co-operation<br><br>Response to change pressures |

Culture and values

Structural focus

Minicase 5.4 looks at the attributes of a learning organization in the context of Team New Zealand, the sailors who took the America's Cup from the US. Clearly, the team was relatively small in size and it must be appreciated that creating a learning organization in a large company is no easy task. However, wherever it can be achieved to some creditable degree, there are likely to be substantial benefits.

## Minicase 5.4  Team New Zealand

The America's Cup series of yacht races, between the current holder and a preselected challenger, lasts over several weeks and requires considerable preparation and dedication. When New Zealand won in 1995 it was only the second time a team from outside America had won in 144 years, the first being Australia in 1983. Moreover in the final races, New Zealand won 41 races and lost just one, an incredible margin of victory. The team had 'continually expanded its ability to create its destiny'. There had been a driving vision throughout the preparation and the race series: 'to build, modify and sail the fastest boat on any given day'. This vision had brought together the (technical) designers with the users, the sailors, and created synergy where often there is conflict. Their respective perspectives are, quite simply, different. Team New Zealand was successful in defending the trophy in 2000, but then events would take an unexpected turn.

There are 17 sailors on board an America's Cup race boat. The skipper has overall responsibility and is the leader whilst the team are at sea. He relies on his tactician (who keeps the boat on course) and navigator (who looks after the sophisticated electronic tracking instrumentation). A helmsman drives the boat and a strategist monitors the slightest changes of wind speed and direction. Decisions to alter course or rigging are often made very quickly and they need implementing instantaneously. There are then 11 sailors with specific roles mainly related to the deployment of the huge sails. The seventeenth man is really something of a spectator and is often a team sponsor.

Several factors, all characteristic of a successful learning organization, have been put forward as important contributors to the success of Team New Zealand in 1995 and 2000:

■ There was an *inspirational leader* in the form of Sir Peter Blake, who was an experienced sailor, but not the skipper of the actual crew. Nor was he an experienced boat designer. Blake convinced everyone that winning was possible, and he then made sure that happened. The skipper was Russell Coutts. Blake had built his reputation as a round-the-world challenge sailor and he has been described as a 'meticulous planner and gifted leader who inspired loyalty'. Coutts, 33 years old in 1995, was an Olympic gold medallist for sailing (in 1984) and a previous winner of many leading races. He was 'obsessive about detail and technically very skilled'. Blake and Coutts became a formidable partnership who provided leadership on shore and at sea.

■ There was a *strong sense of community* in the team. Blake was visible in driving this, leading from the front. He ensured that the designers were not allowed to drive the agenda without challenge from the sailors.

■ *Open communications* were sponsored, in the form of free-flowing ideas. No hidden or undeclared agendas were permitted. Resources had to be shared. Blake held meetings between the designers and sailors at regular intervals during the build-up period and ran them without ceremony or hierarchy. He encouraged people to be creative in their search for different and unusual answers to problems and issues. It was noted that the secretary at one meeting felt comfortable contributing an idea that turned out to be really valuable.

■ There was a *sustained record of improvement* in product design and racing skills right through to the end of the race series. Team

▶

New Zealand did not stop searching for improvements even when they were winning every race! They built on their successes to reinforce their advantage. There was a willingness by the sailors to accept design modifications if they made the boat go more quickly, even where it made their task of sailing it more difficult or uncomfortable. During the pre-race trials Team New Zealand sailed two identical boats, rather than two different designs in competition. Their choice of design had been made by simulation. Because the two boats began as identical, any successful modifications to the design of one could be copied by the team sailing the other. As a result, considerable emphasis was placed on improving sailing skills as well.

- There was clear evidence of a very *strong commitment* by the individual team members, who were convinced that winning the America's Cup mattered immensely to the whole country, which was drawn behind the team in a positive and supportive way.

- The *team* was *carefully selected* to ensure that they were people who would 'own' what they were taking on. They needed to have individual sailing skills and experience, but they had to be able to interact well with others. They also had to demonstrate they were able to handle disappointment and quickly put it behind them. Outstanding individuals who might be reluctant team players, however good they were personally, were rejected by Blake, who built his team around the tasks. (Interestingly, and in contrast, it sometimes appears that certain footballers are selected for the England football team because of their individual skills, and then asked to play out of position. Right-footed players play on the left of the field, for example, and then do not play to their potential.)

Could this successful combination defend the America's Cup for a second time in 2003? After the victory in 2000 both Russell Coutts and tactician Brad Butterworth 'defected' to Alinghi, a team bankrolled by Swiss billionaire and yachting fanatic Ernesto Bertarelli, who would sail as the navigator. The final Alinghi team for 2003 would include seven New Zealanders and just two Swiss sailors. Its successful challenge was devastating for New Zealanders as really it was the core of the previous winning teams that won for a third time. Blake, unfortunately, was unable to contribute to either team. In December 2001 he was shot on board his boat by people described as pirates whilst sailing up the Brazilian Amazon.

At the same time as its film industry has benefited from the success of the *Lord of the Rings* trilogy, the New Zealand marine industry has grown dramatically on the back of these successes. In value terms it is now on a par with wool and twice as significant as wine.

## Questions

1. Do you agree that Team New Zealand is a learning organization?
2. How important do you think individuals are in building such a team?

## Source of basic material

Maani, K and Benton, C (1999) Rapid team learning – lessons from Team New Zealand's America's Cup campaign, *Organizational Dynamics*, Spring.

**Team New Zealand**
http://www.xtramsn.co.nz/teamnewzealand

## 5.5 Information and information technology

### 5.5.1 The strategic value of information

People make decisions, but information is the fuel they use in decision-making; it can also be an important source of competitive advantage in certain circumstances. It must be stressed that IT, per se, is rarely a source of advantage, but information management can be. So, what exactly do we mean by 'information' and how might it be exploited?

Information has been defined as 'some tangible or intangible entity that reduces uncertainty about a state or event' (Lucas, 1976), which is a way of saying that information increases knowledge in a particular situation. When information is received, some degree of order can be imposed on a previously less well-ordered situation.

Information is needed for, and used in, decision-making. Information, information systems and information technology are all aids to decision-making. The more information managers and other employees have about what is happening in the organization, and in its environment, the more strategically aware they are likely to be. Information about other functional areas and business units can be particularly helpful in this respect.

Ackoff (1967), however, suggested that management information systems can easily be based on three erroneous assumptions:

- Managers are short of information. In many cases managers have too much irrelevant information.

- Managers know the information they require for a decision. However, when asked what information they might need, managers play safe and ask for everything which might be relevant, and thereby contribute to the overabundance of irrelevant information.

- If a manager is provided with the information required for a decision he or she will have no further problem in using it effectively. How information is used depends on perceptions of the issues involved. Moreover, if any additional quantitative analysis or interpretation is required, many managers are weak in these skills.

Nevertheless, decisions and decision-making do involve both facts and people. While the right information available at the right time can be extremely useful, the real value of information relates to how it is used by decision-makers, particularly for generating and evaluating alternative possible courses of action. In designing and introducing IT and management information systems into organizations it is necessary to consider the likely reaction of people as well as the potential benefits that can accrue from having more up to date and accurate information available. Information gathering should never become an end in itself, for the expertise and experience in people's heads can be more useful than facts on paper.

Moreover, it is important to evaluate who actually needs the information, rather than who might find it useful for increasing awareness, and to ensure that those people receive it. Although information technology and information systems can be expensive to introduce, those organizations that receive information, analyse and distribute it to the appropriate decision-makers more quickly than their competitors can achieve a competitive edge, particularly in a turbulent environment. Hence, the structure and culture of the organization should ensure that managers who need information receive it, and at the right time. However, while information can lead to more effective decision-making, it remains a manifestation of power within the organization, and this aspect needs monitoring. If information that could prove useful is withheld from decision-makers, negligently or deliberately by political managers pursuing personal objectives, the effectiveness of decision-making is reduced.

Information is used through a filter of experience and judgement in decision-making, and its relative value varies between one decision-maker and another. In certain instances the available information will be accurate, reliable and up to date. In other circumstances the information provided may already be biased because it is the result of the interpretation of a situation by someone who may have introduced subjectivity. Some managers, perhaps those who are less experienced, will rely more heavily on specific information than others, for whom experience, general awareness and insight into the situation are more important.

To complicate matters further, Day (1996) argues that organizations do not know what they know. In other words, they are awash with data that do not get translated into valuable information and hence real organizational knowledge. Linked to this, it is clear that quite frequently they also fail to realize the value of some of the information that some people in the organization possess. This can be taken even further. If organizations do not know what they know, it must follow they do not know what they do not know. They remain unaware of certain opportunities that others will seize and that they would have found valuable if they knew of their existence. Correspondingly, they do not find out about certain threats until it is too late to act.

## 5.5.2 Decision-making and the interpretation of information

Spear (1980) argues that when information systems and the provision of information for managers are being considered it is important to bear in mind how people make decisions, interpret data and information, and give meaning to them. In decision-making managers sometimes behave in a stereotyped way and follow past courses of action; sometimes they are relatively unconcerned with the particular decision and may behave inconsistently. In each case they may ignore information which is available and which if used objectively would lead to a different conclusion and decision. At other times information is used selectively and ignored if it conflicts with strongly held beliefs or views about certain things. In other words, information may be either misused or not used effectively.

Moreover, when considering a problem situation managers have to interpret the events that they are able to observe and draw certain conclusions about what they believe is happening. The question is: do managers perceive reality? Is there even such a thing as reality, or are there simply the meanings that we give to events? The following example will explain the point. Worker directors, popular in some other European countries, have always been a controversial issue among managers and trade union officials in the UK, with some of them supportive and others, in reality a majority, strongly opposed to their introduction. Managers who oppose them argue that they will reduce managerial power to run an organization; union opponents argue they would increase managerial power because the directors would be carefully selected or co-opted to include mainly those who were antagonistic to many of the aims of the union. These views represent meaning systems. The idea of worker directors, and what they are, is definite and agreed; their meaning and the implications of using them are subjective and interpretative.

A parallel situation would concern the interpretation of economic data. If, say, interest rates are rising, share prices are falling or the value of the pound is strengthening, do economic analysts agree or disagree on their meaning?

### 5.5.3 Counterintuitive behaviour

A failure to think through the implications of certain decisions on other managers, departments or business units can have effects that are unwelcome. The same can happen if there is an inability to appreciate the consequences because of a lack of information, or if there is a misunderstanding resulting from the wrong interpretation of information. Such an event is known as counterintuitive behaviour, and it often creates a new set of problems that may be more serious than those that existed originally.

Jay Forrester, in his book *Urban Dynamics* (1969), discusses how a strategy of building low-cost housing by the US equivalent of a local authority in order to improve living conditions for low-income earners in inner city areas has done more harm than good. The new houses draw in more low-income people who need jobs, but at the same time they make the area less attractive for those employers who might create employment. General social conditions decline. The area becomes even more destitute, creating again more pressure for low-cost housing. 'The consequence is a downward spiral that draws in the low-income population, depresses their condition, prevents escape and reduces hope. All of this done with the best of intentions.'

A more recent and real example concerns horse racing. It has always been the case that flat racing is cheaper and easier to stage than National Hunt racing over hurdles. Generally, but not exclusively, and dictated by ground conditions, flat racing is focused on the summer with National Hunt in the winter months. Weather conditions are more likely to be adverse in the winter, and so artificial turf all-weather surfaces were put on trial to test their value in overcoming the problem for horses of hard, frozen ground. The intention was to make National Hunt economically more attractive. Paradoxically, the all-weather surfaces proved too tough for chasers and hurdlers when they landed from jumping, but they proved ideal for flat racing. The outcome is that the flat racing season can be extended, giving it even more of a relative advantage over National Hunt.

Related problems occur with misinterpretation of information. Consider the example of a small independent retailer who finds that he is selling more of a particular item than normal and more than he expected to sell. Deliveries from his wholesaler or other suppliers require a waiting period. Does he simply replace his stock, or increase his stockholding levels? How does he forecast or interpret future demand? When he starts ordering and buying more, or buying more frequently, how do his suppliers, and ultimately the manufacturer, respond? On what do they base their stockholding and production decisions, given that there will be penalties for misunderstanding the situation? Such problems are made worse by time-lags or delays. The use of IT by major retail organizations has proved that the impact of this dilemma can be reduced.

Summarizing, the fact that information is available does not necessarily mean that more effective decisions will result.

*Information technology is a solution looking for a problem.*

Donald Jones, CEO, ETSI (Consultants in call centre technology)

## 5.5.4  Information systems and information technology: a cautionary comment

IT can be regarded as 'the application of hardware (machinery) and software (systems and techniques) to methods of processing and presenting data into a meaningful form which helps reduce uncertainty and is of real perceived value in current or future decisions'.

A management information system collects, processes and distributes the information required for managers to make decisions. It should be designed to be cost-effective, in that the additional revenue or profits generated by more effective decisions exceed the cost of designing, introducing and running the system, or that the value of management time saved is greater than the cost of the system. In addition, the information provided should be valid, reliable and up to date for the decisions concerned.

It should be realized that while computers and IT might be an essential feature of a management information system, the basic ideas behind an information system have little concern with computers. The terms are not synonymous.

Earl and Hopwood (1980) expressed a concern that there would be a tendency for the potential of IT to lead to an increasingly technological perspective on the way in which information is processed by managers. This would lead to increasingly formal systems and bureaucratic procedures which 'neither fit nor suit the realities of organizational activity'. On many occasions, informally exchanged information between managers who trust and respect each other is extremely important, and in some organizations political activity and power is important in certain decisions. In addition, organizations can become overloaded with information that they cannot utilize effectively.

In the mid-1990s Tesco introduced its customer loyalty card, Clubcard, and was later followed by Safeway (ABC card) and Sainsbury (Reward Card). Every time shoppers pass through a till their card is swiped to record their purchases. Customers build up points which can be used as a discount on future purchases either with the supermarket in question or with partner organizations. At the same time the computer records every item the customer has bought. The idea was that this could be used to profile people's

---

### Minicase 5.5  Tesco                                              GB

Tesco is the UK's leading supermarket group, and as we shall see later in Chapter 13, it has expanded successfully overseas. Tesco was founded by Sir Jack Cohen and grew during the 1980s with a philosophy of 'pile it high, sell it cheap'. In the early years the emphasis was on small stores, town centre locations and low prices. Its image was somewhat downmarket.

In the 1990s, however, driven by two new strategic leaders, Ian MacLaurin and later Terry Leahy, Tesco was transformed and became the market leader. Sainsbury was deposed from the number one position, and later overtaken by ASDA after its acquisition by Wal-Mart.

Tesco has refocused on large out-of-town superstores, 'everyday low prices' and given its brand high prominence, with high profile television advertising featuring Prunella Scales and Jane Horrocks as a sparring mother and daughter. It also pioneered refrigerated lorries for transporting food and developed large distribution depots, also with multi-temperature storage facilities. The logistics were, however, managed by specialist providers. Tesco has increasingly used IT to share its current sales data with its suppliers, requiring them to track sales trends and use the information to ensure warehouses are restocked as and when necessary to ensure individual stores never run out but never have to hold significant inventories. IT has also been utilized to allow Tesco to develop a home delivery arm for goods ordered over the Internet.

Tesco has been renowned for its range of wines and spirits for a number of years, and its drinks-only superstore near the Channel Tunnel terminal at Calais is hugely popular with UK day trippers. Tesco has, moreover, continually increased the percentage of space it gives over to non-food items. Books, magazines, stationery, music and DVDs have joined clothing and electrical goods. Another major 'loser' as Tesco has grown has, therefore, been WH Smith.

In 2002 Tesco acquired T&S stores, a chain of some 850 'small' stores, many of which it would rebrand as limited-concept, restricted range, Tesco Express stores. Local neighbourhood convenience stores saw this move as threatening as it allowed Tesco to become number two to the Co-op (linked with Alldays) in this sector of the market.

Tesco continues to experiment with other uses and opportunities for exploiting IT more extensively. It has developed a small computer which shoppers can attach to their trolleys and use it for bar-scanning every item they select from the shelves. This provides both price checks and an accumulating spend total. It can also be used to check both shelf locations in the store and on product availability. Customers will be notified of special offers and promotions as they shop.

It has also developed:

- new scales which photo-identify fruit and vegetables, weigh, price and label them
- vending machines for fresh products and
- self-service exit scanning.

Some or all of these developments will be rolled out in the future.

**Tesco** http://www.tesco.com

habits and preferences so that special promotions could be targeted, instead of the more traditional 'blanket coverage' approach. Safeway invested £50 million a year for five years to run its system and then abandoned it. Customers had used the cards, but many possess more than one supermarket card in any case, reducing the value of the loyalty element. Safeway also admitted that it had underestimated the scope of the systems needed to handle, analyse and exploit the data it was collecting. In the end, Safeway concluded the £50 million per year would be better spent on reducing prices. A company survey of 5500 shoppers in 1999 was used to justify this decision: only five wanted a loyalty card, they said! ASDA, incidentally, as did William Morrison, opted not to go down this route. Minicase 5.5 looks at IT in supermarkets in greater detail.

With the complexities discussed above as a backcloth, it is now important to examine the strategic information challenge facing organizations.

### 5.5.5 The strategic information challenge

Why do some organizations, which are currently enjoying success and high profits, fail to realize when products, services or strategies are about to lose customer support? Why do they fail to anticipate competitor initiatives? Why are others able to be more pro-active?

Being close to customers, and in touch with new developments in a dynamic and possibly chaotic marketplace, requires information, intelligence and learning. Successful organizations monitor the activities of their customers, suppliers and competitors; they ask questions and test out new ideas. They express a willingness to learn and to change both their perspective on competition – their mindset concerning which factors determine competitive success – and the things they actually do. Sophisticated analyses and models of past and current results and behaviour patterns make an important contribution but, as Day (1996) argues, it is also necessary to think through how a market might respond to actions designed to retain existing customers and win new business, while outflanking and outperforming competitors. One of the reasons for Canon's continued success has been its ability to spot new market opportunities for its advanced technologies and exploit them early. Canon is also adept at reducing its dependency on products/markets as competition intensifies and demand plateaus. In the 1970s, for example, Canon successfully and systematically switched emphasis away from cameras (while remaining active and innovatory in the market) to photocopiers, and then to computer printers and facsimile machines, always adopting the same focus principles. Canon now has a range of digital cameras and accessories.

In order to become and remain strategically successful, organizations must create and sustain competitive advantage. They must continue to enjoy E–V–R congruence, frequently in a dynamic and turbulent environment. To achieve this, information must be gathered and shared, but this is not merely a question of designing a new information system.

Day (1996) contends that many organizations 'do not know what they know' either because data and signals are misinterpreted or because the flows are inadequate. Decision-makers do not receive the information that they need, or they fail to learn about things that might prove useful. Organizations that prioritize vertical channels and ignore horizontal flows are the ones most likely to fail to learn. The important elements for strategic success are:

- tracking events in the market and the environment, choosing responses (both proactively and reactively) and monitoring the outcomes of the actions which follow. Competitor initiatives must be dealt with; benchmarking best practices and general awareness can suggest new ideas
- making sure that important information from the questioning and learning from these emergent changes is disseminated effectively
- reflecting upon outcomes in the context of E–V–R congruence to ensure that the organization can sustain an effective match with its environment
- where appropriate, adapting policies and procedures to better guide future decisions.

The implication is a constant willingness to be flexible and to change as necessary. Companies must work from the twin perspectives of opportunity and threat. First, a willingness to learn and grow and, second, a realization that without appropriate and timely change a company is likely to face a crisis. Gilbert (1995) further argues that strategically successful organizations **leverage** their innovative competitive ideas with speed and act quickly.

They obtain market feedback continuously and rapidly and adapt to the feedback ahead of their rivals. They exploit the potential of strategic as well as competitive and operating information systems.

## Three levels of information

- *Operating information systems* – Cost accounting systems, sales analyses and production schedules are essential for efficiency and control. Used creatively as, for example, is the case with airline reservation systems, they can create competitive advantage, but they are not designed to drive strategic change.

■ *Competitive information systems* – Important elements of the various operating systems need to be integrated and synthesized to ensure that the organization is using its resources both efficiently and effectively. Specifically, it is meeting the needs and expectations of important external stakeholders. Competitive information systems, therefore, relate to competitive advantage and E–V–R congruence. They require managers to think and work across functional boundaries and consider the total service package provided to customers, encapsulating all the ways in which an organization can add value in a co-ordinated way.

However, Gilbert (1995) argues that managers will not always be aware of the information they have used in arriving at a competitively successful formula. Where organizations do not fully understand why they are successful, that success may be fragile.

■ *Strategic information systems* – While competitive information systems will typically focus on existing competition, organizations must also be able to learn about the business environment in order that they can anticipate change and design future strategies. Marchand (1995a) stresses that strategic information management should not be confined to the level of the strategic leader, but rather dispersed throughout the whole organization. This implies an innovative culture and an organization structure which facilitates the sharing of information – one essential element of a learning organization. A learning organization requires considerable decentralization and empowerment, which must not be at the expense of control. Centralized systems are often required for sound control and effective co-ordination, thus presenting organizations with the dilemma of how to obtain the speed and flexibility benefits of decentralization without sacrificing control.

It is important to stress that appreciating the significance of particular events, and assessing the potential significance of opportunities and threats which have been spotted often requires judgement, which will be discussed at greater length in Chapter 11.

Hence, as one moves up these three levels of decision-making, the contribution of IT and information systems to decision-making changes. Once operating systems are established, they can be used to make a number of decisions and drive the operations. By measuring performance, the systems can again make a valuable contribution and highlight when things are going wrong. For strategic decisions, however, IT is primarily an aid to decision-making. Systems cannot realistically make the decisions, and consequently interpretation and meaning systems are particularly important. For such decisions the systems should be designed to provide information in a form that is useful to decision-makers.

**Information uses** Expanding this point, Marchand (1995b) distinguishes among four important and distinct uses for information at the operating, competitive and strategic decision-making levels.

■ *Command and control* – The formal gathering of information to allow centralized control and decentralized accountability. Budgeting and resource allocations will typically be included. Command and control is valuable for managing resources efficiently but, used in isolation, it does not drive rapid change. Many organizations use tight financial targeting and monitoring as an essential driver of their competitiveness. Command and control invariably requires an organization to be broken down into subunits, such as independent businesses, divisions or functional departments.

- *Improvement* – Here the emphasis is on integrating the functions to improve both efficiency and effectiveness through better all-round service. Processes that link the functions are often the focus of attention, and initiatives such as total quality management and business process improvement will be integral.

- *Opportunities for organizational synergy* – If complex multibusiness organizations can find new opportunities for internal synergy, sharing and interdependency, they can clearly benefit. Teamworking and special project teams are one way of doing this. This can be particularly important if the organization acquires another business which needs to be integrated.

- *Environmental opportunities* – Market intelligence, competitor monitoring and benchmarking best practice can generate new ideas and opportunities, as we have seen. This requires that managers are vigilant and enquiring. Critically, ideas spotted by one part of an organization, and of no discernible use to that business, might be valuable for another business or division, and consequently the ability to share – based on an understanding of needs and a willingness to trust and co-operate – is essential.

Figure 5.6 illustrates that an organization must be able to manage all four information needs simultaneously and harmoniously if it is to benefit from improved efficiencies and manage change both continuously and discontinuously. Herein lies the real strategic information challenge. The deployment of organizational resources, the corresponding style of management and the cultural implications vary between the four information needs and the decision-making processes that they support. Command and control management requires the organization to be separated into functions, businesses and/or divisions for clarity; the others demand different forms of integration, both formal and informal, to share both information and learning.

**Figure 5.6** The strategic information challenge

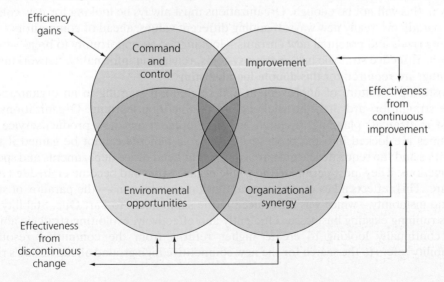

**Figure 5.7** Single- and double-loop learning and strategic change

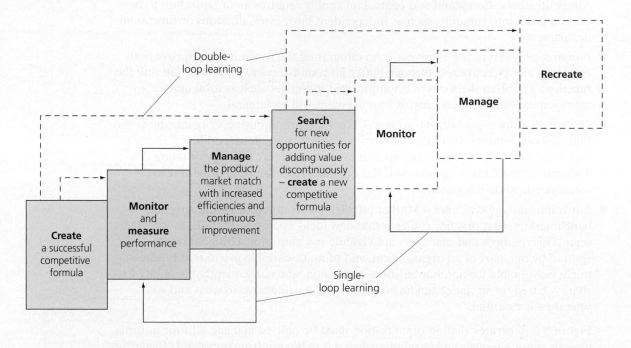

Figure 5.7 illustrates how organizations need first, to develop a perspective on how they can add value and create competitive advantage. Through monitoring, measurement, continuous improvement and innovation they should seek to become increasingly efficient and effective. This continual process represents **single-loop learning** and it is essential if competitive advantage is to be sustained in a dynamic environment. This requires sound operating and competitive information systems. However, over time, on its own, this will not be enough. Organizations must always be looking for new competitive paradigms, really new ways of adding different values, ahead of competitors – both existing rivals and potential new entrants – looking for an opportunity to break into the market. Effective strategic information systems, relying on informality, networking and learning, are required for this **double-loop learning**.

Fostering a culture of improvement and single-loop learning in an organization is more straightforward than the challenge of double-loop learning. Organizations that invest in strategic planning, research and development and new product/service programmes are locked into the process, but the real benefits cannot be gained if these activities and the requisite learning are confined to head office departments and specialist functions. They must permeate the whole organization and become embedded in the culture. This reflects a key organizational tension and dilemma – the paradox of stability and instability – which was introduced in the supplement to Part One. Stability concerns running existing businesses efficiently and effectively, exploiting strategic abilities and continually looking to create higher returns from the committed resources. Instability refers to the search for the new competitive high ground ahead of one's rivals.

Information, however, as well as being a vital element in decision-making, can also be a source of competitive advantage, as shown in the next section.

## Minicase 5.6  British Airways    GB

British Airways invested some 5 per cent of its gross revenue in IT during the 1990s. IT was first utilized over 30 years ago to streamline the reservations systems. Subsequently, it was used for aircraft scheduling, spares control and crew rostering. BA now obtains many of its supplies by Internet procurement. Improved efficiencies in these areas are critical as cargo and passenger volumes grow, and continue to grow.

Increasingly, IT has also been used to add value and to improve BA's overall service and effectiveness in a very competitive industry. A number of the applications are described below.

Computerized reservation systems now link travel agencies directly with the airlines and provide instantaneous information on availability, followed by reservations and tickets. There are a number of systems but the market is dominated by two, which carry up-to-date information on hundreds of airlines and their flight schedules. Sabre (begun by American Airlines) quickly became market leader for the US market but has a more limited presence in Europe; Galileo/Apollo (two merged systems, owned at one stage by United Airlines and BA together with nine other airlines) was market leader in Europe and second largest in America. Most airlines have sold their stakes in these systems: BA sold its holding in two separate tranches. These systems allow airlines to change prices and pricing policies frequently in their attempt to maximize their yield. In other words, fares for a particular flight can be adjusted in line with demand, and ticket prices can be discounted to try to fill the aeroplane if there are spare seats. The airlines want to sell seats at the highest prices they can obtain, but an empty seat means lost and irrecoverable revenue. This is complex as there are 30 different fares available on a typical transatlantic flight on a Boeing 747.

Travel agents and specialist 'consolidators' (who buy blocks of discounted seats and sell them on either directly or via other travel agents), with access to substantial information, will often shop around for the lowest fares. In addition, computer reservation systems allow passengers to be allocated specific seats well in advance of their flight rather than when they check in at the airport. Clearly, both the airline and the passenger can benefit. The airlines further argue that these systems give them better control over their deliberate overbooking policies. An airline is often willing to sell more seats than they have available on a flight, assuming that some passengers with tickets will not travel, and balancing the cost of compensation and lost goodwill against the lost revenue from empty seats.

BA, like most major international Airlines, has a frequent flyer programme with air miles and various other benefits. Air miles are also available from organizations with whom BA has an alliance, including other airlines, car rental companies and leading hotel chains. Without IT to record the relevant flight and fare details, such programmes would not be feasible.

New ticketing machines at airports enable passengers on certain flights (in BA's case on shuttle services) to buy their ticket and obtain their printed boarding card in 40 seconds. The technology also exists for machines to scan a passenger's thumbprint (assuming that it has been previously verified), issue a ticket and debit that person's bank account. This is seen as more secure than the existing machines, which respond to credit and debit cards, and more likely to generate customer loyalty. Hand-held computers are available to speed up checking-in and reduce queuing. Electronic ticketing takes several forms. Typically with some BA flights passengers are simply provided with a booking reference (after they have paid) which they feed into a machine at the airport, which then issues their boarding card. Some airlines provide passengers with plastic identity cards (the same size as credit cards) which can be swiped through a machine by the gate staff who can then issue the boarding card at the very last minute before boarding the aircraft.

ACARS (Aircraft Communications Addressing and Reporting System) allows fast transfer of information by radio waves between computers on the ground and computers on board aircraft. Data transmitted during a flight can help to plan routine and extra ground maintenance and boarding delays can be reduced. Some of the ground time between flights is spent analysing and responding to information on load and balance.

Personal video players, which are typically standard in first and business class, can be adapted to enable passengers to book hotels and cars during their flights and possibly use their credit cards for mail-order shopping. (Hertz already have touch-panel machines with visual prompt screens at airports to enable passengers to reserve cars at their destination just before they fly. A printed confirmation takes six seconds.)

BA has also harnessed IT to improve its response to complaints. Only three customers in 1000 complain about anything, but this still represents several hundred letters every day. Most people are only looking for an explanation and an apology, but they expect it quickly. If they receive a satisfactory response, they tend to stay loyal to BA, and customer retention is much less expensive than generating new business. Given that the customer's explanation must be checked carefully, it has proved beneficial to link the customer service system with BA's other information systems, such as bookings and flight information. New letters of complaint are scanned in and the relevant records checked quickly before a response is generated. Each letter is given a priority rating.

Prior to his resignation early in 2000, chief executive Robert Ayling committed BA to increasing the percentage of its tickets sold by the Internet from 1 per cent to 50 per cent in less than five years. His successor has reinforced the strategy but trimmed the target. easyJet promotes itself as the 'Web's favourite airline' (as a spoof on BA's claim to be the 'World's favourite airline') and, like Ryanair, sells its tickets only via the Internet or its own telephone call centre.

**Question**

1. Can you think of other opportunities where BA might seek to exploit IT for competitive advantage?

**British Airways** http://www.britishairways.com

## 5.5.6 Information, information technology and competitive advantage

It is clear that IT offers many potential strategic opportunities which go beyond the notion of faster data processing, but that harnessing these opportunities involves changes in attitude and culture among managers. McFarlane (1984) claims that IT strategies should relate to two criteria:

- How dependent is the organization on IT systems which are reliable 24 hours a day, seven days a week? International banks and stock and currency dealers who trade around the clock, and who use IT to monitor price movements and record their transactions, need their systems to be wholly reliable.
- Is IT crucial if the organization is to meet key success factors? If it is, there is an implication that companies can benefit from harnessing the latest technological developments. An obvious example is the airline industry. Minicase 5.6 looks at IT in British Airways, but in fairness it reflects developments by all the leading airlines.

Rayport and Sviokla (1995) argue that competition is now based on two dimensions: the physical world of resources and a virtual world of information. Information clearly supports and enhances every activity in an organization, but it can itself be a source of added value and consequently competitive advantage as long as organizations are able to extract that value.

Michael Porter (1985) had earlier suggested that technological change, and in particular IT, is among the most prominent forces that can alter the rules of competition. This is because most activities in an organization create and use information. Porter and Millar (1985) contend that IT could affect competition in three ways:

- IT can change the structure of an industry, and in so doing alter the rules of competition
- IT can be used to create sustainable competitive advantage by providing companies with new competitive weapons
- as a result of IT new businesses can be developed from within a company's existing activities.

These three themes are examined in greater detail below.

### 5.5.7 Industry structure

As shown in Chapter 4, according to Porter (1980), the structure of an industry can be analysed in terms of five competitive forces: the threat of new entrants; the bargaining power of suppliers; the bargaining power of buyers; the threat of substitute products and services; and rivalry amongst existing competitors. Porter and Millar (1985) suggested that IT could influence the nature of these forces, and thereby change the attractiveness and profitability of an industry. This is particularly applicable where the industry has a high information content, such as airlines and financial and distribution services. Moreover, firms that were either slow or reluctant to introduce IT might well be driven

---

### Minicase 5.7 The Holiday Travel Industry (GB)

Minicase 5.6 showed how airline tickets are increasingly available direct from airline call centres and via the Internet. In recent years holidays, especially last-minute bargains, have been advertised on teletext to encourage direct bookings, and the Internet is also becoming accepted as an appropriate channel for customers to use. Both of these imply that the high-street travel agent is bypassed. However, many people still prefer the personal help and advice provided by a travel agent, but travel agencies have increasingly made use of IT to provide a better, faster and cheaper service. A 1999 MORI survey concluded some 45 per cent of people *would* book a holiday direct via the Internet, but so far only 1 per cent had. Digital television would inevitably have a further impact.

**Thomson Holidays: pioneer of IT for competitive advantage**

The package tour holiday industry is extremely competitive, with pricing an important weapon. The leading holiday companies are vertically integrated and own high-street travel agency chains as well as their own airlines. Thomson, which became the market leader several years ago, believes that much of its early competitive advantage derives from its pioneering of IT-based booking systems, and that further developments with IT have helped it to retain market leadership.

In general, it is difficult to create and sustain competitive advantage in this industry. Package tour companies hire beds and airline seats, put them together, and by adding fringe services market them as a package holiday. Offering better service at airports or a wider range of tours in the various resorts can easily be copied by rivals, and so any competitive edge is quickly eroded. The same is true of different holiday packages such as self-catering apartments as an alternative to a hotel.

Thomson first introduced computers in ten regional offices in 1976, allowing easier access for travel agents. Previously, agents had to telephone one location; now they had access to ten linked centres. The computer generated management information and invoices as well as providing availability data for agents, but the agents still relied on the telephone, backed up by paperwork for confirming bookings.

Thomson recognized that what was needed was a terminal in every travel agent's office, but appreciated that if the system were exclusively Thomson it might be less popular than one that also allowed access to rival organizations. In 1979 they began experimenting (with Prestel), and in 1982 introduced TOP or the Thomson Open-line Programme. Through TOP travel agents enjoyed instant access to Thomson holiday information on their terminal screens, but their terminals also accessed rival and, at the time, less sophisticated, systems. The problem of customers having to wait while telephone calls to check availability ring unanswered because the system is congested had been largely eliminated. This proved particularly valuable on busy Saturdays and enabled Thomson to save on staff costs. The computer could handle both options and confirmed bookings, and customers were encouraged to book because more and better information was being made available to them. The system has been continually improved, and the effect has been reduced booking costs for both Thomson and the travel agents. In addition, the role of the agent has been changed more towards selling than administration. Other operators have followed, but the time-lag clearly proved beneficial to Thomson.

Thomson has also been able to obtain more control and planning information for future capacity planning, and the gradual introduction of terminals linked to the UK in their offices abroad has improved the total service in other ways.

## More recent IT applications

IT has had a major impact on the marketing and selling of holidays because at the booking stage it is information that is being exchanged. Nevertheless, for certain elements of the service, IT has had only limited impact: travel shop windows are invariably filled with hand-written signs for late booking holidays and prices, for instance.

Tour operators move the prices of holidays several times a day when they are chasing last-minute bookings, based on the number of unsold holidays, the current levels of demand and, most importantly, competitor prices for the equivalent holiday. Sophisticated IT systems are essential to facilitate this flexibility. From the customers' position, both teletext and the Internet provide information on the availability of last-minute holidays, as pointed out above. Various e-commerce companies, such as Lastminute.com, offer tickets and holidays at reduced and sometimes bargain prices.

Some travel agencies provide self-service, touch-screen terminals which allow customers to access multimedia information about holidays and talk to sales people via a video-telephone link. Interactive televisions also offer information about hotels in audio, video and text forms. The Internet can be used to acquire information on airlines, resorts and hotels.

The leading travel agents, including Thomson and My Travel (previously Airtours), have invested in Internet booking systems. In most cases they have bought out small, specialist companies that have been set up independently, rather than start their own.

Travel agencies can print airline tickets directly in their branches, rather than simply order them from the airline who would issue them at a later date. However, electronic ticketing is making this less significant. Commissions vary and represent more of a management fee than a percentage commission at a standard rate.

In 2000 Airtours opened a 24-hour telephone call centre in Majorca to provide its customers with help and advice. This implied a reduction in the number of representatives who tour the various hotels and apartments on a routine basis.

### Project

1. Use teletext and the Internet to access and evaluate the holiday bargains that are available.

### Question

1. Can you see a real future for *auctioning* last-minute bargain holidays via the Internet?

**Thomson Holidays** http://www.thomson-holidays.com
**lastminute.com** http://www.lastminute.com
**MyTravel** http://www.mytravel.com

out of the industry, because they would be unable to offer a competitive service. Where the cost of the necessary IT, both hardware and software systems, is high it can increase the barriers to entry for potential new firms.

Minicase 5.7 builds on Minicase 5.6 and explains how holiday companies have made use of IT to lower costs and allow them to compete more aggressively on pricing. The result of the competitive activity has been an increase in concentration, with the largest companies gaining market share at the expense of smaller rivals, many of whom have left the industry.

Porter and Millar show that IT can both improve and reduce the attractiveness and profitability of an industry, and that as a consequence manufacturers should analyse the potential implications of change very carefully.

IT and the Internet – which is discussed below – have transformed such financial services as banking, enabling customers to carry out many of their financial transactions by telephone or personal computer without needing to queue for a cashier. However, there is the disadvantage that certain aspects of banking are being made more impersonal, and the personal service aspect is being reduced.

### 5.5.8 The creation of competitive advantage

**Lower costs** If costs are reduced to a level below competitors' costs and this advantage is maintained, above-average profits and an increased market share can result. Porter and Millar (1985) suggest that while the impact of IT on lower costs has historically been confined to activities where repetitive information processing has been important, such restraints no longer apply. IT can lead to lower labour costs by reducing the need for certain production and clerical staff. As a result, there should be both lower direct production costs and reduced overheads. IT applied to production systems can improve scheduling, thereby increasing the utilization of assets and reducing stocks, and in turn lowering production costs.

**Enhancing differentiation** Differentiation can be created in a number of ways, including quality, design features, availability and special services that offer added value to the end consumer. McFarlane *et al.* (1983) contend that IT offers scope for differentiation where:

- IT is a significant cost component in the provision of the product or service, as in banking, insurance and credit-card operations

- IT is able to affect substantially the lead time for developing, producing or delivering the product (CAD/CAM systems play an important role in this)
- IT allows products or services to be specially customized to appeal to customers individually
- IT enables a visibly higher level of service to customers, say through regular and accurate progress and delivery information, which might be charged for
- more and better product information can be provided to consumers.

Most insurance companies quote rates for insuring property and cars partially based on specified postcode districts. To achieve this they need accurate information on the risks involved in different areas and how these are changing. This in turn requires close liaison and information exchanges with brokers. The insurers, brokers and ultimately customers can all benefit as premiums more accurately reflect risks.

Supermarkets began to use hand-held computers several years ago, and these allowed staff to record the current stock levels each evening. Shelves could then be replenished overnight or the next day from regional warehouses. Sales representatives from, say, food manufacturers who sell extensively to small outlets were able to use similar hand-held computers for entering their orders. The computer could price the order immediately and a confirmation was then printed out. Further cost savings were possible where computer systems could be networked. As we saw in Minicase 5.5, Tesco also sought to establish closer linkages with its suppliers. Orders for immediate delivery were transmitted electronically, although projections based on the latest sales analyses would have been provided some weeks earlier. If supplier delivery notes were sent ahead of the actual delivery these were then used to check the accuracy of the shipment and a confirmation was returned. This represents a promissory note to pay by an agreed date, and no further invoicing is required. These linkages made use of electronic data interchange systems to exchange information. More recently, using the Internet, **e-markets** have begun to appear. These developments clearly saved costs and allowed for lower prices, but they also streamlined the distribution network. Fast replenishment meant that customers should not find that stores have run out of an item; moreover, fresh produce could easily be replenished daily. Overall, the level of service was improved.

**New competitive opportunities** IT has resulted in the creation of new businesses in three distinct ways.

- New businesses have been made technologically feasible. Telecommunications technology, for example, led to the development of facsimile services and organizations that provide fax services. In a similar way microelectronics developments made personal computing possible.
- IT created demand for new products such as high-speed data communications networks that were unavailable before IT caused the demand.
- New businesses have been created within established ones. Several organizations have diversified into software provision stemming from the development of packages for their own use.

There are numerous examples of how competitive advantage has been derived specifically from IT. Debit cards, such as Barclay's Connect, have replaced cash and cheques for many customers; similar to credit cards in format, they allow money to be debited immediately from a bank account. Because computers can store and process information very quickly, they allow the banks and building societies to offer rates of interest which increase and decrease directly in line with the size of a customer's deposit.

The US company McKesson, which supplies over-the-counter pharmaceuticals to retail chemists, used its salesforce to record on a computer the counter and shelf layouts of their customers. This allowed McKesson to pack orders in such a way that customers could unpack them and display them quickly and sequentially.

Most newspapers now enjoy cost and differentiation benefits from computerized typesetting, whereby type is set directly by a journalist typing at a keyboard. The files can now be transmitted electronically via the Internet so the journalist need not be located in the newspaper building. In the case of UK national daily newspapers, and against some trade union resistance, computerized typesetting was pioneered by Eddie Shah, when he established the *Today* newspaper which, after changes of ownership has now been closed down. For the *Financial Times*, IT supports all the share prices, charts and other information included every day.

Most large hotel chains, including Sheraton and Marriott, operate clubs or programmes for their regular visitors. Participants receive such benefits as free upgrades and free meals as well as the programme points which they can exchange later for free stays or air miles. It is quite normal for travellers to prioritize a particular chain because of the perceived benefits of programme membership. These hotel chains typically cover much of the world, and often include independent hotels in franchise arrangements. Loyalty programmes would simply not be feasible without IT.

The US retailer Wal-Mart issues pagers to customers waiting for prescriptions so that they can continue shopping rather than either wait in line or come back speculatively to check whether their package is ready.

In summary, implementing IT for competitive advantage requires:

- an awareness of customer and consumer needs, changing needs, and how IT can improve the product's performance or create new services
- an awareness of operational opportunities to reduce costs and improve quality through IT
- an appreciation of how the organization could be more effective with improved information provision, and how any changes might be implemented. The impact upon people is very significant.

The argument is that competitive advantage can stem from any area of the organization.

## 5.6 The value chain

### 5.6.1 Supply-chain partnerships

In this section we develop the significance of internal and external architecture introduced earlier in the chapter and explain an important analytical framework. Developing his earlier work on industry structure (Porter 1980 – Chapter 4), where he highlights the significance of the relative power of buyers and suppliers, Porter (1985) argues that in the search for competitive advantage a firm must be considered as part of a wider system:

**suppliers > firm > distributors > consumers.**

As well as seeking improvements in its own activities, a firm should assess the opportunities and potential benefits from improving its links with other organizations. A firm is linked to the marketing and selling activities of its suppliers, and to the purchasing and materials handling activities of its distributors or customers.

The supply chain, then, is a process, and managing it is a key *strategic capability*. Cost savings and service differentiation can be achieved.

Organizations can create synergy, and enjoy the appropriate benefits, if they can successfully link their value chain with those of their suppliers and distributors. Just in time (JIT) deliveries integrate a supplier's outbound logistics with the organization's inbound logistics. Stock and costs can be reduced for the manufacturer, whose delivery lead time and reliability should also be improved. Set up properly, a JIT system can enable suppliers to plan their work more effectively and reduce their uncertainty. This requires an open exchange of reliable, up-to-date information and medium- to long-term supply arrangements. When Nissan was developing the supply chain for its UK manufacturing plant in Sunderland, it deliberately forged links with its suppliers' suppliers in its search to control costs without sacrificing quality and service. A retail bookseller, taking orders for non-stock items, needs to be sure of the delivery lead time from his publishers or wholesaler before quoting a date to the customer. This again demands accurate information, supported by reliable supply.

Carphone Warehouse, a leading retailer of mobile phones, has retailed telephones at prices ranging from 50p to over £300. Where the phone is sold as part of a package which involves a monthly line rental, the phone will typically have been provided free to the Carphone Warehouse by one of the major networks, such as BT, Orange or Vodafone, who in turn will have a supply arrangement with a manufacturer, perhaps Nokia or Motorola. The retailer will later receive a share of the future call revenues, normally between 3 per cent and 5 per cent. The ultimate value to Carphone Warehouse of the sale will average £300, regardless of the apparent selling price. In the case of phones used for prepaid calls without any monthly line rental, a typical sale will yield £200.

Organizations looking to launch a new product need to ensure that their supply and distribution networks are properly in place; given this, all interested parties can benefit. Retailers will need to be convinced of a new product's viability and potential before they agree to stock it, normally at the expense of taking something else off their shelves. Manufacturers must be sure that stocks are available where customers expect to find them before they proceed with launch advertising.

The key lies in an integrated network, where all members of the supply chain see themselves as mutual beneficiaries from an effective total system; however, this does not always happen.

Supply-chain management issues become increasingly important where organizations seek to reduce the number of their suppliers, buying as many items as possible from each selected supplier. It is quite feasible that these major suppliers will have to buy-in products that they do not make themselves in order to create the 'basket' of items demanded by their customer. This strategy has been adopted by the leading oil companies and car manufacturers. In 1994 Ford in the USA included components from 700 US suppliers in its Tempo model; in 1995 the company's equivalent Mercury Mystique was using 227 suppliers worldwide. One supplier, for example, was now required to provide a fully assembled dashboard, ready for immediate installation; it is likely that the electronic instrumentation will be bought-in by the relevant supplier. In 1999 Ford of Brazil went further. For the first time a supplier was given responsibility for part of the production line in a Ford assembly plant. Simply, the workers are employed by the supplier but work inside a plant owned by Ford.

Preece *et al.* (1995) use the value chain to explain how Levi Strauss, producer of the internationally successful Levi's jeans, has created value and used its value-creating activities carefully to establish a distinctive corporate reputation, which is a form of competitive advantage. Key aspects include:

- established links with suppliers from around the world
- team manufacturing (underpinned by training and empowerment) and linked to high-technology equipment and sophisticated information support
- global advertising and branding
- alliances with retailers who concentrate on Levi's jeans and do not stock competitor products
- a programme of 'marketing revitalization' designed to reduce lead times and improve the availability of the products.

We look at other developments with Levi's in Minicase 5.9 at the end of this chapter.

Strengthening the processes involved in managing the supply chain relates to the level of service that companies are able to offer their customers and to total quality management.

*Corporate restructuring to improve international competitiveness is a vital priority for British and European businesses in the 1990s. However, such restructuring must be a continual process of change and revitalization if we are to consistently satisfy the consumer's need for the highest quality products and services at the most competitive cost. The leadership of this process is the primary role of management in the modern company.*

Ian G McAllister, when Chairman and Managing Director, Ford Motor Company Limited, UK

When ICI had an Explosives division, which manufactured a range of explosive products, managers also developed expertise in detonating explosions. Quarry managers, who buy the products, really want stones and rocks on a quarry floor rather than the explosives. As a consequence ICI offered to produce a three-dimensional map of a quarry for their customers, indicating where the charges need to be placed, and then, when suitable holes have been drilled in the quarry face (by the quarry owners), carry out controlled explosions. In this way they add value for their customers and link the two value chains.

## 5.6.2 The organization's value chain

While strategic success depends upon the way in which the organization as a whole behaves, and the ways in which managers and functions are integrated, competitive advantage stems from the individual and discrete activities that a firm performs. A cost advantage can arise from low-cost distribution, efficient production or an excellent sales force that succeeds in winning the most appropriate orders. Differentiation can be the result of having an excellent design team or being able to source high-quality materials

**Figure 5.8** The value chain

Adapted from Porter, ME (1985) *Competitive Advantage: Creating and Sustaining Superior Performance*, Free Press, Michael E Porter © 1985. Adapted with the permission of the Free Press

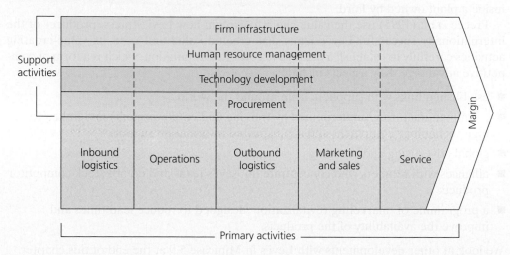

or high-quality production. Value-chain analysis is a systematic way of studying the direct and support activities undertaken by a firm. From this analysis should arise greater awareness concerning costs and the potential for lower costs and for differentiation. Quite simply, argues Porter (1985), competitive advantage is created and sustained when a firm performs the most critical functions either more cheaply or better than its competitors. But what are the most critical factors? Why? How and where might costs be reduced? How and where might differentiation be created?

### 5.6.3  Activities in the value chain

The value chain developed by Michael Porter is illustrated in Figure 5.8. There are five primary activities, namely inbound logistics, operations, outbound logistics, marketing and sales, and service. In the diagram they are illustrated as a chain moving from left to right, and they represent activities of physically creating the product or service and transferring it to the buyer, together with any necessary after-sale service. They are linked to four support activities: procurement, technology development, human resource management, and the firm's infrastructure. The support activities are drawn laterally as they can affect any one or more of the primary activities, although the firm's infrastructure generally supports the whole value chain. Every one of the primary and support activities incurs costs and should add value to the product or service in excess of these costs. It is important always to look for ways of reducing costs sensibly; cost reductions should not be at the expense of lost quality in areas that matter to customers and consumers. Equally, costs can be added justifiably if they add qualities that the customer values and is willing to pay for. The difference between the total costs and the selling price is the margin. The margin is increased by widening the gap between costs and price. The activities are described in greater depth below.

## Primary activities

- *Inbound logistics* are activities relating to receiving, storing and distributing internally the inputs to the product or service. They include warehousing, stock control and internal transportation systems.
- *Operations* are activities relating to the transformation of inputs into finished products and services. Operations includes machining, assembly and packaging.
- *Outbound logistics* are activities relating to the distribution of finished goods and services to customers.
- *Marketing and sales* includes such activities as advertising and promotion, pricing and sales force activity.
- *Service* relates to the provision of any necessary service with a product, such as installation, repair, extended warranty or training in how to use the product.

Each of these might be crucial for competitive advantage. The nature of the industry will determine which factors are the most significant.

## Support activities

- *Procurement* refers to the function or process of purchasing any inputs used in the value chain, as distinct from issues of their application. Procurement may take place within defined policies or procedures, and it might be evidenced within a number of functional areas. Production managers and engineers, for example, are very important in many purchasing decisions to ensure that the specification and quality are appropriate.
- *Technology development*: technology is defined here in its broadest sense to include know-how, research and development, product design and process improvement and information technology.
- *Human resource management* involves all activities relating to recruiting, training, developing and rewarding people throughout the organization.
- *The firm's infrastructure* includes the structure of the organization, planning, financial controls and quality management designed to support the whole of the value chain.

Again, each of these support activities can be very important in creating and sustaining competitive advantage.

**Subactivities**  Porter argues that it can often be valuable to subdivide the primary and support activities into their component parts when analysing costs and opportunities for differentiation. For example, it is less meaningful to argue that an organization provides good service than to explain it in terms of installation, repair or training. The competitive advantage is likely to result from a specific subactivity. Similarly, the marketing mix comprises a set of linked activities which should be managed to complement each other. However, competitive advantage can arise from just one activity in the mix, possibly the product design, its price or advertising, technical support literature, or from the skills and activities of the sales force.

### 5.6.4 Linkages within the value chain

Although competitive advantage arises from one or more subactivities within the primary and support activities comprising the value chain, it is important not to think of the chain merely as a set of independent activities. Rather, it is a system of interdependent activities. Linkages in the value chain, which are relationships between the activities, are very important. Behaviour in one part of the organization can affect the costs and performance of other business units and functions, and this quite frequently involves trade-off decisions. For example, more expensive materials and more stringent inspection will increase costs in the inbound logistics and operations activities, but the savings in service costs resulting from these strategies may be greater. The choice of functional strategies and where to concentrate efforts will relate to the organization's competitive and corporate strategies concerning competitive advantage.

Similarly, several activities and subactivities depend on each other. The extent to which operations, outbound logistics and installation are co-ordinated can be a source of competitive advantage through lower costs (reduced stockholding) or differentiation (high quality, customer-orientated service). This last example uses linkages between primary activities, but there are also clear linkages between primary and support activities. Product design affects manufacturing costs, purchasing policies affect operations and production costs, and so on.

Having introduced and discussed the concept of the value chain, it is now important to consider how it might be applied in the evaluation of costs and differentiation opportunities.

## 5.7 The value chain and competitive advantage

### 5.7.1 Cost leadership and differentiation strategies

In the next chapter we discuss how differentiation and cost management are two key themes in competition and also introduce Porter's generic strategies built around cost leadership and differentiation (Porter, 1985). Here, though, we look at how these themes relate to the value chain framework.

**Cost leadership** Chapter 6 discusses the argument of Porter (1985) that the lowest cost producer in either a broad or narrow competitive scope (the broad market or specialist segments):

- delivers acceptable quality but produces the product or service with lower costs than competitors
- sustains this cost gap
- achieves above-average profits from industry-average prices.

This cost advantage will be achieved by the effective management of the key determinants of costs.

**The differentiation strategy** Similarly, Porter argues that the successful application of a differentiation strategy involves:

**Table 5.2** Indicative cost breakdown of a manufacturing and a service business

| | Manufacturing firm (% of total) | Professional firm of accountants (% of total) | |
|---|---|---|---|
| *Primary activities* | | | |
| Inbound logistics | 4 | 8 | (data collection for audits) |
| Operations | 64 | 26 | (actual auditing) |
| Outbound logistics | 1 | 5 | (report writing and presentations) |
| Marketing and sales | 7 | 21 | (getting new business) |
| Service | 1 | 3 | (general client liaison) |
| | 77 | 63 | |
| *Support activities* | | | |
| Procurement | 1 | 1 | |
| Technology development | 10 | 8 | (IT development) |
| Human resources management | 2 | 16 | |
| Firm's infrastructure | 10 | 12 | |
| | 100 | 100 | |

These figures are only indicative, and should not be seen as targets for any particular firm.

- the selection of one or more key characteristics which are widely valued by buyers (there are any number of opportunities relating to different needs and market segments)
- adding costs selectively in the areas perceived to be important to buyers, and charging a premium price in excess of the added costs.

The success of this strategy lies in finding opportunities for differentiation which cannot be matched easily by competitors, and being clear about the costs involved and the price potential. Costs in areas not perceived to be significant to buyers must be controlled, and in line with competitor costs, for otherwise above-average profits will not be achieved.

The successful implementation of both of these strategies therefore requires an understanding of where costs are incurred throughout the organization. Understanding costs and the search for appropriate cost reductions involves an appreciation of how costs should be attributed to the various discrete activities which comprise the value chain. Table 5.2 compares a possible cost breakdown for a manufacturing firm with that for a firm of professional accountants. If an analysis of the value chain is to be meaningful, it is important that the costs are genuinely attributed to the activities that generate them, and not simply apportioned in some convenient way, however difficult this might prove in practice. Given the figures in Table 5.2 one might question whether the manufacturing firm is spending enough on human resources management and marketing, and the accountancy practice too much.

## 5.7.2 Cost drivers

It is important to appreciate which cost drivers are the most significant. The following cost drivers can all influence the value chain.

- Economies of scale and potential experience and learning curve benefits.

- Capacity utilization, linked to production control and the existence of bottlenecks.
- Linkages – Time spent liaising with other departments can incur costs, but at the same time create savings and differentiation through interrelationships and shared activities.
- Interrelationships and shared activities – Shared activities, possibly a shared sales force, shared advertising or shared plant, can generate savings. Close links between activities or departments can increase quality and ensure that the needs of customers are matched more effectively.
- Integration – This incorporates the extent to which the organization is vertically integrated, say manufacturing its own component parts instead of assembling bought-in components, or even designing and manufacturing its own machinery. This again can influence costs and differentiation, and is an important element of the strategy of YKK, which is featured as an example later in this chapter.
- Timing – Buying and selling at the appropriate time. It is important to invest in stocks to ensure deliveries when customers want them, but at the same time stockholding costs must be monitored and controlled.
- Policies – Policy standards for procurement or production may be wrong. If they are set too low, quality may be lost and prove detrimental. If they are too high in relation to the actual needs of the market, costs are incurred unnecessarily.
- Location issues – This includes wage costs, which can vary between different regions, and the costs of supporting a particular organization structure.
- Institutional factors – Specific regulations concerning materials content or usage would be an example.

Porter argues that sustained competitive advantage requires effective control of the cost drivers, and that scale economies, learning, linkages, interrelationships and timing provide the key opportunities for creating advantage. In the case of a cost leadership strategy, the cost advantage is relative to the costs of competitors, and over time these could change if competitors concentrate on their cost drivers. Consequently, it is useful

## Box 5.3 Cost Drivers – an Application

A key challenge for motor car manufacturers is one of reducing new product development times and costs while increasing the number of models that they offer their customers. To succeed, a car must look and feel different from its rivals, but the manufacturers have found that they can save both time and cost if they share components *which are hidden from view*. Examples would include floor pans (or platforms), engines and chassis. As a consequence, in recent years, there has been a tendency for new partnerships to emerge, as well as a number of important mergers.

Fiat, for example, owns the Alfa Romeo and Lancia marques and uses the same platforms for similar-sized models with the Fiat, Alfa Romeo and Lancia names.

Similarly, Volkswagen has acquired Audi, Seat and Skoda and adopts similar strategies. The platforms account for one-third of the costs incurred in designing a new car.

Manufacturers trade engines. Ford, for example, sells engines to other companies, as well as sharing components across the businesses it owns, which now include Jaguar, Land Rover and Volvo. In the same way, Peugeot diesel engines are common to Citroën and Peugeot cars.

to attempt to monitor and predict how competitor costs might change in the future linked to any changes in their competitive and functional strategies.

Box 5.3 provides details of some cost drivers in the car industry.

### 5.7.3 Common problems in cost control through the value chain

It was mentioned above that it can prove difficult to assign costs to activities properly, and this is one of the difficulties likely to be encountered in using value-chain analysis as a basis for more effective cost management. Porter contends that there are several common pitfalls in managing costs for competitive advantage:

- misunderstanding of actual costs and misperceptions of the key cost drivers
- concentrating on manufacturing when cost savings are required. Often it is not the area to cut if quality is to be maintained, especially once a certain level of manufacturing efficiency has been achieved
- failing to take advantage of the potential gains from linkages
- ignoring competitor behaviour
- relying on small incremental cost savings when needs arise rather than introducing a long-term, permanently installed cost-management programme.

### 5.7.4 Differentiation opportunities

It has been mentioned on a number of occasions that competitive advantage through differentiation can arise from any and every area of the business. In relation to the component parts of the value chain, the following are examples of where differentiation might originate.

#### Primary activities

- *Inbound logistics* – careful and thoughtful handling to ensure that incoming materials are not damaged and are easily accessed when necessary, and the linking of purchases to production requirements, especially important in the case of JIT manufacturing systems.
- *Operations* – high quality; high-output levels and few rejections; delivery on time.
- *Outbound logistics* – rapid delivery when and where customers need the product or service.
- *Marketing and sales* – advertising closely tied to defined market segments; a well-trained, knowledgeable and motivated sales force; and good technical literature, especially for industrial products.
- *Service* – rapid installation; speedy after-sales service and repair; and immediate availability of spare parts.

#### Support activities

- *Procurement* – purchasing high-quality materials (to assist operations); regional warehousing of finished products (to enable speedy delivery to customers).
- *Technology development* – the development of unique features, and new products and services; the use of IT to manage inbound and outbound logistics most

effectively; and sophisticated market analyses to enable segmentation, targeting and positioning for differentiation.

- *Human resources management* – high-quality training and development; recruitment of the right people; and appropriate reward systems which help to motivate people.

- *Firm's infrastructure* – support from senior executives in customer relations; investment in suitable physical facilities to improve working conditions; and investment in carefully designed IT systems.

In searching for the most appropriate means of differentiating for competitive advantage it is important to look at which activities are the most essential as far as consumers and customers are concerned, and to isolate the key success factors. It is a search for opportunities to be different from competitors in ways which matter, and through this the creation of a superior competitive position. The Japanese zip manufacturer YKK, the world market leader, grew to enjoy a superior competitive position, and the

**Figure 5.9** YKK's competitive advantage

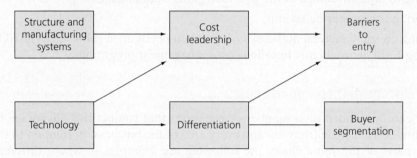

**Figure 5.10** YKK's competitive advantage and the value chain
Developed from Channon, DF and Mayeda, K (1979) Yoshida Kogyo KK 'A' and 'B' Case Studies.
Available from The European Case Clearing House. The dotted lines illustrate the linkages

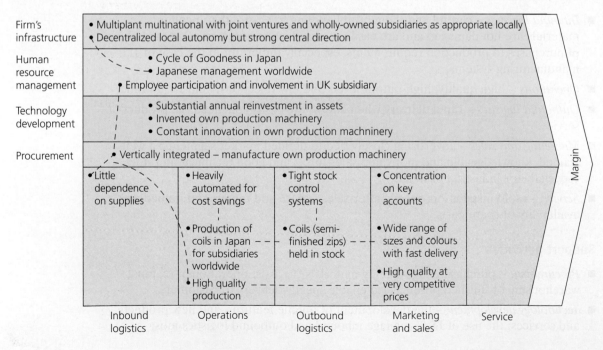

company's strategy is analysed against the value chain in the next section. The underlying philosophy of YKK, the 'Cycle of Goodness', is illustrated in Chapter 7, Box 7.3.

### 5.7.5 An application of the value chain

YKK has arguably succeeded in creating both cost leadership and substantial differentiation with its corporate, competitive and functional strategies, and these have resulted in effective barriers to entry into the industry and close relationships with customers. The idea might be illustrated in Figure 5.9.

The essential components of the strategy, summarized below, are illustrated in Figure 5.10, which places them in the context of the value chain and highlights the linkages.

YKK is structured as a multiplant multinational company with both wholly owned subsidiary companies and joint ventures throughout the world. The latter organizations are primarily the result of local politics, particularly in low labour cost countries in the Far East. While the subsidiaries are decentralized and enjoy some local autonomy, they are invariably managed at the top by Japanese executives on a period of secondment. Consequently, there is substantial influence from the Japanese parent.

YKK invests a significant percentage of after-tax profits back in the business, and as a result is heavily automated and able to enjoy the benefits of the experience/learning curve. Moreover, YKK prices its finished products very competitively both to generate customer satisfaction and to create barriers to entry. The company is vertically integrated, designing and manufacturing its own production machinery, and this gives it a unique competitive edge. It is also particularly innovative as far as both machinery and finished products are concerned.

Coils of semi-finished zips are produced in the Far East, particularly Japan, and exported to such countries as the UK, where they are cut to size and finished in response to customer orders. This results in both cost advantages and speedy deliveries from semi-finished stocks. A wide range of colours and sizes is kept ready for finishing. In the UK the key garment manufacturers and the retail outlets that they serve are targeted by YKK and are given special service.

The 'Cycle of Goodness' philosophy has not been exported in its complete form, but employee relations are an important aspect of the human resources strategy. Participation and involvement are essential features, and total quality management is a key feature.

Conceptually, the value chain is a useful way of analysing resources and functions within the organization in the context of how they might individually contribute to competitive advantage. At the same time the linkages between them should be assessed, because it is from these interrelationships and linkages that synergy in the form of additional cost savings or differentiation is created.

To apply the value chain properly it is important also to allocate costs to activities, and to evaluate whether costs could be saved in various areas or whether additional spending on certain activities might yield additional benefits by adding value in ways which are important to consumers. In practice it can be difficult to assign costs accurately. In this respect the actual application, rather than the concept, of the value chain is more applicable for managers than for students of this subject. In the authors' experience, applications of the value chain pose difficulties for managers, primarily because the management accounting systems in many organizations do not readily provide the data in the form required. Developing this theme, Johnson and Kaplan (1987) contend that certain costs are extremely difficult to allocate to certain individual products, but they are the costs of activities which are very significant in relation to total quality and in turn competitive advantage. Machine failures are one example, and they affect a number of products and can mean that deliveries are late and possibly priorities are changed. But how should the costs be allocated? As production systems become increasingly sophisticated, overheads, as a proportion of total costs, increase relative to the direct costs of labour and materials. Genuinely allocating these production overheads is difficult.

Nevertheless, the value chain can provide an extremely useful framework for considering the activities involved in producing products and services and considering their significance for customers.

> *We are students of Japan here in General Electric. We think they're marvellous, marvellous industrialists. We like their new product development, we like their speed, we like their quality focus. I put them at the pinnacle, and we're working every day to learn everything we can from them.*
>
> John F Welch, ex-Chairman and CEO, General Electric

We continue this chapter by returning to Kay's (1993) framework and looking at reputation, but before we do this it is important to cross reference activity mapping. In a 1996 *Harvard Business Review* article, Michael Porter developed activity maps as an adjunct to the value chain. The challenge is to produce a framework of the critically important activities, together with those that support them, and show how they all link together.

## 5.8   Reputation and branding

Reputation and branding are clearly linked but they are not one and the same. In a sense, a brand is a label that is attached to an organization's reputation. Kay (1993) contends that reputation is a key element of differentiation and that both reputation and branding are key **intangible resources**. What matters with differentiation is the customers' perception of the difference and what it means or conveys. It is, therefore, a qualitative indicator of quality; where quantitative measurement is difficult it can be a significant variable in decision-making and choice.

The reputation of Sir Richard Branson's Virgin brand has allowed him to diversify into a wide range of activities – customer confidence in the brand provides reassurance and allows him entry into areas where he has little if any previous experience or expertise. It is critically important, therefore, never to disappoint customers in ways which tarnish a reputation; somewhat paradoxically, this means that there can be a huge downside risk for companies with the strongest reputations if they make strategic errors of judgement.

In similar vein, a strong reputation provides a safe choice for customers who are new entrants to a market. A strong reputation therefore can help to sustain and build a strong position in a market. Moreover, it can sometimes be used to justify a premium price.

Famous-name endorsements provide an ideal opportunity for enhancing a company's reputation. Ownership of an endorsed product makes a statement about a person. People hold certain personalities in very high regard and would find it hard to imagine that they would endorse anything that was not good, even the best in the market. Whether such people actually use the products and services that they endorse is an entirely different matter!

## 5.8.1 Branding

Many differentiated products, and some services, are identified by brand names. These brand names, and/or the identity of the companies that own them, convey an image to customers. Simply, brands reflect reputations; and advertising is often used to create and reinforce this image and reputation. As competition intensifies, more and more products are perceived as commodities, sold essentially on price. When this happens, differentiation and branding become increasingly significant. The product needs a clear brand identity; a supportive corporate image, a company brand, is also valuable.

Minicase 5.8 illustrates how Britt Allcroft has built a very successful business by exploiting a number of children's character brands.

Brands add value, possibly the promise of some particular satisfaction or experience, a 'guarantee' of a specific level of quality, or reliability. Consequently, a brand can be seen as an actual product or service augmented by some additional added value. Branding is important and valuable; the drive to establish and maintain a recognized brand image can bring about differentiation and innovation. Nescafé, for example, has had several variants and improvements over the years. However, the value added must be real, as informed customers today will quickly see through any marketing hype. Moreover, the distinctiveness will not be achieved without investment, in both research and development and advertising, an issue which is taken up later.

Ideally, successful branding will generate customer loyalty and repeat purchases, enable higher prices and margins, and provide a springboard for additional products and

---

### Minicase 5.8  Britt Allcroft    (GB)

CASE

Britt Allcroft, who became a producer of television programmes, went to the same school at the same time as Anita Roddick, founder of the Body Shop. She always had a passion for storytelling. In her younger days she wrote several short stories, but none of them was ever published. Instead she found her way into television, and in 1978 she was asked to make a film about the British passion for steam engines.

There can be few better-loved children's characters than Thomas the Tank Engine, created originally by the Reverend W. Awdry in his spare time. As well as this series of illustrated books for children, Awdry wrote serious, adult books on steam railways. Although the Thomas books were no longer enjoying the popularity they initially had, Awdry was invited to appear in the film. He agreed, but inclement weather held up the project for several days. Awdry and Allcroft spent two days talking to each other. Although others had tried unsuccessfully to animate Awdry's characters – essentially a fleet of steam engines with distinc-

tive faces and personalities – Britt Allcroft became determined to succeed where others had failed.

*You need courage when people tell you you are off your head ... Thomas is much more than just a steam train having adventures – it is a way of life for me.*

Together with her business partner, who at the time was her husband, she approached venture capitalists, but the general reaction was that the time for Thomas had passed. Eventually, a bank loan from Barclays, supplemented by a second mortgage, allowed her to agree a licensing deal with publishers Reed Elsevier, who owned the master rights to the character, and to make her first film, which was broadcast on network television in 1984. Supported by a range of toys and clothing, the film was an instant success.

Her business now grew rapidly. More films were completed, with ex-Beatle Ringo Starr doing the narrating, the books were all reissued and character merchandising mushroomed. The films

▶

found an audience in 43 countries, including the US where, for political correctness, the Fat Controller was renamed Sir Topham Hat! When Britt Allcroft's company went public in 1996, it was valued at £31 million. In 1998 she posted a profit of £3 million, roughly 10 per cent of this coming from the films and 90 per cent from merchandising. A total of 1800 different items – books, videos, toys, clothes, bags, party supplies, bakewear, computer games, puzzles, models and carpets – was being manufactured by 400 sublicensees. Thomas had become the seventh most valuable toy brand in the US.

In 1997 Britt Allcroft acquired the worldwide rights to another past-glory character, Captain Pugwash, for £1.5 million, and set about resurrecting a programme that had first appeared on television in 1957 and disappeared in 1975. In the following year she bought all the rights to Thomas from Reed Elsevier (for £13.5 million) and no longer has to pay an annual licence fee. In 1999 Britt Allcroft formed an alliance with the two venture capital businesses which own the rights to Sooty, a hugely popular puppet character since its creation by Harry Corbett in 1952. Allcroft would merchandise the characters around the world and receive a management fee. In 2000 this deal was followed up with the acquisition of the company which produces Art Attack, then the second most popular children's television programme in the UK. Britt Allcroft has also opened a Thomas World theme park in Japan and acquired the rights to Guinness World Records.

Britt Allcroft herself stepped down from the Board of the business she founded in September 2002 and moved to Los Angeles, from where she intended to provide creative television and film inputs from the company's American office. The business was renamed Gullane Entertainment.

## Questions

1. Character merchandising can clearly be very lucrative, but how would you set about putting a value on a particular character?
2. Can you think of other ways Gullane/Britt Allcroft might exploit its brands and strengthen the synergy between them?
3. Were they to be available, what others could be usefully added to the portfolio?

**Thomas the Tank Engine**
http://www.thomasthetankengine.com

services. Customers expect to find the leading brand names widely available in distribution outlets but, in the case of, say, grocery products, the supermarkets will typically only offer the number one and number two brands alongside their own-label competitor. In the case of groceries, strong branding has been essential for enabling the leading manufacturers to contain the growing power of the leading supermarket chains. Nevertheless, branding has not exempted them from tight pricing strategies. Edwin Artzt, until the mid-1990s a powerful and renowned Chief Executive of Procter and Gamble, has stated that 'winning companies offer lower prices, better quality, continuous improvement and/or high profits to retailers'.

The quality of own-label products has increased, and consequently the magnitude of the premium that customers will pay for the leading manufacturer brand has declined in recent years. Procter and Gamble, which is not alone in this strategy, has adopted perpetual 'everyday low prices' for all of its products. Marlboro cigarettes, the world's leading cigarette brand, were reduced in price dramatically in the mid-1990s. In the competitive food sector, product innovation, quality, specific features and, to a lesser extent, packaging are seen as the most effective means of distinguishing brands from own-label alternatives.

## 5.8.2 Examples of leading brands

- *Persil* and *Pampers*: brand names not used in conjunction with the manufacturer's name – they are produced by Unilever and Procter and Gamble, respectively.

- *Coca-Cola*: manufacturer's name attributed to a product. *Levi's* is derived from Levi Strauss. Minicase 5.9 (at the end of the chapter) on Levi's looks at how a company with a significant brand and image has changed tactics in a dynamic and competitive environment.

- *Cadbury's Dairy Milk* and *Barclaycard Visa*: the first is a combination of a company and a product name, the second a combination of an organization (Barclays) and a service provided by a separate business.

- *St Michael*: the personalized brand name used historically on all products sold by Marks and Spencer.

- *Hoover*: a company name which historically became irrevocably associated with a particular product, although it is just one of a range of products produced by Hoover.

Several large organizations have, through strategic acquisitions and investments in brands, established themselves as global corporations. Examples include:

- *Unilever*: now owns a variety of food (Bird's Eye, Batchelors, Walls, John West, Boursin, Blue Band, Flora), household goods (Shield soap, Persil, Lux and Surf detergents) and cosmetics (Brut, Fabergé and Calvin Klein) brands.

- *Philip Morris*: US tobacco company which has acquired General Foods (US; Maxwell House coffee) and Jacobs Suchard (Switzerland; confectionery and coffee).

- *Nestlé*: including Chambourcy (France), Rowntree (UK) and Buitoni (Italy).

- *LVMH*: discussed earlier, in Chapter 3.

These companies can afford substantial investments in research and development to innovate and:

- strengthen the brand, say by extending the range of products carrying the name

- develop new opportunities, for example, Mars Bars ice cream, which was launched simultaneously in 15 European countries and priced at a premium over normal ice-cream bars

- transform competition in the market. Pampers disposable nappies have been developed into a very successful range of segmented products selling throughout the USA and Europe.

Strong brand names are clearly an asset for an organization. The value of the brand, the so-called brand equity, relates to the totality of all the stored beliefs, likes/dislikes and behaviours associated with it. Customer attitudes are critical; so too are those of distributors. The fact that a brand can command a certain amount of shelf space in all leading stores carries a value. However, creating and maintaining the image is expensive. It has been estimated that manufacturers spend on average 7 per cent of sales revenue to support the top ten leading brands, covering all product groups; this percentage increases as the brand recognition factor decreases. Because of this, manufacturers need to control the number of brands that they market at any time; Procter and Gamble withdrew over 25 per cent of their brands in the 1990s. Similarly, new product launches need to be managed effectively.

There is a so-far unresolved debate concerning how these assets might be properly valued in a company balance sheet. In the mid-1990s the US magazine *Financial Week* postulated that the world's most valuable brand name was Marlboro (owned by Philip Morris) and that it was then worth in excess of $30 million. In terms of monetary value, Coca-Cola was perceived to be second, although it is generally accepted that it is better known. The most valuable European brand is Nestlé's Nescafé; the three leading British brands (worldwide) are Johnnie Walker Red Label whisky (owned by Guinness), Guinness itself and Smirnoff Vodka (Diageo). Where the most recognized brand names are tied to high market shares and above-average margins, they are typically valued at over twice their annual revenues.

However, not all brand names are strong and effective. Prudential, best known as an insurance business, launched its Internet bank in 1999. The company opted to call it 'Egg' partly to provide a distinctive and unusual launch platform. The business has been a success and in 2004 Egg had between three and four million customers. Recognizing that Egg needed investment at a level that would stretch its own resources, Prudential attempted to find a buyer for the business, but none was forthcoming at the right price. This provided wonderful ammunition for some to criticise the name 'Egg', which had never been universally popular. Phrases such as 'egg on its face', 'half-baked' and 'gone off the boil' all appeared in the press.

Sometimes companies change their brand names – and not always for the better. In recent years The Post Office changed its corporate identity to Consignia. Unquestionably some design team created a clever play on the word 'consignment' but the public reaction was hardly supportive. There have been rumours that many people inside the company would prefer to see the name changed back!

### 5.8.3 Celebrity brands

High profile media figures have always been able to exploit their name and image by endorsing products. Actresses such as Liz Hurley (cosmetics) and footballers like David Beckham (sportswear) are well-known examples. But celebrities have finite life cycles. Sports stars are not necessarily high profile once they stop playing; supermodels 'get old' and are replaced by younger models. The more astute celebrities have found new ways to exploit their name and reputation. Elle McPherson, supermodel and actress, for example, launched her own range of lingerie from a base in her native Australia. More recently Claudia Schiffer has opted to go down a similar route. The 33-year-old (in 2004) supermodel has promoted brands and products such as Revlon, Chanel and L'Oréal cosmetics, Citroën cars, Ebel watches and Ferrero Rocher chocolates over several years. She set out to find a business partner to help her develop her own products – 'perhaps in beauty, fragrance or children's clothing'.

### 5.8.4 Relationship marketing

Branding helps to establish, build and cement relationships among manufacturers, their customers and their distributors. The term 'relationship marketing' is used to reinforce the argument that marketing should be perceived as the management of a network of relationships between the brand and its various customers. Marketing, therefore, aims

The new look Citroën Xsara.
Travel in a safer world.

In the new Citroën Xsara you're protected in style. Four airbags as standard. Option for two, extra, side window airbags. Three rear seats, each with a 3-point seat belt. Variable power steering. ABS with electronic brakeforce distribution (EBD) to maximise braking and steering efficiency. New, more powerful, 1.6i and 2.0i 16v petrol engines. And our revolutionary 2.0 HDi diesel. The new look Xsara boasts more specification and now, with prices starting from only £10,295,* Citroën is making better cars more affordable. For more information visit www.citroen.co.uk or call free on 0800 262 262.

**NOW WITH 3 YEARS' WARRANTY.\***

☆ CITROËN XSARA
NOTHING MOVES YOU LIKE A CITROËN

Manufacturer's recommended on the road retail price for car shown, new look Xsara 1.6i 16v SX hatchback, £12,995. On the road price includes £690 for delivery, VAT, number plates, 12 months' road fund licence and Government first registration fee. Optional metallic paint, alloy wheels and side window airbags available at extra cost. *Model range starts at £10,295 for the 1.4i L hatchback. ♠Warranty offer applies to vehicles registered from 23 October 2000. Warranty is only on vehicles sourced from Citroën UK Limited. 1 year's manufacturer's warranty and no-fee customer option of 2 years' extended warranty. Contact your dealer for terms and conditions. Prices correct at time of going to press.

**Claudia Schiffer** advertising Citroën Xsara  – example of celebrity branding © The Advertising Archive Ltd

to enhance brand equity and thus ensure continued satisfaction for customers and increased profits for the brand owner. Implicit in this is the realization that new customers are harder, and more expensive, to find than existing ones are to retain. This potent mix of brand identity and customer care is clearly related to the whole service package offered by manufacturers to their customers, and to total quality management.

> *We always travel with our teddy bears. When we got back to our room at the hotel we saw that the maid had arranged our bears very comfortably in a chair. The bears were holding hands.*

> *I needed a few more minutes to decide on dinner. The waitress said: 'If you would read the menu and not the road map, you would know what you want to order'.*

Binter et al., 1990

## 5.9 The impact of the Internet

The emergence and rapid growth of the Internet and the World Wide Web during the 1990s spawned a number of new and very entrepreneurial businesses. It is easy to be seduced by Internet possibilities and, supported by venture capital, many new Internet companies have grown rapidly. Few, however, have turned growing revenues into profits. At the same time, it has also demanded that every organization develop a strategy for harnessing its potential: it will not go away and, for some, will completely transform their ways of operating and doing business. This section briefly explores some of these issues.
The Internet:

- provides information – which can make decision-making much easier, but is potentially in quantities so great that it is hard to assimilate
- allows a company to advertise and promote itself and its products and services
- speeds up communication by replacing printed memos and telephone calls
- enables electronic trading. This again can take several forms. For consumer sales, information on a product (such as a book) can very readily be provided, along with reviews; moreover, in the case of a compact disc, sample tracks can be played. Virtual reality can be employed to move people around either a shopping mall or a supermarket.

Minicase 7.1 in Chapter 7 shows how certain organizations have been able to secure very large amounts of capital to pursue an apparent good idea for an e-commerce business. However, it also shows how volatile the traded shares of these businesses can be as they grow in size but fail to post any profits.
The fundamental principle behind many new *e-commerce businesses* is trading without either manufacture or long-term inventory. E-commerce cuts out the retail store element. New organizations dedicated to e-commerce are similar in principle yet distinctly different from the situation where established organizations (for example, Tesco and Waterstone's) sell via the web as well as through their own high-street outlets. The large retailers are increasingly moving in this direction because of the impact of the specialist e-commerce companies on customer buying habits. While the new businesses may own warehouses for collecting stock for onward transmission and holding limited numbers of fast-moving items, there will rarely be any need for them to employ either

sales or production staff, and this element can be outsourced to specialists in logistics, leaving the e-commerce company to focus on creating and maintaining a successful web site once the supply chain is set up. Simply, they are a virtual company.

The transaction begins when a potential customer uses a home computer to check out the web site of the e-commerce business, selects an item and places an order electronically. Typically, credit-card information will be requested, and an instant credit check will be carried out by contacting the computer system of the relevant credit-card company. Once the payment details have been confirmed, an order is transmitted to the manufacturer of the product in question. If the e-commerce company is holding the product in stock, this would be replaced by an order to the company's own warehouse, who will later reorder from the manufacturer. Delivery to the customer can be direct from the manufacturer or via the e-commerce business who will receive bulk supplies and post out individual parcels.

Their fundamental advantage is their ability to reach a wide customer audience at low cost, as long as they can be attracted in the first place and then retained as a regular customer. Relatively specialist items can thus be made available to people who find it difficult to visit the shops that sell them directly. One key disadvantage is that the goods cannot be touched and inspected, which matters more for some customers and products than it does for others. The main infrastructure requirements for a successful e-commerce business are appropriate managerial and technical skills, venture capital to set up a sophisticated supply chain and secure payment systems. They also need customers who can and do access their site, recognize the convenience and benefits being offered, and believe that the payment systems are private and secure.

Every business needs an Internet strategy; it has to decide upon the extent to which it intends to use the Internet for promotion and for commercial transactions. For many organizations, it is far more important for business-to-business transactions than it is for direct sales to customers.

The ultimate popularity of Internet trading for consumer products remains difficult to predict for a number of reasons. More and more households are on-line but the penetration is uneven. While all age groups are involved, younger people are more likely to use the Internet than older generations. Men seem more comfortable with the technology than women in many cases, and there is a greater incidence when people have enjoyed higher education and have above-average earnings. The geographical coverage in the UK is biased to the southern counties. But this is now. Various predictions for future take-up have been offered and they are not all in accord. Some customers are keen to use the Internet for information gathering but stop short of buying electronically. This is partly linked to a reluctance to input credit-card details into a personal computer.

However, the potential of the Internet to link business with business is enormous and it offers both cost savings and service improvements. The term *e-markets* is normally used for this linkage. E-markets:

- link computers and databases
- constitute virtual and private networks where companies and their suppliers can share vital information
- allow easy and fast transfer of up-to-date information on current orders, contracts, prices, inventory, deliveries and so on – access can be controlled through passwords
- monitor and analyse activities
- have a facility for transactions

- enable cost reductions together with better information and a faster response time
- allow suppliers to auction any surplus stock, and
- allow buyers to ask for bidders against a special or an emergency need.

## 5.10 Conclusion: Information, knowledge and corporate capital

Information, then, is required to support the decision-making processes related to strategic change – both formally planned changes and emergent, adaptive, incremental change – at all levels of the organization. Figure 5.11 summarizes the key points. Information, itself supported by IT, is used by people to help them to make decisions. History and experience qualify the information and analysis. The information, and the way in which people use it, comprises the organization's knowledge.

Figure 5.12 attempts to draw together those elements and resources which comprise the organization's corporate capital. It is a summary of many of the points and issues raised and discussed in Parts One and Two so far. Part Two opened by distinguishing between opportunity-driven and resource-based strategy. Figure 5.12 is a comprehensive summary of all the resources that an organization possesses and which it should lever and exploit to create and sustain competitive advantage and strategic success.

### Minicase 5.9 Levi's ⬤ US

Levi's, a global business with a base in San Francisco, has built an established brand and image which allows it to sell at premium prices and still command a sizeable market share for its jeans. During the 1990s two significant events took place. To protect its image Levi's took out a legal action against Tesco in the UK to stop the supermarket group selling imported Levi's 501s at reduced prices. In a sense Tesco was offering the same service as the outlet stores which sell branded products (often last year's ranges) at substantial discounts. In addition, the market for denim fashions began to fall away. As an initial response to this Levi's moved further upmarket and launched a new range in the £175 per pair price bracket.

Meanwhile competitor brands such as Lee and Wrangler, which sold at lower prices, were doing well. Levi's concluded it had to respond and decided it would switch its emphasis and target the mass market through supermarkets. In 2003 the company launched a new range in Europe, priced at around 60 per cent of the price for its traditional branded jeans. Its Signature Range had already been made available in the US through Wal-Mart. The target customers were people in their thirties with mortgages and families, people who had earlier been fashion-conscious but were now less so for economic reasons. The implied price was around £25 per pair, compared with a typical Levi's price between £40 and £45. At this time some 25 per cent of jeans customers were willing to pay £30 and above; just 8 per cent were in the £45 plus sector of the market. The lowest priced jeans available from Tesco in 2003 were £6.

### Questions

1. In the circumstances do you think this was a sound or a risky tactic for Levi's to adopt?
2. To what extent do you believe the quality difference between various brands of jeans is based on design and fashion as distinct from workmanship and higher quality materials?

**Levi's** http://www.levis.com

Logically, it can be argued that a company which aims to build and sustain competitiveness and success will audit these elements and use this analysis as a source of ideas for attention and improvement.

**Figure 5.11** Using knowledge for competitive success

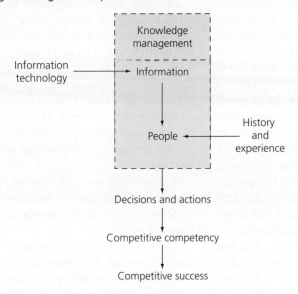

**Figure 5.12** Corporate capital
Developed from ideas contained in the 1994 and 1995 Annual Reports of Skandia

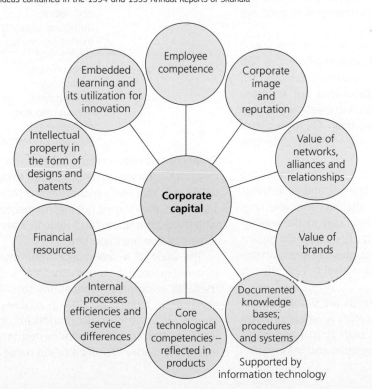

# SUMMARY

Acquiring, deploying and exploiting key resources in an individual and effective way is the source of important differences and, in turn, competitive advantage. The resource-based view of strategy looks at how organizations *individually* respond, and at how their core competencies and strategic capabilities determine their success as a competitor.

A simple *resource audit* is an attempt to assess the strengths and weaknesses of an organization; typically it will be carried out in conjunction with an assessment of opportunities and threats. However, any evaluation should be relative. The assessment should be in the context of, first, the key success factors for the markets and industries in question and, second, the comparable strengths and weaknesses of competitors for the same customers.

*Strategic architecture* refers to the linkages inside the organization (between different divisions, departments and managers) and the relationships, possibly partnerships, that an organization has with other members of the relevant value chain, such as suppliers and distributors. Synergy, mutual dependency and trust are key issues in the relationships.

People who contribute as innovators and intrapreneurs must be in a position where they feel stretched and rewarded. For some organizations, *empowerment* is a wonderful idea but no more than that. They find it difficult to create the appropriate climate and culture; their employees may not wish to be empowered to some considerable degree.

Emergent strategy possibilities are enhanced where people work well together and collectively. There is a team spirit, sharing and learning. *Synergy* is the outcome. Extended to the level of the organization, this constitutes a learning organization. Like empowerment, this can seem attractive as a theoretical idea and ideal but be difficult to implement effectively.

The information that feeds the whole process of decision-making comes from a variety of internal and external sources, both formal and informal. Formal information systems and *information technology* can both make a valuable input, but information is more than information technology.

However much information they have, managers are still not 'seeing reality', rather they are put in position where their perception of events can be more informed and hopefully more insightful. Because issues of meaning are crucial, it is possible that decisions lead to counterintuitive behaviour with unanticipated outcomes.

Nevertheless, as well as informing decision-making, information and information technology can be a source of competitive advantage in its own right.

The emergence of the *Internet* has spawned a host of new businesses. It has also required every company to formulate a strategy for harnessing its potential effectively.

Michael Porter has provided a useful value-chain framework for helping to understand where differences are created, where costs are incurred and how synergy might be generated through linkages. His value chain comprises:

Five primary activities – inbound logistics; operations; outbound logistics; marketing and sales service; and

Four support activities – procurement; technology development; human resource management; the firm's infrastructure.

Organizations must understand and manage their cost drivers. They should not attempt to cut corners with things that really matter for customers; at the same time, they should not incur unnecessary costs with things that do not add value in ways that customers believe are important.

The value of a strong reputation must not be underestimated. A sound corporate reputation reassures customers. It generates sales and, very significantly, repeat sales. It can enable price premiums. It is a crucially important intangible resource. It is frequently manifested in a strong, visible and readily identified brand name.

## QUESTIONS AND RESEARCH ASSIGNMENTS

1. What are the opportunity-driven and resource-based views of strategy? Where and why are they different? Why is it important for organizations to embrace both views simultaneously?

2. Think about your own buying habits and choices. Where do you specifically choose high-profile branded items, and where are you less concerned? Why? What do you think this behaviour is saying about you?

3. Consider how strategic changes in one retail sector, from an emphasis on hardware stores that specialize in personal service and expert advice to customers from all employees, to a predominance of do-it-yourself supermarkets and warehouses, might have affected issues of staff motivation, personal development needs and appropriate reward systems.

4. Albeit by rule of thumb, take a team of people with whom you associate closely and evaluate their behaviour characteristics Where is the team strong? Where is the team weak? Do you believe it is balanced? If not, what might be done to change things?

5. Consider how the increasing utilization of information technology in retailing has affected you as a customer. Do you feel that the major retail organizations who have introduced and benefited from the greater utilization of IT have attempted to ensure that the customer has also benefited and not suffered?

6. Consider why it is argued that the increasing utilization of IT by organizations is a cultural issue. How might managers be encouraged to make greater use of the technology which is available?

7. How do you personally use the Internet? Do you feel you are exploiting its potential?

## INTERNET AND LIBRARY PROJECTS

1. Using the Internet to look at the current status of Dyson and the other main manufacturers of vacuum cleaners, to what extent has James Dyson transformed an industry? How has he now extended the product range for his dual cyclone cleaners? In what ways are his washing machines different?

   **Dyson** http://www.dyson.com

2. Selecting an organization of your choice, and ideally one with which you are familiar, carry out a resource audit. Make sure that you take account of industry key success factors and competitors' relative strengths in your evaluation.

3. Using the same organization, apply Porter's value chain. As far as you are able, and accepting that there may be elements of subjectivity, allocate the costs and consider whether your breakdown matches your initial expectations. Where are the all-important linkages?

4. For an organization of your choice ascertain the range of products and services offered and answer the following questions:

   ■ What are essential information needs from outside the organization (the environment) for managing these products and services both now and in the future?

   ■ Where are the limitations in availability?

   ■ What role might IT play in improving availability?

5. By visiting and talking to staff at an appropriate level and with several years work experience in that environment, in both a travel agency and a retail store which makes extensive use of an EPOS (electronic point of sale) system, ascertain the effect that IT has had on their decision-making. Do the staff feel they are more aware strategically? If so, has this proved valuable?

## Further reading

Garvin, DA (1984) What does product quality really mean?, *Sloan Management Revue*, Fall.

McFarlane, FW (1984) Information technology changes the way you compete, *Harvard Business Review*, May–June.

Drucker, PF (1988) The coming of the new organization, *Harvard Business Review*, January–February.

Kanter, RM (1989) The new managerial work, *Harvard Business Review*, November–December.

Senge, P (1990) The leader's new work – building learning organizations, *Sloan Management Review*, Fall.

Miller, D (1992) The Icarus paradox – how exceptional companies bring about their own downfall, *Business Horizons*, January–February.

Rayport, JF and Sviokla, JJ (1995) Exploiting the virtual value chain, *Harvard Business Review*, November–December.

Porter, ME (1996) What is strategy?, *Harvard Business Review*, November–December.

Porter, ME (2001) Strategy and the Internet, *Harvard Business Review*, March–April.

Part 1 Supplement 2 listed the McKinsey 7-S framework for resource analysis. Details can be found in: Peters, TJ and Waterman, RH Jr (1982) *In Search of Excellence: Lessons from America's Best Run Companies*, Harper & Row.

## References

Ackoff, RL (1967) Management misinformation systems, *Management Science* 14, December.

Belbin, RM (1981) *Management Terms: Why They Succeed or Fail*. Heinemann.

Binter, MJ, Booms, B and Tetreault, MS (1990) The service encounter: diagnosing favourable and unfavourable incidents, *Journal of Marketing*, 54, January.

Buckingham, M and Coffman, C (1999) *First, Break all the Rules*, Simon and Schuster.

Capelli, P and Crocker-Hefter, A (1995) HRM: The key to competitive advantage, *Financial Times Mastering Management Series*, No. 6, 1 December.

Cummings, TG (1981) Designing effective work groups. In *Handbook of Organizational Design* (eds PC Nystrom and WH Starbuck), Oxford University Press.

Day, G (1996) How to learn about markets, *Financial Times Mastering Management Series*, No. 12, 26 January.

Earl, MJ and Hopwood, AG (1980) From management information to information management. In *The Information Systems Environment* (eds HC Lucas, FF Land, JJ Lincoln and K Supper), North-Holland.

Forrester, J (1969) *Urban Dynamics*, MIT Press.

Gilbert, X (1995) It's strategy that counts, *Financial Times Mastering Management Series*, No. 7, 8 December.

Hersey, P and Blanchard, K (1982) *The Management of Organisational Behaviour,* 4th edn, Prentice-Hall.

Hertzberg, F (1968) One more time how do you motivate employees? *Harvard Business Review*, January–February.

Johnson, HT and Kaplan, RS (1987) *Relevance Lost: The Rise and Fall of Management Accounting*, Harvard Business School Press.

Kay, JA (1993) *Foundations of Corporate Success*, Oxford University Press.

Kelly, FJ and Kelly, HM (1987) *What they Really Teach you at the Harvard Business School*, Piatkus.

Kotter, JP and Heskett, JL (1992) *Corporate Culture and Performance*, Free Press.

Lucas, H (1976) *The Analysis, Design and Implementation of Information Systems*, McGraw-Hill.

Maitland, A (1999), Strategy for creativity, *Financial Times,* 11 November.

Marchand, DA (1995a) Managing strategic intelligence, *Financial Times Mastering Management Series*, No. 4, 17 November.

Marchand, DA (1995b) What is your company's information culture? *Financial Times Mastering Management Series*, No. 7, 8 December.

McClelland, D and Winter, D (1971) *Motivating Economic Achievement*, Free Press.

McFarlane, FW (1984) Information technology changes the way you compete, *Harvard Business Review*, May–June.

McFarlane, FW, McKenney, JL and Pyburn, P (1983) The information archipelago – plotting a course, *Harvard Business Review*, January–February.

McGregor, DM (1960) The Human Side of Enterprise, McGraw-Hill.

Peters, TJ and Waterman, RH Jr (1982) *In Search of Excellence: Lessons from America's Best Run Companies*, Harper & Row.

Porter, LW, Lawler, EE and Hackman, JR (1975) *Behaviour in Organisations*. McGraw-Hill.

Porter, ME (1980) *Competitive Strategy: Techniques for Analysing Industries and Competition*, Free Press.

Porter, ME (1985) *Competitive Advantage: Creating and Sustaining Superior Performance*, Free Press.

Porter, ME (1996) What is strategy? *Harvard Business Review*, November–December

Porter, ME and Millar, VE (1985) How information gives you a competitive advantage, *Harvard Business Review*, July–August.

Prahalad, CK and Hamel, G (1990) The core competency of the corporation, *Harvard Business Review*, May–June.

Preece, S, Fleisher, C and Toccacelli, J (1995) Building a reputation along the value chain at Levi Strauss, *Long Range Planning*, 28, 6.

Rayport, JF and Sviokla, JJ (1995) Exploiting the virtual value chain, *Harvard Business Review*, November–December.

Roffey Park Management Centre (1995) *Career Development in Flatter Structures.* Research report.

Schein, EH (1983) The role of the founder in creating organizational culture, *Organisational Dynamics*, Summer.

Senge, P (1991) *The Fifth Discipline – The Art and Practice of the Learning Organization,* Doubleday.

Skandia (1994, 1995) *Annual Reports and Accounts.*

Spear, R (1980) *Systems Organization: The Management of Complexity*, Unit 8, *Information*, The Open University T243.

# The Dynamics of Competition

## Learning objectives

Having read to the end of this chapter you should be able to:

- explain the notion of dynamic, tactical change in a competitive environment
- define product (service) differentiation and cost leadership and explain their role in the creation and maintenance of competitive advantage; and
- show how Michael Porter used these themes to create four important generic strategies
- appreciate why competitive strategies must be changed in a dynamic environment if any advantage is to be sustained
- describe a number of key competitive platforms
- show how an organization can evaluate its competitive strategies against those of its competitors.

Few companies enjoy the luxury of having no serious competitors or little likelihood of any need to change their competitive strategy. It is essential for companies to look for opportunities to create – and sustain – a competitive edge over their rivals and build customer loyalty that provides something of a comfort zone. Logically this should lead to superior profits.

However, competitive advantage, as a term, is easily misunderstood. Some organizations clearly believe, and thus delude themselves, that a clear competitive strategy constitutes advantage. It does not. Advantage comes from being better or different in some meaningful way.

Even the strongest companies cannot afford to stand still, as shown in Minicase 6.1. A cynic would argue that a company must change more rapidly than its rivals can steal its ideas!

This chapter begins by looking at the nature of competition in general, before discussing models and frameworks which help us to understand competitive strategy, competitive advantage and competitive dynamics.

## Minicase 6.1  Coca-Cola                                   US    Int

Although it is typically priced higher than many competing products, Coca-Cola (Coke) remains the world's best-selling soft drink and the world's best-known brand name. Coca-Cola is reputed to see its only serious competitor as water! Ideally an adult requires a daily liquid intake of 64 ounces, and overall Coke provides just two of these. The soft drinks industry has been categorized in the following way:

- Refreshment – typical carbonated drinks, such as Coke
- Rejuvenation – ready-to-drink teas and coffees, for example
- Health and nutrition – juices and milk drinks
- Replenishment – bottled water and sports drinks

The Coca-Cola company was founded over 100 years ago, and today it remains largely focused; Columbia Pictures was acquired some years ago, but later sold to Sony. Seventy per cent of Coke's sales and 80 per cent of its operating profits are now earned outside the US. The company has a 50 per cent share of the world market for carbonated drinks, including 44 per cent of the US market. A typical American adult who drinks Coke will consume 400 eight-ounce servings in a year, just over one a day. Because Americans own very large refrigerators which can store the largest bottles available, this can work out relatively inexpensive. By contrast, a regular British Coke drinker consumes 120 eight-ounce servings in a year, from smaller and more expensive bottles and cans. The UK is still perceived to be a developing market for the product. Other established territories, which include Switzerland, Chile and Mexico, have a consumption of 300 eight-ounce servings per year.

Over the years critics have predicted that something would happen to stem the continual and successful growth of the business, possibly changing tastes, stronger competition or market saturation. This really has not happened; Coca-Cola has continued to increase worldwide sales through clever marketing and occasional new products. In

1996 Coca-Cola was America's most admired company in the *Fortune* rankings but, as will be seen in Chapter 7, it has not sustained this position in the late-1990s and early 2000s, although it continues to enjoy high global admiration. In terms of increases in shareholder wealth, Coca-Cola was unrivalled in the US throughout the leadership of its charismatic chief executive, Roberto Goizueta. Goizueta was the strategic leader from 1981 until his death in post in 1997. Nevertheless, Coca-Cola still made a number of strategic misjudgements during this time.

### Competitive strategies

Coke had successfully established Fanta (the fizzy orange drink launched in 1960) and Tab (sugar-free Coca-Cola, 1963) when Goizueta took over. In 1982 Diet Coke was launched. Diet products are particularly important for the American market, but generally less significant elsewhere.

However, in 1985, New Coke was launched to replace the original blending, but subsequently withdrawn after a consumer outcry. It was sweeter and some critics suggested it had been developed because of the increasing popularity of the sweeter Pepsi Cola. One lady Coke fan who lived on the east coast went round all the local stores in her district buying up all their remaining stock of the original blend. Two middle-aged men on the west coast started a society pledged to restore the original taste. Members from across the nation paid to join and the group organized demonstrations. Inevitably there was huge publicity. The company eventually backed down and relaunched the original blend as Coca-Cola Classic. Some time later New Coke was withdrawn. Whilst one might have imagined the company would be damaged, it actually benefited from the enormous publicity it generated. The debacle cost money, but sales increased.

The Fresca range has also been launched. Sprite is another famous Coca-Cola brand, as are Minute Maid fruit juices. In 1998, an agreement to buy the Schweppes soft drinks businesses outside the

US from Cadbury's was thwarted by the European regulatory authorities. Coca-Cola has also been affected by economic crises and recessions in countries where it is particularly popular, especially Russia and Asia. In 1999 it was forced to withdraw the product in Belgium after a health scare resulting from minor contamination. Arguably, the company's public relations could have been better.

In 2001 Coca-Cola formed a joint venture with Procter and Gamble to link its soft drinks with P&G's snacks, such as Pringles. This was really following a strategy developed by PepsiCo. Also in 2001 Coca-Cola allied with Disney to allow it to use Disney characters for promotional purposes. The company has also extended its product ranges into Fruitopia, a 'new age' fruit drink, bottled water (Dasani brand) and lemon and vanilla Coke.

Coke had really became popular overseas when it was shipped out to GIs during the Second World War, and systematically it has been introduced to more and more countries. For many years its stated goal was to 'always have Coca-Cola within an arm's reach of desire' and preferably in chilled storage, whether this was on retail shelves or through vending machines. It has benefited from being associated with the image and persona of America. When GIs drank it during the Second World War – and subsequent wars in Korea and Vietnam – it was seen as a reminder of exactly what they were fighting for. Early in 1999 Coca-Cola's name was linked to a line of fashion and sports clothing, the first significant extension of the brand.

Coca-Cola controls production of the concentrated syrup from Atlanta; mixing, bottling/canning and distribution is franchised to independent businesses worldwide. In truth, the issue of the 'secret formula' is more mystique than necessity, but it provides another valuable story to reinforce the brand and its image.

Goizueta inherited a distribution network which was underperforming and he set about strengthening it with proper joint venture agreements and tight controls. Effective supply management is absolutely vital for the business. Goizueta chose to acquire its smaller, underperforming bottlers, invested in them and, when they were turned around, sold them to stronger anchor bottlers – specifically those with the financial resources to invest in developing the business. 'Coca-Cola's distribution machine is [now] the most powerful and pervasive on the planet.'

Coca-Cola has always advertised heavily and prominently; and Goizueta has also negotiated a number of important promotional agreements. Coca-Cola has special aisles in Wal-Mart stores; Coke's Hi-C orange juice is supplied to McDonald's, for example. In recent years there has been increased emphasis on branding and packaging at the expense of pure advertising. 'We had really lost focus on who our customer was. We felt our customer was the bottler, as opposed to the McDonald's and the Wal-Marts' (Goizueta).

Faced with increased competition from retail own-label brands sold mainly through supermarket chains, Coca-Cola has carefully defended and strengthened its other distribution outlets such as convenience stores, fast-food restaurants and vending machines.

## Competition

Coca-Cola's main rival is Pepsi Cola, which has a 30 per cent share of the US market and 20 per cent of the world market. Its share has been growing since the 1993 introduction of Pepsi Max, a sugar-free product with the taste of the original Pepsi. Pepsi diversified into snack foods (Frito-Lay in the US, Walkers and Smiths crisps in the UK) and restaurants (Pizza Hut, Taco Bell and Kentucky Fried Chicken in the US); just one-third of global profits came from soft drinks in the mid-1990s. Pepsi also owns much of its bottling network. In 1996 the Pepsi brand was relaunched with a massive international promotional campaign. The new Pepsi colours, predominantly blue, were chosen to appeal to the younger buyer. In 1997 PepsiCo divested its restaurants into a separate business, and followed this up with the acquisition of the French company, Orangina – after the European competition regulators had prevented Coca-Cola from buying the business. A year later Pepsi acquired Tropicana, the world's largest marketer of branded juices, which it bought from the

Canadian company Seagram. With this purchase, Pepsi controlled 40 per cent of the US chilled orange juice market, twice the share of Coca-Cola.

Another significant competitor is Cott of Canada, which produces discounted colas with acceptable alternative tastes. Cott produces concentrate for Wal-Mart in the US and for Sainsbury and Virgin in the UK.

In 2004 Douglas Daft, the second CEO since Goizueta, announced he would retire at the end of the year. He would be 61 and have completed five years in charge. The company had a succes-sion problem all over again. It was rumoured it might seek to split the Chairman and CEO posts.

**Questions**

1. Why is Coca-Cola 'number one' in its industry?
2. Where is its competitive advantage?
3. If it avoids serious mistakes, does it need to do anything radically different to retain its position?
4. Can you think of anything its leading rivals might do to upset the applecart?

**Coca-Cola** http://www.coca-cola.com

*One advantage when you're No. 1 or 2 in an industry is that you can really have a hell of a lot of say in what the future's going to be like by what you do. I'm not a believer in always forecasting the future. But if you take actions that can create that future, at least shape it, then you can benefit from it.*

*They say: 'Do you sleep well at night with all the competition?'*
*I say: 'I sleep like a baby'. They say: 'That's wonderful'.*
*I say: 'No, no. I wake up every two hours and cry!'*
*Because it's true, you know. You have to feel that restlessness.*

Roberto Goizueta, late Chief Executive, Coca-Cola Corporation

## 6.1  Competition: an introduction

Causes generate effects. Actions lead to outcomes. On occasions companies may attempt to seize the competitive initiative and introduce an innovatory change. An action by one competitor which affects the relative success of rivals provokes responses. One action can therefore provoke several reactions, depending on the extent of the impact and the general nature of competition. Each reaction in turn further affects the other rival competitors in the industry. New responses will again follow. What we have in many markets and industries is a form of *competitive chaos*. Figure 6.1 shows a competitive business environment which is permanently fluid and unpredictable. For example, British Telecom (BT) continues to face competition from cheap phone call and Internet service providers as well as demands that it provides free access to its network. This is considered a restrictive act and has slowed down the development of both the Internet in the UK and of broadband services. BT must adapt and respond to defend its place in the market, or eventually the government will force regulatory change on them.

It is important to differentiate between two sets of similar, but nevertheless different, decisions. First, some actions are innovatory and represent one competitor acting upon a perceived opportunity ahead of its rivals; other actions constitute reactions to these competitive initiatives. Second, some decisions imply incremental strategic change to

**Figure 6.1** Dynamic competition

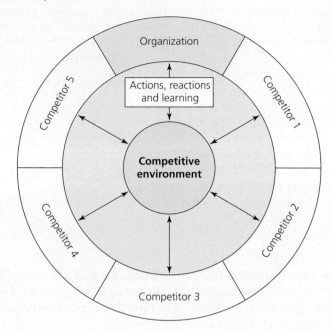

existing, intended strategies; on different occasions companies are adapting their strategies (**adaptive strategic change**) as they see new opportunities which they can seize early, or possible future threats which they are seeking to avoid. The process is about *learning and flexibility*. Often, as shown in Chapter 10, they involve an *intrapreneur*, an internal entrepreneur.

The skills required by organizations are:

- the ability to discern patterns in this dynamic environment and competitive chaos, and spot opportunities ahead of their rivals
- the ability to anticipate competitor actions and reactions
- the ability to use this intelligence and insight to lead customer opinion and outperform competitors.

Ocean Spray has been cited by Rosabeth Moss Kanter (1990) as another US company which spotted a potentially lucrative competitive opportunity missed by its rivals. Small 'paper bottles' for soft drinks were being used in Europe, but the leading US manufacturers did not see them taking off in America and were not enthusiastic. Ocean Spray, which manufactures a range of products, including drinks, from cranberries (sometimes mixed with other fruits) had empowered a middle manager from engineering to look for new ideas for the company – an aspect of their planned strategy – and he saw the potential. The result was an 18-month exclusive rights agreement. The packaging concept proved attractive and the final outcome was a substantial increase in the popularity of cranberry juice drinks. Simply, children liked the package and came to love the drink. Ocean Spray products are now much more evident around the world.

The Ocean Spray example illustrates how competition can come from unexpected sources. It is dangerous for any organization to assume that future competitive threats will only come from rivals, products and services that they already know and understand;

in reality, it can be the unrecognized, unexpected newcomers which pose the real threat because, in an attempt to break into an established market, they may introduce some new way of adding value and 'rewrite the rules of competition'.

Bill Gates' view of the future, based on personal computers on every desk, was radically different from that of long-time industry leader, IBM, and it enabled Microsoft to enter and dominate the computer industry. British Airways was surprised by the entry and success of Virgin Atlantic Airways on profitable transatlantic routes, as it perceived its main competition to come from the leading US carriers. Virgin was adding new values, offering high and differentiated levels of service at very competitive prices. The success of Direct Line, with telephone insurance services at very competitive prices, has provoked a response from existing companies; telephone banking is having a similar effect. In both cases the nature of the service has been changed dramatically, and improved for many customers.

Figure 6.2 shows how organizational resources need to be used to drive the competitive cycle. Constant, or ideally growing, sales and market share can lead to economies of scale and learning and, in turn, cost reductions and improved profits. The profits could, in a particularly competitive situation, be passed back to customers in the form of

**Figure 6.2** The competitive cycle

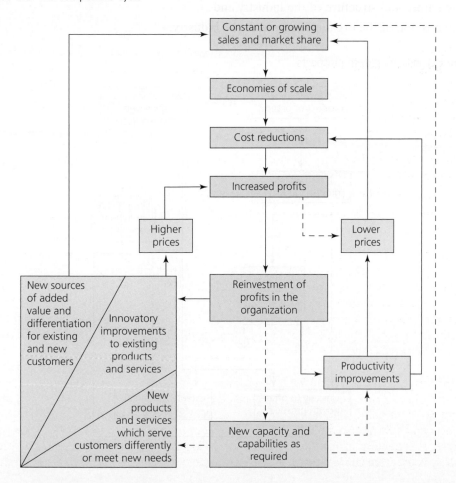

lower prices, but more normally they will be reinvested in the organization. This can generate productivity improvements, sometimes with new capacity and, then, lower prices and/or further cost reductions. The investment can also bring about new sources of added value and differentiation, possibly allowing higher prices and further profit growth. The improved competitiveness should also increase sales and market share and drive the cycle round again. These changes might take the form of gradual, continuous improvements or radical changes to establish new rules of competition.

In this regard the market for DVD players has shown both dramatic growth and massive price reductions. When first introduced, a DVD player was a premium item. Now they are being sold in supermarkets for a fraction of the initial entry price.

### 6.1.1 Competitive themes and frameworks

According to Michael Porter (1980) effective strategic management is the positioning of an organization, relative to its competitors, in such a way that it outperforms them. Marketing, operations and personnel, in fact all aspects of the business, are capable of providing a competitive edge – an advantage which leads to superior performance and superior profits for profit-orientated firms.

Two aspects of the current position of an organization are important:

■ the nature and structure of the industry and
■ the position of the organization within the industry.

**Figure 6.3** Industry growth prospects

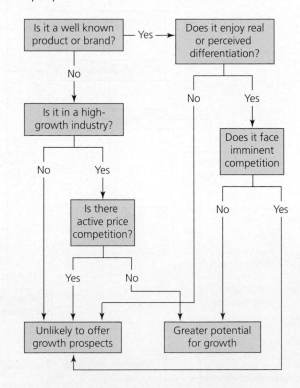

1. The number of firms, their sizes and relative power, the ways they compete, and the rate of growth must be considered. An industry may be attractive or unattractive for an organization. This will depend on the prospects for the industry and what it can offer in terms of profit potential and growth potential. Different organizations have different objectives, and therefore where it is able an organization should be looking to compete in industries where it is able to achieve its objectives. In turn, its objectives and strategies are influenced by the nature of the industries in which it does compete. Porter (1980) has developed a model for analysing the structure of an industry, which we discussed in Chapter 4. The flow chart illustrated in Figure 6.3 reinforces the basic principles.

2. The position of a firm involves its size and market share, how it competes, whether it enjoys specific and recognized competitive advantage, and whether it has particular appeal to selected segments of the market. The extent of any differentiation, which is discussed below, is crucial here.

An effective and superior organization will be in the right industry and in the right position within that industry. Size can matter, as we see in Figure 6.4. The largest of the mainstream competitors, as long as it is run effectively and efficiently, will be able to enjoy superior margins in comparison to its nearest rivals because it can generate scale economies. However, at the other end of the scale, the small competitor with a very carefully and defended niche can also enjoy superior margins.

An organization is unlikely to be successful if it chooses to compete in a particular industry because it is an attractive industry which offers both profit and growth potential but is one for which the organization has no means of obtaining competitive advantage. Equally, a company should not concentrate only on creating competitive advantage without assessing the prospects for the industry. With competitive advantage a company can be profitable in an unattractive industry, but there may be very few

**Figure 6.4** Market share and profit margin
Developed from ideas provided by George Buckley, Brunswick Corporation

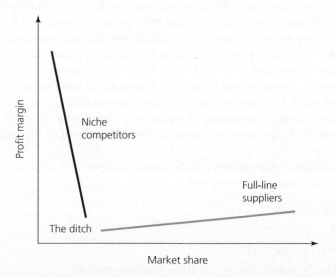

- Markets, except truly global ones, almost always have three full-line suppliers
- Competition between no. 1 and no. 2 always impacts negatively on no. 3
- Size matters …!

growth opportunities if the industry is growing at a slower rate than the economy generally. Much depends on objectives and expectations.

In the economy profit is the reward for creating value for consumers; and in individual businesses profits are earned by being more successful than competitors in creating and delivering that value. Profit may or may not be an end in itself, but profits are important for achieving other objectives and for helping to finance growth. The profit remaining after interest and tax can be paid in dividends or reinvested in the firm (an issue explained later in Chapter 7). A firm will be healthier in the long run if it can invest as it wishes and finance the investments without building up too substantial a debt. In the same way, a not-for-profit organization may not have a profit-orientated mission, but it must generate revenue to stay viable and a surplus over expenditure to develop the organization.

The most successful competitors will:

- create value
- create competitive advantage in delivering that value and
- operate the business effectively and efficiently.

For above-average performance all three are required. It is possible to run a business well – efficiently – but never create competitive advantage. Here we are introducing the concept of 'doing the right thing as opposed to doing things right'. There is no point being the most efficient producer of diesel train engines when demand is for electric. Burtons were very good at making made-to-measure suits for men. Once the demand for these suits declined this became increasingly pointless. Like Burtons, certain products and services may have competitive advantage and yet be produced by organizations that are not run well. In both, potential is not fully exploited. Moreover, competitive advantage must be sustained. A good new product, for example, may offer the consumer something new, something different, and thus add value; but if it is easily imitated by competitors there is no sustainable competitive advantage. For example, Freddie Laker pioneered cheap transatlantic air travel but went out of business in the face of competition and management weaknesses.

In the authors' experience sustaining competitive advantage, rather than creating it initially, presents the real challenge. Competitive advantage cannot be sustained for ever and probably not for very long without changes in products, services and strategies which take account of market demand, market saturation and competitor activity. People's tastes change, the size of markets is limited not infinite, and competitors will seek to imitate successful products, services and strategies. Competitive advantage can be sustained by constant innovation. Companies that are change orientated and seek to stay ahead of their competitors through innovatory ideas develop new forms of advantage. Minicase 6.1 earlier considers how Coca-Cola retains global leadership of the soft drinks market.

Heller (1998) has suggested that organizations which sustain competitive advantage over time will be addressing seven questions effectively:

1. Are we supplying the 'right' things?
2. In the most effective way?
3. And at the lowest possible economic cost?
4. Are we as good as – and ideally better than – our strongest competitor?
5. Are we targeting and serving the widest possible market?

6. Do we have a unique selling proposition – something which will persuade customers to buy from us rather than anyone else?

7. Are we innovating to make sure the answer to all these questions will remain 'yes'?

## 6.1.2 Differentiation and market segmentation

A product or service is said to be differentiated if consumers perceive it to have properties which make it distinct from rival products or services, and ideally unique in some particular way. Differentiation is most beneficial when consumers value the cause of the difference and will pay a premium price to obtain it, and where competitors are unable to emulate it.

Differentiation recognizes that customers are too numerous and widely scattered, and with heterogeneous needs and adequate spending power, for them all to prefer exactly the same product or service. Hence competitors will distinguish their brand, product or service in some way, perhaps size, quality or style, to give it greater appeal for certain customers. Those customers who value the difference will be willing to pay a premium price for it and ideally buy it consistently in preference to the alternatives.

Consequently, effective organizations will be both customer-driven (responsive) and customer-driving (innovative).

### Sources of differentiation

- *Speed* – High-street opticians and photo developers compete on their speed of service; courier businesses are successful because of the speed at which they can move items.

- *Reliability* – Consistent quality and the ability to keep promises: providing what customers want, where, when and how. One example is McDonald's.

- *Service* – Adding extra values to augment the service and thereby satisfy customers. Staff in certain hotels illustrate this point; some years ago Xerox provided a new level of service by incorporating a self-diagnostic computer chip in its copying machines.

- *Design* – both in the product itself (Bang and Olufsen hi-fi equipment, for instance) and in its reparability. This also relates to:

- *Features* – such as cordless irons, kettles and drills. The balance, though, is critical; some video cassette and DVD recorders now have too many features for most customers.

- *Technology* – which, say, led to the development of laser printers.

- *Corporate personality*. There is a value in certain corporate names and images, such as the Body Shop.

- *Relationships with customers* – through effective supply-chain management.

The differentiation need not be clearly tangible as long as customers believe that it exists.

Where specific groups of customers with broadly similar needs can be identified and targeted they are known as market segments, and often products and services are differentiated to appeal to specific segments. The segmentation might be based on ages, socio-economic groups, lifestyle, income, benefits sought or usage rate for consumer markets, and size of buyer and reasons for buying in the case of industrial markets. To be viable the segment must be clearly identifiable, separated from other segments, easily reached with advertising and large enough to be profitable. Given these factors and a differentiated product, prices, distribution and advertising can all be targeted specifically at the segment.

Successful differentiation and segmentation require that products and services are clearly positioned. Toyota, for example, wanted to appeal to the lucrative executive market with a car that offered the 'ultimate in quality' and succeeded against BMW, Mercedes and Volvo. The car needed to be differentiated from the main Toyota brand and consequently it was named Lexus.

## 6.2 Competitive strategy

As far as customers are concerned, the link between price and perceived quality must make sense. Products and services should be neither overpriced (resulting in a loss of goodwill and often lost business) nor underpriced. In this latter case, potential profits must be lost and, perversely, orders may be lost as well – people may become suspicious of the unexpectedly low price and begin to question their perception of the relative quality. Companies must, therefore, also be realistic about customer perception of the relative quality of their products and services and neither overestimate nor underestimate the situation. Companies may think, or wish to believe, that they are 'the best'; customers may disagree.

Figure 6.5 offers a simple matrix of competitive strategies developed from this reasoning.

Porter (1985) developed his earlier work on industry analysis to examine how a company might compete in the industry in order to create and sustain a position of strength. In simple terms, he argued, there are two basic parameters:

■ Parameter 1. A company can seek to compete:
by achieving lower costs than its rivals and, by charging comparable prices for its products or services, creating a superior position through superior profitability,

**Figure 6.5** Simple competitive strategy matrix
Based on an idea found on the Abram Hawkes plc web site

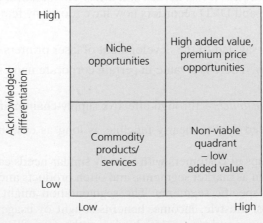

or through differentiation, adding value in an area that the customer regards as important, charging a premium price, and again creating a superior position through superior profitability.

■ Parameter 2. The arena in which the company seeks to compete can be a broad range of segments or a narrow range, perhaps just one.

These arguments led to Porter's valuable model of generic strategies, which is discussed below. It also focused attention on the relevance of differentiation, adding value and cost management for helping to create – and sustain – competitive advantage. It is important, first, to appreciate that the generic strategy framework is a reflection of current (or targeted) positioning, and that competitive advantage is by nature a relative (to other competitors) and dynamic notion. Second, as mentioned briefly before, it is essential to realize that competitive strategy and competitive advantage, although clearly linked, are not one and the same. Competitive strategy concerns the way in which organizations choose to compete and position themselves – competitive advantage may or may not be an outcome of this. To achieve true advantage an organization must find opportunities to be different in ways which are meaningful for customers. The activities which create the position are the key to advantage.

## 6.2.1. Generic competitive strategies

Porter's two parameters, then, lead to the three generic strategies illustrated in Figure 6.6(a). **Cost leadership** is where the company achieves lower costs than its rivals and competes across a broad range of segments. **Differentiation** occurs when the company has a range of clearly differentiated products which appeal to different segments of the market. **Focus strategies** are where a company chooses to concentrate on only one segment or a limited range of segments. With this approach it can again seek either lower costs or differentiation.

Before considering these generic strategies in greater detail it is useful to apply them to particular industries. Porter argues that in the motor vehicle industry (Figure 6.6b) Toyota became the overall cost leader. The company remains successful in a number of segments with a full range of cars, and its mission is to be a low-cost producer. Minicase 6.2 outlines Toyota's competitive strategy. In contrast, General Motors (GM) also com-

**Figure 6.6(a)** Porter's model of generic strategies

Adapted with the permission of Simon and Schuster from Porter, ME (1985) *Competitive Advantage: Creating and Sustaining Superior Performance*, Free Press

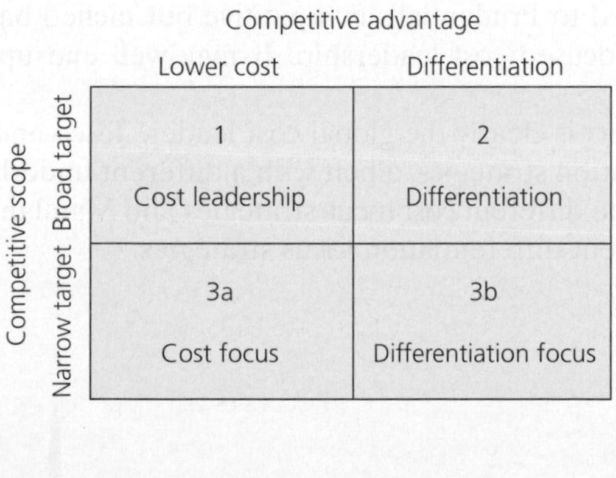

Competitive advantage

|  | Lower cost | Differentiation |
|---|---|---|
| Broad target | 1<br><br>Cost leadership | 2<br><br>Differentiation |
| Narrow target | 3a<br><br>Cost focus | 3b<br><br>Differentiation focus |

Competitive scope

**Figure 6.6(b)** Porter's model of generic strategies applied to the world motor industry
Adapted with the permission of Simon and Schuster from Porter, ME (1985) *Competitive Advantage: Creating and Sustaining Superior Performance*, Free Press

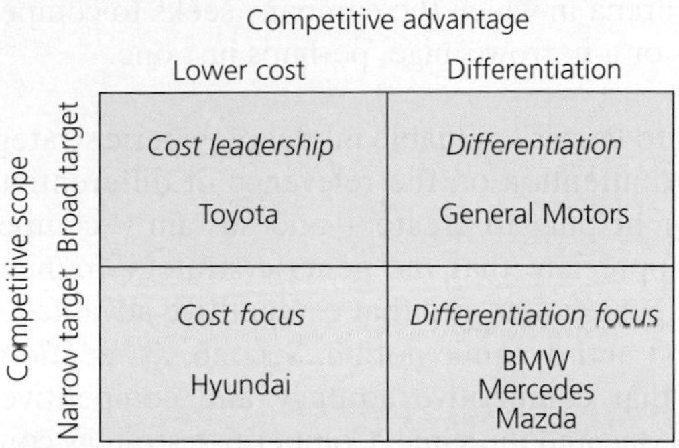

Competitive advantage

|  | Lower cost | Differentiation |
|---|---|---|
| **Broad target** | *Cost leadership*<br><br>Toyota | *Differentiation*<br><br>General Motors |
| **Narrow target** | *Cost focus*<br><br>Hyundai | *Differentiation focus*<br>BMW<br>Mercedes<br>Mazda |

Competitive scope

petes in most segments of the market but seeks to differentiate each of its products with superior styling and features. GM also offers a wider choice of models for each car in its range.

Hyundai became successful around the world with a restricted range of small- and medium-size cars which it produced at relatively low cost and priced competitively. It should be noted that neither Toyota nor Hyundai markets the *cheapest* cars available. BMW and Mercedes have both succeeded historically by producing a narrow line of more exclusive cars for the price-insensitive, quality-conscious customer. Both companies have widened their ranges in recent years without fundamentally changing their basic strategy. There are several cars available from both companies but they are clearly targeted at people who are willing to pay premium prices for perceived higher quality. Mazda was similarly successful with a narrow and sporty range.

It is never going to be easy to identify who the true cost leader is in any industry or segment. To ascertain this we need accurate information on gross margins and profitability together with an acceptance of the relevant segment boundaries. We can, nevertheless, make educated guesses.

Applying the same ideas to credit cards, it is quickly and readily appreciated that Barclaycard, by offering both Visa and Mastercard credit cards, together with platinum, gold and special business versions, is differentiated and covers most segments of the market. American Express, and the increasingly popular affinity cards, such as those linked to football clubs, are focused differentiators because they concentrate on identifiable interest groups. Some would argue that MBNA, because of its international coverage and strategy of persuading other cardholders to transfer, has become the overall cost leader. Egg, linked to Prudential's competitive but niched banking activity, is following a strategy of focused cost leadership. It may well end up part of the MBNA stable.

In retailing Wal-Mart is clearly the global cost leader. Tesco and Marks and Spencer both follow differentiation strategies, albeit with a different underlying promise. Toys R Us and Aldi adopt quite different cost focus strategies and Matalan and Harvey Nicholls pursue radically different differentiation focus strategies.

## Minicase 6.2  Toyota's Cost Leadership Strategy

■ Toyota historically has enjoyed a 40 per cent plus market share in Japan, supplemented by 7.5 per cent of the US market (where it also manufactures) and 3 per cent of Europe – Toyota followed Nissan in manufacturing in the UK.

■ Toyota has focused on organic growth and avoided the acquisition and alliance strategies of its major rivals. It has invested in local plants in key countries around the world. Its European plants, however, are less profitable than those in the US and Japan.

■ Toyota has sought to sell a range of cars at prices marginally below those of comparable Ford and GM cars. Ford and GM both sell more cars than Toyota worldwide. However, Toyota's operating profits have exceeded those of its rivals because it has ruthlessly controlled its costs.

■ Production systems, based on JIT supply of components, are very efficient. Toyota claims fewer defects than any other manufacturer, resulting from the vigilance of each worker on the assembly lines. The Lexus range of top-quality cars requires one-sixth of the labour hours used to build a Mercedes. During the mid-1990s the best Toyota plant was assembling a car in 13 person-hours, whereas Ford, Honda and Nissan all required 20. Its sophisticated assembly techniques eliminate waste at every stage and are driven by strong JIT delivery systems.

■ 'Toyota does not indulge in expensive executive facilities'.

■ Toyota also spends 5 per cent of sales revenue on research and development (as high as any major competitor), concentrating on a search for continuous improvements 'to inch apart

**Toyota car**

from competitors', rather than major breakthroughs.

- Continuous improvement is a 'way-of-life' as Toyota strives to ensure its costs are always below the prices customers are willing to pay.

- There is a policy of fast new model development. In the 1990s Toyota models had an average age of two years; Ford and GM cars averaged five years. Many cars tend to be a refinement of previous models rather than revolutionary designs. Some would argue this implies many Toyota cars lack passion, of course.

Revenues, however, began to fall back in 1995. Sales of Toyota's new, revamped version of its best-selling Corolla saloon were disappointing. 'In its hot pursuit of cost savings, Toyota had produced a car that lacks character.' Overall cost leaders, slicing through the competitive middle market, must still produce distinctive, differentiated products to justify their near-market-average pricing policy. More recently Toyota has launched the Yaris, which has received wide acclaim. In addition, the growing popularity of four-wheel drive recreational vehicles affected saloon car sales, but Toyota responded with its own models, especially the popular Rav 4.

Chairman Hiroshi Okuda describes Toyota as a 'clever engineer that is quick to spot consumer trends and which captures customers with high quality products'.

All quotations are from Hiroshi Okuda.

### Question

1. What do you believe the competitive position of Toyota to be now?
   (To answer this it would be useful to look at the margin and profitability figures for the leading manufacturers.)

   **Toyota** http://www.toyota.com

## 6.2.2 The cost leadership strategy

To achieve substantial rewards from this strategy Porter argues that the organization must be *the* cost leader, and unchallenged in this position. There is room for only one; and if there is competition for market leadership based on this strategy there will be price competition.

Cost leadership as a generic strategy does not imply that the company will market the lowest price product or service in the industry. Quite often the lowest price products are perceived as inferior, and as such appeal to only a proportion of the market. Consequently, low price related to lower quality is a differentiation strategy. Low cost therefore does not necessarily mean 'cheap' and low-cost companies can have upmarket rather than downmarket appeal. Equally, low cost does not imply lower rewards for employees or other stakeholders, as successful cost leaders can be very profitable. Their aim is to secure a cost advantage over their rivals, price competitively and relative to how their product is perceived by customers, and achieve a high profit margin. Where this applies across a broad range of segments turnover and market share should also be high for the industry. They are seeking above-average profits with industry-average prices.

Cost focus strategies can be based on finding a distinct group of customers whose needs are slightly below average. Costs are saved by meeting their needs specifically and avoiding unnecessary additional costs.

Figure 6.7 illustrates the above points and relates the generic strategies to efficiency and effectiveness.

There is little advantage in being only one of a number of low-cost producers. The advantage is gained by superior management, concentrating on cost-saving opportunities, minimizing waste, and not adding values which customers regard as unimportant to

**Figure 6.7** Competitive strategies

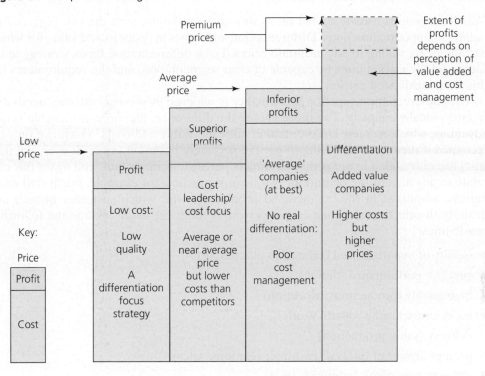

the product or service – many products do have values added which are not regarded as necessary by the market. Cost savings can generally be achieved in any and every area of the business, and quite often they begin with the strategic leader. Senior executives who enjoy substantial perks are unlikely to pursue a cost leadership strategy. Porter suggests that it is a mistake to believe that cost savings are only possible in the manufacturing function and that this strategy is only applicable to the largest producers in an industry. However, where cost leadership generates market share and volume production opportunities, economies of scale in manufacturing do apply.

### 6.2.3 The differentiation strategy

Cost leadership is usually traded off against differentiation, with the two regarded as pulling in opposite directions. Differentiation adds costs in order to add value for which customers are willing to pay premium prices. For a differentiation **focus strategy** to be successful the market must be capable of clear segmentation, and the requirements for this were highlighted earlier.

With differentiation superior performance is achieved by serving customer needs differently, ideally uniquely. The more unique the difference, the more sustainable is any advantage which accrues. Differentiation must inevitably add costs, which can only be recouped if the market is willing to pay the necessary premium prices. It is crucial that costs are only added in areas that customers perceive as important, and again this can relate to any area of the operation. A solicitors' practice, for example, might find competitive advantage in the manner and promptness with which customer queries are dealt, both over the telephone and in person. A fuller list might include the following possibilities:

- quality of materials used (related to purchasing)
- superior performance (design)
- high quality (production; inspection)
- superior packaging (distribution)
- delivery (sales; production)
- prompt answer of queries (customer relations; sales)
- efficient paperwork (administration).

Furthermore, it is insufficient merely to add value; customers must recognize and appreciate the difference.

The differentiation strategy can be easily misjudged, however, for a number of reasons, including:

- by choosing something that buyers fail to recognize, appreciate or value
- by over-fulfilling needs and as a consequence failing to achieve cost-effectiveness
- by selecting something that competitors can either improve on or undercut
- by attempting to overcharge for the differentiation
- by thinking too narrowly, missing opportunities and being outflanked by competitors.

Minicase 6.3 illustrates four distinct differentiation strategies.

### 6.2.4 A critique of Porter's generic strategies

Care must be taken not to misunderstand the implications of delineation. Porter has stated that successful organizations will select and concentrate their efforts on effectively implementing one of the generic strategies that he identified; they will avoid being 'stuck in the middle'. However, it does appear that while cost leadership and differentiation may be seen as mutually exclusive, successful strategies can be based on a mix of the two. YKK, the Japanese zip manufacturer and world market leader, achieves both cost leadership and significant differentiation, as we saw in Chapter 5.

Hendry (1990) has suggested that as there can be only one cost leader, cost leadership is not so much a strategy as a position that one company – which is almost certainly differentiated – enjoys. Toyota may be overall cost leader, but it still differentiates all of its cars. There are different models for different market segments, as well as the associated Lexus range. Because it is a position, and because competitors are always likely to be following cost reduction strategies, it can be a very risky and precarious position if other opportunities for adding value are ignored. Simply, cost leadership is based on efficiencies and sound cost management, but being different still matters.

Similarly, differentiation may be concerned with adding value, and therefore costs, but costs must still be managed. We must understand the cost drivers for any business. It is important to incur and add costs only where they can be recouped in the form of premium prices. Yet, where a company is particularly concerned with issues of size and market share it may deliberately choose to charge relatively low prices and not attempt to recover the extra costs it has added in its search to be different. It sacrifices superior profits, at least in the short term while it builds a power base.

Hendry also questions the value of broad and narrow focus, arguing that internal industry boundaries are always changing, enhanced by the speed of technological change. New niches are emerging all the time, such that what appears to be a solid niche can quickly become a tomb.

To summarize, while the ideas of Michael Porter can be questioned and debated, they nevertheless provide an extremely useful framework for analysing industries and competitive strategy. It is important not to take them simply at face value and assume that the idea of generic strategies is the key which unlocks the secret of competitive advantage. They are not prescriptive.

---

## Minicase 6.3 Four Differentiation Strategies: BMW, Miele, Bang & Olufsen and James Purdey

CASE

### BMW

BMW follows a number of strategies designed to protect its market niche, especially from Japanese competition. Notably, these cover both the cars and the overall service package provided by BMW for its customers.

- Cars can be tailored and customized substantially. Customers can choose any colour they want, a benefit normally restricted to Rolls Royce and Aston Martin; and there is a wide range of interior options and performance extras.

- Safety, environment, economy and comfort are featured and stressed in every model.

- National BMW sales companies are wholly owned, together with strategically located parts warehouses. The independent

distributors place their orders directly into BMW's central computer.

- There are fleets of specially equipped cars to assist BMW motorists who break down.

- In 1994 BMW became the first European car manufacturer to produce in the US.

- Historically, BMW chose to ignore sports cars and hatchbacks, which it saw as downmarket from luxury saloon cars. However, market trends and preferences brought a change of heart. The 1994 BMW Compact was launched as a hatchback version of the successful 3-series; a BMW sports model was used for the James Bond film *Goldeneye*.

The acquisition of Rover gave BMW a range of successful, smaller hatchbacks, along with Land Rover recreational and multipurpose vehicles. But the two companies, with their very different histories and cultures, were not easily integrated. In 2000 Rover was bought back by a financial consortium and Land Rover was sold to Ford.

When BMW divested Rover it retained the rights to the Mini, which it has redesigned and successfully relaunched. It is quite normal for demand to exceed supply, such that there is a waiting list for new models. It is significant that, although they may be adjacent on the same site, mainstream BMW and Mini models are typically sold from separate showrooms.

**BMW** http://www.bmw.com

## Miele

The German company Miele is a global leader in high quality domestic appliances – washing machines, vacuum cleaners and dishwashers. The business was formed in 1900 and it is still run by two great-grandsons of the founding partners. Around 90 per cent of the sales are in Europe, where the company has a 6 per cent market share. The other 10 per cent come from America. It does not look to compete on price – indeed the prices of a Miele can be up to 70 per cent higher than some rival branded products. The brand stands for quality. The typical life of a Miele machine is 20 years, and the company enjoys a tradition of loyal customers and repeat purchases.

Most of the products are manufactured in Germany, regarded as a relatively high wage country. Miele even manufactures its own motors at a plant near Cologne. However, as a result of the German recession at the end of the 1990s/early 2000s, Miele has established a small production plant in the Czech Republic – where wages are one quarter of those it is paying in Germany. It already had one plant in Austria and a joint venture in China. Some 12 per cent of revenues are re-invested in product development, a figure much higher than the industry average. The company has around 700 different patents to protect its designs. There is a strategy of rigorous and lengthy product testing.

Innovation is simply seen as routine and significant. The drums in large front-loading washing machines, for example, have some 4000 holes for letting the water in and out. Miele reduced this to 700 without reducing performance, thus making the drums both stronger and easier to manufacture at the same time. Interestingly Miele has not copied the principle of the Dyson vacuum cleaner (Minicase 5.1) – it continues to believe bags are superior.

## Bang & Olufsen

Now 75 years old, Bang & Olufsen is a Danish manufacturer of hi-fi equipment and televisions, which enjoys an elite reputation and status worldwide for the quality of its products. Its customers tend to be very loyal.

The company has adopted sleek, tasteful designs, clever technologies and high standards of manufacture for many years. During the 1980s its performance deteriorated because it was seen as too much of a niche competitor. As a response, ranges of slightly less expensive – but still exceptionally high-quality – products were launched. From this a new philosophy has emerged – that the products are about lifestyle and technical excellence is more of a given.

Company advertising uses the slogan 'a life less ordinary' to suggest that 'distinctiveness is a value in itself'. Clearly, this fits with the paradigm of the dream society discussed in Chapter 7.

Bang & Olufsen never asks its customers about future designs and products. Instead, its 'free-thinking designers plant their ideas in the marketplace'. The company sees itself as a fashion leader. In addition, the company is very concerned to maintain control over who retails its products and how they are displayed in stores.

The company's niche must be potentially under threat if its rivals are able to improve the quality and reliability of their designs and exploit the manufacturing competencies of lower-cost labour countries.

**Bang & Olufsen** http://www.bang-olufsen.com

## James Purdey

Purdey firearms would be classified as a super-luxury product; they retail at 'prices more normally associated with small houses'. The company manufactures something in the order of 60 guns per year, 90 per cent of which are sold abroad.

There is close attention to detail, and quality control is incredibly tight. Every order is perceived as a special; nothing is seen as standard. The stocks are oil polished rather than varnished in a lengthy, labour-intensive process; and buyers can choose almost any special, idiosyncratic feature as long as they are happy to pay the appropriate premium. Typically, orders are placed two years in advance of delivery.

Because they appeal to a very limited market segment, and because they literally last a lifetime (and sometimes longer), growth potential for James Purdey, without diversification, is clearly limited.

**James Purdey** http://www.purdey.com

### Question

1. Are these companies successfully defending their differentiation focus strategies?

## 6.3  Competitive advantage and competitive success

So far it has been argued that competitive strategies are *built around* differentiation and cost leadership. Competitive advantage is *reflected in* and accrues from perceived differences and real cost advantages, both of these relative to competitors. Hence, competitive advantage is *dependent upon* strategic positioning, but the two are not the same.

**Table 6.1** Functional strategies and competitive advantage

| | Competitive strategy | |
|---|---|---|
| *Functional strategy* | *Low cost* | *Differentiation* |
| Marketing | Large companies can obtain media discounts | Image – reinforced by well-known strategic leader |
| Operations | Efficient plant management and utilization (productivity) | Low defect rate and high quality |
| | Re-engineered processes which reduce costs | Re-engineered processes which add extra value |
| Human resources | Training to achieve low rejections and high-quality policies which keep turnover low | Incentives to encourage innovation |
| Research and development | Reformulated processes which reduce costs | New, patented breakthroughs |
| Finance | Low-cost loans (improves profit after interest and before tax) | Ability to finance corporate strategic change, investments and acquisitions |
| Information technology | Faster decision-making in flatter organization structure | Creative use of information to understand customer needs, meet them and outperform competitors |
| Distribution logistics | Lower stock-holding costs | Alliances with suppliers and/or distributors which are long-term and mutually supportive |

This list of examples is indicative only, and not an exhaustive set of possibilities.

Competitive advantage will normally, at least in the long term, result in superior margins. Table 6.1 shows that any individual functional area, or a combination of several functions, can be the actual source of the advantage.

Porter (1996) later reinforced these points, and attempted to answer some of the criticisms of his generic strategy approach, when he restated that competitive success is based on one of two alternatives. First, an organization can aim to be better than its rivals and focus on operating efficiencies to achieve this. Second, it can seek either to do different things, or to do things differently. This concerns effectiveness, and it relates to strategic positioning. He identified three broad approaches to positioning:

■ An organization can focus on a particular product or service – or an identifiable and limited range – and sell it to every customer who is interested. This is the approach favoured by BMW and easyJet.

■ It can, alternatively, target a segment group and provide a wider range of products which can serve a variety of their needs. This is the IKEA approach.

■ Third, it can identify and focus on a carefully defined niche with a single product or service. James Purdey (Minicase 6.3) provides an ideal example.

**Activity maps** Porter pointed out that it is activities – what the organization actually does both directly and indirectly for its customers, its functional strategies – that create and build value and, in turn, advantage. Together these activities determine the strategic position that an organization enjoys, and competitive advantage comes from the strength of the position. While being able to do something better or differently is essential, the way in which the activities are combined to generate synergy is also critical. Most individual activities can be copied, but it is much more difficult to replicate what might be a unique combination of activities. Porter (1996) developed activity maps as a way of capturing this. An activity map is a diagramming technique where the most critical activities are shown as a core series of related actions into which every other activity feeds. In many ways this is an alternative to the notion of value chain linkages we discussed in Chapter 5.

Consequently, organizations must choose what to do and what not to do, which activities to undertake and which to ignore, and how they might be fused into a powerful mix. Activities that affect the value proposition must not be neglected, but those that have little impact should not consume resources. Critical trade-offs must be made in an attempt to find a unique position. It can be expensive, even self-destructive, to try and do too much and not focus on what does make a difference.

IKEA has chosen to trade-off in a number of ways, for example. It sacrifices being able to offer a wide range of bought-in products by designing and manufacturing its own. By choosing to hold stock in all of its stores and warehouses IKEA sacrifices the low inventory costs some of its competitors enjoy by only delivering against orders. It sacrifices the use of the highest quality materials in favour of function and affordable prices. IKEA also sacrifices sales assistance in favour of self-service; and it opts for only out-of-town locations.

*Many companies spend a lot of time and money researching customers' views, but most spend nothing like enough on observing competitors. The main reason for change is to keep ahead of competitors or to catch up on the complacent market leaders. Companies must invest in development – it's a case of 'duck or no dinner'.*

Sir Simon Hornby, ex-Chairman, WH Smith plc

*When I'm on a plane, I prowl around and talk to passengers and ask the staff about everything. I normally come back with a hundred notes in my pocket scribbled on little pieces of paper. Direct feedback is far better than market research.*

Sir Richard Branson, Chairman, Virgin Group, quoted in Ferry (1989)

The strategy of Virgin Atlantic Airways is built around quality service and differentiation. Virgin's 'Upper Class' aims to offer a first-class-equivalent service at business-class prices and has provided for a number of years, for example, electrostatic headphones that customers can keep afterwards, a large selection of films to watch on personal mini video-cassette players, and chauffeur-driven rides to and from airports.

### 6.3.1 Sustaining competitive advantage

Few positions are defensible long term against rivals. Competitors will copy good ideas and maybe even improve on them. Change is the key. Competitors, having created a competitive advantage, will stay ahead if they innovate and look for improvements on a continuous basis and, at the same time, look for discontinuous opportunities to effect change on industries and markets.

Figure 6.8 combines a number of the points made here, emphasizing that successful companies create advantage and success by being committed to their customers through careful positioning and managed change. The differences and cost advantages which

**Figure 6.8** Competitive advantage through customer commitment
Developed by John Thompson from material in Silver, M (1997) *Strategy in Crisis*, Macmillan

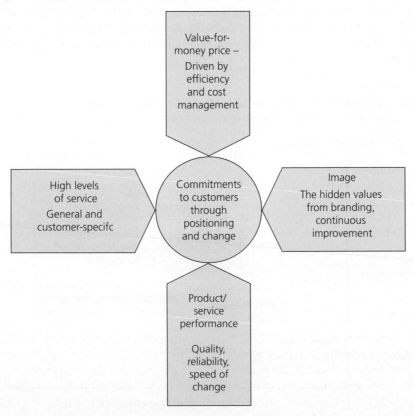

create a position must be supported by high levels of service in strategy implementation and ideally by a strong reputation and brand, as discussed earlier in Chapter 5.

Figure 6.9 shows that competitive advantage can be rooted in technology, organization and people, but that it is people and people-driven processes that are the real source of *sustained* advantage, because it is these that are most difficult for rivals to copy. People must be convinced that they are important, and that their contribution is valued – logically through an appropriate reward system – as otherwise they may not deliver and improve the all-important service. This will always prove difficult in a culture where cost management and resource savings have become dominant.

There are many examples where once-powerful and prominent companies have lost their edge and failed to sustain their competitive advantage:

- Minicase 1.2 showed how Marks and Spencer took its eye off the ball and allowed some of its ranges, particularly clothing, to become tired. Large retailers such as M&S normally control buying, product and range selection for every store centrally, because this can save costs. In an attempt to re-establish its position, M&S is allowing individual store managers to have more of an input than in the past. After all, they are closest to local customers.

- With Next, George Davies opened a niche for stylish clothing for slightly older age groups. However, once such a niche has been opened it is relatively easy for rivals to copy the broad strategy, and they did. When Next failed to defend its position by improvements, and instead committed resources to the acquisition of other retail brands and formats, its early advantage was lost. Davies was a corporate casualty. However, as a designer, George Davies has proved much more resilient than many retailers with successful retail clothing developments within both ASDA and Marks and Spencer. His Per Una range of fashionable clothing designed exclusively for M&S provided one of the few welcome highlights for the embattled retailer in 2003.

**Figure 6.9** Sustainable competitive advantage – the need to grow the business
From Simon, H (1996) *Hidden Champions*, Harvard Business School Press

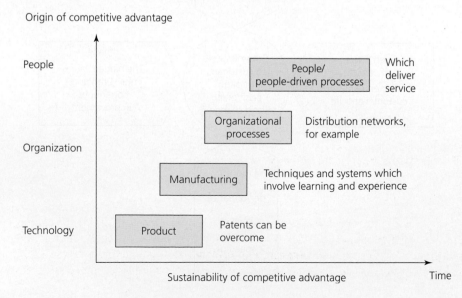

**Per Una range** Designed by George Davies for Marks and Spencer

- Toys Я Us are the American toy superstores who grew at the expense of independent retailers. More recently, Toys Я Us has suffered at the hands of Wal-Mart, which has used its purchasing power to compete on price and gain a significant market share. Wal-Mart simply focuses on the best-selling toys which it offers at rock-bottom prices. Toys Я Us has a wider choice but that clearly is not what every customer wants. According to Tomkins(1998), 'the company's big mistake was complacency ... they stopped renewing and refreshing their stores', and thus provided a way in for Wal-Mart. Toys Я Us became 'stuck in the middle'. The remaining high-street independents are often more convenient and the discounters are cheaper. Their demise was exacerbated by a reputation for relatively poor in-store service.

## 6.4 The dynamics of competition

### 6.4.1 Competitive platforms

Building on issues incorporated in Figure 6.9, George Buckley (2003), Chairman and Chief Executive of the Brunswick Corporation, contends that costs, technology and people provide the three key **competitive platforms** for strong competitors to build on. He suggests, however, that six platforms should always be considered. These are:

■ The best (not the lowest) cost manufacturing when set alongside direct competitors. Cost, after all, is the ultimate competitive weapon as it becomes increasingly significant in the toughest trading conditions. If demand falls away and especially if this means supply exceeds demand, price competition becomes inevitable as rivals vie for market share. When this happens and margins tighten, the higher-cost manufacturers suffer before their lower-cost rivals. In theory (and excluding the complexity introduced by cross-subsidy opportunities in large corporations) prices can easily be driven down to the break-even cost level of the second to lowest-cost competitor. At this stage only the lowest cost company is making money. Emphasizing again the points we have made earlier, lowest cost does not imply lowest quality – it means lower costs than rivals for comparative perceived quality. Companies following differentiation strategies must remain vigilant with costs.

■ Technology, innovation and styling. Good design and style does not have to cost a great deal but it can be an ideal differentiator.

■ Customer service.

■ Brands, marketing and reputation.

■ Distribution. The best products in a design sense will be wasted opportunities if their manufacturers cannot put them in front of potential customers where and when they expect them. Entrepreneurs developing new ideas must always address this key issue of how to reach the market. It is clear that there are better alternatives to many of the products and services we consume on a regular basis, but our choice is affected by availability.

■ People. Competitors can acquire equivalent technology and tooling and copy processes, but it is much harder to replicate the contribution made by people. Minicase 6.4, which concludes the chapter, considers the extent to which technology and design can be a barrier against competition.

### 6.4.2 Competitor benchmarking

Again recapping key points from earlier in the chapter, a true cost leader will also enjoy some form of differentiation, and successful differentiators will be effective cost managers. Differentiation and cost control are compatible. All companies should continually search for innovatory differentiation opportunities and for ways of improving their cost efficiencies. As seen in earlier chapters, leveraging resources and setting stretching targets for employees can help to bring about innovation and savings; benchmarking good or best practice in other organizations (a process of measurement and comparison) can also provide new ideas and suggestions for reducing costs and improving efficiency. Organizations from different sectors and industries can be a useful source of ideas if they have developed a high level of expertise. It should be stressed that this process is a search for ideas that can be customized for a different organization rather than an exercise in simply copying. Managers should be open-minded and inquisitive and look *everywhere* for ideas.

At the same time, it is vital for an organization to understand clearly its position relative to its competitors. Table 6.2 provides a general framework for considering competitive strategies and Figure 6.10 shows how we might benchmark competitors for comparison with an organization and with customer preferences. The key order criteria – key success factors – are listed down the left-hand side and ranked in order of their

**Table 6.2** A framework for evaluating competitive strategies

| | |
|---|---|
| Scope | Global; industry-wide; niche |
| | Single or multiproduct/service |
| | Focused or diversified |
| | Vertical linkages with suppliers/distributors |
| Objectives | Ambitious for market or segment leadership |
| | Market presence just to support other (more important) activities |
| Success | Market share |
| | Image and reputation |
| | Profitability |
| Commitment | Aggressive – willing to acquire to grow |
| | Passive survivor |
| | Willing to divest if opportunity arises |
| Approach | Offensive – attacking other competitors |
| | Defending a strong position. Note that the same strategy (new products, price cuts) can be used both offensively and defensively |
| | Risk-taking or risk averse |
| | Teasing out new segments or niches |
| Strategy | High quality – perhaps with technological support |
| | High service |
| | Low price |
| Position | Cost advantage or even cost leadership enjoyed |
| | Clearly differentiated |
| Competitive resources | High-technology base; modern plant |
| | Location relative to markets |
| | Quality of people (ability to add value) |
| | Reputation |

The examples provided for each of the eight criteria are not offered as an exhaustive list.

importance to customers. Their relative significance is plotted against the horizontal axis. The ability of different competitors to meet these key success factors is illustrated by the dotted lines. Competitor A is clearly relying on its quality and technical back-up, for which it has a good reputation, but is it truly satisfying customer needs? Competitor B seems to offer an all-round better service, and in a number of areas is providing a service beyond that demanded. Given the areas, this may be good as it will indicate a reliable supplier.

*How would our customers rank our products/services in relation to those of our competitors?*

- *Not as good as. We must improve!*
- *No worse than. This implies a general dissatisfaction, so there must be real opportunities to benefit from improvement and differentiation.*
- *As good as the others, no better, no worse. Again opportunity to benefit if new values can be added and real differentiation perceived.*
- *Better than. We must still work hard to retain our lead.*

*I subscribe absolutely to the concept of stealing shamelessly! Wherever you come across a good idea, if it's likely to work, pinch it. There's nothing wrong with that.*

**Figure 6.10** Competitor analysis

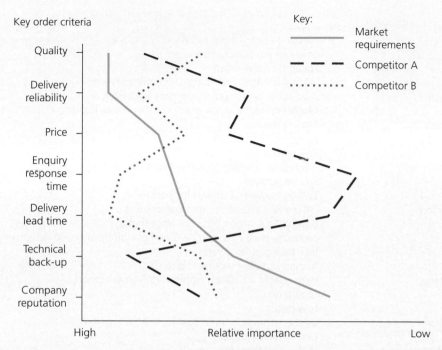

> *There is a quite respectable word – benchmarking – which is the same thing if you think about it.*
>
> Bill Cockburn, British Telecom, when Group Chief Executive, WH Smith plc

### 6.4.3 Changing competitive positions

A successful competitive position implies a match between customers' perceptions of the relative quality or value of a product or service – in comparison to rival offerings – and its price, again in relation to the prices of competing products or services. The relevant area of **competitor gap analysis** is the segment or segments in which an organization chooses to compete; and, in addition, the total price should be used for comparison purposes. Customers, for example, may willingly pay a premium purchase price initially for a particular brand of, say, an electrical good or car if they believe that over its life it will incur lower maintenance and service costs than competing brands. Products offered at initially lower prices may be perceived to be more expensive overall.

Figure 6.11 (which develops Figure 6.5) features a competitive positioning grid. Three basic positions are shown by sectors 1, 2 and 3. Sector 6, high perceived prices but only average (at best) quality, is an untenable position in the long run. Sector 4 illustrates a company competing on price, which can be a successful strategy, but it can provoke competitive responses; in which case, it may only serve in driving down all prices and making all competitors less profitable. Do-it-yourself chains, such as B&Q, have come to believe that the key to survival in a crowded market is to offer permanently competitive prices as well as developing a unique identity. Sporadic high discounts are being replaced by 'everyday low prices'; success is more dependent on volume sales than the actual margins on individual products.

**Figure 6.11** A competitive position matrix

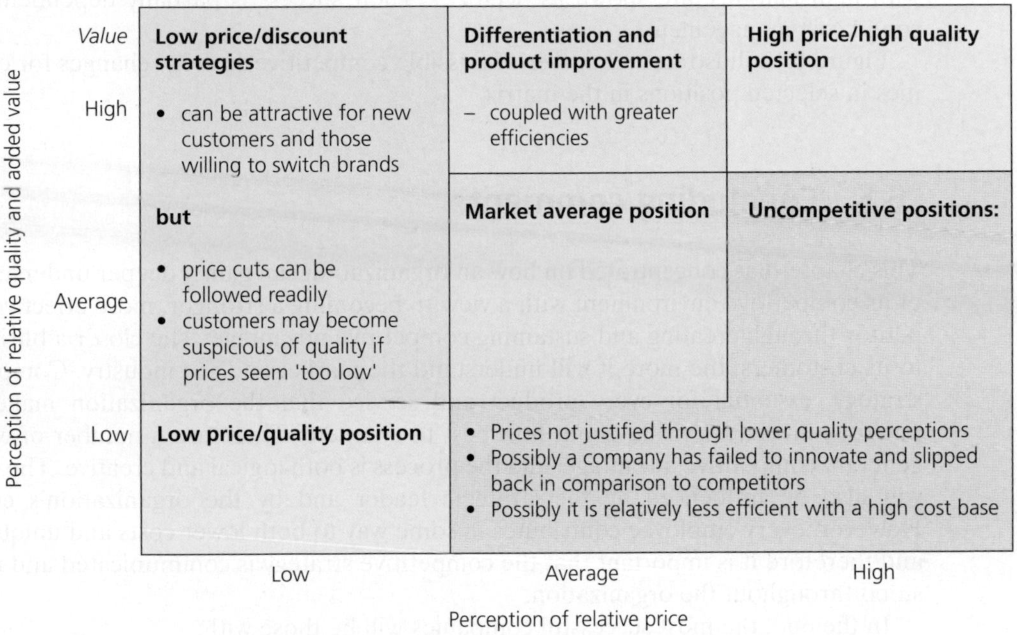

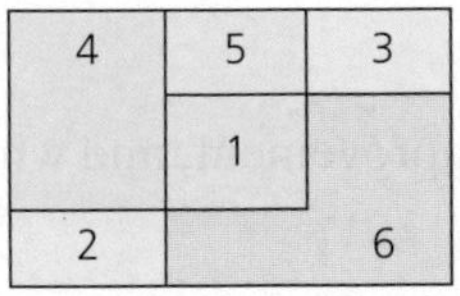

| | Low price/discount strategies | Differentiation and product improvement | High price/high quality position |
|---|---|---|---|
| **Value** **High** | • can be attractive for new customers and those willing to switch brands | – coupled with greater efficiencies | |
| | **but** | **Market average position** | **Uncompetitive positions:** |
| **Average** | • price cuts can be followed readily<br>• customers may become suspicious of quality if prices seem 'too low' | | |
| **Low** | **Low price/quality position** | • Prices not justified through lower quality perceptions<br>• Possibly a company has failed to innovate and slipped back in comparison to competitors<br>• Possibly it is relatively less efficient with a high cost base | |
| | Low | Average | High |

*Perception of relative quality and added value* (vertical axis)

Perception of relative price

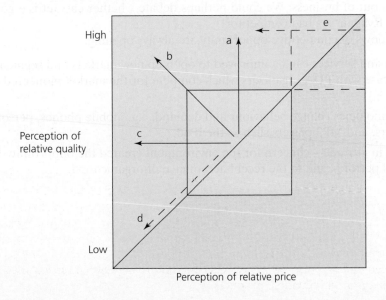

| | | |
|---|---|---|
| 4 | 5 | 3 |
| | 1 | |
| 2 | | 6 |

1, 2, 3  Acceptable strategies and positions
4      Competition on price – successful if not copied and costs controlled
5      Effective differentiation
6      Uncompetitive, unsustainable positions

**Figure 6.12** Possible competitive strategy changes

High

a
b
Perception of relative quality
c
d
e

Low

Perception of relative price

Effective differentiators, commanding premium prices and earning superior profits with high margins, are shown as Sector 5. Their success is partially dependent upon sound cost management.

Figure 6.12 illustrates a number of possible competitive strategy changes for companies in selected positions in the matrix.

# 6.5  Concluding comments

This chapter has concentrated on how an organization can gain a deeper understanding of its competitive environment with a view to becoming a stronger, more effective competitor through creating and sustaining competitive advantage. The closer a business is to its customers, the more it will understand the market and the industry. Competitive strategy, essential for every product and service that the organization makes and markets, involves a vision about how best to compete. There are a number of ways to generate competitive advantage, and the process is both logical and creative. The choice will also be influenced by the strategic leader and by the organization's culture. However, every employee contributes in some way to both lower costs and uniqueness, and therefore it is important that the competitive strategy is communicated and understood throughout the organization.

In the end, the most successful companies will be those with:

- differentiated products and services which are recognized for their ability to add value, and are:
- produced efficiently
- upgraded over time through innovation and improvement, and which
- prove relevant for international markets.

Porter contends that competitors can be viewed as good or bad. Good ones differentiate, innovate and help to develop an industry; bad ones just cut prices in an attempt to drive others out of business. We could perhaps debate whether easyJet is a good competitor and Ryanair is a bad competitor!

New windows of competitive opportunity are always opening:

- Products and services can be improved to open up new markets and segments, as was the case with PDA organizers which compete for the market pioneered by Filofax.
- New technologies change behaviour and demand, e.g. mobile phones, personal computers, and MP3 players such as the iPod.
- Changes in attitude – concern for the environment created the opportunity for unleaded petrol – and to the recent acceptance of organic food.

## Minicase 6.4  Schick versus Gillette

US

Gillette is a well-known brand, recognized around the world for its shaving products. Its main rival in America is Schick, which trades in the UK as Wilkinson Sword, a company it acquired some years ago.

The Chairman of Gillette is Warren Buffett, one of the world's richest men and known as the 'Sage of Omaha' for his astute shareholdings in a wide range of businesses through his investment company Berkshire Hathaway. Coca-Cola is one company in which he has a substantial holding. Buffett championed the appointment of a new CEO in 2001 – Jim Kitts, who had built his reputation with Kraft Foods/Nabisco. Between 1996 and 2001 Gillette had experienced five years of stagnating revenues and profits; Kitts was able to restore growth and profitability almost immediately.

He strengthened the company's working capital by better debt collection and tighter inventory controls. He championed the launch of the Mach 3 razor, which utilized three blades carefully positioned to produce a truly close shave. Gillette also introduced a range of battery-operated toothbrushes. He appeared to be able to reinvigorate brands and exert financial control at the same time. He was a proactive marketer, whereas Gillette had become somewhat reactive with an 'if you build it, they will come' approach to new product marketing. The company had become sleepy. In part this had resulted from Gillette enjoying a reputation for superior technology with its products and being able to charge relatively high prices. It had also acquired Duracell, manufacturer of high-quality premium price batteries. However, superior quality razors and superior quality batteries require a different approach to marketing. Customers are clearly willing to pay premium prices for superior quality razors; they are more resistant and price-conscious when it comes to replacement batteries.

In 2002, the Mach 3 generated revenues in excess of $2 billion. Schick (which also markets Energizer batteries) launched a competitive product in 2003. Its Quattro razor uses four blades. Both razors position the blades sequentially closer to the skin such that each ones gives a closer shave. Gillette has claimed its patent has been infringed because it is about positioning principles and not about the actual number of blades. Schick has countered by querying why Gillette then opted for three and not four blades.

### Questions

1. How important is technological innovation as a competitive platform?
2. Can and should any company ever rely on patent protection as a competitive weapon?
3. If you were involved in product development at either of these businesses, what do you think the next development might be?
4. Will it continue to be incremental or might something more revolutionary be feasible?

**Schick** http://www.schickquattro.com
**Gillette** http://www.gillette.com

## SUMMARY

Many industries and markets are characterized by competitive 'chaos' – they are dynamic and uncertain. All the time rivals may be trying out new initiatives which cannot be ignored. To succeed long term, organizations must be able to manage both continuous and discontinuous change pressures. This is achieved with a mix of incremental and more dramatic changes to competitive and corporate strategies.

In an endeavour to manage in, and manage, their competitive environment, organizations must understand the nature and attractiveness of their industry, and their relative position in it.

Positioning can be examined against a framework of generic strategies, which are based on differentiation and cost leadership. The issue of a broad or narrow market focus is another important consideration.

Michael Porter has provided two useful frameworks to help with these assessments.

However, competitive positions, per se, do not yield competitive advantage. Advantage is a reflection of a strong position, but it is the result of the activities which create the position and, in particular, the synergistic links between them. Successful organizations achieve a unique mix which is hard to replicate, although the individual activities, at a basic level, can be copied.

While competitive advantage comes from technologies, organization and people, it is the people-driven processes that enable advantage to be sustained and extended.

All the time the pace of change and competition is speeding up in many markets and industries. To deal with this it is essential for organizations to benchmark both their competitors and other high-performing organizations in a search for good ideas and best practice. Specifically, they are looking for new opportunities to add or build value in ways that are meaningful for customers.

## QUESTIONS AND RESEARCH ASSIGNMENTS

1. Study Figures 6.6 (a) and (b) and consider where you would place British Airways and other major carriers such as Air France as opposed to easyJet and Ryan Air.

2. Apply Figures 6.11 and 6.12 to this industry.

## INTERNET AND LIBRARY PROJECTS

1. Take an industry of your choice and analyse one or more of the major competitors in terms of their chosen competitive strategies.
   As well as the Internet the following library sources might prove useful sources of information:

   - *Business Monitors* (PA and PQ series)
   - *Annual Report of the Director General of Fair Trading* (as a source of ideas)

   - Monopolies and Mergers Commission reports, and Competition Commission reports, which usually feature a comprehensive industry analysis
   - McCarthy's (or similar) Index (press-cutting service for firms and industries).

2. How successful has Porsche been since the introduction of its new models? Do you

believe that the size of its niche is viable, or might the company have to extend its range?

**Porsche** http://www.porsche.com

3. In the 1970s, Apple ignited the personal computer revolution with the Apple II and reinvented the personal computer revolution in the 1980s with the Macintosh Now in late 2003, Apple has launched its lastest versions of its pocket sized iPods, which are linked to Apple's iTunes Music Store. Steve Jobs revealed in January 2004 at the MacWorld Expo in California that two million iPods had been sold since its launch in 2002. The iPod is being hailed by the music industry as the most promising 'legal' digital consumer music service to date. At the same event, Jobs also revealed a deal with HP (Hewlett Packard) to produce a HP-branded version of the iPod and preinstall Apple iTunes software on all HP's customers' PCs and notebooks. According to Jobs, Apple's goal is to get iPods and iTunes into the hands of every music lover around the world. Jobs is the original comeback kid. He was only 13 when he teamed up with Steve Wozniak to invent the world's first PC in Jobs' stepfather's garage. The rest is history. Jobs left Apple in 1986 to set up a new computer company to do it all again. The alternative version is that Jobs was booted out because Apple was a managerial mess. He called his company NeXT. Although it was not successful, Jobs' other development was Pixar Studios. He returned to Apple as chief executive in 1997 at the request of a board desperate for innovation and for someone to salvage their fortunes.

Jobs' new gamble is taking Apple into digital music. It is considered to be both hugely risky and highly profitable for someone who can get it right. He faces competition from Dell, Wal-Mart and Microsoft. It also depends on Jobs, and anyone else in the business, understanding the fickle tastes of teenagers and college students. Jobs loves music and is a big fan of Bob Dylan and the Beatles. However, today Apple is a midget compared to Microsoft. For all Jobs undoubted creative talent, Apple has not amounted to much in fiscal terms. In 2003 it reported sales of $6.3 billion, most of it from the sales of computers. The company that started the PC revolution is a lowly ninth behind competitors such as Dell, HP and IBM.

'Innovate', an unshaven Jobs bellowed from the stage to a gathering of French elite at a swell party in the Musée d'Orsay in Paris in September 2003. 'That's what we do – we innovate'. Of course, he is right and that may be the trouble. It is possible to innovate pointlessly. Darwin and others described the virtues of creative destruction. At Apple, it may have an evil twin: destructive innovation.

## Source

*Scotland on Sunday*, Business Agenda, January 11, 2004

What do you think is the current position with Apple under Steve Jobs? Has the company been turned around or is it still struggling to find a strong competitive position?

**Apple** http://www.apple.com

## Further reading

Porter, ME (1979) How competitive forces shape strategy, *Harvard Business Review*, March–April.
Clarke, CJ (1988) Using finance for competitive advantage, *Long Range Planning*, 21 (2).

Stalk, G (1988) Time – the next source of competitive advantage, *Harvard Business Review*, July–August.
Hamel, G and Prahalad, CK (1994) Seeing the future first, *Fortune*, September 5.

## References

Buckley, G (2003) Presentation at the University of Huddersfield, November.

Ferry, I (1989) Branson's misunderstood Midas touch, *Business*, November.

Heller, R (1998) *Goldfinger – How Entrepreneurs Grow Rich by Starting Small*, HarperCollins.

Hendry, J (1990) The problem with Porter's generic strategies, *European Management Journal*, December.

Kanter, RM (1990) Strategic alliances and new ventures, Harvard Business School Video Series.

Porter, ME (1980) *Competitive Strategy: Techniques for Analysing Industries and Competitors*, Free Press.

Porter, ME (1985) *Competitive Advantage: Creating and Sustaining Superior Performance*, Free Press.

Porter, ME (1996) What is strategy? *Harvard Business Review*, November–December.

Tomkins, R (1998) Trouble in toyland pushes Toys R Us on the defensive, *Financial Times*, 29 May.

# Success, Culture and Values

The performance of a company, the outcomes of the strategies that it is pursuing, is typically evaluated by financial ratios and other quantitative measures. In this chapter it is argued that while these are an essential element of the evaluation process, alone they are inadequate. We need to take a more holistic perspective which embraces both subjective performance indicators and also recognizes the underlying causes of relative success and failure. We cannot, therefore, ignore culture and values in the process. Culture affects every element of strategy and strategic management.

We show how different measures and assessments can provide conflicting conclusions and provide a comprehensive model based on E–V–R (environment–values–resources) congruence.

Because culture and values influence strategic positioning, the strategic choices that are made and the feasibility of change – which in turn help determine success – this chapter looks into these implications and into the determinants of culture and cultural differences. The culture varies between organizations, although some elements will be common and transferable. It also varies between countries, influencing the relative competitiveness of industries and organizations in different countries.

Financial ratio analysis, however, remains an important aspect of management case-study analysis; consequently a section explaining the main ratios is appended to this chapter.

## Minicase 7.1 The New Internet Businesses  (GB)

As we get into the new millennium, cyberspace and e-commerce are providing another Klondike gold rush. Using the 'gold-rush' metaphor is interesting; it conjures up thoughts of huge fortunes and, without question, these fortunes are being made. The Internet is a wonderful and attractive opportunity, but it will prove disappointing, even cruel, to many of those would-be entrepreneurs that it attracts. The commercial potential of new creative, innovative ideas is always difficult to evaluate.

Brady (1999) argues that the success of any e-commerce business is dependent upon several factors. The idea must be innovatory, and while the business should be clearly focused it must be able to change and evolve speedily if it is to sustain growth. The people behind the business, their plans and their grasp of the issues, together with their ability to raise the necessary finance, are obviously critical issues. It is also essential that they develop a strong brand and, on the back of this, create and maintain very high levels of service. The site must be readily accessible, orders must be simple to place and then easily tracked while they are in the system, and deliveries should be on time.

How, then, might we evaluate these new businesses, remembering that at the moment only a minority is profitable? Partly concerned not to be left behind in this new gold rush, some financiers and venture capitalists have been willing to back some very high-risk proposals if they believe in the idea and the entrepreneur. Amazon.com, the most substantial and famous e-commerce company in the world, has secured enormous funding but has yet to declare a meaningful profit. The theoretical value of the company, a reflection of its current share price, varies dramatically – and many analysts have suggested that it is overvalued because of the relative uncertainty. It is perhaps significant that three of the most profitable businesses –

Hotmail (e-mail services), Google (search engine) and eBay (online auction) are not selling products in the way that Amazon is.

*Management Today* (see Gwyther 1999) offers the following set of evaluation criteria.

### Three factors which determine the extent and value of the opportunity

1. The concept or idea
   - How *value* is created and built
   - The potential for profit, based on costs and revenues
   - The size of the potential market
   - The potential to establish an advantage and reap the rewards, specifically the presence of effective barriers to entry by direct competitors.

2. Innovation
   - The initial difference and the potential to build new values and thus sustain any early advantage.

3. Engagement and implementation
   - The ability to set up the infrastructure and the business, which inevitably depends on the people behind the business.

### Three further factors which reflect the project or business outcomes

4. Traffic
   - Numbers of customers generated – linked to the extent of repeat business, which in turn is dependent on service levels achieved. Although web congestion can be a constraint, the fact that people recommend web sites by word of mouth is a major opportunity.

▶

5. Financing
- Financial resources secured, to fund continued expansion as well as start-up. Setting up a robust business and infrastructure on the web is expensive.

6. Visibility
- The critically important brand identity and image, remembering that a strong public profile and visibility can also act as a barrier to entry. This will often be in the form of media coverage for either an exciting new idea or the recognition of a new, successful entrepreneur or even web millionaire.

## Lastminute.com

Lastminute.com deals in products and services with a finite shelf-life that are close to their sell-by date and are sometimes candidates for distress pricing. Seats for flights, sporting events, theatres and holidays would all qualify. Events in the UK, France and Germany are included. The business model is simple: Lastminute.com brokers a deal and then takes a commission. Clearly this web company is not the only potential outlet for the products in question, and consequently its success will depend on the variety it can offer, the extent of the business it can generate through its site and its ability to bring buyer and seller together. The target market is cash-rich, time-constrained professionals who would like a bargain but who cannot invest the time and effort to find it personally.

The company was founded in November 1998 by two ex-consultants in their late twenties, Brent Hoberman and Martha Lane Fox. The basic idea was Hoberman's, who had become increasingly irritated with the process of price haggling with individual hotels and airlines when he was travelling. Mid-way through 1999 the two partners had raised over £6 million from, amongst others, Intel and Deutsche Telekom, and they were constantly seeking new backers to help to develop the scope and extent of the business. At this time it was being speculated that the company would be floated in 2000. A potential valuation of £400 million was featured in the reports. The two partners would be able to retain 45 per cent of the equity. In mid-1999 Lastminute.com was declaring 300,000 registered subscribers with an average of almost 15 site visits per month. Revenues amounted to some £6 million, and no direct American equivalent had been identified.

Having expanded its activities into France, Germany and Sweden, the company was floated in early 2000. The valuation was now some 50 per cent higher than the 1999 indication and the shares were oversubscribed. Investor allocations had to be rationed and the price soared immediately. The uncertainty of this sector ensured that they fell just as quickly and soon they were trading at just one-third of their post-flotation high. After all, for some, Lastminute.com is 'nothing more than an upmarket bucket shop'. Brent Hoberman reacted to the adverse publicity that the company was beginning to attract and commented: 'People have chosen to focus on personalities and the share price, but the results should focus people's minds on the business and we have shown real growth.'

To date Lastminute has accumulated losses in excess of £70 million. The figures for 1999–2002 respectively are: £5 million, £35 million, £30 million and £7 million. All the time the company has been growing. Late in 1993 Martha Lane Fox announced her departure from the company.

**Lastminute.com** http://www.lastminute.com

## References

Brady, G (1999) The new rules for start-ups, *e-business*, December.

Gwyther, M (1999) Jewels in the web, *Management Today*, November.

## Questions

1. Is Lastminute.com a successful company? If yes, on what criteria are you judging it? If not, why not?
2. Access the web site and look into the activities and organizations with which Lastminute has reached agreements. Do you believe the package is too diversified or are there opportunities to grow and maybe diversify further?

## 7.1  Introduction

### 7.1.1  Defining success

An organization is successful if it is meeting the needs and expectations of its stakeholders. This implies a mixture of common sense and competency. These two simple, bold statements explain how we should seek to measure the success of an organization. We certainly need to know how well the stakeholder expectations are being met; we also need to understand the 'why' and 'how' behind the 'how well', as otherwise we will not be in a strong position to remedy weaknesses or sustain success.

We may feel that we know instinctively whether an organization is doing relatively well or relatively poorly, but realistically we need to be more precise than this. For one thing, we could be deluding ourselves or misjudging a situation. We could be seduced into feeling complacent and ignoring environmental changes. Success, assuming the success is real and not imagined, can be transient.

Figure 7.1 therefore implies that it is essential that organizations and their managers know where, how and why a company is doing relatively well or relatively poorly and that they use this information to sustain success by improvement and change or remedy weaknesses by remedial action. Otherwise, if relative success is taken for granted, or if relative failure is not understood, the organization will experience decline, whether this is slowly or rapidly.

It is quite normal to look for explanations when results or outcomes are disappointing or below target. Attention is quickly focused on failure. This is not always the case

**Figure 7.1** Success and failure

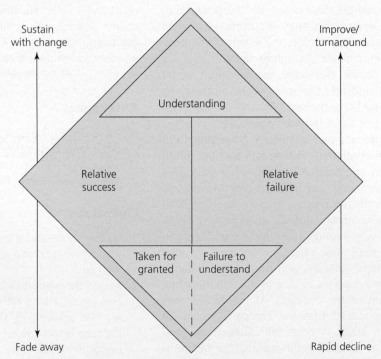

Can thinking ever be a luxury?
But... do successful businesses always appreciate why they are successful?

with success. It is not unusual for a group of managers proverbially to pat themselves on the back and assume that the success is a result of their personal abilities and brilliance. The reality could be that the success lies more in good fortune and an absence of any strong, threatening competitors. Such advantages can prove very short-lived. Success, when taken too much for granted, can quickly turn to failure. The issues, of course, are a manifestation of the prevailing culture.

It is also necessary to face up to the real issues and not attempt to 'spin' the figures to provide an attractive, but not entirely honest, explanation. Companies like to present and discuss their results in terms of absolute figures for revenue and profits, and the media seem happy to report these figures, frequently headlining any growth. Absolute growth in this form can – and can be used to – hide a deterioration in true performance. Profitability, for instance, is more important than profit per se for understanding how well a company is doing. Growth alone can be a very dubious and misleading measure of success. Always remember – *sales revenue is vanity; cash flow is clarity; profits are sanity.*

Taking this point further, it is also not unusual for companies to concentrate measurement on factors that can be measured most easily or readily. Typically, these will relate to inputs, resources and efficiencies, because outcomes and effectiveness are more difficult to measure. Yet, as we have already seen, satisfying the needs and expectations of key stakeholders is critical for long-term prosperity. Box 7.1 on efficiency and effectiveness reinforces the point. Minicase 7.2 then looks at efficiency and effectiveness measurement for the British Tourist Authority.

Thompson and Richardson (1996) have shown how generic strategic competencies can be categorized into three broad groups which influence the organization's efficiency and effectiveness and have a relevance for all of its stakeholders. *Content* competencies reflect the ways through which organizations add value, differentiate and manage their costs. They include functional and competitive strategies. *Process* competencies deal with the ways by which these content competencies are changed and improved in a dynamic and competitive environment, while *awareness and learning* competencies inform the change management process. Process competencies relate, for example, to strategy implementation and to quality and customer care; awareness and learning competencies include the ability to satisfy stakeholders, ethical and social issues and the ability to avoid and manage crises.

## Box 7.1 Efficiency or Effectiveness?

There are three important measures of performance:

- Economy, which means 'doing things cost effectively'. Resources should be managed at the lowest possible cost consistent with achieving quantity and quality targets.
- Efficiency, which implies 'doing things right'. Resources should be deployed and utilized to maximize the returns from them.

Economy and efficiency measures are essentially quantitative and objective.

- Effectiveness, or 'doing the right things'. Resources should be allocated to those activities which satisfy the needs, expectations and priorities of the various stakeholders in the business.

Effectiveness relates to outcomes and need satisfaction, and consequently the measures are often qualitative and subjective.

Where economy, efficiency and effectiveness can be measured accurately and unambiguously it is appropriate to use the expression 'performance measures'. However, if, as is frequently the case

**KEY CONCEPT**

▶

with effectiveness, precise measures are not possible, it can be more useful to use the term 'performance indicators'.

As the following grid indicates, only efficient and effective organizations will grow and prosper. Effective but inefficient businesses will survive but underachieve because they are not using minimum resources; efficient but ineffective companies will decline as they cease to meet the expectations of their stakeholders – simply, the things they are doing are wrong, however well they might be doing them.

|  | Ineffective | Effective |
| --- | --- | --- |
| Inefficient | Corporate collapse | Survival |
| Efficient | Gradual decline | Growth and prosperity |

## Possible performance measures for British Airways – an application

An airline is a people-dependent service business. Unquestionably its revenue, profits, profitability, liquidity and market share (explained and discussed in the supplement to this chapter) are all important. But alone they are inadequate for assessing the overall performance.

The following list contains examples of appropriate measures that might also be used.

*Economy measures*
- Costs, e.g. the cost of fuel
- The cost of leasing aircraft
- Staff levels and costs – slimming these is acceptable as long as the appropriate quality of service is maintained. This could be measured as an overhead cost per passenger.

*Efficiency measures*
- Timekeeping/punctuality
- Revenue passenger kilometres (RPK), the number of passengers carried multiplied by the distances flown

- Available seat kilometres (ASK), the number of seats available for sale multiplied by the distances flown
- The overall load factor = RPK/ASK. (Similar measures for freight are also relevant.)

Solid performance with these measures is essential if the airline is to run at all profitably, but increasing them requires the airline to be more effective in persuading more customers to fly, utilizing marketing and consistently good service.

A related measure is:

- Passenger revenue per RPK. Improving this implies increasing the return from each flight, given that on any aircraft there are likely to be several pricing schemes in operation. We shall see later how BA has changed its strategy to address this issue (Minicase 12.3).
- Income (from all sources) related to the numbers of employees
- Reliability of the aircraft, i.e. continuous flying without breakdown (as a result of efficient maintenance, see below)
- The average age of the aircraft in the fleet.

*Effectiveness*
- Ability to meet all legislative requirements
- Image – which is based on several of the factors listed in this section
- Staff attitudes and contributions – both on the ground and on board the aircraft: care, courtesy, enthusiasm, friendliness, respect and efficiency
- The aeroplane – does it look and feel new and properly looked after?
- Other aspects of the on-board service, such as the cleanliness of the seating and toilet areas, food and entertainment
- Innovation – new standards of passenger comfort
- Safety record
- The number of routes offered, the timing of flights and the general availability of seats (this requires good links with travel agents)

- Recognition of, and rewards for, regular and loyal customers, reflected in the accumulation of air miles by passengers and the numbers of passengers who become 'gold-card' holders in regular flier schemes
- Having seats available for all people with tickets who check in. While airlines, like hotels, often overbook deliberately, they must ensure that they are not 'bumping' people onto the next available flight at a level which is causing ill-will and a poor reputation
- The compensation package when people are delayed
- Time taken at check-in
- Reliability of baggage service, particularly making sure that bags go on the right flight. This also involves the issue of bags being switched from one flight to another for transit passengers
- The time taken for baggage to be unloaded (this is partially in the hands of the airport management)
- The absence of any damage to luggage
- The systems for allocating particular seats in advance of the flight and at check-in
- The number of complaints; the number in relation to the number of passengers
- The way in which complaints are handled
- The ability to balance the cost of maintenance with the costs incurred if things go wrong. If there is inadequate maintenance there are likely to be incidents or accidents which are costly in lost revenue and goodwill. At the same time airlines could overmaintain to a level where they are no longer able to compete because of too-high costs.

The additional factors below are not wholly the responsibility of airlines as they also involve the airport owners:

- Terminal provisions and comfort – seating, escalators, restaurants, duty-free shopping and toilets
- Security – evidence of security and the perception that it is being taken seriously
- Availability of trolleys and wheelchairs for disabled passengers.

## Endnotes

It is also important to consider how all these factors might be measured and evaluated. Observation, passenger surveys, complaints and comparisons with other airlines are all possibilities.

The distinction between indicators – aspects of service which are actually difficult to measure – measures and performance targets – standards to measure against – needs to be recognized.

The following points are also worth noting:

- it is sensible not to be overambitious with both measures and targets
- if something cannot be measured it is perhaps better to leave it out
- the chosen measures must be relevant and easily understood; hopefully the very act of measurement will foster improvements.

## Minicase 7.2  The British Tourist Authority (BTA)   **GB**

CASE

The *mission* of the BTA is 'to strengthen the performance of Britain's tourist industry in international markets by encouraging people to visit Britain and encouraging the improvement and provision of tourist amenities and facilities'.

### BTA objectives

The BTA has agreed the following long-term objectives:

1. Maximize the benefit to the economy of tourism to Britain from abroad.

2. Ensure that the Authority makes the most cost-effective use of resources in pursuing its objectives.

Resources are constrained by grants and the ability to agree joint venture projects; and therefore the benefits generated are inevitably limited. With more money benefits could be increased, but when do they become less cost-effective to create?

3. Identify what visitors want and stimulate improvements in products and services to meet their needs.

4. Encourage off-peak tourism.

5. Spread the economic benefit of tourism more widely, and particularly to areas with tourism potential and higher than average levels of unemployment.

Objectives 3, 4 and 5 may well prove contradictory. Moreover, there will always be considerable elements of subjectivity and value judgement in establishing priority areas.

## Measures of corporate performance

BTA could be judged to be successful if visitors (business people and tourists) come to Britain, if they come both off-season and in-season (objective 4), if they spend increasing amounts of money while they are in Britain, if they spend in the preferred places (objective 5), and if they go home and tell other people to come – and over a period this increases the number of visitors and their expenditure (objective 1 explicitly and objective 3 implicitly).

These are all measures of effectiveness, whilst objective 2 addresses resource efficiency. However, there is a problem of cause and effect. While the criteria listed above can all be measured, the net contribution of the BTA cannot be so easily ascertained. Tourists and business people would still

**Houses of Parliament and Big Ben, London** A leading tourist venue ©Midnight Blu Design Ltd

come, regardless of the existence of the BTA. In addition, many of the reasons for them choosing to come, or not to come, are outside both the control and influence of the BTA. The cause and effect of BTA initiatives is consequently very difficult to ascertain without extensive tracking studies, which can be prohibitively expensive. However, research in the early 1990s showed that at that time 27 per cent of all visitors to the UK had visited a BTA office abroad.

It is believed implicitly that the activities undertaken around the world contribute to corporate objectives and performance, but often it is the activities (efficiencies) which are measured rather than the outcomes. Are particular promotions actually implemented? Are planned brochures published? Are desirable workshops and seminars attended? In fairness, despite the difficulties, BTA does attempt to measure the impact of the special promotions that it undertakes on the numbers of visitors to the UK.

**Questions**

1. Can you suggest any other/better measures of performance than those mentioned?
2. How difficult do you think it might be to track the effectiveness of the BTA?

**British Tourist Authority** http://www.bta.org.uk

## 7.1.2 Improving competency

Where organizations need to become more successful and less crisis prone, it will be necessary for them to improve and/or reprioritize their competencies. Thompson and Richardson (1996) argue that it is necessary, first, to evaluate which competencies are critical for strategic and competitive success and, second, to ensure that the organization possesses these competencies at an appropriate level. To facilitate this, and to ensure that there is improvement and change, it will clearly be necessary for organizations to measure their competencies. Figures 7.2 and 7.3 expand the strategic implications of these points on competency for organizations.

**Figure 7.2** Conscious and unconscious competency

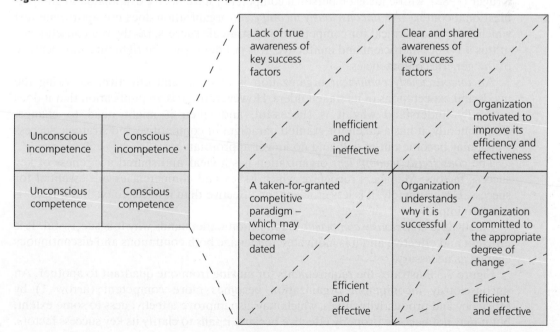

**Figure 7.3** Improving competencies

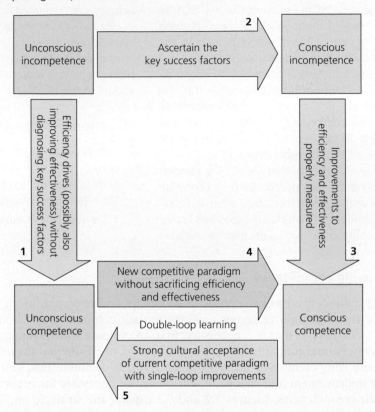

The four-quadrant box on the left of Figure 7.2 has been adapted from May and Kruger (1988), whose ideas on personal competency have been extrapolated to an organizational context. An *unconsciously incompetent* organization does not appreciate just which factors are critical for competitive and strategic success; partly as a consequence of this it is both inefficient and ineffective. It is not deploying the right mix and measure of the generic competencies.

An *unconsciously competent* organization is efficient and effective, satisfying the needs and expectations of its stakeholders. However, there is an implication that it does not fully understand why it is successful, and when it might need to change. Consequently, it has a taken for granted paradigm of competitive and strategic success which may become out of date and no longer appropriate.

The *consciously incompetent* organization has a clear and shared awareness of key success factors. Managers recognize which issues and competencies are essential for success. Unfortunately, it is less efficient and effective than it needs to be, but it is motivated to improve.

Finally, the *consciously competent* organization understands why it is successful. It is efficient and effective and it is motivated to manage both continuous and discontinuous change as necessary.

Figure 7.3 illustrates the requirements for moving from one quadrant to another. An unconsciously incompetent organization becomes more competent (arrow 1) by efficiency and productivity drives, which may also improve effectiveness to some extent, but it may not become properly effective because it fails to clarify its key success factors.

The same organization, alternatively, may become more conscious by attempting to clarify the key success factors (arrow 2). This, later, needs to be accompanied by a determined effort to improve efficiency and effectiveness (arrow 3) to generate competency.

Arrows 4 and 5, linking the bottom two quadrants, indicate an organization with E–V–R congruence. Once an organization has become consciously competent, these competencies and the associated competitive paradigm need to be fully accepted and absorbed into the organization's culture and values. Satisfying the key success factors happens almost automatically and unconsciously (arrow 4), and there is an ongoing commitment to continuous improvement. However, this state of affairs is only satisfactory while the underpinning competitive paradigm remains appropriate. Competitive pressures will at some stage require most organizations to search for a new perspective of effective competition, and ideally reach the new competitive high ground ahead of their rivals. This means that the competency package – and key success factors – should be evaluated constantly to ensure that they remain appropriate. When the competitive strategy is changed, efficiency and effectiveness must not be sacrificed (arrow 5).

## 7.2 What should we measure?

*The three most important things you need to measure in business are customer satisfaction, employee satisfaction and cash flow.*

Jack Welch, ex-Chief Executive Officer, General Electric (US)

The ultimate measure of success for any organization will invariably have a quantitative element. For profit-seeking businesses it will concern revenue growth, profits and profitability. For non-profit-seeking concerns it will relate to an ability to raise sufficient funding to fulfill its purpose and objectives effectively. However, simply focusing on financial measures, important as they are, is woefully inadequate as they pay insufficient regard to issues of cause and outcome.

### 7.2.1 A holistic model

Accepting these reservations, it is next important to look at performance measures within a comprehensive cause and outcome framework. Manfred Kets de Vries (1996) argues that strategic leaders have two key roles to play. First, a charismatic one, through which they ensure that the organization has an understood vision and direction, people are empowered and as a consequence they energize, stimulate and galvanize change. Second, an architectural role of establishing an appropriate structure and style for both control and reward. Effective leaders succeed when strategies are owned by those who must implement them, customers are satisfied, people enjoy their work and things happen in the organization – specifically, the necessary changes are quick and timely. These issues will be explored more fully in Chapter 10.

Extending the themes, Figure 7.4 reinforces earlier comments about how strategic leadership is crucial for establishing (and changing) both competency and the corporate strategic logic of the organization. With the latter we are considering whether or not the organization's corporate portfolio and its competitive strategy or strategies make sense and can be justified, or appear to be a recipe for poor or disappointing performance.

**Figure 7.4** Strategic performance evaluation

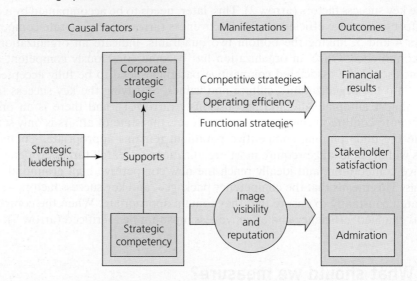

A strong and well-managed portfolio will be reflected in successful and effective competitive and functional strategies and in operating efficiency. Equally important and relevant manifestations are the image, visibility and reputation of the organization, its strategic leader and its products and services, factors which can be managed and can have a bearing on many things, but which are tricky to evaluate and measure, particularly by the organization itself. Largely, they are the subjective opinion of external experts and stakeholders.

There are three distinctive broad approaches to measuring outcomes. These are:

■ *Financial results* and other market-driven quantitative measures such as market share

■ *Stakeholder satisfaction*, reflected in the balanced scorecard and similar packages

■ *Admiration*, for example the annual reviews carried out by *Fortune* in the US and *Management Today* in the UK.

This chapter now looks briefly at corporate logic, and then at admiration, image and reputation, financial measurement and stakeholder measures, to explain the linkages in Figure 7.4.

### 7.2.2 Corporate strategic logic

Caulkin (1995) stresses that the average life expectancy of successful UK companies is some 40–50 years. He has shown how only nine of the 30 companies used to make up the first *Financial Times* share index in 1935 still existed in their own right 60 years later. Several others were still in existence, but under new ownership. Some had been liquidated; many had been acquired and absorbed by their new corporate parents. It is inevitable that every one of the companies will have seen major strategic and/or structural changes of some kind.

Sadtler *et al.* (1997) defend the case for a clear focus built around a defensible core of related activities, and in this they reflect current practice. These issues are debated further in Chapter 12.

### 7.2.3 Admired companies

Sound profits and a strong balance sheet are very important, but alone they will not necessarily lead to a company being 'admired'. In the 1980s, and based on research in the USA by *Fortune*, *The Economist* began to investigate which companies are most admired by other business people, particularly those with whom they compete directly. More recently, *Management Today* has taken over the project in the UK and the *Financial Times* in association with Price Waterhouse later initiated a parallel European and then a global study. Business people are asked to allocate marks against certain criteria for their main rivals. The criteria used in the UK survey are as follows: quality of management; financial soundness; value as a long-term investment; quality of products and services; the ability to attract, develop and retain top talent; capacity to innovate; quality of marketing; and community and environmental responsibility. These reflect multiple perspectives and stakeholder interests; and consequently *The Economist* (1991) argues that admiration encourages customers to buy more and to stay loyal, employees to work harder, suppliers to be more supportive and shareholders also to remain loyal.

Table 7.1 features a selection of the most admired British companies for the period 1994–2002, tracking the relative progress in the charts of the top five businesses in both 2002. Tesco stands out as the one business which has been ranked consistently over this period of years; the other winners have enjoyed more mixed fortunes, although BP has been particularly strongly regarded in recent years. In 2002 BP's CEO, Lord (John) Browne was also recognised as Britain's most admired corporate leader. It is very unusual for a company and its leader to receive such joint honours. In contrast, Marks and Spencer has declined dramatically. Positioned between 3 and 7 between 1994 and 1997, M&S dropped to eleventh place in 1998 and then fell out of the top 100. The explanation can be found in Chapter 1. In general, British service businesses also score very highly in the European poll but, significantly, the manufacturing sections are normally dominated by German, Swedish and Swiss companies.

Listed below are the ten most admired American companies in 2003 on the *Fortune* web site – if they had a top ten place in 2002 these are in brackets:

1. Wal-Mart (5)
2. Southwest Airlines (16)
3. Berkshire Hathaway (7)
4. Dell Computers (3)

**Table 7.1** Britain's most admired companies, 1994–2002. Selected results for the 2002 Top 5

|  | *1994* | *1995* | *1996* | *1997* | *1998* | *1999* | *2000* | *2001* | *2002* |
|---|---|---|---|---|---|---|---|---|---|
| Tesco | 31 | 4 | 1 | 2 | 1 | 1 | 5 | 4 | 3 |
| BP |  |  |  |  |  |  | 2 | 3 | 1 |
| Glaxo Wellcome | 2 | 13 | 11 | 4 | 6 | 3 |  |  |  |
| Glaxo SmithKline |  |  |  |  |  |  | 1 | 5 | 5 |
| SmithKline Beecham | 4 | 14 | 7 | 8 | 5 | 2 |  |  |  |
| Cadbury Schweppes | 7 | 1 | 5 | 16 | 2 | 5 | 4 | 7 | 2 |
| Unilever | 5 | 2 | 16 | 6 | 7 | 7 |  | 13 | 4 |

Source: *Management Today*

5. General Electric (1)
6. Johnson & Johnson
7. Microsoft (2)
8. Federal Express
9. Starbucks
10. Procter and Gamble

A number of observations can be made:

■ In an era of strategic focus, an extensively diversified company, GE, was the most admired – and globally the most respected – for a number of years. GE was only deposed when its highly regarded chief executive, Jack Welch, retired. The important contribution made by Jack Welch, in ensuring that there is a cohesive and synergistic link between strategy, structure and style will emerge throughout this book.

■ In 2000 the chart of winners was dominated by computing, networks and semiconductor companies, of which there were five in the top ten. Cisco, Intel and Lucent have since disappeared and been replaced by a mixture of service businesses and long-established manufacturers.

■ The extremely successful and remarkable Berkshire Hathaway is included. Run by entrepreneur Warren Buffett, Berkshire Hathaway is neither a manufacturing nor a service business; instead it is an investment vehicle for its shareholders' funds. Minority shareholdings in a range of companies, including Coca-Cola, are typically held for the long term. Notably, high-technology companies are avoided because of their perceived inherent uncertainty.

Table 7.2 shows the world's most respected companies for 1998 and 2002. Notably, General Electric tops this poll in both years, with Microsoft following up. The other American giants included here, Coca-Cola and IBM are, interestingly, not in the US top

**Table 7.2** The world's most respected companies. Selected placings, 1998 and 2002

|  | *1998* | *2002* |
| --- | --- | --- |
| General Electric | 1 | 1 |
| Microsoft | 2 | 2 |
| IBM | 4 | 3 |
| Coca-Cola | 3 | 4 |
| Toyota | 5 | 5 |
| *Selected UK companies* | | |
| Shell | 12 | 18 |
| Unilever | 35 | 12 |
| Marks & Spencer | 35 | 19 |
| BP | | 20 |
| Tesco | | 24 |
| Glaxo SmithKline | | 41 |
| Cadbury Schweppes | | >100 |

Source: *Financial Times*

ten listed above. It is also noticeable that the British companies which enjoy the most respect globally are quite different from those admired 'at home'. Shell and Marks and Spencer both enjoy greater respect abroad than they do at home.

The Top 30 for the World's Most Respected Companies includes 17 US corporations, 2 from Japan (Toyota and Sony, fifth and sixth respectively), 3 completely UK companies, 2 which are joint UK/Netherlands (Shell and Unilever) and 6 from the rest of Europe. These six are: Nestlé, Daimler/Chrysler, BMW, Mercedes, Nokia and L'Oréal.

An earlier survey in the UK by BMRB/Mintel (see Summers 1995) asked a sample of consumers which companies they perceive offer good value for money, understand their market, are trustworthy and care about the environment. Boots won every category except for environmental concern, where it came second to the Body Shop. Inevitably, the winning companies in a poll such as this will be those with high visibility and presence, especially retailing organizations, reflecting the value of a good corporate image. Ironically, Marks and Spencer did not appear in the top ten in any category.

Yet another related survey is the British Quality of Management awards (see Houlder, 1997), where Marks and Spencer were again placed first for three consecutive years in the mid-1990s, this time followed by British Airways and Glaxo Wellcome. The polling here is conducted by MORI, who seek opinions on a selection of key issues from institutional investors, company chief executives and business journalists. One significant fact to emerge is that different categories of judges prioritize the significant issues in different ways. Journalists see innovation as vitally important, whereas it receives much lower priority from industrialists in the MORI poll. By contrast, Price Waterhouse concluded that both industrialists and analysts see innovation as the most important factor of all.

Interestingly, strategic leadership is not recorded as a particularly high priority for fund managers by MORI but the following comment was made about ABB's success in the European poll for several years in the 1990s:

*The biggest asset may well be the charismatic figure of its chairman [Percy Barnevik] … who is identified as an outstanding business leader.*

Asea Brown Boveri (ABB) is a Swedish–Swiss engineering conglomerate

Financial success alone certainly does not guarantee admiration from competitors and popularity with all the stakeholders; at the same time, as evidenced by the Body Shop over a period of years, deteriorating financial returns will bother shareholders far more than customers! Fisher (1996) has argued that admiration placings in the US can certainly affect the stock price both positively and negatively, yet the extent to which financial performance affects the admiration marks remains less clear.

While several tentative conclusions might be drawn from these polls, prolonged debate is outside the scope of this book. However, it is worth emphasizing three points: first, fortunes can change very quickly; second, admiration seems to be affected by short-term changes of fortune; and third, the various polls on the same themes are themselves not always consistent, although some patterns can be traced.

## 7.2.4 Image and reputation

A well-recognized and positive image and reputation appear to improve the admiration rankings; and, correspondingly, linkage with a major corporate mistake or mishandled crisis has a negative effect, especially if social and ethical responsibilities are involved.

The next issue to be addressed, therefore, concerns the relative value of a good reputation and high visibility. Could reputation, inevitably a subjective judgement, actually help to cover up a relatively poor financial performance, itself a more objective measurement? Fombrum (1996) contends that reputations create economic value, and that image, because it embodies the company's uniqueness, is a key competitive tool. He uses this as an argument in favour of benchmarking those companies perceived to be the leading performers, to ensure that no critical gaps are left open.

Brands can give a company visibility, sometimes international visibility. When a prominent brand becomes associated with trust and quality, its corporate owner should be in a position to command premium prices, although some of this is needed to cover the extra promotional costs required to sustain the brand's visibility. Companies are increasingly including their brands as balance-sheet assets and attempting to place a value on them. Usefully for consumers, sensible companies will invest in their brands in order to improve them and sustain their competitive leadership.

> *Virgin may be innovative and Body Shop may be ethical, but the main thing that distinguishes these companies from the pack is how hard they shout about their achievements.*
>
> Columnist Lucy Kellaway writing in the *Financial Times*, 23 September 1996

The relative value of a charismatic, high-profile and media-friendly – or even media-chasing – strategic leader such as Richard Branson is more difficult to quantify, although the reality of their impact is not in question.

### 7.2.5 Financial measures

A plethora of financial performance measures has long been used to help evaluate the relative success and progress of a business; there is no suggestion here that this should cease to be the case. These measures include ratios such as return on capital employed and return on shareholders' funds, earnings per share, the share price itself and the price to earnings ratio. Typically, a company's share price performance will be evaluated against the relevant industry average and against one of the *Financial Times* indices. While these are objective within the constraints of accounting practice and convention, there are two points to note. First, although analysts always seem to stress profitability, relating pre- or after-tax profits to either sales, capital employed or shareholders' funds, press headlines are more likely to focus on the specific growth or decline in revenues and actual profits made. Second, share prices are also affected by future expectation, and a plausible and convincing strategic leader can be persuasive about 'better times being on the way'.

An analysis of financial ratios is useful for a number of reasons.

- It enables a study of trends and progress over a number of years to be made.
- Comparisons with competitors and with general industry trends are possible.
- It can point the way towards possible or necessary improvements – necessary if the organization is performing less and less well than competitors, useful if new opportunities are spotted.
- It can reveal lost profit and growth potential.

- It can emphasize possible dangers – for example, if stock turnover is decreasing or ratios affecting cash flow are moving adversely.

Financial analysis concentrates on efficiency rather than effectiveness unless the objectives are essentially financial or economic ones. The real measures of success, as far as the strategic leader and the various stakeholders are concerned, is whether or not the objectives that they perceive as important are being achieved.

Outside analysts, such as students and interested readers, can gain some insight into the apparent objectives of an organization by reading annual reports, articles, press releases and so on, but only the people involved in decision-making know the real objectives and whether they are being achieved. Financial analysis from the published (and easily obtained) results can be very informative and lead to conclusions about how well a company is performing, but certain aspects remain hidden. Decision-makers inside an organization use financial analysis as part of the wider picture, but outsiders are more restricted. Financial analysis, then, is a very useful form of analysis, and it should be used, but the wider aspects should not be overlooked.

More recently, *economic value added* (EVA; see, for example, Lynn 1995) has been adopted as another measure. EVA compares a company's after-tax operating profits with its cost of capital.

A more detailed treatment of financial measures is included as a Finance in Action supplement to this chapter.

## 7.2.6 Stakeholder measures

The important *Tomorrow's Company* report (RSA 1995), written in an attempt to improve the competitiveness of UK industry in global markets, concluded that there is:

- complacency and ignorance about world-class standards
- an overreliance on financial measures which often focus attention on the short rather than the long term
- a national adversarial culture which fails to integrate stakeholders into a cohesive network of interdependent organizations.

The preferred solution lies in a more holistic approach which incorporates the interests of multiple stakeholders. Implicit here is a clear realization that both measurement and organizational learning must encompass both what is happening inside an organization and what is emerging in the outside environment. This accords with the ideas behind the '*balanced scorecard*' approach of Kaplan and Norton (1992, 1996).

Kaplan and Norton suggest that organizations should focus their efforts on a limited number of specific, critical performance measures which reflect stakeholders' key success factors. In this way managers can readily concentrate on those issues which are essential for corporate and competitive success.

Kaplan and Norton use the term 'balanced scorecard' to describe a framework of four groups of measures, and argue that organizations should select critical measures for each one of these areas. The four groups, and examples of possible measures, are:

- financial – return on capital employed; cash flow
- customers – perceived value for money; competitive prices
- internal processes – enquiry response time; enquiry to order conversion rate

**Figure 7.5** Stakeholder measures

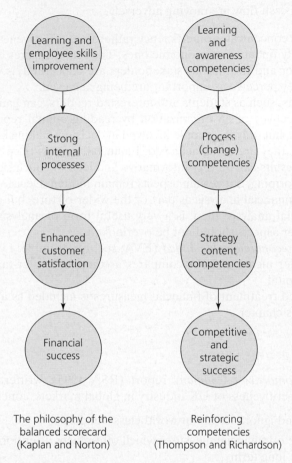

The philosophy of the
balanced scorecard
(Kaplan and Norton)

Reinforcing
competencies
(Thompson and Richardson)

- growth and improvement – number of new products/services; extent of employee empowerment.

These measures encapsulate both efficiency and effectiveness. Figure 7.5 illustrates the synergistic dependencies and linkages between the four groups of measures. These have a close relationship with the competency linkages mentioned in the Introduction to this chapter, and featured on the right-hand side of the figure.

Measuring effectiveness requires a recognition that quality does not mean the same things for every customer. Organizations must determine what will generate repeat business and seek to provide it. Supermarkets, for example, can offer service in the form of a wide range of products, brand choice for each product in the range, low prices, fast checkout and ample car parking. Stores can focus aggressively on one or more of these or seek a balanced profile. The major chains will have a basic competitive posture and then tailor each store to meet local conditions.

Minicase 7.3 – Classic FM – describes how a radio station has introduced classical music to millions of new listeners, and caused an increase in classical CD sales, whilst not meeting all its own financial expectations. It has also been criticized by 'musical purists'.

## Minicase 7.3 Classic FM GB

Owned by radio group, GWR, Classic FM was launched in 1992. It is now a 24-hour commercial radio station which plays exclusively classical music in typically four minute extracts. As its audience ratings have continued to grow – they now exceed seven million – and making extensive use of its web site, Classic FM has increasingly involved its listeners in choosing the playlist. This began with an annual popularity poll for people's favourite classical music; now people vote for their favourites from a predetermined list every day of the week. As with popular music, there is also a Classical Top 20 (best-selling CDs) which is featured every week.

In the beginning some 'purists' were incensed. This was different from the approach of the 70-year-old BBC Radio 3 which had always targeted highbrow listeners. Opera and theatre director, Jonathan Miller commented that he saw it as part of a 'global decline where all thought is reduced to soundbites'.

*The Times* feared it would 'relegate serious music from high art to low entertainment'.

Diarist and playwright Alan Bennett described Classic FM listeners as 'Saga-louts'.

But there have been some notable achievements:

- Classical music has acquired a mainstream audience
- Classic FM is one of the best-known brands in the UK
- The company has found opportunities to diversify – into a magazine, retail organization, record label, credit card and dating agency

- Compilation albums of favourite classical music have been spawned and sold in large numbers by both Classic FM and mainstream labels
- Record stores feature classical music more extensively, especially the chart albums
- Classic FM has helped launch the careers of such popular artists as Russell Watson, Andrea Bocelli, Bond and The Opera Babes
- It has also popularized the soundtracks of films such as *Titanic*, *Lord of the Rings* and *Harry Potter* – all of which have sold in huge quantities.

Although turnover exceeded £30 million by the early 2000s, with the company profitable from 1997, advertising revenues have fallen short of early targets. Part of the issue lies with the age profile of the listeners it attracts. The median age is 52; half are over 45, half under. There is a strong student audience, but students are not big spenders! Indeed much of this book has been written with the station playing quietly in the background. Simply, the biggest spending advertisers want to see evidence of the key 35–44 age group.

### Questions

1. Visit the Classic FM web site and tune into the station (101 fm) and consider what options Classic FM might have for increasing its popularity with the key 35–44 age group.

Sanghera, S (2002) Gentle ways to make ears pay, *Financial Times*, 23 July.
**Classic FM** http://www.classicfm.com

## 7.3 The measurement of success in not-for-profit organizations

It was suggested in Chapter 2 that the objectives of not-for-profit organizations are often stated in terms of resource efficiency because of the difficulty of quantifying their real purpose. As a result, the measures of their success that are used in practice may not be closely related to their real mission and purpose. Where this happens, financial and other quantitative measures are being used as the measures of performance, and efficiency, not effectiveness, is being evaluated. In other words, performance and success is being measured, but despite the usefulness of, and need for, the measures being used, they may not be assessing strategic performance directly in relation to the mission. These points are expanded below.

Drucker (1989) comments that many not-for-profit organizations are more money conscious than business enterprises are because the funding they need is hard to raise. Moreover, they could invariably use more money than they have available. Money, however, is less likely to be the key element of their mission and strategic thinking than are the provision of services and the satisfaction of client needs. Given this premise, the successful performance of a not-for-profit organization should be measured in terms of outcomes and need satisfaction. Money then becomes a major constraint upon what can be accomplished and the appropriate level of expectations.

The outcomes, in turn, must be analysed against the expectations of the important stakeholders. For many organizations in this sector this involves both beneficiaries of the service and volunteer helpers as well as financial supporters and paid employees. Typically their personal objectives and expectations will differ.

But what is the case in reality?

The performance and effectiveness of the education system relates to the impact on pupils after they leave the system, their parents, the taxpayers who fund education and future employers. Their perspectives will differ, and their individual aspirations and expectations will be difficult to quantify and measure. It is far easier to measure efficiency in the way that resources are utilized, for example by class sizes, staff/student or staff/pupil ratios, building occupancy and examination performance.

Similarly, local authorities exist to serve local residents, and their mission is concerned with making the area a better place in which to live. Would all the residents agree on what is implied by 'a better place in which to live', and could changes be objectively measured and evaluated? Because of the difficulties, value for money from the resources invested is more likely to be considered, and improvements in the efficiency of service provision sought.

If a charity seeks to save money by minimizing administration and promotion expenditures it is focusing on short-term efficiency. If it concentrates on long-term effectiveness it may well be able to justify investing in marketing and administration in order to raise even more money. A charity that spends some 60 per cent of its current income on administration and marketing (and the rest on its directly charitable activities) could well, in the long run, be more effective than one that spends only 20 per cent in this way. The aim is to establish the most appropriate structure, administration network and promotional expenditure to achieve the purpose, and then run it efficiently.

The not-for-profit sector is increasingly attempting to measure effectiveness in terms of impacts and outcomes rather than efficiency alone. The task is not straightforward.

Value for money looks at the relationship between the perceived value of the output (by the stakeholders involved) and the cost of inputs. Essentially it is used as a comparative measure. There are too many uncertainties for there to be any true agreement on the magnitude of 'very best value', and consequently one is seeking to ensure that good value is being provided, when measured against that of other similar, or competitive, providers.

If we consider both inputs and outcomes then we are considering the efficiency and effectiveness of the organization's transformation processes, its ability to add value. With certain non-profit organizations, such as the UK National Health Service (NHS), it is also tempting to make international comparisons. How much per head of the population is spent on health care? What percentage of gross domestic product does this represent? Again, these are input measures when it is outcomes that matter. The life expectancy of British people and the infant mortality rate are critically important outcomes but, while health care makes an important contribution, it is not the only causal factor.

Jackson and Palmer (1989) emphasize that if performance is to be measured more effectively in the public sector, then the implicit cultural and change issues must also be addressed, a point that was addressed in Chapter 2. The climate must be right, with managers committed to thinking clearly about what activities should be measured and what the objectives of these activities are. This may well involve different reward systems linked to revised expectations. This approach, they suggest, leads managers to move on from measuring the numbers of passengers on the railway network to analysing how many had seats and how punctual the trains were; and measuring and analysing the numbers of patients readmitted to hospital after treatment, rather than just the numbers of patients who are admitted and the rate of usage of hospital beds. Jackson and Palmer also emphasize the importance of asking users about how effective they perceive organizations to be.

## 7.4 A holistic framework of measures

Figure 7.6 offers an outline framework for reflecting on the measurement demands facing an organization. It is based on the premise that a competitive and strategically successful organization will achieve and, with changes, sustain, a congruency among its environment (key success factors), resources (competencies and capabilities) and values (the ability to manage appropriate and timely continuous and discontinuous change). A small reminder of this E–V–R congruence model is provided in the top right corner.

While corporate strategic success is concerned with the mission and purpose of the organization, it will frequently be assessed by financial measures of some form, as highlighted earlier. Long-term strategic success requires that the interests of stakeholders are met, and are seen to be met, that this is accomplished efficiently with capable resources, and that there is a commitment to the mission reflected in organizational values. The implication is that in addition to resource efficiency and stakeholder satisfaction, organizations should attempt to measure values to ensure that the culture is appropriate. However, the true complexity of this task is realized when we question whether we really know what the culture of an organization in an era of continuous change – and incorporating periodic restructurings and downsizings – should be like.

*In a very turbulent, rapidly changing time what we need to give people is something they can depend on, something lasting. Every company needs to rethink what are the values and what are the operating principles that will be unchanging in time so that we can truly establish a new contract with all employees.*

George Fisher, Chairman, Eastman Kodak

Research can capture a snapshot of currently held values and the extent to which particular behaviours are being manifested. Some organizations will prefer to use volunteers from among the workforce rather than select a sample. The findings should be evaluated against a set of expectancies, and follow-up research can track both positive and negative developments. The organization must then decide what action to take if there is any deterioration or the initial absence of a critical value or behaviour pattern. Changing the culture of the organization is dealt with later in this chapter.

It will, therefore, be realized that the Figure 7.6 framework implies a series of both hard and soft measures and indicators. Some will be straightforward, others far more difficult and subjective. Arguably the real key to success lies in those issues that are most difficult to assess. This is no excuse for not attempting a robust assessment of some form, even though it is sometimes easy to argue a case based on unsubstantiated opinion which, when rigorously probed, turns out to be a delusion. It is all too easy for senior managers to argue for what they would like to believe is a reality: that their company is

**Figure 7.6** A holistic framework of measures

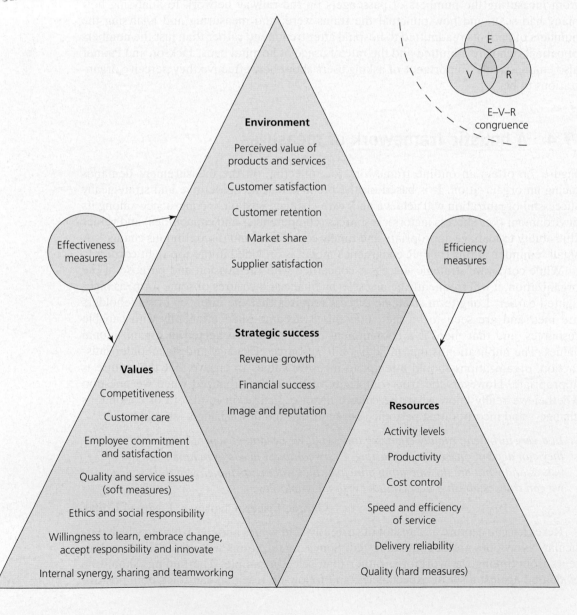

competitive, that it is committed to quality and service, and that their employees are committed and supportive. They need to check these things out!

We have now established that culture and values are important for establishing, sustaining and changing winning strategic positions, and that their assessment and measurement can be tricky. It is, therefore, now appropriate to examine the subject in greater depth.

## Minicase 7.4  The Body Shop  GB  Int

The Body Shop, which sources and retails (directly and through franchises) naturally inspired lotions and cosmetics, has been a highly successful business with a price to earnings ratio which stayed well above the retail sector average throughout the 1980s, before declining as a result of expansion and increased competition. Until 1999, The Body Shop also manufactured at least half of the products it sold.

The Body Shop was started in England in 1976 by Anita Roddick and her husband Gordon, as a means of supporting Anita and their two daughters while Gordon went to fulfil a dream, riding horseback across the Americas. Gordon helped Anita get a bank loan of £4000 to open the first shop and shortly afterwards while Gordon was away the first franchise was agreed. Stores have subsequently been opened in over 40 countries – there are now over 1700 stores – and The Body Shop was floated on the UK Stock Exchange in 1984. Well renowned for its environmental and ethical stance and strategies, The Body Shop has made an impact around the world. 'If you think you are too small to have an impact, try going to bed with a mosquito' (Anita Roddick).

Anita's motivation for starting her business was always influenced by her personal commitment to education and to the environment and social change. Simply, her talent for entrepreneurism was channelled into a cause. The business and its financial success has been a vehicle to achieve other, more important, objectives. 'Profits are perceived as boring, but business as exciting.' The Body Shop's declared 'reason for being', 'dedicates the business to the pursuit of social and environmental change'. Anita Roddick was concerned to do something that was 'economically, socially and ecologically sustainable, meeting the needs of the present without

compromising the future'. Her ideas were the outcome of her world travels. She had visited many developing countries, 'living native', and had seen how women used natural products efficaciously and effectively. She noticed how women in Tahiti rubbed their bodies with cocoa butter to produce soft, satin-like skin despite a hot climate. She realized that women in Morocco used mud to give their hair a silky sheen. She also saw Mexicans successfully treat burns with aloes, the slimy juice from cactus leaves. From these observations and experiences she conceptualized, and realized, her opportunity. She would use natural ingredients from around the world to produce a range of new products. People in villages were asked to supply her with the natural ingredients she needed – a form of community trade.

The Body Shop has always aroused enthusiasm, commitment and loyalty amongst those involved with it. 'The company must never let itself become anything other than a human enterprise.' Much of this has developed from the ethical beliefs and values of Anita and Gordon Roddick, which have become manifested in a variety of distinctive policies. Gordon oversaw many of the operational aspects of the business.

The Body Shop adopts an environmentally responsible approach, offering products in minimal or no packaging. Posters in the shops have been used to campaign, among other things, to save whales and to stop the burning of rain forests. Packaging is simple, yet the shops are characterized by strong and distinctive aromas. The packages, together with posters and shelf cards, provide comprehensive information about the products and their origins and ingredients. This has created a competitive advantage which rivals have at times found difficult to replicate.

CASE

▶

The sales staff are knowledgeable, but they are not forceful and do not sell aggressively, generally offering advice only if it is requested. Marketing themes concern 'health and well-being rather than glamour, and reality rather than instant rejuvenation'. The Body Shop chose to avoid advertising for many years, preferring in-store information and word of mouth to attempts at persuasion. More recently, and especially in the US, informative advertising has been used. The Body Shop states that neither ingredients nor final products have been tested on animals. Despite the company's active stance on ethical issues, there have been accusations to the contrary, and The Body Shop was forced into litigation (which it won) in 1992. The business has always been controversial in some circles and attracted hostility. When the first shop opened local morticians were horrified at the name: The Body Shop!

Employees are provided with regular newsletters and training packages. Anita Roddick contributes regularly to the newsletters, which concentrate on The Body Shop campaigns and products. Employees are given time off during working hours, to do voluntary work in the community.

The Body Shop was initially able to integrate manufacturing and retailing effectively and was efficient and operationally strong. Fresh supplies could be delivered to its UK stores with a 24-hour lead time. These strategies, policies and beliefs generated substantial growth and profits in the 1980s. In the year ended 28 February 1991 turnover exceeded £100 million with trading profits of some £22 million. When these results were announced the UK share price exceeded 350 pence. Between 1984 and 1991, against the *Financial Times* All Share index of 100, The Body Shop shares rose from an index figure of 100 to 5500. However, by mid-1995 the share price had fallen to 150 pence. Profits had fallen; new professional senior managers had been brought in to add strength. One dilemma concerned whether the culture and quirky management style was still wholly appropriate as The Body Shop became a much bigger international business. Global scale brings global competition. As the business grew it lost some of its entrepreneurial spirit.

In addition, The Body Shop had attracted more and more competition. Leading UK retailers such as Boots, Marks and Spencer and Sainsbury's introduced natural ingredients in their own-label ranges; further competition arrived in the form of the US Bath and Body Works chain, whose early trial stores in the UK were a joint venture with Next. Bath and Body Works is renowned as a fast-moving organization, quick to innovate new ideas – and aggressive at advertising and promotion. Among its responses in the UK, The Body Shop began trials of a party plan operation. The first Values Report was published by The Body Shop in 1995 and detailed independently verified information relating to the company's social and ethical performance.

In October 1995 The Body Shop announced its intention to reprivatize the company by buying back shares. The shares would then be placed in a charitable trust, which would be able to make donations to humanitarian and environmental causes. The plan was abandoned in March 1996 because The Body Shop would have had to borrow heavily to finance the plan. In 1998, Anita joined Gordon as a co-chairman and a new chief executive (Patrick Gournay) was recruited from outside the company. The loss-making US business was separated out and a joint venture agreement was established; a non-executive director injected $1 million in exchange for an option to acquire 49 per cent of the US business. In 1999 The Body Shop withdrew from manufacturing and established a strong supply network instead, enabling it to concentrate on the retail end of the business.

Profits grew steadily throughout the 1990s, reaching almost £40 million in 1998. However, by 2001/2 they had fallen to £13 million and disappointed shareholders wanted changes. Gournay was dismissed; the Roddicks stepped down from their co-chairman role, although Anita was retained as a creative consultant. The US joint venture partner was bought out. Takeover rumours came and went. The new chief executive, Peter Saunders, proclaimed that his strategic priorities were new products (for new customers) and tighter cost controls.

Simply, the 'green market' for cosmetics had changed as it had grown, albeit that that growth had been prompted by the success of The Body Shop. Competitors such as Aveda had seized the premium end of the market; at the same time the leading supermarket chains had taken sales of lower price items. The Body Shop had lost something of its distinctive edge.

The Body Shop is an idiosyncratic, unusual and high-profile business; Anita Roddick, like Richard Branson, is an entrepreneur who has made a very individual contribution. It has not been easy and has required courage in the face of criticism, hostility and setback.

**Questions**

1. How different do you believe it would feel to work for The Body Shop as distinct from a retailer without the same manifest commitment to environmental and ethical issues?
2. In what ways might this commitment prove disadvantageous?

To answer these questions you are encouraged to visit a Body Shop and other rival stores and consider the culture against the framework presented in Figure 7.7.

3. What do you think The Body Shop should do next? Is there a future without Anita Roddick? In this regard examine what happened to Laura Ashley as a business after the unexpected death of its founder.

**The Body Shop** http://www.bodyshop.com

## 7.5  Culture – an introduction

When any group of people live and work together for any length of time, they form and share certain beliefs about what is right and proper. They establish behaviour patterns based on their beliefs, and their actions often become matters of habit which they follow routinely. These beliefs and ways of behaving constitute the organization's *culture*.

Culture is reflected in the way in which people in an organization perform tasks, set objectives and administer resources to achieve them. It affects the way that they make decisions, think, feel and act in response to opportunities and threats. Culture also influences the selection of people for particular jobs, which in turn affects the way in which tasks are carried out and decisions are made. Culture is so fundamental that it affects behaviour unconsciously. Managers do things in particular ways because it is implicitly expected behaviour.

The culture of an organization is therefore related to the people, their behaviour and the operation of the structure. It is encapsulated in beliefs, customs and values, and manifested in a number of symbolic ways.

The formation of, and any changes to, the culture of an organization is dependent on the leadership and example of particular individuals, and their ability to control or influence situations. This is itself dependent on a person's ability to obtain and use power.

Minicase 7.4, The Body Shop, shows how the values of the founder, Anita Roddick, inspired employees and attracted customers. The distinctive culture enabled The Body Shop to grow and prosper, but it was not totally appropriate for the large, international business that The Body Shop became. As a consequence, Anita Roddick has relinquished day-to-day control and a number of changes have been made to the strategies.

Culture and power, then, affect the choice, incidence and application of the modes of strategy creation, which will also reflect the values and preferences of the strategic leader. The preferred mode must, however, be appropriate for the organization's strategic needs, which are affected by competition. Moreover, culture and power are such strong forces that, if the prevailing culture is overlooked, implementation may not happen. Strong cultures can obstruct strategic change, particularly if companies are in decline and people feel vulnerable.

Quite simply, culture is at the heart of all strategy creation and implementation. Organizations are seeking to respond to perceived strategic issues. Resources must be deployed and committed, but successful change also requires the 'right' attitude, approach and commitment from people. This mindset, which might, for example, reflect a strong customer and service focus, could imply further empowerment and consequently cultural change.

In the early 1980s, Berry (1983) claimed that after some 20 years of emphasis on analytical techniques in strategic management, the concentration switched to the softer aspect of culture. The emphasis was no longer on the marketplace, but on what managers could do to resolve internal problems; by using culture, companies could become more strategically effective. The perspective of this book is that both the hard and soft aspects of strategy have important roles to play in strategic management.

Strong cultures, then, are an important strategic asset. Internalized beliefs can motivate people to exceptional levels of performance. An effective strategic leader will understand and mould the culture in order that a vision can be pursued and intended strategies implemented. Most successful companies develop strong cultures; the major doubt concerns an organization's ability to change the culture.

Moreover, large organizations formed by a series of acquisitions will frequently exhibit different cultures in the various divisions or businesses; in many international businesses this is inevitable. The challenge for corporate headquarters is to ensure that certain critically important values are reflected in all branches of the corporation and cultural differences do not inhibit internal architecture and synergy. The acquisition of Compaq by Hewlett-Packard in 2002 (Minicase 7.5) provided exactly this challenge.

CASE

## Minicase 7.5 Hewlett-Packard                                                  US

Hewlett-Packard (HP) began life in a garage in Palo Alto, California, in 1939. It happened because Stanford Professor Fred Terman brought together two of his Ph.D. students, Bill Hewlett and Dave Packard, and encouraged them to start a business based on their research. HP not only became a leading computer company, it was also the foundation upon which Silicon Valley was built. Some 60 years later HP was probably best known for its computer printers – it had some 40 per cent of the world market and also earned substantial revenues from sales of replacement ink and toner cartridges. But HP was a diversified business and also supplied PCs, laptops, servers, scanners and digital cameras as well as providing IT consultancy services. In 1999 Carly Fiorina became the new CEO and she was determined to strengthen HP's posi-

tion in the market and make it the number two company behind IBM. She launched an agreed $1.9 billion bid for Compaq. The opposition to this strategy was led by Walter Hewlett, the son of Bill Hewlett, who believed that instead of moving further into computers, HP should become more focused on printers and associated digital businesses. Fiorina's logic was that sales of computers, scanners and digital cameras drive printer sales. HP had a special range of photo printers.

In contrast Compaq was a much younger company which had been founded in 1982 by three senior managers from Texas Instruments. They set out to make affordable and portable PCs to run the software being developed for the IBM PC. These were commonly known as IBM clones,

▶

and the design for the first model was sketched out on a restaurant placemat.

The emphasis was on volume production and managed costs to fuel competitive prices.

The company became one of America's fastest growth businesses. Over 50,000 were sold in the first year of operations. By 1994 Compaq was the world's leading PC supplier. However, in 1998 Compaq acquired Digital Equipment for $9.6 billion in cash. Digital provided high-end servers, operating systems and chip technology. It might have been complementary, but it was certainly not a direct competitor. At the same time Compaq was experiencing more intense competition from the aggressive Dell, started in Texas by the entrepreneurial Michael Dell, whose business model relies on sourced-in components and direct sales. There were post-acquisition problems and soon Compaq was carrying expensive excess inventory. The product lines and distribution had to be rationalized. Jobs, including senior executives, were lost. Fast, aggressive and competitive, for some analysts the company had lost its way strategically. Under a new CEO, however, the decline was staunched and the situation was stabilized with a stronger focus on services – but not sufficiently to withstand a market slump in 2001, when more jobs were lost.

> *Compaq Computer lived the Hank Williams life – it ran hard, got famous and died before its time*
>
> CNET News.com

HP's values, known widely as 'The HP Way' were based on trust, respect, passion for customers, speed and agility of service. They had evolved over 60 years. The company saw itself as process-intensive and very much technology-based.

> *At HP we believe ideas thrive on teamwork. Everyone at every level in every function is encouraged to have original ideas and to share them. We believe anything can be achieved if you really believe in it and will invest in your ideas to change lives and*

> *working practices. That's because we work across borders and without limits. Global virtual teams share resources and pool their brainpower to solve business issues and meet personal goals. You will be valued for your unique skills, experiences and perspective. You will add value with every idea you have.*
>
> Statement to employees

One analyst, John Madden (Summit Strategies, Boston) mused that it was unclear whether a combined HP-Compaq would have a cohesive strategy but acknowledged that 'culture issues aside, services for both companies are at the heart of the bulls-eye'.

One interesting and perhaps significant development in 2004 was HP's decision to launch a range of notebook computers with the Linux open-source operating system installed. Started by Finnish entrepreneur, Linus Torvalds, Linux has been made available either free of charge or for a small licence fee from certain organizations who will provide technical support. It is a growing competitor to the ubiquitous Microsoft Windows, but, as yet, has only had a limited impact on the market. Leading rival, Dell, sells 'naked' machines – with no operating system installed – but it has yet to offer Linux pre-installed, possibly concerned about its long-term relationship with Microsoft. HP is the first to do so. The price saving is not huge – some $60 in a $1000 plus notebook; the real issue is one of consumer choice.

## Questions

1. How different do you imagine the HP and Compaq cultures were when Compaq was thriving as a manufacturer of PCs and laptops?
2. How difficult might it be to reconcile the differences and create a cohesive culture?
3. What do you think the decision to launch a Notebook with Linux installed is saying about the HP culture?

**HP** http://www.hp.com

At the same time, cross-border mergers and alliances promise to fuse together the best features of different cultures, but this may prove more idealistic than realistic. For example, the acquisition of Rover by BMW appeared to offer an opportunity to bring together the longer-term German perspective on investment, training and employee consultation and the UK's flexibility in working practices and lower manufacturing costs. In the event the marketing aspects were ineffective and well-reviewed Rover cars did not sell in the showrooms. In spring 2000 Rover was resold by BMW to the specially formed Phoenix Group.

## 7.6 Aspects of culture

The points discussed in this section are summarized in Figure 7.7.

### 7.6.1 Manifestations of culture

Edgar Schein (1985) contends that it is important to consider culture as having a number of levels, some of which are essentially manifestations of underlying beliefs.

**Figure 7.7** Aspects of culture – the culture grid

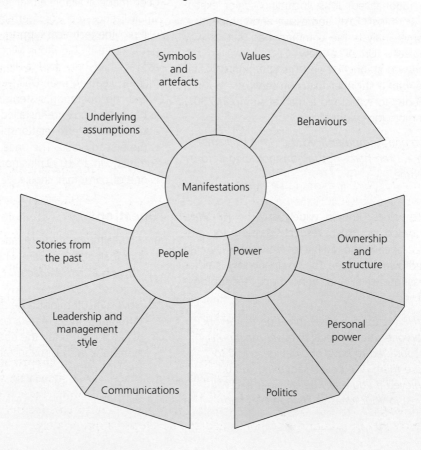

The first and most visible level Schein terms '*artefacts*'. These include the physical and social environment and the outputs of the organization. Written communications, advertisements and the reception that visitors receive are all included.

*Values* are the second level, and they represent a sense of 'what ought to be' based on convictions held by certain key people. For example if an organization has a problem such as low sales or a high level of rejections in production, decisions might be made to advertise more aggressively or to use high-quality but more expensive raw materials. These are seen initially as the decision-maker's values, which can be debated or questioned. Many of the strategies followed by organizations start in this way, and many will reflect values held by the strategic leader.

If the alternative is successful it may well be tried again and again until it becomes common practice. In this way the value becomes a belief and ultimately an assumption about behaviour practised by the organization. These basic *underlying assumptions* are Schein's third level, and they represent the taken-for-granted ways of doing things or solutions to problems.

One belief accepted by employees within a bank might be that all lending must be secure. A football team could be committed to always playing attractive, open football. A university might be expected to have clear beliefs about the relative importance of research and teaching, but this is likely to be an issue where employees 'agree to disagree', leading to a fragmented culture. Examples of *behaviours* are speedy new product development, long working hours, formal management meetings and regular informal meetings or contacts with colleagues, suppliers and customers.

It is also important to appreciate that certain organizations may state that they have particular values, but in reality these will be little more than verbal or written statements or aspirations for the future.

Schein argues that cultural paradigms are formed which determine how 'organization members perceive, think about, feel about, and judge situations and relationships' and these are based on a number of underlying assumptions.

## 7.6.2 People and culture

For Schwartz and Davis (1981) culture is 'a pattern of beliefs and expectations shared by the organization's members, and which produce norms that powerfully shape the behaviour of individuals and groups in the organization'. They argue that the beliefs held by the company are seen as major aspects of corporate policy as they evolve from interactions with, and in turn form policy towards, the marketplace. As a result, rules or norms for internal and external behaviour are developed and eventually both performance and reward systems will be affected. These aspects of the culture are often transmitted through *stories* of past events, glories and heroes.

Success is measured by, and culture therefore becomes based on, past activities. Current decisions by managers reflect the values, beliefs and norms that have proved beneficial in the past and in the development and growth of the organization. Moreover, they reinforce the corporate culture and expected behaviour throughout the organization.

The culture affects suppliers and customers, and their reactions are important. They will feed back impressions about the organization, and their views should be sought. Successful organizations will ensure that there is congruence between these environmental influences and the organization culture. In this way key success factors can be met if resources are administered, controlled and developed appropriately.

Organizations need a cohesive blend of the philosophies introduced earlier. A cohesive culture would exhibit strong *leadership*, whereby the strategic leader is sensitive to the degrees of decentralization and informality necessary for satisfying customer needs efficiently, and managing change pressures, in order to keep the business strong and profitable. At the same time a centralized information network will ensure that communications are effective and that managers are both kept aware and rewarded properly for their contributions. A fragmented culture, in contrast, would suggest that the needs of certain stakeholders were perhaps not being satisfied adequately, or that strategies and changes were not being co-ordinated, or that managers or business units were in conflict and working against each other, or that the most deserving people were not being rewarded.

Linked to this is *communication*, an essential aspect of culture. The organization might be seen as open or closed, formal or informal. Ideally, employees from different parts of the business, and at different levels in the hierarchy, will feel willing and able to talk openly with each other, sharing problems, ideas and learning. 'Doors should be left open.' Employees should also be trusted and empowered to the appropriate degree. Good communications can stop nasty surprises. It is helpful if employees know how well competitors are performing, where they are particularly strong, so they can commit themselves to high levels of achievement in order to outperform their rivals.

Communication is clearly essential for creating effective internal and external architecture.

Hampden-Turner (1990) argues that culture is based on communication and learning. The strategic leader's vision for the organization must be communicated and understood; events and changes affecting the organization also need to be communicated widely. Managers should be encouraged to seek out new opportunities by learning about new technology and customer expectations, and to innovate. The organization should help them to share their experiences and their learning.

### 7.6.3 Power and culture

Power is reflected in the *ownership* of the business. It may be a family company with strong, concentrated power. A small group of institutional shareholders could control the business, in which case it is conceivable that short-term financial targets will dictate strategies. *Structural issues* include the extent to which the organization is centralized or decentralized, the role and contribution of corporate headquarters, and control and reward systems. *Personal power* is discussed later in this chapter; *politics* refers to the ways in which managers use power and influence to affect decisions and actions.

Minicase 7.6 analyses IKEA against this model. IKEA focuses on being a low-cost competitor and achieves this while maintaining a complex supply-chain network. IKEA also has an ability to be flexible in response to local opportunities, which could easily add costs as well as value. The company is product and production driven, but able to capture and use ideas from customers and employees.

## Minicase 7.6  IKEA  (Eur)  (Int)

IKEA was started in Sweden by Ingvar Kamprad, who pioneered the idea of self-assembly furniture in handy packs. His vision of 'a better, more beautiful, everyday life for the many' led to 'a wide range of home furnishings, of good function and style, at low prices, for mass consumer markets'. Kamprad began with a mail-order business in 1943; the first IKEA store was opened in 1958. Every year IKEA prints over 110 million catalogues – this is by far the single largest print run of any comparable item anywhere in the world.

Growth has been carefully regulated. IKEA waited for seven years before opening a second branch; the first branch outside Sweden was in the early 1970s; the first US store opened in 1985, with typically one new store being added every year. This approach allows IKEA to establish local supply networks and ensures that it does not become stretched financially. The expansion programme has always been funded from cash generated by the retail activities. IKEA does not have a large market share in any single country; instead, it has a global brand and an intriguing reputation which draws customers from substantial distances away.

By the early 2000s, IKEA had some 175 shops in 31 countries, 21 of them franchises, and 70,000 employees worldwide. IKEA's strategy has always involved high-quality merchandise at prices which undercut the competition. In the mid-1990s IKEA's annual turnover passed the $5 billion mark; after-tax profits were estimated to be 8 per cent of revenue. Sales have risen in every year of its existence, and by 2001 revenues had doubled to $10 billion. Reputedly worth at least $25 billion, IKEA has always been reticent about the financial data it releases. Moreover, as IKEA has only recently started to target Russia and China, growth prospects appear to remain healthy.

IKEA stores focus on sales of self-assembly packs which customers take away themselves. IKEA will, however, deliver fully assembled pieces for a premium price. The stores have a wide range of facilities, typically including restaurants and games and video rooms for children; these are normally on the top floor, which is where customers come in. People are then routed carefully through a series of display areas to the downstairs purchase points which resemble a typical discount warehouse.

The furniture packs are commissioned from over 2300 suppliers in some 70 countries, many of them low labour-cost countries in the Far East and Eastern Europe. IKEA has an equity stake in several of its suppliers and insists on tight stock control programmes to reduce costs through the whole supply chain. IKEA designs all its own products and aims to lead customer taste. There is just one range of products for the global market, but not every country and store stocks the full range. IKEA chooses not to have mini-ranges for specific countries and prides itself on an ability to respond to local fashion and opportunities by quickly adjusting the range in any one store. Sales per square foot invariably exceed industry averages.

### Manifestations of IKEA's distinctive culture

The *artefacts* clearly include the stores, the products and the prices. There are no brands other than IKEA's own. There are no annual or seasonal sales; prices stay valid for a whole year. There is a plethora of in-store information and communications, but no commissioned sales people.

*Values* – IKEA use the word 'prosumers' to imply that value is added by both IKEA and their customers in partnership. Employees are empowered to be innovative and helpful and challenged to 'dare to be different'. IKEA recognizes that always offering prices substantially below those of its competitors places considerable pressure on its staff. IKEA also expect, and get, some complaints about busy stores and slow checkout service – a price that they claim has to be paid for low prices. Even though IKEA prices could easily have been increased, Kamprad has stuck with his original approach and mission.

*Underlying assumptions* can be summarized in the following quotes:

> *We do not need to do things in traditional ways (window manufacturers have been*

*approached to make table frames; shirt manufacturers for seat cushions).*

*Break your chains and you are free; cut your roots and you die. IKEA should look for constant renewal.*

*Experiments matter; mistakes (within reason) will be tolerated.*

*Behaviours* – Every IKEA manager flies economy class and uses taxis only if there is no suitable alternative. In the Netherlands, managers have been encouraged to stay with typical IKEA customer families to learn more about their needs. Kamprad himself, despite his enormous wealth (estimated at £9 billion), drives a ten-year-old Volvo car. In this respect he can be likened to the late Sam Walton of Wal-Mart, who opted for a pick-up truck.

## People

A variety of *stories* permeates the IKEA culture. Initially customers in the US stores were simply not

**Ikea store**

buying any beds – there had been no market research into US tastes; it was IKEA's global product. Eventually, it was realized that Americans sleep in bigger beds than Swedes. Similarly, kitchen units had to be adjusted to handle extra-large pizza plates.

Kamprad denies that there is any truth in the story that his parsimony stretches to him buying cans of Coca-Cola from local supermarkets to replenish hotel room mini-bars because he is reluctant to pay hotel prices for soft drinks.

*Leadership and management style* – Kamprad rarely shows his face to the public. At one stage there was some adverse publicity concerning alleged wartime allegiances, but no lasting damage. The lack of published financial information reinforces this hidden aspect of IKEA. Now well into his 70s, Kamprad has declared his three sons will take over the business from him.

*Communications* – Both customers and employees are encouraged to provide ideas and suggestions, which may be translated into new products. Information enters the system from several points. When Kamprad visits stores he encourages staff to use his Christian name and he spends time with them and IKEA customers receiving feedback.

## Power

*Ownership and structural issues* – IKEA remains a private company which owns all of its sites. It pays for new sites in cash: 'We don't like to be in the hands of the banks.' There are no plans to become a limited company either; Kamprad has criticized the short-term interests of many investors.

The company operates as three distinct activities. The core retailing business is now a Dutch-registered charitable foundation. The profits of the operations are subjected to a top-slice of 3 per cent to fund a separate business which has responsibility for managing the brand and IKEA's franchisees. The third arm is a banking and finance business; IKEA, for example, owns a majority shareholding in Habitat in the UK.

*Power* – The organization is structured as an inverted pyramid and based on managers and co-workers. 'Employees are there to serve customers.' Kamprad was always concerned that IKEA should not become inflexible as it grew in size. There are no directors, no formal titles and no dining rooms or reserved parking spaces for executives. Managers are quite likely to switch between functions and countries. The organization is fundamentally informal with 'few instructions'. Every year there is an 'anti-bureaucracy' week when everyone dresses casually.

**Questions**

1. IKEA believes that fashionable and modern furniture and furnishings can be affordable for most families. It need not be prohibitively expensive. How does it achieve this?
2. Do you believe IKEA enjoys E–V–R congruence? If so, what are the key congruency themes? If not, in what way is it incongruent?

**Ikea** http://www.ikea.com

## 7.7 Determinants of culture

Deal and Kennedy (1982) argue that employees must be rewarded for compliance with the essential cultural aspects if these values are to be developed and retained over time; and they conclude that people who build, develop and run successful companies invariably work hard to create strong cultures within their organizations.

From their research Deal and Kennedy isolated five key elements or determinants of culture.

- The environment and key success factors: what the organization must do well if it is to be an effective competitor. Innovation and fast delivery are examples quoted.

- The values that the strategic leader considers important and wishes to see adopted and followed in the organization. These should relate to the key success factors, and to employee reward systems.

- Heroes: the visionaries who create the culture. They can come from any background and could be, for example, product or service innovators, engineers who build the appropriate quality into the product, or creative marketing people who provide the slogans which make the product or brand name a household word.

- Rites and rituals: the behaviour patterns in which the culture is manifest. Again there are any number of ways in which this can happen, including employees helping each other out when there are difficulties, the way in which sales people deal with customers, and the care and attention that go into production.

- The cultural network: the communications system around which the culture revolves and which determines just how aware employees are about the essential issues.

When the culture is strong, people know what is expected of them and they understand how to act and decide in particular circumstances. They appreciate the issues that are important. When it is weak, time can be wasted in trying to decide what should be done and how. Moreover, it is argued that employees feel better about their companies if they are recognized, known about and regarded as successful, and these aspects will be reflected in the culture.

There can be a number of separate strands to the culture in any organization, which should complement each other. For example, there can be aspects relating to the strategic leader, the environment and the employees. There could be a strong power culture related to an influential strategic leader who is firmly in charge of the organization and whose values are widely understood and followed. This could be linked to a culture of market orientation, which ensures that customer needs are considered and satisfied, and to a work culture if employees feel committed to the organization and wish to help in achieving success.

## 7.8 Implications of culture

Pümpin (1987) suggests that seven aspects comprise the culture of an organization, and that the relative significance of each of these will vary from industry to industry. The seven aspects are:

1. The extent to which the organization is marketing orientated, giving customers high priority.
2. The relationships between management and staff, manifested through communication and participation systems, for example.
3. The extent to which people are target orientated and committed to achieving agreed levels of performance.
4. Attitudes towards innovation. It is particularly important that the risks associated with failure are perceived as acceptable by all levels of management if innovation and entrepreneurship are to be fostered.
5. Attitudes towards costs and cost reduction.
6. The commitment and loyalty to the organization felt, and shown, by staff.
7. The impact of, and reaction to, technology and technological change and development. One major issue concerns whether or not the opportunities offered by information technology are being harnessed by the firm.

Many of these aspects are developed further in later chapters of the book.

Hampden-Turner (1990) believes that the culture is a manifestation of how the organization has chosen to deal with specific dilemmas and conflicts. Each of these can be viewed as a continuum, and the organization needs a clear position on each one. As shown earlier, one dilemma might be the conflict between, on the one hand, the need to develop new products and services quickly and ahead of competitors and, on the other hand, the need for thorough development and planning to ensure adequate quality and safety. Another dilemma is the need for managers to be adaptive and responsive in a changing environment, but not at the expense of organization-wide communication and awareness. Such change orientation may also conflict with a desire for continuity and consistency of strategy and policy.

Tables 7.3 and 7.4 take this idea further. Table 7.3 highlights how every apparent virtue also has a 'flip side', and consequently something which is positive at one point may suddenly prove disadvantageous. Table 7.4 looks at the advantages and drawbacks of three business paradigms: a market-orientated business, an organization focused on resource efficiency, and a growth-driven business. Taken together, these confirm that there can never be one best or ideal culture. The culture needs to be flexible and adaptive as circumstances change. The cultural factors that bring initial success may need to

**Table 7.3** Every coin, every virtue, has a flip side!

| | |
|---|---|
| Team players | May be indecisive and avoid risks |
| Customer focus | Can lead to reactivity and lack of innovation |
| Action orientation | Can become reckless and dictatorial |
| Analytical thinking | Can result in paralysis |
| Innovation | Which is impractical, unrealistic, ill thought-through, wastes time and money |
| A global vision | May mean valuable local opportunities are missed |
| Being a good 'people manager' | May allow someone to become soft and walk away from tough decisions |

Developed from ideas in McCall, MW (1998) *High Flyers*, Harvard Business School Press.

**Table 7.4** The imperfect world of organizations

| A market-driven business is likely to be: | An efficient operations-driven business is likely to be: | A growth-orientated business is likely to be: |
|---|---|---|
| Resourceful | Efficient | Competitive |
| Entrepreneurial | Strong on teamworking | Strong on targets and achieving results |
| Risk oriented | Good at executing plans | Full of hard-working people |
| Pragmatic in terms of getting things done | Sophisticated with its systems and procedures | Flexible |
| | | Changing quickly |
| *But it may not be:* | *But it may not be:* | *But it may not be:* |
| Consistent | Responsive to customers | Taking a long-term perspective |
| Disciplined in what it does | Good at managing change | Offering a balanced lifestyle for its employees |
| Adhering to systems and procedures | Able to see 'the big picture' | Sensitive to people's needs |
| Strong on teamworking | | |

Developed from ideas in McCall, MW (1998) *High Flyers*, Harvard Business School Press.

be changed if success is to be sustained. Similarly, it is not enough simply to look at what other successful organizations are doing and copy them. Benchmarking and teasing out good practices is both important and beneficial, but these practices again need customizing and adapting to the unique circumstances facing an individual organization.

## 7.9 Culture and strategy creation

We have already seen that the essential cultural characteristics will dictate the preferred mode of strategy creation in an organization; all the modes are likely to be present to some degree.

The culture will influence the ability of a strategic visionary to 'sell' his or her ideas to other members of the organization and gain their support and commitment to change. The planning mode is most suitable in a reasonably stable and predictable environment, but a reliance on it in a more unstable situation can lead to missed opportunities. It is an ideal mode for a conservative, risk-averse, slow-to-change organization. Where environmental opportunities and threats arise continuously in a situation of competitive chaos an organization must be able to deal with them if it is to survive. It is the culture, with its amalgam of attitudes, values, perceptions and experiences, which determines the outcomes and relative success. The structure must facilitate awareness, sharing and learning, and people must be willing and able to act. People 'learn by doing' and they must be able to learn from mistakes. Peters (1988) states that 'managers have to learn how to make mistakes faster'. The reward system is critical here. Managers and employees should be praised and rewarded for exercising initiative and taking risks which prove successful; failures should not be sanctioned too harshly, as long as they are not repeated!

Berry (1983) argues that if a strategic leader really understands the company culture they must, by definition, be better equipped to make wise decisions. They might conclude that 'cultural change will be so difficult we had better be sure to select a business or strategy that our kind of company can handle well'. This is just as valid as, and perhaps more useful than, believing that one can accomplish cultural change in order to shift the firm towards a new strategy.

Moreover, if business strategies and culture are intertwined, the ability to analyse and construct strategies and the ability to manage and inspire people are also intertwined. Hence, a good strategy acknowledges, 'where we are, what we have got, and what therefore managerially helps us to get where we want to be' and this is substantially different from selecting business options exclusively on their product/market dynamics. In other words, developing and implementing strategy is a human and political process that starts as much with the visions, hopes and aspirations of a company's leaders as it does with market or business analysis. Ideas drive organizations.

With ever-shortening product life cycles, intense global competition and unstable economies and currencies the future is going to require organizations that are ready to commit themselves to change. Strategy is going to be about intertwining analysis and adaptation. The challenge is to develop more effective organizations.

Miles and Snow (1978), whose research has been used to develop Table 7.5, have suggested a typology of organizations which can be looked at in relation to culture and strategy formation. The typology distinguishes organizations in terms of their values and objectives, and different types will typically prefer particular approaches to strategy creation. Defenders, prospectors and analysers are all regarded by Miles and Snow as positive organizations; reactors must ultimately adopt one of the other three approaches or suffer long-term decline. Suggested examples of each type are as follows. GEC, despite being in high-technology industries, was relatively conservative and a defender. The risk-oriented, innovative Amstrad has always been a prospector. The respective strategic leaders of these organizations, the late Lord Weinstock (until his retirement in 1996) and entrepreneur Sir Alan Sugar adopted different styles of management and exhibited different corporate values. Weinstock's successor, Lord Simpson, adopted a far higher risk 'prospector' strategy, divesting defence businesses and acquiring telecommunications companies. The outcomes were disappointing and led to the collapse of the company, which had been renamed Marconi.

**Table 7.5** Organizational values and strategies

| Type | Characteristics | Strategy formation |
|------|-----------------|--------------------|
| Defenders | Conservative beliefs<br>Low-risk strategies<br>Secure markets<br>Concentration on narrow segments<br>Considerable expertise in narrow areas of specialism<br>Preference for well-tried resolutions to problems<br>Little search for anything really 'new'<br>Attention given to improving efficiency of present operations | Emphasis on planning |
| Prospectors | Innovative<br>Looking to break new ground<br>High-risk strategies<br>Search for new opportunities<br>Can create change and uncertainty, forcing a response from competitors<br>More attention given to market changes than to improving internal efficiency | Visionary mode |
| Analysers | *Two aspects: stable and changing*<br>Stable: formal structures and search for efficiencies<br>Changing: competitors monitored and strategies amended as promising ideas seen (followers) | Planning mode<br><br>Adaptive/Incremental mode |
| Reactors | Characterized by an inability to respond effectively to change pressures<br>Adjustments are therefore forced on the firm in order to avert crises | Adaptive mode |

Historically, many public-sector bureaucracies have been stable analysers, while Marks and Spencer has long been a changing analyser. Prior to its decline and acquisition by BTR, Dunlop, in the 1970s, exhibited many of the characteristics of a reactor organization, and failed to change sufficiently in line with environmental changes.

Miles and Snow argue that, as well as being a classification, their typology can be used to predict behaviour. For example, a defender organization, in a search for greater operating efficiency, might consider investing in the latest technology, but reject the strategy if it has high risk attached.

> *The power of 'corporate culture' should not be underestimated, both for a company's success and, if it is inappropriate, in frustrating change. Values, strategies, systems, organization and accountabilities – the components of culture – are a very strong mix which can either make a company successful or, alternatively, lead to its decline. The task of corporate leadership is to apply energy and judgement to the corporate culture to ensure its relevance.*
>
> Sir Allen Sheppard, when Chairman, Grand Metropolitan plc

# 7.10 Culture, structure and styles of management

Charles Handy (1976), building on earlier work by Harrison (1972) has developed an alternative classification of organizations based on cultural differences, and this is illustrated in Figure 7.8.

## 7.10.1 The club culture or power culture

In the club culture type of organization, work is divided by function or product and a diagram of the organization structure would be quite traditional. There would be departments for sales, production, finance and so on, and possibly product based divisions or strategic business units if the organization was larger. However, this structure is mostly found in smaller firms.

These functions or departments are represented in Handy's figure by the lines radiating out from the centre; but the essential point is that there are also concentric lines representing communications and power. The further away from the centre, the weaker is the power and influence. This structure is dominated from the centre and therefore is typical for small entrepreneurial organizations. Decisions can be taken quickly, but the quality of the decisions is very dependent on the abilities of managers in the inner circle.

In its heyday Hanson was described by a former director as a 'solar system, with everyone circling around the sun in the middle, Lord Hanson' (see Leadbeater and Rudd 1991). This analogy suggests both movement and dependency. The Hanson story is discussed in detail in Chapter 16 and in a full-length case on the accompanying web site.

**Figure 7.8** Handy's four cultures

Apated from Handy, CB (1976) *Understanding Organizations*, Penguin

| Culture | Diagrammatic representation | Structure |
|---------|-----------------------------|-----------|
| Power or club |  | Web |
| Role |  | Greek temple |
| Task | 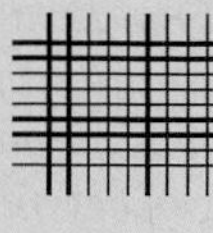 | Net |
| Person or existential | 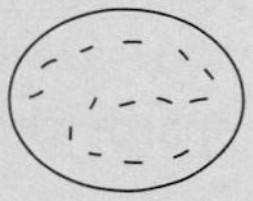 | Cluster |

Decisions depend a great deal on empathy, affinity and trust, both within the organization and with suppliers, customers and other key influences.

People learn to do instinctively what their boss and the organization expect and require. Consequently, they will prove reliable even if they are allowed to exercise a degree of initiative. Foreign-exchange dealers provide an illustration of this point.

For this reason the culture can be designated either 'club' or 'power'. Employees are rewarded for effort, success and compliance with essential values; and change is very much led from the centre in an entrepreneurial style.

A culture such as this may prevent individual managers from speaking their minds, but decisions are unlikely to get lost in committees.

### 7.10.2   The role culture

The role culture is the more typical organization as the culture is built around defined jobs, rules and procedures and not personalities. People fit into jobs, and are recruited for this purpose. Hence, rationality and logic are at the heart of the culture, which is designed to be stable and predictable.

The design is the Greek temple because the strengths of the organization are deemed to lie in the pillars, which are joined managerially at the top. One essential role of top management is to co-ordinate activity, and consequently it will be seen that both planning systems and incremental changes can be a feature of this culture. Although the strength of the organization is in the pillars, power lies at the top. As well as being designed for stability the structure is designed to allow for continuity and changes of personnel, and for this reason dramatic changes are less likely than more gradual ones.

High efficiency is possible in stable environments, but the structure can be slow to change and is therefore less suitable for dynamic situations.

Aspects of this culture can prove beneficial for transport businesses such as railways and airlines, where reliability and timekeeping are essential. Unfortunately, it is not by nature a flexible, service-orientated culture. Intrapreneurship or elements of the task culture are also required for effectiveness.

### 7.10.3   The task culture

Management in the task culture is concerned with the continuous and successful solution of problems, and performance is judged by the success of the outcomes.

The challenge is more important than the routine.

The culture is shown as a net, because for particular problem situations people and other resources can be drawn from various parts of the organization on a temporary basis. Once the problem is dealt with people will move on to other tasks, and consequently discontinuity is a key element. Expertise is the major source of individual power and it will determine a person's relative power in a given situation. Power basically lies in the interstices of the net, because of the reliance on task forces.

The culture is ideal for consultancies, advertising agencies and research and development departments. It can also be useful within the role culture for tackling particularly difficult or unusual problem situations.

In dynamic environments a major challenge for large organizations is the design of a structure and systems which allow for proper management and integration without losing the spirit and excitement typical of small, entrepreneurial businesses. Elements of the task culture superimposed over formal roles can help by widening communications and engendering greater commitment within the organization. One feature is cost. This culture is expensive as there is a reliance on talking and discussion, experimentation and learning by trial. Although Handy uses the expression problem solving, there can be problem resolutions or moves towards a solution along more incremental lines, as well as decisions concerning major changes. If successful changes are implemented the expense can often be justified.

### 7.10.4 The person culture or existential culture

The person culture is completely different from the other three, for here the organization exists to help the individual rather than the other way round. Groups of professional people, such as doctors, architects, dentists and solicitors, provide excellent examples. The organization with secretarial help, printing and telephone facilities and so on provides a service for individual specialists and reduces the need for costly duplication. If a member of the circle leaves or retires, he or she is replaced by another who may have to buy in.

Some professional groups exhibit interdependencies and collaboration, allocating work among the members, although management of such an organization is difficult because of individual expertise and because the rewards and sanctions are different from those found in most other situations.

However, in an environment where government is attempting to increase competition between professional organizations, and in some cases to reduce barriers to entering the profession, it is arguable that effective management, particularly at the strategic level, will become increasingly necessary. Efforts will need co-ordinating and harnessing if organizations are to become strong competitors.

## 7.11 Management philosophies

Press (1990) suggests that the culture of an organization is based upon one or more philosophies. His ideas are developed in Figure 7.9. The specific philosophies are related to the various stakeholders in the business, and are determined by two intersecting axes. One relates to whether the business is focused more internally or externally; the other is based on performance measures. Do they concentrate more on resource management and efficiency, or outcomes and effectiveness? This creates four discrete philosophies:

- the resource focus, which concentrates on internal efficiencies and cost management
- the shareholder focus, which sees the business as a portfolio of activities which should be managed to maximize the value of the business for its shareholders
- the people focus, which emphasizes the skills and contribution of employees, and their needs and expectations
- the market focus, which stresses the importance of satisfying customers by adding value and differentiating products and services.

All of these are important; none of them can be ignored. The culture can be analysed in terms of how these four philosophies are perceived and prioritized. As pointed out earlier, the philosophy may have to change if success is to be sustained.

**Figure 7.9** Organizational philosophies

Adapted from Press, G (1990) Assessing competitors' business philosophies, *Long Range Planning*, 23 (5)

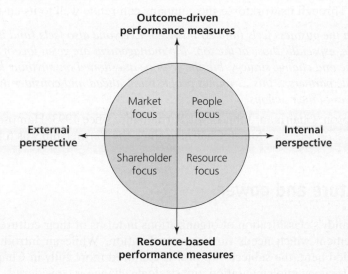

A company which relies heavily upon formal strategic planning, for example, is likely to concentrate more upon shareholders and resources. It may be argued that at a corporate level Hanson was similarly inclined; the individual subsidiary businesses typically had a resource focus supported by people and market philosophies. (Hanson was ultimately split into five separate businesses: the strategy, structure and style are all explained in more detail in Chapter 16.) General Electric (GE) of the US (see Chapters 15, 16 and 17) is another diversified conglomerate but with a different policy and style from Hanson on empowerment and decentralization. GE places most emphasis upon people and its style and culture has proved more enduring. Japanese companies, discussed later in this chapter, exhibit a particular blend of people, markets and resources.

## 7.12 Styles of management

The style adopted by the strategic leader can have a strong influence on the culture of the organization. Individual leaders can, for example, be relatively autocratic or democratic, visionary or essentially champions of the past, orientated more towards markets or more towards financial controls.

Styles which differ from the 'normal and traditional' can prove to be very effective in particular circumstances. The John Lewis Partnership, Britain's third largest department store chain after Debenhams and House of Fraser, practises worker participation and democracy. John Lewis is also diversified into supermarkets with its Waitrose chain. The company has a chairman, a board of directors and a management structure, as do most companies, but parallel to this commercial structure stands a second structure which represents the interests of the ordinary worker who is also a partner in John Lewis. While a partner working in a department in a store cannot directly influence management decisions, as a result of the partnership and its constitution the ordinary workers are again in ultimate control of the company for which they work. This is supplemented by a profit-sharing scheme. Decision-making and communications within the organization must be affected by high levels of participation. John Lewis's motto of 'never knowingly undersold' is based on value for money which is helped by employee involvement. Through its workforce the company can relate well to its customers.

*Everyone in the business feels (and is) involved. Everyone also feels (and is) accountable, especially those at the top. Top management are given lots of freedom to determine and change strategy, but they can be questioned on anything by the rank-and-file partners… this … makes people think ahead and consider the consequences of their actions.*

Stuart Hampson, Chairman, John Lewis Partnership, since 1993. Hampson is only the fourth Chairman since the Partnership was formed in 1929

## 7.13 Culture and power

In Charles Handy's classification of organizations in terms of their culture, power is an important element which needs further consideration. While an introduction to the topic is included here, the subject of power is explored more fully in Chapter 17 when its impact on strategy implementation and strategic change is considered.

Power is related to the potential or ability to do something. Consequently strategic change will be strongly influenced by the bases of power within an organization and by the power of the organization in relation to its environment.

### 7.13.1 Internal power

Change is brought about if the necessary resources can be harnessed and if people can be persuaded to behave in a particular way. Both of these require power. Power results in part from the structure of the organization, and it needs exercising in different ways in different cultures if it is to be used effectively. At the same time power can be a feature of an individual manager's personality, and managers who are personally powerful will be in a position to influence change.

The ways in which managers apply power are known as 'power levers'; Box 7.2 describes seven major sources of power. The classifications of power bases produced by a number of authors differ only slightly. Box 7.2 has been developed from a classification by Andrew Kakabadse (1982), who has built on the earlier work of French and Raven (1959).

In order to understand the reality of change in an organization and to examine how change might be managed, it is important to consider where power lies, which managers are powerful, and where their sources of power are. While a visible, powerful and influential strategic leader is often a feature of an entrepreneurial organization, the nature and direction of incremental change will be influenced significantly by which managers are powerful and how they choose to exercise their power.

A power culture has strong central leadership as a key feature and power lies with the individual or small group at the centre who controls most of the activity in the organization. In contrast, role cultures are based on the legitimacy of rules and procedures and individual managers are expected to work within these. Task cultures are dependent on the expertise of individuals, and their success, in some part, depends on the ability of the individuals to share their power and work as a team. Managers are expected to apply power levers in ways that are acceptable to the predominant culture of the organization,

## Box 7.2 Power Levers

1. **Reward power** is the ability to influence the rewards given to others. These can be tangible (money) or intangible (status). Owner managers enjoy considerable reward power, managers in larger public sector organizations very little. For reward power to be useful, the rewards being offered must be important to the potential recipients.

2. **Coercive power** is power based on the threat of punishment for non-compliance, and the ability to impose the punishment. The source can be the person's role or position in the organization, or physical attributes and personality.

3. **Legitimate power** is synonymous with authority, and relates to an individual manager's position within the structure of the organization. It is an entitlement from the role a person occupies. The effective use of legitimate power is dependent on three things: access to relevant information; access to other people and communication networks inside the organization; and approaches to setting priorities – this determines what is asked of others.

4. **Personal power** depends on individual characteristics (personality) and physical characteristics. Charm, charisma and flair are terms used to describe people with personality-based power. Physical attributes such as height, size, weight and strength also affect personal power.

5. **Expert power** is held by a person with specialist knowledge or skills in a particular field. It is particularly useful for tackling complex problem areas. It is possible for people to be attributed expert power through reputation rather than proven ability.

6. **Information power** is the ability to access and use information to defend a stance or viewpoint – or to question an alternative view held by someone else – and is important as it can affect strategic choices.

7. **Connection power** results from personal and professional access to key people inside and outside the organization, who themselves can influence what happens. This relates particularly to information power.

and at the same time the manner in which power levers are actually used affects what happens in the organization. Power is required for change; change results from the application of power. Hence the implementation of desired changes to strategies requires the effective use of power bases; but other strategic changes will result from the exercise of power by individual managers. It is important for the organization to monitor such activity and ensure that such emergent changes and strategies are desirable or acceptable.

### 7.13.2 The relative power of the organization

The ability of an organization to effect change within its environment will similarly depend on the exercise of power. A strong competitor with, say, a very distinctive product or service, or with substantial market share, may be more powerful than its rivals. A manufacturer who is able to influence distributors or suppliers will be similarly powerful. The issue is the relative power in relation to those other individuals, organizations and institutions – its stakeholders – on whom it relies, with whom it trades, or which influence it in some way.

## 7.14 Culture and competitive advantage

Barney (1986) has examined the relationship between culture and 'superior financial performance'. He has used microeconomics for his definition of superior financial performance, arguing that firms record either below-normal returns (insufficient for long-term survival in the industry), normal returns (enough for survival, but no more) or superior results, which are more than those required for long-term survival. Superior results, which result from some form of competitive advantage, attract competitors who seek to copy whatever is thought to be the source of competitive advantage and generating the success. This in turn affects supply and margins and can reduce profitability to only normal returns and, in some cases, below normal. Therefore, sustained superior financial performance requires sustained competitive advantage. Barney concluded that culture can, and does, generate sustained competitive advantage, and hence long-term superior financial performance, when three conditions are met.

- The culture is valuable. The culture must enable things to happen which themselves result in high sales, low costs or high margins.
- The culture is rare.
- The culture is imperfectly imitable, i.e. it cannot be copied easily by competitors.

Peters and Waterman's (1982) research-based book *In Search of Excellence* identified a number of factors which appeared to explain the success of a number of large American businesses. Although this work was in part discredited, as some successful companies experienced declining fortunes, the book focused on aspects of corporate culture and emphasized its impact on corporate performance. At the time the question raised was: if the cultural factors identified by Peters and Waterman were in fact transferable easily to other organizations, could they be the source of superior financial performance? Barney contends that valuable and rare cultures may be difficult, if not impossible, to imitate. For one thing, it is very difficult to define culture clearly, particularly in respect of how it adds value to the product or service. For another, culture is often tied to historical aspects of company development and to the beliefs, personality and charisma of a particular strategic leader.

Minicase 7.7, Club Méditerranée – at the end of the chapter – and Minicase 7.4 earlier (The Body Shop) both provide examples of companies which have gained success and renown with a culture-based competitive advantage. While maintaining the underlying principles and values, both companies have had to rethink their strategies to remain competitive.

**The limits to excellence** To summarize, some firms do appear to obtain superior financial performance from their cultures, but it does not follow that firms who succeed in copying these cultural attributes will necessarily also achieve superior financial results. Organizations which pursue the excellence factors must surely improve their chances of success, but clearly there can be no guarantees. Ignoring these issues will, however, increase the chances of failure.

The need to maintain E–V–R congruence in a dynamic, competitive environment must never be forgotten. During the early 1980s Jan Carlzon turned around the struggling SAS (Scandinavian Airlines System) by focusing on improvements in service and communications. Profits were restored with improved revenues, but costs later increased as well. As a driving philosophy, the service culture had to give way to a focus strategy and rationalization.

## 7.15 Changing culture

The culture of an organization may appear to be in need of change for any one of a number of reasons. It could be that the culture does not fit well with the needs of the environment or with the organization's resources, or that the company is not performing well and needs major strategic changes, or even that the company is growing rapidly in a changing environment and needs to adapt.

Ideally, the culture and strategies being pursued will complement each other and, again ideally, the organization will be flexible and adaptable to change when it is appropriate. But these ideals will not always be achieved.

The culture of an organization can be changed, but it may not be easy. Strong leadership and vision is always required to champion the change process. If an organization is in real difficulty, and the threat to its survival is clearly recognized, behaviour can be changed through fear and necessity. However, people may not feel comfortable and committed to the changes they accept or are coerced into accepting. Behaviour may change, but not attitudes and beliefs. When an organization is basically successful the process of change again needs careful management – changing attitudes and beliefs does not itself guarantee a change in behaviour. It is not unusual for a team of senior managers to spend time, frequently at a location away from the organization itself, discussing these issues and becoming excited about a set of new values that they proclaim are the way forward. After the workshop any commitment to the new values and to change can be easily lost once managers return to the daily grind and they become caught up again in immediate problems and difficulties. Their behaviour does not change and so the culture remains largely untouched.

The potential for changing the culture is affected by:

- the strength and history of the existing culture
- how well the culture is understood
- the personality and beliefs of the strategic leader and
- the extent of the strategic need.

Lewin (1947) contends that there are three important stages in the process of change: unfreezing existing behaviour, changing attitudes and behaviour, and refreezing the new behaviour as accepted common practice.

The first steps in changing culture are recognizing and diagnosing the existing culture, highlighting any weaknesses and stressing the magnitude of the need to change.

One way of changing behaviour would be the establishment of internal groups to study and benchmark competitors and set new performance standards. This would lead to wider discussion throughout the organization, supported by skills training – possibly including communication, motivation and financial awareness skills. People must become committed to the changes, which requires persistence by those who are championing the change and an emphasis on the significance and the desired outcomes.

Unless the changes become established and part of the culture, there will be a steady drift back to the previous pattern. While critical aspects of the culture should remain rock solid and generate strategic consistency, this must not mean that the organization becomes resistant to change without some major upheaval. Competitive pressures require organizations to be vigilant, aware and constantly change-orientated, not change-resistant.

Resistance to change should always be expected. People may simply be afraid because they do not understand the reasons behind the proposed changes; they may mistrust colleagues or management because of previous experiences; communications may be poor; motivation and commitment may be missing; internal architecture may be weak, causing internal conflict and hostility; and the organization may simply not be good at sharing best practice and learning. This topic is revisited in Chapter 17, Leading Change.

## 7.16 Culture – an international dimension

There are cultural differences between nations and ethnic groups. What constitutes acceptable behaviour in one country (for example, bribes) would be totally unacceptable in others. Ways of conducting discussions and deals vary – Indians always like and expect to negotiate, for instance. Some countries, such as France, have a high respect for tradition and the past, while others, such as the US, are more interested in future prospects. This influences the extent to which both individuals and organizations are judged on their track record and on their promise. These differences are important because business is conducted across frontiers and because many organizations have bases in several countries. Organizations, therefore, have to adjust their style for different customers and markets and accept that there will be cultural differences between the various parts of the organization. This reality affects the ability of the strategic leader to synthesize the various parts of the organization and achieve the potential synergies.

Related to these issues, research by Kanter (1991) drew out different perspectives on competitive success between the leading nations, where she argued that these stemmed from national cultures and cultural differences. Her findings indicated the following priorities:

- Japan
  - Product development
  - Management
  - Product quality
- USA
  - Customer service
  - Product quality
  - Technology
- Germany
  - Workforce skills
  - Problem-solving
  - Management.

These conclusions may be summarized by arguing that Japan is driven by a commitment to innovation, America by customers and Germany by engineering.

Interestingly, the report highlighted how UK competitiveness had been enhanced by its drive to privatize public services and other state-owned organizations, the opening up of its capital markets and its encouragement of inward investment. At the same time it is arguably inhibited by an education system which discourages rather than encourages creativity, individualism and entrepreneurship, by a general lack of language skills and, for many, a preference for leisure over work. While a case can be made that these issues are being addressed in various ways, they remain relative weaknesses.

Differences in international cultures have been examined by various authors, including Hofstede (1991), Kluckhohn and Strodtbeck (1961) and Trompenaars and Hampden-Turner (1997). The following points have been distilled from their findings. From these points general conclusions may be drawn about cultural differences between nations; but it must also be recognized that certain organizations in the same country do not automatically fit the national picture in every respect. In some respects, for example, Sony is typically Japanese. In other respects it behaves more like an American company, such that research has confirmed that many US citizens think that Sony is American!

- Some countries and cultures prefer a watertight contractual approach while others are more comfortable with trust and a handshake. The appropriate way of conducting business therefore varies accordingly.

- In some countries managers operate with individual freedom and responsibility, and negotiations are on a one-to-one basis. In others there will invariably be a team of people involved. Where there are multiple decision-makers like this, there will sometimes be a clear hierarchy and recognition of the relative power of various individuals. On other occasions such demarcations will be less obvious or visible.

- In addition, individual managers can be relatively selfish in their outlook, or far more corporate. This can have a particular bearing on where managers' natural competitive energy is channelled. Is it directed at outside competitors, as realistically it should be, or at perceived internal rivals? Simply, would a culture of internal rivalry inside an organization be typical or rare?

- There is also an issue of women managers. In some countries they will not be found, either at all, or at least in positions of real authority.

- Leisure activities can play a relatively minor or more prominent role in business. The image of the British bank manager who enjoys long lunches and regular golf matches with clients has been largely confined to history, but negotiations and networking away from the place of business can still be important. Corporate hospitality at major sporting events would be one example, but it is not practised universally.

- Senses of humour also vary, which begs the question: is creativity more likely to be found in some countries than others? Creativity implies elements of fun and irreverence, challenging existing ways and looking for new and different alternatives. Certainly humour, together with other issues, such as the symbolism of certain objects and colours, affects advertising and promotion. The same campaigns cannot necessarily be used on a global scale.

- This leads on to a final point: do managers in different countries have similar or different perspectives on uncertainty? Some countries, organizations and managers are relatively risk orientated and view environmental turbulence as a source of opportunity. They look to be proactive. Others seek to be more reactive and adaptive, attempting to find positions of stability amongst the perceived chaos.

Since the end of the Second World War Japan has risen to become a major economic force around the world, with some Japanese companies extremely prominent in certain industries. The Japanese style of management is very different in some respects from that found in most Western countries and, while it cannot simply be copied – largely because of cultural differences – it offers a number of important and valuable lessons. Consequently, this chapter finishes with a section on Japanese culture and management style.

## 7.17  The Japanese culture and style of management

Without question, Japanese companies have become formidable competitors in several industries. We saw earlier that Toyota and Sony were the only two non-American businesses to appear in the World's top ten Most Respected Companies. For many years they have been the principal challengers of Western firms serious about world markets. More recently domestic recession, a high yen and intensifying competition from other Pacific Rim countries (many with lower wages) have restrained Japan's global expansion. However, a study of the philosophies, strategies and tactics adopted by Japanese companies will yield a number of valuable insights into competitive strategy, even though it is impractical to suggest that Western businesses could simply learn to copy their Japanese rivals. This section looks at some of the reasons for Japan's economic rise and success; it has to be acknowledged that in the 1990s some of the practices have changed. 'In the long-run the only feasible response is to do better what the Japanese are doing well already – developing management systems that motivate employees from top to bottom to pursue growth-oriented, innovation-focused competitive strategies' (Pucik and Hatvany, 1983).

Deal and Kennedy (1982) have argued that 'Japan Inc.' is a culture, with considerable co-operation between industry, the banking systems and government. For this reason certain aspects of the Japanese culture are difficult to imitate. For example, banks in the UK are public companies with their own shareholders and they borrow and lend money in order to make profit; this is their basic 'mission'.

Another key structural feature historically has been the *keiretsu*, or corporate families, whereby a unique mix of ownerships and alliances makes hostile takeovers very unlikely. At its height, for example, the powerful Mitsubishi *keiretsu* represented 216,000 employees in 29 organizations as diverse as banking, brewing, shipping, shipbuilding, property, oil, aerospace and textiles. The companies held, on average, 38 per cent of each other's shares; directors were exchanged; and the fact that 15 of the companies were located together in one district of Tokyo facilitated linkages of various forms, including intertrading wherever this was practical. The *keiretsu* influence is fading as Japanese companies are locating more and more production overseas in their search for lower manufacturing costs. Mitsubishi's shipping company, for instance, has begun to buy vessels manufactured in Korean yards; Japanese shipbuilders are no longer an automatic low-price competitor.

Culture plays a significant role at the heart of the Japanese strategy process.

In Japan the historic focus has been on human resources (Pucik and Hatvany, 1983) and this became the basis for three key strategic thrusts which are expressed as a number of management techniques. These have acted as key determinants of the actual strategies pursued (Figure 7.10). The three strategic thrusts are the notion of an internal labour market within the organization, a unique company philosophy, and intensive socialization throughout the working life.

The internal labour market is based on the tradition of lifetime employment whereby young men (not women) who joined large companies after school or university were

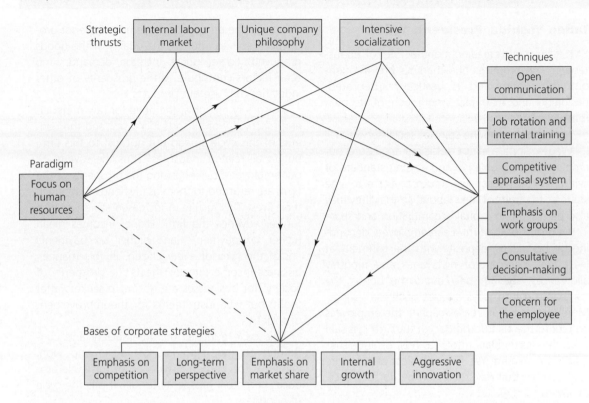

**Figure 7.10** The Japanese management system
Developed form Pucik, V and Hatvany, N (1983) *Management Practices in Japan and Their Impact on Business Strategy*, JAI Press

expected to remain with them for life and in return were offered job security. Commitment and loyalty to the employer result. With recession in recent years this practice has been less widespread.

The articulated and enacted unique philosophy is again designed to generate commitment and loyalty with the argument that familiarity with the goals of a company helps to establish values and provides direction for effort and behaviour. YKK's 'Cycle of Goodness' (Box 7.3) is an excellent example.

The potential benefits of a company philosophy will only be gained if the philosophy is communicated to employees and demonstrated by managers. Hence this is a key aspect of company socialization in Japan, which starts with initial training and continues with further training throughout the working life.

These three strategic thrusts are closely linked to six management techniques used extensively in Japanese firms.

Open communication and sharing information across departmental boundaries aims to develop a climate of trust and a team spirit within the organization. This is enhanced by close integration between managers and employees. Job rotation and the internal training programmes supplement this communication system because through them employees become more aware of what happens throughout the organization. Because of relatively low labour turnover, promotion opportunities are very limited and advancement is slow and often based on seniority. However, performance is essential, and employees are carefully and regularly appraised in their abilities to get things done and to co-operate with others.

## Box 7.3 The Cycle of Goodness

### Tadeo Yoshida, President, YKK

YKK is the world's leading manufacturer of zip fasteners. YKK produces and markets zips throughout the world, and is vertically integrated, designing and manufacturing much of its own machinery.

I firmly believe in the spirit of social service.

Wages alone are not sufficient to assure our employees of a stable life and a rising standard of living. For this reason we return to them a large share of the fruits of their labour, so that they may also participate in capital accumulation and share in the profits of the firm. Each employee, depending on his means, deposits with the company at least ten per cent of his wages and monthly allowances, and 50 per cent of his bonus; the company, in turn, pays interest on these savings. Moreover, as this increases capital, the employees benefit further as stockholders of the firm. It is said that the accumulation of savings distinguishes man from animals. Yet, if the receipts of a day are spent within that day, there can be no such cycle of saving.

The savings of all YKK employees are used to improve production facilities, and contribute directly to the prosperity of the firm. Superior production facilities improve the quality of the goods produced. Lower prices increase demand. And both factors contribute to the prosperity of other industries that use our products.

As society prospers, the need for raw materials and machinery of all sorts increases, and the benefits of this cycle spread out not just to this firm, but to all related industries. Thus the savings of our employees, by enhancing the prosperity of the firm, are returned to them as dividends that enrich their lives. This results in increased savings which further advance the firm. Higher incomes mean higher tax payments, and higher tax payments enrich the lives of every citizen. In this manner, business income directly affects the prosperity of society; for businesses are not mere seekers after profit, but vital instruments for the improvement of society.

This cycle enriches our free society and contributes to the happiness of those who work within it. The perpetual working of this cycle produces perpetual prosperity for all. This is the cycle of goodness.

**YKK** http://www.ykk.com

This is particularly important as Japanese companies revolve around groups rather than individuals, with work being assigned to teams of employees. This, together with the use of quality circles (whereby groups of employees are encouraged to discuss issues and problems and suggest improvements), is seen as a key motivator. There is considerable emphasis on consultative decision-making, involving these working groups, and a desire for consensus decisions. This generates greater loyalty to the decisions and to implementation. Finally, managers are encouraged to spend time with employees discussing both performance and personal problems. Companies have also frequently provided housing and various other services for employees.

Several Japanese companies have invested in manufacturing plants in the US and Europe in recent years. In a number of cases they have selected industries where the country had already ceased to manufacture products because of an inability to compete (e.g. television sets and video recorders) or where the competitive edge had declined. Motor vehicles is an example of the latter. The British car industry fell behind the Japanese and German producers in terms of quality and productivity and has struggled to catch up. The first Japanese car plant in the UK was built by Nissan near Sunderland and, using a Japanese approach – rather than adopting all the techniques described in this section – it has become the most productive car plant in the UK, and one of Nissan's most efficient anywhere in the world.

Hill (1990) explains that the key human resources aspects of the Nissan UK strategy are as follows.

- There is a single union agreement, with the AEU.
- All employees (including managers) have the same conditions of employment, and wear similar blue overalls at work.
- There are no (inflexible) written job descriptions.
- There is no clocking on and no privileged parking.
- Absenteeism has remained very low.
- There are daily communications meetings – searching for continuous improvement.
- Employees often go to Japan for training – skilled workers learn both operational and maintenance skills.
- The training budget, equivalent to 14 per cent of sales revenue, is exceptionally high for a British company. A typical employee will receive 9 days on-the-job and 12 days off-the-job training each year.
- Supervisors are empowered managers. They recruit and select their own staff (individually they are responsible for about 20 employees), and they control the layout and operation of their own part of the production line.

*The core of management is the art of mobilizing every ounce of intelligence in the organization and pulling together the intellectual resources of all employees in the service of the firm. We know that the intelligence of a handful of technocrats, however brilliant and smart they may be, is no longer enough. Only by drawing on the combined brain power of all its employees can a firm face up to the turbulence and constraints of today's environment.*

Mr. Konosuke Matsushita, Matsushita Electrical Industrial Company Ltd

**Quality and competition** Prahalad and Hamel (1985) have suggested that the Japanese 'rewrite the rules of the game to take their competitors by surprise'. Through technology, design, production costs, distribution and selling arrangements, pricing and service they seek to build 'layers of competitive advantage' rather than concentrate on just one aspect. Many competitors in the West think more narrowly. Prahalad and Hamel suggest that Japanese companies are successful in part because they have a clear mission and statement of strategic intent, and a culture which provides both opportunity and encouragement to change things incrementally. Getting things right first time and every time – total quality management – is endemic in the culture.

Internationally, Japanese companies may not be consistent with their strategies; instead they will seek the best competitive opportunities in different places and they will change continually as new opportunities arise and are created.

Japanese companies benchmark against the best in the world and willingly customize their products to meet local market demand.

**Long-term perspective** It was shown in Chapter 2 that while many Western companies concentrate on short-term strategies, influenced often by financial pressures, the Japanese take a long-term perspective.

**Emphasis on market share** Japanese companies are competitive, growth orientated and anxious to build and sustain high market shares in world markets. This will enable them to provide the job security that is a fundamental aspect of the culture. They often use their experience curve (which is examined in detail in the supplement to Chapter 4) to develop strategies aimed at market dominance with a long-term view of costs and prices.

**Internal growth** Mergers, acquisitions and divestitures are relatively uncommon in Japan – the Japanese favour the internal production system and innovation.

In a book on Japanese manufacturing techniques, Schonberger (1984) argued that a major reason for Japan's success has been its ability to use its resources well, better than many Western competitors. In many factories, he contends, the equipment is no better than that used elsewhere in the world, but wherever they can Japanese companies invest in the best equipment available. Managerial skills are used in improvement drives, a search for simple solutions and, in particular, a meticulous attention to detail. Simplicity is important since management and shop floor can relate better to each other; and flexible techniques and workforces result in low stock production systems, efficiency and lower costs.

The ability to trust and establish close links with other companies in the supply chain allows focused specialization and just in time manufacturing with low inventories. However, this type of dependency can act as a hindrance to global expansion until comparative supplier links can be established.

**Innovation** Research and development is deemed important and funded appropriately. As a result much of Japan's technology has advanced quickly, and firms who fail to innovate go out of business. Ohmae (1985) has described Japan as a 'very unforgiving economy', with thousands of corporations destroyed every year through bankruptcy. He points out that Japan is selective about the industries in which research and development will be concentrated. Japan has, for example, spent a relatively high proportion of its research and development money in ceramics and steel, and as a result has become a world leader in fibre optics, ceramics and mass-produced large-scale integrated circuits. For similar reasons the US is world leader in biotechnology and specialized semiconductors, and Europe in chemicals and pharmaceuticals.

Product innovation in Japan is fast and competitive. For example, Sony launched the first miniaturized camcorder (hand-held video camera and recorder) in June 1989. Weighing less than 700 g (1.5 lb) it was one-quarter of the size of existing camcorders. Within six months Matsushita and JVC had introduced lighter models. Within a further six months there was additional competition from Canon, Sanyo, Ricoh and Hitachi. Sony introduced two new models in summer 1990. One was the lightest then available; the other had superior technical features. More recent models feature larger viewfinders and allow the user to hold the camcorder at arm's length instead of up to the eye. In recent years we have seen exactly the same trend with laptop computers.

This faster model replacement is linked to an ability to break even financially with fewer sales of each model. Japan has achieved this with efficient and flexible manufacturing systems and a greater willingness to use common, rather than model-specific, components.

Individual Western companies have proved that it is possible, with determination and distinctive products, to penetrate Japanese markets successfully, but contenders can expect fierce resistance and defensive competition.

We conclude the chapter with a case on Club Méditerranée, a company whose strategy was built around values. The case highlights how difficult it can be to sustain competitive success when values are core but the competitive environment changes. This case also brings out the use of power by external shareholders to change the strategic leader when the strategy is proving unsuccessful.

## Minicase 7.7  Club Méditerranée   (Eur)  (Int)

Club Med, founded in 1950 in France, became Europe's largest tour operator with a clearly distinguished product.

The original Club Med represented 'beautiful people playing all sorts of sports, white sand beaches, azure sky and sea, Polynesian thatched huts, free and flowing wine at meals, simple yet superb food' (*The Economist*, 12 July 1986). It was an 'organized melange of hedonism and back to nature'.

The organization systematically spread around the world, opening over 100 holiday villages and over 60 holiday residences (hotel/sports complexes) for both summer and winter vacations. Organizers were present in a ratio of 1:5 with guests, for whom they provided sports tuition and organized evening entertainment. Traditionally all tuition, food and drinks with meals were paid for in advance in the holiday cost, and guests were provided with beads which they used as they chose to buy extra drinks and so on. Clothing was permanently casual.

Club Med has traditionally charged prices above the average for package holidays, its clientele have been mainly above-average income earners, and the organization has enjoyed a reputation for delivering customer service and satisfaction. The strategy was developed and maintained by one of the two the founders of the business, Gilbert Trigano. Although Trigano was always an influential strategic leader, Club Med is a public company, with most of its equity held by institutional shareholders.

A culture of creativity and teamworking has long been encouraged at all levels in Club Med. Gilbert Trigano always saw the organization as 'one big, happy family'. No employee should feel as if they are simply a pawn; promotions are typically from within. The loyalty of Club Med staff has typically been very high, making it difficult for outsiders to come in as managers. Trigano and his partner, Gerald Blitz, set up Club Med as an organization 'without rules – in a world where most companies operate with fixed rules and structures. Everyone is under an obligation to create, but, of course, not every idea is a success'.

The company grew successfully for over 30 years with little change to the basic strategy. By the mid-1980s, however, occupancy rates had fallen, and profits declined and then stagnated. While the underlying concept was still sound, people's tastes were changing. Holidaymakers increasingly sought higher-quality facilities than the straw huts provided. Many Americans wanted televisions and telephones – yet it was the absence of these which helped make Club Med unique.

Building on the original concept and strategy, Club Med developed new products in order to better satisfy selected audiences around the world. In addition to the traditional villages, where in some cases straw huts were replaced by bungalows, Club Med introduced cheaper, half-board holidays in newly acquired hotels and villages, at the same time as it opened more expensive properties. This latter development was pioneered at Opio, near Cannes, which opened in 1989. Opio has expensive rooms with facilities, and, unusually, is open 12 months of the year. The international conference trade was being targeted. A limited number of villages experimented with a multilingual staffing policy to ensure that visitors from different European countries could all be greeted in their own language. Attempts have been made to attract more American visitors, but there has always been some scepticism. Americans are more puritanical in their tastes and expectations, and Club Med's sexy image has not proved as successful in the US.

There have also been problems with certain other strategic developments:

- Profitability at the Vienna City Hotel and from two cruise ships was never adequate.
- New developments in Japan were delayed.
- In 1991 Club Med bought a controlling stake in a second charter airline – its first airline came when Club Med acquired a competitor in the 1980s. Combined the two could fly to 100 destinations spread over 20 countries on four continents. In reality, Club Med had too much capacity and ended up selling 80 per cent stakes in both airlines.

In 1993, with European occupancy rates depressed, Club Med recorded its worst ever results to date. Gilbert Trigano (then aged 72) partially retired and was succeeded by his son, Serge, who was determined to:

- accelerate developments in new territories such as Asia and
- reduce costs to allow for more competitive prices, still with quality and innovation – it was 'time to realize people would not always come just because it is Club Med'.

'It is by focusing on our core business that we will return to profit.'

Nevertheless, Rosemary Astles, Marketing Director at Thomson Holidays, was quoted as saying 'Club Med has a reasonably unique formula that has worked well in a number of markets … but there will be [only] limited growth for the club concept in the future. It's a fairly mature market.'

Serge Trigano resigned after losses in 1995. Interestingly – and unusually – Serge Trigano had no personal shareholding; and his father owned just 0.8 per cent of the business. He reflected: 'Perhaps I was not quick enough to take the necessary measures … perhaps we should have closed loss-making villages more quickly.'

Club Med appointed a new Chief Executive in February 1997; Philippe Bourguignon had previously been Chairman of Euro Disney.

Club Med reportedly 'began preparing for a future of tougher professional management' while conscious of the need to retain the important aspects of its culture, image and strategy. After all, the company was still successful. There had been 20 million customers in its 47 years and 1.4 million of those holidayed at Club Med villages and hotels in 1995–96. New imitations were happening all the time as the idea of the 'all-inclusive' holiday has grown in popularity. Nevertheless, the emphasis has been changing. Telephones in rooms and tables for two instead of eight, for example, were becoming increasingly normal as the average age of customers increased.

The first main change announced by Bourguignon implied the abandonment of the ubiquitous beads (for purchasing extra drinks) in favour of smart cards, which would enable tighter management controls. The fully inclusive package concept was retained; earlier trials with à la carte alternatives had not proved successful. Bourguignon commented:

*Club Med is a well known product but with a fuzzy identity. It is far too French in an international context. We need a complete recreation of the group. The concept is not outdated but the image is stuck in the 1970s.*

After a period of review it was decided to abandon the Club Aquarius budget format, re-creating most of these villages in the traditional Club Med style. At the other end of the scale, the most luxurious five-star villages were phased out in favour of the typical mid-range three-star village. Between 1998 and 2000 some 74 out of a remaining 120 villages were renovated. Some now had a more limited range of activities. Linked to this was a major price restructuring – low-season holidays in particular were discounted by up to 30 per cent – and new advertising was targeted directly at younger people.

In 2001 Bourguignon announced a new diversification – into entertainment centres in or near the world's largest cities, beginning with Paris. Bookshops, travel agencies, restaurants, gymnasiums, restaurants, concert halls and nightclubs would all fit the concept.

A year later Club Med saw jobs being axed as profits fell back again – the first recorded loss since 1997. Bourguignon left just before the end of the year. Not for the first time the powerful Agnelli family – the Italian family behind the Fiat and Ferrari empire – had exercised their power as leading shareholders. Together with others they had not been sold on the entertainment centre strategy. The new Chief Executive was Henri Giscard d'Estang, son of the former French President, who opted to focus more on the core product. The fundamental business model 'was not broken'. In 2004, after experiencing financial difficulties with their mainstream businesses, the Agnelli family sold its stake to Accor, the French hotel chain, perhaps best known for its Sofitel brand.

After a period of consolidation, leaving 95 villages, Giscard announced a new line of super deluxe boutique hotels, beginning with a 60-bed property in Marrakesh, The Riad. Some 40 poorer-grade properties had been closed down and the remaining 95 had been or were being refurbished. The idea behind the boutique properties is to locate them close to the traditional villages. That way, residents can enjoy luxury and privacy but still use the sports and other leisure facilities at the villages whenever they want.

## Questions

1. Is Club Med now realistically a limited-appeal niche product?
2. If so, what are the implications of this fact? If not, how might the business be expanded?
3. Is there actually any real future for the Club Med business model?

**Club Med** http://wwwclubmed.com

## SUMMARY

At a most basic level of argument, an organization is successful if it is meeting the needs and expectations of its stakeholders, such that their support and commitment are maintained.

Strategically, this will imply a clear direction, from which are derived corporate, competitive and functional strategies, the implementation of which brings about the desired results. This needs both common sense and strategic competency.

Measurement matters. Apparent success cannot, and must not, be taken for granted. Nor must weaknesses be overlooked. We must measure those issues which really matter. The act of measurement focuses attention and endeavour on that which is being measured: being brilliant at things that do not really matter to stakeholders will not add and build value.

Some key elements will, through their very nature, be difficult to measure. They are essentially subjective and qualitative issues rather than objective and quantifiable. This is no excuse to avoid tackling them; instead we have to rely on indicators rather than measures of performance.

In some cases attention is focused on efficiency measures, which largely concern the utilization of resources. We are evaluating whether or not we are 'doing things right'. Measures and indicators of effectiveness look more at outcomes (for stakeholders) and provide a check on whether we are 'doing the right things'.

Most organizations use a raft of quantitative measures, embracing sales and production. Analysts external to the organization, such as students – and lecturers, come to that – will not normally have access to this information to draw conclusions from. However, financial data have to be published and can be used to calculate a number of valuable ratios which provide some insight into organizational performance. In the supplement to this chapter investment, performance, solvency and liquidity ratios are explained.

The balanced scorecard approach provides a more comprehensive set of measures which cover stakeholders. The four categories for measurement are: finance; customers; internal processes; and growth and improvement.

It is also relevant to look at issues of admiration, image and reputation. These evaluations are normally by people inside the relevant industries and therefore provide an insight into how organizations are rated by their competitors and peers. There is, however, a short-term focus in this approach. Companies that are highly regarded will not necessarily be those with the strongest financial results. Although there is some link between the most admired American and the most respected global companies, those British companies that enjoy the greatest international admiration are not those held in the highest regard at home.

In isolation, therefore, any single measure or type of measure must be treated cautiously.

Consequently, this part of the chapter concluded with a holistic framework of measures derived from the E–V–R congruence model.

Culture is the way in which an organization performs its tasks, the way its people think, feel and act in response to opportunities and threats, the ways in which objectives and strategies are set and decisions made. It reflects emotional issues and it is not easily analysed, quantified or changed. Nevertheless, it is a key influence on strategic choice, strategy implementation and strategic change – until we understand the culture of an organization we cannot understand strategic management in that organization.

A large organization is unlikely to be just one single, definable culture. It is more likely to be a loose or tight amalgam of different cultures.

It is quite normal for the culture to be influenced by a strong strategic leader and his or her beliefs and values.

In a very broad sense we can think of culture as a mixture of behaviours (manifestations) and underlying attitudes and values. It is easier to change one of these rather than both simultaneously.

There is no 'ideal culture' as such. Key elements typically have a flip side and, therefore, a style and approach that is appropriate at a particular time can quickly become out of date and in need of change.

▶

A useful grid for analysing the culture of any organization would comprise:

- Manifestations – artefacts; values; underlying assumptions; behaviours
- People – stories; leadership; communications
- Power – ownership and structure; personal power; **organizational politics**.

Charles Handy proposes four cultural types which help to explain the culture, style and approach of different organizations. These are the power culture (typical of small, entrepreneurial organizations), the role culture (larger and more formal organizations), the task culture (the complex organization seeking to achieve internal synergies through effective linkages) and the person culture (built around the individual managers' needs).

In an alternative and equally significant contribution Miles and Snow differentiate among *defenders* (conservative and low-risk organizations), *prospectors* (innovative and entrepreneurial), *analysers* (limited change with measured steps) and *reactors* (followers). These can be readily linked to styles of strategy creation.

We can only understand culture when we understand power inside an organization. Who has power, how do they acquire it and how do they use it?

A number of books on the general theme of 'organizational excellence' have highlighted how it is culture that is at the heart of success. Although general themes and lessons can be teased out, an organization cannot simply replicate the culture of another successful organization and become successful itself.

There are important cultural differences between nations. This has implications for businesses which operate or trade globally.

## QUESTIONS AND RESEARCH ASSIGNMENTS

1. The purpose of the Metropolitan Police Service is to: 'uphold the law fairly and firmly; to prevent crime; to pursue and bring to justice those who break the law; to keep the Queen's peace; to protect, help and reassure people in London; and to be seen to do all this with integrity, common sense and sound judgement'.

   How might they measure their success?

2. The Royal Charter for the Royal National Institute for the Blind (RNIB), granted originally in 1949, states that the RNIB exists in order to:

   - 'promote the better education, training, employment and welfare of the blind
   - protect the interests of the blind; and
   - prevent blindness.'

   How might they assess how well they are doing?

3. Use the text in Minicase 7.6 (IKEA) to complete a culture grid (Figure 7.7) for IKEA.

4. Take an organization with which you are familiar and evaluate it in terms of Handy's and Miles and Snow's typologies.

5. List other organizations that you know which would fit into the categories not covered in your answer to Question 4.

   For both Questions 4 and 5 you should comment on whether or not you feel your categorization is appropriate.

6. Considering the organization that you used for Question 4, assess the power levers of the strategic leader and other identifiable managers.

7. Thinking of the identified cultural priorities for Japan, Germany and the US, listed in the text, what do you think the cultural priorities of UK businesses are?

# INTERNET AND LIBRARY PROJECTS

1. In early 2000 Microsoft was judged by the American courts to have been operating as a monopoly and stifling competition. How have its reputation, respect and admiration been affected by this judgement and also by subsequent moves by both the company and the competition authorities in both America and Europe?

    **Microsoft** http://www.microsoft.com

2. Select a number of organizations from Tables 7.1 and/or 7.2 (or the *Fortune* list), picking out ones that interest you personally. Obtain their financial results for at least two years which correspond with the admiration rankings. To what extent are financial performance and admiration linked? By also checking the movements in the company's share prices over the same period, does the company's market valuation more closely reflect financial performance or a wider perception of its relative performance?

3. The National Health Service

    British Prime Minister John Major announced a new Citizen's Charter in July 1991. This implied a change of attitude for the NHS: patients should be seen as customers with rights, rather than people who should be grateful for treatment, however long the wait. From April 1992 hospitals would have to set standards for maximum waiting times.

    This followed on from the 1989 NHS White Paper, Working for Patients, which was designed to achieve:

    ■ raising the performance of all hospitals and general practitioners (GPs) to the level of the best (significant differences existed in measured performances)

    ■ patients receiving better health care and a greater choice of services through improved efficiencies and effectiveness in the use of NHS resources

    ■ greater satisfaction and rewards for NHS staff.

    In subsequent years, how did this impact on NHS strategies?

    In 1997 a Labour government was elected and it set about changing the Conservative philosophy, dismantling and replacing a number of strategies.

    What was the Labour approach? How have these changes impacted upon performance measurement? Can the relative success of the NHS ever be evaluated effectively without imputing political concerns?

    **Citizen's Charter** http://www.cabinet-office.gov.uk/servicefirst
    **NHS** http://www.nhs50.nhs.uk

4 From the 1980s to the mid-1990s Rover had a strategic alliance with Honda. When its then owner, British Aerospace, sold Rover to BMW this alliance was wound down and then terminated. A Japanese influence was replaced by a German one. Rover developed a number of new models but by early 2000 its trading losses were so significant that BMW decided to 'sell or close'. The Phoenix group was pulled together by a previous Rover manager, John Towers, and he acquired the business for a mere £10. Rover became British once more. Since then Rover has resurrected the MG name and used it to brand a number of its models. Rover has also developed strategic alliances with manufacturers in India and China.

    How has the culture and style been affected by these various changes?

    **Rover Group** http://www.mg.rover.com
    **Honda** http://www.honda.com
    **British Aerospace** http://www.baesystems.co.uk
    **BMW** http://www.bmw.com

5. Research how profitable John Lewis and Waitrose have been in comparison with their major competitors in the last ten years. What conclusions can you draw?

    **John Lewis Partnership** http://www.johnlewis.co.uk
    **Waitrose** http://www.waitrose.com

6. Find out where your nearest John Lewis or Waitrose store is and if possible visit it. Can you detect any differences in attitude between the John Lewis staff and those who work in similar stores?

    **John Lewis Partnership** http://www.johnlewis.co.uk
    **Waitrose** http://www.waitrose.com

## Further reading

Harrison, R (1972) Understanding your organization's character, *Harvard Business Review*, May–June.

Miles, R, Snow, C, Meyer, A and Coleman, H (1978) Organizational strategy structure and process, *Academy of Management Review*, July.

Waterman, R, Peters, T and Phillips, J (1980) Structure is not organization, *Business Horizons*, June.

Peters, TJ (1980) Putting excellence into management, *Business Week*, July 21.

Schein, EH (1984) Coming to a new awareness of culture, *Sloan Management Review*, 25 (2).

Barney, JB (1986) Organizational culture – can it be a source of sustainable competitive advantage?, *Academy of Management Review*, 11 (3).

Bourantes, D and Mandes, Y (1987) Does market share lead to profitability?, *Long Range Planning*, 20 ( 5).

Johnson, G (1988) Rethinking incrementalism, *Strategic Management Journal*, January–February.

Kono, T (1990) Corporate culture and long range planning, *Long Range Planning*, 23 (4).

Kaplan, RS and Norton, DP (1992) The balanced storecard – measures that drive performance, *Harvard Business Review*, January–February.

Kaplan, RS and Norton, DP (1996) Using the balanced scorecard as a strategic management system, *Harvard Business Review*, January–February.

Atkinson, AA *et al.* (1997) A stakeholder approach to strategic performance management, *Sloan Management Review*, Spring.

Kaplan, RS and Norton, DP (2000) Having trouble with your strategy? Then map it, *Harvard Business Review*, September–October.

Huffman, B (2001) What makes a strategy brilliant?, *Business Horizons*, 44 (4).

## References

Barney, JB (1986) Organization culture: can it be a source of sustained competitive advantage? *Academy of Management Review*, 11 (3).

Berry, D (1983) The perils of trying to change corporate culture, *Financial Times*, 14 December.

Caulkin, S (1995) The pursuit of immortality, *Management Today*, May.

Deal, T and Kennedy, A (1982) *Corporate Cultures. The Rites and Rituals of Corporate Life*, Addison-Wesley.

Drucker, PF (1989) What businesses can learn from nonprofits, *Harvard Business Review*, July–August.

*Economist, The* (1991) Britain's most admired companies, 26 January.

Fisher, AB (1996) Corporate reputations, *Fortune*, 4 March.

Fombrum, CJ (1996) *Reputation – Realising the Value from the Corporate Image*, Harvard Business School Press.

French, JRP and Raven, B (1959) The bases of social power. *In Studies in Social Power* (ed. D Cartwright), University of Michigan Press.

Hampden-Turner, C (1990) Corporate culture – from vicious to virtuous circles, *The Economist*.

Handy, CB (1976) *Understanding Organizations*, Penguin. The ideas are elaborated in Handy, CB (1978) *Gods of Management*, Souvenir Press.

Harrison, R (1972) Understanding your organization's character, *Harvard Business Review*, May–June.

Hill, R (1990) Nissan and the art of people management, *Director*, March.

Hofstede, G (1991) *Cultures and Organization: Software of the Mind*, McGraw Hill.

Houlder, V (1997) What makes a winner? *Financial Times*, 19 March.

Jackson, P and Palmer, R (1989) *First Steps in Measuring Performance in the Public Sector*, Public Finance Foundation, London.

Kakabadse, A (1982) *Culture of the Social Services*, Gower.

Kanter, RM (1991) Transcending business boundaries: 12000 world managers view change, *Harvard Business Review*, May–June.

Kaplan, RS and Norton, DP (1996) *The Balanced Scorecard*, Harvard Business School Press.

Kaplan, RS and Norton, DP (1992) The balanced scorecard – measures that drive performance, *Harvard Business Review*, January–February.

Kets de Vries, M (1996) Leaders who make a difference, *European Management Journal*, 14 (5).

Kluckhohn, C and Strodtbeck, F (1961) *Variations in Value Orientations*, Peterson.

Leadbeater, C and Rudd, R (1991) What drives the lords of the deal? *Financial Times*, 20 July.

Lewin, K (1947) Frontiers in group dynamics: concept, method and reality in social science, *Human Relations*, 1.

Lynn, M (1995) Creating wealth: the best and the worst, *Sunday Times*, 10 December.

May, GD and Kruger, MJ (1988) The manager within, *Personnel Journal*, 67 (2).

Miles, RE and Snow, CC (1978) *Organization Strategy, Structure and Process*, McGraw-Hill.

Ohmae, K (1985) *Triad Power*, Free Press.

Peters, TJ (1988) *Thriving on Chaos*, Knopf.

Peters, TJ and Waterman, RH Jr (1982) *In Search of Excellence: Lessons from America's Best Run Companies*, Harper and Row. Original article: Peters, TJ (1980) Putting excellence into management, *Business Week*, 21 July.

Prahalad, CK and Hamel, G (1985) Address to the Annual Conference of the Strategic Management Society, Barcelona, October.

Press, G (1990) Assessing competitors' business philosophies, *Long Range Planning*, 23 (5).

Pucik, V and Hatvany, N (1983) Management practices in Japan and their impact on business strategy, *Advances in Strategic Management*, vol. 1, JAI Press.

Pumpin, C (1987) *The Essence of Corporate Strategy*, Gower.

Reid, W and Myddelton, DR (1974) *The Meaning of Company Accounts*, 2nd edn, Gower. The quotation in the supplement was taken from this second edition, but there are later editions.

RSA (1995) *Tomorrow's Company: The Role of Business in a Changing World*, Royal Society of Arts.

Sadtler, D, Campbell, A and Koch, R (1997) *Break-up. When Large Companies are Worth More Dead Than Alive*, Capstone.

Schein, EH (1985) *Organizational Culture and Leadership*, Jossey Bass.

Schonberger, RJ (1984) *Japanese Manufacturing Techniques*, Free Press.

Schwartz, H and Davis, SM (1981) Matching corporate culture and business strategy, *Organizational Dynamics*, Summer.

Summers, D (1995) Boots comes top in corporate image poll, *Financial Times*, 23 October.

Thompson, JL and Richardson, B (1996) Strategic and competitive success – towards a model of the comprehensively competent organization, *Management Decision*, 34 (2).

Trompenaars, F and Hampden-Turner, C (1997) *Riding the Waves of Culture: Understanding Cultural Diversity in Business*, Nicholas Brealey Publishing.

# Finance in Action: Financial Statements

## Learning objectives

Having read to the end of this section you should be able to:

- describe the key parts of a balance sheet, profit and loss account and cash flow statement

- calculate and evaluate a number of ratios relating to investment, performance and financial status

- discuss how profitability might be improved.

This supplement is a simple guide to aspects of financial accounting. For those readers familiar with the subject it serves as a short reference guide: for others, it provides a brief and straightforward summary of the critical issues.

The purpose of including it is to enable readers to be able to analyse and make sense of published financial data and the financial appendices which accompany many strategy case studies.

The content is:

- Financial statements – profit and loss accounts; balance sheets; cash flow statements

- Investment, performance, solvency and liquidity ratios.

## Financial analysis

The published financial accounts of a company, as long as they are interpreted carefully, can tell a good deal about the company's activities and about how well it is doing. This section concentrates on three main aspects, examining the financial measures and what they can tell us, and considers the strategic implications. The three aspects are as follows.

- *Investment*: How do the results relate to shareholders and the funds they have provided, and to the company's share price?

- *Performance*: How successfully is the business being run as a trading concern? Here we are concerned not so much with profit as with profitability. How well is the company using the capital it employs to generate sales and in turn profits?

- *Financial status*: Is the company solvent and liquid? Is it financially sound?

The ratios calculated in each of these categories have relevance for different stakeholders. Shareholders, and potential investors, are particularly concerned with the investment ratios. Performance ratios tell the strategic leader how well the company is doing as a business. Bankers and other providers of loan capital will want to know that the business is solvent and liquid in addition to how well it is performing.

This form of analysis is most relevant for profit-seeking businesses, although some of the measures can prove quite enlightening when applied to not-for-profit organizations.

Ratios are calculated from the published accounts of organizations, but an analysis of just one set of results will only be partly helpful. Trends are particularly important, and therefore the changes in results over a number of years should be evaluated. Care should be taken to ensure that the results are not considered in isolation from external trends in the economy or industry. For example, the company's sales may be growing quickly, but how do they compare with those of their competitors and the industry as a whole? Similarly, slow growth may be explained by industry contraction, although in turn this might indicate the need for diversification.

Hence, industry averages and competitor performance should be used for comparisons. One problem here is that different companies may present their accounts in different ways and the figures will have to be interpreted before any meaningful comparisons can be made. Furthermore, the industry may be composed of companies of varying sizes and various degrees of conglomeration and diversification. For this reason certain companies may be expected to behave differently from their competitors.

In addition, it can be useful to compare the actual results with forecasts, although these will not normally be available to people outside the organization. The usefulness is dependent on how well the forecasts and budgets were prepared.

## Financial statements

The two most important statements used for calculating ratios are the profit and loss account and the balance sheet, simplified versions of which are illustrated in Tables 7.6 and 7.7. The full accounts may be required in order to make certain adjustments.

**Table 7.6** Simplified profit and loss account

|       | Sales/turnover        |   |                                                  |
|-------|-----------------------|---|--------------------------------------------------|
| less: | Costs of goods sold   | = | Gross profit                                     |
| less: | Depreciation          |   |                                                  |
|       | Selling costs         |   |                                                  |
|       | Administration costs  | = | Profit before interest and tax*                  |
| less: | Interest on loans     | = | Profit before tax                                |
| less: | Tax                   | = | Profit after tax                                 |
| less: | Dividends             | = | Retained earnings (transferred to balance sheet) |

*In published accounts this figure will not always be shown. It is required, however, for the calculation of certain ratios.

**Table 7.7** Simplified balance sheet

| Information required for ratio calculations | | Conventional presentation of figures in published accounts | |
|---|---|---|---|
| Fixed assets | Land; property buildings; plant and equipment | Fixed assets | |
| + Current assets | Stock; debtors; cash and investments | + Current assets | |
| less Current liabilities | Creditors: amounts falling due within one year; specifically trade creditors, overdraft, taxation not yet paid | less Current liabilities | |
| = Net assets | | = Total assets less Current liabilities | |
| Long-term loans | Generally termed creditors: amounts falling due after more than one year | plus long-term loans | |
| | | = Total net assets | |
| + Shareholders' funds | Called-up share capital: share premium account; revaluation reserve; profit and loss account | Shareholders' funds | |
| = Total capital employed | | | |
| Net assets equals | Total capital employed | Total net assets = Shareholders' funds | |

From the profit and loss account (Table 7.6) we wish to extract a number of figures. Gross profit is the trading profit before overheads are allocated. It is the difference between the value of sales (or turnover) and the direct costs involved in producing the product(s) or service(s), which is known as the contribution. In the case of multiproduct or multiservice organizations, where it may be difficult to attribute overheads to different products and services accurately, comparison should be made between the contributions from different divisions or strategic business units.

When depreciation and selling and administrative overheads are subtracted from gross profit the remainder is profit before interest and before tax. This is the net profit that the organization has achieved from its trading activities; no account has yet been taken of the cost of funding. This figure is not normally shown in published accounts; it has to be calculated by adding interest back onto profit before tax.

Profit before tax is the figure resulting when interest charges have been removed. Tax is levied on this profit figure, and when this is deducted profit after tax remains. This represents the profits left for shareholders, and a proportion will be paid over to them immediately in the form of dividends; the remainder will be reinvested in the future growth of the company. It will be transferred to the balance sheet as retained earnings (or profit and loss) and shown as a reserve attributable to shareholders.

This simplified outline excludes the need to, and value of, clearly separating the revenue and profits from ongoing businesses or continuing activities, recent acquisitions and discontinued activities.

Balance sheets are now normally laid out in the format illustrated on the right in Table 7.7. Assets are shown at the top and the capital employed to finance the assets below.

Fixed assets comprise all the land, property, plant and equipment owned by the business. These will be depreciated annually at varying rates. Balance sheets generally reflect historical costs (the preferred accounting convention), but occasionally assets may be revalued to account for inflation (land and property values can increase significantly over a number of years) and any ratios calculated from an asset figure will be affected by this issue of up-to-date valuations.

Current assets, assets which are passing through the business rather than more permanent features and which comprise stocks (raw materials, work-in-progress and finished goods), debtors (customers who are allowed to buy on credit rather than for cash), investments and cash, are added on. Current liabilities, short-term financial commitments, are deducted. These include the overdraft, tax payments due and trade creditors (suppliers who have yet to be paid for goods and services supplied).

The left-hand column of Table 7.7 shows the resultant figure as net assets, which is equal to the total capital employed in the business, or the sum of long-term loans and shareholders' funds. The right-hand column differs slightly and presents net assets as total assets minus the sum of current liabilities and long-term loans – and therefore equal to shareholders' funds. This is the normal way in which a company will present its accounts, leaving us to calculate a figure for total capital employed.

Long-term loans are typically called 'creditors: amounts falling due after more than one year'. Shareholders' funds are made up of the called up share capital (the face value of the shares issued), the share premium account (money accrued as shareholders have bought shares for more than their face value, dependent on stock market prices at the time of sale), any revaluation reserve (resulting from revaluation of assets) and retained earnings (past profits reinvested in the business).

Balance sheets balance. Net assets are equal to the capital employed to finance them.

## Investment ratios

The five key investment ratios are explained in Table 7.8, and the linkages between four of them are illustrated in Figure 7.11.

The return on shareholders' funds deals with the profit available for ordinary shareholders after all other commitments (including preference share dividends) have been met; and it is divided by all the funds provided both directly and indirectly by ordinary shareholders.

*The return on shareholders' funds is probably the most important single measure of all. It takes into account the return on net assets, the company's tax position, and the extent to which capital employed has been supplied other than by the ordinary shareholders (for example by loans).*

Reid and Myddelton, 1974

Earnings per share indicates how much money the company has earned in relation to the number of ordinary shares. Taken in isolation this measure is useful if considered over a number of years. Companies can be compared with each other if the ratio is linked to the current market price of shares. This calculation provides the price-to-earnings ratio – P/E.

**Table 7.8** Investment ratios

| Ratio | Calculation | Comments |
|---|---|---|
| Return on shareholders' funds (%) | $\dfrac{\text{Profit after tax}}{\text{Total shareholder's funds}}$ | Measures the return on investment by shareholders in the company.<br>The more unstable the industry and the company, the higher this will be expected to be |
| Earning per share (pence) | $\dfrac{\text{Profit after tax}}{\text{Number of ordinary shares issued}}$ | Profit after tax represents earnings for the shareholders. It can be returned to them immediately as dividends or reinvested as additional shareholders' funds (retained earnings) |
| Price-to-earnings ratio (P/E) | $\dfrac{\text{Current market price of ordinary shares}}{\text{Earnings per share}}$ | Indicates the multiple of earnings that investors are willing to pay for shares in the stock market<br>The higher the ratio, the more favourably the company is perceived |
| Dividend yield (%) | $\dfrac{\text{Dividend per share}}{\text{Market price per share}}$ | Equivalent to rate of interest  per cent paid on the investment<br>Shareholders will not expect it to equal say building society rates – reinvested profits should generate longer-term increases in the share price |
| Dividend cover (number of times) | $\dfrac{\text{Earning per share}}{\text{Dividend per share}}$ | The number of times the dividends could have been paid from the earnings: the higher the better |

**Figure 7.11** Linkages between four investment ratios: the squares represent the investment ratios; the circles represent the figures required for calculating ratios. (Note: the two figures required to calculate each ratio are shown leading into the box.)

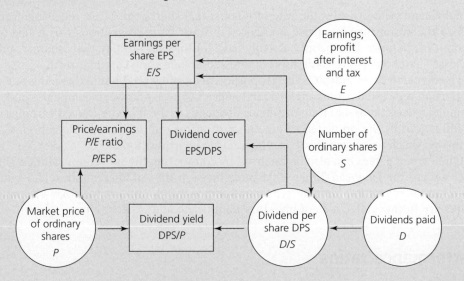

The P/E ratio indicates the amount (how many times the current earnings figure) that potential shareholders are willing to pay in order to buy shares in the company at a particular time. It is affected by previous success and profits, but really it is an indication of expectations. The more confidence the market has in a company, generally the higher will be its P/E. It can also indicate relatively how expensive borrowing is for the company. If the company opts to raise money from existing shareholders by offering new shares in a rights issue (the shareholders are invited to buy new shares in fixed proportion to those they already hold) the higher the P/E is, the cheaper is the capital. A high P/E implies that shareholders will pay many times current earnings to obtain shares.

The P/E ratio is also very important in acquisition situations. Consider two companies as an example. Company A has issued 500,000 ordinary shares with a face value of 25p and their current market price is 600p. Current earnings per share are 20p (£100,000 in total). Hence, the P/E is 600/20 = 30. Company A looks attractive to the shareholders of company B when it makes a bid for their shares. B also has 500,000 shares issued, again with a face value of 25p, but they are trading at only 150p as company B has been relatively sleepy of late and growth has been below the average for the industry. With earnings per share of 10p (£50,000 in total) the P/E is 15. A offers one new share in company A for every three shares in B (perhaps more generous than it need be), and the shareholders in B accept. A–B now has 666,667 shares issued; at the moment the combined earnings are £150,000. If the stock market, and the shareholders, are confident that A can turn B round and increase earnings significantly the current P/E of 30 could remain. If so, the new price of shares in the combined A–B is 675p. Earnings per share are 22.5p (£150,000/666,667 shares).

A's share price has in effect risen, possibly making it appear an even more successful company. Any company wishing to acquire A will now have to pay more. Equally, A's ability to acquire further companies on the above lines has been enhanced.

The price-to-earnings ratio and earnings per share are measures which are most applicable to companies whose shares are traded on the stock market.

### Two dividend ratios

The dividend yield provides the rate of interest that shareholders are receiving in relation to the current market price for shares. It must be used cautiously as it takes no account of the price that people actually paid (historically) to buy their shares; and in any case shareholders are often more interested in long-term capital growth.

The dividend cover indicates the proportion of earnings paid out in dividends and the proportion reinvested. Company dividend policies will vary between companies and, for example, a decision to maintain or reduce dividends in the face of reduced earnings will be influenced by the predicted effect on share prices and in turn the valuation of the company, which as we saw above can be an issue in acquisitions.

Quoted companies can also be analysed by considering the movement of their share price against the *Financial Times* 100 Shares Index or the All Shares Index, and against the index of shares for their particular industry. Under- and overperformance of the shares are further reflections of investors' confidence and expectations.

## Performance ratios

Tables 7.9 and 7.10 explain the various performance ratios.

**Table 7.9** Performance ratios

| Ratio | Calculation | Comments |
|-------|-------------|----------|
| Return on net assets Return on capital employed (%) | Profit before interest and before tax / Total capital employed in the business | Measures the relative success of the business as a trading concern Trading profit less overheads is divided by shareholders' funds and other long-term loans Useful for measuring and comparing the relative performance of different divisions/strategic business units |
| Profit margin (%) | Profit before interest and before tax / Sales (turnover) | Shows trading profit less overheads as a percentage of turnover Again useful for comparing divisions, products, markets |
| Net asset turnover (number of times) | Sales / Total net assets or capital employed in the business | It measures the number of times the capital is 'turned over' in a year Or: the number of pounds of sales generated for every pound invested in the company |

## Profitability

The return on net assets or the return on capital employed uses profit before interest and before tax and compares it with the assets, or capital employed, used in the business to create the profit. Actual profit is important as it determines the amount of money that a company has available for paying dividends (once interest and tax are deducted) and for reinvestment. But it is also important to examine how well the money invested in the business is being used – this is profitability. This particular ratio ignores how the business is actually funded, making it a measure of how well the business is performing as a trading concern. It was mentioned earlier that contributions from different products or strategic business units should be compared in the case of multiproduct organizations. The return on net assets should also be used to compare the profitabilities of products and strategic business units. In this way the ratio can be used for evaluating particular competitive strategies and the relative importance to the business of different products. However, this measure should not be used in isolation from an assessment of the relative importance of different products in terms of turnover. High-volume products or divisions may be less profitable than smaller volume ones for a variety of reasons, which are examined in the section on **portfolio analysis** in Chapter 9.

This ratio is particularly useful when it is examined in the light of the two ratios that comprise it. The return on net assets is equal to the profit margin times the net asset turnover. The profit margin is the proportion of sales revenue represented by profits (before interest and tax); the net asset turnover illustrates how well the company is utilizing its assets in order to generate sales.

Certain companies will adopt strategies that are designed to yield good profit margins on every item sold, and as a result probably add value into the product or service in such a way that their assets are not producing the same amount of sales per pound sterling as is the case for a company which uses assets more aggressively, adds less value and makes a lower profit margin. Particular industries and businesses may offer little choice in this respect; others offer considerable choice.

If a decision is reached that for the business as a whole, or some part of it, the return on net assets (profitability) must be improved, there are two approaches. Either profits

**Figure 7.12** Improving profitability

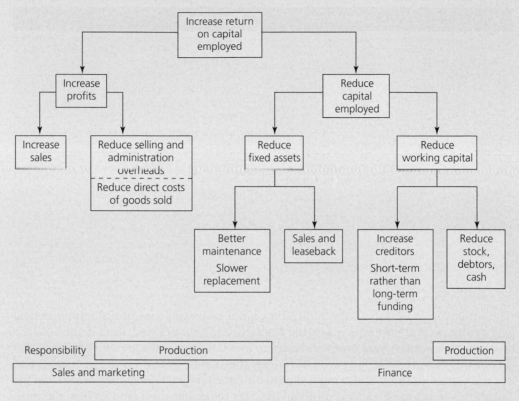

must be increased, or assets reduced, or both. Figure 7.12 illustrates the alternatives available to the organization, and at the bottom the functional responsibilities. Hence, a corporate or competitive strategy change will result in changes to functional strategies.

## Other useful performance ratios

Table 7.10 explains stock turnover and debtor turnover, which both indicate how well the company is managing two of its current assets. The stock turnover will depend on how the company is managing its operations – different strategies will lead to higher or lower stocks. Low stocks (high stock turnover) save costs, but they can make the business vulnerable if they are reduced to too low a level in order to save money and result in production delays. Debtor turnover, for certain types of business, looked at over a period can show whether the company is successful at persuading credit customers to pay quickly. This can affect the marketing strategy if decisions have to be taken not to supply certain customers who are slow payers.

The gross profit margin and the selling and administration costs to sales ratio are useful for indicating the percentage of turnover attributable to overheads. If a company has a high gross profit margin but is relatively unprofitable after accounting for overheads it is a sign of poor management. The product or service is able to command a price comfortably in excess of direct costs (direct labour and materials) but this contribution is being swallowed by overheads which are possibly too high and in need of reduction. Such a company is appropriate for restructuring and perhaps acquisition.

**Table 7.10** Other useful performance ratios

| Ratio | Calculation | Comments |
|---|---|---|
| Stock turnover (number of times) | $\dfrac{\text{Turnover}}{\text{Stock}}$ | Shows how quickly stocks move through the business. Logically the quicker the better – as long as it does not result in stock shortages. Most accurate measurement from average stock level over the year rather than the balance-sheet figure |
| Debtor turnover (number of times; or days of credit given) | $\dfrac{\text{Turnover}}{\text{Debtors}}$ | Shows how quickly credit customers pay. Again, use average debtors. Retail organizations, such as Marks and Spencer, sell mostly for cash, or charge interest for credit through their credit cards |
| | $\dfrac{\text{Debtors}}{\text{Turnover} \times 365}$ | A similar measure, credit purchases/average creditors, shows how much credit time is received by the company |
| Gross profit margin (%) and | $\dfrac{\text{Gross profit}}{\text{Turnover (sales)}}$ | Indicates percentage profit before overheads |
| Selling and administration costs to sales (%) | $\dfrac{\text{Selling and administration costs}}{\text{Turnover (sales)}}$ | Shows overheads (indirect costs) in relation to turnover |

Again, these ratios should be examined over a period of years to ensure that the overhead burden is not creeping up without just cause. In terms of increasing profits (to improve profitability; Figure 7.12) it may be easier to reduce overheads than to reduce direct costs.

# Measures of financial status

Measures of financial status can be divided into two groups: solvency and liquidity. The ratios are explained in Table 7.11.

## Solvency

The major ratios are the debt ratio and interest cover. The debt ratio relates to the company's gearing – how much it is funded by equity capital (shareholders' funds) and how much by long-term loans. Loans generally carry fixed interest payments, and these must be met regardless of any profit fluctuations; a company can elect not to pay dividends to shareholders if profits collapse, which gives it more flexibility.

Managers and investors will both be wary of the debt ratio creeping up, as it does when companies borrow money from the banking system to finance investment or acquisitions. In fact, acquisitive companies must relate their acquisition strategies to their ability to finance them. Sometimes money can be raised from shareholders, but the company must be confident that shareholders will subscribe to rights issues. If not, and the shares have to be sold to the banks who underwrite the issue (who then sell them

**Table 7.11** Measures of financial status

| Ratio | Calculation | Comments |
| --- | --- | --- |
| *Solvency* Debt ratio (%) | Long-term loans / Total capital employed | The lower the debt ratio the more the company is cushioned against fluctuation in trading profits |
| Interest cover (number of times) | Profit before interest and before tax / Interest on long-term loans | Indicates how many times the interest is covered by earnings It is sometimes argued banks expect a figure of at least three times |
| *Liquidity* Current ratio (ratio x:1) (also known as working capital ratio) | Current assets / Current liabilities | Shows the extent to which short-term assets are able to meet short-term liabilities 1.5:1 and 2:1 both suggested as indicative targets. Also suggested that working capital (current assets minus current liabilities) should exceed stock |
| Liquidity or acid test ratio (ratio x:1) | Liquid assets (i.e. current assets less stock) / Current liabilties | This shows how liquid the company is relative toshort-term liabilities. Stock is excluded as it can take months to turn into cash |

when the price is appropriate), blocks of shares can be bought up by other acquisitive companies and this can pose a threat. The alternative is long-term loans, and the higher the proportion these constitute, the more stable profits need to be. This is taken up later in the book (in a Finance in Action supplement to Chapter 11).

Interest cover shows by how much the interest payments are covered by profits.

## Liquidity

The two main liquidity ratios, the current ratio and the acid test (liquidity) ratio, relate to working capital. Has the company sufficient money available to meet its short-term commitments? They are determined by the flow of cash in and out of the business. A shortage of cash, and commitments to meet, will push the company towards increased borrowings (say a larger overdraft), and this will increase interest commitments.

While targets of 1.5:1 and 2.0:1 are sometimes quoted for the current ratio, these should be treated with some caution. Companies who trade mainly in cash, rather than allow credit, are likely to have a ratio much nearer 1:1 and still be perfectly liquid. Retailers and breweries are cases in point.

A company will experience liquidity problems if it invests in stock and then fails to win orders or if it fails to control its debtors. Conversely, a successful company can have cash problems. Success at winning orders may require investment in machinery or stocks and labour, and these may have to be paid for before and during production and before the goods are delivered and paid for by customers. This can lead to temporary illiquidity, and is known as overtrading.

# Managing cash

Cash flow, therefore, can be just as important as profitability. Where demand is seasonal for certain products production may take place when sales are low, in advance of peak demand. This puts pressure on cash flow in the way outlined above. A perfect example of this is Standard Fireworks, a largely focused business, whose sales are concentrated in the weeks before bonfire night (5 November), but who produce all through the year.

Cash reserves built up in good years can be run down to finance a company during lean years or a recession.

Cash-flow issues affect corporate strategy in terms of the range of products, services and businesses selected, competitive strategies in terms of the way they are marketed (to avoid the worst implications of seasonal fluctuations) and functional production, marketing and financial strategies.

It is not unusual for companies to be slow in paying their bills when their performance is poor. This impacts upon their suppliers, and highlights the importance of cash flow, particularly in a recession. Table 7.12 shows how cash is generated and spent.

Cash flow can be improved in a number of ways, for example, by

- increased turnover – but only if linked to
- effective management of debtors and creditors
- higher operating profit margins
- reduced tax payments
- reduced investment in working capital and/or fixed assets
- improved gearing to reduce interest payments.

Simply, a company must be able to produce cash in order to finance future investments and acquisitions, meet outstanding payments on earlier acquisitions and cover any unexpected events requiring extraordinary charges.

**Table 7.12** A typical cash-flow statement

| Cash generated by operating activities (including operating profits, changes in stocks, debtors, and creditors and depreciation charged in the accounts) | |
|---|---|
| *Add:* | Interest from investments |
| | Proceeds from any share issues |
| | Receipts from any asset sales |
| | New loans taken out |
| *Deduct:* | Interest paid on loans |
| | Loans repaid |
| | Tax paid |
| | Dividend paid |
| | Fixed assets purchased |
| *Leaving:* | Money available for further investment |

## Accounting for inflation

It is an accounting convention to use historical costs, and within the accountancy profession there is ongoing debate and disagreement about how best to treat inflation. This topic is outside the scope of this book. However, it is important to take some account of inflation when looking at growth rates for actual data such as turnover and profits as otherwise companies appear to be doing far better than in reality they are.

## Other quantitative performance indicators

In addition to all of these financial ratios, businesses will typically collect and evaluate information concerning the performance of all the activities being undertaken. For each functional area there will be a number of measures, such as the value of orders acquired by every salesperson, machine utilization, turnover at every retail outlet, output per shift, productivity per employee and absenteeism. Performance will be evaluated against targets or objectives agreed with individual managers who should be held accountable. These **performance indicators** are measures of resource efficiency. They are important control measures which evaluate the efficiency of each functional area of the business.

Similarly, individual sectors will favour particular measures. Retailers will typically consider sales per square foot of trading space, sales per employee, average shopping spend per trip and the number of new store openings or refits.

Improvements can strengthen the company's competitive capability. In isolation, however, these measures do not indicate how successful the company is strategically. This particular issue is very significant for not-for-profit organizations which cannot use the traditional profitability ratios sensibly and at the same time cannot readily measure their effectiveness in relation to their fundamental purpose. Consequently, they often rely more on quantitative measures of efficiency.

These measures are not developed in the same detail as the financial ones in this chapter and supplement as they will not be available to students tackling management case studies, whereas key financial data are normally obtainable.

## Service businesses

In addition to the above measures, the ability to retain customers is a key requirement for service businesses. Retention implies customer satisfaction and probably word-of-mouth recommendation. It is likely to result in higher profits because of the high costs incurred in attracting new business. Moreover, customers are likely to increase their level of spending over time. For insurance companies the cost of processing renewals is far cheaper than the cost of finding new clients; and many people will take out additional policies with a company on which they feel they can rely.

Key performance measures for solicitors are their ability to achieve results for their clients, and the service they offer, measurable by, for instance, the speed with which they respond to letters and telephone calls.

## INTERNET AND LIBRARY PROJECTS

### Applying the ratios

Table 7.13 provides selected financial data for British Airways in 1994/5, and Table 7.14 a worked analysis of a number of key ratios described in this Finance in Action supplement.

Check how these ratios have been calculated and consider how strong you think BA's performance was at this time. Then update the figures for some (or all) the intervening years and bring your performance evaluation up to date. Where has it improved? Deteriorated?

What factors have affected BA's performance in any meaningful way? The following incidents – which are not an exhaustive list of issues – are examples of things you might look for:

- The launch and subsequent sale of Go, the low-cost airline

- The failure to acquire KLM

- The failure to cement a proposed strategic alliance with American Airlines

- 11 September

- BA's decision to focus more on business and first class passengers than economy cabins

- The Air France Concorde crash and its eventual retirement from service

- The resignation of Chief Executive Robert Ayling and the appointment of his successor, Rod Eddington from Qantas.

**Table 7.13** British Airways: Extracts from profit and loss account and balance sheet, 31 March 1995

| | £ million | | £ million | £ million |
|---|---|---|---|---|
| Turnover | 7177 | Fixed assets | 6163 | |
| | | Investments | 471 | |
| Cost of sales | 6436 | | | 6634 |
| Gross profit | 741 | Current assets | | |
| | | Stock | 70 | |
| Overheads/administration | 123 | Debtors | 1182 | |
| | | Short-term loans | 1099 | |
| Operating profit | 618 | Cash | 64 | |
| Other income/provisions | (76) | | | 2415 |
| Interest | 215 | Current liabilities | 2320 | |
| Tax | 77 | Working capital | 95 | |
| Profit after interest and tax | 250 | Total net assets | | 6729 |
| Dividend paid | 119 | Long-term loans | 4582 | |
| Retained profit | 131 | Provisions for charges | 57 | |
| | | Shareholders' funds | 2090 | |
| Number of ordinary shares | 954,605,000 | | | |
| Year-end share price | 402 pence | Total capital employed | | 6729 |

**Table 7.14** British Airways: worked ratio analysis for 1994–95

### Investment ratios

| | | | | |
|---|---|---|---|---|
| Return on shareholders' funds | = | $\dfrac{250}{2090}$ | = | 11.96 per cent |
| Earnings per share | = | $\dfrac{250}{954.605}$ | = | 26.2 pence |
| Price/earnings ratio | = | $\dfrac{402}{26.2}$ | = | 15.34 |
| Dividend yield | = | $\dfrac{12.46}{402}$ | = | 3.1 per cent |
| Dividend cover | = | $\dfrac{26.2}{12.46}$ | = | 2.1 times |

### Performance ratios

| | | | | |
|---|---|---|---|---|
| Return on net assets | = | $\dfrac{618}{6279}$ | = | 9.2 per cent |
| Profit margin | = | $\dfrac{618}{7177}$ | = | 8.6 per cent |
| Net asset turnover | = | $\dfrac{7177}{6729}$ | = | 1.07 times |
| Stock turnover | = | $\dfrac{7177}{70}$ | = | 102 times |
| Debtor turnover | = | $\dfrac{7177}{1182}$ | = | 6.1 times (or 60 days) |
| Gross profit margin | = | $\dfrac{741}{7177}$ | = | 10.3 per cent |

### Solvency ratios

| | | | | |
|---|---|---|---|---|
| Debt ratio | = | $\dfrac{4582}{6729}$ | = | 68 per cent |
| Interest cover | = | $\dfrac{542}{215}$ | = | 2.5 times |

### Liquidity ratios

| | | | | |
|---|---|---|---|---|
| Current ratio | = | 2415:2320 | = | 1.04:1 |
| Liquidity ratio | = | 2345:2320 | = | 1.01:1 |

# Strategy Creation

This part of the book acts as a transition between the key themes of awareness and change. It looks at the ways in which organizations might, and in reality do, generate new ideas for future strategies.

There are three key elements:

- Planning – based on systems and procedures and which in turn is dependent upon the quality of the available information

- Leadership – to provide both ideas and a clear framework in which other decision-makers can operate effectively. Embraces a visionary element

- Innovation – intrapreneurship within the organization to ensure that new opportunities are found and threats are avoided, such that the organization stays strong, competitive, effective and successful in a dynamic environment. This is again dependent upon communications and information and it relies on effective internal networks.

The following chapters show why it is the case that every manager can be a strategy maker, although it should be said that not every manager can be either a leader or an entrepreneur. Very broadly, Chapters 8, 9 and 10 examine these three elements systematically. Every organization will feature a blend of all three, although one may well be a dominant feature. Chapter 8 provides a short introduction to the whole topic of strategy creation.

# An Introduction to Strategy Creation

This chapter recaps on themes introduced in Chapter 1. Figure 1.8 summarized the situation, by showing the linkages between the ideas of intended strategy (through strategic planning and entrepreneurial leadership) and emergent strategies when intended strategies are changed incrementally as they are implemented and new strategies are created as managers adapt in a changing environment.

> *We're not necessarily great overall strategists [at Virgin] … we often do things and then work out afterwards what the overall strategy was.*
>
> Sir Richard Branson, Chairman, Virgin Group
>
> *If you're in the penalty area and aren't quite sure what to do with the ball, just stick it in the net and we'll discuss your options afterwards.*
>
> Bill Shankly (1914–1981), once Manager, Liverpool Football Club

## 8.1 Introduction

Football, or really any professional sport, provides a useful metaphor for understanding strategy creation. Teams – or, in the case of sports such as tennis, individuals – will begin all important matches with a game plan. They will have studied their opponents, assessed their relative strengths and weaknesses, thought about their natural game and about how they might approach this particular match, and worked out how they might be beaten. Led by the manager, coaches will have helped the players with the analysis and the tactics. Normally, the objective will be about winning. In some instances it can be about not losing (a subtle difference) or winning might be qualified by adding a 'means' objective related to approach and style. These game plans will undoubtedly *inform* the players, but it may be impossible to carry them out to the letter. Unexpected tactics from their opponents will ensure that this is the case.

Once the game is underway, the intended plans and strategies will be adjusted – there will be incremental changes. Broadly, however, they may well be implemented, certainly as long as the game is being won and not lost. At the same time, new, unexpected opportunities will be presented during the game, and good teams will be able to adapt.

Of course, 'the best laid plans o' mice and men gang aft a gley'. The opponents may prove stronger and more disciplined than predicted. They may take the lead in the first minute and seize control of the game. In this case, there will be a need to adapt to the threats and change the tactics. When this happens, the ability to remain cohesive and disciplined as a team is essential. In football pundit terminology this is usually described as 'keeping your shape'.

At any time there is always the opportunity for individuals to show initiative and to shine. A strong, experienced and maybe visionary team manager (the strategic leader in this example) can act as a master tactician and an inspiration both beforehand and from the sidelines during the game. Talented players, with individual goals, spectacular saves or important tackles at key moments, will often make important contributions and, by doing so, encourage their colleagues also to make the extra effort that tips the balance. As they always say, a game is not lost until the final whistle: teams often do go one or two goals down before recovering to win.

It is useful to contrast this metaphor with others. American football resembles rugby in some ways, but it remains a very distinctive game. At any one time a team will be attacking or defending in a series of moves, designed to advance a fixed number of yards – or stop the opposing team advancing. The player pool will contain both attackers and defenders, and players will enter and exit the fray depending on the state of the game. Specialist kickers will only be on the field when a kick needs taking. Coaches can call time-outs and provide tactical advice between plays as players come on and off the field. Tactics and planning clearly have a different role.

Warfare is also a competition in its own way. There are clearly objectives for the conflict. There are plans and tactics. There are visionary leaders and historically there has been considerable emergence, with a reliance on the bravery of men in the field. In the past warfare has often involved a serious degree of slaughter in the attempt to defeat the enemy systematically over a period of time. More recently the strategic intent has been based on demoralization. Combatants will endeavour to make a very powerful early strike of such enormity it destroys the enemy's belief that they can win. This implies an emphasis on vision (the way to achieve this), planning (the tactics) and speedy execution. There is, then, less reliance on emergence.

## 8.2 Strategy creation

Chapter 1 explained how strategy creation involves three strands:

**Figure 8.1** Strategy creation

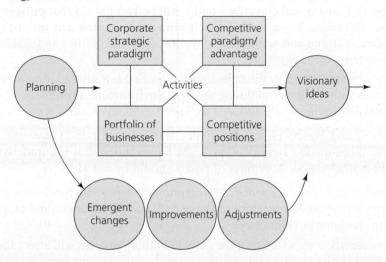

- *planning*, both systematic and formal strategic planning systems and informal, cerebral planning
- *vision* and visionary leadership, and
- *emergent strategies* – incremental changes to predetermined, intended strategies and adaptive additions with learning and responsiveness to opportunities and threats.

Figure 8.1 reiterates that strategy and strategic management embrace the corporate portfolio of businesses and the search for competitiveness and competitive advantage with each business, product and service, and that this competitiveness arises from the functional activities that an organization undertakes. Visionary ideas *pull* the organization forward. Where these result in significant changes, they will often be associated with the strategic leader. Planning *pushes* everything forward. Emergent changes, improvements and adjustments – intrapreneurial changes initiated and implemented by individual managers throughout the organization – *support* and complete the process.

If all strategies were planned formally, then organizations would be able to look back and review the decisions that they had made over a period of time. At some stage in the past there would have been a clear recorded statement of intent which matched these events closely. In reality, stated plans and actual events are unlikely to match closely. In addition to strategies that have emerged and been introduced entrepreneurially, there are likely to have been expectations and planned possible strategies that have not proved to be viable. However, broad directions can be established and planned and then detailed strategies allowed to emerge as part of an ongoing learning experience within the organization.

Idenburg (1993) presents these ideas in a slightly modified way, distinguishing between the following strategies.

- Formal planning systems, through which clear objectives should lead to intended strategies.
- Learning or real-time planning, which represents a formal approach to adaptive strategy creation. Managers meet regularly, both formally and informally, and debate how key strategic issues are changing and emerging. Objectives and strategies will be changed in a turbulent environment.

- Incremental change and logical incrementalism. The organization will have a clear mission and directional objectives, and it will be recognized that pursuing these requires flexibility. Managers will be encouraged to experiment with new ideas and strategies, learning and adapting all the time. Internal politics and systems will play an important role in this mode.

- Emergent strategies. Specific objectives will not be set; instead, organizations will be seen as fully flexible, 'muddling through' environmental turbulence. Opportunism, being ready and able to 'seize the main chance', is critical.

Mintzberg and Waters (1985) and Bailey and Johnson (1992) have also shown how the simple three-mode categorization might be extended, but the underlying implications remain unchanged. A number of points should be noted:

- Although it is not made explicit, some strategies, especially those formulated by a visionary entrepreneur, attempt to shape and change the environment, rather than react to changing circumstances.

- The organization structure and the actual planning process will affect the nature of planned objectives and strategies. Wherever a group of managers is involved in planning, their personal values and relative power will be reflected. See Cyert and March's behavioural theory in Chapter 2.

- Adaptive changes will also reflect the values, power and influence of managers.

It is important to appreciate that the three modes described above are not mutually exclusive, and that one mode frequently leads on from another. The implementation of visionary ideas and strategies typically requires careful planning, for example, and this will invariably bring about incremental changes. In Chapter 1 it was confirmed that all three modes will be found in an organization simultaneously, but the mix and prioritization will be particular to an individual company. This key point is illustrated in Figure 8.2. It was also emphasized that individual managers, depending largely on their position within the organization, will not necessarily agree on the relative significance of each mode. It is essential that managers understand and support the processes.

The mixed approach is both sensible and justifiable. In some manufacturing industries the time taken from starting to plan a substantive innovatory change to peak profit performance can be ten years. This needs planning, although the concept may be vision-

**Figure 8.2** Strategy creation and strategic change

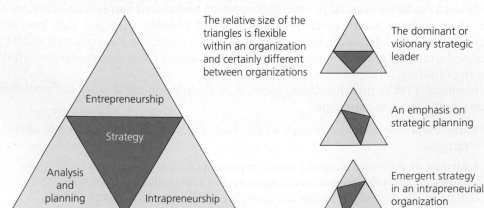

ary. Throughout the implementation there has to be adaptive and incremental learning and change. Where strategies are being changed in a dynamic environment it is also useful, on occasions, to evaluate the current situation and assess the implications. This could well be part of an annual planning cycle.

It is now appropriate to reread Minicase 1.4, which looked at how the three modes can be seen in practice in McDonald's. McDonald's has a clear and understood vision which also embraces its thousands of franchisees worldwide. In the late 1990s its annual rate of global expansion grew to over 3000 new restaurants although this has been trimmed back after some misguided expansion; this required careful planning. This planning, together with arrangements with building contractors and suppliers, has also allowed McDonald's to cut 30 per cent off the cost of opening every new restaurant, through the use of more efficient building systems, standardized equipment and global sourcing. As a consequence, it can now afford to open restaurants in locations which, in the past, had been seen as uneconomical. Given the intense competition in the fast-food industry, it is also essential for McDonald's to remain flexible and responsive, internationally, nationally and locally.

Minicase 8.1 applies these themes to EasyGroup, the collection of businesses started by Stelios Haji-Ioannou on the back of the success of easyJet, which we featured in Minicase 1.1. Stelios had a vision for the airline opportunity and executed it effectively. None of his other businesses have achieved the same level of success. Is he getting the vision and the business model wrong? Is there inadequate preparation and planning? Is there an over-reliance on 'everything working out'? Interestingly, and maybe significantly, this serial entrepreneur continues to start new ventures before his last one has broken even.

Table 8.1 further relates these themes to the three levels of strategy: corporate, competitive and functional. In large organizations much of the responsibility for corporate strategic change will be centralized at the head office, although the businesses and divisions can be involved or consulted. Competitive and functional change decisions are more likely to be decentralized, but again, not exclusively. Corporate policies can require or constrain changes at these levels.

**Table 8.1** Levels of strategy and modes of strategy creation

| | Levels of strategy | |
|---|---|---|
| Modes of strategy creation | Corporate strategy | Competitive and functional strategies |
| Planning | Formal planning systems | Planning the detail for implementing corporate strategies |
| Visionary | Seizing opportunities – limited planning only | Innovation throughout the organization |
| Adaptive/incremental | Reacting to environmental opportunities and threats, e.g. businesses for sale; divestment opportunity | Reacting to competitor threats and new environmental opportunities<br>Learning and adjustment as planned and visionary strategies are implemented |

### 8.2.1 Planning and strategy creation

Mintzberg (1989) contends that the strategic leader should be the chief architect, in conjunction with planners, of corporate plans; the process should be explicit, conscious and controlled; and issues of implementation should be incorporated. Essentially, analysis leads to choice, which leads on to implementation. The process is sequential:

**Analysis → Choice → Implementation**

Certain organizations might claim that detailed long-term planning is essential for them. An airline, for example, must plan capacity several years ahead because of the long delivery lead times for new aeroplanes and the related need to manage cash flow and funding. In addition, resources must be co-ordinated on an international scale. While planes are utilized on most days and fly as many hours in the day as possible, crews work only limited hours, and typically finish a flight or series of flights in a location which is different from their starting point.

However, Mintzberg argues that this is planning the implications and consequences of the strategic perspective, not necessarily the perspective itself. Detailed planning of this type should not inhibit creativity concerning the perspective.

Planning of some form will always be required in large organizations. It forces thinking and enables and supports resource allocation and budgeting. However, the extent and nature of the overall planning contribution will relate to the industry and the environment and be affected by both leadership and culture.

CASE

## Minicase 8.1  easyGroup                                                      GB

### The founder

Entrepreneur Stelios Haji-Ioannou was born in Athens in 1967 – his business card describes him as a 'serial entrepreneur'. His father was a successful businessman. After completing two degrees (in London), and work experience in his father's shipping company, he used family money to start Stelmar Shipping in 1992. Three years later he established easyJet. Both companies have been very successful and continue to prosper.

Minicase 1.1 discusses the growth of easyJet, bringing out its rivalry with Ryanair in the quest to be Europe's leading no-frills airline. easyJet has a clear business model, borrowed in many respects from the pioneering Herb Kelleher and Southwest Air in America. Its growth has been supported by television exposure (a long-running 'docusoap') and the acquisition of Go after this spin-out from British Airways had itself been bought by its managers with substantial venture capital funding.

In 1998 Stelios set up easyGroup as a **holding company** to facilitate the exploration of new venture opportunities through which the 'easy' brand could be extended. Licensing, franchising and alliances have all featured. Although there are clear differences of style and approach, in many respects this was the growth path trodden earlier by Richard Branson with his Virgin brand.

Meanwhile easyJet was floated successfully as a public company (2000) and Ray Webster, an experienced airline executive from Air New Zealand who had joined easyJet in1996, was promoted to run the company for Stelios. Stelios himself began to withdraw from the management of the airline and in 2002 he left completely to concentrate on his new ventures. Because his name is associated with the founding of easyJet, and because he remains a major shareholder, many people would imagine he still runs it.

Stelios argues he looks for business opportunities where 'he can rip the frills out of the industry' and sums up his own contribution as follows:

▶

*I am best at doing research and deciding on the business model ... as soon as I've found the business model I hire a manager to run it ... I learn by doing more and more myself and getting the right people to help.*

Stelios believes it will take between three and five years for one of his new businesses to become profitable. One question is: does he typically get the business model right, especially in the beginning?

## Stelios' other businesses

The second 'easy' business was originally called easyEverything, but it has since been renamed *easyInternetcafé*, which better describes its purpose. The first café was opened in central London in 1999, but others soon followed in other leading European cities. The idea was fast access to the Internet at any time, night or day, seven days a week. The business model was price-driven: basically £1 for 1 hour. Keyboards and screens were provided side-by-side in wide rows. Tutors were available if required, who also doubled as local managers and, when necessary, 'porn patrollers', charged with 'ensuring that the stores remained a welcoming place for their millions of customers'. This did not prevent easyGroup losing a court case in 2003 when it was held liable for customers downloading copyright music illegally. Nowadays the company utilizes automated webfiltering. Coffee and snacks could be bought and consumed on site. easyInternetcafés turned out to have a high cash burn. There were interest charges on the debt capital required for the top-range computers, the sites were centrally located in high lease areas and salaries had to be paid. Customers may have been plentiful but they did not provide enough revenue to meet the costs. The business was unprofitable and Stelios has had to inject additional personal funding to support it. Moreover the business model has been recrafted. Now Stelios focuses on smaller sites and rents space in other retail properties which are managed for him by franchisees. He is not concerned to be the leaseholder. In larger sites that he has retained, space has been sublet to other retailers and fast food providers.

*easyCar* followed in 2000. This rental car company began by focusing on city centre locations and a single model of car – small A series Mercedes. The basic rental charges were way below those of leading names such as Avis and Hertz. Personal and car insurance premiums soon reduced the gap, but a clear gap remained. Customers who were alleged to have scratched their cars (but some of whom disputed this fact) and who were charged a supplementary amount, complained to television consumer programmes – which inevitably brought adverse publicity to the company. In response easyCar stopped charging anyone for any damage to the cars, but that proved prohibitively expensive! At that stage they introduced their £50/30 day automatically refundable deposit. This covered them for damage risks, but it also acted as insurance against unpaid parking tickets and other traffic infringements which tended to result from their concentration on urban sites.

easyCar acknowledges that originally they misunderstood third party contingent liabilities. Initially the cost base for easyCar proved too high for the income being generated and the business was unprofitable. In 2003 plans were being drawn up for a new strategy when the managing director left. The idea for a new rental business would be based on pools of cars which would be parked up in relatively quiet areas and unattended. Customers would book over the Internet and then make their own way to the pool, where they would contact a service centre by mobile phone. The car would be unlocked remotely by radio signal; the keys would already be inside. The idea has not been taken forward; instead easyCar has grown dramatically to 1000 sites worldwide with a brokerage strategy. easyCar provides sales and marketing support to locally based operators, who own their own rental cars.

*easyValue* is an online price comparison service. It was initially an alliance with Kellkoo, but since that business was purchased by Yahoo, easyValue has been powered by Shopping.com. The original business model was based on advertising with the hope that it could be turned into a subscription service. In the beginning it was a struggle to raise sufficient revenue from advertising to break-even, but the business is now profitable.

*easyMoney*, begun in 2001, is a credit card that customers design to suit their own needs. It is operated by Lloyds TSB. Customer numbers were 'disappointing' but are now 'encouraging', so much so that easyMoney also generates a profit for the easyGroup in a very competitive industry. Other established businesses are *easy Bus* and *easyCinema*.

Stelios launched *easyBus* in 2004, to provide short haul low fare services using orange (the traditional *easy* colour) minibuses. The starting fare is £1. At roughly the same time, Stagecoach, a leading bus and coach operator, launched a no-frills cut price service on much longer routes and using double deckers. Brian Souter, founder of Stagecoach, has expressed a doubt that Stelios has a profitable business model as his required revenue per seat mile (to cover costs) is way in excess of the Stagecoach model. However, they are not competing businesses and Stelios, unlike Stagecoach, avoids town and city centre main bus stations, where access charges can be expensive. easyBus argues they have started something really new and different, whilst Stagecoach is new, albeit powerful, competition on existing routes.

There are also plans for a chain of *easyPizza* outlets, a pizza delivery service. Perhaps the nearest rival business model would be that of Domino's Pizza, but Domino's is not exclusively delivery as it has some walk-in trade. The delivery: collection ratio is in the order of 80:20. easyPizza will be exclusively delivery and the first unit is on an industrial estate near Milton Keynes. The idea for easyDorm was budget hotel rooms but this has been abandoned in favour of *easyHotel*: affordable en-suite rooms. *easyCruise* will provide a hop-on hop-off cruise package calling at various Mediterranean ports. Customers pay for a cabin at a daily rate and then everything else on board is chargeable if consumed. Also being planned during 2004 were *easy4Men* male toiletries and *easyMusic* downloads. The toiletries were scheduled to be available in stores in time for Christmas.

## easyCinema

easyCinema may eventually grow into a chain, but at the moment it is a single multiplex cinema in Milton Keynes. Cinemas are attractive to Stelios because they are sometimes full and have rows of empty seats at other times. Popularity is affected by time of day, day of the week and certainly by the film itself. Some blockbusters play in several cinemas in a multiscreen at any one time and run for weeks if not months. Other films last just one week before they are dropped. Whilst there are discounted matinee prices (and, of course, concessions for children and pensioners), unlike the theatre, the prices tend to be standardized and do not vary between different films. Stelios believed there were wasted opportunities for price differentiation. As well as day and time, different film titles and the number of weeks since a film's release are relevant – and naturally cheaper prices could be offered for booking a number of weeks in advance. However, if schedules are not available weeks in advance there could be an element of lottery in this. He believed low prices would stimulate high demand and he wanted 20 pence prices for Internet bookings one month in advance to be his baseline. The starting price is now 50 pence as Stelios has discovered customers do not discriminate when the charge is a single coin under a pound (sterling).

Stelios – assisted by Stuart Niblock, a senior easyGroup executive, and, in effect, a project manager – set out to find a suitable venue to trial his business model. Once they found somewhere, they would 'work out how to do it'. They came across The Point in Milton Keynes, which was closed but which had been a thriving UCI multiplex cinema after it opened in 1985 – it had lost out when competitors opened new complexes. They took it on in 2003 and in a matter of weeks it would be refurbished and open for business.

There was to be no box office and no ice cream, soft drinks or popcorn for sale – but drinks and popcorn are now available at £1.00. People would be asked to carry out and deposit all their rubbish so the downtime between screenings could be minimized. Customers would book in advance on the Internet and once they had paid with their credit card they would be able to print off a bar code on a sheet of paper. When passed over a scanner at the entrance to the relevant cinema screen they would be allowed through a turnstile. Staff would be present to help anyone in difficulty and generally watch over things.

All Stelios needed now was popular films at the time of their release. Six leading distributors control some 90 per cent of film releases and every one of them appeared sceptical about the sustainability of the easyCinema business model. They all refused to supply him with films. Normally they receive a figure approximating to £1.30 per person viewing for the films they supply. Pathé, not one of the six, did agree to supply him with films so he could open his cinema, but they were not the latest mainstream titles. Would people be attracted by 20p prices for films that had been around for a while and that had never been stunningly popular? Stelios offered the leading distributors up-front cash payments and when they refused this he argued they were acting as a cartel to exclude him from the industry. He realized he could sue them in America, where he would not have to pay their legal costs if he lost: there were other litigation possibilities in the European courts. In the end this did not prove necessary.

Staff were recruited and trained in 'easy' procedures. Stelios himself was on hand and he walked around Milton Keynes – and in rival cinemas – with a sandwich board promoting the venture. (He had adopted a similar approach when the airline Go started up and challenged easyJet. He had bought tickets, organized photographers and turned up in an orange easyJet boiler suit and carrying a promotional banner.) One cinema threw him out – whereupon he complained to the police. The scanners did not work altogether smoothly on opening night, but plenty of customers turned up! To the amazement of some of them Stelios went around with a bucket and asked them for more money 'to help him fight his campaign against the leading distributors'. Afterwards he said the money would be topped up by him and given to charity; he just wanted to draw people's attention to the issue.

From the beginning Stelios attracted a steady stream of customers with his very low prices for non-mainstream films, but the venture is not yet profitable. In spring 2004 the leading distributors had partly capitulated, but he was still only able to secure films a month after their initial release. He recruited Charles Wesoky to run easyCinema for him. Wesocky was a 'veteran of the industry'; indeed he had opened The Point for UCI some 20 years earlier. His main role: improve relations with distributors. The situation with films on release has continued to improve. easyCinema now gets a regular supply of first run films which are shown at prices some 30 per cent lower than the local competition. Attendances continue to grow. easyCinema is on the look-out for a second site in the south of England.

**Questions**

1. Picking up on the earlier comment, does Stelios generally 'get the business model right in the beginning'?
2. How much is Stelios an entrepreneurial visionary? Is there sufficient planning of the right type?
3. Is too much left to chance?
4. If it was your decision, would you persist and expand the cinema chain, close the one in Milton Keynes or adopt a different business model?

Stelios Haji-Ioanno http://www.stelios.com

### 8.2.2 The visionary mode

A visionary strategic leader who formulates strategic change in his or her mind may only be semiconscious of the process involved. He or she will clearly understand the current and desired strategic perspective, and ideally the culture of the organization will be one in which other managers are receptive of the changes in perspective. The personality and charisma of the leader, and the ability to sell his or her ideas, will be crucial issues, and as speed of action, timing and commitment are typical features the strategy can prove highly successful.

The visionary or entrepreneurial approach suggests that the strategic leader is very aware of the strengths, weaknesses and capabilities of the organization; the current matching with the environment; a wide range of possibly diverse opportunities for change; and the likely reaction of managers to certain changes. Similar to the 'bird approach' described in Chapter 1, Box 1.3, the selection is made somewhat arbitrarily without careful and detailed planning, and therefore an element of risk is involved. This informality in the process is important to allow for creativity and flair. The strategic leader then sells the idea to other managers, and the strategy is implemented and changed incrementally as experience is gained and learning takes place. In other words, the vision acts as an umbrella and within it specific decisions can be taken which lead to the emergence of more detailed strategies.

Chris Gorman, the new co-owner of the Gadget Shop chain, operates very much within the entrepreneur strategic leader role. Immediately prior to the Gadget Shop, Gorman had the very interesting title of 'Chief Entrepreneur' within Great Universal Stores. GUS had bought the Reality Group from Gorman and after the acquisition Gorman had this new role. However, Gorman did not stay long within GUS because 'it was not my skill set... I am not someone who is comfortable as a manager working through the layers that make up a large PLC.'

With this mode it is difficult to separate analysis and choice, so that

**Analysis (in the form of ongoing awareness)**
**and choice** → **Implementation**

**Dangers** The success of this mode in the long term depends on the continued strategic awareness and insight of the strategic leader, particularly if the organization revolves around a visionary leader and becomes heavily dependent upon him or her. People may be visionary for only a certain length of time, and then they become blinkered by the success of current strategies and adopt tunnel vision, or they somehow lose the ability to spot good new opportunities. It might also be argued that, if luck is involved, their luck runs out. The problems occur if the strategic leader has failed to develop a strong organization with other visionaries who can take over.

On a current basis the strategy requires management as well as leadership. In other words, managers within the organization must be able to capitalize on the new opportunities and develop successful competitive positions within the revised strategic perspective. This might involve an element of planning; equally it might rely more on the adaptive approach described below.

## 8.2.3 The adaptive and incremental modes

Under the adaptive and incremental modes strategies are formed and evolve as managers throughout the organization learn from their experiences and adapt to changing circumstances. They perceive how tasks might be performed, and products and services managed, more effectively, and they make changes. They also respond to pressures and new strategic issues. There will again be elements of semiconsciousness and informality in the process. Some changes will be gradual, others spontaneous, and they will act collectively to alter and improve competitive positions. As individual decisions will often involve only limited change, little risk and possibly the opportunity to change back, this is essentially the 'squirrel approach' described in Chapter 1, Box 1.3. Managers learn whether their choice is successful or unsuccessful through implementation.

Hence this mode implies limited analysis preceding choice and implementation, which are intertwined and difficult to separate. A proper analysis follows in the form of an evaluation of the relative success:

| **Analysis**<br>**(limited)** | → | **Choice and**<br>**implementation** | → | **Analysis** |
|---|---|---|---|---|

Adaptive strategic change requires decentralization and clear support from the strategic leader, who also seeks to stay aware of progress and link the changes into an integrated pattern. It is often based on setting challenges for managers: challenging them to hit targets, improve competitiveness and stretch or exploit internal systems and policies to obtain the best possible returns. The greater the challenge, the more care needs to go into establishing a suitable reward system. When the structure enables effective adaptive change, then intrapreneurship can be fostered throughout the organization and individual managers can be allowed the necessary freedom. However, if adaptive changes are taking place in a highly centralized organization, and despite rigid policies, there is a problem which should be investigated. The major potential drawbacks concern the ability of the organization and the strategic leader to synthesize all the changes into a coherent pattern, and the willingness and ability of individual managers to take an organization-wide perspective. This latter point is examined later in Chapter 10.

Information technology provides opportunities for collecting and co-ordinating information and should be harnessed to support decentralization. In addition, team briefing can prove useful. Here, a strategic leader would regularly brief his or her senior executives, discussing progress and any proposed changes to the corporate strategy and policies. On a cascading basis managers would quickly and systematically communicate this information downwards and throughout the organization by meeting teams of people responsible to them. The secret lies in also using team briefing meetings to communicate information upwards by reporting on new strategic issues and how they are being handled.

Figure 8.3 provides a short summary of the processes. Planning is shown at the top as a 'closed funnel' activity. The entrepreneurial, visionary style is more one of diverging and opening things up, widening the scope of the ideas considered. Adaptive strategy (responding to new opportunities) is, conversely, illustrated as a convergent process. Here, learning and synthesis are required to form cohesive patterns which bind the emerging strategies. In the entrepreneurial mode, planning is required during

**Figure 8.3** Strategy creation processes

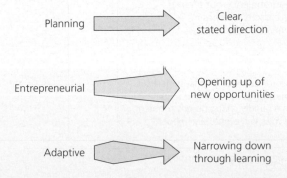

implementation; and in the adaptive mode, individual managers are doing their own planning, sometimes informally, sometimes more formally.

## 8.3 Changing strategies

Two important strategic pressures can leave the unprepared organization weakened: competitive and other environmental pressures, and focusing too much on controls at the expense of flexibility.

Hurst (1995) has shown how management and control becomes increasingly necessary as organizations grow and become more complex, but that this development contains the seeds of potential failure. Figure 8.4 shows that organizations often start life with an entrepreneurial vision but that the significance of this vision soon gives way to learning and emergence as the entrepreneur and the organization learns to cope with the pressures of a dynamic and competitive environment. This flexibility maintains the momentum and the organization grows and prospers. To ensure that the organization is managed efficiently, planning and control systems run by specialist professional managers become increasingly prominent, but this often reduces the flexibility which has proved so valuable. If the flexibility is lost, if the organization fails to address what it is doing wrong while it is still succeeding, some of the momentum for innovation is lost. Unless the entrepreneur and the organization foresee the impending problem and find a major new initiative, a crisis is likely to happen. If the organization is to survive the crisis it will need a substantial new opportunity, together with a renewed reliance on innovation and learning.

**Figure 8.4** Strategic change

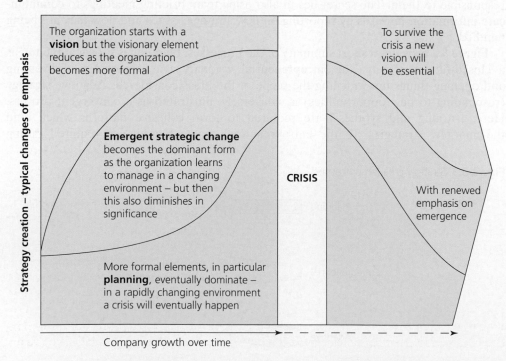

The organization starts with a **vision** but the visionary element reduces as the organization becomes more formal

To survive the crisis a new vision will be essential

**Emergent strategic change** becomes the dominant form as the organization learns to manage in a changing environment – but then this also diminishes in significance

**CRISIS**

With renewed emphasis on emergence

More formal elements, in particular **planning**, eventually dominate – in a rapidly changing environment a crisis will eventually happen

Strategy creation – typical changes of emphasis

Company growth over time

Businesses hit these crisis points when they run short of money, usually because they have failed to remain competitive and to attract sufficient resource contributions from customers and other important resource suppliers. Sometimes turnaround is possible, frequently accompanied by a change of strategic leader to input the new vision and inspiration. On other occasions the intervention is too late, and the organization either collapses or is taken over as a means of providing the necessary new leadership and resourcing.

Businesses in trouble, then, may be realistically irrecoverable, recoverable but only to a level of survival, or capable of genuine renewal. The immediate need is to stop any financial haemorrhaging before new opportunities are sought and pursued. The first step does not need someone with entrepreneurial talent and temperament – it is largely based on technique, backed by a willingness to take tough decisions – but the second stage does.

Hurst further argues that on occasions it can be valuable to engineer an internal crisis and upset in order to drive through major changes in an organization that has lost its dynamism and become too resistant to change. A controlled crisis is better than one resulting from external events as it can be used for positive change rather than constitute a more desperate reaction.

Stasis is less likely to happen if the company employs and encourages creative people who drive innovation and intrapreneurship. But if momentum is lost, the company may need more than creative people: it may need a 'maverick', perhaps someone who is normally ill-at-ease in a typical organization or a new strategic leader who will come in for just a short period. The maverick manager is unorthodox, individualistic and outspoken, someone who will challenge mediocrity and existing ways of doing things and someone who is not afraid to upset others in the drive for change.

Another way of presenting these arguments is the following four-stage model of organizational progression and development.

- The first step is a *creative* one, when new ideas are put forward.

- *Reflection and nurturing* follow as the idea is crafted into a winning opportunity. The person who has the original idea may not be the person who takes it forward in the most opportune way.

Minicase 8.2 examines the difference between a great idea and a true market opportunity.

- The third stage is an *action* stage as the organization grows by developing a business from the opportunity. As the business takes off, and more and more products are sold, some element of order becomes vital if the organization is to control events, manage its cash flow and deliver on time.

- The fourth stage then becomes one of *management* and administration with clear policies and procedures which deliver smooth running and efficiencies. This can become a dangerous stage if stasis sets in and new, creative ideas are not forthcoming.

Clearly, each stage has a downside. A constant stream of new ideas may not constitute entrepreneurial opportunities. Too much deliberation may inhibit action. An overemphasis on 'doing' and competitiveness may mean that inadequate attention is given to structural necessities. Finally, too much bureaucracy can mean missed opportunities. The organization begins to need a fresh input of creative ideas. Individually, we are all different and our affinity and fit with each of these stages varies; some of us are not able to switch styles. While the most successful and habitual entrepreneurs will ensure that there is a constant flow of activity between these stages and the potential downsides do not materialize, other strategic leaders will need to recognize their relative strengths and weaknesses and recruit other people carefully to ensure that there is a balance of skills and constant progression. Moreover, the positive organization implied here will be in a better position to exploit and retain its most talented intrapreneurial managers.

---

**CASE**

## Minicase 8.2  Eclipse Aviation – Great Opportunity or Just a Great Idea?   US

A new jet aeroplane, the Eclipse 500, made its first – and successful – test flight in America in August 2002. Eclipse Aviation was attempting an 'aviation first' with this new aircraft – the first commercial jet priced at under $1 million (approximately £650,000). At this price it would be 75 per cent cheaper than a near rival, the Cessna Citation. To achieve this price, Eclipse would have to sell 1000 aircraft a year. The intention was full airworthiness certification in 2003 with deliveries from 2004. Four separate certifications were required – the aircraft, the engine, the welding technique being used and the avionics.

Industry experts were sceptical about the proposal, but non-experts were in favour.

### The specification

The aircraft has six passenger seats but no toilet. Its flying speed is 400 miles an hour and its range is 1300 miles. It is powered by a new single Williams engine (which, like the plane, has yet to be certified) with double the thrust-to-weight ratio of rival engines.

Eclipse had found a suitable supplier for its avionics, which it believed it could purchase for $50,000, whilst Cessna pay $700,000. Manufacturing processes are based on high-volume techniques, and a new type of welding is being adopted.

Sceptics believe the overall extent of technological change is too ambitious.

### The aims of the business model

Eclipse hopes to expand jet travel beyond 'executive elites' and to open up a new market opportunity for 'taxis in the sky'.

The idea for a taxi service would require an independent operator to create a service which links hundreds of small airports. As a concept it is unproven. Fractional, part-ownership share schemes have been tried out, but they have been largely unprofitable, as much as anything because of the complex logistics. Forecasting demand and dealing with planes flying return or collection journeys without passengers are a big issue.

### Funding

To date some $238 million has been invested in the development. Investors include Bill Gates and an ex-Ford CEO. There has been $25 million in customer deposits which has been used for working capital. Currently the business is burning at least $5 million every month and needs more funding to see it through certification.

### The market

The year 2001 was a record one for business jet manufacture. 738 were built. *Forecast International* suggests a market of 1900 between 2002 and 2011, with Eclipse perhaps achieving 400 of these.

Eclipse aims for sales of 140 in 2004, 500 in 2005, 900 in 2006 and then 1500 by 2007. Where from? The replacement of existing jets as well as new sales and taxis. It claims it already has 1350 firm orders. But mysteries abound.

A Russian entrepreneur, who built a substantial perfume chain, said he had a company called Nimbus which had access to $1.2 billion for an air taxi service with 1000 aircraft. Nimbus turned out to be an online auction business.

▶

Another Swiss entrepreneur announced that Aviace would acquire 112 planes to start a business in Europe. Aviace paid a deposit but the rest of its funding was not yet in place.

### The entrepreneur behind Eclipse

Vern Raburn has a background in technology not aviation. He was, in fact, the eighteenth person to join Microsoft in its early days. He believed he could use his experience in improving value to drive new sales and also drive down costs and prices.

### Additional risks

Since 1960 only one new entrant to the market – Embraer of Brazil – has managed to deliver more than one new business jet per month.

The first Eclipse 500 may have tested successfully but it had not been built with the production tooling that has been put in place subsequently.

Any one of the four areas could fail certification and thus delay the project. Any delay would require even more investment capital to bring the project to market.

### Questions

1. Eclipse has been described as 'the last great dream in aviation' … but does this imply a 'half full' or a 'half empty' perspective? Is it a good dream or a bad dream?
2. Use the Internet to determine what has happened with the venture.

   Eclipse Aviation http://www.eclipseaviation.com

### Source

Daniel C (2002) Eclipse flies in the face of criticism, *Financial Times*, 25 September.

## 8.4  Military strategy revisited

As a conclusion to this short chapter we return to the military metaphor and consider how strategy is planned by the armed forces. This provides a valuable link to Chapter 9 on Strategic Planning.

In today's world the armed forces prefer to win without ever firing a shot. This implies being able to scare the enemy with superior force. Pure strength and hold over a market (or niche) can similarly provide a barrier to entry and is clearly valuable to have. To retain such strength, nations invest and innovate in their defence capabilities; companies have to do the same. Sitting back as others change should never be an option. This links to the resource-based view as you are looking to identify, develop and sustain superior resources.

However, if it becomes necessary to 'engage the enemy', clear operational/tactical planning is essential. The planning is done to a particular level of detail and then handed over for implementation. However, 'no detailed plans ever survive engagement with the enemy' (paraphrasing von Moltke). Therefore, it is perhaps ideal if those carrying out orders clearly understand and subscribe to the broad purpose and appreciate what they are trying to achieve and stick with this – adjusting tactics as necessary to deliver the desired outcomes.

In this context, the military adopt a clear seven-stage approach to planning, based on asking and answering seven questions:

1. What are the enemy (*our competitors*) doing and why? The answer to this will broadly explain why you have a problem or an issue to deal with.

2. In response to this, what are we trying to achieve? What are our desired outcomes – at a broad level. Depending upon the level of management dealing with a problem or issue, this might be rephrased – 'What have we been told to do and try to accomplish?'

3. What specific outcomes are we trying to deliver? What impact do we want to have on our enemy *(rivals)*? Basically dealing with measures of performance and success. How will we know when we have achieved what we are hoping to achieve?

This is a 'bridge' level. These issues remain a given. Further, more detailed planning will take place, but these plans will be flexible and adjustable within this context.

4. Where and how should we act to fulfil these ambitions? Generally these will be based on a series of verbs – military examples might include *find* (the enemy); *deny* (something); *destroy* (either something the enemy has or some part of the infrastructure as a diversion); *block* (and thus prevent the enemy doing something); *protect* (something strategic or valuable); *defeat* (not destroy, thus setting back in some way) .

5. What resources are required for each of these actions and deliverables? Typically the view will always be that they are inadequate and more would be desirable.

6. When and where should the actions take place. This is clearly tactical and it implies sequencing and appreciating dependencies. It is (in part) about project planning. Contingencies are required for when setbacks or unexpected events occur. After all, the enemy is also working to something of a game plan, even if they might have inferior resources. Within the time available, as much conceptual planning as possible should take place, but clearly not every eventuality can be accounted for in advance.

7. What control measures need to be put in place?

The Military would see 1, 2 and 3 as Strategic Planning.
4 and 5 are Operational Planning.
6 and 7 are then Tactical Planning.
The seven stages are based on the premise that:

$$Capability + Intent = Credibility$$

In drawing up clear and strong plans there are three clear issues:

- The moral case for what you are doing – this affects people's will as it is, in effect, the quality of the case or cause
- The broad concept – people's ability to grasp the issues and significance. It often relies significantly upon communication from the top
- The physical aspects – having or acquiring the resources that are going to be required. Only if you have them can you plan how you are going to deploy them to achieve the outcomes.

## SUMMARY

This short chapter has explained the three main strands of strategy creation. Some strategies are intended; others are emergent in real time. Intended strategies can emanate from planning and also from ideas input by key decision-makers or influencers, typically an owner-manager or a visionary strategic leader. Emergent strategies happen when intended strategies are changed incrementally as they are implemented or when organizations respond to environmental opportunities and threats. We would expect to find at least some evidence of all of these modes in every organization – simply the relative significance of each one will vary.

As organizations grow and become more complex, then it is not unusual to find an increasing reliance on planning at the expense of the other modes. This is understandable as there is an increasing need for effective control mechanisms. However, the risk is that bureaucracy and stasis accompanies the reliance on planning, and this must not be allowed to happen.

The section on military strategy and planning highlights the value of preparation whilst retaining the ability to be flexible. There is, however, one typical difference worth mentioning. Military officers and planners will invest time and energy in planning possible campaigns and in establishing contingencies for how they might respond when the unexpected happens after they engage the enemy. Business leaders might well be expected to do the same. However, in the services, once a decision has been reached all personnel will be expected, if not required, to 'own' the strategies, set off to carry them out, passing them on to others without any question or criticism. Of course, they will have authority to change tactics if and when necessary. In business we would not expect to see this happen in quite the same way. It is not unusual to hope that strategies can be sold to others and that the people who must implement them will feel some ownership of them – but we would not expect to find that people don't question them if they remain sceptical. Later in the book, therefore, we will look in greater depth at the whole issue of strategic change.

These themes are now explored in detail in the next two chapters. Chapter 9 focuses on the role and contribution of planning in strategy; Chapter 10 looks at strategic leadership, entrepreneurship and intrapreneurship – picking up the visionary and emergent modes of strategy creation.

## QUESTIONS AND RESEARCH ASSIGNMENTS

1. What is the difference between planned strategy, visionary strategy and emergent strategy? Distinguish between adaptive and incremental change.

2. Thinking about any project or sporting event you have been involved with, how relevant are the introductory comments on professional football? What have you learned about strategy creation from your own experiences in either a business or other context?

## INTERNET AND LIBRARY PROJECTS

1. Use the Internet to look at all Stelios' businesses – other than easyJet – and consider where he might have made a visionary impact. What do you think are the main contributions planning might make to the business? How much have the strategies changed as Stelios has striven to make these various businesses profitable?

   **Stelios** http://www.helios.com

## Further reading

Mintzberg, H and Waters, JA (1985) Of strategies deliberate and emergent, *Strategic Management Journal*, 6.

Mintzberg, H (1987) Crafting strategy, *Harvard Business Review*, July–August.

Peters, T (1993) The transformation of positively everything, *Director*, March.

Stacey, R (1993) Strategy as order emerging from chaos, *Long Range Planning*, 26 (1).

Idenburg, PJ (1993) Four styles of strategy development, *Long Range Planning*, 26 (6).

Mintzberg, H (1999) Reflecting on the strategy process, *Sloan Management Review*, 40, Spring.

## References

Bailey, A and Johnson, G (1992) How strategies develop in organizations. In *The Challenge of Strategic Management* (eds G Johnson and D Faulkner), Kogan Page.

Hurst, DK (1995) *Crisis and Renewal – Meeting the Challenge of Organizational Change*, Harvard Business School Press.

Idenburg, PJ (1993) Four styles of strategy development, *Long Range Planning*, 26 (6).

Mintzberg, H (1973) Strategy making in three modes, *California Management Review*, 16 (2), Winter.

Mintzberg, H (1989) Presentation to the Strategic Planning Society, London, 2 February. Further details can be found in Mintzberg, H (1973).

Mintzberg, H and Waters, JA (1985) Of strategy deliberate and emergent, *Strategic Management Journal*, 6 (3).

# Strategic Planning

## Learning objectives

Having read to the end of this chapter you should be able to:

- distinguish between planning as a cerebral activity carried out by all managers and systematic strategic (or corporate) planning
- describe a number of approaches to corporate planning and, in relation to these, discuss who should be involved in planning
- explain the concept of the planning gap
- discuss what is involved in a contemporary approach to planning
- assess the contribution of a number of planning techniques
- discuss how corporate planning would be used in the public sector
- explain the idea of spheres of influence.

Planning the future – thinking about the most appropriate strategies, and changes in strategic direction – is essential for organizations, particularly those experiencing turbulent environments. Rigid systematic planning, based on techniques and formalized procedures is, however, no longer as fashionable as it was, nor is it the only way in which strategic change decisions are made. There are dangers if organizations become reliant upon professional planners and where the only outcome of planning is a plan. This may not allow for effective strategic thinking, and may not result in a clear direction for the future.

There are dangers, then, in thinking that all strategic changes can be planned systematically and procedurally. Whether it is the result of formal and systematic planning, or much more informal and ad hoc leadership and management – which, paradoxically, still implies an element of planning – an organization will have strategies and processes whereby these strategies are changed. The processes need to be understood, and in many cases improved. It is important to assess where and how the organization should change and develop in the light of market opportunities and competitive threats, but there are lessons to be learnt about their appropriateness to certain strategic opportunities. Managers should know clearly where the organization is, and where it might sensibly go, and start making appropriate changes. They should then monitor progress and be aware of changes in the environment; in this way they can be flexible and responsive. After all, all managers are strategy makers.

In this context, this chapter considers what is meant by the term planning, and what is involved in the systematic planning cycle approach to the management of strategic change. The contribution of a number of planning techniques will be evaluated, and possible pitfalls and human issues in planning will be pinpointed.

Readers may notice that a number of the references in this chapter are rather dated. There is a very good reason for this – whilst at one time strategic planning and strategic management were almost synonymous, this is no longer the case. Relatively little is being written on strategic planning that improves on earlier material. The earlier writings on the topic, however, remain important and valid. The points they make have not changed, although it is imperative that we place strategic planning within the wider context of strategy creation.

## Minicase 9.1 Federal Express  US  Int

Federal Express provides an excellent example of an organization (and an entrepreneur) that opened up an unrealized market opportunity and began a new industry. It has been claimed that the 'greatest business opportunities arise when you spot things your customer didn't have a clue they needed until you offered it to them.'

The idea behind FedEx is simple. It is to provide a speedy and reliable national and international 'overnight' courier service for letters and parcels based upon air cargo. FedEx rightly claim to have invented the concept of overnight delivery, creating a whole new market where previously there was none. The company had a peripheral but significant role in the film *Castaway*, which featured Tom Hanks as a FedEx manager who survived the crash of a FedEx airplane only to spend several years marooned on a desert island. He held on to one of the packages from the plane and finally succeeded in delivering it.

FedEx is, however, unusual in a number of ways. Before it could even begin, FedEx needed a nationwide (North American) distribution system with a fleet of planes and trucks – a huge investment in planning and resources.

The business was the idea of Fred Smith, whose father was also an entrepreneur who had founded and built a successful bus company. When Fred was a student at Yale in the 1960s he wrote a paper outlining his idea for a freight-only airline which delivered and collected parcels to and from a series of hubs. Traditionally parcels were shipped on scheduled passenger airlines as normal mail,

whilst Smith proposed flying at night when the skies were relatively quiet. His paper was graded as a C. After graduating, Smith served as a pilot in Vietnam before he bought a controlling interest in Arkansas Aviation Sales, a company which carried out modifications and overhauls. Determined to implement his idea for a courier service he invested a $10 million family inheritance and raised a further $72 million from various sources, based on a number of independent but positive feasibility studies.

FedEx took to the skies in 1973, offering a service in and out of 25 east coast cities with 14 jet aircraft. The demand was there, as he had forecast. Unfortunately the rise in the OPEC oil price made FedEx uneconomical almost as soon as it started. Two years of losses and family squabbles – Smith was accused of 'squandering the family fortune' – were followed by profits and Smith's belief, courage and persistence were rewarded.

FedEx is successful because it delivers on time and speedily, and because it has a sophisticated tracking system for when something does go astray. There are now over 600 FedEx aircraft flying one million miles every two days. The central hub remains in Memphis in the US, but the flights are international. Three million packages from 200 countries are handled every night. FedEx's courier vans cover another two million miles every day collecting and delivering these parcels. To ensure FedEx can maintain its service it flies empty aircraft every night, which track close to the pick-up airports and which are brought into service if they are needed.

**FedEx** vans cover two million miles every day

Its success has, of course, spawned competition. But with learning and emergence FedEx has stayed at the forefront of the industry it invented.

**Questions**

1. What role did planning play in the beginning of the FedEx story and how do you think it is utilized now?
2. Is it more or less significant than visionary ideas and emergent strategy?

*Federal Express* http://www.fedex.com

**FedEx central hub**

*The planning era, if one may call it that, occurred some time ago, and has been discredited as we have moved on to the greater belief in the development of common values in the organization, and are rediscovering again today the necessity to be close to the market.*

Sir John Harvey-Jones, Past Chairman, ICI, 1987

*Planning is one of the most complex and difficult intellectual activities in which man can engage. Not to do it well is not a sin; but to settle for doing it less than well is.*

Russell Ackoff, 1970

## 9.1   Strategic thinking and strategic planning

The opening case story on FedEx shows two key elements of strategy creation in action and working together – visionary ideas and planning. The planning focuses on the project management and the implementation of a visionary idea. Without sound planning the venture could not possibly have worked. But when we talk about 'strategic planning' this is not exactly what we mean. Planning can also be used to identify future strategies, although it is only one way of identifying future opportunities. This chapter looks at planning's contribution to strategy making.

Robinson (1986) argues that the role of the planner should be not to plan but to enable good managers to plan. It is not the task of the planner to state the objectives; rather he or she should elicit and clarify them. Planning should concentrate on understanding the future, which is uncertain and unpredictable, and helping managers to make decisions about strategic changes. Thus, the aim of planning should be to force people to think and examine, not to produce a rigid plan.

It is worth reinforcing here that the real value of planning is not the plan which emerges, and which might be produced as a summary document which is worth little more than the paper it is printed on! Rather, the value lies in the thinking that the act and process of planning forces people to do.

Undoubtedly, planning techniques, used carefully, can help to provide a valuable description and analysis of where the organization is 'now'. But for managing the future and its inherent uncertainties, vision and flexibility will also be essential, alongside a clear direction and purpose. New thinking is essential for reaching the new competitive high ground first.

Strategic planning systems, popular and dominant in the 1960s and 1970s, became less fashionable in the 1980s and 1990s, but they still have an important contribution to make. In most companies planning had not contributed to strategic thinking and, because strategic thinking is essential, a new role has had to be found for strategic planning.

Strategic planning became fashionable for two basic reasons. First, it provided a means for allocating resources and managing budgets in complex multiproduct organizations and, second, it helped to pull together the disparate activities and businesses in organizations. These needs remain.

The outcome for many organizations was formal planning systems, heavily reliant on financial data, and supported by thick planning manuals. This was the downside.

On the positive side, planning can encourage managers to think about the need and opportunities for change, and to communicate strategy to those who must implement it. This was particularly important in the 1960s and early 1970s when there was an abundance of investment opportunities and a dearth of capital and key priorities needed to be established. In complex multiactivity organizations, decisions have to be made concerning where to concentrate investment capital in relation to future earnings potential, and this has generated a number of portfolio analysis techniques, some of which are studied later in this chapter. Rather than use these techniques for gaining greater awareness and insight, for which they are well suited, managers sought to use them prescriptively to determine future plans.

Formal strategic planning had become unfashionable by the 1980s for a number of reasons:

- Planning was often carried out by planners, rather than the managers who would be affected by the resultant plans.

- As a result, the outcome of planning was often a plan which in reality had little impact on actual management decisions, and therefore was not implemented.

- The planning techniques used were criticized primarily because of the way in which they were used.

- The important elements of culture and total quality management were usually left out.

However, many industries continue to experience turbulent environments caused by such factors as slower economic growth, globalization and technological change, and consequently strategic thinking is extremely important. The following questions must be addressed:

- What is the future direction of competition?

- What are the future needs of customers?
- How are competitors likely to behave?
- How might competitive advantage be gained and sustained?

Organizations must ensure that these questions are constantly addressed rather than addressed occasionally as part of an annual cycle. Line managers who implement plans must be involved throughout the process. Every executive needs to understand how to think strategically. Rigorous frameworks and planning manuals are not necessary as long as the proper thinking takes place.

There should be a strategic plan for each business unit in a complex organization, i.e. clear competitive strategies built around an understanding of the nature of the industry in which the business competes, and sources of competitive advantage. Chosen strategies must have action plans for implementing them, including an assessment of the needs for finance and for staff training and development. This is generally less difficult than formulating a corporate strategy for the whole organization.

## 9.2 Planning and planning systems

### 9.2.1 What do we mean by planning?

All managers plan. They plan how they might achieve objectives. However, a clear distinction needs to be made between the cerebral activity of informal planning and formalized planning systems.

A visionary strategic leader, aware of strategic opportunities and convinced that they can be capitalized upon, may decide independently where the organization should go and how the strategies are to be implemented. Very little needs to be recorded formally. Conversations between managers may result in plans which again exist only in individual managers' heads or in the form of scribbled notes. Equally, time, money and other resources may be invested by the organization in the production of elaborate and formally documented plans.

In all cases planning is part of an ongoing continuous activity which addresses where the organization as a whole, or individual parts of it, should be going. At one level a plan may simply describe the activities and tasks that must be carried out in the next day or week in order to meet specific targets. At a much higher level the plan may seek to define the mission and objectives, and establish guidelines, strategies and policies that will enable the organization to adapt to, and to shape and exploit, its environment over a period of years. In both cases, if events turn out to be different from those which were forecast, the plans will need to be changed.

### 9.2.2 The value of strategic planning

When managers and organizations plan strategies they are seeking to:

- be clearer about the business(es) that the organization is in, and should be in
- increase awareness about strengths and weaknesses
- be able to recognize and capitalize on opportunities, and to defend against threats
- be more effective in the allocation and use of resources.

Irrespective of the quality or format of the actual plans, engaging in the planning process can be valuable. It helps individual managers to establish priorities and address problems; it can bring managers together so that they can share their problems and perspectives. Ideally, the result will be improved communication, co-ordination and commitment. Hence there can be real benefit from planning or thinking about the future. What form should the thinking and planning take? Should it be part of a formalized system making use of strategic planning techniques?

### 9.2.3 Corporate and functional plans

Corporate and strategic plans concern the number and variety of product markets and service markets in which the organization will compete, together with the development of the necessary resources (people, capacity, finance, research and so on) required to support the competitive strategies. Strategic plans, therefore, relate to the whole organization, cover several years and are generally not highly detailed. They are concerned with future needs and how to obtain and develop the desired businesses, products, services and resources. The actual timescale involved will be affected by the nature of the industry and the number of years ahead that investments must be planned if growth and change are to be brought about.

Functional plans are derived from corporate strategy and strategic plans, and they relate to the implementation of functional strategies. They cover specific areas of the business; there can be plans relating to product development, production control and cash budgeting, for example. Functional plans will usually have shorter time horizons than is the case for strategic plans, and invariably they will incorporate greater detail. However, they will be reviewed and updated, and they may very well become ongoing rolling plans. While strategic plans are used to direct the whole organization, functional plans are used for the short-term management of parts of the organization. It is easy to imagine how this would apply to Federal Express.

Competitive strategies and functional strategies and plans are essential if products and services are to be managed effectively, but they should be flexible and capable of being changed if managers responsible for their implementation feel it necessary.

Ohmae (1982) emphasizes that individual products must be seen as part of wider systems or product groups/business units, and that although short-term plans must be drawn up for the effective management of individual products, it is important to ensure that thinking about the future is done at the appropriate level. As an example, a particular brand or type of shampoo targeted at a specific market segment would constitute a product market. The company's range of shampoos should be produced and marketed in a co-ordinated way, and consequently they might constitute a strategic planning unit. The relevant strategic business unit might incorporate all of the company's cosmetics products and there should be a competitive strategy to ensure that the various products are co-ordinated and support each other. In terms of strategic thinking, Ohmae suggests that it is more important to consider listening devices as a whole than radios specifically, and that this type of thinking resulted in the Sony Walkman and similar products. In the same way, the Japanese realized a new opportunity for black and white television receivers in the form of small portable sets, when other manufacturers had switched all of their attention to the development of colour sets. If the level of thinking is appropriate, resources are likely to be allocated more effectively.

## 9.2.4 Alternative approaches to planning

Taylor and Hussey (1982) feature seven different approaches to planning which are detailed briefly below.

- *Informal planning* takes place in someone's head, and the decisions reached may not be written down in any extensive form. It is often practised by managers with real entrepreneurial flair, and it can be highly successful. It is less likely to be effective if used by managers who lack flair and creativity.

- *Extended budgeting* is rarely used as it is only feasible if the environment is stable and predictable. Extended budgeting is primarily financial planning based on the extrapolation of past trends.

- *Top-down planning* relates to decisions taken at the top of the organization and passed down to other managers for implementation. These managers will have had little or no input into the planning process. Major change decisions reached informally may be incorporated here, and then a great deal depends upon the strength and personality of the strategic leader in persuading other managers to accept the changes. At the other extreme, top-down plans may emanate from professional planners using planning techniques extensively and reporting directly to the strategic leader. These are the type of plans that may not be implemented.

- *Strategic analysis/policy options* again uses planning techniques, and involves the creation and analytical evaluation of alternative options. Where future possible scenarios are explored for their implications, and possible courses of action are tested for sensitivity, this form of planning can be valuable for strategic thinking. It is an appropriate use of planning techniques, but it is important to consider the potential impact on people.

- *Bottom-up planning* involves managers throughout the organization, and therefore ensures that people who will be involved in implementing plans are consulted. Specifically, functional and business unit managers are charged with evaluating the future potential for their areas of responsibility and are invited to make a case for future resources. All of the detail is analysed and the future allocation of resources is decided. In an extreme form thick planning manuals will be involved, and the process may be slow and rigid. Necessary changes may be inhibited if managerial freedom to act outside the plan is constrained. A formal system of this nature is likely to involve an annual planning cycle.

- *Behavioural approaches* can take several forms, but essentially the behavioural approach requires that managers spend time discussing the future opportunities and threats and areas in which the organization might develop. The idea is that if managers are encouraged to discuss their problems and objectives for the business freely, and if they are able to reach agreement concerning future priorities and developments, then they will be committed to implementing the changes. However, it is quite likely that not all of the conflicts concerning resource allocation and priorities will be resolved. Clearly, scenario planning can be very useful here.

- The term *strategic review* was coined to take the best features of the other six approaches and blend them together into a systematic and comprehensive planning system.

All of these approaches have individual advantages and disadvantages, and they are not mutually exclusive. The approach adopted will depend on the style and preferences of the strategic leader, who must:

■ clarify the mission and corporate objectives and establish the extent and nature of changes to the corporate perspective

■ approve competitive and functional strategies and plans for each part of the business, however they might be created, and

■ establish appropriate control mechanisms, which may or may not involve substantial decentralization.

It has been established that planning may be either informal or formal. Informal planning, as such, cannot be taught; but formal planning systems can. These are the subject of the next sections.

### 9.2.5 The planning gap

Such authors as Argenti (1980), Hussey (1976), Cohen and Cyert (1973) and Glueck and Jauch (1984) have developed a number of essentially similar models of systematic planning. All of these models use the concept of gap analysis, which is extremely useful for strategic thinking purposes and which is explained in Box 9.1.

The concept of the **planning gap** relates very closely to issues which were raised in Chapter 2 on objectives. It addresses the following questions:

■ Where do we want to go?
■ Where can we go realistically?

When considering where and how an organization might develop in the future, both the desired and realistic objectives are essential considerations. Desired objectives relate to where the strategic leader and other decision-makers would like to take the organization if it is possible to do so. Realistic objectives incorporate the influence of the various stakeholders in the business, and their expectations; the existence of suitable opportunities; and the availability of the necessary resources. The issue of the risk involved in the alternative courses of action that might be considered is crucial. The discussion of the planning gap in Box 9.1 draws attention to the increasing risk typically associated with certain strategic alternatives, in particular diversification, which is often implemented through acquisition. Failure rates with diversification are high, as will be discussed in Chapter 12. However, diversification may be the only feasible route to the achievement of high growth targets or the maintenance of present rates of growth in profits and sales revenues. The strategic leader, perhaps under significant pressure from City investors, shareholders and analysts who expect growth rates to be at least maintained, may be forced to pursue high-risk strategies.

Table 9.1 looks at how three organizations, specifically Virgin, Royal Bank of Scotland, and Sony, have pursued several different strategies over a period of years.

While undue risk should be avoided wherever possible, it is always important to accept a certain level of risk and set stretching targets for managers and businesses.

**Table 9.1** Applications of the simple growth vector

|  | *Virgin* | *Royal Bank of Scotland* | *Sony* |
|---|---|---|---|
| Market penetration | Publicity, self-publicity and exploitation of Virgin name, e.g. Branson's balloon challenges | Sponsorship of major sporting activities. Not closing branches when other banks were closing their branches | Sony as a brand |
| Market development | Before divesting the businesses: opening Virgin Megastores around the world and a music business in the US | Building the credit card business to No. 2 in the UK in partnership with multinationals such as Shell | The Sony Walkman and associated derivatives: existing products repackaged |
| Product development | Music retailing led to music production and publishing and later music videos | Building scale through UK bank acquisitions e.g. National Westminster | Tape recorders to videos; televisions; compact discs (some limited diversification involved) |
| Related diversification | Films, computer games | Insurance: Direct Line; US banking acquisitions | Computers, Sony Playstation (related technologies e.g PDAs) |
| Unrelated diversification | Virgin Atlantic Airways, Virgin Holidays, Virgin Cola, Virgin Financial Services | | CBS Records, Columbia Pictures (vertical integration that some would argue is related dirversification for Sony) |

## Box 9.1 The Planning Gap

The planning gap should be seen as an idea which can be adapted to suit particular circumstances, although gap analysis could be regarded as a planning technique.

An example of the planning gap is illustrated in Figure 9.1. The horizontal axis represents the planning time horizon, stretching forward from the present day; either sales volume or revenue, or profits, could be used on the vertical axis as a measure of anticipated performance. The lowest solid line on the graph indicates expected sales or profits if the organization continues with present corporate, competitive and functional strategies; it does not have to slope downwards. The top dashed line represents ideal objectives, which imply growth and which may or may not ultimately be realized. The difference between these two lines is the gap. The gap is the difference between the results that the organization can expect to achieve from present strategies contin-

ued forward and the results that the strategic leader would like to attain.

The example illustrated in Figure 9.1 shows the gap filled in by a series of alternative courses of strategic action ordered in an ascending hierarchy of risk. Risk is constituted by the extent to which future products and markets are related to existing ones; and this idea of increased risk and strategic alternatives is developed further in Figures 9.2 and 9.3.

The lowest risk alternative is to seek to manage present products and services more effectively, aiming to sell more of them and to reduce their costs in order to generate increased sales and profits. This is termed market penetration in the simple growth vector developed by H Igor Ansoff and illustrated in Figure 9.2. It can be extended to strategies of market and product development, which imply, respectively:

KEY CONCEPTS

**Figure 9.1** An example of the planning gap

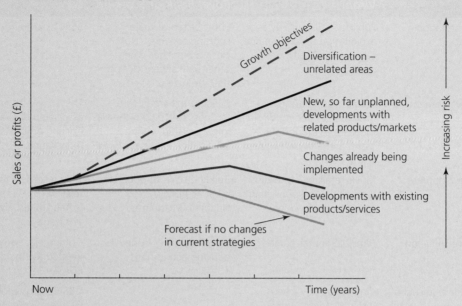

**Figure 9.2** Ansoff's growth vector

Ansoff, HI (1987) Corporate Strategy, revised edn, Penguin

|  | Product Present | New |
|---|---|---|
| **Market** | | |
| Present | Market penetration | Product development |
| New | Market development | Diversification |

■ new customers or even new market segments for existing products, which might be modified in some way to provide increased differentiation; and

■ new products, ideally using related technology and skills, for sale to existing markets.

(In this context 'new' implies new to the firm rather than something that is necessarily completely new and innovative, although it could well be this.) Figure 9.1 distinguishes between market and product development strategies that are already under way and those that have yet to be started.

The highest risk alternative is diversification because this involves both new products and new markets. Figure 9.3 develops these simple themes further and distinguishes between the following:

■ replacement products and product line extensions based on existing technologies and skills, which represent improved products for existing customers

■ new products based on new or unrelated technologies and skills, which constitute concentric diversification (these may be sold to either existing or new customers)

■ completely new and unrelated products for sale to new customers. This is known as

**Figure 9.3** An extended growth vector

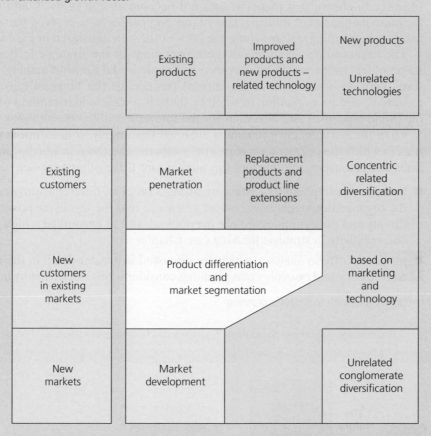

conglomerate diversification and is regarded as a high-risk strategic alternative.

## Using the planning gap

Thinking about the extent of the initial gap between present strategies and ideal objectives enables managers to consider how much change and how much risk would be involved in closing the gap and achieving the target objectives. Some of the strategies considered might be neither feasible nor desirable, and consequently the gap might be too wide to close. Similarly, the degree of risk, especially if a number of changes is involved,

might be greater than the strategic leader is willing to accept. In these cases it will be necessary to revise the desired objectives downwards so that they finally represent realistic targets which should be achieved by strategic changes that are acceptable and achievable.

This type of thinking is related to specific objectives concerning growth and profitability. It does not follow, as was discussed in Chapter 2, that either growth or profit maximization will be the major priority of the organization, or that the personal objectives of individual managers will not be an issue.

### 9.2.6 A contemporary approach to strategic planning

In order to ensure that planning does not become an end in itself, and that planners facilitate management thinking, many large companies have evolved personalized contemporary planning systems along the lines of the one illustrated in Figure 9.4.

The organization's culture and the expectations of the strategic leader and the key stakeholders influence the whole process of analysis and decision-making. The thinking starts with an assessment of the current position of the organization, its skills and resources, and an evaluation of whether there is a clear understanding of the mission, the broad objectives and directions for the future.

Then the business environment is analysed thoroughly, concentrating on the industries in which the organization currently competes and those in which it might apply its skills and resources. Feeding into this analysis are three other analyses:

■ broad scenario planning – conceptualizing a range of different futures with which the organization might have to deal, to ensure that the less likely possibilities, threats and opportunities are not overlooked, and to encourage a high level of flair and creativity in strategic thinking (see Chapter 4)

■ product portfolio analyses, which are discussed in greater detail in the next section; contingency and possible crisis planning considerations can be incorporated in this

**Figure 9.4** A contemporary approach to strategic planning

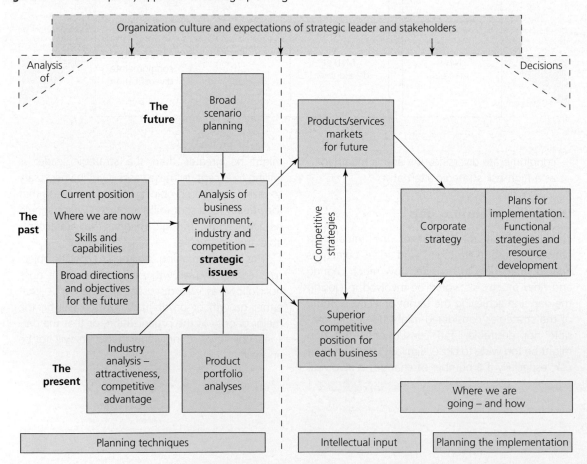

- industry analyses, following the Porter criteria for judging attractiveness and opportunities for competitive advantage (see Chapters 5 and 6).

This environmental analysis should focus on any *strategic issues* – current or forthcoming developments, inside or outside the organization, which will impact upon the ability of the organization to pursue its mission and meet its objectives. Ideally, these would be opportunities related to organizational strengths. Wherever possible any unwelcome, but significant, potential threats should be turned into competitive opportunities. The band across the bottom of Figure 9.4 shows how this contemporary approach blends planning techniques with an intellectual input and later action plans for implementing strategic choices.

It will be seen that the identification of strategic issues is the transition point from analysis to decisions regarding future strategy: it is where techniques give way to more intuition and intellectual inputs before implementation issues are explored.

From these analyses competitive strategy decisions must be reached concerning:

- the reinforcement or establishment of a superior competitive position, or competitive advantage, for each business within the existing portfolio of products and services
- product markets and service markets for future development, and the appropriate functional strategies for establishing a superior competitive position.

Amalgamated, these functional and competitive strategies constitute the corporate strategy for the future, which in turn needs to be broken down into resource development plans and any decisions relating to changes in the structure of the organization – i.e. decisions that reflect where the organization is going and how the inherent changes are to be managed.

Simply, planning techniques and analyses are used to clarify the key strategic issues. Discerning the issues and deciding what should be done to address them requires creativity (the search for something different) and hence a more intellectual input. Once broad strategic directions are clarified, detailed implementation planning will follow. Like the strategies, these detailed implementation plans should not be seen as inflexible.

It is important that new strategic issues are spotted and dealt with continuously, and the organization structure must enable this to happen, either by decentralization and empowerment or by effective communications.

Minicase 9.2 looks at the strategic issues facing high-street banks in the 1990s and how they have affected strategic developments.

The Channel Tunnel between England and France was named the greatest construction achievement of the twentieth century. Passenger and freight shuttles began operating in 1994; Eurostar passenger services began a short while later, but growth was constrained until the fast access route between London and Folkestone began opening (in stages) in 2003. Freight trains also use the tunnel. The tunnel operator, Eurotunnel, has made operating profits since 1997 but other charges have meant net losses. In 2003 Eurotunnel identified the following strategic issues:

- the expensive infrastructure was underutilized
- operator access charges were too high
- there were conflicts between the various stakeholders, many of them caused by the financial losses.

## Minicase 9.2 Strategic Issues and High-street Banking

During the 1990s, and following the worldwide economic recession and the ensuing bad debts, the UK high street clearing banks have changed their strategies as a response to a number of key challenges and issues.

### Strategic issues

■ They faced a need to switch from a position of high overheads with an extensive branch infrastructure and the associated high-risk lending (required to cover the overheads) to one where their (lower) cost base is in equilibrium with the type and volume of lower risk business that can be more readily justified.

■ Information technology, exploited effectively, offered opportunities for providing new and more efficient services without sacrificing either quality or reliability. In addition, the Internet was forecast to attract up to 10 million personal accounts by 2003.

Both of these issues implied restructuring and job losses, although there was always the possibility that once the banks had re-established strong controls and truly efficient systems they would reconsider taking higher risks again.

■ The entry of new competitors, particularly linked to Internet banking (Prudential's Egg) and savings accounts (the leading supermarkets).

■ A prediction that many personal customers would switch emphasis from borrowing to saving as the economy strengthened. The high-street banks were not perceived to be good for savers, offering relatively low rates of interest in comparison to the building societies and PEP-linked (subsequently ISA-linked) unit trusts.

■ A possibility that customers would be more willing to switch bank accounts than has generally been the case historically. The reasoning was that the Internet was making everything, including comparable interest rates, much more visible.

■ Changes in capital markets were taking away some of the bank's leading corporate customers.

### New strategies

■ High-street banks now typically offer a wider range of financial services, which they promote aggressively, often using their extensive databases for direct-mail campaigns.

■ Attempts by certain banks to charge customers from other banks who use their 'hole-in-the-wall' automated teller machines (ATMs) – this strategy provoked considerable controversy.

■ Efforts to reinforce brand names and strengthen reputations – difficult for some who faced customer resistance to branch closures.

■ Stronger credit controls for more effective loan management – implying both improved information and tracking and a reduction in the number of loans.

■ Computerized credit and loan assessments to link charges with risks more closely than in the past. This has changed the role of individual bank managers and, for some businesses, made borrowing more difficult. Many business managers now offer counselling and advice rather than negotiate and track loans.

■ A tighter focus on specific market segments, looking for positions of strength, rather than 'being involved in everything'. In particular, UK banks have reviewed their overseas exposure. The Royal Bank of Scotland is heavily involved in the US.

■ A search for more attractive savings products in an increasingly competitive environment.

■ New forms of service. Following the pioneering work of First Direct (a subsidiary of the old Midland, now owned by HSBC) other clearing banks have introduced telephone banking services. The merged Halifax and

Bank of Scotland Group now offer Intelligent Finance banking online. This would not have been possible without information technology.

- Mergers between banks, building societies and insurance companies to create a more comprehensive financial services corporation. The systematic amalgamation of Lloyds, TSB, Cheltenham & Gloucester and Scottish

Widows is an excellent example of this as is the Halifax merger with the Bank of Scotland.

**Question**

1. From your own experiences, what changes have you noticed in the service and the range of services offered by your bank?

Eurotunnel decided to reduce access charges to stimulate demand. There was a belief that demand was sufficiently price-elastic for this to improve profitability. Debts would have to be restructured – and not for the first time. There would be fresh investment in the Folkestone freight terminal to allow it to handle Continental gauge trains for the first time. And the terminal areas of Kent and the region around Calais would be promoted to stimulate tourism.

**Commentary** A systematic approach to corporate planning may well succeed in the essential task of co-ordinating the plans for all the divisions and businesses in a large organization, enabling the strategic leader to exercise control over a conglomerate – and this is good. However, the system should not prohibit vision and learning within the corporation, which is important as these are the two modes of strategy creation most likely to take the organization forward in a competitive and uncertain environment. Unfortunately, the vision and learning may be concentrated within individual divisions when ideally, it will permeate the whole organization.

Typically, strategic planning systems grew to be very formal. All ideas from the individual businesses had to be supported by comprehensive, documented analyses. Now it is frequently accepted that many proposals cannot be fully justified quantitatively; instead, the assumptions and justifications will be probed and challenged by divisional boards. Care must also be taken to ensure that the evaluation and resource allocation processes do not create too high a level of internal competition. Divisions and businesses should have to justify their intentions and proposals, and it is inevitable they will be competing for scarce resources. Nevertheless, the real enemy is external competitors, not other parts of the organization, and this must never be forgotten.

In addition, some organizations still tend to use the performance targets as the primary means of control, which sometimes results in short-term thinking. Once a business drops below its target it is put under considerable pressure to reduce costs, and this may restrict its ability to be creative and innovative. Many strategic planning systems could be improved if the head office corporate planners had more contact and involvement with the businesses; they sometimes tend to be remote and detached.

In summary, formalized planning systems may be imperfect, but a system of some form remains essential for control and co-ordination. Alone it cannot enable the company to deal with competitive uncertainties and pressures – vision and learning are essential, but planning must not be abandoned.

This section has considered the important role and contribution of strategic planning in large, and possibly diverse, organizations. The next section considers strategic planning in small businesses. Box 9.2 examines a number of relevant planning issues in local government.

**STRATEGY IN ACTION**

## Box 9.2 Strategy and Local Government

A typical UK local authority is likely to perceive the aim of the activities it carries out as the provision of more, and ideally better, services for the local community. These services fall into three broad categories: front line (housing, education and leisure), regulatory (environmental health, planning and building control), and promotional (economic development and tourism).

How does local government 'work' strategically? Strategic decisions at the top policy level demand an input from two groups of people: the elected councillors who exert a controlling influence, and the salaried managers. The councillors may be politically very experienced and, working on behalf of their constituents, they should be in a position to reflect local needs. The specialist expertise is more likely to come from the salaried staff, although there are some very well qualified and expert councillors. There are, therefore, two strategic leaders – the Leader of the Council and the Chief Executive – who ideally will be able to work together harmoniously and synergistically. On occasions there will be clear evidence of visionary leadership. Some leaders, either individually or in partnership, will transform the character and infrastructure of a town or city. At the other extreme, other leaders really do little more than manage budgets and carry through central government initiatives.

There is an obvious role for strategic planning as local authorities have to work within guidelines and budget restraints set by central government. They have to decide upon how, at least, to maintain local services, improve efficiencies and implement any central government requirements.

Councillors will form into policy-making groups, and the salaried employees will operate with some degree of delegated authority in discrete service areas. Each service will have policy guidelines, output targets and a budget. Normally they will be free to develop and adapt strategies as long as they operate within their budget and achieve their outputs.

Many councils will want to increase spending wherever possible, as more or better services are popular with the electorate. In simple terms, spending minus income (including grants from central government) equals the sum to be raised from householders and businesses, and generally more spending is likely to lead to higher local taxes. The freedom to increase these is constrained by central government. Borrowing is used primarily to fund new capital programmes and for managing the cash flow on a temporary basis. It is, for example, being suggested that in the future many more local councils will borrow money to build new roads or improve existing ones and repay the money with congestion charges on motorists, at least in part following the lead of London. Some councils establish partnerships with specific developers. An independent company might, for example, develop a new shopping centre in partnership with a local authority. Together they will put up or raise substantial sums of development capital which will be repaid later through rents and business rates.

It is very difficult to measure quantitatively the benefits that accrue from certain services, such as parks and gardens for public recreation. Information from the Audit Commission enables one authority to compare its costs and spending in total, and per head of the population, for individual services with those incurred by similar authorities in the UK. Where this is utilized it is basically a measure of efficiency, rather than an assessment of the overall effectiveness of the service provision, as shown in Chapter 7.

Until the 1980s it was usual for a local authority to carry out most of its activities in-house. External contractors were used for some building and engineering work, and in other instances where very specialized skills were required. However, the first Thatcher government required that councils put out to tender all major new build projects, together with significant projects in housing and highways maintenance. Later in the 1980s school catering, refuse collection, street cleaning and most white-collar services were also subject to compulsory competitive tendering (CCT). Where services were put out for tender an

▶

authority continued to determine the specific level of service to be provided, and then sought quotations for this provision. Tendering organizations neither suggested nor influenced the actual level of service. This power remained firmly with the local authority. As more and more services were compulsorily put out to tender, local authorities essentially became purchasers of services on behalf of the local community.

The Blair Labour government, elected in 1997, was determined to abolish CCT and replace it with 'Best Value'. CCT was abandoned in 2000. Best Value requires a local authority to review each of its services over five-year periods, assessing whether it should be provided in-house, via the voluntary sector or by private-sector contractors. There are four key themes:

■ challenge

■ consult (stakeholders)

■ compare (by benchmarking external and other local authority providers)

■ compete (with the best providers that can be identified).

In recent years the contribution of the voluntary sector in providing services that local (and national) government cannot or will not provide has grown – without this contribution many individuals and communities would be far worse off.

Local councils are constrained by both central government financial rules and by legislative requirements. Since the Blair Labour government came to power in 1997 it has tightened up on the rules that govern residential care homes for the elderly. Room sizes and facilities must meet certain minimum standards. As a result many have closed, although some have been rebuilt, making homes with fewer but better rooms. In some communities it is significant that it is the public sector homes, rather than those run by the private sector, that have closed down.

**Audit Commission UK** http://www.audit-commission.gov.uk

## 9.2.7 Strategic planning and small businesses

Many small companies stay focused and do not diversify or acquire another business. Their corporate perspective stays the same, but they still need to create some form of competitive advantage and develop and integrate functional plans. In this respect, small business planning is similar to that for an individual business inside a conglomerate. Unfortunately, many small owner–managers misguidedly believe that:

■ strategic planning is too expensive and only belongs in large organizations

■ formalized processes, requiring expert planners, are essential

■ the benefits are too long term and there are no immediate pay-offs.

As a result they adopt a more seat-of-the-pants reactive approach. Both vision and flexibility are important features of most successful small businesses, but these can be built on to provide greater strength and stability. Simply, and reinforcing points made earlier in the chapter, small companies can benefit in the same way as large ones from discerning the important *strategic issues* and from involving managers from the various functions in deciding how they might best be tackled.

Small companies should involve all relevant managers in discussions about priorities, opportunities, problems and preferences. They should look ahead and not just consider immediate problems and crises. Objective information and analyses (albeit limited in scope) are required to underpin the process, which must be actively and visibly supported by the owner–manager or strategic leader, who, in turn, must be willing to accept ideas from other managers. Adequate time must also be found, and sound financial systems should be in place to support the implementation of new strategies and plans.

It is, of course, important to remember that small companies which needed to raise finance from the banking system or elsewhere would have had to draw up a business plan to support their request. All too often these plans are then put in a drawer and largely forgotten rather than being used as a framework for budgeting and monitoring performance. Some small company managers never really develop a discipline of planning.

## 9.3 Strategic planning issues

### 9.3.1 Who should plan?

Among the various authors on corporate planning who have been referred to earlier in this chapter, there is a consensus of opinion that strategic planning should not be undertaken by the chief executive alone, planning specialists divorced from operating managers, marketing executives or finance departments. An individual or specialist department may be biased and fail to produce a balanced plan. Instead, it is important to involve, in some way, all managers who will be affected by the plan, and who will be charged with implementing it. However, all of these managers together cannot constitute an effective working team, and therefore a small team representing the whole organization should be constituted, and other managers consulted. This will require a schedule for the planning activities and a formalized system for carrying out the tasks. As discussed above, it is important that planning systems do not inhibit ongoing strategic thinking by managers throughout the organization. Threats must still be spotted early and potential opportunities must not be lost.

**Planning traps** Ringbakk (1971) and Steiner (1972) have documented several reasons why formal planning might fail and have discussed the potential traps to avoid. Among their conclusions are the following:

- Planning should not be left exclusively to planners who might see their job as being the production of a plan and who might also concentrate on procedures and detail at the expense of wide strategic thinking.

- Planning should be seen as a support activity in strategic decision-making and not a once-a-year ritual.

- There must be a commitment and an allocation of time from the strategic leader. Without this managers lower down the organization might not feel that planning matters within the firm.

- Planning is not likely to prove effective unless the broad directional objectives for the firm are agreed and communicated widely.

- Implementers must be involved, both in drawing up the plan (or essential information might be missed) and afterwards. The plan should be communicated throughout the organization, and efforts should be made to ensure that managers appreciate what is expected of them.

- Targets, once established, should be used as a measure of performance and variances should be analysed properly. However, there can be a danger in over-concentrating on targets and financial data at the expense of more creative strategic thinking.

- The organizational climate must be appropriate for the planning system adopted, and consequently structural and cultural issues have an important role to play.

- Inflexibility in drawing up and using the plan can be a trap. Inflexibility in drawing up the plan might be reflected in tunnel vision, a lack of flair and creativity, and in assuming that past trends can be extrapolated forwards.

- If planning is seen as an exercise rather than a support to strategy creation, it is quite possible that the plan will be ignored and not implemented.

## 9.3.2 The impact of planning on managers

Unless the above traps are avoided and the human aspects of planning are considered, the planning activity is unlikely to prove effective. Abell and Hammond (1979) and Mills (1985) highlight the following important people considerations:

- Ensure the support of senior executives.

- Ensure that every manager who is involved understands what is expected of them and that any required training in planning techniques is provided.

- Use specialist planners carefully.

- Keep planning simple, and ensure that techniques never become a doctrine.

- Particularly where detailed planning is involved, ensure that the time horizon is appropriate. It is harder to forecast and plan detail the further into the future one looks.

- Never plan for the sake of planning.

- Link managerial rewards and sanctions to any targets for achievement which are established.

- Allow managers of business units and functions some freedom to develop their own planning systems rather than impose rigid ones, especially if they produce the desired results.

In summary, planning activities can take a number of forms, and organizations should seek to develop systems that provide the results they want. Ideally, these should encapsulate both strategic thinking and the establishment of realistic objectives and expectations and the strategies to achieve them. Planning techniques can be used supportively, and their potential contribution is evaluated in the next section. Systematic corporate planning, though, should not be seen as the only way in which strategic changes are formulated.

## 9.3.3 The role of planning and planners

In the light of the comments above on strategy formulation, this section concludes by considering further the role of planning and planners. Planning and strategy creation are different in the sense that planners may or may not be strategists but strategists might be found anywhere in the organization. Mintzberg (1989) suggests that planning activities are likely to involve a series of different and very useful analyses, but it does not follow that these must be synthesized into a systematic planning system. Planners can make a valuable contribution to the organization and to strategic thinking by:

- programming strategies into finite detail to enable effective implementation (this will involve budgeting and ensuring that strategies are communicated properly, plus the establishment of monitoring and control processes)
- formalizing ongoing strategic awareness – carrying out SWOT analyses and establishing what strategic changes are emerging at any time
- using scenarios and planning techniques to stimulate and encourage thinking
- searching for new competitive opportunities and strategic alternatives, and scrutinizing and evaluating them.

In other words, all of the activities incorporated in the planning systems discussed earlier in the chapter are seen to be making an important contribution, but they need not be component parts of a systematic model. Rather, they are contributors towards strategic thinking, awareness and insight.

Johnson (1992) further points out that on occasions plans are documented in detail only because particular stakeholders, say institutional shareholders or bankers, expect to see them as justification for proposals. There is never any real intention that they should be implemented in full.

Figure 9.5 draws together a number of these themes and illustrates the various contributions that planning and planners can make. In conjunction with this, the next section considers the relative value and contribution of selected planning techniques.

*The key macro and micro variables of our business are so dynamic that poker becomes more predictable than planning and reactivity more profitable than rumination.*

Dr John White, ex-Managing Director, BBA, whose customers were involved in the motor vehicle industry

**Figure 9.5** The planning contribution. Systematic planning (in isolation) will not create a vision – but you can plan your own way towards a vision. Ideas generated through planning may well change the vision

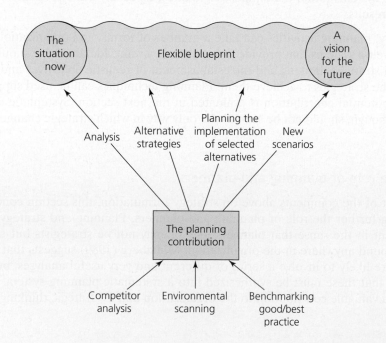

*I have a saying: 'Every plan is an opportunity lost' ... because I feel that if you try to plan the way your business will go, down to the last detail, you are no longer able to seize any opportunity that may arise unexpectedly.*

Debbie Moore, Founder Chairman, Pineapple (dance studios) Ltd

## 9.4 Strategic planning techniques

It has already been explained that different strategists and authors of strategy texts adopt different stances on the significance of vision, culture and strategic planning techniques in effective strategic planning. In this book the view is held that the role of the strategic leader, styles of corporate decision-making and organization culture are key driving forces in strategy creation and implementation. However, strategic planning techniques, which rely heavily on the collection and analysis of quantitative data, do have an important contribution to make. They help to increase awareness, and thereby reduce the risk involved in certain decisions. They can indicate the incidence of potential threats and limitations which might reduce the future value and contribution of individual products and services. They can help in establishing priorities in large complex multiproduct multinational organizations. They can provide appropriate frameworks for evaluating the relative importance of very different businesses in a portfolio.

However, their value is dependent on the validity and reliability of the information fed into them. Where comparisons with competitors are involved, the data for other companies may well involve 'guesstimation'.

Judgement is required for assessing the significance of events and competitor strategies; vision is essential in discontinuous change management.

In the author's opinion strategic planning techniques should be used to help and facilitate decision-makers. They should not be used to make decisions without any necessary qualifications to the data and assumptions.

**Portfolio analysis** The Boston Consulting Group growth-share matrix (Box 9.3) can be very useful for positioning products in relation to their stage in the product life cycle as long as one is both careful and honest in the use of data. It can provide insight into the likely cash needs and the potential for earnings generation. However, while a particular matrix position indicates potential needs and prospects, it should not be seen as prescriptive for future strategy. In certain respects, all competitive positions are unique, and it is very important to consider the actual industry involved and the nature and behaviour of competitors. Business unit and product managers are likely to be able to do this with greater insight than specialist planners as they are in a better position to appreciate the peculiarities of the market.

The product portfolio suggests the following strategies for products or business units falling into certain categories:

- cash cow – milk and redeploy the cash flow
- dog – liquidate or divest and redeploy the freed resources or proceeds
- star – strengthen competitive position in growth industry
- question – invest as appropriate to secure and improve competitive position.

## Box 9.3 The Boston Consulting Group (BCG) Growth-share Matrix

**Figure 9.6** The Boston Consulting Group growth-share matrix

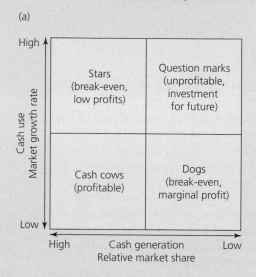

(a)

(b) An example of a balanced portfolio

### Basic premises

Bruce Henderson (1970) of BCG has suggested first that the margins earned by a product, and the cash generated by it, are a function of market share. The higher the market share, relative to competitors, the greater the earnings potential; high margins and market share are correlated. A second premise is that sales and revenue growth requires investment. Sales of a product will only increase if there is appropriate expenditure on advertising, distribution and development; and the rate of market growth determines the required investment. Third, high market share must be earned or bought, which requires additional investment. Finally, no business can grow indefinitely. As a result, products will at times not be profitable because the amount of money being spent to develop them exceeds their earnings potential; at other times, and particularly where the company has a high relative market share, earnings exceed expenditure and products are profitable.

Profitability is therefore affected by market growth, market share, and the stage in the product life cycle. A company with a number of products might expect to have some that are profitable and some that are not. In general, mature products,

where growth has slowed down and the required investment has decreased, are the most profitable, and the profits they earn should not be reinvested in them but used instead to finance growth products that offer future earnings potential.

### The matrix

The matrix is illustrated in Figure 9.6. Chart (a) shows the composition of the axes and the names given to products or business units which fall in each of the four quadrants; chart (b) features 15 products or business units in a hypothetical company portfolio. The sterling-volume size of each product or business is proportional to the areas of the circles, and the positioning of each one is determined by its market growth rate and relative market share.

The market growth rate on the vertical axis is the annual growth rate of the market in which the company competes, and really any range starting with zero could be used. The problem is where to draw the horizontal dividing line which separates high-growth from low-growth markets.

The relative market share on the horizontal axis indicates market share in relation to the largest competitor in the market. A relative market share of 0.25 would indicate a market share one-quarter of that of the market leader; a figure of 2.5 would represent a market leader with a market share that is 2.5 times as big as that of the nearest rival. The vertical dividing line is normally 1.0, so that market leadership is found to the left-hand side of the divider. It is important to consider market segmentation when deciding upon the market share figure to use, rather than using the share of the total market.

The growth-share matrix is thus divided into four cells or quadrants, each representing a particular type of business.

■ Question marks are products or businesses which compete in high-growth markets but where market share is relatively low. A new product launched into a high-growth market and with an existing market leader would normally constitute a question mark. High expenditure is required to develop and launch the product, and consequently it is unlikely to be profitable and may instead require subsidy from more profitable products. Once the product is established, further investment will be required if the company attempts to claim market leadership.

■ Successful question marks become stars, market leaders in growth markets. However, investment is still required to maintain the rate of growth and to defend the leadership position. Stars are marginally profitable only, but as they reach a more mature market position as growth slows down they will become increasingly profitable.

■ Cash cows are therefore mature products which are well-established market leaders. As market growth slows down there is less need for high investment, and hence they are the most profitable products in the portfolio. This is boosted by any economies of scale resulting from the position of market leadership. Cash cows are used to fund the businesses in the other three quadrants.

■ Dogs describe businesses that have low market shares in slower growth markets. They may well be previous cash cows, which still enjoy some loyal market support although they have been replaced as market leader by a newer rival. They should be marginally profitable, and should be withdrawn when they become loss makers, if not before. The opportunity cost of the resources that they tie up is an important issue in this decision.

**Boston Consulting Group** http://www.bcg.com

Given that a dog represents a product or service in a relatively low-growth industry sector, and one which does not enjoy market segment leadership, it follows that many companies will have a number of dogs in their portfolios. **Liquidation** or divestment will not always be justified. Products which have a strong market position, even though they are not the market leader, and which have a distinctive competitive advantage can have a healthy cash flow and profitability. Such products are sometimes referred to as cash dogs. Divestment is most appropriate when the market position is weak and when there is no real opportunity to create sustainable competitive advantage, as long as a buyer can be found. Turnaround strategies for products which are performing very poorly are examined further in Chapter 14.

According to Hamermesch (1986) many businesses that are classified as cash cows should be managed for innovation and growth, especially if the industry is dynamic or volatile, or can be made so. In other words, strategies that succeed in extending the product life cycle can move it from a state of maturity into further growth. One example quoted is coffee. This market experienced renewed growth when the success of automatic coffee makers increased demand for new varieties of fresh ground coffee. The success of Starbucks (Minicase 9.3) shows how a single organization which spots and seizes an opportunity can change an industry and provide an impetus for growth.

## Minicase 9.3 Starbucks

In under 15 years Starbucks grew from a single store on the Seattle waterfront to a chain of over 1600 stores across America, spawning competitors in the US and elsewhere. As part of its drive to expand internationally, Starbucks bought its smaller UK rival, The Seattle Coffee Company, in 1998. Starbucks succeeded because it found the right way to blend sales of top-grade fresh coffee beans with sales of cups of coffee to drink.

Coffee bars have existed for a very long time, but rarely have they featured the strong and distinctive aroma found in stores that sell fresh coffee. The individual drinks in Starbucks are relatively expensive, but they are individualized and made to order. There is a wide range of piping-hot and ice-cold variants to choose from. Although coffee to drink is very much the leading product, fresh coffee beans and a range of related products, such as cakes, biscuits, mugs and coffee makers are also on offer. Customers include shoppers and working people from local stores and offices at lunchtime and teatime on their way home – people who take time to relax and converse over their coffee, as well as people who pop out from work to their nearest outlet when they have a short break because the coffee is perceived to be superior to the instant that they might otherwise have to drink. Outlets can also be found at airport terminals and in those bookstores where people go to browse and relax. Essentially, Starbucks 'sells an emotional experience' and not just a commodity product. It thus adds value.

The success is down to Howard Schulz, the son of a blue-collar worker in Brooklyn. Schulz became a salesman, and when he was working for a houseware products company he visited Seattle and was introduced to the Starbucks Coffee Company, a business that sold imported coffee beans. He joined the business in 1982 with the title of Marketing Director. Enthused by espresso bars on a business trip to Italy, and convinced that a similar concept could be developed for the US, he attempted to sell the idea to his bosses. The family declined to go along with him and he left to start up on his own. He managed to raise enough money to open one outlet and within two years he was in a position to buy out Starbucks.

Schulz claims that his mission has always been to 'educate consumers everywhere about fine coffee'. Customers who visit Starbucks must feel relaxed and enjoy 'a sense of wonder and romance in the midst of their harried lives'. People will pay 'arguably outrageous prices' for their coffee as long as it is seen as an indulgence. If this is to be achieved, staff attitudes and behaviours are critical. Service, therefore, is everything. Schulz has created Starbucks as 'living proof that a company can lead with its heart and nurture its soul and still make money'.

Employees are seen as partners. Including part-timers, they all enjoy free health insurance, stock options (known as bean stock), training programmes and wages above the industry average. Although many are young and fit, students who will not stay long enough to earn stock options and who will not need health care, they still feel valued and consequently deliver the desired service. They matter. In addition, all unsold beans over eight days old are given away free to local food banks. Nevertheless, the company has also been criticized for exploiting cheap labour in coffee-growing countries.

### Questions

1. How would you summarize the opportunity that Starbucks has identified and exploited?
2. How has Starbucks developed and changed its business model as new competitors have entered the attractive market?

**Starbucks** http://www.starbucks.com

When 'milking' products care also has to be taken not to reduce capacity if there is a chance that demand and growth opportunities might return as a result of scarcities or changes in taste. When restrictions on the import of Scotch whisky into Japan were eased in the late 1980s, the product enjoyed star status, even though it was seen as a cash cow in the UK.

Strategic decisions based on portfolio positions may also ignore crucial issues of interdependence and synergy. Business units may be treated as separate independent businesses for the purposes of planning, and this can increase the likelihood of the more qualitative contributions to other business units, and to the organization as a whole, being overlooked when decisions are made about possible liquidation or divestment.

### 9.4.1 Directional policy matrices

The best-known directional policy matrices were developed in the 1970s by Shell and General Electric and the management consultants McKinsey. They are broadly similar and aim to assist large complex multiactivity enterprises with decisions concerning investment and divestment priorities. A version of the Shell matrix is illustrated in Figure 9.7; a fuller explanation can be found in Robinson *et al.* (1978).

In using such a matrix there is an assumption that resources are scarce, and that there never will be, or should be, enough financial and other resources for the implementation of all the project ideas and opportunities which can be conceived in a successful, creative and innovative organization. Choices will always have to be made about investment priorities. The development of an effective corporate strategy therefore involves an evaluation of the potential for existing businesses together with new possibilities in order to determine the priorities.

The matrix is constructed within two axes: the horizontal axis represents industry attractiveness, or the prospects for profitable operation in the sector concerned; the vertical axis indicates the company's existing competitive position in relation to other companies in the industry. New possibilities can be evaluated initially along the vertical axis by considering their likely prospects for establishing competitive advantage. It will be appreciated that Michael Porter's work links closely to this.

In placing individual products in the matrix the factors shown in Table 9.2 are typical of those that might be used.

**Table 9.2** Factors in the directional policy matrix

| | |
|---|---|
| Industry attractiveness | Market growth |
| | Market quality, or the ability for new products to achieve higher or more stable profitability than other sectors |
| | Supplier pressure |
| | Customer pressure |
| | Substitute products |
| | Government action |
| | Entry barriers |
| | Competitive pressure |
| Competitive position and relative strength | Competition |
| | Relative market shares |
| | Competitive postures and opportunities |
| | Production capability |
| | Research and development record and strengths |
| | Success rate to date, measured in terms of market share and financial success (earnings in excess of the cost of capital) |

**Figure 9.7** The directional policy matrix developed by Shell – two presentations

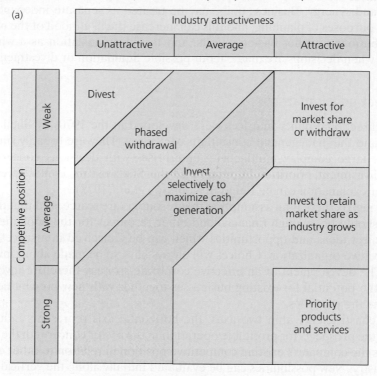

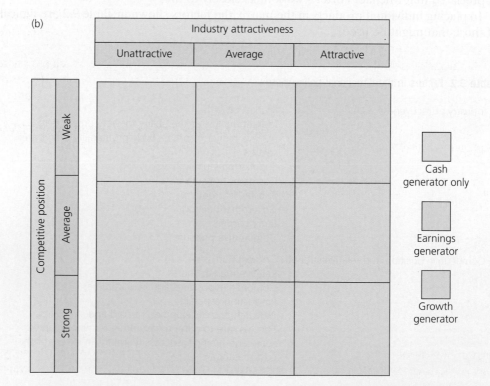

Each factor would be given a weighting relative to its perceived importance, and each product being evaluated would be given a score for every factor. The aggregate weighted scores for both axes determine the final position in the matrix.

**Using the matrix** Figure 9.7 (a) illustrates that the overall attractiveness of products diminishes as one moves diagonally from the bottom right-hand corner of the matrix to the top left. Priority products, in the bottom right-hand corner, are those which score highly on both axes. As a result they should receive priority for development, and the resources necessary for this should be allocated to them.

Products bordering on the priority box should receive the appropriate level of investment to ensure that at the very least market share is retained as the industry grows.

Products currently with a weak competitive position in an attractive industry are placed in the top right-hand corner of the matrix. They should be evaluated in respect of the potential to establish and sustain real competitive advantage. If the prospects seem good, then carefully targeted investment should be considered seriously. If the prospects are poor it is appropriate to withdraw from the market. A weak position in an attractive industry might be remedied by the acquisition of an appropriate competitor.

Products across the middle diagonal should receive custodial treatment. It is argued that a good proportion of products is likely to fall into this strategic category, which implies attempting to maximize cash generation with only a limited commitment of additional resources.

Currently profitable products with little future potential should be withdrawn gradually, but retained as long as they are profitable and while the resources committed to them cannot be allocated more effectively elsewhere.

Products for divestment are likely already to be losing money if all of their costs are properly assigned.

Figure 9.7 (b) provides an alternative presentation and flags that products should been seen as either cash generators at best, earnings generators or true growth generators, dependent upon their relative positioning.

The **directional policy matrix**, like other matrices, is only a technique which assists in determining the industry and product sectors that are most worthy of additional investment capital. Issues of synergy and overall strategic fit require further managerial judgement before final decisions are reached.

Minicase 9.4 (at the end of the chapter) shows how Unilever has utilized portfolio management to focus attention on selected brands with high growth potential.

## 9.4.2 SPACE (strategic position and action evaluation)

Rowe *et al.* (1989) have developed a model based on four important variables:

- the relative stability/turbulence of the environment
- industry attractiveness
- the extent of any competitive advantage
- the company's financial strengths – incorporating profitability, liquidity and current exposure to risk.

Scores are awarded for each factor, and then put into a diagram (see Box 9.4). This particular illustration features a financially strong company (or division or product) enjoying competitive advantage in an attractive industry with a relatively stable environment.

## Box 9.4 SPACE: Strategic Position and Action Evaluation

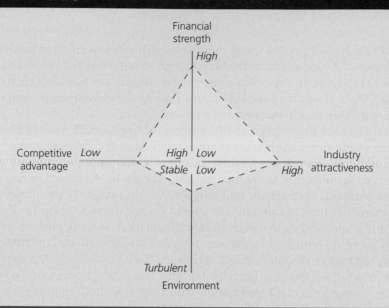

| Strategic thrust | Aggressive | Competitive | Conservative | Defensive |
|---|---|---|---|---|
| **Features:** | | | | |
| Environment | Stable | Unstable | Stable | Unstable |
| Industry | Attractive | Attractive | Unattractive | Unattractive |
| Competitiveness | Strong | Strong | Weak | Weak |
| Financial strength | High | Weak | High | Weak |
| **Appropriate strategies** | Growth, possibly by acquisition | Cost reduction, productivity improvement, raising more capital to follow opportunities and strengthen competitiveness | Cost reduction and product/service rationalization | Rationalization |
| | Capitalize on opportunities | | Invest in search for new products, services and competitive opportunities | Divestment as appropriate |
| | Innovate to sustain competitive advantage | | | |
| | | Possibly merge with a less competitive but cash-rich company | | |

Source: Rowe, AJ, Mason, RO, Dickel, KE and Snyder, NH (1989) *Strategic Management: A Methodological Approach*, 3rd edn, Addison-Wesley

The appropriate strategy is an aggressive one. The table shows the appropriate strategies for four clearly delineated positions, and judgement has to be applied when the situation is less clear cut.

This technique usefully incorporates finance, which will affect the feasibility of particular strategic alternatives and the ability of a company to implement them. It has similar limitations to directional policy matrices. Box 9.4 can be applied very effectively to the banking industry in the UK.

Scottish and Newcastle is a large UK brewing business which in 2003 sold its 1450 pubs in the UK to Spirit for £2.5 billion. It is following a strategy of concentrating on brewing rather than be diversified by owning the outlets for its products. It is also rationalizing the location of its brewing activities and going into partnerships with smaller scale real ale brewers such as the Caledonian Brewing company in Edinburgh, who brew the award-winning Deuchar's IPA. At the same time the CEO of S&N (Tony Frogatt) is pursuing a strategy of 'turning its back on acquisition activity and focusing on operational efficiencies, increased marketing investment and improved utilization of capital' (Source: Ian Shackleton, Credit Suisse First Boston.) It could be argued that S&N is pursuing all four of the strategic thrusts identified above.

## 9.5 Spheres of influence

According to D'Aventi (2001), **spheres of influence** relate to the building of an arsenal of products and services that enable and support real influence across a wide range of critical interests – they imply consideration of the so-called wider picture. Building this bigger picture implies planning linked to a vision. Although companies may focus on a core (or heartland) of activities, they must not neglect to build a portfolio of logically-related interests, even if some of them are clearly peripheral. The basic idea is to create or restore order in an industry in times of complexity and chaos. After all, more chaos and uncertainty equates to lower profits. It is about strategic logic and it mimics how nations have behaved historically. Under traditional portfolio theory, investment decisions do not require a consideration of the strategic logic for supporting a business, even though it could be relatively low profit, whereas spheres of influence looks at why organizations might choose to be in particular businesses.

The desired outcomes are:

- Competitors are manoeuvered into corners
- Rivals are encouraged to focus on areas which do not conflict with your interests directly
- There is less destructive price competition lowering profits
- There are fewer opportunities for new, rule-changing competitors to enter an industry.

There are five key planning elements:

1. *Core geographic and product markets.* The centre of the sphere of influence and where a company is seeking domination.
2. *Vital interests.* Geographic or product zones which are critical for protecting the core. These activities would include complementary products, key supplies and providers of valuable resources such as know-how or employee skills. Sometimes, but not always, they exploit competencies and capabilities associated with the core.
3. *Pivotal zones.* Markets that could, in the long term, tip the balance of power or control away from a company in favour of a rival, were it/they to be freely dominated by a competitor. A position is needed more for defensive purposes than dominance.
4. *Buffer zones.* Positions in expendable, non-committed, markets simply to constrain competitor activities. They are an important bargaining weapon – as are

5. *Forward positions.* Front-line products located close to the core activities of key rivals. These can be used for purposes of attack, but they are mostly defensive. They cause competitors to think carefully about attacking any company which has them in place – there is a fear of a possible response.

We can apply these five elements to Microsoft as follows.

- *Core* – desktop operating systems; graphical user interfaces; Internet browsers.
- *Vital interests* – where it seeks to be a winner – operating systems for networks and for portable devices.
- *Pivotal zones* – e-portals and e-commerce businesses.
- *Buffer zones* – computer games and the X-Box, because rivals might use their dominance of this sector to develop operating systems.
- *Forward positions* – initially bundling Explorer with Windows was a forward position, partly synergistic, partly competitive, to deter Netscape – but it became core.

It is interesting that much of Microsoft's history – and phenomenal success – is characterized by 'catch-up' strategies where it has been quick to capitalize on rival initiatives, but then overtake them with alternative products and services. The Windows computer operating system lagged behind – but grew to dominate – Apple's MacIntosh, which at one time was market leader. Whilst it remains the system of choice for some, especially designers, MacIntosh now has only a fraction of the market share of Windows. Word similarly grew to dominate and displace WordPerfect. Its commercial database SQL was developed to take on Oracle; Windows (Internet) Explorer eventually sidelined Netscape's Navigator although some believe there was an element of 'foul play' in the way Explorer was bundled with other Microsoft products. The Pocket PC was launched as a rival to the Palm hand-held organiser, and its Internet portal MSN was a follower of AOL. X-Box, of course, is designed to rival the Sony PlayStation, but in this case Microsoft continues to lag well behind the market leader.

**Other examples** Wal-Mart focuses on establishing and sustaining dominance of key product markets and territories around the world by, in part, establishing and nurturing relationships with key suppliers, which it then exploits through its huge buying power to force its rivals into niches that are either unoccupied or in which Wal-Mart is not particularly interested. This, of course, is a very typical retail strategy.

Disney retains a presence in children's book publishing and in branded retail stores to give it countervailing bargaining power against potential rivals should it ever need to use it.

Johnson & Johnson (J&J) is perhaps describable as 'The Baby Company' and Procter and Gamble (P&G) 'The Soaps and Shampoo Business'. These two businesses have activities and interests which overlap, but they avoid destructive rivalry. J&J opts not to compete directly with P&G's diaper business and its powerful Pampers brand, a massive baby product; and, similarly, P&G focuses on adult soaps and shampoos and does not address the children's market. Why? Because J&J owns the Neutrogena brand of mild adult soaps and shampoos, which are tightly niched and not mainstream – but they provide the company with competencies and capabilities which it could use to expand if it wished. Equally P&G has the competencies and capabilities to produce children's soaps and shampoos. Competition from powerful rivals in core areas could destroy position and power; there would be no winner as any victory would be pyrrhic. Simply, potential threats are keeping rivals at bay.

## Minicase 9.4 Unilever  GB  Eur

Unilever is an Anglo-Dutch multinational corporation with manufacturing activities and markets all round the world. In 1999 50 per cent of Unilever's turnover came from food products, 23 per cent from personal care products and the remaining 27 per cent from home care products and dry cleaning services. In 1999 the portfolio was restructured into 13 categories, with different priorities, and these are listed later. The main brands at the time included:

- *Food products* – Wall's ice cream, sausages, etc.; Bird's Eye frozen foods; Stork, Flora and other margarines and spreads; Brooke Bond (PG Tips) and Lipton teas
- *Personal care* – Timotei and Sunsilk shampoos
  Sure deodorants
  Signal and SR toothpastes
  Elizabeth Arden, Brut, Karl Lagerfeld, Fabergé and Calvin Klein fragrances
- *Home care* – Persil, Lux, Fairy and Dove branded products.

Many of the products are subject to constant innovation. Persil washing powder, for example, lost its market leadership position to Procter and Gamble's Ariel brand in the 1980s and Unilever was determined to fight back. Liquids and concentrates had already taken market share from traditional powders when Unilever launched its new Persil Power in 1994 (branded Omo Power in continental Europe). This new powder product was claimed to wash clothes cleaner than rival brands, which it did. Unfortunately, the special cleaning agent was particles of manganese, and Unilever misjudged the amount. Procter and Gamble were able to demonstrate that some clothes were damaged after multiple washes, and finally the product was abandoned. Other Persil products, specifically for colour and fine wool and silk garments, followed before Unilever pioneered its new – and this time very successful – Persil tablets.

In 1998 Unilever had charged 20 of its younger managers (their average age was 32) to spend six months on a special project designed to identify new opportunities:

- One outcome was a new way of thinking about products and brands. Unilever, they concluded, was in 'the business of selling dreams of healthy eating, clean living and fragrant sex appeal'. People no longer really want soap powder, instead they want clean clothes, ideally without the hassle of using a washing machine! Unilever's future might well be in services rather than products.

- It was decided that Unilever should be seen as a brand marketing group that makes some of its products, as distinct from a manufacturing organization. Did this imply a new business model?

- The divestment of non-core products was completed. Over a period of years, Unilever has divested plantations, shipping lines and speciality chemical companies.

- The number of global manufacturing sites was reduced from 400 to fewer than 300. Of these 150 were designated key sites; the rest are ancillary. Most divestment was in food processing.

- At the same time, the number of suppliers was reduced to provide a more streamlined supply chain.

- The number of global brands was to be reduced from 1600. The top 400 (which, in classic Pareto style, contribute 90 per cent of annual turnover) would receive serious investment to generate a targeted annual growth rate of 6 per cent (although this would later be reduced for particular years) and higher profit margins. Of the remaining 1200, some would be dropped altogether, some harvested and abandoned when they are no longer profitable, and others marketed without promotion of any consequence. This strategy was known as 'The Path to Growth'.

The 13 new product groups were classified as offering either superior growth (number 1 in the table below), steady growth (number 2) or selective growth only (number 3).

| Activity | Product category | Growth prospects |
|---|---|---|
| Food | Tea | 1 |
| | Culinary products | 1 |
| | Ice cream | 1 |
| | Spreads and cooking products | 2 |
| | Frozen foods | 3 |
| Personal care | Hair care products | 1 |
| | Skin care products | 1 |
| | Deodorants | 1 |
| | Toothpaste and oral products | 2 |
| | Fragrances | 3 |
| Home care | Laundry products (soap powders, etc.) | 2 |
| | Household care products | 2 |
| | Professional cleaning | 3 |

In 2000 Unilever announced that it would split its businesses into two separate companies: foods and home products. Unilever then started a new round of acquisitions and divestments. First it acquired Slimfast Foods, and followed this with Ben and Jerry's premium ice-cream business (featured in Minicase 2.1). Later it agreed to buy the American Bestfoods, which constituted the biggest global acquisition in the food industry for 12 years. With an annual turnover of $8 billion, Bestfoods was approximately one-fifth the size of Unilever. Bestfoods provided a number of important brands to complement Unilever's portfolio: Knorr soups, Hellmann's mayonnaise, Mazola oils and Bovril stock cubes and concentrate. To ensure that the acquisition was not blocked by the European competition authorities, Unilever agreed to seek a buyer for its Batchelor's and Oxo branded products. With these acquisitions Unilever became the world's second largest food business, second only to Nestlé. At the same time as acquiring new food brands, Unilever divested its main bakery business for £440 million. As Bestfoods also owns

bakeries (producing, for example, Entemann's cakes) it was assumed these might later be sold as well. It also sold the Elizabeth Arden cosmetics business. Unilever was now far more exposed to the food industry than in the past; it had to exploit the brands it owned.

In 2001 professional cleaning services were divested. Unilever had experimented with MyHome domestic cleaning services (using its own branded products of course) but was unhappy with the outcomes. Mazola cooking oils also went. The remaining perfume brands were offered for sale in 2002, but there were no immediate takers. Ambrosia (creamed rice) was sold in 2003.

At the same time certain brands were being deliberately extended. The Dove name belonged to a mild cleansing bar launched in the 1950s – it was now extended to shampoos, conditioners and a deodorant. Ice cream was also an investment priority. Unilever was already the leading company in this industry around the globe, with a 17 per cent share. Its main brands were Magnum and Cornetto as well as the ubiquitous Wall's – plus Ben and Jerry's premium ice cream. There were to be 1000 new ice cream cabins on popular beaches around the world, and new Ben and Jerry's parlours would be built. Advertising would be stepped up and a clothing range (featuring the Wall's heart-shaped logo) launched.

In 2003 ice cream did well – but Knorr hot foods suffered – with the record hot temperatures across Europe. With a cooler and wetter summer in 2004, ice cream did much less well. Frozen foods and fragrances were also disappointing in 2003 – both of course were relatively low priority groups. One problem with frozen foods is that customers now perceive chilled foods to be fresher and healthier and Unilever has recognized it must act to try and redeem their image. But the worst fall was suffered by the recently acquired Slimfast products, where sales fell by 30 per cent. The problem – the popularity of the Atkins diet which recommends a low intake of carbohydrates but regular consumption of meat and protein. The general view was that Unilever had failed to generate the returns it had hoped for from the Bestfoods brands it had acquired.

In summary: Unilever certainly seemed able to slim down its portfolio of brands, shed staff and shut factories, but its ability to increase sales to the targets it originally set was more questionable. The recorded growth rates for sales of its leading brands was as follows:

| Year | Percentage |
|------|------------|
| 1999 | 3.8 |
| 2000 | 3.8 |
| 2001 | 5.3 |
| 2002 | 5.4 |
| 2003 | 3.0 |

The target for 2004 was 2.5 per cent but half way through the year this was looking very optimistic. Unilever was coming up to the end of five years of its 'Path to Growth'. It seems significant that further restructuring was being planned in an attempt to simplify management structures. The new intention was one operating company (embracing all brands) in each country.

## Questions

1. In the light of its new product prioritization, do the acquisitions of Ben and Jerry's and Bestfoods make strategic sense?
2. Can you identify any problems or risks in Unilever's strategy of focusing on just 400 of its previous 1600 brands?
3. Do you agree with the decision to split the business into two?

**Unilever** http://www.unilever.com

# SUMMARY

Planning techniques, then, can be extremely useful, particularly as they force managers and organizations to ask themselves many relevant and searching questions and compile and analyse important information. But the techniques do not, and cannot, provide answers: they merely generate the questions. The danger is that some managers may perceive the output of a technique such as matrix analysis as an answer to strategic issues.

*Strategic planning* – using techniques and formalized procedures – is just one of the ways in which strategies are created. Strategies can also be provided by the strategic leader and be decided by managers in real time. Intended strategies, say those selected by the leader or a formal planning system, have to be implemented, and during this implementation they may well be changed incrementally. After all, intended strategies imply forecasting, and, to some extent, all forecasts are wrong. In addition, flexible organizations will adapt all the time by responding to new opportunities and threats.

In the 1960s and 1970s the predominant view with academics and organizations was that formalized strategic planning was at the heart of strategy creation, and should be used to manage future direction. It became clear, however, that a planning approach that relies on quantitative data, forecasts and manuals, can restrict creativity, thinking, flexibility and, critically, the support and engagement of the managers who must implement strategy. Many organizations fell into the trap of believing the key outcome of planning is the plan!

Nevertheless, it is important to realize that all managers plan, all the time. Evaluating the current situation, and discussing possible changes and improvements with colleagues, implies planning. Simply, this is informal planning rather than the formalized systems implied by the term strategic planning.

There are at least seven approaches to planning, which should not necessarily be seen as mutually exclusive. Formal planning is separate from informal planning. The process can be largely top-down or bottom-up. It can take the form of extended budgeting and be numbers driven, or be more behavioural in approach, possibly using scenarios.

The '*planning gap*' is a very flexible concept and technique which can be used in a variety of ways. Broadly, it is used to clarify the extent of the revenue or profits gap that might emerge if current strategies are left largely unchanged. The more ambitious the objectives set by the company, the greater the risk that is likely to be involved in the strategies required to close the gap.

Our contemporary approach to strategic planning is based on a mixture of planning techniques, intellectual input and action plans for implementing strategies; and central to the whole process are current strategic issues.

With any form of strategic planning it is important to decide upon who should be involved and what they should contribute. Professional or specialist planners have an important role to play, but others must be involved as well. Where there is an over-reliance on planners, or where there is inadequate flexibility with the plan itself, the organization is likely to fall into one of the obvious planning traps.

Planning has a number of important contributions to make and individual organizations will not all adopt the same approach.

There is a number of useful planning techniques, specifically:

- The Boston Consulting Group (BCG) 2 × 2 matrix
- Directional policy matrices
- SPACE

In various ways all of these techniques can be valuable. They will always be dangerous if they are used too rigidly and allowed to drive decisions without reference to, or qualification by, managerial judgement.

The thinking behind spheres of influence concerns the big picture, and contends that companies should look to develop a portfolio of products that strengthen its all-round ability to compete by opening up competitive fronts both proactively and reactively.

## QUESTIONS AND RESEARCH ASSIGNMENTS

1. Mintzberg has distinguished between 'grass-roots' strategies (which can take root anywhere in the organization but eventually proliferate once they become more widely adopted) and 'hothouse' strategies which are deliberately grown and cultured. What do you think he means?

2. Who should plan? What should they plan, how and when?

3. A manufacturer of industrial products is structured around five separate strategic business units (SBUs).

| SBU | Sales (£ million) | Number of competitors | Sales of top three companies (£ million) | Market growth rate (%) |
|-----|------|------|------|------|
| A | 0.4 | 6 | 0.8, 0.7, 0.4 | 16 |
| B | 1.8 | 20 | 1.8, 1.8, 1.2 | 18 |
| C | 1.7 | 16 | 1.7, 1.3, 0.9 | 8 |
| D | 3.5 | 3 | 3.5, 1.0, 0.8 | 5 |
| E | 0.6 | 8 | 2.8, 2.0, 1.5 | 2 |

Use the data below to construct a Boston matrix and assess how balanced the portfolio seems. Where are the strengths? Where are the weaknesses?

4. In the context of the Boston matrix, is the Big Mac a cash cow? What do you feel McDonald's competitive strategy for the Big Mac should be?

## INTERNET AND LIBRARY PROJECTS

1. For an organization of your choice, ideally one with which you are familiar:
   (a) Ascertain how the planning, entrepreneurial and emergent modes might apply currently to strategic change in the organization. Which mode is predominant? Why do you think it is the preferred mode? How successful is it?
   (b) What would be the opportunities and concerns from greater utilization of the other modes?
   (c) As far as you are able, draw up a directional policy matrix for the products and services of the organization. (Use your own judgement in assigning weights to the various factors for assessing industry attractiveness and competitive position.)

2. Compare and contrast the fortunes of Abbey National with the Royal Bank of Scotland. Just how strong is RBS and how balanced is the portfolio? What could go wrong?
   **Royal Bank of Scotland** http://www.rbs.co.uk
   **Abbey National** http://www.abbey.com

3. In 1975 the Boston Consulting Group wrote a report for the British government concerning the penetration of Honda motorcycles in the USA. They concluded that the success was the result of meticulous staff work and planning.
   Pascale (1984) disagrees and argues that the success was entirely due to learning and persistence, and that it was Honda's learning experience concerning operating in the USA that eventually led to a more rationally planned approach.
   Both arguments are documented in Pascale, R (1984) Perspectives on strategy – the real story behind Honda's success, *California Management Review*, 26 (3). Read this article and assess the points that Pascale makes.
   **Boston Consulting Group** http://www.bcg.com
   **Honda** http://www.honda.com
   **California Management Review**
   http://www.haas.berkeley.edu/news/cmr/

4. Case 9.4 mentions that Unilever launched Persil Power in the early 1990s but had to withdraw it when it was shown to damage clothes that were washed repeatedly. Did the company make serious errors of judgement, or was it out-manoeuvred by the aggressive response of its leading rival in this industry, Procter and Gamble?
   **Unilever** http://www.unilever.com

5. Overall, has the Channel Tunnel been a success or a failure? Can you identify additional strategic issues to those listed in the text? What alternative strategies might be considered to improve the fortunes of Eurotunnel?
   **Eurotunnel** http://www.eurotunnel.com

## Further reading

Ringbakk, KA (1971) Why planning fails, *European Business*, Spring.

Hedley, B (1977) Strategy and the 'business portfolio', *Long Range Planning*, 10.

Abell, D (1978) Strategic windows, *Journal of Marketing*, 42, July.

Haspeslagh, P (1982) Portfolio planning – uses and limits, *Harvard Business Review*, January–February.

Bryson, JM (1988) A strategic planning process for public and non-profit organizations, *Long Range Planning*, 21 (1).

Hamel, G and Prahalad, CK (1989) Strategic intent, *Harvard Business Review*, May–June.

Sahlman, WA (1997) How to write a great business plan, *Harvard Business Review*, July–August.

Williamson, PJ (1999) Strategy as options on the future, *Sloan Management Review*, 40, Spring.

## References

Abell, DF and Hammond, JS (1979) *Strategic Market Planning*, Prentice-Hall.

Ackoff, RL (1970) *A Concept of Corporate Planning*, John Wiley.

Ansoff, HI (1987) *Corporate Strategy*, revised edn, Penguin.

Argenti, J (1980) *Practical Corporate Planning*, George Allen & Unwin.

Buzzell, RD and Gale, BT (1987) *The PIMS Principles – Linking Strategy to Performance*, Free Press.

Cohen, KJ and Cyert, RM (1973) Strategy formulation, implementation and monitoring, *Journal of Business*, 46 (3), 349–67.

D'Aventi R A (2001) *Strategic Supremacy – How industry leaders create growth, wealth and power through spheres of influence*, The Free Press.

Glueck, WF and Jauch, LR (1984) *Business Policy and Strategic Management*, 4th edn, McGraw-Hill.

Hamermesch, R (1986) Making planning strategic, *Harvard Business Review*, July–August.

Henderson, B (1970) *The Product Portfolio*, Boston Consulting Group.

Hussey, D (1976) *Corporate Planning – Theory and Practice*, Pergamon.

Johnson, G (1992) Strategic direction and strategic decisions, presented at 'Managing Strategically: Gateways and Barriers', Strategic Planning Society Conference, 12 February.

Mills, DQ (1985) Planning with people in mind, *Harvard Business Review*, July–August.

Mintzberg, H (1989) Presentation to the Strategic Planning Society, London, 2 February. Further details can be found in Mintzberg, H (1973).

Ohmae, K (1982) *The Mind of the Strategist*, McGraw-Hill.

Ringbakk, KA (1971) Why planning fails, *European Business*, Spring.

Robinson, J (1986) Paradoxes in planning, *Long Range Planning*, 19 (6).

Robinson, SJQ, Hitchens, RE and Wade, DP (1978) The directional policy matrix – tool for strategic planning, *Long Range Planning*, 21, June.

Rowe, AJ, Mason, RO, Dickel, KE and Snyder, NH (1989) *Strategic Management: A Methodological Approach*, 3rd edn, Addison-Wesley.

Steiner, G (1972) *Pitfalls in Long Range Planning*, Planning Executives Institute.

Taylor, B and Hussey DE (1982) *The Realities of Planning*, Pergamon.

# Strategic Leadership, Entrepreneurship and Intrapreneurship

## Learning objectives

Having read to the end of this chapter you should be able to:

- define the term strategic leadership
- explain how a strategic leader is responsible for the meta-strategy which embraces creation and implementation
- identify factors which contribute towards effective strategic leadership
- differentiate between a number of different leader styles
- discuss a number of critical leadership issues such as finite shelf-lives and succession
- explain visionary leadership, entrepreneurship and intrapreneurship
- describe the conditions for making an organization intrapreneurial.

Strategic leaders 'come in all shapes and sizes'. They have to be able to think, make things happen, engage the support of other people and, on occasions, be the public face of the organization. It is optimistic to believe that all strategic leaders will be good at all four of these tasks. Some, such as Sir Richard Branson and Sir John Harvey-Jones in the past, are very visible and have an influence which extends well beyond the organizations that they run. Others are far more anonymous as far as the public are concerned but are excellent leaders of their organizations. There is no 'right' style or personality but there are certain roles that must be fulfilled effectively, regardless of the type or size of organization. The strategic leader has an overall responsibility for clarifying direction, for deciding upon strategies by dictating or influencing the relative significance of the modes of strategy creation discussed in this part of the book, and for ensuring that strategies are implemented through the decisions that he or she makes on structure, style and systems.

Some leaders are entrepreneurial and visionary, but this is not a requirement. In turn these visionary leaders may be very effective entrepreneurs but they may not be the people to manage the business at a particular point in time. This requirement to try and balance the leadership needs of a business with the need for effective management is at the heart of the success or failure of any business.

As well as leading from the front it is also important for a leader to create a climate that facilitates emergent change – appropriate employees should be empowered, encouraged and energized. Intrapreneurs then lead the emergent change initiatives. Leadership is both a job and a process – a process concerned with influence and change. It requires both personal characteristics and leadership skills. The skills can be learned, but effective leaders need to possess certain characteristics in the first place. Successful leaders also tend to build effective teams to support them. Before reading on, readers might wish to revisit Chapter 5 and re-read the sections on empowerment and learning organizations.

In exploring these issues, this chapter also looks at how some leaders are perceived to fail and fall from grace, and at the vital issue of leadership succession.

## Minicase 10.1  Sam Walton and Wal-Mart                    US

Sam Walton was a truly great retailer. His Wal-Mart stores provide huge ranges and choices of household goods. Prices are kept low through scale economies and a first-class supply-chain network. Despite their size, the stores-seem friendly and Walton employed people simply to answer customer queries and show them where particular goods were shelved. A visionary, he was focused and dedicated. He worked long hours and 'talked retailing outside work'. Strong on the people and team elements, and willing to take measured risks, Walton sought to learn from other organizations. In this respect he was opportunistic, but reflective. He never claimed to be an original thinker and he networked widely to find his new ideas.

Born in 1918 (in Missouri, USA) and raised in relative poverty, Walton started earning money from selling newspapers when he was very young. As a footballer he showed he was highly competitive, a trait which again proved valuable when he started his career in retailing. After he graduated in 1940 he began selling shirts in a J.C. Penney store. Because of a minor heart murmur he was not drafted for the war effort and instead worked in a gunpowder factory. Afterwards, and in partnership with his brother, he took on the franchise for a Ben Franklin five-and-dime store in Arkansas. The two brothers bought additional outlets, abandoned counters in favour of self-service, established central buying and promotion, and quickly became the most successful Ben Franklin franchisees in America. In 1962, the same year that K-Mart began opening discount stores in larger cities, Walton began with discount stores in small towns. Both had seen the concept pioneered elsewhere. Walton's principle was simple: mark everything up by 30 per cent, regardless of the purchase cost. This proved to be a winning formula. He toured, observed, absorbed and learned to develop his 'buy it low, stack it high, sell it cheap' strategy. Walton's first Wal-Mart store opened in Arkansas in 1962; turnover now exceeds the figures for McDonald's, Coca-Cola and Walt Disney combined! With 3600 stores in the US alone, and with annual sales of $85 billion, Wal-Mart is the world's largest retailer. It is exceeded by only the Indian National Railways, the Russian Army and the British National Health Service in terms of numbers employed. Yet the wealthy Sam Walton is alleged to have always driven himself around in a pick-up truck and to have been a mean tipper until the day he died!

Growth was gradual in the early years, but there were 30 Wal-Mart stores by 1970. Once Walton opened his own distribution warehouse (another idea that he copied) growth would explode. In addition, Wal-Mart was the first major retailer to share sales data electronically with its leading suppliers. 'We got big by replacing inventory with information.' Wal-Mart has always been careful to contain the risk 'by not investing more capital than is justified by results'. But Sam Walton was always willing to try out new ideas, quickly abandoning those that did not work. He successfully combined emergent strategy with his vision to create a potent organization and formula.

Walton's very strong ego drive was manifested in three guiding principles: respect for individual employees, service to customers ('exceed their expectations') and striving for excellence. An intuitive and inspirational retailer, Walton was also a cheer-leading orator and inspirer. He preached that 'extraordinary results can come from empowering ordinary people'. His showman style was

▶

also reflected in 'glitzy store openings'. He created a 'culture that in many ways represents a religion – in the devotion it inspires amongst its associates and in the Jesuit-like demands it makes on its executives'. Following the lead of the John Lewis Partnership in the UK, Walton called his employees 'associates' and personally spent much of his time in stores exchanging ideas with them. Profits were shared with employees. 'Ownership means people watch costs and push sales.' Sam Walton provided support for many good causes, but largely anonymously. Recognizing his own weaknesses, Walton recruited an analytical businessman, David Glass, to be his number two. Glass commented once that Walton 'wasn't organized – I saw one store he was running with water melons piled outside in temperatures of 115 degrees'. Glass has continued as Chief Executive after Walton's death.

Founded by a truly individual and visionary entrepreneur, Wal-Mart has become an entrepreneurial business; its growth and prosperity have continued after the death of the founder. Wal-Mart is now expanding selectively into other countries and, in 1999, it acquired ASDA in the UK. Since then, ASDA has grown rapidly with a programme of store openings and extensions.

## Questions

1. In terms of leadership styles and characteristics, how would you describe Sam Walton?
2. Why do you think Wal-Mart has been able to grow into the world's largest retailer in a relatively short space of time? Is there a 'secret formula' which is hard to copy, and is it reflected in Wal-Mart's strategy creation?

**Wal-Mart** http://www.walmart.com

*The most important quality of a CEO (Chief Executive Officer) is communicating a clear vision of the company's strategy – and the reputation of the CEO directly contributes to the company's ability to attract investment, recruit talent and survive crises.*

Burson-Marsteller, US public relations business

# 10.1 Introduction

*The task of leadership, as well as providing the framework, values and motivation of people, and allocation of financial and other resources, is to set the overall direction which enables choices to be made so that the efforts of the company can be focused.*

In this quotation, Sir John Harvey-Jones emphasizes the need for a clear direction for the organization.

It is the responsibility of the chief executive to clarify the mission and objectives of the organization, to define the corporate strategy which is intended to achieve these and to establish and manage the organization's structure. Personal ideas, vision and planning systems are all involved in defining the strategy.

The corporate strategy will be implemented within the structure, and the ways in which people behave – and are allowed to behave – within the organization structure will impact upon changes in competitive and functional strategies. The chief executive will also be a major influence on the organization's culture and values, which are key determinants of the ways in which strategies are created and implemented.

However, the chief executive is not the only creator of strategic change. Managers who are in charge of divisions or strategic business units (normally referred to as 'general managers') are also responsible for strategic changes concerning their own products, services or geographical territories. Functional managers will make and carry out decisions which result in strategic change. In many firms the chief executive will also act as chairman of the board, but in others he or she will be supported by a part-time, non-executive chairman who will contribute actively to corporate strategy decisions and external relations. In a limited number of large companies, particularly those which are diverse and multinational, a chief operating officer will report directly to the chief executive. He or she will be responsible for ensuring that the operating parts of the business perform effectively, and consequently will influence changes in competitive and functional strategies. Throughout this book the term *strategic leader* is used to describe the managers who head the organization and who are primarily responsible for creating and implementing strategic change, particularly corporate strategic change.

While the strategic leader has overall responsibility for managing strategy in the organization, it should not be thought that they are the sole source of thoughts and ideas. All employees can make a contribution, and should be encouraged to do so. The more that people are invited to participate in debate and discussions concerning products, services, markets and the future, the more likely they are to accept changes. Where people accept empowerment, emergent strategies can make the organization a strong competitor. Simply, leaders should not – and realistically cannot – do everything themselves, but they remain the catalyst for what does happen.

The strategic leader is in a unique position to gather and receive information about all aspects of the business, and it is incumbent on him or her to monitor the environment and the organization and watch for important opportunities and threats that could affect the whole business. He or she will need both analytical skills and insight (or awareness) to provide an intuitive grasp of the situation that faces the organization.

The way in which the organization manages to grasp opportunities and overcome potential threats will be very dependent on the personal qualities and values of the strategic leader.

Power is irrevocably associated with leadership. Strategic leaders are put in a position of power, but they have discretion over how they use this power. Some leaders, but not all, will be very motivated by the power that the position gives them. However, as explained in Chapter 7, there are many sources of power and many ways in which it can be obtained and used. Some strategic leaders will use it to impose their own ideas; others will seek to share power and responsibility with others, empowering them and encouraging them to make decisions without always referring back for advice and guidance. Everyone who becomes a strategic leader will have some experiences and expertise on which they call. The nature of their background and experience will have some impact upon their relative preference for analysis and planning or for working through people and allowing them individual freedom in strategy creation.

These are the key themes of this chapter.

The strategic leader is responsible directly to the board of directors of the organization, and through the board, to the stakeholders in the business. The responsibilities of the board and, in effect, the strategic leader, could be summarized as follows:

1. Manage the business on behalf of all the stakeholders (or interested parties).
2. Provide direction in the form of a mission or purpose.
3. Formulate and implement changes to corporate strategies.
4. Monitor and control operations with special reference to financial results, productivity, quality, customer service, innovation, new products and services and staff development.

**Figure 10.1** The strategic leader's contribution

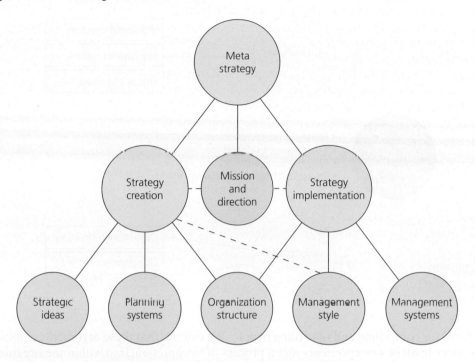

5. Provide policies and guidelines for other managers to facilitate both the management of operations and changes in competitive and functional strategies.

Responsibility 5 is achieved through the organization structure; 2 and 4 are dependent on an effective communications network.

Figure 10.1 summarizes these points by explaining that, essentially, the strategic leader has a meta-level responsibility for deciding how strategies are to be created and implemented to pursue the mission and direction. He or she may impose strategies and at the same time decide upon the nature, scope and significance of strategic planning systems. The choices of structure and management style will affect emergent strategy making, as will be seen in Chapters 15 and 16. The structure, style and management systems provide the implementation framework, a subject explored in detail in Part Five. Minicase 10.1 shows how Sam Walton provided this metastrategy for Wal-Mart and built the world's largest retail group.

## 10.2  Strategic leaders and strategic leadership

Kets de Vries (1996) concludes that the most successful strategic leaders perform two key roles, a charismatic role and an architectural one, effectively (see Figure 10.2). As a result, their strategies are owned, customers are satisfied, employees enjoy work and things can, and do, happen and change quickly. The charismatic role involves establishing and gaining support for a (winning) vision and direction, empowering employees and energizing them, gaining their enthusiastic support for what has to be done. The architectural role concerns building an appropriate organization structure, together with

**Figure 10.2** Strategic leadership roles

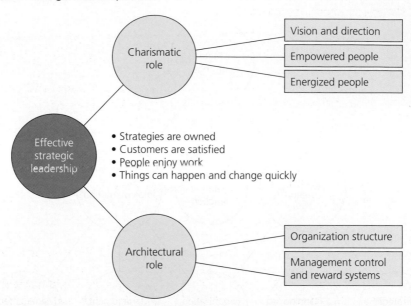

systems for controlling and rewarding people. We can see that these arguments embrace visionary leaders, entrepreneurs and a process of intrapreneurship within the organization.

Related to this latter point, Hamel (1999) distinguishes between stewardship and entrepreneurship. Stewardship concerns the continued exploitation of opportunities spotted in the past. Costs will be managed for efficiencies; some incremental changes and improvements will be made to reinforce the strategic position in a competitive environment. On its own, however, in an increasingly dynamic environment, this may well prove inadequate. Hamel uses the metaphor of Silicon Valley to contend that organizations need to bring together new ideas, talented and entrepreneurial managers, and the resources that they need in order to exploit new opportunities in an entrepreneurial way. The style of these people is dictated more by aspiration than it is by analysis.

By way of illustration, Table 10.1 features ten quite different strategic leaders who have made a real impact. They have made their difference in a variety of ways. Most of the companies are featured in Minicases at various points in the book. Anita Roddick built The Body Shop around her personal vision and refused to abandon this vision when the company experienced trading difficulties. She accepted a new role in the organization which continues successfully. Another visionary, Sir Richard Branson, accepted that parts of the Virgin empire that he built up needed to be sold off at different times, partly to secure the future for that particular business and also to provide funding for new business ideas which he wished to pursue. Sir Alan Sugar similarly chose to separate Viglen from Amstrad, the company he founded – but this was a corporate split, not a sale, and he retained an influence over both businesses. Tim Waterstone, having been made redundant by WH Smith, opened the first Waterstone's store using ideas he spotted in the US. Having built up a chain of bookshops he sold them all to WH Smith, with whom he stayed for a period of years. He resigned and, in true entrepreneurial fashion, began a series of new ventures. When Waterstone's was merged with EMI's Dillons and HMV music stores, and then floated off as a separate business, Tim

**Table 10.1** Ten strategic leaders, each of whom has or had a vision, and is linked irrevocably with their company's strategy, structure and performance

| | | |
|---|---|---|
| Anita Roddick | The Body Shop | Built up and 'stuck with it' |
| Richard Branson | Virgin | Built up and sold parts |
| Alan Sugar | Amstrad | Built up and split up |
| Tim Waterstone | Waterstone's | Built up, sold off and started again |
| Archie Norman | ASDA | Turned around and rejuvenated |
| Jack Welch | General Electric | Transformed |
| Percy Barnevik | ABB (Asea Brown Boveri) | Integrated |
| Gerald Ratner | Ratner's | Inherited, grew and lost |
| Freddie Laker | Laker Airways (Skytrain) | Built up, lost and retired eventually |
| Stelios Haji-Ioannou | easyGroup | Built up; stepped down from original business |

Waterstone returned as Chairman. He later tried to separate Waterstone's from the group and take it independent again – but he was unsuccessful in this.

Archie Norman was recruited to ASDA when it was in trouble. Together with Allan Leighton, whom he recruited, ASDA was turned around and rejuvenated before being sold to Wal-Mart. As we see later in the chapter (Minicase 10.11) two ASDA managers from this era are now running Sainsbury's and Boots. Jack Welch similarly transformed General Electric in the US, but GE is a hugely successful diversified conglomerate in an era when such conglomerates are unfashionable. Percy Barnevik integrated the Swedish Asea engineering business with Swiss Brown Boveri to create a powerful business that stretches around the globe, although its success has faded in recent years.

Gerald Ratner inherited a family business, built it up rapidly and then fell from grace when he spoke out of turn at a conference and rubbished his company's products. The business, renamed Signet, has survived and thrived without him. Sir Freddie Laker built his Skytrain business and then went out of business through a series of strategic misjudgements and very aggressive competition. Stelios Haji-Ioannou built up easyJet but 'had to step down' from being the chief executive once it was floated on the London Stock Exchange. Ratner, Laker and Stelios, again typical of a true entrepreneur, have all made comebacks with ambitious ventures.

*The problem is not to get people to work. It is to get them working together for the same damn thing.*

Sir John Harvey-Jones, retired Chairman, ICI

*Strategic awareness and change involves: becoming aware – listening, being on the shop floor more than in the office whilst, most important of all, staying humble – and taking action – sharing with others.*

Michel Bon, PDG, Carrefour SA

*As a strategic leader … one must organize oneself to have as much time as possible to see colleagues in the firm, and to be known to be available to them, for talking face-to-face is more valuable than a long memo. One must go and see others in their offices. This is the only way to stay in touch with what is going on and to ensure that an agreed plan is being carried out.*

François Michelin, PDG, Michelin et Cie

### 10.2.1  The role of the strategic leader

The strategic leader must *direct* the organization and must ensure that long-term objectives and strategies have been determined and that they are understood and supported by managers within the organization who will be responsible for implementing them. The more feasible and achievable the objectives and strategies seem, the more likely they are to be supported.

These intended strategies will be implemented through the *organization structure* adopted by the strategic leader. Some intended strategies will prove not to be feasible, as the assumptions on which they are based may be wrong, and circumstances can change, and they will be discarded or postponed. Decisions taken by general and functional managers within a decentralized structure will lead to new, incremental and adaptive changes in competitive and functional strategies. A third major responsibility of the strategic leader is a system of *communications* which first enables managers throughout the organization to be strategically aware, and second ensures that the strategic leader stays informed of the changes that are taking place.

**Strategic vision – thinking**  At the heart of everything is the need for a clear, understood and supported mission for the organization. Employees must appreciate the fundamental purpose and be committed to its achievement; the mission will provide guidance and direction when managers make decisions and implement strategies determined by others. The mission and vision may be those of the current strategic leader; equally they may have been established by a predecessor. Similarly, the actual strategies – corporate and competitive – for achieving long-term objectives may be created personally by a strong or visionary strategic leader, or they may be ideas from anywhere inside the organization.

It is important to appreciate that strategic leaders need not be personally visionary, the type of visionary leader discussed later, but they must ensure that the organization has a clear direction and resources are committed to its achievement.

Figure 10.3 develops the ideas behind the E–V–R (environment–values–resources) congruence framework introduced in Part One. Effective strategic positioning is seen as being central and reflecting competitive advantage. It has to be recognized that positions have to be changed. Sometimes the situation will be improved with innovation and incremental changes, and functional upon the culture and values, and the ways in which managers work and make decisions about possible changes. On other occasions the changes will be more dramatic and discontinuous and reflect a change in the vision. Hence, the strategic leader dictates changes to both the vision and values.

In Chapter 1 we explained that strategy comprises four visions – for corporate strategy, competitive strategy, synergy and change. Making sure these are in place is the first task of the strategic leader.

> *Until kings become philosophers and philosophers kings, things will never go well in the world.*
>
> Plato

**Pragmatism – doing**  This is the ability to make things happen and bring positive results. This implies that the organization's resources are managed efficiently and effectively. Some strategic leaders will be *doers*, active in carrying strategies through; others will be delegators who rely instead on their skills for motivating and inspiring. Control systems for monitoring results and strategic effectiveness are also important.

**Figure 10.3** Strategic leadership and E–V–R congruence

Some corporate leaders, then, will be strategic visionaries who are also active in operations; others will contribute ideas and leadership but be happy to devolve operational responsibility. It is possible for pragmatic but non-visionary leaders to be highly effective as long as they ensure that the organization has a clear and appropriate purpose and direction. The dangers here are, first, that short-term success can sometimes be the result of efficient management against a background of friendly market forces (which can, of course, quickly become less friendly) and, second, that when previously successful strategies are in need of renewal, a non-visionary may fail to provide the appropriate leadership and champion the necessary changes. Consequently, Bennis (1988) suggests that vision is crucial and that the most effective leaders are those with ideas. This accords with the view of Sir Winston Churchill, who believed that the 'emperor of the future will be the emperor of ideas'.

The strategic leader's vision and his or her record of achievement are critical for obtaining and maintaining the confidence and support of influential stakeholders, especially the very important institutional shareholders. The willingness of large shareholders to hold or sell their shares, and their expressed support for company strategies, are essential for maintaining a healthy share price and reducing the likelihood of a takeover. Their confidence in the ability of the leader is a major determinant; on occasions it is shareholder pressure which forces a change of leadership.

As well as vision and pragmatism it is necessary for the leader to build a structure and culture that captures the abilities and contributions of other managers and employees.

**Structure and policies**  It is the strategic leader who decides on the appropriate structure for carrying out existing strategies and ensuring that there is proper momentum for change.

The issues are as follows:

■ Should the organization be relatively flat and informal or have several layers of management and more formality?

■ Should it be split into individual businesses or divisions?

**Churchill**  © Bettman/Corbis

- How much power and responsibility should be delegated and decentralized?

- What is the appropriate role for the corporate headquarters?

- How might planning systems be used to direct and co-ordinate the various parts of the organization?

- To what extent should managers and other employees be empowered to take more responsibility?

- What structures and mechanisms are required to ensure that managers in different business areas and different functions integrate and plan how they can help each other? In other words, planning synergies through effective organizational teamworking.

- What policies are necessary and appropriate for guiding and directing decision-making?

These issues are explored in greater detail in various parts of the book.

**Culture** To a great extent the culture of the organization is dictated by the strategic leader. The attitudes and behaviours of people are affected, as well as their willingness to accept responsibility and take measured risks.

The strategic leader may have very clear or specific values which influence his or her style, and the culture of the organization. For example, if the leader has a financial background and orientation, this may prove important. Financial targets and analysis may be crucial elements in the management of strategy. Similarly, if the leader has a marketing background this could result in a different style of leadership, with perhaps more concentration on consumers and competition. An engineer may be very committed to product design and quality. These comments are generalizations, and will not always prove to be true; over a period of time a strategic leader is likely to become more of a generalist and less of a specialist. If a new strategic leader is appointed from another company it is inevitable that he or she will bring values which have been learned elsewhere, and these may involve change. Logically, the person will be chosen because of his or her successful record in one or more previous companies, and the newcomer may be determined to establish his or her presence by introducing changes.

Figure 10.4 delineates six key leader styles, each of which makes an important contribution. It may be argued that every leader will have a dominant style, but must make sure that the others are not neglected because all of the contributions are required. The balance between the six, which ones are strong relative to the others, will affect the culture and management style of the whole organization. Arguably, use of this framework can help us to understand why things happen as they do in any organization being analysed. It will certainly help to explain the relative balance between visionary, planned and emergent strategy creation.

**Figure 10.4** Strategic leadership style

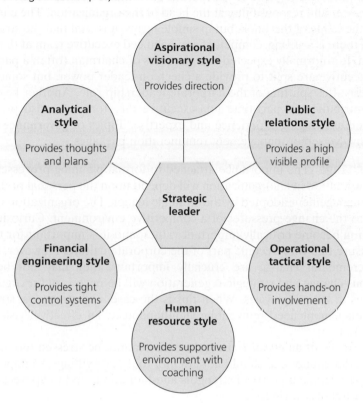

**The communications network** Effective communication systems, both formal and informal, are required to share the strategic vision and inform people of priorities and strategies and to ensure that strategies and tasks are carried out expeditiously. Where the organization is decentralized an effective communications network is vital for feeding information *upwards and laterally* inside the organization; without this control will be lost. In quite different ways, both 'managing by wandering around' and budgetary control systems can help to achieve this co-ordination. Good lateral communications also help managers to learn from other parts of the business; this in turn can lead to best practices being shared.

In addition, the strategic leader must champion the relationships between the organization and its important stakeholders, particularly its financiers, suppliers and major customers. Effective communications with government agencies and the media may also prove to be critically important.

> *Two-way communication is at the heart of successful management of change. Top management must beware of the conceit that it has all the answers. Having identified a problem, it will often be very rewarding to put to those in middle management a challenge to suggest a solution. Being nearer to the 'sharp-end' of the business in practical terms, it is surprising how frequently and rapidly they will provide an answer; and, since it comes from the heartland of the business, its implementation will find easier acceptance.*

> Peter Smith OBE, when Chairman, Securicor Group plc

**Governance and management** **Corporate governance** relates to the location and exercise of power and responsibility at the head of the organization. The complex issues are beyond the scope of this book, but in simple terms, it is vital that the strategic leader ensures that there is a strong, competent and balanced executive team at the head of the organization. It is normally expected that the roles of chairman (often a part-time post) and chief executive are split to provide a check on leader power, but some companies choose to resist this splitting of the corporate leadership role. Another key issue is the role and contribution of part-time non-executive directors, who also provide reality checks as well as bringing experience and expertise. Topics of **governance** controversy frequently involve senior management remuneration packages.

**Managing change** The importance attached to formal planning processes and emergent strategy creation in an organization will depend upon the personal preferences and the style of management adopted by the strategic leader. The organization must be able to respond to the change pressures of a competitive environment. Curiosity, creativity and innovation become critically important values, and it is important for the strategic leader to ensure that they become part of the corporate culture. However, while learning and incremental change are crucially important, they may not be sufficient. Discontinuous change and strategic regeneration will be necessary for organizations at certain stages in their life cycles. When this is the case, and strategies, structures and styles of management need reinventing simultaneously, an effective, visionary leader will be essential.

The importance of an *effective* strategic leader cannot be stressed too highly, but an individual leader cannot and should not attempt to do everything. An important skill is the ability to understand personal strengths and limitations and to appreciate the most appropriate ways of contributing.

There is no single, recommended behaviour for effective strategic leadership. Some leaders are autocratic, others democratic in the way they make decisions. Some rely on planning and analysis, while others are more intuitive and visionary. Leaders vary in the degree of risk they will accept willingly. Some look for consistency as far as is practicable in today's dynamic environments, while others are constantly opportunistic and driving change. Some pursue growth through efficiency and cost savings, others by adding new values in an innovatory climate. Some set very ambitious growth objectives, and others are more modest. All of these styles can prove effective; the challenge lies in creating and maintaining E–V–R congruence.

It is always important to evaluate the leader's position and situation. A strategic leader may be the founder of an organization and still in control, or they may be a later family generation. The leader may have 'risen through the ranks' to take control, or may have been brought in specially, possibly to turn around a company in difficulty. The leader may be relatively new or have been in post for some time. The style of leadership adopted will depend upon the leader's preferred style, their background and the situational circumstances.

Box 10.1 provides a summary of the qualities and skills required for effective leadership, together with a list of the factors that typically characterize ineffective leadership. Figure 10.5 features those requirements that will determine the extent of the impact made by a strategic leader. The model presents the issues in three clusters:

- Drive – concerns motivation and ambition and a person's ability to accept demanding targets and achieve results

## Box 10.1  Effective and Ineffective Leadership

### Qualities and skills for effective leadership

- A vision – articulated through the culture and value systems.
- The ability to build and control an effective team of managers.
- Belief in success and in corporate strengths and competencies that can be exploited.
- The ability to recognize and synthesize important developments, both inside and outside the organization. This requires strategic awareness, the ability to judge the significance of an observed event and conceptualization skills.
- Effective decentralization, delegation and motivation (the appropriate extent will vary).
- Credibility and competence. Knowing what you are doing and having this recognized. This requires the abilities to exercise power and influence and to create change.
- Implementation skills; getting things done, which requires drive, decisiveness and dynamism.
- Perseverance and persistence in pursuing the mission or vision, plus mental and physical stamina.
- Flexibility; recognizing the need (on occasions) to change strategies, structures and style. Some leaders are single style and inflexible.

### Characteristics of ineffective leadership

After a period in office some leaders appear to coast, enjoying their power and status, but no longer adding any real value to the organization. Specifically:

- There are few new initiatives; instead there is a reliance on tinkering with existing strategies to try and update past successes.
- Good new products and services are not developed.
- The leader surrounds himself or herself with loyal supporters, rather than enjoying the stimulus of newcomers with fresh mindsets.
- Moreover, discordant views are either ignored or not tolerated.
- Cash reserves, beyond those needed to sustain a period of depressed sales, are allowed to accrue.
- The leader becomes out of touch with the views of customers and the activities of competitors.
- Too much time is spent by the leader on external activities, without ensuring that other managers are dealing with important organizational issues.

- Judgement – related to decision-making style and abilities. The softer or more conceptual issues of opportunity spotting and problem framing (awareness and insight into a situation) blend with harder analytical abilities
- Influence – a person's appreciation of how others might be influenced and their way of doing it. Networks and contacts are an important element of this.

A number of these themes is also illustrated in Minicase 10.2 on Sir Tom Farmer, founder of Kwik Fit. Tom Farmer imported his vision for Kwik Fit from the US; success has involved opportunism and innovation backed up by sound business sense.

Sir Tom Farmer could legitimately be described as an entrepreneur. The next section looks at the link between entrepreneurs and strategy before examining visionary strategic leadership.

CASE

## Minicase 10.2 Tom Farmer and Kwik-Fit  GB

Tom Farmer was born into a working-class family in Edinburgh, Scotland, in 1940; he was the seventh child. Brought up a Roman Catholic in a largely Protestant city, he left school at the age of 15 and began working in a tyre company. In 1964 he set up his own business, retailing tyres at discount prices. New legislation on minimum tyre depths opened a window of opportunity and he quickly expanded from one to four outlets. After four years he sold the whole business for £450,000 to Albany Tyres, 'retired' and went to live in California. Within three years he and his wife were bored. He returned to Scotland but, because of his agreement with Albany, he could not start a new tyre-retailing business until a number of years had elapsed.

Instead, he brought over an idea he had seen in the US: a fast-change exhaust shop. Again, he quickly expanded from one to four outlets, so that he could re-employ a number of his old friends! Tyres were added later. As for the Kwik-Fit name, he just dreamed it up. The distinctive blue and yellow colours, pervasive to this day, were chosen because these were the colours of some paint that someone would give him free of charge!

Farmer is a workaholic and was always very committed to his business and his employees. All of Tom Farmer's employees were put on profit-share schemes; about half became individual shareholders in the business. Private garages and repair shops are often thought to involve dubious commercial practices; one of Tom Farmer's major achievements has been to bring a high level of perceived (and real) integrity into the industry. He places a strong emphasis on good customer service and friendliness, attributes which are featured in distinctive Kwik-Fit advertisements.

By the early 1980s there were 200 depots; arguably the business grew too quickly. Inadequate management control left the company vulnerable to takeover for a while, but it managed to retain its independence. For 29 years the company grew organically and stayed focused. There was some geographical expansion, successfully in Belgium and the Netherlands, but Kwik-Fit entered and then withdrew from France. 'There are cultural differences. The French want to close for lunch. French managers are reluctant to bond with their employees. These are key Kwik-Fit values.'

In 1994 Kwik-Fit acquired 105 Superdrive Motoring Centres from Shell, a related business. In 1995 Kwik-Fit Insurance was launched, exploiting Kwik-Fit's large customer database. Farmer argues that it is based on the same principles: high service using someone else's products. In 1999 Kwik-Fit was sold to Ford for £1 billion. By this time there were 1900 outlets, 10,000 employees and 8 million customers a year. Tom Farmer, by this time Sir Tom, stayed active in the business for a some time after the sale to Ford, before effectively retiring for a second time. But he remains active, encouraging other young entrepreneurs.

Yet Farmer has always been seen as a demanding man to work for, and many employees have been 'rather frightened of him'.

In an interview with *Management Today* (August 1995) Tom Farmer made the following comments.

> *If the customer is king, the staff are emperors.*
>
> *We don't have a head office; we have a support office. We don't have senior management; we have support management.*
>
> *All sound businesses are built on good Christian ethics: don't steal, don't exploit your customers or your people, always use your profits for the benefit of your people and the community.*
>
> *We are in business to make a profit and we should not be ashamed of that, provided we stick to sound principles, and, at the end of the day, do proper things with that profit.*

### Questions

1. Why is Kwik-Fit so successful?
2. Is Tom Farmer a visionary leader, an entrepreneur or both?
3. Does the fact that he lives in a large house and owns both a corporate jet and a helicopter contradict any of his stated beliefs?

**Kwik-Fit** http://www.kwik-fit.com

**Figure 10.5** Leadership requirements
Based on a framework devised by Kingfisher plc in conjunction with occupational psychologists YSC

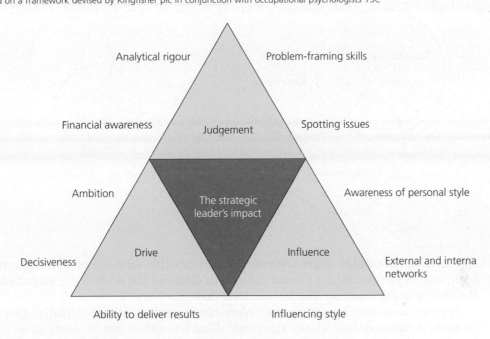

## 10.3 Entrepreneurs and entrepreneurship

Bolton and Thompson (2000) define an entrepreneur as a person who 'habitually creates and innovates to build something of recognized value around perceived opportunities'. Entrepreneurs can be found starting organizations, running organizations and working in organizations as employees. In the latter case they are typically called intrapreneurs, i.e. internal entrepreneurs. Two issues now need to be examined:

■ the strategic leader as an entrepreneur
■ whether the strategic leader has built an organization which fosters intrapreneurship.

Strategic management is concerned with environmental fit and it is important to achieve congruence between environment, values and resources for both existing and potential future products and services. Figure 10.6 revisits the model of E–V–R congruence and presents it in a marginally different way, one which implies action rather than being an expression of a state. The environment is presented as a number of windows of opportunity, and resources are represented by organizational competencies and capabilities. The argument is that entrepreneurship in the organization, both at the level of the leader and throughout the whole organization, is required to ensure that resources are developed and changed and used to exploit the windows of opportunity ahead of rival organizations.

The management of existing businesses should ensure that attention is focused on costs and prices (as they determine profits) and on ways of reducing costs by improving productivity. Technology changes and new operating systems, may reduce costs; equally they may improve product quality, for which premium prices might be charged.

**Figure 10.6** E–V–R congruence and entrepreneurship

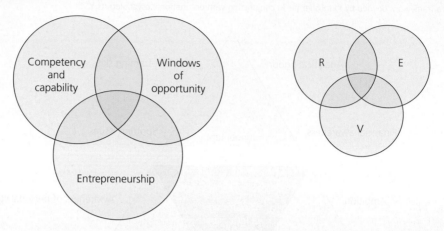

Future developments might concern new products (or services) or new markets or both, and they might involve diversification. For different alternatives the magnitude of the change implied and the risk involved will vary.

For both areas the changes that take place can be gradual or incremental, or they can be more dynamic or individually significant. Real innovation can be costly in terms of investment required, and consequently can involve a high level of risk, but sometimes it is necessary.

Figure 10.7 shows alternative development paths for a business. We normally think of entrepreneurs as the people who develop new ideas and new businesses, but there are different views on the implications of an entrepreneurial start-up. Schumpeter (1949), for example, argues that entrepreneurs bring innovative ideas into a situation of some stability and create disequilibrium. The so-called Austrian School of economists (see Kirzner, 1973) suggests that entrepreneurs create equilibrium (in the form of E–V–R congruence) by matching demand and supply in a creative way. However, it is the path of future progress that really matters.

From its initial position the business could at first be successful but then fade away without further innovation and renewal (Path I). The original window of opportunity closes and the business fails to find or capitalize on a new one.

Some businesses never really improve and grow (Path II), sometimes by deliberate choice, sometimes through lack of insight and awareness; however, they survive as long as they can satisfy a particular niche or localized market. If one window of opportunity closes they find a new one, but in this respect they are more likely to be reactive rather than proactive. It is quite feasible for Path II businesses to *expand*, as distinct from true growth based on improvement and excellence. In reality, many businesses fall in this category. They are the archetypal small business – and they are not run by 'real' entrepreneurs as they fail the 'habitual' requirement included in the definition. They can legitimately be called lifestyle businesses and their founders are sometimes described as lifestyle entrepreneurs.

Paths III and IV feature more proactive entrepreneurial businesses which *grow* via productivity improvements and/or by leveraging their resources to develop new products and service opportunities. Sometimes, but certainly not always, such businesses will be decentralized, empowered and *intrapreneurial*.

**Figure 10.7** Business development paths

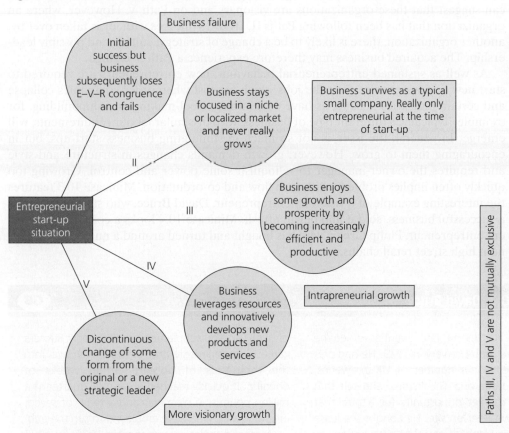

Path V implies discontinuous change and requires visionary leadership, either from the original founding entrepreneur or a new strategic leader, which Mintzberg (1973) summarizes as follows:

- Strategy making is dominated by the active search for new opportunities.
- Power is centralized in the hands of the chief executive – certainly as far as corporate strategy changes are concerned.
- Strategic change is characterized by dramatic leaps forward in the face of uncertainty.
- Growth is the dominant goal of the organization.

Implicit is an attempt to be proactive and manage the environment. Paths III, IV and V are clearly not mutually exclusive; they can all be present simultaneously in an organization.

Sustained entrepreneurial behaviour is required for a successful economy; organizations must innovate and search for opportunities to rewrite the rules of competition. In this way home industries can succeed against foreign competitors (whose products and services may be differentiated successfully or priced very competitively because of cost advantages such as low wages) and find overseas markets. Paths I and II are not entrepreneurial businesses; in a different way, nor is an organization which grows via acquisitions but then fails to add new values and drive improvements along either Paths III or

IV. Ironically, the nature of the strategic changes and the increases in size and revenue can suggest that these organizations are visionary and on Path V. However, where an organization that has been following Paths II, III or IV merges with, or is taken over by, another organization, there is likely to be a change of strategy, culture and possibly leadership. The acquired business may therefore experience a Path V change.

As well as sustained entrepreneurial behaviour, new entrepreneurs are required to start new businesses to replace the jobs which are lost when other companies collapse and certain industries decline, as have coal mining, steel-making and shipbuilding, for example. Typically, a different type of business, with dissimilar labour requirements, will emerge. In general, the issue is not so much in stimulating business start-ups, but in encouraging them to grow. However, growth demands changes in structure and style and requires the owner-manager to relinquish some power and control. Growing too quickly often implies problems with cash flow and co-ordination. Minicase 10.3 features the interesting example of a visionary entrepreneur, David Bruce, who started and grew a successful business, sold it and began afresh. Minicase 10.4 looks a completely different entrepreneur, Philip Green, who has bought and turned around a number of prominent high street retail chains.

**CASE**

## Minicase 10.3 David Bruce    GB

David Bruce was in his late twenties when he opened his first pub-brewery in 1979. He had previously worked for a number of UK breweries, including Courage and Theakstons, and felt that there was a market opportunity for a pub that brewed its own beer on site. He bought the lease on a site at the Elephant and Castle in London, an existing pub which was being closed down, and renamed it the Goose and Firkin. The pub was completely remodelled with one large bar with wooden seats, bare floorboards and several decorations such as a stuffed goose. The aim was to recreate a traditional drinking house. Brewing took place in the cellar, which had a production capacity of 5000 pints per week. In addition, other real ales were sold. Lloyds Bank lent £10,000 for this new venture, but Bruce was turned down by others whom he approached. He had to take a second mortgage on his house to provide collateral for his overdraft and he borrowed some money from a friend of his wife.

Three types of real ale were brewed and sold, all with individual brand names and varying in strength. These were Bruce's Borough Bitter, Bruce's Dog Bolter and Bruce's Earth Stopper, which at o.g. 1075 was claimed to be the strongest draught beer in Britain. Traditional food

of high quality supplemented the beer. Success came instantaneously and the turnover was into the thousands of pounds within weeks of opening. It quickly reached an annual quarter of a million pounds. A manager and a team of seven, including a brewer, were employed to run the pub.

A second outlet was opened in 1980; by 1985 there were seven, with the total reaching 11 in 1987. All 11 were in the Greater London area, and nine of them had in-house breweries. The last two were called the Fuzzock and Firkin and the Flamingo and Firkin. By the mid-1980s Bruce was the fifth largest operator of breweries in the UK. All of the pubs had Firkin in the name, and by this time a number of new real-ale brands had been introduced, including Spook, brewed exclusively in the Phantom and Firkin. Bruce had also developed a reputation for promotional slogans for each pub. The Flounder and Firkin was a 'plaice worth whiting home about' and at the Phantom and Firkin you could 'spectre good pint when you ghost to the Phantom'.

Sales in 1986–87, with eight outlets operating, were £4 million. Bruce had sold 10 per cent of the equity to Investors in Industry for £100,000, and they also provided additional loan facilities. There had been difficulties, however. In 1982 Bruce had obtained a pub-brewery with additional warehouse capacity in Bristol. His aim was to distribute his real ales to West Country pubs. But the company was already experiencing problems from the rapid growth. Beer quality was inconsistent, there were cash-flow problems, and David Bruce's own role was unclear. A microbiologist and an accountant were brought into the business, which relieved the first two of these. However, Bruce still faced the problem that, while there were managers in every outlet, he was personally responsible for ensuring that his original success formula at the Goose and Firkin was implemented and maintained in all of the pubs and at the same time was seeking new opportunities for growth and development. Once the company spread outside London Bruce felt that he was no longer able to pay sufficient attention to detail throughout the organization. Essentially the problem was one of managing growth and at the same time retaining the 'personal touch', a key success factor for this type of service business. The Bristol site was sold.

Bruce had hoped to take the company to the Unlisted Securities Market in 1987, but this never happened. Further growth, he felt, was inhibited by a lack of equity capital and the problems of interest charges on loans. In March 1988 Midsummer Leisure, an expanding public house, snooker club and discotheque business with some 130 outlets, bought Bruce's Brewery, comprising 11 outlets and one site for development, from David Bruce for £6.6 million in cash. The business had a number of different owners in the 1990s, during which period it continued to expand to a chain of 179 pubs, not all of which brewed on site. It was sold again in 1999, this time by Allied Domecq to Punch Taverns, who plan to close some outlets and take on-site brewing out of all the others. Punch had little choice in this, because of legislation and their present mix of activities; but the brand will be preserved. Is it the end of an era?

After paying off loans and capital gains tax, Bruce was left with £1 million in 1989, part of which he used to establish a charitable trust to provide canal holidays for disabled people. In 1990 David Bruce started brewing again. Two pubs, both named The Hedgehog and Hogshead, and

offering beers such as Hogbolter and Prickletickler, were opened in Hove and Southampton. The conditions of sale of Bruce's Brewery prevented Bruce from opening in Greater London. Key staff were recruited back from Midsummer Leisure, the sites were leased rather than freehold, and borrowing was kept to a minimum. Bruce personally invested £500,000. He later moved to other ventures before entering a joint venture with WH Brakspear in September 1999. Brakspear has brewed in Henley-on-Thames since 1779. One of his other ideas has been the Bertie Belcher brand, 'pubs that brew the beer you'll want to repeat'.

The name for the new venture is Honeypot Inns; David Bruce is chief executive. Brakspear has put seven managed pubs into the venture (six more will be added every year) and they will be retained as independent pubs which reflect the character of the building and their local communities. They will be a loose chain, linked by a common brand name but they will all be individual. The new additions will be unusual sites rather than typical high streets.

Brakspear believes that Bruce has 'tremendous skills for identifying opportunities for the development of retail operations that catch the imagination of consumers'. He is certainly a master of the weak pun. Bruce asserts that 'creating the right ambience is an innate skill – not something I can explain'. He fully intends to move on again when the venture is properly up and running …'I put my all into these ventures for up to five years and then I have to do something else'.

## Questions

1. Following the growth of the chain and its associated changes of ownership, can an individual 'Firkin' pub be the same as the original that David Bruce opened back in the 1980s?
2. Is this necessarily a disadvantage?
   (Additional questions on David Bruce are included at the end of the chapter.)

   **Hogshead** http://www.hogshead.co.uk/hogs.html
   **WH Brakspear & Sons plc** http://brakspear.co.uk

It is, therefore, important for us to understand the motivation of entrepreneurs and how they see and activate opportunities.

### 10.3.1 Achievement and power motivation

McClelland and Winter (1971) have argued since the 1950s that all managers, in fact all workers, are influenced and motivated by three desires: the desire to achieve, the desire for power, and the desire for affiliation at work. The relative strength of each of these three desires or motives will vary from individual to individual, and what matters as far as management is concerned is to understand what does motivate people, rather than to believe that all people can be motivated in the same way.

Entrepreneurial behaviour is characterized by high achievement motivation, supported by a power motive, and with affiliation very much third.

Achievement motivation is characterized by concern to do a job well, or better than others, with the accomplishment of something unusual or important, and with advancement. Such managers thrive where they have personal responsibility for finding answers to problems, and they tend to set moderate achievable goals and take calculated risks. If the targets are too modest, there is little challenge and little satisfaction, but if they are too high they are too risky.

Actually achieving the goal is important. They also prefer constant feedback concerning progress. Achievement motivation is closely linked to the desire to create something.

Entrepreneurial behaviour also features a desire for power, influence and independence.

Entrepreneurs need both creativity and confidence if they are to seek out and exploit new ideas; and they must be willing to take risks. While McClelland and Winter describe achievement-motivated people as those who take very measured risks, there are some entrepreneurs who thrive on uncertainty and are successful because they take chances and opportunities that others would and do reject. They will not always succeed, however.

In contrast with this business 'analysis, one might expect to see people who aspire to be leaders to be driven more by a desire for power.

---

**CASE**

## Minicase 10.4 Philip Green　　　　　　　　　　　　　　　　**GB**

Philip Green is 'Britain's biggest private retailer', having completed a number of very successful deals, using largely his own money.

His business career began in 1973, when, at the age of 21, he took over the family property company. His move into retailing came in 1985, when he invested £65,000 to buy the Jean Jeanie chain of shops. He sold it five months later for £3 million. Three years later he invested in the Amber Day retail chain, a quoted company. After running the business for four years he resigned when he was under pressure following a profits decline. He later bought the Owen Owen department store chain

(1994) and Mark One discount clothing (1996), of which he still owns 50 per cent of the shares.

In 1997 he bought Shoe Express from Sears for £8.3 million, and followed this up by purchasing the whole Sears empire for £550 million in 1999. He set about splitting the Sears retail conglomerate and ended up with a profit of some £180 million. When Marks and Spencer was in difficulty in 1999/2000, Philip Green was clearly interested – but never made a formal bid. Instead, and using £50 million of his own money, he bought British Home Stores for £200 million. By 2002 BHS was estimated to be worth £1.2 billion – 'the fastest billion pounds ever made in retailing'. In 2002 Philip Green bought Arcadia for £850 million. Arcadia had divested the Debenhams chain but it still comprised the Top Shop, Top Man, Miss Selfridge, Dorothy Perkins, Wallis, Evans and Burtons brands.

Green was rebuffed by Marks and Spencer in 2000, but four years later he returned. This time he did make a formal proposition to the board and asked that they recommend it to their shareholders. He was not minded to enter a hostile takeover situation. As we saw in Minicase 1.2, the M&S board responded by replacing their Chairman and Chief Executive. They refused to support Green's bid, although the largest institutional shareholder had agreed to sell to Green if the bid was recommended by the board.

Green has been described as a 'born trader'. He is clearly enthusiastic and energetic; and he believes businesses are built on relationships and a small top team. As far as he can, he shuns the services of 'so-called experts'. He is incredibly focused and he understands customers and their expectations. Somewhat predictably he has strong self-belief and (like Tom Farmer) is rumoured to be a hard man to work for. Very hands on, he is always likely to turn up unannounced at one of his stores.

His leadership style involves tight control and centralization of key decisions. Each store group, such as Burtons, is a profit centre. It has its own Brand Director and Finance Director and these two are largely in control. Whilst the Brand Director will control styles, designs and ranges, he or she will be required to buy from approved suppliers wherever possible – and these suppliers will also supply other groups in the Green empire, thus enabling substantial discounts and scale economies. Information technology, human resources and financial services are all centralized.

It is, of course, impossible to say what he might have done with Marks and Spencer had he been able to take it over. Some critics of M&S, who believed the company had lost its way, thought he should be given a chance. Others felt he was simply not 'the right person' for M&S; he was culturally inappropriate.

### Questions

1. Use the Internet to help determine why Philip Green has been as successful as he has. How have the fortunes of all the businesses he has owned in recent years fared under his leadership?
2. Can you identify other retail chains that might benefit from the 'Philip Green touch'?

**Arcadia** http://www.arcadia.co.uk
**British Home Stores** http://www.bhs.co.uk

## 10.4 Intrapreneurship

Entrepreneurial activity, innovation and growth are affected greatly by the ambition and style of the strategic leader, their values, and the culture that they create, but arguably they should be spread throughout the organization. Intrapreneurship is the term given to the establishment and fostering of entrepreneurial activity within large organizations. Many new ideas for innovation, for product or service developments, can come from managers within organizations if the structure and climate encourage and allow them to contribute. There are a number of ways. Special task forces and development groups are one alternative. Allowing individual managers the opportunity, freedom and, if necessary, the capital to try new ideas is another. Success requires that change is perceived more as an opportunity than a threat, that the company is aware of market opportunities and is customer orientated, and that the financial implications are thought through.

*In times of discontinuity and accelerated change, survival depends on flexibility, on our ability to learn to adapt. Organizations which learn fast will survive.*
*Management must take the lead. We must mobilize our greatest asset, our people,*

*invest in their training and orchestrate their talents, skills and expertise. Their commitment, dedication, quality and care will build the competitive advantage of a winning team. Only they can provide our customers with the best product and service in the industry. The management of change takes tenacity, time, talent and training.*

JFA de Soet, President, KLM Royal Dutch Airlines

## 10.4.1 Building the organization

Effective leaders possess a number of characteristics, they set direction and they inspire others. However, their strong leadership should not throttle flexibility and learning by a resistance to trusting other managers and involving them in key decisions. The most successful strategic leaders realize that they cannot do everything on their own and build a team to whom they can delegate important decisions and contributions. While some of these people will, by necessity, be specialists, professionals and technocrats, Horovitz (1997) stresses the importance of also recruiting or developing entrepreneurial managers to ensure the flow of innovation and change and prevent entropy. He argues that one of the reasons for Club Méditerranée losing momentum in the 1990s was the result of a failure to accomplish this back-filling effectively (see Minicase 7.7). Quinn (1980) also emphasizes the importance of innovation and ongoing learning by this team because not all of the issues and difficulties that will have to be faced can be foreseen.

*The aim in a global business is to get the best ideas from everywhere. [In General Electric] each team puts up its best ideas and processes – constantly. That raises the bar. Our culture is designed around making a hero out of those who translate ideas from one place to another, who get help from somebody else. They get an award, they get praised and promoted.*

Jack Welch, Chief Executive, General Electric

Horovitz (1997) contends that organizations should look for the problems before they even arise, by questioning what the (possibly very successful) organization is doing wrong. At times it is important to abandon products, services and strategies which have served the organization well in the past, as they are not the future. de Geus (1997) contends that businesses need to become 'living organizations' if they are to enjoy long and sustained success. This requires that the company:

- knows 'what it is about'
- understands where 'it fits in the world'
- values new ideas, new people, and fresh views and opinions
- manages its resources (especially financial resources) in a way which places it in a position to govern its own future; in other words, it is prudent and does not spend beyond a level it can earn.

These requirements are manifest in:

- clear direction and purpose (awareness of its identity)
- strategic positioning (its sensitivity to its environment)
- the management of change (its tolerance of new ideas) and
- the efficient use of its capital investment.

People, then, must be seen as key assets and managed accordingly; controls must have some element of looseness and flexibility; and constant learning must be possible.

Rosabeth Moss Kanter (1989) clearly supports this view when she argues that the whole organization holds the key to competitive advantage. She suggests that five criteria are found in successful, entrepreneurial organizations:

- *focused* on essential core competencies and long-term values
- *flexible* – searching for new opportunities and new internal and external synergies with the belief that ever-increasing returns and results can be obtained from the same resources if they are developed properly and innovative
- *friendly* – recognizing the power of alliances in the search for new competencies
- *fast* and able to act at the right time to get ahead and stay ahead of competitors
- *fun* – creative and with a culture which features some irreverence in the search for ways to be different; people feel free to express themselves.

In her earlier work, Kanter (1983) warned about the potential for stifling innovation by:

- blocking ideas from lower down the organization, on the grounds that only senior or very experienced managers are in a position to spot new opportunities. On the contrary, she argues, younger people with fresh minds are in an excellent position to question and challenge the status quo
- building too many levels in the hierarchy so that decision-making is slowed almost to a point of non-existence
- withholding praise from people who do offer good, innovative ideas, and instilling a culture of insecurity so that people feel too terrified even to question authority, policies or procedures
- being unwilling to innovate until someone else has tried out the idea – a fear of leading change.

Minicase 10.5, Richer Sounds, illustrates an organization that has benefited substantially from involving employees widely in new strategy creation.

While robust questioning and assumption-testing of new ideas is crucial, it is particularly important to remember that many people fear change, partly because of uncertainty about its impact on them personally. As a result, some people will seek to resist valuable change initiatives, and may even attempt to mount an active and orchestrated opposition. Managing change effectively, therefore, requires continuous effort and sometimes patience, reinforcing the significant contribution made by the project champion.

## 10.4.2 The process of intrapreneurship

Bridge *et al.* (1998) highlight the importance of recruiting, spotting and using people with entrepreneurial talent who are motivated to use their abilities and initiative and do something on their own, but who may not want to start their own business. These internal entrepreneurs have been called *intrapreneurs* by Pinchot (1985). Intrapreneurship, then, is the term given to the establishment and fostering of entrepreneurial activity in large organizations which results in incremental improvements to existing products and services and occasionally to brand-new products. Box 10.2 presents an idealized version of this situation.

## Minicase 10.5 Richer Sounds GB

Electrical goods retailers are not new. The dominant names in the UK are Comet and Curry's, but Richer Sounds is different, and very successful. Richer is more focused than its main rivals, specializing in hi-fi, especially separate units. According to the *Guinness Book of Records*, Richer achieved the highest sales per square foot of any retailer in the world. Sales per employee are also high. Stock is piled high to the ceilings in relatively small stores in typically low-rent locations. All the main brands can be found; the latest models feature alongside discontinued ones, these at very competitive prices. 'We just aren't that ambitious [to justify diversifying] ... we feel that by staying with what we know best we can concentrate our effort and resources in one field and hopefully do it well.'

Julian Richer was born in 1959; his parents both worked for Marks and Spencer. He was just 19 when he opened his first shop at London Bridge: 'seventy thousand commuters passed the shop every day'. He now owns 39 stores in the UK and Eire and two more in the Netherlands. Apart from Christmas, Richer will not open on Sundays. His employees are known as colleagues and they are empowered to work 'The Richer Way'. He claims that his suggestion scheme has generated the highest number of suggestions per employee of any scheme anywhere in the world, and the best

ideas are rewarded with trips on the Orient Express. The most successful employees (in terms of sales) can win free use of a holiday home; the most successful shops earn the free use of a Bentley or Jaguar for a month. Every employee is allowed £5 per month 'to go to the pub and brainstorm'. Julian Richer has advised ASDA on suggestion schemes, and ex-ASDA Chairman, Archie Norman, has said: 'Julian has gone to great lengths to create a system that works without him, but, to a great extent, his business is his personality.'

Richer has established a parallel consulting arm, with eight consultants who offer 'The Richer Way as a philosophy for delighting customers.' Consultancy is provided free to charities and good causes. Richer has also established a foundation to help selected good causes, and he owns a number of other small businesses. These include a retail recruitment agency, a property portfolio, and an award-winning tapas bar in Fulham. He has, however, 'one business and a number of hobbies'.

### Questions

1. Is 'The Richer Way' a key to sustained competitive advantage?
2. Why do you think it has been successful?

**Richer Sounds** http://www.richer-sounds.co.uk

Figure 10.8 shows that both entrepreneurship (creating outcomes which imply a real difference) and intrapreneurship (less ambitious changes which are more likely to be based around improvements than major changes of direction) are broadly similar. They both begin when someone has a personal vision from which an idea and a related opportunity emerge. The opportunity must then be engaged and resources acquired as prerequisites to action and implementation. Intrapreneurship happens as individual managers promote and sell their ideas inside the organization and build a team of supporters. They drive change.

This was illustrated with the example of 3M and Post-It Notes, but realistically this is an extreme case. The innovation is more likely to be a minor, but significant improvement to a product or service or process: anything that makes a valuable difference. Box 10.3 illustrates how Shell has attempted to foster intrapreneurship with a special programme.

Intrapreneurs, typically, are strategically aware, ideas-driven, creative, flexible, innovative, good networkers, individualistic but also able to work well in a team, persistent

**Figure 10.8** The entrepreneur: seeing and activating opportunities

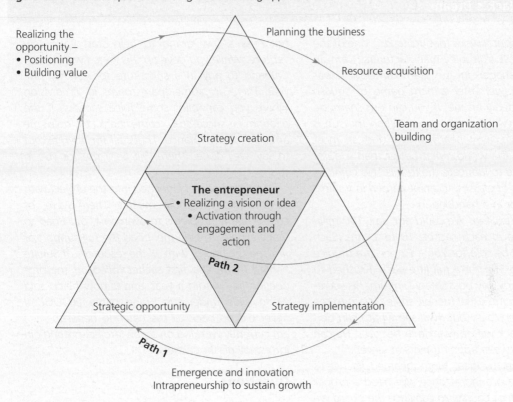

Realizing the
opportunity –
• Positioning
• Building value

Planning the business

Resource acquisition

Team and organization
building

Strategy creation

**The entrepreneur**
• Realizing a vision or idea
• Activation through
engagement and
action

*Path 2*

Strategic opportunity

Strategy implementation

*Path 1*

Emergence and innovation
Intrapreneurship to sustain growth

**Path 1:** Intrapreneurship/corporate entrepreneurship.
A flow of ideas from inside the organization

**Path 2:** Fresh ideas from an entrepreneurial strategic leadership

and courageous. If frustrated by a lack of freedom they will underachieve or possibly leave. But they are volunteers; intrapreneurship is not right for everyone.

According to Pinchot (1985), the key lies in engaging people's efforts and energy for championing, capturing and exploiting new ideas and strategic changes. This must stretch beyond the most senior managers in the organization, who do not have a monopoly on good ideas. On the contrary, the potentially most valuable and lucrative ideas are likely to come from those people who are closest to the latest developments in technology or to customers. Suggestion schemes are linked in, but on their own do not constitute intrapreneurship. The ideas need to be taken forward, and they can only be developed if the potential intrapreneurs are able to obtain the necessary internal resources and, moreover, they are willing to do something. This in turn requires encouragement and appropriate rewards for success. People must feel involved in the process and comfortable that they are being supported. Intrapreneurship cannot work where people feel frozen out or dumped on. Churchill (1997) summarizes the philosophy as skills following opportunities. People in entrepreneurial businesses see the opportunities and set about acquiring the necessary resources. The whole process of change then becomes gradual and evolutionary. The momentum for change and improvement is

## Box 10.2 Jack's Dream

*I'm Jack Dupont. I work for Sunlite PLC, one of the world's largest fruit juice manufacturers. I am an assistant manager in the staff canteen. I was having a shower after a hard game of squash when it suddenly hit me. If you can put shampoo in a sachet, why not fruit juice? When the sun is beating down, as it nearly always does in most countries of the world, what better than a quick squirt of juice to lubricate the tonsils? No cumbersome bottles or glasses, it can be carried in a shirt's top pocket or in a handbag.*

*I became excited. We could put, say, 100 millilitres of juice in each sachet. 10 to a litre. Each sachet could be sold for 20p – £2 per litre of juice compared to 50p for a full litre pack. I rushed to see Jim McIlroy, my boss. Mary Dignum, his secretary, gave me her usual friendly smile. 'Want to see Jim? He is very busy but I will see what I can do.' She came back with a twinkle in her eye. 'He can fit you in between appointments at eleven.'*

*I explained my idea. 'Hum' beamed Jim. 'Let's get it off the ground at once. We need a proper business plan of course, to convince the board we have done things properly. Ring James Petrie at Price Waterhouse (Mary has the number) and ask him to do a market assessment for us. Harry in Packaging will know who to contact for the machinery to sachet the juice. You'll need money. We were about to launch a campaign to expand our market in Singapore, but I am sure they would*

*not miss a few grand to help start your new venture. While you develop this idea, I will instruct Catering to buy in a substitute for you for one year. There are some spare rooms in 'D' division where you can pilot some juice sachets. If the piloting is successful, come back to help me arrange further finance. That's all for now, except to say, well done. There will be a rise for you in this'.*

*I felt inspired as I launched into the project with all the energy I could muster. There were, of course, many problems to overcome, but I had so many experts to help me. I had the full support of Jim and the board, with all the resources of Sunlite behind them. The first sachet rolled off the production line within a year, and is now being sold world wide under the brand name 'KOOOL'. I never did go back to the catering department. I am currently working on a new project putting gin into small plastic sachets.*

### Questions

1. Have you ever had an idea and a dream like Jack's? If so, how did you feel?
2. What were you minded to do about it?

Developed from ideas contained in Pinchot's *Intrapreneuring*: 'How to succeed against the odds'.

---

never lost and the organization is less likely to be exposed and weakened by its competitors, resulting in it having to cross a 'bridge too far'.

Maitland (1999) has described how Bass developed new pub brands. In the early 1990s Bass' traditional customers (older people, and more working than middle class) were deserting pubs; young people became the new target. '[Bass] needed a radical "break-out" strategy of new product development and concept innovation.' Bass spotted the new It's A Scream format, conceived by entrepreneur David Lee and popular with students. Lee was a builder in Farnham who had been given a pub in lieu of an unpaid debt and had transformed it. Bass bought the pub and the concept and recruited Lee as a consultant with a profit-share and a fixed fee for every new It's A Scream pub which opens. The All Bar One theme pubs, an upmarket, well-lit, city-centre chain with large windows which attracts groups of young female drinkers, reflects a similar story. Other initiatives have been developed from ideas put forward by existing managers, who have been offered secondment to champion their project ideas. Bass recognized the impor-

## Box 10.3 Shell's GameChanger

Royal Dutch Shell, with revenues of around £85 billion and over 100,000 employees worldwide, is an industrial giant in an established industry: petroleum. Historically, access to capital has been carefully controlled and radical ideas from internal entrepreneurs have been rare. Managers switch between divisions and countries for experience and promotion, but they are generally disciplined and loyal to corporate policies and procedures. In 1996, Tim Warren, Director of Research and Technical Services in Exploration and Production (Shell's largest division), was determined to change this, and to free up ideas, talent and resources. He was concerned that competition was intense in the dynamic and turbulent oil industry and Shell was 'not inventing radically new businesses'. Moreover, he firmly believed that Shell possessed the talent to drive a different behaviour.

In November 1996 he secured the resources to launch *GameChanger* and £12.5 million was set aside to fund radically new ideas submitted by employees. A group of key people would evaluate the ideas put forward by their peers. Consultants were brought in to run a series of creativity laboratories for volunteers; 72 turned up to the first one.

The focus was on:

- identifying and challenging industry conventions
- identifying emerging discontinuities

- leveraging and exploiting existing competencies to create new competitive opportunities.

The ideas began to flow from the laboratories and their interactive sessions. Some of the money set aside was used to ensure that the ideas which passed the first selection and screening were put into action. The creativity laboratory was supplemented by further work on project management.

As the programme has developed, Shell's intranet has been used increasingly to move ideas around the organization. Initial funding has averaged some £60,000 per project selected, but it has been as high as £350,000. Employees are encouraged to stay involved. Once the concept is proven, further funding can be arranged. A number of important new Shell initiatives have emerged from *GameChanger*.

### Questions

1. Why do you think many large organizations ignore the potential of initiatives such as this?
2. What are the dangers in their approach?

### Source

Hamel, G (1999) Bringing Silicon Valley inside, *Harvard Business Review*, September–October.

Shell (Royal Dutch Shell) http://www.countonshell.com

**STRATEGY IN ACTION**

tance of visible support and encouragement from the top, so this became an engineered and not a random process. Bass ensured that adequate financial resources were available and also utilized sophisticated computer mapping systems to help with location issues. The two parallel questions are: Where are the ideal places for siting a particular format? What would be the best format for a site they already own? The key variables are age, affluence and car ownership, linked to how far people are willing to travel to eat or drink out. In other words, Bass brought together ideas, talented intrapreneurs and the resources that they needed.

To summarize these points, Hurst (1995) likens entrepreneurial strategic leaders to gardeners. They prune. They clear out. They plant, by recruiting other entrepreneurial managers. They feed, by encouraging and rewarding managers for being creative and innovative. Simply, they nurture and manage the organization as they would a garden. Paradoxically, many good ideas begin in the same way that weeds emerge in a garden, i.e. randomly. They then need spotting and looking after – the equivalent of transfer to a hothouse?

### 10.4.3 The intrapreneurial organization

Fradette and Michaud (1998) describe four main elements to an organization which succeeds with intrapreneurship. First, the strategic and structural environment is 'right'. The purpose and direction implies a realistic vision and it is widely understood and shared. Formal systems and controls do not stifle innovation and people are free to make limited changes. Inhibitive internal chimneys are pulled down so that people can collaborate and share ideas readily. Second, an appropriate workforce has been built. Enterprising people have been recruited. They have been trained in key skills and there is an appropriate reward system. The organization's main heroes are the entrepreneurial ones. Third, the workforce is backed by the necessary support systems. Teamworking is commonplace, people collaborate and network naturally, information is shared and learning is fostered. After all, several people in the organization may be thinking along the same lines at the same time concerning future possibilities. Fourth, successes are visibly rewarded and mistakes are not sanctioned so harshly that people are dissuaded from further initiatives. These points are discussed further later in this chapter.

An intrapreneurial organization will often feature a relatively flat structure with few layers in the hierarchy; too many layers tend to slow decision-making down. The culture and atmosphere will be one of collaboration and trust. The style of management will be more coaching than instructional, and mentoring will be in evidence. Ideally it will be an exciting place to work. The entrepreneur's enthusiasm will have spread to others. In other words, it will be have to be 'contagious'.

Terazano (1999) also reminds us that effective intrapreneurship is not that easily achieved, and that many organizations set off down the road but fail to reap the anticipated rewards. Balancing control (to ensure that current activities and strategies are implemented efficiently) with flexibility (to foster and embrace changes to the same strategies) can imply different cultures, which are difficult to achieve without tension and conflict. Another difficulty frequently lies with finding the appropriate reward and remuneration systems to ensure fairness. It is a brave organization which only awards bonuses to the visibly entrepreneurial people. Managers in established companies often find it difficult to handle setbacks and disappointments when initiatives fail. But there always has to be the risk of failure, albeit temporary, when experimenting with new and unproven ideas. While intrapreneurs often have the security of large company employment, such that the penalty for failure is to some extent reduced, the rewards for real success are unlikely to equal those of the true entrepreneur. Nevertheless, 'increased competition in global markets and the pressure for innovation is forcing Britain's large companies to look for methods to stimulate ideas for new products' (Terazano 1999).

## 10.5 Visionary leadership

Visionary leadership is often associated with an organization that might be described as entrepreneurial, and many visionary leaders are legitimately entrepreneurs, but not always. Moreover, it is not a requirement that, to be effective, a strategic leader has to be personally visionary.

Mintzberg *et al.* (1998) contend that for a visionary strategic leader, strategy is a mental representation of the successful position or competitive paradigm inside his or her head. It could be thought through quite carefully or it could be largely intuitive. This representation or insight then serves as an inspirational driving force for the organization. The vision or idea alone is inadequate; the leader must persuade others – customers, partners, employees and suppliers – to see it, share it and support it. Flexibility will always be an inherent factor, and detail emerges through experience and learning.

For Mintzberg *et al.* (1998), visionary entrepreneurs often, but not always, conceptualize the winning strategic position as a result of immersion in the industry. They may simply have a genuine interest; equally they may have worked in the industry for some length of time. Their secret is an ability to learn and understand, making sense of their experiences and the signals they see. While some people would never be able to make sense of a pattern of strategic signals pertinent to an industry, others learn very quickly.

*There are two types of people in the world – reasonable and unreasonable. A reasonable man adapts himself to the world; the unreasonable man persists in trying to adapt the world to himself.*

George Bernard Shaw

This quotation from Shaw appears to reinforce the relative merits of two schools of thought concerning what entrepreneurs are actually doing: Schumpeter's (1949) belief that entrepreneurs disturb the existing market equilibrium and stability with innovation, contrasted with the Austrian contention that entrepreneurs actually create equilibrium and market stability by finding new, clear, positive strategic positions in a business environment characterized by chaos and turbulence. The Austrian perspective is that of the reasonable man who observes chaos and uncertainty and looks for an opportunity gap that others have missed. Schumpeter's innovators are unreasonable; they are trying to disturb the status quo, turn things upside down, find new strategic positions and make life hard for any existing competitors. Blanchard and Waghorn (1997) claim that Ted Turner (with CNN 24 hour network news) and Steve Jobs (Apple, a case discussed in Chapter 17) are unreasonable men who, like entrepreneurs in the mobile phones business, have been instrumental in changing the world we know.

Successful visionary, aspirational leaders and entrepreneurs are clearly not all from the same mould. The authors believe that there is a hypothetical well of talent and as individuals we possess the potential most suitable for us to become either a leader, an entrepreneur, an intrapreneurial manager, an inventor, a follower or whatever. We remain in the well until we are released. We can, of course, propel ourselves out with sheer determination; equally, if we are fortunate, we can be spotted, nurtured and encouraged. It is not inconceivable that our true talents will lie buried for many years. The point is that when people with entrepreneurial talents emerge from the so-called well, they follow different paths. In Figure 10.9, hard entrepreneurship represents the paradigm of the independent, pragmatic, opportunistic and competitive entrepreneur. These achievement-orientated people are the typical managed risk-takers and natural networkers in search of a deal. Not every entrepreneur fits this pattern. Some present a softer image. They operate in a more informal manner; they are strong on communication and they sell their vision to engage and motivate others. The hard and soft approaches lead to quite different cultures.

Some visionary, adventurous entrepreneurs set out to change the world. These are people with a real ability to galvanize others; they work hard, play hard and operate at the leading edge. They have to have enormous energy and generally they would be described as 'having a presence'. Again, this approach is not, and need not, be ubiquitous. The fourth arm, innovation, still requires imagination, creativity, passion and a commitment to bring about change (see Lessem, 1986, 1998).

**Figure 10.9** Four dimensions of entrepreneurship

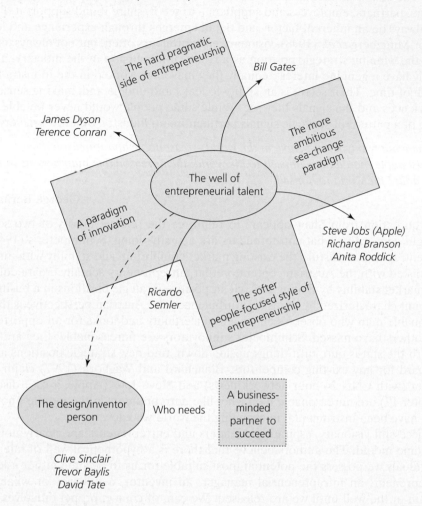

It may be suggested that Bill Gates (Minicase 10.6) is a typical hard adventurer – Microsoft has literally changed the world of computing – while James Dyson (Minicase 5.1) is a hard innovator. Steve Jobs (Apple – Minicase 17.1 later), Richard Branson (Minicase 1.3) and Anita Roddick (Minicase 7.4) are certainly visionaries, whose products have again had a major impact on our lives, but they have all adopted a softer style and approach. Ricardo Semler (Minicase 5.3) is a visionary as far as management style is concerned, but Semco's engineering products, including pumps and industrial dishwashers, are hardly revolutionary. He appears to typify the soft innovator.

There is, however, one final category: the designer–inventor who lacks the necessary business acumen or interest to build the business on his or her own, but who can, with help, be part of a successful and entrepreneurial business. Sir Clive Sinclair is a designer–inventor who has come up with a number of truly innovative ideas and products, but he has never found the right partner and built a winning business. Trevor Baylis also fits here. He did find the right partner and his BayGen radio has provided the foundation for a successful business. This story is also discussed in Chapter 11.

## Minicase 10.6  Bill Gates

US

Bill Gates had a vision for transforming the lives of ordinary people, 'foreseeing a single operating system for every personal computer around the world' to complement Steve Jobs' (Apple) vision of 'a personal computer on every desk in every home and office around the world'. Dedicated pursuit of this focused vision through Microsoft has made him the world's richest person. At the beginning of 2000 Microsoft was valued at $600 billion; Gates' personal wealth exceeded $85 billion. Gates was born to wealthy parents; he was energetic and inspired to work 'ridiculously long hours', and he has inspired criticism and, inevitably, jealousy.

There are several reasons behind Gates' phenomenal success. Among them are his ability to absorb information quickly and his technical expertise – he can actually write computer code. He understands consumers and is uncannily aware of market needs. He has an eye for the main chance coupled with an ability and will to make things happen. Moreover, he is an aggressive defender of his corner, which in the end may work against him with the American anti-trust authorities.

Born in 1955 in Seattle, Gates quickly became interested in science fiction and unusually went to a school which had a computer that students could use. A 'nerd' from an early age, it has been said Gates 'preferred playing with computers to playing with other children'. He nevertheless teamed up with his friend, Paul Allen, and together they 'begged, borrowed and bootlegged' time on the school computer, undertaking small software commissions. Gates and Allen went to Harvard together, where Gates proved to be an unpopular student because of his high self-opinion. Surreptitiously using Harvard's computer laboratories they began a small business on the campus. Gates later left Harvard to start Microsoft, never completing this formal part of his education. Allen was his formal partner in the venture, but Gates always held a majority control. Bill Gates' visionary contribution was the realization that operating systems and software (rather than the computer hardware) held the key to growth and industry domination.

Gates took risks in the early days but, assisted by some good luck, his gambles largely paid off. When the first commercial microcomputer (the Altair) needed a customized version of the BASIC programming language, Gates accepted the challenge. His package was later licensed to Apple, Commodore and IBM, the companies which developed the personal computer market. When IBM decided to attack seriously the personal computer market Gates was commissioned to develop the operating system. Innovatively improving an existing off-the-shelf package and renaming it MS-DOS (Microsoft Disk Operating System) Gates was now on his way. Since then Windows has become the ubiquitous first-choice operating system for most PC manufacturers.

By and large, his success has depended on his ability to create standard products, the benchmark against which others are judged.

Gates hires the 'best and brightest' people and he has made many of them millionaires. He prefers a college-style working environment with a culture dedicated to learning, sharing and overcoming hurdles. Gates personally thrives on combat and confrontation. His colleagues have to be able to stand up to him, but it does generate creative energy. However, he is also seen as enormously charismatic, and employees desperately 'want to please him'. In his younger days he was branded a risk-taker; stories are told of his love of fast cars and his tendency to leave late for meetings in order to provide him with an excuse for driving quickly. After a two-year investigation by the American anti-trust authorities it was ruled (in 2000) that Microsoft should be split into two businesses – one for operating systems and one for applications, including the Internet – and should also be required to give away some of its coding. Gates and Microsoft had been found guilty of exercising monopoly power to the detriment of their competitors. Gates was incensed and appealed against the verdict, which was largely overturned in a higher court. In 2004 the European Competition Commission also ruled against Microsoft, arguing that it had created an

▶

effective monopoly by bundling its own Media Player with Windows. Microsoft said that again it would appeal the verdict.

Since the US ruling Gates has announced two key things. First, in the future Microsoft will focus its resources and energies on developing software that will be delivered as services via the Internet rather than loaded into individual PCs. Second, he was standing down as chief executive. He would continue as chairman and adopt a new role as the company's top software architect. He was returning to his roots.

*I'm returning to what I love most – focusing on technology. These are dramatic times in our industry. We recognize that we must refocus and reallocate our resources and talents.*

The new role also allows him more time to write and to work with his $17 billion Foundation, set up to support initiatives in health and learning.

The new CEO is Steve Ballmer, who had joined Gates during the Harvard days, where he was a fellow student. Having been a successful vice president for sales, support and marketing he had later been appointed president. Ballmer is recognized as an aggressive hardliner: Gates 'respects his ability to clearly discern key strategic issues'.

**Questions**

1. What are the strategic issues that confront Microsoft today?
2. Does it make sense for Bill Gates to adopt his revised role?
3. What exactly did the European Competition authorities decide and what has developed since the announcement in March 2004?

**Microsoft** http://www.microsoft.com

## 10.5.1 Visionary leadership and strategy creation

Visionary leadership, then, implies a strategic leader with a personal vision for the future of the organization and at least a broad idea of the strategies for pursuing the vision. Such leadership often appears to be based on intuition and possibly experience rather than detailed analysis, but truly visionary leaders possess strategic awareness and insight, and do not require extensive analyses to understand key success factors and how the organization can use its abilities and competencies to satisfy needs and expectations. There is a 'feel' for which strategies will be appropriate and feasible and for the potential of the opportunity.

When a visionary leader pursues new opportunities and introduces changes the detailed plans for implementing the new strategies are unlikely to be in place; instead, there will be a reliance on incremental learning, flexibility and adaptation. For the approach to succeed, the leader must be able to inspire others and persuade them of the logic and merits of the new strategies. This is true for all important strategic changes, but when new proposals have emerged from a more formal strategic planning system there will be substantive detail and analysis to justify the case instead of a strong reliance on vision and intuition.

Where major changes to the corporate strategy are being considered it may be necessary for the strategic leader to convince other members of the board of directors and, if new funding is needed, the institutional shareholders and bankers.

The strategy cannot be successful until it has been implemented and has brought the desired results and rewards. Such outcomes require the support and commitment of other managers, and consequently effective visionaries are often articulate, communicative and persuasive leaders.

In simple terms, then, visionary strategic leadership implies three steps: step one is the vision, step two is selling it to other stakeholders and managers; and step three is making sure it happens – aspects of vision, communication and pragmatism.

Richardson (1994) suggests that the following factors are typical of visionary leadership:

- 'covert' planning – planning is often cerebral rather than formal and systematic, such that planning *systems* are not a major aspect of strategy creation
- a passion about what they are doing and their business
- they are instrumental in creating and fostering a particular culture
- they are highly persuasive when encouraging others to implement their ideas and strategies
- they rely on charisma and personal power.

Although visionary leaders are sometimes entrepreneurs, and some entrepreneurs are visionary leaders, the two terms are not synonymous. In this book a visionary strategic leader is seen, typically, as someone who is a persuasive and charismatic agent of change, either starting a new, differentiated business which takes off, or changing the direction and corporate strategy of a business in order to maintain or improve its rate of growth. Major, discontinuous change is implied. The growth can be fuelled by astute acquisition. While entrepreneurship again implies growth, the growth need not always be visionary or discontinuous. Equally, many entrepreneurs are not, and need not be, charismatic figures. The key element of visionary strategic leadership is a visionary impact on strategy creation.

Remember, however, that a strategic leader who succeeds in turning around a company in crisis and *restores growth* – a process sometimes called corporate entrepreneurship – can be a visionary. At the same time, it does not follow that visionary leadership is necessary for either new ventures or successful turnaround situations. When a company is in trouble, a good, analytical 'company doctor' who can restructure, rationalize and refocus the business can be very effective. An example of this can be found in the management buy-in to Clyde Blowers plc orchestrated by Jim McColl OBE, provided as Box 10.4.

## 10.5.2 Narcissistic leaders

Maccoby (2000) has highlighted how strategic leaders, especially those whom we would describe as visionary, are typically more visible today than they ever have been in the past. Some are excellent self-publicists to begin with, and the media are generally more interested in business stories, especially where they concern new industries. Partly as a result of this, Maccoby concludes that an increasing number of strategic leaders are narcissists, inspirational personalities who have a major impact upon culture and style, who enjoy the visibility and notoriety, and who often believe that they are 'something special'. Prior to his retirement (in 2001), Jack Welch, who we mentioned earlier and who we also talk about later in this chapter, negotiated an advance of several million dollars for his autobiography. Richard Branson published his own best-selling autobiography and Bill Gates wrote a successful book on how digital processes can solve business problems.

## Box 10.4  Jim McColl

Jim McColl had spent 17 years (1968–1985) working as an engineer in various UK companies. He followed this with a period of three years as a senior consultant with Coopers and Lybrand working mainly in corporate care work. From 1987–1992 he worked as an independent company doctor. In his own words 'all the time looking for an opportunity to buy into an engineering business'. In 1992 he was offered that opportunity when he bought a 29.9 per cent stake in Clyde Blowers, a public listed engineering company whose principal business activity was sootblowing from coal-fired boilers. Established in 1924 as a family firm, Clyde Blowers in 1992 was still controlled and run by the original family. Instead of being an engineering business, Clyde Blowers had become a property company which also earned some revenues from sootblowing. McColl set about 'realising the value in the engineering business' by selling off the property interests and investing the cash in the engineering business which had been starved of investment. Additionally, he set about building up the business through a series of acquisitions. During the period 1992–1997, seven companies were acquired worldwide which took the market share enjoyed by Clyde Blowers to over 25 per cent of the world market for sootblowing. In 1992, the turnover of Clyde Blowers was £3.3 million and 100 per cent within the UK. By the year 2000, the geographical spread of sales was: 56 per cent US, 34 per cent Europe, 7 per cent UK and 3 per cent China on a total turnover of £70 million. McColl describes his strategy for Clyde Blowers as a classic example of textbook consolidation involving: rationalizing of activities; simplified product lines; 43 per cent reduction in manpower, elimination of the competition; and internationalizing the business.

Described thus it all looks very simple. However, it was McColl who spotted the opportunity and had the vision and drive to see the strategy through to completion, including delisting Clyde Blowers from the London Stock Exchange and taking the company private when the share price of the business was marked down by analysts.

### Question

1. What has happened to Jim McColl and Clyde Blowers in recent years?

   **Clyde Blowers** http://www.clydeblowers.co.uk/

---

*A lot of people want to be led – yet there are very few leaders in life. When people have a good leader who instils team spirit, and they work in an environment that demands excellence, energy, and the keeping of momentum in order to achieve a goal, then they want to stay … or, if they leave, they want to come back!*

Linda J Wachner, when CEO, Warnaco (US)

*To be effective, leadership has to be seen, and it is best seen in action. Leadership must be communicated in words, but even more importantly in deeds. Leaders must be seen to be up-front, up to their jobs and up early in the morning.*

Lord Sieff of Brimpton, Chairman, Marks and Spencer, 1972–1984

What we have in these three cases are big-picture visionaries who are associated with risks and who also come across as being charming personalities. They are typically entrepreneurial and competitive.

There is, however, a potential downside to the narcissist. He or she can be an unrealistic dreamer who has delusions of grandeur. They might also be a poor listener and a relatively isolated loner who is uncomfortable with challenge or criticism.

Richard Branson, for example, has sued the author of an unauthorized biography which questions some of his strategies and claims.

# 10.6 Issues in strategic leadership

### 10.6.1 A precarious position?

Chief executives of large UK businesses (ones in the top 100 in the *Financial Times* index) stay in post for an average of just four years, while their equivalents in the US last, on average, a year longer. Simply, partly because of the visibility mentioned above, perceived poor performers are dismissed more readily than in the past. A price has to be paid for perceived failure.

Charan and Colvin (1999) suggest that these people are normally bright and experienced executives who can articulate a vision and strategy for their organization. This is not their failing. Instead, their shortcomings lie in an inability to implement strategy. This makes sense. In an age of visibility, visions and broad strategies soon become public property. Rivals can attempt to copy them if they wish. Hence, as was shown earlier (see, for example, Chapter 6, Figure 6.9) sustained competitive advantage lies not in ideas and strategic positions, but in the way strategies are executed.

Charan and Colvin specify a number of typical strategic leader misjudgements:

- underestimating the importance of people – a topic taken up in Chapter 5
- failing to put people in the right jobs – Buckingham and Coffman (1999) emphasize the importance of ascertaining people's individual strengths and natural behaviours and using these to judge where they are most likely to make their best contribution
- failing to deal with underperforming managers, especially if they are people they have appointed and who remain loyal
- not stretching people to the highest levels of performance that they can reach
- failing to put in effective decision-making processes – such that important decisions are either not made or not carried through. This relates to empowerment, another topic discussed in Chapter 5
- misjudging the balances between strategy and operations and between the external and internal focus of their efforts. Often this is linked to poor corporate governance, a topic taken up at the end of the chapter. The outcome may well be that a good vision and broad strategy is neither implemented effectively nor updated in changing circumstances.

In the remainder of this section several of these points are taken up.

### 10.6.2 Finite shelf lives?

All leaders, including the most successful, have finite shelf lives, periods of time when they can contribute effectively to an organization. Some know when to step down and either retire or move on, before they cease to be effective. Others stay too long and risk being remembered for their later shortcomings rather than their earlier successes. Churchill was at his peak at the end of the Second World War; Margaret Thatcher achieved her zenith once the main planks of Thatcherite reform were in place. When she stayed on, opposition to her later policies began to ferment, and the details of her downfall will be remembered at least as much as her achievements. Recently Sir Alex Ferguson, who has been the manager of Manchester United for 14 years and brought to the football club a long run of unprecedented success, is now the subject of speculation

**Figure 10.10** Intrapreneurship and entrepreneurship

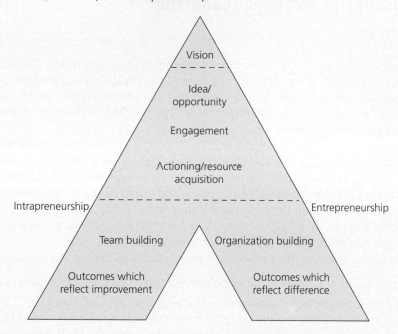

that perhaps he has stayed too long. Minicase 10.7 (Volvo) looks at another long-standing strategic leader who eventually lost the confidence of his board.

Kets de Vries (1994) argues that chief executives who fail to make a timely exit go through a three-phase life cycle. As we progressed through the 1990s, the length of this life cycle was shortening. The first stage is the entry of a new strategic leader into the organization, which is followed by experimentation with new strategies. Downsizing, acquisitions, re-engineering and a drive for improved service and quality are likely. The newcomers make their mark; results improve, certainly in the short term. This becomes the second stage of consolidation, when it is likely that the changes are cemented in a new culture. If an organization was in crisis, the risks are now perceived to have fallen back, and herein can lie the seeds of a new crisis. The third stage, then, is one of decline and a new crisis.

**CASE**

## Minicase 10.7 Volvo

Volvo was led from 1971 to 1993 by Pehr Gyllenhammar, a lawyer who was married to the daughter of the previous chief executive. Gyllenhammar has been credited as a visionary leader who failed to implement many critical strategic proposals.

In the early 1970s he concluded Volvo was reliant on a limited product range (essentially large cars, trucks and buses) and constrained by Sweden not being a member of the European Union. He acquired Daf from the Dutch government; a prolonged period of learning curve was required before Volvo's subsequent range of small cars proved successful. He began to build the first foreign-owned car assembly plant in the US, but production never started. He opened the revolutionary Kalmar assembly plant in Sweden in 1974, based on autonomous work groups rather than the traditional assembly line; the idea was successful, but not outstandingly so, and Kalmar was closed in 1993. In 1977 a proposed merger with Saab-Scania was abandoned when Saab had second thoughts. In 1978 Gyllenhammar agreed to sell 40 per cent of Volvo to the Norwegian government in exchange for oil rights, but Volvo's shareholders revolted.

In the 1980s Volvo acquired the US White truck business and diversified into the food and drug industries in Sweden, but not without some friction with the Swedish government. Throughout this period Volvo's car subsidiary enjoyed continuing success, albeit with its relatively staid image and reputation.

In 1989 Volvo and Renault cemented a strategic alliance with the exchange of minority shareholdings, and in 1993 a full merger was proposed. Fearing the future role of the French government (Renault was nationalized but due for privatization), Volvo's shareholders again refused to back Gyllenhammar. After this defeat he resigned but has since been active in other business and civil engineering ventures. Despite all the setbacks, Volvo proved to be robust and, under Gyllenhammar, grew into one of Sweden's leading businesses.

The diversification strategies had been focused on less cyclical industries to offset the uneven cash flow characteristics of car manufacturing, but a new corporate strategy was announced in April 1994. Non-vehicle interests would be divested systematically. Vehicle joint ventures with a series of companies worldwide would be sought.

Gyllenhammar's immediate successor as chief executive, Sören Gyll, appeared to be adopting a different style. He was more of a team player. The new strategy for cars became the responsibility of a new divisional head. In 1995 Volvo changed the marketing strategy for its cars, attempting to shift away from an image built wholly on safety, reliability and (more recently) environmental friendliness, to one of 'safe but sexy'. Advertisements claimed that (when accelerating in top gear) a Volvo 850 could outpace a Ferrari. The aim was to attract younger 'pre-family' and older 'post-family' buyers without losing the core family customers, and increase output by one-third.

In 1999 Volvo's car division was sold to Ford, which was concerned that 'Volvo had failed to attract younger buyers' and this needed addressing urgently. There would be further changes of management. The sale was possibly inevitable – the group was no longer generating an adequate cash flow for sustainability.

In 2000 Volvo – which by now was largely trucks – bought Renault's truck businesses (which included the American Mack business) and became Europe's largest heavy truck maker. Some time earlier Volvo had been prevented by the European competition authorities from acquiring Swedish rival Scania. In recent years the business has suffered from declining demand in key American and European markets.

Perhaps ironically Volvo cars – under Ford ownership – has prospered and become a very profitable brand. Quality, design and profits have all improved. Some analysts insist this is the result of its managers being allowed to focus exclusively on cars.

## Questions

1. Do you think that those who criticize Gyllenhammar for being an overambitious and individualistic strategic leader are being altogether fair?
2. What do you think his strengths and his failings might have been?

**Volvo** http://www.volvo.com

## 10.6.3 The appropriate style

Visionary leadership is frequently associated with entrepreneurial strategies for companies enjoying prosperity in growth markets. As the organization continues to grow, a more formal structure, together with robust control systems, will be required. The leader must therefore be flexible, capable of adapting and willing to relinquish some personal control. Ideally, other managers will be empowered and encouraged to be entrepreneurial and visionary.

This will not always happen, as some visionary leaders tend to be inflexible. In such circumstances a change of leader would benefit the organization.

Similarly, companies in trouble, facing a strategic crisis or which need rationalizing require a leader who is skilled at managing detail and resources to generate productivity improvements – again different characteristics from the visionary. However, as highlighted earlier, once such an organization has been successfully rationalized, fresh growth requires vision, and here a more visionary leader can again prove ideal.

### 10.6.4 Succeeding a visionary

Unless proper plans are made, succession can be a critical issue. Unfortunately, many visionary leaders are driven by personal ambition and a personal vision; they are difficult to work with and they do not share their game plan. As a consequence, they fail to build a pipeline of managers ready for succession. This raises a number of possible problem scenarios:

- owner-managed businesses may need to be sold, but once an entrepreneurial leader has left, what is the true value of the remaining assets?
- on a visionary's retirement a complete outsider may be needed, implying major change
- the leader could have an accident or illness, leaving a yawning gap which cannot be filled in time to prevent a crisis.

The very successful diversified American conglomerate, General Electric (GE), is discussed at various points in this book. Comments from its visionary strategic leader, Jack Welch, also appear regularly. One apocryphal story of Welch concerns an alleged conversation with a New York yellow cab driver, who claimed he sold his GE shares every August and bought them back in September. 'Jack goes on holiday in August and who knows what might happen when he's away.'

When Welch gave GE advance notice that he would retire in April 2001, succession planning got underway. Three internal divisional heads, those for GE Medical Systems, GE Power Systems and GE Aircraft Engines, were identified as possible successors. They were all interviewed by GE main board members, as were the key staff who reported to them, to assess their style and suitability. To ensure that one of them could be moved up without leaving a gap at the top of their division, a new chief operating officer was appointed in each case, to provide for a second-stage orderly succession. 'Few large companies approach their succession planning with such care.' Of course, they do not always have as much notice!

Welch's successor has proved to be effective – but in a different way. The two disappointed executives both left to take up CEO roles at other companies, both in retailing: Albertson's and Home Depot. Both businesses were in trouble and have been turned around successfully by their new startegic leaders – the stories of both are featured later in the book.

In contrast, Minicase 10.8 at the end of the chapter looks at how succession issues have contributed to the declining fortunes at Sainsbury's and Boots.

When a new strategic leader is appointed, things may not be the same, strategically, culturally and stylistically. This can be good or bad. If real changes are required because the company has lost momentum or is in difficulty, then logically a new leader with a different style is being brought in to make changes. Where a company is successful, then 'change for the sake of change' may be a mistake. But it would not be unusual for a new leader to want to be seen to be his or her own person and to make an early mark. Returning to Figure 10.4, it is quite normal for any new leader to have a different preferred style.

## 10.6.5 Leadership and corporate failure

Businesses 'fail' when they fail to meet the needs and expectations of their key stakeholders, or when decisions that they take lead to outcomes which are unacceptable to the stakeholders. These failings may generate crises with which the business is able to deal, usually at a cost; they may also lead to the ultimate collapse of the organization. The outcomes can take a variety of different forms, but authors such as Slatter (1984) have clearly identified three main, direct causes of corporate failure and collapse:

- weak or inappropriate strategic leadership
- marketing and competitive failings
- poor financial management and control.

It can be seen how these failings imply an *incongruency*, or lack of fit, between environment, values and resources, resulting from a lack of strategic awareness. Leadership issues also underpin the marketing and financial weaknesses.

Richardson *et al.* (1994) have identified a number of discrete failure crisis situations, against which we can consider strategic leadership.

A *niche becomes a tomb* when a small company, locked into a successful product or service, lives in the past and fails to change. This is invariably a sign of poor leadership, and quite frequently it will be tied in to succession problems. When *markets are not understood* small companies will fail to establish a position in the market they have targeted and simply not take-off and grow. Sometimes this will be the result of attention being concentrated on the production aspects of the business, where the would-be entrepreneur may have expertise but may not satisfy customer needs and expectations. Equally, sales may be achieved, but not in sufficient volume.

*Strategic drift* with larger organizations is the result of introversion and inertia in a changing environment. Complacency from past success, or a concentration on day-to-day reactive or crisis management, can lead to a failure situation. Minicase 10.8 on Sainsbury's and Boots provides a clear example of a previously successful large business having problems adapting to a changing environment.

*Overambition* can be seen in the guise of the failed entrepreneur and the failed conglomerate kingmaker. The former enjoys early success and rapid growth on the back of a good product or service, but the desire to maintain high growth encourages the entrepreneur to diversify into less profitable areas. A downward spiral begins. The conglomerate kingmaker wants to build a large and powerful corporation and is tempted to acquire businesses that cannot be justified financially. Specifically, they pay a price which either overvalues the assets or which cannot be recouped from earnings, or they overestimate the potential for synergy with the existing businesses. Vodafone plc is a possible case in point. It was been built up by Sir Christopher Gent through a series of major acquisitions. Yet in 2002 Vodafone plc lost £12.7 billion on a turnover of £22.8 billion, despite enjoying a gross margin of 40 per cent. In 2003 the company had a turnover of £30.37 billion and lost £10.97 billion.

Failures of this nature are frequently characterized by strong, powerful strategic leaders and inadequate attention to critical financial measures and controls. In some instances the result is inadequate governance. The business does not appear to be looking after the interests of all its stakeholders, but instead is driven by the strong, selfish and personal motives of the leader. Small business people will sometimes borrow money on the strength of the business and then milk it dry. Because they enjoy total control, their judgement is not questioned. Some leaders of large corporations, Robert Maxwell was an example, rule by fear and coercion, and as a result their actions are largely unchecked. Maxwell was driven by the desire to build a global empire and to receive recognition and acceptance. In the end he was seen as something of a villain for taking money out of a pension fund to shore up another business in his empire. In the early part of the twenty-first century a number of so called corporate scandals have been widely publicized and generated considerable cynicism about the world of business and especially about high-profile, celebrity leaders. Creative accounting practices at Enron, alleged greed at Tyco, and convicted insider dealing by Martha Stewart are three examples. Trust is becoming an increasingly significant issue in leadership.

**CASE**

## Minicase 10.8  Sainsbury's and Boots – Changes at the Top    GB

**Sainsbury's** began in 1869 in London's Drury Lane, as a shop which sold dairy products – butter, milk and eggs. Expansion of the stores and the range of products really began in the London area in the 1880s. It was 50 years later when the company moved north into the Midlands. The company was floated in 1973. The first Savacentre (an extra large supermarket which sells non-food as well as food products) opened in 1977 and the first Homebase (DIY and gardening products) followed in 1981. Sainsbury's later acquired Shaw's, a relatively small supermarket chain located in the eastern states of the US.

After the flotation the Sainsbury family still owned 39 per cent of the shares, and a family member was chairman of the board from 1869 until 1998. Sainsbury's became grocery market leader in the 1980s and then lost its leadership to Tesco in the 1990s. At the beginning of the new millennium it was also under some threat from a revitalized ASDA, now owned by Wal-Mart – and which is now ahead of Sainsbury's in market share. Profits were falling and its margins are lower than those of its rivals. The acquisition of Safeway by Morrison's is a further threat and some analysts expect Sainsbury's to drop another place to fourth position.

In 1998 the then chairman David (Lord) Sainsbury stepped down to become a government Minister; one year later Sir Tim Sainsbury resigned as a director and for the first time ever there was no family member on the Sainsbury board. The family then sold three-quarters of its 39 per cent shareholding for £2 billion.

The next chairman was Sir George Bull, recruited from Grand Metropolitan (now called Diageo), the spirits and foods group. Sir Peter Davis (ex-Prudential insurance) was appointed chief executive. In 2004 Davis was controversially moved to the chairman role (many investors would have preferred an outsider) and Justin King recruited to the CEO position. King came from Marks and Spencer, where he headed the Foods Division, but previously he had worked for ASDA.

One analyst's view was that 'Sainsbury's no longer appears to have a strategy to secure a place in the aggressive new world of grocery retailing.'

An opposing view suggested that 'Sainsbury's is still a strong brand and can be revived if it returns to its roots as a high quality grocer' ... territory currently held by the considerably smaller Waitrose, a subsidiary of the John Lewis Partnership. This strategy might well require the divestment of Savacentre, Homebase and Shaw's.

▶

Both Homebase and Shaw's have subsequently been sold, Shaw's to Albertsons of the US. Meanwhile, in 2004, Waitrose has bought a number of stores from Morrisons.

Davis was known as someone with a strong leadership style based on a clear vision for any business he was running, backed up by a personal characteristic of being known for having a quick temper. As well as divesting certain businesses, Davis also increased the number of non-food ranges, especially developing a clothes range from designer Jeff Banks. This forced major changes to store layouts. Small specialist stores were opened on Shell garage forecourts and the whole supply chain was streamlined. Millions of pounds were spent on overhauling the company's distribution and IT systems. Sales growth reached a ten-year high; Jamie Oliver, the celebrity chef, was recruited for the advertising campaign. But Sainsbury's continued to be less profitable than all its leading rivals.

In the end, and whichever of the two analysts' views might ultimately prevail, there continues to be a real challenge for the new strategic leadership. King believes the culture is wrong and that far too many managers oppose change. The communication links between head office and the stores are too fragmented. In 2004 the company was failing to achieve the 2002 level of sales. Profits are much the same as they had been in 1989.

What had gone wrong? A number of issues seems to have played a part.

■ The patriarchal family culture, style and control, so valuable for so long, proved restricting when competition really intensified. Until the 1990s members of the family retained their own private entrance to the company's head office and were deferentially called Mr John, Mr David and so on.

■ During the 1970s, 1980s and into the 1990s Lord John Sainsbury of Preston Candover was the strategic leader. A 'true grocer' he was very successful, but he left a huge gap to fill. He had, moreover, been very powerful and autocratic in style.

■ By the late 1980s, under his leadership, the stores were trading profitably and to their full capacity and Sainsbury's was market leader but, with hindsight, the expansion plans in place would prove inadequate for a market that was beginning to change. With a new strategic leader of its own, Ian MacLaurin, Tesco was setting new standards. It had seized the initiative for developing large out-of-town superstores with extensive parking, and when the government began to restrain planning permission for new sites, Tesco already owned a number of new sites that it could develop. Sainsbury's lost out by being reactive. Tesco was also developing new IT-based supply-chain initiatives to strengthen its links with its suppliers and distributors. It is an interesting contrast that when Ian MacLaurin retired in 1997 he was replaced by an insider, Terry Leahy, who had been with the company since 1979. Tesco's leaders have been successful at conveying that the brand is more important than who runs the company.

■ The new Chairman (in 1992), David Sainsbury, who had been Finance Director, was not 'an instinctive retailer' like his predecessor. His style was more consensual and he was more cerebral. 'For the first time he began to ask managers to think for themselves.'

■ In 1995 Tesco launched its Clubcard loyalty scheme. David Sainsbury dismissed it as a gimmick, a reaction that came back to haunt him when it proved successful and Sainsbury's had to follow it with their own scheme 15 months later. The press was rather unkind about the U-turn!

■ Sainsbury's rivals were now proving to be more innovative in several ways, including 24 hour shopping, smaller specialist stores in the high street to complement the superstores and home shopping. Simply, Sainsbury had become a follower, whose stores and supply-chain infrastructure needed major investment.

■ David Sainsbury's initial choice of chief executive, Dino Adriano from Homebase, failed to achieve the turnaround he was brought in to deliver.

**Boots** is another leading high street chain that has 'lost its gloss'. Boots grew out of its origins in pharmacies to become a department store chain – but it has always been recognized as a chemist and optician. It also diversified into unrelated products, such as Halford's (car spares, bicycles etc) and Do It All (a joint venture with WH Smith) which competed with Sainsbury's Homebase and the market leader, B&Q. These businesses have largely gone.

Competition was already beginning to affect Boots when Lord Blyth, who had been in charge for thirteen years, retired in 2000. He left an 'insular, change-resistant culture', having focused his efforts on maintaining the share price. After all, he was one of Boots' leading private shareholders! A significant setback for his successor would occur a year later when resale price maintenance on branded pharmaceuticals was abandoned – retailers could now charge whatever price they liked. Tesco saw this as a wonderful opportunity and led the way, discounting and seizing market share – they also opened their own in-store pharmacies for dispensing prescriptions.

Steve Russell, who took over in 2000, had built his career at Boots. One key plank of Russell's strategy had been the creation of centres of expertise in health and well-being. Manicure, dental and laser eye treatment services had been introduced in some large stores – but later abandoned. Boots had acquired the US company, Clearasil, which many readers will recall fondly

from the days when they had acne! To many observers though, from 2000–2003 the company simply lurched from crisis to crisis. Russell opted to retire early and was succeeded by Richard Baker.

At 40 years old Baker is marginally younger than Justin King. They had worked together at ASDA. Baker quickly decided the supply chain was inadequate, customer service was not good enough and the stores were not open late enough. When he announced some 60 new edge-of-town stores were to be opened, there was speculation that some high street stores would be shut. One-third of head office jobs were to go, and more responsibilities devolved to store managers. An all new top-management team would tackle the corporate culture. Prices were to be cut to deal with competition from Tesco.

## Questions

1. Which of the two scenarios presented in the case for the future of Sainsbury's do you believe is more realistic?
2. Are the situations at Sainsbury's and Boots broadly similar or fundamentally different?
3. Can you think of any other companies where a dominant family influence has finally left a huge gap?

Sainsbury's http://www.sainsburys.com
Boots http://www.boots.com

Source for some of the material: Cope, N (2000) Checking out Sainsbury's, *Management Today*, February.

# SUMMARY

The *strategic leader* of an organization affects both strategy creation and strategy implementation. He or she is responsible for establishing the basic direction of the organization, the communications system and the structure. These influence the nature and style of decision-making within the firm. In addition, decision-making and change is affected by the personal ambitions of the strategic leader, his or her personal qualities such as entrepreneurialism and willingness to take risks, the style of management adopted and the management systems used. Power – how it has been obtained and how it is used – will also affect the style and approach of the strategic leader.

Strategic leaders come in 'all shapes and sizes'. Some are personally visionary, but this is not a prerequisite for effective leadership. It is, however, incumbent on the strategic leader to ensure that the organization has a vision and clear direction and that resources are committed towards its achievement.

Strategic leaders must perform four key tasks or, at least, ensure that they are performed by someone. They must ensure that the organization thinks strategically, that people are engaged and committed and that as a result there is positive action, and that the organization has an appropriate public face and visibility.

The leader can contribute by starting a new business or venture, by turning around a company in trouble, by transforming an already successful company or even by splitting up a company to exploit the true value of its subsidiary parts.

Six different *leadership styles* were identified, often related to past experiences. The leader's natural or preferred style will have a major impact upon the culture of the organization. The six are: analytical, aspirational, public relations, financial engineering, operational and people-based.

Visionary leaders typically provide a strategic vision and rely less on formal planning systems. They are persuasive and charismatic and operate through the culture.

*Entrepreneurs* are similar in many respects, but they are different. Entrepreneurs build value around opportunities. Internal entrepreneurs (intrapreneurs) will be provided with opportunity and encouragement in some organizations where they will drive emergent strategic change.

Clearly, some strong leaders are instrumental in the success and prosperity of organizations. On other occasions they are perceived to fail. In reality, the shelf-life of many large company chief executives is relatively short. Where they are seen to fail it is often the result of poor implementation, which implies that leaders are more likely to know what they would like to achieve than how to do it. This has a further implication: it suggests that it is easy to think that success lies in a good idea, in a strategic position; but ideas and positions can be copied. Sustained competitive advantage lies in the ways in which things are done. Processes and behaviours are harder to replicate.

*Succession* is a crucial issue, particularly succession for someone who has been especially successful or charismatic. It would not be unusual for a newcomer to want to make changes, possibly for no other reason than to stamp his or her personality and preferences on the organization.

## QUESTIONS AND RESEARCH ASSIGNMENTS

1. Using the Volvo case (Minicase 10.7) as a background, discuss why effective leadership involves both strategy creation and strategy implementation. From your experience and reading, which other well-known strategic leaders do you believe are strong on
   (a) creation
   (b) implementation
   (c) both?

2. Minicase 10.3 (David Bruce).
   (a) Do you think David Bruce's approach to growth and change was appropriate for the business he first began? Do you see it as opportunistic or incremental or planned?

   (b) Why do you think Bruce's brewery ventures have been successful?
   (c) Do you think David Bruce's approach of starting off a venture and then leaving to start something else confirms that he is a habitual entrepreneur?

3. Where do the entrepreneur and the visionary leader overlap and where are they different?

4. Apply Figure 10.4 (alternative styles of leadership) to any strategic leader whom you are in a position to evaluate.

## INTERNET AND LIBRARY PROJECTS

1. What has happened to David Bruce recently?

2. Please examine Figure 10.4. Can you attach a particular entrepreneur to each one of the six key leader styles?

3. The following facts relate to Sir Alan Sugar, founder of Amstrad, and one of Britain's richest businessmen.

   | | |
   |---|---|
   | 1947 | Born Hackney, East London |
   | 1963 | Left school |
   | 1966 | Began selling car aerials from a van |
   | 1968 | Founded Amstrad to sell plastic covers for record players. Involvement in televisions, video receivers and CB radio led to |
   | 1985 | Launch of a low-cost word-processor and compact disc player |
   | 1986 | Acquisition of the intellectual property rights of Sinclair computers from Clive |

   | | |
   |---|---|
   | | Sinclair and launch of an IBM-compatible microcomputer |
   | 1988 | Entered satellite dish market |
   | 1991 | Entered laptop computer market. |

   Research the growth and success of Amstrad in the consumer electronics and microcomputers markets and assess what has happened to Alan Sugar in the past 10 years since his company entered the laptop computer market.
   What can you conclude about his style of leadership? Is he an entrepreneur?
   **Amstrad** http://www.amstrad.com

4. How has the General Electric succession issue been resolved?
   **General Electric** http://www.ge.com

5. In the text, Enron, Tyco and Martha Stewart are cited as recent cases of corporate excess. What happened in each of these cases?

## Further reading

Weinshall, TD and Vickery, L (1987) Entrepreneurs: a balanced view of their role in innovation and growth, *European Management Journal*, 5 (4).

Morris, E (1987) Vision and strategy – a focus for the future, *Journal of Business Strategy*, 8 (2).

Pearson, EA (1988) Tough minded ways to get innovative, *Harvard Business Review*, May–June.

Richardson, W (1994) Towards a profile of the visionary leader, *Small Business Enterprise and Development*, 1 (1).

Kets de Vries, M (1994) CEOs also have the blues, *European Journal of Management*, September.

Ginsberg, A and Hay, M (1994) Confronting the challenges of corporate entrepreneurship, *European Management Journal,* 12 (4).

Kets de Vries, M (1996) Leaders who make a difference, *European Management Journal*, 14 (5).

De Geus, A (1997) The living company, *Harvard Business Review*, March–April.

Brody, P and Ehrlich, D (1998) Can big companies become successful venture capitalists?, *McKinsey Quarterly,* 2.

Zack, MH (1999) Developing a knowledge strategy, *California Management Review*, 41 (3).

Hansen, MT (1999) What's your strategy for managing knowledge?, *Harvard Business Review*, March–April.

Eisenhardt, KM (1999) Strategy as strategic decision making, *Sloan Management Review*, 40, Spring.

Hamel, G (1999) Bringing Silicon Valley inside, *Harvard Business Review*, September–October.

Maccoby, M (2000) Narcissistic leaders, *Harvard Business Review*, January–February.

Goffee, R and Jones, G (2000) Why should anyone be led by you?, *Harvard Business Review*, September–October.

# References

Bennis, W, Interview recorded in Crainer, S (1988) Doing the right thing, *The Director*, October.

Blanchard, K and Waghorn, T. (1997) *Mission Possible*, McGraw Hill.

Bolton, WK and Thompson, JL (2000) *Entrepreneurs: Talent, Temperament, Technique*, Butterworth-Heinemann.

Bridge, S, O'Neill, K and Cromie, S (1998) *Understanding Enterprise, Entrepreneurship and Small Business*, Macmillan.

Buckingham, M and Coffman, C (1999) *First, Break all the Rules*, Simon and Schuster.

Charan, R and Colvin, G (1999) Why CEOs fail, *Fortune*, 21 June.

Churchill, NC (1997) Breaking down the wall, scaling the ladder. In *Mastering Enterprise* (eds S Birley and D Muzyka), Financial Times/Pitman.

De Geus A (1997) The living company, *Harvard Business Review*, March–April.

Derr, CB (1982) Living on adrenaline – the adventurer entrepreneur, *Human Resource Management*, Summer.

Ettinger, JC (1983) Some Belgian evidence on entrepreneurial personality, *European Small Business Journal*, 1 (2).

Fradette, M and Michaud, S (1998) *The Power of Corporate Kinetics – Create the Self-adapting, Self-renewing, Instant Action Enterprise*, Simon and Schuster.

Hamel, G (1999) Bringing Silicon Valley inside, *Harvard Business Review*, September–October.

Horovitz, J (1997) Growth without losing the entrepreneurial spirit. In *Mastering Enterprise* (eds S Birley and D Muzyka), Financial Times/Pitman.

Hurst, DK (1995) *Crisis and Renewal – Meeting the Challenge of Organizational Change*, Harvard Business School Press.

Kanter, RM (1983) *The Change Masters – Innovation and Entrepreneurship in the American Corporation*, Simon and Schuster.

Kanter, RM (1989) *When Giants Learn to Dance*, Simon and Schuster.

Kets de Vries, MFR (1994) CEOs also have the blues, *European Journal of Management*, September.

Kets de Vries, M (1996) Leaders who make a difference, *European Management Journal*, 14 (5).

Kirzner, IM (1973) *Competition and Entrepreneurship*, Cambridge University Press.

Lessem, R (1986) *Enterprising Development*, Gower.

Lessem, R (1998) *Managing Development Through Cultural Diversity*, Routledge.

Maccoby, M (2000) Narcissistic leaders, *Harvard Business Review*, January–February.

Maitland, A (1999) Strategy for creativity, *Financial Times*, 11 November.

McClelland, D and Winter, D (1971) *Motivating Economic Achievement*, Free Press.

Mintzberg, H (1973) Strategy making in three modes, *California Management Review*, 16 (2).

Mintzberg, H, Ahlstrand, B and Lampel, J (1998) *Strategy Safari*, Prentice-Hall.

Pinchot, G III (1985) *Intrapreneuring*, Harper and Row.

Quinn, JB (1980) *Strategies for Change: Logical Incrementalism*, Irwin.

Richardson, B (1994) Towards a profile of the visionary leader, *Small Business Enterprise and Development*, 1 (1).

Richardson, B, Nwanko, S and Richardson, S (1994) Understanding the causes of business failure crises, *Management Decision*, 32 (4).

Schumpeter, J (1949) *The Theory of Economic Development*, Harvard University Press; original German edition, 1911.

Slatter, S (1984) *Corporate Recovery: Successful Turnaround Strategies and their Implementation*, Penguin.

Terazano, E (1999) Fresh impetus from the need to innovate, *Financial Times*, 25 June.

# Corporate Strategy

This part of the book is about choices.

Chapter 11 provides an outline of the whole range of strategic alternatives, together with the alternative means of implementing them, only some of which will be relevant for a particular organization at a particular time, although organizations often pursue different strategies at different times. It also looks at strategy selection criteria.

Chapter 12 concentrates on managing growth by discussing diversification, acquisition strategies and strategic alliances.

Chapter 13 covers the broader topic of international strategy. It is broader in the sense that all of the growth strategies discussed in Chapter 12 can have an international dimension. Therefore internationalization needs to be examined as a strategic action in its own right.

Finally, Chapter 14 looks at business failure, consolidation and recovery strategies. If anything in human life is certain then it is death. This applies to many businesses. At some point in the life of any business, elements of Chapter 14 will be relevant. Corporate level failure is a fact of life; no business of any size is immune to this possibility and just as failure can happen so can it be avoided or recovered from by the correct strategic actions.

In Part Two we explored the roots of competitive advantage and hence strategy – difference, cost and speed. Now we look at strategic routes and consider both growth and retrenchment options. We also discuss the means of implementing the choices once they are made.

# Corporate Strategy

# Strategic Alternatives, Strategy Evaluation and Strategy Selection

## Learning objectives

Having read to the end of this chapter you should be able to:

■ identify and describe a number of possible strategic alternatives, separated into limited growth, substantive growth and retrenchment clusters

■ define and discuss innovation and show how it is essential for sustaining competitiveness

■ explain how selected strategies might be implemented through internal or external growth

■ show how organizations pursue different strategic alternatives and means at various times in their development

■ define the key criteria for evaluating the appropriateness, feasibility and desirability of a particular strategic alternative

■ discuss why there might be a trade-off between these factors

■ explain the contribution to this evaluation of techniques described earlier in the book

■ summarize a number of alternative theories of decision-making and explain why subjectivity can sometimes result in poor decisions

■ explain the role of judgement in strategic choice.

This chapter outlines the various strategic alternatives that might be available to an organization in thinking and deciding where it wants to go, and for helping to close the planning gap. The attractiveness of particular alternatives will be affected by the objectives of the organization. While a whole range of options is discussed, it does not follow that they will all be available to an organization at the same time. Because of the costs or risks involved, particular alternatives might be quickly rejected. The appropriate strategy always matches the environment, values and resources congruently.

As shown in Minicase 11.1, Diageo, organizations change their strategies over time, and from this the corporate profile takes a new shape.

In their consideration of strategic alternatives, some organizations will be entrepreneurial and actively search for opportunities for change. Others will only consider change if circumstances dictate a need. Some organizations will already have sound and effective strategies that are producing results with which they are satisfied. Others may ignore the need to change. Some texts have quoted the example of the typewriter companies who thought they knew instinctively that electric typewriters, let alone word processors, would never catch on.

The essential criteria for strategy evaluation and selection are appropriateness, feasibility and desirability. These involve a mixture of objective and subjective factors. Not every strategic decision will be objective and consequently we need to understand how managers (and in turn organisations) make decisions and the impact of uncertainty and judgement on these decisions.

**CASE**

## Minicase 11.1 Diageo     GB   US

By the early 1990s Grand Metropolitan (GM) had become the world's leading manufacturer and distributor of spirits, through its IDV (International Distillers and Vintners) subsidiary, and an important manufacturer of foods, particularly in the USA. GM owned Pillsbury, the Jolly Green Giant foods company. The strategic perspective had changed dramatically in the previous 25 years, influenced markedly by three strategic leaders, and it was about to change again!

In the early 1960s, led by Sir Maxwell Joseph, GM, then known as Grand Metropolitan Hotels, was a leading hotel company and was specialized. Through a series of acquisitions GM then diversified into restaurants, dairies and supermarkets, leisure activities, brewing and spirits. Additional hotel chains were also acquired. This external growth activity slowed down in the 1970s because GM had become highly geared and was affected by the international oil crisis and high interest rates. When Joseph retired in 1980 three strategic problems could be identified:

■ GM was overreliant on the UK (90 per cent of turnover)

■ IDV was inadequately represented in the US, a key market for spirits

■ many hotels needed upgrading if they were to capitalize upon the increase in tourism, especially from the US.

The new chief executive, Stanley Grinstead, sought mainly to consolidate and build, concentrating on the USA. GM acquired its US spirits distributor, Liggett and Myers, in 1980. Liggett also manufactured cigarettes but the tobacco interests were quickly sold off. GM bought Inter-Continental hotels from Pan American and adopted a strategy of repositioning its hotels. Lower grade properties were divested. GM concentrated on exploiting its major brand names and also bought Pearle Health Products in the US. By the mid-1980s hotels contributed 19 per cent of turnover and 6 per cent of profits. The breweries were suffering as lager became more popular at the expense of bitter beers.

Sir Allen Sheppard, who took over in 1986, chose to focus on those businesses where GM could obtain world market strength and divest everything else. The major acquisitions were Heublein (1987), owners of Smirnoff Vodka, the world's second largest spirits brand, Pillsbury, whose main brands are Green Giant, Burger King and Häagen Dazs ice cream, and Pet, which includes Old El Paso Foods (USA) and Shippam pastes in the UK. Mexican food is an important growth sector in the US. After divestments over half of GM's revenue was now being earned in the US.

The true synergy potential of food and drinks was always debatable – while food is essentially a necessity, drinks are more aspirational – but both businesses feature strong, international brands. GM essentially had developed competencies in people, management and control systems, and operational effectiveness, and used these to add value to its businesses.

Sir Allen Sheppard retired as chief executive in 1996 and was replaced by George Bull, an internal promotion. One year later, Grand Met merged with Guinness, and the group was subsequently renamed Diageo. The name was a combination of the Latin *dia*, meaning day, and the Greek *geo*, meaning world. Diageo therefore symbolized 'everyday pleasure, everywhere'.

A number of important changes happened in 2000. Principally, Burger King (which had been acquired with Pillsbury) was lined up to be floated off as an independent business, and the remaining food businesses (Pillsbury and Pet primarily) were sold to General Mills. It was then speculated that if a suitable joint venture partner could be found (as a way of overcoming potential resistance from the relevant competition authorities) Diageo would bid for the drinks businesses owned by the Canadian conglomerate Seagram. These included Chivas Regal brandy. In the event Diageo joined forces with Pernod of France to follow up this opportunity. The joint bid was successful, but Pernod acquired Chivas Regal – Diageo obtained Captain Morgan rum and several prominent American and Canadian whiskies.

Paul Walsh replaced George Bull as chief executive.

In essence, this left Diageo more focused as the world's leading spirits business together with additional interests in wine and brewing (Guinness). IDV's leading brands are: J&B and Bells (whisky), Smirnoff (vodka), Gilbey's (gin), Bailey's and Piat d'Or. The merger with Guinness added UDV (United Distillers and Vintners) and the following brands: Dewar's and Johnnie Walker (whisky) and Gordon's gin.

The following time-line traces the main acquisitions (normal case) and *disposals* (shown in italics).

1957  Origin of Grand Metropolitan in hotels
1966  Chef and Brewer (restaurants)
1969  Express Dairies (Eden Vale and Ski products)
1970  Berni Inns (restaurants)
      Mecca (including William Hill) – leisure activities (bingo), casinos and betting shops
1971  Truman Hanbury Buxton (brewers)
1972  Watney Mann (brewing)
1973  IDV (spirits)

1980  Liggett and Myers (US) – tobacco plus spirits distribution
      *Liggett and Myers tobacco interests*
1985  Pearle Health Care (US) – eye products
1987  Heublein (US spirits, including Smirnoff)
      *Beginning of divestment of hotel portfolio*
1988  Pillsbury – including Green Giant foods, Häagen Dazs ice cream and Burger King
1989  Wimpey restaurants
      *Mecca and William Hill*
1990  20 per cent stake in Rémy Cointreau
      *Pubs put into Inntrapreneur, a joint venture with Courage*
      *Brewing interests sold*
      *Wimpey restaurants*
      *Berni Inns*
1992  Cinzano
      *Express Dairies*
1993  Glen Ellen – US wineries
      *Chef and Brewer*
1995  Pet (US foods, including Old El Paso and Shippam's pastes)
1996  *Pearle Health Care*
1997  Merger with Guinness and creation of Diageo
1999  *Cinzano*
2000  *Unsuccessful attempt to float off Burger King*
      *Pillsbury and Pet (to General Mills).*
      Spirit brands from Seagram – including Captain Morgan Rum and Seagram's whiskies
2001  Bid for Californian wine business, Kendall Jackson
2002  *Malibu auctioned off – a regulatory outcome of the Seagram acquisitions*
      *Burger King also auctioned off*

## Questions

1. Is a focused spirits business with brewing interests strategically more defensible than a diversified food and drinks business?
2. Was synergy between food and drinks – two consumer products sold through overlapping outlets – realistic or opportunistic?

**Diageo** http://www.diageo.com

## 11.1 Introduction

Figure 11.1 provides a summary of the main strategic alternatives, which are separated into three clusters: limited growth, substantive growth and **retrenchment**. In addition, an organization can opt to do nothing; and on occasions the whole business will be sold or liquidated.

**Figure 11.1** Strategic alternatives

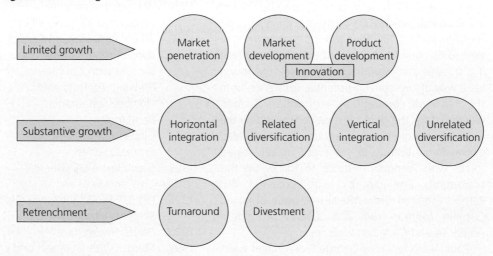

**Figure 11.2** Market entry strategies

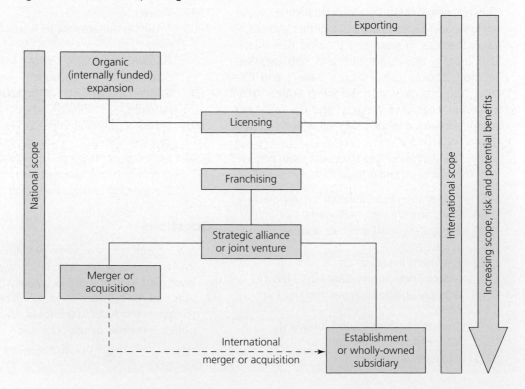

From origins in a single business concept, market penetration and product and market development are shown as limited growth strategies as they mainly affect competitive strategies rather than imply major corporate change. Invariably they involve innovation. The substantive growth strategies imply more ambitious and higher risk expansion which is likely to change the corporate perspective or strategy. These options, explained below, may involve either a strategic alliance or an acquisition, and these *strategic means* are discussed later in the chapter. It was established in Chapter 1 that it is important for organizations to seek competitive advantage for each business in the portfolio. Consequently, once an organization has diversified, it will be necessary to look for new competitive opportunities, or limited growth strategies, for the various individual businesses.

The bottom section of Figure 11.1 shows the main strategies for corporate reduction, namely turnaround and divestment which are discussed in detail in Chapter 14.

Figure 11.2, market entry strategies, summarizes the various ways in which an organization might implement its chosen strategies. It should be appreciated that any strategic alternative can be international in scope, rather than focused on a single country or market, and that as we move from the top to the bottom of the chart the inherent scope, risk and potential benefits all increase. The content of Figure 11.2 is discussed in this chapter and Chapters 12 and 13.

The choice must take into account the risk that the strategic leader considers acceptable given any particular circumstances, and the ability of the organization to deal with the risk elements. Some organizations will not select the most challenging and exciting opportunities because they are too risky.

The options should not be thought of as being mutually exclusive – two or more may be combined into a composite strategy, and at any time a multiproduct organization is likely to be pursuing several different competitive strategies.

Table 11.1 combines the themes of this chapter. It provides examples of seven growth directions related to three alternative means of pursuing each of these strategic alternatives. Many of the examples included are discussed in greater detail throughout the

**Table 11.1** Examples of strategic growth and change

| | | Direction of growth | | | | | |
|---|---|---|---|---|---|---|---|
| | | Inventing a new way of doing business | Market penetration/ development | Globalization | Vertical integration/ diversification | Related diversification | Unrelated diversification | Focus by divestment |
| **Means of growth** | Organic/ internal | Southwest Air Amazon.com Hotmail | Toyota (with Lexus) | McDonald's Canon | Exxon (with refineries) Disney (with stores) | Sony Disney (with cruise ships) | Tata* (India) Virgin Atlantic Airways | Hanson Burton/Debenhams |
| | Strategic alliance | Bennetton and IKEA (with their supply chains) | General Motors and Saab | Star Alliance[†] Coca-Cola and its bottlers | MBNA/Co-op Bank credit cards | Nokia and 3 Com (Internet mobile phones) | Siam Cement[‡] (Thailand) | Yorkshire Water's onion outsourcing strategy |
| | Merger, acquisition takeover | Royal Bank/Direct Line | Ford with Jaguar, Land Rover, Volvo, Daewoo | Astra/Zeneca | Merck with Medco, a distributor | Disney/ABC Television; Wal-Mart and ASDA | General Electric (GE) and NBC Television | ICI's sale of non-core businesses after splitting from Zeneca |

*Tata: construction machinery, engineering, locomotives; tea (where it has global leadership).
[†]Airline code sharing alliance: includes United Airlines, Air Canada, Air New Zealand, British Midland, Lufthansa, SAS.
[‡]Siam Cement: also pulp and paper, construction materials, machinery and electrical products, marketing and trading.

book. The one strategy not discussed in detail here is inventing a new way of doing business. On relatively rare occasions a newcomer to an industry or market will have a disruptive influence through real innovation and, in effect, rewriting the rules of competition. They thus force other competitors into a defensive reaction. The prime example of this is Ryanair and easyJet forcing British Airways and other major European carriers into a whole series of actions including setting up their own budget airlines (Go, Buzz, bmi baby). While the real significance of this possibility is recognized, and discussed in other chapters, it is not realistically an alternative open to a normal organization.

## 11.2 Limited growth strategies

### 11.2.1 The do-nothing alternative

This do-nothing alternative is a continuation of the existing corporate and competitive strategies, whatever they might be, and however unsuccessful the company might be. The decision to do nothing might be highly appropriate and justified, and the result of very careful thought and evaluation. However, it can also be the result of managers lacking awareness, being lazy or complacent, or deluding themselves into believing that things are going well when in fact the company is in difficulties. Doing nothing when change is required is a dangerous strategy.

A company might appear to an outsider to be doing nothing when in reality it is very active. Some companies, for example, prefer not to be the first to launch new product developments, especially if they know that their competitors are innovating along similar lines. A product may be developed and ready to launch but be held back while another company introduces its version into the market. This allows the initial reaction of consumers to be monitored and evaluated, and competitive and functional strategies reviewed before eventual launch. Timing is the key to success with this strategy. A company will want sufficient time to be sure that its approach is likely to prove successful; at the same time it must react sufficiently quickly that it is not perceived to be copying a competitor when that competitor has become firmly established. In general, the rather more theoretical than realistic do-nothing alternative could conceivably be viable in the short term but is unlikely to prove beneficial or plausible in the long term as environmental factors change. Marks and Spencer has been trying to change to cope with the severe competition it now faces. However, the changes have been criticized as essentially reactive. Named fashion ranges Per Una and Autograph, store credit cards, contemporary store fit-outs, adding furniture to the mix and cutting food prices with special offers are all reactions to what the competition is doing.

We next discuss internal growth strategies – market penetration, market development, product development (all of them dependent upon innovation) and **combination strategies**. It should be appreciated that the strategies described are typically organic in nature (namely, growth from within) and they are not fully discrete and independent of each other. The ideas behind them are closely linked, and it may be very difficult to classify a particular strategic change as one of these strategies rather than another. They can all be linked to the idea of the product life cycle, for they provide suitable means of extending the life cycle once it reaches a stage of maturity and potential decline. It will also be appreciated that they are the key elements of the Ansoff grid introduced in the discussion of the planning gap in Chapter 9. At the heart of all these competitive strategies are customers. It is essential that organizations develop strategies for:

- simply retaining existing customers, which may itself require innovation in a competitive market or industry

- expanding the relationship with existing customers by providing them with additional products or services. Direct Line began with car insurance, but soon realized that there was an opportunity to provide home and contents insurance for its existing client base. Kwik Fit also realized that it had a valuable database of motorists and diversified into providing them with insurance as well as tyre and exhaust services. Sometimes the relationship can be expanded by providing more specialized product and service alternatives to target quite narrow niches

- winning new customers (and hence market share) from competitors.

Consequently, the important issue is the line of thought and the reasoning behind the strategy in question, and the objectives.

## 11.2.2 Market penetration

This strategy can have one of two broad objectives. First, to seek assertively to increase market share; and second, and more defensively, to hang on to existing customers by concentrating, specializing and consolidating, which implies what Peters and Waterman (1982) designated 'sticking to the knitting' in their book *In Search of Excellence*.

It involves concentrating on doing better what one is already doing well, and quite frequently involves an investment in brands and brand identity. Although it may seem similar to doing nothing, growth is an objective and there is an implicit search for ways of doing things more effectively. In this respect, and because market environments are invariably dynamic, it overlaps with the ideas of market and product development described below.

Resources are directed towards the continued and profitable growth of a 'single' product in a 'single' market, using a 'single' technology. This is accomplished by attracting new users or consumers, increasing the consumption rate of existing users and, wherever possible, stealing consumers and market share from competitors. The word *single* needs careful interpretation, in the context of the limited growth strategies, as companies such as Kellogg (breakfast cereals) and Sony (music) would be classified as organizations which have succeeded with specialization strategies based around a core brand identity. An extensive product line of differentiated brands designed to appeal to specific market segments would periodically have new additions and withdrawals.

At the same time, productivity and more effective cost management can make significant contributions. Sometimes this will be achieved by investing in new technology at the expense of labour.

The two main advantages are, first, that the strategy is based on known skills and capabilities and in this respect it is generally low risk. Second, because the organization's production and marketing skills are concentrated on specialized products and related consumers, and not diversified, these skills can be developed and improved to create competitive advantage. The company has the opportunity to be sensitive to consumer needs by being close to them, and may build a reputation for this.

Market penetration strategies generally have a high likelihood of success, greater in fact than most other alternatives. There are important limitations, however. Alone they may be inadequate for closing an identified planning gap.

Whilst market penetration is a growth strategy, the long-term growth is likely to be gradual rather than explosive. This should not be seen as a disadvantage, because steady growth can be more straightforward in managerial terms. Any firm pursuing this strategy is susceptible to changes in the growth rate or attractiveness of the industry in which it competes, and therefore the strategy can become high risk if the industry goes into recession. There is also a constant need to monitor competitors and ensure that any innovations do not constitute a major threat.

This strategic alternative is particularly applicable to small businesses which concentrate their efforts on specific market niches.

### 11.2.3 Market development

Market development, together with product development which is considered next, is very closely related to a strategy of specialization. All of these strategies build on existing strengths, skills, competencies and capabilities. Market development is generally another relatively low-risk strategy; and the idea behind it is to market present products, with possible modifications and range increases, to customers in related market areas. This may imply broadening a product range to increase its attractiveness to different customers in different market segments or niches. Clearly, therefore, this strategy is about modifications to strategic positioning. Changes in distribution and advertising will also typically support this strategy.

In summary, the key themes are:

- modifications to increase attractiveness to new segments or niches
- new uses for a product or service
- appropriateness for different countries with particular tastes or requirements.

One example of a market development strategy, then, would be a firm which decided to modify its product in some minor way to make it attractive to selected export markets where tastes and preferences are different. This would be supported by advertising and require the opening of new channels of distribution.

In the last 20 years China has become an increasingly attractive market for specialised children's products, including nutritional supplements and certain upmarket toys. This is the period during which the Chinese government restricted families to a single child as a form of population control. Two parents and four grandparents for each child amounts to some significant purchasing power. And 20 million babies are born in China every year.

### 11.2.4 Product development

Product development implies substantial modifications or additions to present products in order to increase their market penetration within existing customer groups. It is often linked to an attempt to extend or prolong the product life cycle, and typical examples would include the second and revised edition of a successful textbook, or the relaunch of a range of cosmetics with built-in improvements which add value. As product life cycles contract and time becomes an increasingly important competitive issue, this strategy becomes more significant. Minicase 11.2 looks at how Lego has built its success around constant product development and questions whether this strategy has proved adequate.

Operational issues cannot, however, be ignored. For example, when Lesney Products was developing its range of Matchbox Toys in the 1960s and 1970s it withdrew and

## Minicase 11.2 Lego — Eur Int — CASE

*In a volatile and competitive environment we
have concentrated and used our strength to
go deeper into what we know about.*

Kjeld Kirk Kristiansen, President

Lego, the brightly coloured plastic building bricks,
was launched in 1949, and has always proved
popular in an industry renowned for changing
tastes and preferences and for innovation. The
name was derived from Leg Godt, which is Danish
for 'play well'. Ironically Lego in Latin means 'I put
together'. On the strength of this one product
Lego has become Europe's largest and the world's
fourth-largest toy maker. Lego is Danish, family
owned and based on strong principles. For
example, no toys will be developed that have a
military theme. Lego has five stated values: creativity, innovation, learning, fun and quality.
Historically it has been relatively secretive, hiding
its actual sales and profit figures. The company
admits to exceeding sales of 10 billion Danish
Kroner (£830 million) in 2002.

The basic strategy is one of product development, with Lego developing an enormous number
of variations on its basic product theme. Wheels
and electric motors were added in the 1960s. By
the mid-1990s some 300 different kits (at a wide
range of prices) were available worldwide. There
were 1700 different parts, including bricks, shapes
and miniature people, and children could use
them to make almost anything from small cars to
large, complex, working space stations with
battery-operated space trains. Brick colours were
selected to appeal to both boys and girls; and the
more complex Lego Technic sets were branded
and promoted specially to make them attractive to
the young teenage market. Over 200 billion plastic
bricks and pieces have been produced since Lego
was introduced.

In a typical year Lego has replaced one-third of
its product range, with many items having only a
short lifespan. New ideas are developed over a
two- to three-year period and backed by international consumer research and test marketing. Lego
concentrates on global tastes and buying habits.

The Pacific Rim was perceived to offer the highest
growth potential during the 1990s. 'If you differentiate too much you start to make difficulties for
yourself, especially in manufacturing.' Competition has forced Lego to act internationally and
aggressively. One US company, Tyco, markets
products that are almost indistinguishable from
Lego. Lego has attempted unsuccessfully to sue
for patent infringement and now views this competition as undesirable but stimulating. More
recently new competition has come from another
rival construction product, K'Nex, again American.

In the mid-1990s sales were being affected
adversely by changing tastes and by the growing
popularity of computer games. In 1997 Lego
opted for a new range extension. A new kit, especially for girls, was launched – a doll's house series
complete with miniature dolls and furniture. Lego
also began to market construction kits with
microchips and instructions on CD-ROMS. In 1998
the company introduced a new Mindstorms range,
built around a brick powered by AA batteries,
which could be incorporated into a variety of different models that could then be instructed to
move with the aid of an infrared transmitter and a
typical personal computer. Lego had had the technology for some while but had been waiting until
it could reduce costs to a realistic level. More
recently, Lego has ventured into the computer
games market with CD-based products enabling
users to 'build' train sets, vehicles, etc., on screen.
It has also agreed licensing deals for kits based on
Bob the Builder, Star Wars and Harry Potter.

When Lego launched Serious Play in 2002, a
corporate training package, it was capitalizing on
Lego-based activities developed by independent
trainers over many years. Vision Lab is a new
research centre built in 2002 to develop scenarios
on future families and play.

Lego manufactures in Switzerland, the Czech
Republic, South Korea and the USA as well as
Denmark, making its own tools for the plastic
injection moulding machines. Bricks are only
moulded in Denmark and Switzerland but there
are finishing factories in other countries. Tool-

making could easily be concentrated in one plant, but takes place in three to engender competition and to emphasize quality. Lego deliberately maintains strong links with its machinery suppliers. In this and other respects Lego sees itself as being closer culturally to a Japanese company than a US one. Investments in production and improvements are thought to be in the region of at least £100 million per year.

Some years ago, in 1968, Lego diversified with a theme park, featuring rides and displays built with Lego bricks, in Denmark. This has been followed with a similar development on the site of the old Windsor Safari Park in the UK and followed by a third in San Diego, California, and a fourth in Gunzburg, Germany. In the late 1990s the UK park was attracting 1.5 million visitors every year.

Lego recorded record trading losses in 2000 and set about restructuring. Jobs and plants were lost. There was a new logo – with a new strapline, 'Play On' – and new packaging. Diversification trials for clothing, bags and accessories were abandoned. In 2001 the company was profitable again. Unfortunately this would only last two years, before Lego plunged into loss again. Many believed it had been over-ambitious with its licensing agreements as many of these were only short-term windows of opportunity. There has been further restructuring 'in a drive to remain independent'.

## Questions

1. Can Lego realsitically anticipate further growth and prosperity if it relies on its focused strategy or will it become increasingly vulnerable to competitive threats? What would you recommend?
2. Should Lego consolidate or continue to seek to grow?

**Lego** http://www.lego.com

![Lego diversified into clothing]

**Lego** diversified into clothing © Lego 2004

**Legoland** on the site of the old Windsor Safari Park
© Lego 2004

replaced two miniature car models every month to maintain an evolving range of 72 models. Had it increased the number in the range the production complexities would have threatened both controls and profits. Moreover, research and development issues are critical as often new manufacturing competencies have to be developed.

### 11.2.5  Innovation

Innovation is linked to the three strategies described above but it often involves more significant changes to the product or service. It is explored further in Box 11.1. As a strategy it can imply the replacement of existing products with ones which are really new, as opposed to modified, and which imply a new product life cycle. An excellent example of this is Smirnoff Ice from Diageo (Minicase 11.1) in 1998. This vodka-fruit mix 'alcopop' exploits the Smirnoff brand and also takes sales away from bottled beers. The original target market was young female drinkers who wanted to drink from a bottle rather than a glass (which is easier for someone to 'spike' with a drug) but who didn't particularly like beer. Other successful alcopops – or RTD's (Ready to Drink) as they are more properly known – include Bacardi Breezer and Archer's Aqua. Diageo also tried Gordon's Edge (made from gin) but it was withdrawn. One problem is that these innovative drinks have been linked to young 'binge drinkers'. As a consequence some European governments have increased the tax on them, thus hitting sales.

The line which differentiates a really new product from a modification is extremely difficult to quantify. In the case of cars such as the Ford Escort or Ford Fiesta, for example, which appeared in new forms every few years, the changes for each new model were typically marked differences rather than essentially cosmetic. Each new model was very different from the existing model, simply the name was the same.

Similarly, it is important to consider which product life cycle is being addressed. The Sony Walkman and similar personal cassette players have enjoyed their own successful life cycle; at the same time they have extended the product life cycle of cassette players in general far beyond their technical life. As shown in Table 11.1, innovation can be behind the invention of a new way of doing business. Box 11.2 on Dyson, Flymo and Honda provides a brief look at one of the most successful introductions of innovation into an existing business sector, the Dyson vacuum cleaner.

It can be risky not to innovate in certain industries as a barrier against competition. Innovatory companies can stay ahead by introducing new products ahead of their rivals and concentrating on production and marketing to establish and consolidate a strong market position. All the time they will search for new opportunities to innovate and gain further advantage by limiting the market potential for retailer own-brands.

Constant innovation is likely to be expensive and will require other products and strategies to be successful in order to provide the funding. Flymo looks at innovation and product development by a discrete business within a more diversified conglomerate – Flymo is a subsidiary of Electrolux. It emphasizes the importance of design for competitive advantage.

### 11.2.6  Combination strategies

A firm with a number of products or business units will typically pursue a number of different competitive strategies at any time. Product development, market development and innovation may all be taking place. Box 11.2 on Honda shows how three different,

## Box 11.1  Innovation

Innovation takes place when an organization makes a technical change, e.g. produces a product or service that is new to it, or uses a method or input that is new and original. If a direct competitor has already introduced the product or method then it is imitation, not innovation. However, introducing a practice from a different country or industry rather than a direct competitor would constitute innovation.

Innovation implies change and the introduction of something new. Creating the idea, or inventing something, is not innovation but a part of the total process. While at one level it can relate to new or novel products, it may also be related to production processes, approaches to marketing a product or service, or the way in which jobs are carried out within the organization. The aim is to add value for the consumer or customer by reducing costs or differentiating the product or total service in some sustainable way. In other words, innovation relates to the creation of competitive advantage; and, to summarize, there are four main forms of innovation:

■ new products, which are either radically new or which extend the product life cycle

■ process innovation leading to reduced production costs, and affected partially by the learning and experience effect

■ innovations within the umbrella of marketing, which increase differentiation

■ organizational changes, which reduce costs or improve total quality.

Where the innovation reflects continuous improvement, product or service *enhancement*, and only minor changes in established patterns of consumer behaviour, the likelihood of success is greater than for those changes that demand new patterns of usage and consumption. Examples of the latter include personal computers and compact disc players. Discontinuous innovations such as these are more risky for manufacturers, but if they are successful the financial payoffs can be huge. By contrast, continuous improvements –

which, realistically, are essential in a dynamic, competitive environment – have much lower revenue potential.

Innovation can come about in a variety of ways:

■ Ideas can come out research and development departments, where people are employed to come up with new ideas or inventions. Some would argue that there is a risk that departments such as this are not in direct touch with customers; however, while customers may sense that a product or service has drawbacks, they may have no idea how it might be improved. This requires a technical expert.

■ People from various parts of an organization working on special projects.

■ Employees being given freedom and encouragement to work on ideas of their own, e.g. the 3M approach.

■ Everyday events as people interact and discuss problems and issues.

There is a mix of routine, structured events and unstructured activities.

Changes in the service provided to customers and the development of new products and services imply changes in operating systems and in the work of employees, and some of the proposed changes may well be the result of ideas generated internally. However, many of the ideas for innovations come from outside the organization, from changes in the environment. This emphasizes the crucial importance of linking together marketing and operations and harnessing the contribution of people. For example, Ford in the US realized some years ago that a number of its engineers had a tendency to 'over-engineer' solutions to relatively simple problems. As a result, its costs were higher than those of its rivals, particularly Japanese and Korean companies, and its new product development times were considerably longer. Instead, the company needed 'creative engineers' with a fresh perspective and greater realization of customer expectations.

## Box 11.2  Three Innovation Strategies: Dyson, Flymo and Honda

*James Dyson is the subject of Minicase 5.1.*

The profile of James Dyson is one which shows someone with a long history of trying to incorporate degree training in design into viable industrial products and to create within his business an environment which stimulates innovation.

*We were hell bent on doing something different, creating better technology, and designing and engineering a radically different product. It was absolutely in our blood. There should be no fear of doing something that is not normal or sensible.*

### James Dyson CV

Born 1947.

1966–1970 Attends Royal Collge of Art, studying furniture and then interior design.

1970 Joins Rotork in Bath to manage its Marine Division, invents the Sea Truck and develops product sales to 40 different countries.

1974 Invents the Ballbarrow.

1979 Sells shares in the Ballbarrow for £10,000 to support development of his bagless vacuum cleaner.

1979–1984 Builds 5127 prototypes of the Dual Cyclone vacuum cleaner.

1985–1986 Launches the G-Force machine through a Japanese company.

1993 Sets up Dyson Ltd in the UK with Japanese, American and Canadian royalties, and opens R&D centre and factory in Chippenham, Wiltshire.

1995 The Dyson Dual Cyclone becomes the best selling vacuum cleaner in the UK. Buys a larger factory in Malmesbury.

2000 Launches the Contrarotator washine machine.

2002 Transfers vacuum cleaner manufacturing to Malaysia.

2003 Transfers washine machine manufacturing to Malaysia.

2003 Enters the US market and exceeds targets by 180 per cent. The aim for 2006 is for the US to account for a third of Dyson business.

### Reference

*Growing Business for Entrepreneurs*, Issue 28, April 2004.

### Questions

1. The UK has a long history of inventors whose inventions were never capitalized on and turned into major businesses. Why did James Dyson manage to do what many had failed to achieve?
2. His vacuum cleaner is a commercial success. What has happened to the Contrarotator washine machine?

    Dyson http://www.dyson.co.uk

### Flymo

Flymo was started in the 1960s in the north east of England by a Swedish inventor who adapted hovercraft technology for use in lawnmowers. Initially his Flymos were powered by petrol; the electric versions came later.

The company remained focused on lawnmowers for over 20 years before it added additional, but related, garden products. Trimmers came first, in 1988, designed to capture the grass around trees and along lawn edges more easily. In the 1990s Flymo introduced garden vacuum cleaners, using a design that had been brought to them by a British inventor. The company has, however, continually developed and improved its lawnmowers and has over 70 patents registered. Two examples of valuable improvements are first the mower that can compact grass cuttings tightly in a box so that the machine needs emptying less frequently and second the models with simple reel-in electric cables. Anyone who has used an electric mower understands how easily the cable can become twisted! 'The innovation comes from focusing on customer needs, not product features.'

Flymo's design approach is based on teams which embrace research and development, marketing and manufacturing as well as their key suppliers.

## Question

1. Can you think of any sensible new product that Flymo might add to its range?

**Flymo** http://www.flymo.com

## Honda

In an era of cross-border mergers and alliances Honda has made a determined effort to remain independent. In fact, of the main Japanese car manufacturers, only Honda and Toyota are presently not allied in some significant way to an American or a European producer.

'Success is not related to size – it is about satisfying customers.'

Honda's strategy has focused on related high added-value products from a limited number of platforms. Traditionally they have earned above-average margins for their industries. They manufacture outside Japan, and have significant plants in both the UK and US.

There are three main divisions:

■ *Cars* – Honda currently concentrates on cars which (a) are very reliable and comfortable and (b) models which have a sporty image and high performance. As well as cars there is a very successful range of people carriers. The strategic focus for cars is reliability and *innovation mainly through engine technology.*

■ *Motorcycles* – although Honda has a comprehensive range it is probably more associated with smaller versions. The current focus is on *revitalization*.

■ *Power products* – which include lawnmowers, marine engines and agricultural equipment. Honda is looking to *strengthen* its position in these markets.

Honda has developed core competencies in engine technology and power transmissions and has found it valuable (and synergistic) to transfer its learning and technology across the three divisions.

## Questions

1. Might Honda be in danger of becoming a niche player with relatively high costs in the motor vehicle industry if it remains independent?
2. Would this necessarily be a disadvantage in an industry plagued by overcapacity?

**Honda** http://www.honda.com

**Honda** Honda's strategic focus for cars is reliability and innovation, mainly through engine technology

but related, divisions pursue different strategies because of different competitive circumstances.

The internal growth strategies discussed in this section are primarily concerned with improving competitive strategies for existing businesses. Such changes may not prove adequate for closing the planning gap, and consequently higher risk external growth strategies may also be considered. They are also likely to involve a new strategic perspective.

# 11.3 Substantive growth strategies

While this section provides an overview of four substantive growth strategies – horizontal integration, vertical integration, related and unrelated diversification – many of the key issues are discussed in more detail in Chapter 12.

Substantive growth strategies are frequently implemented through acquisition, merger or joint venture rather than organic growth. Franchising can provide another means of generating external growth, but it is only likely to be applicable for certain types of business.

External growth can involve the purchase of, or an arrangement with, firms that are behind or ahead of a business in the added value channel, which spans raw material to ultimate consumption. Similarly, it can involve firms or activities that are indirectly related businesses or industries, those which are tangentially related through either technology or markets, and basically unrelated businesses. The key objectives are additional market share and the search for opportunities that can generate synergy. The outcome from this will be larger size and increased power, and ideally improved profitability from the synergy. In reality, as will be explored in greater depth in Chapter 12, the outcome is more likely to be increased size and power than improved profitability. Synergy often proves to be elusive.

## 11.3.1 Horizontal integration

Horizontal integration occurs when a firm acquires or merges with a major competitor, or at least another firm operating at the same stage in the added value chain. The two organizations may well appeal to different market segments rather than compete directly. Market share will increase, and pooled skills and capabilities should generate synergy. Horizontal integration is, therefore, concerned with issues of critical mass, which are discussed later in this chapter.

Numerous examples exist. Rover Cars, recently part of BMW and previously known as Austin Rover, and before that British Leyland, was the result of a series of amalgamations over many years. Such brand names as Austin, Morris, MG, Wolseley, Standard, Triumph and Rover, which were all originally independent car producers, became combined. Jaguar was also included until it was refloated as an independent company in the mid-1980s and later bought by Ford. The new owners of Rover, a financial consortium, are anxious to resurrect some of the older brand names. BMW have very successfully resurrected the Mini both as a brand and as a very desirable car.

In 1998 Enso (Finland) merged with Stora (Sweden) to create the world's largest forest products (paper making) company. Interestingly, the company enjoyed only a 4 per cent share of the global market, although holding strong positions in certain

## Minicase 11.3 Electrolux

In 1970 Electrolux was a Swedish-based manufacturer of mainly vacuum cleaners, supported by refrigerators. A new chief executive introduced a strategy of horizontal integration and acquisition, and within 20 years Electrolux became the world's leading manufacturer of white goods: refrigerators, freezers, washing machines, tumble dryers and dishwashers. The company also owns Flymo (garden products) and Husqvarna (chain saws).

Major acquisitions included:

| | |
|---|---|
| 1984 | Zanussi (Italy) |
| 1986 | White Consolidated (third largest US producer) |
| 1987 | Tricity (UK, from Thorn-EMI) |
| 1988 | Corbero/Domar (Spain) |
| 1991 | Lehel (largest producer of white goods in Hungary – providing a base for expansion in Eastern Europe) |
| 1994 | AEG. |

Electrolux bought 400 companies over 20 years, with unrelated businesses and surplus assets often being sold off to recoup part of the purchase price.

Production has been rationalized, with many parts standardized, in an attempt to reduce costs, but Electrolux remains a global manufacturer. Wherever possible the best practices from new acquisitions are shared across frontiers, and clearly Electrolux has faced a series of challenges in integrating the new businesses with their distinctive, national cultures. The integration strategy is based upon speed and the immediate input of a small task force to search for synergy and divestment opportunities.

The ultimate success will depend upon the ability of Electrolux to integrate its marketing, particularly in Europe, which accounts for some two-thirds of the sales. In fact 90 per cent of the sales come from mature European and US markets. Product differentiation is possible, but the fact that competing white goods invariably look alike in many respects adds difficulties. In addition, tastes and preferences concerning particular features vary from country to country.

In 1991 products carrying the Electrolux brand name were relaunched as a pan-European upper mass-market brand, with new design features and common advertising and promotion. A similar strategy, but with a more downmarket image, was to follow for Zanussi-branded products. Local brands have also being retained, targeted at individual country preferences: for the UK this means Tricity and Bendix, and for the US, Frigidaire. This dualistic strategy, involving up to four distinct brands in most countries, differs from that of Whirlpool, the US company which acquired Philips' white goods business, and is Electrolux's main rival. Whirlpool is more reluctant to differentiate between countries.

In June 1992 Electrolux agreed a joint venture with AEG, a smaller European competitor and a subsidiary of Daimler-Benz. Electrolux then acquired the whole AEG appliance business in 1994. The AEG brand is particularly strong in Germany, and this final acquisition gave Electrolux individual country shares of some 35% in France, Germany, Italy and the UK. The Electrolux brand is most popular in northern Europe and Zanussi in southern Europe.

However, the concentrated white goods industry has oversupply and fierce price competition; in 1997 Electrolux announced the closure of 25 plants around the world and a workforce reduction of 11 per cent. Electrolux admitted that Whirlpool was enjoying higher operating efficiencies because it had fewer brands. One analyst commented that 'Electrolux has been good at acquiring companies but not so good at integrating them into one unit.' While the challenge seemed to be one of reducing the number of different brands, the trick is to find the right number. Whirlpool had attempted to design a 'world washing machine' to a single specification, and failed. Of course, it doesn't help that the Electrolux brands convey different messages to customers. AEG is associated with German engineering efficiency; Zanussi with Italian style; whilst Electrolux 'conjures up the 1940s and 1950s'.

In 1999 Electrolux settled on a reduced number of global platforms. Dishwashers were reduced from 4 to 1; refrigerators from 46 to 17; and washing machines from 13 to 6. Ovens for much of Europe would be to a common size, but have special features for individual countries. Italians insist on a special pizza setting, for example. Similarly, in France refrigerators have special compartments for fish and shellfish. Figure 4.2 showed how design preferences for washing machines vary between European countries. There are to be fewer brands and the Electrolux name will be featured on every appliance. But which should be retained, and which can be abandoned?

Production is increasingly being switched to lower labour cost countries whilst designers are being challenged to be more innovative. A talking washer – the 'Washy Talky' – has been developed for India. There are refrigerators which can contain smells in separate compartments. The so-called 'Holy Grail' is a washer/dryer that washes clothes but finishes them in such a way that ironing is not required. Electrolux is very aware that if its products are ever seen as commodities its margins will reduce dramatically.

## Questions

1. Are the barriers to global products insurmountable in this industry?
2. Are the preference differences too great to overcome?
3. Has Electrolux found an ideal compromise?
4. Can you see any parallels with motor cars?
5. What impact might the new Dyson washing machine have? (See Minicases 5.1.and Box 11.2.)

**Electrolux** http://www.electrolux.com

segments, particularly newsprint, fine paper and liquid-beverage packaging board. The aim was to provide a stronger base for expansion in South-East Asia where wood fibre is cheaper than it is in Europe.

In the financial services sector, the National Westminster Bank was created by the merger of the National Provincial Bank and Westminster Bank. In early 2000 NatWest was itself acquired by the Royal Bank of Scotland, but this was a hostile take-over in competition with the Bank of Scotland which in turn was taken over by the Halifax Building Society. NatWest had failed to implement a number of strategies over a period of years and had become vulnerable. Shareholders were promised cost savings and profit increases from the larger group, which would be in a position to close some branches and consolidate overlapping activities. Similarly, a number of building society mergers has taken place. The Alliance and Leicester and Nationwide Anglia are typical examples.

Insurance has also been affected. In 1998 Commercial Union and General Accident merged; two years later the new CGU merged with the floated Norwich Union. In 1997 BAT (British American Tobacco) merged its insurance activities (Eagle Star and Allied Dunbar in the UK, Farmers in the USA) with Zurich of Switzerland. Two years later, BAT's residual tobacco interests were merged with Rothman's to create a company large enough to compete seriously with global market leader, Philip Morris. The larger company might also be in a stronger position to deal with the increasing litigation resulting from tobacco-related illnesses.

Minicase 11.3, Electrolux, is an example of international horizontal integration and it shows how difficult it can be to pull everything together and achieve synergy, despite broadly similar competencies and products.

### 11.3.2 Vertical integration

Vertical integration is the term used to describe the acquisition of a company which supplies a firm with inputs of raw materials or components, or serves as a customer for the firm's products or services (a distributor or assembler). If a shirt manufacturer acquired a cotton textile supplier this would be known as **backward vertical integration**; if the supplier bought the shirt manufacturer, its customer, this would constitute **forward vertical integration**.

At times firms will reduce the extent to which they are vertically integrated if they are failing to obtain the appropriate benefits and synergy from the fusion of two sets of skills and capabilities. In 1988 the UK clothing retailer Burton Group sold the last of its suit-making factories in order to concentrate on retailing. At one time Burton had been one of the leading clothing manufacturers in Europe, but that was before made-to-measure suits were substantially replaced in popularity by ready-made suits.

Backward vertical integration aims to secure supplies at a lower cost than competitors, but after the merger or acquisition it becomes crucial to keep pace with technological developments and innovation on the supply side, or competitive advantage may be lost.

In 1987 Rover divested its parts distribution business, Unipart – an example of vertical disintegration. Eight years later, after its acquisition by BMW, Rover sought unsuccessfully to buy Unipart back, arguing that it needed to control its parts distribution to support its increasingly international role.

Forward vertical integration secures customers or outlets and guarantees product preference, and it can give a firm much greater control over its total marketing effort. At the consumer end of the chain, retailers generally are free to decide at what final price they sell particular products or services, and their views may not always accord with those of the manufacturer. However, greater control over distribution might mean complacency and a loss of competitive edge through less effective marketing overall. In addition, manufacturing and retailing, if these are the two activities involved, require separate and different skills, and for this reason synergy may again prove elusive.

Many of the benefits of vertical integration can be achieved without merger or acquisition. Joint ventures, discussed later, are one option. In addition, there may simply be agreements between companies who appreciate that there can be substantial gains from proper co-operation. Marks and Spencer (Minicase 1.2) provide an excellent example historically. Marks and Spencer have benefited from long-term agreements with their suppliers with whom they have worked closely. Many suppliers of a wide variety of products sold by Marks and Spencer rely very heavily upon them, as they are their major customer. At the same time Marks and Spencer set exacting standards for cost, quality and delivery, and guarantee to buy only when these standards are met continuously; and there will always be competitors who would like them as a customer.

The effect of vertical integration can be created organically, without merger or acquisition, but this is likely to be more risky. New skills have to be developed from scratch. Examples of this would be a manufacturer deciding to make components rather than buying them from specialist suppliers, or starting to distribute independently rather than relying on external distributors.

Because new and different skills are involved, vertical integration really implies diversification, but normally these strategic change options are considered separately. The growth and development – and later contraction – of Airtours (now called My Travel) as a vertically integrated holiday company is outlined in Minicase 11.4.

## Minicase 11.4  Airtours/My Travel

In 2000 Airtours was Europe's second largest tour operator, some way behind Germany's Preussag which had recently acquired the UK market leader, Thomson. Founded in 1972 by David Crossland, who remained chairman and chief executive, Airtours could boast 900 customers in 1980. In 2000 that number exceeded 15 million. But things were about to change.

Ten years before, in 1990, Airtours was still a relatively small but fast-growing package tour operator. Based in Lancashire, it offered low-price holidays in cheaper resorts and for a while had a reputation for carrying rowdy youngsters. Most of its customers were based in the north, and Airtours benefited competitively when the impact of the recession was felt first in the south. When bookings fell dramatically before and during the Gulf War (in Airtours' case, by 40%), the company pulled out of selected markets, slowed down its planned move to new premises and froze capital expenditure on new information technology. Airtours was, however, building an airline, and was committed to taking delivery of five McDonnell Douglas aircraft on lease which would operate from Manchester (three planes), Birmingham and Stansted.

Airtours successfully predicted the collapse of International Leisure Group, which included Intasun, the second largest package tour operator. When ILG ceased trading in March 1991 Airtours had agents in place in targeted resorts (the Balearic and Canary Islands, Portugal and Greece) who were ready to buy up all of the released Intasun beds. Striking early, and with the Gulf War still an issue, Airtours obtained good price deals. Within just one week Airtours booked 90,000 new holidays and quickly became the third largest package tour operator. The company had no debt. In 1992 Airtours bought Pickfords, the third largest travel agency in the UK with 333 branches, using its own cash reserves.

In 1993 Airtours narrowly failed to acquire Owners Abroad, then marginally the second-largest UK package tour operator ahead of Airtours. Together the two businesses would have been bigger than the existing market leader, Thomson. However, Airtours did buy the 214 Hogg Robinson travel agencies to add to Pickfords, giving it number two position in this sector of the market – the travel agency sector leader was Thomson subsidiary Lunn Poly. Pickfords and Hogg Robinson have subsequently been combined and renamed Going Places.

Further acquisitions of small UK tour operators soon gave Airtours second position in the package tour market; the company also expanded in Europe by buying the leisure activities of SAS (Scandinavian Airline Systems). At the time of acquisition, SAS Leisure owned or managed 14 resort hotels and also had a substantial interest in its own charter airline.

Airtours diversified into the cruise business in 1994 when it bought two cruise ships and began to provide its own holidays in the Mediterranean and Canaries. In 1996, Carnival, the leading US cruise company, set out to acquire a 29.6 per cent stake in Airtours, firmly linking the two businesses. Together, as a joint venture, Airtours and Carnival bought the Italian cruise line Costa.

In 1997 Airtours bought Belgium's largest tour operator and continued to strengthen its presence throughout Europe. A year later it took a 30 per cent stake in one of Germany's largest tour operators, for example. Also in 1998 were acquisitions in Ireland and America and of a Glasgow-based telephone sales business, Direct Holidays.

In 1999 there was a major setback. Airtours launched a hostile bid for First Choice, the fourth largest UK tour operator, but was thwarted by the European competition commissioner. At this time Airtours was credited with an 18 per cent market share, Thomson had 23 per cent, Thomas Cook/Carlson 16 per cent and First Choice 15 per cent.

However, in 2000 Airtours bought an American Internet travel company – a specialist in cruise holidays – to complement its increasing Internet booking in Europe. The company has opted not to supply other competing Internet businesses: 'Airtours is only willing to work with agents who can bring something to the table.' The company also opened a call centre in Majorca to deal with all of its customers and their needs and queries.

In 2001 Airtours' performance deteriorated markedly as a result of problems with its German operations. Carnival decided to sell its 25 per cent shareholding; Airtours' partial shareholding in Costa Cruises had already been sold to Carnival.

David Crossland announced he would step down as Chairman when he reached 55 late in 2002. Tim Byrne had already taken over from him as CEO in 2000. The company would be renamed My Travel at the same time. A new budget airline, MyTravel Lite began flying from Birmingham. But trading difficulties continued, affected in no small part by the reluctance of many people to fly afer 9/11 the year before. Rivals had cut capcity; Airtours did not. There was a series of profits warnings and a realisation that the company's auditors were querying the way certain transactions were booked in the accounts. The share price was collapsing. From a price of over £5.00 per share in 1999 it was soon down at 90 pence.

Crossland deferred his retirement and Tim Byrne left the company. The new CEO was Peter McHugh who had been running the businesses in America. The accounts were published in November; the company recorded its first ever loss. There was also a change of finance director.

David Crossland did finally depart in March 2003, although he remained the largest share-holder. Unfortunately the share price had now fallen to 14 pence. My Travel had to make disposals. The US Internet travel businesses were divested, along with the German and Polish businesses. To make matters worse a computer error that had caused incorrect (low) prices was discovered. Trading losses continued and another substantial loss was recorded for the year.

Early in 2004 My Travel sold its cruise ships, reduced the number of hotel beds it controlled and cut back the number of planes it was leasing. Continuing losses kept the share price down at around 10 pence.

## Questions

1. Given that for many customers a holiday essentially comprises the sale and provision of a package of services, such as hotel beds, apartments, flights and resort services, how much of the supply chain does My Travel need to own?
2. In the case of Airtours do you think the problem was fundamentally one of strategic misjudgements (the wrong strategy) or setbacks in implementation?
3. Do you see resort-based call centres adding more or less value than the more traditional holiday representatives who tour the hotels and apartments?

My Travel http://www.mytravel.com

### 11.3.3 Related (or concentric) diversification

Any form of diversification involves a departure from existing products and markets. The new products or services involved may relate to existing products or services through either technology or marketing; where this is the case, the diversification is known as concentric rather than conglomerate. A specialist manufacturer of ski clothing who diversified into summer leisure wear to offset seasonal sales would be an example. Potential consumers may or may not be the same; distribution may or may not change; the existing production expertise should prove beneficial.

Similarly, when retailers such as WH Smith add new and different lines and products, they are seeking to exploit their resources and their retailing skills and expertise (core competencies) more effectively.

There is an assumption that synergy can be created from the two businesses or activities; and ideally the new, diversified, company enjoys strengths and opportunities which decrease its weaknesses and exposure to risks.

Any organization seeking concentric diversification will look for companies or opportunities where there are clearly related products, markets, distribution channels, technologies or resource requirements. The related benefits should be clear and genuinely capable of generating synergy. However, diversification might be adopted as a means of covering up weaknesses or previous poor decisions. Benefits will not be expected immediately, and the change involved may divert interest and attention away from existing problems or difficulties.

### 11.3.4  Unrelated (or conglomerate) diversification

In the case of conglomerate diversification there is no discernible relationship between existing and new products, services and markets. The diversification is justified as a promising investment opportunity. Financial benefits and profits should be available from the new investment, and any costs incurred will be more than offset. Financial synergy might be obtained in the form of greater borrowing capacity or acquired tax credits.

The strategy is regarded as high risk because the new technologies, new skills and new markets involved constitute unknowns and uncertainties. Moreover, because the change is uncertain and challenging, it can be tempting to switch resources and efforts away from existing businesses and areas of strength, and this compounds the element of risk involved.

Conglomerate diversification is often linked to portfolio analysis, and sometimes the search for businesses which might remedy any perceived strategic weaknesses. A company with reserves of cash to invest, because it has a number of cash cow businesses, might seek to buy businesses with growth potential in new industries. Some acquisitive and financially orientated companies diversify in this way with a view to rationalizing the businesses that they buy. Parts will be retained if they feel they can add value and benefit accordingly; other parts will be divested. In such cases, the critical issue should be the opportunity cost of the money involved. In other words, the long-term return on capital employed should exceed alternative uses for the money, including simply keeping it banked! While some companies build up substantial capital reserves to ensure that they have the resources to manage during the recessionary stage of a business cycle – as was the case with GEC under Arnold (Lord) Weinstock – others will use the cash to buy back equity. Shareholders will like to see a company enjoying sound financial health but may well feel that a 'cash mountain' should be used for something! It can be a difficult balance. Referring to points made earlier, where a company is anxious to grow, it might initially look for closely related acquisitions but find such routes blocked by competition authorities who feel that customers might be disadvantaged. When such companies opt for unrelated acquisitions they are very likely to argue that there is more relatedness than there is in reality!

Unrelated diversification became less popular in the 1990s, especially under the onslaught of management guru thinking that favoured focus. We develop this later in this chapter as well as in Chapter 16. The real issue concerns whether the strategic leadership can deliver value for all key stakeholders from the diversification. See Minicase 11.5 on Granada.

Some conglomerates and their strategies can work successfully because they targeted underperforming companies and turned them around – linkages and synergies were not high on the agenda. Such strategies are only feasible when poorly performing companies are there to be acquired. Sooner or later the opportunities become fewer and fewer. At

## Minicase 11.5  Granada

### Granada's acquisition of Forte

Hostile takeovers had become relatively rare during the recession of the 1990s when Granada launched its unwelcome bid for Forte in November 1995. At this time Forte was the UK's largest hotel group, with a number of divisions and activities. The hotels included Exclusive hotels around the world, the Méridien chain (bought from Air France), the Heritage, Posthouse and Travelodge brands and White Hart hotels. Little Chef-type restaurants and airport catering were the other main activities. Forte's strategic leader was Sir Rocco Forte, son of the chain's founder. He had been chief executive since 1982 and chairman since 1992. The company had recently been growing at a slower rate than Granada and was underperforming against the FTSE index.

Granada was mainly diversified into Granada Television (based in the north-west of England and famous for its long-running *Coronation Street*), London Weekend TV, Granada Rentals and Sutcliffe contract catering. Granada also operated motorway service stations with linked lodge accommodations. The strategic leader was Gerry Robinson, an Irish-born accountant whose first job had been as a cost clerk with Lesney products. Robinson has been described as instinctive and impatient, and under his leadership Granada had outperformed the FTSE index. He was perceived as a success by Granada's institutional shareholders. Granada was run from a small, tight head office of 24 people; Forte's head office, by contrast, employed 290.

Granada stated that if the bid was successful it would seek buyers for a number of Forte businesses and that the intended retentions were Forte Posthouse hotels, Travelodges in the UK and the chain of Little Chef (364), Happy Eater (68) and Côte (30 in France) restaurants. This collection of assets was valued at £1.7 billion and it generated 80 per cent of Forte's profits. Heritage and White Hart hotels might also be retained; a decision would be taken later. Forte's shareholding in the Savoy, a hotel that it wished to acquire but

where it had so far been thwarted, would also be sold.

Forte's defence against the bid was comprehensive:

- Future profit forecasts were raised.
- The hotels were revalued at £3.35 billion – a figure higher than Granada's £3.26 billion bid.
- A share buy-back was proposed at a premium on the current price.
- A dividend increase of 20 per cent for the next three years was promised.

Shortly after the bid, Forte also sold its wine and spirits distribution business, Lillywhite's sports retail store and 490 Travelodges in the USA. It sought buyers for its Savoy shares, the airport catering and White Hart hotels, and later agreed to sell the UK Travelodges and Little Chef-type restaurants to Whitbread if Forte's bid failed. Granada had applied to the UK Take-over Panel to restrain further asset sales during the period of the bid. Forte also announced Britain's largest ever share repurchase, again if the bid failed. Forte was looking to refocus on its core competency in hotels and retain the Exclusive, Méridien, Heritage and Posthouse brands. The company was credited with a creative and positive defence strategy, but maybe the divestments were coming too late.

Granada's initial bid was increased in January 1996 to a figure equivalent to a 35 per cent premium on the share price prior to the initial bid. The offer was a mixture of shares and cash, fully underwritten by a cash alternative. The additional amount represented a special dividend to be paid out of Forte's own assets. The outcome depended upon the attitude of a number of City institutions, many of whom held shares in both organizations. A key player, and one of the last to announce its decision, was Mercury Asset Management (MAM), a shareholder in Granada which also owned 14 per cent of Forte. MAM backed Granada and the bid succeeded.

Granada finally paid £3.9 billion to acquire Forte. Its new balance sheet showed £3.5 billion debt. Granada urgently needed to dispose of some Forte assets to raise cash and then to generate a positive cash flow from the businesses that it retained.

Sir Rocco Forte immediately announced that he was putting together a consortium to try and buy back Forte's Exclusive, Méridien and Heritage hotels; however, he later withdrew.

## Granada after the merger

In 1996 it was being speculated that Granada might be split into two separate businesses: television and media (with rentals a possible disposal), and hotels and catering. This was subsequently ruled out by Granada.

Granada abandoned the Forte structure of multiple business units for the hotels. It reduced a portfolio of 11 discrete units to three geographical divisions, based on London, the rest of the UK and the rest of the world. Granada did succeed in selling some of the hotels that it had targeted for disposal, but by no means all of them. It refocused on three brands: Posthouse, Travelodge and Le Méridien, into which it incorporated all of its four-star hotels. Heritage hotels were retained, as no buyer was found. In addition, this part of Granada included Little Chef, motorway services and Sutcliffe catering.

The remaining part of the group, Granada Media, acquired additional independent UK television franchises, namely Yorkshire, Tyne Tees and Border. It also sold its stake in BSkyB in order to establish a digital television joint venture with rival independent television broadcaster, Carlton Communications.

## Acquisitions and splitting up

In 2000 Granada announced that it was merging with Compass Catering, a company with a strong presence in canteen vending services and out-source catering for businesses. Compass also owned a number of restaurants. Gerry Robinson knew Compass – in the 1980s he had led a management buy-out of the business from Grand

Metropolitan. Since this buy-out the company had expanded dramatically to become one of only two truly global catering businesses.

Shortly afterwards, Granada Media was spun off as a separate business, led by Charles Allen, previously deputy to Robinson. During summer 2000 the Department of Trade and Industry (DTI) relaxed its rules on the ownership of independent television franchises. It was willing to allow further acquisitions as long as at least two major players remained – this ruling recognized the increasing threat of cable and satellite broadcasters. However, an investigation between a proposed merger of the two other main players, Carlton and United News & Media, required the divestment of UNM's Meridian, the franchise for the south-east. The two abandoned their plans and Granada bid for UNM. This time the requirement would be the divestment of the strategically less important HTV, the franchise for Wales. Granada was basically acquiring Meridian and Anglia Television. The general assumption at the time was that the DTI rules would later be relaxed further and Granada would absorb Carlton as well.

Towards the end of the year, with its shares underperforming against the FTSE index, Granada Compass announced it was auctioning off all of its hotels with the exception of Travelodge. By 2001 the programme of disposals was largely complete. Some £5 billion had been raised; just Little Chef remained. Once this amount was discounted back to a net present value for 1996, the year of acquisition, no profit had been made on the deal. The purchase and sale prices were roughly equal. The general view was that the main beneficiaries had been the various advisers and Forte's old shareholders, as Granada had paid a premium price. In the end all that had really happened was that a hotel chain had been broken up and the various parts placed under new ownership. Using the proceeds from the sale of his shares, Rocco Forte had started a new, small premium hotel chain which was performing well.

Granada and Carlton merged in 2003.

## Questions

1. Do acquisitions of this nature make strategic sense – and if so, for whom?
2. Assume that you are a hotel manager who began with Forte before the acquisition by Granada – how do feel your life might have changed?
3. Do you think you would be better off or worse off?

Forte http://www.roccofortehotels.com
Compass Catering http://www.compass-group.co.uk
Granada Food Services
http://www.granadafoodservices.co.uk
Granada Media http://www.granadamedia.com
Granada Rental http://www.box-clever.com
Granada Television http://www.g-wizz.net

**Lowry Hotel**, Manchester – owned by Sir Rocco Forte

this time General Electric (GE) remains a highly successful diversified conglomerate which achieves synergies across unrelated businesses through its ability to operate as a 'learning organization' which exchanges skills and ideas.

Some companies diversify to build a bigger business and thus reduce the likelihood of being acquired by an unwelcome outsider. The argument is, the bigger they become, the fewer companies can afford to buy them. Paradoxically, if they fail to achieve synergy, they may look attractive to an outside bidder who sees value in buying them to split them up.

## 11.4 To diversify or not – and how

The introduction to this topic begins by defining key terms and looking at diversification and acquisition in a wider context.

Figure 11.3 demonstrates that the growth challenge is to find opportunities for developing and deploying technologies, processes and competencies in ways that generate a more effective and beneficial match between the organization's products and services and its customers and markets. Some of the key themes are:

- the potential for synergy from internal and external linkages and alliances
- the diversification/focus dilemma
- opportunities for, and abilities in, transferring skills and competencies
- opportunities to benefit from the exploitation of a successful corporate brand name.

Table 11.2 provides a brief summary of the advantages and drawbacks of the main growth options, namely:

- organic growth – growth from within, utilizing the organization's own resources and developing new competencies as required

**Figure 11.3** The growth challenge

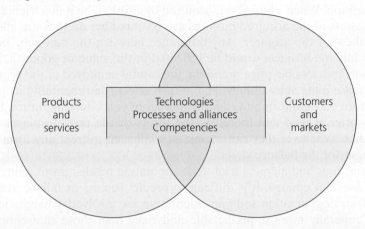

**Table 11.2** Alternative growth strategies

|  | *Advantages* | *Possible drawbacks* |
|---|---|---|
| Organic growth | Lower risk<br>Allows for ongoing learning<br>More control | Slow<br>Lack of early knowledge – may be<br>  misjudgements |
| Acquisition | Fast<br>Buys presence, market share and<br>  expertise | Premium price may have to be paid<br>High risk if any misjudgement<br>Preferred organization may not be<br>  available<br>May be difficult to sell unwanted assets |
| Strategic alliance | Cheaper than takeover<br>Access to market knowledge<br>Useful if acquisition impractical | Possible lack of control<br>Potential managerial differences and<br>  problems |
| Joint venture | As for strategic alliance plus:<br>■ Greater incentive and closer<br>  contact<br>■ Can lock out other<br>  competitors more effectively | As for strategic alliance |

- acquisitions – an umbrella term to encompass the friendly purchase of one company by another, an unfriendly purchase (a takeover) and a straightforward merger of the assets of two or more organizations
- strategic alliances – some form of agreement between two or more companies
- joint ventures – alliances, but where there is the exchange of minority shareholdings between the companies involved or the establishment of an independent company, jointly owned by the organizations who start it.

A merger of two organizations will always be agreed mutually, and in some cases acquisition of one firm by another is friendly and agreed. In other cases proposed acquisitions are opposed and fought bitterly by managers in the threatened firm who try to persuade their shareholders that the company would be better off remaining under their control. These are referred to as takeovers; and when the bid succeeds a premium price is often paid. Although not all acquisitions are aimed at bringing about diversification, the majority appears to represent some form of diversification, related or unrelated.

There is another important reason, a financial one, for differentiating between the types of acquisition. When a business is acquired by another, be it in a friendly or hostile manner, the assets of the acquired business are revalued before they are absorbed into the balance sheet of the acquirer. Any difference between the new valuation and the price paid to buy the business would be reflected in the value of goodwill. Because of this revaluation and possible price premium, the capital employed of the acquiring business may increase quite substantially, and in turn affect (detrimentally) its profitability ratios and return on capital employed for a number of years into the future. In a merger situation, no price is paid and therefore the assets of the two businesses are simply pooled together. Wherever they can, businesses will seek to treat any form of acquisition as a merger for the balance sheet.

Many acquisitions and mergers lead to disappointing results: profitability is reduced and synergy does not emerge. It is difficult to predict success or failure in advance, as issues of both strategy creation and implementation are involved. Changes in corporate strategy are generally more unpredictable and risky than those that concentrate on improving competitive and functional strategies. However, growth opportunities for the present products and markets may be limited and insufficient to fill the planning gap. Few products and ideas cannot be copied and so a company must build and retain a superior competitive position. Experience, applied properly, is of great importance in this. Nevertheless, well-executed acquisitions and diversifications can be sound and very good strategic moves. However, some organizations will turn to strategic alliances or joint ventures as an alternative approach in their attempt to achieve the potential benefits, but avoid some of the potential drawbacks, of acquisitions. In Chapter 12 it is shown that strategic alliances bring their own problems and challenges.

Minicase 11.5 brings out a number of these issues. The acquisition of Forte by Granada represented diversification; the approach was hostile but successful. The subsequent divestment of assets was less extensive than had been predicted and some analysts quickly began to suggest that the new Granada should be split up. The hotel and catering businesses have now been separated from Granada's media activities, which are being expanded with related acquisitions in a changing legislative and competitive environment.

In May 2004 Sir Clive Thompson was ousted as chairman of Rentokil, a company whose growth he had championed over a number of years. He was previously CEO. The apparent reason: disagreements over strategy. His successor as CEO and other executives favoured investing in organic growth, while Sir Clive wanted 'more focus'. By this he meant disposing of certain businesses in order to return some money to shareholders and also to fund 'bold acquisitions'. He was perceived to be thinking more short term than the others.

### 11.4.1   The increasing tendency to diversify

Some years ago, Channon (1983) analysed the extent to which the largest firms in the UK had become increasingly diversified over a 30 year period from the early 1950s. He used *The Times'* Top 200 companies as his database and categorized them as follows:

- *Single-product companies* – Not less than 95 per cent of sales derived from one basic business
- *Dominant-product companies* – More than 70 per cent, but less than 95 per cent, of sales from one major business

- *Related-product companies* – Companies whose sales are distributed among a series of *related* businesses, where no single business accounts for 70 per cent of sales. This would include companies who had pursued strategies of vertical or horizontal integration or concentric diversification

- *Conglomerate/unrelated-product companies* – Companies whose sales are distributed amongst a series of *unrelated* businesses, again where no single business accounts for 70 per cent of sales.

Channon contends that typically a company would start life as a single-product enterprise and then graduate through the dominant-product stage to become a related business, before finally emerging into a conglomerate. However, he emphasizes that companies do not have to follow this particular growth pattern. Some will miss one or more of the natural stages; others will choose to stay in one form and not change.

Table 11.3 illustrates the changes in the structure of the largest UK enterprises between 1950 and 1980, and compares the structural patterns with those of the largest 500 US companies in 1970 and 1980. Utilizing data from Dyas and Thanheiser (1976), some historical comparisons with French and German companies in 1970 are also provided.

In 1950 only 25 per cent of the top 200 companies in the UK had become diversified to the related or unrelated stage, and of these only 5 per cent were classified as conglomerates. By 1980 the respective percentages had increased steadily to 65 and 17 per cent. This compares with percentages of 78 per cent and 24 per cent for the largest 500 companies in the US. Over the same period the number of concentrated single product companies had declined from 35 to 8 per cent.

In contrast with 1970 UK figures of 60 per cent (related and unrelated) and 11 per cent (conglomerate/unrelated) the respective figures for France were 52 and 10 per cent, and for Germany 56 and 18 per cent.

During the late 1980s and throughout the 1990s conglomerate diversification decreased in popularity, and instead companies sought to grow in related areas where skills and competencies are more clearly transferable. Acquirers now typically seek to avoid diversifications that are unrelated to their basic businesses on more than one of the following dimensions: geography, technology, type of product/market or service/market, and the style of corporate **parenting** required (i.e. cultural and leadership issues).

**Table 11.3** Diversification by UK and international companies

| | UK Percentage of top 200 companies | | | | International comparisons | | | | |
|---|---|---|---|---|---|---|---|---|---|
| | | | | | France, percentage of top 100 | Germany, percentage of top 100 | | USA percentage of top 500 | |
| | 1950 | 1960 | 1970 | 1980 | 1970 | 1970 | | 1970 | 1980 |
| Single | 35 | 20 | 11 | 8 | 16 | 22 | | 10 | 0 |
| Dominant | 40 | 43 | 29 | 27 | 32 | 22 | | 41 | 22 |
| Related | 20 | 28 | 49 | 48 | 42 | 38 | | 36 | 54 |
| Conglomerate/unrelated | 5 | 9 | 11 | 17 | 10 | 18 | | 13 | 24 |

Sources: Channon, DF (1983) *Strategy and Structure in British Industry*, Macmillan; Dyas, OP and Thanheiser, HT (1976) *The Emerging European Enterprise: Strategy and Structure in French and German Industry*, Macmillan.

*The minimum scale for effective survival is always rising. A niche can easily become a tomb.*

The late Lord Weinstock, when Chief Executive, GEC

### 11.4.2 Critical mass

As markets and industries become increasingly global a certain minimum size and market share is often thought to be necessary for competitive viability. This is known as critical mass, and it is one explanation for the growing incidence of mergers and alliances between related and competing organizations. Critical mass is important to ensure that:

- there is sufficient investment in R&D to keep pace with the market leader
- the important cost benefits of the experience curve can be achieved
- marketing activities achieve visibility and a competitive presence. This might require a wide product range and good coverage globally.

Lloyds Bank has systematically acquired fellow organizations TSB, the Cheltenham and Gloucester (C&G) Building Society and Scottish Widows (life insurance) to give it a comprehensive geographical coverage in UK financial services; critical mass and cost-reduction opportunities were used to justify the acquisitions. The new company is one of the top three in all of the financial services sectors that it targets. Mortgages are now marketed through C&G; Lloyds was already strong in this segment. Lloyds is also a key player in the small business lending market and TSB is very popular with savers. TSB included an important insurance underwriting business to merge with Lloyds Abbey Life.

Box 11.3 discusses critical mass in greater detail and provides additional examples from the global oil industry.

As stated at the beginning of this chapter, much of the post-Second World War growth and diversification by UK companies has been brought about by merger and acquisition. Some of this has been outside the UK, for a long time, mostly in the US. Statistics from JP Mervis, London-based corporate finance advisers, suggest that, of acquisitions by UK companies in Europe and the USA in the late 1980s, over 90 per cent of the spending was in the USA. Acquisitions involved some well-known companies and brand names. Grand Metropolitan (now Diageo; Minicase 11.1), the leisure and hotels group, took over Pillsbury (the Jolly Green Giant foods group) after an acrimonious battle; and Marks and Spencer bought Brooks Brothers, an upmarket menswear retailer. Marks and Spencer have experienced implementation difficulties with this acquisition, and divested it, and Pillsbury has recently been sold back to the American food business, General Mills.

During the 1990s links with European companies have inevitably grown in popularity. Because of both competitive requirements and regulatory and cultural issues many of these links are between existing competitors, and they often take the form of joint ventures and strategic alliances rather than mergers or acquisitions. On occasions there will be clear arguments in favour of linking two organizations, but pressure from shareholders, managers or governments may mean that acquisition is not feasible.

## Box 11.3 The Significance of Critical Mass

### The reality

The current trend is for horizontal and cross-border integrations:

- to establish critical mass and as
- industry rationalization to create global players.

### *Examples:*

- Airbus (combining the relevant British, French and German interests to create a single business that can compete with Boeing)
- pharmaceuticals companies (as shown in Chapter 4 and prompted by high research costs)
- banking – NatWest's acquisition by the Royal Bank of Scotland for cost-saving potential
- Vodafone/Mannesmann – for European/world power and economies.

Industry concentration in the UK has, however, been stable since the 1970s.

### Points of debate

There is clear evidence that 'big can be best'.

Shell and Exxon (see later in the box) as well as Coca-Cola are long-term survivors. At the end of the 1990s, Lloyds TSB was the best performing British bank.

But do they always stay the best? Are they more vulnerable to the external rule changer? After all, size is no protection against lost competitive advantage.

Glaxo grew from semi-obscurity to become the top pharmaceuticals company in the world on the back of a single new drug, Zantac, but arguably the rules in this industry have changed since then. Governments are cutting back their spending; generic drugs are becoming more popular all the time; and smaller, entrepreneurial biotechnology companies are having an impact on the industry giants.

However, privatization and splitting up of the utilities has improved efficiencies.

At the same time, many dominant industry leaders do falter and fail.

United Steel was once the world's largest company and is now 'nowhere in sight'.

Sometimes an industry declines, but sometimes large organizations become sluggish with power.

Others diversify and get it wrong strategically, and then get taken over and possibly split up.

### What, then, goes wrong?

- lost control
- lack of co-ordination and communication
- lost momentum/motivation/hunger.

### The key issues

Big must think and behave small! Because:
- speed is critical as product life cycles are getting shorter
- information can be dispersed quickly and electronically.

Do alliances make more sense?

### Consolidation and critical mass in the oil industry

During the latter years of the 1990s oil was one industry that has seen a new round of consolidation and merger activity. To a large extent the major players at the end of the twentieth century had dominated the industry from its very beginning.

| | |
|---|---|
| August 1998 | BP (British Petroleum) merges with Amoco |
| September 1998 | Royal Dutch Shell and Texaco discuss (but abandon) plans for a refining joint venture |
| November 1998 | Exxon (already global leader) absorbs Mobil |

| | | | |
|---|---|---|---|
| December 1998 | Total (second largest French oil company) merges with Petrofina (Belgium) | 2001 | Phillips and Conoco merge, creating the world's fifth largest refiner. |

December 1998 — Total (second largest French oil company) merges with Petrofina (Belgium)

July 1999 — TotalFina makes a hostile bid for Elf (number one in France)

Early 2000 — BP/Amoco merges with American Arco

March 2000 — BP/Amoco/Arco acquires Burmah Castrol to 'plug a gap in its portfolio', and later launches a completely new corporate logo

September 2000 — Texaco and Chevron agree to merge

2001 — Phillips and Conoco merge, creating the world's fifth largest refiner.

In mid-2000 the market positions had been:

1. Exxon-Mobil
2. Royal Dutch Shell
3. BP/Amoco/Arco
4. TotalFina + Elf

Chevron (fifth) and Texaco (sixth) were both some way behind the leading four companies.

### 11.4.3 Introducing the diversification/focus debate

Although their popularity has waned in the 1990s, research evidence confirms that *successful* diversified conglomerates can be very profitable at certain times and in certain circumstances. Hanson and BTR (whose histories are discussed in greater detail in Chapter 16) have been notable examples. They succeeded because they:

- carefully targeted their acquisitions
- avoided paying too much (normally)
- adopted an appropriately decentralized structure and control systems; and
- corporately added value.

Implementation is critical. These two conglomerates were structured as holding companies with very slim head offices; individual businesses enjoyed considerable autonomy; and tight financial control systems prevailed. Financial improvements took precedence over a search for skills transfer and synergies. Businesses were sometimes acquired (and divested) more on the logic of their financial contribution than on arguments concerning strategic fit.

Head-office capabilities and contributions for adding value included low-cost financing for the subsidiaries and skills in trading assets and improving operating efficiencies. In simple terms, these organizations developed a strategic expertise in running a diversified conglomerate, skills not matched by many organizations which choose this strategic alternative. During the late 1990s Hanson has been split into five parts and BTR has itself been acquired. Their particular strategies – which relied on finding acquisitions of a suitable size at a favourable price – became increasingly inappropriate as the British economy revived and weak, underperforming companies either became more productive or disappeared. However, as will be seen in later Minicases, the American General Electric (GE) has remained a very successful diversified conglomerate with a completely different style of management. GE does look to transfer ideas and skills to generate synergy between its businesses.

Goold *et al*. (1994) use the term *heartland* to describe a range of business activities to which a corporation can add value rather than destroy value by trying to manage a conglomerate which is too diverse. Key constituents are:

- common key success factors – often market driven
- related core competencies and strategic capabilities
- related technologies.

These issues are debated further in Chapter 16, but, as a final comment here it should not be forgotten that a strategy of focus is not immune from the risk of overdependency. Minicase 11.6 considers the different challenges faced by three focused organizations.

*As soon as things go wrong, companies start talking about focus. Focus is the crutch of mediocre management … If you are trained in the techniques of management … you should be able to apply them across a range of companies. Diversified companies possess both defensive qualities in recession and a springboard for new ventures in more expansive times.*

A comment in defence of conglomerate diversification by
Sir Owen Green, previously a successful Chairman of BTR

Source *Management Today*, June 1994

## Minicase 11.6 Rolls Royce, Kodak and Nokia – Three Focus Strategies

CASE

### Rolls Royce

Rolls Royce had to be rescued with an injection of government funding early in the 1970s; the company had become too dependent financially on the success of one aircraft engine project, the RB211. The aero engine and luxury motor car businesses were separated completely, and the Rolls Royce car brand is now owned by BMW. At the end of the 1990s the company remained focused on the design and manufacture of large, powerful aero engines. Rolls Royce's main two competitors are General Electric (GE) and Pratt & Whitney, both American and both more diverse. Not only is GE a diversified conglomerate, GE Finance controls GPA, the aircraft-leasing company based in Ireland.

Most development funds are committed to high-thrust engines whereby two engines can power large jets over increasingly long distances. Typically, engines are customized for particular aeroplanes, and airline customers normally specify their engine preference from the alternatives available. Rolls Royce's Trent 700, for example, has captured 40 per cent of the engine orders for the

Airbus A330, but initially it was less successful with early orders for the Trent 800, designed specifically for the newest Boeing, the 7E7, seen as a replacement for the 'workhorse' 737, the mainstay of most budget airlines around the world. The competitive arena is now focused on the battle for engine supremacy between the world's leading three producers for both the proposed new giant Airbus A380 (capable of carrying some 550 passengers on two levels) and the 250-seater Boeing 7E7. Early indications are that GE will remain number one, with Rolls Royce second; Pratt & Whitney seems to be the relative loser.

Rolls Royce http://www.rolls-royce.com

### Kodak

Kodak's growth and success over many years has been heavily dependent on photographic film and printing paper. During the 1980s Kodak realized that it faced a possible future threat from digital photography, which had the potential to make traditional film redundant. Half-hearted attempts to develop expertise in digital photography were relatively unsuccessful and consequently Kodak changed to a diversification strategy. In 1988 Kodak bought a pharmaceutical company, Sterling Drug.

Synergy was not forthcoming – the move was not seen as a success – and a new chief executive, George Fisher, was eventually recruited from the electronics company Motorola. Fisher divested peripheral businesses to focus on those related to *imaging*. He rationalized that even when digital cameras were successful and popular, people would still want hard copies of their photographs. Clearly, digital offered important new opportunities; customers could experiment alongside a technician who would be able visibly to enlarge and crop images before a final picture is printed. The technology has existed for a while; the challenge is making it affordable for typical consumers.

In 1998 Kodak acquired Picture Vision, a leading software company which specialized in digital photography. The intention was jointly to develop a strategy that would allow customers to drop their films off at a store and then the developed images would be posted on the Internet for them to download digitally. With this technology customers could then send their pictures electronically to friends and family for them to download as well.

By 2003 Kodak was visibly running down factory space and jobs as digital photography continued to bite in to traditional photography markets. Partly thanks to the acquisition of a Japanese company, Kodak was manufacturing and selling digital cameras – more recently it has added a specialist printer into which its cameras can be docked. But competition remained intense, especially from Japanese companies. Sanyo, Canon, Fuji, Olympus and Sony produce cameras; Hewlett Packard, Sony and Canon dominate in printers.

Kodak bought another business – PracticeWorks, which produces dental imaging software. Related technology but for a radically different market. It also linked with Nokia and Cingular Wireless to develop a new range of mobile phones with inbuilt digital cameras. Using radio waves, the digital images can be sent to Kodak retail kiosks which will print them.

Customers need only make one trip – to collect their pictures. As a consequence Kodak is increasing the number of dedicated kiosks in the US.

It is forecast that by 2007 the percentage of households owning and using digital cameras will exceed those using conventional film. Kodak remains well ahead of its main rival, Fuji, for conventional 35mm film, but it needs a winning strategy for a declining industry to run alongside one for the rapidly growing digital industry. In one it is the leader; in the other it most certainly is not.

**Kodak** http://www.kodak.com

## Nokia

In the early 1990s Nokia of Finland decided to focus on the telecommunications industry. Four key strategic themes were identified: telecommunications orientation, globalization, focus, and value-added products.

Nokia grew rapidly and profitably during 1992 by concentrating on becoming a major player in mobile telecommunications (where it achieved a 20 per cent share of the world market, second only to Motorola) and digital cellular equipment, where it became second to Ericsson of Sweden. The company's origins are in paper and other Nokia products have included televisions, tyres and power, but telecommunications grew from 14 per cent to 60 per cent of the total. Nokia was very successful with its small, lightweight portable telephones; one range competed with Japanese phones by including Japanese numerical characters. Its phones were successful for a number of reasons:

- Small, neat designs
- More user friendly than many rival products
- Good battery life
- Arguably Nokia segmented the market very effectively
- Economies of scale in production and distribution
- Tight control over costs.

Some of the growth was due to weaknesses with two leading rivals, Motorola and Ericsson, but this would not last forever! In 1996 there was a profits warning and a collapsing share price. The growth in demand for mobile phones had led to production bottlenecks, compounded by component supply issues. Nokia was experiencing problems in training its new recruits quickly enough. World prices for analogue phones were falling rapidly; even though market demand was growing healthily, new competitors such as Siemens and Alcatel (Germany and France) were causing supply to exceed demand. Nokia undertook drastic cost reduction programmes and sought to become even more focused on telecommunications. Television manufacture was just one divested activity. The target was for 90 per cent of sales to relate to telecommunications.

By 2000 Nokia was focused on mobile phones together with (a much smaller) networks division. It was the world's leading manufacturer of mobile phones (with a 28 per cent market share) – Motorola (16 per cent) and Ericsson (12 per cent) were some way behind. However, Nokia announced a delay with new models. In this industry, innovation is critical. The original mobile phones remain, but they are much smaller and lighter than they used to be. Camera phones have helped grow the market overall, especially as picture quality has improved. There is a market for phones that provide effective Internet access and others which allow game-playing. There are various views on the market potential for these more sophisticated (and expensive) alternatives. Nokia's 2003 pocket-size folding clam-shell phone (with a picture in the top half and the keys in the bottom half) has, however, proved very successful. As the market grows, prices continue to fall in both real and relative terms. The experience curve has had an effect. After many years of rapid growth there were signs that 2004 might see

**Clam Shell Phone**

some reduction in the rate of growth as the market starts to look saturated. In a number of countries there are now more mobile phones than land lines, despite a considerable differential in call costs.

Between 2002 and 2003 Nokia's market share increased from 32.5 to 34 per cent. Motorola was consistent with 15 per cent in second place. Samsung grew from 8 to 11 per cent; Siemens from 8 to 9 per cent. Sony Ericsson (a joint venture discussed separately in Chapter 12) fell from 6 to 5 per cent. But Sony Ericsson's products are higher price, higher value products; Nokia is particularly strong with lower price phones.

**Nokia** http://www.nokia.com

### Questions

1. Should all three companies remain focused?
2. Would any form of real diversification make sense for any one of them?
3. If so, why?

## 11.4.4 Causes and effects of diversification activity

Constable (1986) argues that the UK experienced the highest rate of diversification among the leading industrial nations between 1950 and 1985, and as a result developed the most concentrated economic structure. Coincidentally, this concentration was accompanied by a trend to the weakest small company sector.

The process of diversification was achieved largely through acquisitions and mergers, which have taken place at a higher rate than that experienced in other countries, especially Japan where there are few large-scale acquisitions. Constable contends that Japan, the US and Germany have concentrated more on product and market development and on adding value to current areas of activity, and that partly as a result of this they have enjoyed greater economic prosperity. Hilton (1987) has suggested that one reason behind this is that in Germany and Japan there is a greater emphasis on the respective banking systems providing funding, rather than shareholders, and this has influenced both the number of take-over bids and expectations of performance.

Diversification and acquisition strategies and tests to establish whether or not a proposed diversification seems worthwhile will be considered further in Chapter 12.

This section of Chapter 11 concludes by emphasizing that organizations change their strategies, either regularly or occasionally, to pursue different alternatives at different times. Figure 11.4 tracks a range of possible moves. For many, the most logical strategic choices are built around relatedness and the consequent synergy. The central spine of the chart shows that product and market development are used to extend a single product range while retaining a clear focus. Chapter 16 looks in greater detail at the idea of a 'heartland' of related businesses which all benefit from belonging to one particualar organization. On occasions, acceptable diversification strategies will also be followed, but sometimes these will later be reversed as the organisation returns to a more focused alternative. Returning to Minicase 11.1, Diageo – when it was Grand Metropolitan – diversified before refocusing, but it refocused on a new heartland, one quite different from where the company had begun. The three tests – appropriateness, feasibility and desirability – listed at the bottom of the chart are the subject of the next part of this chapter.

**Figure 11.4** Changing strategies

**Growth drivers:** – Organic investments – Merger, acquisition, takeover

**Reduction drivers:** – Cut back – Divestments

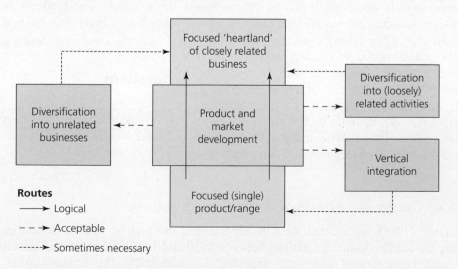

**The tests:** – Appropriateness – Feasibility – Desirability

# 11.5 Introducing strategy evaluation

There is no single evaluation technique or framework as such that will provide a definite answer to which strategy or strategies a company should select or follow at any given time. Particular techniques will prove helpful in particular circumstances.

A sound choice will always address four issues:

1. competitiveness and competitive advantage
2. strategic logic and synergy
3. the financial returns, which should normally exceed the cost of capital
4. the ability to implement.

Several frameworks and techniques which are often classified as means of evaluating strategy have been discussed in earlier chapters and are listed in Box 11.4, together with a number of additional financial considerations which are explained and discussed in the Finance in Action supplement at the end of this chapter.

Certain essential criteria, however, should be considered in assessing the merits and viability of existing strategies and alternatives for future change. This chapter considers how one might assess whether or not a corporate, competitive or functional strategy is effective or likely to be effective. The issues concern *appropriateness*, *feasibility* and *desirability*. Some of the considerations are likely to conflict with each other, and consequently an element of judgement is required in making a choice. The most appropriate or feasible option for the firm may not be the one that its managers regard as most desirable, for example.

In many respects the key aspects of any proposed changes concern the *strategic logic*, basically the subject of this book so far, and the *ability to implement*. Implementation and change are the subject of the final chapters.

Strategic logic relates to:

- the relationship and fit between the strategies and the mission or purpose of the organization; and the current appropriateness of the mission, objectives and the strategies being pursued (synergy is an important concept in this)
- the ability of the organization to match and influence changes in the environment
- competitive advantage and distinctiveness
- the availability of the necessary resources.

## Box 11.4 The Main Strategy Evaluation Techniques

SWOT analysis
E–V–R congruence
Planning gap analysis
Porter's industry analysis and competitive
   advantage frameworks
Portfolio analyses
Scenario modelling

Break-even analysis
Investment appraisal techniques using discounted
   cash flows
Net present value
Internal rate of return
Payback
Cash-flow implications
(The public sector often also uses cost–benefit
analysis)

**KEY CONCEPTS**

**Figure 11.5** E–V–R congruence restated

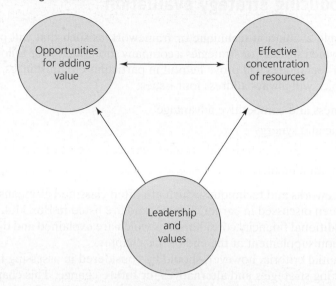

Figure 11.5, which recrafts the earlier model of E–V–R (environment–values–resources) congruence, shows that organizations must seek and exploit opportunities for adding value in ways that are attractive to customers. This can be at both the corporate and competitive strategy levels. At the corporate level, the organization is looking to establish a heartland of related businesses and activities; at the competitive level, the challenge is to create and sustain competitive advantage. Resources must be deployed to exploit the new opportunities, and this is driven or, in some cases, frustrated by strategic leadership and the culture of the organization.

Implementation concerns the management of the resources to satisfy the needs of the organization's stakeholders. Implicit in this is the ability to satisfy customers better than competitors are able to do. Matching resources and environmental needs involves the culture and values of the organization, and decisions about future changes involve an assessment of risk. Relevant to both implementation and strategic logic is the role and preference of the strategic leader and other key decision-makers in the organization.

This chapter addresses the following questions:

- What constitutes a good strategic choice?
- What can the organization do and what can it not do?
- What should the organization seek to do and what should it not seek to do?

The last question should not be treated lightly. there will always be options available which are not appropriate for the organization as a whole, even though they might be attractive to some managers and could be readily implemented. This point is brought out in Minicase 11.7 on Peugeot–Citroën.

When evaluating any corporate, competitive or functional strategy it is worth considering ten strategic principles, all of which are discussed in detail elsewhere in the book. Where these principles, which are listed in Box 11.5, are evident, and particularly where they are strong and powerful forces, the likelihood of strategic success and effectiveness is enhanced. In addition, the financial returns should always exceed the costs involved, unless there is a defensible strategic reason for cross-subsidization.

## Box 11.5 Ten Principles of Strategy

1. Market orientation and customer relevance
2. Innovation
3. Distinctiveness – relating to differentiation and competitive advantage
4. Timeliness (appropriate for the current situation) and
5. Flexibility (capable of change)
6. Efficiency – relating to cost control and cost efficiency, particularly in production and operations

7. Building on strengths and competencies
8. Concentration and co-ordination of resources (rather than spreading them too widely) to achive synergy
9. Harmonization of strategy creation and implementation
10. Understanding – remembering that if a strategy is to be supported by employees who are motivated and enthusiastic it must be communicated and understood.

**Table 11.4** Evaluating strategies in terms of objectives

| Strategic alternative | Objectives* | | | | | |
| --- | --- | --- | --- | --- | --- | --- |
| | Ability to achieve specific revenue or growth targets | Ability to return specific profitability targets | Ability to create and sustain competitive advantage | Synergy potential – relationship with other activities | Ability to utilize existing (spare) resources and skills | and so on |
| Existing competitive strategies for products, services, business units | Score out of say 10 | | | | | |
| *and* | *or* | | | | | |
| Possible changes to corporate and competitive strategies | rank in order of preference | | | | | |

*For evaluation purposes, each objective could be given a relative weighting.

### 11.5.1 Corporate strategy evaluation

Rumelt (1980) argues that corporate strategy evaluation at the widest level involves seeking answers to three questions:

- Are the current objectives of the organization appropriate?
- Are the strategies created previously, and which are currently being implemented to achieve these objectives, still appropriate?
- Do current results confirm or refute previous assumptions about the feasibility of achieving the objectives and the ability of the chosen strategies to achieve the desired results?

It is therefore important to look back and evaluate the outcomes and relative success of previous decisions, and also to look ahead at future opportunities and threats. In both cases strategies should be evaluated in relation to the objectives that they are designed to achieve. A quantitative chart along the lines of Table 11.4 could be devised to facilitate this. In this illustration, and in order to evaluate current and possible future strategies and help to select alternatives for the future, the objectives are listed at the top of a series of columns. It will be appreciated from the sample objectives provided that some can have clear and objective measurement criteria, while others are more subjective in nature. The alternatives, listed down the left-hand side, could be ranked in order of first to last preference in each column, or given a numerical score. In making a final decision based on the rankings or aggregate marks it may well prove appropriate to weight the objectives in the light of their relative importance. This table could simply be used as a framework for discussion without any scoring or ranking, if this approach is preferred. In terms of assessing the suitability of strategic alternatives in particular circumstances, Thompson and Strickland (1980) suggest that market growth and competitive position

---

**CASE**

## Minicase 11.7 Peugeot-Citroën

Jean-Martin Folz, the new president, appointed in 1998, inherited what he saw as three weaknesses in this well-known and largely focused French car manufacturer which competes in a European car industry plagued by overcapacity:

- a lack of volume
- a lack of innovation, and
- a lack of profitability.

One key dilemma was the extent to which the merged Peugeot and Citroën businesses should be kept separate. They compete in the same segments of the market. Their designs may be different but technologies are shared. In many respects this is a potential advantage. Research confirms that 75 per cent of car buyers think they will be able to find what they are looking for in most models of a particular car size just by opening the door. It is the looks and feel – the aesthetics, which are often associated closely with the actual brand name – that determine the perception of difference.

As an immediate strategic change, Folz established a corporate Innovation Directorate to collect a library of ideas upon which everyone in the corporation could draw.

Shortly afterwards he decided upon a number of strategies that Peugeot-Citroën would *not* contemplate in the immediate future. Folz opted not to:

- build a plant in Eastern Europe – where other competitors have 'gone before'. When these countries ultimately join the European Union, these plants will simply add to the existing overcapacity
- build a plant in America, where, again, others have 'gone before'. The US would be too expensive and the domestic market is very mature
- develop a 'world-car' as the various markets are too different
- acquire any specialist, niche company
- merge with France's largest car manufacturer, Renault – which is strongly linked to Nissan. The only real savings would be on components, something that can be easily acquired with a strategic alliance or a joint venture.

### Question

1. What would you do if you were the strategic leader of Peugeot-Citroën? In answering this question you might also like to read Minicase 12.5 which looks at the alternative strategic approaches of Ford and General Motors.

**PSA Peugeot-Citroën** http://www.psa-peugeot-citroen.com

**Table 11.5** Strategic alternatives: their appropriateness in terms of market growth and competitive position

| Strategy | Market growth | Competitive position |
|---|---|---|
| Concentration | High | Strong |
| Horizontal integration | High | Weak |
| Vertical integration | High | Strong |
| Concentric diversification | Not material | Not material |
| Conglomerate diversification | Low | Not material |
| Joint ventures into new areas | Low | Not material |
| Retrenchment | Low | Weak |
| Turnaround | High | Weak |
| Divestment | Not material | Weak |
| Liquidation | Not material | Weak |

Developed from ideas in Thompson, AA and Strickland, AJ (1980) *Strategy Formulation and Implementation,* Irwin.

are important elements. Table 11.5 summarizes their argument. Concentration, for example, is seen as an appropriate strategy where market growth is high and the existing competitive position is strong. By contrast, where market growth is slow and the competitive position is weak, retrenchment is likely to be the most suitable strategy for the organization. Where 'not material' is listed in a column, the contention is that the strategy is appropriate for either high or low growth or strong or weak competitive positions.

# 11.6 Criteria for effective strategies

When assessing current strategies, and evaluating possible changes, it is important to emphasize that there is no such thing as a right or wrong strategy or choice in absolute terms. However, certain factors will influence the effectiveness of strategies and the wisdom of following certain courses of action. A number of authors, including Tilles (1963) and Hofer and Schendel (1978), have discussed the factors that determine the current and future possible effectiveness of particular strategies.

The factors that they suggest, and others, are considered in this chapter in three sections: appropriateness, feasibility and desirability. This categorization has been selected for convenience, and it will be appreciated that there is some overlap between the sections.

The major issues are summarized in Figure 11.6 and are discussed below. A number of factors have been linked to each of the three main criteria or sections. These linkages are not fully cut-and-dried. Some of the factors clearly impact upon more than just one of the criteria.

## 11.6.1 Appropriateness

In reviewing current strategies, assessing the impact of adaptive incremental changes that have taken place and considering strategic alternatives for the future it is important to check that strategies are consistent with the needs of the environment, the resources and

**Figure 11.6** Criteria for effective strategies

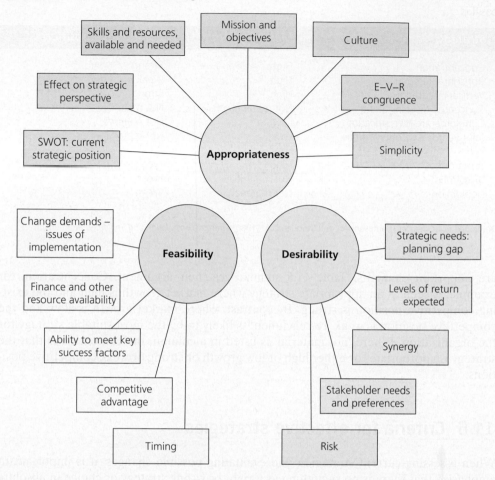

values of the organization, and its current mission. These general points are elaborated below. For the rest of this section the term 'the strategy' is used to refer to each particular strategy being considered, be it a current one or a proposed change or addition.

**Mission and objectives** Does the strategy fit the current mission and objectives of the organization? Is it acceptable to the strategic leader and other influential stakeholders? (This issue is developed further in the Desirability section below.)

**Effect on the strategic perspective** Does the strategy proposed have the potential for improving the strategic perspective and general competitive position of the organization? In other words, will the individual business not only have a strong competitive position (possibly drawing upon strengths and competencies from elsewhere in the organization) but also be able to make a positive and synergistic contribution to the whole organization?

The company, then, must be responsive to changes in the environment and it may wish to be proactive and influence its market and industry. All the time it should seek to become and remain an effective competitor.

**SWOT – current strategic position**  Is the strategy appropriate for the current economic and competitive environment?

Is the strategy able to capitalize and build on current strengths, competencies and opportunities, and avoid weaknesses and potential threats?

To what extent is the strategy able to take advantage of emerging trends in the environment, the market and the industry?

**Skills, competencies and resources: available and needed**  Are the strategies being pursued and considered sufficiently consistent that skills, competencies and resources are not spread or stretched in any disadvantageous way?

Does any new proposal exploit key organizational competencies? For current businesses and strategies: can the organization effectively add value, or would a divestment strategy be more appropriate?

It will be appreciated that this consideration embraces both the opportunity-driven and resource-based perspectives on strategy.

**Culture**  Does the strategy fit the culture and values of the organization? If not, what are the implications of going ahead?

**E–V–R congruence**  Summarizing the above points, is there congruence between the environment, values and resources?

**Simplicity**  Is the strategy simple and understandable? Is the strategy one which could be communicated easily, and about which people are likely to be enthusiastic? These factors are also aspects of desirability.

### 11.6.2   Feasibility

**Change demands – issues of implementation**  Is the strategy feasible in resource terms? Can it be implemented effectively? Is it capable of achieving the objectives that it addresses?

Can the organization cope with the extent and challenge of the change implied by the option?

**Finance and other resource availability**  A lack of any key resource can place a constraint on certain possible developments. The cost of capital is explained in the Finance in Action supplement at the end of this chapter.

**The ability to meet key success factors**  A strategic alternative is not feasible if the key success factors dictated by the industry and customer demand, such as quality, price and service level, cannot be met.

**Competitive advantage**  The effectiveness of a strategy will be influenced by the ability of the organization to create and sustain competitive advantage. When formulating a strategy it is important to consider the likely response of existing competitors in order to ensure that the necessary flexibility is incorporated into the implementation plans. A company which breaks into a currently stable industry or market may well threaten the market shares and profitability of other companies and force them to respond with, say, price cuts, product improvements or aggressive promotion campaigns. The new entrant should be prepared for this and ready to counter it.

**Timing** Timing is related to opportunity on the one hand and risk and vulnerability on the other. It may be important for an organization to act quickly and decisively once an opening window of opportunity is spotted. Competitors may attempt to seize the same opportunity.

At the same time managers should make sure that they allow themselves enough time to consider the implications of their actions and organize their resources properly. Adaptive incremental change in the implementation of strategy can be valuable here. An organization may look to pursue a new strategy, learn by experience and improve by modification once they have gone ahead.

Strategic leadership and the structure, culture and values of the organization are therefore important.

Timing is also an implementation issue; Minicase 11.8 on Next provides one illustration of its significance. This case shows how Next introduced a number of successful strategic changes which resulted in growth and increased profitability, but then overstretched themselves by pursuing strategies for which they had insufficient resources at the time. This theme relates to the theory of growth and the existence of the receding managerial limit suggested by Edith Penrose (1959), which was discussed in Chapter 2.

Minicase 11.8 also addresses an important paradox of resource management. Resources must be stretched if they are to achieve their full potential, but if the targets set for them imply a 'bridge too far' there is a real danger of both underachievement and damage to the rest of the organization. Here, resources might have to be redeployed, which will have consequences for the business from which they are taken. The reputation of the organization might easily be tarnished. Clearly, the decisions reached will reflect the risk perspective of the managers concerned.

CASE

## Minicase 11.8  Next    GB

At the end of 1988 George Davies lost the chairmanship of Next, the retail company that he had built which had experienced rapid growth and success during the 1980s. Recent strategic changes had failed to provide the desired level of success. Arguably, the speed of the growth and the extent of the diversification had been too great for Next's resources, and profits had fallen as a result. Over four years and with a series of strategic moves, Davies had transformed the relatively dowdy menswear retailers J Hepworth into Next, a group which was innovative, design led and fashion orientated. J Hepworth had started trading in 1864 and had divested into womenswear only in 1981 when it bought Kendalls. The Next brand began life a little later.

Next segmented the retail market, selling fashionable clothing to younger men and women, as well as for children, and jewellery and furniture. However, alone a strategy of targeting new segments is not a source of sustained advantage. Rivals will soon see the new opportunity and seek to move in. In addition, Next had diversified into general mail order by the acquisition of Grattan, one of the largest catalogue retail operations.

The moves which proved problematical occurred in 1987 and 1988. In 1987 Next took over Combined English Stores (CES), a large and already diversified retail group which included Biba (the West German fashion retailer), Zales (jewellery), Salisbury's (luggage, handbags and the like), a chain of chemist's shops, a carpet business and a

▶

holiday company. This gave Next a substantial high-street presence, together with the problem and expense of converting a large number of stores to the fashionable Next image and format, which was regarded as a key factor in their record of success. Critics argued that Next had acquired too many stores, however, and Zales and Salisbury's were sold to Ratner's in autumn 1988. This reduced the extent of Next's diversification, and helped to reduce the gearing from 125 per cent.

In January 1988 the Next Directory, an exclusive mail-order catalogue, was launched and *sold* to potential customers through advertising and direct mail. At this time catalogues were normally free. The product range in the Directory was designed to appeal to upmarket buyers, not the traditional mail-order customers, who could specify when they wanted their goods delivered. The launch and the new concept proved less successful than fore-casts and expectations. Moreover, in 1988 there was growing friction between Next and Grattan. Grattan disagreed with Next's plans to redevelop their product line. Davies has claimed that in October 1988 there were serious discussions about splitting Next and Grattan, as happened with ASDA and MFI.

At the end of 1988 Next's profitability had declined, its strategy was not co-ordinated, and there were concerns about a fall in demand in 1989 as a result of increased interest charges and inflation.

*Question 1*
Had the diversification into mail order and the acquisition of Combined English Stores been appropriate and feasible?

Next was unable to provide all of the necessary resources at the time they were required; and George Davies was quoted in the *Financial Times* on 5 December 1988 as saying, 'The lesson that I've learnt this year is that you must stick to the markets you know.'

Next, also, was a highly innovative company, yet Davies was seen as an autocratic strategic leader who had failed to develop an appropriately supportive team of managers and an organization that was sufficiently decentralized.

After Davies' departure Next concentrated on two principal businesses:

- retailing ladies', men's and children's clothing, accessories and home furnishings – the remaining retail businesses were divested
- the Next Directory – Grattan was sold to Otto Versand, the German mail-order company.

George Davies, whose collaborative alliance with ASDA has been successful, was replaced as chief executive by David Jones, who had joined Next when it acquired Grattan. Jones has been described as a cautious, conservative accountant.

*I probably gamble a little more than people think, but only when I have the information to ensure it is a safe bet.*

David Jones

Jones' strategies for rationalizing and consolidating the business proved very successful and by the end of 1995 Next had been turned around.

| | Index of sales revenue (1986 = 100) | Trading costs as a % of turnover | Return on capital employed |
|---|---|---|---|
| 1986 | 100 | 88 | 11.4 |
| 1989 | 500 | 97 | 6.7 |
| 1992 | 255 | 93 | 19.2 |
| 1994 | 344 | 86 | 33.6 |

The figures show how quickly sales revenue rose during the 1980s with the acquisitions and the more aggressive retailing style, but costs were also rising and profitability was falling. With divestments sales then fell, before rising again. Under Jones the return on capital advanced steadily. In 1995 Next was not only profitable, it had accrued cash reserves of £150 million.

*Question 2*
What strategies would be appropriate, desirable and feasible for utilizing these resources effectively?

In the event, there was some international expansion but no major acquisitions. Paradoxically, once there were no major crises to deal with, some complacency set in. Next sales fell back during 1998, the first reduction during the 1990s.

■ There had been operational misjudgements – resulting in inadequate stocks of the best-selling lines of women's and children's wear.

■ By switching its range emphasis to provide a stronger appeal to 'higher fashion' customers, Next had partially taken its eye of its core customers.

■ The problems were compounded by complacency over issues at the store level. After the run of success Next management had turned its attention more to improving its warehousing and logistics.

Jones commented: 'We do not have a divine right to be successful.'

The real danger was that some customers might have been lost permanently to rival high-street retailers.

### Question 3

David Jones has clearly been successful – and he remained as strategic leader. But: could a case be made for ensuring that he had a 'partner' with a greater willingness to take risks and who would deliberately seek to stretch the organization more?

In 1999 Internet selling was added to the Next Directory operations; and in 2001 flowers were added to the Internet product range.

Next began to experiment with a new larger store format. It was successful and several more have been opened. At the same time some of the smallest stores have been closed down. As a result the average store size has gradually increased from 5000 to 7000 square feet.

David Jones became Executive Chairman in 2002 and Simon Wolfson (from a family of renowned retailers linked previously to Great Universal Stores) was appointed as CEO in his place. The first true overseas branch of Next was opened in Denmark in 2004; previously Next had operated through franchises. The company was also offering call centre service facilities to customers such as British Gas through its Ventura subsidiary.

Between 2002/3 and 2003/4 the company was clearly growing. UK Retail now accounted for some 72 per cent of turnover and profits. The Next Directory (21 per cent), Ventura (5 per cent) and overseas franchises made up the rest.

### Question 4

It has been said that whilst David Jones has been in charge, Next has not been very exciting in terms of acquisitions and divestments – but it has seemed to have a clear strategy. But maybe this is just what it needed. What do you think?

**Next** http://www.next.co.uk

### 11.6.3 Desirability

**Strategic needs – the planning gap** The ability of the strategy to satisfy the objectives of the organization and help to close any identified planning gap are important considerations. Timing may again be an important issue. The ability of the strategy to produce results in either the short or the longer term should be assessed in the light of the needs and priorities of the firm.

**The level of returns expected** Decisions concerning where a company's financial resources should be allocated are known as investment or capital budgeting decisions. The decision might concern the purchase of new technology or new plant, the acquisition of another company, or financing the development and launch of a new product.

Competitive advantage and corporate strategic change are both relevant issues.

The ability to raise money, and the cost involved are key influences, and should be considered alongside two other strategic issues:

- Does the proposed investment make sense strategically, given present objectives and strategies?
- Will the investment provide an adequate financial return?

The latter question is partly answered by the company's cost of capital and the whole topic of investment decisions is explored in the Finance in Action section at the end of this chapter. Strategic fit is a broad issue and is addressed in the main part of the chapter.

**Synergy**  Effective synergy should lead ideally to a superior concentration of resources in relation to competitors. The prospects for synergy should be evaluated alongside the implications for the firm's strategic perspective and culture, which were included in the section on Appropriateness. These factors in combination affect the strategic fit of the proposal and its ability to complement existing strategies and bring an all-round improvement to the organization. Diversification into products and markets with which the organization has no experience, and which may require different skills, may fit poorly alongside existing strategies and fail to provide synergy.

**Risk**  It has already been pointed out that risk, vulnerability, opportunity and timing are linked. Where organizations, having spotted an opportunity, act quickly, there is always a danger that some important consideration will be overlooked. The risk lies in these other factors, many of which are discussed elsewhere, which need careful attention in strategy formulation:

- the likely effect on competition
- the technology and production risks, linked to skills and key success factors. Can the organization cope with the production demands and meet market requirements profitably? Innovation often implies higher risks in this area, but offers higher rewards for success
- the product/market diversification risk – the risk involved in overstretching resources through diversification has been considered earlier in this chapter
- the financial risk – the cash flow and the firm's borrowing requirements are sensitive to the ability of the firm to forecast demand accurately and predict competitor responses
- managerial ability and competence – the risk here involves issues of whether skills can be transferred from one business to another when a firm diversifies, and whether key people stay or go after a takeover
- environmental risks – it is also important to ensure that possible adverse effects or hostile public opinion are evaluated.

Many of these issues are qualitative rather than finite, and judgement will be required. The ability of the organization to harness and evaluate the appropriate information is crucial, but again there is a trade-off. The longer the time that the organization spends in considering the implications and assessing the risks, the greater the chance it has of reducing and controlling the risks. However, if managers take too long, the opportunity or the initiative may be lost to a competitor who is more willing to accept the risk. The subject of risk is revisited in Chapter 16.

*In my experience those who manage change most successfully are those who welcome it in their own lives and see it as an opportunity for stimulation and learning new things. Implicit is the willingness to take risks, including making intelligent mistakes.*

*I am much more interested in important failures that prepare the way for future success than I am in cautious competence and maintaining the status quo.*

Robert Fitzpatrick, when President Directeur Général, Euro Disneyland SA

**Stakeholder needs and preferences** This relates to the expectations and hopes of key stakeholders, the ability of the organization to implement the strategy and achieve the desired results, and the willingness of stakeholders to accept the inherent risks in a particular strategy.

Strategic changes may affect existing resources and the strategies to which they are committed, gearing, liquidity and organization structures, including management roles, functions and systems. Shareholders, bankers, managers, employees and customers can all be affected; and their relative power and influence will prove significant. The willingness of each party to accept particular risks may vary. Trade-offs may be required. The power and influence of the strategic leader will be very important in the choice of major strategic changes, and his or her ability to convince other stakeholders will be crucial.

# 11.7 Decision-making

It has already been emphasized that strategies can form or emerge as well as be formulated or prescribed. Strategic change results from decisions taken and implemented in response to perceived opportunities or threats. The management of change therefore requires strategic awareness and strategic learning, which implies the ability to recognize and interpret signals from the environment. Signals from the environment come into the organization all the time and in numerous ways. It is essential that they are monitored and filtered in such a way that the important messages reach decision-makers. If strategic change is to some degree dependent on a planning system, then that planning system must gather the appropriate data. Equally, if there is greater reliance on strategic change emerging from decisions taken within the organization by managers who are close to the market, their suppliers and so on, these managers must feel that they have the authority to make change decisions. In both cases appropriate strategic leadership is required to direct activity.

This section looks at decision-making in practice, at how decisions are taken and might be taken, and at why some bad decisions are made.

## 11.7.1 Decision-making and problem-solving

Decision-making is a process related to the existence of a problem, and it is often talked about in terms of problem-solving. A problem, in simple terms, exists when an undesirable situation has arisen which requires action to change it. In other words, a problem exists for someone if the situation that they perceive exists is unsatisfactory for them. They would like to see something different or better happening and achieving different results.

However, in many instances the problem situation is very complex and can only be partially understood or controlled, and therefore decisions are not so much designed to find ideal or perfect answers but to improve the problem situation. In other instances, managers may find themselves with so many problems at any time that they can at best reduce the intensity of the problem rather than systematically search for a so-called right answer.

Russell Ackoff (1978) distinguishes between solving, resolving, dissolving and absolving problems. A *solution* is the optimum answer, the best choice or alternative, and rational decision-making (developed below) is an attempt to find it. A *resolution* is a satisfactory answer or choice, not necessarily the best available, but one that is contingent upon circumstances, such as time limitations or lack of real significance of the problem. This will again be developed below. A *dissolution* occurs when objectives are changed in such a way that the problem no longer seems to be a problem. Feelings about what *should* be happening are changed to bring them in line with what *is* happening; current realities are accepted. Typically managers accept new, weaker objectives which allow them to feel that there is no longer a problem. For example, achieving a target revenue growth of 5 per cent in a static market might be proving difficult; a revised (downwards) figure of 2 per cent would be much more achievable! *Absolution* happens when problems are simply ignored in the hope that they will rectify themselves. Some people tend to treat minor illnesses in this way.

While there will always be an objective element in a strategic decision, other more subjective influences will also play a part. Figure 11.7 shows that the ultimate decision will have been affected by three elements:

- the results of whatever analyses have been used to evaluate the data available

- the intuition and perspective of the person or people involved. Past experiences and their willingness to trust the reliability and validity of the information that they have will both be influential issues. Some managers and strategic leaders, particularly those whom we would describe as entrepreneurial, often have an uncanny and difficult-to-explain understanding of a market or industry and of which strategy would work. They do not appear to carry out any formal analysis or use any of the techniques described here. But such managers are a minority and others are well advised to use formal analysis!

**Figure 11.7** Decision-making

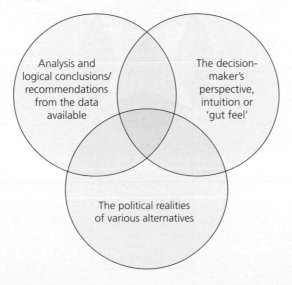

■ the political realities of the various alternatives. The contingent decision is the one that people believe can be implemented. It is not necessarily the alternative that on paper promises the highest rewards. To be effective, all managers must be able to handle the relevant political issues, as discussed in Chapter 17.

Figure 11.8 presents these themes in a different way by illustrating the four key issues in any decision:

1. the nature of the actual intervention. The idea of 'meaning systems' means that the person or people involved will be involved for a reason. Maybe it is their direct responsibility. Perhaps they have been asked to advise and help. Possibly they have been brought in because those whose responsibility the problem is are simply not coping. Regardless, they bring their own perspective, interpretation and objectives to the situation. Naturally this will have an important bearing on:

2. the relevant power issues and political realities

3. the quality and reliability of the information available

4. cultural issues, in particular norms, values and key roles. The decision taken should never ignore the likelihood of it being implemented successfully. If people oppose the changes or strategy proposed, for whatever reason (again discussed in Chapter 17), they may be minded to try and block its implementation. Where the change

**Figure 11.8** Key issues in decision-making

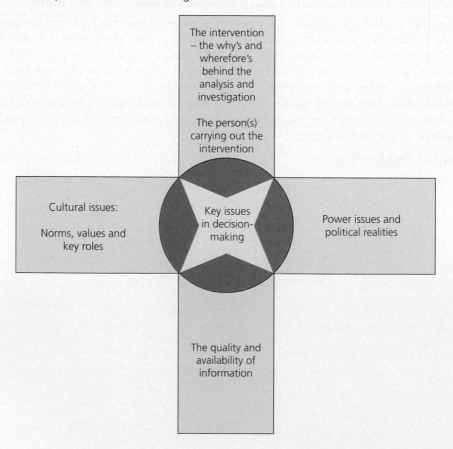

complements existing values and practices it should be more acceptable than if it implies a change of culture and behaviour. Radical change is sometimes essential, and should not be avoided simply because it is likely to attract opposition. However, it must be realized that it will take longer to implement.

### 11.7.2 'Good' and 'bad' decisions

Decision-making, then, involves both information and people. While the strategic leader must develop an appropriate information system, he or she must also ensure that a good team of people has been gathered and manage them well.

*The conductor is only as good as his orchestra.*

André Previn

Considerable research has been carried out into group behaviour, and it is not within the scope of this book to examine it in detail. But no leadership style is universally better than the others. Much depends on the personality, power and charisma of the leader.

In just the same way that we might like to see evidence of more objectivity in some decisions, we would also like to see organizations being proactive as well as reactive in their decision-making. In the latter case, there is a real risk that they are missing new windows of opportunity because they are perpetually 'crisis fighting'. Table 11.6 lists the characteristics of a fragmented organization, where decision-making is likely to be inadequate for internal cohesion and synergy and where there is likely to be considerable crisis fighting. Organizations should usefully evaluate the extent to which any, or all, of these factors are present in the decisions that their managers are making. Improvements could then foster increased co-operation and sharing and allow managers who do seem to be perpetually crisis fighting to be more proactive in seizing new opportunities.

Because of the nature of the issues, it is not being suggested that there are obvious and quantitative measures available for assessing them. Rather, managers should be encouraged to confront and discuss the ways in which they behave, make decisions, carry out the decisions they make and, in the process, help or hinder their colleagues and other stakeholders. Hopefully, this will persuade people to reflect on the inherent style weaknesses without the process being either hostile or confrontational. While a personal self-audit is possible, the process is enhanced with groups of managers and frank exchanges. How often, when managers gather for a meeting, is the purpose task-orientated, with the process element being either ignored or taken for granted? Increased attention to

**Table 11.6** Manifestations of a fragmented organization

- Irrational decision-making (processes)
- Weak decision-making/leadership (people)
- Rigidity, reluctance to change and negative politics
- Conflicting perspectives and interests
- Over-hasty decisions (decisive!) which are difficult to implement
- Lack of clear purpose
- Dissolution and absolution (of problems) instead of resolution and solution
- Unhelpful personal objectives
- Stakeholder conflicts
- Poor information
- Inadequate measurement and control
- Managerial inability to take a holistic perspective

process can strengthen the decision-making. There is nothing new in this argument, but the very fact that is frequently missing requires that it is restated.

**Irrational decision-making** The notion of a rational decision-making process would include the following stages, not necessarily in this sequential order:

- clarify the problem, which implies more than a statement of the obvious symptoms and manifestations
- establish clear objectives for the desired outcome
- generate possible alternative courses of action
- assess the probable outcomes for each alternative
- select a course of action, by considering likely outcomes and desired objectives
- implement this choice and
- monitor and evaluate progress.

It is clear that most decisions and managerial actions do not follow a sequence such as this, or incorporate all of these stages. Short-cuts are taken, often because of a lack of time or a lack of information, and sometimes through laziness. A number of explanations for this is available. Simon (1976) offers the idea of 'satisficing', the acceptance of a satisfactory course of action (not necessarily the best solution) which at least deals with the problem. Lindblom (1959) and later Quinn (1980) offer alternative theories based around the concept of trial and error in incremental, learning stages as distinct from a more hands-off decision. Etzioni (1967) argues that managers make a judgement on the relative importance and priority of an issue or problem, and then base the time and attention that they give to the issue on this judgement. All of these are logical and defensible. The issue concerns the extent to which managers are avoiding – consciously or unconsciously – the elements of the rational approach, especially in the case of major, serious problems and, in the end, making poor decisions which fail to deal adequately with the problem.

**Weak decision-making** Here we are looking for managers to realize and discuss the extent of their:

- tunnel vision, leading to a lack of internal synergy
- information flows and communications which prevent the right information reaching the people who need it when they can make best use of it
- personal objectives and agendas which lead to subjectivity, selfishness and internal tensions
- willingness to ignore the potential downside impact of their actions on other managers and other parts of the organization
- unwillingness to compromise to reach an accommodation with other managers.

Many of these issues are always likely to be present. Are they being ignored – causing frustration and maybe even despair – or dealt with? It is important here to stress the idea of *accommodation* among managers, as distinct from consensus, where multiple objectives and perspectives are present.

**Resistance to change** Heirs and Farrell (1987) identify three 'destructive minds', the impact of which organizations must minimize if they are to manage change effectively:

- the rigid mind which stifles originality and creativity and ignores the need to change
- the ego mind which fosters subjectivity and makes collaboration very difficult
- the 'machiavellian mind' which uses political activity to achieve personal objectives at the expense of others.

All effective managers will be political; they will use their power and influence to bring about decisions and actions which serve the needs and interests of the organization. Negative politics occurs when this power and influence is used against the best interests of the organization.

How many of these minds are evident in a crisis fighting organization that is largely reactive to events?

**Over-hasty decisions** Crisis fighters are typically pragmatic and decisive. Sometimes, though, decisions taken in haste prove difficult to implement, as valuable time is spent trying to justify the decision. Taking time initially to search for support and agreement, involving a range of people and opinions in the process, can be hard to justify when time pressures are tight. However, if decisions enjoy people's support because they have been consulted and understand the background, implementation can be smoother, actually saving time in the end. We can learn a great deal from the Japanese here – but in many organizations, are managers listening and learning?

**Stakeholder conflicts – the need for a holistic perspective**
It is unlikely that all the preferences of every internal and external stakeholder can be met in full and, as we saw earlier, accommodation is necessary. The issue here concerns the ability of managers to appreciate and accept that different people have different perspectives, and they do not see problems and issues in the same way. There is a saying: 'the way we see the problem is the problem'. Too narrow a perspective leads to a poor decision with adverse impacts on others. Taking account of different perspectives demands dialogue and sharing.

### 11.7.3 Implementing decisions

The implementation aspects of the decision are of vital importance. Simply, a decision can only be effective if it is implemented successfully and yields desirable or acceptable results. It may prove very sensible to spend time arriving at a decision by, say, involving the people who must implement it, aiming to generate a commitment at this stage even though it may be time-consuming. Such a decision is likely to be implemented smoothly. One alternative to this, the speedy decisive approach, may prove to be less effective. If it is not supported, the alternative chosen may result in controversy and reluctance on the part of others to implement it. Vroom and Yetton (1973) have developed a model of five alternative ways of decision-making.

**Vroom and Yetton's model** A short summary of the five approaches is as follows.

1. The leader solves the problem or makes the decision him or herself using information available at the time.
2. The leader obtains necessary information from subordinates and then decides on the solution to the problem him or herself. Subordinates are not involved in generating or evaluating alternative solutions.

3. The leader shares the problem with relevant subordinates individually, obtaining their ideas and suggestions without bringing them together as a group. Then the leader makes the decision, which may or may not reflect the influence of subordinates.

4. The leader shares the problem with the subordinates as a group, collectively obtaining their ideas and suggestions. Then he or she makes the decision, which again may or may not reflect their influence.

5. The leader shares the problem with the subordinates as a group, and together the leader and subordinates generate and evaluate alternatives and attempt to reach an agreement on a solution.

(Vroom and Yetton use the expression 'solve' throughout.)

Vroom and Yetton contend that the choice of style should relate to the particular problem faced, and their model includes a series of questions which can be used diagnostically to select the most appropriate style. While the model is useful for highlighting the different styles and emphasizing that a single style will not always prove to be the most appropriate, it is essentially a normative theory – 'this is what you should do' – and in this respect should be treated with caution.

## 11.8 Judgement

*The judgement dilemma*
*Judgement, per se, cannot be taught or learned; instead it comes from experience. Experience is gained by making mistakes, which, of course, are the result of poor judgement! Managers exercise poor judgement because it cannot be taught or learned.*

Strategic changes can be selected by an individual manager, often the strategic leader, or a team of managers, and Vickers (1965) stresses that three contextual aspects have a critical impact on the decision:

■ the decision-makers' skills and values together with aspects of their personality (*personal factors*)

■ their authority and accountability within the organization (*structural factors*)

■ their understanding and awareness (*environmental factors*).

Related to these, the decisions taken by managers are affected by their personal judgemental abilities, and understanding judgement can, therefore, help us to explain why some managers appear to 'get things right' while others 'get things wrong'.

Vickers suggests that there are three types of judgement:

1. *Reality judgements* – Strategic awareness of the organization and its environment and which is based upon interpretation and meaning systems.

2. *Action judgements* – What to do about perceived strategic issues.

3. *Value judgements* – Concerning expected and desired results and outcomes from the decision.

Figure 11.9 shows how these are interconnected. Decision-makers need to understand 'what is' (*reality*), 'what matters' (*values*) and 'what to do about it' (*action*). Their choice will be based upon a conceptualization of what might or what should be a better

**Figure 11.9** Judgement and strategic decision-making – I

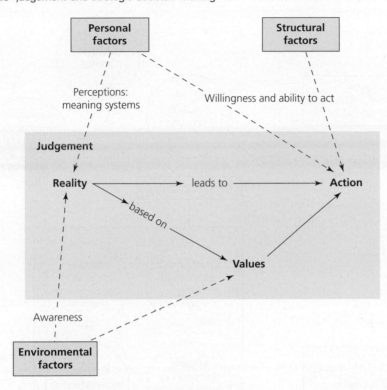

alternative to the current situation. Ideally, it will incorporate a holistic perspective, implying either an understanding or a personal interpretation of the organization's purpose or mission, and it also requires an appreciation that what matters is a function of urgency and time horizons. A company with cash difficulties, for example, might need a strategy based upon immediate rationalization or consolidation; a liquid company evaluating growth options has greater flexibility. The choice will also be affected by managers' relative power and influence, their perception of the risks involved, and their willingness to pursue certain courses of action.

To conclude this chapter, Figure 11.10 draws together key points from the sections on decision-making and judgement. The top part of the diagram explains that managers have to assess any problematical situation and determine the extent to which it is normal or unusual. This is their reality judgement of the situation. Where they perceive that there is a real degree of normality to the events, the likelihood is that they will continue to rely on traditional routines and approaches. However, where the situation is seen as more unusual a decision has to be made about how to deal with it. This choice reflects action judgement, and there are six (and possibly more) alternatives to choose from:

1. Continue to rely on approaches which have worked well in the past.
2. From a position of leadership, take decisive action – reflecting an entrepreneurial style.
3. Involve others in formal analysis, discussion and planning.
4. Possibly involving others, adopt a trial-and-error approach to craft a new strategy adaptively or incrementally.
5. Seek input from an expert, maybe an external consultant.

**Figure 11.10** Judgement and strategic decision-making – II

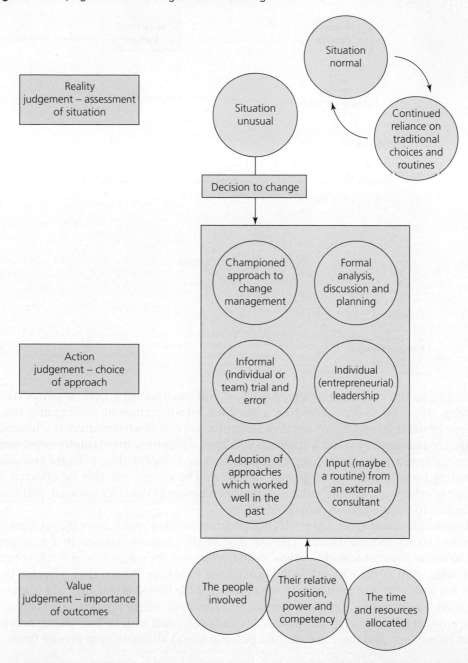

6. Establish that there is a change project under way and follow a 'textbook' approach – along the lines of the one explained in Chapter 17.

The outcomes are going to be dependent upon the people who become engaged and involved, their relative positions, power and competency and the time and resources allocated to the decision taking and implementation. This final part is the relevant value judgement.

# SUMMARY

There is a range of strategic alternatives and strategic means that organizations might review and possibly choose at any time. Organizations will change their directions and strategies and they do not always pursue the same strategy in the same way. Normally, they will aim to be proactive and purposeful about this. Sometimes, however, they are constrained: an option that they would like to pursue is unrealistic. This would be the case if the Competition Commission blocked a proposed acquisition. Similarly, the Commission might insist on a particular divestment in return for permission to proceed with a merger.

Over time, the corporate portfolio migrates. It should be built around a defensible heartland of related businesses, accepting that at times there will be diversification into related and unrelated activities. We cannot finally judge the worthiness of a particular choice until we take account of the organization's ability to implement the strategy that it has chosen.

The key strategic alternatives are limited growth, substantive growth and retrenchment.

## Limited growth:

- market penetration, either in a deliberate attempt to build market share or as a form of consolidation to protect a customer base

- market development – opening up new opportunities with different customers, possibly in overseas markets

- product development – extending the range in order to expand the level of business with existing customers.

## Substantive growth:

- horizontal integration – generally merging with a direct or indirect competitor, again to increase market share

- vertical integration – linking with another company in the same supply chain

- related diversification – moving into an area where either marketing or technology issues are similar, often by acquisition, merger or strategic alliance

- unrelated diversification – the higher risk strategy involving new markets, new products and new technologies.

The key strategic means (which are discussed next) are:

- organic growth – internal investment to develop new competencies

- acquisition (friendly purchase), merger (two companies simply joining together) and take-over (hostile purchase)

- strategic alliances (partnerships, whatever the form) and joint ventures (alliances which involve a major financial investment by the parties concerned).

When evaluating and selecting strategies, it is important for organizations to address the following questions:

- What constitutes a good strategic choice?

- What can the organization do and what can it not do?

- What should the organization seek to do and what should it not seek to do?

An effective strategy is one that meets the needs and preferences of the organization, its key decision-makers and influencers – ideally better than any alternatives – and can be implemented successfully.

The techniques introduced in earlier parts of the book can all make a contribution, but there are likely to be subjective elements as well.

There are three broad criteria for evaluating strategies:

*Appropriateness*
- Does the proposal fit – and strengthen – the existing portfolio of activities?

- Is it compatible with the mission of the organization?

- Does it address any targeted opportunities or help redress any critical weaknesses?

## SUMMARY (cont.)

- What impact would the change have on E–V–R congruence?

- Is this an opportunity for stretching the organization's resources and exploiting core competencies further? Or does it imply diversification?

*Feasibility*
- Can the strategic change be implemented successfully – and without any detrimental impact upon present activities?

- Does the organization possess the skills and competencies required? If not, can they be acquired in a relevant timescale?

- Can the implied costs be met?

- Is there an opportunity to build and sustain a strong competitive position?

*Desirability*
- Does the option truly help to close the planning gap?

- Is the organization comfortable with the risks implied?

- Is this a justifiable (and, in certain cases, the most profitable) use of organizational effort and resources?

- Is there potential synergy?

- Which stakeholder needs will be met and satisfied?

When reviewing options, it is unlikely that one will turn out to be the most appropriate, the most feasible and the most desirable. Trade-offs will have to be made.

The decision-making processes used will inevitably have elements of subjectivity. Judgement will have to be applied alongside any technique-driven strategic analyses. Decision-making, therefore, must embrace issues of intuition and political reality alongside the available information and analyses. There are a number of explanations – all easily appreciated – for 'poor' decision-making.

Judgement comprises three key elements:

- a *reality judgement* of the situation and the implied problem

- an *action judgement* about what to do

- *value judgements* concerning expected and desired outcomes.

## QUESTIONS AND RESEARCH ASSIGNMENTS

1. For each of the following strategic alternatives, list why you think an organization might select this particular strategy, what they would expect to gain, and where the problems and limitations are. If you can, think of an example of each one from your own experience:

   - do nothing; no change

   - market penetration

   - market development

   - product development

   - innovation

   - horizontal integration

   - vertical integration

   - concentric diversification

   - conglomerate diversification.

2. What are the relative advantages and disadvantages of organic growth as opposed to external growth strategies?

3. Which of the evaluation techniques listed in the chapter (Box 11.4) do you feel are most useful? Why? How would you use them? What are their limitations?

4. From your experience and reading, which evaluation criteria do you think are most significant in determining the effectiveness of strategies? List examples of cases where the absence of these factors, or the wrong assessment of their importance, has led to problems.

## INTERNET AND LIBRARY PROJECTS

1. For an organization of your choice, trace the changes of strategy and strategic direction over a period of time. Relate these changes to any changes in strategic leadership, structure and, wherever possible, culture.

2. Walt Disney Corporation became hugely successful and influential on the back of cartoon films, beginning with Mickey Mouse. In more recent years theme parks and 'straight' movies have also been vitally significant. In addition a number of proposals have bitten the dust. As a consequence, in 2004, the CEO Michael Eisner was under considerable pressure from some shareholders to resign. Research and evaluate the various strategic options pursued by Disney. Where should it seek to develop next?

3. In 1996 Walt Disney Corporation was thought by analysts to be a prospective buyer for EMI Music after its split from the Thorn Rentals part of Thorn EMI. Would music have been an appropriate and desirable addition to the Disney portfolio? Do you think that the acquisition of an essentially British company would have been difficult for Disney to absorb?

   What in fact has happened with EMI Music? Was the actual outcome more appropriate, feasible and desirable for EMI?

   **Walt Disney Company** http://www.disney.go.com
   **EMI Group** http://www.emigroup.com

4. In 1983 Tottenham Hotspur became the first English football club to be listed on the Stock Exchange. Subsequently, the club diversified, acquiring a number of related leisure companies. The intention was to subsidize the football club with profits from the new businesses. Initially this happened, but in the recession of the late 1980s football had to prop up the other activities. Businesses were closed or divested, and the ownership of Tottenham Hotspur changed hands in 1991. During the 1990s entrepreneur Alan Sugar acquired the club, only to relinquish control when he proved unpopular with many Spurs fans. Since then Tottenham Hotspur has struggled but managed to retain its place in the Premiership. Research the various changes and evaluate the strategies. Was it appropriate and desirable for Tottenham to become a public limited company at the time it did?

   How different was the approach taken some years later by Manchester United? What strategies have made Manchester United the richest football club in the world?

   **Tottenham Hotspur plc** http://www.spurs.co.uk
   **Manchester United FC** http://www.manutd.com

## Further reading

Tilles, S (1963) How to evaluate corporate strategy, *Harvard Business Review*, July–August.

Markides, CC (1999) A dynamic view of strategy, *Sloan Management Review*, 40, Spring.

## References

Ackoff, R (1978) *The Art of Problem Solving*, John Wiley.

Channon, DF (1983) *Strategy and Structure in British Industry*, Macmillan.

Constable, CJ (1986) Diversification as a factor in UK industrial strategy, *Long Range Planning*, 19 (1).

Etzioni, A (1967) Mixed scanning: a third approach to decision making, *Public Administration Review*, 27, December.

Goold, M, Campbell, A and Alexander, M (1994) *Corporate Level Strategy*, John Wiley.

Heirs, B and Farrell, P (1987) *The Professional Decision Thinker*, Sidgwick and Jackson.

Hilton, A (1987) Presented at 'Growing Through Acquisition', Conference organized by Arthur Young, London, 31 March.

Hofer, CW and Schendel, D (1978) *Strategy Evaluation: Analytical Concepts*, West.

Lindblom, CE (1959) *The Science of Muddling Through*, reprinted in *Organization Theory*, Pugh, DS (ed.) 2nd edn (1987) Penguin.

Penrose, E (1959) *The Theory of the Growth of the Firm*, Blackwell.

Peters, TJ and Waterman, RH Jr (1982) *In Search of Excellence: Lessons from America's Best Run Companies*, Harper and Row.

Quinn, JB (1980) *Strategies for Change: Logical Incrementalism*, Richard D Irwin.

Rumelt, R (1980) The evaluation of business strategy. In *Business Policy and Strategic Management* (ed. WF Glueck), McGraw-Hill

Simon, HA (1976) *Administrative Behavior: A Study of Decision Making Processes in Administrative Organizations*, 3rd edn, Free Press.

Thompson, AA and Strickland, AJ (1980) *Strategy Formulation and Implementation*, Richard D Irwin.

Tilles, S (1963) How to evaluate corporate strategy, *Harvard Business Review*, July–August.

Vickers, G (1965) *The Art of Judgement: A Study of Policy Making*, Chapman & Hall.

Vroom, V and Yetton, P (1973) *Leadership and Decision Making*, University of Pittsburgh Press.

# Finance in Action: Financial Management

## Learning objectives

Learning objectives

Having read to the end of this supplement you should be able to:

- discuss the advantages and disadvantages of different sources of investment capital
- apply a number of different investment appraisal techniques and evaluate their contribution to investment decisions
- calculate the optimal capital structure for a firm and its weighted average cost of capital
- describe the capital asset pricing model
- explain how a company might be valued, say for acquisition purposes.

## Financing the business

The various sources of funds to support a growing business and their relative cost. Calculating the cost of capital, taking into account the various funding sources.

## Investments and capital budgeting

Alternative ways of calculating the real cost and returns from investment opportunities.

# Financing the business

## Sources of funds

Most funds used by established UK organizations are normally generated internally through retained profits, but from time to time it is necessary to raise funds externally. This applies to both the public and the private sectors. In general, loan capital or borrowing has been used more extensively than equity, which might take the form of new equity issued openly or rights issues to existing shareholders.

At present in the UK and USA, equity funding is proving more significant than borrowing; the reverse is the case for Germany, France and Japan, partially as a result of different regulations. In the 1990s some UK companies used new equity to compensate for reduced cash flows and retained earnings, and US companies bought back shares and returned funds to their shareholders. This strategy is a form of defence against possible unwelcome bids. Regulations reduce the likelihood of German, French and Japanese companies being acquired by unwelcome predators.

Investment funding, then, is available through borrowing or increased equity, but assets can be increased without investing to the same extent. This is accomplished by leasing them rather than purchasing them.

**Equity capital**  In general, equity capital would be increased by a rights issue of ordinary shares to existing shareholders. As an example, holders of ordinary shares might be offered one new share for every two or three that they already own, at a price equal to or below the current market price. At a higher price people would be unlikely to purchase. If all shareholders take up the offer then the percentage breakdown of the shareholders' register will remain the same; if they are not taken up by existing shareholders they will be offered to the market by the institutional underwriters, and the share register profile may change. Blocks of shares could be built up quite readily, and at a price below the current market price; and depending upon who was buying them threats to the organization from powerful shareholders could emerge.

Rights issues will not be successful without the support of institutional shareholders. This requires investor confidence in the company's strategy and strategic leadership.

Although many shareholders buy and retain shares with a view to a long-term capital gain, resulting from their sale at a price higher than the one at which they were bought, dividend policy is important. Dividends represent a rate of return on shareholders' investments. Although dividends are not fixed and can theoretically be raised or lowered freely and in relation to increases or decreases in profits, and to any changing need for retained earnings for investment, companies generally seek stability.

**Loan capital**  There are various forms of loan capital, but they all have one essential characteristic. They do not carry ownership, which ordinary shares do. Loans might well be for a definite period, after which they are repayable, and with a fixed rate of interest for each year of the loan. Hence, interest payments come out of profits, but they cannot be reduced if profits decline through unfavourable trading conditions. Overdrafts provide flexible short-term funding up to an agreed limit, and their cost will vary both up and down as the prevailing market rate of interest changes. Loans are invariably secured against assets, which reduces the risk for the lender. If interest payments are not met, the bank, or whoever has loaned the money, is free to appoint a receiver and effectively take over day-to-day control of the company. Interest is paid out of profits before they are assessed for taxation, and they can thereby reduce the company's tax burden; dividends for ordinary shareholders are paid after tax.

Generalizing, the cost of borrowing can be expected to rise as the degree of risk for the lender increases. Lenders will expect higher returns from higher risk investments. Government securities are considered very safe, for example, and consequently the anticipated rate of return will typically be lower than for other investments. Secured loans are safer than ordinary shares, as mentioned above, and therefore borrowing should normally prove cheaper than equity.

The ability to obtain either – and the cost – are likely to be dependent on how well the company has been performing, and how well it has been perceived by the market to have been performing. Opportunity, ability and cost are therefore essential criteria in deciding upon a preference between equity and loan funding, but this decision should be related to the decision concerning whether to invest at all. Investments, which are discussed later in this Appendix, should be analysed by comparing their returns, discounted for the period they are earned, with the cost of financing them, or the opportunity cost of the money being used. The viability of an investment is therefore dependent upon the cost of the capital used. The cheaper the cost of capital, the more likely it is that an investment is viable and profitable. Hence if the cost of obtaining investment funding is high, opportunities might be lost.

Moreover, the capital structure of the company determines the impact of profit fluctuations on the money available after tax for paying dividends and for reinvestment. Large loans and high interest payments absorb profits, and this can be crucial if profits fluctuate significantly for any reason. The more that is paid out in dividends, the less is available for reinvesting, and vice versa. In turn, dividend payments are likely to affect the view held by shareholders and the market of the company's performance, and this will affect their willingness to lend more.

**Leasing**  In many cases organizations are more concerned with using assets than actually owning them. Leasing assets is one way of acquiring them without paying their full price at any one time; the popularity of leasing has grown since the late 1970s.

When an asset is leased there will normally be an agreed annual charge for a fixed number of years, and possibly there will be an arrangement whereby the company obtains ownership of the asset for a residual price at the end of the period of the lease. In aggregate terms leasing is unlikely to be cheap, but it can have a significant effect on cash flow. In addition, there have been advantageous tax regulations. Leasing is generally low risk for the lessor, who retains legal ownership of the asset and can reclaim it if the lease payments are not met.

Leasing has offered strategic opportunities, as well as financial benefits, for certain organizations. Some companies have chosen to sell and lease back property that they owned, for example, finding willing partners in property companies and institutional investors. The funds released have then been available for other investments.

## The cost of capital

**The optimal capital structure**  In theory there is an *optimal capital structure* (OCS) in terms of debt and equity for any firm, and it will depend on:

- the amount of risk in the industry
- the riskiness of the company's corporate and competitive strategies, and their potential impact on profits
- the typical capital structure for the industry, and what competitors are doing – the cost of funding can provide competitive advantage
- management's ability to pay interest without too serious an impact on dividends and future investment
- both the owners' and the strategic leader's preference for risk, or aversion to it.

**The weighted average cost of capital** In considering, or attempting to decide, the OCS it is important to evaluate the *weighted average cost of capital* (WACC). The WACC, again in theory, is the average rate of return that investors expect the company to earn. In practice it is the average cost of raising additional investment funding. If a company used only loan funding the WACC would be the after-tax cost of borrowing more; but most organizations have a complex structure of debt and equity, each of which carries a different cost. The WACC is therefore an attempt to approximate what more funding would cost if it were raised proportionately to the percentages of debt and equity in the OCS. In practice it will relate to the current capital structure.

**Determining the weighted average cost of capital** The formula is:

WACC = (Percentage of long-term debt in the OCS × After-tax cost of debt)

*plus*

(Percentage of ordinary shares in the OCS × After-tax cost of equity)

As mentioned above, the WACC will normally be calculated in terms of the firm's current capital structure rather than the theoretical OCS.

The *cost of long-term debt* is the weighted average of the various interest rates incurred on existing loans, after accounting for tax. Hence, for a company which pays 10 per cent interest on 40 per cent of its loans, 12 per cent on the other 60 per cent and tax at an effective rate of 30 per cent, the cost of long-term debt is:

$$((10\% \times 40) + (12\% \times 60)) \times (1 - 0.3) = 7.84\%$$

The *cost of equity* is more difficult to calculate. One popular model for estimating it is the capital asset pricing model (CAPM), which is described here only in outline.

**The capital asset pricing model** In theory the cost of equity for an individual company should equal the rate of return that shareholders expect to gain from investing in that company. This is based on their perception of the amount of risk involved. The CAPM attempts to capture this. The formula is:

$$R = F + \text{beta}\ (M - F)$$

$R$ is the expected earnings or return on a particular share and $F$ represents the risk-free rate of return expected from the most secure investments such as government securities, where the likelihood of default is considered negligible. The expected risk-free rate is determined by the current interest rate on these securities and expected inflation. $M$ is the average rate of return expected from all securities traded in the market and beta is a measure of risk based on the volatility of an individual company's shares compared with the market as a whole. A beta of 1.6 (empirically high) means that a company's share price fluctuates by 1.6 times the market average. In other words, if the market average rises or falls by 10 per cent, the company's share price increases or decreases by 16 per cent. A low beta might be 0.3. Low beta shares in a portfolio reduce risk, but in general high beta shares do little to reduce risk.

Research at London Business School yielded the following betas in the mid-1990s:

| | |
|---|---|
| Hong Kong and Shanghai Banking Corporation | 1.6 |
| J. Sainsbury | 0.6 |
| Manchester United Football Club | 0.4 |

Large organizations evaluating possible investments for different divisions or business units should consider the estimated rate of return from each proposal, the current returns being obtained in each division and the company's average cost of capital, as well as any strategic issues. Take the following two possibilities:

|  | Division A | Division B |
|---|---|---|
| Rate of return on proposal | 20% | 13% |
| Current returns | 25% | 9% |

Division A's proposal could seem unattractive as it offers a lower return than existing projects, while B's investment offers an improvement to current returns. If the company's cost of capital is 15%, A's proposal is profitable and B's proposal is not.

## QUESTIONS AND RESEARCH ASSIGNMENTS

1. Calculate the weighted average cost of capital given the following information:

   Optimal capital structure 50:50

   Debt funding: half is at 10% interest, half at 12%

   Effective tax rate 30%

   Risk-free rate 8%

   Return expected in the stock market 12%

   Company's beta 1.2.

2. A firm has two investment opportunities, each costing £100,000 and each having the expected net cash flows shown in the table below. While the cost of each project is certain, the cash-flow projections for project B are more uncertain than those for A because of additional inherent risks. Those shown in both cases can be assumed to be maxima. It has therefore been suggested that while the company's cost of capital is of the order of 10 per cent, B might usefully be discounted at 15 per cent.

   (a) For each alternative calculate the net present value, the internal rate of return and the payback.

   (b) On the data available what would you advise the firm to do?

   (c) How limited do you feel this analysis is?

Expected cash flows

|  | Project A (£) | Project B (£) |
|---|---|---|
| Year 1 | 50,000 | 20,000 |
| Year 2 | 40,000 | 40,000 |
| Year 3 | 30,000 | 50,000 |
| Year 4 | 10,000 | 60,000 |

# Strategic Growth

External growth strategies continue to be popular alternatives for many companies, particularly larger ones, but research suggests that they often fail to meet expectations. Growth strategies need careful, thorough and objective analysis before they are pursued, and care and attention in implementation. This chapter explores diversification and acquisition strategies adopted by UK companies and considers how to manage these strategies effectively.

Acquisitions happen for a number of reasons, some strategic, others more personal to a strategic leader. There is a strongly held view that the strategic argument of synergy should only be used to justify an acquisition which implies real diversification if the companies concerned are somehow blocked from working together in some form of partnership, alliance or joint venture. Simply, there is an argument that alliances and joint ventures are often a better alternative than a full acquisition, merger or takeover for generating synergy and fuelling growth. Alliances and joint ventures are not, however, without risks and they can sometimes be problematical in the implementation stages. However, they will generally offer more flexibility. Their downside for many strategic leaders is that they do not create a larger and more powerful organization.

This relatively short chapter explores these issues by looking at different forms of partnering and the various reasons for doing so. Franchising and licensing are also considered briefly.

Strategies can only be judged to be relatively successful or unsuccessful when implementation issues are also considered. Therefore, corporate strategy is explored here in the context of both the strategy and its implementation.

## Minicase 12.1 Daimler-Chrysler   (Eur) (US)

This case charts the German company Daimler-Benz's search for synergy in its quest to create an integrated transport company.

Daimler-Benz has long been renowned for engineering excellence, product quality and marketing. At the beginning of the 1990s it was Europe's largest manufacturing group, and comprised:

- Mercedes-Benz – commercial vehicles and passenger cars
- AEG – electrical and electronic products
- Dasa – aerospace
- Debis –financial and information services.

Vehicles were responsible for two-thirds of annual sales revenue; AEG and Dasa each generated approximately 15 per cent.

The majority of the non-vehicle businesses had been acquired systematically during the 1980s; the intention had been to create an 'integrated technology' group. Daimler-Benz's stated objectives for the acquisitions were, first, to offset stagnating vehicle sales by expanding into high-technology growth markets, and second, to strengthen the automotive businesses by applying advanced technologies from the new acquisitions. The challenge was always to achieve this potential synergy; the time-scale to realize the benefits was set at ten years, and the important institutional shareholders allegedly pledged their support for the strategy.

Initially, vehicles had to subsidize the new businesses; but critics argued that the second of the two objectives did not require ownership and that in reality the synergy argument was being used as an afterthought to justify the diversification.

Daimler-Benz's strategic dilemma was that both AEG and Dasa required turning around at the same time that vehicles were under threat from Japanese car manufacturers, who were becoming increasingly competitive in the more upmarket sectors. Mercedes needed new, more competitive models to prevent being squeezed into too small a niche. An alliance with Mitsubishi was mooted as one suitable way forward.

AEG, which Mercedes had rescued from near bankruptcy, was already diversified (it included white goods, typewriters and traffic-control systems) and was itself searching for synergies. Some AEG business areas were losing money, and in 1994 AEG's appliance business was sold to Electrolux (see Minicase 11.3). AEG's railway equipment division became a 50:50 joint venture with ABB (Asea Brown Boveri). Daimler-Benz actually had to pay ABB as AEG's division was currently losing money and its new partner was profitable. The two businesses complemented each other well: ABB focused on heavy locomotives, high-speed trains and signalling; AEG was concentrated on light and urban railways and airport transit systems.

Dasa (Deutsche Aerospace) comprised a number of separately acquired companies and there was some duplication of activities. Messerschmitt has always been a major supplier to the European Airbus project, but its contribution, rear fuselages, is technically less sophisticated than Aerospatiale's forward fuselages and flight decks and British Aerospace's wings. Further alliances with other members of the Airbus consortium, to develop commuter aircraft and helicopters, were discussed. In 1992 Daimler-Benz added to this division when it acquired a 78 per cent shareholding in the Dutch aerospace company, Fokker. The Dutch government held the remaining shares but, again, the company was already in difficulty.

The promised synergies simply did not materialize as Germany suffered its deepest recession in manufacturing since 1945. Mercedes-Benz began to trade at a loss in 1993, and this led to job reductions and investment in plants outside Germany (to avoid the difficulties of high domestic wage rates and a strong Deutschmark). Development work on new four-wheel drive vehicles and a micro car (eventually launched as the Smart car) were already under way, the latter in conjunction with SMH of Switzerland, best known as the manufacturer of Swatch watches.

A new chairman was appointed in the summer of 1995 and later that year Daimler-Benz announced a trading loss equivalent to £2.7 billion, 'the worst non-fraudulent result ever recorded by a German company'. A leading analyst commented that the company was 'so bogged down with aerospace and AEG it had missed important opportunities in the automotive arena'. Drastic action was anticipated.

In January 1996 further AEG divisions were sold to Alcatel Alstom (France); the remainder were to be fully absorbed into Mercedes-Benz. Daimler-Benz also announced the withdrawal of further financial support for Fokker, making its collapse inevitable unless a new buyer came forward.

Daimler-Benz redefined itself as a 'transportation group' and restructured into 25 operating units in seven main divisions. All operating units had to fit the core strategy and achieve a target of 12 per cent return on equity. Failure to achieve would result in sale or closure. The future of Dornier (manufacturer of regional aircraft) and MTU (Daimler aero engines) thus looked particularly precarious unless alliance partners could be found to help.

In 1997 Daimler-Benz increased its already dominant presence in the global heavy trucks industry by acquiring Ford's activities. In the same year Mercedes launched its first small car, the 'A' class hatchback. Almost immediately the car was withdrawn from sale when a motorist, admittedly

driving in unusual and extreme conditions, had turned one over. The car was redesigned and relaunched. The launch of the even smaller Smart micro car was also delayed for safety reasons. As a consequence Mercedes bought out its partner in this venture to take total control.

In 1998 Daimler-Benz announced a 'merger of equals' with America's third largest, and most profitable car manufacturer, Chrysler. The new company would be called Daimler-Chrysler, but ownership was split 57:43. It would be the fifth largest in the world, after General Motors, Ford, Toyota and Volkswagen. There was no product overlap, as Chrysler's Dodge and Plymouth cars were less luxurious than Mercedes, which also had the monopoly on small cars. Chrysler was prominent in pick-up trucks and four-wheel drive vehicles (the Jeep brand), which were new to Mercedes. However, it was arguable that together the two companies would have too many platforms and some rationalization would be required. The intention was to retain separate brands, plants and dealerships. The synergy would come from administration, shared skills and (later) common platforms. Chrysler, however, was less global than Daimler-Benz and the cultures of the two companies were very different. Daimler-Chrysler subsequently bought minority stakes in Mitsubishi and Hyundai. However, towards the end of 2000 it was clear that there were significant implementation problems with the Daimler-Chrysler merger. Meanwhile, Dasa had been merged with British Aerospace, its partner in the Airbus project.

In 2000 Kirk Kerkorian, a US billionaire who had been the largest individual shareholder in Chrysler and who remained the third largest shareholder in Daimler-Chrysler, began a legal action (which is still ongoing) against three Daimler-Benz executives. He is alleging fraud in the takeover – which he claims was not a merger of equals. A structure which reflected equality had been promised; in the end the business was controlled from Germany.

Meanwhile restructuring continued. Chrysler was being dramatically rationalized on the grounds that it had ageing product lines which had to be axed. Before the merger the company had been discounting heavily and investing significantly in new products at the same time. Financially it was weak. The intention was to replace 80 per cent of its product range over five years. Jobs were lost and the ex-Chrsyler shareholders had seen the value of their investments collapse. By 2002 it was clear that Chrysler were refocusing on saloon cars at the expense of light trucks and SUVs – sports utility vehicles. Both of these had been growing but competition, especially from Japan, had intensified.

In 2003 BMW cars outsold Mercedes for the first time in six years. Customer complaints were increasing. Jeremy Clarkson even described a new Mercedes as 'crap' on a UK 'Top Gear' television programme. Why? The smaller car strategy had failed to meet hopes and expectations. The new BMW Mini was more popular than the Smart car.

Sales of new Mercedes SUVs were also below target.

By 2004 Mitsubishi Motors (in which Daimler-Chrysler retained a minority stake) was in trouble. Daimler-Chrysler declared they had no resources to invest to help it out. The company also decided to sell its stake in Hyundai. Mercedes were also to be assembled in China for the first time.

### Questions

1. Do you believe that the Daimler-Chrysler merger can eventually unlock the synergy which Daimler-Benz had earlier found elusive?
2. Where do you think the problems and difficulties might lie?

**Daimler-Chrysler** http://www.daimlerchrysler.com

**Mercedes** have seen a decline in sales and customer complaints have increased due to failed expectations and hopes

## 12.1 Introduction

Organizations can opt to grow organically, by investing their own resources to develop new competencies and capabilities and open up new market opportunities, but this is always going to take time. There is also an implicit assumption that the necessary competencies can actually be developed. It could be that aspects of the intellectual property involved are elusive. Equally, potential customers have to be persuaded to buy from a new and possibly unproven provider. Again this may prove elusive. Acquisitions, joint ventures or strategic alliances have the advantage of linkages with a proven supplier who has already developed the appropriate competencies and the necessary customers. They will also typically be faster – but they are often going to imply higher risk because they involve partnerships that have to be worked out. The successful implementation of an acquisition can easily take longer than anticipated. These themes, together with the issue of diversification, were introduced in Chapter 11 and they are illustrated in Minicase 12.1 on Daimler-Chrysler. Because many organizations continue to prefer 'external' means to the internal, organic option, diversification (a route) and acquisition (a means) often go hand-in-hand. They both imply some uncertainty and risk, risks that roll together.

As a result of the diversification, merger and acquisition activity the UK (for one) has developed a number of large companies with sizeable asset bases and domestic market shares, but few which are dominant in their industries or sectors at a world or even a European level – points that were also discussed earlier in the book (see Chapter 7). Constable (1986) argues that the high level of strategic energy devoted to these strategies created an illusion of real growth, with an emphasis on the shorter-term financial aspects of strategic expertise as opposed to the operational and market-based aspects which, long term, are of great significance. Arguably, too much top management time and effort has been spent on seeking and implementing acquisitions, and avoiding being acquired.

Although the nature of investment funding and stock market expectations have been significant influences behind the diversification and acquisition activity in the UK, there are other explanations. If a company has growth objectives and there are finite limits to the potential in existing markets, as well as barriers to becoming more international in order to penetrate related markets abroad, diversification may be an attractive option. However, there may already be intense competition in domestic markets which the company considers entering, especially if the industries involved are attractive and profitable. The competition may be both UK producers and imported products and services and may be compounded by active rivalry for share and dominance. In such circumstances, direct entry may seem less appropriate than acquisition of an existing competitor.

As acquisitions and mergers increase industrial concentration and the power of certain large organizations, government policy on competition may act as a restraint on particular lines of development for certain companies. Large firms may be encouraged to diversify into unrelated businesses where there is little apparent threat to the interests of consumers, rather than attempting horizontal integration which might be prevented by the intervention of the Competition Commission. Joint ventures offer another way round this constraint.

A contrasting argument suggests that a company which has grown large, successful and profitable in a particular industry is likely to seek diversification while it is strong and has the resources to move into new business areas effectively. The benefits of such a move are likely to seem more realizable by the acquisition of an existing organization than by the slower build-up of new internal activities. This type of growth requires finance, which generally has been available for successful companies.

When companies are acquired then both sales and absolute profits increase quickly, and sometimes markedly. But does profitability also increase? Are assets being utilized more effectively in the combined organization? Is synergy really being obtained? Or are the increased sales and profits merely an illusion of growth?

Finally, Constable offers two further arguments to explain the strategic activity in the UK. First, strategic leaders of large organizations are typically aggressive in nature, and acquisition is an expression of aggression. Second, there is a commonly held belief that the larger a company becomes the less likely it is to be a victim of a takeover bid. Hence, while diversification is essentially offensive and designed to bring about expansion and growth, it could be argued that on occasions it is a defensive strategy.

In choosing whether to diversify or not, Markides (1997) recommends that organizations should address five key questions:

1. What can we do better than our competitors? This, of course, is the area around which to focus and build.
2. What strategic resources are required in the possible new areas? What are the implications of this?
3. Can we beat the competition and become a strong player?
4. Is there a downside risk? In particular, might existing businesses be affected in any detrimental way?
5. What learning potential is there? Can the new business enhance synergy and improve our existing businesses and the organization as a whole? This assumes, of course, that the organization is able to exploit the learning potential.

### 12.1.1   Reasons for diversification and acquisition

There are, then, a number of sound and logical reasons why a firm might seek to diversify through acquisition. Some of these have been mentioned above; others are discussed below. Most are economic. The fact that diversification and acquisition strategies often prove less successful than the expectations for them is more likely to result from the choice of company to acquire and from issues and problems of implementation than the fact that the idea of diversification was misguided. This will be explored further later in the chapter.

Diversification may be chosen because the existing business is seen as being vulnerable in some way: growth potential may be limited; further investment in internal growth may not be justified; the business may be threatened by new technology. Some businesses are undervalued by the stock market, making them vulnerable to take-over if they do not diversify. Some products and businesses may currently be valuable cash generators, but with little prospect of future growth. In other words, they may be cash cows generating funds that need to be reinvested elsewhere to build a future for the company. Leading on from this, the company may have growth objectives that stretch beyond the potential of existing businesses.

Diversification may occur because a company has developed a particular strength or expertise and feels that it could benefit from transferring this asset into other, possibly unrelated, businesses. The strength might be financial (high cash reserves or borrowing capacity), marketing, technical or managerial. If genuine synergy potential exists, both the existing and newly acquired businesses can benefit from a merger or acquisition.

A company which has become stale or sleepy, or which has succession problems at the strategic leader level, may see an acquisition as a way of obtaining fresh ideas and new management, and this may seem more important than the extent to which the businesses are related.

Some diversification and acquisition decisions are concerned with reducing risk and establishing or restoring an acceptable balance of yesterday's, today's and tomorrow's

**Figure 12.1** Diversification alternatives

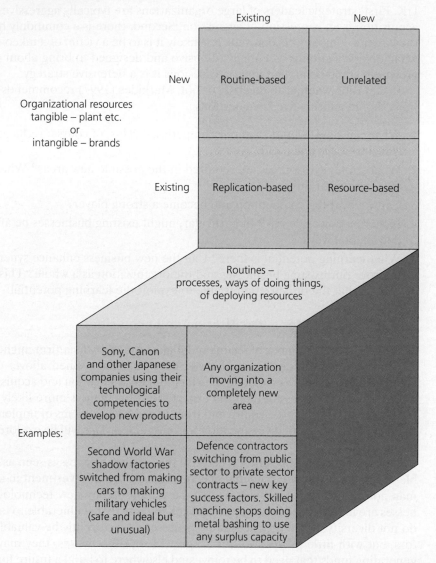

Developed from Chiesa, V and Manzini, R (1997) Competence-Based Diversification, *Long Range Planning*, 2 June.

products in a complex portfolio. This will be especially attractive where a company is relying currently on yesterday's products.

Some strategic changes in this category will result from the ego or the ambitions of the strategic leader, who may feel that he or she can run any type of business successfully, regardless of the degree of unrelatedness. Some may be very keen to grow quickly, possibly to avoid takeover, and acquisitions may happen because a company is available for purchase rather than as the outcome of a careful and detailed analysis.

It will be suggested later that the major beneficiaries of an acquisition are often the existing shareholders of the company being acquired. Consequently, it is sometimes argued that the self-interest of the City and large institutional shareholders might be behind certain mergers and acquisitions.

Figure 12.1 provides a useful summary of related and unrelated diversification opportunities. The top part of the diagram suggests that the degree of unrelatedness increases when:

- the **tangible resources** involved, both plant and equipment and intangible brands are different rather than similar, and
- the processes – the ways in which these resources are deployed and utilized – also changes.

The bottom part provides examples of each situation. It will be appreciated that the strategic risk increases as the extent of the newness and learning increases.

## 12.2 Research into diversification and acquisition

### 12.2.1 The relative success of diversification and acquisition

A number of research studies have been carried out in both the UK and the US on the relative success of diversification and acquisition strategies. There are some general conclusions as well as specific findings, and the major ones are documented here. In the main, most of the findings are consistent.

It is important to emphasize, however, that this is a particularly difficult area to research because of problems with data availability. If, for example, one is attempting to study the change in a company's performance before and after an acquisition, then one needs several years of data to ensure that longer-term effects are studied once any teething problems of early implementation are overcome. However, company W may have acquired company X in, say, 1995 and as a result been included in a research study which began in the same year. Ideally, the performance of the combined company WX would be compared with the previous performance of W and X as independent companies. If company W is naturally acquisitive it may divest some unattractive businesses from X during 1996 in order to raise money to help to finance the purchase of company Y in 1998 and company Z in 1999. An ongoing programme of this nature means that it is impossible to compare the long-term effects of one particular acquisition on an organization. The original sample continually reduces. In the same way, a comparison of the performance over a period of time of companies which might be classified as single, dominant, related and unrelated product (terms explained in Chapter 11) will be affected by firms which change category as a result of the strategies they follow. The relevance of these points can be seen in Minicase 11.5, Granada.

General conclusions from the research suggest that no more than 50 per cent of diversification through acquisition strategies are successful. Quite simply, the synergies that were considered to exist prior to acquisition are frequently not realized. There is also agreement that shareholders in a company which is taken over or acquired benefit from selling their shares to the bidder, who often pays an unwarranted premium. Shareholders who accept shares in the acquiring company instead of cash, together with the existing shareholders in that company, tend to be rewarded less in the longer term using share price appreciation as a measure. As mentioned earlier in the chapter, the research findings also support the contention that the profitability gains attributable to internal investments in companies are generally much greater than those accruing to acquisition investments.

Lorenz (1986) suggests that research in this field can be classified into four schools: accounting, economic, financial and managerial. The accounting school have concentrated on post-merger profitability in the 1970s, and their general conclusion, accepting sampling problems, is that few acquisitions resulted in increased profitability and for most the effect was neutral. Some had negative effects. Cowling *et al.* (1979), members of the economic school, concluded that there has been an increase in market power but no increase in economic efficiency.

The financial school has analysed share price movements and concluded that bid premiums are often as high as 20–40 per cent. Many takeovers in both the UK and the US are hostile and opposed aggressively, and this often leads to the payment of high premiums. Five years after acquisition, half of the US acquirers had outperformed the stock market; the other half had performed below average. The success rate is thought to be lower in the UK. One issue in this type of research concerns whether or not stock market prices and performance accurately reflect economic performance.

Kitching (1973), categorized in the managerial school, has concluded that the less related an acquisition is, the more risky it is. In addition, it is more risky to move into new markets than into new technology, assuming that the two are not achieved together. Critics of this conclusion argue that related acquisitions are more likely to be in attractive industries, and consequently more likely to succeed for this reason.

### 12.2.2 Specific research findings

**British research** Reed and Luffman (1986) analysed the performance of 349 of the largest 1000 companies in the UK between 1970 and 1980. These 349 were selected because their product base did not change during the decade. They concluded that the more diversified companies grew most rapidly in terms of sales and earnings, and the capital value of their shares declined by the lowest amount. The respective figures, after accounting for inflation, were 2.1 per cent average annual growth in sales and 1.3 per cent average annual growth in earnings before interest and tax. The capital value of their shares declined by 3.44 per cent per year on average. Dominant-product companies were the next most successful group against these measures, followed by related companies and finally single-product companies.

> There is a 'gin rummy school of management' … you pick up a few businesses here, discard a few there. The sad fact is that most acquisitions display an egregious imbalance – they are a bonanza for the shareholders of the acquiree; they increase the income and status of the acquirer's management; and they are a honey pot for the investment bankers and the other professionals on both sides. But, alas, they usually reduce the wealth of the acquirer's shareholders, often to a substantial extent.
>
> Warren Buffett, Chairman, Berkshire Hathaway, an investment business which buys minority stakes in a range of non-technical businesses and holds them for relatively extended periods

However, the return on capital employed ratios were not consistent with the growth figures. Dominant-product companies were the most profitable (19.1 per cent on average), followed by single-product companies (18.1 per cent), related-product companies (16.9 per cent) and finally unrelated-product companies (16.7 per cent). Reed and Luffman conclude that this is a result of the complexities of the inherent changes rather than of the strategy itself.

These findings replicated earlier US research by Rumelt at the Harvard Business School (1974), and they suggest that the contention by Peters and Waterman (1982) that successful companies 'stick to the knitting' is justified.

Meeks (1977) looked at post-merger profitability during the late 1960s and early 1970s. He started with a sample of 213 firms, reducing the sample size annually as the organizations concerned changed their strategies again in some significant way. In four years the sample halved; and after seven years there were only 21 companies left from the original 213. Meeks looked at the percentage of remaining firms each year and considered whether their profitability had increased or decreased. In the first year after the merger 34 per cent of the firms exhibited lower combined profitability than they had enjoyed previously as independent companies. This percentage increased during the first four years to a high of 66 per cent, with half the original sample left. At the end of seven years of research, 62 per cent of the remaining 21 companies were showing reduced profitability.

Meeks concluded that mergers which involved related businesses increased market power, but this was not the case for conglomerate mergers. All types experienced lower profitability and reflected reduced efficiency as a result of the merger activity. Greater size primarily yields higher salaries for executives, a generally more stable corporate performance and increased immunity from takeover.

Houlder (1997) reports on research from Warwick University which concludes that acquisitions are prone to fail where the acquirer neglects the new business after the acquisition. In such cases, the managers in the acquired business become frustrated and depressed – they feel that they have been left to 'operate in a vacuum'. Their subsequent underperformance increases the likelihood that the business will be sold again. Therefore, a careful balance needs to be struck between independence and 'arm's-length freedom' and determined integration with the parent. The appropriate style will depend upon the extent and the nature of the fit between the two. The research also distinguishes between repeat acquirers, who have learned about integrating new businesses into a corporate whole and have developed key implementation skills, and occasional, even first-time, acquirers who are at the start of a learning curve.

**US research** Salter and Weinhold (1982) studied 36 widely diversified US companies between 1967 and 1977 and concluded that 'diversification strategies designed to raise performance actually brought return on equity down'. In 1967 the companies concerned were producing returns which were 20 per cent above the *Fortune* 500 average, and consequently they could afford to diversify. In 1977 they were 18 per cent below average.

Porter (1987) analysed the strategies and performance of 33 large US conglomerates during the 1970s, and based his general conclusions upon the pattern of later divestment of the acquisitions. Well over half his sample divested at least some of their acquisitions, and a typical retention period seemed to average five to six years. Companies which moved into related activities generally performed better than those which diversified into unrelated areas. From this research Porter suggested three tests for successful diversification, and these are discussed later in this chapter (see p. 570).

McKinsey, in research published in 1988, documented the performance of 116 large UK and US companies since 1972. Sixty per cent had failed to earn back the cost of capital on the funds invested in acquisitions, and this figure rose to 86 per cent for large unrelated acquisitions.

Nesbitt and King (1989) examined the progress of 1800 US companies between 1978 and 1988 and concluded that corporate performance is dependent on strategy implementation rather than the strategy itself. The degree of diversification as opposed to specialization, taken in isolation, has little impact.

Burgman (1985) studied 600 US acquisitions which took place between 1974 and 1978 and concluded that:

- the higher the premium paid to acquire a company, the less likely it was to be successful
- prospects for success were greater where the acquirer had a functional appreciation of the business being acquired
- success depended upon the ability to retain key managers in the acquired company
- larger acquisitions were often more successful, possibly because the sheer size and financial commitment necessitated a thorough appraisal beforehand.

Further research, some of it more recent, confirms these key findings.

These research programmes and papers by Biggadike (1979) and Kitching (1967) suggest a number of reasons why acquisitions fail, and these are considered below.

### 12.2.3 Why acquisitions fail

It has been mentioned previously that a key reason why acquisitions fail is that they do not generate the synergy that was anticipated or at least hoped for. This is particularly true for conglomerate rather than concentric diversification. Minicase 12.1 looks at the search for synergy by Daimler-Benz. In general, it is easier to gain synergy from production and operations than it is from marketing. It is difficult to gain real additional benefit from selling more than one product or service into one market.

Linked to this issue is the reality that in many cases the real weaknesses of the acquired company are hidden until after the acquisition, and consequently are underestimated. Also underestimated are the cultural and managerial problems of merging two companies and then running them as one. As a result insufficient managerial resources are devoted to the process of merging, and hence the hoped-for synergy remains elusive.

This problem typically arises because the acquiring company concludes that the skills which were to be transferred to the new acquisition in order to generate the synergy are in reality not available. They are already fully committed and in the end are not transferred.

Key managers who have been responsible for the past growth and success of the company being acquired may choose to leave rather than stay with the new conglomerate. Where this happens, and depending on the extent of the contribution of these managers, past successes may not be repeatable.

Further reasons concern the amount paid for the acquisition, and the extent of the premium. For a contested take-over in particular, the bidding company may become overenthusiastic and optimistic about the prospects, overstretch itself financially and then not be able to afford the necessary investment to generate benefits and growth in the new company. When a premium is paid the acquirer is likely to set high targets initially for the new company in order to try and recover the premium quickly. When these targets are missed, because they are unrealistic, enthusiasm is lost and feelings of hostility may develop. It can be argued that if synergy really is available, price is less significant as an issue, and a premium may well be justifiable. However, if an acquisition is fundamentally misconceived a low or a cheap price will not make it successful at the implementation stage.

Finally, the reaction of competitors may be misjudged.

The difficulties apply in service businesses as well as manufacturing, as the following examples illustrate. Some years ago the long-established and family-owned Cadbury was persuaded by management consultants to believe that 'successful managers can manage anything' and diversified into Schweppes soft drinks (related distribution channels) and the unrelated Jeyes (disinfectants). Jeyes was quickly divested when it became clear that the core chocolate business was suffering as managers became preoccupied with the new activities. Interestingly, the same consultants also persuaded Cadbury to abandon its paternalistic style of management, manifested in the Bourneville village and community which the Quaker family had built for its workforce. General Accident acquired a related insurance business in New Zealand in 1988 and as part of the purchase inherited the NZI Bank. The loan book deteriorated in the worldwide recession and, lacking the necessary turnaround skills, General Accident decided to close the bank. The Prudential similarly chose to exit estate agencies after incurring huge losses. They had overpaid for their acquisitions and the anticipated learning and synergy was slow to materialize. Some would argue that the strategy of linking insurance with estate agencies was misjudged; others that the problems were really those of implementation. In particular, the Prudential attempted to exercise central control over a disparate group of acquisitions.

In reality, acquisition is an uncertain strategy. However sound the economic justification may appear to be, implementation or managerial issues ultimately determine success or failure. These issues are the subject of the next section.

### 12.2.4  Issues in diversification and acquisition

Where two companies choose to merge there is the opportunity for a reasonably comprehensive assessment of relative strengths and weaknesses, although it does not follow that one or both will not choose to hide certain significant weaknesses. In the case of a contested takeover less information will be available. UK takeover law requires that once a company has built up a shareholding of a particular size in another company it must offer to buy the remaining shares, at which stage, the targeted company must make certain information available through the process of due diligence. (Since 1989 one company must inform another if it builds up a share of three per cent or more. When the ownership reaches 10 per cent a company has to declare its intent – preparation for a later bid or a mere investment. Companies will be held to this declaration. If one says that it is merely investing it will not then be able to launch a bid for at least one year. A company can own up to 29.9 per cent without making a bid for the remainder, but once

**Table 12.1** Information available before and after an acquisition

| Before | After |
|---|---|
| Organization charts | Inner philosophy and culture |
| Data on salaries of top management | Real quality of staff in decision roles |
| Reasonably detailed information on board members and key executives – but only brief details on middle management | Salary and reward structures and systems Decision processes |
| Products | Interrelationships, power bases, hidden conflicts and organizational politics |
| Plants | Individual objectives being pursued |
| Corporate identity, image and reputation | |
| Past record, especially financial | |

**Figure 12.2** Strategy creation and implementation
Based on a matrix devised by Booz, Allen and Hamilton

|  | Vision | |
|---|---|---|
|  | Good | Poor |
| **Good** | Effective strategic management | Opportunist and likely to underperform |
| **Poor** | Wasted opportunity | Ill-conceived mistake |

**Implementation** (row labels Good / Poor)

this figure is exceeded a bid for the rest must follow.) Crucially, however, the information that will affect the ease or difficulty of merging the two cultures and organizations, and implementing the changes, is less freely available than financial data.

It is never easy to determine from outside an organization what the style of management is, its managers' attitude to risks, how decisions are made and whether managers are largely self-reliant. In the final analysis, the success of an acquisition or merger will be influenced markedly by the way the companies fit (or do not fit) together as well as by the logic used to justify the strategy (see Figure 12.2). As a result financial analysis may be used to justify the acquisition, but it will not answer questions relating to implementation. Table 12.1 highlights the significant information that is unlikely to be available until after the acquisition.

The following list of questions and issues indicates the key considerations which should be addressed by a company before it acquires another:

■ how the acquiring company should restructure itself in order to absorb the new purchase, and what implications this will have for existing businesses and people
■ what acceptable minimum and maximum sizes are for proposed diversifications in relation to present activities
■ what degree of risk it is appropriate for the company to take
■ how to value a proposed acquisition and how much to pay
■ how to maintain good relationships with key managers during negotiations to try to ensure that they stay afterwards
■ how to maintain momentum and interest in both companies after a successful offer
■ how quickly to move in merging organizational parts and sorting out problems
■ reporting relationships and the degree of independence allowed to the acquired company, particularly where the business is unrelated
■ whether and how to send in a new management team.

Some of these issues are considered in the next section where effective acquisition strategies are discussed, but many of them are taken up in later chapters which consider the implementation aspects of strategic change. Figure 12.2 illustrates that an effective strategy is one that is based upon good vision and sound implementation prospects. Vision is in relation to the organization's strengths and market opportunities, and an effective strategy will match these. In the context of diversification and acquisition, implementation relates to a consideration of how the two organizations will be merged together and the changes required to structures, cultures and systems in order to ensure that potential synergy is achieved. Poor vision and poor implementation will both cause strategic management to be less than effective. If the logic behind an acquisition is poor, then the merged corporation is likely to underperform, however well the two companies might be managed as one corporate whole. If the vision is good but implementation is weak, underperformance is again likely because synergy will not be created.

If companies develop by a series of acquisitions it is quite typical for several banks to become involved. These could be spread worldwide; their cultures and lending philosophies may differ; their levels of exposure will vary; the assets securing the loans will not be the same; and certain banks may see themselves as lenders to just one company rather than the whole organization. Problems are likely to arise if one of the banks gets into financial difficulties or if the company seeks to extend a loan or adjust the terms.

## 12.3  Effective acquisition strategies

A number of authors have suggested ways of improving the effectiveness of acquisition strategies.

Drucker (1982), for example, argues that there are five rules for successful acquisitions.

1. It is essential for the acquiring company to determine exactly what contribution it can make to the acquired company. It must be more than money.
2. It is important to search for a company with a 'common core of unity', say in technology, markets or production processes.
3. The acquiring company should value the products, services and customers of the company that it is taking over.
4. Top management cover for the acquired company should be available in case key managers choose to leave after the acquisition.
5. Within a year managers should have been promoted across company boundaries.

In a report entitled *Making Acquisitions Work: Lessons from Companies' Successes and Mistakes*, Business International (1988) offers the following guidelines.

- *Plan first* – As a company, know exactly what you are going to do. Ascertain where the company being acquired has been, and maybe still is, successful, and ensure that it can be maintained – taking special account of any dependence on key people. Appreciate also where it is weak. It is quite possible that it will have good products but overheads which are too high.
- *Implement quickly* – People in the acquired company expect decisive action, and delay prolongs speculation. At the same time it is important not to act without thinking things through first.

**Figure 12.3** Effective acquisition strategies

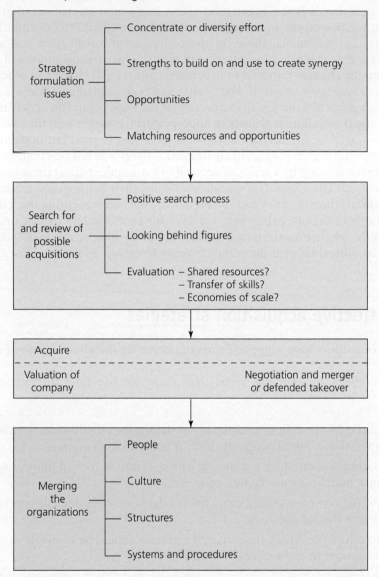

- *Communicate frankly* – Explain the acquisition or merger, the expected benefits and the changes which will be required. In addition, it is useful to ensure that there is an understanding of the values and expectations of the acquiring company.

- *Act correctly*, particularly as far as redundancy is concerned.

Ramsay (1987) argues that effective acquisition strategies have four stages, which are illustrated in Figure 12.3:

- the need to formulate a clear strategy
- the search for possible acquisitions
- the acquisition
- the merger of the organizations following acquisition.

These four stages are now discussed in detail.

## 12.3.1    The formulation of a clear strategy

An effective, well thought through diversification and acquisition can constitute real strategic growth by providing entry into a new market, a new opportunity to build on competitive strengths, an opportunity to create and benefit from synergy, and the possibility of removing some element of competition. This, however, implies more logic behind the acquisition than mere sales growth or the purchase of a profit stream. Hence there are a number of issues to consider in attempting to formulate an effective strategy for acquisition.

- First, the issue of how much to concentrate and how much to diversify must be examined. We mentioned earlier that research indicates that concentration is generally superior but that the opportunities available may not be sufficient to fill the planning gap. A major advantage of concentration, and a limit on diversification, is that experience is difficult to copy. Learning and experience can lead to superior competitive positions through an understanding of customers and how to satisfy their needs through production and service. Horizontal integration and concentric diversification can both provide opportunities to capitalize on learning and experience.

- Second, a good strategy will build on existing strengths and develop synergy around them. This requires an opportunity to transfer skills and competencies and achieve economies of scale. This issue is discussed further below.

- Third, it is important to be able to spot an opportunity and act quickly and decisively to capitalize on it. It has been argued, for example, that, once legislation permitted it in the mid-1980s, the building societies that moved quickly into estate agencies benefited far more than those that lagged behind, because the cost per site increased with the acquisition activity. Such a strategic move would be classified as vertical integration because an estate agency is really a channel of distribution for mortgages.

- Fourth, resources (strengths) and opportunities need to be matched. The ability to do this effectively relates to the way the company is managed, and to the culture and values.

## 12.3.2    The search for, and review of, possible acquisitions

- There should be an active and positive search process. Acquisitions are difficult, diversification is risky, and the decisions can prove expensive if they are wrong. Strategic leaders should track and carefully analyse possible acquisitions rather than rely on opportunities which might arise.

- It is essential to be realistic. Where there is a friendly merger, or the acquisition of a company in difficulties, it is possible that certain key weaknesses may be hidden; and in the case of a hostile bid situation it is important not to become unrealistic through determination and, as a result, pay too much.

- Before acquiring it is crucial to assess just how resources are going to be shared, where and how skills are going to be transferred, and where and how economies of scale are going to be obtained. If such an analysis is left until after an acquisition, synergy is likely to prove more elusive.

The price paid to acquire a company relative to its earning potential, and the ability to generate synergy through shared activities or transferred skills, are the key determinants of likely success.

Porter (1987) contends that a portfolio of unrelated companies is only a logical corporate strategy if the aim is restructuring. Restructuring is the strategy pursued by conglomerates such as Hanson, and it requires the identification of companies which are underperforming and which can be transformed with new management skills. Ideally, they are valued below their real potential when acquired. The new owner seeks to improve the competitive position of the organization and improve its profitability. Logically, companies or business units are sold when they no longer have potential for increasing earnings further. The opportunity to pursue this strategy effectively lies in the ability to spot and acquire undervalued companies cheaply and to manage unfamiliar businesses better than the existing managers.

In any acquisition, Porter argues, three tests should be passed.

1. The industry involved should be or could be made structurally attractive. In other words, the potential returns exceed the company's cost of capital.

2. The entry cost should not be so high that future profit streams are compromised. As well as the purchase price, the cost must also take account of professional fees involved in the merger or acquisition.

    Granada incurred professional fees exceeding £100 million for its takeover of Forte. Forte's defence costs, post-acquisition divestment fees, together with other payments and provisions, built up an accumulated total of some £250 million. Granada paid £3.9 billion for Forte.

3. One of the companies should be able to gain competitive advantage, and the newly acquired business should be better off in the new corporation than elsewhere. In other words, the interrelationships, based on shared activities and transferred skills, must give added value which outweighs the costs incurred. These benefits are often not gained for two main reasons. The new, more diverse, more complex, organization is likely to be decentralized, but the business units may be independent in practice rather than interdependent. Managers may not be able to understand and implement the interrelationships.

Minicase 12.2 evaluates the ASDA-MFI merger against these three tests and argues that it did not pass them all, in that the expected synergy was not achieved.

Van de Vliet (1997) reports on research from Mercer Consulting which confirms the switch during the 1990s from conglomeration to mergers with a more defensible strategic logic, but also confirms a concurrent increase in hostile takeovers. The implication is that higher premiums are being paid. This seems to be a situation of gain against one test and deterioration against another!

Some commentators have also argued that a fourth test should be added to Porter's three: how much will have to be invested in the future, post-acquisition? The experience of BMW with Rover is testimony to the significance of this test. BMW underestimated the investment requirements and eventually sold the business 'for a song' to avoid further spending.

Figure 12.4 attempts to pull these points together diagrammatically.

Hence companies that are seeking to grow through acquisition and the consolidation of the acquired and existing businesses should ensure either that skills can be transferred or that activities can be shared, i.e. clear interrelationships can be identified.

## Minicase 12.2 The ASDA–MFI Merger/Demerger         (GB)

ASDA – now owned by Wal-Mart – enjoys second position in the UK groceries market. Its large stores also sell a wide range of non-food products, including clothing and electrical goods.

Its real growth into one of the UK's largest food retail chains began in the mid-1960s when it first recognized the potential for out-of-town sites with large car parks. ASDA remain strongest in the north of England; the head office is in Leeds. ASDA's other main retailing activity in the 1980s, however, was carpets and furnishings, which it entered with acquisitions. ASDA tried unsuccessfully to divest Allied Carpets in the mid-1980s, but then opted to support it by buying two-thirds of Waring & Gillow (furniture shops) and forming Allied Maples – again in 1989. Allied Maples was finally sold to Carpetland in 1993.

In 1985, with a welcome bid, ASDA acquired MFI, the nationwide retailer of self-assembly furniture. This represented concentric diversification as, although the products were different, the customer base was seen as essentially the same. Synergy was expected between the food superstores and MFI rather than through the furniture links, as both were professional edge-of-town retailers in complementary businesses. Both were innovators and their management teams could learn from each other. There was an additional hidden motive. The Chairman of ASDA, Sir Noel Stockdale, was approaching retirement and there was no natural successor. Derek Hunt of MFI was thought to be an ideal replacement. Hunt became Chief Executive of ASDA–MFI in 1986, but retained his working base in the south of England where MFI headquarters had been.

The expected benefits and synergy did not accrue. In 1984 the return on net assets of ASDA was 43 per cent and of MFI 38 per cent. In the three years that the companies were merged the relevant figures for the group dropped from 40 per cent in 1985 to 27 per cent in 1987.

In 1987 MFI was sold in a management buy-out to a consortium led by Derek Hunt, but ASDA retained a 25 per cent interest. Since the demerger MFI has acquired its main supplier of furniture packs, Hygena, and this backward vertical integration quickly brought some tangible financial benefits. However, the improvement was temporary – in the recession at the end of the 1980s/early 1990s MFI traded at a loss. Interest costs arising out of the buy-back and a reputation for poor quality compounded their trading difficulties.

At ASDA, John Hardman took over as chairman in 1987, but he resigned in 1991 when ASDA also started losing money. The losses continued in 1992. The company was trading profitably but exceptional charges were leading to pre-tax losses. ASDA had paid too much for 60 Gateway stores in 1989 and still owned 25 per cent of the debt-ridden MFI. The MFI shares have since been sold, but the Gateway stores were valued in the balance sheet at just two-thirds of their acquisition price. Moreover ASDA lacked an effective competitive identity and was perceived to be a less successful retailer than its main rivals, who were also proving more successful in obtaining the premium sites for new stores. ASDA had centralized its distribution into a limited number of regional warehouses, but had been a follower rather than a leader in this key strategic development. In 1990 ASDA formed a joint venture with George Davies (ex-Next) in an attempt to revive its non-food activities with a range of designer clothes.

The new chairman (Patrick Gillam) and 'youthful' chief executive (Archie Norman, then aged 37) embarked on a three-year programme which 'would not produce significant results in the immediate future'. Their aim was to turn back the clock and return to 'meeting the weekly shopping needs of ordinary working people and their families'. ASDA saw itself positioned and differentiated as 'the store for ordinary working people who demand value'. The market was carefully segmented and prices made keener; ASDA set out to be some 5–7 per cent below Sainsbury and Tesco to drive higher volumes. Productivity has been improved and service quality stressed; supplier arrangements have been strengthened; and there is an increased emphasis on fresh foods and clothing, where ASDA believes it has a relative strength. There are also regional variations in stocking policy. Norman perceived the increasing success of the discount-price food retailers to be a threat as ASDA has retained a number of small stores in less affluent areas.

When Gillam and Norman took over, the *Financial Times* suggested that ASDA's institutional investors 'would be persistently whispering thoughts of mortality into the ears of ASDA's new emperors'. In the event ASDA was successfully turned around.

The culture also changed. ASDA now has a huge open-plan head office and managers are asked to wear ASDA baseball caps at their desks if they do not want to be disturbed. In its attempt to strengthen its customer focus, ASDA has increasingly pushed head office managers out into the stores. Internal communications have been fostered. Archie Norman became non-executive chairman when he became a Conservative MP in 1997, but gave this up some time after the Wal-Mart acquisition. His previous deputy, Allan Leighton, took over for a period and consolidated ASDA's strengthening position.

## Applying the acquisition tests to ASDA-MFI

### The attractiveness of the kitchen furniture industry

In the case of kitchens supplied direct to individual customers (as opposed to sales to building contractors) the actual suppliers of kitchen furniture did not enjoy as strong a market profile as did MFI, and buyers individually had very little power. En masse they are influential. Any competitor wanting to enter the market on the MFI scale would require massive investment; substitute products were often units which were already assembled, such as those sold by Magnet Southern. Increases in disposable income might make these more attractive. There was intense rivalry for market share, however, as sales of kitchen furniture were flat in the 1980s.

On balance the industry was not unattractive, and MFI was a past 'winner'. Profits had grown 87 per cent in real terms between 1980 and 1985.

### The cost of entry

MFI cost ASDA £570 million, which represented 5.5 times net assets and 14 times 1984 pre-tax profits. It was a 31 per cent premium on the current market capitalization, and it measured MFI on a price to earnings ratio of 22 rather than the 18 that it had been before the bid. Debt and equity funding were both involved; and ASDA's gearing increased from little more than zero to 40 per cent. Both sets of shareholders were supportive, but with hindsight it seems a high price.

### Increased competitive advantage

There was no real benefit to be gained from common purchasing, no site sharing, and the two companies enjoyed different geographical concentrations. ASDA was northern and MFI national.

After the merger the companies were run autonomously with few activities shared. Prior to merging it had been argued that there would be intangible benefits from shared expertise. In the event, there was little cross-flow of managers, product innovation, marketing or operations skills. The cultures remained separate; and Derek Hunt, who became chief executive, worked from London despite ASDA's northern base.

While ASDA did compete with Sainsbury's, who at the time had a chain of Homebase DIY stores, this was not seen as a threat that MFI would address; and in any case MFI was very narrowly focused within the DIY sector.

While the industry was not unattractive the merger proved expensive for ASDA, and the potential synergy used to justify the merger to shareholders seemed not to be there in reality.

## Questions

1. Do you agree with this final assessment of the ASDA-MFI merger? Could this merger ever have been successful or was it always misguided strategically?
2. Why do you think that ASDA's acquisition strategies typically failed whilst the acquisition of ASDA itself (by Wal-Mart) has been an outstanding success?
3. Since its demerger, has MFI also proved to be 'better-off'?

ASDA http://www.asda.com
MFI http://www.mfi.co.uk

**Figure 12.4** The effective acquisition

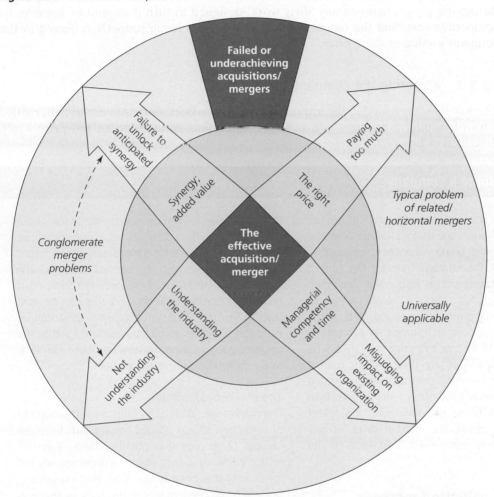

These can relate to any part of the value chain. The aims are greater economies of scale, lower costs or enhanced differentiation through sharing activities, know-how or customers, or transferring skills and know-how. The research findings quoted earlier suggest that these opportunities are more likely to be found in industries which are in some way related. Tobacco companies in both the UK and the US, for example, when faced with declining demand and hostile pressure groups, realized that they would have to diversify if they were to avoid decline. They chose such industries as food, wine and brewing initially because they felt that they could transfer their skills and expertise in marketing consumer products.

Acquisitions are likely to prove disappointing if the opportunity for such synergy is not evaluated objectively in advance, or if the companies convince themselves that synergy must be possible without establishing where and how.

It is also vital to check carefully for any skeletons prior to an acquisition. In 1990 ICI Explosives bought Atlas Powder in the US. In the same year, a US rival of Atlas, Thermex Energy, was declared bankrupt, and when, some years later, Atlas was found guilty of conspiring to drive Thermex out of business, ICI was held responsible by the US courts. Substantial, but contested, damages were awarded against ICI.

One final point worth making is on timing. The ideal time to bid for a company is during the period between any 'dirty work' designed to turn it around or improve its competitiveness, and the outcome of these strategies being properly reflected in the company's value or share price.

### 12.3.3 Acquiring the company

The key issues involved in the acquisition itself have been discussed earlier; alternative ways of valuing a business – in order to determine an appropriate bid price – are described in Box 12.1.

---

## Box 12.1 Valuing a Company

Acquisition of another company constitutes an investment, although one major strategic objective might be to avoid being taken over by another firm. Whatever the strategic reason, the current value of an organization is important. Assuming that we are not talking about a merger (of assets), a company will normally be acquired when another company buys an appropriate percentage of its shares. While the bid price will always be influenced substantially by their current market price in trading, the likely purchase price in both a hostile and a bidding situation (where more than one prospective buyer is in evidence) will reflect a premium. However, the market price at any time may or may not reflect the value of the organization.

### Alternative valuation methods

#### Rule of thumb

A typical rule of thumb valuation of a company would be to multiply the most recent annual profits (or an average of the last few years) times an *x* factor. Relatively small *x*s will be selected for small companies (which have fewer customers and fewer key people) and service businesses, where it is easier for key people to be lost during or after the acquisition. The *x* factor might vary from 3 up to 13 for large, established manufacturing businesses.

#### The balance sheet valuation

The balance sheet value of a company is normally taken from the value of the net assets. Divided by the number of ordinary shares issued, this yields the asset value behind every ordinary share, and it can therefore be useful in assessing what an appropriate bid price for the ordinary shares might be. However, caution is needed because the balance sheet traditionally records historical costs rather than present values, and this can be misleading in the case of property. In addition, although some companies do account for this, the value of such intangible assets as brand names is rarely reflected in the balance sheet.

#### The market valuation

The market valuation of a company is the number of ordinary shares issued multiplied by their present price plus the inherited debt. This will reflect the likely lowest cost to a buyer, as any bid for shares at a price below their existing price is unlikely to succeed. In reality, the price of shares is likely to increase during the period between when current shareholders realize that a bid is likely, or when one is announced, and when control is finally achieved by the bidder.

The current share price and the asset value of shares should be looked at together.

#### Earnings potential

Many contend that it is future earnings potential that determines how valuable a company is, not historical results – see, for example, Allen (1988). An analysis of past and current performance is therefore limited in its usefulness. In isolation, a high return on capital employed, for example, can hide the reality of an asset base which is declining in real terms. Therefore, one should estimate the future cash flows that the company is capable of generating and discount these by the cost of capital. The current value of the company is determined by this net present value calculation.

The decision to acquire a company, however, will not be based solely on the discounted future earnings, nor the purchase price, but both of these are very important. Future earnings potential for both the acquiring and the acquired companies could be improved with a merger if valuable synergy of some form is derived, and for this potential a premium price might be justified.

### A multifactor approach
Consequently, Copeland et al. (1990) recommend a five-level valuation approach:

- The first level is the current market value, described above.
- The second level is the earnings potential, the value of the projected cash flow, discounted.

- The third level projects a value once internal improvements have been undertaken. New business processes, for example, could improve the cash flow.
- The fourth level is the value after restructuring, when non-core or poorly performing activities have been sold or divested.
- The fifth level combines level three and four benefits. Significantly, the improvements implied in these three levels may require a fresh management team and style.

### References

Allen, D (1988) *Long Term Financial Health – A Structure for Strategic Financial Management*, Chartered Institute of Management Accountants (CIMA).

Copeland, T, Kotter, T and Murrin, J (1990) *Valuation: Measuring and Managing the Value of Companies*, John Wiley.

It was emphasized above that it is important to look for hidden weaknesses in friendly mergers and avoid paying too much in a contested take over bid. It was also mentioned earlier that if too high a premium is paid the acquisition is less likely to be successful (Burgman 1985), and a vicious circle of disillusionment can easily be created. If the acquisition is overvalued or a substantial premium is paid, the expected early returns on the investment will be very high. An acquisition involves an investment that must be paid back by generating returns which exceed the cost of capital involved. If targets are missed the possible disillusionment and loss of confidence may mean that additional investment to develop the business, which really is needed, will not be forthcoming. Consequently, performance will deteriorate further and the business will run down. A likely outcome of this will be its sale at a discounted price, and the acquirer will have lost money from the acquisition. The payment of any premium should be related to the ability of the acquirer to add value by sharing activities or transferring skills.

There are a number of ways of *paying for the business*. Clearly cash is one alternative. In this case, the likely return should exceed either the return that could be earned if any surplus cash were invested elsewhere, maybe in government securities, or the cost of borrowing the cash required for the purchase. The other option is to use equity, whereby a predator or acquirer simply offers its shares in exchange for those in the targeted business. This is perfectly feasible as shares normally have a trading value, but invariably it will be necessary to offer more than the current value of the shares in the business being acquired. Sometimes a mixture of shares and cash will be chosen. The decision will be influenced by:

- whether there is surplus cash in the balance sheet
- the prevailing rate of interest

- the impact on the acquirer's debt ratio and gearing.

In the UK a company cannot use the assets of a targeted business as collateral for a loan, although this is permissible in the US. It is also legal in the US to buy shares in another business with the later intention of selling them back to the company for a profit, an action sometimes called 'greenmail'.

**Unwelcome bids** Organizations which find themselves the object of an unwelcome bid can defend themselves in a number of ways. A revised profit forecast, promising improvements, can prove effective – but subsequently the improvement must be delivered. This will sometimes be linked to a promise to restructure and divest parts of the business which are not core and not contributing synergy. An appeal to regulatory bodies may at least impose a delay; and finally, the company can seek a white knight, a preferred friendly bidder. Jenkinson and Mayer (1994) have shown, first, that white-knight interventions normally succeed but, of course, the company's independence has still been lost and, second, that where there is no white knight cash bids are more difficult to defend against than equity bids.

On other occasions a targeted company will seek the support of its employees or trade unions, on the grounds that it is their jobs that could be affected detrimentally. The outcome of this strategy is variable and unpredictable. Another popular strategy is to acquire fresh assets which make the acquisition less attractive to the predator but, of course, there might be a strategic price to pay later if the bid does not go through and if this is purely defensive in nature! A number of defensive strategies by Forte is evident in its attempt to avoid take-over by Granada (Minicase 11.5).

These issues are explored further in Box 12.2.

## Box 12.2 Hostile Takeovers

**KEY CONCEPTS**

In a research sample year (1989) in the UK there were 161 bids for publicly listed companies; 35 of these were hostile takeover attempts as distinct from agreed or friendly acquisition bids. In one sense the year was seen as typical: some 70 per cent of the largest acquisitions/takeovers were hostile. Of these about half will normally succeed; in the other cases the target company will be able to mount an effective defence strategy.

By contrast, Germany had experienced just three hostile takeover bids since 1945. They are equally rare in France and almost unheard of in Japan. They remain popular in the US, where a larger number of defence mechanisms are available than is the case in the UK.

### Alternative defence strategies

(Listed in order of popularity in the UK)

1. *Financial responses* Companies will hope to be able to announce forthcoming profit improvements – they have been targeted because, although fundamentally competitive and sound, recent profits have been disappointing. They may also seek to revalue their assets to make the bid appear to be undervaluing the true worth of the business.
2. *Legal and political tactics* Political lobbying and attempts to get a bid referred to the competition authorities, the latter to, at the very least, buy time and allow a company to mount a stronger defence.
3. *Attempted white-knight bids* An alternative, preferred, outside bidder is sought.
4. *Corporate restructuring* As seen in Minicase 11.5, disposals are announced. Bidders will claim that attempts to rationalize and downsize, while appropriate and desirable,

have been provoked by the bid and are indicative of reactive senior management. Sometimes the strategic leadership will attempt to mount a management buy-out as an alternative to the outside bid.

5. *Poison pills* This strategy, most popular in the US, describes shareholder rights plans which effectively increase the price to the bidder. An example would be preferentially priced stock being available to existing shareholders, giving them a later right to new ordinary shares. Similarly, the term *golden parachutes* describes special departure terms for directors in the event of an unwelcome acquisition.

In 1999, for example, American Airlines (linked to Canadian Airlines and allied with British Airways in the Oneworld alliance) was interested in bidding for Air Canada, which was experiencing financial difficulties. However, Air Canada was part of the Star Alliance, dominated by American's main rival, United Airlines. A poison pill was in evidence – whoever might own Air Canada, it would remain a member of the Star Alliance for ten years or United and its partners would be entitled to huge damages. The presence of this arrangement was sufficient to deter American.

## Outcomes

In general a well-formulated and strategically logical bid for a poor performer should succeed; a strong performer will clearly be in a stronger position to defend itself and its record. However, in isolation, a strong financial performance is not everything – simply, there may appear to be more strategic logic in the business being parented by the bidder instead of staying as it is.

Cash bids have the greatest likelihood of success. In 1989, 21 per cent of the 161 bids were equity based and just 11 per cent of these succeeded; 43 per cent were cash only with a 56 per cent success rate; the remaining 36 per cent were mixed cash/equity bids and 53 per cent of these succeeded. Normally, the value of a hostile bid will be increased once the nature and robustness of the defence is revealed.

Cash bids are most likely to fail if an alternative white knight bidder is found. The likelihood of the success of equity and mixed bids appears to depend upon the quality of the financial defence.

## Source

Jenkinson, T and Mayer, C (1994) *Hostile Takeovers: Defence, Attack and Corporate Governance*, McGraw-Hill.

**Abandoned discussions** There are occasions when merger talks fail and are abandoned. Walton and McBride (1998) provide a number of possible reasons for this, few of which relate to the actual strategic logic of the merger:

- There is a reluctance on the part of one company to accept that they are in reality number two and that it is not a partnership of equals.
- There is disagreement on future strategic leadership – who will run the new merged company. Egos get in the way. There was a delay in the merger between Glaxo Wellcome and SmithKline Beecham for exactly this reason (Minicase 4.1).
- There is inadequate consultation with key shareholders – typically institutions – who then intervene.
- There is an insistence on preserving too many elements from the past – often things related to a strategic leader who is reluctant to let them go.
- Relationships and trust simply break down as negotiations proceed.

### 12.3.4 Implementation issues

Ernst and Young (1995) argue that the nature of the post-acquisition challenge depends upon the type of acquisition and the objectives behind it. They identify four alternatives:

1. *Financial acquisitions* are companies brought into a holding company, sometimes for the purpose of restructuring. The main objectives for the acquisition are the financial opportunities from cost (overhead) eradication, cost reduction and improved efficiencies. Those parts of the business which do not offer these opportunities are likely to be offered for sale; and, in fact, any part of the business is likely to be available for sale to a buyer offering a premium price. The critical implementation issues concern timing and decisiveness.

2. *Geographical acquisitions* are intended to expand the acquirer's core business across new frontiers. Merging different country cultures is the key challenge, but this is generally regarded as manageable as long as the strategic logic for the merger is sound. One dilemma concerns cuts and job losses in the acquired business; alleged national bias may well cause resentment.

3. *Symbiotic acquisitions* describe situations where newly acquired products and competencies are absorbed into the parent's business but the acquired company retains some independence. Abbey National's purchase of Scottish Mutual is an example. The establishment of an appropriate new structure, culture and communications system are the implementation issues.

4. *Absorption acquisitions* imply that the two businesses are fully integrated, with one effectively losing its identity. Such acquisitions are particularly challenging to implement as really everything changes.

For any acquiring company to gain financially, sales must be increased and costs reduced to a level which compensates for any price premium paid. Researchers suggest that this is rarely less than 20 per cent. Easy savings are rare, particularly in the case of many hostile bids, where the target is often a high, rather than a poor, performer. Too many companies, apparently, pursue the elusive synergistic opportunities and do not act on the cost base quickly and decisively. They also tend to postpone the difficult issues relating to culture and style. Successful acquisitive companies such as Hanson and BTR did act quickly, concentrating on cost eradication and reduction; they also imposed their own style of management on their new businesses, top-down from the centre.

Clearly, the type of acquisition and the rationale behind it must influence the appropriate implementation strategy; as noted already, Hanson and BTR were restructuring organizations. Where genuine synergy potential exists, a more participatory style is likely to prove appropriate and foster the necessary learning and skills transfer.

### 12.3.5 Merging the two organizations

Merging two organizations involves decisions about the integration of strategic capabilities, in particular:

- operating resources – sales forces, production facilities
- functional skills – product development, R&D
- general management skills – strategy development, financial control, human resource strategies.

The speed and pattern of the integration will be dependent on the desired interdependency of the businesses, and the opportunities for synergy. It is essential that there is a strategy for the implementation, and ideally this will be developed after the merger or acquisition when fuller details are available. Moreover, important issues concerning people, culture, structure, systems and procedures must be thought through.

- *People* – It is accepted that many chief executives and other senior managers leave acquired companies either immediately or within one to two years after the acquisition, especially where the acquisition was contested. This may or may not be significant, depending on the strengths of the acquiring company. In some cases it will prove crucial, particularly where the managers have been the major source of competitive advantage. The managers in the two organizations being merged may well have different values, ethics and beliefs in quality and service, and these will somehow have to be reconciled.

- *Culture* – It is quite possible that the two organizations will have different cultures, which also must be reconciled. One may be a large company and the other small, with typical role and power cultures, respectively. Managers will be used to different levels of responsibility. One may be much more formal and procedural than the other. One may be entrepreneurial and risk orientated, and the other cost conscious and risk averse. These cultural issues should be considered when the post-acquisition structure is designed, and in the new systems and procedures.

- *Structure, systems and procedures* – While mentioned here, this issue is the subject of Chapter 15, and it concerns the degree of decentralization. As companies become larger and more complex they must be broken down into business units, and managers must be given some degree of independence – to motivate them and to ensure that functional and competitive strategies can be adapted in response to environmental changes. However, if activities are to be shared, or skills transferred, it is essential to ensure that independence does not inhibit, or even prohibit, the implementation of the necessary interdependencies.

McLean (1985) contends that six factors determine whether the integration of two or more companies is a success or a failure:

- first, active leadership by the strategic leader of the acquiring company in conveying objectives and expectations, and in redesigning the structure of the organizations
- second, the conscious development of shared values and a transfer of the important aspects of the culture of the acquiring firm
- third, an appropriate interchange of managers between the firms, which can be one way of retaining valuable managers from the acquired company
- fourth, proceeding with caution (although some changes may have to be implemented quickly, say to reduce costs in certain areas, others will be less urgent; this provides an opportunity to learn about the underlying strengths of the new business which might be capitalized on)
- fifth, relationships with customers must be protected until decisions about future products and market priorities are taken
- sixth, rigid new systems, which might be inappropriate for the new business, should not be imposed too ruthlessly or too quickly. Where there are differences in, in particular, culture, technology and marketing needs, managers in the acquired

company should be allowed the necessary freedom to manage the competitive and functional strategies and respond to market pressures.

To summarize this section, it could be argued that:

- the price paid for an acquisition should reflect the ability of the acquirer to add value, share resources and transfer skills
- the strategy for achieving this should be soundly based, and the potential synergy real rather than imagined
- post-acquisition management should recognize that, while changes will have to be made in order to add value, two cultures have to be integrated if the strategy is to be implemented effectively.

Finally, five factors for implementing acquisitions and mergers successfully can be identified:

1. Tread warily and carry out sufficient analysis – especially where there is a hostile reaction from the target.
2. Evaluate any prospective partner fully, carrying out a culture and style assessment as well as a financial evaluation.
3. Take on board the best practices from both (all) businesses to increase the prospects for synergy. It is highly unlikely that one partner will have a monopoly on good ideas.
4. Communicate with those people affected to the maximum extent that is expedient.
5. Ensure that key people are identified and stay.

## 12.4   Strategic alliances – an introduction

While some form of partnership can be one of the quickest and cheapest ways to grow or develop a new and maybe global strategy, it is also one of the toughest and most risky. Many alliances fail. The needs of both partners must be met, and consequently three important questions must be answered satisfactorily:

1. *Why* use an alliance?
2. *Who* to select as a partner?
3. *How* to implement the agreement?

Garrette and Dussauge (1999) argue that many European companies have tended to think about alliances from a defensive perspective rather than as a proactive growth opportunity. All too often they are a fall-back when the competition authorities stand in the way of a merger or acquisition. Many of the examples referred to throughout this chapter indicate that several successful American and Japanese companies have adopted a different perspective. In the late 1990s, for example, research into the largest 1000 American companies revealed that 20 per cent of their revenues came directly from alliances.

Minicase 12.3 shows how British Airways (BA) has mixed mergers and alliances, together with both positive and reactive strategies for its alliances, in an attempt to create the world's first truly global airline. BA has not succeeded in its quest.

## Minicase 12.3 British Airways  (GB)

John King (later Lord King) was recruited from outside the industry to become Chairman of the then nationalized British Airways (BA) in 1981. Supported by Chief Executive, Sir Colin Marshall, he turned the ailing company around and, in 1987, BA was successfully privatized. By the early 1990s, BA was ranked seventh in the world in terms of revenue, but fifth in terms of passenger miles flown (behind the four leading American carriers with their huge domestic networks). Only Swire Pacific (of Hong Kong) and Singapore Airlines were more profitable. In fact, many of the world's largest airlines were being run at a loss, many of them subsidized by their governments.

By 2000, Lord King had retired. He had been succeeded by Marshall, who had in turn been replaced by Robert Ayling. Marshall is still chairman in 2004. Growth and prosperity had fluctuated in the intervening years. BA had been affected by the expansion of Virgin Atlantic and had 'lost the war of words' between these two rivals, fuelled originally by the tension in the relationship between Branson and King. Capacity globally had expanded to exceed demand, but airlines were still being propped up – as a result prices had fallen, in some cases to uneconomic levels. BA had changed many of its tailplanes, using designs from around the world to replace the Union Jack symbol. Popular outside the UK, unpopular at home, criticized by Margaret Thatcher, this was always controversial. An acrimonious strike by cabin crew, handled clumsily by BA, left Ayling's reputation tarnished. After BA's profits and profitability fell dramatically, Ayling resigned. His replacement, Rod Eddington, came from Qantas. The general consensus, nevertheless, was that BA's corporate and competitive strategies remained strong.

Whatever the general consenses, there were two key problems. First, BA's costs remained high. When demand dropped after 9/11, and prices fell across the world, BA struggled to make a decent margin. Second, regulation in the UK and US has prevented BA from developing the global alliances it sought and probably needed.

### The corporate strategy

Lord King always wanted BA to become the 'world's first truly global airline'. Progress has been made towards this vision, but it has not been achieved. Maybe it is not even achievable. In line with this, BA adopted the advertising slogan: 'The world's favourite airline' which has on occasions come back to haunt its managers.

King and Marshall realized that BA needed to establish a strong presence in Europe, North America and Asia/Pacific if it was to be a global carrier. It endeavoured to achieve this with a series of acquisitions, alliances and franchise arrangements.

BA purchased 25 per cent of US Air, then America's fifth largest airline, which has hub bases in four eastern American cities: Pittsburgh, Philadelphia, Baltimore and Charlotte. BA crew then flew the existing scheduled US Air services between London Gatwick and these American cities; joint ticketing arrangements allowed BA's passengers to enjoy easier onward travel, albeit not across the whole of the US. The benefits, therefore, were clear but limited. In 1996 BA began to talk with American Airlines, number two in the market, with a view to a much stronger and more beneficial arrangement.

Combined, these two would have enjoyed enormous power, and consequently the American and European competition authorities were interested. America wanted a more open-skies arrangement allowing more US airlines access to Heathrow as well as Gatwick; the European Competition Commissioner was insisting that BA give up slots at Heathrow. London Heathrow is the busiest international airport in the world, and the fourth busiest overall. It is the preferred port of entry to the UK and is also a gateway to and from the rest of Europe. BA has control over some 36 per cent of the flight slots in and out of Heathrow – a hugely valuable asset, but one which has proved a drawback with certain negotiations. This discussion partly involved a debate over whether they could be sold or had to be given away. In the

▶

event the alliance that BA and American envisaged has never happened, but seven years later (in 2003) they were allowed to sell seats on each other's flights.

Meanwhile, BA sold its shareholding in US Air, which objected to the ongoing discussions with American. In addition, in 1999, BA, American, Canadian Airlines, Cathay Pacific and Qantas formed the Oneworld alliance, and they have since been joined by Iberia (Spain) and Finnair. Arguably this alliance (like the rival Star Alliance) provides seamless global travel for passengers through interchangeable ticketing, shared air mile programmes and the use of each other's lounges. Passengers can reach a wide variety of destinations with what amounts to a single ticket.

In 1992, BA bought a 25 per cent stake in the Australian national airline, Qantas, from the Australian government. In the same year it acquired 49.9 per cent of the French regional carrier, TAT. BA bought the remaining shares in 1997 and linked TAT with Air Liberté, which it had acquired in 1996. In 2000 the subsidiary was sold to SAir Group in Switzerland. Again in 1992 BA purchased a German airline, Delta, which it rebranded Deutsche BA. This has also been sold – to a German company, although at one stage EasyJet was the preferred buyer. A minority stake in Iberia followed in 1998 – and this grew into a formal joint venture to consolidate their operations in 2003. In 2004 a year-old alliance with Swiss International Airlines collapsed – SIA had pulled out as they were unwilling to join the larger Oneworld alliance of which BA is a leading player. One positive outcome for BA was that they had been able to buy eight pairs of take-off and landing slots at Heathrow.

Once Rod Eddington became the new Chief Executive (in 2000), he struck quickly. A merger with KLM (of the Netherlands) had been discussed and abandoned in 1992, but the idea was resurrected in a different market situation. Together they would be the third largest airline worldwide when measured by passenger miles. Clearly, there is some route overlap, and it was anticipated that the European Commission would, at the very least, require BA to divest Go and KLM its similar

no-frills subsidiary, Buzz. Again the merger plans were abandoned largely because of reservations from the European Competition Commission – and yet Air France and KLM have since been allowed to merge.

By this time BA also owned a minority stake in Eurostar and it had divested both its in-flight catering business and its ground fleet services. These are now both bought in from the specialist alliance partners to whom it sold the businesses.

BA also opted to give up operating a number of short-haul domestic UK and European routes – in part to reduce overheads but also to allow concentration on major European cities and the long-haul routes to the rest of the world – and entered into franchising arrangements with other airlines who would fly the routes but retain BA flight numbers and use BA's livery on their aeroplanes. These arrangements included British Mediterranean Airways (who fly some London to Middle East routes), British Regional Airways (Scottish routes), Brymon (Channel Islands) and Comair (internal routes in South Africa). BA has since bought Brymon and British Regional Airways (2001) but they remain relatively independent subsidiaries. It also owns CityFlyer Express, which flies to Europe from Gatwick and which Virgin was interested in acquiring.

In the late 1990s BA established Go as an independent, low-price, low-cost, no-frills airline which would fly within the UK and between the UK and Europe from Stansted, in competition with Ryanair and easyJet. After two years of trading losses, Go started breaking even. Go soon carried some two million passengers a year between its 20 destination airports. This move arose hostility, especially from easyJet, which believed Go would be unfairly subsidized by BA. In the end BA decided to sell Go, and it was acquired by venture capitalists, 3i, who encouraged the existing management to stay on and to become shareholders. Barbara Cassani, an ex-BA employee, was CEO. Within a couple of years 3i agreed to sell Go to easyJet for a handsome profit. Cassani left the company.

All in all, these strategic moves provide BA's international passengers with access to a very wide spectrum of routes and destinations.

## The competitive strategy

As well as opting to focus on major world cities, and cover the rest with a variety of different arrangements, BA wanted to increase its flight revenues on its major long-haul routes in particular. Overall capacity was cut. Some routes were abandoned; others had a reduced frequency. In 2002 the in-flight service package was cut on a number of short-haul routes to cut costs and improve BA's competitiveness against the no-frills carriers.

In 1999 a decision was made to increase the number and quality of first- and business-class seats on each aeroplane, in particular business class: BA's Club Class has been given flat bed seats. The intention was to reduce by 15 per cent the number of heavily discounted economy tickets being sold. This was combined with a stated intent gradually to change the fleet and replace some larger Boeing 747s with smaller aircraft such as the new Boeing 777. In addition, a new class and cabin, World Traveller Plus (for full-fare economy passengers) would provide a higher level of economy service in a segregated and quieter area on the plane.

BA has also found an Internet booking partner in its quest to sell more tickets over the Internet and thereby reduce costs.

Changing relatively expensive work practices, that were once the heart of its high service offering, has proved troublesome for BA in recent years. Go staff, for example, were on lower pay rates that mainstream BA staff when that airline was set up. Ground staff walkouts have brought bad publicity as flights have been cancelled and passengers left temporariliy stranded.

### Questions

1. Why do you think BA's alliance strategies have changed as much as they have?
2. Given national resistances, and the desire of many countries to have their own international airline, has BA developed as far as any airline might in the quest to become global?

**British Airways** http://www.britishairways.com

**British Airways** increased the number of first and business class seats, reducing the number of discounted economy seats available

There is evidence of some disagreement amongst strategy authors concerning the meaning of the terms 'joint venture' and 'strategic alliance'. Here, *strategic alliance* is used to encapsulate all forms of agreement between partners, and *joint venture* for those agreements which involve either the establishment of a new, independent company owned jointly by the partners, or the minority ownership of the other party by one or both partners.

The term 'consortium' is also used in this context. One instance would be where companies in an industry generally collaborate or share, maybe through a trade association. The Japanese *keiretsu* (or family of businesses) is another, but quite different, example. Here companies, often in a geographical cluster, own stakes in each other and share and collaborate wherever possible. This might take the form of intertrading; it might equally be by seconding staff to help with a particular problem or difficulty.

An alliance (or joint venture) could involve:

1. direct competitors, maybe sharing common skills, and with the objective of increased market share

2. less direct competitors with complementary skills – where the intention is more likely to be benchmarking and learning for mutual benefit, and the possible development of new ideas

3. related companies sharing different skills and competencies. Here organizations might well be linked in the same added-value chain (e.g. a manufacturer and either a supplier or a distributor). Such an alliance should generate synergy through co-operation, innovation and lower costs while allowing each partner to concentrate on its core competencies.

The intention will invariably be to increase competitive advantage without either merger or acquisition. As we move from an alliance to a joint venture and from 1 to 3 in the above hierarchy, the significance increases for the partners involved. Some companies will be involved in several alliances with different companies at the same time – this is not a one-off strategy for them. As an example, Toshiba (Japanese manufacturer of heavy electrical apparatus, electronic devices, information systems and consumer products such as televisions, videos, kitchen appliances and white goods) has created a global network of allies for different products and technologies, including Alstom, Siemens, Ericsson, General Electric, Motorola, Time Warner and Apple. Toshiba sees this 'circle of friends' as an opportunity for sharing ideas to obtain the latest technology and to gain competitive advantage through learning.

Minicase 5.2 showed how Benetton has built strong partnership sourcing agreements and a network of retail franchisees who together yield economies, speed and competitive advantage. Here, the ability to manage a network of partners is a core strategic capability and source of competitive advantage. Minicase 12.4 describes how Yorkshire Water adopted an onion strategy to allow it to concentrate more on its core service competencies; as a result it had to form a network of partnerships.

**CASE**

## Minicase 12.4 Yorkshire Water's Onion Strategy ⓖⓑ

Since being privatized in 1989 most of the ten water companies in the UK have pursued diversification strategies. The core business activities are water supply and the management of waste water (i.e. sewage treatment). Prices and quality standards are closely regulated, and consequently the diversification is aimed at offsetting the perceived risks and constraints inherent in regulated businesses. The most popular activity has been waste management, the collection and disposal of industrial and domestic waste. For example, Severn Trent Water acquired Biffa, and Wessex formed a joint venture with Waste Management of the US, one of the world's largest companies in the industry. South Staffordshire diversified into Homeserve, which organises plumbing services for clients who

take out insurance policies with them. Yorkshire Water developed a similar business but sold it to South Staffs. Homeserve has been split off from its original parent and is thriving.

Yorkshire Water (YW) basically created two separate, but linked, businesses: Yorkshire Water Services to control the core businesses, and Yorkshire Water Enterprises, later renamed Yorkshire Environmental Solutions, for other commercial ventures.

### Yorkshire Water Enterprises

This business became active in the following areas:

- *Waste management* – Industrial effluents and clinical waste. This was sold in 1998 to Waste

Recycling, but Yorkshire Water retained a 46 per cent shareholding in the enlarged Waste Recycling business – until recently, when it was sold off completely.

■ *Engineering consultancy and support* – A joint venture with Babcock International. Since 1989 YW have been investing in treatment plants (mainly) and water-distribution networks, the latter to free up engineering resources which the joint venture would seek to deploy and exploit.

■ *'Pipeline Products'* – The sale of existing stores items to external customers.

■ *'Waterlink'* – A network of approved subcontractor plumbers. YW provided an arrangement service before selling the business to South Staffordshire Water.

■ *Laboratory services* – Providing analytical services and environmental testing to a range of businesses and agencies – before being sold.

■ *Loop* – A separate subsidiary to provide customer service management, billing, payment and debt collection. Services are sold to external customers.

■ *Management training* – Primarily exploiting existing markets and competencies.

■ Key Land Developments – Property development and representing 'real' diversification.

The Director General of OFWAT, the industry regulator, emphasized that he was not going to ignore these strategic developments. 'Customers of core services must not be affected adversely.' For example, the water companies were prevented from selling services from the associated businesses to the core at contrived prices which benefited shareholders at the expense of captive water customers. In addition, 'the required investment funds for the water supply services must not be put at risk'.

**Yorkshire Water Services**

YW stated quite early that it did not intend to build and then manage a diversified corporation.

Once the appropriate business had been constructed, with YW's resources deployed effectively, the layers would be peeled away systematically – an onion focus strategy – until only the core business remained. The defined core activity was *water delivery*, which incorporated the removal of sewage and water treatment. The pursuit of this strategy entailed divesting certain non-core or support activities into either wholly owned subsidiaries or independent contractors (in properly negotiated alliances), and possibly more joint ventures, but only where there were providers able to deliver the range and quality of services.

Four alternative implementation approaches for this strategy are illustrated in Figure 12.5.

The services divested by YW are also highlighted. Where there were agreements with multiple outside contractors (Approaches 2 and 3), separate geographical regions were typically the predominant logic. For example, the pipework to sewage treatment works was divested to individual local authorities.

This corporate onion strategy aims to improve a company's competitiveness with the premise that non-core services can invariably be acquired more effectively from an experienced outside provider, selected because it already has competitive advantage. It is essential to define the core carefully and to establish the appropriate ongoing relationships in order to minimize risk. The order and timing of each divestment is also an important issue. The company benefits because it can concentrate on its core activities; it has access to a wider skill and resource base, which should promote best practice, enable greater service flexibility and lead to overall quality improvements. Resources should match needs more effectively. In addition, clearer accountability should foster cost reductions, and the introduction of controlled competition should enhance the quality of in-house service provision and act as a catalyst for change throughout the organization. To implement the strategy successfully the central organization must develop competency in network management. Effective partnership sourcing such as this requires unambiguous long-term agreements, clear performance measures and shared risk. It is most appropriate

**Figure 12.5** Four alternative onion-focus strategies applied in Yorkshire Water Services

**Strategy 1**

Examples: Stores
Fleet service

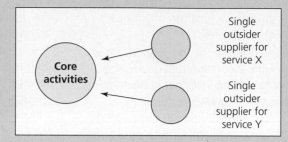

**Strategy 2**

Examples: Pipe manufacture
Electrical spares

*Key success factor:*
Partnership sourcing, establishing
firm alliances with each supplier

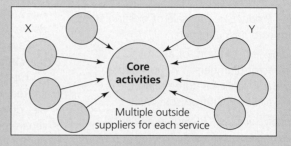

**Strategy 3**

Examples: Sewerage management
(pipework to the sewage
treatment works)

*Objective:* Develop the in-house
capability into a centre of excellence

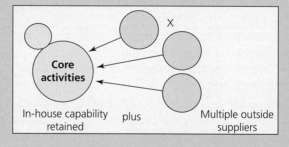

**Strategy 4**

Examples: Electrical and
mechanical maintenance

*Objective:* Form an alliance with an
outside expert and benchmark to
drive internal improvement

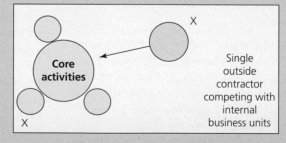

where the service is a core activity for the contracted supplier. The partners should engage in ongoing dialogue and maybe even exchange personnel periodically.

However, in the mid-1990s a summer drought caused Yorkshire Water considerable embarrassment. Public relations were clumsy; the managing director suggested people could easily wash with just a basin of water as opposed to having a bath, for example. The company ended up hiring road transporters to move water from north-east England to its own reservoirs, but supplies were never cut off. In the end the chairman and managing director both retired and, with a new strategic leader, the parent company was renamed Kelda.

Approach 3 in Figure 12.5, sewage management, has subsequently been taken back from local authority control, and the company bought Aquarion, an American water company, in 2000. Since then this New England business has been active acquiring related businesses in other New England states. But price regulation continued to bite, and profits and the shareholder value of Kelda were hit for a time.

In 2000 Kelda announced a radical proposal. It indicated an intent to sell all of its physical assets (pipes, sewage works and reservoirs) to a new mutual company, which would be owned by Kelda's customers and financed with debt capital. Kelda would simply lease back the assets and employ contractors. Other activities would also be sold to leave a water *services* company. Aquarion and the 46 per cent of Waste Recycling would not be sold. Environmental groups, customers and the water regulator all opposed the plan, which was subsequently abandoned.

**Question**

1. Can alliance-based networks such as the one developed (and proposed) by Yorkshire Water deliver the equivalent or even greater value to customers than a company which owns and manages all of its activities?

**Yorkshire Water** http://www.yorkshirewater.com

### 12.4.1 Reasons for joint ventures and strategic alliances

- The cost of acquisition may be too high.
- Legislation may prevent acquisition, but the larger size is required for critical mass.
- Political or cultural differences could mean that an alliance is more likely to facilitate integration than would a merger or acquisition.
- The increasing significance of a total customer service package suggests linkages through the added value chain – to secure supplies, customize distribution and control costs. At the same time individual organizations may prefer to specialize in those areas where they are most competent. An alliance provides a solution to this dilemma.
- The threat from Japanese competition has driven many competitors into closer collaboration, but they may not wish to merge. For example, American and European car manufacturers have taken stakes in Japanese businesses, where outright acquisition is unlikely.
- Covert protectionism in certain markets necessitates a joint venture with a local company. This has been particularly true in China, one of the world's fastest growing economies.

Developing these points, Minicase 12.5 contrasts the acquisition approach of Ford with the alliance strategy of General Motors as they have both become increasingly global in their endeavours to remain the world's largest car manufacturers.

### 12.4.2 The likely outcomes

- In simple terms, increased competency, synergy and a stronger global presence are the potential outcomes targeted most frequently by alliance and joint venture partners.
- Greater innovation could well accrue from the pooling and sharing of ideas and competencies, which in turn enables greater focus (by each partner) combined with resource leverage.

## Minicase 12.5  General Motors and Ford     US  Int

The American General Motors (GM) is the world's largest car manufacturer; Ford is second. Toyota is smaller but the most profitable. The third-largest US car manufacturer is Chrysler, which we dicussed in Minicase 12.1. In the early 2000s GM has enjoyed higher operating margins than its leading rival, but this has not always been the case. Over the last 30 years GM's performance has been steadier and more predictable than Ford's. In some years Ford has exceeded GM's operating profits; in other years it has lagged markedly. Both GM and Ford have their corporate headquarters in Detroit, Michigan. In fact they are less than ten miles apart. But these two companies have followed quite different strategies in their quest for globalization.

### General Motors

GM has formed a loose network of international partners. 'We can realize synergies faster than in a full buy-out situation – we get most of the gain and less of the pain.'

GM's joint ventures have included the following:

- GM bought 20 per cent of Fiat Auto (Italy) with an option to buy the remaining 80 per cent should it so wish – a reflection of Europe's overcapacity. As part of the deal, GM helps Fiat to market its Alfa Romeo brand in America, but the expensive Ferrari and Maserati brands are excluded from the alliance.

- GM also owns 20 per cent of Fuji Heavy Industries, which includes Subaru cars and major components businesses.

- GM has 10 per cent of Suzuki and 49 per cent of Isuzu (trucks as well as cars). Suzuki sells GM products in Japan.

In all of these cases, GM gains access to technology and platforms that would be hugely expensive to develop in-house.

- GM has relatively recently bought the remaining 50 per cent of Saab to give it total

control – it had held the first 50 per cent for over ten years. Subaru has helped Saab to develop its newest models.

- In 2002 GM acquired 67 per cent of Daewoo (South Korea). Ford had been the preferred bidder for Daewoo at one stage, but had withdrawn.

GM's philosophy is one of accord and it is generally opposed to hostile takeovers, but GM is on a learning curve for yielding the potentially elusive synergistic benefits of these alliances.

### Ford

Ford, meanwhile, after many years of fundamentally organic growth, made a series of acquisitions in the late 1990s: Jaguar, Land Rover, Aston Martin and Volvo. Ford also bought Kwik-Fit, the tyre and exhaust replacement specialist, but later sold it at a substantial loss – a diversification that did not pay off.

Ford's strategy has been to buy and own *strong brands*, which it could position and market as it liked to complement the complete Ford portfolio. Chief Executive in the 1990s, Jacques Nasser, claimed that GM would also have bought brands like these if it had been able. Ford dismissed Nasser and replaced him with Bill Ford Jr, a direct descendant of founder Henry Ford.

There are though, a number of parallel alliances. Ford is allied with Peugeot-Citroën for diesel engine development, and with Yahoo!, Oracle and Microsoft for Internet services of various forms. It also has joint ventures in China, India and Turkey.

An earlier alliance with Volkswagen to build people carriers on a common platform failed to deliver the anticipated results and was abandoned. In addition, Ford took a 33 per cent shareholding in Mazda (in 1996) and accepted a major role in the control and running of the Japanese company. Importing American techniques into Japan is difficult, and Mazda's fortunes have fluctuated. Ford's dilemma concerns whether the Mazda brand should stand apart or be integrated into the rest of the Ford portfolio.

Ford is now perceived to have fallen behind GM is rationalizing its ranges and platforms and in new product development. Recently its (acquired) luxury brands have been subsidizing the mainstay Ford product ranges. It is perhaps ironical that integrating the acquisitions has not been easy (and has perhaps diverted attention away from issues with Ford cars and trucks) but the acquired up-market brands are the most profitable parts of the group. A major and high profile recall of Ford Explorers – SUVs – because of problems with its standard Firestone tyres has been embarrassing and again diverting.

**General Motors** http://www.gm.com
**Ford Motor Company** http://www.ford.com

## Questions

1. Whose approach do you believe is the better one? Why?

- The partnership and sharing could also result in lower costs. A virtual circle of learning, where each partner learns new skills and competencies from the other, contributes to this.
- Finally, the linkage could provide access to new markets and technologies.
- Simply, an alliance is a means to an end. It is not necessarily going to be seen as a permanent arrangement, and it most probably can be changed as time goes on.

Developing these outline points, Connell (1988) contends that companies collaborate strategically for primarily three reasons:

1. To gain access to new markets and technologies as markets become increasingly international.

   In 1989 Pilkington, the UK float glass manufacturer and world market leader, sold 20 per cent of its US vehicle glass subsidiary to Nippon Sheet Glass of Japan. Pilkington had 17 per cent of the world market for vehicle glass, Asahi of Japan 19 per cent. Nippon already had 9 per cent and manufactured float glass under licence from Pilkington. Nippon gained access to the US market; Pilkington was looking to build a customer base in Japan, arguing that as car manufacture becomes increasingly global they needed a presence in all major markets. Pilkington already supplied the Toyota plant in the US.

2. To share the costs and risks of increasingly expensive research and development.

   Nippon Steel (a related business) has another strategic alliance – designed to cut production costs – with Posco (South Korea's Pohang Iron and Steel). Nippon and Posco are the world's largest steelmakers (a joint market share of just 7 per cent, nevertheless) and wish to retain their positions of leadership. When the South Korean government privatizes Posco, which is imminent, Nippon is expected to buy a stake. Research and development resources are pooled but so far there is no collaboration on either production or marketing. Suppliers are concerned that the partners might use their alliance to drive down prices.

3. To manage innovation more effectively.

   This is important because of high R&D costs and greater globalization, which together often ensure that any competitive advantage gained from technology is relatively short-lived. Both the opportunities and threats require that companies are able to be flexible and change quickly.

In 1995 Motorola joined with IBM, Siemens and Toshiba (an existing alliance) to develop the next generation of advanced memory chips, which are highly complex and extremely costly to develop and make. There is arguably a fourth reason – an attempt to regain lost competitiveness in a marketplace. This is thought to be the cause of a series of agreements among European electronics manufacturers, and links between them and Japanese and US competitors.

While there are a number of reasons and justifications for such strategic alliances, they can again be difficult strategies to implement effectively, as shown later in the chapter.

## 12.5  Forms and examples of strategic alliances and joint ventures

Strategic alliances and joint ventures can take a number of forms. The six categories which follow should not be seen as mutually exclusive; some joint ventures will cover more than one.

### 12.5.1  Component parts of two or more businesses might be merged

GEC Alstom was a 50:50 joint venture company formed in 1988 when the power systems divisions of GEC (the UK General Electric Corporation) were merged with the Alstom subsidiary of France's CGE. The company, the largest manufacturer of generating equipment in the EU, was created to allow GEC and CGE to compete more effectively with ABB (Asea Brown Boveri), the Swedish/Swiss multinational and the world's biggest electrical engineering group. The companies competed directly in a number of sectors, such as railway equipment and rolling stock. More recently an alliance between GEC Alstom and Siemens was mooted, to develop the high-speed trains of the future. The intention here would have been to reduce risk in an industry bedevilled by political issues. Governments around the world are inevitably involved and projects are frequently delayed or even cancelled for both political and financial reasons. In the event, GEC Alstom was floated off as an independent business when George Simpson replaced Lord Weinstock as Chief Executive of GEC – explored in Minicase 14.3.

### 12.5.2  Companies might agree to join forces to develop a new project

Club Méditerranée and Carnival Cruise Lines (US) joined forces to provide cruise-based holiday packages for Europe and Asia.

Philips and Nintendo have jointly developed a new generation of video games on compact discs compatible with Philips' CD-i (compact disc-interactive) players which link up to high-definition televisions.

Airbus Industrie was formed because no partner alone could afford the development costs of large passenger aircraft, and because of pressure from European governments who wanted to reduce the predominance of the large US companies.

Psion, UK manufacturer of palm-size computers and electronic organizers, has joined forces with the world's largest mobile telecommunications companies, Nokia, Motorola and Ericsson, to develop Internet-linked mobile phones and other products which use WAP (wireless application protocol) technology. This alliance was seen as a means of counteracting the power of Microsoft in one of the fastest growing areas of the computing industry.

Sony has been an innovative company throughout its 50-plus years of existence. Using its competencies in miniaturization it has developed a vast range of home electronics products, including the Walkman (in its many variants) and the PlayStation games consoles, sales of which now exceed 75 million units worldwide. Sony has recently joined forces with Intel (manufacturers of sophisticated memory chips) to develop applications that can again be linked to the Internet. One example is the Memory Stick, which stores images, music and computer files and then allows them to be used in various electronic devices. Sony is also partnered with DoCoMo, another Japanese company which has 17 million subscribers and specializes in delivering computer games and other services directly over the Internet.

### 12.5.3 Companies might agree to develop a new business jointly

Sony and Apple (computers) of the US earlier formed a new multimedia company as a joint venture. The aim here was to produce a 'palm-size, wire-less personal communication device with digital audio and visual functions'.

Sony Ericsson is a 50:50 joint venture for developing upmarket mobile phones. There have been problems integrating teams from two distinct backgrounds and cultures, but the business is beginning to develop products that can compete effectively in this very competitive industry. Some phones are being assembled in China, which has, of course, introduced new issues to deal with.

Cereal Partners World-wide is a joint venture designed to strengthen market access for the two companies involved. General Mills, an American rival to Kellogg, had developed a number of popular products (particularly Cheerios), but was not geared up to distribute them outside America. Nestlé owned a formidable distribution network and could provide access to most of Europe. Nestlé had earlier tried to break into this industry without any marked success.

### 12.5.4 There might be specific agreements between manufacturers and their suppliers

Some years ago a new chief executive was appointed at the American electronics company NCR. As well as making sure that he formed a personal relationship with all of the company's major business customers (a very typical approach) he set up a programme of visits to every major supplier, which is more unusual. As a result, relationships have been strengthened for mutual benefit. Typical outcomes have been extended contracts but a reduction in the number of suppliers. Learning about each other's needs has delivered both service differentiation and lower costs.

American Express (AMEX), like many other large corporations, had a travel department which organized the global travel arrangements for its managers. They developed a competency which they now provide as a service to other corporations who prefer to outsource this task when they can find someone with the appropriate expertise. AMEX developed this competency further and moved into consumer travel as well.

### 12.5.5  A company might make a strategic investment in another firm

Several years ago Guinness and LVMH exchanged shareholdings and formed a whole series of distribution joint ventures around the world. There were efficiency savings and marketing advantages from combining, in particular, the spirits brands of the two companies. LVMH owns the world's leading cognac brand, Hennessy, as well as its leading champagnes; Guinness, through its United Distillers subsidiary, owned a portfolio which includes Johnnie Walker, the world's best-selling Scotch whisky, and Gordon's gin, another international best-seller. However, Guinness merged with Grand Metropolitan (see Diageo – Minicase 11.1) and this put enormous stress on the joint venture. In fact, LVMH was able to dictate certain terms of the merger agreement.

British Telecom (BT) sees minority stakes and joint ventures as its path to a global presence. It has used this strategy to become the second largest competitor in several European countries, namely Sweden, France, Germany, the Netherlands, Spain, Portugal and Italy. BT, which has the most extensive portfolio of assets in the European telecommunications industry, claims that acquisitions were 'never on the cards' but does not rule out increasing its stake in the partner organizations.

### 12.5.6  Companies might form international trading partnerships

Fujitsu of Japan has owned 80 per cent of ICL, the UK computer manufacturer, for many years, but runs it as an independent subsidiary. However, they are allied in the form of joint retailing and servicing in North America and Australia.

Disney Corporation, McDonald's and Coca-Cola, owners of three of the most important brands in the world, have a loose partnership which varies from country to country, depending upon how local managers wish to exploit its potential. There are several aspects to the partnership:

- McDonald's is Coca-Cola's largest customer and buys its soft drinks exclusively from Coca-Cola
- McDonald's sponsors activities and exhibits at Disney attractions as well as running restaurants on site
- Disney collaborates with McDonald's on special worldwide promotions which feature Disney characters, especially when new movies are released
- Coca-Cola is also the sole supplier of soft drinks to Disney's theme parks.

## 12.6  Key Issues in joint ventures and strategic alliances

This concluding section summarizes the views of a number of key authors who have examined the relative success of alliances and joint ventures.

Kanter (1990) offers the following criteria as key determinants of their success:

- The alliance or joint venture must be important strategically for both partners.
- Ideally they should bring complementary, rather than exactly the same, competencies to the arrangement.
- Information must be shared openly.

- There should be genuine integration to create linkages, even though this may be across divergent cultures. Trust becomes essential.

- The arrangements should become institutionalized into some framework which can demonstrate a clear identity and a position of importance.

Kanter reinforces the point that alliance management needs to become a key strategic capability.

Ohmae (1989) argues that the following issues are significant and help to determine whether the agreement is likely to prove effective:

- Successful collaboration requires commitment on both sides. Without sufficient management time, trust and respect the agreement is likely to fail. In reality, all the required resources must be committed. Either for managing linkages, or for managing a new joint venture company, capable managers must be transferred or seconded. The outcome of the alliance will depend upon both the commitment of the partners and the emergent power and influence they exert.

- There must be mutual benefits, the attainment of which may well involve sacrifices on both sides. Both partners should appreciate clearly what the other party wants from the agreement, and their objectives. If the commitment of each ally is uneven, the keener partner or the faster learner is likely to assume control. This might mean that the interests of the weaker partner are either bought out or simply taken over.

- If circumstances change during the period of the alliance, flexibility may be required as the objectives and priorities of either or both partners may change.

- Cultural differences, which might be either geographic or corporate in origin, will have to be reconciled.

In addition, it is sensible if alliance partners see their joint involvement as an opportunity to learn new skills and good practices. Partners are not simply there to plug gaps or weaknesses. Analysts acknowledge that the Japanese have been very good at learning from their alliances, and that Western companies have been slower to exploit the learning opportunities.

Badaracco (1991) differentiates between:

- migratory knowledge – easily transferred technical skills, and

- embedded knowledge about how a company does business, which is particularly useful for deepening insight into new markets.

Where companies do enter an alliance through weakness rather than strength, it is vital that they use the partnership for learning and development. In 1991 Ford formed an alliance with Yamaha to develop a new engine for its Fiesta and Escort ranges. While such high-performance engines as the Ford Cosworth are the outcome of past joint ventures, this was the first incidence of an alliance for mainstream car engines. Analysts have commented that Ford needed an agreement because they had become weak in a rapidly changing industry, stimulated by new materials, higher fuel consumption expectations and tighter emission standards. 'Ford must learn from the deal, and not subcontract their engine technology for the long term.' Ford prefers acquisition to alliances (see Minicase 12.5 earlier).

Acquisitions should be evaluated in terms of their ability to generate synergy. Joint ventures and strategic alliances should be regarded in the same light. Devlin and Bleackley (1988) argue that the key issues are the strategic wisdom behind the decision to form an alliance in the first place, the choice of partner, and the management of the alliance once it has been agreed. The position of both parties to the agreement should be improved from the alliance. If there is a real opportunity for synergy, joint benefits and mutual trust and commitment by both parties, joint ventures can be an effective means of implementing strategic change. However, although some of the inherent difficulties of acquisition are avoided by this type of agreement, there will still be implementation issues. Unless these are tackled properly, the joint venture is likely to prove expensive and tie up resources which might otherwise be deployed more effectively.

Alliances can fail and/or be dismantled for a number of reasons; consequently the extent to which any organization is dependent upon its alliances should be carefully monitored.

## 12.7 Franchising and licensing

Finally in this chapter we look at two other means of growing the organization which avoid the risks and pitfalls of acquisitions and joint ventures, but which still require relationship building and trust.

### 12.7.1 Franchising

Franchising again takes many forms, and it provides an opportunity for rapid growth for established businesses and a relatively low risk means of starting a small business. Service businesses are more common than manufacturing in franchising, and as the UK continues to switch from a manufacturing to a service economy they may well become even more important. Tie Rack is one example of a retail organization which has concentrated on specific market segments and grown rapidly with franchising. Thornton's chocolate shops, Fastframe picture framing, Prontaprint printing and copying shops, Body Shop and the British School of Motoring are other examples. Although McDonald's is franchised throughout the US, many restaurants in Britain are owned by the company. Subway, Kentucky Fried Chicken, Burger King and Spud-U-Like, however, are franchised.

A company which chooses franchising as a means of strategic growth enters into contractual arrangements with a number of small businesses, usually one in each selected geographical area. In return for a lump sum initial investment and ongoing royalties the typical franchiser provides exclusive rights to supply a product or service under the franchiser's name in a designated area, know-how, equipment, materials, training, advice and national support advertising. This allows the business in question to grow rapidly in a number of locations without the investment capital which would be required to fund organic growth of the same magnitude. Another advantage for the franchiser is the alleviation of some of the need for the development of the managers, skills and capabilities required to control a large, growing and dispersed organization. Instead efforts can be concentrated on expanding market share. It is essential, though, to establish effective monitoring and control systems to ensure that franchisees are providing the necessary level of quality and service.

The small business franchisee needs sufficient capital to buy into the franchise, but the risk is less than most independent starts because the business is already established. As a result a number of small independent businesses operate as part of a chain and can compete against larger organizations.

## 12.7.2 Licensing

Licensing is an arrangement whereby a company is allowed to manufacture a product or service which has been designed by someone else and is protected by a patent. Companies in different countries are often involved. Pilkington, for example, patented float glass and then licensed its production throughout the world. Pilkington earned money from the arrangements and established world leadership; they would not have been able to afford to establish production plants around the world. In contrast Mary Quant, designer of cosmetics, tights, footwear, beds and bed linen, never manufactured the products she designed. They were all licensed; and some were marketed under the Quant name and some under the manufacturer's name (Myers beds and Dorma bed linen, for example). Licensing also provides an ideal opportunity for the owners of valuable **intellectual capital** (such as Disney with their characters) to earn revenues from their knowledge-based resource without having to invest in manufacturing. One argument in favour of this arrangement has been that production and labour relations problems are avoided, enabling the business to concentrate on the areas in which it has expertise and competitive advantage.

# SUMMARY

Periodically, organizations must make decisions about how focused and how diversified they wish to be. Horizontal integration, such as acquiring or merging with a competitor, will engender critical mass but may be restrained by the relevant competition authorities. Diversification can be into related or unrelated businesses, or vertically forwards or backwards in the supply chain.

Where a company does choose to diversify it is more likely to implement this strategy through acquisition (friendly purchase), merger (bringing together the assets of two businesses) or takeover (hostile purchase) than it is through organic growth.

Unrelated diversification is invariably high risk, but it may be justified or chosen for one of the following reasons:

- weakness of the present businesses
- existing businesses having strengths and competencies that could be exploited in other industries
- the ambitions of the strategic leader.

Research in both the UK and US consistently indicates that diversification through acquisition has only a 50 per cent likelihood of success, specifically delivering the hoped-for benefits. The typical reasons for failure are:

- the synergy potential is overestimated
- managerial problems and issues are underestimated
- key managers leave after the acquisition
- hidden weaknesses are not spotted until it is too late
- too much money is paid and the premium cannot be recovered.

The companies that succeed with this strategy tend to follow a number of simple rules:

- they carefully target their acquisitions
- they learn from previous experiences and become 'professional acquirers'
- they avoid paying too high a premium
- they adopt an appropriate post-acquisition structure and style and ensure that the businesses are integrated effectively
- corporately, they add value.

Strategic alliances and joint ventures (a stronger type of alliance where shares are exchanged or an independent company is set up) provide an alternative to an acquisition or merger. While they are designed to deliver synergy, cost savings and access to either technology or markets, they are not without their own implementation challenges.

It is generally acknowledged that the Japanese in particular have developed real capabilities in alliance management and that many Western companies have looked upon them from a more defensive perspective. For example, they are an alternative when an acquisition is not feasible for whatever reason.

There are three main reasons behind this strategy:

- to gain access to new markets and technologies
- to share expensive research and development costs
- to manage innovation more effectively.

Clearly these reasons overlap.

There are six particular, and again overlapping, forms of alliance and joint venture:

1. the merging of component parts of two or more businesses
2. companies joining forces to develop a new project
3. companies joining forces to develop a new business together
4. agreements between partners in the same supply chain
5. where companies purchase a stake in another business for strategic, rather than purely financial, reasons
6. international trading partnerships.

▶

For alliances and joint ventures to work successfully, commitment from all parties is required. Everyone must appreciate that they can benefit and commit accordingly. Trust, sharing and collaboration become essential, even though different cultures and languages might be involved.

Franchising and licensing can sometimes provide valuable means of growing. The risks are different but the capital required is considerably less.

## QUESTIONS AND RESEARCH ASSIGNMENTS

1. From the various points and issues discussed in this chapter list the possible advantages and disadvantages of diversification and acquisition strategies, and from your experience list one successful and one unsuccessful example of this strategy. Why have you selected these particular cases?

2. What are the key arguments for and against strategies of unrelated diversification and focus? Again, from your own experience, list examples of each.

3. What exactly is the difference between a strategic alliance and a joint venture? Can you provide examples of each – in addition to those included in the text?

4. Do you agree with the view that, if they are established and managed carefully, strong alliances can provide all the benefits of an acquisition or merger without most of the drawbacks?

## INTERNET AND LIBRARY PROJECTS

1. Obtain statistics on either a selection of large companies which interest you, or the largest 20 companies in the UK, and:

   (a) ascertain the extent to which they are diversified and classify them as either single, dominant, related or conglomerate product companies

   (b) determine their relative size in relation to their competitors in the US, Japan and Europe.

2. In 2003 Cadbury Schweppes became more diversified – albeit relatedly – when it acquired Adams Confectionery, a leading manufacturer of chewing gum. Was this a justifiable move? Why? Why not? Has it turned out to be a successful strategy?

3. Enron and Tyco are two US companies that pursued high growth strategies which ended up with senior executives being prosecuted. Were the failings ones of poor strategic choice or simply individual greed?

4. Take any well-known Japanese manufacturer, such as Toshiba or Sony, and determine how many alliances and joint ventures they have and what they are designed to contribute strategically.

5. Using actual examples as your base point, could the high-technology things we currently take for granted (such as mobile phones, personal computers and the Internet) have been developed to the stage they have if companies had worked in isolation? Has the co-operation approach been more sensible and realistic than a series of cross-border mergers?

## Further reading

Biggadike, R (1979) The risky business of diversification, *Harvard Business Review*, May–June.

Devlin, G and Bleackley, M (1988) Strategic alliances – guidelines for success, *Long Range Planning*, 21 (5).

Clarke, CJ and Brennan, K (1990) Building synergy in the diversified business, *Long Range Planning*, 23 (20).

Kanter, RM (1994) Collaborative advantage: the art of alliances, *Harvard Business Review*, July–August.

Caulkin, S (1996) Focus is for wimps, *Management Today*, December.

Markides, C (1997) To diversify or not to diversify, *Harvard Business Review*, November–December.

# References

Badaracco, JL (1991) *The Knowledge Link: How Firms Compete Through Strategic Alliances*, Harvard Business School Press.

Biggadike, R (1979) The risky business of diversification, *Harvard Business Review*, May–June.

Burgman, R (1985) Research findings quoted in McLean, RJ How to make acquisitions work, *Chief Executive*, April.

Business International (1988) *Making Acquisitions Work: Lessons from Companies' Successes and Mistakes*, Report published by Business International, Geneva.

Chiesa, V and Manzini, R (1997) Competence-based diversification, *Long Range Planning*, 2 June.

Connell, DC (1988) Strategic partnering and competitive advantage, Presented at the 8th Annual Strategic Management Society Conference, Amsterdam, October.

Constable, CJ (1986) Diversification as a factor in UK industrial strategy, *Long Range Planning*, 19 (1).

Cowling, K, Stoneman, P and Cubbin, J (eds) (1979) *Mergers and Economic Performance*, Cambridge University Press.

Devlin, G and Bleackley, M (1988) Strategic alliances – guidelines for success, *Long Range Planning*, 21 (5).

Drucker, PF (1982) Quoted in Drucker: The dangers of spoonfeeding, *Financial Times*, 15 October.

Ernst and Young (1995) Key success factors in acquisition management, Research project with Warwick Business School, Ernst and Young, London.

Garrette, B and Dussauge, P (1999) Strategic alliances – why Europe needs to catch up, *Financial Times Mastering Global Business*, No. 5.

Houlder, V (1997) Neglect of the new addition, *Financial Times*, 5 February.

Jenkinson, T and Mayer, C (1994) *Hostile Take-overs: Defence, Attack and Corporate Governance*, McGraw-Hill.

Kanter, RM (1990) *Synergies, Alliances and New Ventures*, Harvard Business School video package.

Kitching, J (1967) Why do mergers miscarry? *Harvard Business Review*, November–December.

Kitching, J (1973) *Acquisitions in Europe: Causes of Corporate Successes and Failures*, Report published by Business International, Geneva.

Lorenz, C (1986) Take-overs. At best an each way bet, *Financial Times*, 6 January.

Markides, C (1997) To diversify or not to diversify, *Harvard Business Review*, November–December.

McLean, RJ (1985) How to make acquisitions work, *Chief Executive*, April.

Meeks, J (1977) *Disappointing Marriage: A Study of the Gains from Merger*, Cambridge University Press.

Nesbitt, SL and King, RR (1989) Business diversification – has it taken a bad rap? *Mergers and Acquisitions*, November–December.

Ohmae, K (1989) The global logic of strategic alliances, *Harvard Business Review*, March–April.

Peters, TJ and Waterman, RH Jr (1982) *In Search of Excellence: Lessons from America's Best Run Companies*, Harper & Row.

Porter, ME (1987) From competitive advantage to corporate strategy, *Harvard Business Review*, May–June.

Ramsay, J (1987) The strategic focus: deciding your acquisition strategy, Paper presented at 'Growing Through Acquisition', Conference organized by Arthur Young, London, 31 March.

Reed, R and Luffman, G (1986) Diversification: the growing confusion, *Strategic Management Journal*, 7 (1).

Rumelt, RP (1974) *Strategy, Structure and Economic Performance*, Division of Research, Harvard Business School.

Salter, MS and Weinhold, WA (1982) *Merger Trends and Prospects for the 1980s*, Division of Research, Harvard Business School; quoted in Thackray, J (1982) The American take-over war, *Management Today*, September.

van de Vliet, A (1997) When mergers misfire, *Management Today*, June.

Walton, C and McBride, J (1998) Broken engagements, *Financial Times*, 26 February.

# International Strategy

## Learning objectives

Having read to the end of this chapter you should be able to:

- show how the issues covered in Chapters 11 and 12 can be applied at an international level
- explain what is meant by a global strategy
- appreciate why internationalism is essential for many organizations
- discuss the important considerations in international strategies
- explain a simple stage model of international development
- evaluate the value and relevance of different market entry strategies in an international context
- appreciate how franchising has been behind the growth of a number of well-known international brands
- discuss a number of constraints and outline a selection of possible future influences on international growth.

We have discussed in Chapters 11 and 12 the various strategic alternatives that might be available to an organization in thinking and deciding where it wants to go, and for helping to close the planning gap. In this chapter we look at the issues in the international context. Options range from 'simply' exporting to a fully-fledged global strategy and structure. The attractiveness of particular alternatives will be affected by the objectives of the organization. Some companies will be proactive; others reactive. Not all organisations need to, or should, take advantage of every international opportunity which comes their way. The appropriate strategy always matches the environment, values and resources congruently.

## Minicase 13.1 Tesco's International Strategy

Tesco is the UK's leading supermarket chain and its largest private sector employer – and it is diversified into several non-food lines. It has also expanded overseas in a careful and systematic manner. By 2004 some 20 per cent of its revenue was earned outside the UK. This also represented 15 per cent of total pre-tax profits but from 50 per cent of the floor space. In global terms, Tesco is sixth largest. The five larger supermarket groups are Wal-Mart (including ASDA and which earns 21 per cent of its revenues outside America); Carrefour (48 per cent outside France); Ahold (84 per cent outside the Netherlands); Metro (47 per cent outside Germany); and Kroger (entirely US).

Chronologically the Tesco story is as follows:

The first 'foray' overseas was the Republic of Ireland, when Tesco acquired an existing retail chain in 1978 – which it later divested in 1986.

In 1993 the company acquired a French rival, Catteau, but never really consolidated the business and sold that in 1997.

Since then it has been more successful. In 1994 Tesco purchased a majority share in the Hungarian retailer, Global (41 supermarkets), and followed that with acquisitions in Poland (1995), the Czech Republic and Slovakia (1996). Prior to these moves, Tesco had employed a Hungarian to do ground research in Eastern Europe. Tesco is now the largest private employer in this part of the world as well. With the exception of Slovakia, it is the market leader, but it wasn't the first overseas grocer to enter the market. Although it has yet to make a move, it has Romania, Bulgaria and Russia 'in its sights'.

Tesco returned to Ireland (both Northern Ireland and the Republic) when it bought the retail interests of Associated British Foods in 1997.

The next ventures were largely in the Far East. An acquisition in Thailand (1998) was followed by a joint venture with Samsung in South Korea in 1999. Tesco opened its own business in Taiwan in 2000, entered into a joint venture with Sime Darby in Malaysia in 2002 and then acquired a chain in Japan in 2003. There has also been an acquisition

in Turkey (2003) and a joint venture in the US with Safeway (2001). In 2004 Tesco entered China.

Japan is an unusual retail market in some respects, but it is the world's second largest. Luxury brands such as Louis Vuitton, Prado and Gucci do well, but from the UK both Boots and Prêt a Manger have entered and exited. Operating costs are high and consumers are fastidious. The message has to be right! But in addition shopping by car is hardly ubiquitous – many people shop on their bikes. Consumers often buy food every day and they happily visit several stores and shop around.

In 2003 Tesco bought a chain of 80 discount convenience stores in the Tokyo region – not its usual supermarkets-hypermarkets by any means. This approach had already been taken by Wal-Mart in Japan – but Carrefour was operating a limited number of successful hypermarkets. Tesco was able to export its Tesco Metro (small, localized) store format to some degree.

It was clear for a while that Tesco was 'looking to buy' a stake in a Chinese food retail chain, and it found a receptive business (25 hypermarkets) in 2004. Hymall is Taiwanese-owned and concentrated in east, north and north-east China. Ten new stores are in the offing. Tesco acquired a 50 per cent stake at a cost of £140 million. Again Wal-Mart and Carrefour are already there.

The company has also moved towards global sourcing, and has established four sourcing centres in Hong Kong, India, Thailand and Central Europe. These currently source 50 per cent of Tesco non-food products, excluding health and beauty products.

Since the mid 1990s Tesco has sent experienced UK managers overseas to work with locals to get the business model right. Whilst each country has a strong element of local taste in the product range and store ambience, they are Tesco stores. There is a common philosophy globally – '*Every little helps*'. From this stem price discounts and a high level of customer service.

The company appears to be following a classic 'think globally, act locally' strategy, by having a format which is internationally transferable, but which at the same time can be adapted locally. Thus, the stores in central Europe and Asia tend to have more products on sale, with a higher proportion of non-food ranges. The whole operation is geared towards a single shopping trip. Tesco combines its retailing skills and high service standards to serve these markets, and at the same time acquires local knowledge which it uses to good effect. Tesco's chief executive, Terry Leahy, has stated that successful retailers will be those which can manage changes in domestic and foreign markets to emerge as global forces.

**Questions**

1. Why do you think that after its earlier disappointments Tesco has managed to develop a strong global strategy?
2. Would it make any sense for Tesco to want stores in countries where it sources products for sale in the UK?
3. Where do you think Tesco should seek to venture next?
4. Should it expand where it is or disperse itself further?

Tesco http://www.tesco.com

*Globalization is now no longer an objective, but an imperative, as markets open and geographic barriers become increasingly blurred and even irrelevant. Corporate alliances, whether joint ventures or acquisitions, will increasingly be driven by competitive pressures and strategies rather than financial structuring.*

John F Welch, Chairman and CEO, General Electric – quoted in *Fortune*, 26 March 1990

*In future we will have local [retail] companies and global companies and not much in-between. Globalization pressures will lead to those who are not in the first division and those who are purely national to make alliances.*

David Bernard, Chairman, Carrefour hypermarkets

## 13.1 Introduction

Internal growth, external growth and disinvestment strategies may all involve an international dimension with special complexities. Countries differ economically (variable growth rates), culturally (behaviours, tastes and preferences) and politically. National politics can dictate the appropriate strategy – some markets cannot be penetrated effectively without joint ventures with local companies.

Internal growth might involve exporting to new markets overseas and the development of special varieties of a product or service in order to target it to the specific needs and requirements of overseas customers. External growth can range from the creation of distribution or assembly bases abroad, to joint ventures and licensing agreements with foreign companies, to the establishment of a comprehensive global organization. The latter can be accomplished through both acquisition and strategic alliances. The opening Minicase shows how Tesco's international strategy has emerged over a period of time.

Kay (1990) recommends that organizations should seek to determine the smallest area within which they can be a viable competitor. Whilst a retail newsagent can still succeed by concentrating on a local catchment area, most car manufacturers, in common with many other industries and service businesses, now see their relevant market as a global one. The term 'multinational' is generally applied to any company which produces and distributes in two or more countries; a transnational, global, corporation is one which has a large proportion of its sales, assets, and employees outside its home base. Using these criteria, Nestlé is the most global business in the world.

Porter (1990) believes **global strategies** essentially supplement the competitive advantage created in the home market. Firms must retain their national strengths when they cross over borders. Ohmae (1990) disagrees and argues that global firms should shake off their origins. Managers must take on an international perspective, avoiding the near-sightedness which often characterizes companies with centralized and powerful global headquarters. Markets, he says, are driven by the needs and desires of customers around the world, and managers must act as if they are equidistant from all these customers, wherever they might be located.

Ohmae is perhaps presenting a futuristic vision of how he believes things will be as global forces strengthen. At the moment, whilst world leaders like IBM, Sony and Nestlé are spread around the world and substantially dependent on non-domestic customers, their underlying cultures and competitiveness remain rooted in the US, Japan and Switzerland, respectively.

Chandler (1990) stresses the continuing importance of economies of scale (cost advantages with large scale production) and economies of scope (the use of common materials and processes to make a variety of different products profitably). This implies carefully targeted investment in large-scale operations and a search for international marketing opportunities.

### 13.1.1 Definitions of internationalization

One problem with attempting a definition of internationalization is trying to find one on which everyone can agree. A brief review of the literature will reveal that such a definition does not exist. Instead there are almost as many definitions as there are contributions to the body of research knowledge on this topic. Following a study in 1988, the following useful definition was produced: 'Internationalization may be viewed as an approach to management which allows an organization to integrate domestic and international opportunities with internal resources' (Janacek 1988). Each new study on the topic tends to have a different perspective and so it is difficult to point to a simple coherence in the literature on the subject of internationalization. But then again, why should there be any simple solution to such a complex process?

The origin of much of the work on internationalization stems from studies in the 1960s on the nature of export behaviour, when the promotion of an 'international outlook' or 'internationalization' among managers was identified as a more successful route to increasing exports than any appeal to nationalistic motives. This work became formalized into models of export behaviour, mainly by a number of Swedish researchers including Johanson and Wiedersheim (1975). For them it was the interaction of these attitudes and actual behaviour which describe the internationalization process. These attitudinal and behavioural themes continued to be echoed in the literature by Joynt and Welch (1985). More importantly they also state that a crucial component of the whole internationalization process is the 'internationalization of people and their attitudes'.

Another theme apparent in some of the definitions of internationalization is that it is a gradual process during which firms acquire, integrate and utilise their knowledge about foreign markets and operations. As this happens over time, the firms gradually increase their commitment to international markets. Some research work on this topic has suggested that internationalization evolves as firms gradually increase their commitment and exposure to risk. This is reflected in their market entry mode which may progress through (i) exporting, (ii) agency representation, (iii) overseas licensing, (iv) overseas sales subsidiary, and finally (v) the establishment of an overseas production subsidiary.

Apart from these recurrent themes there remains no one agreed definition. Part of the problem is that few studies use identical methodologies, and therefore cross-cultural or longitudinal studies are rare. Other criticisms of the work into internationalization have included its over-association with the exporting mode, lack of empirical evidence for the stages model (discussed in Section 13.3), discrepancies based on the unit of observation, and a neglect of service-based companies and of purchasing behaviour.

## 13.1.2 Motives for internationalization

Generally speaking the first decision go international is a specific one based on an actual opportunity rather than a decision to look around the globe for investment opportunities (Ghauri, 2000). At this stage the company has limited knowledge but will benefit from its early experiences in its subsequent investment decisions. What is needed is a strong push and/or commitment to go abroad. Ghauri sees the decision to go international as being strongly influenced by three organizational and three environmental factors:

| *Organizational* | The ambitions of the management team |
| | The objectives and motives of the organization |
| | The company's success record in its home market |
| *Environmental* | Unsolicited proposals |
| | The bandwagon effect |
| | Strong overseas competition in the home market |

Most of these factors are self-explanatory, but it may be worth noting that the unsolicited proposal can come from a foreign government, distributor or customer. The bandwagon effect can be created by competitors going international or a general belief that a presence in a certain market is somehow a must. Examples of the latter include investment in the former communist states of Eastern Europe post-1989 and the current fascination for China.

In this context, the crucial importance of spending significant amounts of time on relationship building and on being sensitive to the cultural differences in both business and personal relationships cannot be stressed too highly.

**Market entry** Firms enter into the international arena, then, for a variety of reasons. No classification can be regarded as inclusive of all possible reasons; instead they act as a shorthand guide to be adapted to all sorts of situations. Likewise, all firms operate within a framework of constraints; not all opportunities can be responded to positively, and they need to be evaluated within the overall context of the businesses aims. Motives are also directly related to the mode of market entry adopted by a company.

There are a range of generally recognized export motives, but ways of classifying them vary and in some cases it is not always clear which category a particular motive belongs in. The traditional way in the literature is to regard export motives as push (internal) and pull (external) factors.

The main *push factors* are:

- Excess capacity
- Having a unique product
- Having a company-specific advantage
- Having a marketing advantage
- Being driven by the ambitions of the strategic leader.

And the main *pull factors* are:

- Receiving an unsolicited order
- A saturated domestic market
- Competitive pressures
- Attractive export development or incentive programmes.

Some find this a difficult classification to endorse, since the difference between a pull and a push can be difficult to judge. For example, a saturated home market could really be seen as both a pull and a push factor. Perhaps greater clarity is offered by the use of the terms proactive and reactive, which can be cross-tabulated against internal and external – see Table 13.1.

Proactive internationalization is then seen as being in line with the ambitions of the strategic leader (the owner–manager in a small organization) and it follows a strong market development in the domestic market that provides finance for international activities. Alternatively the company may internationalize rapidly because of a strong product concept, brand or service. Internationalization in this context is deliberate and planned, reflecting the owner's commitment to the process and the associated risks. Quite often proactive internationalization can be the result of a conscious policy of

**Table 13.1** A classification of international involvement motives

|  | Internal | External |
|---|---|---|
| Proactive | <ul><li>driven by owner–manager/key decision-makers</li><li>desire to increase profits</li><li>to increase market share/market power</li><li>having a unique product/service/brand</li><li>extend life cycle or seasonality</li><li>new product/service development</li><li>having a company-specific advantage, e.g. in marketing, technology</li><li>to serve customers better by being closer to where they are.</li></ul> | <ul><li>perceived international market opportunities, e.g. removal of trade barriers</li><li>export development activity by governments, trade associations, banks</li><li>improvements in IT, physical infrastructure e.g. transport links</li></ul> |
| Reactive | <ul><li>excess production capacity</li><li>spreading costs and risk</li></ul> | <ul><li>unsolicited order</li><li>small domestic market</li><li>declining domestic market</li><li>saturated domestic market</li><li>peer competitive pressure</li><li>service existing customers who have gone international</li></ul> |

recruiting people, often younger graduates, who have a positive attitude to international business and to 'dealing with foreigners'.

Reactive internationalization tends to be based, at least initially, on an extension of domestic marketing practice with very little adaptation to local customer needs. The whole internationalization process tends to be more gradual and it emerges in an ad hoc and incremental way. This is often based on a chance order from abroad which the company follows up without any grand design. Market spreading tends to be more common than concentration as opportunities are followed without, at least initially, any strategic plan in mind.

Two examples from the north of Scotland are given below:

**Proactive internationalization** – a weaving company was founded in the far north of Scotland in 1991 and it is involved in the production of fashion accessories. The key influence here on their exporting activity was that a previous company had existed from 1986–1990. Crucially, the international networks developed by the designer associated with the original company were maintained by the new company as a part of their business strategy. This planned use of networks paved the way for the international success and the company now has agents in France, Italy, Japan and the US. Indeed the company's entire turnover has traditionally come from export markets. It is only since 1995 that the domestic market has been given serious marketing consideration.

**Reactive internationalization** – a second company, founded in 1995, is located north of Inverness and is involved with jewellery design and making. The entry to the export market occurred when the owner attended a trade fair in London. The entrepreneur was approached by a Japanese buyer for a small gallery in Yokohama City. The buyer 'liked the design, then the price'. The gallery has since reordered and the company is seeking to extend its business in Japan. Clearly in this case attending the trade fair was a crucial catalyst for starting exporting, but, from the entrepreneur's point of view, it was an unplanned development.

## 13.2 International strategies

Developing new markets for existing products and diversification are the options most likely to be associated with international business. Diversification is the highest risk strategy since it takes the company furthest away from its core expertise in production and domestic distribution.

For some growth companies, being global is the 'holy grail' and it is a central part of the business strategy from the formation of the company. Going global may seem ambitious but it is also a viable strategy, if it is well managed by the leadership team. This is akin to portfolio management and involves the simultaneous entry in to a number of different markets geographically. Clearly the option is most viable for companies (or entrepreneurs) that have technology- or knowledge-based products that are transferable across international boundaries.

Globalization is a business philosophy that is based on the belief that the world is becoming more homogeneous and that distinctions between national markets are not only fading but, for some products, will eventually disappear. It is argued that companies need to globalize and standardize their international strategy by formulating it across country markets in order to take advantage of underlying market, cost, environmental and competition factors.

Companies such as Coca-Cola and Levi Strauss have based their global marketing effort over the past decades on the premise that universal appeal exists. Coke's *'one sight, one sound, one sell'* was a legend among global marketers. But the world is continually changing, and with it the need to revise global marketing strategies. If cultural and competitive differences are less important than similarities, a single advertising approach can exploit the similarities to stimulate sales everywhere. This can be done at far lower cost than if campaigns were developed for each market.

Organizations which develop their corporate strategy internationally have to consider in particular:

- marketing and financial strategies
- the structure of the organization – including location issues
- cultural and people issues.

Before discussing these factors individually, Figure 13.1 endeavours to link them together and implicitly reinforce the notion of E–V–R (environment–values–resources) congruence. The situational factors have to be right for an international strategy to make sense. Specifically, the returns must exceed the investment. We can see this illustrated in Figure 13.2.

Gupta and Govindarajan (1998) argue that the potential pay-off can be assessed by addressing a number of obvious questions:

**Figure 13.1** International strategy

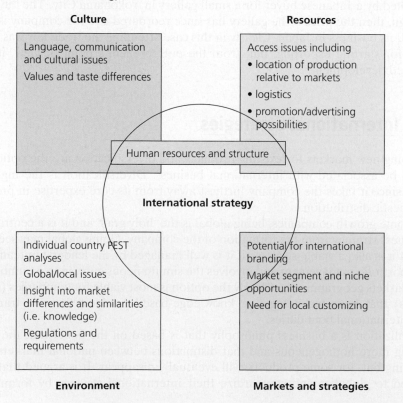

| Culture | Resources |
| --- | --- |
| Language, communication and cultural issues<br><br>Values and taste differences | Access issues including<br>• location of production relative to markets<br>• logistics<br>• promotion/advertising possibilities |

Human resources and structure

**International strategy**

| Environment | Markets and strategies |
| --- | --- |
| Individual country PEST analyses<br><br>Global/local issues<br><br>Insight into market differences and similarities (i.e. knowledge)<br><br>Regulations and requirements | Potential for international branding<br><br>Market segment and niche opportunities<br><br>Need for local customizing |

**Figure 13.2** The attractiveness of the international opportunity

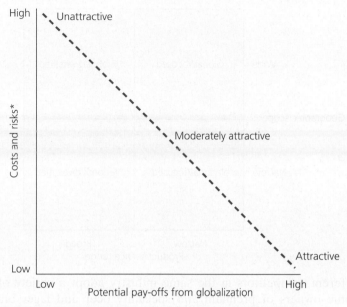

*The costs and risks relate to entry barriers, local regulations (e.g. the need for a local partner)
and the extent of investment required to make products/services suitable for individual markets

- Which product lines are (most) suitable for internationalization?
- Which markets should be targeted – and in what order of priority?
- What are the most appropriate ways of entering these target markets?
- How rapidly does it make sense to expand? Does a fast-track approach (such as Glaxo licensing Zantac for production in various countries simultaneously) make more sense than a slower approach (IKEA deliberately restricting the number of new branch openings every year to retain tight control)?

## 13.2.1 Marketing

The issue of how global products and services can be made, and the extent to which they have to be tailored to appeal to different markets, is critical. Markets vary from those termed multi-domestic (where the competitive dynamics of each separate country market are distinctive and idiosyncratic) to global (where competitive strategies are transferable across frontiers). Coca-Cola, Levi jeans and the expensive perfumes and leather goods marketed by LVMH, Louis Vuitton Moët Hennessy, do attract a global consumer with identical tastes, but they are more exceptional than normal. The challenge to design the 'world car', for example, remains unresolved. Honda initially hoped to achieve this when it began redesigning its Accord range in the mid-1980s, but concluded that international performance expectations, and in turn components, are irreconcilable. In Japan the Accord is seen as a status symbol car for congested roads where driving is restricted; in the US it is a workaday vehicle for travelling long distances on open highways. Standardizing platforms and hidden components for different models and countries has provided a suitable compromise.

**Figure 13.3** Competitor analysis in a global context

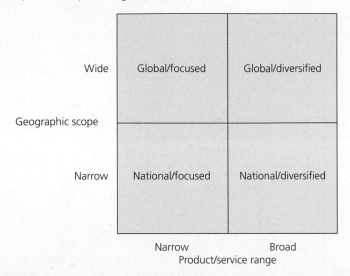

Clearly different competitors in the same industry adopt a variety of competitive strategies. Some owners of premium and speciality beer and lager brands elect to control the brewing of their product and rely on local, individual country brewers for distribution; others license the actual brewing to these national companies. Grolsch, recognizable by its distinctive bottles with metal frame tops, is brewed and bottled in Holland and exported. Most UK premium beers which succeed in the US are similarly exported to that country. Guinness is brewed in Dublin and exported for bottling in the US, whilst Fosters and Budweiser are both brewed under licence in the UK.

There is a follow-up issue concerning the appropriate range of products or services. The following framework (illustrated as a 2 × 2 four-quadrant matrix in Figure 13.3) could be a useful starting point for analysing both opportunities and competitor strategies:

| | Product/service range | Geographic scope |
|---|---|---|
| 1 | Narrow | National |
| 2 | Broad | National |
| 3 | Narrow | Global |
| 4 | Broad | Global |

Where organizations find it necessary to be located close to customers in order to provide the delivery and other services demanded, this can be achieved with strategic stockholding rather than manufacturing.

Globalization differs from a multilevel domestic approach in three basic ways:

1. The global approach looks for similarities between markets. The multilevel domestic approach ignores similarities.
2. The global approach actively seeks homogeneity in products, image, marketing, and advertising message. The multilevel domestic approach results in unnecessary differences from market to market.
3. The global approach asks: *'is this product or process suitable for world consumption?'* The multilevel domestic approach, relying solely on local autonomy, never asks the question.

In a multilevel domestic strategy, marketing is typically the most localized of the business functions. Even within marketing, however, differences exist in marketing mix elements and between companies. Elements that are strategic – such as positioning – are more easily globalized, while tactical elements – such as sales promotions – are typically determined locally. Interestingly, adaptation is present even at Coca-Cola, which is acknowledged to be one of the world's most global marketers. The key is the worldwide use of ideas and methods rather than absolute standardization.

Globalization, by contrast, means the centralization of decision-making – something that is invariably beyond the resource or management capability of a small fast growth company.

Adaptability – or localization – invariably takes place influenced by three factors:

■ The markets targeted and their level of sophistication

■ The product and its ability to transfer across boundaries, to include issues of conformity and supply-chain management

■ Company culture including factors such as resources and experience in overseas markets.

On this basis it is possible to be a global company, providing that a company has the vision and means to adapt products or services to suit local circumstances. This means that the process of being a global company involves an infinite number of alterations to the marketing mix.

The characteristics of a global business are summarized in Table 13.2.

**Table 13.2** Characteristics of a global business

| Criteria | Measurement |
|---|---|
| Mission | Clear mission statement signalling that the company has significant international ambitions |
| Objectives | Quantifiable objectives showing ambition to operate or market on two or more continents |
| Size | >£5m turnover<br>Minimum 30 per cent turnover from overseas |
| International markets | Sales: minimum two continents |
| Overseas operations | On a minimum of two continents:<br>Employment or assembly or manufacture or distribution channels |
| HQ | CEO based in and board meetings held in founding country<br>Overall operational control there |
| Strategic independence | Strategic decision-making in 'home' country |
| Growth | Five year turnover growth |
| Influence on markets | Global market share<br>Global brands |
| Integration of operations | Operational control<br>or<br>Brand management on at least two continents |
| International recruitment | Significant numbers of non-home nationals at senior managerial level |
| International sourcing | Company seeks inputs worldwide |

### 13.2.2  Finance

The management of currency transfers and exchange rates adds complexity. Floating exchange rates imply uncertainty, although companies can, and do, reduce their risk by buying ahead. The European Exchange Rate Mechanism (superseded by the single European currency, the Euro) was originally designed to minimize currency fluctuations, but economic pressures still cause periodic devaluations. Predictable or fixed rates benefit, for example, a car manufacturer which produces engines and transmission systems in one country, transfers them to assembly plants in a second and third country, each specializing in different cars, and then finally sells them throughout Europe. Costs and estimated profits must be based on predicted currency movements, and any incorrect forecasting could result in either extra or lost profits.

Where such an organization structure is created, transfer pricing arrangements are required. If managers of the various divisions or business units are motivated or measured by their profitability figures there will be some disagreement about the **transfer price** which affects their value added figures. Equally the organization may be seeking to manage transfer arrangements for tax purposes, seeking to show most profit where taxes are lowest.

Companies with a main base in a country whose currency is strong and appreciating may find their international competitiveness weakened. Exported products will become relatively expensive, competing imports cheaper. Such companies may be tempted to invest and relocate elsewhere. In 1995, for example, Toyota, which already had a number of manufacturing plants around the world, began to seriously consider closing down plants in Japan because of the high yen. Companies must also see financial markets as global, seeking to borrow where loans are cheapest – as long as the source is not too risky.

Whilst both governments and companies would ideally like a strong local currency and to be able to export at high prices to earn substantial wealth internationally this may not be practical. It certainly requires high added value and very clear differentiation.

### 13.2.3  Structure

The two key questions are:

1. Where to make the various products and services to obtain the necessary people and other resources required, to be as close as appropriate to each defined geographic market and to manage costs efficiently; and

2. How best to structure the organization in order to control it effectively but, at the same time, ensure it is sufficiently responsive to changing environments. The speed and nature of change pressures may be uneven. IT increasingly offers opportunities for more effective control of globally dispersed businesses.

One obvious way for a firm to expand is by offering its existing products in foreign markets. This can be done by exporting from its domestic production base, and employing the services of agents and distributors to handle its products in export markets. Alternatively, and implying greater commitment, the firm may decide to relocate production itself by establishing manufacturing plants in selected overseas markets.

The company may decide to become vertically integrated on a global basis, sourcing some of its raw material requirements and intermediate products from overseas subsidiaries or suppliers, and establishing overseas sales subsidiaries in order to put its international marketing operations on a more dedicated footing. Likewise, the company may choose to diversify its business by acquiring suitable foreign companies. These multichannel strategies are consistent with becoming a global entity.

The structural alternatives available are:

- A globally centralized organization, remote from markets, and relying on exporting. This is likely to prove cost-efficient but possibly out of touch.

- Manufacturing plants located close to markets in order to satisfy local needs and preferences. This structure, known as both international and multi-domestic, could still be controlled centrally, or substantially decentralized into fully autonomous units, in which case the plants may be independent or co-operate in some way. This is a more expensive structure, but one which can offer higher levels of service. Unilever, which relies on localized manufacturing and marketing, is an example. Whilst cement is an international commodity product, companies are structured in this way because there is no benefit to be gained from transporting cement across frontiers.

- Centralized manufacture of key components, possibly in a low-wage country, with final assembly or finishing nearer to markets. Caterpillar Tractors utilize this strategy.

- An integrated global structure with production locations chosen on resource or cost grounds. Finished goods will be transported to markets. In this structure the organization will have an international presence, but in say Country X its sales could consist mainly of products imported from other locations, whilst most of Country X's production is exported. Marketing, production *control*, purchasing and research and development will all be co-ordinated globally if they are not centralized.

Centres of excellence may be established where cultural values and behaviours are most appropriate. Philips chose to concentrate technology development in the Far East, where a long-term perspective is natural; IBM have established R&D facilities in Italy, which they regard as suitably intuitive and innovative. However, if national preferences and requirements are markedly different, there is an argument in favour of establishing dedicated R&D facilities in several countries. ICI opened a technical centre in Japan for developing special chemicals and materials in collaboration with the major car and electronics manufacturers. The intention was to sell their products to Japanese plants throughout the world. 'Japanese companies prefer to collaborate with chemicals suppliers which have scientists and engineers in Japan, and a factory to produce material locally.' General Motors strengthened its Opel technical development centre in Frankfurt to spearhead its expansion in all international markets outside the US. Eastern Europe and the Pacific Rim are targets for growth in respect of both production and sales. Meanwhile Ford has sought to integrate product development globally in its search for a range of world cars.

- A global network via strategic alliances.

This alternative has many strategic advantages, but it can be complex to control and costly in overheads. Typical companies are Sony and Coca-Cola. Coca-Cola, based in Atlanta, commands 50 per cent of the world's soft drinks market and 44 per cent of the US domestic market. The key success factor is obtaining distribution and access to markets, and because Coca-Cola is mostly water this is decentralized. Branding and marketing is global and centralized. The strategy is to sell concentrate or syrup to local bottlers, be they independent businesses or joint venture partners. Pricing is based on what can be afforded locally, and a variety of support mechanisms are offered. Coke is frequently promoted with local endorsements, but marketing and advertising also features sponsorship of international sporting events. The evolving international strategies of Matsushita and Canon are discussed in Minicase 13.2.

## Minicase 13.2  Matsushita and Canon                    (AS)  (Int)

**Matsushita**, whose brands include Panasonic, National and Technics, is the world's largest consumer electronics company. JVC is a subsidiary business. The product range includes video and audio products, electronic components, batteries, home appliances and kitchen equipment.

In the early 1990s Matsushita operated 150 plants in 38 countries including Brazil, the US, Austria, Tanzania, Malaysia and China. 'The sun never sets on its holdings.' Products are moved widely across frontiers, some even back to Japan, but 70 per cent of Matsushita's employees still work in Japan.

Matsushita has become international for a variety of reasons, not least the strength of the yen, but its growth overseas has been measured and careful.

Initially a plant would be opened in a country to manufacture specifically for that market. The next stage during the 1980s was to move these plants away from merely replicating products designed and manufactured in Japan to the production of variants which had been adapted for local markets. Exporting from these overseas plants then followed. One example here was microwave ovens. European customers like their ovens to finish meat in different ways; the UK, for example, has a preference for crispy fat and consequently needs microwaves with extra strong heating elements. 'It is difficult for product engineers in Japan to understand all the differences and to respond accordingly.'

A further stage involved export centres where all the design and development of a range of products is now based outside Japan, often using lower cost labour. Malaysia now produces 25 per cent of all Matsushita's televisions, and 90 per cent of that country's production is exported, mostly to

other countries in South-East Asia and the Middle East. It is argued that Malaysian television plants outperform those back in Japan in terms of both quality and efficiency.

Typical of Japanese companies, Matsushita remains strongly centralized. Subsidiaries cannot deposit or borrow money locally; all financial transactions are handled through a central treasury in Japan. One reason for the caution has been the difficulty in transferring important Japanese values to certain other countries. China is said to be relatively poor on punctuality; the Chinese are not natural teamworkers and do not share their knowledge readily. Matsushita's US employees have very high technical skills, higher than their colleagues in Japan, but they are apparently less willing to take responsibility for changing things and to tinker with manufacturing processes.

Nevertheless, there have been problems and relative failures. Following the lead of Sony, which bought Columbia Pictures and CBS Records, Matsushita acquired MCA film studios and music interests. The deal did not prove successful because of the cultural differences and the real difficulty in trying to manage a business such as this, focused in Hollywood, from a base in Japan. MCA managers were refused investment money to buy either Virgin Records or a stake in NBC Television. The subsidiary was eventually sold to Seagram. Sony too experienced problems with this type of diversification but was willing to decentralize more power and responsibility to local managers.

Schlender (1994) offers six lessons from the international approach and experience of Matsushita:

1. Be a good corporate citizen in every country; respect local cultures, customs and languages.

▶

2. Export your best manufacturing technology to overseas subsidiaries, not second-hand equipment.
3. Minimize the number of expatriate managers and groom local talent to take over.
4. Allow plants to establish their own rules and procedures, fine tuning the manufacturing processes to match the skills of the local workforce.
5. Invest in local R&D facilities to tailor products to markets.
6. Encourage competition between those plants located overseas and those back home.

**Canon** has adopted a different approach to globalization. Canon began after the Second World War, manufacturing cameras. Systematically it has used its technological competencies to move into related areas, each time seeking market leadership for its new product but never abandoning its previous interests as long as they are still relevant for the market. Canon invented the bubble-jet and laser printers for computers; it has also been successful with desk-size photocopiers.

Since the mid-1980s Canon has devolved more and more responsibility overseas. Manufacturing was migrating in any case, as Japan was becoming a relatively high-cost producer. Canon increased the numbers of foreign managers employed to a level higher than is normal for Japan and watered down some Japanese practices in favour of the 'best of the rest'. By the mid-1990s 30 per cent of manufacturing was overseas, with the percentage rising every year. Of Canon's overseas staff only 20 per cent were Japanese.

In 1995, again unusually, world responsibility for key research projects was shifted from Tokyo:

research and development consumes some 7 per cent of annual revenues, more than Canon spends on capital investment. The US became the new base for software research, France for telecommunications, and the UK for automated language translation. Canon was projecting that some years hence it would have a global set of Canon regional headquarters each with world responsibility for development, manufacturing and sales of particular products 'Tokyo cannot know everything.' Instead, the role of the head office should be to:

- provide low-cost capital
- move top management around and
- come up with investment initiatives.

Previously, Canon had trawled the world for ideas and then sought to develop them in Tokyo, an approach which was becoming more difficult as the US in particular was more vigilant to the potential of good new ideas. Canon believes that 'Americans are more creative.'

Quotations are from Schlender (1994).

## Question

1. In the end, do you think that the Canon approach (also favoured by Sony) is inevitable for any company seeking world domination in a particular industry?

**Canon** http://www.canon.com
**Panasonic** http://www.panasonic.com

## Reference

Schlender, BR (1994) Matsushita shows how to go global, *Fortune*, 11 July.

### 13.2.4 International location

The international location decision is affected by a number of key issues, including:

- The existence of any national resources which influence competitive advantage in any significant way. Nike and Reebok have built factories in China, Thailand and the Philippines for labour cost savings. A number of leading computer and semiconductor businesses are located in California's Silicon Valley because of the pool of skilled labour and acquired expertise to support research and development. Consumer electronics and pharmaceuticals are further examples of industries where

Infosys is a software business based in India, but which targets markets around the globe. It was set up with this strategy in mind.

Infosys was started in 1981 with 10,000 (Indian) Rupees, equivalent to some US$1200; it is now one of India's most dynamic wealth generators. The company was floated in 1993; within six years, and after growing by some 50 per cent per year, the share value had increased 85 times. Infosys has become the fifteenth largest company quoted on the New York NASDAQ and the first Indian business to be listed there.

Founder Narayana Murthy, who was around 35 at the time, left an American computing business, together with six Indian colleagues, and they started Infosys in Murthy's home in Poona, near Bombay. Infosys would write software for established businesses in the G7 countries, and also provide systems integration and consultancy services. Murthy was the son of a teacher, and, although he had been working abroad extensively, particularly in Paris, he was to be the only one of the seven to stay based in India. The others would work in America, close to their key clients. The business would be global from day one; there was no local market of any consequence for what they were doing. Their first major client was Reebok.

> *The market for the idea did not exist in India ... we had to embrace globalization. I believe globalization is about sourcing capital from where it is cheapest, producing where it is most cost-effective and selling where it is most profitable, all without being constrained by national boundaries.*
>
> Murthy

India was able to offer well-educated, English-speaking staff who were proficient in IT. They had a strong work ethic and the prevailing salaries were well below those of their client countries. America has generally provided two-thirds of the company's revenues. Infosys was able to offer very competitive prices for high quality work.

But things were not altogether smooth. 'It took one year for a specialist telephone connection, two years to get a license to import a computer and two weeks every time we needed foreign currency to travel abroad.'

In 1987 Infosys began a joint venture with a management consultancy based in Atlanta. The US staff would seek out business; Infosys would provide the skilled personnel to deliver the product. This gave Infosys market credibility and opened up a host of fresh opportunities. New clients included Nestlé, General Electric and Holiday Inn.

The joint venture was abandoned in 1995 when Infosys felt it was sufficiently established and well-known to open its own offices in the US. In 1991, back in India, Infosys had moved from Poona to a new 55-acre complex in Bangalore, home of India's burgeoning software industry.

There was now to be a focus on a broader product range with an extended set of staff skills and competencies; this would involve selective acquisitions. The company was restructured around strategic business units. The emphasis would be on service and customer focus. Additional business from existing clients was sought energetically – it amounted to 80 per cent of revenues – as well as the active search for new clients.

There are a number of reasons why Infosys has been as successful as it has:

- World-class operations and high quality products and service
- A recognition that in software human resources are the core resources and they must be nurtured. Systems and conditions were created which would attract and retain the best. Good young talent was sought and, unusually for India, Western-style stock options offered
- Expertise in project management
- A clear structure (in Bangalore) that was dedicated to servicing overseas clients. However, as relative salaries in India have risen (albeit still well below those of the US and UK!) Infosys has started to set up overseas supply operations. It now employs software

writers at its operation in Shanghai, China, for example.

■ Ensuring that whilst large clients are sought, Infosys avoids dependency on any single client. At one time GE provided 25 per cent of revenues; this has been reduced to 10 per cent over time as the company has grown.

Infosys has not been without its critics in India. Its social perspective on working conditions and rewards has not endeared it to everyone. Murthy has proclaimed that 'all profitable exporters should give 20 per cent of their earnings before interest and tax to help fund higher education in India', which has detractors as well as supporters.

As for Murthy himself, he has stepped down from the chief executive position he held for over 20 years but he remains as chairman. In 2003 he became the company's 'Chief Mentor' responsible for helping to 'create future leaders' within Infosys.

### Questions

1  What factors might threaten the type of global strategy practised by Infosys?
2. What do you think are the most realistic growth options available to Infosys?

**Infosys** http://www.infosys.com

the headquarters of the leading companies are concentrated in one or a few countries. Minicase 13.3 shows how Infosys chose to locate where specialist people resources were available and affordable.

■ Scale economies from key resources in, say, production or technology. Toyota, Honda and Nissan preferred to produce in Japan and export for many years, but the strong yen eventually encouraged them to locate abroad.

■ Transport considerations.

■ The availability of a suitable supply chain.

■ Political issues.

Whatever the structural format, a truly international business must develop a global mission and core values (such as consistent quality worldwide), and achieve integration through effective communications. The corporate strategy must be centralized even if the company has a number of independent subsidiaries and operates in several multi-domestic markets. However, the organization must be able to embrace the different national cultural traits and behaviours, and this presents an important managerial challenge. Decisions have to be made concerning the balance of local managers and mobile 'international' managers who are easily transferable between divisions and countries.

Bartlett and Ghoshal (1989) summarized the above points as three potentially conflicting issues which must be reconciled. These are:

■ the need for efficiency through global centralization

■ the need to respond locally through decentralization

■ the need to innovate and transfer learning internationally.

Bartlett and Ghoshal (1992) have also concluded:

■ There can be no such thing as a 'universal international manager'. Large global companies will need functional specialists (such as production experts) and national managers (committed to one country and most familiar with that culture) as well as those executives who are able to switch readily between divisions and countries. International managers are responsible for corporate and competitive strategies within the organization, whilst national managers ensure that the needs of local customers, host governments and employees are satisfied effectively. The organizational challenge in respect of functional managers is to ensure that best practices are learned and spread throughout the organization.

■ The attempts to integrate all the global operations (products, plants and countries) should be concentrated towards the top of the organizational hierarchy. At lower levels managers should have clear, single-line, responsibilities and reporting relationships.

■ One benefit of adopting these recommendations is a limited requirement for international managers, who, inevitably, are in short supply because of the qualities they are required to have. Some industrialists would argue that this supply constraint is the deciding force, and that a successful global matrix structure would be preferable. One such structure is described in a later case on ABB (Asea Brown Boveri). ABB's managers were encouraged to 'think globally but act locally'. Their key measure was profitability and this can be enhanced if managers respond effectively to local employee and customer needs, seeking to satisfy different aspirations and requirements, whilst thinking globally about, say, sourcing and supply flexibility to take advantage of price and currency opportunities.

### 13.2.5 Culture

It is important to consider cultural issues in the process of globalization from two points of view – a national perspective as well as a policy perspective. The outcome is strategies that allow entrepreneurial companies to think globally and still deliver products and services that are locally suited. One of the key contributions to the understanding of culture and its influence comes from Hofstede (1991) who states that differences, and specifically cultural differences, reveal themselves in various ways through values, rituals, heroes and symbols. Expanding issues we raised in Chapter 7, Hofstede developed five dimensions to describe the culture of 58 countries.

These are:

1. *Masculinity* – specifically values associated with earnings, advancement and assertiveness – *versus femininity* – values associated with a friendly atmosphere, nurturing and relationship building.

2. *Individualism* – a concern for oneself – *versus collectivism* – a concern for the priorities of the group or team to which one belongs

3. *Uncertainty avoidance* – preferring formal rules and not tolerating ambiguity

4. *Power distance* – the extent to which hierarchy is a fact of life

5. *Long-term versus short-term orientation.*

In terms of masculinity, for example, it was found that within Europe Austria, Italy, Switzerland, the UK, Ireland and West Germany (as it was at the time) had the highest scores, while feminine cultures where found in Scandinavia, Holland and the former Yugoslavia. Better off nations were found to be more individualistic and the poorer ones more collective orientated. Uncertainty avoidance is higher in the Latin European and Mediterranean countries than in the English speaking countries. Latin countries also score highly on the power distance dimension while most of the countries studied scored highly on the short time dimension.

Separately, colleagues teaching international MBA students have commented that western European students are more comfortable with group working than many people from the former communist Eastern European countries.

Wherever this type of analysis is used, cultural differences must influence the market entry strategies of firms. McAuley (2001) notes that:

> the European retailers prefer to enter geographically close countries first and often, but not always, these were culturally close. It was also found that standardized retail formats are first exported to culturally close countries (Ikea). In addition those countries (France, Germany and Belgium) with a high degree of uncertainty avoidance apply entry modes giving them a high degree of control. The same was true for power distance in the case of the examples from France and Germany.

## Minicase 13.4 Constellation Wines

US ANZ Int

CASE

Constellation Wines came about when two of the 'new world's' leading wine producers merged in March 2003. The Constellation Group of California effectively acquired Australia's BRL Hardy Group (which already had interests in New Zealand) to create the world's largest producer. Constellation's leading brands include Hardy's, Ravenswood, Nobilo and Banrock Station. However, it chose Adelaide for its headquarters. The new CEO was Stephen Millar, an accountant recruited from General Motors. His credo is that 'business culture is the one competitive advantage any business has. Brands and vineyards can be bought and sold'.

Constellation's market position is as follows:

| Country | Position | per cent share |
|---|---|---|
| Australia | 1st | 24 |
| US | 2nd | 20 |
| New Zealand | 2nd | 14 |
| UK | 1st | 10 |

The second largest producer is Gallo, another Californian business – reflecting the growing popularity of new world wines in recent years. It is, in fact, these wines that have underpinned the growth in wine drinking around the world. Many consumers see Australian wine as the all-round best value. These new world producers have a radically different business model from the archetypal small French vineyard that grows and presses its own grapes. Competitive success comes from astute grape buying and blending, efficient processing and distribution and branding based on grape varieties rather than regional or even district origins.

Australia came 'from nowhere' to be the world's fourth largest exporter of wine in a period of some 20 years at the end of the last century. Over this time production tripled. It is particularly famous for its Chardonnay (white) and Shiraz (red) grapes. Its main export market is the UK, followed by the US. Constellation is the leading distributor but the second largest Australian producer – Southcorp (brands – Lindemans, Rosemount and Penfold) is number one.

Ninety-five per cent of American wine is produced in California, where Gallo is the leading producer and distributor, and 75 per cent of the wine drunk in America is home-produced. The leading importer is Italy, followed by Australia. Just 15 per cent of wine production is exported.

The industry has grown remarkably in recent years, but where next? France is a leading producing and drinking country, but French people are fiercely loyal to French wine. Germany is the world's biggest importer, but 'the bastion of old world wine'.

### Question

1. What do you think Stephen Millar's strategy should be if Constellation is to reap the potential benefits of the 2003 merger?

**Constellation Wines** http://www.cbrands.com

This approach, though, creates a dilemma for firms seeking rapid internationalization – is it better to opt for an efficient distribution network and tackle countries that are closer or better to account for cultural similarities? Whilst it is not possible to be predictive about cultural differences, it can be suggested that geographic proximity and logistics can be overridden by cultural empathy – an understanding of a particular market or a feeling of national closeness.

Minicase 13.4 touches upon the cultural differences between the so-called 'old world' and the new world wine producers.

## 13.3 Stage models

Stage model frameworks such as the one featured in Figure 13.4 are based on the premise that internationalization is a process. It is viewed as an evolutionary development over time and consists of a number of phases. Two concepts strongly associated with the models are psychic distance and geographic proximity. Psychic distance refers to the tendency for those people involved in first time exporting to trade with countries with which they feel comfortable culturally. So, for example, English speaking nations will be more likely to trade with each other initially, even if the geographic distance is greater than their nearest neighbour. The issue of geographic distance is straightforward in that the initial exporting will take place to countries in close proximity. Both concepts work together to influence the destination of the first export order.

The models draw on organisational behaviour and learning theory to capture both firm behaviour and managerial learning over time – as the following story illustrates.

**Figure 13.4** A stage model framework

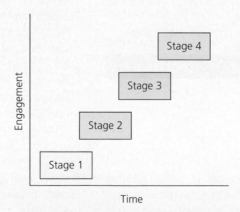

Stage 1: No regular export activities
Stage 2: Export via independent representatives
Stage 3: Establish a marketing/sales subsidiary
Stage 4: Establish a manufacturing facility

### 13.3.1  Ensuring successful market entry

*A company was founded in 1981 in Newcastle, England, UK – its set-up was, in itself, an interesting process. It was started by a Swedish entrepreneur and, because of patent protection in the UK, was immediately forced to export – a truly international firm from the outset. Whilst not directly reflecting the classic stages model, its history does help to illustrate stages of gradual market expansion and product development. The first main products which the company marketed were surf boards and surf skis. These were sold into identified markets in France, Australia and the United States. Five years after it was founded, the company acquired a clothing manufacturer in order to develop a range of leisure wear, which it again sold to the same markets where it had successfully marketed its surf boards. This time, of course, it had benefited from the market knowledge and experience gained from the first round of international involvement. Further new product development produced a kayak which again was to be sold into the company's already established key markets.*

Much of the conceptual and empirical foundation in this school of research was initiated by Johanson and Wiedersheim-Paul (1975), who developed a model which suggests that internationalization activities occur incrementally, and are influenced by increased market knowledge and commitment. The basic theory is that the perceptions and beliefs of managers both influence, and are shaped by, incremental involvement in foreign markets. This results in a pattern of evolution, from the managers having little or no interest in international markets, to trial initiatives in, and evaluation of, psychically close markets. Managers then pursue active expansion into more challenging and unknown markets, becoming increasingly committed to international growth.

Since the late 1980s research has shown that many companies are engaging in rapid and more direct forms of internationalisation. The stage models are ill-equipped to deal with this dynamic process. Many of the early models were based on very small samples of large firms, whose wider relevance must be questioned. Further, the implied sequential process is not inevitable and there is evidence of companies moving backward and forwards or even jumping stages within the model. Evidence of rapid internationalization by high-technology products, whose window of opportunity on the world market can be quite limited, has further added to the criticism.

Why, then, has this theory survived so long? One reason is that nothing better has come along. The model remains intuitively appealing to our search for order and neat explanations in the chaos of the international environment. However, while elements of the model may provide useful insights to our understanding, it is long past the time when the stages approach should be accepted as the best explanation of the internationalization process.

## 13.4  Market entry strategies

Selecting international markets in which to operate is a crucial element of international activity. In Minicase 13.5 we can see how Volkswagen has entered different countries to acquire both existing brands and assembly plants and for sourcing components.

Any company will have a number of broad strategic choices which it will have to address including: is a domestic export-based strategy, or a production-based strategy in the host country, more appropriate? It may be that the host country will only welcome the exporter if it involves a presence in the host market. Such a presence will require a commitment, at the very least, to international marketing or a production plant, unlike a pure domestic export-based strategy. For many years China, for example, required joint venture arrangements with a local Chinese company as a condition of market entry. Under such a strategy the responsibility could be devolved to the intermediary being used.

Table 13.3 shows that there are a number of ways to classify the options open to companies, and no one method is correct or perfect. The approach used in this chapter is to look at indirect and direct market entry together with strategies which do or do not involve foreign investment. This is outlined in Table 13.3 and some of the strategies are discussed in greater detail. We concentrate on those not discussed in detail in Chapter 12, although some of these, especially acquisitions, joint ventures and strategic alliances, are very significant in international strategy.

**CASE**

## Minicase 13.5 Volkswagen

Volkswagen (VW) Europe's leading car manufacturer, has pursued a number of international strategies. But are they all positive and do they fit together cohesively? The name 'Volkswagen' translates into 'People's Car' – and this company name was, in fact, coined first by Adolf Hitler in 1924.

Historically many people would instinctively think of the 'Beetle' when confronted with the name Volkswagen – although this will have changed in recent years. This is the car which helped the company grow and prosper after the Second World War as Germany revived. It has been described as 'the most popular car in history' and, of course, it featured as *Herbie* in the various *Love Bug* movies. The original-design Beetle was taken out of production in Europe many years ago but since then has been produced under licence in Mexico and exported from there. An updated, modern design is now available but it is nowhere near as popular as the original was.

The Beetle was effectively replaced by the Golf which has been hugely popular and is now at the fifth generation level. The best sales have typically been of the higher specification models. The Golf GTi has always been popular.

VW has acquired Audi (more upmarket German cars that allow VW to overlap with BMW and Mercedes to some extent), Seat (Spain) and Skoda (Czech Republic). Seat assembled outdated Italian designs under licence before being acquired –

since when the business has been transformed with new, modern designs and a reputation for high quality. Skoda was one of those Eastern European manufacturers whose cars were the butt of many jokes for poor design and quality. That is no longer the case! VW shares platforms across its various brands to drive scale economies, and operates price differentials based on finishing touches and reputation.

At the same time VW has acquired the really upmarket Lamborghini (Italy) business with its associated Bugatti brand and introduced some expensive top-end-of-the-range cars. It also owns the UK's Bentley business (which was separated out of Rolls Royce) and which it has used to produce six Le Mans (24-hour endurance race) winners.

More recently VW has launched the Phaeton under its own brand. Some believe this is a 'bridge too far' for the company and thus very high risk. The Phaeton is custom-built. Buyers can opt for almost any feature imaginable – if they are willing to pay for it! They are invited over to the factory in Dresden where they select their ideal design and colour – their car is then completed within 48 hours. Its price is £68,000 – which some believe is too high for a car with the VW name on the front. China is a key target market. This development was championed by CEO Bernd Pischetsrieder who joined the company from BMW. He carried the responsibility for BMW's expensive investment in Rover, before it was divested for next to nothing.

▶

To put the company in context:

- VW sales have fallen as the German economy has stagnated
- The company has been forced to pursue extensive cost-cutting
- Luxury cars are cross-subsidized by mid-range models
- Productivity is clearly lower than that of Toyota and other sizeable mid-range producers
- The development costs of its new cars are relatively high
- Overheads in its relatively opulent factories are also high
- The reliability of VW cars is not as high as it used to be; and, somewhat inevitably
- Profits have fallen.

Supporters argue that VW has simply taken its eye off the ball in recent years and that with the new global strategies it can recover in strength. Opponents are more critical and believe VW has lost the plot, especially with the Phaeton. They believe VW should not have started manufacturing the Polo in China, which has brought about a number of problems, and that it should have developed a sports utility vehicle (SUV) or a 4-wheel drive model sooner than it did. The new Touareg off-road vehicle is a recent development.

In June 2004 VW announced it was proposing to move some components production to the United Arab Emirates in exchange for an equity investment. Some believed it was really being driven out of Europe by new EU regulations on carbon emissions which would place upward pressures on costs which VW could not readily embrace. Energy costs for manufacturing in the Gulf States are relatively low.

At the same time VW has expanded its car leasing activities – it now has the world's second largest vehicle leasing portfolio. VW believes there are two basic types of car buyer. First, those for whom cars are a means of transportation from A to B, with the least hassle. Brands are not that important when set alongside functionality and value. Second, those who enjoy cars and often drive from A to A for fun and enjoyment. Brands really do matter to them. Leasing can be ideal for the former customers. In addition, most profits in the industry do not come from the basic sale of the car in the first place, but from all the other associated activities.

## Questions

1. Do you believe VW has a cohesive, global strategy?
2. What suggestions do you have for future developments?

**Volkswagen** http://www.vw.com

**The Phaeton**

For more information call 01908 601187       © Copyright free for editorial purposes only

**Press and Public Relations**

**VW Phaeton**, a custom built luxury car. Have Volkswagen gone too far?

**Table 13.3** Classification of modes of market entry

| Indirect market entry | Strategies without foreign investment |
|---|---|
| ■ Unsolicited orders<br>■ Domestic-based intermediaries<br>    Courier/express services<br>    Export management companies<br>    Export houses<br>    Trading companies<br>    Piggybacking<br>    Brokers<br>    Jobbers | ■ Licensing<br>■ Franchising<br>■ Management contracts |
| **Direct market entry** | **Strategies with foreign investment** |
| Domestic-based intermediaries<br>■ Freight forwarders<br>■ Consortium exporting<br>■ Export department<br>Foreign-based intermediaries<br>■ Agents<br>■ Distributors | ■ Marketing subsidiary<br>■ Manufacturing subsidiary<br>■ Joint ventures<br>    Joint equity venture<br>    Contractual joint venture |

## 13.4.1 Ensuring successful market entry

Of course nothing can guarantee success; not even a monopoly situation in the long term, as many state-owned businesses have found to their cost throughout the world. The environment does not stand still. Market awareness and knowledge is important, as the following story illustrates.

> *For one company that attempted to exploit the Dutch market from a base in the UK, failure was based on poor market research. A showroom was opened in Holland to sell female clothing. The company attempted to simply transfer the product to the new market, and in so doing made the mistake in marketing of giving the market the wrong product. Colours and styles which had gone down well in England were found to be unacceptable in the Dutch market. The company also encountered problems with regard to the size of its garments. It did not take into account the difference in stature between customers in the two markets. The company found, too late, that the Dutch customer was taller and larger than its UK market. Formal market research would have revealed the special characteristics of the new market, and allowed the company to adapt its products to the fashion tastes of the Dutch buyers.*

> *In hindsight the company accepted it had learnt a lot:*

> *I think that if the company is going to go into the Dutch market then you have to sort of cater for their way of thinking. You maybe have to hire Dutch designers if you go into things like that because it's so specialized. They're different people – it's like the French, they have a different attitude towards fashion.*

However, the very best information-gathering exercise is only as good as the interpretation or spin put upon it by the individuals concerned. There is perhaps a rather understated view, which says that marketing cannot guarantee success, but that an enterprise will fail less badly because of it. Not everything goes smoothly all the time for market entry and the literature is full of famous errors. Failure can occur for all sorts of reasons e.g. poor intermediaries, poor communication, or not getting paid.

### 13.4.2 Export readiness

Few companies have the management resources, experience or financial resources to launch products globally. It is therefore inevitable that the choice of market entry options is more restricted for smaller and newer companies. It is also not possible to be prescriptive about the method of entry chosen. Different international markets require different solutions!

The starting point for understanding market entry decisions is the play-off between having a high level of control set against the cost of achieving this status. Most writers on this subject make the distinction between indirect and direct modes of entry. The difference between the two centres on the level of foreign (or direct) investment that is available for overseas expansion. For example, a new firm or a firm new to exporting may, for financial reasons, choose to use domestic intermediaries to respond to unsolicited orders. As these types of order grow in numbers and regularity, the company may then choose to appoint a representative in-country who will be given the task of actively seeking new orders.

**Indirect exporting**  According to McAuley (2001) 'the indirect method of exporting is often referred to as passive exporting or as being a result of an 'export pull' effect, since people outside the company stimulate the activity'. He goes on to suggest that the strategies that come under this category are 'responding to unsolicited or chance orders'. For some companies, this is the first introduction to international markets, which may stimulate them to explore the feasibility of exporting more seriously as the stage models would suggest. It does have that advantage of being new, unexpected business. It illustrates the fact that there are potential, as yet unreached, customers in the world, and it involves no product adaptation costs or promotion costs. The downside of this approach is that the company

> is not geared up for exporting, and therefore there are relatively high costs involved because of the learning curve which has to be gone through. For example, a one-off distribution channel will be relatively expensive as no economies of scale are available. The potential benefits of this initial involvement depend on the company's medium-term response to the unsolicited order.

### 13.4.3 Direct entry

The direct approach centres on finding and appointing in-country representatives, usually in the form of agents or distributors. This is an active form of exporting and it relies on using in-country intermediaries. Inevitably the commitment and investment required are greater than in direct exporting, but then again, the rewards are potentially greater.

The options involved are as shown in Table 13.4.

Whilst agents and distributors are the most common form of entry by newer growth firms, this form of representation requires management and control. Sometimes this is learnt the hard way!

The major limitation of working through an intermediary is that a firm will not own its distribution network or its customers within a foreign market. The most significant

**Table 13.4** Options for direct entry

| Agents | Generate customers for products on a commission basis | Exporter's control is high but the method involves close management if market coverage is to be achieved |
|---|---|---|
| Distributors | Take title of goods and earn a profit from the mark-up<br>Handle local distribution and marketing | Low level of initial control but offers rapid coverage |
| Direct selling | Supply to direct customers who order through catalogues, online or through trade fairs | Potentially high level of control but lack of country presence may limit penetration |
| Sales office | Exporter's own personnel actively target customers<br>Office handles all sales functions | Country presence helps develop sales but coverage may not be sufficient for larger markets such as the US |
| Subsidiary | Dedicated sales and operations may range from assemblage to locally sourced manufacturing | High potential control but coverage can be limited |

impact of this is that the exporter can be starved of information on market trends and competitor activities. This is because it is in the interest of an intermediary to control that information.

It is worth noting that in fast-moving markets or with products at the early stages of growth, access to information can be crucial to gaining entry. For this reason, licensing and joint ventures are more common methods of entry for technology-based businesses.

Agents and distributors will usually seek exclusivity for a territory. The difference between an agent and a distributor is that the distributor will, like a foreign customer, be placing orders, holding stock and accepting responsibility for the sale of goods. Despite best intentions, a growth business with a limited track record and product innovation is less likely to attract a distributor who is willing to hold stock. Agency agreements are, initially, the more common form of entry, especially where more than one market is being addressed. In this case, most agreements are set out between sole agents rather than the larger multichannel agency that is more likely to deal with public limited companies.

It is always important to find an agent for whom the company's business is significant – such that they will provide adequate support and prioritize the products amongst the range they represent and promote. At the same time it is important to remember that no agent will willingly expose himself to the risk of being supplanted by a branch of the company's own sales organization. Exclusivity is usually central to negotiations for the agency agreement, but many unsuspecting firms give away too much territory to a single agency.

In market situations where there is slow growth for the company's product in an otherwise high growth market – which does happen – there is a real likelihood the agent concerned is either overstretched or the wrong agent. By this we mean someone for whom the products and the business are insignificant or low priority.

On the other hand, high market growth can create pressures within the company to take over the territory or replace the agent. This may often require compensating the agent handsomely, especially where local legislation exists to protect his position. Elsewhere, the situation may arise where the company wishes to expand its product line or else diversify into a quite different product. If the local agent finds himself unable to meet this new expansion, but still holds a company agreement to exclusivity of sales territory, then contracts will need renegotiating or terminating.

These factors may explain why, when entering a new market, it is comparatively easy to find an agent but extremely difficult to find the one that is right for the company. An agent is paid commission only on sales, so loyalty rests purely on the company currently providing him with the greatest earnings. As agents may represent a number of separate companies and product lines, this may be – or it may become – a problem. Meanwhile, the company holds responsibility for whatever unsold inventory is held by the agent, while at the same time being virtually deprived of market information. This can be frustrating and points to the need for preparation when recruiting agents.

Other direct entry choices tend to rely on strategic alliances or partnering relationships, which can take many forms.

### 13.4.4 Other direct entry choices

**Licensing** refers to agreements that provide unilateral technology access, frequently through patents, to a licensee in return for a fee. Cross-licensing is a bilateral form of licensing where companies usually swap packages of patents to avoid patent infringements or to exchange existing, codified technological knowledge.

**Second-sourcing agreements** regulate the transfer of technology through technical product specifications in order to produce exact copies of products. In the case of mutual second sourcing this transfer takes place between two or more companies that transfer technical specifications of different products.

**Customer-supplier relationships** are co-production contracts and co-makership relations that basically regulate long-term contracts between vertically-related, but independent, companies that collaborate in production and supply. A specific case of customer–supplier relationships are R&D contracts where one company is subcontracted by another company to perform particular R&D projects.

**Joint R&D** pacts and joint development agreements are contractual relationships through which companies perform jointly funded R&D projects, or in the case of joint development agreements, jointly work on the development of new products or processes.

**Joint ventures** are the combinations of the economic interests of at least two separate companies in a distinct organizational entity, where profits and losses are usually shared in accordance with the equity investments by the parent companies. Joint ventures act as separate organizations that have regular company objectives such as production, marketing and sales, but if relevant also R&D, as a specific objective of the partnership.

It is not always possible to distinguish between these alternatives, and experienced companies will often mix and match the methods according to their market and their resources. The characteristic that all the methods share is that they promote collaboration through two or more firms. The main factor which increasingly encourages and enables this form of businesses activity is information communications technology (ICT). This not only allows businesses to trade (electronically) across boundaries, it has also facilitated new forms of organisations such as virtual companies.

It can be argued that the world has become too large and the competition too strong for even the largest multinational corporations to do everything independently! Technologies are converging and markets becoming integrated, making the costs and risks of both product and market development ever greater. Partly as a reaction to and partly in order to exploit these developments, entrepreneurial management has become more pragmatic about what type of alliance it takes to be successful in global markets.

The emerging business model, especially amongst technology-centred companies, favours the formation of strategic alliances with suppliers, customers, competitors, and companies in other industries. These alliances can take many forms, ranging from informal co-operation to joint ownership of plants and operations.

We might contrast this with the approach of Sanyo (Minicase 13.6) which has chosen to supply other companies with more recognizable names.

## Minicase 13.6 Sanyo

Sanyo is an innovative and pioneering Japanese electronics company, and a global leader for certain consumer electronics goods. Once best known for its low prices, Sanyo is described as unusual amongst Japanese businesses – it drops products and businesses that underperform rather than persisting with them. Sanyo is the world's leading manufacturer of digital still cameras, a very high growth business – it has a 30 per cent share. This fact would not be realized by looking at the camera displays in stores around the world – the vast majority (95 per cent) of the cameras it makes are marketed with other leading brand names attached. This approach helps overcome the relative weakness of its own brand, when compared with other leading Japanese electronics companies – and also provides a revenue stream to fund research and investment. It is also a leader with optical pick-ups, a key component of CD and DVD players, where it has a 40 per cent share. Some 40 of its various semiconductor products enjoy niche dominance and it produces the rechargeable batteries for 50 per cent of the world's mobile phones.

Sanyo is successful because it focuses its resources on carefully identified opportunities:

■ It concentrates on where it can be number one globally. 'Unless you choose what to focus on, you will not survive' (Yukinori Kuwano, CEO).

■ It rates all its businesses by their growth potential and achievable margins – basically following the portfolio approach discussed in Chapter 9.

■ It constantly searches for new opportunities, especially acquisitions that would strengthen critical mass and market (segment) dominance.

■ Sanyo has also developed a joint venture in China with Haier, China's largest consumer electronics group, to provide access to this important and growing market.

### Question

1. What do you think are the relative merits and disadvantages of Sanyo's strategy of producing digital still cameras for some of the leading brand names?

**Sanyo** http://www.sanyo.com

## 13.5 Franchising

A number of prominent companies have used franchising to open up access to a global market without the financial and other resource implications of, say, acquisitions. We mentioned it earlier in this part of the book and here we explore it in greater detail.

In most developed economies franchising is widely used for operating businesses. It is a system that has enabled organisations to develop some of the largest brands around, for example, McDonald's, Dyno-Rod and Holiday Inn. Moreover, the governments of some developing countries actively encourage business people to use franchising as a way of fostering entrepreneurship. The franchisor gains national and international distribution for the business idea much more quickly than if the expansion had been undertaken through fully-owned outlets. Also, as self-employed individuals, the franchisees, who supply most of the capital for the expansion, are usually more motivated to work hard at building their businesses.

Franchising is not new; the emergence of the modern concept of franchising occurred in the United States just after the Civil War with the activities of the Singer Sewing Machine Company. However, it was not until the beginning of the twentieth century that this method of business development gained wider acceptance. The automobile industry and the soft drink industry were the first to adopt the so-called product and trademark franchising. These include arrangements in which franchisees are granted the right to distribute a manufacturer's product within a specified territory or at a specific location, generally with the use of the manufacturer's identifying name or trademark, in exchange for fees or royalties.

By the 1930s the petroleum industry was franchising gasoline/petrol service stations. The real expansion of franchising, though, took place in the US in the1950s, with the appearance of 'business format franchising'. This type of franchising is also known as second generation franchising, and it is characterized by an ongoing relationship between the franchisor and the franchisee. This includes the product or service, the trademark and effectively the entire business concept – a marketing strategy and plan, operating manuals and standards, quality control and a continuing process of assistance and guidance. In the 1970s companies increasingly saw the international potential of business format franchising.

Under a business format franchise the franchisees operate the franchise in a standard way under a common trademarked name. The kinds of businesses operating under such a system can include fast food restaurants, courier services, cleaning services, employment or estate agents, kitchen or bathroom installers.

Initially the expansion took place in markets which were most accessible or had good market potential, low cultural distance and the existence of a developed service sector. Thus, Canada became a prime target for international expansion, followed later by the UK and Australia. Development of franchising in Japan was facilitated by the use of a master franchise agreement, which reduced the need for direct involvement in the development of operations in what was, especially for Americans, a very unique culture. A master franchisee usually has responsibility for more than one outlet and is commonly totally responsible for the development of the franchised business (through other franchisees) in an area.

There are, then, a number of other models which are dependent on franchise relationships:

1. *Manufacturer-Retailer* – Where the retailer, as franchisee, sells the franchisor's product directly to the public (for example, new motor vehicle dealerships).
2. *Manufacturer-Wholesaler* – Where the franchisee, under licence, manufactures and distributes the franchisor's product (for example soft drink bottling arrangements).
3. *Wholesaler-Retailer* – Where the retailer, as franchisee, purchases products for retail sale from a franchisor wholesaler (typically a wholesale co-operative set up by the franchisee retailers, who are contractually obliged to purchase from it). Examples include hardware and automotive product stores.
4. *Retailer-Retailer* – Where the franchisor markets a service or a produce under a common name and standardized system through a network of franchisees. This is the classic business format franchise.

**Why businesses franchise** Companies can expand in a number of ways, and full ownership of new outlets is perhaps the most obvious way forward. However, having fully assessed the costs and risks of expansion, some organisations decide to follow the franchising route. Why? Three key reasons are resource scarcity, agency theory and risk spreading.

*Resource scarcity* means that a company needs access to management talent or other knowledge not available to them, and at the same time may not have a large amount of money to invest in the expansion. *Agency theory* is about the way in which those people who manage the outlet are motivated and monitored. Because franchisees have considerable financial investments at stake, and because they receive profits from the outlet, they are more motivated than managers of company-owned units to work hard to make the franchise profitable. *Risk spreading*, compensating for the decisions surrounding any expansion, is accomplished through franchising. The investment risk is lowered through franchising compared with joint ventures, which can involve large capital investments and legal complications. Franchising creates sales and brand recognition at a much lower cost. In international expansion the political risk and the overall risk of failure are primarily borne by the franchisee.

The timescale required by franchising is seen as faster than self-owned expansion, which will often require more monitoring. The process of establishing a chain of franchises increases the knowledge of the franchisor, and the time required for each new outlet is reduced as expertise increases. With experience the franchisor develops sensitivity to site selection, store layout, procurement and operating policies appropriate to particular environmental settings.

## 13.6 Constraints on internationalization

It is worth bearing in mind that not all companies are in a position to take advantage of all the international opportunities which may present themselves. Indeed, it is possible that not all opportunities will even be recognised by the decision-makers in the company. It is this perceptual variation and ability to process information which helps to create the variability on the map of international activities.

Morgan and Katsikeas (1997) identified four barriers that explain why business owners are discouraged from participating in international business:

■ First, an insufficient pool of resources can create strategic obstacles.

- Second, a firm's cost base and margins can lead to operational (and logistical) obstacles.

- Third, a lack of fit between a firm's strategy and its environment may result in limited knowledge of market opportunities, creating informational obstacles.

- Fourth, a firm may be unable to maintain necessary interactions with key parties because of limited resources leading to process-based obstacles.

Little, quoted in Yanacek (1988), has identified ten constraints faced by companies marketing products or services internationally. These are:

- Building distribution networks
- Designing market entry strategies
- Identifying market opportunities
- Dealing with political and commercial risks
- Obtaining information on alternatives to direct exporting
- Securing working capital and export financing
- Collecting foreign receivables
- Providing after-sales customer service
- Dealing with tariff barriers and quotas
- Dealing with export laws, regulations and procedures.

Of course, it is also worth remembering that not all companies wish to become internationally active. This can occur for a variety of reasons, some of which, particularly in smaller companies, can be associated with the personal characteristics of the strategic leader or founding entrepreneur. Some find it difficult to delegate responsibility and, therefore, it is difficult for the company to grow. Others have reached what some authors have called the 'comfort level', and do not wish to see an expansion of the business. While outsiders may wish to see growth, and while it may be frustrating to watch a company effectively underachieve, it is also dangerous to force change upon such a company.

In the Western Isles of Scotland there is a company which produces soft toys, particularly teddy bears. This is a small company operating in a remote area where any employment is welcomed. Production is limited as the toys are hand-made. During a visit to Scotland executives from Disney who had seen the company's products, and liked them, approached the company to investigate the possibility of them becoming a supplier to Disney. The executives were taken aback to find that the person they spoke to had never heard of Disney – nor was the company interested in doing a deal on the grounds the volume Disney required was way beyond their capacity. This story raises a number of interesting points. For one thing, it shows that even a global brand as powerful as Disney can still be taken down a peg or two. More significantly, there is the lost potential for bringing new business to a remote community. Had the motives and personal attitudes been different at the company, then perhaps an opportunity might have been explored to machine-make the teddy bears as a special line for Disney. There could be marketing kudos in the fact that they were linked to a hand-made tradition. This would require knowledge of branding and product line differentiation, but unfortunately this option was never explored.

As well as what might be termed these 'softer' constraints, there are the more traditional ones related to worries about:

- Resources – mainly finance and people
- Time available
- Market uncertainties
- Marketing costs
- Payment terms
- Exchange rates
- The cost of insurance
- Information shortages
- Political uncertainties
- Cultural differences.

Any organization, then, faces many decisions in its attempt to internationalize its activities:

- what volume of trade is desirable?
- how many countries to market in?
- which countries to select?

The degree of market attractiveness will be influenced by a number of factors related to geographic, demographic, economic, technological and sociocultural characteristics. Once it has evaluated the relative attractiveness of the potential markets in relation to the company's product/service a company should be better placed to select those markets where the 'fit' is apparently best. For each business, the selection of entry mode will then be linked to their international strategy, which in turn is influenced by motives and constraints. For example, the use of export or international production strategies, the use of intermediaries or how much control over marketing activities the business wishes to retain. There will be also issues regarding expected payback on the investment, the degree of flexibility required and how the strategy fits with broader business objectives. All of these issues prepare the way for one of the dominant decisions of the internationalization process, namely, the mode of market entry decision.

In briefly exploring the constraints on internationalization, it is clear that they can act as barriers to the initiation of international activity as well as affecting the process of international business by influencing the choice of market entry.

## 13.7 Future influences on international business

The international business environment will continue to evolve and the activities of individual firms will be shaped by the interaction of external and internal forces. Within Europe, for example, the current expansion of the EU and the further development of the Russian Federation will have a significant impact. More generally, global trends will include the creation of enterprises based on the knowledge-based economy. The preceding discussion has described the background against which managers and marketers act their part in the global economy. This background, as we have seen, is complex, full of uncertainty and subject to change which is often rapid and unpredictable. Organizations must be alive to the opportunities which come along and be prepared to take advantage of windows of opportunity as they open. This is just as relevant for **small and medium-sized enterprises** as it is for the multinational.

Three decades of constant progress in information and communication technologies have triggered a complex pattern of change in international business relationships. This technological revolution is shaping the process of globalization by providing new tools and infrastructures with which entrepreneurial companies capture global opportunities. Unlike previous transformations, the international economy now encompasses global consumers who have local tastes, preferences and servicing requirements. The concluding section in this chapter looks at the knowledge economy and how this will affect business models and business methods in the coming years. Particular attention is paid to sectors of the economy that are already global in their scope of operations. It also examines the 'virtual firms'. The virtual firm is seen as an embodiment of the entrepreneurial business in a global economy.

## 13.7.1  The knowledge economy

In 1988, Peter Drucker wrote an article in the *Harvard Business Review* entitled 'The Coming of the New Organisation' in which he defined the term knowledge management as being the criteria that would define companies in the next 20 years. The knowledge economy differs from the traditional economy in several key respects. The most significant influence is that knowledge is measured not of scarcity, but rather of abundance. Unlike most company resources that deplete when used, information and knowledge can be shared, and actually grow through application.

This has the effect of encouraging business alliances across international frontiers. In this sense, the effect of location is diminished. Using appropriate technology and methods, virtual marketplaces and virtual organisations can be created that offer benefits of speed and agility, of round the clock operation and of global reach. These characteristics require new thinking and approaches by entrepreneurial companies, policy-makers, senior executives and knowledge workers alike. To do so, though, requires leadership and risk taking, against the prevailing and slow changing attitudes and practices of existing institutions and business practice.

There are several types of knowledge – 'knowing' a fact is little different from 'information', but 'knowing' a skill, or 'knowing' that something might affect market conditions is something that, despite attempts of knowledge engineers to codify such knowledge, has an important human dimension. It is some combination of context sensing, personal memory and cognitive processes. Measuring the knowledge asset, therefore, means putting a value on people, both as individuals, but, more importantly, on their collective capability, and other factors such as the embedded intelligence in an organisation's computer systems. Unlike information, knowledge is less tangible and depends on human cognition and awareness.

Like most assets, knowledge is only valuable if it can be transmuted into goods and services that people will pay for. Here we get into leveraging knowledge, looking at adding value through its development.

## 13.7.2  Virtual companies

Knowledge management combined with the enabling technology associated with e-business is changing nearly all that companies do, from the procurement of supplies to the delivery of finished products and services. New types of competitors, value-added services and new delivery channels are shifting the boundaries between customers, suppliers, partners and competitors, and profoundly altering industry value chains.

Arguably, web-based organizations exist because market conditions are changing. Customers demand more specialized products which means that companies have to develop a wider range. At the same time they expect a high degree of customization as well as localization to suit conditions that prevail in any particular market. Virtual companies are able to command resources beyond those immediately available to them through collaboration and alliances – a strategy ideally suited to those organizations who wish to cross geographic frontiers.

Specialization and individualization of products leads to shorter production cycles which in turn increase the investment and costs of R&D, production, and sales. As a counter balance to this trend, information communications technology (ICT) has dramatically improved the speed, quantity and quality of communication and especially the co-ordination of economic actions and transactions. In this respect ICT can be viewed as an enabler and at the same time as a driving force towards the virtual organization. A key objective of a virtual company is to improve its flexibility – the kind of flexibility needed to meet the fast changing market conditions. In order to decrease complexity and increase flexibility companies seek to create, nurture and exploit relevant core competencies. This strategy means that companies concentrate on what they can do best – they specialise in certain areas, they develop and constantly improve their core competencies.

However, as we pointed out in Part Two, a core competence on its own does not create any value; therefore, companies have to search internationally for value chains where they can integrate their core competencies. Those core competencies are then flexibly configured in different value chains whereby those value chains are made of many different core competencies provided by different economic actors, which leads theoretically to an optimum value creation process.

In conclusion, the evolution of virtual organisations is forced by changing market conditions: in particular, the increased requirement to offer specialized products, to reduce the time to market process, the increased international competition (globalization), and the need to satisfy individual customer needs to which organizations have to respond. Some commentators expect multinationals to be losers in this world order. Others anticipate that the large global companies will form strategic alliances with the small technology innovators and between them they will have the capability to squeeze out the existing market leaders. This process of change offers an increasing number of opportunities for entrepreneurial firms that are knowledge-based and willing to play on the global stage.

# SUMMARY

All strategic options can have an international dimension – ranging from exporting to a global corporation where products are manufactured in various places around the world and then marketed globally as appropriate.

Some companies will 'go global' with existing products and services they market overseas – others will tailor complete strategies for local markets.

The motivation to 'go international' can be internal (organization-driven) or external and driven by environmental opportunities. The deciding factors can thus be push or pull and involve either a proactive or reactive stance.

The key issues in developing an international strategy concern:

■ Products
■ Markets
■ Entry considerations
■ Timing.

The main considerations then are:

■ Marketing – the global and multi-domestic approaches
■ Finance
■ Structure and location – where to produce in relation to market opportunities
■ Culture – which differs between countries.

There are useful stage models which provide some insight into a typical (if not universally adopted) path to internationalization.

Similarly there are a number of market entry opportunities, although sometimes there will be a given element which acts as a constraint.

Entry into a market can be either direct or indirect and it may or may not require foreign investment.

Good overseas agents (a crucial element of the direct approach) are worth their weight in gold, but it is all too easy to appoint the wrong agent.

Strategic alliances can also be very significant in developing internationally.

Franchising is an approach used by many countries to develop internationally. It can allow for controlled investment and more limited resource implications.

Not all options are always going to be available or suitable. Constraints thus limit opportunities – here resources, costs and knowledge may be relevant. The ability to gain market access will always be critical.

Some companies will deliberately avoid the risks and uncertainty associated with internationalization.

Finally, we outlined how e-commerce and the knowledge economy is changing the nature of global strategy by opening up new and exciting opportunities.

## QUESTIONS AND RESEARCH ASSIGNMENTS

1. Revisiting Chapter 11, for each of the following strategic alternatives, list why you think an organization might select this particular strategy as a means of international growth. What would they expect to gain, and where are the problems and limitations? If you can, think of an example of each one from your own experience:

   ■ market development
   ■ product development
   ■ innovation
   ■ horizontal integration
   ■ vertical integration
   ■ concentric diversification
   ■ conglomerate diversification.

2. What are the relative advantages and disadvantages of direct market entry as opposed to indirect entry strategies?

3. What are the essential differences between an export, an international and a global organization?

## INTERNET AND LIBRARY PROJECTS

1. Consider the most appropriate strategy for a sizeable UK-based company with international ambitions in the following industries (assume that your choice could be implemented):
   - steel
   - pharmaceuticals
   - civil aircraft
   - ladies' cosmetics/fragrances.

2. For an organization of your choice, trace the changes of international strategy and strategic direction over a period of time. Relate these changes to any changes in strategic leadership, structure and, wherever possible, culture.

3. Sony is renowned as an innovative company within the consumer electronics industry, and its success has depended substantially on televisions, videos and hi-fi equipment. In recent years Sony has followed a strategy of globalization and diversification, arguably in related product areas. The international strategy has been called global localization; Sony aims to be a global company presented locally, and this involves devolving authority away from Tokyo and expanding manufacturing and R&D around the world.

   How does Sony achieve this?

   **Sony** http://www.sony.com

4 Abrakebabra is Ireland's premier fast food chain. It has grown through franchising, but in the early days it struggled to get the franchising arrangements correct. Can you ascertain why? How 'international' could this business be?

   **Abrakebabra** http://www.abrakebabra.com

5. Find two businesses that have grown internationally through franchising, one a product business and the other a service business. Compare and contrast their development. To what extent are they similar and to what extent different?

## Further reading

Levitt, T (1983) The globalization of markets, *Harvard Business Review*, May–June.

Douglas, S and Wind, Y (1987) The myth of globalization, *Columbia Journal of World Business*, Winter.

Bartlett, C and Ghoshal, S (1987) Managing across borders – new organizational responses, *Sloan Management Review*, Fall.

Porter, ME (1990) *The Competitive Advantage of Nations*, The Free Press.

## References

Bartlett, C and Ghoshal, S (1989) *Managing Across Borders: The Transnational Solution*, Harvard Business School Press.

Bartlett, C and Ghoshal, S (1992) What is a global manager? *Harvard Business Review*, September–October.

Chandler, AD (1990) The enduring logic of industrial success, *Harvard Business Review*, March–April.

Drucker, PF (1988) The coming of the new organization, *Harvard Business Review*, January–February.

Ghauri, P (2000) internationalization of the firm, in Tayeb, M (ed.) *International Business – Theories, Policies and Practices*, FT-Prentice Hall.

Gupta, A and Govindarajan, V (1998) How to build a global presence, *Financial Times Mastering Global Business*, No 1.

Hofstede, G (1991) *Cultures and Organization: Software of the Mind*, McGraw Hill.

Johanson, J and Wiedersheim-Paul, F (1975) The internationalization of the firm – four Swedish cases, *Journal of Management Studies*, 12 (3).

Joynt, P and Welch, L (1985) A strategy for small business internationalisation, *International Marketing Review*, 2 (3).

Kay, JA (1990) Identifying the strategic market, *Business Strategy Review*, Spring.

McAuley, A (2001) *International Marketing – Consuming Globally, Thinking Locally*, John Wiley.

Morgan, RE and Katsikeas, CS (1997) Obstacles to export initiation and expansion, *International Journal of Management Science*, 25.

Ohmae, K (1990) *The Borderless World*, Harper.

Porter, ME (1990) The *Competitive Advantage of Nations,* Free Press.

Yanacek, F (1988) The Road to Exports, *Transportation and Distribution*, 29 (2).

# Failure, Consolidation and Recovery Strategies

Ultimate business failure implies closure or liquidation – the organization has failed to satisfy certain key stakeholders and it has ceased to be financially viable. It is beyond turning around by new management. This happens with many small businesses and it also happens with much larger and established organizations. However, the larger the organization the greater the general likelihood that at least some part can be rescued. Where the fortunes of a business have sunk to a crisis level and radical changes of strategy are required, this clearly also represents failure – even if with sound retrenchment and turnaround strategies the business can be rescued. It is a failure of strategic management because mistakes have been made, in the form of either poor judgement or relative inactivity in the face of a need to change. If a business, or a part of a business, is sold because it is unprofitable, this may well represent failure by the current management team. The assumption is that the business has a stronger future in different hands. However, one should not assume that all divestments of this nature imply failure – they may simply represent poor strategic fit and perhaps a past misjudgement. Hence the study of failure here concerns why the performance of a business can sink to a crisis level which demands either drastic remedial action, sale or closure.

Poor strategic leadership, insufficient control of the essential aspects of financial management and the failure to be competitive are the key issues behind corporate decline and failure. All of them are manifested in the opening case on Laker Airways.

At any given time certain industries will provide attractive growth prospects for those companies who already compete in them, and for potential newcomers. At the same time, however, other industries will be in terminal decline. This might be taking place slowly or rapidly. In the case of slow decline, profitable opportunities may still exist for those companies that can relate best to changing market needs. Where decline is rapid, prospects are likely to be very limited. A third group of industries might be undergoing significant change, and the companies that can adapt effectively will be able to survive and grow. An example of this can be found in shipbuilding, an industry which has migrated to yards in the Far East. Some European yards have thrived by switching to building modern cruise ships for an industry now flourishing by adapting to changes in holiday patterns and the age profile of the population at large.

Any recovery from a difficult situation will be related to, first, improved marketing effectiveness, competitiveness and revenue, and second, managing the organization more efficiently in order to reduce costs. Where these changes in functional and competitive strategies prove inadequate, something more drastic will be required. Retrenchment strategies aim to increase revenue and reduce costs by concentrating and consolidating – these involve changes in functional strategies. Turnaround strategies relate to changes in competitive strategies and frequently feature repositioning for competitive advantage. Retrenchment and turnaround strategies are often collectively called recovery strategies. Divestment occurs when part of an organization is sold, normally because it is diverting resources which could be used more effectively, but sometimes just to raise money. These result in changes to the company's corporate strategy.

This chapter ends by exploring recovery and divestment strategies in greater detail, considering first the overall feasibility of recovery and different recovery situations. These issues are of primary concern to companies that are already experiencing difficulties and showing symptoms of decline. The last section looks at strategic alternatives for declining industries, which is relevant for companies that may be currently successful or unsuccessful in a situation of change. The closing Minicase (Arcadia) emphasizes just how difficult sustained turnaround can be.

**CASE**

## Minicase 14.1  Laker Airways

Freddie Laker, who became Sir Freddie in 1978, was an entrepreneur and a pioneer in the competitive international air transport industry. He was a well-quoted self-publicist whose commercial exploits brought him fame and recognition. He introduced cheap transatlantic air travel, providing travel opportunities for many people who previously had not been able to afford the fares, but his business collapsed in the early 1980s. At the time he blamed others for his demise and, while there is substance in his argument, the fact remains that he had personally sown the seeds of his downfall

with a flawed strategy. However, he would later bounce back again.

Laker was born in 1922 in Canterbury. His trigger for a life in aviation was a sight of the Hindenberg and a Handley-Page biplane flying over his house when he was still a boy. He subsequently learned to fly and served with the Air Transport Auxiliary in the Second World War. In 1953 he began his first business, Channel Air Bridge Ltd, to sell air transportation of vehicles, passengers and cargo (including live animals) on the same aircraft. He was involved in the design

▶

and development of Gatwick Airport, before he helped to develop and run British United Airways (BUA) in 1960. At this time BUA was the largest aircraft company in the private sector. His next venture, Laker Airways in 1966, was a small independent company 'operated on a shoestring' which offered inclusive package holidays and provided charter flights for organizations who could book all the seats on a plane and flights for tour companies who did not own their own airline. He was the first all-jet carrier in the UK. Laker's stated intention was to stay small: 'If we get any bigger than six planes you can kick my arse.' From a marketing perspective, Laker was always pioneering new ideas.

In the 1970s his ambitions changed and he became determined to 'try a new market and offer transport to a lot more people'. At this time the only cheap air fares across the Atlantic were charter flights, whereby travellers had to be a member of some sponsoring organization for at least six months before flying. The international carriers operated a price-fixing cartel organized by the International Air Transport Association (IATA) with the connivance of all governments concerned. Charter flight regulations tended to be abused, and consequently the major carriers fought for stricter monitoring which brought about a decline. Laker conceived Skytrain, a 'no booking, no frills' operation with prices significantly below those offered by the major airlines, who naturally opposed his idea.

Laker first applied to the Civil Aviation Authority (CAA) for a licence in 1971 and was refused. In late 1972 he was given permission as long as he flew out of London's Stansted airport, although his base was on the other side of London at Gatwick. Delaying tactics involving British and US airlines, the UK Labour government, the US government and the American equivalent of the CAA meant that the first flight did not take place until September 1977, when Skytrain was launched with enormous publicity, this time from Gatwick. In this period oil prices had increased dramatically and Skytrain, although still under £100 for a single fare, was double the price estimated in 1971. In turn, the Skytrain fare was well

under half the cost of the cheapest fare offered by IATA carriers, who subsequently had to reduce their fares in the face of this new competition.

Although they claimed that they did this reluctantly, it had a devastating impact on Laker, who accused them of adopting a predatory pricing strategy purely to try and drive him out of business. Skytrain's competitive strategy, and apparent advantage, was its low price resulting from its low cost base, but its service package was clearly inferior to that of the major carriers. When the price gap was narrowed, Skytrain became less attractive to customers and its early competitive advantage was not sustainable.

Skytrain made £2 million profits in its first year of operation, but difficulties experienced when it was extended to Los Angeles in 1978 effectively wiped out the profitability. In 1979 Laker became a fully licensed transatlantic carrier and for the first time was able to pre-sell reserved seats. Laker's confidence grew, and anticipating that he would be given permission to fly more routes around the world he ordered ten Airbus A-300s and five McDonnell Douglas DC10s at a total cost of £300 million. Eventually this was to bring about his downfall. Laker was already using DC10s for Skytrain and when the US government grounded all DC10s for checks in 1979 Laker lost £13 million in revenue. In 1980 he failed to win licences to fly Skytrain in Europe and to Hong Kong, although he did begin services from Prestwick and Manchester and to Miami.

Profits of £2.2 million were reported for 1980–81, but significantly three-quarters of this came from favourable currency movements. By 1981 the pound was falling against the dollar, demand was declining, revenue was down, but the debt interest payments, mostly in dollars, were rising. There were, in effect, too many planes and not enough passengers flying the Atlantic. The major airlines wanted fares to rise, but Skytrain remained the force that kept them low. Laker managed to renegotiate some interest payments and a cash injection from McDonnell Douglas, but he also had to increase fares and sell his Airbuses. He was left with a break-even level of virtually all the seats on every Skytrain, but was able to fill only one-third of them. When the receiver was called in (February 1982) Laker had debts of some £270 million.

Laker had pioneered cheap transatlantic air fares, which have stayed in different guises since his collapse, but he made the mistake of becoming overconfident. The man who originally intended to stay small went for growth. At the same time he was determined to retain total control of his company and therefore raised loan capital against very limited assets rather than seeking outside equity funding. The interest payments brought him down, particularly as he raised most of the money in dollars without adequate cover against currency fluctuations. Finally, as something of a buccaneering character described by one airline executive as a man who 'a few hundred years ago would have brass earrings, a beard and a cutlass', he underestimated the power of the vested interests who opposed him. Had their opposition not delayed the introduction of Skytrain by six years, maybe things would have turned out differently.

A bitter Sir Freddie moved to Florida, and by the early 1990s he was back. In 1992 he began regular flights to and from the Bahamas from his new hub; and then, in 1996, he returned to the UK with return charter flights to Gatwick from Orlando. This time he intended to compete on service as well as discounted prices – he had learned a hard lesson. He negotiated convenient take-off and landing times and offered above-normal baggage allowances. His drinks (in crystal glasses) and food (served on china with stainless steel cutlery) were to be superior to most other charter flights. Would the package prove sufficiently different and would he be able to fly his small fleet of DC10s reliably? Yet again, all would not go smoothly.

**Questions**

1. How much of Freddie Laker's downfall was the result of his own misjudgements and how much external forces?
2. To what extent were the pluses and minuses of Freddie Laker's business career built into his entrepreneurial personality?

## 14.1 Introduction: failure in context

In broad terms it could be argued that a company is failing if it does not meet the objectives set for it by its stakeholders, or if it produces outputs that are considered undesirable by those associated with it. The outcome may not be ultimate failure, closure or liquidation, however. When the failure or the decline reaches a certain level, or continues for a certain length of time: this should act as a trigger for remedial action. Such action might be spurned, of course, or prove inadequate, such that the business deteriorates and is finally liquidated.

A company which polluted or harmed the natural environment in some way would be classified as unsuccessful – and maybe even perceived as a failure – by certain stakeholders, but it would not necessarily fail financially and go out of business. Companies sometimes develop and launch new products that fail because very few people buy them – the Ford Edsel car and Strand cigarettes are well-quoted examples. In this respect the companies are unsuccessful with particular competitive strategies, but again they may not necessarily experience corporate failure as a result.

Corporate failure, liquidation and the lack of success should not then be seen as synonymous terms. A private-sector, profit-seeking organization would certainly be classified as a failure if it ended up in liquidation and was closed down with its assets sold off piecemeal. A similar company might be unsuccessful and in decline, but able to avoid liquidation. Appropriate strategic action that addresses the causes of the decline may generate recovery. For example, the major shareholders might insist upon the appointment of a new strategic leader, or the financial or competitive weaknesses might be acted upon. Such a company might also be acquired by another, and this may be because the shareholders are happy to sell their shares or because the company has been placed in receivership and the receiver has arranged the sale of the business as a going concern. Receivership occurs when a business is unable to pay its creditors, for example its suppliers or bank loan interest. The receiver is normally a professional accountant and is charged with saving the business if it is possible to do so.

In a similar way a non-profit-seeking organization could be closed down or provided with new leadership and direction on the insistence of its major financial stakeholders or trustees.

A company might be relatively unsuccessful compared with its competitors for a prolonged period if the key stakeholders allow it, but it is never perceived to be failing. For example, a small private company whose shares are not quoted on the stock exchange might be making only very limited profits and growing at a rate slower than its industry, but its owners may be happy for it to stay in existence as long as it is solvent. This could be because the owners are drawing substantial earnings and not reinvesting to build a future – for them the business exists to provide them with a lavish lifestyle. In the English football league a large number of clubs, particularly outside the Premier League, fail to make any profit on their footballing activities because their crowds are too low, but other commercial activities, sponsorship, sales of players – and particularly benevolent directors – keep them in business. However, such a lack of success consistently will weaken the company, cause it to exhibit symptoms of decline (discussed below) and may ultimately lead to failure. Top football league clubs in countries such as England, Italy and Spain have all been living beyond their means, particularly in paying players a far greater salary than normal cash flow management would dictate. Inflated and unpredictable television and Champions League revenues have all led to potential major failures for clubs such as Leeds United, Barcelona and Lazio. Minicase 14.2 looks in detail at the rapid collapse of Leeds United.

The forthcoming sections look at what factors typically lead to corporate decline and failure and at how managers might realize that their company is heading for failure unless remedial action is taken. A **turnaround strategy** for companies in trouble will be considered in detail in this chapter.

## Minicase 14.2  Leeds United Football Club                                    GB

Under manager Don Revie, Leeds United enjoyed their so-called 'Glory Days' in the 1960s and early 1970s, when they were successful in both England and Europe. In 1974 Revie left to become England manager. Six years later – after five changes of manager – the club was relegated from the first to the second division. In 1982, with Eddie Gray (a star player from the Revie era) now installed as manager, crowd trouble and continuing poor performance made this a low period in the club's history. Another ex-star player, Billy Bremner, who lasted until 1987, replaced Gray. Gray retained a support role and in 2004 was again caretaker manager as Leeds struggled to avoid relegation from the (now) Premier League, having just been sold in a last ditch attempt to avoid possible liquidation.

With Howard Wilkinson as manager, Leeds gained promotion and became League Champions in 1991/2, the season before Division One became the Premier League. Fortunes continued to be cyclical and George Graham, who left in 1996 to manage Tottenham Hotspur, replaced Wilkinson. David O'Leary, who was deputy manager, took over in 1998. By this time Leeds United had been acquired by external investors and was, in reality, a PLC, Leeds Sporting. The new chairman, Peter Ridsdale, had been managing director of a retail chain which was a major club sponsor. Some commentators were astonished that Ridsdale reportedly offered George Graham a salary package of £1 million a year in an attempt to persuade him to stay. O'Leary's contract was, however, also worth £6 million over five years. Leeds was successful, in part due to a number of young players who had been recruited as youths in the Graham years. However, by 1999, leading players were asking for £50,000 per week salaries. The wage bill was spiralling upwards and the club also began to spend millions of pounds to bring in new players. Both Ridsdale and O'Leary were gambling on success, which, really, they were attempting to buy. In one respect, it made sense – if it was achievable. The winning Premier League clubs attract the most television income and success opens up a variety of commercial and sponsorship opportunities. At the very least, to remain financially viable, Leeds United had to qualify for a place in the very lucrative European Champions League and this meant either winning the FA Cup or finishing in the top three of the Premier League. In 2001 Leeds United were beaten semi-finalists in the European Champions League. In one sense getting as far as they did was a real achievement. In another sense, defeat was a setback – but less of a setback than failing to qualify for the competition in the following season.

Leeds Sporting was profitable until 2000, but the financial situation began to deteriorate in 2001, which coincided with yet another decline in the club's playing success. During this period Manchester United was the dominant club in England, although Arsenal enjoyed some more limited success. Manchester United, of course, is a hugely successful global brand which opens up a myriad of income-generating opportunities. The situation had been made worse for Leeds United in 2000 when two players, Lee Bowyer and Jonathan Woodgate, were charged with assault outside a nightclub in Leeds city centre.

In 2001 Ridsdale began to receive hate mail from fans who opposed his proposal to move Leeds United out of their Elland Road ground to a new purpose-built stadium. He was now England's highest-paid football club chairman. Bowyer and Woodgate were acquitted, but Ridsdale disciplined Bowyer, which again angered certain fans. The club was beginning a spiralling cycle of decline.

Results on the field were poor, despite some European success. O'Leary was sacked (with a multimillion pound pay-off). Terry Venables and Peter Reid preceded Eddie Gray's second chance as manager. The tendency to replace the manager when results are poor was continuing. Recent signing Rio Ferdinand was sold to Manchester United for £30 million, yielding a £12 million profit. But he was just one of several players divested to help offset the now unprofitable club's debts, which were growing rapidly as Leeds United was unable to generate an adequate cash flow without European football.

Ridsdale himself resigned in March 2003. To many outsiders he had enjoyed too much power and his willingness to spend money on players and wages had been largely unchecked. Within 12 months, and with debts approaching £100 million, Leeds United's leading creditors accepted a deal and new owners bought the football club from Leeds Sporting, whose shareholders lost everything they had invested. It was now crucial the club avoided relegation at the end of the 2003/4 season. But this was not to happen. Rumours that the club was to be sold again (literally within months) came to nothing when one interested businessman could not secure the necessary funding. Gray was sacked as manager and it was obvious that a number of players would be sold to raise money and reduce the wage bill. What was going to be required now to secure promotion back to the Premier League, let alone to restore the 'Glory Days'?

David O'Leary, also seen by many as a culprit for spending money to build a winning side that

▶

failed to deliver results, is now manager at Aston Villa – who almost qualified for a place in the European Champions League in 2004. Peter Ridsdale was chairman of Barnsley FC for a spell, which is another club that has experienced financial difficulties in recent years.

2. How different is the situation at Chelsea – a club which is also gambling on success by investing over £100 million on players from around the world? Although there is a wealthy benefactor, he could change his mind if the club doesn't win trophies.

Leeds United http://www.leedsunited.com

**Question**

1. What exactly had gone wrong? Is it ever possible to apportion blame in circumstances like these?

## 14.2 Symptoms of decline

Symptoms of decline are not the causes of failure but indicators that a company might be heading for failure. They will show when a company is performing unsuccessfully relative to what might be expected by an objective outsider or analyst. As mentioned above they will indicate the outcome of poor strategic leadership, inadequate financial management or a lack of competitiveness. Slatter (1984), building on the earlier work of Argenti (1976), analysed 40 UK companies in decline situations which have either been turned around or have failed. He concluded that there are ten major symptoms. In the same way that relative success can be evaluated from financial analysis, several of these symptoms of decline are finance based:

1. falling profitability
2. reduced dividends, because the firm is reinvesting a greater percentage of profits
3. falling sales, measured by volume or revenue after accounting for inflation
4. increasing debt
5. decreasing liquidity
6. delays in publishing financial results, a typical indicator that something is wrong
7. declining market share
8. high turnover of managers
9. top management fear, such that essential tasks and pressing problems are ignored
10. lack of planning or strategic thinking, reflecting a lack of clear direction.

If any of these symptoms are perceived it will be necessary to identify the underlying causes before any remedial action can be attempted. Slatter concluded that a number of causal factors recurred on several occasions in the companies that he studied, and these are summarized below, but categorized in terms of issues of leadership, finance and competitiveness.

Although Slatter's work is two decades old, it remains definitive. More recent research affirms the arguments. For example, The Society of Practitioners of Insolvency (1995) investigated some 1000 insolvencies in 1994 and determined that the greatest single cause of business failure was loss of market, which was responsible for 29 per cent of the insolvencies. Inadequate cash flow accounted for a further 25 per cent and leadership failings 16 per cent. Earlier analyses by the SPI placed greater emphasis on inadequacies in the financial structure of organizations.

### 14.2.1 Signals of weak strategic leadership

This list of warning signals has been largely derived from Heller (1998) and Oates (1990) and it relates mainly, but not exclusively, to smaller organizations.

1. *The existence of (too many) 'would-bes'* – Something critical is missing. Possibly the interested people have a will to do something different but lack a good new idea; some key competence is missing, making implementation difficult; or there is a lack of true commitment to an idea, opportunity or venture.

2. *The single-dimension paradox* – The start-up stage for a small business has progressed well, but there is a lack of ability or opportunity to grow the business beyond the initial stages. The idea might only be viable in the short term; there may be inadequate funding; the entrepreneur may be unwilling to let go at the critical time; the initiative could simply run out of steam. The paradox is that the clear focus and individual drive that get the initiative moving in the first place can be what brings it down, through a lack of necessary flexibility.

3. *The business is a half-way house* – In other words it is a franchise or co-operative (or something conceptually similar) and critically dependent upon the continued support and engagement of others who may be outside the business.

4. *The business is impoverished* – Specifically, it fails to achieve, or it loses, a winning strategic position – it is not sufficiently different. Funding is difficult or mismanaged and the business is undercapitalized. Insufficient attention is given to getting the quality right to delight customers. The management team has not developed in the appropriate way, or it has been weakened by people leaving, such that key skills are missing. The business cannot cope when succession becomes an issue.

5. *The business is blinkered* – There is too much self-belief, perhaps driven by an orientation to production rather than customers – the 'we know best' syndrome. The strategic leader is unwilling to accept outside views and advice.

6. *The business is technology shy* – There is a tension here – the business needs capital and technology, but it all costs money. The key questions are just when do you invest and how much do you spend?

7. *The business has become smothered* – Specifically, it has become too bureaucratic, either because of government or even European legislation/rules and regulations, or because it has become bigger and more structured and has lost its creative spark. This latter issue is debated in greater depth in Chapter 8.

8. *The business is (now) run by a crisis manager* – a manager who relies too much on an ability to deal (or not deal!) with setbacks and crises as they arise, often implying the wrong trade-off between reactive and proactive strategies.

9. *The business has started making (too many) mistakes* – Possibly it has become too ambitious, say with misjudged diversification or acquisition. Perhaps it has ignored warning signs such as a cash shortage. Perhaps it is simply too greedy.

The next section discusses how these signals are often the prelude to decline and failure.

# 14.3 Causes of decline

## 14.3.1 Inadequate strategic leadership

**Poor management** It was shown in Chapter 10 how inadequate strategic leadership can be manifested in a number of ways, which in turn cause key strategic issues to be neglected or ignored. The company could be controlled or dominated by one person whose pursuit of particular personal objectives or style of leadership might create problems or lead to inadequate performance.

The organization might fail to develop new corporate or competitive strategies such that previous levels of performance and success are not maintained when particular products, services or strategies go into decline. This issue can be compounded or alleviated by weak or strong managers, respectively, supporting the strategic leader, and by the quality of non-executive directors on the board.

Poor strategic leadership in terms of building an appropriate organization might mean that key issues or key success factors are ignored or are not given the attention they deserve. A company that is dominated by accountants or engineers might, for example, fail to pay sufficient attention to changing customer requirements and competition. Equally, a company without adequate financial management might ignore aspects of cost and cash-flow management – a factor which will be explored next. Similarly, a company that is undergoing rapid change and possibly diversification might concentrate its resources in the areas of development and neglect the core businesses which should be providing strong foundations for the growth.

**Acquisitions which fail to match expectations** As shown in Chapter 12, companies seeking growth or diversification may acquire or take over other companies, or merge with them. Research consistently confirms that in many cases the profits and successes anticipated from the acquisition fail to materialize. This can be the result of a poor choice by the strategic leader, who overestimates the potential, or an inability to manage the larger organization effectively because the problems are underestimated. It is not unusual for companies which fail to have sought fast growth, often following strategies involving major acquisitions.

**Mismanagement of big projects** This is related to the previous point, but incorporates a number of other possible strategic decisions. By big projects is meant any really new venture for an organization, including developing new and different products and entering new markets, possibly abroad. It is essential to forecast potential revenues without being unrealistically optimistic, and to control expenditures and costs, but this does not always happen. It seems that companies often:

■ underestimate the capital requirements – through poor planning, design changes once the project is under way, and inaccurate estimations of the development time that will be required

■ experience unforeseen start-up difficulties – sometimes resulting from lack of foresight and sometimes from misfortune

■ misjudge the costs of market entry because of customer hostility or hesitation, or the actions of competitors.

Companies should be careful not to stretch their financial and managerial resources with big projects as they can cause other healthier parts of the business to suffer.

Minicase 14.3 General Electric Corporation (GEC) illustrates these points.

## Dishonesty

There is no doubt that some strategic leaders and businesses take chances and risks which amount to sharp practice and rely on not being found out. However, if there is real dishonesty, and it is found out, then ultimately the business may find survival difficult. The story of the collapse of Robert Maxwell's business empire, after his untimely death by drowning, is well known – he had been using funds from the Mirror Group pension fund to shore up other businesses which needed cash. Once the real extent of the funding needs became known, the whole empire was in danger. A very astute businessman had become too greedy and then turned to desperate measures.

The earlier classic case of the high profile and media-loving American John de Lorean is another example. Supported with money from the UK government he built a car assembly plant on waste land near Belfast and began to manufacture the gull-wing sports car that was featured prominently in the three *Back to the Future* movies. Sadly a series of financial scandals helped finish the venture. De Lorean himself was charged with possessing drugs but the case was eventually dismissed on the grounds of 'federal entrapment'.

More recent cases in the United States featuring huge businesses such as Enron (creative accounting) and Tyco (misuse of corporate funds as well as creative accounting), and entrepreneur Martha Stewart (insider trading), indicate what can happen when corporate governance and greed are allowed to manifest themselves.

**De Lorean car** as featured in the *Back to the Future* films © Amblin Universal/The Kobal Collection

## Minicase 14.3  The General Electric Corporation (GEC)          GB

The growth years of GEC are really the story of Arnold (Lord) Weinstock who was once described by fellow industrialist Lord Hanson as 'the best manager Britain has produced'. Born in 1924, Weinstock died in 2002. Until his retirement in 1996 he was 'the dominant figure in the British electrics and electronics industries'. Weinstock was recognised for his strong focus on cost control and his sustained ability to deliver on profitability and shareholder value. He was criticized by some for his caution and for avoiding risks by staying away from the fastest growing sectors of electronics. 'He was good at generating cash but less good at spending it.' One might expect bankers and financiers to criticize businessmen who don't borrow money but instead build up reserves – there is no profit for them in that! But the empire he built so carefully would crumble in the years after his retirement.

Weinstock first worked for the Admiralty and then as an estate agent before he joined his father-in-law's business in 1954. Michael Sobell owned Radio and Allied, which manufactured radios and televisions. Weinstock soon took over the business and improved its profitability – before selling it to GEC in 1961, when he became a director of the new owner. By 1963 he was managing director of GEC. He established a small top team to run the company and set out to reduce bureaucracy. He also switched the focus from heavy industry to consumer products. In 1967, and with connivance from the Labour government of the time, GEC absorbed AEI. One year later GEC was a 'white knight' bidder for English Electric, which was being stalked by Plessey. English Electric had earlier acquired telecommunications business, Marconi. Between 1970 and 1977, and with rationalization, profits increased fivefold.

In 1985 GEC bid for Plessey, but this time the Monopolies Commission stood in the way. Plessey was acquired though in 1988, when GEC put in a joint bid with Siemens of Germany. Around this time GEC also collaborated with Alstom of France (in power engineering) and GE (the American General Electric) in domestic appliances. By 1990 GEC had also bought important parts of defence business, Ferranti. Some time later Weinstock considered bidding for British Aerospace (BAe) but didn't. Instead he acquired Vickers Shipbuilding in 1995.

When he retired (in 1996) GEC was a diversified conglomerate in an era when focus was becoming strategically more acceptable. He favoured 'eggs in several baskets'. Power engineering, telecommunications and domestic appliances accounted for 40 per cent of the company, and they were all joint ventures. Defence electronics, semiconductors, shipbuilding, elevators and wire cables were other important activities. GEC was the UK's second largest defence supplier (after BAe) with 'a number of excellent businesses with stable cash flows'. Profts amounted to £1 billion a year from a turnover of £11 billion. There were 80,000 employees,

Weinstock controlled the empire from his London head office, rarely visiting the factories themselves. He relied on detailed financial reports and regular phone calls to his managers. He had a telephone switchboard on his desk to facilitate instant access. He set out to build and hold cash reserves – they amounted to £1.4 billion in 1996 – to help the company through business downturns and cyclical variations. The diversified portfolio meant his businesses were not all in recession at the same time. Outside work he was passionate about the opera and horseracing. A bloodstock owner, his horse won the Derby in 1979. He had 'little enthusiasm for conventional business school strategy and even less for exploring synergies … he allowed the businesses to operate with autonomy'.

Weinstock recruited a Scottish accountant to succeed him. George (Lord) Simpson has built his career in the car industry. He had spent several years at British Leyland/Rover before its acquisition by British Aerospace, which he joined and became Deputy CEO. In this role he engineered the sale of Rover to BMW. He then left to join Lucas, which, in turn, he sold to Varity of America.

Once installed at GEC Simpson recruited John Mayo as his Financial Director. Mayo had worked for S.G. Warburg (investment bankers) and Zeneca (pharmaceuticals) and was described as 'brilliant but utterly ruthless'. His view was that if any business produced below 7 per cent cash flow returns on investment, after inflation and tax, it must cut costs. But if earnings exceeded 12 per cent a business should grow as fast as possible, using the cash it was generating.

Simpson and Mayo concluded the existing management had 'got it all wrong'. They simply did not have a risk-taking approach to growth. They quickly abandoned the joint ventures, divesting most but buying out Siemens' share in telecommunications, and sold the defence businesses to BAe to build up an acquisitions war chest of £5 billion. The new focus was to be on high growth telecommunications and they looked for acquisitions in America, although, because of the dot.com bubble (which had yet to burst), prices were inflated. The two major buys were Beltec (a network and access specialist) for $2.1 billion and Fore Systems (Internet switching and networking) for $4.5 billion. In no time the company had debts of some £3 billion. But, as Simpson pointed out, 'cash in the bank earns a very low return'. One critic suggested that GEC was 'buying from the Americans businesses no other Americans wanted'.

In 1999 GEC opted to change its name to Marconi to reflect its new focus. The share price – £3.50 before the change of strategy – was on the rise, reflecting favourable investor reactions. By late 2000 the price had more than tripled to £11.50. But in 2001 telecom shares everywhere began to fall when investors concluded they had grown too rapidly.

Marconi declared poor results in May 2001 but Simpson and Mayo were promising renewed growth. The reality was that the company was running out of cash. When a serious profits warning was issued in July, the share price had

fallen back to £3.75. Chairman Sir Roger Hurn tried to persuade institutional investors to adjust the Directors' share option scheme to allow them to buy at lower prices and he continued to promise 'gold around the corner'. Was this credible when 4000 job cuts were announced? In the end over 10,000 jobs would be lost in the UK in 2001. Shareholders were 'outraged at the duplicity' and the share price was soon down to £1. Mayo was forced to resign. To many he was the real culprit for bringing the company to its knees. Initially Arnold Weinstock (a leading shareholder and non-executive director) continued to back George Simpson, but by September both Simpson and Hurn were gone. In 2002 another 4000 jobs would be lost.

When Mike Parton took over as CEO – an internal promotion – debts had risen to £4.4 billion and the shares stood at 50 pence. There was an exceptional profit charge of £3.5 billion because of the fall in value of the US acquisitions. Future and planned capital expenditures were slashed. There would be further disposals and Marconi would focus on network communications.

## Questions

1. What do you think might have happened if Weinstock's strategy and style of management had been retained?
2. Was he correct to avoid risky industries or is this inevitably a flawed strategy in the long run?

## Project

1. Use the Internet and other sources to check the progress of Marconi in recent years. What has happened to the businesses GEC sold?

**Marconi** http://www.marconi.com

### 14.3.2  Poor financial management

**Poor financial control** This can manifest itself in a number of ways. Particularly important are the failure to manage cash flow and the incidence of temporary illiquidity as a result of overtrading. Inadequate costing systems can mean that companies are not properly aware of the costs of the different products and services that they produce, and as a result they can move from profit to loss if the mix of products that they produce and sell is changed.

If an organization invests in expensive equipment for potentially lower costs or product differentiation, then it automatically increases its fixed costs or overheads. This will increase the break-even point and consequently make the company more volume sensitive. Investments of this nature should not be undertaken lightly and without a thorough and objective assessment of market potential; but some companies do invest without adequate analysis and create financial problems for themselves.

Finally, some companies in decline situations appear not to budget properly. Budgets are short-term financial plans which forecast potential demand and sales revenue, the costs that will be incurred in meeting this demand, and the flow of cash in and out of the business. If budgeted targets are not being met it is essential to investigate why and take any steps necessary to improve the situation. Without proper budgeting companies cannot estimate profits and cash needs adequately and can therefore experience unexpected financial difficulties. Minicase 14.2 on Leeds United deals with this.

**Cost disadvantages**   In addition to the problem of breaking even and covering overheads, described above, companies can experience other cost disadvantages which result in decline.

Companies without scale economies can be at a cost disadvantage relative to larger competitors and suffer in terms of low profit or a failure to win orders because their prices are higher.

Other companies which are vertically integrated and able to exercise control over their supplies, or which are located in areas where labour or service costs are relatively low, can enjoy an absolute cost advantage over their rivals and thereby put pressure on them.

Company structure can yield both cost advantages and cost disadvantages. Large multiproduct companies can subsidize the cost of certain products and again put pressure on their rivals; or conversely they can find that their costs are higher than their smaller competitors because of the overhead costs of the organization structure, say through an expensive head office.

Finally, poor operating management can mean low productivity and higher costs than ought to be incurred, and thereby cause decline. These cost problems all affect competitiveness and they are therefore linked to the additional competition factors discussed below.

**Other issues**   The debt ratio should be controlled so that companies do not risk embarrassment through not being able to pay interest charges because of low profits. Companies which rely on loan capital may find that in years of low profits they are unable to invest sufficiently and this may lead to decline. Conversely, other companies may decline because they have not invested as a result of conservatism rather than financial inability. This reflects another weakness of strategic leadership.

### 14.3.3  Competitive forces

Porter's model of the forces that determine industry profitability was discussed in Chapter 4. While all the relevant forces can be managed to create competitive advantage, each of them could cause a weak competitor to be in a decline situation.

**The effect of competitive changes** Primarily, companies can find themselves in decline situations if their products or services cease to be competitive. Their effective life and attractiveness to customers might be ending; or their competitors might have improved their product or introduced something new, thereby strengthening their product differentiation and competitive edge and inevitably causing demand for other products to fall. In other words, decline can result from a loss of clear differentiation and in turn a failure to maintain competitive advantage.

If costs increase, say because of increased labour costs which competitors manage to avoid, then pressure will be put on prices or profit margins, and it may no longer be worthwhile manufacturing the product or service.

**Resource problems** It was mentioned above and in Minicase 14.2 that increased labour costs can render a company uncompetitive; other resources controlled by strong suppliers can have a similar effect. In addition, a company can experience cost problems as a result of currency fluctuations if it fails to buy forward appropriately to offset any risk, and with property rents if leases expire and need renegotiating during a period of inflation.

**Inadequate or badly directed marketing** This factor relates to issues of rivalry between competitors. Companies whose competitive strategies rely on differentiation must ensure that customers recognize and value the source of the differentiation. This requires creative and effective advertising and promotion targeted to the appropriate segments and can be very expensive, especially if the industry is characterized by high advertising budgets. Companies who fail to market their products or services effectively may decline because they are failing to achieve adequate sales.

Minicase 14.1, Laker Airways, illustrates a number of the above points. Freddie Laker, when he launched his Skytrain, undercut the prices of the major airlines and appealed to a distinct sector of the market, but he was overconfident and committed too many resources to his new venture and to possible growth which did not materialize. His financial arrangements constituted his downfall. The case also illustrates the importance of understanding and not underestimating the environmental forces that influence the organization.

## 14.4 Predicting a failure

Financial databases, such as Datastream, typically provide an index known as a $Z$-score, which was originally devised by Edward Altman (1968) and which purports to predict potential corporate failure as a result of insolvency. Altman's research in the USA in the 1960s found the $Z$-score to be a good indicator of potential bankruptcy, but further research in the UK by Argenti (1976) and others suggests that the index should be used cautiously. The $Z$-score, which is explained in Box 14.1, is thought to be more appropriate in the last two years before bankruptcy when it could be argued that a good financial analyst should be able to see clearly that a company is experiencing difficulties and is in decline. Box 14.1 also includes details of a refined version developed by Taffler (1977). The attractiveness and potential value of these indicators remain, despite their limitations, and Urry (1999) reports a more recent framework, an $H$-score, from Company Watch, which increases the number of ratios to seven. The $H$-score again relies on profits in relation to current liabilities, liquidity and the adequacy of the long-term capital base.

Argenti argues that managers rarely look for symptoms of decline, and consequently the $Z$-score can be a useful indicator of when such an analysis might be appropriate. If a company appears to be in decline and the trend is identified soon enough, then recovery strategies can be initiated.

## Box 14.1 *Z*-scores

The original $Z$-score of Altman (1968) is:

$$Z = 1.2 \times W^1 + 1.4 \times W^2 + 3.3 \times W^3 + 0.6 \times W^4 + 1.0 \times W^5$$

Where

$W^1$ = working capital divided by total assets
$W^2$ = retained earnings divided by total assets
$W^3$ = earnings before interest and tax divided by total assets
$W^4$ = market value of equity divided by book value of total debt
$W^5$ = sales divided by total assets

and

- working capital is current assets less current liabilities

- total assets is fixed assets plus all current assets

- retained earnings is accumulated profits in the business

- market value of equity is the number of ordinary shares × their current market price + the value of preference shares

- book value of total debt is long-, medium- and short-term debt, including overdraft.

For US companies. Altman argued that if $Z$ is less than 1.8 they are 'certain to go bust' and if it exceeds 3.0 they are 'almost certain not to'. Argenti (1976) suggests that the appropriate UK figures are more of the order of 1.5 and 2.0, respectively.

Companies with a strong asset base will tend to have a high $Z$-score under the Altman formula, but such businesses do fail, generally then being sold as going concerns.

Taffler (1977) has devised an alternative formula which places greater emphasis on liquidity:

$$Z = 0.53 \times W^1 + 0.13 \times W^2 + 0.18 \times W^3 + 0.16 \times W^4$$

Where

$W^1$ = profit before tax divided by current liabilities (incorporating profitability)

$W^2$ = current assets divided by total debts (working capital)

$W^3$ = current liabilities divided by total assets (financial risk)

$W^4$ = the no credit interval (liquidity)
and the 'no credit interval' is defined as:

$$\frac{\text{Immediate assets} - \text{current liabilities}}{\text{Operating costs} - \text{depreciation}}$$

Using Taffler's formula a score in excess of 0.2, and certainly 0.3, indicates a company with good long-term prospects; below 0.2, and definitely below 0.0, is a score characteristic of companies which have failed in the past.

### Sources

Altman, E (1968) Financial ratios, discriminant analysis, and the prediction of corporate bankruptcy, *Journal of Finance*, 23 (4), September.

Argenti, J (1976) *Corporate Collapse*, McGraw Hill.

Taffer RJ (1977) Going, going, gone, *Accountancy*, March.

KEY CONCEPTS

## 14.5 Reprise

Ultimate business failure happens when a business is liquidated or sold. Its managers have made strategic errors or misjudgements; maybe they simply avoided the need to change in a dynamic environment. However, a business can similarly fail to meet the needs and expectations of key stakeholders, experience financial difficulties but be saved. In this latter case, one or more factors might be involved. A new strategic leader might be appointed who succeeds in turning the company around. Part, or all, of the business might be sold.

There are several signals of a company in difficulty – they constitute symptoms of the failing situation. These should normally be easily discerned by vigilant managers who are tracking a company's performance although, on occasions, circumstances can change quickly. It is the actions which follow that are critical. At the end of this chapter a summary of $Z$-scores is included; these are sometimes used as a predictor of failure.

Companies fail for a variety of reasons, and normally more than one factor is in evidence. The main ones are:

- *Poor management* – either at strategic leader level, or through the heart of the organization. The latter is also indicative of weak leadership.

- *Poor financial control* – weak budgeting and cost management; an inability to cover overheads.

- *Competition* – the company has become relatively weak in comparison to its competitors.

- *Decline in profits* – meaning that there is inadequate funding to meet the business' commitments (suppliers' bills and interest on loans, for example), let alone reinvest in the business. This can be the outcome of lost competitiveness or poor financial management.

- *Decline in demand for the product or service* – which implies a need to change and suggests an inadequate response by the company's managers. These last three factors all imply *poor marketing*.

- *Misjudged acquisitions or other changes in corporate strategy* – implying that the company's resources have been overstretched and attention has been diverted away from the needs of existing products and services.

Minicase 14.4, which discusses the decline of H P Bulmer, a long-established family company, illustrates many of these points.

## 14.6 The feasibility of recovery

When sales or profits are declining because a company is uncompetitive or because an industry is in decline, recovery may or may not be possible. If a company is a single-product firm, or heavily reliant on the industry in question, then it may be in real difficulties and in danger of liquidation unless it can diversify successfully. If profits are declining, such a strategy may be difficult to fund. Where the situation applies to one business unit in an already diversified company, the company as a whole may be less threatened. However, a change of strategy will be required, and the issue concerns whether or not a successful recovery can be brought about and sustained.

## Minicase 14.4   H P Bulmer GB

The UK is the world's leading producer of cider, with France in second place. H P Bulmer is the leading UK producer with nearly two thirds of the UK market. It manufactures some 480 million of the 800 million pints sold every year. The major brands are Strongbow, Woodpecker and Scrumpy Jack. The company was first established in 1887 when the son of a local vicar began using the apples from the vicarage orchard. To many, cider was an efficacious cure for a number of ailments. His first brand was Woodpecker, in 1894. Some 50 per cent of the shares remained in family hands or family control up to 2003 and descendants of the Bulmer family retained seats on the Board. The company's objectives were listed in Box 2.1.

The company began losing money in the early years of the twenty-first century and Bulmer's was forced to call in a turnaround specialist. Corporate debts amounted to £100 million against a capitalization of £67 million. A profit write-off was required to cover capitalized product development costs and goodwill on recent acquisitions in America. There was also a shortfall in the pension fund to deal with – caused by the decline in the value of equities generally.

The real, underlying problem is that the cider industry has never been particularly big and had become vulnerable to competition from new alcopop drinks such as Smirnoff Ice in the 1990s. In an attempt to deal with the impact of these issues, the CEO at the time (Mike Hughes) sought expansion overseas. He grew the activities in selected European countries and South Africa and embarked on a joint venture in China. He also bought two American cider producers, both based in Vermont, and who, between them, commanded 50 per cent of the American market. But cider was only 0.16 per cent of the market for long alcoholic drinks in the US.

During 2002 and early 2003 the workforce was reduced from 1000 to 800, but there was a further impact on the local economy. Most of the apples came from Herefordshire (where Bulmers is based), Worcestershire and Gloucestershire – although concentrate is imported from overseas.

After disposing of the Australian interests to Fosters, the rest of Bulmers was sold to Scottish and Newcastle (S&N) Breweries in April 2003. S&N believed it had the scale and power to exploit the potential market.

### Questions

1. Do you believe Bulmer's will be safer as a small cog in a large wheel than as an independent business?
2. As a family company, was a sale into corporate ownership always inevitable for the market leader in the niche market that cider enjoys as a long alcoholic drink?

**H P Bulmer** http://www.bulmer.com

**Bulmers** and other cider producers have become vulnerable due to competition from alcopop dinks
© The Advertising Archive Ltd for Alcopop

**Figure 14.1** The feasibility of recovery

(a) Adapted from Slatter, S (1984) *Corporate Recovery*, Penguin.
(b) Adapted from Weitzel, W and Johnson, E (1989) Decline in organizations – a literature integration and extension. *Administrative Science Quarterly*, 34 (1)

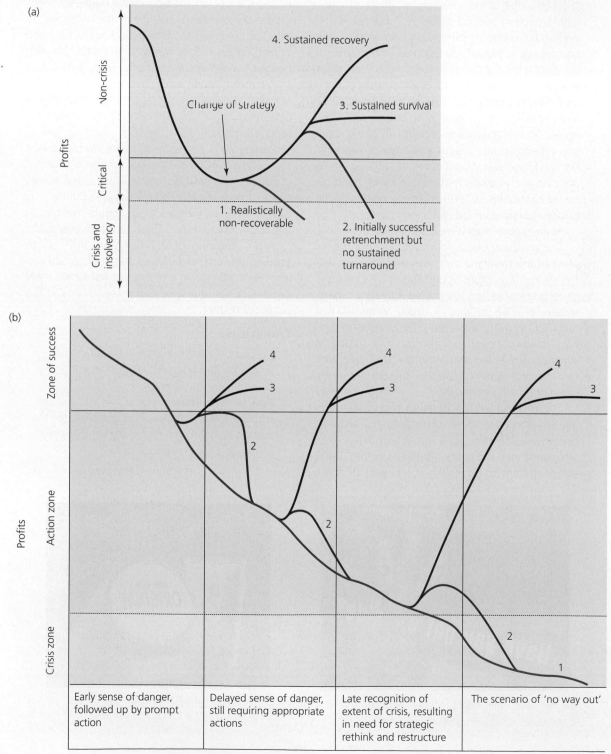

The likelihood of a possible recovery improves where:

■ the causes of the decline in the firm's sales and profits can be tackled and the problems overcome – this depends upon how serious and deep-rooted they are

■ the industry as a whole, or particular segments of the industry which might be targeted, remains attractive

■ there is potential for creating or enhancing competitive advantage.

### 14.6.1 Recovery situations

Slatter (1984) has postulated that there are essentially four types of recovery situation, and these are illustrated in Figure 14.1(a). Once the profits of the firm or business unit have declined to a crisis stage, then a change in strategy is essential. However, the industry and competitive factors might be such that recovery simply is not feasible. Insolvency is inevitable, whatever alternative strategies might be tried. Successful retrenchment strategies might be implemented and profits improved to a non-crisis level again. However, unless the industry remains in some way attractive and potentially profitable, or the firm retains its competitive advantage, the retrenchment might subsequently fail. A third alternative is a successful turnaround but no real growth and sustained recovery. Possibly in a low-profit industry insufficient funds are generated to finance investment for further growth and diversification. A sustained recovery implies real growth, and possibly further changes in functional, competitive and corporate strategies.

Weitzel and Johnson (1989) drew attention to the issue of timing and highlighted that the later an organization leaves it before it attempts to recover itself from a downward trend, the more difficult the task. Figure 14.1(b) shows that sustained survival or sustained recovery is a much steeper challenge (with less likelihood of success) when remedial action is delayed. There is a point in time – shown as a 'crisis zone' – when recovery is unrealistic.

**Non-recoverable situations** Slatter argues that in situations where there is little chance of survival and the likelihood that both retrenchment and turnaround strategies will fail, a number of characteristics are likely to be present.

■ The company is not competitive and the potential for improvement is low. This might be the result of a cost disadvantage that cannot be remedied. Certain businesses and industries that have declined in the face of foreign competition, especially from countries with low wage costs, are testament to this.

■ The company is not diversified and lacks both the resources and access to resources to remedy this weakness.

■ Demand for the basic product or service involved is in terminal decline.

**Temporary recovery** Where a retrenchment strategy is implemented successfully it may or may not be sustained. If new forms of competitive advantage are found and sustained, or the product or service is effectively repositioned, subsequent insolvency may be avoided. However, if costs are reduced or additional revenues are generated in an essentially unattractive and declining industry, the effect will be limited. In such cases it will become important for the company to invest the cash generated from the retrenchment to diversify, if that is possible.

If an organization has captive customers who are in some way dependent and face high short-term exit costs, possibly because of agreed specifications, they can exploit them for a period by charging high prices. There will be a temporary profit improvement, but the customers will be lost in the medium to long term. Companies following this strategy need to use the extra revenue and the time that they buy to develop new strategic opportunities.

Minicase 14.9 (at the end of this chapter) illustrates a temporarily successful turnaround by the Burton Group which was not sustained. Further retrenchment has been required.

**Sustained survival** Sustained survival implies that a turnaround is achieved but there is little further growth. The industry may be in slow decline, or generally competitive and unprofitable. Survival potential and limited profit opportunities continue to exist, but little more. Sustained survival would also apply where a company failed to use its increased earnings effectively and did not diversify into new, more profitable opportunities which could provide growth prospects.

**Sustained recovery** A sustained recovery is likely to involve a genuine and successful turnaround, possibly new product development or market repositioning. In addition, the turnaround may well be followed by a growth strategy, perhaps acquisition and diversification.

The recovery is helped if the industry is strong and attractive and the company's decline has been caused by poor management rather than because the industry itself is in a decline.

Both a sustained survival and a sustained recovery may involve divestment of assets or part of the business to enable the company to concentrate on selected market segments or products.

Slatter (1984) studied a number of successful and unsuccessful attempts at turnaround, and concluded that there are three main features of a sustained recovery:

1. Asset reduction is invariably required in order to generate cash. Quite frequently this will be achieved by divestment of part of the business.

2. A new strategic leader is usually necessary. The new strategic leader will typically be associated with a restructuring of the organization, the introduction of new strategies and a redefinition of roles and policies.

3. Better financial control systems are also a normal feature.

While retrenchment and initial survival can be achieved by concentrating on improving efficiencies, sustained survival and recovery will invariably require more effective competitive and corporate strategies. Minicase 14.5, Pringle, provides an example of a more sustained recovery.

To summarize this section, the opportunities for sustained recovery, or at least survival, improve where:

- there are fewer causes of the decline
- the crisis is not deep-rooted, perhaps because the decline is the result of poor management rather than an unattractive declining industry
- there is support from key stakeholders for the changes required (this may involve understanding by financiers and the commitment of managers and other employees to the necessary changes)

## Minicase 14.5  Pringle     GB

Pringle is a long-established clothing and knitwear manufacturer based in the Scottish borders. Formed in 1815, Pringle is believed to be the UK's oldest clothing brand. The company became known for the 'twinset' matching jumper and cardigan for ladies – which was worn and popularized by movie stars such as Audrey Hepburn, Vivienne Leigh and Margaret Lockwood in the 1950s – the shruggie 'ballet cardigan' and the Argyle check sweater worn by golfers.

In 2002 the current owner, Dawson International, a Scottish yarn and clothing manufacturer, was keen to refocus its business around cashmere products, and opted to sell Pringle for £10 million to Fang Brothers Knitting of Hong Kong. At the time Pringle was in decline. A number of reasons were cited. Sales had fallen in key Asian markets; the value of sterling was high; the clothes were staid and unfashionable; the brand had failed to keep up with changing tastes. Dawson had closed the Pringle factory in Berwick and reduce the headcount elsewhere – but the overall health of the business had not improved markedly. New owner Kenneth Fang decided he needed a fresh chief executive if the brand was to be rejuvenated.

He recruited Kim Winser, at the time a marketing director with Marks and Spencer, where she had worked since she was 18. Feisty, she had once criticized M&S chief, Lord Sieff, in a meeting, arguing against his plan to appoint a female board director. The argument is that she herself wanted to be the first woman on the M&S board! She had been promoted through the ranks and was credited with turning around the womenswear business in the 1990s. She came with a reputation for being driven, career-minded and organized. Fang was willing to give her considerable autonomy.

She concluded the brand needed reconceptualizing and repositioning in a short period of time – her target was just three months. She set out to simultaneously lower costs and develop new products and market opportunities. More jobs, including senior management posts, were lost. The long-standing retail concession with Edinburgh Woollen Mills was abandoned in favour of high end/high fashion outlets such as Selfridges and Harvey Nichols. A celebrity endorsement deal with golfer Nick Faldo was terminated.

A new collection was quickly designed – with a more modern look – although the product range overall was being reduced. Aspects of the past – the Argyll check, the twinset and the cashmere yarns – were retained, but new colours, new styles and new ways of displaying the famous Pringle motifs were sought. The range was promoted in glossy fashion and lifestyle magazines; model Sophie Dahl was recruited for the campaign. The effect was instantaneous and sales jumped 30 per cent. A confident Pringle joined the London catwalk for the first time in its history. When Madonna, David Beckham and Robbie Williams were all seen in public wearing Pringle clothes (a hugely valuable free endorsement) the brand was 'hot'. It was now 'nightclub' rather than 'golf club'.

Winser decided to enter retailing, another first for Pringle. She began with a shop at Heathrow Airport, but with plans for Central London, New York, Tokyo and other European cities. The range has also been extended beyond knitwear into complementary skirts, trousers, dresses, coats, swimwear and accessories. Baby wear and homewear are on the future agenda. It helps that any spare capacity in the Pringle factories can be used to manufacture other products for the Fang Brothers.

### Question

1. Given that in the world of high fashion little stays still for long, what would you recommend Kim Winser should do in the future to make sure Pringle does not once again switch from growth into decline?

**Pringle** http://www.pringle-of-scotland.co.uk

- strategic opportunities exist to differentiate, refocus and create competitive advantage
- the company has the ability to reduce costs.

Rescue, to provide a platform for recovery, could well take 12–18 months and the key themes are:

- making the business cash rich by: selling assets, obtaining a new injection of funding and restructuring debt; and
- tightening operations by: strengthening margins, better cost control, better working capital management and better information.

True renewal and recovery could then require a further 3–5 years.

The skills required for the rescue and recovery stages are different. There may be a requirement or a logic in changing the strategic leader – as happened at Pringle – to find the most appropriate person at any time.

It is worth remembering that a vision for recovery is of little use until the business has been rescued and consolidated; equally, consolidation without a future vision is likely to show only limited and short-term benefits.

## Minicase 14.6 Ministry of Sound

**GB**

Ministry of Sound is a multimedia business founded by ex-Etonian entrepreneur James Palumbo, despite him being described as 'media shy and someone who loathes dance music'. It began in 1991 when a south London warehouse was transformed into London's first 'superclub'. The brand was extended and the business diversified into CD compilations, magazines, holidays, a music Internet site and clothes. Ministry of Sound also started an independent record label. Its 'Relentless' label (a joint venture) recorded Daniel Bedingfield.

In 2000 Palumbo was able to sell 15 per cent of the business to 3i for £24 million.

But by 2002 dance music was less popular and the dedicated magazine *Ministry* was closed down. Ten per cent of the staff were made redundant and a planned move into radio was abandoned. Then the record label failed. Palumbo opted to step up to the chairman role and promoted marketing manager Mark Rodol to be CEO. Rodol was charged with finding a 'focused, long-term, brand-led strategy'; he was seen as closer to the customers than Palumbo himself.

What had gone wrong? The business had perhaps expanded too quickly in too many directions. It pursued an idea if Ministry 'could make money out of it' regardless of whether it added value to the corporate brand or even had distinctive competitive advantage.

Rodol wanted to focus on clubs, CDs, the popular Internet site, events and relevant licensing deals. The flagship London nightclub, which was still attracting between 5000 and 7000 clubbers every week, was refurbished. A new magazine deal was established with publishers, Condé Nast. Ministry of Sound licensed its name to electronics company, Bush, for a new range of hi-fi equipment. Annual sales of £20 million were expected.

### Questions

1. Has Rodol found a defensible 'focused, long-term, brand-led strategy'?
2. What future changes/additions would you recommend?

**Ministry of Sound** http://www.ministryofsound.com

Van de Vliet (1998) provides the following list of useful questions for attempting to assess the situation and the recovery potential:

1. Is there some part of the business worth rescuing?
2. What are the key core activities in the business?
3. Does the organization have the people it is going to need, people who truly understand the business at an operational level?
4. Do these managers have the freedom to manage?
5. Are there ways in which the product(s) and/or service(s) could be improved?
6. Can the necessary resources (other than people) that are going to be required be secured?

Minicase 14.6 – Ministry of Sound – deals with these points.

Having considered the background feasibility of recovery, the actual recovery strategies are now examined in greater detail.

# 14.7 Retrenchment strategies

In this section organizational and financial changes, cost and asset reduction and strategies aimed at generating revenue are considered. Retrenchment strategies are essentially functional, rather than competitive or corporate, and are aimed at making the company more productive and profitable while retaining essentially the same products and services, although there might be some rationalization. By concentrating on financial issues, they often address major causes of the company's decline.

## 14.7.1 Organizational changes

It was emphasized above that a change in strategic leadership is frequently involved in recovery strategies. In addition, there might be a need to strengthen the management team in other areas. The fact that there are personnel changes is not the important issue. The subsequent changes to strategies, structure and policies, and the effect on the existing staff and their motivation, are what matter. Reorganizations are likely to take place, involving new definitions of roles and responsibilities. Policies and management and control systems may also be changed to give managers new opportunities to achieve, and to convince them that recovery prospects are real.

## 14.7.2 Financial changes

Poor financial control systems, say a badly managed cash flow, are often a feature of companies in difficulties. In addition, overheads may have been allowed to become too high in relation to direct production costs, and the company may not know the actual costs of producing particular products and services or be able to explain all expenditures. The establishment of an effective costing system, and greater control over the cash flow, can improve profitability and generate revenue.

Another retrenchment strategy is the restructuring of debt to reduce the financial burden of the company. Possibly repayment dates can be extended, or loan capital converted into preference shares or equity, thereby allowing the company more freedom through less pressure to pay interest. Eurotunnel provides an excellent example of this: loans were rescheduled and some were transferred into equity to reduce the interest burden as the company struggled to generate enough revenue to cover its costs. Operationally, Eurotunnel is now a success. Passenger and freight traffic, supported by income from Eurostar, delivers a trading profit – but the cost of its debt, required for the enormous construction project over several years, drastically reduces this.

### 14.7.3 Cost-reduction strategies

When the acquisition strategies of such companies as Hanson and BTR are discussed later in Chapter 16, it is emphasized that they historically looked for companies with high gross margins and relatively low after-tax profitability. These are indications of overheads which have been allowed to grow too much, thereby providing opportunities for improving profits by reducing organizational slack and waste.

Companies can address the overheads issue for themselves, without being acquired, if they recognize the extent of the problem and are determined to reduce their costs in order to improve their competitiveness and profitability. This happened increasingly in the late 1980s and 1990s, reducing the number of attractively priced acquisition targets. By and large those companies that could not reduce their costs were liquidated as the economy tightened.

In terms of reducing costs, the normal starting place is labour costs. In many cases opportunities will exist to reduce labour costs and improve productivity, but if the reductions are too harsh there can be a real threat to the quality of both the product and the overall service offered to customers. One opportunity is to examine working patterns and attempt to manage overtime, part-time arrangements and extra shifts both to meet demand and to contain costs. Companies can slip easily into situations where overtime and weekend working are creating costs which cannot be recovered in competitive prices.

Redundancies may be required to reduce costs and bring capacity more into line with demand. Again this can be implemented well or poorly. In most cases the issue is not losing particular numbers of people and thereby saving on wages, but losing non-essential staff or those who fail to make an effective contribution. There is always the danger in a voluntary redundancy programme that good people will choose to leave or take early retirement.

Costs can be reduced anywhere and everywhere in the value chain. Better supply arrangements and terms can reduce costs; products can be redesigned to cost less without any loss in areas significant to customers; and certain activities, such as public relations, training, advertising and research and development (R&D) might be cut. The argument here is that these activities are non-essential, and this might be perfectly plausible in the short term. It may not be the case for the longer term, and therefore they would need to be reinstated when extra revenues had been regenerated.

### 14.7.4 Asset-reduction strategies

*Divestment* of a business unit, or part of the business, is an asset-reduction strategy but is considered in greater detail later. It is really more of a corporate than a functional strategy, and the decision should not be made on financial grounds alone. While the sale of a business can raise money, this gain may be more than offset if there is existing synergy with other parts of the company which suffer in some way from the divestment.

*Internal divestment or rationalization* can take a number of forms. Plants might be closed and production concentrated in fewer places; production might be rescheduled to generate increased economies of scale. The idea is to reduce both overheads and direct costs.

*Assets might be sold and leased back* – As far as the balance sheet is concerned, assets have been reduced and in turn cash has been generated. The scope and capacity of the business may be unaffected; the changes are exclusively financial.

### 14.7.5 Revenue-generating strategies

The marketing strategies considered in the next section on turnarounds are essentially revenue-generating strategies, and they frequently involve changes in competitive strategies. However, revenue can also be generated by improving certain management control systems. If stocks are reduced by better stock management or by a review of the whole production system and a move towards just in time, cash is freed. In the same way, if debtors can be persuaded to settle accounts more speedily, cash flow can be improved.

> *We weren't making money at SAS [Scandinavian Airlines System] when I came here. We were in a desperate situation, and that's the worst time to focus on preventing mistakes and controlling costs. First, we had to increase revenues. We had to decide what business we were going to do – before you can start managing effectively you must know who is your customer and what is your product – and go to work on the revenue side. Then we could think about cutting costs, because only then would we know which costs could be cut without losing competitiveness.*

> Jan Carlzon, when President and Chief Executive Officer,
> Scandinavian Airlines System

# 14.8 Turnaround strategies

Retrenchment strategies will usually have short time horizons and they will be designed to yield immediate results. Turnaround strategies are likely to address those areas which must be developed if there is to be a sustained recovery. They involve changes in the overall marketing effort, including the repositioning or refocusing of existing products and services, together with the development of new ones. They are designed to bring quick results and at the same time contribute towards longer-term growth. They overlap with the internal limited growth strategies outlined in Chapter 10, and they may also be a stepping stone to growth through diversification.

Retrenchment strategies do not affect customers directly, but the following turnaround strategies are designed to improve the effectiveness of the company's marketing. Consequently, they are addressing customers and consumers directly, and for this reason some degree of caution is required in implementing the changes involved.

### 14.8.1 Changing prices

Prices can be changed at very short notice, and price increases or decreases can result in increased revenue. Price rises can increase revenue as long as the elasticity of demand ensures that sales do not decline unacceptably with the price increase. Price decreases can improve demand and hence revenue, again depending on the elasticity of demand.

Hence, it is important to have an insight into the demand elasticity for individual products and services, although forecasting the effect of price changes will be subject to some uncertainty. In general, the opportunity to increase prices is related to the extent of existing differentiation, and the opportunity to differentiate further and create new competitive advantage.

It is important to remember that unless particular products and services are regarded as underpriced by customers in relation to their competition, a price rise should be accompanied by advertising support and possibly minor changes and improvements in the product or packaging. The price change must be justified.

It is also important to consider the likely reaction of competitors, which in turn will be influenced by the structure of the industry and the degree and type of competitive rivalry. Markets with an oligopoly structure, an essential feature of UK industry, were introduced in Chapter 3, when it was emphasized that oligopoly competitors tend to follow price decreases but not price rises.

In relation to the concept of price changes, discount structures might be altered to favour certain groups of customers at the expense of others. Such a strategic move can both raise revenue and improve the attractiveness of a company to certain market segments. Any negative effect on other customer groups should be monitored carefully.

However, on occasions, some companies will be seen to increase their prices immediately after being acquired by a new parent. When this happens there is often an assumption that existing customers are, at least for a time, committed and locked in – finding a new supplier will take time – and so they can be 'exploited'. The new parent is willing to lose them in the medium term as it has other plans for the business, which it might well involve rationalization and selling on.

### 14.8.2  Refocusing

The idea behind refocusing is to concentrate effort on specific customers and specific products, relating the two closely together. The strategy requires careful thought and attention in relation to why people buy and opportunities for differentiation, segmentation and competitive advantage. The selection of particular product/market and service/market niches for concentrating effort will depend upon revenue and growth potential, gross margins, the extent and type of competition for the segment or niche, and the potential to create a response to marketing activity, such as advertising.

In the short term products or services that sell quickly and generate cash quickly may be attractive opportunities even if their gross margin is small; and there may well be a group of customers for whom an appropriate package can be created.

### 14.8.3  New product development

The replacement of existing products with new ones may be required to effect a turn-around if a company has been losing competitiveness in an attractive industry by falling behind competitors in terms of innovation and product improvement. Equally, product improvements, designed to prolong the product life cycle, can be extremely useful in low-growth or declining industries. They can be used to help a company to concentrate on the particular segments of the market that are remaining relatively strong.

## 14.8.4  Rationalizing the product line

Variety reduction can similarly be useful for concentrating efforts on the stronger market segments and opportunities, particularly where the industry overall is losing attractiveness. Such a strategy needs a proper understanding of costs, and which individual products and services are most and least profitable. In a multiproduct organization, with interdependencies between the business units, for example, transfer price arrangements can distort profitabilities. As mentioned earlier, certain products and services can be vital contributors to overall synergy, but individually not very profitable, and care needs to be taken with these.

## 14.8.5  Emphasis on selling and advertising

An emphasis on selling and advertising might take the form of selected additional expenditure in order to generate greater revenue, or the examination of all current marketing expenditure in order to try and ascertain the best potential returns from the spending.

Expenditure on advertising, below-the-line promotions and the sales force is used to promote products and services in order to generate sales revenue. However, all of these activities are investments, and their potential returns should be considered. The increased revenue expected from any increased spending should certainly exceed the additional costs incurred, and there is an argument that the opportunity cost of the investment funds should also be assessed.

While five alternative approaches to improving marketing effectiveness have been considered in this section, a number of them may be used in conjunction at any time. Moreover, these turnaround strategies may also be combined with the retrenchment strategies discussed earlier, the aim being both to reduce costs and to improve revenue at the same time.

It has already been explained that the divestment of products or business units can be useful for reducing assets in retrenchment strategies. Divestments can also be used to rationalize the product line, as discussed above.

Minicase 14.7, Albertson's and Home Depot, illustrates many of these issues.

## Minicase 14.7  Albertson's and Home Depot  US

Albertson's and Home Depot are both large American retail chains. They are in separate industry sectors; they do not compete with each other. They are, however, connected. When Jeff Immelt was chosen by General Electric to replace legendary CEO Jack Welch when he retired – see Minicases 16.1 and 17.4 – two other nominated contenders for the post were disappointed and they sought other senior positions. One, Bob Nardelli, was recruited to be CEO at Home Depot; the other, James McNerney, left to run 3M. At around the same time, a third GE Divisional Head,

Larry Johnson, left to take over the hot seat at Albertson's.

**Albertson's** is the second largest grocery retailer in America. It achieved this position with the acquisition of American Stores in 1999. The combined turnover was some $38 billion from 2400 stores and 220,000 employees. Albertson's is larger than Tesco, even when all Tesco's interests around the world are included.

The acquisition in reality merged three supermarket brands, Albertson's, Jewel and Acme, with two drugstore chains, Osco and Sav-On. The

▶

Jewel-Osco stores had been a mixture and foods and drugs. Fusing all these interests was tricky as there were both cultural clashes and intensified competition from Wal-Mart, which was aggressively growing its food interests.

In April 2001 Albertson's appointed a new chief executive, Larry Johnson, who inherited the challenge of completing the effective integration of the merged businesses. Johnson came from General Electric (GE) where he had been for 28 years and had risen to be general manager of GE's Appliances Division. He was, of course, steeped in the Jack Welch style of management, and it seemed inevitable he would bring at least some of this style to Albertson's.

In his first nine months he spent some 170 days on the road visiting stores and motivating staff. It was commented that he ran the business from a hand-held e-mailer which he used at airports whilst waiting for connections.

In reality he introduced a number of important changes to simplify the business before experimenting with a new style of store.

He closed 165 underperforming outlets and came out of certain cities where he thought the competition was too intense.

He cut 20 per cent of management above the store level. He placed much greater emphasis on information technology for streamlining the supply chain – an area where the US had tended to lag behind the UK, but something upon which Wal-Mart had focused aggressively. It seems inevitable there would be potential savings from linking the distribution of the two groups of products.

He tightened the communication links between the stores and head office staff.

He started up 'Swift quality teams' (along the lines of GE's Six Sigma programme) in a search for efficiency improvements.

He focused determinedly on 'quality, choice and convenience' to position Albertson's as different from the price-led Wal-Mart strategy. It is estimated that 35 per cent of American customers put price first in their purchasing decisions.

He tailored product ranges to local neighbourhoods with greater precision.

Johnson then began to experiment with new combo-store formats. He wanted to combine the supermarket and drugstore formats in a single outlet and yet keep them separate. The combo stores have two names and two separate entrances but it is easy to walk through from one to the other. Shoppers can pay for everything they pick at a single checkout point; they do not need to queue twice. The return on capital employed percentage from these combo stores is greater than the average for either the existing specialized supermarkets or drugstores when examined individually.

**Home Depot** saw its share value halve in 2002 as sales revenue fell. To some analysts the chief culprit was new CEO, Bob Nardelli, who had been recruited from General Electric in 2000. He had been head of GE's Power Systems. But Nardelli was part-way through his turnaround strategy; and in 2003 sales rose rapidly once again.

Home Depot had been founded in 1978 by two entrepreneurs – Bernie Marcus and Arthur Blank – and it held the record for having reached sales of $50 billion faster than any other retailer in history. The stores were in reality huge warehouses which sold broad ranges at very low prices. The nearest UK equivalent would be a B&Q Warehouse, selling a complete range of home improvement products. But Home Depot 'never put in place the necessary systems, processes and disciplines' (Buckley and Liu 2003) for the business it became. The 1500 store managers still ran largely independent businesses, typically setting their own prices. Although buying was not at store level – it was, in fact, done by nine separate (and independent) regions – stores chose their own product ranges. Whilst this devolution encouraged local enterprise, it was an atypical retail model. Home Depot was not achieving the maximum purchasing economies, and margins were compromised with the very tight pricing strategies. As a consequence there was a lack of investment in the stores and many looked shabby. Because the company had grown as fast as it had nobody had worried too much about this detail! But Nardelli did.

He began by:
■ centralizing purchasing and merchandising

- appointing new directors for marketing, finance and human resources
- introducing overnight replenishment of shelves in stores to free up staff to concentrate on customer service during trading hours
- refitting many stores.

Initially there were stock-outs and so it seemed inevitable that sales would fall – but they would recover just as quickly. Rather than feeling he did too much too fast (which some accused him of) Nardelli felt 'he did not do enough quickly enough'. In particular he felt he should have speeded up the introduction of new computer systems.

In 2003 more upmarket brands were introduced. Home Depot also grew to be number three in the market for home appliances. In some cities older stores were closed and replaced by newer and bigger ones. The company also stated it was considering targeting professionals as well as the domestic DIY (do-it-yourself) customer. In the UK this market is largely separate. In 2004 Home Depot diversified into installation services. It did not employ the workmen it used; rather it acquired service businesses which worked on behalf of independent tradesmen, acquiring business on their behalf, mainly from the retailers of the products they installed. Replacement windows, external wall coverings and roofing were all involved. Home Depot simply takes a margin for bringing two parties together – a potentially very lucrative business. But this strategic development was not welcomed by everyone – after all, Home Depot's reputation might suffer if these subcontract installers let customers down or provide poor service.

## Questions

1. Evaluate the strategies followed by Johnson at Albertson's. Whilst they might be expected to yield cost savings, how effective do you think they might be for integrating the two businesses, generating synergies and encouraging new growth?
2. Do you agree with Nardelli's decisions to target professional builders, plumbers and electricians and to diversify into installation services? Can a single store service both the professional and domestic markets effectively or is there a real risk of losing focus?

**Albertson's** http://www.albertsons.com
**Home Depot** http://www.homedepot.com

## 14.8.6 Rejuvenating mature businesses

Pulling these points together, Baden-Fuller and Stopford (1992) define a mature business as 'one whose managers believe themselves to be imprisoned by their environment and unable to succeed'. As a consequence they are invariably giving poor service to their customers and achieving financial returns that are barely adequate. Often, with a more creative, entrepreneurial, innovative approach, they can be rejuvenated. The challenge, simply, is to become a stronger competitor. This transformation is likely to require a number of developmental steps over an extended period, rather than be achieved with a one-off major project; it implies a change of culture and style. Success will not be instantaneous; it will need building. Baden-Fuller and Stopford have developed a four-stage model for rejuvenation, which is summarized in Figure 14.2.

1. *Galvanization* comes when there is a clear recognition of the true state of the business and the establishment of an able management team which is committed to dealing with the problem. This may only need a change of strategic leader; on other occasions the changes will be more extensive. If those managers who are responsible for bringing about the crisis, through poor decisions and judgement, or negligently allowing the situation to deteriorate, stay, they will need to change.

**Figure 14.2** Rejuvenating the mature business
Adapted from Baden-Fuller, C and Stopford, J (1992) *Rejuvenating the mature business*, Routledge.

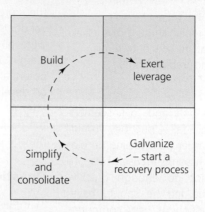

Progress then requires resources. Independent businesses are likely to require fresh capital and possibly new owners. Subsidiaries of larger organizations will have to justify new, corporate investment.

2. *Simplification* follows, implying a clearer focus and the concentration of scarce resources on a smaller agenda to build a strong and sustainable core. Strategies, structures and styles may all have to change. This level of change is sometimes termed strategic regeneration, and the demands and implications are looked at further in Chapter 17. The business must next

3. *Build* new competencies and competitive advantages. Because of resource pressures this is again likely to take time and prove highly challenging. Finally, true rejuvenation requires it to

4. *Exert leverage* to extend its new competencies and capabilities into new products, services, markets and opportunities.

Total quality management initiatives and business process re-engineering programmes can make a major contribution, but alone they will not make an organization more innovatory. The whole enterprise must become more customer focused, committed to efficiency and improvement, and responsive to environmental demands.

It would be useful at this point to return to Figure 5.7, p. 244. Through double-loop learning an uncompetitive firm has found new opportunities for adding value and creating advantages; it has then used single-loop learning initially to leverage this new advantage.

### 14.8.7 Turnaround themes

To round off this section, van de Vliet (1998) suggests that the following themes determine the likelihood of turnaround success:

■ the existence of 'some fat to live off'. An organization which has reached a certain size, perhaps a turnover of some £10 million, and has a strong customer base, will have a more realistic chance than a much smaller organization without an equivalent customer base

- some identifiable potential, such as market leadership in a niche or segment
- the consistency or focus in the portfolio – and the potential for synergy. If there has been a series of non-synergistic acquisitions, divestments should be straightforward
- the opportunity for a fresh perspective from a new strategic leader
- the existence of a strong management team, or one with potential, even if they are currently underperforming
- the existence of a clear structure and communications
- the ability to eradicate any overtrading quickly to strengthen the cash position.

# 14.9 Divestment strategies

Divestment can be essentially *internal*, the closure of a plant as part of a rationalization programme, or *external*, the sale of part of the business. The justification will be similar for each, and any resources saved or generated should be reallocated.

Davis (1974) argues that divestments are often sudden decisions rather than decisions reached as part of a continual evaluation process which reviews all of the products and services in the firm's portfolio periodically. Companies that utilize portfolio analysis as part of their planning will be in a position to identify which parts of the business are the poorest performers and possible candidates for divestment. However, Devlin (1989) contends that effective divestment is a skill that few strategic leaders actually possess. This, he suggests, is a critical strategic issue, given that many acquisitions fail to achieve their expected returns. While divestment may suggest an admission of failure, it can be used positively. After Boots (Minicase 10.8) divested Halfords (car spares, bicycles etc.) the 'business that did not fit' has thrived under new ownership.

There will be an obvious reluctance to sell a business unit to another company, especially a competitor, who might succeed and transform the business into an effective performer. This will be particularly important if such success could pose a future threat to business units that have been retained. For these reasons divestments are often associated with a change of strategic leader, as an outsider is less likely to feel any loyalty to past decisions.

## 14.9.1 Issues in selecting a divestment candidate

A number of possible considerations might be relevant in selecting a product, service or business unit for divestment. Both financial and strategic aspects are important:

- the current position in the product lifecycle, and the likely future potential for further growth and profitability
- the current market position, and opportunities for competitive advantage
- taking these two points further and considering portfolio analyses, the future potential for cash generation and future investment requirements in order to remain competitive (linked to this is the opportunity cost of the resources being utilized)
- identified alternative uses for the resources which could be freed up, and in certain cases the extent of the need to free up resources for relocation
- the ability to find a suitable buyer willing to pay an acceptable price.

In Chapter 12 we saw how Daimler-Benz decided to withdraw funding from its Fokker aircraft subsidiary. Realistically, a new owner was required for Fokker. One possibility was Bombardier, the Canadian company which had already rescued Shorts (Belfast, and a major subcontractor to Fokker), de Havilland and Learjet. Bombardier's post-acquisition strategy is to invest heavily to restructure, modernize and extend the product line. It weighs the turnaround chances carefully, looking for good management and stable employee relations, sound technologies, products with competitive advantage and long-term growth potential, component orders to offset cyclical downturns and tight cost management. In the event, Bombardier decided that Fokker was not an appropriate purchase.

### 14.9.2 Issues in the divestment

Once the decision to divest has been taken, there is a number of further considerations.

First, there is the issue of how active and how secretive the search for a buyer should be. It can be argued that there should be an active search for an acceptable buyer who is willing to pay an appropriate premium, on the grounds that it is all too easy to sell a business cheaply. A low price might be expected where the sale is hurried, perhaps because there is a pressing need to raise money or where a first offer is accepted without an exploration of other options. There is also an argument in favour of secrecy and speed as opposed to prolonged and publicized negotiations. Employees may leave if they feel that their company is no longer wanted by its existing parent, and relationships with important suppliers and customers may also be affected.

In addition, simply offering a business for sale may not be productive. Sales must be negotiated and potential buyers must be vetted. The terms of the sale should be financially acceptable, and the buyer should not be an organization that can use the newly acquired business to create a competitive threat to retained activities.

Devlin (1989) suggests that in general speed is of the essence. Long delays are likely to mean lost confidence. However, some businesses may be difficult to sell.

Second, buyers can be categorized into different types, and the potential of the business for them needs careful consideration during negotiations:

- *Sphere-of-influence buyers* might expect immediate synergy from the acquisition. These would include competitors for whom it would be horizontal integration, and buyers and suppliers for whom it would imply vertical integration. These are the buyers who are most likely to pose future threats unless the divestment removes any involvement in the industry in question.

- *Related industry companies* – these might not be current competitors but companies for whom it might be possible to share activities and transfer skills.

- *Management buy-outs* – discussed in Box 14.2 and supported by additional material on the web site.

- *Management buy-ins* – where a business is acquired by a group of external investors (not an existing trading business) who appoint a new management team. Minicase 14.8 describes a buy-in at Debenhams.

Third, there is an argument that the cash raised from the sale should be deployed effectively and without undue delay. If a company is decreasing in size, building up reserves of cash, and can find no suitable investment opportunities, it might become vulnerable to acquisition. Ideally, a use for the cash will be determined before the sale, but

## Box 14.2  Management Buy-outs in the UK

*Management buy-outs* involve the purchase of a business from its existing owners by the current managers in conjunction with one or more financial institutions.

In Europe the proposal to purchase a business from its existing owners has typically come from the managers; in the US, where the investment banks play a more aggressive role, the idea has often originated with the financial institutions. In the US the sales have often been associated with a need to reduce borrowing; in the UK this has been less of a necessity. Sales have been aimed at generating greater focus and concentration and divesting businesses which are not producing acceptable financial returns or generating synergy. Some buy-outs occur because family owners have no organized succession and a sale to the existing managers is seen as more desirable than sale to an unknown outsider.

*Management buy-ins* occur when a group of outside managers is brought in to run a company which is sold to them and their backers rather than to existing managers. The disadvantage is the loss of continuity and the lack of insight and experience in the particular company; a possible advantage in certain circumstances is the influx of fresh ideas.

Management buy-outs generally involve three parties:

1. *Managers* acquire control of their own business, often with a substantial equity stake while investing only a small proportion of the total funding involved.
2. *Vendors* divest businesses which may be performing poorly or failing to create synergy with their other activities, and they frequently accomplish this amicably and profitably.
3. *Financiers* are attracted to management buy-outs because they offer the potential to earn higher financial returns than investing in large companies and lower failure rates than traditional start-up businesses.

### Objectives and key success factors

While there are important issues of managers wanting to own their own businesses, and possibly preserve their jobs when their company is in difficulties, management buy-outs are characterized by important financial objectives and constraints. Buy-outs typically have unusual financial structures and high gearing, and the financial institutions which back them have financial targets and expectations. Management buy-outs are expected to prove to be profitable for their shareholders and other backers by earning out the debt assumed when the company is bought out and by improving the company's performance in comparison with the results achieved by the previous owners. The banks will normally agree to a higher percentage of debt in relation to equity (gearing) or in relation to total capital employed (the debt ratio) than is conventional, and will look for a cash flow that can both pay the interest and repay the debt after an agreed number of years.

It is important that managers are able to make the business more competitive and overcome the constraints imposed by the high debt burden. In addition, they must be able to generate a positive cash flow.

### Advantages to the vendor

- The cash is from a willing buyer who has knowledge of the business. If the price is acceptable, the cash is neither better nor worse than cash from elsewhere, but such a sale is good for the corporate image.

- It can reduce borrowings, divest a loss-making activity, or enable specialization and concentration.

- Because of the existing knowledge of the buyers, the negotiations will concentrate on the financial package rather than any possible hidden truths about the business.

- If there are any interrelationships or interdependencies with activities which are being retained, continuity should be maintained.

## Advantages to the managers

- There is continuity of employment, and also continuity of both management and trading relationships for suppliers and customers.
- There is commitment to the business because of personal financial involvement, providing real incentives to succeed. This is often used to justify the high gearing allowed by financiers.
- They know the problems, and probably how to improve productivity and reduce overheads. The latter is often crucial for transforming a marginal business into a profitable operation.
- It could lead to real substantial long-term gains if a flotation results.

## Three issues

1. A company or business unit which a vendor is willing to sell at a particular price may be seen as incapable of being turned round sufficiently to meet the needs of potential financiers.
2. The vendor has the problem of ensuring that he or she obtains a good deal, if not the best deal, for existing shareholders, and at the same time takes appropriate account of other stakeholders. The managers may not be the only bidders.
3. A company is possibly unwilling to sell a business to its existing managers and then watch them improve performance and thereby expose the previous failings. This is regarded as less of an issue than it used to be.

## Success and failure

The success rate tends to be relatively high – many end up being floated or sold on for a substantial premium. Where this happens the key managers tend to become very rich people.

There are cases of failure, though. The main funders accept that they will back a mixture of winners and losers and balance their portfolio accordingly. A buy-out is not guaranteed to succeed.

## Exit routes

One important consideration for all parties investing in a buy-out is their ability to withdraw their money at any time. Exit routes are particularly important for financiers, who are likely to want some flexibility.

The main exit routes are:

- liquidation
- sale to another business
- flotation
- earn out – the managers buy out their financiers.

## Notable examples

- Charles Letts (diaries)
- Dolland and Aitchison (opticians)
- Hornby Hobbies, the long-established toy company
- Parker Pen
- Premier Brands, the foods and confectionery arm of Cadbury Schweppes which produces Cadbury's drinking chocolate, biscuits and Smash instant mashed potato
- Standard Fireworks

Virgin and Andrew Lloyd Webber's Really Useful Group were management buy-backs of publicly quoted companies.

## Minicase 14.8  Debenhams  ⒼⒷ

The hostile acquisition of Debenham's department stores by Burtons – which later changed its own name to Arcadia – is described in Minicase 14.9 at the end of this chapter. Debenhams was owned by Burton for 12 years (1985–1997) before it was demerged as an independent company with a separate listing on the Stock Exchange. It was generally acknowledged that it had not been able to prosper as part of the larger group. At this time sales exceeded £1 billion from the 92 stores. The managing director in post at the time, Terry Green, stayed on until 2000, when he left to run British Home Stores (Bhs).

Belinda Earl was then promoted to the top job: at 38 years old, she had extensive experience in trading but was less experienced in the property and financial aspects. Her strategy was focused on improving customer service and introducing a wider, more differentiated product range. The ranges would not be the same in every store; she wanted the individual units to be as flexible as possible and able to respond to regional taste variations. She also wanted to increase the number of stores to 150 – but gradually over a period of time. She also opted to join Barclaycard, BP and Sainsbury in the Nectar loyalty card scheme.

Prices were reduced in 2001 and 2002 to boost sales; and by 2002 turnover had risen to £1.7 billion. Pre-tax profits were £150 million. Many analysts believed Debenhams was being set up for sale.

In 2003 two prospective external buyers came on the scheme. Both were venture capitalists, anxious to buy a successful business. First to bid was Permira, once called Schroder Ventures. It offered 425 pence per share, valuing the business at £1.54 billion. Permira were experienced in these deals, having bought Homebase from Sainsburys and strengthening it for sale on to Great Universal Stores (GUS). In two years Permira generated a cash return of six times its original investment. Belinda Earl and her finance director were given permission by the Debenham's board to co-operate fully; and it was assumed that if Permira were successful, Earl would stay on as managing director and as a substantial shareholder.

The alternative bidder was CVC Capital Partners in association with Texas Pacific Group. They bid 455 pence per share, valuing the business at £1.65 billion. Some independent non-executive directors on the Debenhams board backed them, but it was clear CVC would not be retaining Belinda Earl if they succeeded. CVC were successful and they installed a new management team. In charge was Rob Templeman, who was currently the Chairman of Halfords, which CVC had bought from Boots. He had also been in charge of Permira's turnaround of Homebase after its purchase from Sainsbury.

The business changed hands in December 2003. The buy-in team had four main planks to its strategy: improve cash management; cut costs; increase top-line sales – the new target audience was to be young females interested in fashion; and better supply-chain management. Head office staffing levels were soon reduced and supply chain costs saved through inventory reductions of £50 million, coupled with an increased stock turn. By mid 2004 sales were running some 5.5 per cent ahead of 2003 levels; profits were up by round 14 per cent. Five new outlets are planned for 2005. New overseas suppliers are being targeted. It seemed only a matter of time before Debenhams followed Halfords and Homebase as a sale or flotation business in a relatively short space of time.

### Question

1. Clearly when strategic leaders fail, their replacement by someone capable of turning around the business can be justified. But Belinda Earl was successful. In whose interests is a management buy-in along the lines described here?

### Project

1. By either visiting a Debenham's store or using the Internet (or both) try and ascertain what benefits have accrued from this change of ownership and management.

**Debenhams** http://www.debenhams.com

implementation of a combined sale and investment may prove difficult. Devlin argues that where these changes can be managed effectively, divestment can provide a source of new competitive advantage.

Having explored retrenchment, turnaround and divestment strategies, these strategies are discussed specifically in the context of an economic recession, and this chapter concludes by considering alternative strategies for declining industries and how the most appropriate strategy might be selected.

*We have used the recession as a time to bring new products out.*

*It shows you're not demoralized, and it's something new to go to customers with.*

*Being private has enabled us to plough our own furrow through the good and the bad times and not be swallowed up. All our capital investment would be looked at in a different way if we were a public company.*

Sir Anthony Bamford, Chairman, JC Bamford (JCB Excavators),
quoted in the *Financial Times*, 2 June 1993

## 14.10 Managing in a recession

The early 1990s was characterized by an economic recession. This was not unusual; economies experience cycles. Typically, the latter years of the decade provided clear evidence of an economic recovery in the UK, but this time the real beneficiaries were service businesses rather than the manufacturing sector, which was affected by the high value of the pound sterling. This early 1990s recession was global and it affected most countries, industries and businesses, regardless of size or sector. Since then other world economies have performed worse than the UK, which has benefited from low inflation and low interest rates and from investment in the public sector. It is highly likely that another recession will occur at some stage in the future, but the unpredictable issue is its possible extent.

In a recession, retrenchment strategies are frequently required as demand falls and costs need containing; at the same time there is a need, wherever practical, to invest and prepare the organization to benefit from the recovery when it comes.

Recession alone will not necessarily put a company into a crisis or turnaround situation; rather, it highlights existing weaknesses either created in, or hidden in, boom conditions. The organizations that are best prepared to cope with a recession are those with relatively low borrowings. Highly geared companies may be forced to divest assets in order to raise cash to cover their interest and repayment needs.

Clifford (1977) has suggested that companies that survive a recession most successfully are characterized by superior management which emphasizes the protection of margins, the efficient use of capital, and a concentration on markets or segments where distinctive competitive advantage is possible. Such competitive advantage will result from more effective cost control, innovative differentiation, a focus on service and quality and speedy reaction and change in a dynamic environment. An economic recession will typically force organizations to be creative in their search for cost reductions, especially if productivity drives have already eliminated many operational inefficiencies. Information technology (IT) has provided some valuable opportunities in recent years. Cost savings must then be controlled to ensure that they do not creep up again. The focus of the cost-cutting is critical. Training and R&D, for example, should not be sacrificed unnecessarily because new ideas and service quality are increasingly important for adding value, helping customers to find new competitive opportunities themselves and persuading consumers to buy when their spending power is limited. R&D, then, should be managed better rather than cut, and directed more towards short-term improvements. However, the long-term needs should not be wholly ignored. In particular, the development time for new products and services should be speeded up.

Dividend payments and investment funding may have to be traded off against each other. Some organizations will reduce dividends when profits fall to conserve their resources; others will maintain them to appease shareholders.

Moreover, increasing global competition has forced companies to target markets and niches more effectively and, in many cases, increase their marketing rather than cut expenditure. The emphasis has typically focused on efficiencies and savings rather than luxury – consumers with less discretionary purchasing power have been more selective.

Whittingham (1991) reinforces points made earlier in the book and contends that innovation and product and service improvement is a more effective use of scarce resources in a recession than is diversification, and that cutting back too much leaves companies exposed and under capacity for the recovery. Ideally, organizations will consult and involve employees, looking to, say, negotiate pay freezes and reduce hours rather than make staff redundant. This provides greater flexibility to grow. Nevertheless, many firms will not have sufficient resources to pursue their preferred option.

When companies emerge from a recession and attempt to satisfy increasing demand there is a fresh challenge: the need to control events, monitor the cash flow and guard against overtrading.

Paradoxically, a recession can be an ideal time to invest for the future, to ensure that the organization is in a state of readiness to capitalize fully when the economic recovery begins. This could imply investing in new plant and equipment, in R&D or in new IT at a time when the company is struggling. The secret is money. If a company builds up a cash mountain when its revenues and profits are high, there is a real likelihood that it will be criticized for not finding opportunities to spend it. It may even come under pressure to return some of it to shareholders. It might also be persuaded to diversify or acquire unnecessarily. It is such a cash mountain that helps to pay staff when future revenues and profits are restrained. This can allow an organization to hang on to the people whom it does not want to lose rather than face enforced redundancy programmes. It can also be used for investments when the timing is most appropriate. See Minicase 14.3 on GEC.

Accenture (2003) suggest the following companies as examples of strategic successes during the 1990s. Nokia divested a range of businesses and invested in mobile telephones, becoming the world's leading manufacturer of handsets. Southwest Airlines continued to expand through the recession, opening up new routes and cities, but never deviating from its winning competitive formula. It was consistently profitable when other airlines were losing money. Wal-Mart also grew (opening up more and more new stores) and remained focused on its existing strategies, whilst many other rivals changed their strategy in an attempt to boost sales. In contrast Samsung restructured, decentralizing to give managers more autonomy. In every case we can see evidence of investment in a clear business model. The conclusion: successful companies do not spend excessively in boom times; instead they generate cash, reduce debt and build up their resource base. This provides them with flexibility. Of course, at the same time, a recession provides new opportunities for alert businesses. The online auction house, eBay, made a lot of money by helping companies clear their surplus stocks.

**Table 14.1** Managing in a recession

In a recession, companies should:
- Determine and clarify strategic priorities
- Be willing to act rather than procrastinate with some tough decisions
- Stay fully informed about trends and changes in relevant industries, making use of IT for this and other potential benefits
- Monitor gross profits and cash flow very carefully
- Identify where there is any overcapacity
- Spend carefully
- Seek to extend payment times to creditors
- Look for possibilities to reduce overheads or fixed costs
- Cut back on borrowings if at all possible
- Monitor currency fluctuations if the company trades in foreign currencies, buying forward where appropriate
- Recognize that high prices may be unsustainable and act sooner rather than later
- Keep staff informed of the situation, taking as positive a stance as is realistic
- Tighten staffing levels where appropriate, but not by losing key people
- Make any necessary redundancies all at once
- Invest in training for those who remain and look to retain morale
- Stay in close contact with customers and look for opportunities where both parties can help each other
- Seek out relevant marketing opportunities at home and abroad – recessions are uneven in their impact
- Accept that flexibility and innovation are crucial

Table 14.1 provides a useful summary of these and other points.

## 14.11  Strategies for declining industries

Rarely is an industry unattractive for every company competing in it; mature and declining industries can be made attractive for individual competitors if they can find appropriate and feasible opportunities for adding value and creating competitive advantage. Although tea is a more popular drink than coffee in the UK, consumption has been declining for a number of years. Tetley became the market leader in the 1990s and it has adopted a number of strategies to retain its leadership. For example, it promoted more specialist teas such as Earl Grey and Lapsang and it introduced draw-bag tea bags. After being bought out by its managers (from Allied Domecq) in 1995, Tetley formed a joint venture with Indian tea grower, Tata – which is now its new owner.

Some firms experiencing decline in a mature industry will be the cause of their own demise, through their persistence with dated, inappropriate competitive strategies; and in some cases, an innovatory new strategy by one competitor can rejuvenate the whole industry.

When an industry has reached maturity or begun to decline, a number of issues must be faced. Generally:

- while demand overall is declining, the pattern can vary markedly – some sectors or segments may be static or expanding

- consumers will be knowledgeable because the product or service has been around for a while

- many customers will become increasingly price conscious and prices will tend to fall in real terms
- the 'commodity' perception of products will increase
- distribution is likely to become more concentrated.

Companies will again be attempting to find new ways of adding value and differentiating, but as time goes on the opportunities become increasingly limited. Paradoxically, they will often find it harder to justify both R&D spending (to develop new variations) and marketing expenditure to inform and persuade customers of the differentiation. However, as the decline continues and overcapacity emerges, there will be a tendency for the weakest or least profitable producers to withdraw from the industry. This relieves some of the pressure on those who remain.

Harrigan (1980) draws upon the themes outlined when portfolio analysis was discussed in Chapter 9 and considers whether retrenchment, turnaround or divestment is the most appropriate strategy for an individual competitor in a declining industry. Strategies of leadership and **niche marketing** (turnaround), exploiting or harvesting (retrenchment) and divestment are considered in the light of the overall attractiveness of the industry while it is declining and the opportunities for an individual competitor to create and sustain competitive advantage. These are illustrated and defined in Figure 14.3.

**Figure 14.3** Strategies for declining industries. The asterisks indicate the terms that are used in the directional policy matrix discussed in Chapter 9 (Figure 9.7)
Developed from Harrigan, KR (1980) *Strategies for Declining Businesses*; Heath, Harrigan KR and Porter, ME (1983) End-game strategies for declining industries, *Harvard Business Review*, July–August

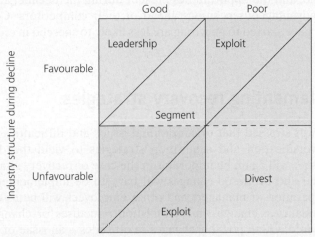

| Leadership | Selective investment*: turnaround<br>Invest as appropriate to give real competitive advantage<br>Idea: Become one of the strongest competitors in the declining industry with either the lowest costs or clear differentiation |
| Segment or niche | Selective investment*: turnaround<br>Identify one or more attractive segments, those with greatest potential for longer-term survival or short-term returns, and seek a strong position whilst divesting in other segments |
| Exploit or harvest | Phased withdrawal*; retrenchment<br>Controlled disinvestment, reducing product alternatives, advertising and so on in order to cut costs<br>Problem: losing the confidence of suppliers and buyers as they witness the obvious reduction of commitment<br>Must lead eventually to divestment or liquidation |
| Quick divestment | Immediate sale or liquidation |

Harrigan contends that the most appropriate strategy is dependent on four factors:

1. the nature of the decline, and the causes – the speed at which decline is taking place, and whether specific segments are still surviving and offering differentiation and niche marketing opportunities for companies who can create and sustain competitive advantage. These factors affect the attractiveness of the industry

2. the ability of a company to target these market segments effectively and create consumer preference. This is affected by company strengths and weaknesses

3. the exit costs for all competitors. Exit costs influence the degree of urgency that companies feel towards finding a way of remaining competitive rather than simply withdrawing. Exit costs relate to:
   - the inability to find a buyer for the business, and the cost of closure
   - the strategic significance for the company as a whole, particularly if vertical integration strategies are affected
   - the possible effect upon key stakeholders, such as shareholders, managers and the strategic leader, especially if they have had a long-term commitment to the product service or business unit.

4. linked to all these, the opportunities or threats which exist as a result of competitor activities, what they choose to do and why. If the product is strategically significant, certain competitors may choose not to withdraw, accepting very low profits or even no profits, and thereby making it more difficult for others.

Figure 14.3 encapsulates the first two points above; the decision will also involve the last two points.

Competitive advantage is likely to be attained by those companies who are aware early of the decline, and the opportunities present during the decline, and who seek to create the most advantageous positions ahead of their competitors. Companies who react when things have started to go wrong are less likely to succeed in creating an effective strategy.

## 14.12 Implementing recovery strategies

In Chapter 12 it was stressed that organizational issues and difficulties often result in failure of the diversification and acquisition strategies to yield the desired results. Organizational issues will again be important in the case of recovery strategies. Time is likely to be limited and proposed changes will have to be implemented quickly. The support and co-operation of managers and other employees will be essential, particularly where redundancies, changes in organization structures or changes in working practices are required. Quite possibly changes in attitudes – an issue of organizational culture – will be involved. Although the gravity of the situation may be visible, and the dangers of failing to change clearly understood, the changes will need managing properly if they are to prove effective. The issues involved in managing change are discussed in Chapter 17.

We finish the chapter with Minicase 14.9 on Arcadia, a retail group that has experienced turbulent times. Attempts to revive the fortunes of once-famous brands have proved how difficult sustained turnaround is. The company is now owned by the entrepreneur Philip Green.

## Minicase 14.9  Arcadia  (GB)

Arcadia was previously known as the Burton Group of retail outlets.

### Origins and diversification

The Burton Group became a retailer of fashionable clothing for men and women through a number of branded outlets. The company was started as a single shop in 1901 by Montague Burton, who had built the company into a vertically integrated organization of factories and some 600 stores when he died in 1952. The main product area had been made-to-measure suits for men.

In the late 1960s the company had problems of management succession and it was basically stagnant with underutilized assets. Burton was also experiencing a number of specific problems:

- The menswear market was switching in preference from made-to-measure to ready-made suits.

- The company had a large manufacturing base in relation to the falling demand for its products. Moreover, the factories were inefficient and insufficiently capital intensive.

- There was growing competition from such stores as Marks and Spencer.

- The company had an old-fashioned image, made worse by stores which were not designed or fitted for the growing market for ready-made clothes.

A new management team was appointed and their strategy was one of diversification. In the early 1970s Burton acquired five new businesses:

- Evans – outsize fashions for women with fuller figures
- Ryman's – office supplies
- St Remy – clothing stores in France
- Green's – cameras and hi-fi equipment
- Trumps – an employment agency.

Burton also opened a chain of womenswear shops with the Top Shop brand name.

### Divestment and turnaround; the acquisition of Debenhams

The diversification strategy failed in overall terms, although parts did prove successful, and divestment began in the mid-1970s.

In addition:

- Branches were modernized and some were enlarged. The aim was to make Burton stores more appealing to younger buyers. Some stores, though, were closed.

- A new chain of Top Man stores was opened to complement Top Shop.

- There was greater emphasis on the womenswear market, with more Top Shops and the acquisition of Dorothy Perkins.

- The Principles chain was developed.

- Manufacturing was pruned and the final factory was disposed of in 1988.

Between 1976 and 1979 the number of employees was reduced from 21,400 to 11,000.

These changes were led by Ralph Halpern, who became chief executive in 1977 (and executive chairman in 1981), and the result was revitalization, new growth and profitability. The Burton Group built up a 12.5 per cent share of the UK clothing market, second only to Marks and Spencer. Halpern was fêted as a retailer of genius, and rewarded with a million pound salary, a knighthood and celebrity status. However, when this expansion required consolidation in the 1980s, a number of strategic misjudgements were made.

- In 1985 Burton took over Debenhams after a fierce and very acrimonious battle. The new department stores required expensive revamping and the payback was slower than anticipated. Moreover, different retailing skills were involved.

- Burton diversified into shopping-centre development, and was financially exposed when property prices fell.

- The growth led to overexpansion and the acquisition of new sites with very high rent and lease charges. These proved too expensive in the retail recession of the late 1980s.

Profits and the share price collapsed and Halpern departed in November 1990, to be replaced as chief executive by his deputy, Lawrence Cooklin. In mid-1991 Burton sought to raise money in a 'desperate rights issue', imposed a pay freeze and looked to rationalize by reducing both the number of stores and head-office administration.

The company traded at a loss during 1991–1992; a new, experimental, out-of-town discount format, branded IS, was introduced and the flagship Harvey Nichols London department store was sold for £51 million in August 1991. (Harvey Nichols was floated on the stock exchange in 1996 with a valuation of £150 million.) Analysts commented that Burton was still searching for a retail format suitable for the 1990s and estimated the odds of a second successful recovery to be no better than 50:50. Cooklin was replaced in February 1992 by American John Hoerner from Debenhams.

### A second turnaround

Hoerner was determined to tackle two key strategic issues:

1. The Burton brands/businesses saw themselves in competition with each other; they frequently targeted the same customers
2. The company was too willing to discount its prices when trading levels were disappointing.

Three years later Burton was profitable again. What had happened? Initially:

- Hoerner initiated a cross-formats review of target markets, design, merchandising, pricing strategies, visual marketing and buying.
- The formats were then refocused, some more than others, and new strategies trialled. Top Shop, for example, targeted 16–19-year-olds by experimenting with a 'funky, grungey' look. Those targeted loved the new image;

unfortunately Top Shop's other customers did not, and they voted with their feet. Top Shop switched to a less radical look which had appeal for all ages up to 30.

- Locations were reviewed from a corporate perspective. Some sites were closed and replaced with new ones, although not as many. In addition, some formats were exchanged for other Burton brands to try and achieve the most appropriate location for each one.
- The new but unprofitable IS format was abandoned in 1994.
- The head office was reduced in size and numbers. In the branches there was a programme of switching employees from full-time contracts to flexible part-time hours.

Hoerner then turned his attention to supplier relationships and to the links and interdependencies between the Burton formats. The future strategy was to be based on building the strength of the various brand names.

During 1996 mail order (or home shopping) began to play a more prominent role in Burton. Two acquisitions: first, the Innovations (unusual and inventive household and leisure products) and second, the Racing Green (smart casual clothes) catalogues were added to Hawkshead and McCord which Burton already owned.

### Demerger

In July 1997 Burton Group announced that it was to demerge the department store chain Debenhams into an independent business. It was generally acknowledged that it has not been able to prosper in a Burton Group beset with other high-street problems. In recent months Debenhams had been growing much more quickly than Burton's other brands. Burton's menswear sales in particular were being affected by the increasing success of specialist designer menswear brands and branded sportswear companies.

John Hoerner would remain as chief executive of Burton – which was to be renamed Arcadia – and which now comprised the Burton, Dorothy

Perkins, Evans, Principles, Miss Selfridge, Top Shop and Top Man high-street stores, together with Burton Home Shopping. The new chief executive of Debenhams was to be Terry Green, who was currently in charge within Burton's. Shareholders should benefit from identified cost savings amounting to £30 million. There would be job losses as the operating and administration systems for all the Burton stores would now be amalgamated and centralized. Each store chain would retain its independence for product sourcing, range building, supplier development and customer relations.

It is invariably possible to reduce costs after a strategic change such as this. The real challenge lies in finding new opportunities for adding value and differentiating to give fresh life to the brands and stores concerned. The prediction was that both Burton Group and Debenhams could benefit and grow after this split. Time would tell.

An argument was put forward that department stores such as Debenhams could prove to be the new retail force for 'thirty-something and forty-something' shoppers as they would be able to offer designer brands (concessions), smart cafés, baby changing rooms and affordable own-label products in a single store, and thus provide convenience for the whole family.

In 1999 Burton extended its women's wear chains by buying Wallis, Warehouse and Evans (again, having sold it) from Sears.

## Arcadia/Burton in 2000

In April 2000 Arcadia announced that 400 shops would be closed and 3500 jobs lost. Casualties included all of the Principles for Men and Top Shop branches and some Miss Selfridge and women's Principles stores. In addition, Burton stores would be paired with Dorothy Perkins rather than remain as stand-alones. The reason was intense discounting in the clothing sector in late 1999. Arcadia was trading at a loss and could no longer afford the rents and rates that it was paying.

Customer comments reinforced Arcadia's difficulties: it was often difficult to differentiate between the product ranges in the various high-street chain stores. Cut-price warehouses (such as Matalan) were also making real inroads into the market.

In 2002 the entrepreneur Philip Green bought the business for £850 million (see Minicase 10.4).

## Questions

1. Given the fact that in June 2000 rival C&A announced it was also closing all of its high-street stores, and the ability of relative newcomers such as Gap and Matalan to grow rapidly, what is the future for specialist clothing retailers such as Arcadia and its long-established brands?
2. If you were new owner, Philip Green, what would you do to try and secure Arcadia's future?

## Project

1. What has happened to Harvey Nichols since its sale by Burton in 1991. Are such specialist brands better off with greater autonomy?

Arcadia (Burton Group) http://www.arcadia.co.uk
Harvey Nichols http://www.harveynichols.com

# SUMMARY

Ultimate business failure happens when a business is liquidated or sold. Its managers have made strategic errors or misjudgements; maybe they simply avoided the need to change in a dynamic environment. However, a business can similarly fail to meet the needs and expectations of key stakeholders, experience financial difficulties but be saved. In this latter case, one or more factors might be involved. A new strategic leader might be appointed who succeeds in turning the company around. Part, or all, of the business might be sold.

Companies fail for a variety of reasons, and normally more than one factor is in evidence. The main ones are: poor management; competition; a decline in profits; a decline in demand for the product or service; misjudged acquisitions or other changes in corporate strategy.

At any time certain industries will be declining and others will be relatively unattractive as far as particular companies are concerned, generally because of intense competition. Individual companies might be performing poorly and in need of either a recovery strategy or an appropriate divestment.

When this is the case, the feasibility of recovery will vary from situation to situation, and the four possible outcomes of a change in strategy are:

■ a failure to recover

■ temporary recovery

■ sustained survival, and

■ sustained recovery.

The likely outcome is inevitably affected by the timing of the intervention. If a company realizes the gravity of a pending situation at an early stage, it will be better placed to deal with it. Recovery will be more difficult to achieve if the organization waits until it facing a real crisis.

In simple terms, *retrenchment* – to create a platform for possible expansion later on – concerns stronger cash management and tighter operations. Renewal brings in marketing and the search for new opportunities for adding value and differentiating. It is about building new forms of competitive advantage.

*Divestment* can be an important theme in retrenchment and consolidation. Management buy-outs are sometimes used as a convenient means of divesting a business which has the potential to grow but which is no longer core to its existing parent.

A four-stage model of the process can be summarized as:

1. galvanization – engaging the problem
2. simplifying the situation so it can be dealt with
3. building new competencies
4. exerting leverage to develop and sustain new competitive advantages.

From time to time economies move from boom conditions into recessions, the depth and length of which vary markedly. In a recession company revenues and profits will fall and a number of the issues and strategies discussed in relation to retrenchment and consolidation become relevant. Paradoxically, an economic recession is often an ideal time for a company to invest if it has the appropriate resources. If it can afford to hold on to its staff, the chances are that they will have time to deal with the implied changes. New plant, equipment and technology could then be in place in time for when the economy turns around – placing the organization in a strong position.

There are several possible strategies for individual competitors in mature and declining industries. Some companies will withdraw from the industry. Others will find attractive niches. The fact that an industry is in decline does not automatically make it unattractive for everyone.

## QUESTIONS AND RESEARCH ASSIGNMENTS

1. Do the causes discussed in this chapter provide an adequate explanation for any corporate failure with which you are familiar?

2. Why might a company wish to remain a competitor in an industry despite low or declining profitability? Classify your reasons as objective or subjective. Can the subjective reasons be justified?

3. What factors do you feel would be most significant to all parties involved in a proposed buy-out during the negotiations? Where are the major areas of potential conflict?

## INTERNET AND LIBRARY PROJECTS

1. In the 1980s, *Z*-scores provided by Datastream suggested that the following companies (amongst others) were in decline:

   - Rover Group (then British Leyland)
   - British Aluminium
   - Renold (chainmakers)
   - Acrow (cranemakers)
   - Dunlop
   - Lucas
   - Tube Investments.

   The companies listed below are considered vulnerable to acquisition or even failure which might happen because their share price is low in comparison with the book value of their assets (House of Fraser and Debenhams) or because of the level of their debts (Vodafone and Eurotunnel).

   - House of Fraser
   - Debenhams (Minicase 14.8)
   - Vodafone
   - Eurotunnel.

   Look up the financial data on these companies, and based on your findings, decide how valuable you believe the Z-score might be.

   You will realize that several of these organizations are used as examples in different parts of the book.

   **Datastream** http://www.dstm.com

2. What has happened to the jewellery retail group Signet since Gerald Ratner was forced to resign after his infamous quote that Ratner's crystal glass decanters were priced as cheaply as they were because they were 'total crap'? In the event, were his comments a 'minor blip' or a much more serious strategic issue that needed careful handling if a recovery were to be engineered? (At the time the company was called Ratners.)

   **Signet Group** http://www./hsamuel.co.uk

3. Hornby is one of the few survivors in the UK toy industry, but it has experienced some dramatic changes in strategy and ownership. Hornby was acquired by Lines in 1964; in 1971 Lines was in liquidation. Dunbee-Combex-Marx then bought Hornby, but DCM itself collapsed in 1981. At this stage Hornby was bought out by its managers. Its main products are still electric train sets and Scalextric, but production in the UK has been replaced by foreign sourcing to improve the quality without increasing costs – in China over two hours labour can be afforded for every one hour in the UK and this has allowed improvements in finishing and detail. Some models now emit actual steam for the first time. Hornby has also benefited from the success of Harry Potter and the Hogwarts Express.

   - What has happened to the company since 1982?
   - How successful has the MBO been?
   - What are Hornby's current products and strategies?

   **Hornby Hobbies** http://www.hornby.co.uk

## Further reading

Harrigan, KR and Porter, ME (1983) End game strategies for declining industries, *Harvard Business Review*, July–August.

Clarke, CJ and Gall, F (1987) Planned divestment – a five-step approach, *Long Range Planning*, 20 (1).

Stopford, JM and Baden-Fuller, C (1990) Corporate rejuvenation, *Journal of Management Studies*, July.

Kanter, RM (2003) Leadership and the psychology of turnarounds, *Harvard Business Review*, May–June.

## References

Accenture (2003) *Investing for the Upturn*. Summarized from the Accenture web site at the time: www.Accenture.com/upturn

Altman, EI (1968) Financial ratios, discriminant analysis and the prediction of corporate bankruptcy, *Journal of Finance*, 23(4), September. The Z-score is explored further in Altman, EI (1971) *Corporate Bankruptcy in America*, Heath.

Argenti, J (1976) *Corporate Collapse*, McGraw-Hill.

Baden-Fuller, C and Stopford, J (1992) *Rejuvenating the Mature Business: The Competitive Challenge*, Routledge.

Buckley, N and Liu, B (2003) Fixer puts the final touches to a DIY refit, *Financial Times*, 8 July.

Clifford, DK (1977) Thriving in a recession, *Harvard Business Review*, July–August.

Davis, JV (1974) The strategic divestment decision, *Long Range Planning*, February.

Devlin, G (1989) Selling off not out, *Management Today*, April.

Harrigan, KR (1980) *Strategies for Declining Businesses*, Heath.

Heller, R (1998) *Goldfinger – How Entrepreneurs Get Rich by Starting Small*, Harper Collins.

Oates, D (1990) *The Complete Entrepreneur*, Mercury.

Slatter, S (1984) *Corporate Recovery: Successful Turnaround Strategies and Their Implementation*, Penguin.

Society of Practitioners in Insolvency (1995) *Personal Insolvency in the UK*, SPI, London.

Taffler, RJ (1977) Going, going, gone, *Accountancy*, March.

Urry, M (1999) Early warning signals, *Financial Times*, 3 October.

Van de Vliet, A (1998) Back from the brink, *Management Today*, January.

Weitzel, W and Johnson, E (1989) Decline in organizations – a literature extension and integration, *Administration Science Quarterly*, 34 (1).

Whittingham, R (1991) Recession strategies and top management change, *Journal of General Management*, 16 (3).

# PART FIVE

# Strategy Implementation

Parts One and Three – an introduction to strategy and a consideration of strategy creation – have addressed a number of important 'how' questions, in particular, how strategies are created, while Parts Two and Four have been more focused on 'what' and 'where' issues. This final part of the book addresses a number of additional 'how' questions regarding the management of strategy and strategic change.

In particular, the following questions are asked:

■ How are intended strategies implemented? (Chapter 15)

■ How does emergent strategy actually happen? (Chapter 15)

■ How should the organization be structured and designed to ensure that both happen? (Chapter 15)

■ How should resources be deployed and managed? (Chapter 16)

■ How can the organization manage risk and avoid and manage crises? (Chapter 16)

■ How can the strategic leader manage both the organization structure and resources to achieve corporate-level synergy? Are the various functions, activities and businesses co-ordinated and contributing towards clearly understood objectives? (Chapter16)

■ How should the organization seek to deal with the pressures and demands of change, appreciating that cultural and behavioural changes may be required? (Chapter 17)

# Strategy Implementation

It was emphasized in Chapter 11 that to be considered effective a chosen, intended strategy must be implemented successfully. The prospects for effective implementation are clearly dependent upon the appropriateness, feasibility and desirability of the strategy. At the same time, competency in implementation – the ability to translate ideas into actions and generate positive outcomes, sometimes swiftly, can itself be a major source of competitive advantage. Internal processes can add value by creating high levels of customer service and/or saving on costs by, say, removing any unnecessary delays or duplication of activities. In this last section of the book, therefore, we consider issues of strategy implementation and control. Reed and Buckley (1988) suggest that new strategies are selected because they offer opportunities and potential benefits, but that their implementation, because it involves change, implies risk. Implementation strategies should seek to maximize benefits and minimize risks. How might this be accomplished?

The final section examines the linkages between strategy and structure by examining a number of alternative structural forms and by considering the key issues of centralization and decentralization. The forces that influence and determine the structure are discussed. The structural challenges of global and small, entrepreneurial businesses, manufacturing and service companies and organizations in the public sector are also covered.

## Minicase 15.1  Amstrad  GB

Amstrad, the UK-based producer of personal computers and other electrical and electronic products, has been run since 1968 by its founder, entrepreneurial businessman Sir Alan Sugar, who, until 2001, was also the chairman and leading shareholder of Tottenham Hotspur football club. Amstrad was floated in 1980 but, when Sugar tried to buy it back in 1992 – offering investors a lower price per share than they had paid originally – he was frustrated by the company's institutional shareholders. Corporate and competitive strategies have changed creatively over the years, but Amstrad has experienced a number of implementation difficulties.

Amstrad's real success began when Sugar identified new electronics products with mass market potential, and designed cheaper models than his main rivals were producing. Manufacturing was to be by low-cost suppliers, mainly in the Far East, supported by aggressive marketing in the West. Expenditure on high-profile marketing was possible because little or no capital was tied up in plant and machinery. Central overheads were kept low and potential suppliers were played off against each other in order to reduce direct costs.

Sugar does not have a background in engineering, and when he bought Sir Clive Sinclair's computer business in 1986 he is reported to have said: 'For God's sake, Clive, I don't care if they have rubber bands in them as long as they work.' Instead, Sugar has a flair for understanding the *external* design requirements of electronic products and the price points that will attract large numbers of customers.

In 1988 the flexibility that Amstrad had built into this strategy turned from a strength to a weakness. There were five main reasons for this:

■ In 1987 there was a worldwide shortage of memory chips, essential components for Amstrad. Some chip prices were doubled and others trebled, and in order to maintain production Amstrad had to pay whatever suppliers asked. The production of certain products was cut back deliberately.

■ The launch of a new personal computer was delayed because a sophisticated chip, designed by Amstrad, failed to work when full production began.

■ Labour shortages in Taiwan led to a reduced supply of audio products.

■ A joint venture with Funai of Japan for the production of video recorders in the UK took off more slowly than anticipated. Previously all Amstrad's videos had been manufactured for them in Japan, by Funai.

■ Amstrad established its own distribution network in West Germany, replacing an existing agreement with a third party. However, the previous distributor was left with surplus, unwanted, stock which it sold off cheaply, undercutting Amstrad's own price.

### Changing strategies

As a consequence Sugar began to move production to higher cost locations in Europe, and Amstrad became a manufacturer. However, the recession of the early 1990s affected Amstrad's sales and the company traded at a loss for the first time in 1991–92; it was to record three consecutive years of losses. Sales of personal computers suffered when manufacturers of higher quality and more expensive machines, including IBM and Compaq, slashed their prices to try and stimulate demand and Amstrad's competitive edge (its price advantage) was lost. Alan Sugar's dilemma was that if he withdrew from the market he had nothing really new to replace PCs.

Amstrad had earlier withdrawn from computer games, unable to compete successfully with the aggressive Nintendo. Satellite dishes (introduced in 1988), however, seemed safer with continental sales buoyant; and the increasing involvement of BSkyB in major sporting activities (exclusive coverage of the cricket world cup and live football from the Premier League) augured well for the 1990s. Amstrad's word processors and fax machines (introduced in 1989) were continuing to sell satisfactorily; and although demand for video cassette recorders (VCRs) had fallen, Amstrad had successfully innovated a new double-decker machine which allows users to edit their own tapes and to record from two television channels at the same time. The company had launched a new laptop computer in 1991.

Sugar's initial reaction was to consolidate and to minimize inventories in order to strengthen Amstrad's balance sheet. He commented: 'We have no intention of moving into technology-led businesses or the high end of the market. Our vocation is always in the lower end of the market.'

The appropriateness of the strategy for the 1990s was questionable. Although new electronics products were in the development pipeline, Amstrad's basic problem was that the markets in which it competed were already crowded. It needed to find new market niches with real growth potential. It was at this stage, and faced with these issues, that Sugar attempted unsuccessfully to reprivatize Amstrad.

Late in 1993 Amstrad acquired Viglen, a rival manufacturer of personal computers, but a company which focused on direct sales and corporate customers. Within a year Amstrad had reduced its high-street sales by withdrawing its products from Dixons, whose margins, it claimed, were too low. To compensate, Amstrad began a direct-selling operation, using the expertise that it acquired with Viglen.

Amstrad bought two other businesses. First, it acquired the loss-making Danish manufacturer of cellular telephones, DanCall, and entered this fast-growth market. DanCall was a high-technology business; Amstrad could offer complementary skills in mass production. Second was a controlling interest in Betacom, another telephone equipment company.

## Restructuring

Also in 1994, Sugar recruited David Rogers from Philips to be his new chief executive and to take over some of the strategic leadership responsibilities. Rogers was mainly responsible for the new businesses, but his brief was to:

- help to introduce more robust management systems
- integrate the new acquisitions to achieve synergies
- help determine new growth areas, and
- foster new strategic alliances that would reduce Amstrad's dependency on personal computers. One alliance was with an IBM subsidiary that manufactured ink-jet printers, and which Amstrad later bought.

Amstrad was restructured into three divisions: ACE (Amstrad Consumer Electronics), personal computers and telecommunications. By early 1995 Amstrad was again profitable, but ACE was making losses. ACE was then split into two divisions, one which would focus on buying in and trading low-price products, mainly from South-East Asia, and one whose main role was to spot and develop new opportunities. ACE was cut back at the beginning of 1996 with a number of job losses.

Late in 1995, history also repeated itself in one respect – new DanCall products were delayed. At this time, after just 18 months with the company, Rogers resigned.

In June 1996 it was reported that Amstrad had been having discussions with Psion, and that Psion was likely to launch an acquisition bid. Psion, founded in 1980 by an academic turned entrepreneur, David Potter, is best known for its palm-size computer diary/organizer. Psion's products are typically high added value and high margin, and the real synergy was thought to be between Psion's data management competencies and DanCall's competencies in mobile telephone technology. New opportunities for combining data and voice technologies were believed to exist. Commentators assumed that Viglen would be retained as a stand-alone subsidiary but that ACE would be divested. David Potter commented: 'Psion has no interest in the consumer electronics side.'

The proposed acquisition of Amstrad by Psion foundered when Alan Sugar refused to accept a price below 'that which he believed Amstrad was worth'. Psion was offering 200 pence per share.

## Corporate split

In April 1997 Amstrad sold DanCall, the Danish mobile telephone business that it had acquired in 1993, to the German company Robert Bosch. Just one month earlier, DanCall had announced the launch of a typical Amstrad product. Its new and innovative mobile phone could be used interchangeably in Europe and America; previously, separate handsets had been required to cope with different transmission systems.

Two months later, in June, Alan Sugar announced that Amstrad would be split up during the summer and two separate companies formed. Viglen Technology would be focused on personal computers; Betacom (which had already absorbed the limited remains of Amstrad's consumer electronics activities, its original business), and which was now built around telecommunications, would comprise (and be known as) the new Amstrad.

Shareholders would be given:

1. One Viglen share for every existing Amstrad share. Because Viglen has no direct competitor in the UK it is a difficult business to value. Analysts' preliminary predictions varied between a value of 50 pence and 110 pence per share. When they opened in August 1997 the early price was around 70 pence
2. A pro-rata distribution which reflected Amstrad's 70 per cent shareholding in Betacom. Assumed value: 28 pence per existing Amstrad share
3. Loan notes, convertible for cash in June 1998, worth 163 pence per share
4. 'Litigation vouchers' which would entitle holders to a proportion of any court awards arising from outstanding cases against two suppliers. The estimated worth at this time was 110 pence per Amstrad share, but the eventual settlement was 43 pence per share. The litigation concerned two suppliers of disc drives; Amstrad blamed faulty parts for the demise of its PC business at the end of the 1980s.

The value of this combined package clearly exceeded the value of Psion's offer. Interestingly, when Alan Sugar tried unsuccessfully to buy Amstrad back from its shareholders in 1992, he was offering just 30 pence per share.

Alan Sugar would remain as chairman of Amstrad but become a non-executive director of Viglen, which had been managed independently ever since its acquisition. Sugar retained a 34 per cent shareholding in Viglen and he personally received over £100 million from the break-up.

## The new Amstrad

From the beginning, the new Amstrad seemed to have a logical growth path – digital television decoder boxes, a natural extension from satellite dishes. But in February 1999 Amstrad launched a new generation of consumer products. Its 'Phone Book Databank' was a telephone with a QWERTY (computer) keypad – up to 500 numbers could be input and stored. The phone also had an integral palm-size organizer. It was priced at under £100.

A year later Amstrad followed this with a new e-mail business, called e-m@iler. The business was built around telephones with e-mail access, courtesy of an integrated screen and keypad. Dixon's bought a 20 per cent stake in this new business. Alan Sugar's earlier disagreement with the retailer over prices and margins was no longer an issue. The phones were sold below their cost price – Amstrad had an agreement with British Telecom, through which it received a share of the call revenues.

In 2000 Amstrad opted to re-enter the mobile phone market with a range of pay-as-you-go telephones, which it would sell to just one network operator in any one country. Amstrad had sold its previous mobile phone business to Bosch in 1997, when it signed an agreement to stay out of the market for three years. However a supply delay meant the lucrative Christmas 2000 sales opportunity was missed.

Amstrad was profitable in 2001, but set-top boxes were subsidizing the e-m@iler. Things were different a year later when the company traded at a loss. Sales of set-top boxes had been adversely affected by the switch from analog to digital television. Sugar, however, was not one to walk away from a setback and a challenge. He launched an upgraded model in February 2002 and then, a year later, he halved the prices to under £50 per unit. By the end of 2003 the e-m@iler was making money. Moreover a third generation model was already in the pipeline.

## Viglen technology

Viglen, meanwhile, was also progressing. In October 1997 an agreement was reached with Microsoft for jointly branded PCs to be sold through Dixons. This represented a first for both organizations. It was the first time that Microsoft had allowed its name to be linked with a particular PC, and it was the first time Viglen had used independent distribution rather than sold direct.

In December 1998 Alan Sugar made a bid for the remaining Viglen shares and he ended up with a 72 per cent shareholding and control. In January 2000 Viglen announced the launch of an investment fund to support embryo start-up proposals for products directly linked to Viglen's business interests. At roughly the same time the name was changed to Learning Technology.

The company was taken private in 2002 when Sugar bought the remaining 28 per cent of the shares. The business now focuses on computer services for the education sector.

## Question

1. How might you judge the relative success of Amstrad's strategy – both ideas and implementation – over its 35 plus years of life?

**Amstrad** http://www.amstrad.com

**Amstrad e-mailer**

# 15.1  Strategy → structure or structure → strategy?

*We trained hard, but it seems that every time we were beginning to form up into teams we would be reorganized. I was to learn later in life that we tend to meet any new situation by reorganizing, and a wonderful method it can be for creating the illusion of progress, while producing confusion, inefficiency and demoralization.*

Gaius Petronius Arbiter, Roman Governor at the time of Nero

The structure of an organization is designed to break down the work to be carried out – the tasks – into discrete components, which might comprise individual businesses, divisions and functional departments. People work within these divisions and functions, and their actions take place within a defined framework of objectives, plans and policies which are designed to direct and control their efforts. In designing the structure and making it operational it is important to consider the key aspects of empowerment, employee motivation and reward. Information and communication systems within the organization should ensure that efforts are co-ordinated to the appropriate and desired extent and that the strategic leader and other senior managers are aware of progress and results.

**Figure 15.1** Strategy implementation

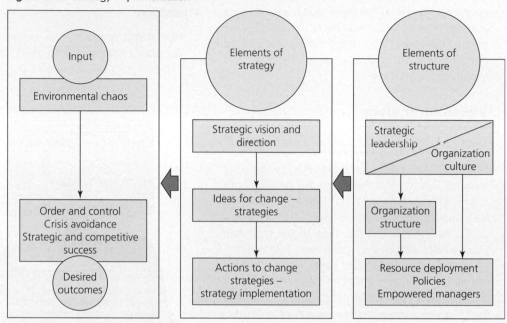

It has already been established that in a competitively chaotic environment one essential contribution of the strategic leader is to provide and share a clear vision, direction and purpose for the organization (see Figure 15.1). From this, and taking into account the various ways in which strategies might be created (incorporating the themes of vision, planning and emergence), actions and action plans need to be formalized – the middle column in the figure. These strategies and proposals for change cannot be divorced from the implementation implications, which are shown in the right-hand column. Is the structure capable of implementing the ideas? Are resources deployed effectively? Are managers suitably empowered? Do organizational policies support the strategies? If the answers to these questions contain negatives, then either the strategic ideas themselves, the structure, organizational policies or aspects of resource management will need to be reviewed and rethought. The final decisions will either be determined or strongly influenced by the strategic leader, and affected by the culture of the organization. Minicase 15.1 describes a number of strategic, structural and managerial changes at Amstrad; Amstrad has always been a strategically creative company but it has sometimes been constrained by implementation difficulties. The case documents a number of changes of fortune and potential crises and describes how Amstrad has managed these various challenges.

If appropriate, feasible and desirable strategies that *are* capable of effective implementation are selected and pursued, the organization should be able to establish some order and control in the environmental chaos and avoid major crises – the left-hand column of Figure 15.1. This still requires that strategies, products and services are managed efficiently and effectively at the operational level. Responsibility for operations will normally be delegated, and consequently, to ensure that performance and outcomes are satisfactory, sound monitoring and control systems are essential.

It is important to appreciate that while structures are designed initially – and probably changed later at various times – to ensure that *determined* or *intended* strategies can be implemented, it is the day-to-day decisions, actions and behaviours of people within

**Figure 15.2** Intended strategy implementation

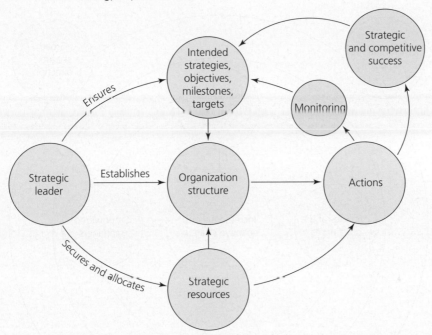

the structure which lead to important *emergent* strategies. There is, therefore, a continual circular process in operation:

Consequently, while issues of structure and implementation are being considered at the end of this book, they should not be thought of as the end point in the strategy process. They may be the source of strategic change.

Figure 15.2 explains the implementation of intended strategies in more detail. The strategic leader is charged with ensuring that there are appropriate targets and milestones, establishing a suitable organization structure and securing and allocating the relevant strategic resources, such as people and money. People then use the other strategic resources, working within the structure, to carry out the tasks that they have been allocated, and their actions should be monitored and evaluated to check that the targets and objectives are being achieved.

Figure 15.3 summarizes the emergent strategy process which, clearly, is less prescriptive. This time the strategic leader provides a broad strategic direction. Empowered managers work within a decentralized structure, but they are constrained by any relevant rules, policies and procedures. The strategies that emerge are affected by the constraints, the extent to which managers accept empowerment and the accumulation, sharing and exploitation of organizational knowledge. The outcome of the strategies is related to the extent to which they deal with the competitive and environmental pressures with which the organization must deal.

To summarize the outcome, in terms of strategic management and organizational success, is dependent upon:

**Figure 15.3** Emergent strategy

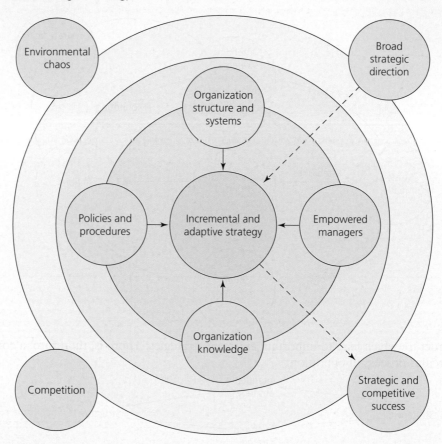

- the direction provided by the strategic leader
- the culture of the organization
- the extent to which managers throughout the organization understand, support and *own* the mission and corporate strategy, and appreciate the significance of their individual contribution
- the willingness and ability of suitably empowered managers to be innovative, add value and take measured risks to deal with environmental opportunities and competitive surprises
- the effectiveness of the information sharing, monitoring and control systems.

*Business is a game, a game to win. My job is to set the strategy and have a team that can deliver it, to review their performance, handle the regulatory issues and set targets and objectives to grow the business.*

Charles Allen, Chairman, ITV

## 15.2 Implementation and change

Implementation incorporates a number of aspects, some of which can be changed directly and some of which can only be changed indirectly. The latter aspects are more difficult for the strategic leadership to control and change. The success of the strategic leader in managing both the direct and indirect aspects influences the effectiveness of:

- the implementation of strategies and strategic changes which are determined through the planning and visionary modes of strategy creation, and
- the ability of the organization, and its managers, to respond to changes in the environment and adapt in line with perceived opportunities and threats.

### 15.2.1  Aspects of implementation that can be changed directly

- The organization structure (the actual, defined structure, not necessarily the way in which people behave within the structure)
- management systems
- policies and procedures
- action plans and short-term budgets
- management information systems.

### 15.2.2  Aspects of implementation that are changed indirectly

**Communication systems** While the management information system can affect formal information flows, the network of informal communications truly determines awareness. Such communications are affected by, and influence, the degree and spirit of co-operation between managers, functions and divisions.

**Managing and developing quality and excellence** Attention to detail, production on time and to the appropriate quality, and the personal development of managers and other employees are all factors in this. As well as developing managers' skills and capabilities generally, it is important to consider the quality of management in particular areas and the cover for managers who leave or who are absent. The organization structure should provide opportunities for managers to grow and be promoted.

**Manifested values and the organization culture** This involves the way in which things are done: standards and attitudes which are held and practised.

**The fostering of innovation** The willingness of people to search for improvements and better ways of doing things. Their encouragement and reward is very much influenced by the strategic leader, with leadership by example often proving significant.

Those aspects that can be changed directly generally imply physical changes in the way in which resources are allocated. Behavioural aspects, which imply changes in beliefs and attitudes, can only be modified indirectly. Both are considered in the forthcoming chapters.

## 15.3  Problems of successful implementation

Owen (1982) contends that in practice there are four problem areas associated with the successful implementation of strategies.

1. At any time strategy and structure need to be matched and supportive of each other. Products and services need to be managed independently, or in linked groups or business units, if they are to be matched closely and effectively with their environments. There may be good reasons for having a structure that does not separate the products, services and business units in this way. The strategic leader might prefer a centralized structure without delegated responsibilities, for example. The organization might possess certain key skills and enjoy a reputation for strength in a particular area, and this might be influential in the design of the structure. Equally, certain skills might be absent and have to be compensated for. Related to this might be the willingness or reluctance of managers to change jobs or location within the structure. Structures cannot be created and activated independently of the people involved; their individual skills may provide either opportunities or constraints. Changing attitudes and developing new skills is accomplished indirectly, as pointed out above, and takes time.

   It is also possible that related products may be produced in various plants nationally or internationally, when a geography-orientated structure, which keeps the plants separate, is favoured for other sound reasons. In addition, it may not prove feasible to change the structure markedly every time there is a change in corporate strategy and, instead, acceptable modifications to the existing structure are preferred to more significant changes.

2. The information and communications systems are inadequate for reporting back and evaluating the adaptive changes that are taking place, and hence the strategic leader is not fully aware of what is happening. Hence the performance of the existing structure is not monitored properly, and as a result control mechanisms may be ineffective.

3. Implementing strategy involves change, which in turn involves uncertainty and risk. New skills may have to be developed, for example. While managers may agree in meetings to make changes, they may be more reluctant in practice to implement them. Motivating managers to make changes is therefore a key determinant.

4. Management systems, such as compensation schemes, management development and communications systems, which operate within the structural framework will have been developed to meet the needs of past strategies. They may not be ideal for the changes that are taking place currently, and again it is difficult to modify them continually.

Alexander (1985) argues that additional factors are also significant, especially:

- The failure to predict the time and problems that implementation will involve, such as the time required for a new business or venture to take off, which is invariably underestimated. This may not seem critical, but it can be. In the early months of a new business, more cash is typically spent than revenue is earned. The accumulating debt is a so-called 'valley of death' that the business must come through and out of before it can start earning real money and (eventually and hopefully) enter the land of plenty.

- Other activities and commitments that distract attention and possibly cause resources to be diverted. Paradoxically, one way of coping with the likelihood of disruptive and distracting events is to ensure that the organization has spare resources in readiness for such emergencies; but slack of this sort can appear to imply inefficiency and underutilized resources, and it can be expensive.

■ The bases on which the strategy was formulated changed, or were forecast poorly, and insufficient flexibility to deal with the change pressures has been built in.

All of these problems presuppose that the formulated strategic change is sound and logical. A poorly thought-out strategy will create its own implementation problems.

## 15.4 Successful implementation

To counter these problems Owen (1982) suggests the following:

■ Clear responsibility for the successful outcome of planned strategic change should be allocated.

■ The number of strategies and changes being pursued at any time should be limited. The ability of the necessary resources to cope with the changes should be seen as a key determinant of strategy and should not be overlooked.

■ Necessary actions to implement strategies should be identified and planned, and again responsibility should be allocated.

■ Milestones, or progress measurement points, should be established.

■ Measures of performance should be established, as well as appropriate monitoring and control mechanisms.

These, Owen argues, can all be achieved without necessarily changing the structural framework but rather by changing the way in which people operate within it.

In addition, Alexander contends that the involvement and support of people who will be affected by the changes in strategy must be considered, and that the implications of the new strategies and changes should be communicated widely, awareness created and commitment and involvement sought. Incentives and reward systems underpin this.

In the same way that no single evaluation technique can select a best strategy, there is no best way of implementing strategic change. There are no right answers, as such. A number of lessons, considerations and arguments, however, can be incorporated into the thinking and planning; and these are the themes of Part Five.

Three final points need to be mentioned to conclude this introduction. First, although there are no right answers to either strategy formulation or strategy implementation, the two must be consistent if the organization is to be effective. Arguably, how the organization does things, and manages both strategy and change, is more important than the actual strategy or change proposed.

Second, the style of strategic leadership will be very influential. We also argue that the preference of the strategic leader affects the desirability of particular strategic alternatives. The structure of the organization, the delegation of responsibilities, the freedom of managers to act, their willingness to exercise initiative, and the incentive and reward systems will all be determined and influenced by the strategic leader. These in turn determine the effectiveness of implementation. The strategic leader's choices and freedom to act, however, may be constrained by any resource limitations and certain environmental forces. These points are picked up in Minicase 15.2, Pilkington.

Third, the timing of when to act and make changes will also be important. In this context, for example, Mitchell (1988) points out that timing is particularly crucial in the implementation decisions and actions that follow acquisitions. Employees anticipate changes in the organization, especially at senior management level, and inaction, say

## Minicase 15.2 Pilkington

St Helens-based Pilkington is a renowned innovator in the glass industry. In the 1950s it invented float glass, which has now become a standard process in the industry worldwide. The idea is to float sheets of glass on molten tin to smooth the surfaces, and this is far more efficient than polishing and grinding. The company opted to license its technology to other manufacturers around the world and critics would accuse it of 'sitting back and enjoying its stream of royalties'. However the company has also since invented fire resistant glass, complex shapes for windscreens and self-cleaning glass (which absorbs ultraviolet light which in turn breaks down dirt).

The issue is that company profitability has failed to reflect its world leadership in glass technology. In the 1980s the company was somewhat fortunate to fight off a hostile takeover bid from the acquisitive conglomerate, BTR. Pilkington also struggled to integrate two businesses it acquired – Flachglas (Germany) and Libbey-Owens-Ford (US).

A new CEO was recruited in 1997. Paolo Scaroni set out to reduce costs (especially targeting overheads) and rationalized operations. He was determined to break down the family traditions, which he blamed for holding back the business. For most of its 175-year history a Pilkington family member had led the company. Scaroni's changes brought about renewed prosperity.

Scaroni chose to move on in 2002 and he was replaced by Stuart Chambers, an internal promotion. Chambers had a marketing background and he was determined that the culture must not be allowed to 'slip back into the old ways'. Managers were given clear objectives, as well as the freedom and authority to take decisions. He was also demanding about performance against objectives. He argued that the strategy and style must work together – perhaps implying entrepreneurial management to exploit the technological innovation.

### Question

1. Whilst licensing is clearly an excellent way to exercise technology leadership in a global industry, can it work in conjunction with an entrepreneurial management style?

**Pilkington** http://www.pilkington.com

---

beyond three months, causes uncertainty and fear. As a result, there is greater hostility to change when it does occur. The dangers of hasty action, such as destroying strengths before appreciating that they are strengths, are offset. Mitchell concludes that it is more important to be decisive than to be right, and then learn and adapt incrementally.

## 15.5 Structural alternatives

We have established in the early pages of this chapter that the organization structure provides the framework through which intended strategies are implemented – or not, as the case may be. However, at the same time, the structure also provides a foundation for emergent strategy creation. By dividing up tasks, the structure places people in certain roles with certain expectations. The accompanying systems, which in part are designed to co-ordinate all of these tasks into a meaningful whole and thus create synergy, help to determine the freedom that individual managers have to change things. It is the style of management, largely dictated by the strategic leader, which finally determines how co-ordinated the efforts are, how co-operative managers, functions and businesses are with each other, and how willing managers are to accept empowerment and make changes.

We now examine the linkages between strategy and structure by examining a number of alternative structural forms and by considering the key issues of centralization and decentralization. The forces that influence and determine the structure are discussed. The structural challenges of global and small, entrepreneurial businesses, manufacturing and service companies and organizations in the public sector are covered.

Lawrence and Lorsch (1967) have argued that the organization should be structured in such a way that it can respond to pressures for change from its environment and pursue any appropriate opportunities which are spotted. Given that strategies are concerned with relating the organization's resources and values with the environment, it follows that strategy and structure are linked. Structure, in fact, is the means by which the organization seeks to achieve its strategic objectives and implement strategies and strategic changes. Strategies are formulated and implemented by managers operating within the current structure. Thompson and Strickland (1980) comment that while strategy formulation requires the abilities to conceptualize, analyse and judge, implementation involves working with and through other people and instituting change. Implementation poses the tougher management challenge.

The essential criteria underpinning the design of the organization structure are:

■ first, the extent to which decision-making is *decentralized*, as opposed to centralized, and

■ second, the extent to which policies and procedures are *formalized*.

Decentralization to some degree is required if incremental and adaptive strategic change is to take place. Issues of centralization/decentralization are explored in Box 15.1. Formality is linked to the extent to which tasks and jobs are specialized and defined, and their rigidity, i.e. the period over which jobs have remained roughly the same. The longer the period is, arguably, the greater will be the resistance to changing them. Clearly, communications and formality are linked. In a formal organization there will be a reliance on vertical communications, with instructions passing downwards and information on results passing upwards. In some organizations, there is a tendency for good news to flow upwards quickly and readily and for bad news to be covered up. The

## Box 15.1  Centralization and Decentralization

Centralization and decentralization relate to the degree to which the authority, power and responsibility for decision-making are devolved through the organization. There are several options, including the following:

■ All major strategic decisions are taken centrally, at head office, by the strategic leader or a group of senior strategists. The size of any team will depend upon the preference of the overall strategic leader together with the size, complexity and diversity of the organization. Strictly enforced policies and procedures will constrain the freedom of other

managers responsible for business units, products, services and functional areas to change competitive and functional strategies. This is centralization.

■ Changes in the strategic perspective are decided centrally, but then the organization is structured to enable managers to change competitive and functional strategies in line with perceived opportunities and threats.

■ The organization is truly decentralized such that independent business units have general managers who are free to change their respective strategic perspectives. In effect they

**KEY CONCEPTS**

▶

run a series of independent businesses with some co-ordination from the parent headquarters.

The extent to which true decentralization exists may be visible from the organization's charted structure. It is always useful to examine the membership of the group and divisional/business unit boards, regardless of the number and delineation of divisions. The organization is likely to tend towards decentralization where there is a main board and a series of subsidiary boards, each chaired by a member of the main board. The chief executive/strategic leader, who is responsible for the performance of each subsidiary, will not necessarily have a seat on the main board. The organization will tend towards greater centralization where the main board comprises the chairperson/chief executives of certain subsidiaries, generally the largest ones, together with staff specialists. Hence decentralization and divisionalization are not synonymous terms.

## The ten main determinants

- the size of the organization
- geographical locations, together with the
  - homogeneity/heterogeneity of the products and services
  - technology of the tasks involved
  - interdependencies
- the relative importance and stability of the external environment, and the possible need to react quickly
- generally, how quickly decisions need to be made
- the workload of decision-makers
- issues of motivation via delegation, together with the abilities and willingness of managers to make decisions and accept responsibility
- the location of competence and expertise in the organization. Are the managerial strengths in the divisions or at headquarters?
- the costs involved in making any changes

- the significance and impact of competitive and functional decisions and changes
- the status of the firm's planning, control and information systems.

## Advantages and disadvantages

There are no right or wrong answers concerning the appropriate amount of centralization/decentralization. It is a question of balancing the potential advantages and disadvantages of each as they affect particular firms.

It has been suggested that companies which achieve and maintain high growth tend to be more decentralized, and those which are more concerned with profits than growth are more centralized. The highest performers in terms of both growth and profits tend to retain high degrees of central control as far as the overall strategic perspective is concerned. Child (1977) contends that the most essential issue is the degree of internal consistency.

## Advantages of centralization

- Consistency of strategy
- Easier to co-ordinate activities (and handle the interdependencies) and control changes
- Changes in the strategic perspective are more easily facilitated.

## Disadvantages of centralization

- May be slow to respond to changes which affect subsidiaries individually rather than the organization as a whole, depending upon the remoteness of head office
- Easy to create an expensive head office that relies on management information systems and becomes detached from customers, and for which there are too many diverse interests and complexities
- General managers with real strategic ability are not developed within the organization. Instead the organization is dependent on specialists and as a result the various functions

may not be properly co-ordinated. Does this achieve a fit between the organization and its environment?

## Advantages of decentralization

- Ability to change competitive and functional strategies more quickly
- Improved motivation
- Can develop better overall strategic awareness in a very complex organization which is too diverse for a head office to control effectively.

## Disadvantages of decentralization

- May be problems in clarifying the role of head-office central services which aim to co-ordinate the various divisions and business units and achieve certain economies through, and the centralization of, selected activities
- Problems of linking the power that general managers need and the responsibility that goes with the power. General managers must have the freedom to make decisions without referrals back.

## Minicase 15.3 The National Health Service　　GB

The UK National Health Service (NHS) is one of the largest employers in the world; it may only be exceeded by the Indian railways in terms of numbers of employees. This makes it inherently complex. Designing a structure to implement government strategies for health is tricky, and successive governments have been criticized for constant changes in structure and expectations. It is, of course, probably impossible to meet most (let alone all) the expectations of the various stakeholders. In some respects, a fundamental role of the NHS is to ration the resources it has available – and thus satisfy some demands at the expense of others.

When they were in power in the 1980s and early 1990s, the Conservatives pursued a strategy of internal competition to drive efficiencies. The system they inherited was essentially centralized. At the core, GP (General Practitioner) Fundholders now bought services from Hospital Trusts, working alongside Health Authorities who guided priorities and provided quality assessment. They were theoretically free to choose which hospitals they sent their patients to.

When Labour came to power in 1997 it set out to dismantle this internal market at the first opportunity. GP Fundholders soon became Primary Care Groups which helped Health Authorities purchase services from Hospital Trusts. Over a period of time

the higher-tier Regional Health Authorities disappeared, and 95 lower-tier Area Authorities became 28 larger ones through consolidation and rationalization. In 2002 these Primary Care Groups became Primary Care Trusts – which purchased care themselves. Labour defended this as a different type of internal market. It was different because it was heavily regulated, and much less 'free' than it had been under the Conservatives. This implied the creation of new managerial and administrative posts. But once again money was related directly to activity.

More recently, and somewhat controversially, Foundation Hospitals have been created. Those Hospital Trusts that score three stars on a raft of key measures can apply for greater independence within the Health Service. They can, for example, borrow money at their own discretion. The catch is, the Treasury monitor this and, by other withdrawals, make sure no extra money is going into the system, beyond that the Chancellor of the Exchequer has decreed is the appropriate aggregate amount. The star rating is monitored on an annual basis, and any Trust that loses its three-star rating loses its Foundation status. From time to time the key measures are changed as well. In 2004, for example, the ability to control the 'super bug' – which leaves hospital patients with secondary infections – became critical for the first time.

Another regulatory arm introduced by Labour has been NICE – the National Institute for Clinical Excellence – which dictates which drugs can and cannot be prescribed.

Alongside the NHS itself, the government has allowed and encouraged Fast Track Surgery Centres, where the private sector provides certain procedures on behalf of the NHS at an agreed charge to the system. The relevant costs are typically less than those of the insurance-based private sector itself. These centres have often attracted surgeons from overseas and they are a threat to the poorest-performing hospitals, those that cannot cope with their waiting lists. Some patients have also been allowed to have treatment in other European countries (paid for by the NHS) where local waiting lists are lengthy.

In summary, centralization gave way to a free market which itself was replaced by regulated devolution.

### Questions

1. What do you think might be the advantages and disadvantages of the current system?
2. Could you design a structure that allows greater decentralization without destroying the ethos of a 'national' health service?

**National Health Service** http://www.nhs.uk

---

greater the informality, the greater the likelihood of strong and effective horizontal communications as people across the organization are encouraged to talk and share.

Minicase 15.3 illustrates the difficulty in finding a balance between central government centralization and local hospital decentralization in managing the National Health Service.

The challenge for most organizations, then, is to find the appropriate degrees of decentralization and informality, to enable them to maintain control while innovating and managing change in a dynamic and turbulent environment. In turn, this requires that managers are *empowered*. (Empowerment was explained in Box 5.1, p. 222.)

It would not be unusual for an organization to be centralized and informal when it first starts up. Afterwards, as limited power and responsibility is devolved to identifiable managers, the structure becomes more formalized, but the central power of the strategic leader remains strong. As the organization grows beyond a stage where one person can really remain in effective control, the switch is to decentralized with formal controls through policies, procedures and reporting relationships. It is not difficult to imagine how the need for a formal structure developed and became urgent as Nantucket Nectars (Minicase 15.4) grew in size.

These structural types, then, will be evidenced in the organization frameworks and structural designs which are explored in detail in the next section of this chapter. It is

---

CASE

## Minicase 15.4 Nantucket Nectars

US

Nantucket Nectars is an unusual but very successful business which was started by two friends. When Tom First and Tom Scott graduated from Brown University in Rhode Island they decided they wanted to live on Nantucket Island, off the New England coast, and find some way of earning a living. In the summer of 1989 they started a small business for servicing the yachts belonging to visitors to the island. This was always going to be seasonal. They travelled around the harbour in a distinctive red boat, delivering newspapers, muffins, coffee, laundry and any other supplies for which there was a demand. They also washed boats, emptied sewage and shampooed dogs. This seemed to lead naturally to them later opening the Nantucket Allserve general store, which still exists. They used the following promotional slogan in the early days: 'Ain't nothing those boys won't do.'

Once the summer was over, demand for their services fell as the yachts disappeared. They decided to experiment with fruit juices, mixed in a household blender. They first sought to replicate a peach-based nectar that they had sampled in Spain. During the following summer they sold their bottled juices from their red boat. They always produced distinctive flavours from the best quality ingredients. By investing their joint savings they were able to hire a bottler to produce 1400 cases. Overall, though, the business merely struggled on for a couple of years, until one wealthy yacht owner offered them a $500,000 loan to develop the business. They seized the opportunity. Nantucket Nectars then expanded quickly to cover a number of states on the American east coast. Initially they did their own bottling, but this is now subcontracted.

> If I were on the outside looking in, I'd say Nantucket Nectars was an overnight success. Being on the inside, it's been a long, long time. We almost went out of business a thousand times.
>
> Tom Scott

By the late 1990s Nantucket Nectars employed over 100 people and sold in over 30 US states and a number of selected export markets. Values were always a key element, the partners remained determined to 'create the best quality product in the juice market', and yet the company remained enigmatic. The bottle labels stated: 'We're juice guys. We don't wear ties to work'; folksy radio commercials were utilized extensively in America; but the new head office is in an old Men's Club near Harvard University. It is furnished with antiques and managers have private offices instead of the open-plan arrangement which is increasingly popular in many informal organizations. First and Scott typically took their dogs into work. Each week every head-office manager focused on talking personally with one of their salespeople in the field, staff who would otherwise have little contact with head office.

The founders claim that the company was always run on gut instinct and trial and error. Few people had any formal business qualifications. In 1997 Nantucket Nectars was awarded a contract to provide juice for Starbucks, and later that year Ocean Spray – leading manufacturer of cranberry juices and other products – acquired a 50 per cent stake. The companies believed that they could make extensive savings on supplies if they joined forces. First and Scott continued to run the business that they founded.

### Questions

1. How easy will it be for First and Scott to maintain their informal style and culture as Nantucket Nectars grows further?
2. Will more formality be required?

### Task

Apply Figures 15.1–15.3 to this case.
1. How are strategy and structure linked?
2. What is the balance between intended and emergent strategy?

**Nantucket Nectars** http://www.juiceguys.com

important to appreciate that structure involves more than the organization chart or framework which is used for illustrative purposes and to explain where businesses, products, services and people fit in relation to each other. Charts are static; structures are dynamic and involve behaviour patterns.

## 15.6 Structural forms

A number of discrete structural forms can be adapted by an organization when attempts are made to design an appropriate structure to satisfy its particular needs. The following are described in this section:

- the entrepreneurial structure
- the functional structure
- the divisional structure
- the holding company structure
- the matrix structure.

This is not an exhaustive coverage, in the sense that personalized varieties of each of these alternatives can easily be developed.

Chandler (1962) and subsequent authors such as Salter (1970) have suggested that as firms grow from being a small business with a simple entrepreneurial structure, a more formal **functional structure** evolves to allow managers to cope with the increasing complexity and the demands of decision-making. As the organization becomes diversified, with a multiplicity of products, services or operating bases, a different structure is again required, and initially this is likely to be based on simple **divisionalization**. In other words, there are stages of structural development which evolve as strategies change and organizations grow. Chandler contends, however, that while strategy and structure develop together through a particular sequence, structures are not adapted until pressures force a change. The pressures tend to relate to growing inefficiency resulting from an inability to handle the increasing demands of decision-making. **Matrix organizations** have been designed to cope with the complexities of multiproduct, multinational organizations with interdependencies which must be accommodated if synergy is to be achieved. However, matrix organizations are difficult to manage and control. Large organizations in particular change their structures (at least in part) quite frequently as they search for one that allows effective implementation of intended strategies while permitting emergent strategy creation to a desired level.

*In my experience, the key to growth is to pick good managers, involve them at the outset of discussions on strategy and objectives, and then devolve as much responsibility as they will accept. That's the only way you know if they are any good.*

Michael Grade, BBC Chairman, when Chief Executive, Channel Four Television

*Autonomy is what you take, not what you are given.*

Roy Watts, when Chairman, Thames Water

*Organizational flexibility is essential. Rates of change have speeded up. The hierarchical organization is slow to respond. Decisions taken at the  centre are too far away from the coal face. While the centre seeks local and relevant understanding, delays in decision making result. In today's turbulent business environment speed of decision making is critically important … decisions should be pushed down the organization and as close to the customers as possible.*

Sir John Harvey-Jones MBE, quoted in The responsive organization, *BIM*, 1989

It has been emphasized earlier (see Chapter 12) that many organizations fail to achieve the anticipated synergy from strategies of diversification and acquisition, and as a result divest the businesses to which they cannot add value. Implementation difficulties are often linked to a failure to absorb the new acquisition into the existing organization, and this is likely to involve changes in the structure.

It is important to appreciate that the structural forms described in this section are only a framework, and that the behavioural processes within the structure, the way in

**Figure 15.4** The entrepreneurial structure

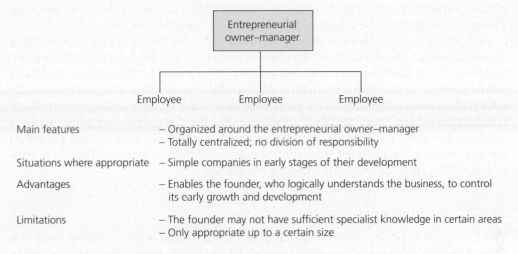

| Main features | – Organized around the entrepreneurial owner–manager<br>– Totally centralized; no division of responsibility |
|---|---|
| Situations where appropriate | – Simple companies in early stages of their development |
| Advantages | – Enables the founder, who logically understands the business, to control its early growth and development |
| Limitations | – The founder may not have sufficient specialist knowledge in certain areas<br>– Only appropriate up to a certain size |

which resources are managed and co-ordinated, really determines effectiveness. In turn, this is related to the way in which authority, power and responsibility are devolved throughout the organization, and whether generally the firm is centralized or decentralized. These themes were explored in Box 15.1, where it is emphasized that decentralization and divisionalization are not synonymous. The establishment of a divisionalized structure does not necessarily imply that authority to adapt competitive and functional strategies is freely delegated; the firm could remain centralized.

### 15.6.1 The entrepreneurial structure

The entrepreneurial structure, built around the owner–manager and typically utilized by small companies in the early stages of their development, is illustrated in Figure 15.4. The structure is totally centralized. All key decisions are made by the strategic leader, and employees refer everything significant back to him or her. It is particularly useful for new businesses as it enables the founder, who normally will have some expertise with the product or service and whose investment is at risk, to control the growth and development.

There is an argument that this is not really a formal structure as all responsibility, power and authority lie with one person. However, in some small companies of this nature, selected employees will specialize and be given job titles and some limited responsibility for such activities as production, sales or accounting. In this respect the structure could be redrawn to appear more like the functional organization discussed below. The functional form only really emerges when *managers* are established with genuine delegated authority and responsibility for the functions and activities that they control.

New firms with entrepreneurial structures are likely to be established because the owner–manager has contacts and expertise in a particular line of business and, for whatever reason, wishes to establish his or her own business. While the entrepreneur will want to control the early stages of growth, it does not follow that he or she will have expertise in all aspects of the business. Many start-ups occur because the founder understands the technology and production or operational aspects of the business. Marketing, sales and financial control may well be areas of potential weakness with a consequent reliance on other people together with an element of learning as the business develops. This need can prove to be a limitation of the entrepreneurial structure.

Another limitation relates to growth. At some stage, dependent on both the business and the founder, the demands of decision-making, both day-to-day problem decisions and longer-term planning decisions, will become too complex for one person, and there will be pressure to establish a more formal functional organization. The owner–manager relinquishes some responsibility for short-term decisions and has greater opportunity to concentrate on the more strategic aspects of the business. This can prove to be a dilemma for some entrepreneurs, however: particularly those who started their own business because they wanted total control over something, or because they were frustrated with the greater formality of larger companies.

### 15.6.2  The functional structure

The functional structure, illustrated in Figure 15.5, is commonplace in small firms that have outgrown the entrepreneurial structure and in larger firms that produce only a limited range of related products and services. It is also the typical internal structure of

**Figure 15.5** The functional structure

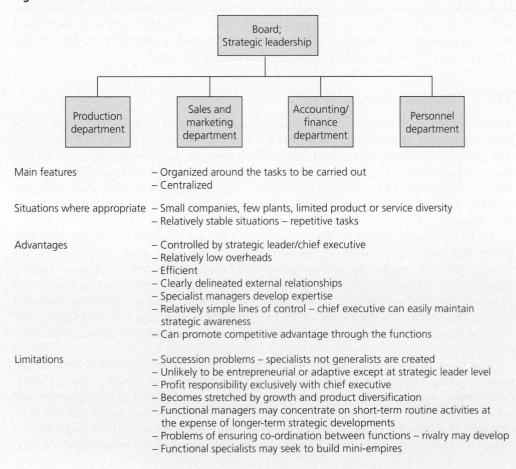

Main features
- Organized around the tasks to be carried out
- Centralized

Situations where appropriate
- Small companies, few plants, limited product or service diversity
- Relatively stable situations – repetitive tasks

Advantages
- Controlled by strategic leader/chief executive
- Relatively low overheads
- Efficient
- Clearly delineated external relationships
- Specialist managers develop expertise
- Relatively simple lines of control – chief executive can easily maintain strategic awareness
- Can promote competitive advantage through the functions

Limitations
- Succession problems – specialists not generalists are created
- Unlikely to be entrepreneurial or adaptive except at strategic leader level
- Profit responsibility exclusively with chief executive
- Becomes stretched by growth and product diversification
- Functional managers may concentrate on short-term routine activities at the expense of longer-term strategic developments
- Problems of ensuring co-ordination between functions – rivalry may develop
- Functional specialists may seek to build mini-empires

the divisions and business units that comprise larger diversified organizations. It is more suitable in a stable environment than a turbulent one, as it is generally centralized with corporate and competitive strategies again being controlled substantially by the strategic leader.

The structure is built around the tasks to be carried out, which tend to be split into specialist functional areas. Managers are placed in charge of departments which are responsible for these functions, and they may well have delegated authority to change functional strategies. Consequently, the effectiveness of this structure is very dependent on the ability of these specialist managers to work together as a team and support each other and on the ability of the strategic leader to co-ordinate their efforts.

The functional structure can be highly efficient with low overheads in comparison with divisional structures, which have to address the issue of functions duplicated in the business units and at head office. Functional managers will develop valuable specialist expertise which can be used as a basis for the creation of competitive advantage, and the relatively simple lines of communication between these specialists and the strategic leader can facilitate a high degree of strategic awareness at the top of the organization.

There are some limitations, however. The concentration on the functions tends to lead to managers with greater specialist expertise rather than a more corporate perspective. General managers who can embrace all of the functions are not developed, and consequently any internal successor to the chief executive is likely to have a particular specialist viewpoint, which may involve cultural change. This might conceivably mean a change from a financial orientation to a customer-led organization, for example, or vice versa.

**Figure 15.6** Growth strategies and related structural formats

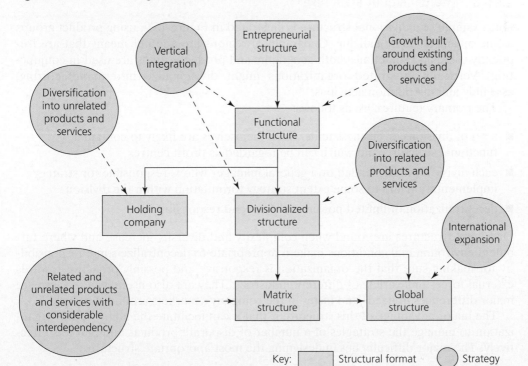

Functional organizations are less likely to be entrepreneurial throughout the company than is the case in more decentralized forms, although the strategic leader could be personally dynamic and entrepreneurial. Because corporate and competitive strategy changes are generally the responsibility of the strategic leader, functional managers may concentrate on short-term issues at the expense of longer-term strategic needs. The tendency for profit responsibility to lie primarily with the strategic leader compounds this. Functional managers may seek to build mini-empires around their specialism, and this can lead to rivalry between departments for resources and status and make the task of co-ordination and team-building more difficult.

The structure is stretched and becomes more inefficient with growth and product or service diversification. As the firm grows from a limited range of related products to unrelated ones, co-ordination proves increasingly difficult. Hence, a need grows for some form of divisionalization, together with a revised role for the strategic leader. The strategic leader is now responsible for co-ordinating the strategies of a series of business units or divisions, each with a general manager at their head, rather than co-ordinating specialist functional managers into a cohesive and supportive team. Financial management skills become increasingly necessary. Adaptive changes in competitive strategies are now likely to be delegated.

Once organizations reach the functional stage, their choice of future corporate growth strategy will have a major bearing upon the structural developments. Figure 15.6 shows the structures discussed in this section linked to relevant growth strategies. These linkages must be seen as indicative; it does not follow that organizations must follow these routes. Figure 15.6 additionally includes the global structure which was discussed in Chapter 13 and, for this reason only, is excluded from this chapter.

### 15.6.3  The divisional structure

One example of a divisional structure is illustrated in Figure 15.7, using product groups as the means of divisionalizing. Geographical regions are another means that are frequently used, and sometimes both geography and product groups are used in conjunction. Vertically integrated organizations might divisionalize into manufacturing, assembly and distribution activities.

The primary features are as follows:

- a set of divisions or business units which themselves are likely to contain a functional structure, and which can be regarded as profit centres
- each division will be headed by a general manager who is responsible for strategy implementation and to some extent strategy formulation within the division
- decentralization of limited power, authority and responsibility.

Divisional structures are found when complexity and diversity increase and where turbulent environmental conditions make it appropriate to decentralize some responsibility for making sure that the organization is responsive and possibly proactive towards external forces in a variety of different industries. They are also useful where there are major differences in needs and tastes in the company's markets around the world.

The major advantage of this structure is that it can facilitate the ability of the organization to manage the strategies of a number of disparate products and markets effectively. The major difficulty lies in designing the most appropriate structure.

**Figure 15.7** The divisional structure. A product divisional structure is illustrated. Geographical divisions, or a mixture of the two, are also used

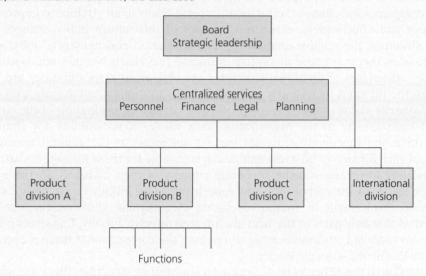

| | |
|---|---|
| Main features | – Divisions are likely to be profit centres and may be seen as strategic business units for planning and control purposes<br>– Divisions/business units are headed by general managers who enjoy responsibility for their own resources<br>– Decentralized |
| Situations where appropriate | – Growing size and complexity<br>– Appropriate divisional/business unit splits exist<br>– Organizations growing through merger and acquisition<br>– Turbulent environments<br>– Product/market divisions/business units most appropriate where there is a diverse range of products<br>– Geographic divisions are common where there are cultural distinctions between the company's markets – especially if distances are great<br>– Divisionalization may also be a mix of products and geography or based on different production processes |
| Advantages | – Spreads profit responsibility<br>– Enables evaluation of contribution of various activities<br>– Motivates managers and facilitates the development of both specialist and general managers<br>– Enables adaptive change<br>– Chief executive can stay away from routine decisions and concentrate on corporate strategy<br>– Growth through acquisition more readily implemented<br>– Can be entrepreneurial throughout the organization<br>– Divestment can also be handled relatively easily |
| Limitations | – Conflict between divisions, say for resources<br>– Possible confusion over locus of responsibility (head office and divisions) and duplication of efforts and resources<br>– Divisions may tend to think short term and concentrate on profits<br>– Divisions may be of different sizes and some may grow very large – evaluation of relative performance may be difficult<br>– Co-ordinating interdependent divisions and establishing transfer prices between them |

There is no one best way of dividing a business into divisions, especially if the composition of the whole corporation changes with acquisitions, divestments and closures. Large companies will change their structures periodically in an attempt to improve both efficiency and effectiveness. Structural changes of this nature imply changes in the power structure, the relative amount of decentralization and managers' jobs, and for these reasons they may prove disruptive. Minicase 15.5 charts Nestlé's approach.

Other advantages of divisional structures are that profit responsibilities are spread between the divisions or business units. This helps to motivate managers who can be given authority and responsibility for profit, and enables an evaluation of the contribution of each activity to the organization as a whole. Responsibility for changes in competitive and functional strategies can be delegated to the general managers in charge of each division or business unit; and it is feasible for these managers also to have responsibility for changes in the corporate strategy of their divisions. In this way the strategic leader of the corporation can concentrate substantially on corporate strategy and avoid involvement in routine decisions. Acquisitions and divestments can be handled so that only parts of the firm are affected directly. Finally, this structure facilitates innovation and intrapreneurship throughout the corporation if there is encouragement for this by the strategic leader.

In addition to the difficulty of designing an appropriate structure, there are problems of implementation. It was highlighted above that divisions are normally seen as profit centres, and consequently their profit targets will be used as a basis for assessing performance and effectiveness. There may be problems in establishing profit targets which are seen as equitable, given that divisions (a) may well be of uneven sizes, (b) are likely to be operating in markets which differ in their attractiveness, (c) may have strong or weak relative market shares, (d) may be interdependent upon each other, and (e) have to compete with each other for scarce corporate resources. Where there are interdependencies the corporate policy on transfer prices will favour certain divisions at the expense of others, which again can cause conflict. Wherever profits are a key measure, buying divisions will look for discounts and favourable treatment from within the corporation; selling divisions will expect other parts of the company to pay the going market price, or they will prefer to sell outside. Such profit orientation may also encourage divisions to think in terms of short-term financial measures rather than address more strategic issues.

Where an organization has a variety of different products, all of which depend on core skills and technologies, the challenge is to harness and improve the skills (which are, in effect, corporate resources) while ensuring competitiveness and operating efficiency for each product range. Canon, for example, has developed a range of discrete products (cameras, copiers, printers, etc.) around three core competencies: precision mechanics, fibre optics and microelectronics.

Finally, each division is likely to contain a functional structure, and there is also likely to be functional support from headquarters. The corporation as a whole may be able to negotiate better borrowing terms than an individual division could; personnel policies may need to be consistent throughout the firm; and head-office planners may provide support to divisional planners. Reconciling any conflicts between these divisional and head-office groups, together with the need to minimize the potential waste from duplicate resources, can be a limitation of this structural form. The problem can be more difficult to resolve where there are layers of divisions, as discussed below.

# Minicase 15.5  Nestlé

**Eur**  **Int**

Nestlé began in the 1860s as a condensed milk factory in Switzerland, where it still has its global headquarters. Having developed largely by acquisition (followed by organic growth) Nestlé now produces in 500 factories in 60 countries and sells in over 100 countries, many of which have strong local preferences. Only 2 per cent of its sales now originate in Switzerland. It aims to be number one or number two in all the markets it targets, and consequently invests in branding. The main products and brands are as follows:

**Beverages** – coffee (its Nescafé brand is ubiquitous around the world), mineral water (Perrier carbonated water was acquired in 1992 to add to Vittel still water) and fruit juices

**Milk products** – based on its original brand name, Carnation but also including Libby's

**Ice cream, chocolate** (Rowntree and Kit Kat, for example, both acquired in 1988) **and confectionery** (Smarties)

**Prepared dishes** (Crosse and Blackwell), frozen foods (Findus), **sauces and condiments** (including Maggi and Buitoni)

**Pet foods** – Spillers was acquired in 1998 to supplement the existing business

Nestlé also owns a substantial stake of the French cosmetics business, L'Oréal.

Its corporate headquarters was slimmed down in the early 1990s in an attempt to be more innovative and more customer-focused. There are now seven strategic business units (including coffee and beverages; foods, etc.) which have worldwide *strategic* responsibility. Operations in the various countries are co-ordinated through a regional network. Six business unit head offices are co-located at corporate headquarters in Switzerland; Nestlé's mineral water interests, including Perrier, are run from Paris. There were plans to locate the global confectionery business in York (where the

**Nestlé brands**

Rowntree business was built and based) but these were abandoned because of the travel implications.

Each strategic business unit is free to operate in the most appropriate way – there is no longer a 'central way of doing things'. The style and approach appears to vary with the degree of novelty/maturity of the business, its market share and technological intensity, and the need to be localized. The intention is to establish the most appropriate cost structure and decision-making procedures. The requirements for E–V–R congruence vary between the divisions. There are, however, inbuilt mechanisms to try and spread best practices and to overcome a past tendency to resist adopting ideas developed in other countries.

## Question

1. Does this structure make sense for the scope and diversity of the businesses? Why? Why not?

**Nestlé** http://www.nestle.com

Where organizations grow very large, complex and diversified it may be necessary to establish a number of layers of divisions or business units within larger divisions. Each business unit or subdivision may also be a profit centre with its own general manager.

As organizations develop globally the structural issues are compounded. It was shown in Chapter 13 that Porter (1990) and Ohmae (1990) disagree about how a company should transform itself into a successful global firm. Ohmae argues that it should shake off its origins, whereas Porter thinks they must be preserved. Should all of the high added value activities (such as design, development and engineering) be centralized at a global company's home base or spread around the world? Ohmae advocates decomposing the central head office into a number of regional headquarters, with the control of different functions (marketing, production, etc.) being dispersed to different extents and to different locations. Minicase 15.6 (later) discusses ABB, a company which deliberately followed a strategy of devolution when it was growing and diversifying.

### 15.6.4 The holding company structure

The holding company structure, illustrated in Figure 15.8, is ideal for diversified conglomerates where there are few interdependencies between the businesses. The small

**Figure 15.8** The holding company structure

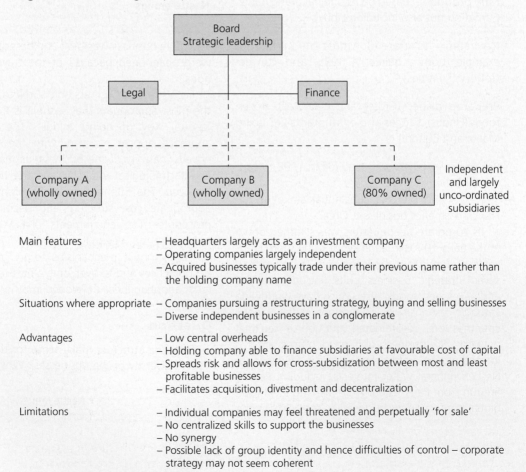

| Main features | – Headquarters largely acts as an investment company<br>– Operating companies largely independent<br>– Acquired businesses typically trade under their previous name rather than the holding company name |
|---|---|
| Situations where appropriate | – Companies pursuing a restructuring strategy, buying and selling businesses<br>– Diverse independent businesses in a conglomerate |
| Advantages | – Low central overheads<br>– Holding company able to finance subsidiaries at favourable cost of capital<br>– Spreads risk and allows for cross-subsidization between most and least profitable businesses<br>– Facilitates acquisition, divestment and decentralization |
| Limitations | – Individual companies may feel threatened and perpetually 'for sale'<br>– No centralized skills to support the businesses<br>– No synergy<br>– Possible lack of group identity and hence difficulties of control – corporate strategy may not seem coherent |

head office acts largely as an investment company, acquiring and selling businesses and investing money as appropriate. The subsidiaries, which may or may not be wholly owned, are very independent, and their general managers are likely to have full responsibility for corporate strategy within any financial constraints or targets set by headquarters. It is quite common to find that the subsidiaries trade under individual names rather than the name of the parent organization, especially where they are acquisitions who may at any time be sold again.

The holding company structure is particularly appropriate for companies pursuing restructuring strategies, buying, rationalizing and then selling businesses when they can no longer add further value. The advantages of this structural form are that it implies low central overheads and considerable decentralization but enables the head office to finance the subsidiaries at a favourable cost of capital. In fact, low-cost finance can reduce the total costs for a business and thus help to provide competitive advantage. In addition, risks are spread across a wide portfolio, and cross-subsidization is possible between the most and least profitable businesses. This again raises the issue of ascertaining a fair reward structure for the general managers.

The limitations relate, first, to the vulnerability that general managers may feel if they suspect that their business may always be for sale at the right price. There are fewer centralized skills and resources supporting the businesses, little co-ordination and therefore few opportunities for synergy. In addition, there may be no group identity among the business units and a lack of coherence in the corporate strategy. The potential benefit to headquarters lies in their ability to earn revenue and profits from the businesses, ideally in excess of pre-acquisition earnings, and being able to sell for a real capital gain.

> *The constituent companies [in LVMH, Louis Vuitton Moët Hennessy] have asked for the following: simplified structures, autonomy for the operational units and a method of administration in keeping with their particular culture.*
>
> *I am convinced that the success of our group and its subsidiaries is due to the fact that we trust the operational teams to carry out their own quest for quality.*
>
> *We keep these companies autonomous at middle management level so that they can have the advantages of medium size companies as well as the advantage of belonging to a powerful group that can fund their development.*
>
> Bernard Arnault, Group Chairman, LVMH,
> Louis Vuitton Moët Hennessy

Several control issues which face head offices of divisionalized and holding company structures have been mentioned in the above sections, and these will be explored in greater detail in Chapter 16.

### 15.6.5   The matrix structure

Matrix structures are an attempt to combine the benefits of *decentralization* (motivation of identifiable management teams; closeness to the market; speedy decision making and implementation) with those of *co-ordination* (achieving economies and synergy across all the business units, territories and products). They require dual reporting by managers to, say, a mix of functional and business unit heads or geographical territory and business unit general managers.

The matrix structure is found typically in large multiproduct, multinational organizations where there are significant interrelationships and interdependencies, as illustrated

**Figure 15.9** The matrix structure

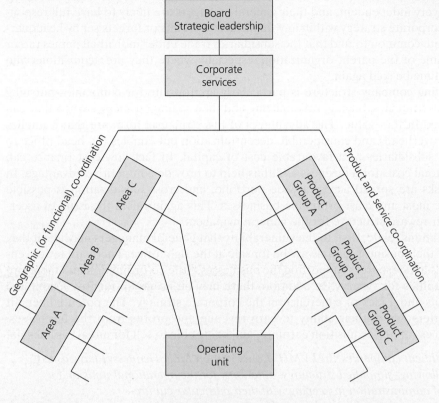

Main features
- Double definition of profit centres
- Permanent and full dual control of operating units – although one wing will generally be more powerful than the other
- Authority and accountability defined in terms of particular decisions

Situations where appropriate
- Large multiproduct, multinational companies with significant interrelationships and interdependencies
- Small sophisticated service companies

Advantages
- Decisions can be taken locally, decentralized within a large corporation which might otherwise be bureaucratic
- Optimum use of skills and resources – and high quality informed decisions reconciling conflicts within the organization
- Enables control of growth and increasing complexity
- Opportunities for manager development

Limitations
- Difficult to implement
- Dual responsibilities can cause confusion
- Accounting and control difficulties
- Potential conflict between the two wings, with one generally more powerful
- High overhead costs
- Decision-making can be slow

in Figure 15.9 and Minicase 15.6, and in small sophisticated service businesses such as a business school. The matrix structure in Figure 15.9 illustrates an organization which is split into a series of divisions, based on both products and geographical territories. The product groups would be responsible for co-ordinating the production and marketing of their particular products in a series of plants which might be based anywhere in the world. The geographical divisions would have responsibility for co-ordinating the sales, marketing and distribution of all of the corporation's products, regardless of where they are manufactured, within their territorial area. The operating units would be the production plants, who were members of one or more product groups, depending upon the range of products manufactured in the plant, and whose products are marketed in more than one territory or geographical region. Consequently, the general manager in charge of each operating unit is responsible in some way to a series of product and territory chiefs (four in the illustration), all of whom will have profit responsibility. The matrix is designed to co-ordinate resources and effort throughout the organization. Structures such as this evolved in the 1960s and 1970s because of the need to establish priorities in multiproduct, multinational organizations. Should the resources and efforts be concentrated on the product groups or in the geographical territories? The ideal answer is both.

## Minicase 15.6  Asea Brown Boveri (ABB)

### Barnevik's matrix structure

ABB was formed in 1988 when the Swedish company ASEA merged with Brown Boveri of Switzerland to create a global electrical engineering giant. At the time this was the largest cross-border merger in modern history. ABB would later acquire over 100 additional, but smaller, businesses in Europe and America, all of which have needed integrating effectively. The chief executive who masterminded the merger and consequent restructuring was Percy Barnevik (of ASEA), who realized that he had a major challenge if he was to maintain both drive and dynamism during the integration. He became committed to an individualized matrix structure and his aim was to make ABB the global low-cost competitor. His creation has been declared 'the ultimate global organization' – a decentralized structure with centralized control over information and knowledge development. Simply, ABB became a 'multinational without a national identity'.

Barnevik is Swedish and he has been described as soft spoken, intense and philosophical. He was noticeably strong on information technology (IT) and he was very committed to the economic development of Eastern Europe and to the fostering of clean energy and transportation. During his eight year reign as chief executive revenues doubled and net profits trebled. The share price rose by 20 per cent every year.

Under Barnevik ABB was divided up into 1300 identifiable companies and 5000 profit centres. These were aggregated into eight business segments and 59 business areas. There were over 200,000 employees worldwide.

The eight segments were:

- power plants, further subdivided into
  - gas turbine plants
  - utility steam plants
  - industrial steam plants
  - hydro power plants
  - nuclear power plants
  - power plant controls
- power transmission
- power distribution
- electrical equipment
- transportation (such as high-speed trains)
- environmental controls
- financial services
- other activities.

The segments were responsible for organizing manufacture around the world and for product

**Figure 15.10** Component businesses in the ABB matrix

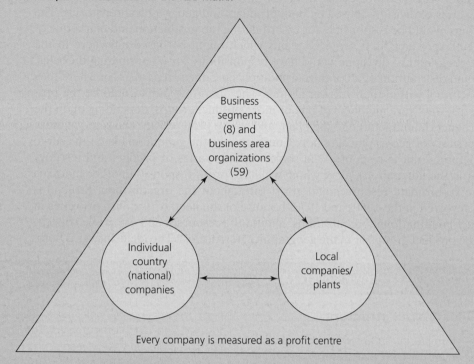

Every company is measured as a profit centre

development. Horizontally, ABB was divided up into a mix of countries and regions. Figure 15.10 summarizes the basics of the matrix. There was a 12 member executive board representing products, regions and corporate operations, and a slim head office (under 200 employees) in Zurich. It was not seen as essential that the divisional headquarters for the eight business segments were located in Zurich. Some years earlier ASEA had had a head office staff complement of 2000; Brown Boveri employed 4000 in its head office.

Zurich essentially retained control over:

■ acquisitions
■ shifting production to Asia and Eastern Europe
■ raising and managing corporate finance.

Financial reporting and evaluation was on a monthly basis.

The basic structure, therefore, was based on small units (of 50 people each on average) supported by good communications and IT. Although ABB comprised distinct businesses, both technology and products were exchanged. Under Barnevik, every employee had a country manager and a business sector manager. Dual responsibilities such as this are often key issues in matrix structures which fail. However, Barnevik insisted that ABB's version was 'loose and decentralized' and that it was easily recognized that the two bosses are rarely of equal status.

Barnevik was obsessed with the idea of creating a small-company and entrepreneurial climate within his large corporation. Extra costs and some fragmentation in the structure were seen as 'a small price to pay for speed and flexibility, with employees staying close to customers and understanding the importance of their own individual efforts for the success of their profit centre'. He also believed that if a large company is to manage internal communications effectively it must develop a 'horizontal integration process'.

The front-line managers, the heads of the 1300 businesses, were no longer implementers of decisions from the strategic leader; instead they were initiators of entrepreneurial action, creating and chasing new opportunities. The role of middle managers – in this flatter structure – concerned coaching and technology and skill transfer. Strategic leadership was about creating purpose, challenging the status quo and setting stretching, demanding targets for front-line managers; it was not simply, as historically it was, to allocate corporate resources and resolve internal conflicts.

Barnevik also commented that the biggest problem was 'motivating middle and lower level managers and entrenching corporate values – particularly a customer and quality focus'. He believed that his executives should see the business as their number one priority and assumed that high-fliers would spend up to 30 hours a week (in addition to their regular tasks) travelling, attending conferences and evening seminars and lectures.

*It is the responsibility of every manager to network within the family of companies, developing informal relationships and looking for synergistic opportunities.*

Barnevik

## Life – and structure – after Barnevik

In 1997 Barnevik gave up the chief executive role and became non-executive chairman of ABB. His successor was Göran Lindahl, perceived as more of a detail and less a concept person. Under Lindahl the process of transferring manufacturing to Asia and Eastern Europe from America and western Europe accelerated. He initially reduced the importance of those executives with geographical responsibilities to focus more emphasis on manufacturing and to iron out some of the complex, dual-reporting issues. But he waited eighteen months before dismantling the matrix struture of his predecessor. He was, however, anxious to retain the learning style and the concentration on small units.

Lindahl decided to take ABB out of capital-intensive and low margin activities, here targeting transportation and power generation. He wanted to focus more on automation businesses. In three years the number of employees would fall from 215,000 to 160,000. Lindahl resigned in 2000 after initiating these changes of strategic direction. When he left the share price was half the value when he took over. At this time there were four industrial divisions – power transmission; power distribution; building technologies; and automation.

In fairness to Lindahl, some of ABB's markets had been declining and many agreed the company had diversified too quickly and too far. Adverse interest rate movements affected pre-tax profits and an ill-judged acquisition in America left ABB saddled with asbestos liabilities.

His successor, Jörgen Centerman, opted to restructure ABB again, this time around four consumer segments – utilities; process industries; manufacturing and consumer industries; oil, gas and petrochemicals – and two product segments – power technology and automation technology. The product divisions both provided technology support to all the consumer divisions. It took him just one month to instigate this change. In recent years, sales growth had fallen back and Centerman believed ABB had to focus more on its customers. However he also created a stronger central executive team. The general assumption was that he would focus even more on automation and exit power transmission and distribution.

In November 2001 Barnevik resigned as chairman, 'accepting responsibility for the collapse of the business'. The share price was now back to the 1988 merger value. Barnevik was replaced by Jurgen Doorman, who was recruited from Avensis (created through the merger of German and French chemical/pharmaceutical companies Hoechst and Rhône Poulenc). He was a 'hard-headed numbers man'.

*You may have a brilliant vision ... but if your bottom line is bad, your vision will be called into question very quickly ... you have to implement your ideas.*

Doorman

When Centerman also left in September 2002, Doorman took over his role as well.

Almost immediately, ABB's financial services business was sold to General Electric and oil and petrochemicals were put up for sale. A deal was concluded in 2003. ABB was to be structured around two core activities: automation technologies and power technologies. There would be twelve business areas. Current staff levels of 150,000 would shrink further. ABB was now a 'mid-size engineering group with a lot of debt and a list of disposable assets'.

ABB had once been renowned for its growth and imaginative structure, for which it had sought publicity and notoriety. But

> *arrogance and complacency are contagious ... successful organizations have a tendency to become bureaucratic. The company went from the very entrepreneurial spirit under Percy [Barnevik] in his early days to then having become too successful. People felt there was too much power out there and wanted to centralize management control. This went far beyond what should have happened. It's operational excellence that's required now ... and improving operating margins ... some might say that's [more] boring [than in the past].*

Doorman

ABB began its recovery in 2003, but it was a dramatically different company from when Asea and Brown Boveri were merged. Fred Kindle (from Sulzer) was appointed in 2004 to succeed Doorman as CEO from 1 January 2005. Doorman would progressively reduce his commitment to the business. There were 115,000 employees and the 2003/4 financial year showed a profit after three consecutive trading losses.

### Questions

1. While the idea of a matrix structure is very attractive, it is inherently complex. Why do you think Barnevik's structure has been described as the 'ultimate global organization'?
2. How do you think it would feel to work within a structure such as this?
3. Is the swing between decentralization and centralization flagged in the final quote at the end of the Minicase an inevitability?

**ABB** http://www.abb.com

Figure 15.11 is a more straightforward illustration of how the staff in a business school might be organized. It is assumed that all of the academic staff would have a specialization which would fit into one of the six columns shown, and that expertise and development in their subject specialism would be important to the staff. At the same

**Figure 15.11** Possible matrix structure for a business school

| | Human resources | Marketing | Operations | Finance and accounting | Business policy/ strategy | Information technology |
|---|---|---|---|---|---|---|
| Undergraduate courses | | | | | | |
| Postgraduate and post-experience courses | | | | | | |
| Research | | | | | | |
| Executive courses | | | | | | |

time the business school would offer a series of products or services, which are shown as four rows. Staff from each subject group would be allocated to each of these areas. Each product group, and possibly each course within the group, would have a leader with responsibility for delivering a quality product and earning revenue; each subject group would also have a leader responsible for allocating resources and ensuring that staff develop academically.

The potential advantages of a matrix are that responsibility and authority are delegated and spread throughout a complex organization and the stifling tendencies of a bureaucracy are avoided. Because of the flows of information, and the establishment of priorities, decisions are informed and quick. Conflicts between the various groups are reconciled within the structure by the establishment of the priorities and objectives. In addition there are numerous specialist and generalist development opportunities for managers.

**Alternatives to the matrix**   In many cases, then, the matrix has proved to be too complicated to be effective. The primary reason has been the inability to deal with the issues of dual responsibility. Henri Fayol (1916) established a number of basic management principles, one of which was 'unity of command', the need to be responsible to only one manager; and the matrix has challenged this premise. Fayol's contention, however, has not been overturned. Decisions have been stifled by confusion, complexity and delay because managers have not been sufficiently sophisticated to operate effectively within this theoretically ideal structure. The need for a structural form which offers the potential advantages of the matrix to large complex multiproduct, multinational organizations, and which can be implemented, remains. If an organization is unable to design and operate a structure that enables the effective linking of a diverse range of related interests to achieve synergy, and at the same time permits the various business units to be responsive to environmental change, the organization may need to be split up.

Hunsicker (1982) quotes Philips, Ciba-Geigy and Texas Instruments as examples of multinationals that introduced and then retreated from the pure matrix structure. ABB (Minicase 15.6) changed its matrix to adjust the balance of power and then largely abandoned it. Hunsicker argues that matrices were designed to co-ordinate activities, and that the real strategic need has now become the development of new initiatives. This suggests a greater emphasis on temporary project teams, and the development and encouragement of managers within the organization so that they are more innovative and intrapreneurial. This implies that attention is focused more on changes in behaviour than on changes in the structural framework.

Pitts and Daniels (1984) list the following opportunities for obtaining the benefits of a matrix-type structure within more unitary forms:

- Strengthen corporate staffs to look after corporate strategic developments. They might, for example, search for new opportunities that existing business units could exploit.

- Rotate managers between functions, business units and locations. This increases their awareness and provides inputs of fresh ideas.

- Locate those executives responsible for product co-ordination in geographical territories physically closer to those managers responsible for production of the key products. Quite often such territory managers are based in their territories, close to their customers and somewhat divorced from manufacturing.

- Create some form of liaison groups which meet periodically and whose brief is to co-ordinate related issues. Such a group might attempt to co-ordinate the global strategies of a number of related products in a search for synergy and mutual benefits.

- Build the notion of agreed contributions between business units into both the management by objectives systems and the compensation schemes.

- Periodically review and amend the constitution of the divisions without restructuring the whole organization.

These suggestions again concentrate more on the processes within the structure than on the framework itself.

To conclude this section and chapter, it is worth recapping an earlier argument. Drucker (1988) suggested that the organization of the future would have fewer managers and fewer layers in the management hierarchy. He believed that IT would lead to more autonomy for individual managers and more informed decision-making when specialists have decentralized responsibility for key activities within the organization. Strategy co-ordination would still constitute a major challenge, however. We are now in a position to judge his prediction. Virtually every manager has access to a personal computer, an organizational intranet and the Internet. For many, letters, memos and phone calls have been replaced by e-mails. In reality what has really changed?

# SUMMARY

To be successful an intended strategy must be implemented.

This requires that the organization's strategic resources are developed, deployed and controlled appropriately. This is accomplished through the design of the organization (the structure) and the processes encapsulated within the structure.

The structure can be described as the *means* by which an organization seeks to achieve its strategic objectives. However, the structural processes are a reflection of culture, power and political activity, and where people are empowered in a decentralized organization, it is these processes which determine the actual (adaptive and/or incremental) strategies pursued.

Consequently the structure must be capable of both creating and implementing strategy. The key issues which impact upon strategy creation and implementation are the extent of any decentralization, the need for co-ordination and the relative degree of formality–informality.

Organization structures are designed to ensure that intended strategies can be implemented effectively. The processes within the structure also affect and facilitate emergent strategy. Particularly significant for ensuring that both happen is the location of power, responsibility and authority in the organization and the extent to which these are centralized and decentralized. In large organizations the relationship between the head office and the various subsidiaries (businesses or divisions) relates to this issue.

*Centralization* yields consistency and control, but it can result in an organization being slow to respond to the pressures for change in its external environment. In addition, entrepreneurial managers may feel constrained. *Decentralization* enables flexibility, but control is more difficult. It is dependent upon an effective information system which can gather together the various changes that are taking place as empowered managers make and take decisions.

Centralization/decentralization and formality/informality (the nature of control mechanisms and communications) determine the broad structural type.

There are five main structural forms:

- The *entrepreneurial structure* is found in the typical small business where everything is centred around a key person, often the owner–manager.

- The *functional structure* emerges as departments and managers are created to deal with the increasing number of tasks.

- The *divisionalized structure* is a popular structure for organizations with several products or services which may or may not be related.

- The *holding company* is adopted by a diversified business with largely unrelated activities or businesses which can advantageously be kept separate for control purposes.

- The *matrix structure* – or some variant of it – is most frequently used where there is a need to co-ordinate both products and countries in a business which manufacturers and markets worldwide. Because of its inherent complexities alternative forms of integration might be sought.

Organizations change their structures as they grow. They may also be changed in line with alterations to the corporate portfolio to try and keep the two in balance.

The main determinants of structure are: size, tasks to be carried out, environment and ideology.

The basic structure divides up the tasks but, of course, the structure is merely a framework for allocating tasks and roles and positioning people. The real follow-up challenge is one of integration.

# QUESTIONS AND RESEARCH ASSIGNMENTS

1. It was stated in the text that decentralization and divisionalization are not synonymous. What factors determine the degree of decentralization in a divisionalized organization?

2. For an organization with which you are familiar, obtain or draft the organization structure. How does it accord with the structural forms described in the text? Given your knowledge of the company's strategies and people, is the structure appropriate?

Why? Why not? If not, in what way would you change it?

3. How uncertain and traumatic might it be to work in a middle or senior management position in a large organization which changes its structure relatively frequently? Despite this, is change inevitable?

# INTERNET AND LIBRARY PROJECTS

1. Evaluate the divisionalized or holding company structure of a large, diverse, multiproduct multinational, considering the main board status of the key general managers. Does this suggest centralization or decentralization? If you are familiar with the company, do your findings accord with your knowledge of management styles within the organization?

2. In the last ten years WH Smith has struggled to clarify its strategic position in the retail industry. There is serious competition for all its products. As a consequence its performance has both improved and deteriorated. There have been changes of leadership and rumours of a possible takeover. The table below provides a summary of the organization structure in 1995, 1999 and 2003. Research the company's progress over this period. Has the structure merely changed to reflect changes of strategy? Or might the structural changes have been a serious attempt to drive the business both competitively and in fresh directions?

## WH Smith: Group Structure, 1995, 1999 and 2003

### 1995

**1. Retailing: UK and Europe**

| | |
|---|---|
| WH Smith Retail | High street stores – books, sounds, stationery |
| | Airports and stations |
| | Specialist Playhouse video stores |
| Virgin Our Price (75 per cent holding) | Virgin Megastores – *sold 1998* |
| Waterstone's | Specialist booksellers – large towns and cities – *sold 1998* |

**2. Retailing: USA**

| | |
|---|---|
| WH Smith Inc | Gift shops, typically in hotels and airports |
| The Wall Inc | Specialist bookselling in major cities and airports – *sold 1998* |

**3. Distribution: UK and Europe**

| | |
|---|---|
| WH Smith news and books | Newspaper and magazine wholesaling and distribution |
| | Book distribution to retailers, schools and libraries |
| WH Smith business supplies | Five acquired suppliers of commercial stationery and office products amalgamated under the Nice Day brand – *sold in 1996 to Guilbert of France* |

**4. Do It All**

| | |
|---|---|
| | DIY retailers, at this time a 50:50 joint venture with Boots – *sold to Boots in 1996* |

## WH Smith: Group Structure, 1995, 1999 and 2003

### 1999

| | |
|---|---|
| WH Smith High Street | 545 stores – books, sounds, stationery in the main |
| WH Smith Europe Travel Retail | 183 station and airport stores |
| WH Smith USA Travel Retail | 412 gift shops mainly in hotels and airports |
| WH Smith Asia Travel Retail | Hong Kong, Singapore and Sydney airports |
| WH Smith Direct | Internet retailing, with terminal access in selected stores |
| Hodder Headline | Consumer books publisher – with an 8.5 per cent share of the relevant market segment |
| WH Smith News Distribution | 51 depots, making WHS the UK's leading wholesaler of newspapers and magazines. (The High Street and Europe Travel Retail included the rebranded John Menzies stores acquired by WH Smith in 1998) |

### 2003

| | |
|---|---|
| UK Retailing | The high street, airport and station stores plus WH Smith Direct |
| WH Smith Asia Pacific | Stores in Australia (Angus & Robertson) and New Zealand (Whitcoulls) had been acquired – *but they would be sold in 2004. The US Travel Retail Business was sold in 2003* |
| WH Smith News Distribution | |
| Publishing | Publishers John Murray and Robert Gibson had been acquired to strengthen Hodder Headline. *Publishing was floated off as an independent business in 2004.* |

## Further reading

Greiner, LE (1972) Evolution and revolution as organizations grow, *Harvard Business Review*, July–August.

Pitts, RA and Daniels, JD (1984) Aftermath of the matrix mania, *Columbia Journal of World Business*, Summer.

Handy, C (1989) End of the world we know, *Management Today*, April.

Mintzberg, H (1991) The effective organization – forces and forms, *Sloan Management Review*, Winter.

## References

Alexander, LD (1985) Successfully implementing strategic decisions, *Long Range Planning*, 18 (3).

Chandler, AD (1962) *Strategy and Structure: Chapters in the History of the American Industrial Enterprise*, MIT Press.

Child, JA (1977) *Organization: A Guide to Problems and Practice*, Harper & Row. (A more recent edition is now available.)

Drucker, PF (1988) The coming of the new organization, *Harvard Business Review*, January–February.

Fayol, H (1916) *General and Industrial Administration*, Pitman, 1949 (translation of French original).

Hunsicker, JQ (1982) The matrix in retreat, *Financial Times*, 25 October.

Lawrence, PR and Lorsch, JW (1967) *Organization and Environment*, Richard D Irwin.

Mitchell, D (1988) *Making Acquisitions Work: Lessons from Companies' Successes and Mistakes*, Report published by Business International, Geneva.

Ohmae, K (1990) *The Borderless World*, Harper.

Owen, AA (1982) How to implement strategy, *Management Today*, July.

Pitts, RA and Daniels, JD (1984) Aftermath of the matrix mania, *Columbia Journal of World Business*, Summer.

Porter, ME (1990) *The Competitive Advantage of Nations*, Free Press.

Reed, R and Buckley, MR (1988) Strategy in action – techniques for implementing strategy, *Long Range Planning*, 21 (3).

Salter, MS (1970) Stages in corporate development, *Journal of Business Policy*, Spring.

Thompson, AA and Strickland, AJ (1980) *Strategy Formulation and Implementation*, Richard D Irwin.

# Managing Strategy in the Organization

## Learning objectives

Having read to the end of this chapter you should be able to:

- describe and explain a number of alternative approaches to the management of a corporate portfolio
- distinguish between the alternative control mechanisms which large, diverse organizations might use
- define the terms 'heartland' and 'corporate parenting' and explain their significance and implications
- explain the role and contribution of corporate headquarters to large, multibusiness organizations
- discuss the role and skills of general managers in these organizations
- consider organizations at the beginning of the twenty-first century
- distinguish between resource allocation issues at corporate and business unit level
- define risk, identify the risks faced by organizations and discuss how they might be approached and managed
- identify the main issues in crisis avoidance and management.

Growth is often an important objective for organizations. Frequently this growth has involved diversification and acquisitions in either related or unrelated areas. In recent years the strategic logic of large, diversified conglomerates has been questioned as many organizations have instead chosen to focus on related businesses, technologies or core competencies, where they can more readily add value across the businesses and generate synergy. Whatever the strategic choice, though, it must be implemented successfully. The opening case looks at how GE has become the world's leading company (by asset value) whilst remaining extensively diversified. Conglomerate, diversified businesses cannot be dismissed automatically; they can be both successful and profitable if they can find new, suitable businesses to acquire, opportunities for growth with their subsidiary businesses and if their strategic control system is appropriate. Simply, the strategy can still be justified if it can be implemented successfully. This chapter explores alternative approaches to strategic control and applies these issues to diversified conglomerates. The relationship between the corporate centre and individual businesses is examined. Typically, in recent years, corporate had offices have been slimmed down as organizations have become more decentralized.

The implementation of intended strategies, and the ability of the organization to be responsive in a dynamic, competitive environment, require the organization's strategic resources to be deployed and managed both efficiently and effectively. It is also vital for the organization, on the one hand, to seek to be crisis averse rather than crisis prone and, on the other hand, to be able to deal with crises if and when they do occur. All of these issues are a reflection of the organization's ability to appreciate and manage risk and they are also discussed in this chapter.

This is a chapter of debates, opinions and interpretations, but few clear-cut answers. Simply, both the strategy and the structure need to change but stay complementary as the business environment changes. If accomplishing this was straightforward and clear-cut many organizations would be more successful than they actually are.

**CASE**

## Minicase 16.1 General Electric (GE)    **US**

General Electric (GE) is diversified into four 'long cycle businesses' – power systems, aircraft engines, defence electronics and medical systems (such as brain and body scanners) – four 'short cycle businesses' – plastics engineering, household consumer goods, lighting and NBC Television in the USA. GE also provides financial services (through the specialist GE Capital subsidiary) – which in terms of monetary assets is effectively the fourth largest bank in America. GE Capital has annual revenues of $60 billion (45 per cent of GE's total revenues) and profits of $5.6 billion (27 per cent of the total).

The company is truly global – it sells more in Europe than British Aerospace, one of the UK's leading manufacturers and a direct competitor. GE, under Chief Executive Jack Welch, proved that a business does not have to be 'focused on one or two related activities' to be successful and profitable. Before he retired Welch:

- Changed the culture
- 'Turned people on' and
- Delivered results through carefully crafted incentives.

Welch delayed his planned retirement by a year whilst he attempted to acquire Honeywell, only to be thwarted by the European Competition Commission – which feared there was a conflict of interests between GE Finance (which has a huge aircraft leasing arm) and Honeywell Engines.

(Welch's succession was mentioned in Minicase 14.7 where it was highlighted that a number of those executives who were overlooked have gone on to run other large and very successful organizations. A second Minicase on GE in Chapter 17 discusses the culture change programme.)

Unlike the companies featured in Minicase 16.2, GE has sought to gain maximum value from its disparate activities by investing to provide a platform for growth. GE wants to be number one or number two in every market segment in which it competes. It seeks to exploit the breadth and diversity of its portfolio to find new ways for adding value and new customers.

*Being a conglomerate makes no sense unless you can leverage the size and diversity of the company and spread learning and best practices across the company.*

Larry Johnston, ex-GE Executive

The company is decentralized and employees are encouraged to speak out and pursue ideas. External contacts and sources are constantly monitored for new leads and opportunities. 'We'll go anywhere for an idea.' Welch always believed 'the winners of the 1990s would be those who could develop a culture that allowed them to move faster, communicate more clearly, and involve everyone in a focused effort to serve ever more demanding customers'. GE has its own 'university' and brings managers of various levels in all the businesses together regularly to explain what they are doing and to share new ideas.

*We have this incredible intellect in GE ... we are exposed to so many industries that when we [senior managers] all get together we have the opportunity to maximize our intellect. That's the advantage of a multibusiness company ... we can share ideas.*

Welch

Much of this is facilitated through Management Councils – comprising people from different businesses and divisions – who meet quarterly. Every member of a council must bring to every meeting at least one idea from which other managers could learn something valuable or useful. One notable example was the idea of 'reverse mentoring' to deal with the demands of e-commerce. Older managers were encouraged to use younger and more aware managers as their mentors, even though they might be lower in the current hierarchy.

*Fortune* magazine declared Welch to be the 'manager of the century' for his achievement in turning a 'slumbering dinosaur' into a 'lean and dynamic company with a paradigm of a new management style'. Whereas Percy Barnevik (Minicase 15.6) redesigned the ABB structure, Welch transformed GE through management style. They both believed 'small is beautiful' and that innovation and intrapreneurship is critical. The decentralization at GE aims to 'inject down the line the attitudes of a small fast-moving entrepreneurial business and thereby improve productivity continuously'. Integration strategies promote the sharing of ideas and best practices.

There is a developed strategy of moving managers between businesses and countries to transfer ideas and create internal synergy, together with a reliance on employee training. It has been said that 'if you sit next to any GE executive on a plane they will all tell the same story about where the company is going'. There is a shared and understood direction and philosophy, despite the diversity. Promotion is normally given to those managers who can prove they are 'boundary-less'.

Welch regularly attended training courses to collect opinion and feedback. 'My job is to listen to, search for, think of and spread ideas, to expose people to good ideas and role models.' GE's *'work out'* programme involves senior managers presenting GE's vision and ideas to other managers and employees, and then later reconvening to obtain responses and feedback on perceived issues and difficulties. All employees in a unit, regardless of level, are thus provided with an opportunity to review and comment upon existing systems and procedures. The check is always based on whether they add value. External advisers (such as university academics) monitor that communications are genuinely two-way. GE also developed *'Six Sigma Quality Management'* which has been adopted by companies around the world.

Managers are actively encouraged to work closely with suppliers and customers, and they have '360 degree evaluations', with inputs from superiors, peers and subordinates. 'People hear things about themselves they have never heard before.' Products and businesses should be number one or number two in a market, and if they are not achieving this, their managers are expected to ask for the resources required to get there.

Welch summarized his philosophy as follows:

*If we are to get the reflexes and speed we need, we've got to simplify and delegate more – simply trust more. We have to undo a 100-year-old concept and convince our managers that their role is not to control people and stay on top of things, but rather to guide, energize and excite. But with all this must come the intellectual tools, which will mean continuous education of every individual at every level of the company.*

It was inevitable that people would question whether GE could survive when Welch retired. His chosen successor, Jeffrey Immelt, has made changes – but only limited ones to the structure and style – and the company continues to thrive and prosper. In 2003 GE acquired the UK healthcare group, Amersham, which has a number of important biotechnology activities. This was followed, in 2004, by a leading airport security scanning system business. Since 9/11 airport security has been a growing business around the world.

**Questions**

1. Do you think Welch's management style could be easily copied?
2. Why? Why not?

Follow-up questions when you have read more of the chapter:

3. Just how different is the GE approach from that adopted by BTR and Hanson?
4. Where does GE fit in our framework of corporate management styles?

**General Electric** http://www.ge.com

## 16.1 Introduction: corporate strategy and implementation

There are a number of key themes to a synergistic, successful and profitable portfolio of businesses:

- related competencies and capabilities, which can be transferred between businesses and between each of these businesses and the corporate headquarters, or the overall strategic leader
- the ability to create and build value, both individually and collectively, by the businesses and the corporate headquarters
- the ability to implement strategies and strategic ideas to achieve their potential. This contribution is again individual (in, say, the form of profit streams because of a strong competitive position) and collective, through learning, sharing and the transfer of skills and resources.

In this chapter, therefore, a number of key themes are brought together.

First, the relatedness of the actual businesses in the portfolio. Where technologies or markets are similar or even the same, there must be relatedness. However, some diversified conglomerates have shown that they can relate unlike businesses to create value – see Minicase 16.1. This relates to issues of style and culture, rather than basic strategic logic.

Second, the management of the portfolio of activities to ensure that strategies are implemented effectively. As a result, the overall organization should be demonstrably better off from the existence of the businesses and strategies involved. Its is clearly possible for a problematical business to be a distraction which draws resources (people, money and time in particular) away from potentially more lucrative opportunities.

Figure 16.1 shows how strategy and implementation must work together harmoniously for competitive, strategic and (where relevant) financial success. Where the strategy is stretched or particularly demanding for the resources possessed by the organization, there is still likely to be underachievement even where there is sound implementation. If the accompanying implementation is also weak, the organization is likely to seem fragmented and fragile. A basically sound strategy, poorly implemented, would typically suggest structural and stylistic flaws.

The basic dilemma for many organizations is understanding why, when something is wrong. If performance is below expectations, is it the strategy or the implementation which is mainly to blame? The reaction of many businesses to the very competitive and

**Figure 16.1** Strategy and implementation

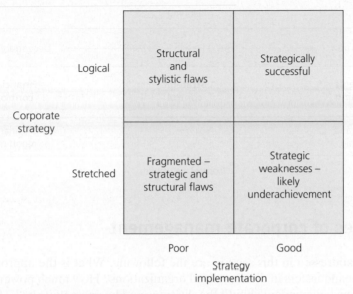

increasingly global business environment of the 1990s has been to work on both. Strategies have typically become more focused and structures less hierarchical.

Richter and Owen (1997) show how there has been:

- refocusing – organizations have reduced the number of industries in which they compete, and
- simpler structures – characterized by smaller head offices and fewer layers of management.

In the end we are left to question whether there has been too much reaction and an over aggressive response, partly the result of pressure from institutional investors and the financial markets, which have tended to be intolerant of diversity. Yet one of the most valuable and respected business in the world, General Electric, remains a very diversified conglomerate. We have tended to assume that diversified conglomerates are strategically illogical, and yet it could be that many managers have simply been unable to manage them in the 1990s when a radically different approach was required from that which succeeded with diversified conglomerates in the 1980s.

Richter and Owen (at the London School of Economics and Public Science) used primary research and secondary data to track the strategic progress of large UK and German companies between 1986 and 1996. They found that over this decade 75 per cent of British companies became more focused compared with only 50 per cent in Germany. The figure for the US was even lower. Only 16 per cent of acquisitions (32 per cent for Germany) were in unrelated businesses. Germany experienced more vertical integration than the UK, where it was almost non-existent.

At the same time large UK businesses experienced:

- head-office personnel reductions, from an average of 175 to 100
- the number of business heads reporting to boards coming down from eight to six and
- the number of layers of management in the operating businesses being reduced from seven to five.

**Figure 16.2** Corporate management style

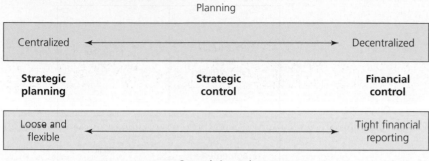

**16.2 Styles of corporate management**

The questions addressed in this section are the following. What is the appropriate role for corporate headquarters in divisionalized organizations? How much power should be centralized? How independent should the divisions and business units be? These relate to the difference between the divisional and the holding company structures and styles of management, and the themes of integration and behavioural processes within the structural framework are explored further.

In relation to these issues Goold and Campbell (1988) have contrasted the views of Sir Hector Laing, ex-chairman of United Biscuits, with those of Lord Hanson. Laing contended that it takes a number of years to build a business, and that during this period corporate headquarters should help the general managers of business units to develop their strategies. Hanson argued that it is more appropriate for head office to remain detached from operations, and instead of involvement to set strict financial targets. All Hanson businesses were reputedly for sale at any time. Both approaches have been shown to work, but with different levels of overall performance and strategic growth patterns. In essence it is all down to the quality of management! The Hanson approach typified that of many diversified conglomerates in the 1980s, but it lost favour with investors in the 1990s. This fact alone was cause enough for many of them to refocus or break up, as Minicase 16.2 shows.

These two approaches represent two ends of a spectrum, and a third approach is a compromise between the two. This spectrum is illustrated in Figure 16.2. The determining variables are the extent of centralization and decentralization (which influences the nature and role of strategic planning in the organization) and the nature of key reporting systems (the extent to which they are loose and flexible or tight and financial). Goold and Campbell use three terms – financial control, strategic planning and **strategic control** – to categorize large UK companies against these criteria.

### 16.2.1 Financial control companies

Financial control is seen as an ideal approach for a holding company where the businesses are independent and unrelated. Hanson and BTR, discussed in Minicase 16.2, were excellent examples and advocates of this style, which for many years under the leadership of Lord (Arnold) Weinstock was also preferred by the more focused GEC.

■ Strategy creation is heavily decentralized to business unit managers. Within their agreed financial targets they are free to develop and change their competitive and functional strategies.

---

## Minicase 16.2 Four Diversified Conglomerates: BTR, Hanson, Tomkins and Williams Holdings (GB)

This case tracks the strategic development of four leading acquisitive UK diversified conglomerates. At different times in the 1980s and early 1990s, all four companies were very successful, typically using a 'hit squad' approach by a small team of turnaround specialists who were expert in evaluating recent acquisitions, setting demanding (financial) targets, rewarding success and dismissing managers who could not perform. In the second half of the 1990s, BTR was merged with another conglomerate, Hanson was broken up, and Tomkins and Williams have pursued more focused strategies. Their fortunes can be usefully contrasted with ABB (Minicase 15.6) and GE (Minicase 16.1). In every instance two major challenges were:

■ the ability to find and fund a suitable acquisition at the appropriate time and stage of corporate development, and then

■ finding opportunities to add value.

Here there is evidence of a concentration on mature industries where the right competitive strategy could bring high rewards but where there was only limited growth potential.

### BTR

BTR grew strongly in the 1970s and 1980s under the strategic leadership of Sir Owen Green. By the early 1990s the company was diversified into control systems, polymers (including factories in Taiwan), electrical products (Hawker Siddeley motors as well as Newey and Eyre), construction (Tilcon*, Graham Builders Merchants*, Pilkington Tiles* and aggregate businesses in the US), transportation (railway equipment), packaging (Rockware Glass), paper technology and consumer products (Dunlop Slazenger* and Pretty Polly lingerie).

Alan Jackson succeeded Sir Owen Green as chief executive in 1991 (Green remained as chairman for some time afterwards) and instituted a strategy of withdrawal from non-manufacturing interests. The companies marked with an asterisk were sold to other parents or to their existing managers. At the same time Jackson made a number of acquisitions, including Varta, the German battery manufacturer and Gencorp, a US company which produces vibration controls. Hawker Siddeley (1991) was the last *major* acquisition by BTR.

Goold *et al.* (1994) examined the parenting style of BTR. They concluded that the company's underlying belief or paradigm was that businesses can benefit from pressure on costs and productivity; focused, mature, businesses which are pushed to increase prices and margins (at the expense of market share and growth) can be made more profitable. BTR's parenting skills were intensive profit planning, the ability to manage a decentralized business with multiple profit centres, low central overheads, and skills in acquiring and turning around acquisitions. This last point includes the ability to introduce the BTR culture into the new business.

BTR's heartland was based on manufacturing businesses, industrial customers, low to moderate technology and capital intensity, relatively stable environments with only limited impact from economic cycles and niche markets. Critics of BTR claimed that the strategy was unco-ordinated and based on cost-cutting and price rises during periods of inflation. The prospects for both of these strategies largely disappeared in the 1990s.

Jackson's successor in 1996, Ian Strachan, continued with the strategy that he inherited, declaring that BTR was to be focused on four core activities: automotive components, power drives, control systems and other specialist engineering

▶

products. Several remaining businesses were targeted for divestment, but there were to be accompanying acquisitions of related businesses and new joint ventures overseas. Strachan advised institutional shareholders that 'BTR's day as an acquisitive conglomerate is over' and that organic growth around its core strengths was to be a priority. In the past BTR had not invested heavily in organic growth.

At this time BTR still comprised over 1000 business units worldwide. Turnover approached £10 billion, although at the peak of it success revenues had reached £14 billion. The style of corporate management was changed from financial control to strategic control in order to encourage business managers to take a longer-term and more strategic view. Instead of annual profit planning being the key focus, growth priorities for up to five years were sought.

As disposal followed disposal, Jackson, now retired and living in Australia, expressed his belief that BTR was being reduced to too tight a core. Whoever was correct in his belief, the share price continued to fall through 1997 and 1998.

In November 1998 BTR was merged with fellow engineering conglomerate, Siebe, and the new business eventually renamed Invensys. The chief executive of Siebe, Allen Yurko, was to be the strategic leader and Strachan his deputy. Based on share distribution, Siebe comprised 55 per cent of Invensys and BTR 45 per cent. There were now five broad and complementary divisions: intelligent automation, controls, power systems, industrial drives and equipment and automotive components. The combined revenues were around £9 billion. In portfolio terms, both BTR and Siebe contributed 'cash cows' but BTR had more of the 'dogs' and Siebe more 'stars'. Some BTR businesses were still for sale – but, and somewhat controversially, Invensys bought Boan, a Dutch software business in trouble.

There were profits warnings in both 2000 and 2001 and the share price continued to underperform the main indeces. More jobs were lost and Yurko resigned. His replacement, Rick Haythornthwaite, was seen as a turnaround expert. Disposals continued to leave a declared new core – control systems, for running factories and process plants, and for managing energy. Everything else was available for sale.

There was yet another profits warning in 2003. Amongst a range of problems, Boan was still in trouble – it was inadequately competitive and it was sold on.

Some of the businesses, but not all that were available for sale, were sold. As a consequence, Invensys announced a further restructuring. There were to be six divisions, including some of those that had been for sale. Control systems were still at the heart, but more markets were being targeted, including home appliances and railways. Haythornthwaite declared that 'slimming down was not what Invensys actually wanted – it had been forced on it by market conditions and shareholder pressure'. The latest change was now possible as the UK economy was strengthening. The new sales target was £3.8 billion, a considerable reduction on previous years. But the earlier plan had been only half that!

### Hanson

Hanson was essentially a company which pursued a restructuring strategy. It was based in the UK and US and led by partners Lord James Hanson and Lord Gordon White. Over a period of some 20 years Hanson was involved in 35 agreed acquisitions, six hostile takeovers and 15 unsuccessful bids. Following the 41 acquisitions there were 40 business disposals. Hanson also bought sizeable stakes in 22 other companies. On a number of occasions (in particular the acquisitions of SCM and Imperial Group) Hanson raised more money from business disposals than it paid to acquire the companies in the first place, and in each case it was left with a valuable core business – SCM Chemicals and Imperial Tobacco, respectively.

This 'Hansonizing' strategy was based on three essential principles:

- The key objective is to maximize shareholder value.
- Many companies do not do this and are therefore run badly.

- Such companies are good buys because their assets can be made to create more value for shareholders.

James Hanson always argued the strategy could be applied successfully in any industry, and consequently Hanson diversified into a number of unrelated areas including construction, bricks, textiles, animal foods and meat processing, pulp, coal, gold, tobacco and chemicals. Hanson did not always stay in an industry, and instead divested companies and business units when appropriate for its basic strategy.

Typically, businesses in competitive industries, and which required investment, were sold, and mature, slow-growth companies retained. Cyclical businesses were also attractive targets for Hanson. In the early 1990s some 90 per cent of Hanson's profits were from mature industries. Despite the lack of growth potential in these businesses the Hanson restructuring strategies generated a high and consistent growth in group profits. Hanson believed that earnings per share were maximized when business units achieved the highest possible sustainable return on capital employed. Earnings per share could be improved by increasing returns from existing capital or by reducing capital and maintaining earnings. The latter theme encapsulates divestments.

Although it does not always happen, it could be argued that in an organization such as this, which is not primarily concerned with staying in particular industries, business units should be sold when their earnings cannot be increased further and should be replaced by others with greater potential. Shareholders who support such organizations expect the increased returns to be generated quickly, and consequently Hanson was not thought to be interested in companies that could not be improved within three to four years. Although earnings per share could be improved by investing and using debt financing, rather than equity, Hanson was basically risk averse and sought to constrain its gearing. The companies in the group also benefited from low-cost finance and astute tax management, which helped to lower their total costs.

Business units were decentralized and given strict targets to achieve, but all capital investments were carefully scrutinized at board level. Profits from the businesses were returned to the parent, who decided how they would be used and spent. General managers in charge of businesses could not spend over £500 without the approval of James Hanson (in the UK) or Gordon White (in the US). Within these financial constraints businesses could adapt their competitive and functional strategies as they wished.

For many years Hanson was acknowledged to be a very successful company from which many other organizations could learn some important lessons. Up to the mid-1980s Hanson consistently outperformed the stock market. However, once the acquisition trail became more difficult, with a series of well-publicized hostile bids failing to result in takeovers, the strategy was questioned. When Lord Hanson's partner, Lord White, died, Hanson himself was over 70 years old and succession became a real issue of concern.

In 1995 it was announced that the American businesses were to be floated off as US Industries, and the remaining activities split into four separate businesses. Existing shareholders would receive stock in each of the new, more focused, companies. The four were:

- Millennium Chemicals (based around SCM and Quantum in America)
- The Energy Group (Peabody Coal and Suburban Propane (US) and Eastern Electricity (UK))
- Imperial Tobacco
- Hanson (based on bricks and aggregates in the UK and US).

Imperial continues to thrive with several new brands – it has increasingly targeted markets outside the UK. The new Hanson has pursued the old strategy of acquisition and divestment, but this time based around a tighter, more focused core of activities. It has also been successful. Lord Hanson died in 2004.

## Tomkins

This conglomerate grew out of a buckle-manufacturing business based in Walsall, UK; acquired businesses included Smith and Wesson handguns, Hayter lawnmowers, Murray bicycles (in the US) and a range of different industrial products. The chief executive – from 1983 until 2000 – Greg Hutchings, was ex-Hanson.

In 1992 Tomkins acquired Rank Hovis McDougall (the milling and baking business which owns the Bisto, Paxo and Mr Kipling brands), beating off a rival bid from Hanson. Four years later, after successfully absorbing RHM, Tomkins bought the US company Gates Rubber, the world's largest manufacturer of power transmission belts and industrial hoses. RHM cost £93.5 million; Gates was roughly the same. In 1997 Tomkins added a US manufacturer of windscreen wipers (Stant) to bolt on to Gates. At this time Tomkins was building up a cash pile which it used to buy back shares – it was not finding suitable new acquisitions and there were few investment opportunities in the businesses that it owned.

In 1998 Tomkins opted to dispose of its distribution businesses to focus on manufacturing. Tomkins bought a US tyre-valve manufacturer and sold the original buckle company. In the same year it was a loser in the auction for Dalgety Foods, which was bought by the Kerry Group of Ireland. However, Kerry sold Dalgety's Spillers flour mills to Tomkins. This provoked an investigation by the UK competition authorities who demanded that Tomkins sell four of the six Spillers mills that it had bought.

In 1999 Tomkins bought Aquatic, a Texas-based manufacturer of whirlpools, but opted to divest all of its baking and foods businesses to concentrate on automotive and building products. This was completed in summer 2000.

Hutchings resigned after an investigation into how he and his family had been using corporate assets for private benefit. It appeared the company had bought properties for their use and was also paying for their domestic staff. In addition, corporate jets were used as private taxis.

His replacement, Jim Nicol, a Canadian, began a disposal programme. Murray Bicycles (2000), Hayter lawnmowers (2000) and Smith and Wesson (2001) began the process. The new focus was to be on innovative products and developments in the core engineering and industrial businesses.

## Williams Holdings

Built by accountants Nigel Rudd (a deal-maker) and Brian McGowan (acknowledged to be good at handling City institutions), Williams grew during the 1980s from an English Midlands base in foundries. McGowan left in 1993; Rudd remained as strategic leader. The acquisition strategy in the 1980s was based largely on good opportunities for restructuring, but Williams quickly realized the value of established brand names and concentrated on businesses where it could exploit its brand management skills.

Through the 1980s and early 1990s the acquisitions included: Fairey Engineering, Rawlplug, Polycell, Crown Berger paints, Smallbone (kitchen units), Amdega (conservatories), Dreamland (electric blankets), Kidde (from Hanson – aerospace and fire extinguishers), Yale (locks) and Valor (locks and heating). Several of these were then sold as Williams chose to focus on three business areas: building products (including DIY), fire protection and security (locks). Other UK fire-equipment companies were added to the portfolio: Angus, Rockwell and a Thorn-EMI subsidiary. These were followed by related fire and locks acquisitions in Italy and the US, and in 1996 Williams bought Sicli and Siddes, the largest fire-protection company in France. At £175 million, Sicli was its largest purchase for five years.

At this stage in its development Williams claimed to be Britain's first focused conglomerate, but some critics argued that focus requires more than the structural 'bundling of a number of businesses into separate divisions'. The fire and security businesses helped to offset the economic cycles of the construction and building industries, and Williams (with 12 per cent of the world market) offered a wider range of fire-protection products than any of its rivals. As fire-regulations were tightened around the world, this industry was enjoying a high growth potential; it had yet to reach the maturity stage.

*(Tomkins, Hanson, BTR and Williams) ... all started in the same place; buy what you can, sort it out and move on. Now our aspirations are to build businesses internationally.*

Roger Carr, Chief Executive, Williams, in 1996

In 1997 Williams acquired Chubb Security (alarms and locks) on its second attempt and in 1998 it began to divest its home-improvements businesses, a move that it completed in late 1999. Now it was focused on fire and security. In 2000 the company was split into two: Chubb Security Services and Kidde Fire Protection. Yale was sold to a Swedish company.

**Invensys** http://www.invensys.com
**Hanson** http://www.hanson.co.uk
**Tomkins** http://www.tomkins.co.uk
**Kidde** http://www.kidde.co.uk
**Chubb Security** http://www.chubbsecurity.co.uk

## Question

1. Why exactly did the conglomerate diversification strategy of these businesses lose favour with shareholders?

## Tasks

1. Track the share price movements of these businesses during the 1990s and check their progress against the all-share index. What has happened in recent years?
2. Which companies have managed to change and adapt effectively, and which have not?

- Budgets and targets – and their achievement – are critically important control mechanisms.

- The small head office monitors financial returns closely and regularly, intervening when targets are missed – head office is a 'controller'.

- Head office also acts as a corporate investment banker for investment capital.

- Achievement is rewarded, and units are encouraged to put forward and chase ambitious targets. Underperforming managers are likely to be removed.

- The head office adds value by acquiring and improving underperforming businesses; if additional value cannot be added it may well sell off businesses.

- There will, typically, be few interdependencies and links between the businesses.

- Growth is more likely to be by acquisition than organic investment, with many financial control companies taking a short-term view of each business and being reluctant to invest in speculative research and the development of longer-term strategies.

Owen Green, chief executive and architect of BTR, had the following philosophy:

1. Never pursue extra sales at the expense of profit margins.
2. Raise prices whenever there is an opportunity.
3. Investment should never exceed the amount written off in depreciation.

The result was high profit margins but a lack of capital investment; growth was mainly by acquisition rather than by investing in the existing businesses. Herein lay the ultimate limitations.

## 16.2.2 Strategic planning companies

Strategic planning tends to be adopted in organizations which focus on only a few, and preferably related, core businesses. Examples include Cadbury Schweppes, United Biscuits and BP. Historically it has been the favoured approach for most public-sector organizations.

- Strategic plans are developed jointly by head office and the business units, with head office retaining the final say. Strategic planning is centralized.
- Day-to-day operations only are wholly decentralized.
- Head office sets priorities and co-ordinates strategies throughout the organization, possibly initiating cross-business strategies, and thereby acts as an orchestrator.
- A long-term perspective is realistic, and the search for opportunities for linkages and sharing resources and best practice can be prioritized. This normally requires central control. Individually the businesses would tend to operate more independently; organization-wide synergies may involve sacrifices by individual businesses.
- Goold and Campbell conclude that there are co-ordination problems if this approach is used in truly diversified organizations.
- Budgets are again used for measuring performance.
- The tight central control can become bureaucratic and demotivate managers, who may not feel *ownership* of their strategies.

Other dangers are that thinking may become too focused at the centre, with the potential contributions of divisional managers underutilized; and that the organization may be slow to change in response to competitive pressures. Value can be added successfully if corporate managers stay aware and expert in the core businesses and if the competitive environment allows this style to work.

## 16.2.3 Strategic control companies

Financial control and strategic planning are appropriate for particular types of organization, but both styles, while having very positive advantages, also feature drawbacks. The strategic control style is an attempt to obtain the major benefits of the other two styles for organizations that are clearly diversified but with linkages and interdependencies. Value is added by balancing strategic and financial controls.

- Strategy creation involves decentralization to the business units, although head office still controls the overall *corporate* strategy.
- The role of head office is to review divisional and business plans, and approve strategic objectives and financial targets, accepting that they may need to be changed in a competitive environment. Performing a coaching role, head office encourages businesses to achieve their potential by active involvement and by fostering the spreading of learning and good practice through the organization.
- Strategy creation and budgetary control can be separated, allowing for more creative performance measurement. Sometimes competitive pressures and misjudgements mean strategies have to be changed, and hoped-for financial targets may be missed. A strategic control style can recognize this and deal with the implications.

- Head office does, however, monitor and control financial performance and success against strategic milestones and objectives.

Although decentralization is a feature, head office still requires considerable detail about the various businesses if it is to ensure that the synergy potential is achieved and very short-term thinking is avoided. Political activity will be prevalent as individual businesses compete with each other for scarce corporate resources.

It was mentioned earlier (Minicase 14.3) that GEC, under Lord Weinstock – who was in charge for 32 years – adopted a financial control style. When he retired (in 1996) and was replaced by Lord George Simpson the style was quickly changed to strategic control. Simpson inherited a GEC that was diversified and financially sound, but it was risk averse and experiencing relatively low growth. It was also in possession of a legendary cash mountain of £2.5 billion. Simpson created a new agenda for growth. With divestments and acquisitions the portfolio was changed. The style also changed. There was to be more focus on customers and people and less on cost control. There was greater decentralization, accompanied by robust reporting systems. It is not unusual to see changes of strategy, structure and style accompanying a change of leadership, especially if a company is in difficulty or the predecessor has been in place for a long time.

Two leading organizations that utilized the strategic control style – ICI and Courtaulds – both concluded that they were overdiversified. This belief was strongly reinforced by institutional investor pressure. The attitude of the stock market and their shareholders meant that their share prices were underperforming against the index, the average of the UK's largest companies. There were numerous businesses in each organization, although some were clearly interlinked. At the same time these clusters had little in common and featured different strategic needs and cultures. Because of these differences, and the inevitable complexity, corporate headquarters could not add value with a single entity. Both companies split into two distinct parts to enable a stronger focus on core competencies and strategic capabilities. Courtaulds was split into Courtaulds Chemicals (subsequently acquired by Akzo Nobel of Germany) and Courtaulds Textiles (sold to Sara Lee of the US). ICI separated its chemicals and pharmaceuticals businesses. The former remain as ICI, but many of the activities have been divested and replaced by more consumer-focused businesses. ICI continues to struggle. The others were renamed Zeneca, which soon merged into Astra Zeneca.

### 16.2.4  Levels of success

Goold and Campbell (1988) studied 16 large UK companies, including those given as examples above, and concluded that each style has both advantages and disadvantages and that no one style is outstandingly the most successful.

*Strategic planning companies* proved to be consistently profitable during the 1980s, mainly through organic growth. Head office corporate staff tended to be a quite large group and differences of opinion with general managers sometimes caused frustration within the divisions and business units. *Financial control companies* exhibited the best financial performance. In a number of cases, particularly BTR and Hanson, this resulted from acquisition and divestment rather than organic growth. Short-term financial targets were felt to reduce the willingness of general managers to take risks. There were few trade-offs whereby short-term financial targets were sacrificed for long-term growth. A general manager, for example, might consider a programme of variety reduction and product rationalization with a view to developing a more consistent and effective portfolio. In the short term this would result in reduced revenue and profits before new orders and products improved overall profitability. This temporary fall might be unacceptable in the face of short-term financial targets. *Strategic control companies* also performed satisfactorily but experienced difficulties in establishing the appropriate mix of strategic and financial targets for general managers. Financial targets, being the more specific and measurable ones, were generally given priority.

Goold and Campbell concluded that while the style of management adopted within the structure determines the strategic changes that take place, the overall corporate strategy of the company very much influences the choice of style. Large diverse organizations, for example, will find it difficult to adopt a strategic planning approach. Equally, where the environment is turbulent and competitive, increasing the need for adaptive strategic change, the financial planning approach is less appropriate. Not unexpectedly, Hanson's main acquisitions were of companies in mature, slow-growth sectors.

While companies may appreciate that there is a mismatch between their corporate strategy and style, changing the style can be difficult. Moreover, many organizations will not be able to implement a new style as effectively as the one that they are used to.

Goold *et al*. (1993) revisited the organizations and their research five years later, partly stimulated by the change in fortunes in some of the companies involved. This review reinforced the conclusion that financial control is ideally suited to a group of autonomous businesses in a conglomerate, but it is less suitable for a portfolio of core businesses or ones seeking to compete globally. In 1988 Goold and Campbell had argued that the adoption of a hands-off, financial control style by GEC and other electronics companies in the UK had hindered their development as globally competitive businesses. Global development demands synergy between a number of national businesses. BTR and Hanson had already begun to focus more on selected core businesses, and their relative performance was deteriorating.

Strategic planning continued to add value as long as corporate managers had close knowledge and experience of their core businesses. Where their portfolio was arguably too diverse – although not so diverse that they could be classified as diversified conglomerates – strategic control companies were experiencing difficulties. The researchers poured scorn on the idea that a decentralized structure, supported by a modern budgeting and planning system, would enable a competent management team to add value to almost any new business. Strategic control can only work with an effective mix of tight financial control and devolved authority to instigate emergent strategic changes; to achieve this successfully, head offices again need to appreciate the detail of competitive strategies in the subsidiaries.

Appreciating the specific problems and opportunities faced by subsidiary businesses is particularly important for establishing fair reward systems.

Reward systems are likely to be based on specific performance targets, but these could relate to growth in revenue, absolute profits or profitability ratios. Stonich (1982) has suggested that business units might be categorized as having high, medium or low growth potential. Four factors could be used in evaluating their relative performances: return on assets; cash flow; strategic development programmes and increases in market share. The relative weighting attributed to each of these four factors would be changed to reflect their specific objectives and whether they were of high, medium or low-growth potential. Return on assets and cash flow would be critical for low growth business units, and market share and strategic development programmes most important for those with high growth potential. The factors would be weighted equally for medium growth. This approach would be particularly relevant where general managers were changed around to reflect their particular styles of management and the current requirements of the business unit.

One question left unanswered concerns the extent to which the conclusions of Goold and Campbell are a result of British management strengths, weaknesses and preferences. Certain Japanese companies appear to grow organically at impressive rates while maintaining strict financial controls and directing corporate strategic change from the centre. This tendency, however, is affected by legislation which restricts the ability of Japanese companies to grow by acquisition and merger. Without this control Japanese firms may have followed different strategies.

The next section endeavours to pull together the lessons from this and other research and the cases quoted herein.

## 16.3 Diversification or focus: a key corporate dilemma

It is now appropriate to look in greater detail at corporate strategic trends in the UK. The emphasis seems to be on 'divest unrelated activities; acquire related ones'. Restructuring to take out costs has been emphazisedemphasized, but many organizations have simply downsized; they have not *rightsized* to create an organization with the necessary competencies and motivation to stimulate renewal and new growth. In addition, a more recent trend has been share buy-backs, as company after company changes its gearing to make it less vulnerable to shareholder pressure. Really, this is an admission that they cannot find desirable growth opportunities where any accumulated cash might be deployed and used for long-term growth and effectiveness.

As seen in Chapter 12, acquisition and diversification strategies are frequently linked together. Acquisitions (agreed corporate purchases), takeovers (hostile buys) and mergers (the joining of two organizations) fuel organizational growth and, quite often, the necessary capital is available from the City if the organization does not have sufficient reserves. With such strategies, organizations are likely to be able to grow much more quickly than by investing in organic growth to build existing activities and businesses. While organic growth is always going to be important, there is often a dearth of inspirational ideas.

The downside of acquisitions is that often two (or even more) cultures need to be integrated. Growth in size happens, but it may not be accompanied by increased profitability and the synergy required to generate real growth. There is also a paradox of timing and opportunity. An acquisition will use up any spare cash, managerial expertise and managerial time – all scarce resources. Until the businesses have been integrated, resources are stretched and the organization would find it difficult to deal with a further acquisition. Do the best opportunities occur when the organization is ideally prepared or ill prepared?

Diversification implies new products, services and markets. The extent of the differences implies that the diversification is either related in some way, or unrelated. Where new technologies, new skills, new resources, new distribution channels and new markets are all implied, the learning challenge is considerable, together with the inherent uncertainty. However, related diversification, perhaps by the acquisition of an existing competitor, can provoke interest from the competition authorities in individual countries or the European Commission, which can result in its being stopped. Whatever the strategy, in the end its relative success or failure depends upon the ability of the managers involved to generate greater returns from the assets, possibly implying restructuring and some asset sales, and certainly requiring that any anticipated synergy is delivered. This in turn demands that too high a price is not paid for the acquisition in the first place.

At different times, different strategies and approaches enjoy greater or lesser favour. Strategies that are popular today may be unfashionable next year; when this happens those pursuing unfashionable strategies are subjected to considerable scrutiny from the media and from analysts.

The systematic cross-border acquisitions of Rowntree and Perrier by Nestlé have contributed to the growth of a successful international foods business. There are some links between the products, with opportunities for sharing and learning. This strategic approach continues to be fashionable. Reed Elsevier (joint UK and Netherlands) merged with the Dutch company Wolters Kluwer to create the world's largest scientific and professional publishing business. Other similar examples are:

- Glaxo Wellcome's merger with SmithKline Beecham to create Glaxo SmithKline
- the acquisition of Mannesmann by Vodafone – unusual as it is rare for German companies to be acquired by non-German predators.

In contrast, in the mid-late 1990s, conglomerate diversification – building a corporation with unrelated acquisitions – became much less fashionable than it was a decade ago. There are strong arguments in favour of this change of popularity but, nevertheless, it can still be a successful strategy if it is supported with appropriate implementation skills, and it may well become more fashionable again in the future.

As seen earlier, the outstanding example of a successful diversified conglomerate in recent years is General Electric. On the whole, however, GE is not acquisitive on a regular basis; there are frequent bolt-on acquisitions and very occasional major purchases which imply further diversification. Its success comes largely from its ability to foster sharing and learning among its disparate businesses and, most significantly, leverage its existing resources to create new forms of competitive advantage.

> *Our intellectual capital is not US-based … we aim to get the best ideas from everywhere. Each team puts up its best ideas and processes – constantly. That raises the bar. Our culture is designed around making a hero out of those who translate ideas from one place to another, who help somebody else. They get an award, they get praised and promoted.*

> Jack Welch, Chief Executive, GE

This philosophy is in stark contrast to the finance-driven holding company style of Hanson and BTR (in the past), an approach which saw each business as a very independent activity and shunned major investment. The GE philosophy has also been seen to be successful at other diversified American conglomerates. Another example is United Technologies, which comprises Otis, Carrier and Sikorski – respectively, the world leaders for elevators, air conditioners and helicopters – Pratt and Whitney (jet engines), aerospace and automotive components. Here again, there is emphasis on segment leadership.

> *If one of the companies needs some new ideas, they should go and grab them from wherever is appropriate.*

> George David, President and CEO, United Technologies

Focus, then, is unquestionably fashionable. Caulkin (1996) argues that if you have relatively poor management, focus makes absolute sense as focused companies are easier to manage. Unfortunately focus, per se, is unlikely to create new value. The dilemma with diversification lies in establishing clearly whether it is the corporate logic of the diversification strategy itself which is in question, or the inability of many companies to add value to a disparate range of activities and sustain real growth in some way. Sadtler *et al.* (1997) defend the case for a clear focus, built around a defensible core of related activities, arguing that focus is now a more popular corporate strategy for a number of important reasons:

- It allows greater control. Diversified conglomerates must decentralize to allow flexibility and this can imply a trade-off with central control unless the organization can truly share information and learn.
- Divesting unrelated businesses can provide the finance necessary to strengthen the core.
- It often builds shareholder confidence, supporting the share price and making the organization less vulnerable to takeover.
- In increasingly competitive markets and industries poor performance is harder to hide. Focus can ensure that the weakest companies are divested and stronger businesses not held back because of the need to cross-subsidize.

For Sadtler the activity core is built around similar critical success factors (what the businesses have to be good at) and similar improvement opportunities (what they are going to have to do in the future). A corporate centre must be able to add value to every constituent business; every business in the portfolio should add value by contributing to the success of the whole organization.

Detailed criteria can be readily and sensibly established to justify what should and what should not be in the core. The factors embrace financial performance over a number of years, the company's stated mission, the relatedness of tasks and technologies, customer requirements and the opportunities for internal sharing and trading. These points are taken up later.

From their objective analysis based on these criteria, Sadtler *et al.* produced a list of American organizations which they believed were candidates for breaking up. All of the following featured prominently:

- Ford and General Motors have adopted different growth strategies in recent years. Ford has continued to struggle in recent years, and has acquired a number of up-market brands to broaden its product range
- PepsiCo, which has divested its fast-food restaurants to concentrate on snack foods and soft drinks – a strategy which, with hindsight, has worked!
- Exxon, Amoco and Chevron, competitors in the global oil industry, which has been characterized by horizontal integration and consolidation
- Berkshire Hathaway, the investment company run by Warren Buffett which invests long term in other businesses. Its performance did deteriorate for a short period, but its shareholders remained very loyal and supportive. The company is strong again.

In contrast, strategic leaders who have grown successful diversified businesses continue to disagree. Harold Geneen (1997), who died in 1997, is often credited as the founder of truly diversified conglomerates. Geneen's ITT at one time included telecommunications, hotels, baking, cosmetics and lightbulbs, book publishing and Avis Rent-a-Car.

ITT has been comprehensively broken up – although Geneen's tight financial control style worked, when he retired there was no natural succession. However, Geneen continued to claim:

> *To succeed in business it is essential to take risks. But they must be smart risks – researched, understood, survivable. The conglomerate is a good vehicle for identifying and exploiting them… but … running a conglomerate requires working harder than most people want to work and taking more risks than most people want to take.*

Sir Owen Green (1994), ex-BTR, has defended conglomerates even more strongly:

> *As soon as things go wrong, companies start talking about focus. Focus is the crutch of mediocre management … if you are trained in the techniques of management … you should be able to apply them across a range of companies. Diversified companies possess both defensive qualities in a recession and a springboard for new ventures in more expansive times.*

This argument is further borne out by the success of the US conglomerate, Textron, which outperformed the Wall Street stock index by 50 per cent during the 1990s. Textron manufactures light aircraft (Cessna), helicopters (Bell), machine tools, automotive components, lawnmowers, watch straps and Sheaffer pens, as well as owning a consumer finance business. The company argues that its balanced diversity (not being overdependent on any one product) allows it consistently to improve its overall earnings through economic cycles. This case has always been used as an argument to defend diversity, while recognizing that with the wrong approach it can become dangerously short-termist. To succeed it needs a particular management style.

Summarizing this section of the chapter, most strategies can be made to work effectively and efficiently, but the ultimate success of any strategy lies in its implementation. Decisions concerning the implementation issues of structure and management style, as well as those affecting the competitiveness of each product or service in the portfolio, provide additional dilemmas which need to be investigated further.

It should not be forgotten that concentrating the debate on this manifestation of corporate strategy can draw attention away from the real strategic issue, which is creating new values. With Hanson and BTR, once businesses had been turned around and profitability restored, little new value was being added, and so there was an argument that the individual businesses might be better off on their own or with a new parent. Is this an argument for focus or for a different style of corporate management? Reinforcing earlier points, Hamel and Prahalad (1994) contend that today there is too much strategic convergence. High-performance organizations reinvent industries and regenerate core strategies. They innovate around the theme of positioning.

> *If the past couple of years have taught anything about corporate structure, it is that broad generalizations about integration versus specialization, or conglomeration versus focus, are worthless. Everything depends on the pressures affecting individual industries: and within them, the different circumstances of the companies themselves.*

Jackson (1995)

# 16.4 Managing the corporate portfolio

Porter (1987) argues that corporate strategy is that which makes the corporate whole add up to more than the sum of its parts, but further contends that the corporate strategies of too many companies dissipate rather than create shareholder value. He comments:

> *Moving from competitive strategy to corporate strategy is the business equivalent of passing through the Bermuda Triangle. The failure of corporate strategy reflects the fact that most diversified companies have failed to think in terms of how they really add value.*

Porter's arguments are as follows. Corporate strategy involves two key questions or issues. First, what businesses should the company choose to compete in; second, how strategically distinct businesses should be managed at the corporate level?

When the debate on corporate strategy opened in Part Four of this book, synergy was held out as the justification for strategic changes, especially if they involved diversification. The ideas behind synergy are defensible, but synergy *potential* alone cannot justify change. Implementation matters and, being realistic, synergy is frequently based on intangibles and possibilities rather than definites. When we look back on acquisitions that fail to deliver the promised synergies, we can never be sure how much the problem was the strategic logic and how much was implementation. For these reasons, portfolio management, backed by the analytical techniques discussed in Chapter 9, was attractive when it was developed by management consultants.

## 16.4.1 Portfolio management

The basic premise of portfolio management is that competition occurs at the business level and this is where competitive advantages are developed. Businesses should compete for centralized corporate investment resources, and they should be divested if there are no further opportunities for developing new values. To facilitate this, a cost-effective organization structure should enable cross-fertilization between the businesses while maintaining overall control. The role of the corporate headquarters was to seek and acquire attractive (potentially highly profitable) businesses, fit them in to the organization, assess their requirements and allocate strategic resources according to their position in the relevant matrix. Of course, in reality, many low-performing businesses were retained, diluting the earnings potential and, as a consequence, shareholders sometimes became sceptical. Their belief was that they could diversify their own portfolio of investments as a hedge against risk – they did not need the businesses to do this on their behalf.

In addition:

- undervalued companies were not always easily acquired – they were simply not available
- all too often excessive premiums were paid when businesses were acquired
- professional management and capital resources alone do not build value and yield competitive advantage
- businesses are often interdependent for all sorts of reasons and therefore strategies cannot be ring-fenced and set in isolation

■ some businesses (and their managers) are defeated by the complexity and diversity of the portfolio.

However, one variant of portfolio management, restructuring, does have its logic and attraction.

### 16.4.2 Restructuring

Restructuring requires the identification of industries and companies with the potential for restructuring and transformation with new technologies, new people and/or consolidation. There is no need for them to be related to the existing businesses in the portfolio. The new parent intervenes to turn around the business: first, by cost-cutting and increased efficiency, and second, by adding new values to build a stronger competitive base and position. Once there are no further opportunities to add value the business should be sold to raise money for further acquisitions. Restructuring is not about hoarding businesses to build an empire and never divesting anything which, clearly, some strategic leaders have been prone to do.

Clear elements of restructuring can be seen in the Hanson approach. Certainly, efficiencies were increased as businesses were slimmed down, and businesses were always for sale at the right price. However, Hanson did not invest substantially to build new competitive advantages.

Restructuring works well when the strategic leadership can spot and acquire undervalued companies and then turn them around with sound management skills, even though they might be in unfamiliar industries. In a sense, there is an underlying belief that good managers can manage anything, and to a degree there is some truth in this assertion. The issue is whether they manage the renewal as well as the consolidation. The appropriate structure and style of corporate management are clearly critical. Naturally, if suitable undervalued businesses cannot be found – which is typically the case when a country's economy has been tightened and weak competitors have already disappeared as closures or acquisitions – restructuring has no basis.

### 16.4.3 Sharing activities and transferring skills

Porter's three tests for a successful acquisition were explained in Chapter 12. He argues that they are most likely to be met where there is some interrelationship between the existing and new businesses. The basis for this might be tangible or intangible, and therefore it is easy to be deluded into thinking that there are similarities when in reality there are differences. Minicase 16.3 looks at this issue in relation to the recent acquisitions of the UK's three leading roadside-assistance businesses: the AA, RAC and Green Flag.

Interrelationships are defined as 'connections among distinct businesses that lead to competitive advantage from being in both'. Hanson found a connection in low-cost capital and astute tax-avoidance strategies, but it would be more typical to see them in marketing or technology. The search for these synergies begins with an analysis of the value chains and the objective is to find opportunities for lowering costs and creating or enhancing differentiation. Activities, know-how, customers, distributors and competitors can all be shared. The benefits must outweigh the costs involved, for while there are always opportunities to share they may not lead to any competitive advantage. The outcome of sharing can be clearly tangible (such as better capacity utilization) or more intangible where it comes through learning and intelligence.

There is invariably a difficult balancing act involved. A shared sales force is often a possibility, for example. Where this happens, higher calibre people can sometimes be recruited as there are more promotion prospects, buyers can be more easily accessed as more products are being sold at any one time, and less time is spent travelling between calls. However, different selling skills may be required for different products – some are sold on price, others on performance differences – and the attention given to certain ones may be inadequate.

## Minicase 16.3  The AA, RAC and Green Flag – Changes of Ownership  (GB)

These three organizations dominate the roadside-assistance industry in the UK. In 1999 they had the following numbers of members:

| | |
|---|---|
| AA | 9.4 million |
| RAC | 5.5 million |
| Green Flag | 2.3 million. |

In 1998 and 1999 they all experienced a change of ownership. Would their new parents be able to share resources or transfer skills to improve their performance?

The first to be acquired was Green Flag, once known as National Breakdown. Unlike the AA and RAC, which employ their own staff and repair fleets, Green Flag is really a central marketing agency for local, independent roadside-assistance specialists. Along with Capital Logistics (an airport coach business) Green Flag was already owned by National Parking Corporation, known as NCP, which runs 500 town and city car parks in the UK. Recently, NCP had been struggling to find good new sites through which to expand. NCP was bought by the American company Cendant in 1998. Through a series of acquisitions Cendant had grown into the world's largest provider of consumer services, embracing hotels (Ramada and Howard Johnson), car rental (Avis) and real-estate agencies. Its strategic logic was to 'provide its marketing machinery with new products to sell to its existing customers'. Green Flag has formed alliances with motor insurers such as Direct Line, which sells its own branded receovery service which is provided by Green Flag members.

In 1998 Cendant was also believed to be a possible bidder for the RAC – the Royal Automobile Club. At the time the RAC was 'owned' by the existing members of the RAC. A bid was pre-vented by government intervention, on the grounds that prices would probably rise and quality and innovation reduce if the industry was dominated by just two competitors. In the end the RAC was sold to Lex Service Group, a group focused on vehicle distribution and contract hire. Lex Service Group was a decentralized service operation. Its business units were relatively small and operated in local markets with considerable autonomy. The parent provided central services and systems. Some years previously Lex had believed that this style of management lent itself to hotels and acquired eight upmarket hotels, four in the UK and four in the US. Lex found it difficult to acquire additional suitable properties for its portfolio, failed to reach what it believed was critical mass, and systematically divested every property. Again, Lex was looking for opportunities in consumer service businesses. Vehicle distribution (where Lex Service Group began) has now been divested and the name of the whole business changed to RAC (2002). The intention now is to build a business around motoring and vehicle solutions. Financial services (car financing), motor and extended warranty insurance and personal injury claims management are seen as appropriate. The company is expanding into the under-exploited French market, to, in part, capitalize on the number of UK holidaymakers who take their cars to France.

By 1999 the AA (the Automobile Association) had divested its previous retailing and travel businesses but it still provided insurance services. Like other organizations such as Kwik Fit and Virgin, the AA was simply exploiting its brand and its customer database. The AA does not underwrite insurance, it merely sells policies. Other specialist insurers are the real providers of the actual insurance. The business was acquired by Centrica, the trading arm of British Gas. Centrica sells gas to 15 million customers, and installs and maintains central-heating systems. Centrica also offered a Goldfish credit card and marketed insurance. Centrica believed that it was widening its product offering for its huge customer database and could exploit shared support services, especially centralized call centres and billing systems. In 2001 Centrica also acquired Halford's garages (from Boots) which it immediately re-branded AA Service Centres, to build on the used car check-up service the AA already provided. The business concentrates on tyre and exhaust replacement and on MOT testing. The Halfords shops were not included in the deal – they were bought by venture capitalists who have since looked to re-float the business.

### Question

1. Which of these three new parents – Cendant, Lex Service Group and Centrica – has the best opportunity for sharing resources and transferring skills to a roadside-assistance business?

AA http://www.theaa.com
RAC http://www.rac.co.uk
GreenFlag http://www.greenflag.co.uk

The greatest returns should normally be found where activities are actually shared, but where this is not feasible, transferring skills can also be beneficial. The thinking here begins with a clear appreciation of strategic capabilities and the search for related industries in which these skills and capabilities could be usefully applied – again for savings or differentiation. The businesses must be sufficiently similar that sharing expertise is meaningful, and the potential advantage will always be greater if the capabilities involved are fresh to the new industry.

Where activities are to be shared and/or skills transferred, the corporate structure must be one that encourages it to happen and actively encourages managers to search out for opportunities. Many are actually structured in ways that erect barriers to sharing.

Finally, one key challenge in organizations that are heavily diversified and decentralized is to ensure that there is a shared corporate identity, which goes beyond the structural framework and comes down to the style of leadership and management. Porter concludes that diversification, decentralization and sharing can be complementary, although they may appear contradictory. They simply demand a sophisticated approach to the management of diversity.

## 16.5 Corporate parenting

Goold *et al.* (1994) reinforce Porter's arguments when they contend that acquisitions can be justified where the corporation can add value to the business, generating either synergy or valuable emergent properties. Any business must add value to its parent corporation; in turn, the corporation must add value to the subsidiary. The company is better off with its existing parent than it would be with another parent or on its own. Parenting skills, therefore, relate to the ability of a head office and strategic leadership to manage a portfolio of businesses efficiently and effectively and to change the portfolio as and when it is necessary. It is quite conceivable for head offices to destroy value if a subsidiary simply does not fit with the rest of the portfolio and is consequently held back.

Parenting skills vary between countries and cultures. In Japan, for example, the most successful companies are skilled at:

**Figure 16.3** Corporate parenting

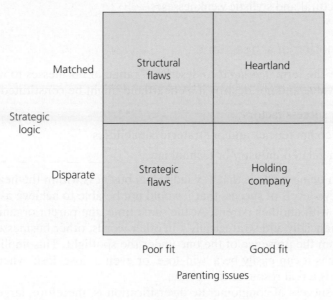

Strategic logic –   Link between products, services, competencies and
key success factors across the portfolio

Parenting issues –   The fit between the needs of individual businesses
and the capabilities of the parent

- securing and sustaining access to government, power and influence
- accessing investment capital, and
- retaining skilled managers.

Much of this is facilitated by the *keiretsu*, families of companies interlinked by share ownership and characterized by intertrading, regular meetings of senior executives and sometimes geographical proximity in a single 'corporate village'. Interestingly, and significantly, these companies are interwoven but there are no corporate headquarters.

Figure 16.3 builds on the arguments of Goold *et al.* and draws these points together. On one axis is strategic logic, the link between products, services, competencies and key success factors across the corporate portfolio. On the other axis are the parenting issues, the fit between the needs of individual businesses and the corresponding capabilities of the parent organization. Where they fit together well, there is a heartland of related businesses, which is explained below. Where there is no natural synergy between the businesses, the organization can be successful to some degree if the parent company uses a *holding company* structure. This implies strong individual companies that could survive elsewhere, but which are managed in a hands-off way. In this respect it is interesting that both Lord Hanson and Lord Weinstock had a reputation for rarely visiting the subsidiary businesses in the conglomerates that they ran.

Where the parenting issues are not addressed properly evidence will be seen of either strategic or structural flaws and the consequent underperformance. Here, *strategic flaws* again implies fragmented businesses with no real synergy potential but this time linked to an inappropriate structure and style. There is a real likelihood of poor performance.

*Structural flaws* reflect a potential for synergy but a potential that is not being realized because of structural and stylistic weaknesses.

### 16.5.1   The notion of a heartland

Goold *et al.* use the term *heartland* to describe a range of businesses to which a corporation can add value and not destroy it. A heartland might be constituted by:

- common key success factors
- related core competencies and/or strategic capabilities
- a common or related industry or technology.

The assumption being made is that any individual business within the heartland should be able to achieve levels of success that it would not be able to achieve as an independent business or with another parent. At the same time, the parent organization should benefit both financially and strategically – in other words, other businesses in the portfolio benefit from the presence of the one under the spotlight. This implies a 'win–win' situation, whereas it can easily be a 'win–lose' or even a 'lose–lose' where the fit is so poor that there is a real resource distraction.

The relative success of conglomerate diversification is, therefore, largely an issue of strategy implementation, specifically the parenting skills of the acquirer, and the ability to add value for both the subsidiary and the parent. The basic argument is that the corporate portfolio should be based around a heartland of businesses that are in some way related. Any which are not, and especially where they are a potential or actual distraction, should be divested. As an organization divests in this way to refocus it is quite normal for this to be followed by, or concurrent with, acquisitions of related businesses to strengthen the core of the new focus. These points are illustrated in Minicase 16.4.

Figure 16.4 offers a framework for assessing the strategic logic of a proposed addition to the corporate portfolio. On one axis is the extent of the linkages and synergy in

**Figure 16.4** Changing the corporate portfolio

Synergy in current portfolio i.e. the relationships and linkages between products and services, competencies and key success factors

High: Potential to dilute value and synergy | Heartland reinforcement
Low: Problem enhancement | With divestment, potential to improve balance of portfolio

New proposal – relationship with existing competencies (Low / High)

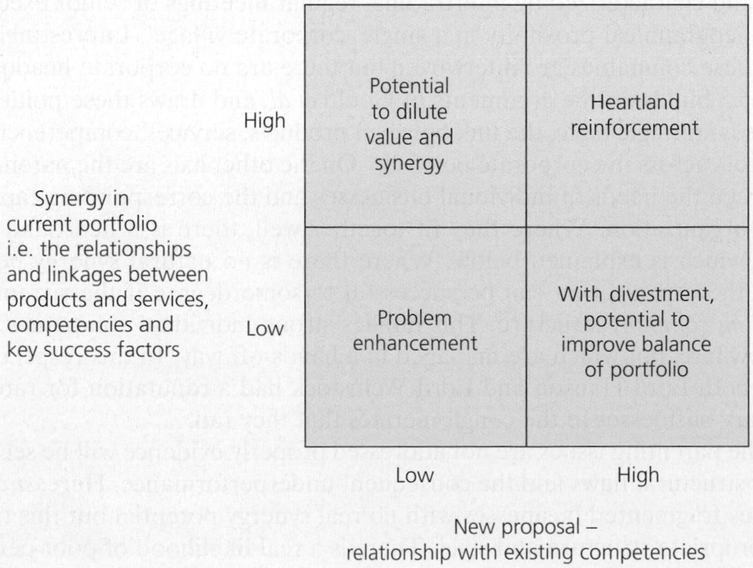

the existing portfolio; on the other axis is the relationship between the competencies required to run the new business effectively and the organization's existing competencies and capabilities. Logically, we are looking for a match – the top right quadrant. Where the existing match is low but the newcomer has similar competencies to certain existing businesses, there could be a logic in going ahead and divesting non-related activities at the same time – the bottom right quadrant. This could have the effect of strengthening the portfolio. In the top left quadrant there is the potential for an unrelated business to dilute value and synergy. An unrelated business added to a non-synergistic portfolio would merely enhance the strategic problems.

## 16.5.2 Determining the heartland

The issues concern:

- first, whether the parent is able to provide – and is actually providing – the services and support the individual businesses need, and

- second, whether the businesses have the people and competencies to fulfil the expectations of the parent.

Goold *et al.* (1994) offer the following framework as a starting point for assessing the existence of, or potential for, a heartland.

---

### Minicase 16.4 Smith's Industries – Developing A New Heartland

CASE

In the 1990s Smith's Industries owned an 'apparently widespread portfolio of engineering businesses' but argued that there was a related heartland. The Stock Exchange categorized Smith's as an aerospace business, but it comprised:

- aerospace components
- telecommunications products
- flexible hoses for vacuum cleaners
- medical products
- electrical instruments for cars.

Structurally, there were three divisions:

- aerospace – civil, military and after-sales service
- medical – equipment and consumables
- industrial.

A chief executive, Keith Butler-Wheelhouse, was recruited from Saab and he argued the company was about 'clever engineering'. Between 1996 and summer 2000, under his leadership, there were 26 acquisitions, mainly bolt-on related businesses. The company delivered 'above average returns and profit growth from some unpromising sectors' and its share price performance was better than most engineering companies.

Butler-Wheelhouse argued that Smith's was:

- focused on niche markets and relatively small businesses
- spread across eight distinct markets such that no single business could make or break the whole organization
- able to generate a cash flow which can fund both organic growth and further acquisitions.

In 2000 Smith's acquired a 'big one'. Tube Investments, long associated with motor vehicle components, was diversified into seals (mechanical and polymer), fluid storage (cars and refrigerators) and aerospace (landing gear and general systems).

Smith's would continue to build its heartland around clever engineering but the business was to be reinvented as an aerospace engineering business with interests in other high-growth niche

▶

opportunities – such as medical equipment and systems for detecting explosives. Various automotive businesses were put up for sale, with mixed success. In the end those that wouldn't sell were floated off as an independent group. Polymer seals were sold in 2003 – at a loss because of an anxiety to divest this non-core activity.

Butler-Wheelhouse commented in 2003 that 'in the past year we've spent five minutes wondering whether we've got a balanced portfolio of businesses and the rest of the time being concerned about how to run the company and generate profits'.

**Questions**

1. How would you summarize the 'heartland' of Smith's Industries before and after the acquisition of Tube Investments?
2. What are your views on the final quote from Keith Butler-Wheelhouse?
3. How significant (relatively) is corporate strategy and how significant is operational strategy to deliver results?

Smith's Industries http://www.smiths-group.com

1. Mental maps (or philosophies) of the parent, incorporating issues of culture and values and broad policies for dealing with events and opportunities.
2. Issues of structure, systems and processes – incorporating the style of corporate management. This would include: procedures for appointing, promoting and rewarding people; the relative significance of budgeting and financial reporting; strategic planning systems; and capital allocation procedures.
3. Central services and resources – what is provided centrally and what is devolved.
4. Key people throughout the organization; key functions; key skills and competencies.
5. The nature of any decentralization 'contracts' and expectations – linked to issues of power, responsibility and accountability; reward and sanction systems; and the expectations that subsidiaries can have for the support they receive from corporate headquarters.

### 16.5.3    The role and contribution of corporate headquarters

This section draws together many of the above issues by considering the role and contribution of company head offices. Typically, these will be larger and grander in centralized organizations; but historically powerful centres have generally been reduced in size, and their work distributed to subsidiaries, as corporations have become more decentralized and adopted flatter organization structures.

There are two fundamental purposes of corporate headquarters:

- serving the global legal and financial needs of the business, and
- supporting strategy making.

In general, this means that they:

- add and subtract businesses from the corporate portfolio
- create linkages to drive synergy throughout the organization – this can include rules or intercompany trading, opportunities for exchanging knowledge and ideas, and facilitating the sharing and transfer of assets

- design, support and maintain the organization structure – this will incorporate communications, the extent of the decentralization, the formality of systems and procedures, and systems for feedback and reward
- provide certain key services – at a minimum this will be a treasury and corporate secretarial service, but others can be added as well.

However, many head offices have historically provided a more extensive range of services to their constituent businesses, including for example:

- marketing
- management development and personnel
- property management
- centralized research and development
- corporate public relations
- industrial relations.

There is a clear need for head offices to add value to the corporation and not simply to spend the money earned by the businesses. With the recent trend for organizations to slim down the size and scope of head offices, in many cases only corporate strategy, financial reporting and control and secretarial/legal services remain centralized. Some head offices retain a responsibility for *policies* but not the activities.

Summarizing points made earlier, large, centralized head offices where all the key business heads are located in one place – Unilever has been a good example until recently – can control the corporation *efficiently*, but strategies can easily become top-down and slow to change. Decentralized organizations such as ABB in the 1990s (Minicase 15.6) push profit responsibility down to the businesses and empower managers. The head office provides more of a support role with few discrete functions. The new challenge is one of co-ordination.

In considering how head offices can best add value to the business as a whole, four broad issues must be addressed:

- how to control and co-ordinate the constituent businesses – issues of structure, corporate leadership and internal communications and synergy
- how to advise the strategic leader and keep him or her strategically aware
- driving performance and improvement through effective reward systems
- deciding which activities should be
  - provided from head office – for which a fee should be levied
  - devolved to the individual businesses
  - bought in from outside specialists.

The alternative approaches include the stand-alone holding company, financial control approach; centralizing specific functions and services; controlling strategic change at the corporate level; and fostering linkages, learning and sharing good practices.

Head offices can destroy value if they:

- become established as *the* perceived centre for expertise in the corporation – they cannot understand all of the important detail about competitiveness in their constituent businesses, whose managers will become demoralized if their potential contribution is not acknowledged

- assume that potential linkages and synergy will happen automatically
- duplicate effort and costs unnecessarily
- buy and sell businesses at the wrong prices
- create or perpetuate a culture where internal competition takes precedence over the need to compete with external rivals.

> *Here at head office, we don't go very deep into much of anything, but we have a smell of everything. Our job is capital allocation – both intellectual and financial capital. We smell, feel, touch, listen, then allocate.*
>
> John F Welch, when Chief Executive Officer, General Electric

## 16.6 The role of general managers

Basically, general managers co-ordinate the work of subordinate specialist managers; they are responsible for the management of strategy implementation and, in certain cases, strategy formulation. The chief executive or managing director of the company, the overall strategic leader, is a general manager. So too are the heads of divisions and business units, and the heads of operating units in a matrix structure. Their task is to match the resources they control with their particular environment effectively and to achieve E–V–R congruence.

Divisionalized organizations were examined in Chapter 15, where it was shown that the degree of decentralization and the power, authority and responsibility enjoyed by general managers will be affected by their relationship with head office and headquarters corporate staff. Whatever the extent of the decentralization from head office to business units, the business units themselves might be highly centralized. This depends on the style of management adopted by the particular general manager in charge.

Each division or business unit is part of a larger organization and corporate structure, and consequently it is not fully autonomous. While the organization as a whole has an external environment comprising customers, suppliers, competitors and shareholders among other influences, each division will have corporate headquarters as part of its environment. Business units may have both divisional headquarters and corporate head office in their environment. General managers in divisions and business units therefore do not have full responsibility for strategy creation and implementation. They can be pressurized by corporate headquarters, and they can turn to head office in their search for additional finance and other resources. The provision of finance within the organization may operate differently from the external market, but justification should still be required.

The relationship between general managers and head office will determine whether they are free to change their portfolios of business units and products or just adapt competitive and functional strategies. Performance measures and expectations will also affect this. Where specific short-term objectives and targets are set, and monitored strictly, general managers are less likely to focus on corporate changes and instead will concentrate on more immediate changes which can yield faster results. Their flexibility to make changes will increase as their targets become more vague and directional and less specific. Even though the general managers of business units may not be responsible for the formulation of changes in the corporate strategy which will affect their sphere of influence, they will invariably be responsible for the implementation of the changes.

## 16.6.1 General management skills and values

It has been established, then, that effective strategic management concerns issues of formulation and implementation. Strategic choices concern:

- the nature and orientation of the organization – the strategic perspective
- the deployment of its resources, ideally to achieve and sustain competitive advantage.

The strategic choice is implemented by the strategic leader, either the chief executive, the owner–manager in the case of a small business, or a general manager. It was pointed out in Chapter 10 that different strategic leaders (a) exhibit different patterns of behaviour and styles of management, and (b) will have different technical skills and biases as a result of their background. Arguably, alternative general managers would seek to implement basically the same strategy in different ways. The views of a number of authors concerning the relationship between general manager skills and particular strategies are discussed below.

Herbert and Deresky (1987) have examined the issue of match between the general manager and the strategy, concluding that the orientations and styles given below were important for particular strategies:

| Strategy | Styles and qualities required |
|---|---|
| *Development* (start-up and growth) | Aggressive, competitive, innovative, creative and entrepreneurial |
| Stabilizing (maintaining competitive position) | Conservative, careful and analytical |
| Turnaround | Autonomous, risk and challenge oriented and entrepreneurial |

Herbert and Deresky contend that financial skills are important for all strategies, with marketing skills being particularly important at the development stage and production and engineering skills invaluable for stabilizing strategies. This raises three issues.

1. Which specialist functional managers might be most appropriate for promotion to general management in particular circumstances? More recent research in the US confirms that the most typical background for large company chief executives is finance; the same pattern applies in the UK. Marketing, technical and manufacturing specialisms also feature but it is rare for a manager with a human resources background to become the strategic leader.
2. Is a change of general manager appropriate as products and businesses grow and decline and need changes in their strategies?
3. As strategies evolve and change should general managers adapt their styles of management accordingly?

Dixon (1989) suggests that *innovatory general management skills* are most required in the early and late stages of the life of a business or product in its present form. These skills are required to establish or recreate competitive advantage and, in the case of terminal decline, to find an alternative product, service or business. These changes are often best accomplished by outsiders with fresh ideas. Correspondingly, the constant search for efficiencies and improvements while an established product or business is maturing is normally best carried out by specialists.

A major problem with this type of innovation lies in the fact that changes in senior management, structure or values may be involved. The outlook and styles of general managers are likely to be different, and their responses to different sets of expectations and performance targets will vary. Again, this raises the issue of which managers are most appropriate for managing particular strategies.

There are similarities and differences in these various conclusions, reflecting again that there is no one best answer. The issue of match between general manager and strategy is important, and consequently one might expect that changes in one will lead to changes in the other.

Clearly, as organizations become flatter and more decentralized skills in synthesis and integration are critically important.

# 16.7 The modern organization

## 16.7.1 Kanter's view

Developing these arguments further, Rosabeth Moss Kanter (1989) has researched the general management skills required to run businesses effectively in the competitive environment of the late 1980s and the 1990s. Large companies, she contended, must be able to match corporate discipline with entrepreneurial creativity in order to become leaner and more efficient whilst being committed to both quality and innovation.

Three strategies are particularly important:

1. restructuring to improve synergy from diverse businesses
2. the development of joint ventures and strategic alliances to input new ideas
3. the encouragement of intrapreneurship within organizations.

These points are explained in greater detail in Box 16.1.

Kanter's main conclusion is that *process is more important than structure*. She suggests that:

- general managers must be able to balance maintenance and entrepreneurial skills
- internal competition (typically fostered in organizations which are divided into discrete divisions and business units) can be harmful and impede synergy
- incentive and reward schemes should reflect the need for co-operation and support between business units
- the increasing incidence of joint ventures, which requires the forging of closer links with other external businesses, suggests that structures may need revision if the potential and desired synergy is to be achieved.

## 16.7.2 Handy's view

Charles Handy (first articulated in 1994, 1995) continues to contend that in order for companies to remain competitive internationally they have had to rethink their basic structures. 'Fewer key people at the heart of the organization, paid very well, producing

## Box 16.1 Rosabeth Moss Kanter on Competitiveness

Future success lies in the capability to change and to accomplish key tasks by using resources more efficiently and more effectively. Organizations must be innovative and, at the same time, control their costs. Sustainable competitive advantage, however, does not come from either low costs, or differentiation, or innovation alone. It needs the whole organization to be *focused, fast, flexible and friendly*.

Being *focused* requires investment in core skills and competencies, together with a search for new opportunities for applying the skills. Intrapreneurship should be fostered to improve the skills constantly; and managers throughout the organization should be strategically aware and innovative. They should own the organization's mission, which, by necessity, must be communicated widely and understood.

*Fast* companies move at the right time, and are not caught out by competitors. New ideas and opportunities from the environment will be seized first. Ideally, they will be innovating constantly to open up and sustain a competitive gap, because gradual improvements are likely to be more popular with customers than are radical changes. However, instant success takes time – the organization culture must be appropriate.

*Flexibility* concerns the search for continual improvement. The implication is a learning organization where ideas are shared and collaboration between functions and divisions generates internal synergy. This, in turn, suggests that perform-

ance and effectiveness measures, and rewards, concentrate on outcomes.

Internal synergy can be achieved with cross-functional teams and special projects, and by moving people around the organization in order to spread the best practices. General Motors allows components and assembly workers, who work in separate plants in different locations, to contact each other by telephone to sort out problems and faults without relying on either written communications or messages which go 'up, across and down again'. These workers see each other as 'colleagues in the *whole* organization'. It is important that internal constraints (imposed by other functions and divisions) and which restrain performance are highlighted and confronted. To be effective this requires a clear and shared vision and purpose for the organization, decentralization and empowerment.

*Friendly* organizations are closely linked to their suppliers and customers to generate synergy through the added value chain. Such external collaboration may be in the form of strategic alliances.

### Reference

The material in this box is summarized from: Kanter, RM (1989) *When Giants Learn To Dance*, Simon and Schuster, but the points remain pertinent and relevant some 15 years later.

far more value.' Handy acknowledges that it is quite feasible that corporations will continue to grow, either organically or through acquisition, but believes that either physically or behaviourally they need to be in small units, focused and closely networked to their suppliers and customers. More activities and components will be bought in from specialists than is the case at the moment; internally, they will also comprise networks characterized by subsidiarity, with the centre (as distinct from a traditional head office) doing only what the parts cannot do themselves. The real power will switch from the top of the organization to the businesses, and consequently a co-ordinating mission and purpose will be essential. Handy favours 'federalism' or reverse delegation – the centre acts on the bidding of, and on agreement with, the parts. Basically, Handy is supporting the decentralization trend, but going much further.

Supported by sophisticated information technology and systems, people will become recognized as the most important strategic resource and, because their expertise and intelligence is an intangible asset, largely unquantifiable, it will become harder to value the *real* assets of a business. Consequently, the appropriate measures of performance must be carefully evaluated, and reward systems will have to be derived which motivate and keep those managers who are potentially the most mobile. The valuable managers will not all be at the most senior levels. Disagreeing with many strategic leaders of global organizations, Handy believes that switching jobs regularly and moving people between different parts of the organization, perhaps to other countries, can be dysfunctional. Simply, they will not be in place long enough to become known and, in the future, trust will be an essential element in management, strategic change and strategy implementation.

*We have designed organizations based on distrust. We have designed organizations so that people will not make mistakes. And, of course, we now encourage people to make mistakes because that is how they learn.*

Handy

Handy's arguments imply major changes to strategies, structures and styles of management for many organizations. Where these changes are simultaneous – amounting to *strategic regeneration* in effect – the changes are dramatic, painful and often difficult to carry through. This is discussed further in Chapter 17.

*Perhaps the most apposite definition of strategy for me is drawn from the world of chess. Strategy is knowing what to do when there is nothing to do; tactics is knowing what to do when there is something to do.*

Sir Trevor Holdsworth, ex-Chairman, GKN, quoted in the
*Strategic Planning Society News*, 1991

*On 25 June 1876 General George Armstrong Custer was informed that a significant number of Indians were gathering at Little Big Horn. Without further intelligence or analysis, he decided he would ride out with his 250 men to 'surround the Indians'. It is difficult for 250 soldiers to surround 3000 Indians – Custer made a serious error of judgement.*

## 16.8 Strategic resource management

Figure 16.5 recapitulates how the corporate mission and purpose provide the basis from which corporate and competitive strategies are derived. The corporate portfolio provides a number of ways for the organization to pursue its mission – but each business in the portfolio will require different levels of attention and resourcing. These decisions relate to priorities linked to the potential of, and desired outcomes from, each business. The achievement of competitive advantage and success comes down, in the end, to individual contributions, and to guide and manage these, objectives, targets and milestones will be set.

Once intended strategies have been determined, either in broad outline or in greater detail, the organization must plan their implementation. This means, first, that the resources required for implementation – including capital equipment, people and finance – are available where and when they are needed. Resources need to be *allocated*

**Figure 16.5** Strategy implementation and resource management

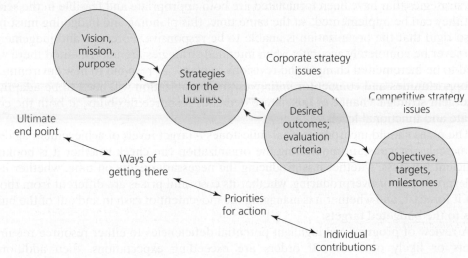

to different managers, functions and businesses, and then *co-ordinated* to generate synergy. Second, the managers responsible for implementation must understand what is expected of them and be empowered and motivated to take the necessary decisions and actions. In addition, *monitoring and control* systems are required.

At the corporate strategy level, organizations might establish priorities for different divisions and businesses using portfolio analysis, and evaluate the strategic and financial implications of alternative investments. Decisions may be taken within the constraints of existing capital, financial and human resources; if they demand new resources, then these must be obtained in an appropriate timescale. Proposed acquisitions may require an organization to raise funding externally; organic development of new products may require new skills and competencies. Resources can be switched from one part of a business to another.

At the functional level, *policies* and procedures can guide managers and other employees in the utilization of these corporate resources to add value, create competitive advantage and achieve the desired objectives. These policies can be tightly defined to maintain strong, central control, or very loose and flexible to enable people to use their initiative and be flexible. The ongoing management of the resources will then use action plans and budgets.

*Action plans* relate to the detailed strategies and plans for the various key functions, the activities which must be carried out if competitive and corporate strategies are to be implemented successfully; *budgets* add a crucial financial dimension to these plans. Together they attempt to integrate sales, supply potential, production activities and cash flow to ensure that resources are available to produce goods and services where and when they are required. The organization would like to avoid a situation where it has requests that it would like to take, or worse, it has booked orders, but it does not have the resources to enable production or supply. The potential danger here is one of over-trading and overcommitment. Both its bank and its customers can easily end up disappointed. It would also wish to avoid situations where it has idle capacity and no orders, or instances where it is producing for stock rather than for customers. This dilemma is one faced all the time by many small businesses, and in it we can see an endeavour to balance the resource-based perspective of strategy with the opportunity-driven approach.

This planning process then provides a useful check that the corporate and competitive strategies that have been formulated are both appropriate and feasible in the sense that they can be implemented. At the same time, this planning and budgeting must not be so rigid that the organization is unable to be responsive. Forecasts and judgements will never be completely accurate; when intended strategies are implemented there will need to be incremental changes and revisions to plans. To respond to new environmental opportunities and competitor initiatives, the organization will need to be adaptive. Emergent strategic change of this nature demands resource flexibility, at both the corporate and functional levels.

The plans should incorporate clear milestones – target levels of achievement against a timescale. By constant monitoring the organization can check whether it is booking sufficient business, whether it is producing the necessary quality on time, whether it is underproducing or overproducing, whether its costs and prices are different from those that it forecast, and whether it is managing the movement of cash in and out of the business to the budgeted targets.

A review of progress can highlight potential deficiencies to either resource requirements or likely outcomes. If orders are exceeding expectations, then additional resources may be required if the organization is to properly satisfy the new level of demand. If these cannot be found, schedules will need to be changed and maybe future supplies rationed. If orders are below expectations, then either new business opportunities will need targeting at short notice, possibly implying very competitive prices and low margins, or end-of-year targets revised downwards. Vigilance and pragmatism here can help to ensure that the organization does not face unexpected crises. Effective communications and management information systems are essential for planning, monitoring and control.

The allocation of resources at a corporate level is closely tied in to the planning system through which priorities must be established. Portfolio analyses such as the directional policy matrix may well be used to help to determine which products and business units should receive priority for investment funding; and any new developments that are proposed will require resources. An acquisition, for example, will need to be financed, but the integration of the new business after the purchase may also involve the transfer of managers and other resources.

### 16.8.1 Corporate resource planning and organization growth

Corporate resources may be allocated in different ways in line with the speed of growth of the organization and the degree of instability in the environment.

**Rapid growth** Where the business overall, or selected business units within it, are growing rapidly the resource allocation process must be able to accommodate this growth and the consequent and possibly continual demand for additional resources. The process could be either centralized or decentralized, or a mixture of the two, influenced by the management style of the overall strategic leader and the interdependencies between the various parts of the organization.

If the process is centralized, priorities will be established by head office corporate staff using some formal planning system and periodic review of the potential of all business units. Business units will need to provide the necessary information. With a decentralized approach the priorities would again be decided centrally, but after allowing all divisions and business units to formulate their own preferred strategies and make their case for the corporate resources that they would require to implement their preferences. A mixed approach would involve resources for continuing activities being allocated through centralized mechanisms and incremental additions funded through a bidding process.

In all cases the decisions should balance the potential financial gains with the strategic logic implied. While divisions or business units may be making individual requests for resources to support certain programmes, the opportunities for synergy, sharing activities and transferring skills across activities should be assessed. In addition, the desirability of the implications of the various proposals for the overall strategic perspective of the organization should be considered.

**Limited change and stability**  Where businesses are growing more steadily and in a relatively stable environment, resource allocation for continuing programmes could be a straightforward extrapolation of previous budgets, incorporating an allowance for inflation. However, a mere continuation of present strategies without evaluation and proper review may lead to ineffectiveness.

Established policies, such as fixing advertising budgets at an agreed percentage of projected sales revenue or maintaining particular levels of stocks, are likely to be a key feature of this approach.

**Decline situations**  Where businesses or business units are in decline some quite tough decisions often have to be taken. Where the organization as a whole is in difficulty the strategic leader must search for new opportunities for redeploying resources. In the case of selected business units that are experiencing decline, unless there are opportunities for turnaround, resources should be transferred to activities with better growth and profit potential. In both cases the decisions are likely to be centralized, particularly as there may have to be structural changes to accommodate the rationalization, divestment or other strategic changes.

Once resources are allocated to divisions, business units and functions there will be further allocations to individual managers within each area; and this to a greater or lesser extent will be delegated to the general manager or functional manager in charge of each one. This is known as functional or operational resource planning; in the process it is important not to overlook any interdependencies between the budget holders.

### 16.8.2  Functional resource planning

When resources are allocated to functions, and to particular activities within functions, there are a number of essential considerations.

1. It is important to consider the relative importance of each function; the concept of the value chain, explained in Chapter 5, could prove helpful in establishing this.
2. Competitive advantage is established within functional activities; consequently, an appreciation of key success factors and competitive opportunities is crucial if the resource allocation is to lead to strategic effectiveness.
3. The important linkages between functions, which are the sources of potential synergy, should be considered. Any appropriate sharing of resources should be encouraged. To this end, activities should be complementary and supportive.
4. Where there are sequential dependencies, the whole resource allocation process must take account of these. For example, if activity Z is dependent upon activity X

which precedes it, then it is both inefficient and ineffective to allocate resources to Z unless adequate resources are also given to X. An obvious application of this would be production activities which must be built around any bottlenecks. Similarly, the capacity of hospital operating theatres should be consistent with the number of beds available for recuperation.

Minicase 16.5 looks at the particular resource and co-ordination problems of Standard Fireworks, a company which manufactures fireworks for ten months of the year but delivers virtually all of its production during a one-month period.

### 16.8.3 Efficiency and effectiveness in resource allocation and management

It is important to consider both efficiency and effectiveness measures in relation to the allocation and deployment of resources. An examination of the way in which resources are employed and managed in the production and marketing of existing products and services can be used to search for improvements. Savings in time and costs (without threatening quality) lead to higher productivity, higher profits and the freeing up of resources which can be deployed elsewhere. This is essentially a search for greater efficiency.

At the same time, it is also useful to consider whether resources are being allocated to those products, services and activities which are most important for the organization as a whole and for the achievement of its objectives. This analysis is applicable at organizational, divisional and business unit level – wherever there is an opportunity cost of the resources in question. If resources are finite and limited to the extent that choices have to be made concerning which products to concentrate resources on and which to give low priority to, then the opportunity cost of the resources should be considered. If growth or profitability or both are important objectives, the resources should be allocated to those products and services which can best fulfil the objectives. This is an assessment of effectiveness. However, as discussed above, it is important to ensure that sufficient resources are allocated to development programmes that will lead to growth and profits in the future.

If decisions are made to alter resource allocations and concentrate them in different areas, issues of managing change arise; these are considered in Chapter 17. It should be appreciated that particular business units, products and services are likely to have their champions within the organization. Resource reductions in favour of alternative products may be resisted by certain managers. Their ability and willingness to resist change pressures from higher management will be related to their power bases and their ability to influence decisions. These issues also are considered in Chapter 17.

It is now appropriate to consider in more detail how resources are allocated to managers and how policies influence the way in which resources are used. Put simplistically, managers are allowed certain resources, which represent costs to the organization, and are then expected to use them to generate revenues and profits. The budgeting process determines how many of which resources managers are allocated. Their agreed objectives and targets concerning particular products and services determine how the resources are further deployed, and established policies influence the way in which they are deployed and managed.

Too many businesses spend money they have yet to earn to buy things they don't need to impress people they don't even like.

# Minicase 16.5  Standard Fireworks    GB   AS

Standard began manufacturing fireworks in the UK in the 1890s. By the 1960s the number of UK producers had declined to 11, and Standard was one of the largest. In the mid-1990s, with factories in Huddersfield and Doncaster – as well as a joint venture in China – it was the only UK *manufacturer*. Standard (with its subsidiary, Brock) had some two-thirds of the UK market; imported brands such as Astra and Black Cat, mostly from China, but with some from Hong Kong, constitute the remainder. Europe has tighter regulatory standards than the Far East, where labour costs are also lower. Simply, UK manufacture is less profitable than production in China, but in the past it has offered more political stability. The quality of UK production is higher in the case of the more sophisticated fireworks; for lower-price items quality differences are not an issue. Quality control is always important.

Standard has 17,000 customers in the UK, many of them small, independent retailers, who buy over 80 million fireworks each year. The UK's biggest demand for fireworks is on 'bonfire night', 5 November each year, which marks the anniversary of Guy Fawkes' ill-fated attempt to blow up the Houses of Parliament. Although Standard's team of eight salesmen collects provisional, indicative orders all through the year, confirmed orders tend to be placed during October for immediate delivery. Virtually all deliveries are made in the three to four weeks which precede bonfire night; all payments are due in late November. For many years the company was very profitable, but this would change with competition.

The company was controlled by its founding family for over 90 years before it was acquired by the mini-conglomerate Scottish Heritable Trust in 1986. SHT's other businesses included hospital beds, golf clubs, sock manufacture and gravel pits. Standard acquired its competitor, Brock, in 1987, and chose to utilize the Brock brand for the fireworks that it manufactured in China. Standard was bought out by its managers in 1992 but then sold to its Hong Kong-based rival, Black Cat, in 1997. Black Cat already had a UK base in Burton

upon Trent which it set about consolidating on to Standard's Huddersfield site. The company is now called Black Cat Fireworks.

Historically, Standard decided what it would make in any one year, and essentially told its retail customers what they could have. This is no longer the case. Production takes place mainly between January and September; Standard does not manufacture any fireworks in November and December, the last two months of its financial year. The product mix, and the numbers of each firework, are initially based on the previous year's delivery pattern, and then adjusted in line with the indicative orders received. Production is constant, rather than loaded at the end of the period, and there are no night shifts. Safety considerations rule out a last-minute rush. It is a 'one-shot' business, with little opportunity to alter the product mix at the end of the cycle if forecasting has been poor.

Fireworks are not produced in a typical factory, again for safety reasons. Teams of one to three employees work in small huts which are geographically separated on the site. If there is an explosion, the hut roof blows upwards and the sides outwards; only a limited number of people are at risk. Gunpowder is delivered in small quantities to each hut on a regular basis, and finished products are taken away for storage elsewhere. Transport is by rubber-wheeled hand carts; there are no petrol-driven vehicles within the confines of the production area. The amount of gunpowder and fireworks that can be stored in any one building and on any one site is regulated and restricted. Standard hires secondary storage facilities near Gretna Green and in Staffordshire.

Standard cannot physically distribute all of its fireworks itself during October. It has to hire capacity from independent carriers. Standard delivers large loads to the carriers who then take the fireworks (in small packages) to the retailers. Co-ordinating this network is critical for success. A few years ago, for example, there were problems with one carrier who was simply unable to deliver the packages on time; given the tight deadlines, this constituted a crisis for Standard.

▶

Managing the cash flow is also critical. The bulk of Standard's inward cash flow is in November; by February the cash reserves have been spent and the overdraft then grows steadily and remorselessly until the following November. There is some limited flexibility in that low-cost fireworks can be manufactured early in the cycle, leaving the most expensive ones until the end.

Looking ahead, it is not inconceivable that resins could replace gunpowder in fireworks, in which case many of the current production constraints would disappear. Production in factory units could be more mechanized. An interesting opportunity for the company concerned the demand for fireworks for the new millennium celebrations, New Year 1999/2000. It was clear in advance that there was going to be a huge demand. But when should Standard manufacture – and what should it produce?

**Questions**

1. What would you have done about the new millennium demand?
2. Given that most European manufacturers focus almost exclusively on high added value (and premium price) display fireworks, what is the future for Standard/Black Cat?

**Standard Fireworks** http://www.standardfireworks.com

## 16.9  Policies, budgets and control

### 16.9.1  Policies

Policies are designed to guide the behaviour of managers in relation to the pursuit and achievement of strategies and objectives. They can guide either thoughts or actions, or both, by indicating what is expected in certain decision areas. Over time they establish the way in which certain tasks should normally be carried out, and place constraints upon the decision-making freedom that managers have. In this respect they imply that the implementation of strategies formulated by strategic leaders is a planned activity, and recognize that managers may at times wish to make changes and pursue objectives which are personally important to them. Policies, therefore, should be related to stated objectives and strategies and assist in their implementation; at the same time they should not restrict managers to the extent that they are unable to make incremental and adaptive changes when these are appropriate or necessary. Managers should be offered sufficient inducements to comply with organizational policies, and sanctioned when they fail to comply without justification.

Policies need not be written down or even formulated consciously. They may emerge as certain behaviour patterns become established in the organization and are regarded as a facet of values and culture. A policy can exist simply because it is the perceived way that something has always been done. Policies are particularly significant in the case of recurring problems or decisions as they establish a routine and consistent approach.

Policies can be either advisory, leaving decision-makers with some flexibility, or mandatory, whereby managers have no discretion. Koontz and O'Donnell (1968) suggest that mandatory policies should be regarded as rules rather than policies. They argue that mandatory policies tend to stop managers and other employees thinking about the most efficient and effective ways in which to carry out tasks and searching for improvements. Policies should guide rather than remove discretion.

Koontz and O'Donnell further argue that advisory policies should normally be preferred because it is frequently essential to allow managers some flexibility to respond

and adapt to changes in both the organization and the environment. Moreover, mandatory policies are unlikely to motivate managers, while advisory guides can prompt innovation.

## 16.9.2  The creation and use of policies

It has already been mentioned that policies may be created both consciously and unconsciously.

The main stated policies are those that the managers of the company draw up in relation to their areas of discretionary responsibility. Certain key policies will be established by the overall strategic leader and will be filtered down the organization. It is important that when general managers create policies for their divisions and business units, and functional managers for their departments, there is some consistency between them.

Some policies will be forced on the company by external stakeholders. Government legislation upon contracts of employment, redundancy terms and health and safety at work all affect human resource policies, for example. The design of certain products will have to meet strict criteria for safety and pollution. The fabric used for airline seats in the UK must be fire resistant, and there are similar restrictions upon the type of foams that can be used in furniture. Car engines must be designed to meet certain emission regulations. In some cases financial policies can be dictated by powerful shareholders or bankers.

It is useful, then, if the major functional areas of the business are covered by explicit policies which are known to all employees who will be affected by them. Where they exist in this form they provide a clear framework in which decisions can be made; and they also allow people to understand the behaviour patterns that are expected of them in particular circumstances. However, the policies should not be too rigid and prevent managers making important change decisions. Changes in strategies may require changes of policy if they are to be implemented successfully.

## 16.9.3  Examples of functional policies

Policies can exist for any functional task undertaken by the organization, and consequently the following examples are merely indicative.

In *finance* the dividend policy constitutes one example. It is typical for dividends to be held constant or increased gradually even though annual profits may be moving upwards and downwards quite significantly. This is meant to convey confidence when profits are falling and prudence when they are rising. Similarly, there may be policies for assessing the viability of proposed investments and ranking a set of alternatives. Where the firm has a financial strategy of investing cash balances on a short-term basis there may well be policies and criteria for evaluating appropriate opportunities.

*Human resource* policies would include the following:

- the type and qualification of employees for particular jobs
- the recruitment activities and procedures that will take place
- the training and development of particular skills and competencies in relation to specified jobs
- communicating to employees how well (or poorly) the company is performing
- policies concerning overtime and bonuses.

Policies with regard to quality and meeting delivery dates are examples from the *operations* function. Policies may also establish who has the authority to change production schedules; and in a retail organization there are likely to be policies concerning the reordering of stock, the refilling of shelves, and the ways in which merchandise should be displayed both in-store and in the windows.

*Marketing* policies are related to the four components of the marketing mix: product, price, promotion and distribution. One product policy of a car manufacturer might establish which models are made in anticipation of sale and displayed in distributor showrooms and which ones are only made when orders have been placed for them. A pricing policy of certain retailers is to reduce prices to the level of their competitors when customers highlight the differential. A preference for advertising in certain magazines or the use of a particular layout would constitute examples of promotional policies. The willingness of Marks and Spencer to exchange goods on demand, regardless of whether they are faulty, is a merchandising policy.

### 16.9.4 Budgets

Budgets, quite simply, are plans expressed in numerical terms, usually in financial terms. They will indicate how much should be spent, by which departments, when, and for what purpose.

Pearce and Robinson (1985) distinguish between three types of budget. *Capital budgets* concern the allocation of resources for investment in buildings, plant and equipment. These new resources will be used to generate future revenues. *Sales budgets* reflect the anticipated flow of funds into the organization based on forecast sales; and *revenue or expense budgets* concern the operating costs that will be incurred in producing these products and services. Because of such factors as seasonal demand, the need to hold stock, and the fact that the final payment for goods and services is likely to occur after all operating expenses have been paid, the flows of cash in and out of the business need to be controlled through these budgets.

Budgeting the direct costs of producing certain products and services requires an estimate of the raw materials, components, labour and machine hours that are likely to be needed. Standard costing techniques usually form the basis of this, with analyses of any variances being used to measure both performance and the reliability of the standard costs.

People are a crucial strategic resource, and their physical contribution in terms of hours of work can be budgeted. Work study and other techniques will be used to establish the standard times required to complete particular tasks, which can then be costed. While such standards, and the wage rates which are used to determine the payment for these inputs, are likely to be common throughout the organization, and in many cases agreed centrally, the selection and training of the people in question are likely to be decentralized. While the skills and capabilities of staff should be considered when the budgets are quantified, the process of budgeting can be useful for highlighting weaknesses and deficiencies.

Developing from this, another expense that needs to be budgeted is training and management development programmes. This involves the utilization of funds which are currently available to improve the long-term contribution and value of people. Training and development should therefore be seen as an investment. However, the anticipated returns will be difficult to quantify, and as a result the investment techniques considered earlier may be of only limited use. Moreover, the contribution of people will also depend

upon their commitment to the organization, which in turn will be influenced by the overall reward and incentives packages which are offered and the ability of the organization structure to harness and co-ordinate their various contributions.

## 16.9.5   The budgeting process

All managers who spend money, and whose departments consume resources, should ideally be given a budget. These budgets should represent agreed targets that relate closely to the manager's objectives, again agreed with his or her superior. In the same way that individual manager objectives contribute towards the objectives for departments, business units, divisions and ultimately the organization as a whole, individual budgets will be part of a master budget. Activities that constrain other activities, because they involve scarce resources for which demand exceeds supply capability, should be budgeted early.

Budgets and objectives are clearly related, and consequently resources should be allocated to those areas and activities in the organization that are seen as priorities. If important objectives are to be achieved, and priority strategies implemented, resources must be provided. Where growth and profits are important organizational objectives, those business units and products that are best able to contribute to their achievement should be funded accordingly. This approach suggests that the strategies being implemented have been formulated to satisfy corporate objectives, and personal objectives have been contained. However, the process of budgeting can facilitate the ability of managers to pursue personal objectives. Moreover, budgeting can be perceived as a technique for short-term financial management rather than a key aspect of strategy implementation. These contentions are expanded below.

Where resources are available and new developments are being considered, the previous record and contribution of managers is likely to have an influence. Rather than select strategies on merit and then allocate the most appropriate managers to implement them, the strategies championed by successful managers may be preferred.

Furthermore, the ability of certain managers to exercise power and influence over resource allocations within the organization, issues discussed in the next chapter, may result in allocations to areas and activities that potentially are not the most beneficial to the organization as a whole. Bower (1970) points out that where the objectives of the organization are difficult to agree and quantify, as is the case in many not-for-profit organizations, the political ability of managers to defend existing allocations and bid for additional resources grows in importance. Wherever this is evident, the resource allocation process becomes a determinant of the objectives and strategies pursued by organizations.

## 16.9.6   Flexibility with budgets

The budgeting process will normally take place on an annual basis, but as the targets will be utilized for regular performance reviews there should be scope to adjust budgets either upwards or downwards. While sales and revenue budgets are by nature short term, capital budgets have long-term implications. Investments may be paid for in instalments, and their returns are likely to stretch over several years. The budgets are interrelated. Once capital investment decisions have been taken there are immediate implications for revenue to support them.

The allocation of resources to managers is dependent upon the strategies that the organization has decided to continue and develop, but adaptive changes require flexibility which must be accounted for. Where resources are limited and finite, strategic opportunities may be constrained. New alternatives may only be feasible if other activities are divested. Flexed budgets are designed to allow for changes in the level of activity, which might result from adaptive changes in functional and competitive strategies. Managers would realize that, if they were able to sell in excess of their targets, then resources would be found to facilitate increased production. The assumption would be that more sales equals more profit, which may well be true. However, if the implication is that resources would be diverted from other activities, issues of opportunity cost are again relevant; and the resources should only be diverted from activities which are either less profitable or strategically less important to the organization in the long term.

### 16.9.7  Zero-base budgeting

Where a traditional approach to budgeting is adopted, once the continued production of a product or service has been assumed or decided, demand prospects are forecast. Against these are set expense budgets based on standard costs. Overhead contributions are most probably adjusted for volume changes and inflation. Previous experiences are therefore carried forward and used as a base. With zero-base budgeting no previous experience is assumed, and every proposed activity must be justified afresh.

It was suggested earlier that many local authorities have, historically, sought to continue with existing service provisions, supplemented by new and additional services when resources could be found to fund them. Local authorities who make use of zero-base techniques start with the assumption that all services must be justified and priorities established on merit. Existing services might well be replaced rather than continued simply because they already exist, or better ways of providing the services might be found.

Under traditional budgeting methods it is easy to carry forward past inefficiencies which result in overspending. Zero-base budgeting should prevent this and offer opportunities for reducing expenses by searching for improved efficiencies. Moreover, the establishment of priorities on merit can result in greater effectiveness, depending on the assessment criteria selected for evaluation.

Zero-based budgeting is conceptually very attractive as it distinguishes between high- and low-priority areas and constrains the pursuit of personal objectives by managers. Its implementation presents a number of difficulties, however, which often result in traditional budgeting being preferred. The most serious problems concern the administration, paperwork and time required to implement it effectively and establish priorities objectively. In large, complex organizations the decision-making burden concerning low-level priorities, which individually may not be very significant, can draw senior management attention away from the overall strategic needs of the organization. Finally, zero-based budgeting implies that any job might be declared redundant at any time, and this causes both uncertainty and increased political activity.

### 16.9.8  Measurement and control systems

The need to measure and evaluate performance, and to make changes when necessary, applies at all levels of the organization. Budgets establish quantitative targets for individual managers, departments, business units and divisions. Progress against these

**Figure 16.6** Monitoring and control

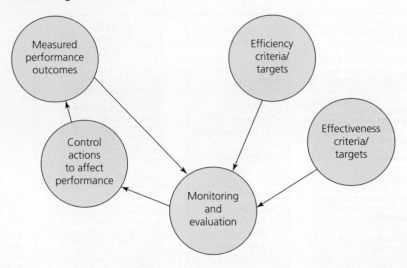

targets can be measured through the information system; and the feedback should be both fast and accurate to enable any corrective actions to take place quickly. The ability of all of these budget holders to achieve their targets will be useful when reviewing their futures.

When establishing budgets and performance targets it is, however, important to ensure that the attention of managers is not focused too narrowly on only their areas of responsibility. Their contributions to other managers and their commitment to the overall interests of the organization are the sources of synergy. While these measures of individual performances are crucial, the effectiveness of all functional, competitive and corporate strategies and their abilities to achieve corporate objectives are the ultimate measures.

The effectiveness of the contribution of such activities as research and development is difficult to assess, but this is no excuse for not trying.

Figure 16.6 summarizes these ideas and Figure 16.7 charts a number of possible performance measures – those on the right focus on efficiency and reflect a financial control culture; those on the left are crucial indicators of a commitment to service, quality and excellence. The culture of the organization will dictate which measures are given priority. Establishing such excellence measures requires a real attempt to reconcile the different expectations of the stakeholders. Where there is no common agreement, the objectives and measures selected will reflect the relative power of the various stakeholders. In any case, commercial pressures invariably focus attention on resource management and efficiencies, which are easier to set and monitor. There is then always the danger that because efficiency measures are possible, and often straightforward, they may become elevated in significance and, as a result, begin to be seen as the foundation for the objectives. In other words, measurement potential rather than stakeholder satisfaction dictates objectives.

**Figure 16.7** Some possible measures of performance

| Stakeholder satisfaction/competitive success/excellence measures | Decision areas | Financial control measures/ resource management |
|---|---|---|

Success implies a strategic perspective which is 'right for today' and developing in line with future needs, linked to a clear mission or purpose which is communicated and understood and the provision of quality products and high levels of service

M e a s u r e s   o f   e f f e c t i v e n e s s

Nos of new products services/markets. High level of service provision. Image/reputation. Responsiveness to (and awareness of) change opportunities.

**Supplies**
Exploiting new opportunities for adding value and competitive advantage.

**Operations**
Provision of total quality. Innovation/ intrapreneurship.

**Capital**
Using capital for competitive advantage. Using capital to fund investment opportunitites – inc. acquisition/ diversification.

**Assets**
Harnessing information technology.

Morale/motivation. Commitment. Leadership qualities in evidence. Flexibility and willingness to change. Pursuit of organizational goals.

**Marketing**
Product/service
– Range/mix
– Quality/specification
Price – cost/competition
Distribution
– Availability and service level
Sales and promotion

**Operations**
– Make or buy
– Delivery lead times
– Capital intensity
– Quality control
Research and development activity

**Finance**
Sources and costs of funds. Information and control systems

**People**
– Decentralization and responsibility
– Rewards
– Selection
– Development
– Management styles

Sales growth. Market share. Length of order book. Customer retention/repeat business. Debtor turnover ratio – some of these relative to competitors.

**Supplies**
Input costs. Lead times, overdues, creditor turnover ratio. Rejections.

**Operations**
Output/time period. Rejections. Variances against standards. Stock turnover ratio. Overheads to total costs. Delivery on time.

**Capital**
Return on shareholder funds. P/E ratio; EPS, interest cover debt ratio; WACC; flexibility. Share price against indices. Share price in relation to asset values.

**Assets**
Return on capital employed. Net asset turnover. Profit margin. Liquidity ratios and cash flow.

Absenteeism and turnover. Productivity. Output/sales per employee. Achievement of agreed targets. Training expenditure per employee.

M e a s u r e s   o f   e f f i c i e n c y

Success implies the organization is well managed and administered, supported by sound budgetary and control systems underpinned by a good information system

| The excellence service-orientated culture | The challenge: Balancing right and left | The financial control culture |
|---|---|---|

## 16.9.9 Performance expectations

Arguably the central issue in measurement and control is what is communicated to managers in terms of performance expectations, and how they are rewarded and sanctioned for their success or failure to achieve their targets. The two issues are linked, and resources should be allocated to enable managers to perform as required and, at the same time, to motivate them.

Reed and Buckley (1988) argue that when this is handled effectively then strategy implementation through action plans can be proactive, and strategies can be adapted in line with changes in the environment. Where it is poorly thought through there is likely to be more reaction to events and external threats. Research indicates that this aspect of implementation is difficult to achieve, however.

Wernham (1984) contends that managers benefit from an appreciation of 'superordinate organizational goals' and the overall strategic perspective, and that any perceived

internal inconsistencies between the performances expected of different managers can be demotivating. Communication and information systems should therefore seek to make managers aware about where the organization is going strategically and how well it is doing. Wernham's argument also implies that resource allocations and strategic priorities should be seen as fair and equitable, and that political activity to acquire or retain resources for the pursuit of personal objectives, or to support ineffective strategies, must be contained.

McMahon and Perrit (1973) have demonstrated that the effectiveness of managers in achieving their objectives is enhanced when the control levers are high, but Lawrence and Lorsch (1967) indicate that these controls also need to be loose and flexible if the environment is volatile.

It has been argued that resources are allocated through the budgeting process and that this establishes a quantitative short-term link between expectations and resources. It has also been argued that managers need to be aware of wider strategic issues, and that their attention should be focused on long-term strategies as well as short-term tactics and actions designed to bring immediate results. This necessitates that managers are aware of the key success factors for their products and business units, and of how their competitive environments are changing. While it is important to achieve budget targets, it is also important that there is a continuing search for new ways of creating, improving and sustaining competitive advantage.

Reed and Buckley (1988) suggest that implementation can be made more effective by addressing the following issues:

- establishing the *strategic benefits* that the organization is hoping to achieve from particular strategic options – both immediate and long-term benefits
- clarifying the managerial actions that will be required if these benefits are to be attained, and using these as a basis for action plans
- incorporating the matching of resources with key success factors, and the development of sustainable competitive advantage, in the objectives and targets that are agreed with managers
- appraising and rewarding the ability of managers to contribute to the development of sustainable competitive advantage and not merely their ability to meet short-term budget targets
- ensuring that sufficient flexibility is built in.

These arguments emphasize that, while budgeting is essential for allocating resources on a short-term basis and progress against budget targets is a vital efficiency measure, organizational effectiveness also depends on longer-term flexibility. New developments and strategies, and improved ways of doing things, must also be considered. These may well involve changes in structures and policies as well as in the status of individual business units and managers. Issues in the implementation and management of change are the subject of Chapter 17.

## 16.10 Risk management

The key elements in risk are the potential upside and downside from future events and the likelihood of certain things happening. Although forecasting and scenario planning are uncertain, they are still important as managers exercise judgement in the decisions

that they take. The greater their awareness, insight and understanding of emerging trends and opportunities, the more informed their decisions should be. Decisions and risk are linked irrevocably as the strategic decisions made by organizations and managers reflect their management of the risks they face. When organizations are managing risks effectively they will be less crisis prone and in a stronger position to deal with potential crises and unexpected events when they do occur. In Minicase 16.6 we show how two airlines, Air France and British Airways, reacted differently to the Air France Concorde crash in July 2000. There is always uncertainty following a disaster such as this, but BA believed that its safety preparations were robust and it kept its Concordes in the air. Air France opted to ground its planes until it had more knowledge. Both airlines were fully aware of the interest of the world's media but they had different perceptions of the risk.

---

## Minicase 16.6  Air France, British Airways and the Concorde Disaster

To understand the impact of a major accident with Concorde a number of background factors must be remembered.

- Concorde became a symbol of pride for Britain and France.

- Technologically it was a triumph.

- People have always made efforts to see it, let alone wanted to fly in it.

- The project helped to cement Anglo-French relations when the UK was wanting to be seen to be European.

- It proved that two countries could work together and challenge American dominance of the aerospace industry. In this respect it was a forerunner to the Airbus consortium.

- The project ran late and was heavily over budget.

- The plane was barred from flying overland at supersonic speeds because of the noise factor.

- Only two airlines ever flew it – when it began both were nationalized. British Airways (BA) has since been privatized.

- The BA Concorde services paid their way operationally, but all of the development costs were absorbed by the British and French governments – in today's money some £9 billion was absorbed.

- The services were mainly London and Paris to New York, but there were some UK to West Indies flights and a wide range of charter opportunities.

- In 1999 BA earned £140 million in revenues and Air France £70 million from Concorde – BA's services were marginally profitable; Air France lost money.

The first crash of a Concorde plane happened on the last Tuesday of July 2000. The passengers on the Air France flight from Paris to New York were German tourists flying out to meet a cruise ship. The plane was seen to be on fire before it even left the ground at Charles de Gaulle airport, but once Concorde has reached a certain speed on the runway take-off cannot be aborted. Two minutes later it had crashed onto a hotel on the outskirts of Paris. Altogether 113 people, the bulk of them passengers and air crew, died. The whole sequence of events was filmed by two amateur video-makers and so the disaster was very high profile.

Immediate speculation blamed an engine fire. There are two engines slung under each wing and those on one side had been clearly on fire. Moreover, the flight had been delayed in Paris while one of these engines was repaired. However, the landing gear was still down: in the little time he had available the pilot had reported that the hydraulics had also failed. Why?

In the event it was to transpire that a rogue strip of metal on the runway had punctured a tyre, and then tyre debris had punctured a fuel tank

incorporated in the wing. It later became apparent that the metal strip had probably been jettisoned from a Continental Airlines DC10 a few minutes earlier. The escaping fuel was ignited by the heat of the adjacent engines. The engines, and in turn the engineers who had repaired one of them, were not to blame. But, of course, the fact the fuel container could be punctured in the way it was caused huge concern.

## The Air France response

- The chairman went to the crash site immediately, signalling a personal involvement.
- All five remaining Concordes were grounded immediately, communicating that safety was the first priority.
- Later, the chairman attended a number of the family funerals and was available to talk to families of the victims.
- Air France provided free flights for relatives to and from Germany.
- Interim compensation payments were offered.

## British Airways

BA opted to keep its seven Concordes flying, although flights were suspended for the first 24 hours. This determination continued even when one had to make an emergency landing in Newfoundland after passengers complained that there was a smell of smoke in the cabin.

BA's pilots were happy about this – they had no fears for the aircraft's safety. Their representatives, together with retired pilots, were all happy to be interviewed by television reporters to confirm this view. Passengers were generally undeterred as well.

It transpired that in 24 years of flying there had been 70 previous incidents where tyres had burst, but never with catastrophic consequences. As a result of this BA had made certain modifications to the wheels which Air France had not copied. In addition, BA used new tyres (Air France used remoulds) which it changed regularly, after a fixed (and limited) number of take-offs or landings.

On 15 August, some three weeks after the crash, BA announced that it too was grounding its Concordes. This pre-empted the withdrawal of its Certificate of Air Worthiness by the Civil Aviation Authority (CAA) on 16 August. Air France commented that it was surprised that it had taken as long as it had.

Senior BA pilots demanded an immediate reprieve and suggested that it could be a ploy by France to end Concorde flights altogether because they were afraid of the cost of possible modifications that might be necessary.

## The UK Civil Aviation Authority

The CAA duly withdrew the Certificate of Air Worthiness, in reality a very rare event. The only time this had happened before as the result of a civil accident was when McDonnell Douglas DC10s were grounded temporarily in 1979. As shown in Minicase 14.1, this contributed to the failure of Laker Airways.

The CAA was asked why it had not acted earlier. The reply was that there had been speculation but no concrete evidence. Only now was the cause of the accident clear. The CAA emphasized its belief that Concorde remained a safe aircraft but that (as yet unspecified) modifications would be required. There was, however, a real concern that a tyre burst had been able to trigger the catastrophic chain of events that followed. Some commentators believed that the reluctance of Air France to restore Concorde services implied that there was an unacceptable risk with the plane.

## Final Outcomes

Ways to protect the fuel containers were devised – based on a kevlar protective lining – and modifications were made by British Airways. Concorde was allowed to fly again – and did. Services to New York were restored. But in the meantime 9/11 had happened, affecting demand for air transportation. And passengers had become more accustomed to (cheaper) first class travel in 'ordinary' aircraft. Transatlantic flights might take longer, but the new first class cabins had private sleeping areas and completely flat beds. One downside to

**Concorde**

Concorde was the relative lack of seating space – it was not a large aircraft. Ticket sales did not reach the levels enjoyed before the crash. BA decided that maintenance and other costs did not justify keeping Concorde in the air and its final flight was in October 2003. The remaining aircraft are grounded museum pieces.

**Questions**

1. Regardless of the actual facts and motives, whose reputation do you think might be most enhanced (or at least protected) by its reaction and behaviour?
2. Did BA do the right thing in the circumstances or should it have reacted differently?
3. Did this disaster merely accelerate the inevitable? Had it not happened, would Concorde still be flying today?

### 16.10.1 Strategic risks

Risk can be best understood as an uncertain prediction about future behaviour in a market or industry, with a chance that the outcome of this behaviour could be detrimental to an organization. Clearly, an organization must try to manage these risks to reduce both the likelihood of a particular event and the extent of any possible downside. In turn, this demands a clear understanding of the inherent risks in decisions and situations.

Minicase 16.7 Jollibee highlights the wide range of uncertainties that a company faces as it grows.

Opportunities and strategies that involve new customers, new markets, new countries and/or new competencies all imply risk – an element of chance that something can go wrong. The greater the potential impact (the downside) of what could go wrong, the greater the risk. This reinforces the value of a heartland of related businesses, which in turn should reduce the number of risk variables. When a company moves away from what it knows it increases its risk because there are more unknown factors. At the same time, not changing in a dynamic environment can also be very risky! Futures, simply, are uncertain.

Companies, then, must make strategic choices – and sometimes they get it wrong. Sometimes what appears to be a poorly judged choice can be turned around with appropriate changes during the implementation phase. It follows, therefore, that risk is best managed in an organization that has a culture of flexibility and innovation and is successful at getting its people involved and committed.

Certain business environments involve higher risks than others. High-technology industries, where there is constant innovation and technological change, involve high levels of risk. In pharmaceuticals it takes a number of years to develop and test a new drug before it can be introduced on to the market, and for much of this time there will be a real possibility that the new drug may never become a commercial success. A third example is oil exploration. Oil companies have to invest several million pounds in the hope of finding oil. While they can reduce their risk with sophisticated geological surveys before full exploration is embarked upon, there is always a risk of failure and loss of investment.

## Minicase 16.7 Jollibee (AS) (Int)

Jollibee, based in the Philippines, became the most rapidly expanding fast-food chain in Asia. It was established in 1978 by five Chinese-Filipino brothers, the Tan Caktiong family, since when it has acquired well over half of the fast-food market in the Philippines. At the beginning of the twenty-first century, there were over 400 branches worldwide, with half of these in the Philippines – of which one-third of this 200 are in Manila. McDonald's had 84 outlets; Wendy's and Kentucky Fried are also active competitors.

Boosted by a relaxation of laws concerning the extent of foreign investment in Filipino companies, Jollibee expanded abroad. An Australian, Tony Kitchener, was appointed to spearhead international developments. The early concentration was in South-East Asia and the Arab Gulf states, targeting especially Filipinos living in Indonesia, Malaysia, Brunei, Bahrain and Dubai. The number of overseas branches soon began to expand at a rate of 30 each year, with Hong Kong, China, Los Angeles and Rome high on the list of later priorities. Vietnam would follow. Increasingly, non-Filipinos are being attracted by the chain's individual products, which have been designed for low- to middle-income families with a sweet tooth, and for children's parties. Prices are kept slightly below those of McDonalds. The main product is an Asian-style hamburger, distinctive because it is cooked *with* the spices rather than them being placed on top afterwards – McDonald's has countered this with its local McDough brand. In addition, there are Spaghetti Fiesta (a Chinese-type mixed chow), salads and mango pie (a locally popular dish). While the hamburger tends to be ubiquitous, different countries have separate menus. Chicken masala is the most popular product in Malaysia and the Gulf. The bulk of the beef is imported from Australia and Jollibee makes all its own bread.

Jollibee waited for critical mass before announcing that 'its burgers are THE Asian fast food'. The company has also diversified, beginning with the acquisition of a pizza chain in the Philippines in 1993.

Expansion is now with joint ventures and franchising such that capital for growth is not a big problem. Some 50 per cent of the outlets are now franchised. It also takes some account of the fact that Jollibee's first independent overseas development in Taiwan (in 1988) was not altogether successful. The chosen location was wrong.

In 1997 Jollibee had to overcome one interesting setback. After the company opened a branch in Port Moresby in Papua New Guinea someone, possibly a competitor, placed the following advertisement in a newspaper: 'Wanted urgently, dogs and cats, any breed. Will pay 40 toea (equivalent to 24 US cents) per kilo live weight. Apply to the Jollibee …'. The company described this as a criminal attempt to try and sabotage their business, but failed to track down the instigator.

In 1998 and 1999 Jollibee, like many Asian businesses, had to deal with what might have been a far bigger potential crisis – the uncertainty caused by high domestic inflation and drastic falls in the value of local currencies. In the event this turned into a wonderful opportunity for Jollibee – whose growth continued unabated. Redundant, experienced executives were keen to buy franchises – in part because the demand for fast food grew. In a part of the world where eating out is normal, the lower-priced fast food outlets took business away from the more expensive restaurants.

### Questions

1. Can anything sensible be done to *prevent* an incident such as the rogue advertisement, or does it always come down to effective reaction?
2. Do you think this amounts to anything more than bad luck?

**Jollibee** http://jollibee.com.ph

Summarizing the points so far, risk occurs whenever anyone must make a choice and the potential outcomes involve uncertainty. If a manager is faced with a decision and the alternative choices involve estimated potential gains and losses which are not certainties, the situation involves risk. The outcome of a typical decision will be dependent on a number of factors, such as customer reaction, levels of demand and competitor responses. Some managers will understand the situation better than others might, and partly for this reason be happier to accept the risk involved in a particular choice. Personality also affects the willingness to accept and take a particular risk. It is important that there is compatibility between the strategic leader's attitude towards risk and the demands of the industry. A risk-averse strategic leader in a high-risk industry may miss valuable opportunities.

Risk increases as the amount of potential loss increases. As a simple example, a person might be offered a ticket in a raffle which costs £1.00, and the chance of winning the first prize of £150 might be 1 in 200. Another person might be offered the opportunity to invest £100 with a similar 1 in 200 chance of winning £15,000. Although the odds of winning and losing are identical, the risk involved in each situation is different. The potential loss in the second case is 100 times greater than in the first, and it consequently involves greater risk. The key issues are the uncertainty (the odds of certain eventualities, and which may or may not be predictable) and the amount that could be lost.

The following four criteria are important in the decision:

- the attractiveness of each option to the decision-maker
- the extent to which he or she is prepared to accept the potential loss in each alternative
- the estimated probabilities of success and failure
- the degree to which the decision-maker is likely to affect the success or failure.

### 16.10.2 Risk, entrepreneurship and decision-making

In considering risk in an organization a number of factors are worth investigating. It may well have an effect if the strategic leader is a significant shareholder rather than a minor one. Similarly, in the case of managers throughout the organization who are involved in strategic decisions in various ways, the culture and values of the organization with regard to reward for success and sanction for failure will be important. Here we are returning to the subject of entrepreneurs and intrapreneurs.

Entrepreneurs are often described as risk takers. Indeed, they do take risks, including a personal risk – it is their business, often their money and sometimes their reputation that is at stake. This personal risk can increase as the business becomes more successful and visible. The rewards for entrepreneurial success can be very high; the social stigma of a major failure can be traumatic.

The issue of entrepreneurs and risk is a complex one. There is an argument that risk awareness and opportunity awareness should be separated. Risk then concerns that which can be quantified, and opportunity that which is much more judgemental. A professional manager, trained in a business school, may well seek to measure and evaluate the risk in the decisions that he or she has to take. Where there is an uncertain opportunity he may well perceive the risk to be too great. There is a potential downside that he is anxious to avoid. Entrepreneurs are aware of both but are attracted by the opportunity.

In chasing an uncertain opportunity, then, the entrepreneur is taking a risk. Sometimes entrepreneurs have a feel for, or an insight into, a situation and an opportunity. This may be the outcome of learning from previous experiences. Basically, though, they know what they are doing; and in many instances they do not see themselves taking major risks; in which case, they are really *managing* the risks, even though they may not be able to quantify them. They are accepting and retaining the inherent risk and going ahead. Other people, whose understanding of the situation, and perception of the inherent risk, is different, may be unwilling to take the same risk. They do not pursue the opportunity.

Some successful entrepreneurs also recognize when an opportunity is beginning to disappear and they time their exit carefully, and focus their endeavours on a new opportunity. This is an excellent illustration of risk management, for they are seeking to avoid future risks.

A case can also be made that entrepreneurs have a lack of risk awareness. In other words, they either elect not to quantify the risks, or they simply turn a blind eye to them. Their philosophy is one of 'take things as they come'. They accept that things will not proceed straightforwardly or go according to plan, and so they brace themselves to deal with the setbacks and challenges as they occur. They have a great faith in their courage and their ability to deal with these setbacks – and in many instances this is good judgement on their part. They are creative and innovative and they do overcome the difficulties, often turning a potential threat into a new opportunity.

Their perception of risk will change over time and with experience. Once an entrepreneur has grown one venture successfully he or she is likely to develop confidence alongside their experience. The canny entrepreneur will accumulate a 'pot of capital' that can be reinvested in a way that does not imply bankruptcy if something goes wrong. Some entrepreneurs, however, start with a failure. Kets de Vries (1997) articulates a view that many entrepreneurs do indeed start in this way but are then determined to start all over again with a fresh risk. They are convinced that the world is against them – there is a resentment of people who succeed – and so failure can be expected. Their challenge is to have another go, but this time to succeed. 'The b\*\*\*\*\*\*s won't get me a second time.'

Attitudes towards risk affect the way in which all managers make decisions. Dunnette and Taylor (1975), whose research involved industrial managers, concluded:

> *High risk takers tended to make more rapid decisions, based on less information than low risk takers, but they tended to process each piece of information more slowly… although risk-prone decision makers reach rapid decisions by the expedient of restricting their information search, they give careful attention to the information they acquire.*

Environmental factors may prove significant. The availability and cost of finance, forecasts of market opportunities and market buoyancy, and feelings about the strengths and suitability of internal resources will all be important. For other managers within the organization the overall culture and styles of leadership and the reward systems will influence their risk taking.

### 16.10.3 Managing risk

The term 'risk management' is often associated with the idea of insurance and, indeed, insurance is relevant, but it is too narrow a perspective.

Organizations will often pursue strategies that seek to manage or minimize risk. Hanson (Minicase 16.2), for example, always investigated the downside in any strategy or proposed deal. Lord Hanson said of his late partner, Lord White: 'We would actually have done a lot more deals if Gordon did not have so many worries. He is constantly looking for the potential trouble in a deal.' The whole Hanson strategy was based on spreading risk. The small corporate headquarters retained the overall financial risk for the organization; all of the market risks were delegated to the individual businesses. When Richard Branson started Virgin Atlantic Airways, clearly a high-risk venture, he was cautious and spread his risk in a different way. He began with just one Boeing plane on sale or return for one year.

The first main step in risk management is clarifying the risks involved. There are four elements:

- personal risk
- opportunity risk
- (business) environmental risks, and
- resource-based risks.

Table 16.1 provides a framework for evaluating the environmental and business risks.

The second step is deciding what to do about the various risks, selecting from a number of alternatives:

- *retain* the risk and prepare for possible eventualities – some risks have to be taken or an opportunity or a venture would have to be abandoned
- *transfer* the risk – this could be achieved by switching it to someone else (divesting a business), diluting it (through a joint venture or strategic alliance) or insuring against it
- *regulate* the risk, perhaps by investing to reduce it.

*If you make a mistake in the UK you have had it … consequently we have a low expectation of achievement and too many people try and survive by not making a screw-up. In America they don't consider you're a businessman until you've screwed something up, because by definition you are not pushing at the frontiers. Almost everything done in the UK, by banks as well as companies, is an endeavour not to make a mistake – and when this happens we are never in front.*

Sir John Harvey-Jones, ex-Chairman, ICI

*Silicon Valley is a graveyard … failure is Silicon Valley's greatest asset*

There is a belief that in some instances organizations do not take certain risks sufficiently seriously. They place people's lives in danger – either by not appreciating the existence of a risk, or by ignoring the dangers. With some health and safety regulations it is clearly cheaper to ignore and pay a fine if caught out rather than invest to regulate the risk in the first place. Safety demands on the railways were stepped up after the tragic crashes at Paddington and Hatfield – the downside is delays and increased costs. In 2000 UK civil servants began drafting a new bill to revise the law on corporate manslaughter. The proposal is that where a company can be shown to have been negligent, and lives have been lost, individual senior managers could be held accountable and sentenced to imprisonment. The intention is to circumvent the 'collective failure' defence. The legislation has yet to reach the statute books, however.

**Table 16.1** Assessing business risks

| Type of risk | Example |
| --- | --- |
| *External environmental risks* | |
| Supply risks | Overdependency on a supplier<br>Outsourcing something which is strategically critical |
| Market/demand risks | Customer preference changes |
| Stakeholder risks | Misjudged priorities |
| Social responsibility and ethical issues | Failure to deal effectively with a chemical spill or a major incident |
| Politico-economic risks | Turbulence in an overseas market |
| Innovation risks | Misjudging market acceptance for a new idea |
| Competitive risks | Existing competitors 'out-innovate' the business<br>Price competition<br>Powerful new rivals enter the industry |
| *Resource-based risks* | |
| Materials risks | Need to handle/transport dangerous materials |
| Process risks | Corner-cutting to save time and money |
| Managerial risks | People's ability to cope with the dynamics of change in the organization |
| People risks | Inadequate or inappropriate training |
| Commitment risks | Individuals do not pull their weight, especially in a crisis |
| Structural risks | Inappropriate balance between centralization (for control) and decentralization (for flexibility)<br>Internal barriers to co-operation |
| Complexity | The spread of activities is too complex and leads to fragmentation and internal conflict |
| Financial risks | Undercapitalization<br>Cash-flow problems |
| Technology risks | Inadequate information systems |

Clarke and Varma (1999) argue that changes in the external business environment mean that satisfying stakeholders effectively is more risky and uncertain for organizations than it was in the past. Risk management has really become a strategic issue but too many organizations still treat it tactically and piecemeal. As a consequence they are more crisis prone than ideally they should be. This is the subject of the next section.

### 16.10.4  The risk-taking organization

Drawing together a number of points discussed earlier in the book, Birch and Clegg (1996) list a number of characteristics that will restrict risk taking by individual managers and employees:

■ centralized and/or committee decision-making
■ adherence to formal systems and budgets

- reliance on performance rewards based on preset (and inflexible) plans
- early evaluation of new ideas and proposals
- mistakes being sanctioned too readily (arguably making the same mistake more than once should be punished, of course!)
- management by fear
- a culture of caution.

Risk taking can be encouraged by:

- decentralization and informality
- initiatives and projects which cut across organizations
- rewarding managers and employees for new initiatives which have succeeded
- providing resources to develop new ideas
- limited adherence to 'badges of office' and job titles
- encouraging and respecting learning
- trusting people and encouraging them to enjoy what they do – a culture with an element of fun.

*Remember chaos in time of order. Watch out for danger and chaos while they are still formless.*

Sun Tzu, some 2000 years ago

## 16.11 Crisis avoidance and management

Crisis management concerns the management of certain risks and future uncertainties. Organizations should be ready to deal with both opportunities and surprises, and resources should be managed to cope with unexpected and unlikely events in the organization's environment: E–V–R (environment–values–resources) congruence again. It is important strategically because failure to deal effectively with crises can lead to losses of confidence, competitiveness, profits and market share.

Crisis management involves elements of planning and management. Planning constitutes crisis prevention or avoidance – the search for potential areas of risk, and decisions about reducing the risks. Management is being able to deal with crises if and when they occur. The way in which organizations do deal with crises can either enhance or damage their reputation. After all, there is always going to be an economic cost and there is little logic in trying to avoid it. Minicase 16.8 looks at how Swissair and TWA reacted to two separate air crashes, with different outcomes for each airline. Swissair was judged to have coped well and received considerable praise for its behaviour. However, this did not prevent the company becoming insolvent and ceasing to trade.

Simplified, there are three decision areas in determining the crisis strategy:

1. Decisions concerning what can go wrong, the probability of it happening, and the impact it will have if it does happen.
2. Crisis planning – decisions about investing in prevention in order to reduce or minimize the risk. Invariably this implies cost increases; and for this and other reasons less is often done than it conceivably could be done.
3. Mechanisms for contingency management.

## Minicase 16.8  TWA and Swissair – Two Different Responses to a Crash

In 1996 a TWA jet en route from New York to Europe came down off Long Island shortly after take-off. TWA was accused of incompetence and insensitivity for the way in which it responded to queries from families of the victims. The Mayor of New York and the media were both critical of TWA. Lasting damage was done to the airline's reputation. What had happened?

- Publication of the passenger list was delayed until every victim's family had been contacted.

- A special toll-free number was set up but calls went unanswered.

- Only limited help was provided for families of the victims who wanted to travel to the crash scene.

In reality, TWA was not a wealthy airline and it had only limited resources with which to respond to an incident of this nature. Moreover, there was immediate speculation that the crash might be the work of terrorists and, consequently, government agencies intervened and banned relatives from the crash site.

Several years after the crash there was still uncertainty as to its cause. Terrorism had been ruled out and an electrical fault is thought to be the most likely explanation.

Two years later, in September 1998, a Swissair flight out of New York plunged into the sea off the coast of Nova Scotia. Swissair was praised for its efficiency and compassion; public confidence in the airline remained intact. This time the Mayor of New York was full of praise.

- The passenger manifest was published within hours.

- Families were provided with quick access to crisis counsellors.

- Flights from Switzerland to the crash site were organized, and families were provided with expenses for the trip.

Swissair was provided with support from its code-share partner, Delta Airlines, which immediately seconded its full crisis team. Moreover, the response was affected by new legislation which had been enacted after the TWA crash.

The issues from the two contrasting incidents are:

1. The speed of response in the first 24 hours is critical. This is the 'make-or-break' period. If confidence is not built with the affected families in this time then conflict will follow.
2. Rehearsal really helps.
3. Money has to be found and spent to do what is necessary. This is clouded by a cultural issue in America, where there is a fear that providing financial assistance for travel and accommodation could merely provoke additional litigation as it implies an admission of guilt.

### Source

Tomkins, R (1998) Moments that build or destroy reputations, *Financial Times*, 29 September.

### Questions

1. What are the key lessons for all organizations from the alternative reactions illustrated here?
2. Are there any comparisons or contrasts with the situation described in Minicase 16.6, the Concorde crash?

**The Flight 800 Investigation** http://www.twa800.com

The decisions involve trade-offs between costs and risks in an attempt to find the best balance between points 2 and 3. The successful management of crisis situations involves both awareness and the ability to deal effectively with unexpected change pressures.

Fire provides a useful example of these points. Fires are caused by such events as smoking, overheating machinery and electrical faults. All of these are predictable. The

likelihood of a fire happening will differ from situation to situation, and the potential damage will similarly vary. Smoking can be banned and all conceivable safety measures can be invested in, if necessary, in order to minimize the risks. However, these may not always be practical or affordable, and consequently detectors, sprinklers and fire doors to isolate areas are used as contingency measures. Nuclear power generation and airlines are examples of businesses which invest substantially in safety and prevention, often led by legislation. Situations are, however, frequently unclear. In 1991, following research after the 1985 fire on board a Boeing 737 at Manchester Airport, the Civil Aviation Authority (CAA) ruled out the use of passenger smoke hoods on aircraft. The CAA argued that they delayed the time required to evacuate an aircraft and thereby risked causing more deaths. The Consumers' Association is one group who disagreed, saying that it was 'outraged' at the decision.

Similarly, and as an outcome of 9/11, there have been demands for armed sky marshals to travel on aircraft on certain routes. This has been standard practice on El Al (Israel's national airline) for many years. The reaction of American airlines to this suggestion has been much more supportive than most European airlines.

### 16.11.1  Defining crises

The word *crisis* covers a number of different issues and events, and it includes a mixture of technical and managerial elements. Some incidents are clearly 'thinkable' and efforts can be made to avoid them or reduce their potential impact. Others remain more unthinkable. Fires, fraud and computer failure are typical crises that might affect any organization almost any time. Poisoning scares or contamination with food products, and oil or chemical spillages, are foreseeable crises for particular companies. Major transport accidents, when they happen, are crises for the railway, shipping company or airline involved. Sometimes, but not always, the accident will prove to have been preventable. In relation to these there is an obvious logic in making contingency plans and being prepared. In addition, organizations can sometimes be affected by natural disasters, events outside their control.

Shrivastava *et al.* (1988) provide us with a valuable definition for a major crisis: 'Organizationally-based disasters which cause extensive damage and social disruption, involve multiple stakeholders, and unfold through complex technological, organizational and social processes.'

Figure 16.8 provides a framework for categorizing different incidents. On one axis is the issue of 'thinkability', while the horizontal axis separates the planned from the unplanned response. Here the terms 'crisis management' and 'disaster management' are used as a convenient form of separating the planned and unplanned response to a major event.

Knight (2000) reports on research at Oxford University which confirms that catastrophes – defined as man-made, rather than natural, crises or disasters – invariably have an immediate negative effect on share prices. Over time, the share prices either recover or stay depressed. The long-term impact is rarely neutral.

In a quite different way, strategic changes can also lead to crises of confidence, particularly amongst employees. Rumours that a firm might be taken over often imply redundancies; falling sales and profits suggest possible cutbacks or closure. Good internal communications and openness are required to minimize the potential damage, especially as competitors might see these situations as competitive opportunities.

**Figure 16.8** A framework for crises and disasters

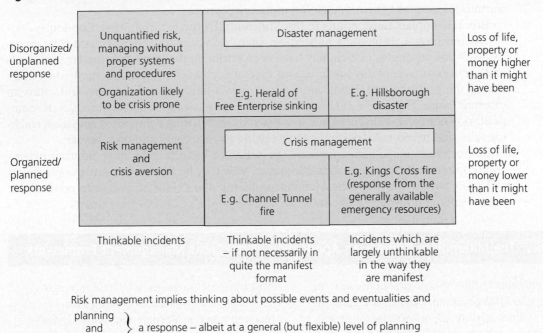

Risk management implies thinking about possible events and eventualities and
planning
and     } a response – albeit at a general (but flexible) level of planning
organizing

### 16.11.2 Understanding crises

Smith (1990) identifies three levels that help to explain why some crises happen when they might have been avoided.

The first level is a set of organizational problems which make the organization crisis prone. These relate to issues of culture and power, misguided strategies and poor control systems. There might be evidence of dangerous cost-cutting or simple neglect.

The second level is the incident itself, often provoked when particular external events clash with the organizational problems.

The third level is one of legitimation. When the incident or crisis is investigated there is a ready willingness to apportion blame and a failure to learn properly from the experiences. Organizational change does not take place and consequently the problems are merely reinforced. The same type of crisis could easily happen again.

Smith concludes that many organizations are actually frail, rather than strong, and relatively crisis prone. There is often an overinflated view of their strengths and competencies and too much belief in their infallibility. If this is linked to arrogance – as seen many years ago with the sinking of the 'unsinkable' Titanic – it can be very dangerous. Smith provides us with a 7-Cs framework for investigating crises. His elements are as follows:

**Table 16.2** The 7-Cs framework

| Warm factors – people related | Culture<br>Communications<br>Configuration – issues of power and influence |
|---|---|
| Cold factors – technocratic | Control<br>Coupling and complexity – the nature of the event itself<br>Costs<br>Contingency planning. |

He argues that we tend to focus our interest on the cold factors, and by ignoring the warm ones we make the organization more crisis prone.

Box 16.2 applies these points to the Millenium Dome in Greenwich. London.

Organizational difficulties and crises, then, occur in several ways and take many forms. Weak strategies (which may have been strong in the past), substandard products and services, unacceptably low prices or excessive costs can often be remedied by diagnosing the problem and acting on it. They have a hard or cold element and often an external focus. They are a relative weakness because of the relative strengths of competitors. They can be observed and measured by monitoring competitor activities, tracking sales and market shares, and simply talking to customers and distributors.

Ineffective management practices, the softer or warmer side, have internal origins and require a different approach. Moreover, they may be hidden because people divert attention away from them by blaming problems and crises on external, competitive factors and on unexpected events.

## Box 16.2 The Millennium Dome – an Application of the Crisis Management Framework

**STRATEGY IN ACTION**

The intention with the Millennium Dome was to build a lasting structure in Greenwich, London, funded with a mixture of government funding, lottery money and private sponsorship. It would be opened on the evening of 31 December 1999 to celebrate the new millennium and then used for one year as a special exhibition with individual zones designed and funded by the sponsors. It was not to be a theme park, but it was to be a signal to the world that Britain could manage a major and ambitious celebratory project 'as well, if not better, than anyone else in the world'. After 2000 the Dome would be sold to a private company for a use to be determined later. The whole project was tied in to public-transport developments, notably the Jubilee Line Extension of the London Underground – for parking at the Dome was to be severely limited.

### The initial outcomes

- The Dome was opened on time.
- However, many of the guests for the special opening night ceremonies had not received their tickets and had to queue for them at an underground station.
- There was hostile media criticism from the moment the Dome was opened. Many visitors commented on the lack of any 'wow' factor. Ironically, the London Eye (the viewing wheel

built by British Airways), which experienced technical difficulties and a delayed start, received a better reaction and has proved very popular and lucrative.

- It quickly transpired that the sales and revenue projections were over-optimistic and were never going to be met. They have been revised downwards more than once.
- Additional money from the National Lottery has been provided on more than one occasion to prevent bankruptcy.
- The person appointed as chief executive of the New Millennium Experience Company (which managed the whole project), Jennie Page, was forced to resign, as was the non-executive chairman of the board, Robert Ayling of British Airways. Jennie Page was replaced by Pierre-Yves Gerbeau from EuroDisney; Ayling by David Quarmby, chairman of the British Tourist Authority. After just a few weeks in the post, Quarmby returned to his original non-executive role on the board. David James, an experienced 'company doctor', was recruited to rescue a rapidly deteriorating situation. James took over some of Gerbeau's responsibilities.
- After just one day in the post James commented publicly that he was 'appalled' at the financial systems that he had inherited.

▶

Controls were inadequate and there was no proper register of assets. Visitor projections (already reduced substantially) were still unrealistic and yet more lottery funding was required if the Dome was to remain open until the end of 2000.

- The Conservative (opposition) party called for the Dome to be closed early and for political resignations. Both demands appeared to 'fall on deaf ears', although Prime Minister Blair acknowledged that mistakes had been made. It was also commented that the Dome 'had always been a regeneration project and not a visitor attraction'.

- Nomura (the Japanese Bank) initially agreed to buy the building, to develop theme park activities in 2001, but pulled out of negotiations when it was unable to gain access to the financial information that it needed for its planning.

## Applying the crisis management framework

### Culture
- Arrogant assumptions about what people (paying customers) would want.
- Arrogance about British achievements – in the event France's lighting of the Eiffel Tower received more praise.
- There was a clear culture of blame.
- There was a failure to synthesize the political agenda of the government and private sector project management.

### Communications
- Clearly fragmented.
- Lack of cohesion amongst the stakeholders.
- Some 'truths' were kept hidden.
- Arguably, the general public was never fully clear about the project and what it stood for.
- What was to be a triumph has become an embarrassment linked to face saving and damage limitation.

- The media generally became hostile towards the project.

### Configuration
- There was a clear political agenda, driven by the early leadership of Peter Mandelson. The project had to be seen as a success.
- There was also a secondary agenda – it was to be linked with public transport developments. The Jubilee Line itself was fraught with problems and was handed over to American contractors to complete.

### Control
- There was a lack of clear governance and responsibility – who actually 'owned' the project?
- Financial controls were inadequate.
- The immovable completion deadline added a new dimension with extra pressures.

### Coupling and complexity
- There were too many perspectives and expectations.
- This was exacerbated by the underlying desire to demonstrate creativity, innovation and 'great achievement'.

### Costs
- Poor forecasting – especially concerning paying visitors – meant that the costs and break-even projections were never realistic.
- There was a very visible need to 'beg' for more subsidy which reinforced a perception of mismanagement.

### Contingency planning
- An early closure was never a realistic option for the government.
- This made cost overruns more likely and sponsorship more difficult.
- Revenue shortfalls would be allowed, but only in a culture of blame.

### Final outcomes

A number of potential bidders – interested in developing both homes and leisure facilities – came forward after the Dome closed, only to either withdraw or be rejected by the Government. After protracted negotiations a developer has been found for the Dome site, which is to become a 20,000 seat concert arena. An initial opening date of 2006 has already been put back to at least 2007. There are also provisional plans for a Las Vegas-style casino to be added to the project.

When the Dome closed some £800 million had been sunk in to the project. The proposed developments should recoup some £550 million of this. Meanwhile ongoing management and maintenance cost the taxpayer £10 million per year.

**Millennium dome**

© Midnight Blue Design Ltd

### 16.11.3 Crisis fighting in organizations

It is generally accepted that organizational environments have become increasingly dynamic and turbulent in recent years, and that as environments spring more and more shocks and surprises on them, organizations must develop new ways of dealing with the uncertainty. Some organizations actively seek to influence and even manage their environments; others rely more heavily on their ability to react and respond quickly. These latter organizations, in particular, may well make a virtue out of their ability to crisis fight. After all, crisis situations often bring out the best in people who call on their reserves of inner strengths. However, extensive crisis fighting carries a downside risk. It is time-consuming, reducing the time and space available for wider strategic thinking, and consequently real growth opportunities may well be missed.

It is unrealistic to think that a 'perfect' organization which is successful, seen as successful, and unaffected by crises, can be created. But most organizations could manage their resources more efficiently and more effectively and, as a result, be less prone to crises. Sometimes an externally generated crisis occurs; on other occasions, the organization actually creates the crisis. As shown above, the long-term situation is made worse when an organization, having somehow dealt with a crisis, fails to learn and make itself less crisis prone for the future.

Crisis aversion demands both single-loop and double-loop learning. Programmed responses to perceived events, the acceptance of current operating practices, norms and policies, can be speedy and efficient. They can reflect the organization's ability to share and learn and to benefit from its experiences. However, there is an important distinction between 20 years of accumulated learning and one year's experiences repeated 20 times over. The danger signals are present when 'we've seen it all before; this is the way we do it here' is utilized too readily and without checking the current circumstances. Double-loop learning demands that managers question why things are done in a particular way, paying attention to environmental changes whose impact will require more than a programmed response.

It is both significant and salutary to emphasize that managerial competency in crisis fighting will often be perceived as a strength and a virtue. People complain about stress levels but paradoxically enjoy the challenge of a crisis. Dealing with the problem quickly and pragmatically gives people satisfaction and a sense of achievement. Even laid-back people can find new motivation and strength. It is human nature. We have all seen television programmes which report how passers-by willingly help in an emergency situation, sometimes improvising on the spot, and frequently with only limited regard for their own safety, until expert help can be called in. In turn, those with expertise also have to improvise on many occasions; instructions and procedures cannot predict every eventuality. At the Hillsborough football stadium disaster in 1989, traumatized people who had just escaped the crush themselves returned to the terraces to help other victims.

People prove themselves to be naturally inventive in particular circumstances. Yet how difficult might it be to persuade many of the same people to be more innovative and intrapreneurial on a day-to-day basis, and to try and move away from the crisis-fighting paradigm?

Crisis fighting in organizations takes up time. Managers are pragmatic but often not thoughtful beyond the confines of their immediate span of responsibility. Internal rivalry may well be reinforced such that people's competitive energy is focused on beating other parts of the organization (who are perceived as rivals rather than colleagues) instead of the real external competitors.

It forces a short-term time horizon on many issues and decisions. People then become frustrated and lose confidence in their organization because they seem to be operating in an organizational darkness where, metaphorically, the right hand does not know what the left hand is doing. It was mentioned earlier that one major retailer recently ran a special promotion where people who spent a certain amount on anything could buy an extra item at a very substantial discount. Unfortunately, the supply chain let the stores down; there were insufficient stocks of the discounted item. A disillusioned staff simply gave out vouchers for use when stocks were renewed.

Ironically, though, crisis fighting can be very customer orientated as managers react to customer pressures and requests. Consequently, the long-term damage to the organization, which it is fostering through a failure to learn properly, can be hidden behind

short-term successes. This is further reinforced by people using the short-term successes to hide and ignore the deeper problems.

In contrast, trying to eliminate the regular and ubiquitous crisis fighting and replace it with a more harmonious culture where people share information and trust and help each other may seem positively boring. However, success with this frees up time and can foster valuable innovation. It goes further than opening up new windows of opportunity for an organization; it can elevate it to a new level of opportunity which previously it could not access. In this respect it is like promotion from the First Division in English football to the Premier League. Here, promotion opens the door to millions of pounds of television and sponsorship money which hopefully will be invested sensibly to strengthen both the team and ground facilities. It is a world inhabited by only the privileged clubs, who will work hard to maintain their status and position. Over time, the gap between the Premier League and the other divisions widens and the poorest clubs inevitably become more crisis prone.

Organizations must invest in people if they are to prevent a competitive gap, let alone a chasm, developing between them and the industry leaders internationally. While organized programmes such as *Total Quality Management* and *Investors in People* have a relevance, the emphasis must be on cultural rather than procedural change. Scenario building, contingency planning and crisis management strategies can all help with unexpected events, which to some large extent are often foreseeable but not necessarily avoidable. Well-managed innovation and new product and service developments can strengthen an organization's competitiveness and reduce its crisis proneness. Internal crises generated by complacency with current good fortune, a reluctance to change, poor decisions and weak management demand a change in culture and style. Understanding, trust and commitment must be fostered.

### 16.11.4 Crisis proneness and crisis aversion

There are, then, several characteristics which indicate crisis proneness in an organization, and these are listed in Table 16.3. Organizations need to determine the extent to which they are manifest.

Managers often believe that they are better at knowing what needs to be changed than in actually managing and implementing the changes. However, this may well be based too much on personal opinion and judgement. Without openness, trust, sharing and learning it is highly likely that organizations will not realize what they already know; consequently, they will not be able to leverage and exploit a critical strategic resource,

**Table 16.3** The crisis-prone organization

- Specialist functions that cannot or do not think and act holistically
- A tendency to look inwards at the expense of looking outwards – internal-competition not external-competition focus
- A strong, rigid belief in present (even past) competitive paradigms
- A reluctance or inability to properly embrace the demands of a changing environment
- Inadequate communications – e.g. vertical but not horizontal; horizontal at discrete levels but only vertical downwards
- An inability correctly to interpret triggers and signals
- Willingness of individuals to break rules and procedures readily for short-term results – and hide the detail

**Figure 16.9** Strategy implementation and crises

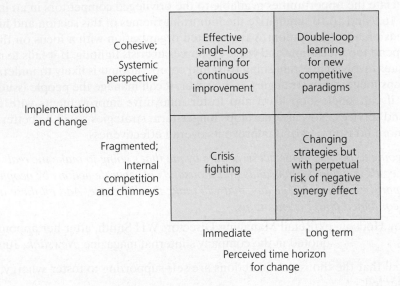

**Figure 16.10** Strategy implementation and crisis avoidance

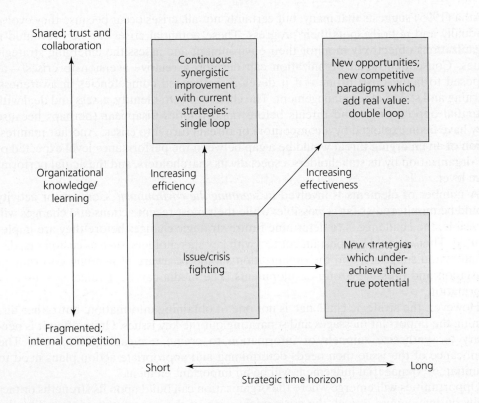

their knowledge. Moreover, they will not realize what they do not know – they will not fully appreciate the opportunities available to the privileged competitors in an industry.

Figures 16.9 and 16.10 summarize the important themes of this section and highlight the demands on an organization. A fragmented organization with a focus on the short term will spend too much time and waste resources in crisis fighting. If it fails to manage the soft issues involved in establishing trust and co-operation it is likely to underachieve as it develops longer-term strategies. If, however, it can manage the people issues more effectively it can single-loop learn and foster innovative improvements with existing products and services. Now as it develops longer-term strategies it will be better placed to take a more holistic view and improve its overall effectiveness.

> *It's not going to be one heroic act or gesture by me that's going to make the real difference; it's going to be thousands and thousands of separate actions by people in the company, every hour of the day, that will make the difference. Add all these up and the combined power is enormous.*

Beverley Hodson, ex-Retail Managing Director, WH Smith, after her appointment, quoted in the company's internal magazine, *Newslink*, June 1997

It is essential that the thousands of actions are self-supporting to foster synergy, rather than fragmented.

## 16.11.5 Crisis avoidance

Bartha (1995) suggests that many, but certainly not all, crises occur because they evolve gradually and nobody spots their progress. These potential crises can be prevented if organizations objectively monitor their environment and assess the emerging strategic issues. Consequently, an organization can develop a relative aversion to crises – as opposed to being crisis prone – if it develops associated competencies in awareness, learning and stakeholder management. The challenge is to identify, assess and deal with potential opportunities and threats before opportunities disappear (perhaps because they have been exploited by a competitor) or threats turn into crises. Another manifestation of an emerging threat would be a gap between the performance level expected of the organization by its stakeholders, especially its shareholders, and the actual performance level.

A number of elements is involved in *scanning the environment*. Competitor activity should be monitored as far as possible; while their most recent actions and changes will be visible, the challenge is to determine future strategic changes before they are implemented. There should be constant contact with key stakeholders, such as customers, distributors and suppliers; and the organization should be aware of pending government legislation and pressure group developments. The media can be a valuable source of information.

However, the strategic challenge is not one of obtaining information, but rather discerning the important messages and separating out the key issues. Quite often it is necessary to synthesize snippets of information to create a meaningful pattern. The significance of the issue then needs determining and appropriate action plans need to be initiated. Managerial judgement will be an important element.

Opportunities will emerge where the organization can build upon its strengths or tactically outmanoeuvre a rival; the crisis might occur if the opportunity is missed by the organization but picked up by a competitor. A potential threat can be present in a number of ways: new legislative restrictions, a disappearing market, financial difficulties

for an important supplier or distributor. Information and triggers can be received anywhere in the organization at any time; making sure that their significance is appreciated and that they are channelled to those people, functions and businesses who could benefit is the next critical step. Communication systems are crucial, together with the ability of individual managers to take an organization-wide, or holistic, perspective.

*The fact you may get knocked down is not the issue – what matters is whether you get up again.*

Based on a quote from a US football coach

*If you think education is expensive, think what ignorance might cost you.*

The ability of managers to act upon the information will, in turn, depend upon organizational policies and the extent of their empowerment; their willingness to act will be affected by their personality, their competencies, their motivation and the reward/sanction system practised by the organization.

### 16.11.6 Crisis management

There are a number of identifiable steps in attempting to manage crises effectively:

- Initially it is necessary to identify the most obvious areas of risk.

- Following on from this firms should establish procedures and policies for ensuring that risks do not become crises. Discussing possible scenarios, training sessions and actual rehearsals can all contribute, in addition to the investment in physical prevention.

- A crisis management team should be identified in advance, trained and prepared to step aside from all normal activities in the event of a crisis occurring. Experience suggests that the expertise required will be primarily communications and public relations, financial and legal. Clear leadership of the team by the strategic leader will be expected; and personnel, operations and marketing skills can be added as required. Secretarial support is sometimes overlooked.

- Building the team is one aspect of a planning process which should also cover how to get hold of key people over weekends and during holidays, how to restore critical facilities that might go down, and how to gain fast access to important regulatory bodies.

- Stakeholder analysis is another crucial aspect of the planning. It is vital to clarify which stakeholders are most likely to be affected by particular crises – and how. After a crisis customers either exhibit loyalty or switch to competitors; the confidence of distributors and the banks may also prove important. The media often play a significant role and their stance is likely to influence the confidence of other stakeholders. Where stakeholder perspectives and expectations differ it may be necessary to deal with each group on an individual basis.

   In 1991 the insurance brokers Sedgewick showed that while 75 per cent of Britain's largest companies claimed to have contingency plans for dealing with sudden crises when they occur, few had plans to cover the follow-up implications. Plans should also be in hand for relaunching products that might have to be withdrawn and for dealing with investors and possible litigation. 'Most companies only find out about the cost of a crisis once it's over.' Infoplan International (1997)

state that 84 per cent of the UK's leading 500 companies then saw crisis management as a senior management responsibility, up from 58 per cent in 1995. Seventy-five per cent had experienced a crisis and put their strategies into action.

■ Finally, a clear communications strategy is essential. Ethical issues may be involved, and the company will be expected to be co-operative, open, honest, knowledgeable and consistent. They must be seen to be in control and not attempting to cover up. The media will want to know what has happened, why, and what the company intends to do about the situation. 'No comment' may well be interpreted as defensive or incompetent. An effective information system will be required for gathering and disseminating the salient facts.

Regester and Larkin (1997) offer the following advice to organizations:

1. Be prepared.
2. Demonstrate human concern when something happens.
3. Consider the worst possible outcomes.
4. Communicate at all times, at all levels.
5. Avoid obsequious people as spokesmen or women.
6. Do not believe that procedure manuals prevent incidents.
7. Do believe 'there is a first time for everything'.

### 16.11.7  Strategies and examples

The most proactive strategy for crisis management can be compared with the notion of total quality management. The organization is looking for a culture where all employees think about the implications and risks in everything they do.

Reactions when a crisis has happened can prove to be effective or ineffective. Effective management is likely to mean that confidence is maintained and that there is no long-term loss of customers, market share or share price. Booth (1990) quotes research which indicates that this is more likely to happen in an open, flexible structure than it is in one which is bureaucratic.

Kabak and Siomkos (1990) offer a spectrum of four reactive approaches. At one extreme (and normally ineffective) is *denial of responsibility*, arguing the company is an innocent victim or that no harm has been done. Similarly, some organizations will attempt to pin the blame on identified individuals (who possibly did make mistakes), or argue that the general public must share the risks. Where individual errors do lead to crises there may well be a lack of effective organizational control systems; and equally the public can only be expected to share the risk if they have available all the information required for decision-making. Much of this is likely to be exclusive to the company, and quite possibly buried away in files.

A better, but still ineffective, approach is *involuntary regulatory compliance*. Exxon's reluctant acceptance of responsibility after their tanker *Exxon Valdez* ran aground and spilled oil off North Alaska in 1989 is given as an example. The incident was the result of human error rather than poor systems, but the company is still held accountable. Bad weather prevented Exxon's chief executive from reaching the site, and consequently a local manager stood in for him. Whatever the reason, unfortunately the wrong message was conveyed, and Exxon's reputation was damaged.

Kabak and Siomkos offer Perrier as an excellent example of the third strategy, *voluntary compliance*. Here there is a positive company response towards meeting its responsibilities (see Minicase 16.9). The incident highlights that even though companies may have crisis management strategies unforeseen difficulties are likely to be encountered.

The other extreme strategy is the *super effort*, whereby the company does everything it can, openly and honestly, and stays in constant touch will all affected stakeholders. In 1982 an extortionist succeeded in introducing cyanide to packs of Tylenol in America. Tylenol is manufactured by Johnson and Johnson and at the time it was the country's leading painkiller with a 35 per cent market share. Six people died.

All stocks were recalled immediately 'to contain the crisis and demonstrate responsibility'. The media were provided with constant up-to-date information. The product was relaunched in tamperproof containers and the associated heavy advertising featured the new containers rather than simply claiming that the product was safe. The incident was costly, but market share was quickly regained. Some had suggested that Johnson and Johnson should drop the Tylenol brand name, but this was resisted. Interestingly, the name Townsend Thoresen was dropped by its parent company, P&O, after the ferry *Herald of Free Enterprise* capsized off Zeebrugge in 1987.

While there is little argument against the logic of planning ahead of a crisis, some organizations are cautious about the extent to which one should attempt to plan.

*The scale of the Bhopal [Union Carbide chemical plant in India] disaster [gas leak in 1984] was unimaginable. There is simply no way anyone could have anticipated it.*

Union Carbide Director of Corporate Communications, quoted in Nash (1990)

While the extent and magnitude of a disaster may be unexpected, events such as Bhopal are predictable, often because there have been similar incidents in the past. Union Carbide argued that they tried to be as honest as they could, but they were limited by the lack of hard facts from a remote area of India. Nash comments that the organization appreciated the need to act quickly and develop effective communications but, after the event, remained sceptical about establishing rigid guidelines, arguing that one can never be certain in advance about the actual nature and detail of any crisis.

## Minicase 16.9 Perrier   Eur US

In 1989 Perrier was the world leader in the fast-growing market for bottled water. In the UK, for example, the Perrier brand accounted for over one-third of the market for sparkling water, which represented 20 per cent of the whole market. Perrier also owns Buxton, which is second to Evian in the still water segment. The name 'Perrier' had become synonymous with bottled water.

In February 1990 minute traces of benzene were discovered in a sample during routine tests in North Carolina, America. The trace, six parts per billion, did not represent any discernible health risk. Within one week every Perrier brand world-wide had been withdrawn from sale. This amounted to 160 million bottles in 110 countries

*Even if it is madness, we decided to take Perrier off the market everywhere in the world. I don't want the least doubt, however small, to tarnish our product's image of quality and purity.*

Gustave Leven, then Chairman, Perrier

Leven, 77 years old in 1990, had built Perrier from a run-down business to world leadership over 40 years. He retired later in 1990.

*Perrier had created crisis management strategies some years earlier ... 'Everyone knew what they were supposed to do ... in spite of this we never, ever, imagined a world-wide withdrawal. We'd never dreamed of a problem of such magnitude.' Only Tylenol had previously been withdrawn on such a scale; and in that crisis people had died.*

## Actions in the UK

Local tests were arranged as soon as news spread from the US. The tests took a normal 48 hours, and benzene was again found in the sample. Unfortunately, during this period a Perrier spokesman in Paris speculated prematurely that a greasy rag might have introduced the wrong cleaning fluid onto bottling equipment. Moreover, when the worldwide withdrawal was announced to the world's press in Paris – rather than local press conferences – the room was too small for the press and television crews attending.

On the following day advertisements appeared around the world, explaining the situation, and clarifying what people, including retailers, should do. The 24-hour emergency telephone network in the UK 'received mostly friendly calls'.

A major problem in the UK concerned the disposal of all the water and the further disposal or recycling of the bottles. A large proportion of the stocks was in the distinctive Perrier green glass which, recycled, has few alternative uses.

The source of the contamination was quickly traced to a filter at the bottling plant in France, a filter used to purify carbon dioxide being added to the water. This revelation suggested that Perrier is not 100 per cent naturally carbonated, although the label on the bottles stated 'naturally carbonated natural mineral water'. It transpired that the gas used is collected underground with the water and added back after purification. Only the gas, not the water, is purified. Nevertheless the publicity caused Sainsbury's to refuse to stock Perrier for a period after it was relaunched in April 1990.

One month after the relaunch Perrier was already selling at half its previous volume; and market leadership was quickly regained. The worldwide cost was estimated to be £125 million.

Competitors had not attempted to exploit the situation, possibly believing they might spread a scare by association and affect the market for all bottled water.

It has been suggested that the very popularity of Perrier had caused the problem. Demand worldwide had put pressure on the supply side. Some years earlier, and before the increased consumer awareness and concern with health issues, the problem would probably have been contained on a smaller scale.

The balance of opinion seems to be that Perrier got the big decisions right. It adopted a worst case scenario, acted fast, and spoke out honestly.

Shortly after the crisis Perrier was bought by Nestlé, which already owned the Vittel brand and the top US bottled water, Poland Spring.

## Sources

Butler, D (1990) Perrier's painful period, *Management Today*, August.
Caulkin, S (1990) Dangerous exposure, *Best of Business International*, Autumn.

## Footnote – A parallel case?

Dasani is Coca-Cola's bottled still water brand. Some 200 million cases are sold every year around the world, but principally in America, where it has been available since 1999. Dasani was launched in the UK in January 2003 – in March the same year all stocks were removed from shelves. The water had been found to contain an illegal level of bromate, which could increase the risk of cancer. However, the levels did not pose any risk to public health or safety. The company seemed to have acted quickly and positively. However it would soon emerge that instead of being natural spring water, Dasani *in the UK* is purified tap water, using a process perfected by NASA. There was something of an outcry and many remembered an

episode of *Only Fools and Horses* where a scam had been run selling untouched bottled tap water as 'Peckham Spring'. Interestingly one month later, in April, Dasani was launched in France, the home of Perrier and Evian (the most popular brand of still water). The public were assured that this time it was natural spring water!

## Question

1. Do you agree that Perrier 'got the big decisions right'?

**Perrier** http://www.perrier.com

## Tasks

1. Ascertain the current situation with Dasani and compare and contrast the relevant marketing and crisis strategies of Nestlé and Coca-Cola.
2. Earlier, in 1999 Coca-Cola withdrew its Coke product from shelves in Belgium. What caused the incident and how well did Coca-Cola deal with it?
3. To what extent do you think it contributed to the early retirement of chief executive Douglas Ivester at the end of that year?

**Coca-Cola** http://www.coca-cola.com

## 16.11.8  A crisis management framework

Companies succeed if they meet the needs and expectations of their stakeholders; companies which fail to meet these needs and expectations, long term, must be in trouble and they may collapse. Perception of relative success and failure is critical. Companies that are succeeding need to be recognized for this. Companies that are not succeeding will want to cover up their weaknesses if they can.

The simple matrix illustrated in Figure 16.11 is based on these premises. Companies that satisfy their stakeholders, and are seen to do so, are classified as crisis avoiders. Crisis-prone organizations fail on both counts. Companies with a strong reputation they do not wholly deserve are termed 'thin high profile' as the situation is likely to be very fragile and fluid. The fourth quadrant contains 'unsung heroes', companies whose reputation does not do justice to their real achievements.

It is worth considering in which quadrant the following two companies should be placed.

The Body Shop saw its share price and price to earnings ratio fall in the 1990s as it faced increasing competition internationally. In 1996, disillusioned with City investors, the Body Shop looked at the viability of reprivatization, but concluded that it would not be an appropriate strategy to follow. Nevertheless, its customers and employees remained loyal and supportive, and, despite some cynicism and criticism, the company's reputation as an environmentally concerned organization also remained strong. However, in recent years, the founders, Anita and Gordon Roddick, have systematically seen their power and influence wane.

In 1995 Shell, one of Europe's most successful and respected companies, was forced to change an important strategic decision following a high-profile campaign by a leading pressure group. Shell had chosen to sink its redundant Brent Spar oil platform in deep seas some 150 miles west of Scotland. It had reached an agreement with the UK government that, scientifically, this was the most appropriate means of disposal for the platform. Greenpeace objected and protesters boarded the platform, claiming that it still contained 5000 tonnes of oil which would eventually be released to pollute the sea. The ensuing and professionally orchestrated publicity fuelled public opinion, and there were protests in a number of European countries, including attacks on petrol stations in Germany. Shell backed down and agreed to investigate other possibilities for disposal.

**Figure 16.11** A crisis-management framework

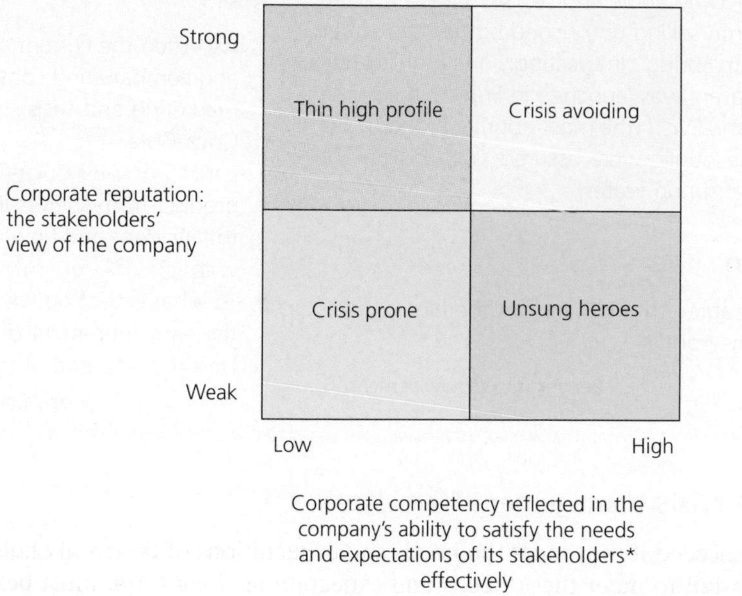

*The stakeholders: customers; employees; investors; suppliers; environmentalists

The UK government expressed both anger and disappointment with this decision. Independent inspectors later proved that Greenpeace's claims were gross exaggerations – the residual oil was much, much less than 5000 tonnes. The press concluded: 'Shell went wrong in spending too much time convincing government of the case for sea-bed dumping, but not attaching enough importance to consulting other stakeholder groups.' Shell had been made to appear socially irresponsible, even though the ethics of the Greenpeace campaign are questionable.

# SUMMARY

Strategies must be implemented if they are to be judged successful and effective. This is accomplished through the structural framework, as we have seen earlier. There are two key variables:

- First, the logic of the *corporate portfolio*. Is synergy a realistic possibility? Is the range too diverse? Is the portfolio built around activities and businesses with overlapping or similar competencies?

- Second, are the *structure and style* of management appropriate for the actual portfolio and its diversity? Does the style of managing the corporation ensure that the potential synergies are achieved?

Goold and Campbell (1988) have described three broad styles of corporate management. The *financial control style* is akin to a holding company, where the head office adopts a very decentralized approach to manage a portfolio where there is (normally) little natural interdependency between the businesses. The *strategic planning style* is based on centralization – the strategic leader believes that he or she is in the best position to dictate strategy for all the businesses in the portfolio. The *strategic control style* is a sort of half-way house that attempts to build on the strengths of the other two.

Defining corporate strategy as the overall strategy for a diversified firm, Michael Porter described four approaches to managing a corporate portfolio. *Portfolio management* is the approach whereby each business is looked at independently to assess its worth to the firm. The assessment is based on industry attractiveness and competitive strengths. Investment should be targeted at priority businesses. *Restructuring* is the attempt to make both an industry and a business more attractive by improving competitiveness – when an organization can no longer add any further value, the business should be divested. *Sharing assets* offers the best opportunity for creating and exploiting synergy across a range of businesses, but *transferring skills* can also prove valuable.

Goold *et al*. (1994) have highlighted the importance of *corporate parenting* – essentially the fit between a head office and the subsidiary businesses in an organization and the opportunities for two-way benefits. Where each business can benefit from being part of an organization, and at the same time make a positive contribution to the whole organization, we have what Goold *et al*. call a *heartland* of related businesses. Businesses should be acquired and divested to strengthen the heartland.

The *corporate headquarters* drives the strategy of the business and provides the structural framework. The range of services which remain centralized is a reflection of the adopted style of corporate management. Head offices should add value and not merely spend money earned by the subsidiaries. In recent years, head offices have been slimmed down.

In conjunction with decentralization, an appropriate role must be found for the general managers in charge of each subsidiary business.

To cope with the pressures and demands of contemporary business environments Rosabeth Moss Kanter (1989) argues that the organization must be *focused, fast, flexible and friendly*. She argues that competitive advantage comes from the way in which everything is integrated and works together.

Charles Handy (1994, 1995) puts forward a more radical thesis and argues for *federal organizations*, where head offices are merely there to serve the needs of subsidiaries.

Successful strategy implementation requires that strategic resources are allocated and controlled efficiently and effectively. In reality, the availability and suitability of resources is a determinant of the feasibility of a particular strategic option. Of course, the existence of resources does not, in itself, guarantee effective implementation – they have to be managed. In addition, resources should be flexible to allow adaptive and incremental change.

We can think of *resource allocation* at two key levels:

- The allocation of *corporate* resources to particular businesses or divisions, based on perceived needs and priorities, and often linked to the growth of the business or industry in question

- The allocation of *functional* resources to build and add value in order to create and sustain competitive advantage.

*Policies* are designed to guide the use of resources by managers.

*Budgets* are used to allocate resources for particular activities and tasks. Budgets, however, are often short term in scope and the measurement of performance against budget targets may be more an evaluation of efficiency in the use of resources than of longer-term strategic effectiveness.

*Resource allocation and management* – and the inherent decisions – reflect the way in which the organization and its managers are dealing with the risks that they face. The key dimensions of risk are:

- the likelihood of certain eventualities – some of which could imply a detrimental impact for the organization, and

- the extent of the downside (perhaps a loss of orders, revenues or confidence) if the particular incident in question does occur.

While there is always a personal risk for entrepreneurs and strategic leaders in corporate strategy changes, a useful framework for clarifying and analysing risks is based on external (environmental) and internal (resource-based) factors.

Risks can be retained, transferred or regulated.

The relative success or relative failure of an organization to deal with the risks that it faces determines the extent to which it is crisis prone or crisis averse.

Crises can be major or minor, 'thinkable' in advance or more realistically unforeseeable. Consequently, organizations need strategies for avoiding crises in the first place and then for dealing with those crises that do occur. Handled well, a crisis can enhance the reputation of an organization. Handled badly, the impact can be substantial and prolonged.

Crises and disasters contain a mixture of 'cold' (technocratic) and 'warm' (people-related) elements. All too often organizations focus their attention on the cold elements when it is the warm ones that hold the key. By not learning lessons and by apportioning blame too readily organizations can legitimate crises and simply increase the likelihood of them happening again.

It remains a paradox that many managers are proud of their ability to crisis fight and deal with problems as they arise. This merely reinforces a reactive attitude and a short-term perspective, and it can be short-sighted.

## QUESTIONS AND RESEARCH ASSIGNMENTS

1. For which (general) corporate strategies are the financial control, strategic planning and strategic control styles of corporate management most appropriate?

2. How do you think the need for general managers might have changed as organization structures have generally been flattened and delayered?

3. Reflect on the work of Kanter and Handy in the late twentieth century – sections 16.7.1 and 16.7.2 in the text. What view if any has best profiled the nature of the modern organization?

4. Are you personally risk averse or perceived as a risk taker? On what evidence are you drawing this conclusion?

## INTERNET AND LIBRARY PROJECTS

1. Update the material on any or all of the four conglomerate businesses discussed in Minicase 16.2.

   Using this and details of the corporate strategies pursued by other large companies with which you are familiar, which of the following two statements do you most agree with?

   'Conglomerate diversification has now given way to focus strategies – focus is here to stay.'

   'Focus strategies cannot generate sufficient growth long-term to satisfy shareholders – diversification will make a comeback.'

2. Take any large organization with which you are familiar. How have its head office structure and roles changed in recent years?

3. For an organization with which you are familiar, ascertain the main stated policies for finance, production, personnel and marketing.

   How are these policies used? How were they created? How do they rate in terms of the principles of good policies discussed in the text?

4. Ascertain the budgeted resources and targets allocated to one manager whom you are able to interview.

   What measures of performance are utilized? What feedback is provided? What does the manager do with the feedback? What do you believe is the personal impact of the budget and measures of performance on the manager? Is he or she motivated? Rewarded or sanctioned for success or failure?

5. Either by contacting a local councillor or using the Internet, ascertain how planning and budgeting are managed in your local authority. What have been the priority areas in the past? What are the current priorities? How have the changes in priority been decided?

6. In August 2000 the Russian nuclear submarine Kursk sank in the Barents Sea after an internal explosion. The whole crew was lost and the Russian government was criticized for not calling on foreign help and expertise as quickly as it might have done. What are the lessons in risk and crisis management from this incident?

7. Use the Internet to assess the possible long-term damage to Ford Motors when it was discovered (in 2000) that the Bridgestone/Firestone tyres used on its Explorer four-wheel drive vehicles were potentially dangerous and had been the cause of a number of accidents over a period of time. How do you think both Ford and Bridgestone handled the crisis – effectively or ineffectively?

## Further reading

Ford, JD (1981) The management of organizational crises, *Business Horizons*, May–June.

Porter, ME (1987) From competitive advantage to corporate strategy, *Harvard Business Review*, May–June.

Goold, M and Campbell, A (1987) Managing diversity – strategy and control in diversified British companies, *Long Range Planning*, 20 (5).

Bishop, JD (1991) The Moral Responsibility of Corporate Executives for Disasters, *Journal of Business Ethics*, 10.

Goold, M and Campbell, A (2002) Parenting in complex structures, *Long Range Planning*, 35.

# References

Bartha, P (1995) Preventing a high-cost crisis, *Business Quarterly*, Winter.

Birch, P and Clegg, B (1996) *Imagination Engineering*, Pitman.

Booth, S (1990) Dux at the crux, *Management Today*, May.

Bower, JL (1970) *Managing the Resource Allocation Process: A Study of Corporate Planning and Investment*, Division of Research, Harvard Business School.

Caulkin, S (1996) Focus is for wimps, *Management Today*, December.

Clarke, CJ and Varma, S (1999) Strategic risk management – the new competitive edge, *Long Range Planning*, 32 (4).

Dixon, M (1989) The very model of a mythical manager, *Financial Times*, 10 May.

Dunnette, MD and Taylor, RN (1975) Influence of dogmatism, risk taking propensity and intelligence on decision making strategy for a sample of industrial managers, *Journal of Applied Psychology*, 59 (4).

Geneen, H (1997) *The Synergy Myth*, St. Martin's Press.

Goold, M and Campbell, A (1988) *Strategies and Styles*, Blackwell.

Goold, M, Campbell, A and Luchs, K (1993) Strategies and styles revisited: strategic planning and financial control, *Long Range Planning*, 26 (5); Strategies and styles revisited: strategic control – is it tenable? *Long Range Planning*, 26 (6).

Goold, M, Campbell, A and Alexander, M (1994) *Corporate Level Strategy*, John Wiley.

Green, O (1994) Quoted in *Management Today*, June.

Hamel, G and Prahalad, CK (1994) *Competing for the Future*, Harvard Business School Press.

Handy, C (1994) *The Empty Raincoat*, Hutchinson.

Handy, C (1995) *Beyond Certainty: The Changing Worlds of Organizations*, Hutchinson.

Herbert, TT and Deresky, H (1987) Should general managers match their business strategies?, *Organizational Dynamics*, 15 (3).

Infoplan International (1997) *Review of Crisis and Risk Management*, London.

Jackson, T (1995) Giant bows to colossal pressure, *Financial Times*, 22 September.

Kabak, IW and Siomkos, GJ (1990) How can an industrial crisis be managed effectively? *Industrial Engineering*, June.

Kanter, RM (1989) *When Giants Learn to Dance*, Simon & Schuster.

Kets de Vries, M (1997) Creative rebels with a cause, in Birley, S and Muzyka, D, *Mastering Enterprise*, Financial Times/Pitman.

Knight, RF (2000) Recovering well from tragedy, *Financial Times*, 3 August.

Koontz, H and O'Donnell, C (1968) *Principles of Management*, 4th edn, McGraw-Hill.

Lawrence, PR and Lorsch, JW (1967) *Organization and Environment*, Richard D Irwin.

McMahon, JT and Perrit, GW (1973) Toward a contingency theory of organizational control, *Academy of Management Journal*, 16.

Nash, T (1990) Tales of the unexpected, *The Director*, March.

Pearce, JA and Robinson, RB (1985) *Strategic Management*, 2nd edn, Richard D Irwin.

Porter, ME (1987) From competitive advantage to corporate strategy, *Harvard Business Review*, May–June.

Reed, R and Buckley, MR (1988) Strategy and action: techniques for implementing strategy, *Long Range Planning*, 21 (3).

Regester, M and Larkin, J (1997) *Risk Issues and Crisis Management*, Institute of Public Relations.

Richter, A and Owen, G (1997) The UK cut down to size, *Financial Times*, 10 March.

Sadtler, D, Campbell, A and Koch, R (1997) *Break Up! When Large Companies are Worth More Dead Than Alive*, Capstone.

Shrivastava, P, Mitroff, I, Miller, D and Miglani, M (1988) Understanding industrial crises, *Journal of Management Studies*, 25 (4).

Smith, D (1990) Beyond contingency planning – towards a model of crisis management, *Industrial Crisis Quarterly*, 4 (4).

Stonich, PJ (1982) *Implementing Strategy*, Ballinger.

Wernham, R (1984) Bridging the awful gap between strategy and action, *Long Range Planning*, 17.

# Leading Change

Having read to the end of this chapter you should be able to:

- appreciate the dynamics of change and change management and why organizations must be change-oriented if they are to grow and prosper
- describe the major forces for change and types of change situation, and draw up a hierarchy of levels of change
- understand that change can be incremental or more discontinuous and transformational
- explain why people frequently resist change
- summarize alternative ways of overcoming resistance
- identify a number of different approaches to the planned management of change
- assess the importance of power and how it is used in change situations
- describe ways in which managers can improve their political effectiveness in organizations.

Organizations and managers face change on a continuous basis, especially in volatile environments. Some changes are reactions to external threats; others are proactive attempts to seize opportunities and manage the environment. Organizations should seek to obtain and maintain a congruence between their environment, values and resources, making changes when there are pressures from either the environment or their resources. It is crucial that organizations seek to create and sustain competitive advantage, and wherever possible innovate to improve their competitive position. This implies a readiness to change within the organization and the ability to implement the proposed changes.

At times there will be a perceived need to try and change values and culture. Towards the end of the twentieth century the pressures for change in a wide cross-section of businesses were clearly visible. Food manufacturers and retailers were affected by changing consumer attitudes to their diet. Mutual societies and banks were responding to changes in the competitive regulations that directly affect them, generally seeing the changes as opportunities. Technological change is at the heart of upheavals in the film and music industry. Many see the changes as threats; others as opportunities.

This chapter looks at various issues and problems in the management of change.

The first and perhaps most important element in the change process is that of leadership. When a major business organization is under pressure it is the chief executive who feels the heat. Organizations must be reactive to external change pressures and proactive in seeking to take advantage of opportunities and shape their environment if they are to be effective strategically. Cultural and power considerations are important variables in the management of change. It is particularly useful at this point to refer back once again to the earlier discussions of intrapreneurship, empowerment and learning organizations.

The opening Minicase looks at a series of strategic, structural and leadership changes at Apple Computers. The case charts the story of Apple over some 25 years and shows how the company has enjoyed mixed fortunes. Sometimes highly innovative and successful, Apple has also been affected by competitor initiatives which have changed the personal computer industry in dramatic ways. Some of the changes documented were therefore reactive while others were more proactive.

CASE

## Minicase 17.1  Apple Computers                                    US

Apple was started in 1976 by a young entrepreneur, Steven Jobs, and his partner, computer nerd Stephen Wozniak. They began by making personal computers (PCs) in a garage. In 1983 the company's turnover, from essentially one model – the distinctive Apple computer – was approaching $1 billion. Apple had ignited the personal computer revolution of the 1970s. At this stage in the company's development Wozniak had already left and Jobs had been quoted as saying that he was no longer able to do what he most enjoyed, working with a small group of talented designers to create new innovative products. To overcome his frustration with an increasingly bureaucratic organization Jobs had formed a new team of designers and set about developing the company's second major product, the Apple Macintosh, away from corporate headquarters and the production plant. The Macintosh was regarded as very user friendly and featured an illustrated screen menu and a hand-held mouse unit for giving instructions. It was launched in 1984 and sold immediately. However, it was launched at a premium price, which remained high as sales took off. This niche-marketing approach left a wide-open gap which was ultimately filled by Microsoft.

Jobs had actually seen the first graphical user interface being demonstrated at Xerox PARC (Palo Alto Research Center) where it had been developed by a Xerox scientist in the 1970s. At this stage, Xerox failed to appreciate the value of the idea they had; Jobs immediately saw the potential of this new technology and set about developing a PC which used it. Jobs used Bill Gates to help with some of the development work – and this was the birth of Windows. Had Xerox executives been more visionary, they would probably have driven the PC industry instead of Microsoft.

John Sculley, previously CEO of PepsiCo, was recruited by Jobs to be Apple president in 1983 and he took over executive control. Sculley reports that Jobs challenged him: 'Do you want to spend the rest of your life selling sugared water or do you want a chance to change the world?' His initial priorities were to co-ordinate product development activities, which he felt were fragmented, and to integrate these developments with existing programmes. To achieve this, power was centralized more than it had been in the past and was supported by formalized reporting procedures and new financial control systems.

Sculley was regarded as being more marketing orientated than Jobs, and their business philosophies clashed. Jobs resigned in 1985, together with a number of other key employees, deciding to concentrate his efforts on the development of sophisticated PCs for university students in a small, entrepreneurial organization environment.

Despite the increased business discipline, Sculley attempted to preserve important aspects of the original Apple culture. Informal dress codes, a 'fun working environment' and elaborate celebra-

tions when targeted milestones are reached were all considered important. Apple retained a structure with few layers of management, few perks and few status-carrying job titles.

Sculley's challenge was to move the company away from an informal and entrepreneurial management style to a more functional and later (1988) a divisionalized structure, while retaining the important aspects of the culture. In addition, Sculley felt that Apple needed to be repositioned in the market in order to overcome the competitive threats from the Far East.

With new versions of the Macintosh, Apple moved from an education and home computer base into a business computer company which also sold to schools and universities. Apple was a major innovator in desktop publishing, pioneering the market in advance of competition from IBM and Xerox.

Apple prospered in the late 1980s, but its strategy began to appear inappropriate for the recession and the 1990s. Apple had concentrated on, and succeeded with, high-margin products which were substantially differentiated. However, Sculley claimed that Apple's ideas were being copied and used in cheaper rival products – Apple began a legal action against Microsoft, alleging that its Windows software used ideas from the Macintosh. Moreover, PCs have become more of a commodity product in a maturing market. Although Apple had sold 22 million Macintosh computers at this time, the continued success of Microsoft has been very damaging to the company.

In 1991 Apple agreed a series of strategic alliances, mostly with IBM, historically its main rival. The alliances concentrated on areas where Apple lacked either development skills or the ability to fund the research and development independently. New PC technology and operating systems software were key areas. Cultural and other differences between Apple and IBM have led to their alliances being relatively unsuccessful.

Coincidental with its agreements with the global IBM Apple's culture had actually been changing. Empowerment, flexibility and freedom remained important, but 'there had to be more discipline. Our cost structure was out of line. We

did not know how to meet schedules. We were a benevolent company that sponsored people to work on things they were interested in' (Sculley).

Apple reduced the prices of its existing products, hoping for higher volumes which would more than compensate for the lower margins, and introduced a range of cheaper, lower-performance Macintosh computers. In terms of new products Apple was arguably two years late with its laptop computer. Other new products concentrated on personal electronics devices and included electronic books and a notebook computer. In 1993 Apple launched *Newton*, a $7 \times 4\frac{1}{2}$ inches black box with a $5 \times 3$ inches screen; users could jot down ideas on the screen and draw sketches as they talked and thought, and record notes and appointments. The machine could translate the images, store and organize. In addition, electronic data, such as a map, could be input. Sales of the Newton were disappointing and it failed to live up to Apple's early expectations.

As market shares and gross margins fell during the early 1990s, Apple's pre-tax profits and share price were both erratic. Sculley, the Newton product champion, was accused of neglecting the main hardware products to push the new idea, and his position was threatened. Sculley was in fact replaced by Michael Spindler in 1993, an internal promotion but, three years later, Spindler also left. Another new strategic leader, Gil Amelio, joined Apple from National Semiconductor in 1996. After his own departure Sculley commented: 'I don't think anyone can manage Apple.'

Amelio decided to halve the Macintosh product range (responsible for 80 per cent of Apple's revenue) in order to reduce costs and help to restore profitability. This controversial cut radically affected Apple's strategy of market segmentation. In addition, six varieties of its software operating system were consolidated into one, which Apple would also seek to license to other manufacturers. Allied with Adobe – which could put on to a laser printer what was appearing on a screen – Apple pioneered desktop publishing. The Macintosh has always been the preferred machine for designers.

The company was also restructured into seven profit-centre divisions: four for different hardware

products, plus software, service and Internet – the Macintosh has always been an ideal machine for creating Internet products.

Amelio recognized that cultural change was again an issue – he believed from one where 'employees felt free to question, and even defy, management decisions' to a more conventional style. Product managers would no longer be 'free to veto the strategic leader'.

Apple's core competency was still its ability to make technology easy to use and Amelio argued that it needed to exploit this in ways that allowed it to move further away from the cut-throat PC market and capitalize upon the new opportunities that were emerging as more and more people worldwide gained access to computers. Currently just 9 per cent of the world's population had access.

Apple's new Macintosh operating system, called Copland, and due around the end of 1996, was being predicted 'to make Windows 95 seem as quaint and feeble as DOS' because of its radical new ability to organize, track and retrieve stored data and files. However, in 1996 Steve Jobs stated:

> If I were running Apple I would milk the Macintosh for all it's worth – and get busy on the next great thing. The PC wars are over. Done. Microsoft won a long time ago.

Declining sales and falling profits were a feature of 1996, and Amelio had to shoulder some of the blame. The new Macintosh operating system, Copland, was not launched on time; the development team had been depleted too much by redundancies and resignations. However, in December 1996, Apple attempted to help rectify these weaknesses by acquiring NeXT Software, the company formed by Apple cofounder Steven Jobs after he was ousted by John Sculley in 1985. The assumption was that Apple should now get the new technology it required for updating the Macintosh. In addition, though, it would obtain the part-time consultancy services of Steven Jobs, who would advise on product strategy.

Jobs commented: 'For the past ten years the PC industry has been slowly copying the Mac's revolutionary graphical user interface. Now the time has come for new innovation …'. The key relationships lay with other software developers who typically produced a Windows version first, and only released Macintosh versions some months later.

NeXT's software had generally been highly acclaimed, but it had enjoyed only limited commercial success. Jobs meanwhile had been more successful with his other company venture, Pixar. Pixar is the film animation company which worked with Disney on *Toy Story* and had a ten-year partnership deal with the Walt Disney Corporation. More recently Pixar has worked on *Finding Nemo* and *Monsters Inc.* Jobs – who to this day remains active within Pixar as well as Apple – quickly began to make an impact. Executives from NeXT took over senior positions at Apple and a close colleague of Amelio was demoted. Jobs' cofounder at Apple, Steven Wozniak, was also brought back as a consultant. Costs and employees continued to be cut back, however. The workforce of 13,000 was reduced to between 10,000 and 11,000. Product development, sales and marketing were streamlined. It was quickly speculated that the Apple Newton would be floated off as a separate business.

Once Amelio had left it was also speculated that Jobs would take over full-time, although he continually denied any interest in the challenge, emphasizing his commitment to Pixar. While some assumed that he would be able to rejuvenate Apple with his renowned entrepreneurial flair, one analyst was sceptical: 'The idea that they are going to go back to the past to hit a big home run to beat Microsoft is delusional.' In addition, there were fresh rumours that the NeXT software was after all proving to be inappropriate for Macintosh.

So, two questions arose. One, where did Apple currently fit in the PC industry? And two, could it continue to survive in its present form? Sales of Macintosh had declined to a level where Apple had less than a 5 per cent share of the US PC market; just two years ago it had an 11 per cent share. The odds on Apple being taken over began to shorten. After all, IBM had already made two unsuccessful offers (in 1994 and 1995) and Sun Microsystems one (in 1996).

Early in August 1997 Steve Jobs announced that Microsoft was to invest $150 million in Apple and the two companies were forming a partnership. The key terms of the agreement were as follows:

- Microsoft would develop and distribute office applications for the Apple Macintosh
- Apple would bundle Microsoft's Internet browser software, Internet Explorer, in future Macintosh products.

For Apple, the alliance clearly provided a positive new lease of life. For Bill Gates and Microsoft, it was more of a defensive strategy. If Apple collapsed, Microsoft would be a monopoly supplier – between them, Apple and Microsoft accounted for virtually all the sales of PC operating systems software around the world – and this might raise issues for the US anti-trust authorities. Moreover, Microsoft's real competitive threat at this time did not come from Apple's software and PCs, but rather from Netscape's rival Internet browser and Oracle's network computer which could grow at the expense of independent PCs. Consequently, this deal was designed to strengthen its overall position.

Early in 1998 Apple became profitable again. A new range of PCs was beating sales forecasts – the latest G3 version of the Mac was faster and cheaper than equivalent Windows-based PCs, a very different situation from the earlier years. Jobs, now firmly in control again, took the credit. Newton was abandoned. One lingering concern, though, was that sales were still to committed Mac users, who were updating, rather than to new buyers.

In May 1998 Apple announced its radical new iMac, an integrated computer and monitor in a single unit and in a bright, translucent housing. A keyboard and mouse could be attached in an instant. The keyboard was also translucent and the mouse lit up. At its launch in August it 'flew off the shelves'. In 1999 Apple launched a new range of notebook computers in a similar style and packaging to the iMac. Jobs appeared to have tapped into a new market segment – 'the Generation Y buyer that likes individuality'. In the end, though,

and however popular its products might be with loyal Apple users, Apple only commands around 3.5 per cent of the PC market.

## Interim questions

1. At this stage would you have thought that Apple's latest turnaround might be real and sustainable?
2. What would be required for sustainability?

## The iPod and iTunes

In recent years Apple's renewed success has been boosted by its leadership of the fast-growing recorded music download industry. The leading music companies (such as EMI, Sony and Time-Warner) have seen sales of recorded music, especially singles, fall – at times quite dramatically. Increasingly consumers were copying CDs and downloading illegally from the Internet. With its innovative iPod and support software, Apple has pioneered legal downloads at 99 US cents per track – around 56 pence. This coincided with the music companies taking legal action (successfully) against companies such as Napster, which were making the illegal downloading possible.

The iPod is a small, stylish portable digital music player – with a significant memory – that has become the 'Sony Walkman for the J-Lo generation', although Sony might dispute this description! This time, though, Jobs was determined not to lose the software battle, as he had done with PC operating systems. By the end of 2000, some 2 million iPods had been sold amounting to a 30 per cent leading share of digital music players.

Supporting the hardware, iTunes is an online music store with which iPods work. It is compatible with Windows PCs. It accounts for some 70 per cent of the legal music downloads around the world. In its first year over 50 million tracks were sold and downloaded. By July 2004 Apple was looking for the person who would download the 100 millionth song – he or she was in line for a special prize!

But how profitable is this business? Of the 99 cents, some 65 cents are given back to the record companies and Apple's direct costs for credit card

transactions and distribution account for another 25 cents. The gross margin is 9 cents. The pricing strategy, however, is set to promote growth in the market – Apple makes a higher margin on the hardware.

Naturally competition would emerge and intensify. In 2004 Sony launched a new 20-gigabyte digital Walkman as a serious competitor to the iPod; and rival products from Philips and Samsung were in the pipeline. Possibly ominously, Microsoft was developing music store software.

**Questions**

1. The music download industry is really still in its infancy – what strategies should Apple adopt if it is to stay ahead of its rivals?
2. In the context of Apple, do you agree with the view that 'the right strategy depends upon personal vision, and personal vision depends upon having the right person'?

**Apple** http://www.apple.com

*There is nothing more difficult to take in hand, more perilous to conduct, or more uncertain in its success than to take the lead in the introduction of a new order of things.*

Machiavelli

*In this race … you run the first four laps as fast as you can – and then you gradually increase the speed.*

William Weiss, when CEO, Ameritech

## 17.1 Introducing strategic change

Figure 17.1 illustrates the strategic change process. The process is driven by the strategic leader and is affected markedly by the organizational culture. The organization is attempting to both manage in (reactively) and manage (proactively) its external environment. The structure, objectives and the related performance measures are determined by the mission and direction and they, in turn, guide the decisions, actions and outcomes. These outcomes can then be compared with performance expectations. The timing of change is critical. If things are not changed at the appropriate time the organization is likely to be reactive and may well end up perpetually crisis fighting.

Strategies, as we have said earlier, follow life cycles. Throughout the life of a strategy it is assumed there will be innovative, incremental improvements in the face of competition. But when industries, markets or technologies are disrupted, companies must adapt and maybe transform themselves if they are to survive. This may be more pronounced if they have been 'betting' as opposed to 'hedging'. Betting implies having pursued a focus strategy and relied on a limited range of related products rather than diversified to spread the risk across a number of industries – which is hedging.

Effective organizations, then, must be able to *manage change*, with managers and employees supportive rather than resistant or hostile. When strategies change, there are often accompanying changes in structures and responsibilities, and people are clearly affected. Kotter and Schlesinger (1979) and later Waterman (1987) suggested that most companies or divisions need to make moderate organizational changes at least every year, with major changes every four or five years. In today's world this demand has certainly not relaxed!

**Figure 17.1** The strategic change process

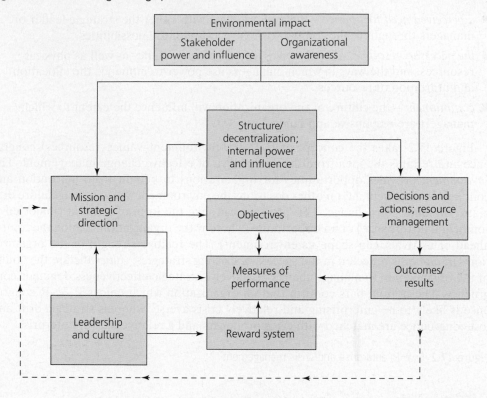

While organizational changes can be reactive and forced by external change, effective strategic management really requires *learning*. Managers must be aware of their environment, assessing trends and deciding in advance what should be done about perceived opportunities and threats. Planning activities and systems should ensure that the future is considered, and the resultant plans should encompass the implementation aspects of any proposed changes and the need to be flexible to accommodate unexpected changes. Moreover, innovation should be possible within the organization. Managers should constantly be looking for ways of being more effective and able to proceed with appropriate changes.

Ideally, the organization will seek to develop a culture where people do not feel threatened when they are constantly asked to question and challenge existing behaviours and acknowledged ways of doing things, and change them – a culture that sees innovation and change as normal; a culture that is ideal for dealing with the competitive chaos that characterizes many industries and markets; a culture where people do not automatically ask: 'Who is already doing this?' when someone proposes an innovative change. This cannot happen without strong strategic leadership which fosters, encourages and rewards intrapreneurial and innovative contributions from managers and other employees throughout the organization.

A culture such as this will frequently be based around a working atmosphere of creativity and fun; people must enjoy doing things differently and originally, actively looking for new competitive opportunities, instead of simply copying others.

A change culture is highly desirable for many organizations but very difficult to achieve.

Hence, the implementation of change requires:

■ *a perceived need for change* – this can originate with either the strategic leader or managers throughout the company who are aware of the possibilities

■ *the necessary resources* – this involves aspects of competency as well as physical resources, and the ways in which managers use power to influence the allocation and utilization of resources

■ *commitment* – the culture of the organization will influence the extent to which managers are responsive and innovative.

Figure 17.2 takes the concept of E–V–R (environment–values–resources) congruence and restates the idea from the perspective of effective change management. The *environment* provides opportunities for organizations to benefit from innovation and continuous improvement; on other occasions the environment will encourage more dramatic, discontinuous change. This pressure can take the form of a threat (major environmental disturbance) or an opportunity (whereby the organization, 'seeing the future' ahead of its rivals, can shape its environment). The relative strength of the organization's *resources* is reflected in the success of existing strategies; *values* dictate the ability of the organization to manage change effectively. Strategic effectiveness demands congruency. The bottom bars confirm that an organization which enjoys E–V–R congruence is likely to be enterprising and relatively crisis averse, whereas strategic drift and lost congruence are matched with crisis proneness and a relative lack of enterprise.

**Figure 17.2** E–V–R, enterprise and crisis management

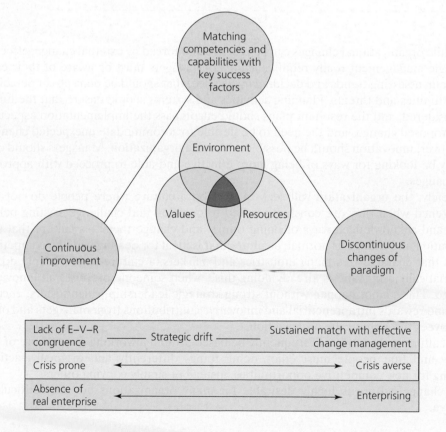

## 17.1.1 The cycle of growth

Figure 17.3 is based around four stages of organizational development and growth: creativity, nurturing, 'doing' and control. Organizations must be able to accomplish all four elements – if any one is relatively overabundant or underachieved, there will be a weakness. Continued progression around and around the loop implies an organization is managing the change agenda; a failure to keep moving perpetually implies a failure to adapt to change pressures.

The model is iterative and systematic. Originally it begins with creativity – new ideas in a somewhat chaotic environment. This active stage should be followed by more passive reflection and nurturing when the idea is crafted into a real opportunity. Often this is where a new business idea springs up. Whilst many organizations and entrepreneurs spend insufficient time carrying out this essential strategic thinking, it is equally possible to become bogged down in planning and not move on to action. Generally it is this action or 'doing' phase that brings about success and growth, demanding proper organization and structure in order that there can be management and control. The danger is that this control can stifle innovation through stasis and a loss of entrepreneurial drive. To ensure the organization can continue to grow, fresh ideas – renewed creativity – is needed once more. We saw earlier in Chapter 8 how some strategic leaders deliberately engineer a (perceived) crisis before a real one takes hold in order to drive the change process.

Ideally an organization will progress from one stage to another and continue around the cycle. However, many people have ideas which never become opportunities, for example. Some opportunities are never enacted; and some entrepreneurial organizations are so involved in the doing stage that they only put in the proper structure when it becomes essential. Once systems, rules and control procedures begin to take hold, fresh creativity can easily be stifled. Naturally creative people may not seem to fit in with the more disciplined approach the organization has adopted. Most of us are capable of being creative, but we need to be working in an appropriate organization culture which encourages us to be creative. Consequently, this progression is unlikely to just happen – movement is likely to require triggers and some clear manifestation of need.

**Figure 17.3** The cycle of growth

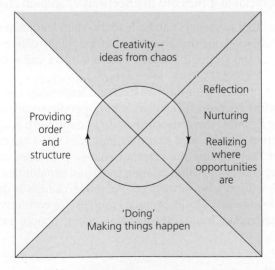

In addition, there are sub-loops in the cycle. Creating and developing an opportunity is often an iterative loop in itself. Strategic thinking and action can be the same. Strategy and structure, as we have seen before, are also linked. Intrapreneurship in large and established organizations is represented by a creativity-reflection-doing sub-loop within an appropriate structure.

As individuals, we are likely to feel comfortable in one or two of these four roles and less comfortable in the others. Hence entrepreneurs and strategic leaders must build management teams to make sure they secure the help they need to overcome their naturally weaker areas.

### 17.1.2  Leading strategic change

We looked at different styles of strategic leadership, at strategic issues in leadership and at intrapreneurial organizations in Chapter 10. We used the term 'meta strategy' for the leader's vision of how strategies should be created, implemented and changed. The leadership contribution of Steve Jobs to Apple over nearly 30 years, and his temporary replacement by others, highlights wonderfully the tension between entrepreneurial vision and bureaucratic discipline. Both are required to some degree, and over time their relative significance waxes and wanes as both strategies and structures change. See Minicase 17.1.

Kotter (1990) argues it is the leader's job to 'create and manage change' and from this he delineated four important differences between managers and leaders:

■ Leaders work with the future in mind and do not always have to be bound by timescales (although sometimes time pressures to deliver are paramount), whilst managers are more concerned with planning and budgeting within defined time frames.

■ Leaders champion organizational communications whilst managers work with the form of the organization.

■ Managers concentrate on problem solving whilst leaders aim to inspire and motivate others.

■ Managers work to targets and can be expected to behave predictably; leaders must at times be unpredictable if they are to effectively champion change.

Kotter acknowledges that managers can be leaders – and leaders managers – at one and the same time. It follows from these points that we might expect changes of strategy and/or structure when the strategic leader changes – as we can see in Minicase 17.2 on Domino's Pizza.

Heifetz and Linsky (2002) caution that strategic leadership can be 'dangerous' [to a leader's mental health] because it involves asking people to adapt. Real leadership – linked to the change agenda – involves confronting people with adaptive challenges that they would often rather ignore. And that they may well rebel against. One problem for some leaders is that they assume the relevant change pressures can be dealt with in a 'technical' (or managerial) way, using existing tools and capabilities – but if this happens any change benefits will only be short-lived. Adaptive change is quite likely to involve restructuring and job losses … hardly popular! Sometimes certainty must be abandoned for uncertainty. Leadership frequently involves giving people news that they would rather not hear.

## Minicase 17.2  Domino's Pizza  (US)

Domino's is the world's biggest pizza delivery company. Pizza Hut is the biggest overall; and recently Papa John's has taken the lead in America for home deliveries. Serving one million pizzas every day, Domino's always specialized in home deliveries rather than providing restaurant facilities although some 20 per cent of the revenues are from 'walk-in' trade. There are 7300 company-owned and franchised outlets in 50 countries. The business model is built around speedy deliveries and consistent quality. Customers were historically offered a generous discount on any home delivery that took longer than 30 minutes. Delivery staff were required to wear trainers and to be fit enough to run between their delivery trucks (or motorcycles) and customers' houses, and to run up apartment stairs rather than wait for lifts. There were competitions between different regions for the best pizzas and fastest service. But the company had to change its promotional message after a delivery cyclist was involved in a nasty road accident whilst endeavouring to deliver a pizza within minutes of a telephone order being placed.

Entrepreneur Tom Monaghan in Ann Arbor, Michigan founded the company, in 1960. He ran the company for 38 years before selling it to a venture capitalist buy-in for $1 billion. The new CEO is David Brandon.

When the business became successful, Monaghan had taken to a 'tycoon lifestyle' with yachts, corporate jets and luxury homes. His personal office was 3000 square foot in size. The headquarters was in farmland he owned and where buffalo roamed quite freely. Yet, paradoxically perhaps, he was a committed Catholic. Later he concluded that he had allowed his personal pride to dominate his actions and he set out to change the culture and style. During the 1990s a new dress code was enforced. Men must wear dark suits and white shirts; women must wear skirts. By the time he sold the business he had divested many of the corporate 'possessions' he had bought. Since 1998 he has devoted his energies – and some of his fortune – to helping social causes. During the 1990s sales increased but Domino's market share declined.

Brandon introduced a series of changes – and in five years managed to increase net profits by 50 per cent. Market share has also recovered. He:

- Abandoned the formal dress code
- Set out to lower (the high) staff turnover and improve service
- Freshened up the stores, refitting many of them
- Added new senior managers to the existing team
- Extended the bonus scheme
- Strengthened top-down communications linked to a personal visible presence and availability
- Became more discerning about overseas locations
- Extended the local-market toppings the company offered.

### Questions

1. Had you been Brandon would you have stuck with the 'delivery only' business model or introduced complementary restaurant facilities?
2. From your own experiences, what might give a pizza delivery company a competitive edge?

**Dominos** http://www.dominos.co.uk

Meanwhile Buchanan *et al.* (1999) put forward the thesis that leaders are courting trouble if they encourage or permit what they term 'initiative overload'. This occurs when individual managers are unable to deal effectively with the uncertainty facing them and it causes them to become cynical about any new change demands. They lose motivation; they become less coherent and less productive; they may even get burnt out. Change is not managed effectively in the organization. When there is any real likelihood

of this happening it is the leader's role to clarify priorities and help people to stay focused on what matters.

The increasing number and popularity of 'my story' books by prominent strategic leaders highlights the potential rewards from organizational success. But, at the same time, strategic leaders may have to pay the price for failure. Shareholders and other stakeholders demand that the leader is held accountable when expectations are not met. That said, they rarely leave empty handed – golden handshakes can be very generous!

Institutional pressures, then, can ensure that the strategic leader is seen to be responsible for his or her strategic decisions and the performance of the company. Three years after the stock market crash of 1987, for example, only one chief executive from the ten worst performing companies (measured by their share price movements) was still in the post. Visible 'losers' included Sir Ralph Halpern of Burton (Halpern had earlier been responsible for turning Burton around after a poor performance during the 1970s) and George Davies, the creator of Next. Halpern largely disappeared from the corporate scene – but Davies reinvented himself as the entrepreneurial designer he really is. He first introduced the hugely successful George clothing range to ASDA before creating the Per Una range for Marks and Spencer. Although almost all of Britain's largest companies are quoted on the stock exchange, in large part due to their need for equity funding at certain stages of their development, some of the country's most dynamic entrepreneurs find this to be an uncomfortable state. They perceive the price of being a public company too high. Richard Branson (Virgin) and Andrew Lloyd Webber (The Really Useful Group) both bought back and reprivatized the successful companies that they had developed.

Another colourful leader to lose shareholder support, and his job, was Gerald Ratner, who had been largely responsible for the rapid growth of the Ratner's jewellery chain after the acquisition of H Samuel. At an Institute of Directors conference in 1991 he claimed that this company was able to sell sherry decanters at really low prices because they were 'total crap'. The tabloid newspapers were very critical and the company's previously strong image was damaged. The group name has subsequently been changed to Signet and it continues to prosper without him. Like George Davies, Ratner too has returned to business – first as the owner of leisure centres and more recently selling jewellery online.

Although sometimes described as losers, many such chief executives resign and receive generous golden handshakes. Interestingly, after Robert Ayling resigned as chief executive of British Airways in 2000, institutional shareholders demanded that the board review the generous payout that was being proposed. This was only the start of this kind of controversy. Very much the same continues to happen elsewhere – most recently in 2004 with Sir Peter Davis at Sainsbury (Minicase 10.11) who was set to receive a final pay package of at least £3.2m. The real losers, of course, are the employees who also lose their jobs in the contraction, and sometimes the shareholders.

Change then can be a risky business. But change remains essential. Would it be unreasonable to argue that for many strategic leaders in dynamic industries with intense competition that they are 'damned if they do' – and yet they would certainly be 'damned if they didn't'?

We look in greater detail at some of these issues in the next sections of this chapter.

# 17.2 Issues in the management of change

It was mentioned earlier that organizations face change pressures from the environment, and the significance, regularity and impact of these pressures will be determined by the complexity and volatility of the environment (see Chapter 4). Box 17.1 examines this issue further. At the same time managers may see opportunities and wish to adapt existing strategies. There are therefore several forces which encourage change, and a variety of different change situations. Change, though, affects people, their jobs and responsibilities and their existing behavioural patterns. It can also lead to changes in the underlying culture of the organization. For these reasons people may be wary or even hostile. This is increasingly likely if they fail to understand the reasoning behind the proposed changes and if they personally feel that they are losing rather than gaining from the changes. The various forces for change, the reasons why people resist change, and an outline framework for the effective management of change are considered in this section.

## Box 17.1 Strategic Inflection Points

**KEY CONCEPTS**

There comes a time in the life of every business when its fundamental *raison d'être* is about to change. This is quite likely to be the result of outside forces at work. New technological developments may be occurring. A competitor may have come up with something that will change the rules of competition; maybe this competitor is a 'breaker-in'. Something could be happening elsewhere in the supply chain, with components or distribution possibilities. Maybe something is changing in a parallel business which could switch demand away from you and others like you; maybe customers are simply changing their preferences for some reason or another.

Whatever the reason might be, the business in question has grown to a particular level and is now approaching a metaphorical fork in the road. Continuing straight on, continuing with existing products, processes and services, is not a realistic option. The business must change direction. If it makes the appropriate decision, it can continue uphill and enjoy renewed growth, albeit with something different. If it makes an inappropriate decision, the route is downhill.

The problem is, the business often reaches this fork relatively suddenly and unexpectedly. **Strategic inflection points** are characterized by uncertainty, but for the ready and flexible organi-

zation, they can be a real new opportunity. Dealing with these change pressures is always going to be hardest for the successful, entrenched business.

IBM was a world leader, vertically integrated into chips, computers, operating systems and software. The strategic inflection point came with the introduction of the microprocessor – computing would never be the same again. IBM with its reliance on mainframe systems could have gone to the wall. Instead it found a new role in a changed industry, one where vertical organizations were no longer the answer. The industry split into five horizontal layers, and businesses opted for focus strategies, such that they could compete to be best in class rather than best at everything. The five layers are chips (where Intel is dominant), computers, operating systems and applications software (both championed by Microsoft) and distribution.

Grove (1996) believes it is important to be a first mover at the strategic inflection point. The secret of the way forward is to find new and appropriate ways of adding value that matter to customers – not simply alternatives that are different from rival organizations – and to price at a level the customer will accept quickly. Somehow costs then have to be driven down to a level where

▶

a margin is possible. This was, of course, always the strategy of Ryanair. The budget airline priced low to attract business and then looked for cost reduction opportunities, without sacrificing safety!

Because the timing of strategic inflection points will always be characterized by uncertainty it is vital to recognize just who in the organization is in the best position to be spotting trends and signals and engage them in discussion. People who seem to be 'off-the-wall' should not be dismissed because they are 'off-line'. Cassandra foretold danger for the Trojans, but they ignored her. Complacent, they never spotted the horse in their midst! Remember the time to worry is when you are doing well! Organizations must somehow recognize when it is essential to give up on analysis (of largely historical data) and rely more on someone's intuition. After all, we can never predict the future with certainty. But we can unlock the secrets of the present if we ask the right questions,

think about the answers we are being given, look at signals and triggers in the environment, think about new resource-based possibilities, properly identify problems and look for creative opportunities to make things more as we feel they should be.

One option is to persist with the silver bullet test. Invite a range of different managers to imagine they have a gun and just one silver bullet – they can eliminate any rival organization. Which one do they choose? Once they have chosen, ask them to think again to be sure they are certain in their choice. If anyone changes his or her mind, or there is noticeable prevarication, maybe there is something to investigate.

**Source**

Grove A S (1996) *Only The Paranoid Survive*, Harper Collins.

### 17.2.1 Forces for change

Five major forces for change are as follows.

1. *Technical obsolescence and technical improvements* – Technical change pressures can stem from outside the organization in the form of new developments by competitors and the availability of new technologies which the organization might wish to harness. Internal research and development and innovatory ideas from managers can generate technical change internally. In high-technology companies and industries, and particularly where product life cycles are becoming shorter, this can be a very significant issue. Some organizations follow product strategies built around short life cycles, product obsolescence (both physical and design) and persuading customers to replace the product regularly. A number of service businesses also find this a useful strategy.

2. *Political and social events* – Many of these change pressures will be outside the control of the firm, but companies will be forced to respond. In the mid-to-late 1980s there was considerable pressure on companies not to trade with South Africa, and in the late 1980s increased public awareness of environmental issues began to place pressure on certain firms. Government encouragement for the use of lead-free petrol, in the form of both media coverage and price advantages from lower taxation, forced car manufacturers to respond. In the 1990s, oil companies such as BP and Shell were forced to respond to the concerns of the public on environmental pollution issues.

3. *The tendency for large organizations and markets to become increasingly global* – While this again has provided opportunities and new directions of growth for many

organizations, others have been forced to respond to changing competitive conditions. The growing incidence of joint ventures and strategic alliances, discussed in Chapter 12, is a feature of this.

4. *Increases in the size, complexity and specialization of organizations* – The growth of organizations, linked to internal changes of structure, creates pressure for further changes. Large complex specialist organizations have made increasing use of information technology (IT) in their operations, introducing automation and just in time (JIT) systems. These create a need for greater specialist expertise from both managers and other employees, possibly necessitating training and changes in their jobs. Effective use of these technological opportunities also requires greater co-operation and co-ordination between functions and managers.

5. *The greater strategic awareness and skills of managers and employees* – Able and ambitious managers, and employees who want job satisfaction and personal challenges, need opportunities for growth within the organization. These can be promotion opportunities or changes in the scope of jobs. Such changes require both strategic development and growth by the company, and appropriate styles of non-autocratic leadership.

## 17.2.2 The current dynamics of change

The strategic environment, especially competitive forces, determines how proactive and change orientated an organization must be if it is to be effective. While the forces and their relative intensity vary between industries and organizations, Peters (1989) suggests that several factors require that most organizations must be receptive to the need for change. Specifically, he highlights the following:

■ the general dynamics and uncertainty of world economies

■ time horizons, which he argues can be a strategic weapon in the face of uncertainty. It was discussed earlier (in Chapter 5) how successful retailers now use IT to monitor demand changes very quickly and to build distribution systems which allow them to respond to changes. As product life cycles shorten, the development time for new products must also be cut

■ organization structures must be designed to enable decisions to be made quickly

■ quality, design and service – which must be responsive to customer perceptions and competitor activities – are essential for competitive advantage.

## 17.2.3 Levels of change

Change decisions can be categorized in terms of their significance to the organization and the appropriate level of intervention (Table 17.1). The six levels form a vertical hierarchy, and it is crucial to clarify and tackle needs and problems appropriately. If the problem is one of operating efficiencies, then the intervention should be at functional strategy level, but this alone would be inadequate for dealing with higher order needs. As one ascends the hierarchy the challenges and difficulties increase – as shown in Chapter 7, changing the culture of the organization can be slow and problematical. Structural changes can sometimes be difficult to implement as well, particularly where individuals perceive themselves to be losing rather than benefiting.

**Table 17.1** Levels of change

| Need | Level of change | Approaches/tactics |
|---|---|---|
| New mission; different ways of doing things | Values; culture, styles of management | Organizational development |
| New corporate perspective/strategy | Objectives; corporate strategy | Strategic planning |
| | Organization structure | New organization design |
| Improved competitive effectiveness (existing products and services) | Competitive strategies; strategic positioning; systems and management roles | Empowerment; management by objectives; performance management; job descriptions; policies |
| | Business processes | Business process re-engineering |
| Improved efficiencies | Functional strategies; activities; organization of tasks | Method study; job enrichment |

In recent years the recession-hit high street banks have introduced major changes in an attempt to protect and consolidate their profits, and these have systematically moved up to the highest level. A variety of approaches has been used to improve productivity and reduce costs, but this alone was inadequate. The services provided to customers have been reviewed, resulting, for example, in new branch interiors and the introduction of personal bankers and specialist advisers. These changes have been linked to restructuring, the closure of some small branches, job losses and increased market segmentation of business clients. More recently the banks have rethought their corporate strategies, having pursued growth through diversification and overseas expansion during the early 1980s. Concentration on core activities is now preferred. During the 1990s the cultural focus saw a reduced emphasis on image and marketing and a return to the more productive utilization of assets, harnessing IT, in order to improve margins.

Minicase 17.3 describes a number of high-level strategic changes at the Halifax. These have been accompanied by the lower-level strategies described above.

### 17.2.4 Types of change

Summarizing these points, Daft (1983) specifies four basic types of change which affect organizations:

- technology – production processes
- the product or service – the output of the business
- administrative changes – structure; policies; budgets; reward systems
- people attitudes – expectations; behaviour.

Invariably, a change in one of these factors will place demands for change on one or more of the others.

When an organization decides to launch a new product it may also need to invest in new technology, modify its existing production plant and either acquire people with, or train existing employees in, the new skills required.

Major changes in the strategic perspective, say the acquisition of a similar sized firm, will force changes in the organization structure, which in turn necessitates changes in jobs and behaviour patterns.

However necessary the changes may be, and however ready the organization might be to implement them, the outcomes will not necessarily be positive for everyone affected.

---

## Minicase 17.3  Halifax plc　　　　　　　　　　　　　　GB

CASE

Several years after the Abbey National Building society had successfully demutualized and become both a bank and a public company, the UK's leading building society, the Halifax, did the same and set about becoming one of the largest financial services providers in the country. When the Abbey floated, the Halifax commented that it saw no need for it to demutualize – but circumstances were to change.

Three key forces have brought about the changes described in this short case:

- Deregulation – discussed below.

- Technological innovation – IT in particular had reduced entry barriers in financial services, fostering such changes as telephone banking, telephone insurance and banking services at the leading supermarket chains.

- Competition – the above changes had introduced new competitors and new forms of competition.

Building societies originally began to grow in the industrial areas of the UK around the middle of the nineteenth century to help to provide houses for the working families who were then benefiting from the industrial revolution. These mutual societies (owned by their members for the benefit of their members, somewhat along the lines of the Co-operative movement), were increasingly regulated in the twentieth century. Exchange controls prevented competition from foreign banks, but their activities were limited to savings and property mortgages.

Things began to change after the election of a Conservative government in 1971. The liquidity ratio for high street banks was eased and they were consequently free to lend out more money, if they could attract savers. Although there was some retightening when the economy boomed the banks had already begun to introduce more attractive, higher interest accounts, thus reducing the gap between themselves and the mutual building societies, which had previously always been perceived as a better alternative for savers. When exchange controls were abolished in 1979–80 the banks additionally became real competitors in the mortgage market; and, to balance things out, the 1986 Building Societies Act widened their range of permitted activities.

The Abbey National was the first leading building society to convert to a plc (in 1988–89), since when it has (in turn) prospered as a bank, an estate agency and a diversified financial services organization. It is now owned by Santander, a Spanish bank. At this time, Halifax was adamant that it intended to retain its mutual status. Views changed, however, and Halifax merged with (and absorbed) the Leeds Permanent Building Society in 1995 as a prelude to a conversion in 1997.

### For and against conversion

The main argument in defence of mutual status is that it allows for higher interest rates for savers and lower charges for mortgage customers; there are no shareholders demanding dividends. However, conversion to a public company brings greater freedom to diversify into more activities. While there is an assumption that diversification into a financial services business is a superior strategy to that of the focused building society, there is

also an argument that the focused building society will become less and less viable in the face of intensifying competition. Conversion raises new capital which can be invested in acquisition and expansion.

## The new Halifax

The key to the new organization is the power and potential of the Halifax brand, which can be applied to a range of related activities.

These activities now comprise:

- mortgages (the UK market leader)
- liquid savings
- long-term protected savings
- retail banking and consumer credit (i.e. loans)
- credit cards – focused on affinity cards for charities and other organizations
- personal and life insurance services
- estate agency services
- treasury activities.

Halifax used acquisitions to help its diversification into insurance and estate agencies. It systematically acquired Clerical Medical Insurance (1996), the Birmingham Midshires Building Society (1998 for £750 million) and the UK credit-card arm of America's Bank One (2000). The activities are distributed to customers in a variety of ways: Halifax branches, independent agents and distributors, independent financial advisers, estate agency branches, automatic teller machines, and direct telephone sales and services.

## A change of leader

In 1998 Mike Blackburn, who had successfully led the Halifax through its conversion, opted for early retirement and was replaced by James Crosby, an internal candidate. The bank had been criticized for:

- lacking ideas for spending the £3 billion plus surplus capital created when it floated. Some analysts believed that this should be used to reduce the Halifax's dependency on mortgages

and savings, two very competitive segments. Some of the money had been spent on the acquisitions, and some on a share buy-back, but by no means all of it

- not articulating clear priorities for its future direction
- losing market share in mortgages
- persisting with a complacent culture.

A merger with another leading bank seemed a quite plausible alternative. This merger happened when Halifax merged with the Bank of Scotland in May 2001 to form HBOS plc.

## The planned transformation

Several changes and intentions were proposed by Crosby when he became the new strategic leader:

- *Strategic changes* – to exploit new technologies to improve the distribution of services. Telephone banking, Internet banking and interactive television all offered real opportunities.
- *Structure* – to help to reduce costs, Halifax anticipated employing fewer and younger people. Responsibilities must increase with greater decentralization.
- *Style* – Crosby wanted the Halifax to become more creative, innovative, fast-moving and flexible. Without this it seemed unlikely that it would be able to take advantage of all the new opportunities which were arising. Halifax recognized that it needed to attract fresh talent and, on occasions, buy in expertise. Peter Wood, founder of Direct Line, joined to help to develop the insurance business. In conjunction with this, Halifax adopted a smart casual dress style for its back-office staff.
- *Image and reputation* – brands are critical, and brand value must be delivered. Halifax began a new series of advertisements featuring some off its own staff. These are undoubtedly irritating advertisements in some people's eyes, but they must work as they have been retained.

### An early setback

In May 2000 Halifax announced that it was trying to patent the account design and software for its new Internet bank – known as IF (Intelligent Finance) – which it planned to launch in July. Commentators were immediately sceptical about how different it might be, doubting that the Halifax was about to 'turn the banking industry upside down'. The idea with IF was that customers would be able to set off savings against borrowings, to achieve the best overall interest rate, without having to combine their accounts into a 'single pot', as was the case with rivals who offered a similar benefit.

The July launch was delayed because of a computer bug. One month later the attractiveness of Internet banking was dimmed when Abbey National's Cahoot product was also experiencing technical difficulties and computer fraud was discovered with the Prudential's online bank, Egg. With the benefit of hindsight, IF seems to have been a good idea and a courageous one at that.

### Question

1. To what extent do you think the Halifax has proactively driven its change agenda, and to what extent do you think it has been responding to external forces and pressures?

**HBOS** http://www.hbos.com

## 17.2.5 The change process

Change frequently disrupts normality. Job security seems threatened; existing behaviour patterns and values are questioned; people are required to be more flexible and to take more risks. While the organization may be facing strong external pressures it is unrealistic to expect managers and other employees not to query or resist the need to change. This is particularly true if individuals feel threatened, or perceive themselves to be losing out rather than benefiting or not being rewarded in some way for co-operating.

It is important to encourage people to recognize the need for change, the benefits, and the external threats from not changing. This can involve the engineered crisis. Managed change should be planned and evolutionary, although some organizations have attempted to become more flexible such that people not only accept change, but constantly seek new opportunities for change and improvement. Although change can be speedy and dynamic – normally when it is forced by powerful external influences – managing change positively in a growth situation, taking advantage of opportunities rather than responding to threats, requires that the process begins gradually and on a limited scale, and then spreads. Advancement needs consolidation and learning. The innovation stage, which can easily go wrong, requires that the change agents (who will not always be the strategic leader) find powerful and influential allies and supporters. Time and effort must be invested in explaining, justifying and persuading. Trial and error leads to incremental learning. Early supporters should be visibly rewarded for their commitment, and this will encourage others and begin to consolidate the changes. Conservative people are inevitably going to be late joiners; and some older people, together with those who are very set in their ways, are likely to be laggards. Because changes can be slow to take off they often appear to be failing once the process is well under way. This will renew opposition and resistance. During the process it is important to continue to monitor the environment. The programme may need amendment if circumstances alter.

*Remember, it is not always the man on the shop floor who opposes change. It can be the second or third tier of management who are the most reactionary.*

Sir Peter Gibbings, ex-Chairman, Anglia Television

*No positive changes will occur within a company unless the chief executive realizes that people are basically opposed to change. A climate for change must be created in people's minds.*

*Changes need to be planned and everyone must be reassured that these changes will be for the betterment of the company, its employees, customers and shareholders. Changes have therefore to be managed against a set of objectives and to a timetable.*

Jacques G. Margry, when Group Chief Executive, Parker Pen Ltd

### 17.2.6 Resistance to change

*People do not resist* change *per se … they resist loss.*

Heifetz and Linsky, 2002

There are several reasons why change pressures might be resisted, and certain circumstances where the implementation of change will have to be planned carefully and the needs of people considered.

■ Some resistance can be expected where people have worked out ways of doing things which are beneficial to them in terms of *their* objectives and preferences. They may see change as a threat. Similarly, when people have mastered tasks and feel in control of their jobs and responsibilities, they are likely to feel relatively safe and secure personally. Again, change may be perceived as a threat to their security, although the aim might be to ensure the security of the organization as a whole.

■ Resistance to 'sideways change' (expanding certain activities while contracting elsewhere) is likely unless the people affected are fully aware of the reasons and implications.

■ Where particular policies, behaviour patterns and ways of doing things have been established and accepted for a long time and in effect have become part of the culture of the organization, change will require careful implementation. The need for change may not be accepted readily.

■ It is not unusual for people to have some fear of the unknown and to feel comfortable with situations, policies and procedures that they know. Awareness and understanding is therefore an important aspect of change.

■ The organization itself, or particular managers, may resist external pressures if the change involves considerable expense, investment in new equipment and the associated risks. This issue can be exacerbated where there has previously been substantial investment in plant and equipment which technically is still satisfactory. Although demand may be falling there may be a reluctance to sell or close.

■ Resistance is likely to be forthcoming where there are perceived flaws or weaknesses in the proposal. Change decisions may be made by the strategic leader and then delegated for implementation. Managers who are closer to the market may have some justified reservations if they have not been consulted during the formulation process.

The opposition may be to the change itself, or to the proposed means of implementation. Both can and must be overcome if changes are to be implemented successfully.

Casualties are, however, possible and sometimes inevitable. Some people will leave because they are uncomfortable with the changes.

## Box 17.2  Six Ways of Overcoming Resistance to Change

1. **Education and communication**
   Education and communication should help people to understand the logic and the need for change. A major drawback can be the inherent time delays and logistics when a lot of people are involved. It also requires mutual trust.

2. **Participation and involvement**
   The contention is that people will be more supportive of the changes if they are involved in the formulation and design. Again, it can be time-consuming; and if groups are asked to deliberate and make decisions there is a risk that some decisions will be compromises leading to suboptimization.

3. **Facilitation and support**
   This can involve either training or counselling but there is no guarantee that any resistance will be overcome.

4. **Negotiation and agreement**
   Negotiation and agreement are normally linked to incentives and rewards. Where the resistance stems from a perceived loss as a result of the proposed change, this can be useful, particularly where the resisting force is powerful. However, offering rewards every time changes in behaviour are desired is likely to prove impractical.

5. **Manipulation and co-optation**
   This encompasses covert attempts to influence people, for example by the selective use of information and conscious structuring of events. Co-optation involves 'buying off' informal leaders by personal reward or status. These methods are ethically questionable, and they may well cause grievances to be stored for the future.

6. **Explicit and implicit coercion**
   The use of threats can work in the short run but is unlikely to result in long-term commitment.

### Source

Kotter, JP and Schlesinger, LA (1979) Choosing strategies for change, *Harvard Business Review*, March–April.

Kotter and Schlesinger (1979) have identified six ways of overcoming resistance to change, and these are described in Box 17.2. They suggest that each method has both advantages and disadvantages and can be appropriate in particular circumstances. Issues raised by some of these alternatives are developed further in this chapter. Organizational development is considered as an approach to gaining support through active participation by managers on a continuous basis; manipulative approaches are discussed as a machiavellian use of power and influence. The next section considers a number of general aspects in the management of change before specific strategies are discussed in more detail.

Argyris and Schön (1978) concluded that it is the most knowledgeable and experienced employees who are most likely to feel inhibited and frustrated by change demands. Their sense of inhibition causes disbelief and distrust; employees lose their sense of commtiment and they develop defensive routines in an attempt to either impede or prevent change. This resistance becomes so embedded it is hard to overcome – and it cannot be defeated by force under any normal circumstances. Instead, the culture must be transformed until it reaches a state where change is welcomed. Argyris and Schön developed 'action science' in an attempt to achieve this.

Fundamentally this requires the generation of powerful, shared knowledge that is relevant to the needs of both the business and its employees. Communications, understanding and trust are at the core.

### 17.2.7 Implementing change: a general overview

Effective change occurs when managers and employees modify their behaviour in a desired or desirable way, and when the important changes are lasting rather than temporary.

Lewin (1947) contends that permanent changes in behaviour involve three aspects: unfreezing previous behaviour, changing, and then refreezing the new patterns. These three stages are crucial if changes in culture are required.

*Unfreezing* is the readiness to acquire or learn new behaviour. People are willing to accept that existing strategies and ways of doing things could be improved and made more effective. Normally this needs a trigger such as declining sales or profits, or the threat of closure or acquisition.

*Change* occurs when people who perceive the need for change try out new ideas. The changes could be introduced gradually or they may be more dramatic. Choosing the appropriate change strategy once the need is clarified may involve the selection of one from a number of alternatives, and consequently there are opportunities for involving the people who are most likely to be affected. Power structures are likely to be altered and consequently resistance might be evident from certain people.

Particularly where the pressures for change are significant, and the likely impact of the changes will be dramatic and felt widely throughout the organization, the change strategy will need a champion. Organizations in difficulty quite often appoint a new strategic leader to introduce fresh ideas and implement the changes. Newcomers are unlikely to be associated with the strategies which now need changing. Similarly, general managers might be moved to different business units when strategic changes are necessary.

*Refreezing* takes place when the new behaviour patterns are accepted and followed willingly. People are supportive and convinced of the wisdom of the changes; ideally the new approaches become established within the culture. Rewards are often influential in ensuring that refreezing does in fact take place.

Whilst this simple model provides an excellent outline of the basic stages in a managed change process, if we want to foster a culture which embraces perpetual change we need to be careful about refreezing new behaviours.

Throughout the change process it is important that people are aware of why changes are being proposed and are taking place, and that they understand the reasons. The key issues are participation, involvement and commitment.

Margerison and Smith (1989) suggest that the management of change exhibits four key features:

1. *dissatisfaction* with the present strategies and styles
2. *vision* of the better alternative – a clear picture of the desired state which can be communicated and explained to others (this again emphasizes the need for a champion of the change)
3. a *strategy* for implementing the change and attaining the desired state
4. *resistance* to the proposals at some stage.

## 17.2.8 Force-field analysis

Lewin (1951) has proposed that changes result from the impact of a set of driving forces upon restraining forces. Figure 17.4 illustrates Lewin's theme of a state of equilibrium which is always under some pressure to change. The extent to which it does change will depend upon whether the driving forces or the restraining forces prove to be stronger. The driving forces, which may be external or internal in origin, are likely to have economic aspects. There may be a need to increase sales, to improve profitability, to improve production efficiencies or to generate new forms of competitive advantage. Corporate, competitive and functional strategies may appear in need of change, but existing strategies may have people who are loyal and committed to them. People will be affected and may feel concerned. Any resistance will constitute a restraining force, seeking to abandon or modify the change proposals.

> *A nursing team in a geriatric hospital wanted the seats of the toilets raised for the comfort of their patients. Hospital management was silent to their pleas. The team re-presented their request and argued that the change would reduce the amount of laundry and in turn the laundry bills. The proposal was approved and implemented.*

Anecdote told by Christine Hancock, ex-General Secretary, Royal College of Nursing

Although the driving forces will be concerned with improving organizational efficiency and effectiveness, the opposition is more likely to stem from personal concerns than from disagreement that improved efficiency and effectiveness are desirable. Lewin suggests that the driving forces are based more on logic and the restraining forces on emotion. However, people who are aware of the situation may seek to argue their opposing case in relation to the relative ability of the change proposal to achieve the required improvements. As a result, the ensuing debate concentrates on these issues. The opponents may choose not to be honest and open about their personal fears, feeling that their arguments must concentrate on the economic issues. When this happens the decision, whatever it might be, has not encompassed important underlying behavioural issues.

Effective managers of change situations will be clearly aware of both the driving forces and the real restraining forces. They will seek to strengthen the justifications by communication and explanation and diffuse opposition by exploring the likely impact with the people affected. Box 17.3 summarizes a number of important issues for the effective management of change.

**Figure 17.4** Force-field analysis

Derived from Lewin, K (1951) *Field Theory in Social Sciences*, Harper & Row.

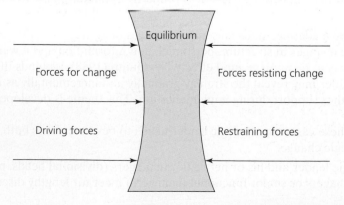

This section has looked generally at the issues which affect and underpin the management of change. Lewin's force-field analysis is particularly helpful for establishing a holistic view of the change situation in terms of cause and likely effect. From this a clearer strategy for implementing the change can emerge. A number of strategies is explored in the following section. Where the extent of the change is substantial, and changes in culture are involved, it is important to ensure that the new behaviour patterns are permanent rather than temporary.

> *To many, uncertainty is a shadow of the unknown, to be avoided; far better, as we are stuck with an uncertain world, is to look upon it as the spice of life.*
>
> Sir Peter Holmes, when Chairman, Shell UK

> *Teach people that change is inevitable and, if embraced, can be fun.*
>
> Leslie Hill, when Chairman and Chief Executive, Central Independent Television plc

## 17.3  Strategies for implementation and change

It is possible to view implementation as an activity which follows strategy formulation – structures and systems are changed to accommodate proposed changes in strategy. However, implementation, instead of following formulation, may be considered in depth at the same time as the proposed strategy is thought through and before final decisions are made. This is more likely to happen where several managers, especially those who will be involved in implementation, are consulted when the strategy is evaluated. Strategies may evolve from the operation of the organization structure. Where managers are encouraged to be innovatory and make incremental changes, elements of trial and error and small change decisions are often found. Implementation and formulation operate simultaneously; the changes are contained rather than dramatic and resistance may similarly be contained. Innovatory organizations can develop change orientation as part of the culture. People expect things to change regularly and accept changes.

Bourgeois and Brodwin (1984) have identified five distinct basic approaches to strategy implementation and strategic change.

■ The strategic leader, possibly using expert planners or enlisting planning techniques, defines changes of strategy and then hands over to senior managers for implementation. The strategic leader is primarily a thinker/planner rather than a doer.

■ The strategic leader again decides major changes of strategy and then considers the appropriate changes in structure, personnel, and information and reward systems if the strategy is to be implemented effectively. Quinn (1988) contends that the strategic leader may reveal the strategy gradually and incrementally as he or she seeks to gather support during implementation. This theme is developed later in this section.

  In both these cases the strategic leader needs to be powerful as both involve top-down strategic change.

■ The strategic leader and his or her senior managers (divisional heads, business unit general managers or senior functional managers) meet for lengthy discussions with

## Box 17.3  Issues in Effective Change Management

- Change programmes must be championed.

- There needs to be a clear purpose to which people can subscribe … which can be justified and defended.

- The change proposals will not be backed by everyone.

- Managers must decide how much to communicate and when – there are dangers in both inadequate information provision and in being too open and candid.

- Senior managers must take responsibility; while empowerment is important, people still need effective leadership.

- Effective change management frequently involves well-led teams and may require process or even structural change.

- Creating and broadcasting early successes speeds up the process, especially as

programmes often lose momentum part-way through.

- Setbacks must be anticipated and managed, and the momentum maintained.

- It is dangerous to claim victory too quickly; the changes must become anchored in the culture.

- The feelings of people who might be hurt by the changes must not be overlooked.

### Sources

Eccles, T (1994) *Succeeding With Change*, McGraw-Hill.

Kotter, JP (1995) Why transformation efforts fail, *Harvard Business Review*, March–April.

---

a view to formulating proposed strategic changes. All of the managers are briefed and knowledgeable, and the aim is to reach decisions to which they will all be committed. Strategies agreed at the meetings are then implemented by the managers who have been instrumental in their formulation. While this approach involves several managers it is still primarily centralized.

- The strategic leader concentrates on establishing and communicating a clear mission and purpose for the organization. He or she seeks to pursue this through a decentralized structure by developing an appropriate organization culture and establishing an organization-wide unity of purpose. While the strategic leader will retain responsibility for changes in the strategic perspective, decisions concerning competitive and functional strategy changes are decentralized to general and functional managers who are constrained by the mission, culture, policies and financial resources established by the strategic leader.

- Managers throughout the organization are widely encouraged to be innovative and come up with new ideas for change. The strategic leader establishes a framework for evaluating these proposals – recognizing that those which are accepted and resourced result in increased status for the managers concerned.

Ghoshal and Caulkin (1998) express a concern that major and dramatic change is often associated with charismatic and tough strategic leaders who attract and reward ambitious high-flying managers who, like them, are willing to subscribe to a dehumanizing style of management to drive through the changes. There is 'a lot of change, a lot of stress and a lot of fear'. Instead, they argue, organizations need either people who can

exercise power robustly but with wisdom, passion and constraint or checks to ensure that people are not forgotten in the drive for change.

Ideas for change, of course, can start at the bottom of the organization rather than always at the top; and change can be seen as both a clearly managed process and the incremental outcome of the decisions taken in an innovative, change-orientated organization where managers are empowered.

These basic approaches highlight a number of general themes and ideas, which are considered below.

### 17.3.1 Top-down strategic change

A number of approaches can be involved in drawing up the strategic plans for the organization, but here changes in strategy are ultimately centralized decisions. This approach can be both popular and viable as long as the strategies that are selected can be implemented effectively. It was mentioned earlier that resistance can be expected if managers who are charged with carrying out changes in strategy feel that there are flaws in the proposals. It is important to ensure that the appropriate level of consultation takes place during formulation.

Capable managers are needed throughout the organization to deal with operational issues, and the quality of the information systems which underpin the planning is a crucial issue. The approach is attractive to strategic leaders who are inclined more towards the analytical aspects of strategy than they are towards behavioural issues.

### 17.3.2 Quinn's incremental model

While Quinn's model is another primarily top-down approach it suggests a high degree of political skill on the part of the strategic leader, who appreciates the difficulties involved in implementing change. These skills are discussed in detail towards the end of the chapter.

Quinn (1988) argues that the hardest part of strategic management is implementation as transition and change impact structures and systems, organization culture and power relationships. The strategic leader is critical in the process because he or she is either personally or ultimately responsible for the proposed changes in strategy, and for establishing the structure and processes within the organization.

Quinn's approach is as follows:

- The strategic leader will develop his or her own informal information and communication channels, both within and external to the organization, and will draw on this as much as using the formal systems.

- The strategic leader must generate *awareness* of the desired change with the appropriate managers within the organization. This involves communication and cultural issues.

- The strategic leader will seek to legitimize the new approach or strategy, lending it authority, if not, at this stage, credibility.

- He or she will then seek to gather key supporters for the approach or strategy.

- The new strategy may be floated as a minor tactical change to minimize resistance, and possibly keep the ultimate aim unclear. Alternatively, the strategy may be floated as a trial or experiment.

- Opposition will be removed by, for example, ensuring that supporters chair key committees, and that stubborn opponents are moved to other parts of the organization.

- The strategy will be flexible so that incremental changes can be made in the light of the trials. There will be a strong element of learning by doing, so that any unexpected resource limitations, such as a shortage of key skills, will be highlighted.

- Support for the change will harden.

- The proposals will be crystallized and focused.

- Finally, the proposed changes will be formalized and ideally accepted within the organization. This should involve honest evaluation and attempts to improve upon the original ideas. It is particularly important to look ahead and consider how the new strategy might be developed further in the future.

Quinn's approach incorporates an appreciation of the likely impact upon people and the culture, and pragmatically searches for a better way of doing things once the decision to change has been made.

### 17.3.4 Empowerment and change

To sustain a culture of change employees must be empowered, but not everyone is comfortable with added responsibilities and accountability. They are risk averse, and again, resistance can be expected. It would seem inevitable that change-focused organizations will be happy to see such people leave, for while they stay they constitute barriers to change. They actively seek to prevent changes which may be essential for the future of the business. Unfortunately, many of these people are likely to be very experienced and knowledgeable, and their underlying expertise is valuable. Their expertise might also be useful – at least temporarily – to a competitor, and for this reason there may be a reluctance to release them.

Empowerment cannot succeed without an appropriate reward system to support it. Financial rewards will remain important, but they are not the complete answer. People must not be rewarded simply because they are holding down a particular job or position; part of their pay must be based on their measured contribution. Outstanding performers must be rewarded for their continuing efforts, and as organizations are increasingly flattened, with fewer layers in the hierarchy, a series of promotions no longer provides the answer.

Empowered middle managers are critically important for the effective management of strategic change, but all too often they are hostile because of fear and uncertainty in a culture of blame. Mistakes are not tolerated, and people are reluctant to take risks. Such managers are portrayed as villains, when really it is the organizational climate which is making them victims. Change and empowerment will only happen when managers are not afraid to 'unfreeze and learn'.

Organizations can benefit from developing people, building their abilities and self-confidence and then providing them with greater stimulation and challenge. Success will yield the opportunity to take on more responsibility. Initially the organization motivates them but they become increasingly self-motivated. Part of their reward package is their enhanced reputation in a successful business, together with increased informal power and influence. They develop the ability to foster and champion innovation and change – strategic changes which they *own*.

A culture of innovation and gradual but continuous change will impact mainly on competitive and functional strategies – the lowest two levels of the hierarchy featured in Table 17.1 earlier. Clearly, they also support corporate strategic changes which may themselves be emergent in nature or the outcome of either a visionary or a planning mode of strategy creation.

### 17.3.5   Organizational development and innovation

The basic underlying theme of organizational development (OD) is that developing an appropriate organizational culture will generate desirable changes in strategy.

Beckhard (1969) defined OD as effort which is 'planned, organization-wide, and managed from the top, designed to increase organizational effectiveness and health through planned interventions in the organization's processes, using behavioural science knowledge'.

OD is, in essence, planned cultural change. The model which has been used to provide the structure for this book shows strategic leadership and culture as being central to both strategic awareness and decision-making. The appreciation by managers of the effectiveness of the current match between resources and the environment, their ability and willingness to make adaptive changes to capitalize on environmental changes, and the formulation and implementation of major changes in corporate strategy are all influenced by the culture of the organization and the style of strategic leadership. Hence, it is crucial for the strategic leader to develop the appropriate culture for the mission and purpose that he or she wishes to pursue. OD helps to develop a co-operative and innovative culture.

The aim of OD is to establish mechanisms that encourage managers to be more open, participative and co-operative when dealing with problems and making decisions. Specifically, the objectives are:

- improved organizational effectiveness and, as a result
- higher profits and better customer service (in its widest context)
- more effective decision-making
- the ability to make and manage changes more smoothly
- increased innovation
- reduced conflict and destructive political activity
- greater trust and collaboration between managers and business units.

Organized OD programmes involve activities such as team building and collaborative decision-making, bringing managers together and encouraging them to share and discuss problems and issues. The thinking is that when managers learn more about the problems facing the organization as a whole, and about other managers who may have different technical or functional perspectives, they become more aware of the impact of the decisions that they make. In addition, if they collaborate and share responsibilities, they are more likely to feel committed to joint decisions.

While one aim is to change the attitudes and behaviour of people in organizations, OD can also allow and encourage the same people to initiate and implement changes through their discussions. Establishing the programmes is likely to involve outside experts who can be seen as objective. OD programmes are not normally a response to

specific problems but rather a general approach to the management of change in the longer term.

Given that one idea behind OD is collaboration and collective responsibility, a key theme is the reduction of conflict between managers, functions, business units or divisions within the organization. A reduction in the use of manipulative styles of management, or dysfunctional political activity, whereby managers pursue personal goals in preference to the wider needs of the organization, is also implied. Functional and dysfunctional political activity is explored in the last section of this chapter, which looks at the bases and uses of power by managers.

## 17.4 Transformational change and strategic regeneration

Powerful environmental issues such as deregulation, globalization, lower trade barriers and economic recessions have combined in the 1990s and beyond to place enormous change pressures on companies. The individual significance of these issues will vary from year to year but, in aggregate terms, the outcome is an increasingly turbulent and uncertain business environment for most organizations, private and public sector, manufacturing and service, large and small, profit-seeking and not-for-profit.

Companies have responded. Many have sought to manage their assets and strategic resources more efficiently and effectively – again the lowest two levels of the change hierarchy. Some have restructured; others have radically changed their processes through business process re-engineering.

However, continuous improvement to an organization's *competitive* capabilities, essential as it is, will not always be sufficient to meet these pressures.

Tom Peters (1992) argues that for some companies the challenge is 'not just about a *programme* of change … strategies and structures need to change perpetually'. Peter Drucker (1993) agrees and contends that 'every organization must prepare to abandon everything it does'. Both authors are implying wholesale corporate renewal or reinvention, which we call transformational change. The terms 'strategic regeneration' and 'discontinuous change' are synonymous.

Successful transformation requires both an external and an internal focus. Externally, organizations must search for new product, new service and new market opportunities, working with suppliers, distributors and customers to redefine markets and industries. Internally, structures, management styles and cultures must be capable of creating and delivering these products and services. Innovation is dependent on processes and people. Strategic awareness, information management and change are critically important if the organization is to outperform its competitors.

Achieving this position may require *simultaneous* changes to corporate strategies and perspectives, organization structures and styles of management. In order to implement **transformational change**, Goss *et al.* (1993) insist that companies must be able to change their *context* – 'the underlying assumptions and invisible premises on which their decisions and actions are based'. Their 'inner nature or being' must be altered. Managers must learn how to think strategically, and be open to new paradigms and perspectives. The requirement is that they change what the company is and not simply the things that it does. Companies are being challenged with changing all the levels of the change hierarchy simultaneously, a huge and complex task for any organization.

Incremental change at the competitive and functional level, trying harder and searching for improvements, must appear to offer an easier, less painful route. The

fundamental question is: alone, is it enough to meet the strategic demands of the contemporary business environment?

Some of the international companies featured in this book have clearly attempted to tackle these important challenges. British Airways (BA) realized in the 1980s that, contrary to much popular opinion at the time, airline customers are willing to pay extra for service. The challenge lies in defining that service and differentiating successfully. BA consequently changed its strategies, structure and culture and became one of the most profitable airlines in the world. The changes at BA have proved successful, but this success has been diminished somewhat by external events post September 11. The move to a more business-orientated clientele has also come under threat from easyJet. General Electric (GE) of the USA is another example. The transformation philosophy and programme at GE is described in Minicase 17.4.

Pascale *et al.* (1997) argue that for effective transformation it is critically important that people understand the organization and its businesses – the big picture. Robust straight-talking should be encouraged to tease out the existing weaknesses in the organization as well as ideas for new opportunities. Transformation then involves 'managing from the future'. A shared purpose and direction sets the agenda. Setbacks must be harnessed in true entrepreneurial fashion. People must accept accountability but, linked to proper rewards, this should be done in an inventive way that ensures that people are engaged in the process. 'There has to be a relentless discomfort with the status quo.'

Hamel (1994) contends transformational change needs vision and perseverance. Companies must invest resources in an attempt to set the new competitive high ground first by changing the key success factors. This inevitably implies time and risk, and it must be a managed and understood process. Speculative investment in the long term must be risky because *spending precedes understanding*; companies are heading into unknown territory. However, companies which choose to avoid the risk, and rely instead on monitoring and copying competitors (such that *understanding precedes spending*) may be caught out.

Hamel cites three important barriers to effective transformational change. First, too many senior managers in an industry have related, often industry-specific, backgrounds, and this inhibits their creative thinking. Second, there are political pressures to maintain the status quo from managers who feel threatened personally, an issue that is looked at next. Third there is the sheer difficulty of creating new competitive strategies in industries that are changing dynamically, continuously and chaotically.

> *The essential prerequisite for an effective change of direction is to create a climate throughout the organization where change is regarded positively.*
>
> *Professor Hague, when he was at Manchester Business School, made the following remark which I have always remembered: 'The successful manager will expect and understand change; the outstanding manager will anticipate and create it.'*
>
> *Once the right climate exists, change must be preceded and accompanied by effective and honest communication, meaningful consultation and sound decision-making. It is not easy and requires genuine top management commitment.*
>
> Tom W Cain, once Director, Human Resources, The Channel Tunnel Group Ltd

However, Abrahamson (2000) implies that major change could be going out of fashion, unless, of course, it becomes essential. Companies that periodically reinvent themselves often face resistance, distress, disaffection and upheaval. All too often the desired or planned changes are not implemented effectively, prompting another pro-

# Minicase 17.4  Transformational Change at General Electric (GE)   US

John F (Jack) Welch became Chief Executive Officer at General Electric in 1981. His structural vision was summarized earlier, in Minicase 16.1. This case describes 'one of the most far-reaching programmes of innovation in business history'.

The programme involved three stages:

1. *Awakening* – the realization of the need for change
2. *Envisioning* – establishing a new vision and harnessing resources
3. *Re-architecting* – the design and construction of a new organization.

Although Welch was the identified strategic leader, several committed senior managers worked together to drive through the cultural changes.

GE has been restructured, and clear progress has been made, but the process of change continues.

## GE in the early 1980s – the need for change

The company had sound assets, reflected in a strong balance sheet, but it was seen as bureaucratic and heavily focused on the US. It was not technologically advanced and it clearly needed a more international perspective.

Specific problems were diagnosed:

- Revenue growth was slow. GE's core business (electrical equipment) was particularly slow.
- As a result, expensive investments were creating cash-flow problems.
- Poor productivity was causing low profit margins.
- Innovation was limited.
- Decision-making was slow.
- Negative internal politics was rife.

## The transformation process

### Awakening
Welch realized that his first challenge was to determine which managers offered the greatest potential as transformational leaders, agents of discontinuous change.

He then sought to clarify and articulate the extent of the need for change, focusing on the above weaknesses. Resistance took three forms:

- Technical – A reliance on existing bureaucratic systems and a fear of the unknown; a distrust of international expansion.
- Political – A desire to protect existing power bases, especially where the strategic value of the particular business was declining.
- Cultural – an unwillingness to accept competitive weaknesses – overconfidence from past successes.

### Changes
- Welch forced people to benchmark competitors' performance standards and achievements, rather than rely only on internal measures and budgets.
- He also took control of external corporate communications, and
- Radically changed GE's approach to management training and development. Rigid rules and procedures about how things should be done were abolished.

### Envisioning
A new vision was developed gradually during the mid- to late 1980s, and it finally became encapsulated in a matrix. Highlights of the new vision are featured in Table 17.2.

Welch saw the technical, political and cultural systems as three strands of a rope which must be changed and realigned together.

### Re-architecting
At the heart of the vision is an 'organization without boundaries' and with an emphasis on internal and external linkages and architecture. Information must flow freely. People must be in a position – and willing – to act quickly. 'A large organization with the speed, flexibility and self-confidence of a small one.'

▶

◄

**Table 17.2** Highlights of GE's corporate vision

|  | Strategy | Structure | Management style |
|---|---|---|---|
| Technical | Focus on market (segments) where the company can be no. 1 or no. 2<br><br>Prioritize high-growth industries | Decentralized<br><br>Foster the sharing of best practices and<br>Pull down internal boundaries | Different reward systems for different businesses, dependent on needs<br><br>Continuous training and development |
| Political | Foster internal and external alliances to harness synergy potential | Flatter, open structure to remove power bases<br><br>Cross-function and cross-business development teams<br>Empowerment to lowest levels of management | Flexible reward systems<br><br>'360 degree evaluations' from superiors, peers and subordinates |
| Cultural | Speedy change to strategies<br><br>Intrapreneurial, innovative, incremental and adaptive change – as a result of – learning from upward, downward and lateral communications | Corporate values but individual business cultures and styles | Track attitudes and values – commitment to customers and quality – and to outperforming competitors |

A number of boundaries had to be removed as part of the Implementation process:

■ vertical/hierarchical – management layers were removed. Welch introduced performance incentives for many more managers and employees; in the past GE had focused on only senior executives

■ horizontal/internal walls – cross-functional project teams were created

■ external – there was a new emphasis on the whole supply or added value chain, alliances were forged with suppliers; customer satisfaction levels were tracked.

Removing these boundaries clearly required radical changes to the ways in which people worked together, made decisions and carried out tasks. Welch believed that the changes must be inspired from the top and that any senior managers who resisted the new style 'would have to go'.

## Reference

Adapted from Tichy, NM (1993) Revolutionize your company, *Fortune*, 13 December.

## Question

1. This case has described a major programme of change and transformation, championed by an exceptional strategic leader, Jack Welch. While it has been reported extensively, and 'the world' knows what Welch has set out to do and what he has achieved, few organizations have been able to replicate his achievement. So how valuable might our insight really be?
2. Why would a programme of this scale and ambition be difficult to replicate?

**General Electric** http://www.ge.com

gramme of change. Abrahamson therefore recommends *'dynamic stability'* – continuous tinkering with existing businesses, alternating occasional major changes with several incremental ones. His research suggests that:

- First, copying can prove very rewarding – there is no need always to be first. This point, though, needs careful interpretation. It is true that major leaps forward can be uncomfortable and disruptive for both customers and employees, and the competitors who follow when the situation has settled down again can enjoy the benefits without incurring the risk of the pioneer. However, sustained competitive advantage often comes from staying just ahead of rivals with constant innovation and leadership. It is a matter of degree.

- Second, home-grown processes are invariably more acceptable culturally than those imported from another country with an 'alien' culture.

Clearly, organizations need to ensure that they change in accordance with real external pressures and to recognize that good ideas can always be found by monitoring the world's best performers. They need to acquire and use this knowledge to craft something that can work for them.

Box 17.4 provides a summary framework for managing transformational change.

## Box 17.4  Twelve Steps in Transformational Change

1. Recognize the scale of the challenge and don't ignore it.
2. Consider where the barriers to change might be strongest.
3. Build a guiding team and establish any necessary partnerships.
4. Establish a sense of urgency and bring the challenge and the issues to the attention of others.
5. Clarify a clear strategic direction or 'vision' for the transformation. This would include a defined business model, key values and drivers and recognition of the relevant strategic competencies required.
6. Communicate this vision, taking ownership and responsibility for it.
7. Seize the initiative as far as barriers to change are concerned.
8. Empower others to act on the vision. Emphasize the need for innovation, emergence and intrapreneurship. The idea is to involve people as widely as possible so the drive to change becomes systemic.
9. Seek to generate short-term wins – which can be publicized and used as a vehicle to reward the change-drivers.
10. Consolidate these short-term wins to increase and maintain the momentum.
11. Monitor and evaluate performance and achievements on an ongoing basis.
12. 'Institutionalize' the changes.

### References

This list of 12 steps has been developed from a number of separate sources, including:

Francis D, Bessant J and Hobday M (2003) Managing radical organizational transformation, *Management Decision*, 41 (1).
Kotter JP (1995) Why transformation efforts fail, *Harvard Business Review*, March–April.

KEY CONCEPTS

## 17.5 Power and politics

*The greatest leader is the one who enables people to say:*
*'We did it ourselves'.*

Chinese proverb attributed to Lao-Tsu

*A leader can stop an organization in its tracks but he can't turn it around on his own. In a year you can change things at a superficial level, using the charismatic model, but you need five to change the culture.*

Morpeth Headmaster, Alasdair Macdonald, discussing change in secondary schools

The management of change requires that managers have the requisite power to implement decisions and that they are able to exert influence. There are several bases of power, both organizational and individual, which constitute resources for managers. The processes that they adopt for utilizing these power bases, their styles of management, determine their success in influencing others. The ability of managers to exert power and influence is manifested in a number of ways, including:

- budgets
- rewards
- organization structure and positions
- promotions and management development
- information systems
- symbols of power and status.

Managers who regularly attempt to get things done, both with and through other people, and introduce changes, have the problem of generating agreement, consent or at least compliance with what should be done, how and when. Typically, opinions and perspectives will differ. Disagreements may or may not be significant, and can range from the polite and friendly to those involving threats and coercion. Each side, quite simply, is attempting to influence the conduct of the other. In this section we consider the power resources that managers are able to use and how they might use them.

Checkland (1986) defines organizational politics as the process by which differing interests reach *accommodation* – a word that he chooses deliberately and in preference to consensus. These accommodations relate to the dispositions and use of power and influence, and behaviour which is not prescribed by the policies established within the organization. It will be shown later that political activity by managers in order to influence others, and ensure that their decisions and strategies are carried out, is essential. Politics can be legitimate and positive, although it can also be more negative and illegitimate. In the latter case managers are seeking to influence others in order to achieve their personal goals. This is often described as machiavellianism and is discussed at the end of this section.

### 17.5.1 The relative power of the organization

The need for change is affected by the relative power and influence of external stakeholders in relation to the organization. Powerful customers, powerful suppliers and changes in government legislation would all represent potential threats and demands for change. In turn, the management and implementation of change is affected by the

relative power of the organization. Some proposed strategies can be implemented because the organization possesses the appropriate power to acquire the resources which are needed and to generate consumer demand. Others may not be feasible.

At the same time the decisions taken within organizations concerning changes of corporate, competitive and functional strategies are influenced by the disposition of relative power between functions, business units or divisions, and the ways in which managers seek to use power and influence.

Internal and external sources of power are discussed further in Box 17.5, based on the work of Mintzberg (1983).

## Box 17.5 Internal and External Sources of Power

Mintzberg (1983) contends that it is essential to consider both internal and external sources of power, and their relative significance, when assessing the demands for, and feasibility of, certain strategic changes.

The organization's stakeholders will vary in terms of their relative power and the ways in which they exert influence. The interests of the owners of the firm, for example, are legally represented by the board of directors. While large institutional shareholders may exert considerable influence over certain decisions, many private shareholders will take no active part. Employees may be represented by external trade unions, who again may or may not exert influence.

The power relationships between the firm and its stakeholders are determined by the importance and scarcity of the resource in question. The more essential and limited the supply of the resource, the greater the power the resource provider has over the firm. According to Mintzberg these external power groups may be focused and their interests pulled together by a dominant power, or they may be fragmented.

Where there are very strong external influences, the organization may seek to establish close co-operation or mutual dependence, or attempt to reduce its dependence on the power source. The historic relationship between Marks and Spencer and many of its suppliers is a good example of mutual dependence of this nature. Marks and Spencer encouraged many of their clothing suppliers to invest in the latest technology for design and manufacturing in order that they can both succeed against international competi-

tion. Marks and Spencer have typically been the largest customer of their suppliers, buying substantial quantities as long as both demand and quality are maintained. However, it is important that their suppliers are aware of fashion changes because they bear the risk of overproduction and changes in taste.

Internal power is linked to the structure of the organization. It is manifested in four ways:

- the personal control system of the strategic leadership
- rules, policies and procedures
- political activities external to these two factors
- cultural ideologies that influence decision-makers.

External and internal power sources combine to determine a dominant source of power at any time, and Mintzberg suggests six possibilities:

- *a key external source*, such as a bank or supplier, or possibly the government as, say, a key buyer of defence equipment – the objectives of the source would normally be clearly stated and understood
- *the operation of the organization structure*, and the strategies and activities of general and functional managers who are allocated the scarce resources: the relative power of business units is influenced by the market demand for their products and services, but generally external sources exert indirect rather than direct influence; functional managers can

enjoy power if they are specialists and their skills are in short supply

■ *strong central leadership*

■ *ideologies* – certain organizations, such as charities or volunteer organizations, are often dominated by the underlying ideologies related to helping others

■ *professional constraints* – accountants' and solicitors' practices, for example, have established codes of professional practice which dictate and influence behaviour. On occasions this can raise interesting issues for decision-makers. A frequently used example is the television journalist or news editor working for the BBC or ITN and able to influence reporting strategies and policies. When assessing sensitive issues does the person see himself or herself as a BBC or ITN employee or as a professional journalist, and do the two perspectives coincide or conflict?

■ *active conflict* between power sources seeking dominance: while this can involve either or both internal and external sources it is likely to be temporary, as organizations cannot normally survive prolonged conflict.

The dominant source of power becomes a key feature of the organizational culture, and a major influence on manager behaviour and decision-making.

### Reference

The source of the basic arguments is Mintzberg, H (1983) *Power In and Around Organizations*, Prentice-Hall.

### 17.5.2  Political activity

Farrell and Petersen (1982) classify political activity in terms of three dimensions:

■ legitimate or illegitimate
■ vertical or lateral
■ internal or external to the organization.

For example, a complaint or suggestion by an employee directly to a senior manager, bypassing an immediate superior, would be classified as legitimate, vertical and internal. Discussions with fellow managers from other companies within an industry would be legitimate, lateral and external, unless they involved any illegal activities such as price fixing. Informal communications and agreements between managers are again legitimate, while threats or attempts at sabotage are clearly illegitimate.

Power and politics are key aspects of strategy implementation because they can enable managers to be proactive and to influence their environment rather than being dominated and manipulated by external events. The issues affect managers at all levels of the organization and decisions concerning both internal and external changes.

### 17.5.3  The bases of power

Seven bases of manager power were introduced and described in Chapter 7: reward, coercive, legitimate, personal, expert, information and connection. The extent to which managers and other employees in organizations use each of these sources of power is a major determinant of corporate culture.

*Reward and coercive power* (the ability to sanction and punish) are two major determinants of employee motivation, and both can be very significant strategically. Thompson and Strickland (1981) argue that motivation is brought about primarily by

the reward and punishment systems in the organization; and Blanchard and Johnson (1982) suggest that effective management involves three key aspects: establishing clear objectives for employees, and rewarding and sanctioning performance against objectives appropriately. Strategic leaders who dominate their organizations and coerce their senior managers can be effective, particularly when the organization is experiencing decline and major changes in strategy are urgently required.

*Legitimate power* is determined primarily by the organization structure, and consequently changes in structure will affect the power, influence and significance of different business units, functions and individual managers.

*Personal power*, which can lead to the commitment of others to the power holder, can be very important in incremental changes. Managers who are supported and trusted by their colleagues and subordinates will find it easier to introduce and implement changes.

*Expert power* can also be useful in persuading others that proposed changes in strategy are feasible and desirable. While expert power may not be real, and instead be power gained from reputation, it is unlikely that managers who genuinely lack expertise can be successful without other power bases. Moreover, expertise is job related. An expert specialized accountant, for example, may lose expert power temporarily if he or she is promoted to general manager. Consequently, an important tactic in the management of change is to ensure that those managers who are perceived to be expert in the activity or function concerned are supportive of the proposed changes.

*Information* and related *connection power* are becoming increasingly significant as IT grows in importance.

These seven power bases are all visible sources. There is, in addition, *invisible power*. One source of invisible power is the way in which an issue or proposal is presented, which can influence the way it is dealt with. Managers who appreciate the objectives, perspectives and concerns of their colleagues will present their ideas in ways that are likely to generate their support rather than opposition. Membership of informal, but influential, coalitions or groups of managers can be a second source of power, particularly if the people involved feel dependent on each other. Third, information that would create opposition to a decision or change proposal might be withheld. In the same way that access to key information can be a positive power source, the ability to prevent other people obtaining information can be either a positive or a negative source of power.

Lukes (1974) has identified three further important aspects of power, namely:

- the ability to prevent a decision, or not make one
- the ability to control the issues on which decisions are to be made
- the ability to ensure that certain issues are kept off agendas.

The use of such power by individuals can inhibit changes which might in the long-term be in the best interests of the organization.

### 17.5.4  Political effectiveness

Hayes (1984) contends that effective managers appreciate clearly what support they will need from other people if proposed changes are to be carried through, and what they will have to offer in return. In such cases they reach agreements (or accommodations) which provide mutual advantages. It is important for the organization as a whole that general and functional managers are effective and politically competent if personal

**Table 17.3** Political power bases and tactics

| Bases of personal power | |
|---|---|
| Expertise | Particularly significant where the skill is in scarce supply |
| | It is possible to use mobility, and the threat of leaving, to gain support for certain changes of strategy – again dependent upon the manager's personal importance to the firm |
| Assessed stature | A reputation for being a winner or a manager who can obtain results. Recent successes are most relevant |
| Credibility | Particularly credibility with external power sources, such as suppliers or customers |
| Political access | Being well known around the organization and able to influence key groups of managers |
| Control over information | Internal and external sources |
| | Information can be used openly and honestly or withheld and used selectively – consequently, it is crucial to know the reliability of the source |
| Group support | In managing and implementing change it is essential to have the support of colleagues and fellow managers |
| **Political tactics to obtain results** | |
| Develop liaisons | As mentioned above, it is important to develop and maintain both formal and informal contacts with other managers, functions and divisions |
| | Again, it is important to include those managers who are most powerful |
| Present a conservative image | It can be disadvantageous to be seen as too radical an agent of change |
| Diffuse opposition | Conflicts need to be brought out into the open and differences of opinion aired rather than kept hidden. Divide and rule can be a useful strategy |
| Trade-off and compromise | In any proposal or suggestion for change it is important to consider the needs of other people whose support is required |
| Strike while the iron is hot | Successful managers should build on successes and reputation quickly |
| Research | Information is always vital to justify and support proposals |
| Use a neutral cover | Radical changes, or those that other people might perceive as a threat to them, can sometimes be usefully disguised and initiated as minor changes. This is linked to the next point |
| Limit communication | A useful tactic can be to unravel change gradually in order to contain possible opposition |
| Withdraw strategically | If things are going wrong, and especially if the changes are not crucial, it can be a wise tactic on occasions to withdraw, at least temporarily |

- Politically successful managers understand organizational processes and they are sensitive to the needs of others.
- Effective political action brings about desirable and successful changes in organizations – it is functional.
- Negative political action is dysfunctional, and can enable manipulative managers to pursue their personal objectives against the better interests of the organization.
- The strategic leader needs to be an effective politician.

Sources: Allen, RW, Madison, DL, Porter, LW, Renwick, PA and Mayes, BT (1979) Organisational politics: tactics and characteristics of its actors. *California Management Review*, 22, Fall and Dixon, M (1982) The world of office politics, *Financial Times*, 10 November.

objectives are to be restrained and undesirable changes, championed by individual managers, prevented. Problems can occur where some managers are politically effective and able to implement change, and others are relatively ineffective and reach agreements with other managers whereby their personal interests, and the interests of the organization, are adversely affected.

Allen *et al.* (1979) and Dixon (1982) point out that certain sources of personal power are essential for managers who are effective politically and able to influence others. In addition, they suggest certain tactics for managing change. These are featured in Table 17.3. It is important that managers are perceived by others to have expertise and ability, and it is useful if they have a reputation built on past successes. Depending on the relative power of outside stakeholders, such as suppliers or customers, external credibility can also prove valuable. It is essential to have access to information and to other powerful individuals and groups of managers.

It can be a disadvantage for a manager to be perceived as a radical agent of change, as this can arouse fear and uncertainty, possibly leading to opposition, in others. As discussed earlier, it can sometimes be valuable to implement a change of strategy gradually and incrementally, allowing people to make adaptive changes as the learning experience develops. At the same time it is important to ensure that opposition is manifested and brought out into the open rather than being allowed to develop without other people being aware.

Managers who are effective and successful politically, and able to implement their decisions and proposed changes, will generally appreciate and understand organizational processes and be sensitive to the needs of others. It is extremely useful if the strategic leader is an able politician. The type and incidence of incremental changes in strategies throughout the organization will also be affected by the political ability of managers. Those with ability will be instrumental in introducing changes. Where the strategic leader wishes to encourage managers to be adaptive and innovative it is important to consider the political ability of the managers concerned. Political ability relates to the use of power and influence in the most appropriate way in particular circumstances. This is the subject of the next section.

## 17.5.5 Uses of power and influence

MacMillan (1978) argues that introducing and implementing change frequently requires the use of power and influence, which he examines in terms of the control of situations and the ability to change people's intentions. Where a person wishes to exercise control over the behaviour of other people, either within the organization or external to it, he or she has two basic options. First, they can *structure the situation* so that others comply with their wishes; second, by communicating with other people, they can seek to change their perceptions so that they see things differently and decide to do as the manager suggests. In other words he or she succeeds in *changing their intentions*. Both of these approaches are categorized as strategies of manipulation.

Where a manager is concentrating on structuring the situation they are using certain power bases as enabling resources; where they are attempting to change intentions they are seeking to use influence. Power, in particular personal power, is again important as a source of influence.

The outcome from both the situational and intentional approaches can be either positive or negative. When the effect is positive the other people feel that they are better off as a result of the changes; the effect is negative if they feel worse off.

MacMillan identifies four tactics in relation to these points:

- *Inducement* – this implies an ability to control the situation, and the outcome is perceived as beneficial by others involved. A large retail organization with several stores might require managers to be mobile as a condition of their employment, and reward them with improved status, salary increases and relocation expenses every time they move. The situation is controlled; ideally the managers concerned feel positive about the moves.

- *Coercion* – the situation is again controlled, but the outcome is perceived negatively. In the above situation the same managers might be threatened with no further promotions unless they agreed to certain moves within the company.

- *Persuasion* – the manager does not try to control or change the situation but argues that the other people can or will benefit by behaving in certain ways. The desired outcome is positive. People might be persuaded to agree to a change which is not immediately desirable by suggestions that future rewards will be forthcoming.

- *Obligation* – this is another intentional tactic, but the outcome is negative. People are persuaded to behave in a certain way by being made to feel that they have an obligation. It might be suggested that people
  - owe the company something for the money that has been invested in their previous training, or
  - owe particular managers a favour for something that has happened in the past, or
  - are obligated to the group of people that they have been working with for some years and should not let them down.

In particular cases, individual managers may or may not have a number of alternative tactics to select from. Tactics that have positive outcomes must normally be preferable to those that cause negative feelings if both are available and likely to yield the desired results. At times managers whose power bases are limited and who need speedy results may have little option but to coerce or obligate people. Kanter (1983) emphasizes that successful managers of change situations are able to keep their power invisible both during and after the change. Participation in the change is then perceived to stem from commitment or conviction rather than from power being exercised over people. Kanter contends that it is very important for middle managers in organizations to be skilful in managing change as they implement the detailed strategies, and that it is important for strategic leaders to ensure that they have support from their middle managers for the overall corporate strategy.

### 17.5.6 Organizational politics and culture

Culture broadly encapsulates manifest actions and behaviours and underlying beliefs, and effective cultural change must include both (see Chapter 7). Where this happens, there will be willing support for, and compliance with, the change. Without a change in beliefs, compliance will be reluctant. Strong, political managers who oppose the changes will show either covert or even overt non-compliance, their choice reflecting their style and power.

Bartlett and Ghoshal (1995) argue that the radical and forced downsizing of the early 1990s left many companies with a context of 'compliance, control, contract and constraint'. Behaviours have changed, but not beliefs; elements of the old culture remain to

create confusion. The challenge for these companies is one of creativity and innovation; they must find ways of adding new values for competitive advantage, which will require a context of support, trust and liberation, and a willingness to accept stretching objectives, alongside appropriate control disciplines.

### 17.5.7  Organizational politics and ethics

It is clear that managers can use political behaviour both for and against the best interests of the organization; at the same time, they can also behave either ethically or unethically. Positive and ethical behaviour is required to satisfy all the stakeholders effectively; negative politics, while ethical, implies that internal stakeholders (maybe even individual managers and functions) receive priority over external stakeholders. Positive politicking which is unethical may well appear successful in the short term, but possibly with a long-term downside risk. Where negative politics combine with unethical behaviour, there is likely to be corruption.

### 17.5.8  Machiavellianism

**Machiavellianism** is the term often used to describe coercive management tactics. Marriott (1908), translating Machiavelli's book *The Prince*, written in the sixteenth century, uses the expression to cover 'the ruthless use of power, particularly coercive power, and manipulation to attain personal goals'. While coercive power can be used effectively by managers it may not always be easy to justify, especially if other alternatives are available. Coercion may not be practical on a repeat basis, and any fear of threats not carried out quickly recedes.

Jay (1967), however, contends that Machiavelli also offers much useful advice for ethical managers. Basing his arguments on Machiavelli's views on strategies and tactics for annexing and ruling nations, Jay argues that chief executive strategic leaders should concentrate their efforts outside the organization, developing and strengthening the strategic perspective. In order for them to feel able to do this, the internal structure and systems must be sound and effective, and managers must be supportive of proposals from the top. General and functional managers should be free to operate and feel able to make certain changes, but their overall power should be contained. They should exercise leadership, which is based on power. This power yields the freedom to decide how things should be done. Managers, though, should be afraid to pursue personal goals against the interest of the organization as a whole. Achieving this requires a clear awareness of what is happening throughout the organization and the appropriate punishment of offenders. Successful managers should be rewarded.

Pearce and DeNisi (1983) stress that most organizations are managed partially by informal coalitions or groupings of managers superimposed on the formal structure. It is particularly important that managers in key positions in the organization, those in charge of important resources or responsible for products upon which the profits or reputation of the organization depend, are known to be committed and loyal to the strategic leader. Moreover, any informal and powerful coalitions that develop should also be supportive. To achieve both of these it may be appropriate for the strategic leader to remove or switch senior managers occasionally as a reminder of his or her overall power. This is particularly likely to happen after an acquisition, during a restructuring exercise, or on the appointment of a new strategic leader.

**Machiavelli** © Archivo Iconografico, S.A./Corbis

Strategic coalitions can be a major force behind strategy formation, especially where the overall strategic leader is relatively weak. An effective leader will therefore seek to use coalitions that already exist, and encourage the formation of other loyal ones.

In considering the feasibility of changes and how to implement them, it is very important to examine the underlying political abilities and behaviour within the firm: who has power, how it is manifested and how it is used. Without taking these factors into account, implementation is likely to prove hazardous.

> *Machiavelli recommended that vanquished foes should be eliminated, but counselled that quite often only the King or Chief needs to be sacrificed; those spared will soon fall into line through fear.*

> *Research into hostile takeovers and acquisitions in the UK between 1990 and 1994 shows that within one year of the takeover 70 per cent of the chairmen of the acquired businesses had left; 57 per cent of the chief executives left within two years.*

> *However it could alternatively be added that in* The Godfather, *the approach of the Don would have been more ruthless to all the family members of the rival gang.*

# SUMMARY

Most organizations must compete or operate in dynamic environments where change is inevitable. Some of this will always be reactive, but the most effective organizations manage, as well as manage in, their environments. Much comes down to the strategic leader and the organization culture, which realistically drive the whole change process.

Effective *change management* requires:

- a clear perception of need – dissatisfaction with the existing status quo
- a way forward – a new direction or perceived opportunity
- the capability to change – the necessary resources
- commitment – change needs managing.

A four-stage cycle of change can be identified: beginning with a creative idea, an opportunity is nurtured before an action stage grows the business. Structure follows to provide control. At this time it is important to find new ideas to maintain the cycle of growth.

There is a number of *levels* of change:

- the corporate culture
- the organizational mission
- corporate strategies
- organization structures, systems and processes
- competitive strategies
- operational tasks and activities.

As we ascend this hierarchy the complexity and the difficulty of the challenge increases.

A simple model of change *management* would have three stages:

- unfreezing existing behaviours
- changing behaviour
- refreezing the new behaviour as common practice.

However, there is an argument that organizations should have a culture that accepts and embraces constant change, and consequently we need to be careful about the implications of refreezing.

There are forces for and against change. There is always likely to be resistance to change – after all, people's jobs are affected and some will perceive themselves to be losing out.

Change can be *continuous*, *innovatory* and *improvemental* – on occasions it will be *discontinuous and transformational*, implying simultaneous changes to strategy, structure and style. Sometimes this is essential, but it can be very disruptive and unsettling for people.

Change management cannot be separated from *power*. Power and influence are required to engineer and effect change – they may also be used in an attempt to stop it. There are two key dimensions: the relative power of the organization in respect of its external environment; and the relative power of different businesses, divisions, departments and individuals within the organization itself.

There are seven key *power bases*: reward, coercive, legitimate, personal, expert, information and connection.

The way that individuals use power and influence is a manifestation of their political abilities. *Organizational politics* can be positive if it is used to carry through and implement decisions that are clearly in the interests of the organization. Negative politics is the tool of machiavellian managers who are minded to pursue self-interest at the expense of other colleagues and maybe at the expense of the whole organization.

## QUESTIONS AND RESEARCH ASSIGNMENTS

1. Describe an event where you have personally experienced forces for change, and discuss any forces that were used to resist the change. What tactics were adopted on both sides?

2. Describe a strategic leader (any level in an organization of your choice) whom you consider to be a powerful person. What types of power does he or she possess?

3. Describe a manager whom you believe is successful at using organizational politics. On what observations and experiences are you basing your decision? How might you measure political effectiveness and the elements within it?

4. As a manager, what are your personal power bases? How politically effective are you? How could you increase your overall power and improve your effectiveness?

## INTERNET AND LIBRARY PROJECTS

1. Select an industry or company and ascertain the forces that have brought about changes in the last ten years. How proactive/reactive have the companies been, and with what levels of success?

2. Analyse the news broadcasts of two rival TV networks, such as the BBC and ITN, or Sky and CNN, and evaluate whether their reporting of industrial and business news is similar or dissimilar. Are they reporting to inform or to persuade about, say, the merits or demerits of government policy? To what extent are they constrained by government?

3. Research and update the Apple Computers case.

How would you evaluate:

(a) The contribution of Steve Jobs?

(b) Jobs as a strategic leader?

(c) Whether Apple is now less crisis prone than it was and more in control of the change agenda?

4. As well as acting as an occasional consultant to Apple, co-founder Steve Wozniak has started two new businesses, one in the 1980s and another in the last few years. How successful were these businesses? Does this picture of Wozniak affect your views on the role and contribution of Steve Jobs?

## Further reading

Salancik, GR and Pfeffer, J (1977) Who gets power – and how they hold on to it: a strategic-contingency model of power, *Organizational Dynamics*, Winter.

Quinn, J (1980) Managing strategic change, *Sloan Management Review*, Summer.

Bourgeois, LJ and Brodwin, DR (1984) Strategy implementation – five approaches to an elusive phenomenon, *Strategic Management Journal*, 5.

Goss, T, Pascale, R and Athos, A (1993) The re-invention roller coaster – risking the present for a powerful future, *Harvard Business Review*, November–December.

Richardson, WA (1994) Comprehensive approach to strategic management – leading across the strategic management domain, *Management Decision*, 32 (8).

Bartlett, C and Ghoshal, S (1994) Beyond strategy to purpose, *Harvard Business Review*, November–December.

Kotter, JP (1995) Why transformation efforts fail, *Harvard Business Review*, March–April.

Hamel, G (1996) Strategy as revolution, *Harvard Business Review*, July–August.

Tichy, N (1996) Simultaneous transformation and CEO succession – key to global competitiveness, *Organizational Dynamics*, Summer.

Pascale, R *et al.* (1997) Changing the way we change, *Harvard Business Review*, November–December.

Abrahamson, E (2000) Dynamic stability, *Harvard Business Review*, January–February.

Francis, D *et al.* (2003) Managing radical organisational transformation, *Management Decision*, 41 (1).

# References

Abrahamson, E (2000) Dynamic stability, *Harvard Business Review*, January–February.

Argyris, C and Schön, D (1978) *Organization Learning: A Theory of Action Perspective,* Addison Wesley.

Allen, RW, Madison, DL, Porter, LW, Renwick, PA and Mayes, BT (1979) Organisational politics: tactics and characteristics of its actors, *California Management Review*, 22, Fall.

Bartlett, C and Ghoshal, S (1995) Rebuilding behavioural context: turn process re-engineering into people rejuvenation, *Sloan Management Review*, Autumn.

Beckhard, R (1969) *Organisation Development: Strategies and Models*, Addison-Wesley.

Blanchard, K and Johnson, S (1982) *The One Minute Manager*, Morrow.

Blanchard, K and Waghorn, T (1997) *Mission Possible*, McGraw Hill.

Bourgeois, LJ and Brodwin, DR (1984) Strategic implementation: five approaches to an elusive phenomenon, *Strategic Management Journal*, 5.

Buchanan, D, Clayton, T and Doyle, M (1999) Organisation development and change – the legacy of the 90s, *Human Resource Management Journal*, 9 (2).

Checkland, PB (1986) The politics of practice. Paper presented at the IIASA International Round-table 'The Art and Science of Systems Practice', November.

Daft, RL (1983) *Organisation Theory and Design*, West.

Dixon, M (1982) The world of office politics, *Financial Times*, 10 November.

Drucker, P (1993) *Managing in Turbulent Times*, Butterworth-Heinemann.

Eccles, T (1994) *Succeeding With Change*, McGraw-Hill.

Farrell, D and Petersen, JC (1982) Patterns of political behaviour in organizations, *Academy of Management Review*, 7 (3).

Ghoshal, S and Caulkin, S (1998) An escape route from ruthlessness, *Financial Times*, 18 November.

Goss, T, Pascale, R and Athos, A (1993) The reinvention roller coaster: risking the present for a powerful future, *Harvard Business Review*, November–December.

Hamel, G (1994) Competing for the Future, Economist Conference, London, June.

Hayes, J (1984) The politically competent manager, *Journal of General Management*, 10 (1).

Heifetz, R and Linsky, M (2002) *Leadership On The Line,* Harvard Business School Press.

Jay, A (1967) *Management and Machiavelli*, Holt, Rinehart & Winston.

Kanter, RM (1983) The middle manager as innovator. In *Strategic Management* (ed. RG Hamermesch), John Wiley.

Kotter, JP (1995) Why transformation efforts fail, *Harvard Business Review*, March–April.

Kotter, JP (1990) *A Force for Change: How Leadership Differs from Management,* The Free Press.

Kotter, JP and Schlesinger, LA (1979) Choosing strategies for change, *Harvard Business Review*, March–April.

Lewin, K (1947) Frontiers in group dynamics: concept, method and reality in social science, *Human Relations*, 1.

Lewin, K (1951) *Field Theory in Social Sciences*, Harper & Row.

Lukes, S (1974) *Power: A Radical View*, Macmillan.

MacMillan, IC (1978) *Strategy Formulation: Political Concepts*, West.

Margerison, C and Smith, B (1989) Shakespeare and management: managing change, *Management Decision*, 27 (2).

Marriott, WK (1908) Translation into English of *The Prince* written by N Machiavelli in the 1500s.

Mintzberg, H (1983) *Power In and Around Organisations*, Prentice-Hall.

Pascale, R, Millemann, M and Gioja, L (1997) Changing the way we change, *Harvard Business Review*, November–December.

Pearce, JA and DeNisi, AS (1983) Attribution theory and strategic decision making: an application to coalition formation, *Academy of Management Journal*, 26, March.

Peters, T (1989) Tomorrow's companies: new products, new markets, new competition, new thinking, *The Economist*, 4 March.

Peters, T (1992) *Liberation Management – Necessary Disorganization for the Nanosecond Nineties*, Macmillan.

Quinn, JB (1988) Managing strategies incrementally. In *The Strategy Process: Concepts, Contexts and Cases* (eds JB Quinn, H Mintzberg and RM James), Prentice-Hall.

Thompson, AA and Strickland, AJ (1981) *Strategy and Policy: Concept and Cases*, Business Publications.

Waterman, RH Jr (1987) *The Renewal Factor*, Bantam.

# Final Thoughts: The Purpose of Strategy

## Learning objectives

Having read to the end of this chapter you should be able to:

- understand the purpose of strategy and why we study it
- list the ten key determinants of strategy
- evaluate the relative significance of various strategic competencies for individual organizations
- revisit the key strategic paradoxes introduced in Part One and debated throughout the book
- draw up a model for a crisis-averse organization.

*Success is never final.*

Winston Churchill

*Things may come to those who wait – but only the things left by those who hustle.*

Abraham Lincoln

## 18.1 Introduction

In these last few pages the main ideas from this book are synthesized in order to reinforce the key ideas and address two questions. First – what is the purpose of strategy? Second – what is strategy?

Many organizations are now operating or competing in dynamic, turbulent, uncertain, chaotic environments. This is partly the result of industries and markets becoming ever more global; it is also driven by continual improvements in technology which, among other things, causes product, service and **strategic life cycles** to shorten. In turn this means that organizations must act, react and change more quickly. Some of these changes will be continuous and emergent, as vigilant, responsive organizations seize opportunities and innovate ahead of their rivals.

Other changes will be discontinuous and imply changes in competitive paradigms. Technology can both create and destroy industries, markets and windows of opportunity; breakpoints – or switches to new competitive rules and agendas – happen increasingly

frequently. Organizations cannot ignore this reality and the pressures that they bring, however disruptive the changes might be.

## 18.2 The purpose of strategy

Famous, and hopefully long lasting organizations, such as Coca-Cola, Apple and Walt Disney, continue to survive these breakpoints – sometimes actually creating them – and, as a result, they thrive, grow and prosper. They are recognized around the world and they exploit their competencies and their reputation. They create E–V–R (environment–values–resources) congruency and sustain it with carefully managed change. These organizations are truly entrepreneurial, but they are exceptional. We can learn from their actions, strategies and behaviours, although it will remain difficult to explain fully all of the reasons for their success. Simply attempting to copy their behaviour is not an adequate answer to the challenges facing organizations.

Other companies grow more steadily and uncertainly; they never seem to have the same command over their environment. Nonetheless, they do survive, partly with innovation, partly with contingent reaction. Others survive for some period of time, but then decline as they lose E–V–R congruency. Some organizations only survive with a change of leadership, style and culture. However, some businesses disappear every year, some to takeover, others to liquidation. It is, therefore, all too easy for currently successful firms to lose their edge and their competitive advantage. Miles and Snow (1994) argue that there are four main reasons for this:

- a lack of awareness and a failure to be alert to new opportunities and threats
- retaining a belief in a successful competitive paradigm for too long. Market leaders seem particularly prone to do this; they tend to rely on *continuous* change to retain their leadership
- an unwillingness to accept the need for structural or cultural change, and
- poor judgement, causing a company to make poor, inappropriate decisions.

There are also important lessons to be learnt from their relative demise.

In looking at strategic effectiveness and success, we can take two related, but distinct, perspectives. The first concerns success: what reasons lie behind the relative prosperity of our most successful organizations, those which continue to add value for their customers, differentiate their products and services, and control their costs? The second perspective concerns survival and environmental management: what factors distinguish a crisis averse from a crisis prone organization? The latter will typically lurch from problem to problem, difficulty to difficulty, crisis to crisis, never really managing its environment. It is fashionable, in the author's opinion, to talk about competitiveness, competitive advantage and success; it is less fashionable, but equally important – and in many cases, more relevant – to explore the issues behind crisis aversion. Too many organizations hover on the narrow line which separates survival from failure.

Organizations are systems that comprise people who are trying to act purposefully rather than thrash around without any real purpose (Checkland 1981). However, people differ in their perspective and perceptions. They use their personal meaning systems to interpret events, actions, opportunities and threats and to decide upon responses. While their personal strengths must be captured and exploited, organizational information systems should ensure that they work within the parameters of the corporate purpose,

vision and policies, and that their initiatives and contributions are shared and understood.

The new technological revolution and the increase in globalization have forced change on organizations everywhere, regardless of their type, size and sector. Few are unscathed. Some have embraced change positively and willingly; others more reluctantly. Those who have failed to change have probably been sold or liquidated. One outcome is a more flexible, but slimmed-down workforce.

On the positive side, many managers and employees are better educated. They are information technology (IT) literate, knowledge workers in a knowledge-based society. Some of them possess scarce skills. In some organizations people have become less constrained and more empowered, willing to be creative and show initiative in a more open, less hierarchical firm. Finally, information often flows more horizontally and freely, enriching and speeding up decision-making.

But this, clearly, is not the case everywhere.

Many workers are now part-time and 'peripheral', as opposed to 'core'. When re-engineering their processes and changing their structures too many companies have gone too far. They have downsized but not rightsized. Important skills and competencies have been lost. Linked to this, strategies of focusing on core activities and competencies, and divesting those which are non-core, have created an increasing incidence of strategic alliances and networks. Managing these networks effectively demands new capabilities, which many organizations have yet to develop fully. People feel under greater pressure and stress; there is more fear and insecurity. Hard as distinct from soft human resource strategies are practised in many companies, and many employees, instead of committing themselves to a single company, look to switch organizations and industries as they take more control of their working lives, and this despite the widespread managerial unemployment and insecurity.

Sadly, many large organizations, composed of very intelligent people, are still slow to respond to change pressures and, when they do, their behaviour is often ponderous. Individuals can, and often do, act dynamically and entrepreneurially; yet many organizations have still to work out how to capture the intelligence and learning in order to facilitate the change process. This is the paradox of the large organization learning how to behave like the archetypal small business.

The challenge of embracing both the hard and soft elements of strategic management in order to increase strategic awareness and manage strategic change more effectively remains a major challenge for many organizations. It is a challenge that is more likely to intensify than to disappear.

This final chapter, therefore:

- identifies ten key elements of strategy
- discusses the idea of strategic competency
- revisits the strategic paradoxes introduced in Part One and which have been debated throughout the book
- presents a model of the crisis-averse organization, and
- finally, offers a view on what strategy is.

## 18.3 Ten key elements of strategy

Figure 18.1 shows ten elements of strategy that have been discussed at various points in the book. The first six are interdependent and if they are interwoven effectively the organization should be more crisis averse than crisis prone. The remaining four impact upon the whole process of strategy creation and implementation.

1. **Perspectives of strategy** Strategy can be about the past (emergent patterns from previous decisions), the present (strategic positions) and the future (strategic plans). It can also be treated at the levels of broad purpose and narrow tactical ploys. All of these perspectives are relevant to the debate about what strategy is. The relevance of strategy will also vary for different people. The main perspective for the strategic leader is the overall corporate strategy for the whole organization, although the other levels are clearly relevant. Other senior managers will be focused on competitive positions and the competitive strategies which determine whether or not the organization enjoys competitive advantage. The activities and functional strategies are perhaps most important to lower-level middle and junior managers but, at the same time, it is vital they understand the wider picture and the contribution that they make.

2. **Corporate strategy and synergy** The issue here, which was discussed towards the end of the book, is whether or not there is a logical and defensible heartland of related businesses comprising the corporate portfolio. Ideally, each business will be

**Figure 18.1** The ten key elements of strategy

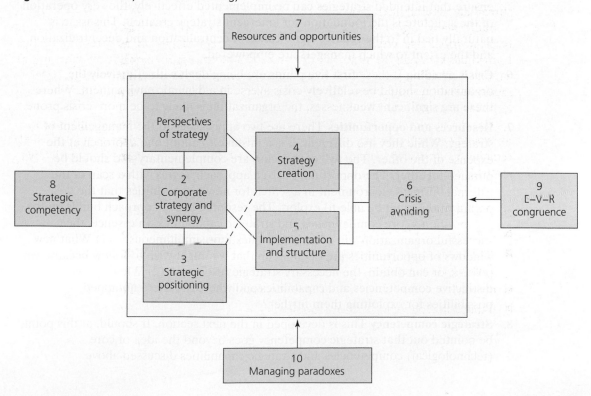

competitive and successful in its own right and, at the same time, contribute synergistically to the corporate parent and to other businesses in the portfolio. The parent organization should equally be able to contribute value to each business.

3. **Strategic positioning and competitive advantage** To be successful, each business or activity will need to establish – and sustain with change – a clear and strong competitive position. Where this position delivers either a cost advantage (when compared with rivals in the market) or a differentiated position which customers perceive as relevant and valuable, or both, then competitive advantage is a real possibility. The advantage does not come from the position itself, but from the activities – competencies and capabilities – which create and sustain the position of advantage.

4. **Strategy creation** Strategy creation is about change. Consequently, the approach that the organization takes to strategy creation is dictated by the strategic leader and influenced, and possibly constrained, by the culture of the organization. Three broad approaches were identified. First, visionary or entrepreneurial strategy creation, itself a reflection of strong strategic leadership. Second, planned strategy, possibly the outcome of a planning system. Together, these reflect intended strategies. Third, emergent strategy creation, which takes two forms: incremental changes to intended strategies during the implementation phase, and adaptive strategy creation in a dynamic and turbulent environment. Organizations need to find an effective blend of the three, all of which are likely to be present to some degree.

5. **Strategy implementation and structure** Strategies must be implemented before they can be deemed successful. While organization structures are designed to ensure that intended strategies can be implemented effectively, the very operation of the structure is the foundation for emergent strategy creation. This issue is naturally tied in to the relative significance of centralization and decentralization, and the extent to which managers are empowered.

6. **Crisis avoiding** If these first five points are being dealt with effectively the organization should be relatively crisis averse in a dynamic environment. Where there are significant weaknesses, the organization is likely to be more crisis prone.

7. **Resources and opportunities** There are two approaches to the management of strategy. While they are different, it is a mistake to adopt one approach at the expense of the other. The two approaches are complementary and should be pursued together. The opportunity-driven approach begins with a scan of the external business environment in a search for new opportunities that the organization might be able to exploit. The resource-based approach builds on the organization's core competencies and strategic capabilities. In essence, the successful organization will address two questions simultaneously. (1) What new windows of opportunities are opening up that we might wish to follow because we possess, or can obtain, the necessary strategic resources? (2) What are our distinctive competencies and capabilities and where are there untapped possibilities for exploiting them further?

8. **Strategic competency** This is developed in the next section. It should, at this point, be pointed out that strategic competency goes beyond the idea of core (technological) competencies and strategic capabilities discussed above.

9.  **E–V–R congruence** Successful organizations create and sustain congruency between the external environment (the source of fresh opportunities and threats), their values and their resources (competencies, capabilities and strengths). It is these values that dictate the ability of the organization to change both continuously (incrementally) and discontinuously (occasionally to new competitive paradigms).

10. **Strategic paradoxes** Again, this is discussed later in the chapter. Simply, the organization must work out a stance for dealing with a whole series of issues and challenges for which there are no clear-cut answers.

## 18.4  Strategic competencies

We believe that strategists should view their organizations as portfolios of strategic competencies which need to be continually reviewed, deployed and developed in ways that enhance the organization's competitive position. Strategic effectiveness, strategic and competitive success in a dynamic and competitive environment, is dependent upon three

**Figure 18.2** Interdependent competencies – I

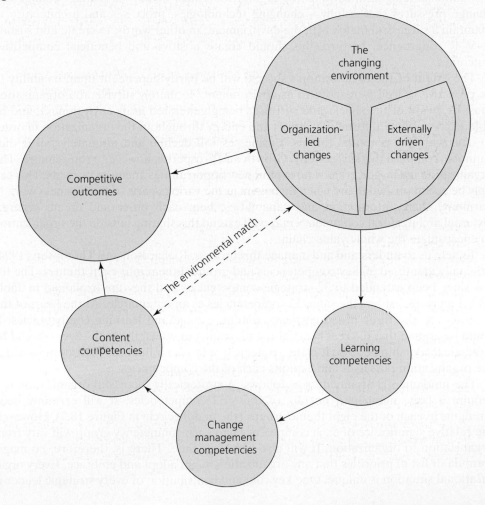

groups of competencies: the *content* of the actual strategies, strategic *change* competencies, and strategic *learning* competencies.

Strong and appropriate *content* competencies will enable the organization to add value, innovate and exploit both its internal and external architecture to gain benefit from its core (technological) competencies and strategic (process) capabilities. From these should come distinct product and service advantages (in the form of differentiation) and controlled costs. In turn, these are the foundations of competitive advantage.

However, the organization must be able to manage both continuous and discontinuous *change* in a dynamic environment, which in turn demands that it understands its environment. This understanding and insight comes from *learning*. The organization can learn from all its stakeholders, including its external suppliers, distributors and customers, as well as from its own employees and from the tactics and strategies of its competitors.

Figure 18.2 draws together these layers of strategic competency as an interdependent and circular process. Organizations must be able to understand the complexity and trends of the changing environment. Some of the changes will be the result of external forces, perhaps competitor actions. Others will be the outcomes of actions taken by the organization itself as it adopts a proactive approach to managing its environment. Using this understanding and learning, the organization must be able to manage change and change pressures successfully – changing technologies, processes and architecture to maintain a successful match with the environment; in other words, to create and sustain E–V–R congruence. In turn, this should create positive and beneficial competitive outcomes.

The extent of the organization's success will be partly dependent upon its ability to be proactive as well as reactive in its environment. To merely survive, the organization must be aware of the shocks and surprises being generated in its environment, and be able to co-ordinate information, effort and energy throughout the organization in order to deal with any potential threats. Businesses will decline and ultimately fail if they cannot accomplish this successfully. Growth and prosperity, however, require more. The organization must spot, create and exploit new opportunities ahead of its rivals. This can only be accomplished if and when managers in the various parts of the business work in harmony, share information and capabilities, help each other and create synergy. External architectural competency may well extend this sharing outside the organization to encapsulate the whole value chain.

To help us to understand and manage this process, Richardson and Thompson (1994) originally identified 30 key competencies and grouped them into eight themes. The list has since been extended to 32 strategic competencies and they are explained in Table 18.1. Figure 18.3 shows the same 32 competencies as an outer circle. At the heart of the diagram are the three broad clusters: content, change and learning competencies. It could be argued that the real heart of the diagram – in effect, the bull's-eye – should be strategic leadership because it is the strategic leader who influences the extent to which the organization possesses and exploits each of the competencies.

The fundamental argument is as follows. A strategically successful organization will require a large number, if not all, of these 32 competencies. It will certainly need strengths in each of the eight theme groups (the middle circle in Figure 18.3). However, the relative significance of each competency and each competency group will vary from organization to organization. It will also vary over time. There is, therefore, no magic formula or list of priorities that any organization might adopt and embrace. Every organizational situation is unique. One key role and contribution of every strategic leader is

**Table 18.1** Thirty-two generic competencies

*Strategic awareness abilities*
1. Think strategically and holistically, encapsulating issues of past, present and future
2. Maintain an awareness of environmental changes and their implications
3. Design and operationalize a 'fitting' organization, the structure and systems of which match its environment(s) and stay matched in times of change and turbulence
4. Avoid the trap of self-enacted reality (whereby an organization would drift into problems because it retains an unrealistic view of its true position) and instead reach more objective, informed and environmentally aware decisions

*Stakeholder satisfaction abilities*
5. Understand the needs and expectations of stakeholders and manage the organization to meet those which must be prioritized
6. Appreciate key success factors (for satisfying stakeholders) and match these with organizational competencies and capabilities, taking into account new opportunities and potential threats

*Competitive strategic abilities*
7. Understand the competitive environment, choose where and how to compete, design effective, winning competitive paradigms and improve these continuously
8. Get and stay close to customers – to understand, attract and satisfy them more effectively than competitors with differentiated, high added-value products and services

*Strategic implementation and change abilities*
9. Establish appropriate objectives, plans and targets and achieve these, while always appreciating the need for flexibility, adaptation and change
10. Implement intended strategies throughout the organization, making (the right) things happen
11. Create, share and implement a winning vision or paradigm
12. Empower people and motivate them towards continuous organizational improvement
13. Foster internal cross-functional and cross-business synergies through co-operation and sharing
14. Co-operate in external strategic alliances for competitive advantage
15. Move to new competitive paradigms discontinuously at timely intervals

*Quality and customer care*
16. Provide excellent quality – as perceived and recognized by customers
17. Continuously improve productivity and cost reductions without ever sacrificing key aspects of quality
18. Invoke a creative, innovative and self-organizing climate in the organization

*Functional competencies*
19. Acquire new, relevant technologies and utilize R&D to help to create a future for the business
20. Develop and launch new products and services both effectively and in the appropriate timescale
21. Develop and introduce new processes for cost savings and speedier decision-making
22. Attract, develop, reward and retain people with appropriate skills and competencies
23. Reach and satisfy customers with effective distribution systems, both nationally and internationally
24. Harness the potential of information technology in design and for fast, efficient and effective information harnessing and sharing
25. Maintain strong financial controls and be able to access capital for future investment programmes

*Failure and crisis avoidance*
26. Avoid business failures by becoming and staying crisis averse
27. Plan for when things do go wrong, and
28. Manage any crises (business and sociotechnical) effectively
29. Turn around a business when there are critical financial, competitive or leadership difficulties

*Ethics and social responsibility*
30. Manage 'green' issues, either to avoid crises or to create competitive advantage
31. Manage socially responsibly
32. Become more ethically aware and manage with an ethical underpinning

**Figure 18.3** Interdependent competencies – II

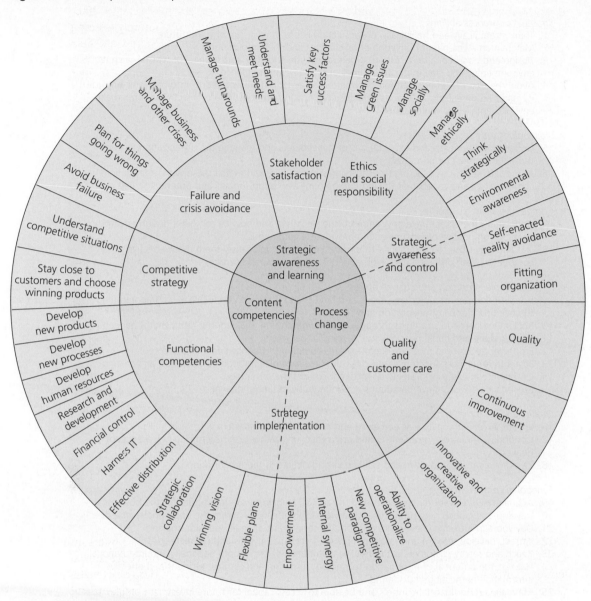

to identify which of these 32 competencies are the ones that can really make a difference for an individual organization in the environment and circumstances that it faces and in which it operates. This list of priorities should be communicated throughout the organization and efforts should be targeted on this list.

Organizations might well be very strong in certain areas but these may not be areas that make a real difference. Weaknesses in some areas will be far more significant than weaknesses in other areas. In an ideal world, areas of organizational strength and competency will be closely matched with those identified as being significant.

Logically, performance measurement will link up with these identified priorities. We all know that when an area is flagged as a priority, and attention is given to it, the likelihood is that results will improve. Again, it could be that organizational energy is being channelled into activities that do not make a real strategic difference, simply because those that truly matter have not been identified and targeted. Research by the author (Thompson and Cole 1997) confirms that in a substantial number of organizations the areas of strongest performance are not coincidental with those competencies believed to be most important for prolonged competitive success. Yet it must be repeated that competitive advantage, the aim of all strategic action, can only be sustained over time by the organization's core competencies, competencies that pervade the whole business. You will note from Table 18.1 and Figure 18.3 how wide-ranging the competencies need to be.

## 18.5 Strategic paradoxes

In Part One a number of strategic issues, challenges or paradoxes were listed, about each of which the organization has to make decisions. Again, the answers are not clear-cut. Rather, the choices that the organization makes – and the relatedness of the decisions that it takes on each of the issues – will have a marked impact upon its strategic effectiveness.

This section recaps the main ones – readers will appreciate how every one of these has been debated at some stage in the book.

**Paradox 1: Past and future**  All organizations build on the past. Sometimes they learn from their successes; on other occasions they learn from their mistakes. Normally, developments from the past will imply continuous improvement around the same competitive paradigm. Sometimes, however, the future requires more dramatic and discontinuous change which implies that past and current competitive paradigms are abandoned. It is a mistake to persist with yesterday's and today's products if their life cycle is heading for decline but, equally, change for the sake of change can be unnecessarily disruptive and threaten control and quality. The challenge, then, is one of balance.

**Paradox 2: Intended and emergent strategy**  Strategic planning plays an important role in strategy, as does the contribution of a strong and charismatic entrepreneurial leader. However, plans must be seen as flexible and there is an inherent danger in being reliant on just one main source of ideas. In a dynamic and competitive environment, learning and emergent strategy will always be vital. The challenge is again one of balance.

**Paradox 3: Reactive or proactive?**  Simply, organizations must be able both to manage in and to manage their environments. They must respond to the unexpected events and surprises; they must at times lead the change agenda.

**Paradox 4: Resource-based or opportunity driven?**  This point was explained earlier in this chapter, when it was highlighted that both need adopting simultaneously.

The chances are that one or the other will take priority – but which, and with what emphasis?

**Paradox 5: Cost or differentiation?**  Again, the answer is both! Organizations, in their search for competitive advantage, can never ignore costs. There is, however, a distinction between striving to be the cost leader (with lower costs than one's main rivals for the same product or service) and effective cost management. Organizations that look to add new values and differentiate their products and services in distinctive ways must invest (and increase their costs) to create this difference – at the same time, there is no benefit in adding costs and benefits that are of little consequence to customers. The secret lies in understanding and managing the key cost drivers.

**Paradox 6: Focus or diversify?**  Contemporary strategic logic says focus. The era of the diversified conglomerate is over, at least for the moment. However, a very tight focus can restrain growth, and consequently most organizations that are seeking to grow will diversify in justifiably related areas. The link might be technology or markets.

**Paradox 7: How big?**  The focus/diversify dilemma is related to growth ambitions. The large organization may be able to claim critical mass, perhaps important in its industry, especially where it has ambitions to be a global competitor. Some very successful organizations deliberately set out to be number one or number two in every market segment in which they compete. Their challenge is to retain the flexibility and the innovation of the small, entrepreneurial business as they grow, to ensure that they do not reach a position of stasis in the cycle of growth and maybe have to engineer a crisis to address the need for renewed creativity. Even the largest, global organizations need to be relevant locally around the world.

**Paradox 8: Centralize or decentralize?**  Centralization certainly retains control at the top of the organization and allows for hands-on leadership from the strategic leader. Unfortunately, it can make the organization slow to respond in a dynamic environment. Decentralization and empowerment can increase flexibility, in conjunction with a hands-off leadership style, but now control has to be achieved through a carefully crafted information system. It seems impossible to balance the two in a totally satisfactory manner and so organizations continually swing from one to the other. Sometimes the adjustments are minor; on other occasions there are major structural changes.

## 18.6  The crisis-averse organization

Figure 18.4 highlights that an organization must meet the needs and expectations of all its stakeholders if it is to survive. It is vital to retain customers; new customers then bring new business rather than merely replace others who have been lost or neglected. Employee support and commitment is essential for delivering the competitive quality and service that customers demand. To achieve this, employees must be motivated and rewarded. In addition, financial targets must be met to ensure shareholder loyalty.

Achieving these outcomes is dependent upon aspects of both strategy and structure, which in turn depend upon effective strategic leadership. A sound, appropriate, commu-

**Figure 18.4** The crisis-averse organization

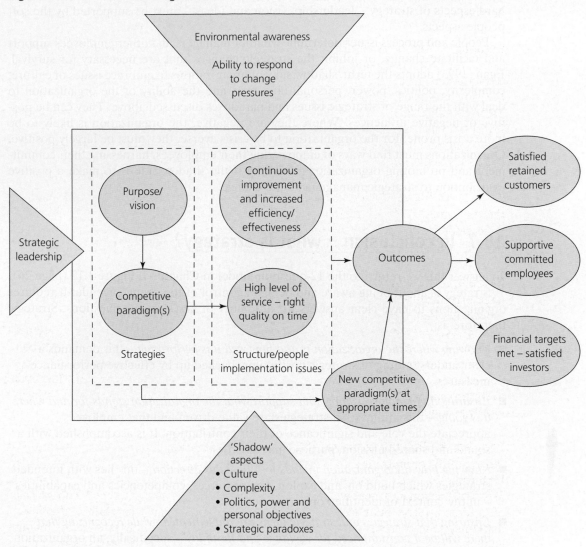

nicated and shared purpose and vision should be manifested in appropriate, feasible and desirable corporate and competitive strategies. These must be:

■ implemented with a high level of customer service

■ improved continuously, and

■ changed to new corporate and competitive paradigms at appropriate times and opportunities.

This demands environmental awareness and the ability of the organization to respond to change pressures and to external strategic disturbances. While we talk about an organization-wide response, the real challenge lies with individual managers and employees, who are closest to customers, suppliers and distributors. Innovative people drive functional-level improvements which can strengthen competitiveness; but they

must be empowered and committed – issues of structure, style and implementation. The hard aspects of strategy – leadership, vision and ideas – must be supported by the soft people aspects.

People and process issues determine whether managers and other employees support and facilitate change, or inhibit the strategic changes that are necessary for survival. Egan (1993) adopts the term 'shadow side' of organizations to embrace issues of culture, complexity, politics, power, personal objectives and the ability of the organization to deal with the range of strategic issues and paradoxes discussed above. They can be positive or negative influences. Where they are negative, the organization is likely to be more crisis prone; for the organization to be crisis averse, they must be largely positive. Organizations must find ways of empowering their employees, harnessing their commitment and promoting organizational learning if the shadow side is to make a positive contribution to strategic management and change.

## 18.7 In conclusion – what is strategy?

To answer this we return to the 12-question model in Chapter 1, Figure 1.12 (page 26).

Strategy is about being aware and being in control of the change agenda. It requires organizations to have clear answers for a number of key strategic questions. Strategy, therefore, is:

- *Knowing where the organization is and how well it is performing* – this demands a clear understanding of strategic positioning, backed up by effective performance measures

- *Ensuring that employees know and support what the organization stands for and where it is going* – this implies that strategies are value driven and that employees appreciate the role and significance of their contribution. It is accomplished with a sound and shared mission, purpose and direction

- *Knowing how the organization intends to follow this direction* – this lies with intended strategies which build on, and exploit, key resources, competencies and capabilities – in the context of identified opportunities

- *Ensuring that strategies and strategic ideas are implemented, while recognizing that there will be a constant need for vigilance and flexibility* – specifically, an organization which can respond to environmental turbulence, competitor actions and occasional setbacks – and innovate to change its strategies; one in which people have some control over the work they contribute.

The appropriate performance measures concern efficiency (doings things right) and effectiveness (doing the right things). Effectiveness encompasses the interests of all key stakeholders – in particular employees, who contribute ideas and ensure that strategies are implemented, customers, for whom the value is created and built, and the shareholders who retain faith in the business and support it financially. Where these are in place we should have an organization which can demonstrate E–V–R congruence and which will be more crisis averse than crisis prone.

In a nutshell, strategy is doing the right things right – and for the right reasons.

## References

Checkland, PB (1981) *Systems Thinking, Systems Practice*, John Wiley.

Egan, G (1993) *Adding Value: A Systematic Guide to Business-driven Management and Leadership*, Jossey-Bass.

Miles, RE and Snow, CC (1994) *Fit, Failure and the Hall of Fame: How Companies Succeed or Fail*, Free Press.

Richardson, B and Thompson, JL (1994) Strategic competency in the 1990s, *Administrator*, July.

Thompson, JL and Cole, ME (1997) Strategic competency – the learning challenge, *Journal of Workplace Learning*, 9 (5).

# Glossary

**acquisition** *(p 20)* the purchase of one company by another, for either cash or equity in the parent. Sometimes the word *takeover* is preferred when the acquisition is hostile, and resisted by the company being bought. Similarly, *mergers* are when two companies simply *agree* to come together as one.

**activities** *(p 20)* those things – acts and tasks – undertaken by an organization which, when aggregated, dictate the strength of a *strategic position*.

**adaptive strategic change** *(p 280)* strategies that emerge and develop on an ongoing basis as companies learn of new environmental opportunities and threats and adapt (or respond) to competitive pressures.

**adding value** *(p 8)* technically, the difference between the value of a firm's outputs and its inputs; the additional value is added through the deployment and effort of the organization's resources. Successful organizations will seek to add value to create outputs which are perceived as important by their customers. The *added value* or *supply chain* is the sequential set of activities from suppliers, through manufacturers and distributors, which is required to bring products and services to the marketplace.

**alliance (strategic alliance)** *(p 118)* an agreement, preferably formalized, with another organization. The alliance might be with an important supplier, with a major distributor, or possibly with a competitor, say for joint research and development.

**appropriability** *(p 193)* the ability of an organization to ensure that at least some of the benefits earned from the value that it creates and adds comes back to the organization, rather than only benefiting others, such as suppliers, customers or even competitors.

**architecture** *(p 117)* a relational network involving either or both external linkages (see *alliance*) or internal linkages between managers in a company or businesses in a conglomerate. The supply chain is one such network. The main benefits concern information exchanges for the mutual gain of those involved, and *synergies* (see below) from interdependencies. Sometimes linked with reputation and innovation as key strategic resources for an organization.

**backward (vertical) integration** *(p 504)* the process by which a manufacturer acquires direct control over its inputs, such that it makes what it previously bought in. See also *vertical integration*.

**benchmarking** *(p 148)* a process of comparative evaluation – of products, services and the performances of equipment and personnel. Sometimes companies attempt to benchmark their competitors; on other occasions they will benchmark those organizations which are seen as high performers.

**branding** *(p 129)* the additional value and reassurance provided to customers through the reputation of the business, represented by the strength and visibility of its brand name.

**break-even** *(p 87)* the level of activity where the total costs incurred in producing and selling a product or service – or pursuing a particular strategy – are equal to the total revenues generated.

**business environment** see *environment*.

**business ethics** *(p 98)* the principles, standards and conduct that an organization practises – and sometimes states formally – for the way in which it deals with its people, its external stakeholders and environmental issues that arise.

**business model** *(p 18)* a concise summary of the organization and its strategy which answers three questions – what, for whom and why? What products and business activities the organization will engage in – and what it will not, who the target market is for each product or business and what their compelling reason to buy is – the why element.

**business process re-engineering** *(p 132)* the analysis and redesign of workflows and processes within organizations and between them (i.e. along the supply chain).

**combination strategies** *(p 492)* term used where more than one discrete strategic alternative is pursued at the same time. Particularly relevant for a mixture of market penetration, market development and product development strategies; and invariably implies innovation.

**competitive advantage** *(p 20)* the ability of an organization to add more value for its customers than its rivals, and thus attain a position of relative advantage. The challenge is to sustain any advantage once achieved.

**competitive platforms** *(p 299)* the important bases of competition in an industry and for an individual competitor.

**competitive strategy** *(p 20)* the means by which organizations seek to achieve and sustain competitive advantage. Usually the result of distinctive *functional strategies*. There should be a competitive strategy for every product and service produced by the company.

**competitor gap analysis** *(p 302)* a comparison of the organization with its leading competitors in terms of their respective ability to satisfy key success factors. Ideally, this will involve an input from relevant customers.

**competitor-influenced strategy** *(p 113)* strategies and tactics that arise from a need to compete in an industry or environment – for both markets and resources. When an organization introduces changes, competitors are likely to react, forcing further incremental changes. At the same time, competitors introduce new strategic ideas that vigilant organizations will respond to.

**concentration ratios** *(p 183)* normally the degree to which added value and/or turnover and/or assets in an industry are concentrated in the hands of a few suppliers. High concentration is reflected in monopoly and oligopoly industry structures. Sometimes measured in terms of aggregate output controlled by the largest companies in a country.

**controls** *(p 95)* means by which progress against stated objectives and targets is measured and monitored, and changed as necessary.

**core competencies** *(p 116)* distinctive skills, normally related to a product, service or technology, which can be used to create a competitive advantage. See also *strategic capability*. Together, they form key resources that assist an organization in being different from (and ideally superior to) its competitors.

**corporate governance** *(p 450)* the selection, role and responsibilities of the strategic leadership of the organization, their conduct and their relationships with internal and external stakeholders. Sometimes responsibility for overall strategy and ongoing operations will be separated.

**corporate strategy** *(p 20)* the overall strategy for a diversified or multiproduct/multiservice organization. Refers to the overall scope of the business in terms of products, services and geography.

**cost leadership** *(p 123)* the lowest cost producer in a market, after adjustments for quality differences. An important source of competitive advantage in either a market or a segment of a market. Specifically, the cost leader is the company that enjoys a cost advantage over its rivals through the

management of its resources, and not simply because it produces the lowest quality.

**cost of capital** *(p 141)* the cost of capital employed to fund strategic initiatives, combining the rate of interest on debt and the cost of equity. The typical formula used is the weighted average cost of capital which encompasses the relative proportions of debt and equity. Should normally be lower than the discounted rate of return from the investment or initiative – see *discounted cash flow*.

**crisis management** *(p 39)* how the organization (a) seeks to reduce the likelihood of, and (b) manages in the event of, a major disturbance which has the potential to damage the organization's assets or reputation. Some crises are the result of mismanagement or inadequate controls; others begin outside the organization and may be unavoidable.

**critical mass** *(p 135)* relates to the actual and relative size of an organization in terms of its ability to be influential and powerful in its industry or environment.

**critical success factors** see *key success factors*.

**culture** *(p 8)* the values and norms of an organization, which determine its corporate behaviour and the behaviour of people within the organization.

**decentralization/centralization** *(p 33)* the extent to which authority, responsibility and accountability are devolved throughout the organization. Centralization should yield tight control; decentralization motivates managers and allows for speedier reactions to environmental change pressures.

**delayering** *(p 132)* the flattening of an organization structure by removing layers of management and administration.

**demerger or divestment** *(p 20)* term used when an organization sells or spins off (or maybe even closes) a business or activity. Usually linked to a strategy of increased focus.

**differentiation** *(p 123)* products and services are differentiated when customers perceive them to have distinctive properties that set them apart from their competitors.

**directional policy matrix** *(p 429)* a planning technique used to compare and contrast the relative competitive strengths of a portfolio of products and services produced by an organization. Used to help in evaluating their relative worth and investment potential.

**discounted cash flow (DCF)** *(p 552)* the sum of the projected cash returns or flows over a period of years from a strategic investment or initiative. Future figures are reduced (specifically, inflation is removed) to bring them into line with present values.

**diversification** *(p 8)* the extent of the differences between the various products and services in a company's portfolio (its range of activities). The products and services may be *related* through say marketing or technology, or *unrelated*, which normally implies that they require different management skills.

**divestment** see *demerger*.

**divisionalization** *(p 700)* a form of organization structure whereby activities are divided and separated on the basis of different products or services, or geographical territories.

**dot.com companies** *(p 45)* organizations that have emerged as the power and potential of the Internet has been realized and exploited. Dot.com companies will normally trade over the Internet, but some are essentially service providers.

**double-loop learning** *(p 244)* an assessment of the continuing appropriateness and value of existing competitive positions and paradigms and the ability to create new competitive positions, ideally ahead of competitors. See also *single-loop learning*.

**downsizing** *(p 132)* sometimes associated with business process re-engineering, downsizing occurs when organizations rationalize their product/service ranges and streamline their processes. People, in particular layers of management, are removed. See also *rightsizing*.

**e-commerce** *(p 161)* short for electronic commerce, and meaning trading over the Internet.

**e-markets** *(p 161)* markets is the term used for when buyers and sellers come together to engineer an exchange. E-markets is the term used when this trading is via the Internet.

**economies of scale** *(p 151)* cost savings accrued with high volume production, which enables lower unit production costs.

**effectiveness** *(p 9)* the ability of an organization to meet the demands and expectations of its various stakeholders, those individuals or groups with influence over the business. Sometimes known as 'doing the right things'.

**efficiency** *(p 60)* the sound management of resources to maximize the returns from them. Known as 'doing things right'.

**emergent strategy** *(p 31)* term used to describe and explain strategies which emerge over time and often with an element of trial and error. Detailed implementation is not prescribed in advance. Some emergent strategies are *incremental changes* with learning as intended strategies are implemented. Other *adaptive strategies* are responses to new environmental opportunities and threats.

**empowerment** *(p 33)* freeing people from a rigid regime of rules, controls and directives and allowing them to take responsibility for their own decisions and actions.

**entrepreneur** *(p 36)* someone who perpetually creates and innovates to build something of recognized value around perceived opportunities.

**entrepreneurial/visionary strategies** *(p 46)* strategies created by strong, visionary strategic leaders. Their successful implementation relies on an ability to persuade others of their merit.

**environment** *(p 16)* everything and everyone outside the organization or organizational boundary – including competitors, customers, financiers, suppliers and government.

**E–V–R (environment–values–resources) congruence** *(p 129)* the effective matching of an organization's resources (R) with the demands of its environment (E). A successful and sustained match has to be managed and frequently requires change; successfully achieving this depends on the organization's culture and values (V).

**experience curve** *(p 173)* the relationship between (reducing) unit costs and the total number of units ever produced of a product. Usually plotted as a graph, and often with a straight-line relationship on logarithmic axes. The percentage unit cost reduction holds steady every time output is doubled.

**financial control** *(p 212)* term used to describe the form of control normally found in a *holding company* structure. Strategy creation is decentralized to independent business units which are required to meet agreed financial targets.

**focus strategy** *(p 287)* concentration on one or a limited number of market segments or niches.

**forward (vertical) integration** *(p 504)* when an organization takes control of aspects of its distribution, transport or direct selling. See also *vertical integration*.

**functional strategies** *(p 20)* the strategies for the various functions carried out by an organization, including marketing, production, financial management, information management, research and development and human resource management. One or more functional strategies will typically be responsible for any distinctive competitive edge enjoyed by the company.

**functional structure** *(p 700)* a structure based around individual functions, such as production, sales and finance, all of which report to an identifiable managing director/chief executive.

**generic strategies** *(p 123)* the basic competitive strategies – based on cost leadership, differentiation and focus – which are open to any competitor in an industry, and which can be a source of competitive advantage.

**global strategies** *(p 602)* strategies for companies which manufacture and market in several countries and/or continents. Issues

concern, for example, the location of manufacturing units and the extent to which control is centralized at a home base or decentralized on a local basis.

**governance** *(p 450)* the location of power and responsibility at the head of an organization. See also *corporate governance*.

**heartland** *(p 118)* term used to describe a cluster of businesses (in a multibusiness organization) which can be justifiably related and integrated to generate synergies.

**holding company** *(p 390)* a structure where the various businesses are seen as largely independent of each other and managed accordingly.

**horizontal integration** *(p 155)* the acquisition or merger of firms at the same stage in the supply chain. Such firms may be direct competitors or focus on different market segments.

**implementation** see *strategy implementation*.

**incremental strategic changes** *(p 229)* changes to intended (possibly planned) strategies as they are implemented. Result from ongoing learning and from changes in the environment or to forecast assumptions.

**innovation** *(p 9)* changes to products, processes and services in an attempt to sharpen their competitiveness – through either cost reduction or improved distinctiveness. Strategically, it can apply to any part of a business.

**intangible (strategic) resources** *(p 262)* resources which have no physical presence, but which can add real value for the organization. Reputation and technical knowledge would be typical examples.

**intellectual capital** *(p 595)* the hidden value (and capital) tied up in an organization's people which can set it apart from its competitors and be a valuable source of competitive advantage and future earnings. Difficult to quantify and value for the balance sheet. Linked to *knowledge*.

**intended strategies** *(p 42)* prescribed strategies the organization intends to implement, albeit with incremental changes. Sometimes the

result of (formal) strategic planning; sometimes the stated intent of the strategic leader. May be described alternatively as *prescriptive strategies*.

**intrapreneurship** *(p 131)* the process of internal entrepreneurship. Occurs when managers or other employees accept responsibility and actively champion new initiatives aimed at making a real difference.

**joint venture** *(p 153)* a form of strategic alliance where each partner takes a financial stake. This could be a shareholding in the other partner or the establishment of a separate, jointly owned, business.

**just in time (JIT)** *(p 114)* systems or processes for ensuring that stocks or components are delivered just when and where they are needed, reducing the need for inventory.

**key (or critical) success factors** *(p 20)* environmentally based factors which are crucial for competitive success. Simply, the things that an organization must be able to do well if it is to succeed.

**knowledge** *(p 36)* an amalgamation of experience, values, information, insight and strategic awareness – which goes beyond the notions of data and information. Retained, managed and exploited it can be a valuable source of competitive difference and advantage. See also *intellectual capital*.

**leadership** see *strategic leader*.

**learning organization** *(p 155)* one which is capable of harnessing and spreading best practices, and where employees can learn from each other and from other organizations. The secret lies in open and effective communications networks.

**leverage** *(p 241)* the exploitation, by an organization, of its resources to their full extent. Often linked to the idea of *stretching resources*.

**life cycle** see *strategic life cycle*.

**liquidation** *(p 425)* the closing down of a business, normally because it has failed. Typically a last resort, when a rescue or sale

has either not been possible or not successful.

**logical incrementalism** *(p 27)* term adopted by John B. Quinn to explain strategy creation in small, logical, incremental steps.

**Machiavellianism** *(p 835)* where individuals use power and influence to structure situations and events, and bring about outcomes, which are more in their own personal interests than those of the organization. Linked to *organizational politics*.

**market development** *(p 141)* continuing with existing products and services but, and possibly with modifications and additions, seeking new market and new market segment opportunities.

**market-driven strategy** *(p 112)* alternative term for *opportunity-driven strategy*.

**market penetration** *(p 141)* persisting with existing products/services and existing customers and markets but accepting that continuous, incremental improvement is possible to strengthen the relevant strategic position. The assumption is that sales and revenue can be increased.

**market segment(ation)** *(p 170)* the use of particular marketing strategies to target identified and defined groups of customers.

**mass marketing** where one product (or service) is sold to all types of customer.

**matrix organization** *(p 700)* a multidivisional organization which seeks to link the various functional activities across the divisions, to achieve the synergy benefits of interdependency.

**merger** see *acquisition*.

**milestones** *(p 8)* interim targets which act as indicators or measures of progress in the pursuit of objectives and the implementation of strategies.

**military strategy** *(p 34)* strategy and planning in the context of warfare through the ages. Strategy has its origins in warfare and consequently a study of military strategy can provide valuable insights into corporate behaviour.

**mission statement** *(p 43)* a summary of the essential aim or purpose of the organization; its essential reason for being in business.

**monopoly power** *(p 183)* the relative power of an individual company in an industry. It does not follow that a dominant competitor will act against the best interests of customers and consumers, but it could be in a position to do so.

**monopoly structure** *(p 182)* term for an industry with a dominant and very powerful competitor. Originally based on the idea of total control, competitive authorities around the world now consider a 25 per cent market or asset share to be a basis for possible monopoly power.

**multinational company** *(p 23)* a company operating in several countries. See *global strategies*.

**niche marketing** *(p 673)* concentration on a small, identifiable market segment with the aim of achieving dominance of the segment.

**not-for-profit organization** *(p 9)* term used to describe an organization (such as a charity) that does not have profit as a fundamental objective. Such organizations will, however, have to achieve a cash surplus to survive.

**objectives** *(p 8)* short-term targets or milestones with defined measurable achievements. A desired state and hoped-for level of success.

**oligopoly** *(p 72)* (structure) an industry dominated by a small group of competitors.

**opportunity-driven strategy** *(p 112)* strategy creation and development that begins with an analysis of external environmental threats and opportunities. See also *resource-based strategy*.

**organizational politics** *(p 365)* the process by which individuals and groups utilize power and influence to obtain results. Politics can be used legitimately in the best interests of the organization, or illegitimately by people who put their own interests above those of the organization.

**outsource/outsourcing** *(p 219)* procuring products and services from independent

suppliers rather than producing them within the organization. Often linked to strategies of focusing on core competencies and capabilities.

**paradigm** *(p 21)* a recipe or model for linking together the component strands of a theory and identifying the inherent relationships, a competitive paradigm explains the underpinning logic of a competitive strategy or position.

**parenting** *(p 513)* the skills and capabilities used by a head office to manage and control a group of subsidiary businesses. The head office should be able to add value for the businesses, while the businesses should, in turn, be able to add value for the whole organization.

**performance indicators or measures** *(p 380)* quantifiable measures and subjective indicators of strategic and competitive success.

**PEST analysis** *(p 111)* An analysis of the *political*, *economic*, *social* and *technological* factors in the external environment of an organization, which can affect its activities and performance.

**plan** *(p 16)* a statement of intent, generally linked to a programme of tactics for strategy implementation.

**planning** see *strategic planning*.

**planning gap** *(p 410)* a planning technique which enables organizations to evaluate the potential for, and risk involved in, seeking to attain particular growth targets.

**policies** *(p 35)* guidelines relating to decisions and approaches which support organizational efforts to achieve stated (intended) objectives. Can be at any level in the organization, and can range from mandatory regulations to recommended courses of action. They may or may not be written down formally.

**portfolio analysis** *(p 375)* techniques for evaluating the appropriate strategies for a range of (possibly diverse) business activities in a single organization. See *directional policy matrix*.

**power** *(p 16)* the potential or ability to do something or make something happen. Externally, it refers to the ability of an organization to influence and affect the actions of its external stakeholders. Internally, it concerns the relationships between people.

**prescriptive strategies** see *intended strategies*.

**product development** *(p 123)* developing additional and normally related products and services to enhance the range available to existing customers and markets, and thereby increase sales and revenue.

**profit** *(p 20)* the difference between total revenues and total costs. Often profit is a fundamental objective of a manufacturing or service business.

**profitability** *(p 28)* financial ratios which look at profits generated in relation to the capital that has been employed to generate them. Two different ratios relate (a) trading profit (or profit before interest and tax) to total capital employed (known as the return on capital employed) and (b) profit after interest and tax to shareholders' funds (known as the return on shareholders' funds).

**public sector organizations** *(p 73–4)* organizations controlled directly or indirectly by government and/or dependent on government for a substantial proportion of their revenue. Includes local authorities, the National Health Service in the UK and the emergency services.

**quality** *(p 19)* strategically, quality is concerned with the ability of an organization to 'do things right – first time and every time' for each customer. This includes internal customers (other departments in an organization) as well as external customers. *Total quality management* is the spreading of quality consciousness throughout the whole organization.

**reputation** *(p 119)* the strategic standing of an organization in the eyes of its customers and suppliers.

**resource-based strategy** *(p 39)* strategy creation built around the further exploitation of core competencies and strategic capabilities.

**retrenchment** *(p 490)* strategy followed when an organization is experiencing difficulties and needs to cut costs and consolidate its resources before seeking new ways to create and add value. Sometimes involves asset reduction (perhaps the sale of a business) and job losses.

**rightsizing** *(p 118)* linked to downsizing, implies the reduction in staffing is to a level from which the organization can grow effectively. On occasions downsizing can mean that strategically important skills and competencies are lost; rightsizing implies this is not the case.

**risk management** *(p 39)* the understanding where and how things can and might go wrong, appreciating the extent of any downside if things do go wrong, and putting in place strategies to deal with the risks either before or after their occurrence.

**scenarios** *(p 39)* conceptual possibilities of future events and circumstances. Scenario planning involves using these to explore what might happen in order to help prepare managers for a wide range of eventualities and uncertainties in an unpredictable future environment.

**single-loop learning** *(p 244)* the ability to improve a competitive position on an ongoing and continuous basis, acknowledging there is always the possibility of improvement. Sometimes the competitive paradigm itself has to be changed – see *double-loop learning*.

**small- and medium-sized enterprises (SMEs)** *(p 630)* term used to embrace new and growing businesses, and those which (for any number of reasons) do not grow beyond a certain size.

**social responsibility** *(p 95)* strategies and actions that can be seen to be in the wide and best interests of society in general and the environment. Sometimes associated with the notion of mutual self-interest.

**spheres of influence** *(p 431)* building an arsenal of products and services that enable real influence across a wide range of critical interests. Routes to growth around a key *heartland.* Also related to protecting existing interests in the face of competition.

**stakeholders** *(p 8)* any individual or group capable of affecting (and being affected by) the actions and performance of an organization.

**strategic alliance** see *alliance.*

**strategic architecture** see *architecture.*

**strategic awareness** *(p 10)* appreciating the strategic position and relative success of the organization. Knowing how well it is doing, why and how – relative to its competitors – and appreciating the nature of the external environment and the extent of any need to change things.

**strategic business unit** *(p 20)* a discrete grouping within an organization with delegated responsibility for strategically managing a product, a service, or a particular group of products or services.

**strategic capability** *(p 39)* process skills used to add value and create competitive advantage.

**strategic change** *(p 10)* changes that take place over time to the strategies and objectives of the organization. Change can be gradual, emergent and evolutionary, or discontinuous, dramatic and revolutionary.

**strategic control** *(p 726)* a style of corporate control whereby the organization attempts to enjoy the benefits of delegation and decentralization with a portfolio of activities which, while diverse, is interdependent and capable of yielding synergies from co-operation.

**strategic inflection points** *(p 807)* introducing important changes at the right moment – related to both competition and customer expectations. Can act as a transformation point in the history of an industry.

**strategic issues** *(p 134)* current and forthcoming developments inside and outside the organization which will impact upon the ability of the organization to pursue its mission and achieve its objectives.

**strategic leader** *(p 16)* generic term used to describe a manager who is responsible for changes in the corporate strategy.

**strategic life cycle** *(p 840)* the notion that strategies (like products and services) have finite lives. After some period of time they will need improving, changing or replacing.

**strategic management** the process by which an organization establishes its objectives, formulates actions (strategies) designed to meet these objectives in the desired timescale, implements the actions, and assesses progress and results.

**strategic planning** *(p 16)* *in strategy creation:* the systematic and formal creation of strategies – to be found in many organizations, and capable of making a very significant contribution in large, multiactivity organizations. *In strategic control:* centralized control, most ideal where there is a limited range of core businesses.

**strategic positioning** *(p 127)* the chosen or realized relationship between the organization and its market. Clearly linked to competitive strategies and competitive advantage. The position itself is not a source of advantage, but the activities that underpin the position are.

**strategic regeneration (or renewal)** *(p 130)* major and simultaneous changes to strategies, structures and styles of management. See also *transformational change*.

**strategic thinking** *(p 147)* the ability of the organization (and its managers) to (a) synthesize the lessons from past experiences and to share the learning, (b) be aware of current positions, strengths and competencies and (c) clarify the way forward for the future.

**strategy** *(p 8)* the means by which organizations achieve (and seek to achieve) their objectives and purpose. There can be a strategy for each product and service, and for the organization as a whole.

**strategy creation** *(p 16)* umbrella term for the formulation and choice of new strategies. Encapsulates direction from the strategic

leader (or an entrepreneur), strategic planning, and emergent strategy. See: *emergent strategy; entrepreneurial strategies; strategic planning.*

**strategy implementation** *(p 25)* the processes through which the organization's chosen and intended strategies are made to happen.

**stretching resources** *(p 48)* the creative use of resources to add extra value for customers – through innovation and improved productivity.

**supply chain** *(p 84)* the linkage between an organization, its suppliers, its distributors and its customers.

**sustainable competitive advantage** *(p 225)* a sustained edge over competitors in an industry, usually achieved by first creating a valuable difference and then sustaining it with improvement and change.

**SWOT analysis** *(p 112)* an analysis of an organization's *strengths* and *weaknesses* alongside the *opportunities* and *threats* present in the external environment.

**synergy** *(p 151)* term used for the added value or additional benefits which ideally accrue from the linkage or fusion of two businesses, or from increased co-operation either between different parts of the same organization or between a company and its suppliers, distributors and customers. Internal co-operation may represent linkages between either different divisions or different functions.

**tactics** *(p 17)* specific actions that follow on from intended strategies but which can also form a foundation for emergent strategy.

**tangible resources** *(p 561)* the organization's physical resources, such as plant and equipment.

**transfer price** *(p 610)* associated with the transfer of products, components or services between businesses in the same organization. A particularly important issue where there are considerable interdependencies between businesses. The (corporately) imposed or agreed transfer price can be of markedly different attractiveness to the buying and

selling businesses and can be a source of friction.

**transformational change** *(p 823)* major and simultaneous changes to strategies, structures and styles of management. See also *strategic regeneration*

**turnaround strategy** *(p 639)* an attempt to find a new competitive position for a company in difficulty.

**value chain** *(p 118)* framework for identifying (a) where value is added and (b) where costs are incurred. There is an internal value chain and one that embraces the complete supply chain. Internally, it embraces the key functions and activities.

**vertical integration** *(p 155)* where firms directly enter those parts of the added value chain served by their suppliers or distributors, the term used is vertical integration. To achieve the potential benefits of vertical integration (specifically synergy from co-operation) without acquiring a business which normally requires specialist and different skills, firms will look to establish strong alliances and networks.

**vision** *(p 16)* a statement or picture of the future standing of an organization. Linked to the mission or purpose, it embraces key values.

# Author index

# Subject index